Gender in Canada

FOURTH EDITION

Adie Nelson
University of Waterloo

Pearson Canada
Toronto

Library and Archives Canada Cataloguing in Publication

Nelson, Adie, 1958–
    Gender in Canada / Adie Nelson. — 4th ed.

Includes index.
ISBN 978-0-13-501041-9

    1. Sex role—Canada—Textbooks. 2. Sexism—Canada—Textbooks. I. Title.

HQ1075.5.C3N44 2010   305.30971   C2008-905780-5

ISBN-13: 978-0-13-501041-9
ISBN-10: 0-13-501041-1

Vice President, Editorial Director: Gary Bennett
Editor-in-Chief: Ky Pruesse
Marketing Manager: Arthur Gee
Assistant Editor: Victoria Naik
Production Editor: Kevin Leung
Copy Editor: Martin Tooke
Proofreader: Elspeth McFadden
Production Coordinator: Lynn O'Rourke
Composition: Laserwords
Art Director: Julia Hall
Cover Design: Jennifer Stimson
Cover Image: Kaadaa/Getty Images

Statistics Canada information is used with the permission of Statistics Canada. Users are forbidden to copy the data and redisseminate them, in an original or modified form, for commercial purposes, without permission from Statistics Canada. Information on the availability of the wide range of data from Statistics Canada can be obtained from Statistics Canada's Regional Offices, its World Wide Web site at http://www.statcan.ca, and its toll-free access number 1-800-263-1136.

1 2 3 4 5   13 12 11 10 09

Printed and bound in the United States of America.

For my children

Contents

Preface

This edition of *Gender in Canada*, like its predecessors, is intended to serve as an undergraduate text in courses on gender relations. The objective has been to create a work that is pedagogically sound, comprehensive, thought-provoking, lucidly written, and engaging to students.

Drawing upon a rich body of quantitative and qualitative research, *Gender in Canada* analyzes the strengths and weaknesses of a wide range of theoretical perspectives. The book is organized into 10 chapters, each introducing the reader to core concepts, theorists, theories, and controversies. Chapter 1 focuses upon the three foundational concepts of sex, gender, and sexuality. It explores gender stereotypes in depth—reviewing the major methods used to investigate them, discussing multiple jeopardies, and examining sex (re)assignment and transsexualism as illustrations of their power. Chapter 1 also alerts readers to the ways in which gender has influenced the development of research and theory.

Chapter 2 examines the basic variables of sex and of gender, both independently and in relation to one another. Disparate theoretical explanations for gender behaviour are explored, including biologically grounded theories (such as sociobiology and psychoanalytic theory), psychological theories, the social-psychological theory of symbolic interactionism, and the gender perspective, which combines elements of social-psychological and structural feminist theories. Chapter 3 explores how a society's structure influences the ways in which gender is experienced and expressed. An overview of the historical development of Canada is provided to illustrate how masculinity and femininity are constructed relative to time and place. The chapter explores mainstream sociological theories (functionalism and conflict theory), and provides a comprehensive review both of feminist theories and of perspectives on men and masculinity.

Chapter 4 examines the dominant themes of gender socialization during childhood and adolescence in Canada, identifying the ways in which messages about gender are transmitted and reinforced within the family, peer group, and school. It discusses the mechanisms that contribute to a child's becoming gendered and suggests how gender ideologies and strategies may impact upon the aspirations of young men and women. Chapter 5 focuses on symbolic representations of gender within language and speech patterns, non-verbal communication, and the media. Attention is directed to the socialization messages conveyed through such media as children's books, comics, television, advertising and commercials, teen magazines, popular music, computers, and the Internet. This examination is designed to stimulate discussion about how the "reality" of gender is created and sustained.

Gender in our society is inextricably intertwined with work and with the family; these social institutions create and sustain gender as much as they are created and sustained by it. Chapter 6 explores paid and unpaid work, probing age and sex differentials in labour-force participation rates; the impact of marital status and parenting upon paid work; occupational segregation; earning differentials; self-employment; part-time work; and the gendered nature of housework. Chapter 7 scrutinizes the subject of intimate relations. Although we may prefer to think of our search for an intimate partner as intensely unique, changing gender expectations and behaviours inescapably condition our options and decisions. This chapter reviews findings on gender differences in friendship, courtship, mate-selection patterns, sexuality, and sexuality scripts; it also highlights the power dimension which is invariably present in intimate relationships. Chapter 8 delves into the topics of marriage and parenting, emphasizing how marriage and gender interact, continually creating and recreating one another. This chapter illuminates how gender and gender inequalities become organizing principles in heterosexual marriages. Readers are challenged to consider the far-reaching significance of our social constructions of motherhood and fatherhood and the ramifications of the new reproductive technologies on families, parenting, and our most basic understandings of gender. This chapter also addresses intimate violence.

Chapter 9 is devoted to selected aspects of the aging process, and, more importantly, the social meanings of that process for each gender. It examines sex ratios, life-expectancy differentials, and gender differences in mortality and morbidity. The chapter follows the paths of gender development through adulthood and old age; topics covered include menopause; men's pause; the double standard of aging; gender depolarization; retirement; widowhood; poverty among the elderly; and the phenomena of displaced homemakers and displaced providers.

Chapter 10 has two different yet related foci. First, using indices created by the United Nations to measure gender equality, it compares Canada's standing with that of other societies; this examination not only helps us to appreciate how far we have come but also leads to questions about where we should go from here. Thus, the second part of Chapter 10 focuses on issues that will undoubtedly influence the future of gender relations in Canada: resistance to feminism, the stalled gender revolution, and new developments within intimate gender relations. The chapter concludes with a discussion of transgenderism.

It is hoped that this text will provide readers with some valuable tools for understanding the past and present of gender relations in Canada, and, perhaps, anticipating some future possibilities.

Supplements

Now available for instructors is a Test Item File, in Word format. Containing multiple-choice questions, short-answer questions, essay questions, and video suggestions, this TIF can be downloaded from a password-protected section of this book's catalogue page at Pearson Education Canada's online catalogue, at **http://vig.pearsoned.ca**. See your local sales representative for details and access.

Acknowledgments

The author wishes to thank the capable staff at Pearson Education for their assistance, especially Victoria Naik and Kevin Leung. In addition, many thanks are extended to copy editor Martin Tooke for his thoughtful remarks and exacting labour.

The publishers would like to thank the following reviewers for their comments: Barbara Hanson, York University, Fiona Green, University of Winnipeg; Leanne Joanisse, McMaster University; and Judith Grossman, University of Lethbridge.

The excerpts from John Money, *Gay, Straight and In-Between: The Sexology of Erotic Orientation*, reprinted by permission of Oxford University Press.

The excerpt from Sherene Razack, "Exploring the Omissions and Silence in Law Around Race," reprinted by permission of Thompson Educational Publishing.

The excerpt from M. Eichler, "Sex Change Operations: The Last Bulwark of the Double Standard," from *The Double Standard* (London: Croom Helm, 1980), reprinted by permission of the author.

The excerpts from J. Henslin and A. Nelson, "Biology versus Culture: Biology Is the Answer," "Biology versus Culture: Culture Is the Answer," from *Sociology: A Down-to-Earth Approach*, reprinted by permission of Pearson Education Canada.

The excerpt from M. Fowler, *In a Gilded Cage: From Heiress to Duchess*, copyright ©1993, reprinted by permission of Random House of Canada.

The excerpt from P. Connelly and L. Christiansen-Ruffman, "Women's Problems: Private Troubles or Public Issues?" reprinted by permission of *Canadian Journal of Sociology*.

The excerpt from Robert Bly, *Iron John: A Book About Men*, reprinted by permission of Addison Wesley.

The excerpt from Kenneth Clatterbaugh, *Contemporary Perspectives on Masculinity: Men, Women, and Politics in Modern Society*, copyright ©1990, reprinted by permission of Westview Press.

The information taken from the website at *http://astro.uwaterloo.ca/u/fich/text/ zazukibirth_announc*, posted March 27, 1995 (no longer available), used by permission of the author.

The excerpt from V. Alia abridged with permission from *Canadian Woman Studies/les cahiers de la femme*, Fall 1994 issue, "Women of the North" (Vol. 14, No. 4).

The excerpt from A. Macklin, "Symes v. M.N.R.: Where Sex Meets Class," reprinted by permission of *Canadian Journal of Women and the Law*.

The excerpt from Julia Wood, *Gendered Lives: Communication, Gender, and Culture*, 2nd ed., reprinted by permission of Wadsworth.

The excerpt from Ralph LaRossa, "Fatherhood and Social Change," reprinted by permission of National Council on Family Relations.

The excerpt from Amartya Sen, "Missing Women—Revisited," abridged and reproduced with permission of the BMJ Publishing Group.

The excerpt from Serena Nanda (2000), *Gender Diversity: Crosscultural Variations*, reprinted by permission of Waveland Press, Inc.

The table from Robert Hopper (2003), *Gendering Talk*, reprinted by permission of Michigan State University Press.

The excerpt from Loren Pedersen (1991), *Dark Hearts: The Unconscious Forces That Shape Men's Lives*, reprinted by permission of the author.

The excerpt from Straus and Gelles, in Hotaling et al., eds. (1988), *Family Abuse and Its Consequences*, reprinted by permission of Sage Publications, Inc.

The excerpt from Gloria Steinem, "Moving Beyond Words," reprinted with the permission of Simon &ampersand; Schuster Adult Publishing Group from *Moving Beyond Words* by Gloria Steinem. Copyright 1994 by Gloria Steinem.

The table from Jean A. Twenge (1997), "Mrs. His Name: Women's Preferences for Married Names," reprinted by permission of Blackwell Publishing.

The figure from Maticka-Tynadale (2001), "Percentage of 15-Year-Olds Who Reported Having Had Sexual Intercourse" reprinted by permission of *The Canadian Journal of Human Sexuality*.

Figures from Canadian Youth, Sexual Health and HIV/AIDS Study (2003), "Reasons Cited for First Sexual Intercourse, Grade 9" and "Reasons Cited for First Sexual Intercourse, Grade 11" reprinted by permission of the Council of Ministers of Education Canada.

Tables 10.1, 10.2, 10.3, 10.5, Figure 10.1 and Box 10.1 from *Human Development Report* (2003) by United Nations Development Programme. Used by permission of Oxford University Press, Inc.

Information from Canadian Institute for Health Information © 2003 CIHI. *Women's Health Surveillance Report: A Multi-Dimensional Look at the Health of Canadian Women.* Used with permission. Published by the Canadian Institute for Health Information, Ottawa, Canada.

Table 10.4, "Women Candidates in Canadian Federal Elections, 1921–2004." On the World Wide Web in "Elections" *www.sfu.ca/~ahead/elections/women.html* reprinted by permission of Andrew Heard.

The excerpt from Dave Barry, *Dave Barry Is Not Making This Up*, copyright © 1994, reprinted with permission of The Ballantine Publishing Group, a division of Random House, Inc.

CHAPTER 1

The Social Construction of Sex, Gender, and Sexuality

BASIC CONCEPTS: SEX, GENDER, AND SEXUALITY

Three concepts, each part of our everyday language, are fundamental to this text. Unfortunately, these basic terms are often used in imprecise and confusing ways. For the sake of clarity, it is essential to first address some definitional issues.

Sex

Sex refers to the condition of being **male** or **female**, as identified from a biological standpoint. The distinction between the two would appear to be simple and obvious. However, defining a person as male or female actually requires making determinations on a number of variable dimensions.

Let us begin by looking at the very nature of categorization. The division of the human population into categories of female or male, sometimes referred to as **sex dimorphism**, rests upon the notion of a *dichotomy* (i.e., "classification by division into two")—in other words, it is based on the assumption that a given phenomenon can be located within one or the other of two mutually exclusive categories. This assumption is the foundation of the belief that only two categories exist—in this case, male and female—and that all persons can be defined as belonging to one or the other.

Dichotomies are integral to the *dualism* that characterizes the predominant patterns of Western thought. Dualism is the doctrine that in any domain of reality there are two separate and distinct underlying principles. Thus, phenomena are conceived dualistically in terms of "either/or" dichotomies: male or female, black or white, good or bad, right or wrong, and so on.

Such conceptions allow us to navigate quickly through social life without having to take myriad complexities into consideration. However, dichotomous thinking has ramifications. A way of thinking that insists that all phenomena must belong to one or the other of two categories tolerates no ambiguous middle ground. In fact, dichotomous thinking encourages us to believe that the elements within each category are different to the point of antithesis. This notion of dichotomies as representing *diametrical opposites* is captured in the expression "opposite sex." A question that immediately presents itself is "who is the *opposite* sex?" At first glance, this may seem to be a joke, but it is a legitimate and meaningful question full of implications for the lives of women and men (Bernhardt-House, 2003; O'Keefe and Fox, 2003). Within our own and many other cultures, males have traditionally been considered the primary or standard sex; females have been defined, analyzed, and interpreted with reference to males—and not the other way around. Consequently, it is females who have been considered the opposite, the different, the deviant, or the "Other" (de Beauvoir, 1961: xvi).

This conclusion is mirrored in Hegarty and Buechel's (2006: 378) content analysis of articles that were published in four American Psychological Association (APA) journals in the period 1965–2004 and which reported differences between males and females. They noted that in both the titles and abstracts of these articles, males were typically portrayed as the norm and females as the "effect to be explained." In 75 percent of the statistical tables that appeared within these articles, data for men were positioned before (or to the left) of the data on women.

Implicit in the idea of "opposite sexes" is the belief and expectation that whatever females are, males are not, and vice versa. Dichotomous thinking leads us to search for and focus upon differences rather than similarities between the sexes.

Gender

Gender refers to **femininity** and **masculinity**, as identified from a sociocultural standpoint. The term "gender" is of relatively recent origin, having been introduced into our vocabulary in 1955 by psychologist John Money. While "there is no linguistic magic that can isolate the strictly social and cultural components of femininity and masculinity in a single operative term" (Komarovsky, 1988: 586), "gender" is the best term available for focusing attention on the socially acquired meanings of being male or female. Unfortunately, a tendency is developing to use the term in a more global, and possibly misleading, way (Kennelly et al., 2001). For example, Udry (1994: 561; 2000) observed that editors of scientific journals regularly strike out his use of the term "sex" and replace it with "gender," even in places where he is specifically referring to the biological designation. Crawford (1995: 3) charged that "[t]he (re)conflation of sex and gender has become ludicrous.... A lengthy report of National Public Radio discusses selective abortion based on the *gender* of the fetus." Chrisler (2007: 444) noted that, in the field of psychology, "one can often find" the authors of conference papers and scholarly articles "discussing their results in terms of the 'gender' of the rats" (see also Haig, 2004). Imprecision in the use of these basic concepts is confusing to researchers, theorists, textbook authors, and students alike.

A major cause of confusion is uncertainty about which of the two concepts—sex or gender—best applies in a particular instance. It is not always clear whether social scientists are examining a biological or a cultural phenomenon (Pryzgoda and Chrisler, 2000). When researchers compare male and female subjects along any particular dimension, are they measuring something that derives from biological maleness/femaleness (best captured by the term "sex") or that is the product of learned feminine and masculine behaviours (best captured by the term "gender")?

Since biology and culture do overlap and interact, the most appropriate term is not immediately obvious. Chrisler (2007: 444), noting that disagreements abound as social scientists and lay persons alike "struggle to decide whether and when to use the words 'sex differences' and 'gender differences,'" suggests that an "ironic embodiment of this disagreement" can be witnessed in one of the most highly regarded scholarly journals which publishes articles on gender, *Sex Roles*, "which, for well over a decade, has had an editorial policy that its authors must use the term 'gender roles,' yet has not changed its name to reflect its own policy." As Unger (in Zurbriggen and Sherman, 2007: 476) has observed, "Despite 25 years of dialogue, psychologists are still unable to distinguish between sex and gender, and most researchers in ... the field as a whole use these terms interchangeably."

Although "it is difficult to avoid confounding sex and gender" (Unger, 1979: 1089), this text will use "gender" to refer to *all expected and actual thoughts, feelings, and behaviours associated with masculinity and femininity*. This definition directs our attention to the fact that gender has external ("expected") and internal ("actual") dimensions. Gender is thus continuously constructed between internal and external sources, and is affirmed or modified through social interaction (Craig and Liberti, 2007; Koenig, 2002; Letendre, 2007; Linstead and Pullen, 2006; Pattinson, 2006).

How Many Genders? The definition of gender in terms of masculinity and femininity suggests that only two, separate and discrete, gender categories exist. Many standard psychological tests, such as the *Minnesota Multiphasic Personality Inventory*, or MMPI, are based upon this assumption of dichotomous genders. However, Bem (1974), introducing the concept of androgyny, argued that masculinity and femininity represent two continua. Suggesting that an individual's location along each continuum may provide an indication of his/her personal combination of masculinity and femininity, she developed a methodological test (the Bem Sex Role Inventory, or BSRI) which yielded a fourfold classification system: (1) **androgynous** individuals rank high on both femininity and masculinity, (2) **feminine** individuals rank high on femininity and low on masculinity, (3) **masculine** individuals rank high on masculinity and low on femininity, and (4) **undifferentiated** individuals rank low on femininity and masculinity. (A simplified version of the BSRI appears in Table 1.1). Thus, Bem conceived of gender as a *pair* of continuous variables: high–low masculine and high–low feminine.

Bem's research provided empirical support for the postulation of four genders. However (partly because of limitations of the English language and partly because of the need to integrate her work into a larger research tradition), Bem's discussion of gender uses only the terms of masculinity and femininity, thereby reinforcing the notion that only two genders exist.

As Heilbrun (1973: xv) acknowledged, "so wedded are we to the conventional definition of 'masculine' and 'feminine' that it is impossible to write about androgyny without using these terms in their accepted, received sense." Without the luxury of a truly neutral, non-gendered language, it is difficult to describe actions, thoughts, and feelings in other than stereotypical terms. Our own linguistic reality is one wherein most behaviour is described with dichotomous gender labels. Yet this is not universally the case. Historical and anthropological records reveal that other cultures have recognized distinctive gender types beyond our own everyday categories of masculine and feminine.

Early European explorers confronted cultures with sex/gender systems very different from their own. Encountering men in Aboriginal societies who dressed as women, performed the work of women, and engaged in sexual relations with men, they derisively labelled them *berdache*—a term derived from an archaic Arabic word for "male prostitute." Reacting out of **ethnocentrism** (i.e., the use of one's own culture as a yardstick for judging the ways of other individuals or societies), they ignored both the cultural meanings and positive value that indigenous peoples themselves attached to gender diversity. Instead, people who did not fit into their dichotomous paradigm were pejoratively described as homosexuals, transvestites, or hermaphrodites. However, as anthropologist Serena Nanda (2000: 12) pointed out,

> the European homosexual/heterosexual dichotomy was not culturally relevant and the European labeling of the berdache as homosexuals resulted from their own cultural emphasis on sexuality as a central, even defining, aspect of gender and on sodomy as an abnormal practice and/or a sin. While berdache in many American Indian societies did engage in sexual relations [with] and even married persons of the same sex, this was not central to their alternative gender role. Another overemphasis resulting from European ethnocentrism was the identification of berdache as transvestites. Although berdache often cross-dressed, transvestism was not consistent within or across societies. European descriptions of berdache as hermaphrodites were also inaccurate.

TABLE 1.1	Bem Sex Role Inventory (Simplified)

Directions: Indicate by writing numbers from 1 to 7 in the blanks below how true of you these various characteristics are. That is: Mark a 1 if the characteristic is never true of you; mark a 4 if the characteristic is true of you about half the time; mark a 7 if the characteristic is always true of you.

___ Self-reliant	___ Yielding
___ Defends own beliefs	___ Cheerful
___ Independent	___ Shy
___ Athletic	___ Affectionate
___ Assertive	___ Flatterable
___ Has strong personality	___ Loyal
___ Forceful	___ Feminine
___ Analytical	___ Sympathetic
___ Has leadership tendencies	___ Sensitive to the needs of others
___ Willing to take risks	___ Understanding
___ Makes decisions easily	___ Compassionate
___ Self-sufficient	___ Eager to soothe hurt feelings
___ Dominant	___ Soft-spoken
___ Masculine	___ Warm
___ Willing to take a stand	___ Tender
___ Aggressive	___ Gullible
___ Acts as a leader	___ Childlike
___ Individualistic	___ Does not use harsh language
___ Competitive	___ Loves children
___ Ambitious	___ Gentle
___ TOTAL = M	___ TOTAL = F

Calculate your total score in each column before reading on.

Interpreting your scores: Your M score indicates the degree to which you perceive of yourself in terms of traditional masculine attributes. Your F score is a self-rating on traditional feminine attributes. Though median scores fall around 100, the main information for the purposes of Bem's classification comes from comparing your F and M scores. If your M score exceeds your F score by more than ten points, your self-perceived gender orientation tends towards the traditionally masculine; if your F score exceeds your M score by over ten points, it tends towards the traditionally feminine. F and M scores that are fairly close together would indicate that you rate yourself about equally on masculine and feminine traits and would be classified on the BSRI as "androgynous."

Source: Adapted from Hopper (2003: 22–23).

Although foreign observers viewed the *berdache* as shameful or "deviant," "mixed gender roles were often central and highly valued in American Indian cultures" (Nanda, 2000: 12; see also Aspin and Hutchings, 2007; Trexler, 2002). Indeed, in many Native American societies, multiple sex/gender roles were normative. The cosmology (system of religious beliefs) of these societies established a "hospitable context" for gender diversity;

in many indigenous cultures, stories of the world's creation involved themes of sex/gender ambiguity, an absence of sexual differentiation, and sex/gender transformation (Nanda, 2000: 20). The assumption of variant gender roles by biological males has been documented in 110 to 150 North American indigenous societies; by biological females, in about one quarter to one half of these societies (Nanda, 2000: 23). In accounting for why female gender variants occurred less frequently than male gender variants, Nanda wrote that "in many American Indian societies women could—and did—adopt aspects of the male gender role, such as warfare or hunting, and sometimes dressed in male clothing, without being reclassified into a different gender."

While the defining criteria, recruitment processes, and behavioural norms of gender-variant roles varied among different indigenous societies, they commonly involved cross-dressing, cross-gender occupation, and same-sex (but different gender) sexuality, as well as "some culturally normative and acknowledged process for recruitment to the role, special language and ritual roles, and associations with spiritual power" (Nanda, 2000: 14; see also Bacigalupo, 2004; Sell, 2004; Walters et al., 2006). In most indigenous societies, gender variants were biologically unambiguous males or females. The Navajo, however, (unlike most other Native American societies) recognized two additional variants: masculine female-bodied **nadleeh** and feminine male-bodied *nadleeh*. Nevertheless, even among the Navajo, where an ambiguous genital configuration was the starting point of a gender-variant role, "it was only a starting point.... American Indian gender variance was defined more by cultural than biological criteria" (Nanda, 2000: 18–19). Moreover, those who occupied these gender-variant roles were regarded by their communities with deference, not disdain, and were considered valuable and gifted members of their social groups.

Some contemporary anthropologists continue to employ the term *berdache* in reference to "people who partly or completely take on aspects of the culturally defined role of the other sex and who are classified neither as women nor men, but as genders of their own" (Nanda, 2000: 12). Others, however, reject the term as insulting in its origins and distorting in its representation of Native American gender diversity. Unfortunately, no unanimously agreed-upon replacement term exists. The most widely accepted term in use today is "*Two-Spirit*," coined in 1990 by urban Native American gays and lesbians (Adams and Phillips, 2006; Calhoun et al., 2007; Fieland et al., 2007; Meyer-Cook and Labelle, 2004). The term seeks to emphasize the fact that in indigenous societies, gender variance was associated with spiritual power (Brotman et al., 2002; Garrett and Barret, 2003; Long, 2004). Nevertheless, this term may itself invite binary thinking about gender and, ironically, reaffirm the Western cultural notion that only two genders exist.

Cross-cultural research challenges us to recognize that "there are many different (though probably not unlimited) ways that societies can organize their thinking about sex, gender and sexuality" (Nanda, 2000: 3; see also DeFrancisco and Palczewski, 2007). The **hijras** (HIJ-ras), for example, are a Hindu caste of men whose religious practice focuses on the worship of Bahuchara Mata, one of the many Mother Goddesses seen as embodiments of female creative power (Nanda, 1990: xi; see also Basu, 2001; Hall, 2002). *Hijras* are biological men who wear female apparel and behave like women. Undergoing surgical emasculation to remove their penis and testicles defines them as *hijras*—"neither men nor women" (Nanda, 1990: xv). Because Indian law prohibits surgical emasculation, not all *hijras* today undergo castration; however, this surgery (often performed by a *hijra* "midwife") continues to be practised in secret (Nanda, 2000: 33; Reddy, 2005). *Hijras* are regarded as "auspicious and powerful ritual figures" (Nanda, 2000: 34); as mediums for the goddesses (Nath and Nayar, 1997: 593), they perform songs and dances at festivals and confer blessings at weddings and on the birth of a child.

The *xanith* (han-eeth) in Islamic Oman are another example of an "intermediate gender" (Wikan, 1977) or "gender pluralism" (Peletz, 2006; see also Chopra, 2006). *Xanith* are males who enjoy all the rights of men under the law, worship in mosques with other men, have male names, and are referred to using the masculine grammatical form. However, *xanith* perform the role of women within their households and their attractiveness is judged by standards of female beauty. In Oman, where the practice of *purdah*, or seclusion, ensures the segregation of women and men, *xanith* are classed with women for most festive occasions and social activities and are allowed to dine and visit with women. Although both men and women generally cover their heads, *xanith* go bareheaded. While both men and women scent themselves with perfume, *xanith* apply perfume more heavily than is typical for either (Nanda, 1990: 131). *Xanith* serve as homosexual male partners, taking the passive role. In Oman, "being a man," or masculinity, is defined by sexual potency in marriage, and a bloodied handkerchief is publicly displayed after the wedding night, to prove, simultaneously, the bride's virginity and the husband's ability to consummate the union. A *xanith* may become reclassified as a man by marrying and demonstrating his potency via a bloodied handkerchief, after which the former *xanith* becomes subject to the same constraints as other men.

In modern-day Hawaii, the term *mahu* (ma-hoo) is used to designate homosexuals. However, in traditional villages of Tahiti and what is now French Polynesia, the *mahu* are a third gender. Unambiguously biologically male, a *mahu* adopts this social and occupational role voluntarily and publicly takes on attributes associated with women. As in the case of *xanith*, *hijras*, and *berdache*, the sexual partners of a *mahu* are not viewed as homosexual, nor is sexual behaviour thought to be the *mahu*'s primary defining characteristic. If, at any time, a *mahu* should feel that he no longer has the calling to continue in the role, he can simply cast it off and resume everyday life as a heterosexual man, performing what are viewed in the village as masculine duties (Nanda, 1990: 134–136). As Nanda (2000: 58–59) noted, in Polynesia the boundaries of gender-variant roles appear to be "porous"; this allows for significant "variability among gender variant individuals, and also within an individual's behavior in different situations and over a lifetime." Some evidence also suggests the availability in Tahiti of female *mahu* roles (Nanda, 2000: 58; Elliston, 1999).

Many additional examples of gender variance may be enumerated, such as Japan's *newhalf* (*nyuuhaafu*)—biological men who view themselves as a "third" or "intermediate sex" and who work "in clearly-defined roles as hostesses, companions, and sex workers within Japan's extensive sex and entertainment industry" (McLelland, 2002); or Brazil's *travesti*—biological males who are centrally defined by their sexuality and their willingness to perform the "feminine," penetrated role in anal intercourse (Nanda, 2000: 43–50); or the *kathoey* of Thailand (Costa and Matzner, 2007); or the *bayot/bantut/bakla* of the Philippines who are "sometimes referred to as a 'third sex'... and who are like women but also are not women" (Nanda, 2000: 71; see also Bacigalupo, 2004).

These examples illustrate the multiplicity of gender variants and illuminate the fact that in Western society, social convention and the nature of the English language limit us to thinking in terms of only two: feminine and masculine. For the moment, we may conceptualize gender in terms of masculine and feminine continua. Individuals may be arrayed along each continuum according to their high–low conformity to the parameters considered prototypical of masculinity and femininity in a given society, culture, and subculture at a particular point in historical time (Lancaster, 2003).

Sex and Gender The nature of the relationship between sex and gender is a fundamental concern for the sociology of gender. Logically, three types of relationships are possible: (1) sex determines gender, (2) sex is arbitrarily related to gender, and (3) sex influences gender (see Chanter, 2000; Kimball, 2007). A fourth possibility, that gender determines or influences sex, exists only in exceptional cases, and will be considered in a later section of this chapter.

The first proposition attributes a causal role to sex and assumes that biological status dictates one's place on the gender continua; in other words, it deems sex both a necessary and a sufficient cause of gender. The second proposition suggests that any apparent relationship between sex and gender is accidental or arbitrary. Some correlation may be found, for example, between being female and being feminine; however, correlation does not imply causality. A correlation may merely be a statistical artifact and not a meaningful reflection of reality; other factors, namely, features of the social environment, may be the real cause. Here, sex is deemed neither a necessary nor a sufficient cause of gender. The third possibility is that sex and gender are related to each other in some necessary fashion, but that gender cannot fully or sufficiently be explained by sex. Additional factors must be taken into account if our goal is to achieve as complete an understanding of the nature of gender as possible.

It is difficult to estimate which of the above views most Canadians subscribe to. Informal observation suggests that most Canadians subscribe to the first, known as **biological determinism**—the belief that biological sex determines masculinity or femininity and that, in fact, the terms "sex" and "gender" are interchangeable. Biological determinism conceptualizes masculinity and femininity in terms of opposite categories, grounded in biology and justified in the rhetoric of "doing what comes naturally." The second position—that sex and gender are related, not intrinsically, but via social learning—is referred to as **social constructionism**. The first and second positions reflect the long-standing "nature versus nurture" (yet another dichotomy) controversy. The third position, rejecting the "either/or" reductionism of the first two, maintains that both biology and the social environment combine to produce gender. This is often referred to as the **interactionist** position.

Money (1988) has made the following criticism of "either/or" conceptualizations:

> Reductionist theory is popular on both sides of the false fence that erroneously claims to separate biology from social learning. It allows its proponents on either side to earn a living by ignoring each other's specialty knowledge, training, and certification. The bureaucracy of scholars is not well suited to inter-disciplinary knowledge, nor to the concept of multivariate, sequential determinants that cross the boundaries of scientific specialties.

In other words, an important factor conducive to the endorsement of the first and second positions, and militating against full acceptance of the third, is the very nature of academic training. The structuring of under- and postgraduate programs within disciplinary lines does not favour the development of multidisciplinary knowledge (Hyde, 2001; Lippa, 2005). Adoption of one of the "either/or" (biological determinist or social constructionist) positions is, therefore, largely a consequence of academic specialization and tends to reflect the researcher's academic roots.

Several recent studies have emphasized the psychological, social, and political consequences of how gender is explained. Experimental research conducted by Dar-Nimerod and Heine (2006) manipulated their participants' beliefs about gender differences in math and then measured their subsequent performance on a math test. Female participants who read an essay that posited a gender divide in mathematical ability stemming from genetics were outperformed by those who read an essay that argued that there were no math-related sex differences or maintained that gender differences in math were caused by experiential factors. The researchers observed that their findings "raise discomforting questions regarding the effects that scientific theories can have on those who learn about them and the obligation that scientists have to be mindful of how their work is interpreted" (p. 435). As they remarked, "Whether there are innate sex differences in math performance remains a contentious question. However, merely considering the role of genes in math performance can have some deleterious consequences" (p. 435).

In a second experiment, conducted by Brescoll and LaFrance (2004), participants were asked to read a newspaper article which contained either a biological or a non-biological explanation of sex differences in the ability to identify plants; a control group was not asked to read a newspaper article. The results indicated that while exposure to the article containing a biological explanation increased test subjects' endorsement of gender stereotypes, exposure to a non-biological explanation increased the likelihood that subjects would believe that people are capable of change. In addition, a content analysis of newspaper reports conducted by these researchers found that the likelihood that biological explanations of sex differences would feature prominently within news reports could be predicted by the degree of political conservatism witnessed in other sections of the newspaper and that "political ideology influenced the translation of scientific research findings" into "news" (Brescoll and LaFrance, 2004: 517). When the science sections of conservative-leaning newspapers were compared to their more liberal counterparts, the former contained a higher proportion of articles that anchored explanations of differences between men and women in biology.

Sexuality

In everyday speech, the terms **sexuality** and **sexual** are often subsumed under the rubric of *sex*. However, the word "sex" may in some cases refer to a biological designation (e.g., her sex is female), and in others to the constellation of feelings, thoughts, and behaviours involved in human sexuality (e.g., he had sex with his lover). Furthermore, the conflation of "sex" and "sexuality" may casually promote the idea that sexuality is biologically determined.

Following Reiss (1986: 31), the words "sexuality" and "sexual" will be used to refer to that range of human activities designed to produce erotic response and pleasure. Reiss defines the universal meaning of human sexuality as "those scripts shared by a group that are supposed to lead to erotic arousal and in turn to produce genital response" (Reiss, 1986: 20). *Scripts* are culturally created guidelines that embody the patterns of behaviour a society or group defines as appropriate in a given social situation. **Sexuality scripts** define how, where, with whom, and under what conditions one is to behave as a sexual being.

How Many Sexualities? Social scientists agree about the existence of certain varieties of sexual scripts: **homosexuality** (a sexuality script oriented towards members of the same sex), **heterosexuality** (oriented towards members of the other sex), and **bisexuality** (oriented towards members of both sexes), although the precise terms used may vary (Money, 1988).

The research of Kinsey et al. (1948, 1953), and others after them, exposed the futility of attempting to divide human beings into two dichotomous categories, "heterosexual" and "homosexual." Yet, even today, many heterosexuals and homosexuals, accustomed to dichotomous thinking, seem to find the notion of a trichotomy threatening (Waites, 2005). People may attempt to dispel the threat by discounting the thoughts and feelings of bisexuals, insisting that "deep down," such individuals are really either straight or gay. However, as Kinsey et al. (1948: 639) pointedly remarked,

> [t]he world is not divided into sheep and goats.... Only the human mind invents categories and tries to force fit individuals into separated pigeon holes. The living world is a continuum in each and every one of its aspects. The sooner we learn this concerning human sexual behaviour the sooner we will reach a sound understanding of the realities of sex.

As Figure 1.1 illustrates, the Kinsey findings and seven-point scale of sexual behaviour emphasize the fluidity of human sexual experience. While 60 percent of their non-random sample of white males had engaged in some form of same-sex experience prior to adulthood and approximately 37 percent had participated in at least one same-sex experience leading to orgasm (including adolescent experiences), only 4 percent proceeded to develop an exclusively homosexual pattern of sexuality. Although approximately 13 percent of women had experienced at least one same-sex experience leading to orgasm, only 2 to 3 percent were mostly or exclusively same-sex in their lifelong sexuality. Bisexuality (positions one through five on the continuum) was much more common than exclusive homosexuality (position six) (Kinsey et al., 1953). (It should be emphasized that all of the statistics reported above refer to sexual behaviour only and do not reflect sexual identity or unacted-upon sexual feelings.)

More recently, in nationwide research on 3432 American adults ages 18 to 59, Michael et al. (1994: 174–177) focused on three measures of homosexuality: sexual attraction to others of the same sex (desire); engaging in same-sex sexual acts (behaviour); and self-identification as homosexual (identity). They discovered that more people found others of the same sex sexually attractive than actually engaged in homosexual acts; men were more likely than women to act on their desires and also to identify themselves as homosexual.

FIGURE 1.1	The Kinsey Continuum of Heterosexuality–Homosexuality					
Exclusively heterosexual			Bisexual			Exclusively homosexual
0	1	2	3	4	5	6

0	Exclusively heterosexual
1	Predominantly heterosexual, only incidentally homosexual
2	More heterosexual than homosexual
3	Equally heterosexual and homosexual
4	More homosexual than heterosexual
5	Predominantly homosexual, only incidentally heterosexual
6	Exclusively homosexual

While 5.5 percent of women reported finding the *thought* of a lesbian sexual experience appealing or very appealing, only 4 percent said they were sexually attracted to other women and less than 2 percent reported having had a same-sex encounter in the preceding year. Although slightly more than 4 percent of the women reported having had a same-sex experience at some point in their lives (rarely prior to age 18), merely 1.4 percent identified themselves as homosexual or bisexual (the researchers combined the two categories when presenting these data). Among the men, approximately 6 percent indicated being attracted to other men, although only 2 percent reported having had a same-sex experience in the past year. Nine percent of the men reported having had a sexual encounter with another man at some point in their lives since puberty. Among those men who had had a same-sex encounter prior to the age of 18, 60 percent continued to engage in homosexual behaviour during adulthood. Still, only 2.8 percent of the male sample identified themselves as either homosexual or bisexual (Michael et al., 1994: 176).

Ellis et al. (2005) conducted a survey of approximately 8000 college students at 20 American colleges and two Canadian universities (University of Lethbridge and University of British Columbia) who were enrolled in social/behavioural sciences courses. The survey employed four measures of sexual orientation:

- a self-identity measure ("How would you describe your sexual orientation: heterosexual, bisexual, homosexual, or uncertain?");
- an attraction measure ("To what degree are you sexually attracted to members of the opposite sex or sexually attracted to members of the same sex [together, the answers should add to 100%]?");
- a fantasy measure ("When imagining sexual interaction with another person, what percentage of the time does this involve a member of the same sex? A member of the opposite sex? Answer each question from 0 to 100% and both should total 100%"); and
- an experiential measure ("Please indicate the number of individuals with whom you have had sexual intercourse [or other sexual contact to the point of one or both climaxing]").

Although the survey did not stipulate any time frame (e.g., one year, five years) for any of the questions posed, the researchers report that "[w]hen the questions were devised, it was assumed that participants would provide responses with reference to the recent past" (Ellis et al., 2005: 571). This survey found that approximately 1 percent of males and females identified themselves as bisexual and another 1 percent identified themselves as homosexual. However, while merely 1.3 percent of males and 0.5 percent of females reported exclusively same-sex sexual attraction, "varying degrees of non-heterosexuality were exhibited by 10.3 percent of males and 13.1 percent of the females." Similarly, while 9 percent of both the men and women in their sample reported exclusively same-sex sexual fantasies, approximately 20 percent of males and 25 percent of females reported occasional sexual fantasies about same-sex others. Among those students who reported having one or more "intimate sexual experiences" (33.5 percent of the men and 31 percent of the women), 13 percent of the sex partners of males and 8 percent of the sex partners of females were same-sex others. Approximately 6 percent of the sexually experienced males, but less than 1 percent of the females (0.5 percent) reported exclusively same-sex sexual experiences.

Ellis et al. (2005: 578) pointedly acknowledged the problematic nature of conducting survey research on sexuality. Thus, they noted that while approximately 15 percent of the men and women in their survey reported being at least occasionally sexually attracted to a member of the same sex... if criteria such as being *predominantly* attracted to the same sex rather than the opposite sex was used, the proportions dropped to approximately 4 percent for males and 2 percent for females. If *exclusive* attraction to the same sex was used, the percentage for males fell to under 2 percent and for females to less than 1 percent.

They also reported that the "most unsettling finding from our study involved the substantial number of inconsistencies in responses to questions that all pertained to sexual orientation," including, "at the extreme, over 200 males and over 400 females [who] ... stated that they were heterosexual" but, nevertheless, reported that "over 90 percent of their sexual fantasies were about members of the same sex."

In the United States, data from the nationally representative General Social Survey reveal that between 1988 and 1998, the percentage of Americans ages 59 and younger who reported having had a same-sex sexual experience in the past five years increased from 0.2 percent to 2.8 percent among women and from 1.7 percent to 4.1 percent among men (Butler, 2000). According to Butler, this increase may be related to diminishing social and legal prohibitions against same-sex sexual behaviour, along with more favourable media images of gay men and women (see also Schiappa et al., 2006). These changes, she suggested, may have made it easier for people to acknowledge and act upon their sexual attraction to same-sex others. However, she emphasized that these figures "should not be taken as estimates of the proportion of the population that is gay or lesbian. Some people may engage in same-gender sexual activity and yet identify as heterosexual, whereas other people may identify as gay or lesbian but may not have been sexually active in recent years" (Butler, 2000: 342; see also Brewer, 2003).

To date, no directly comparable studies have been conducted in Canada. Data from the 2001 Canadian census—the first to include questions recognizing same-sex partner relationships—found that only 3 percent of common-law couples and less than 1 percent of all Canadian couples were of the same sex. More recently, the 2006 Canadian census counted 45 435 same-sex couples, of which 16.5 percent were married (Statistics Canada, 2007a). However, it is not possible to calculate the percentage of homosexual Canadians from this data (as, obviously, not all gays and lesbians live in same-sex married or common-law partnerships). The focus of both the 2001 and 2006 census questions was the domestic arrangements of Canadians, not their sexual behaviour or self-identifications. The first Statistics Canada survey to include a question on sexual orientation was Cycle 2.1 of the Canadian Community Health Survey (CCHS), conducted between January and December 2003 on more than 135 000 Canadians. The target population of the CCHS included household residents age 12 and over in all provinces and territories, excluding Indian reserves and some remote areas; also excluded were full-time members of the Canadian Armed Forces and those residing in health-care institutions.

As previously noted, different concepts can be used to measure sexual orientation, including *behaviour* (over the entire lifetime or during a certain period) or *feelings* (of sexual attraction to a same-sex other). The CCHS, however, used the concept of *identity*—that is, whether an individual considers him/herself to be heterosexual, homosexual, or bisexual. This choice acknowledged that "[d]ata from other countries suggests that the number of people who consider themselves to be homosexual is much smaller than the number who report having had sexual relations with someone of the same sex. However, people are more willing to answer questions about identity than about behaviour" (Statistics Canada, 2004a).

Findings from the 2003 CCHS indicated that merely 1 percent of Canadians ages 18 to 59 considered themselves homosexual, while another 0.7 percent identified as bisexual. "About 1.3% of men considered themselves homosexual, about twice the proportion of 0.7% among women. However, 0.9% of women reported being bisexual, slightly higher than the proportion of 0.6% among men" (Statistics Canada, 2004a). Although these results are similar to those obtained in American studies that have also used the concept of identity, they must nevertheless be regarded with some skepticism. Given this country's long history of antipathy towards homosexuals, it is reasonable to suppose that some may have hesitated to identify themselves as such to a government agency. In consequence, the precise proportion of Canadians who self-identify as hetero-, homo-, or bisexual or engage in homosexual activities cannot be definitively established. However, as the preceding paragraphs suggest, estimates of the distribution of the different kinds of sexuality depend, in part, on the nature of the sample group, and on the kinds of measures used (see Martin and Meezan, 2003; Sullivan and Losberg, 2003).

Heterosexuality, homosexuality, and bisexuality differ from one another in what is known as **sexual orientation**, which refers to the *directionality* of sexuality scripts—that is, whether the primary source of erotic arousal is members of one's own sex, the opposite sex, or both. The term **sexual preference** has sometimes been used interchangeably with "sexual orientation"; however, the term "sexual preference" has fallen into disfavour with some segments of the gay/lesbian rights movement, as it implies that sexual orientation is a matter of choice. Since the mid-nineteenth century, according to Roger Lancaster (2003: 9), "homosexual rights advocates have leaned on innatist paradigms" (i.e., the claim that same-sex desires are inborn and immutable). He noted that "arguments that 'I was born that way' and 'I can't change the way I am' offer ready, economical refutations to conservative and Christian fundamentalist demands that gays abandon their 'unnatural' choices through psychological counseling, religion conversion, or sheer willpower" (Lancaster, 2003: 275). Moreover, because innatist paradigms are compatible with "guidelines established by the bulk of civil rights law, which prohibits discrimination against people on the basis of 'immutable' characteristics (e.g., 'race,' sex, national origin)," they support claims for social acceptance and legal redress (Lancaster, 2003: 275; see also Broad, 2002; Creed et al., 2002; Wozniak, 2003).

In this context, one may consider the results of a 2007 Gallup poll of Americans, which found that those "who believe homosexuals are born with their sexual orientation tend to be much more supportive of gay rights than are those who say homosexuality is due to upbringing and environment (and therefore, perhaps, more of a lifestyle choice).... For example, nearly four in five of those who believe homosexuality is congenital think it should be an acceptable lifestyle. By contrast, only 30% of those who think homosexuality is caused by environmental factors agree" (Saad, 2007; see also Hegarty, 2002). The research of Wood and Bartowski (2004) on the influence of beliefs about homosexuality on attitudes concerning gay rights policy also found a strong positive association between biological attributions of homosexuality and support for gay rights.

Historically, Canada has not been guided by any concept of "different, but equal" in its attitudes to sexual orientation (Goldie, 2001). Heterosexuality has been and remains prescriptively normative; divergence from the heterosexual norm is frequently classified as deviance at best, and a threat to our entire cultural way of life at worst (Garnets et al., 2003; Harper and Schneider, 2003; Ricks and Dziegielewski, 2005; Ryan and Rivers, 2003). From Confederation until 1969, homosexual acts were punishable by up to 14 years in prison under Canadian criminal law. From 1946 to 1977, a practising homosexual faced the possibility of life in prison if decreed a "criminal sexual psychopath" (Kinsman, 1996). It was not until 1969 that homosexual acts, taking place in private between two consenting adults over the age of 21 (later reduced to 18), were decriminalized in our country.

Homophobia (an irrational fear and hatred of homosexuals and homosexuality) is still prevalent in Canada at both the individual and societal levels (EGALE, 2007). Yet, despite widespread use of the term, it may be noted that "homophobia" is actually a misnomer: neither whole societies nor individuals are likely to display the physiological symptoms (e.g., profuse sweating, vertigo, restricted breathing) associated with classic phobias (Gough, 2002). Therefore, other terms, such as *homonegativity, heteronormativity*, and *antigay bias*, have been proposed to refer to negative attitudes towards homosexuals. Another phenomenon that exists at both the societal and individual levels is *heterosexism* (Ellis and Mitchell, 2000: 200; see also Tomsen and Mason, 2001). **Heterosexism** refers to a system of beliefs that asserts the superiority of heterosexuality and a heterosexual way of life and promotes prejudice and discrimination against any other sexual orientation (Russell, 2002).

In both Canada and the United States, **human rights** (sometimes referred to as *civil rights*) have been extended to guarantee equal-rights protection to groups who might be singled out for prejudicial and discriminatory treatment. In 1977, Quebec included sexual orientation in its *Charter of Human Rights and Freedoms*, becoming the first province in Canada to support homosexual civil rights (Gudgeon, 2003: 198); until 1986, Quebec would remain the only jurisdiction in Canada in which "sexual orientation" was a prohibited ground of discrimination under statute law (Yogis et al., 1996: 1). Since then, all provincial and territorial human-rights acts, as well as the federal *Human Rights Act*, have been amended to include sexual orientation as a prohibited basis for discrimination.

Homosexuality (and possibly bisexuality as well) may be said to encompass not only sexual orientation but entire subcultural ways of life. The terms **gay** and **lesbian** have implications that extend beyond the strictly sexual realm. As Thompson (1987: xi) noted, "gay implies a social identity and consciousness actively chosen, while homosexual refers to a specific form of sexuality. A person may be homosexual but that does not necessarily imply that he or she would be gay." Thompson uses the term "gay" to denote homosexuals of both sexes; however, rather than use the term in this generic sense, this text will employ the terms "gay" and "lesbian" when the focus of discussion goes beyond sexual activity.

The Etiology of Sexuality Social scientists have long pondered the relationships between biology, culture and the social environment, and sexuality. The basic question (as discussed earlier) is whether sexuality is determined by, arbitrarily related to, or only influenced by, biology. Our everyday use of language reflects the endemic belief in biological causation (e.g., references to our "sex hormones" or "sex drive"). Gallup poll findings also have revealed that an increasing percentage of the general population believes that homosexuality is inborn—from 13 percent in 1977 to 34 percent in 1999 to 42 percent in 2007 (Gallup Organization, 2000; Saad, 2007). A national U.S. study of homosexual men reported that 90 percent believed they were born with their homosexual orientation; only 4 percent believed environmental factors to be the sole cause (Lever, 1994). Similarly, when a sample of over 2000 American lesbians were asked whether they felt they had a choice about their orientation, 58 percent answered "no," 25 percent believed they had a partial choice, and only 11 percent felt their sexual orientation to be a completely free choice (reported in Lips, 1999: 271). Nevertheless, the findings of empirical research that has sought to isolate a biological basis for sexuality have been less than convincing.

For example, science has yet to identify a "homosexuality gene," despite the claims of researchers such as Hamer et al. (1993) to have discovered *statistical* evidence for its existence. In their examination of 40 pairs of gay brothers, Hamer et al. noted that a significantly higher number (33 out of 40) than expected (20 out of 40) of the pairs shared matching DNA in a region called **Xq28** at the tip of the X chromosome, which males inherit from their mothers. The researchers focused upon this chromosome after noting in previous research that more gay male relatives tended to be found on the mother's side of a homosexual's family (Hamer and Copeland, 1996). However, Hamer and his research team did not actually isolate a specific gene or set of genes; they only provided the statistics-based suggestion that such genes must exist. Their research also failed to account for the homosexuality of those brothers who did not possess the matching DNA (Peele and DeGrandpre, 1995: 64; Lancaster, 2003: 250). More recent Canadian research (Rice et al., 1999), based on a sample of 52 gay male sibling pairs, analyzed four microsatellite markers at position Xq28 but found no support for Hamer's suggestion of an X-linked gene underlying homosexuality (see also Alexander and Yescavage, 2005; McInerney, 2000).

While Pillard and Bailey's (1998) overview of genetics research (based on family, twin, and adoptee studies) concluded that genes account for at least half of the variance in sexual orientation, researchers have yet to discover the existence of a gene or genes for heterosexuality, homosexuality, or bisexuality. As Peele and DeGrandpre (1995: 51) noted, "the search for single genes for complex human traits, like sexual orientation … is seriously misguided." Any attempts to isolate a biological basis for human sexuality cannot account for the tremendous variation in sexual behaviour across the cultures of the world, both currently and historically, nor even for changes in sexual behaviour within the same individual over her or his lifetime. In fact, Canadian and American researchers seeking a biological basis for homosexuality have selected only subjects who self-identity as lifelong homosexuals, ignoring the vast array of potential subjects who have had bisexual experiences (Fausto-Sterling, 2000: 10). It appears that "sexual behaviour is shaped by our social surroundings. We behave the way we do, we even desire what we do, under the strong influence of the particular social groups we belong to" (Michael et al., 1994: 16).

Whatever the findings of empirical research on the etiology of sexuality, it is clear that heterosexuality, homosexuality, and bisexuality are differentially evaluated in our culture (Cameron, 2005; Kitzinger, 2005; Land and Kitzinger, 2005). As Wittig (1992) observed, whether or not homosexuality is regarded as a "sexual preference" or a "sexual orientation," heterosexuality is regarded as both "natural" and "normal" (see Box 1.1).

THE POWER OF GENDER

Gender stereotypes—widely held beliefs about the defining characteristics of masculinity and femininity—exert a very powerful influence upon our expectations, perceptions, and evaluations of ourselves and others (Biernat and Kobrynowicz, 1999). These "lenses of

BOX 1.1

The Heterosexual Questionnaire

The following, which inverts questions that are routinely asked of homosexuals, provides a wry and telling commentary on the pervasiveness of heterosexism in our society.

1. What do you think caused your heterosexuality?

2. When and how did you decide you were a heterosexual?

3. Is it possible that your heterosexuality is just a phase you may grow out of?

4. Is it possible that your heterosexuality stems from a neurotic fear of others of the same sex?

5. If you have never slept with a person of the same sex, is it possible that all you need is a good gay lover?

6. Do your parents know that you are straight? Do your friends and/or roommate(s) know? How did they react?

7. Why do you insist on flaunting your heterosexuality? Can't you just be who you are and keep it quiet?

8. Why do heterosexuals place so much emphasis on sex?

9. Why do heterosexuals feel compelled to seduce others into their lifestyles?

10. A disproportionate majority of child molesters are heterosexual. Do you consider it safe to expose children to heterosexual teachers?

11. Just what do men and women do in bed together? How can they truly know how to please each other, being so anatomically different?

12. With all the societal support marriage receives, the divorce rate is spiralling. Why are there so few stable relationships among heterosexuals?

13. Statistics show that lesbians have the lowest incidence of sexually transmitted diseases. Is it really safe for a woman to maintain a heterosexual lifestyle and run the risk of disease and pregnancy?

14. How can you become a whole person if you limit yourself to compulsive, exclusive heterosexuality?

15. Considering the menace of overpopulation, how could the human race survive if everyone were heterosexual?

16. Could you trust a heterosexual therapist to be objective? Don't you feel s/he might be inclined to influence you in the direction of his/her own leanings?

17. There seem to be very few happy heterosexuals. Techniques have been developed that might enable you to change if you really want to. Have you considered trying aversion therapy?

18. Would you want your child to be heterosexual, knowing the problems that s/he would face?

Source: Rochelin, 1982.

gender" (Bem, 1994) are both descriptive (suggesting what group members are like) and prescriptive (specifying what group members ought to be like) (Glick and Fiske, 1999).

Gender Stereotypes

Ashmore and Del Boca (1979: 222) defined gender stereotypes as "the structured set of beliefs about the personal attributes of women and men." These beliefs focus upon such things as personality traits, attitudes and beliefs, overt behaviour and behavioural preferences, and physical appearance (Eckes, 1994). Empirical research on what are variously referred to as "gender stereotypes," "sex stereotypes," or "sex-role stereotypes" has developed rapidly since the early 1960s (Deaux, 1999: 19; Desert and Leyens, 2006). While several methodologies have been used for gaining access to the content of gender stereotypes, there is much consistency in the sampling techniques. The vast majority of studies are based on **convenience samples** of university and college students. While the use of such samples facilitates the comparison of findings across studies, it does raise questions about their generalizeability.

The three major methodologies used to learn respondents' stereotypes are open-ended questions, rating scales, and adjective checklists. **Open-ended questions** ask subjects to describe, in their own words, the qualities which they feel characterize women and men in general. **Rating scales** typically present a list of personality attributes and ask respondents to indicate (using a five- or seven-point scale ranging from "very much" to "very little") the extent to which they believe each quality is characteristic of each sex. Both of these methods are often used as a preliminary step towards the creation of a more structured adjective list. The **adjective checklist** asks respondents to indicate whether each adjective is more frequently associated with women, men, or neither (i.e., is neutral).

Several such checklists are available and share certain advantages and drawbacks. The greatest advantage of using a single checklist is that it allows comparison of results across studies; the greatest drawback is that such a list limits the respondent's focus to a set of pre-defined qualities. A checklist may contain adjectives that would not spontaneously occur to a respondent as characteristic attributes of gender. While a respondent has the option of indicating "don't know" beside such words, the checklist may simply promote the creation of a more elaborate stereotype in the respondent's mind. Checklists may also omit characteristics that respondents *do* associate with men or women, denying the researcher access to the full content of the gender stereotypes.

Nevertheless, checklists remain the most commonly used method (Six and Eckes, 1991: 59; Auster and Ohm, 2000). Williams and Bennett (1975) administered the 300-item Gough and Heilbrun Adjective Check List (ACL) to 50 male and 50 female psychology students at a private American university. Those adjectives that 75 percent of each set of subjects agreed were characteristic either of men or of women were defined by the researchers as "focused sex stereotypes." Examples of focused sex stereotypes of women are *dependent, dreamy, emotional, excitable, fickle, gentle, sentimental,* and *weak*; stereotypes of men include *adventurous, aggressive, ambitious, boastful, confident, logical, loud, rational,* and *tough*. These results are consistent with the findings of studies conducted from the early 1970s through the late 1990s in Canada, Britain, and the United States (Glick and Fiske, 1999; Lueptow et al., 2001; Spence and Buckner, 1998).

Between 1975 and 1980, Best and Williams (1998) administered the same checklist to equal numbers of male and female students in 30 countries, including Canada. They discovered a high level of similarity among the gender stereotypes of most countries, with the Canadian results strongly paralleling those obtained for the United States. They reported that "in all countries, the male stereotyped items were more active and stronger, whereas the female stereotyped items were more passive and weaker" (Best and Williams, 1998: 109). While the male stereotype is more favourable in certain countries (e.g., Japan, South Africa, Nigeria) and the female stereotype in others (e.g., Italy, Peru, Australia), the relative favourability of the two stereotypes varies from country to country. Further analysis of this data indicated that the pan-cultural male stereotype was rated higher than the pan-cultural female stereotype on extroversion, conscientiousness, emotional stability, and openness to experience, while the pan-cultural female stereotype was rated higher on agreeableness (Williams et al., 1999).

DeLisi and Soundranayagam (1990) devised a method allowing respondents to indicate the degree to which various traits represent "typical" men and women. Findings suggested that the "core" traits for women reside on a niceness/nurturance axis; for men, on a potency/power axis. It was noted that adjectives selected as core traits of one gender were identified as peripheral traits of the other; this seemed to suggest an overlapping of traits between men and women. However, while female respondents augmented the feminine "core" of niceness/nurturance with a second group of adjectives that appeared on the list of male "core" traits (including *competent, dependable, intelligent, responsible, capable*), male respondents did not. Rather, males augmented their lists of female "core" qualities with such adjectives as *attractive, good-looking, sexy*, and *soft* (in Lips, 2001: 7). This study reminds us that not only are some gender-stereotyped qualities considered more important than others, but the meanings of attributed qualities are to be found within larger and different clusters of descriptive terms. Stereotypes of femininity include such positive qualities as helpfulness, kindness, and gentleness—communal or relationship-oriented personality characteristics.

In general, women have been stereotyped as highly likeable but not particularly competent, while men have been stereotyped as ambitious and analytical but insensitive to others (Best, 2001; Lueptow et al., 2001; Prentice and Carranza, 2002). It is important to note that men tend to be described with *agentic* adjectives (i.e., those having to do with "agency" or individual power and control over achievement and success), such as *adventurous* and *assertive*. Consider here that researchers have shown that high-status people are generally judged to be more agentic or self-oriented than low-status people, and that low-status people are generally judged to be more *communal* or relationship-oriented (Pomerantz et al., 2001; Wade and Brewer, 2006). These findings for high- and low-status people parallel the stereotypical characterizations of men and women.

The studies referred to above typically did not ask respondents to report on the beliefs they themselves held about women and men, but on the beliefs they thought others held. Nor did they ask respondents whether they felt that the same stereotyped qualities applied to themselves. However, we do know from other research that when it comes to self-descriptions, "gender stereotypes do not always 'copy' directly onto the self concepts of young women and young men; often times one finds only a 'weak echo' of the stereotypes in the self concepts" (Williams et al., 1999: 524; see also Guimond et al., 2007; McCreary and Rhodes, 2001).

In cross-cultural research, Best and Williams (1998) obtained both "actual" and "ideal" self-descriptions from young men and women in 14 countries. Respondents were presented with the 300 items of the ACL (or its translated equivalent). They were first asked to describe themselves realistically by "selecting adjectives which you consider to be descriptive of yourself as you really are, not as you would like to be." They were then asked to describe their ideal selves by "selecting adjectives that you consider to be descriptive of the person you would like to be, not the person you really are." A mean M percent (masculinity) score was computed for the items that respondents selected as being descriptive of actual self and of ideal self; high M percent scores were indicative of relatively masculine self-concepts, and lower mean M percent scores were indicative of relatively feminine self-concepts (it should be noted that this procedure implies that masculinity and femininity can be represented on a single continuum).

It was found that for both actual and ideal self-concepts, mean M percent scores for both men and women were highest in Italy and lowest in Canada. However, "there were no countries in which the self and ideal self concepts were extremely masculine or extremely feminine" (Best and Williams, 1998: 113). While men's self-concepts were generally more masculine than women's self-concepts, the ideal self for both groups was relatively more masculine than the actual self. "It appears, therefore, that there is a general tendency for both men and women to wish to be more 'masculine' than they are."

The effects of gender stereotypes are significant. Gender stereotypes affect our judgments of individuals in *assimilative* fashion (i.e., by the fitting of data to concepts), disposing us to use *heuristics*—simple formulae that serve as mental shortcuts—in thinking about them. Thus, when we encounter individual men and women, we strive to fit our perceptions of them to our stereotypes (Strub et al., 2006; Torres et al., 2002). For example, Nelson et al. (1990) reported that participants viewing photos of female and male targets consistently judged male targets to be taller—even when the targets were actually matched for height, the participants were informed of this fact, and the participants were offered a cash reward for accuracy! When asked to estimate the personal incomes of 40 men and women based only on head-and-shoulder photographs, participants judged the incomes of male targets to be significantly higher than those of female targets.

In a study on gender stereotypes and competence (Biernat and Kobrynowicz, 1997), participants were asked to evaluate the resumé of a fictitious individual, "Katherine Anderson" or "Kenneth Anderson," for a position as "executive chief of staff" in one version or as "executive secretary" in the other. In actuality, the job descriptions provided to participants were identical, differing only in title. However, when the words "chief of staff" were used, the job was perceived to be more masculine, higher in status, and more likely to merit a higher salary than when the job title was "secretary." Not surprisingly, Kenneth was judged better qualified than Katherine for the chief-of-staff position, and Katherine judged better qualified than Kenneth for the position of executive secretary—despite the fact that the résumés were identical, differing only in the presumed sex of the applicant.

In another study (Biernat and Manis, 1994), participants were asked to read an excerpt of a magazine article, variously attributed to "Joan T. McKay" or "John T. McKay," on a topic area that was judged to be masculine (i.e., bass fishing), feminine (i.e., trends in eye makeup) or neutral (i.e., the mind–body problem). When asked to evaluate the quality, monetary worth, and interest level of the article, gender stereotyping was obvious: participants judged "feminine" articles to be better written when the putative author was "Joan," while "masculine" articles were deemed better written when allegedly authored by John (neutral articles were judged to be equivalently well written, regardless of the author's sex). Participants also judged the monetary worth of an article to be greater when the sex of the author "matched" the article (in other words, John was judged to deserve higher payment than Joan for the same article on bass fishing) (see also Burgess and Borgida, 1999; Foschi, 2000; Steinpreis et al., 1999).

Stereotypes do not merely cramp and distort our perceptions of others, but may constrain others to conform to our expectations (Huston-Comeaux and Kelly, 2002; Madon et al., 2001). By setting in motion a **self-fulfilling prophecy** (Merton, 1968: 475–480), stereotypes ultimately deny individuality. A famous theorem of W.I. Thomas (1928) can help us to understand the self-fulfilling prophecy effect: "If men [sic] define situations as real, they are real in their consequences"; in other words, if people believe something to be real and true, regardless of whether this is objectively the case, they will act upon their belief in such a way as to produce real consequences. Thus, if people believe that men and women possess different gender-specific qualities, they will expect and even pressure them to demonstrate those qualities. To the extent that individuals conform to these expectations, their behaviour will be used as evidence to justify and reinforce gender stereotypes. Thus, the prophecy (the belief that genders are different) itself leads to behaviours that fulfill and perpetuate it (see, for example, Burr, 2002; Madon et al., 2001; Vogel et al., 2003).

Stereotypes prescribe and limit gender behaviour; women and men receive approval for acting in gender-appropriate ways (Prentice and Carranza, 2002; Rudman and Glick, 1999). Departures from stereotypical expectations are judged deviant and labelled as either unmasculine ("effeminate") or unfeminine ("masculine"). Haddock and Zanna (1994) reported that while men negatively stereotyped feminists as aggressive "man haters," they expressed warm and positive feelings towards housewives. Similarly, Glick et al. (1997) found that while homemakers were viewed as interpersonally pleasant (e.g., "warm") but less competent than men, career women were viewed as competent but aggressive, selfish, cold, and "unfeminine." Non-traditional women—career women, feminists, athletes, lesbians—were seen as competent but not likeable (see also Fiske, 1998; Malcolmson and Sinclair, 2007).

These negative judgments operate to force modification of the deviant behaviour and to reinforce the stereotyped standards. Research suggests that, regardless of whether the "ideal" of femininity/masculinity that is contained in the stereotype is accepted or rejected, its contents may command considerable thought and emotion (Krane et al., 2004; Rubin et al., 2004). Cole and Zucker (2007: 1) observed that "even feminists have difficulty renouncing these ideals because women gain power and status through accommodation to them" (see also Black, 2004; Douglas and Michaels, 2004).

Gender stereotypes are complex; as Lips (2001: 10) observed, "[n]ot only do they seem to be made up of different components, they also seem to be organized in terms of specific *type*s of men and women." When Carpenter and Trentham (2001) asked 230 undergraduates to list as many "types" of women and men as they could in two minutes, the students produced 638 subtype terms. Subtypes of women listed by these students included career woman, housewife, athlete, Valley Girl, cheerleader, loose woman, beauty-pageant winner, doormat, and prostitute; subtypes of men included macho man, skirt chaser, businessman, athlete, male chauvinist, womanizer, weight lifter, stuck-up guy, and family man. Vonk and Ashmore (2003) reported that their sample of respondents generated 306 different labels for female types (e.g., femme fatale, secretary, slob) and 310 for male types (e.g., sissy, labourer, workaholic); they found that the most important dimensions of these gender subtypes were young–old, masculine–feminine, and traditional–modern. Other researchers have found that respondents can easily list various "types" of men and women and describe them in some detail (Six and Eckes, 1991; DeWall et al., 2005).

Variations in Gender Stereotypes

Adrienne Shadd, a black woman who grew up in Ontario, has reflected upon the stereotypical and derogatory images she was exposed to during her childhood. She remarked, "I used to wonder if it could really be true that black people the world over were so poor, downtrodden, inarticulate, and intellectually inferior, as the depictions seemed to suggest" (in Schaefer et al., 1996: 196). For Yee (1993: 15), who immigrated to Toronto from Hong Kong at age 2, the Western stereotype of Asian women as "both passive/submissive 'china dolls' and 'dragon ladies' who use their 'exotic' sexuality to manipulate" did not even hint at the strength of Asian women, "the carriers of incredible burdens of family and work, and age-old traditions."

Researchers studying gender stereotypes often ask their respondents to mentally construct a "typical" man or woman and identify the traits that are thought to characterize them. This universal man or woman, according to Lips (1993: 14) is "someone who is relatively young, white, able-bodied, neither too fat nor too thin, neither too short nor too tall, and of average physical attractiveness" (see also Collins, 2004). However, as Razack (1993: 39–40) argued,

> if you isolate gender from race and class (among other things) … you will miss some very important insights into how gender is constructed in specific contexts…. [O]ne can afford to have no clear sense of one's racial or class identity only when those identities never pose a problem, that is to say when one lives close to centre. White, middle-class, heterosexual, non-disabled women can be "simply women," in the same way that white, middle-class, heterosexual, non-disabled men can be simply "human beings."

Inasmuch as "gender is clearly not one identity but a set of relations" (Razack, 1993: 47), it becomes essential to explore the **double** or **multiple jeopardies** created when stereotypes about men and women are enmeshed with stereotypes of race, social class, disability, sexual orientation, age, and attractiveness (Hegarty and Pratto, 2004; Hogan, 2003; McLean, 2003; Wilcox et al., 2006).

Stereotypes must be recognized as consequential, especially for people whose subordinate status is twice-or-more defined. The 1971 murder of a 19-year-old Cree high-school student, Helen Betty Osborne, is an extreme but telling illustration of the double jeopardy faced by Aboriginal women in Canada (Priest, 1990). Abducted by four young white men from the main street of The Pas, Manitoba, in a practice known as "squaw-hopping," Osborne was stabbed over 50 times with a screwdriver when she resisted being raped, and left to bleed to death. For more than 16 years, no charges were laid, although "it was felt that perhaps the majority of people in the town knew about the youths' involvement in the murder" (Griffiths and Yerbury, 1995: 394). Elliott and Fleras (1992: 117) observed that "[i]n the community at the time of the crime, it was an acknowledged practice for white men to harass and sexually assault native women. By applying this derogatory label [squaw-hopping] to the behaviour, the men distanced themselves from its immoral and criminal nature. In effect, they were not with women but with 'squaws.'"

More recently, Goulding (2001) has stated that when Aboriginal women go missing or are discovered to have been murdered, negative stereotypes based on their race, gender, and social class combine and increase the likelihood of an apathetic response from both law enforcement agencies and the Canadian mainstream media. He observed that, in stark contrast to the media frenzy that attended the trial of Paul Bernardo, little media fanfare accompanied the trial of John Martin Crawford, one of this nation's "most prolific serial killers," who murdered his native women victims "in the most horrible fashion imaginable, at times raping, stabbing, strangling, and dismembering them" (Goulding, 2001: 210). However, Crawford's victims were stereotyped as "easy squaws" (Acoose, 1995) and portrayed as participants in a "sleazy downtown street lifestyle"; in the end, each woman was dismissed as "just another dead Indian" (Goulding, 2001).

To test whether stereotypes might be implicitly racist and based upon the construct of an ideal—a typical white, middle-class man/woman—Landrine (1999) asked her sample of 46 undergraduate students to describe, drawing upon a list of 23 adjectives, four "types" of women—black middle-class, white middle-class, black lower-class, and white lower-class. She reported that while all four subtypes were described with stereotypically "feminine" adjectives, white middle-class women were most likely to be so defined; for example, white women were more likely than black women to be described as *dependent*, *emotional*, *status-conscious*, and *passive and concerned*. Since cues provided by physical appearance influence our predictions of a person's traits, occupation, or role behaviours (Sczesny et al., 2006), we might also expect stereotypes of race to modify stereotypes of gender. Physical appearance is undoubtedly a critical aspect of stereotyping; "blond jokes," for example, convey the stereotype that blond women are sexually attractive, eager, but not very bright (Hinz, 2003). Moreover, if our referent for "femininity" is the white middle-class woman, then women of colour, women with disabilities, or women of lower socio-economic status will likely be seen as flawed, inadequate, or less than truly "feminine." As Wolf (1991: 264) observed, in our society, non-white "racial" features have been portrayed as "deformities" to be cosmetically altered in order to achieve the prototypically white ideal of feminine beauty (see also Hall, 2004; Cole and Zucker, 2007; Sekayi, 2003; Thomas et al., 2004).

Research has noted that there is more similarity between the stereotypes about the expressiveness and competence of black American females and males than there is between the stereotypes of white American females and males (Green, 1994; Thomas and Miles, 1995). Black men are more likely than white men to be described as emotionally expressive and less likely to be viewed as competitive, independent, or status-conscious (Niemann et al., 1994; Popp et al., 2003). While less research has been conducted on the gender stereotypes of other racial or ethnic groups, the stereotypes of the "JAP" or "Jewish American Princess" (Beck, 1992), the "ultrafeminine" South Asian woman (Darling-Wolf, 2004; Okazaki, 2002), and the "macho" Hispanic man (Durik et al., 2006) are, unfortunately, all too well known.

Gender stereotypes may, as already suggested, be influenced by variables other than race. Baldus and Tribe (1995) observed that by the time Canadian schoolchildren reach grade 6, the majority have "learned to recognize and classify people and their environment in a context of social inequality." They acquire negative attitudes towards poor people, expecting them to be disagreeable, unlovely, and unlovable (Madon et al., 1998). Lips (2005: 31) reported that lower-class women were more likely than middle-class women to be viewed as "confused, dirty, hostile, illogical, impulsive, incoherent, inconsiderate, irresponsible, and superstitious." Working-class males have been stereotyped as chauvinistic, inarticulate "exemplars of old-fashioned, defiant, aggressive masculinity" (Lips, 2005: 31). These negative stereotypes may influence our beliefs about why the poor are poor, and may result in unwillingness to support progressive welfare policies (Lott, 2002; Scarbrough, 2001). Cozzarelli et al. (2002) examined the views of 206 middle-class undergraduates about the poor, comparing their views of poor people of different sexes. They reported that stereotypes of poor women were both more positive and more consistent with gender stereotypes than were stereotypes of poor men; attitudes towards poor women were significantly more positive as well. Although participants were more likely to attribute the poverty of both men and women to internal rather than external/cultural factors, the content of these attributions differed. All attributions about poor men included references to unwillingness to work. Poor men were held responsible for lack of initiative and self-improvement; poor women were held responsible for non-traditional familial and reproductive patterns.

Snyder and Uranowitz (in Snyder, 2001) examined whether a female's sexual orientation might influence students to construct her in stereotypical terms. In their study, student participants read the biography of a fictitious woman named "Betty K." The researchers had carefully devised her life story to accommodate the stereotyped images of both heterosexual and lesbian women. Thus, Betty had never had a steady boyfriend in high school, but did date, and while she acquired a steady boyfriend in college, it was emphasized that he was more a "close friend" than anything else. A week after distributing this biography to their respondents, Snyder and Uranowitz provided an additional detail: Some students were informed that Betty was involved in a lesbian relationship; others, that she was living with her husband. They then asked students a series of questions about Betty's life. Students' responses revealed that they had retrospectively appropriated the "facts" of Betty's life to "fit" with her new identification as lesbian or heterosexual. Students presented with the lesbian Betty selectively recalled that she had never had a boyfriend in high school, tending to forget that she had dated boys in high school and university. One student pointed to Betty's lack of a steady boyfriend as clear evidence of her sexual disinterest in men; in his mind, Betty had always harboured lesbian tendencies. The heterosexual, married Betty, on the other hand, was seen as just having been choosy in her dating habits. The historical "facts" of the fictitious case were thus reassembled and interpreted to be congruent with what had become Betty's most salient feature: her sexual orientation (see also Miller and Malloy, 2003; Smyth et al., 2003).

Prominent stereotypes of lesbians include that they are masculine and try to seduce heterosexual women (Lancaster, 2003); also, that they are less attractive, more insecure, less loving, less emotional, less stable, and less mentally healthy than heterosexual women (Viss and Burn, 1992; Geiger et al., 2006). Prominent stereotypes of gay men include that they are promiscuous, emotionally unstable, sexually predatory, and "feminine" (Boysen et al., 2006; Fingerhut and Pelau, 2006). In a study investigating whether anti-homosexual prejudice was related to homosexuals' failure to behave in specific "gender-appropriate" ways, respondents were presented with vignettes in which a homosexual target was presented as either "gay-acting" or "straight-acting." It was found that although gender-role characteristics were an important factor in negative attitudes towards both gays and lesbians, "the most important predictor of homophobia is the mere fact that an individual is known to be homosexual" (Schope and Eliason, 2004).

The early research of Storms et al. (1981) revealed the subtle ways in which stereotypes may operate (see also Newman, 2007). In their study, subjects were given written and tape-recorded descriptions of women of two "types": "feminine" (described as emotional, warm towards others, kind, and feminine) and "masculine" (self-important, active, competent, and masculine). Even when the descriptions were identical in every detail, respondents rated the woman identified as lesbian as more "masculine" than the heterosexual woman. What is more, the woman who was described as both feminine *and* lesbian was perceived as having a confused, unstable sexual identity. This study would suggest that even when lesbians do not exhibit stereotypical "masculine" attributes and in fact conform to the prototype of heterosexual femininity, their behaviour is pathologized. It also implies that sexual orientation may override gender in the construction of stereotypes (see also Ewing et al., 2003). The relative importance of gender, as compared to other attributes, in the construction of stereotypes has yet to be fully explored.

CONSTRAINTS AND LIMITATIONS OF GENDER UPON SEX

The power of gender stereotypes is illuminated most dramatically in the phenomena of sex (re)assignment and transsexualism, where gender expectations and beliefs ultimately shape biological sex. For various reasons, infants and children may involuntarily undergo changes to their biological sex. Some persons (usually adults) choose of their own volition to alter their biological sex and may seek medical intervention to accomplish this. All such transformations of biological sex are generically referred to as **sex (re)assignment**. However, the tendency within the literature is to treat voluntary sex (re)assignment separately, describing it using the term **transsexualism**. Regardless of the degree of choice involved, both situations reveal the power of gender beliefs to condition and constrain options and outcomes.

Sex (Re)assignment

Two different conditions occasion sex (re)assignment. Infants born with ambiguous (not clearly male or female) genital configurations (estimated to occur in 2 to 3 percent of all births [Abu-Laban et al., 1994: 231]) are assigned to one sex or the other, based upon the decisions of an attending medical team. These decisions usually result in surgical alteration of the child's genitals. In the very rare second instance, an infant or child initially assigned to one sex must, due to accident or other circumstances, be (re)assigned to the other sex. Once again, further alterations to their biological sex are required.

The biological condition of children born with ambiguous genitalia has been traditionally referred to as **hermaphroditism** or, more recently, **intersex** (Kessler, 1990/1995; Diamond, 1998). True hermaphroditism, or a true intersexed condition, is statistically very rare and occurs when an infant is born with both ovarian and testicular tissues and a genital structure that is unclear upon simple observation by the attending medical team. What is observable looks like either a diminutive penis (sometimes referred to as a *micropenis*) or an enlarged clitoris. The urethral opening is often found somewhere along the shaft of the penis/clitoris. In addition, either the scrotum has not fully closed or the vagina has not fully opened. The more frequently occurring cases, involving ambiguous genitalia along with the presence of either two ovaries or two testes, are referred to as female or male **pseudo-hermaphroditism**.

Being born with ambiguous genitalia is, in itself, rarely harmful to a person's physical health. As noted earlier with regard to *nadleeh*, some societies have accepted persons with ambiguous genitalia as integral members of their communities. In our own society, persons born with ambiguous genitalia are deemed to have an abnormal and problematic condition that calls for medical "correction." Apart from the biological factors, it is "ultimately…cultural understandings of gender" which influence physicians in determining, assigning, and announcing an infant's sex (Kessler, 1990/1995: 8). The most important of these is the belief that only two genders and two biological sexes exist and should be allowed to exist; "physicians hold an incorrigible belief in and insistence upon female and male as the only 'natural' options" (Kessler, 1990/1995: 8).

Contemporary attitudes towards the intersexed condition have been shaped by three developments (Kessler, 1990/1995: 9). First, advances in medical technologies and pharmaceuticals have made possible the extensive alteration of genitalia, reproductive systems, and hormonal balances. Second, the feminist movement has succeeded in challenging traditional gender beliefs according to which the definition of "woman" rested upon reproductive capability; thus, the presence of ovaries is no longer the determining factor in how an intersexed condition will be resolved. Third, social psychological theories (see Chapter 2) stress the importance of a child's gender identity for subsequent gender behaviour. These theories assert that gender identity develops in some form between approximately 18 months and 3 years of age. Since it is assumed that gender identity is based partly upon genital configuration, these theories exert pressure upon attending physicians to establish unambiguous genitalia as soon as possible after birth in order to ensure the child's development of a "healthy" gender identity. As well, physicians assume that parents need and want their child to have an obvious genital configuration.

Guided overwhelmingly by the pioneering work of Money and Ehrhardt (1972), medical decisions are made as quickly as possible after an infant's birth. If the decision is made to assign an infant to the male sex, penis repair is undertaken within the first year; if to the female, vulva repair, including surgical reduction of the clitoris, is begun within three months after birth. Further surgery, if necessary, is performed during early childhood, followed by hormone therapy, particularly around puberty (and in some cases for life). Parents are counselled on what has happened and will happen. Eventually, the children or adolescents themselves are counselled and receive either a full or partial explanation of what has already occurred and will eventually occur (Kessler, 1990/1995: 10–11, 15–17).

What are the medical decisions based upon? While tests are frequently conducted to determine the infant's chromosomal sex, these results do not appear to play a decisive role in the ultimate genital sex assignment. Rather, the *size and functionality* of the real or potential penis appears to be the deciding factor now. Specifically, "[o]ver time the limits to what constituted a large clitoris came arbitrarily to be set as one greater than 0.9 cm and a small penis sufficient to warrant surgery was one smaller than 2.5 cm" (Diamond, 1998: 3).

> Money's case management philosophy assumes that while it may be difficult for an adult male to have a much smaller than average penis, it is very detrimental to the morale of the young boy to have a micropenis. In the former case the male's manliness might be at stake, but in the latter case his essential maleness might be. Although the psychological consequences of these experiences

> have not been empirically documented, Money and his colleagues suggest that it is wise to avoid the problems of both the micropenis in childhood and the still undersized penis postpuberty by reassigning many of these infants to the female gender.... This approach suggests that for Money and his colleagues, chromosomes are less relevant in determining gender than ... the aesthetic of having an appropriately sized penis. (Kessler, 1990/1995: 13)

Existing gender stereotypes about the importance of penis size for masculine identity and behaviour clearly form an important part of the medical decision-making process.

The criterion for sex assignment has shifted from "ovaries equals female" to "penis (large) equals male." Should there be insufficient genital tissue for creation of a sufficiently large penis, the infant will be surgically transformed into a genital female, even though "[t]here is a striking lack of attention to the size and shape requirements... other than that the vagina be able to receive a penis" (Kessler, 1990/1995: 19). Kessler (1990/1995: 16) noted that doctors claim to "reconstruct," not construct, the genitals of intersexed infants. They perceive themselves as acting objectively and only modifying genitals to conform more accurately to what was already there. In this way, they maintain the illusion that subjective beliefs about gender do not play a role in their decision-making processes. Yet the assumption that surgical intervention is necessary reflects cultural beliefs about the dichotomous nature of sex. Ambiguous genitals are perceived to be unnatural, and surgical alteration is performed to create genitals that conform to a "natural," either/or male-or-female state, thereby removing challenges to the belief system and reinforcing the dichotomous conception of sex.

Mackie (1987: 22–23) noted the importance of gender beliefs in the 1984 case of doctors at a Toronto hospital who had to decide the consequences of surgically separating genetically male conjoined twins who shared a common penis. In this case, the more aggressive and physically active twin was "awarded" the penis, while the other was surgically fitted with an artificial vagina and raised as a female. Both decisions reflect dominant beliefs about gender. Masculinity is associated with activity, aggression, and possession of a penis; femininity, ultimately, is associated with the lack of a penis.

A case initially reported by Money and his associates (Money and Tucker, 1975: 91–92; Money and Ehrhardt, 1972) is now famous. In 1967, what was supposed to be a routine circumcision of an eight-month-old male twin at the St. Boniface Hospital in Winnipeg, Manitoba, turned horrific. Whether because of mechanical malfunction, physician error, or some combination of the two, the electric cauterizing machine almost completely burned off the boy's penis. The damage was so severe that existing medical technology was not capable of constructing a penis from the remaining tissue. After consultation with various physicians and with John Money, the parents agreed to have the boy's sex reassigned. Surgical castration was performed when the twin was 22 months of age (Colapinto, 2000). The child's hairstyle and clothing styles were feminized and "Bruce" was given a new, "feminine" name, "Brenda." Hormone therapy was initiated, but further "feminizing" surgery, although planned, was not implemented. The parents were told not to inform their child of his ambiguous sexual status and to treat him as a girl and rear him accordingly. This strategy, they were assured, would lead to the child's establishment of a self-identity consistent with the assigned sex.

Early reports of the child's progress (Money and Ehrhardt, 1972) seemed to give evidence of the primacy of nurture (i.e., environment) over nature (i.e., biology) in the making of boys and girls. In contrast to her biologically identical brother, Brenda, her mother reported, disdained "cars and gas pumps and tools" and was fascinated by "dolls, a doll house and a doll carriage." At the age of $4^{1}/_{2}$, Brenda preferred and took pleasure in her feminine clothing, helped with household chores (while her brother did not), and was neat and tidy. "[S]he is so feminine. I've never seen a little girl so neat and tidy... and yet my son is quite different. I can't wash his face for anything.... She is very proud of herself, when she puts on a new dress, or I set her hair" (Money and Ehrhardt, 1972: 11). These stereotypical preferences and activities were all taken as indicators of successful adaptation to a feminine gender and of the power of gender to override biological sex.

The "twins case" generated worldwide attention, and textbooks in both medicine and the social sciences were rewritten to incorporate Money's reports of the child's progress. For example, in the third edition of his popular introductory textbook, *Sociology*, Ian Robertson (1987: 516) confidently asserted that Money's work proved that "children can *easily* be raised as a member of the opposite sex" (emphasis added). Marlene Mackie's *Gender Relations in Canada: Further Explorations* (1991: 69) also reported that "[t]his oft-cited case... suggests that social assignment outweighs biology in determining gender identity and behaviour."

However, later reports on the reassigned twin began to cast doubt on the transformation's success (Diamond and Sigmundson, 1999). Although feminine in appearance, "by all accounts of family, teachers, guidance clinic workers and relatives, this illusion... disappeared the second Brenda moved, spoke, walked or gestured" (Colapinto, 2001: 57). Brenda insisted on urinating standing up, refused to undergo the further "feminizing" surgeries that had been planned for her, and, from age 7, daydreamed of her ideal future self "as a twenty-one year-old male with a mustache, a sports car, and surrounded by admiring friends" (Colapinto, 2001: 93). She suffered many difficulties, including academic failure and rejection and ridicule from her classmates, who dubbed her "Cavewoman" (Diamond,1982). At age 9, Brenda had a nervous breakdown; at age 14, in a state of acute depression, she attempted suicide (Colapinto, 2001: 96, 262).

At the age of 13, Brenda learned the details of her sex assignment from her father; at age 16, she decided to be reassigned once more and to live as a man rather than a woman. Advancements in medical technology made it possible to construct an artificial penis for the twin, who adopted the name David. Reportedly, at the beginning of the long, slow, and only partly successful process of phalloplasty to construct a penis using skin grafts, David "got himself a van with a bar in it," and, as Dr. Milton Diamond cheerily put it to the *New York Times*, "He wanted to lasso some ladies" (Lancaster, 2003: 294). At age 25, David married a woman and adopted her three children (Gorman, 1997). In 2000, he allowed a journalist to write his biography and reveal his true identity in an attempt to set the published record straight—"a public record which expressly denied the extraordinary torments he had undergone and which, to David's everlasting horror, had led to similar anguish for untold numbers of children" (Colapinto, 2001: 282). David observed, "I don't have the kind of education that these scientists and doctors and psychologists have, but to me it's very ignorant. If a woman lost her breasts, do you turn her into a guy? To make her feel "whole and complete"?... [Y]ou can't be something that you're not. You have to be *you*" (in Colapinto, 2001: 264–265; emphasis in original). This story does not have a happy ending. In 2004, depressed over the suicide of his twin brother and experiencing financial difficulties, David himself committed suicide (Smith, 2004).

Some, including members of David's family, maintain that this tragic example of sex reassignment was doomed from the outset (Colapinto, 2001: xvii). Recalling his brother's conflicted childhood, David's identical twin remarked, "I recognized Brenda as my sister, but she never, ever acted the part. When I say there was nothing feminine about Brenda … I mean there was *nothing* feminine. She walked like a guy. Sat with her legs apart. She talked about guy things, didn't give a crap about cleaning house, getting married, wearing makeup. We both wanted to play with guys, build forts and have snowball fights and play army" (Colapinto, 2001: 57; emphasis in original). The sad history of Bruce/Brenda/David continues to fire debate about the relative importance of nature and nurture. Brym and Lie (2003: 245) suggested that by the time the surgery was performed to transform Bruce into Brenda, the child might already have developed a male gender identity, having been raised as a boy by his parents and treated as a boy by his brother during the first 17 months of his life. Some scientists and physicians still continue to insist that if gender reassignment occurs before the age of 18 months, it can be "successful" (Creighton and Mihto, 2001; Lightfoot-Klein et al., 2000).

However, the question remains: By what criteria should we judge the "success" or "failure" of such attempts? Recall that early pronouncements of "success" directed attention to the fact that "Brenda" exhibited stereotypically "feminine" behaviour and attitudes; the implicit suggestion was that a boy's preference for neatness over filth and his readiness to engage in housework should be taken as evidence of a "gender transformation" and "proof" of the primacy of nurture over nature. Later, evidence that David preferred stereotypically "masculine" behaviours and attitudes was pronounced "proof" of the primacy of nature over nurture—as if the desire to participate in snowball fights or build forts (rather than clean house) was genetically encoded in male DNA. Similarly, Lancaster (2003: 294) pointed out, "'Wanting to lasso some ladies,' of course, is the very definition of natural manhood, or rather, the subject's caricatured performance of heterosexual manhood circa the epoch of *Saturday Night Fever*." It would seem that, behind pronouncements of both success and failure, we witness the power of gender stereotypes to affect our understanding of the connection between gender and sex.

Transsexualism

Transsexuals are individuals with unambiguous genitalia who were assigned at birth to one biological sex and have been socialized in accordance with that assignment, yet choose to be surgically transformed to become as much a member of the other biological sex as possible. Both prior to and in tandem with the physical transformation, transsexuals also engage in a self-socialization process consistent with their desired sex status.

Transsexuals describe having always strongly felt their gender identity to be at odds with their sex assignment and socialization, a condition referred to in the clinical literature as **gender dysphoria**. In other words, they believe they are either a woman trapped in a man's body or a man trapped in a woman's body. Although, throughout history, individuals may have felt "trapped in the wrong body," it is only within the last 50 years that medical technology has provided a medical "solution" to such feelings of distress and unease (Michel et al., 2002; Wilson, 2002). In our gender-dichotomous society, it seems to make perfect sense that if one cannot change the mind to fit the body, one can alter the body to fit the mind (Raymond, 1982). The surgery and accompanying hormonal treatments are supposed to release the inner person and allow self-presentation in a consistent and integrated manner (Campo and Zorggroep, 2003; May, 2002).

> The transexual [sic] applicant has two dogmatic fixations. One is to forfeit those parts and functions of the body that are the somatic insignia of the sex of birth. The other is to simulate the other sex and to pass as a member of that sex, naked and clothed. (Money, 1988: 88)

The Gender Identity Clinic at the Centre for Addiction and Mental Health in Toronto is one of several clinics in Canada which can authorize sex-change operations (others are located in Vancouver and Montreal). Simple desire or financial ability (approximately half of the provinces in Canada cover sex-change operations under Medicare) are not in themselves sufficient to guarantee acceptance for surgery. Candidates must first undertake a "real-life test period" in a cross-gender role before they may receive hormone treatments; a further test period follows before a decision. Test-period length varies across clinics in Canada and the United States; the Gender Identity Clinic requires one year for the first test period and two years for the second (Barrett et al., 1999: 729). Applicants must also demonstrate to the satisfaction of a medical panel that they genuinely suffer from a preoperative condition of gender dysphoria. Medical personnel assume that, through psychological testing, they will be able to distinguish true gender dysphorics from false claimants, such as masochists (who desire the pain occasioned by major surgery) or others who might suffer sex-change delusions as a byproduct of a psychotic condition, such as schizophrenia (Griffiths, 2002; Habermeyer et al., 2003; Kersting et al., 2003). However, these tests may simply measure a would-be transsexual's willingness to abide by gender-role stereotypes.

The California Sex Role Inventory is one of many psychological tests that purport to measure masculinity and femininity. This test presents a series of statements with which the respondent is asked to express agreement or disagreement by answering "true" or "false." Agreement with such statements as "I am somewhat afraid of the dark," "I would find the work of a librarian enjoyable," and "I am afraid of snakes" is taken to indicate femininity; agreement with "I could do a better job than most of the politicians in office today" or "I want to be an important person in the community" is supposedly indicative of masculinity. Should a male-to-constructed-female candidate answer "true" to the questions assessing "femininity" and "false" to questions assessing "masculinity," his chances of qualifying as a gender dysphoric are heightened. It is ironic, considering their willingness to take such drastic measures to escape the constraints of their biological sex, that applicants whose answers demonstrate gender rigidity and reluctance to trespass on conventional boundaries of masculinity/femininity fare better on such tests than those whose answers indicate an acceptance of androgynous or undifferentiated gender.

Research suggests that, despite their ostensible nonconformity, transsexuals are reactionary individuals. A recent study asked 103 male-to-female (MF) transsexuals, 135 control males (CM), and 303 control females (CF) to complete a Sex Role Inventory. On a femininity scale, the scores of MFs actually exceeded not only those of CMs but also those of CFs. On a masculinity scale, MFs rate themselves at a level comparable to CFs and significantly lower than CMs (Herman-Jeglinska et al., 2002; see also Lippa, 2001; Michel et al., 2002). As a group, transsexuals tend to maintain highly conventional notions of gender-appropriate/inappropriate behaviour, and define being "trapped in the wrong body" in ways that reiterate stereotypical images of males and females. The following comments of a male-to-constructed-female transsexual (M-F TS) and a female-to-constructed-male (F-M TS) are illustrative:

> M-F TS: I used to like to play with girls. I never did like to play with boys. I wanted to play jacks. I wanted to jump rope and all those things. The lady in the schoolyard used to always tell me to

go play with the boys. I found it distasteful. I wanted to play with the girls. I wanted to play the girl games.… F-M TS: I have wanted to be a boy ever since I can remember, but there are no logical reasons for what I feel inside.… I used to like playing football. I didn't like being a girl and doing things girls do, and lately, it's gotten more so. I feel very awkward being dressed up and going places as a girl.… [My family] always considered me a tomboy. My mother used to always try to get me to play with dolls and everything, and I wouldn't do it. I played cowboys and Indians with the boys, climbed trees and rode horses, went hunting and fishing with my brothers. I was always out wrestling with the boys. (Green, 1992: 100–102)

During the qualifying period, candidates for transsexual surgery are required to experience themselves, hormonally and socially, as the desired other sex, manifesting comfort in behaviours deemed consistent with that gender. The "real-life test" is based on the premise that the most reversible forms of changing one's gender should precede the most irreversible (Green, 1992: 104). The test mandates, for example, that a candidate for male-to-constructed-female surgery demonstrate facility in adopting "female-appropriate" patterns of dress (including use of the "tuck," i.e., folding the penis back between the legs and eliminating any tell-tale bulge by wearing tight undergarments), deportment, employment, and possibly sexual role (assuming the "passive" position in sexual intercourse).

Hormonal treatments are the first of the medical interventions; these produce relatively consistent effects (Money, 1988: 57–58, 89–90). A female-to-male transsexual is treated with *testosterone*, which promotes the growth of facial and body hair, enlargement of the Adam's apple, lessening of subcutaneous body fat (making the body appear more angular), increase in muscle mass, some shrinkage of the breasts, some enlargement of the clitoris, and eventual dormancy of the ovaries and cessation of menstruation (so long as the dosage of testosterone is maintained, unless a hysterectomy and ovariectomy are performed later). If the hormonal treatments commence after puberty, as is almost always the case, no change will occur to the person's bone structure.

Male-to-female transsexuals are treated with *estrogen*, which promotes breast growth (within the limitations of available glandular tissue), decreases muscle mass, increases subcutaneous body fat (promoting a "softer" or more "rounded" appearance), retards but does not stop the growth of body and facial hair (complete eradication must be accomplished with electrolysis), and also causes shrinkage of the penis with subsequent loss of erectile capacity, shrinkage of the prostate and seminal vesicles (with subsequent loss of the ability to ejaculate), and shrinkage and dormancy of the testicles. Once again, if the treatment is initiated after puberty, bone structure will not change. In addition, voice register and tone will not be affected by post-pubertal hormonal treatments; this accounts for the tendency of male-to-female transsexuals to retain a lower-register voice. Any modulation of one's voice must be accomplished through self-conscious and willful effort (Borsel et al., 2001).

While the transsexual candidate learns to live with the effects of hormonal treatment, deciding if these bodily changes are comfortable and consistent with expectations, behavioural changes must continue. In essence, each transsexual must learn how to conceal the person who—biologically and via socialization—they once were; and how to reveal the person they wish to be acknowledged as. King (2003) suggests that this process can be termed a **gender migration**. He states that, like geographical migrants, gender migrants "often see themselves as beginning a new life; social membership and identity has to be reworked and negotiated, a new way of life has to be learned; the old one has to be left behind" (173). In both cases, the legitimacy of the migrant's settlement in the new country/gender may be challenged and application for full citizenship denied (see also Epstein, 2003; Ellis and Eriksen, 2002; Roen, 2002; Wren, 2002). Perhaps for this reason, transsexuals tend to "go overboard" in their portrayal of an other-gendered person in matters of clothing, cosmetics, and gestures (e.g., Bloom, 2002; Lawrence, 2003). In the process of exchanging one body for another, they appear to exchange one set of gender stereotypes for another. Indeed, they may effect a caricature of the other gender's behaviour, simultaneously reaffirming existing stereotypes.

If, at the end of the waiting period, the applicant still wishes to continue and the medical team at the sex (re)assignment clinic consent, the final, usually irrevocable, surgical step will be undertaken. Up to this point, changes instigated by hormones can be reversed with cessation of treatment and behavioural changes can be unlearned. Surgical changes, however, usually cannot be reversed. Male-to-female transformation is a relatively quick one- or two-stage process, while female-to-male involves a lengthier, multistage series of procedures (Money, 1988: 90–91). To surgically construct a female, the spongy tissue within the penis is removed and the remaining skin of the empty penis is turned outside in, "like the inverted finger of a glove" (Money, 1988: 90), to provide the lining for the new vaginal cavity. If, in the opinion of the surgeons, insufficient skin exists to create a satisfactory vagina, a skin graft from the thigh will be used to lengthen the cavity. The testicles will be removed and skin from the scrotum will be used to fashion the appearance of labia majora, although labia minora will not be created. Although "[s]everal methods have been used to form a clitoris, both cosmetic and functional", including early efforts which saw the implanting of a large silicone chin implant to form a "cosmetic swelling," surgeons now attempt to create a functioning "neoclitoris" that is derived from the glans penis and harvested penile neurovascular bundle (Goddard et al., 2007: 986). However, due to the contraction of perineum muscles surrounding the newly formed vagina, a dilator or "spacer" will have to be used constantly should the transsexual wish to experience vaginal penetration during sexual relations. If desired, implants will be inserted to enlarge the breasts. For a female-to-male transformation, breasts are flattened by mastectomy. Hysterectomy and ovariectomy accomplish a complete cessation of menstruation, or the person may wish to use hormone treatments continuously until menopause. Since the "inverted finger" of a vaginal glove cannot be turned inside out, the vagina is removed.

Until the mid-1980s, skin grafts were used to fashion a penis that was usually "numb and without actual, painful, or erotic sensory feeling" (Money, 1988: 91). The resultant flabby penis was incapable of erection without an additional insertion of a hydraulic device. As well, since the urethral canal was typically left intact, opening at the base of a new penis, using a urinal in the men's washroom was really not an option. Also, in the past, the intact clitoris typically was not removed and remained at the base of the penis, providing for the possibility of orgasm. As a consequence of improvements in microsurgery, a lengthy procedure known as "microvascular right radical artery forearm flap reconstruction" (Colapinto, 2000: 190) can now remove an artery, veins, and flesh from a person's right forearm; with that material, plus some rib cartilage (since erectile spongy tissue cannot be transplanted), a penis can be fashioned that is not only capable of sensation, but is also less flabby and permits stand-up urination. The labia majora can be used to fashion a scrotum and simulated testes can be implanted within. Ejaculation will be impossible unless a hydraulic device, filled with replenishable fluid and complete with a push button attached to either the groin or the scrotum, is also implanted in the penis.

It is indisputable that the surgical procedures required for transsexualism involve the mutilation, removal, and destruction of healthy body tissue for social, psychological, and cosmetic reasons (Eichler, 1980/1995: 30). The surgery is "expensive, time-consuming, arduous, and *painful*" (Richardson, 1988: 12; emphasis in original). Undergoing a transsexual transformation requires a high level of commitment and an intense belief that no other alternative will resolve the personal anguish that is believed to stem from being trapped in a wrong-sexed body. While researchers have sought explanations for this phenomenon in hormonal imbalances and dysfunctional parenting patterns (e.g., Green and Young, 2001; Sadeghi and Fakhrai, 2000; Zucker and Blanchard, 2003), perhaps the most compelling explanation has to do with our culture's rigidly dichotomous gender stereotypes (Cantor, 2002).

Applicants for transsexual surgery as well as the team of clinicians and physicians involved in the sex-change process all endorse the belief that the dichotomy must be upheld and ambiguity not tolerated. As Eichler has noted,

> were the notions of masculinity and femininity less rigid, sex change operations should be unnecessary. Rather than identify somebody with a "gender identity problem" as sick, we could define a society which insists on raising boys and girls in a clearly differentiated manner as sick. What should be treated as a *social* pathology is treated as if it were normal and when it manifests its effect in individuals it is treated as an *individual* pathology, and is "corrected," rather than any attempts being made to combat the issue at its root: the oppressive (non-human) definition of sex roles, and the lack of recognition of intermediate sexes in Western society. (1980/1995: 31; emphasis in original)

Transsexualism is estimated "to occur once among every 20 000 to 30 000 genetic males and once among every 50 000 to 100 000 genetic females" (Lips, 2005: 205). Its higher incidence among males has been attributed to a variety of factors; these include the lower cost and surgical complexity of male-to-female versus female-to-male operations and the relative dearth of men's groups which could provide support for an expanded range of male gender behaviour. However, the "greater sex role rigidity… expected of men" may be of greatest significance in accounting for the preponderance of male-to-female sex changes (Richardson, 1988: 14). To state it somewhat differently: Within a dichotomous gender system, men who are unable or unwilling to fulfill society's stereotype of "real masculinity" may find transsexualism a compelling alternative.

Participants in transsexual transformations—both clients and providers—appear to hold rigid and highly stereotypical views of gender-appropriate behaviour. As the general population becomes aware of transsexualism (primarily from television talk shows), the exaggerated gender-stereotypical behaviour exhibited by transsexuals may serve to reinforce narrow guidelines of gender-appropriate behaviour. Despite an initial impression of extreme deviance, transsexuals and their support teams ultimately reveal themselves to be highly conformist. The phenomenon of transsexualism bears witness to the power of gender stereotypes. As Unger (1993) has remarked, transsexual surgery constructs a context in which gender causes sex. Our culture's intolerance of androgyny curtails and polices "gender-inappropriate" behaviour so relentlessly as to make sex-change surgery seem, to some, a godsend; yet, ironically, gender stereotypes prevail as the new transsexual strives for gender hyper-prototypicality in his/her new role (see also Gilbert, 2000; Kessler and McKenna, 2000).

Sexism in Science

This section focuses on ways in which the gender of researchers and their subjects, as well as certain gender beliefs, contaminate the research process itself and the products of that research. Until relatively recently, the significance of gender was not recognized and its influence upon research processes and theories was largely ignored. However, as we become more aware of the impact of gender, we must guard against the danger of over-emphasizing its influence as a causal factor in various areas of social behaviour. It is essential to strive for a balanced perspective.

Sexism refers to "the belief that innate psychological, behavioural, and/or intellectual differences exist between women and men and that these differences connote the superiority of one group and the inferiority of the other" (Mooney et al., 2004: 209). Margrit Eichler (1984) was among the first Canadian sociologists to write specifically on ways in which sex, gender, and our beliefs about them produce a sexist outcome in the scientific enterprise. According to Eichler (1984: 20), sexism can influence the research process through the use of (1) sexist language, (2) sexist concepts, (3) an androcentric perspective, (4) sexist methodology, and (5) sexist interpretations of results produced by that methodology.

Eichler claimed, first of all, that both English and French are "profoundly *sexist languages*" (Eichler, 1984: 21) and that their uncritical use will continue to lead us into making and accepting statements that are misleading by dint of their sexist nature. A key problem is the use of "generic" male terms (e.g., man, he, his) to refer to humanity; such language either ignores or excludes women. Secondly, *sexist concepts* frame areas of investigation in ways that favour the status quo. Consider, for example, that while the term "maternal deprivation" is common in both popular and scholarly writings, the term "paternal deprivation" seldom appears (Lips, 1999: 29); the implication is that while the absence of mothers is harmful to children, the absence of fathers is not. A third way in which sexism enters the scientific process is via **androcentrism**, a perspective which places males at the centre of all aspects of social and scientific life. Androcentrism not only misrepresents and oppresses women, but is also subtly deleterious to men: in being taken to represent the entire species, many aspects of men's own lives are ignored or distorted; consequently, our understanding of men as men is incomplete. Researchers have historically focused on the public world of men and the private world of women; lacking a coherent awareness of these gender biases, they failed to realize how much of the other realms of men's and women's lives remained unexamined and unknown.

Recognition of androcentric bias in science has heightened our awareness of *sexist methodology*—research methods and models that are influenced by gender and beliefs about gender. The social sciences have long been dominated by *logical positivism,* an approach to knowledge emphasizing the importance of objectivity and favouring methods that preserve distance between researchers and subjects. In keeping with this theory, techniques such as surveys and laboratory experiments have been developed to obtain data that can be *quantified*, or reduced to numbers, mathematical formulae, and statistics. This traditional model of science can be seen "as establishing mastery over subjects, as demanding the absence of feeling, and as enforcing separateness of the knower from the known" (Hess and Ferree, 1987: 13). Feminists, on the other hand—motivated to fill in the gap in the scientific record by allowing previously marginalized parties to be heard—have challenged this androcentric orientation, espousing qualitative research methods that reduce the distance between researchers and subjects and accord pre-eminence to respondents' subjective experience (Morawski, 2001). Case-study approaches (in which a small number of subjects are examined intensively) and non-directive (open-ended) interview strategies are preferred in order to permit respondents to express themselves to researchers as fully as possible (Crawford and Kimmel, 1999; Grossman et al., 1999; Ussher, 1999). Findings are presented using the respondents' own words as much as possible, with a minimum of statistical manipulation or mathematical modelling.

Emphasis on Differences The identification of differences between men and women has been a perennial preoccupation of gender research throughout its history (Deaux, 1999). Kimball (2007: 454) observes that "[b]etween 1974 and 1995, 26,000 studies of sex or gender differences were published, including more than 2000 publications per year in the mid 1990s." Two important reasons for this emphasis on difference are the "politics of publication" and the nature of the scientific enterprise itself. The "politics of publication" refers to the editorial decision-making practices of scholarly journals. Editors and reviewers decide which articles to publish on the basis of a number of criteria, including procedural correctness, coherent presentation, and contribution to scholarly knowledge; however—just as with newspapers, radio, and television—"something different" is more newsworthy than "nothing different" (Bigler, 1999). As a result, gender research has more frequently evinced an **alpha bias**—an emphasis on the ways in which men and women differ (inviting the assumption that one sex is "superior" to the other)—than a **beta bias**, which minimizes gender differences (Hyde, 2001a; Rosenfeld, 2002). In either case, however, the social context of human behaviour is ignored. While men and women may, indeed, differ in many respects, "such differences may reflect their different positions in the social hierarchy of power and status rather than their different 'natures'" (Lips, 1999: 48). It is also important to recognize that even such gender differences as may be identified may only manifest themselves within the scope afforded by the particular social environment. For example, although research has consistently revealed that males of all ages are less law-abiding than females and more likely, in particular, to commit violent crime (Vago and Nelson, 2008), such findings have not led to the preferential hiring of women as police officers, lawyers, or judges.

Focus on Group Averages What kinds of differences is research likely to bring to our attention? The focus of empirical research is typically "group-average differences." Data is first collected from sample groups or social categories. Using scales developed to measure responses along various dimensions, it is then tested and analyzed to determine if any revealed differences are statistically significant (i.e., highly unlikely to have occurred by chance). Usually, the average scores of the groups under examination are compared to determine **group-average differences**. Less often is attention focused upon the *ranges of variation* found within each group or between the groups, or upon the meanings of such variations for our understanding of the group. Consider this example: Height measurements can be taken of a random sample of adult males and a random sample of adult females. Most likely, the average height of the males will be found to be approximately four inches greater than the average height of the females. However, the sample may contain many females who are taller than the average male, and many males who are shorter than the average female; in other words, considerable overlap may exist between the heights of women and of men. Most researchers focus more on the differences between *group averages*, and less on such intra-group variation and inter-group overlapping.

This tendency characterizes research not only on physical characteristics, but on personal and social ones (e.g., empathy, aggressiveness) as well. Research on physical attributes consistently finds that men are, on average, taller, heavier, and more muscular than women, while women are less susceptible to a variety of diseases and illnesses and tend to live longer. However, research into personal and social qualities finds very few consistent average differences and considerable overlap between female and male subjects (Archer, 2004; Eagly et al., 2003; Feingold, 1995; Knight et al., 2002). None of these could be termed *absolute differences* (i.e., cases in which all members of one group invariably outscore all members of another). Hyde's (2005) review of 46 meta-analyses reveals that, with few exceptions, claims of gender differences are often "overinflated" and that there is far more evidence to support a "gender similarities hypothesis" (which holds that males and females are similar on most, but not all, psychological variables) than a model that is predicated on notions of "difference."

The connection between empirical research on gender differences and gender stereotypes is obvious. Both focus upon the average differences between the sexes while essentially ignoring the considerable overlap in their physical, personal, and social qualities (Favreau, 1993). It has been argued that research into female–male differences may be "the proverbial 'wrong question'" (Hare-Mustin and Maracek, 1994: 535), inasmuch as it reinforces categorical thinking about men and women.

Money (1988) declared that **sex-irreducible differences** (i.e., absolute differences between men and women that cannot be broken down into more basic units) are very few and relate solely to biological reproduction:

> [M]en impregnate, and women menstruate, gestate, and lactate. Ovulation is omitted insofar as gestation does not take place without it. Lactation might be omitted insofar as modern nutritional technology has made it possible, though not desirable, for maternal neonatal breast-feeding to be replaced by a formula-milk substitute.... Immutability of the procreative sex difference will undoubtedly remain as if absolute for most men and women forever. However, in the light of contemporary experimental obstetrics, being pregnant is no longer an absolutely immutable sex difference. (Money, 1988: 54)

Statuses and Multiple Occupancy

Status refers to position or location within a group or society. Two characteristics of status are important to note here. First, *the meaning of any status is socially constructed in relation to at least one other status*. Thus, the meaning of the status known as "husband" can only be understood in relation to the status known as "wife." The same is true of student and instructor, child and parent, male and female. It is impossible to meaningfully describe and discuss any status without reference to other related statuses; as Flax (1990: 44) has noted, "each part can have no meaning or existence without the others."

The second characteristic of status is **multiple** (or **simultaneous**) **occupancy**. Each person in a society occupies a number of statuses at any moment and over the course of a lifetime. The same individual occupies a multiplicity of statuses simultaneously: marital (e.g., married, divorced), family (e.g., husband, daughter), religious (e.g., Catholic, Muslim, agnostic), ethnic (including "racial"), social class, age, etc.; these may be long-standing or temporary. At any time, only some of those multiple statuses will be important or relevant. Linton (1945: 78) distinguished between **active status** (relevant) and **latent status**: "[T]he status in terms of which an individual is operating is his [sic] active status at that particular point in time. His [sic] other statuses are, for the time being, latent statuses."

An intriguing question is whether sex is ever a latent, or irrelevant, status. Are there situations in which the sexes of participants are ignored? Freud (1933/1964: 113) observed that "when you meet a human being, the first distinction you make is 'male' or 'female.'" Being female or male is a **master status**, "one which will affect almost every aspect of our lives" (Lindsey, 1994: 2). However, sex is unlikely to be the only active status in any situation; usually at least one other status will be relevant and exert some influence upon the perceptions and behaviours of all parties; recall, for instance, how the status of "lesbian" influenced people's perceptions of a hypothetical female.

New theories are being developed to help us understand how gender interacts with statuses of age, social class, race/ethnicity, sexual orientation, and able-bodiedness to influence an individual's participation in Canadian society. As these theories evolve, we will become less simplistic in our thinking about sex and gender, and better able to discern when a phenomenon is attributable to gender and when it is not.

Sex Roles and Gender Roles Attached to each status is a dynamic element formally known as a **role**. Roles comprise the duties, responsibilities, rights, and privileges associated with occupancy of a status; these are socially constructed in the context of cultural values and beliefs. Generally, "role" is used to refer to what one is expected to do as occupant of a certain status; "role performance," "role enactment," and "role behaviour" are used to refer to what one actually does.

Some confusion and inconsistency surround attempts to apply the concept of roles to the study of sex and gender. Lipman-Blumen (1984: 2; emphasis in original) offered the following discussion of **gender roles**:

> We shall use the better-known term, sex *roles*, to refer specifically to behaviors determined by an individual's biological sex, such as menstruation, pregnancy, lactation, erection, orgasm, and seminal ejaculation. At the same time, we should not forget that even biologically determined phenomena do not escape the influence of cultural attitudes, norms, and values.... Gender roles... are socially created expectations for masculine and feminine behavior. Exaggerating both real and imagined aspects of biological sex, each society sorts certain polarized behaviors and attitudes into two sets it then labels "male" and "female." *Gender roles* are social constructions; they contain self-concepts, psychological traits, as well as family, occupational, and political roles assigned to members of each sex.

Clearly, it is difficult to keep sex and gender roles analytically separate. Given that gender is a social construction and that even sex expectations are strongly influenced by sociocultural forces, a tendency has developed to use just the one general term, "gender roles," to refer to all expectations associated with sex and gender. The concept of gender roles should not mislead us into a deterministic view of gender behaviour. We do not simply learn the roles appropriate to our status and perform them like automatons. As Richardson (1988: 9; emphasis in original) noted,

> Gender behavior is both *prescribed* and *chosen*. On the one hand, appropriate behavior is socially shared and transmitted through the culture: People learn what is appropriate for their gender. But, on the other hand, they choose how to present themselves. Therefore, persons have the option to accept or reject cultural definitions of appropriate gender behavior and, consequently, the ability to change either themselves or the culture.

Some aspects of gender expectations are transmitted to us in such a way that we accept them unthinkingly and therefore uncritically; as a result, some of our gender behaviour involves conformity to prescribed roles. However—particularly today, with our heightened awareness of gender issues—we are also capable of thinking about and consciously accepting or rejecting some aspects of gender expectations. The different ways in which we combine the "prescribed" and the "chosen" account for the variability of gender behaviour that we observe in our lives.

Guidelines for gender behaviour are not uniform throughout an entire culture, but vary across many categories, such as age group, social class, and racial/ethnic group. What is more, each of us occupies a number of statuses and performs a number of roles simultaneously; we are highly unlikely ever to find that only our gender status and role are active—that we are called upon solely to "be a man" or "act like a lady." Rather, our gender role is intertwined with our other roles—age, race/ethnicity, social class, sexual orientation, and so on (Denner and Dunbar, 2004; Lancaster, 1997). Each of us creates our own personal style of gendered behaviour, combining the expectations of relevant social groups and status categories with our own role-skill capabilities (see, for example, Atkinson, 2002; Kennison, 2002; Koenig, 2002; Maltry and Tucker, 2003). The resulting gender behaviours, while diverse, represent variations upon certain themes. These themes will be identified and explored in subsequent chapters.

Key Terms

active status

adjective checklist

alpha bias

androcentrism

androgynous

berdache

beta bias

biological determinism

bisexuality

convenience sample

double jeopardy

ethnocentrism

female

feminine

femininity

gay

gender

gender dysphoria

gender migration

gender stereotypes

gender roles

group-average differences

hermaphroditism

heterosexism

heterosexuality

hijras

homophobia

homosexuality

human rights

interactionist

intersex

latent status

lesbian

mahu

male

masculine

masculinity

master status

multiple jeopardies

multiple occupancy

nadleeh

open-ended questions

pseudohermaphroditism

purdah

rating scales

role

self-fulfilling prophecy

sex

sex dimorphism

sex-irreducible differences

sexism

sex (re)assignment

sexual

sexual orientation

sexual preference

sexuality

sexuality scripts

simultaneous occupancy

social constructionism

status

transsexualism

transsexuals

undifferentiated (gender)

xanith

Xq28

Chapter Summary

1. The term "sex" refers to the biological classification of an individual as male or female; "gender" refers to the social definitions and expectations associated with being male or female.

2. "Sex dimorphism" encourages us to view men and women as fundamentally different, and to search for and focus upon differences rather than similarities between the sexes. Dichotomous thinking is the foundation of the assumption that only two discrete gender categories can exist, "masculine" and "feminine." Cross-cultural research on such distinctive gender types as the *berdache, nadleeh, hijras, xanith,* and *mahu* challenges us to consider how our understanding of the nature and number of genders may be limited by social convention and by the language we speak.

3. "Sexuality" refers to scripted behaviour designed to produce erotic response and pleasure. The term "sexual orientation" refers to the classification of individuals as heterosexual, bisexual, or homosexual on the basis of their emotional and sexual attractions, relationships, self-identity, and lifestyle. "Homosexuality" refers to the predominance of emotional and sexual attraction to persons of the same sex. "Heterosexuality" refers to the predominance of emotional and sexual attraction to persons of the other sex. "Bisexuality" refers to emotional and sexual attraction to members of both sexes. Estimates of the prevalence of various sexual orientations vary due to differences in the way researchers define and measure them.

4. "Gender stereotypes" are widely held beliefs about what women and men are like. Gender stereotypes may result in the expectation and encouragement of "gender-appropriate" behaviour, and in sanctions for engaging in behaviour that defies the stereotypes of how boys and girls, men and women, should or "ought" to act. Gender stereotypes about men and women are enmeshed with stereotypes of race, social class, disability, sexual orientation, age, and attractiveness. The phenomena of sex (re)assignment and transsexualism forcefully illustrate the power of gender stereotypes in Western society.

5. "Sexism" is the belief that there are innate psychological, behavioural, and/or intellectual differences between females and males and that these differences involve the superiority of one group and the inferiority of another. Sexism in research can occur through the use of sexist language, concepts, methodology, and interpretation of results, or the adoption of an androcentric perspective. While "sex-irreducible differences" are very few and relate solely to biological reproduction, gender researchers have historically tended to focus on differences between the sexes, rather than on intragroup variations and inter-group overlapping.

CHAPTER 2

Biological, Psychological, and Social-Psychological Perspectives

SEX AND GENDER: BASIC VARIABLES

Women's track star Stella Walsh won numerous medals in international competitions during the 1930s: five gold (including one for a record-breaking 100-metre dash in the 1932 Olympics), three silver, and one bronze. During her lifetime, Walsh set 20 world records, became the 1954 American women's pentathlon champion, and, in 1975, was inducted into the United States Track and Field Hall of Fame. In 1980, Walsh was shot and killed during a robbery attempt. An autopsy revealed that some of her body cells contained an XY male-sex chromosome pattern and others an XX female-sex chromosome pattern (a condition known as *mosaicism*). Her external (and non-functional) sex organs were male. Further investigation revealed that "Stella" was born in Poland as Stanislawa Walaziewcz. Her former (and dumbfounded) husband from a 1956 two-month-long marriage commented that their lovemaking had always taken place with the lights out. The International Olympic Committee has yet to resolve the dilemmas that these revelations presented them with: Was Stella male or female? Should her medals be confiscated and her championships deleted from the official records (or at least qualified with an asterisk)? Should Canadian Hilda Strike, who in 1932 had tied with Walsh at the 100-metre finish line but only won silver, be posthumously awarded the gold?

Don't fret if you have trouble deciding. After all, it took 30 years for France's Marielle Goitschel to receive her gold medal for the 1966 World Championship downhill-skiing race at Portillo, Chile. The medal had originally been awarded to first-place finisher Erika Schinegger of Austria; however, at the 1968 Winter Olympics in Grenoble, France,

Schinegger was discovered to have male internal organs and a preponderance of male hormones. Erika later underwent a sex-change operation, married, and became a father. Erik Schinegger gave his gold medal to Goitschel in 1988, but the International Ski Federation did not change its mind and make the official presentation until December of 1996.

Dr. Richard Henry Raskind, an ophthalmologist and avid tennis player, was married and the father of a son. However, feeling a central portion of his life to be a lie, he underwent a successful transsexual transformation and became Dr. Renée Richards. Dr. Richards continued to enjoy tennis (even coaching world champion Martina Navratilova) and to compete in professional women's tournaments until 1976, when a protest was lodged to the effect that she held an unfair competitive advantage. Organizers decided to use a buccal smear to establish her eligibility; this procedure, in which a chromosome test is performed on a scraping of cells taken from the inside of the mouth, had been in use since 1968 as a screening device for Olympic competition. Since transsexual transformation does not alter sex chromosomes, Richards could be barred from playing in women's events.

Richards challenged the very idea that chromosomes provide a definitive criterion of sex. She was psychologically female, functioned socially as a female, and possessed female (albeit reconstructed) genitals—all, she argued, more valid parameters of femaleness than chromosomes. However, since transsexual transformation was undertaken after puberty, Renée Richards' bone structure was male, a fact which impacted on her athletic performance. Which test would have been most appropriate for the determination of Renée Richards' sex and eligibility? (Incidentally, the International Olympic

Committee dropped the buccal smear test prior to the 1996 Summer Olympics, and in 1999 suspended, on a trial basis, the mandatory sex-testing of women athletes. Beginning with the 2004 Summer Olympics in Athens, transsexual athletes were allowed to compete in Olympic events in their new gender if they had undergone a minimum two-year period of post-operative therapy and if their new gender had been legally recognized).

Biological sex is not a unitary phenomenon with two simple, dichotomous categories of "male" and "female." Rather, it comprises a number of variables which must be considered together: chromosomal, gonadal, hormonal, reproductive, genital, brain, and assigned sex. Gender, too, has complex dimensions of identity and social behaviour. These variables operate and interrelate in intricate ways.

Biological Sex: Chromosomal and Hormonal Influences

The process of biological sex differentiation begins at the moment of conception, when a male sperm and a female egg (or *ovum*) unite to form a **zygote**. The traditional view of the conception process has reflected gender stereotypes of active male/passive female. This view was humorously presented in a televised beer commercial aired during the 1999–2000 Stanley Cup playoffs: Energetic sperm were shown darting about to a hockey announcer's play-by-play; as one sperm broke out of the pack and streaked forward to touch an unmoving ovum, the voice-over excitedly shrieked,: "He shoots! He scores!"

Despite such renderings, Martin (1989, 2003) challenged the image of sperm as "the nuclear war-head of paternal genes," noting that sperm actually move quite slowly, with more side-to-side than straight-ahead motion; what is more, not only does the egg's adhesive surface aid in the attachment of the sperm, but the egg actively incorporates the sperm's genetic material. For these reasons, Martin argued, sperm and egg are best thought of as mutually interdependent agents.

Chromosomal Sex The zygote contains 46 chromosomes, 23 from each parent; these appear as 23 pairs. Twenty-two of these pairs (known as *autosomes*) contain genetic instructions for various hereditary qualities, such as eye shape, skin colour, and height. Only one of these pairs, the *sex chromosomes*, differs in males and females. A normal female has two X chromosomes; a normal male, one X and one Y; accordingly, the usual genetic code for a female is 46,XX (i.e., 46 chromosomes, including an XX sex-chromosome), while for a male it is 46,XY. The ovum always contains an X sex-chromosome; the sperm, however, can contain either an X or a Y;. Therefore, the father's chromosomal contribution determines a child's sex. Because the larger X chromosome carries more genetic material than does the Y, it is believed that the XX pattern confers advantages to the female immune system, with important ramifications for morbidity and mortality differentials between the sexes. However, in the initial weeks after conception, male and female embryos are anatomically identical in all respects but **chromosomal sex**.

Further sex differentiation *appears to* follow what has been characterized as the **Eve first, then Adam principle** (Money, 1993); "appears to" is emphasized deliberately—researchers have so overwhelmingly focused on male fetal development that they have simply assumed female development to be non-problematic and in need of no separate explanation (Fausto-Sterling, 1993). According to this principle, the "natural" tendency is towards creation of a biological female (Wizeman and Pardue, 2001: 50). For a fetus to differentiate into a biological male, "something" must be added; the specific extra ingredient may be different at different stages of fetal development.

Gonadal Sex The gonads (organs in which reproductive cells develop) begin to develop at around the sixth to seventh week after conception. Male testes and female ovaries, the hallmarks of **gonadal sex**, are *homologous* sex organs; this means that they develop from the same embryonic tissue, known as the primordial or "indifferent" gonad. Without the active interference of masculinizing factors, the indifferent common primordia have an inherent tendency to feminize. While scientists have known for almost half a century that a testis-determining locus, TDF (testis-determining factor), resides on the Y chromosome, it was only about a decade ago that the testis-determining gene was found to be the SRY (sex-determining region Y) gene. The SRY gene, located on the short arm of the Y chromosome in humans, is the inducer of both the differentiation of the indifferent gonad into testes and male sexual development. After expression of SRY in the sexually indifferent gonad, a number of genes encoding transcription factors and growth factors implicated in testis differentiation start to show male-specific expession. "In mammals, gonadal sex is normally determined by the presence or absence of the Y chromosome gene SRY" (Kojima et al., 2007).

Hormonal Sex Subsequent sex differentiation is controlled largely by hormonal mechanisms and is referred to as **hormonal sex**. In our everyday vernacular, **androgens** are commonly referred to as "male sex hormones," while **estrogens** (including progesterone) are referred to as "female sex hormones." Such language implies that only males produce androgens and only females produce estrogens (Roberts, 2002). However, both testes and ovaries produce both. Individuals are arrayed along a hormonal-sex continuum depending upon the proportional balance of these hormones in their bodies: males generally produce a greater proportion of androgens to estrogens, females a greater proportion of estrogens to androgens (Myers, 2007: 124). During fetal development, the absolute amounts of androgens and estrogens produced by males and females are actually very small; greater amounts are produced later in developmental life, around the time of puberty.

Internal Reproductive Sex Meanwhile, other genes have already created the Wolffian and Müllerian duct systems, which have the potential to develop, or proliferate, into the male and female **internal reproductive sex** systems respectively. In the male embryo, the testes begin to secrete two products by the eighth week after conception: androgens—particularly **testosterone**—stimulate the development of the **Wolffian duct system** into *male reproductive-sex* features such as the epididymis, vas deferens, seminal vesicles, and the prostate gland. **Müllerian inhibiting hormone (MIH)** causes the Müllerian ducts to atrophy, or vestigiate, rather than form female internal organs.

If masculinization of the primordial gonad has not occurred around the seventh week, ovaries will typically develop at about the twelfth week of pregnancy. Later, the **Müllerian duct system** differentiates into the *female reproductive-sex* features of the uterus, fallopian tubes, and inner third of the vagina. If not stimulated by sufficiently large amounts of testosterone, the Wolffian duct system in the female atrophies, or vestigiates, into minute fragments and is absorbed into the bloodstream.

External Genital Sex Little differentiation exists in the **external genitals** of a fetus until after the seventh week of development. Androgens (particularly testosterone, which is converted by some body tissues into dihydrotestosterone) appear to be a key factor in the development of the homologous *genital tubercle* into the *male genital-sex* features: the penis and scrotum (Kojima et al., 2007). In the female embryo, the lack of sufficient amounts of these androgens leads to the genital tubercle's development into the *female* *genital-sex* features: the clitoris, inner and outer labia, and outer portion of the vagina. Visible genital differences between the male and female fetus are observable by the fourteenth week after conception.

Brain Sex There is still considerable uncertainty as to whether **brain sex** should be added to the list of biological sex variables. One straightforward example of brain sex as a differentiating variable has to do with a part of the brain called the *hypothalamus*. The presence or absence of fetal androgens influences the number and location of certain types of nerve-cell connections (synapses) that develop in the hypothalamus, eventually affecting its sensitivity to estrogen. The hypothalamus (along with the pituitary gland and the gonads) is involved in a complex feedback loop that becomes operational during puberty. An insufficiency of fetal androgens causes the hypothalamus to become sensitive to estrogen; this sensitivity contributes to the cyclic pattern of sex-hormone production underlying women's menstrual cycles. Sufficient amounts of fetal androgens "masculinize" the hypothalamus to become insensitive to estrogens; as a result, sex-hormone production in post-pubertal men is relatively constant, or *acyclic*. For this reason, men do not have an analogous menstrual cycle, nor do they undergo a biologically based "male menopause" at midlife (Swaab et al., 2003).

Kinsbourne, a leader in brain research, remarked that "many investigators seem determined to discover that men and women 'really' are different. It seems that if sex differences ... do not exist, then they have to be invented" (in Tavris, 1992: 53). These words are as applicable today as they were throughout the twentieth century. The history of research into brain sex has been one of bold pronouncements followed by retractions, based sometimes on the discovery of new information and sometimes on changing gender politics. Researchers in the early 1900s, positing a direct relationship between brain size and intelligence, initially declared that males, possessing the larger brains, possessed greater intelligence. When it was later discovered that brain size was related to the non-sex-irreducible qualities of height and weight, research attention turned to brain lobes instead. When frontal lobes were thought to be the site of intelligence, males were proclaimed to have the larger frontal lobes; when parietal lobes were believed to be its home, scientific opinion changed to assert that men really had larger parietal lobes.

More recently, attention has shifted to the two hemispheres of the brain. Researchers have tried to determine whether a different hemisphere is dominant in each sex and whether specific functions are located in one hemisphere or both. The basic question has been whether male brains are more *lateralized* (i.e., specialized) and female brains more *symmetrical* (meaning that both hemispheres contribute to a wide range of abilities). However, despite the popular press' announcement of seemingly definitive conclusions (e.g., Hales, 1998/1999), existing findings on brain lateralization are either inconsistent or inconclusive (Fausto-Sterling, 2000; Kimura, 2002), as are findings concerning the possibility of sex differences in the *corpus callosum,* the bundle of fibres connecting the brain's hemispheres (Bishop and Wahlsten, 1997; Shin et al., 2005; Myers, 2007: 125).

Over the past decade, a steady stream of best-selling books, including *Sex on the Brain* (Blum, 1997), *Brain Gender* (Hines, 2004), and *Sexing the Brain* (Rogers, 2002) have continued to advance the claim that there are differences in male and female brain structure and hormonal chemistry. For example, psychologist Simon Baron-Cohen's *The Essential Difference* (2003) forwarded an "extreme male brain" theory of autism that built on the hypothesis that male and female brains are significantly different, with the male brain hard-wired for "systematizing" and the female brain hard-wired for "empathizing" (see also

Baron-Cohen et al., 2005). Even more recently, neuropsychiatrist Louann Brizendine's *The Female Brain* (2006) asserted that "the female brain is so deeply affected by hormones that their influence can be said to create a woman's reality." According to Brizendine, the "female brain" possesses "tremendous, unique aptitudes" including "outstanding verbal agility, the ability to connect deeply in friendship, a nearly psychic capacity to read faces and tone of voice for emotions and states of mind, and the ability to defuse conflict." She maintains that while the brains of male and female fetuses are initially the same, male fetuses experience a mammoth surge in testosterone during the eighth week of fetal development that irreparably damages their later ability to process emotions; supposedly, while women "have an eight-lane superhighway" for doing so, men have only a "small country lane."

However, these claims have been hotly disputed by others. Young and Balaban (2006), for example, have accused Baron-Cohen of simply resurrecting the tired clichés of men as "thinkers" and women as "feelers" and adorning them in a pseudo-scientific nomenclature that is "fundamentally non-biological and explains nothing." Similarly, they charge that *The Female Brain* "disappointingly fails to meet even the most basic standards of scientific accuracy;" is "riddled with scientific errors and is misleading about the processes of brain development, the neuroendocrine system, and the nature of sex differences in general;" and exaggerates human sex differences "almost to the point of creating different species ... [even though] virtually all differences in brain structure, and most differences in behaviour, are characterized by small average differences and a great deal of male–female overlap at the individual level."

Even if differences do exist between male and female brains, any connection between such differences and differences in male and female behaviours, abilities, or propensities has yet to be clearly determined. In particular, the *direction* of influence between brain and behaviour is not entirely clear. Brain researchers most often postulate that brain structure and function are established during fetal development and early infancy. However, it has been suggested that the brain may adapt to changes occurring either in other parts of the body or in the environment (Walsh and Cepko, 1992; Tavris, 2005). Learning may also affect brain structures, chemistry, and functioning. At this point, hypothalamic sensitivity to certain hormones appears to be the only area in which brain sex is unmistakably a differentiating variable. See Table 2.1 for a summary of the recognized differentiating variables of biological sex.

TABLE 2.1	Summary of Biological Sex Dimorphism Variables during Typical Fetal Development	
Variable	**Female**	**Male**
chromosomal	XX	XY
gonadal	ovaries	testes
hormonal	more estrogens than androgens	more androgens than estrogens + MIH
internal reproductive	uterus, fallopian tubes, inner third of vagina	epididymis, vas deferens, seminal vesicles, prostate
external genital	clitoris, labia, vagina	penis, scrotum
brain	estrogen-sensitive hypothalamus	estrogen-insensitive hypothalamus

Assigned Sex In the vast majority of cases, a visual inspection of a baby's genitals, usually at birth, provides the basis for **assigned sex**. The observable presence of a penis and scrotum, or of labia and a vagina, is considered sufficient evidence to pronounce the child a boy or a girl. Only in rare instances, as noted in Chapter 1, are further investigations instigated to determine an individual's chromosomal, gonadal, hormonal, and internal reproductive sex. It is simply (and most often accurately) taken for granted that all the variables of an individual's biological sex are *concordant* (i.e., consistent). In other words, it is assumed that an infant possessing an apparent penis and scrotum also possesses a fully developed Wolffian system of vas deferens, epididymis, seminal vesicles, and prostate gland; a proportionally greater balance of androgens to estrogens; testes; and an XY sex-chromosome profile. Similarly, it is assumed that an infant possessing an apparent vaginal opening, labia, and clitoris also possesses a fully developed Müllerian system with the inner third of the vagina, uterus, and fallopian tubes, as well as ovaries and an XX sex-chromosome pattern.

Occasionally, however, there are occurrences of **sex discordance**, which may be identified immediately upon birth or at puberty. The previous chapter noted several examples of intersexed individuals born with ambiguous genital configurations. The clinical literature has identified a number of other types of sex discordance, some characterized by ambiguous genitalia and some not. Ambiguous genitalia are also characteristic of *androgen-insensitivity syndrome* (AIS), *5-alpha-reductase deficiency*, and *androgenital syndrome* (AGS, also known as *congenital virilizing adrenal hyperplasia* or CVAH). In all of these instances, discordance occurs at the hormonal, internal-reproductive, or genital levels, rather than at the genetic or chromosomal level. A sex-linked chromosome may be missing, as in **Turner's syndrome** (with a 45,XO configuration); or an extra sex-linked chromosome may be present, as in **Klinefelter's syndrome** (with a 47,XXY configuration). However, the true incidence of "intersex" is a matter of intense debate, and, as ethicist Alice Dreger (1998: 24) observed, "depends, of course, on how one defines [intersex]":

> Broadly speaking, intersexuality constitutes a range of anatomical conditions in which an individual's anatomy mixes key masculine anatomy with key feminine anatomy. One quickly runs into a problem, however, when trying to define "key" or "essential" feminine and masculine anatomy [see Box 2.1]. In fact, any close study of sexual anatomy results in a loss of faith that there is a simple, "natural" sex distinction that will not break down in the face of certain anatomical, behavioural, or philosophical challenges.

The definition of "intersex" may vary not only between researchers but in the writings of individual authors over the course of time. In her oft-cited article, "The Five Sexes," Fausto-Sterling (1993) used the term "intersex" to refer to individuals having XY chromosomes and predominantly female anatomy, XX chromosomes and predominantly male anatomy, or ambiguous or mixed genitals. However, in more recent writings, she and her colleagues have employed a far broader definition, classifying as intersex any "individual who deviates from the Platonic ideal of physical dimorphism at the chromosomal, genital, gonadal, or hormonal levels;" included within this definition are those who "are undiagnosed because they present no symptoms" (Blackless et al., 2000: 161, 152; see also Fausto-Sterling, 2000: 31). As Sax (2002) pointed out, "A definition of intersex which encompasses individuals who are phenotypically indistinguishable from normal is likely to confuse both clinicians and patients."

It should also be evident that the broader the definition, the more commonly the phenomenon will be reported. Thus, applying Fausto-Sterling's original definition, intersex might be estimated to occur in less than 2 out of every 10 000 live births; applying her

---

BOX 2.1

What Defines Men and Women?

Most folks would define a man by the presence of a penis or some form of a penis. Some would define a woman by the presence of a vagina or some form of vagina. It's not that simple, though. I know several women in San Francisco who have penises. Many wonderful men in my life have vaginas. And there are quite a few people whose genitals fall somewhere between penises and vaginas. What are *they*?

Are you a man because you have an XY chromosome? A woman because you have XX? Unless you're an athlete who's been challenged in the area of gender representation, you probably haven't had a chromosome test.... If you haven't had that test, then how do you know[?]...

Are you a woman because you can bear children? Because you bleed every month? Many women are born without this potential, and every woman ceases to possess that capacity after menopause—do these women cease being women? Does a necessary hysterectomy equal a gender change? Are you a man because you can father children? What if your sperm count is too low? What if you were exposed to nuclear radiation and were rendered sterile? Are you then a woman? Are you a woman because your birth certificate says female? A man because your birth certificate says male?...

I've been searching all my life for a rock-bottom definition of woman, an unquestionable sense of what it is to be a man. I've found nothing except the fickle definitions of gender held up by groups and individuals for their own purposes.

Source: Abridged from Kate Bornstein. 1994. *Gender Outlaw: On Men, Women and the Rest of Us.* New York: Routledge, pp. 56–57.

---

expanded definition, in 1.7 per 100 (Sax, 2002: 3). Relying on the latter figure, Fausto-Sterling (2000: 51) has asserted that males and females should not be viewed as polarized "on the extreme ends of a biological continuum" but as residing upon that continuum. "[We should] lighten up about what it means to be male or female. We should definitely lighten up on those who fall in between because there are a lot of them" (Fausto-Sterling, as quoted in Dreifus, 2001).

Researchers have sought to determine whether the various types of sex discordance can be linked to specific variations in social or psychological *gender behaviour* (e.g., Berenbaum and Bailey, 2003; Hines, 2004; Jurgensen et al., 2007; Reiner and Gearhart, 2004). The results are inconclusive (see Gottschalk, 2003; Lips, 2005: 182–191; Newman, 2002). As one researcher noted, "the history of research on prenatal hormones and human behavior has been typified by reports of suggestive results, followed by realization of potential methodological problems" (Hines, 1982: 73); this observation still holds true, and may be generalized to include research on chromosomal anomalies as well. Although initial studies have suggested that discordant hormonal or chromosomal conditions may have behavioural outcomes, these studies have not held up under scrutiny (Myers, 2007: 124). What discordance does do, however, is dramatically remind us that biological sex is not always a simple concordant variable.

Gender Identity Gender identity is typically defined as one's sense of oneself as being either male or female. From the rudimentary sense evinced by very young children, gender identity becomes increasingly complex and multidimensional by one's late teens (Spence, 1993) and probably continues to evolve over the course of one's life. Males typically equate the sense of maleness with "masculinity," and females their sense of femaleness with "femininity" (Spence, 1993: 633). These labels are applied even though many individuals readily admit that they may be less stereotypically masculine or feminine than other members of their own sex and may, in fact, possess some qualities stereotypically associated with the other sex. Lancaster (2003: 18) pointed out that "[e]ven psychiatrists who treat 'gender dysphoria'—a slick term for rebellion against conventional gender roles—admit that at least 50 percent of children at some point exhibit signs of mixed or crossed gender identity or express a desire to be the 'opposite' sex" (see Chapter 1). Howsoever these "masculine" and "feminine" traits are combined, most individuals in our society maintain and affirm a constant underlying sense of gender identity throughout their lifetimes. We will later review various theories which identify gender identity as the key variable in the ultimate determination of gender behaviour.

Gender Behaviour Gender behaviour, the last of the basic variables of sex and gender, is a general and somewhat vague concept. It is obviously impossible to list all the elements which could fall under this rubric. However, you may begin to explore some of its many dimensions by considering on what basis you identify the sex of a stranger. Unless your meeting takes place in a nudist camp, casual inspection of the person's genitals is probably not an option. So, upon what cues do you rely? In all probability, you rely upon physical appearance and the display of secondary sex characteristics.

We are all aware that appearances can be deceiving. Recall from Chapter 1 that as part of the "real-life test," a candidate for transsexual surgery is required to "pass" as an "opposite"-sexed person; transsexuals, however, are not the only ones who use artifice to project their conformity to gendered expectations. The clothing we wear and the cosmetics we do or do not apply all fall under the heading of gender behaviour and can be used to emphasize or conceal our biological sex (Young, 2000). Furthermore, diet and exercise programs, cosmetic surgery, and "body art" (e.g., tattoos, piercings) all represent ways in which we can alter our physical appearance and influence other people's perceptions of our sex.

If today's unisex fashions, variable hair lengths, and penchant for jewellery frustrate our efforts to distinguish males from females, we may seek other cues. We may scrutinize general demeanour, carriage, and *kinesics* (body movements and gestures). These gender behaviours are learned and can be manipulated to reinforce or modify impressions of gender and sex. Nevertheless, from these we infer the subject's gender identity, genital sex, internal reproductive sex, hormonal sex, and chromosomal sex. All of this is done in a cursory, taken-for-granted manner. Only if we somehow acquire contradictory information will we be motivated to delve beyond our initial assumptions. Most Canadians routinely identify others' biological sex on the basis of appearance—something highly variable and modifiable. Indeed, "it is quite likely that appearance is a core aspect of gender stereotyping" (Lips, 1993: 8). Deaux and Lewis (1984) found that physical cues (e.g., strong and sturdy versus dainty and graceful) invariably outweighed the labels "male" or "female" in respondents' inferences of what a hypothetical person would be like, what traits s/he would possess, and what roles s/he would engage in. In like fashion, we may surmise another person's sexual orientation on the basis of little more than his or her facial appearance. Thus, males with "feminine" faces and females with "masculine" faces are more likely than others to be judged homosexual (Dunkle and Francis, 1990, 1996). Similarly, Madson's (2000) experimental research found that physically androgynous individuals were inferred to possess less gender-typed traits and behaviours than those who were stereotypically masculine or feminine in appearance. Respondents additionally inferred that the physically androgynous were more likely to be homosexual than heterosexual. In this context, one might also consider the semantics of the neologism **metrosexual**. Although early employed by Simpson (2003) to satirize "the effect of consumerism and media proliferation, particularly glossy men's magazines, on traditional masculinity," the term is often employed by the media as a sneer word that suggests that men who are concerned with their appearance, possess a salmon-coloured shirt in their wardrobe, or use multiple hair/skin-care products are other than masculine and/or heterosexual.

As noted in Chapter 1, the immutability of gender identity is still a controversial issue. Of all the sex and gender variables considered thus far, only chromosomal sex, established at conception, is unalterable. Today, we have the ability to alter gonadal sex (via removal of gonads/implantation of non-functioning replicas), hormonal sex, internal reproductive sex, genital sex, assigned sex, and gender behaviour. Thanks to various technologies (including those which allow us to identify more subtle instances of sex discordance), the variability seen in sex and gender will continue to increase. This increase will pose further challenges to theoretical perspectives that strive to establish an all-encompassing explanation of gender; it may be found that current theories best describe a limited set of gender variables.

BIOLOGICALLY GROUNDED THEORIES

Various theories argue that gender behaviour is ultimately a product of human biological nature (see Box 2.2), i.e., that sex determines gender. Among the most prominent of these are sociobiology, evolutionary psychology, and psychoanalytic theory. The three theories selected for consideration here vary in terms of the specific aspects of biology used as a cornerstone for explaining sex and gender differences.

Sociobiology

Introduced by entomologist Edward O. Wilson in 1975, **sociobiology** is "the systematic study of the biological basis of all forms of social behavior" (Wilson, 1978: 16). Sociobiologists claim that at some point in human evolutionary history, certain forms of behaviour (e.g., territoriality, aggressiveness) maximized the reproductive success of the organisms that exhibited them and became genetically encoded within the species through the operation of Darwinian **natural selection**.

According to Darwin (1859), natural selection is based on four principles: (1) reproduction occurs within a natural environment; (2) a species' genes—the basic units of life that are the carriers of heredity—are passed on to offspring; (3) because the members of a species possess different characteristics, some members have a better chance of surviving than others—and of passing their particular genetic traits on to the next generation; and (4) over thousands of generations, those genetic traits that aid survival in the natural environment tend to become common in a species, while those that do not tend to disappear. Natural selection is used to explain both the physical characteristics of animals (including humans) and their behaviour. According to Wilson (1975), human behaviour is no different from the behaviour of rats or mosquitoes—it is bred into *Homo sapiens* through evolutionary principles. "The fundamental assertion of sociobiology is that we are structured by nature with a desire to

BOX 2.2

Biology versus Culture—Biology Is the Answer

Steven Goldberg (1974, 1989, 1993) found it astonishing that anyone should doubt "the presence of core-deep differences in males and females, differences of temperament and emotion we call masculinity and femininity." Goldberg's argument, that it is not environment but inborn differences that "give masculine and feminine direction to the emotions and behaviors of men and women," is summarized as follows.

1. The anthropological record shows that all societies for which evidence exists are (or were) patriarchies (societies in which men dominate women). Stories about past matriarchies (societies in which women dominate men) are myths.

2. In all societies, past and present, the highest statuses are associated with males. In every society, politics is ruled "by hierarchies overwhelmingly dominated by men."

3. The reason for this one-way dominance of societies is that males "have a lower threshold for the elicitation of dominance behavior ... a great tendency to exhibit whatever behavior is necessary in any environment to attain dominance in hierarchies and male–female encounters and relationships." Males are more willing "to sacrifice the rewards of other motivations—the desire for affection, health, family life, safety, relaxation, vacation and the like—in order to attain dominance and status."

4. Just as a six-foot woman does not prove the social basis of height, so exceptional individuals, such as a highly achieving and dominant woman, do not refute "the physiological roots of behavior."

In short, only one interpretation of why every society from that of the Pygmy to that of the Swede associates dominance and attainment with males is valid. Male dominance of society is simply "an inevitable resolution of the psychophysiological reality." Socialization and social institutions merely *reflect*—and sometimes exaggerate—inborn tendencies. Any interpretation other than inborn differences is "wrongheaded, ignorant, tendentious, internally illogical, discordant with the evidence, and implausible in the extreme." The argument that males are more aggressive because they have been socialized that way is the equivalent of a claim that men can grow moustaches because boys have been socialized that way.

To acknowledge this reality is *not* to defend discrimination against women. Whether or not one approves of what societies have done with these basic biological differences is not the point. The point is that biology leads males and females to different behaviors and attitudes—regardless of how we feel about this or wish it were different.

Source: Henslin and Nelson, 1996: 285. Reprinted with permission of Pearson Education Canada Inc.

ensure that our individual genes pass to future generations and that this is a motivating factor in almost all human behavior" (Lindsey, 1994: 41). Sociobiology suggests that within the limitations imposed by our genes (e.g., humans cannot fly like birds) certain characteristics, such as competitiveness and sexual selection, have become part of the human *biogram* (i.e., genetically encoded biological program). The basic message of socio-biology is "genetics is destiny."

Wilson claimed that the sex-based division of labour (in which women look after the home and men assume responsibilities outside the home) is genetically coded, and that, therefore, in future societies, "even with identical education and equal access to all professions, men are likely to continue to play a disproportionate role in political life, business and science" (Wilson as quoted in Doyle and Paludi, 1995: 57). The concept of **parental investment** is used to explain why women in all societies care for children; supposedly, a woman's investment in a child's survival is greater because she contributes more than a man does from the moment of conception. Whereas sperm are "cheap" (each ejaculation may contain as many as a billion sperm cells [Saxton, 1990: 94–95] and can be replicated within 24 to 48 hours), eggs are "precious," not only because just one egg "ripens" per month (unless fertility drugs are used), but because each female possesses only a finite number of eggs.

> Before a baby girl is born, development of future eggs begins in her just-forming ovaries. About halfway through her mother's pregnancy, the girl's ovaries contain 6 or 7 million future eggs, most of which degenerate before birth. About 400 000 immature eggs are present in the newborn girl, and no new eggs are formed after this time. During childhood, continued degeneration reduces the number of eggs still further.... Fewer than 400 follicles [which rupture and release one egg each] are usually involved in ovulation during the female's reproductive years. (Masters et al., 1986: 38, 39)

In addition, eggs provide nourishment for the developing zygote while sperm do not. Eggs, therefore, are larger and more precious than sperm (Dawkins, 1976) and represent a greater genetic investment for the female than for the male biological parent. Noting that a woman invests nine months of her time and bodily resources in carrying a child from conception to delivery, sociobiologists declare that it would be "evolutionary insanity" (Hyde, 1985: 68) for her to relinquish primary responsibility for her genetic child after birth; this "explains" women's primary responsibility for childrearing. Cheap sperm/precious egg theorizing is also used to explain and legitimate the double standard of sexual behaviour: Male promiscuity is held to be evolutionarily adaptive, as it increases the likelihood that a man's genes will survive; women, however, must carefully select the one best partner with whom to mate (Symons, 1979). Sociobiologists also contend that *monogamy* (mating with only one person at a time) evolved to promote infant survival, and that female orgasm evolved to solidify the monogamous bond by sustaining a woman's interest in sexual activity during non-ovulatory times.

Critics argue that sociobiology uses circular reasoning and is simplistic, reductionist, untestable, and inherently conservative (Doyle and Paludi, 1995: 58–59). They point out that sociobiologists have not identified any of the specific genes that supposedly determine social behaviours, and that genetic explanations cannot account for rapid sociocultural changes in such areas as infant-nurturing practices, marital patterns, labour-force participation rates, etc., or for cultural variations in human behaviour. Nevertheless, "[b]y restating age-old claims that human nature is fixed and unchangeable, and that efforts to ameliorate social woes by changing the social environment are doomed to fail, sociobiology gives aid and comfort to supporters of the status quo" (Kamin, 1985: 78).

Hyde (1985) noted that sociobiology is blatantly androcentric and sexist both in its theory and in its choice of examples. Chimpanzees, she pointed out, are indiscriminately promiscuous when in estrous, mating with many males. Sociobiologists might conceivably explain this behaviour pattern as biologically determined to maximize the female's chances of becoming pregnant and ensure preservation of her genetic material. However, since such a claim would challenge the *human* sexual double standard that they hold so dear, sociobiologists typically ignore the sexual behaviour of female chimpanzees (see also Hubbard, 1994; Udry, 1994). Criticism of the selective use of species has been levelled against all research and theorizing that attempts to generalize from animal to human behaviour (Tavris and Wade, 1984: 133–135). Sociobiology has also been faulted for *anthropomorphizing* (i.e., imputing human characteristics or behaviour to) animals and even vegetation. Noting, for example, that Barash (1979) used the term "rape" "to describe what appears to be a male's forcing of sexual advances on an unwilling female among a variety of species," including plants, Lips (1993: 91) queried, "[h]ow ... does a researcher establish that a female flower ... is 'unwilling'?" She remarked, "[a]lthough the use of the word *rape* in such contexts may have an attention-getting function for the scientist, it does little to clarify what is indeed going on."

Most sociologists find the sociobiological position unappealing because it bypasses sociology's essential concern: humans designing their own cultures, their own unique ways of life (see Box 2.3). Sociologists acknowledge that biology underlies human behaviour, in that it takes a highly developed brain to develop human culture and a highly developed cerebral cortex to produce abstract thought. However, they reject the mechanistic claim that human behaviour is attributable to genetic programming (Miller and Costello, 2001). Humans, they argue, are not driven by instincts. Humans possess a sense of self and think abstractly. They create and discuss principles that underlie what they do, develop goals and courses of action, consider, reflect, and make choices. While their creative choices may appear to demonstrate universalities at the most general level, they defy reduction to a simple biological formula.

Evolutionary Psychology

Evolutionary psychology, a theory that Lancaster (2003: 13) has referred to as "sociobiology lite," attempts to blend biology, anthropology, psychology, and psychiatry. Like sociobiology, evolutionary psychology "attributes the origins of human nature to supposed norms of hominid behaviour over eons of evolutionary time" (Lancaster, 2003: 13). It shares sociobiology's bioreductivist assumption that over the course of human evolution, males and females have developed different adaptive strategies, resulting in sex differences in behaviour.

On the basis of a selective examination of cultures and animal species, evolutionary psychology attempts to identify a genetic basis for male promiscuity, female monogamy, male infidelity, and various gendered behaviours, particularly in relation to dating and mating (see, for example, Alexander, 2003; Browne, 2002, 2006; Silverman, 2003). Angier (2000: 156–157) delineates the "cardinal premises" of evolutionary psychology as follows: (1) women are naturally less promiscuous, less approving of casual sex, and more sexually reserved than men; (2) women are inherently more interested in long-term, stable relationships than are men; (3) in seeking mates, women are naturally attracted to the hallmarks of high status (e.g., wealth, professional stature) because of a desire to ensure that they and their children will be provided for, whereas men naturally look for the hallmarks of youth (e.g., smooth skin, virginity) because of a desire for a mate with a long childbearing career ahead of her; and (4) these preferences were "hammered out ... hundreds of thousands of

BOX 2.3

Biology versus Culture—Culture Is the Answer

For sociologist Cynthia Fuchs Epstein (1986, 1988, 2007), differences between males' and females' behaviour are solely the result of social factors—specifically, socialization and social control. Her argument follows.

1. A re-examination of the anthropological record shows greater equality between the sexes in the past than we had thought. In earlier societies, women as well as men hunted small game, devised tools for hunting and gathering, and gathered food. Studies of today's hunting and gathering societies show that "both women's and men's roles have been broader and less rigid than those created by stereotypes. For example, the Agta and Mbuti are clearly egalitarian and thus prove that hunting and gathering societies exist in which women are not subordinate to men. Anthropologists who study them claim that there is a separate but equal status of women at this level of development."

2. The types of work that men and women perform in each society are determined not by biology but by rigidly enforced social arrangements. Few people, whether male or female, can escape these arrangements to perform work outside their allotted narrow range. This gender inequality of work, which serves the interests of males, is enforced by informal customs and formal systems of laws. Once these socially constructed barriers are removed, women can and do exhibit similar work habits as males.

3. The human behaviours that biology "causes" are limited to those involving reproduction or differences in body structure. These differences are relevant for only a few activities, such as playing basketball or "crawling through a small space."

4. Female crime rates, which are rising in many parts of the world, indicate that displays of aggressiveness, often considered a biologically dictated male behaviour, are related to social rather than biological factors. When social conditions permit, such as in the practice of female lawyers, females also exhibit "adversarial, assertive, and dominant behavior." Not incidentally, this "dominant behavior" also appears in scholarly female challenges to the biased views about human nature that have been proposed by male scholars.

   In short, rather than "women's incompetence or inability to read a legal brief, perform brain surgery, [or] predict a bull market," social factors—socialization, gender discrimination, and other forms of social control—are responsible for gender differences in behaviour. Arguments that assign "an evolutionary and genetic basis" to explain gender differences in sex status are simplistic. They "rest on a dubious structure of inappropriate, highly selective, and poor data, oversimplification in logic and inappropriate inferences by use of analogy."

Source: Henslin and Nelson, 1996: 284.

years ago, in the legendary Environment of Evolutionary Adaptedness, or EEA, also known as the ancestral environment, also known as the Stone Age, and they have not changed appreciably since then, nor are they likely to change in the future."

Evolutionary psychologist David Buss (1994, 1995, 1996), while acknowledging that males and females are virtually identical in evolutionary terms, maintained that the case for differential adaptation is particularly strong in the area of mate selection. He argued that males' greater tendency to be jealous and to value sexual loyalty stem from the male desire to ensure the paternity of their mate's offspring. Steven Pinker (1997: 471–472) explained the existence of *Playboy*-type magazines in terms of the biological wiring of men and the supposedly visual nature of their sexuality. He maintained that the male-oriented United States pornography industry—a 10-billion-dollar industry that grosses "almost as much as spectator sports and the movies combined"—fills the same innate need that led men, in foraging cultures, to "make charcoal drawings of breasts and vulvas on rock overhangs, carve them on tree trunks, and scratch them in the sand." He contended that magazines such as *Playgirl* are not intended for a female audience but rather for gay men, and buttresses this claim with the assertion that from an evolutionary perspective, "it would make no sense for a woman to be easily aroused by the sight of a nude male." Pinker accounted for the supposedly non-visual nature of women's sexuality by claiming that a woman naturally desires to find "the best husband available, the best genes, or other returns on her sexual favours. If she could be aroused by the sight of a naked man, men could induce her to have sex by exposing themselves and her bargaining position would be compromised" (Pinker, 1997: 472). As Lancaster (2003: 42) observed, Pinker's explanations may "seem plausible, even convincing—[but] only if they are abetted by the silent labour of the reader, a reader of a certain disposition, who fits familiar form to functional norm, thus converting common sense into analysis, fancy into fact, what conceivably might have been into what indubitably is, and historical contingency into universal biology" (see also Luxen, 2007).

In posing such rhetorical questions as *Why Men Don't Have a Clue and Women Always Need More Shoes* (Pease and Pease, 2006) or *Why Men Don't Listen and Women Can't Read Maps* (Pease and Pease, 2001), best-selling authors in the pop psychology variant of this genre routinely suggest that, as the result of their evolutionary inheritance, men and women are fated to act in very different ways. For example, John Gray's (1993) *Men Are from Mars, Women Are from Venus* argued that the reason why men have difficulty locating items in the fridge is that, as the descendants of "hunters," men's vision has evolved in a way that is best-suited for scanning wide-open spaces. No such disadvantage impacts women, he maintained, because their ancestors were "gatherers." However, other explanations are assuredly possible. As Johnson (2007: 121) wryly observed, given that women often do the grocery shopping, it is not particularly surprising that they may be "more likely to know where they put the butter when they unpacked it."

Evolutionary psychology has been attacked on many of the same grounds as sociobiology. Noting that its core assumption is essentially untestable, Deaux (1999: 17) remarked, "[I]s the distal cause, whose existence can only be hypothesized, preferable to more proximal causes that are amenable to observation and recording?" More emphatic critics declare evolutionary psychology "bad science." Thus, while acknowledging that all science has an ideological component, Lancaster (2003: 353) asserted that "[s]cientists when they practice science well pose hypotheses that are subject to either experimental tests or other systematic checks against empirical evidence. When scientists pose untestable hypotheses ... or when they apply scientific language to problems not commensurate with the methods of scientific investigation ... what they practice is not an ideologically inflected science, but ideology outright."

Evolutionary psychology has also been faulted for its *genecentric* focus on inherited traits and dispositions (Caporael, 1997) and its failure to consider the wide variation in, and plasticity of, human behaviour (Esgate and Flynn, 2005). As di Leonardo (1998: 354–355) stated, "this nouveau sociobiology ... makes no allowance for ubiquitous human homosexuality ... [and] reintroduces the sexist (and anthropologically absurd) notion of a 'bottom line' human nature in which men try to maximize their DNA reproduction through impregnating as many young, nubile women as possible, and women attempt to 'capture' male parental support by enhancing their personal attractiveness." It has been argued that gender socialization and social location, rather than evolutionary forces, are responsible for any sex differences in attitudes about love, sexual fidelity, jealousy, etc. (Angier, 2000; DeSteno and Salovey, 1996).

Psychoanalytic Theory

Initially formulated by Freud (1856–1939), the "father of Western masculinist psychology" (Gerrard and Javed, 1995: 131), **psychoanalytic theory** is essentially *biologically deterministic*; as Freud famously uttered, "anatomy is destiny." It is important to note that Freud's theories of the origin of gender differences, and of female personality in particular, were derived almost exclusively from "talking" therapy with troubled adults.

According to psychoanalytic theory, individuals experience thoughts and feelings at both the conscious and unconscious levels of awareness; in children, Freud believed, most thoughts and motivations occur at the unconscious level. Freud further hypothesized the existence of three mental structures: the **id**, which represents biological influences or drives, governed by the *pleasure principle*; the **ego**, which seeks to impose limits on the id; and the **superego**, which represents society's standards as incorporated into what may be termed the conscience. Although the id is present from birth, every individual must pass through five invariantly sequenced developmental stages (*oral, anal, phallic, latency,* and *genital*) to develop an ego and superego, and to achieve, ultimately, a mature adult personality and behaviour patterns.

Freud believed that human beings are dominated by instincts and that sexuality, fuelled by **libido** (an instinctual craving for sensual pleasure), is one of the key forces motivating behaviour throughout childhood and beyond. During each of the five developmental stages of childhood, libido is centred in a different *erogenous zone*, an area of the body sensitive to sensual stimulation. In the **oral stage** (the first 18 months of life), the infant's mouth serves as the major focus of sexual energy and gratification. In the **anal stage** (18 months to 3 years), sensual pleasure is derived from the region of the anus. Controlling bowel movements gives the child physical and psychological pleasure and provides the first opportunity for freedom from maternal control. According to Freud, the mother is the child's primary love object during the first two stages, and both boys and girls pass through these stages in the same fashion.

However, during the **phallic stage** (ages 3 to 5), when libido focuses on the genitals and masturbation is the source of sexual gratification, boys and girls diverge and follow separate developmental pathways. The young boy becomes fascinated with his penis and develops an unconscious fantasy of possessing his mother sexually. This fantasy creates an

Oedipal complex, which Freud named after the Greek myth of Oedipus, who unwittingly killed his father and married his mother. During this phase, the boy is intensely attached to his mother and resents his father, whom he unconsciously perceives as a formidable rival for his mother's affections. He becomes anxious that his father will castrate him—an anxiety that is further fuelled by his startled observation that girls do not possess a penis, and his assumption that they have been castrated and deprived of a superior sexual organ. Freud considered **castration anxiety** to be a powerful motivating force in male psychosexual development. The young boy, fearful of his father, represses his sexual desires for his mother and identifies with his father as a way of avoiding castration. In seeking to become as much like his father as possible, so that he too will some day be able to satisfy his own sexual cravings, the boy takes on the values, ideas, and gender identity of his father, which leads to his development of an ego, superego, and masculine personality (see also Ross, 2000).

The first critical event for the young girl during the phallic stage is her realization that she does not possess a penis. This awareness immediately creates unconscious feelings of inferiority about herself and envy of boys and men. **Penis envy**, coupled with the girl's belief that her mother must have castrated her, leads her to reject her mother and to unconsciously desire her father sexually and to want impregnation by him. The female parallel to the Oedipal complex is the **Electra complex**, named after the Greek legend of the princess who urged her brother to avenge their father's murder by killing their mother. Freud claimed that a girl could never fully resolve her Electra complex because she can never physically possess a penis of her own. Whereas the boy's powerful fear of castration is resolved by the critical process of identification with his father, the girl is motivated by envy, a less powerful emotion than fear. Eventually realizing that she can never possess her father sexually, the girl comes to identify with her mother as a vicarious way of acquiring her father's penis. Through this weaker identification she takes on her mother's values, ideas, and gender identity and acquires an ego, superego, and feminine personality. As a woman, the wish for a penis finds expression in a desire to bear children. According to Freud, the girl's partial resolution of her Electra complex leaves her with lifelong feelings of inferiority, psychological immaturity, a predisposition to jealousy, intense maternal desires with attendant masochism, a dependence upon men for values, and a less mature sense of conscience or morality (an "immature" superego).

After passing through the phallic stage by age 6, male and female children enter the **latency stage**, in which sexual impulses recede in importance and both boys and girls focus on non-sexual interests. In the **genital stage**, precipitated by instinctual forces at puberty, the adolescent directs his or her sexual interests towards heterosexuality (although Freud did believe all human beings to be potentially bisexual [Lancaster, 2003: 23]) and a mature genital sexuality expressed in different forms, including, in women, a shift of emphasis from the clitoris to the vagina as the mature source of sexual pleasure (Lips, 2001: 47).

Several authors have challenged the basis for Freud's theory, particularly concerning the phallic stage of psychosexual development. As Masson (1985) noted, Freud initially emphasized the alarming prevalence of childhood rape and incest and its pathogenic effects on adult women; however, these revelations led to severe ostracism by his colleagues. It was professional expedience, Masson charged, which led Freud to retract his theory and suggest, instead, that accounts of childhood rape represented the unconscious workings of the Electra complex and repressed, unfulfilled childhood longings from the phallic stage of development. Masson pointed to a letter written by Freud to his friend and colleague Wilhelm Fleiss, in which Freud acknowledged, "[m]y own father was one of these perverts and is responsible for the hysteria of my brother ... and those of several younger sisters." Miller (1990) suggested that Freud may have reformulated his theory to spare his friends the pain of self-examination. She wrote that Fleiss' son, psychiatrist Robert Fleiss, discovered decades after the event that "at the age of two, he had been sexually abused by his father and that this incident coincided with Freud's renunciation of the truth" (Miller, 1990: 56).

Three other major criticisms have been levelled at Freudian theory. First, the theory is both *androcentric* (i.e., male-centred, viewing the world from the vantage point of male experience) and **phallocentric** (i.e., centred and placing inordinate emphasis on the penis). Freud's postulation of profound gender differences in personality and behaviour rests upon the cornerstone of anatomical-sex differences as observed by 3-year-old children who, he alleged, immediately regard the penis as the superior organ. Although Freud studied troubled adults and few children, he confidently asserted that once a girl realizes that she lacks a penis, she "develops, like a scar, a sense of inferiority" (Freud, 1925/1974). This assertion is highly controversial. As Etcoff (1999: 182) observed, "[w]hether or not Freud is right, [it would seem significant that] women, whether out of modesty or lack of inspiration, have not penned paeans to the penis." She directed attention to *The Bell Jar*, in which poet Sylvia Plath memorably described her first glimpse of her lover's genitals as reminiscent of "turkey neck and turkey gizzards"; more recently, Camille Paglia (1991: 17) mused that the male genitals, while boasting a certain "rational mathematical design, a syntax," nevertheless risk "ludicrousness by their rubbery indecisiveness." Steinem's *gynocentric* (i.e., female-centred) spoof of Freud's theory (featured in Box 2.4) satirizes Freud's phallocentrism by focusing triumphantly upon the clitoris, an erogenous organ of the female body whose sole function (unlike that of the phallus) is to provide sensual pleasure.

The second criticism is that in proclaiming biological differences to be the ultimate determinant of social and psychological behaviour, Freud ignored sociocultural influences, not only on the development of gender differences, but also on the creation of his own theory (Mackie, 1991: 63). Influenced by living in a particular historical time (late 1800s–early 1900s) and societal place (Victorian Austria, characterized by a patriarchal authority structure and a strict sex-linked division of labour), Freud generated a polarized depiction of women as "weak, inferior, passive, fragile, soft, vacillating, dependent, unreliable, intuitive rather than rational, castrated and handicapped" and men as "aggressive, controlling, strong, superior, proud, independent, venturesome, competitive, hard and athletic" (Miller, 1974: 367). He then generalized these traits to all women and men in all cultures and eras.

Yet Freud's theory was not entirely biologically determinist. Recall that he portrayed resolution of the Oedipal and Electra complexes as ultimately resting on a child's identification with the same-sex parent—a process that involves *environmental influences* through imitative learning. Psychoanalytic theory thus provided the basis for a later-developed branch of social learning theory known as *identification theory* (Tavris and Wade, 1984: 218). What is more, the "neo-Freudians," such as Erikson (1963) and Horney (1967), later modified Freud's original theory to give more emphasis to the contributions of the sociocultural environment to child development and adult personality.

A third major problem is that the concepts of psychoanalytic theory cannot be evaluated scientifically. Greenglass (1982: 49–50) noted that "[e]mpirical work on many of Freud's

What if Freud Were Phyllis?

The following is a fictional gynocen-tric "rewrite" of Freudian theory, which places women centre stage and men at the problematic margins of social and psychological life.

It's important to understand that when Phyllis was growing up in Vienna, women were considered superior because of their ability to give birth. From the family parlor to the great matriarchal institutions of politics and religion, this was a uniform belief....

Women's superior position in society was so easily mistaken for an immutable fact of life that males had developed exaggerated versions of such inevitable but now somewhat diminished conditions as womb envy. Indeed, these beliefs in women's natural right to dominate were the very pillars of Western matriarchal civilization....

In addition, men's lack of firsthand experience with birth and nonbirth—with choosing between existence and nonexistence, conception and contraception, as women must do so wisely for all their fertile years—severely inhibited their potential for developing a sense of justice and ethics....

Finally, as Phyllis Freud's clinical findings showed, males were inclined toward meanness and backbiting, the inevitable result of having been cut off from the coveted sources of life and fulfillment to which their mates had such ready access within their bodies....

As Phyllis observed ... there was "yet another surprising effect of womb envy, or of the discovery of the inferiority of the penis to the clitoris, which is undoubtedly the most important of all ... that masturbation ... is a feminine activity and that the elimination of penile sensuality is a necessary pre-condition for the development of masculinity."

In this way, Phyllis Freud wisely screened all she heard from her testyrical patients through her understanding, still well accepted to this day, that men are sexually passive, just as they tend to be intellectually and ethically. After all, the libido is intrinsically feminine, or, as she put it with her genius for laywoman's terms, "man is possessed of a weaker sexual instinct."

This was also proved by man's mono-orgasmic nature. No serious authority disputed the fact that females, being multiorgasmic, were better adapted to pleasure and thus were the natural sexual aggressors. In fact, "envelopment," the legal term for intercourse, was an expression of this active/passive understanding. It was also acted out in microcosm in the act of conception itself. Consider these indisputable facts of life: The large ovum expends no energy, waits for the sperm to seek out its own destruction in typically masculine and masochistic fashion, and then simply envelops this infinitesimal organism. As the sperm disappears into the ovum, it is literally eaten alive—much like the male spider being eaten by his mate. Even the most quixotic male liberationist will have to agree that biology leaves no room for doubt about intrinsic female dominance.

What intrigued Freud was not these well-known biological facts, however, but their psychological significance: for instance, the ways in which males were rendered incurably narcissistic, anxious, and fragile by having their genitals so precariously perched and visibly exposed

---

BOX 2.4

What if Freud Were Phyllis? (*Continued*)

on the outside of their bodies.... [M]en's womblessness and the loss of all but vestigial breasts and odd, useless nipples were the end of a long evolutionary journey toward the sole functions of sperm production, sperm carrying, and sperm delivery. Women did all the rest of reproduction. Thus, it was female behavior, health, and psychology that governed gestation and birth. Since time immemorial, this disproportionate reproductive influence had unbalanced the power of the sexes in favor of women.

Finally, there was the unavoidable physiological fact of the penis. Its very existence confirmed the initial bisexuality of all humans. All life begins as female, in the womb as elsewhere (the only explanation for men's residual nipples), and penile tissue had its origin in the same genital nub, and thus retained a comparable number of nerve endings as the clitoris. But somewhere along the evolutionary line, the penis had acquired a double function: excretion of urine and sperm delivery. Indeed, during the male's feminine, masturbatory, clitoral stage of development before young boys had seen female genitals and realized that their penises were endangered and grotesque compared to the compact, well-protected, aesthetically perfect clitoris—it had a

third, albeit immature, function of masturbatory pleasure....

It was almost as if Father Nature himself had paid "less careful attention" to the male. His unique and most distinctive organ had become confused. Was the penis part of the reproductive system or the urinary tract? Was it intended for conception or excretion? How could males be trusted to understand the difference?...

Nonetheless, Freud continued to extend her "Anatomy is destiny" thesis beyond previous boundaries. With the force of logic in combination with clinical evidence of men's greater tolerance for physical as well as psychological pain, she demonstrated that the suicide run of tiny, weak male sperm toward big, strong female ova was the original paradigm of male masochism. There was also the chronic suffering caused by burning urine forced through the residual clitoral nerve endings within the penis. For the next century and perhaps the future of womankind, Freud had brilliantly proved why the pleasure/pain principle of masochism was a hallmark of masculinity.

Source: Steinem, 1994: 32, 33, 35, 36, 48-50, 51, 52, 69. Reprinted with the permission of Simon and Schuster from *Moving Beyond Words* by Gloria Steinem. Copyright © 1994 by Gloria Steinem.

---

assumptions about women has not given support to such ideas as penis envy and the Oedipus complex. For example, little evidence exists that girls and women envy male anatomy, while there is considerable evidence that women and girls envy the masculine role for its greater power and privilege—its greater sociocultural advantages." Lindsey (1994: 38) noted that "[a]lmost a century of empirical research on the foundations of Freud's work has produced more questions than answers and more inconsistencies than agreement." Since Freud's major concepts do not lend themselves to testing, psychoanalytic theory must, like a secular religion, be accepted or rejected on faith.

Psychoanalytic Feminism Drawing upon the work of Horney (1926/1973) and Klein (1957), contemporary **psychoanalytic feminists** or **gynocentric theorists** (Lips, 1999: 85) such as Dinnerstein (1976), Chodorow (1978), Rubin (1983), and Kaschak (1992) have argued that the key personality-shaping events of childhood occur in the "pre-Oedipal" stage of developmental life. The crucial factor, they contend, is that it is women who mother boys and girls. They maintain that child care by mothers produces daughters who want to become mothers and sons who dominate and devalue women.

According to Chodorow (1978), girls' intense bonds with their mothers are never wholly severed. As adults, girls attempt to recreate that emotional closeness in their intimate relationships with men; what is more, their desire for children represents their attempt to reproduce the profound emotional bond they had with their own mothers. However, since masculine identity depends on boys' severing attachment to their mothers and rejecting and devaluing femininity, boys are pushed into a sharp and early separation. This experience, she theorized, may be perceived as abandonment and generate lifelong fears of connecting to another (for fear of being yet again rejected), diffuse feelings of hostility towards women (stemming from unresolved rage against the long-lost love object, the mother), and a turning to the outer world and establishment of a separate, autonomous identity. "The basic feminine sense of self is connected to the world, the basic masculine sense of self is separate" (Chodorow, 1978: 169).

In a complementary theory, Rubin (1983) maintained that the fact that girls and women are of the same sex makes it easier for girls to establish their gender identity, with the result that women develop more permeable ego boundaries and greater empathetic abilities than men. She theorized that differences between boys and their mothers make establishing a gender identity more difficult for boys and promote the development of strong ego boundaries. Thus, women have difficulty maintaining their ego boundaries within a relationship, while men have difficulty breaching their own (Rubin, 1983: 92–96).

According to Kaschak (1992), parenting arrangements in a patriarchal society and the pre-Oedipal attachment of girls to their mothers is consequential in yet another way. In her re-examination of the Oedipus myth, Kaschak directed attention to Oedipus' daughter, Antigone, who devoted herself to being her father's guide and companion. Kaschak argued that early childhood experiences encourage boys to view their mothers as extensions of themselves, whose primary purpose is to gratify their needs. Kaschak contended that males' attitude of "infantile grandiosity" is extended towards other women. The "**Oedipal male**," she wrote, feels entitled to having his needs gratified by women, and this sense of entitlement is supported by a patriarchal society. Women, in contrast, labour under an **Antigone complex**, having learned from early childhood experiences to view women as inferior to men, to treat their own identities and independent existence as of secondary importance, and to view themselves as extensions of the men in their lives. Resolution of the Oedipal complex, according to Kaschak, should require a man to recognize "that he is not a king, just a human being in a world of other humans and living creatures, all of equal importance with him" (p. 73), that women develop an independent identity, and that both resist being "engulfed in masculine meanings."

In various ways, all of these theorists imply that a fundamental reorganization of parenting is urgently desirable and that fathers should become more involved in parenting, at least during the pre-Oedipal stage. However, if the consequences of current parenting arrangements are as these feminists claim, it is unclear how such a reorganization might come to pass. This practical dilemma apart, psychoanalytic feminism is faulted for the same basic problem as psychoanalysis: it is not empirically verifiable. While Chodorow (2002, 2003) maintained that her clinical observations backed up her theory, Renzetti and Curran (2003: 76) emphasized that "the reliability of clinical psychoanalytic data remains a concern; while Chodorow may interpret her patients' statements as supportive ... [of her theory], another clinician—even one who shares a feminist psychoanalytic perspective—may interpret the patients' statements differently." They also noted that Chodorow's theory has been charged with ethnocentrism for its failure to acknowledge that in non-Western societies, child care is not the exclusive domain of one mother, and that even within Western societies, racial, ethnic, and social class variations in child care do occur. Ironically, Chodorow (1996) has herself decried the tendency of psychoanalytic theories about women to "overgeneralize, universalize, and essentialize," and has faulted them for being "permeated with unreflected-upon cultural assumptions" and for their failure to adequately consider "the inextricable cultural aspects in anyone's gender psychology" (see also Chodorow, 1999; 2002a).

PSYCHOLOGICAL THEORIES

It is generally agreed that by the age of 4 or 5, girls and boys demonstrate a preference for same-sex companions and generally seem to prefer activities defined by their culture as sex-appropriate. "The acquisition of sex-appropriate preferences, skills, personality attributes, behaviors, and self-concept is typically referred to within psychology as the process of 'sex typing'" (Bem, 1983/1995: 83; see also Serbin et al., 2002a, 2002b). Several psychological theories consider the processes by which sex typing occurs. This section reviews social learning theory, cognitive developmental theory, and gender schema theory, and concludes with an examination of a social-psychological theory, symbolic interactionism.

Social Learning Theory

Social learning theory (Bandura, 1986) focuses upon the impact of the social environment on human behaviour. This theory has been applied to the development of gender differences, based upon the premise that learning gender follows the same principles as learning any other social behaviour. In explaining the acquisition of gender behaviour, social learning theory stresses the operation of two basic processes. One is **external reinforcement**, or the rewarding of gender-appropriate and punishing of gender-inappropriate behaviour. According to social learning theory, *behaviour is determined by its consequences*. Individuals are likely to repeat behaviours that have elicited a positive response (e.g., praise, smiles of approval) and to desist from those that have elicited a negative response (e.g., criticism, angry looks) (Schwartzman et al., 1995). The second basic process is **modelling**, or the emulation of others' behaviour. Modelling can take either of two forms: **direct imitation**, in which one immediately patterns one's behaviour upon what others are seen doing; and **observational learning**, in which one learns through observation of other people's behaviour (and its consequences), even though the information may not be acted upon until much later. Social learning theorists assume that "knowledge about gender roles either precedes or is acquired at the same time as gender identity" (Intons-Peterson, 1988: 40).

Some social learning theorists (Collins, 2001; Gallahan, 2000; Levy, 1989: 12; Lynn, 1969) have asserted that the mother is the initial and central reinforcer of gender-appropriate behaviour, and that a child learns early in life to exhibit those behaviours that will elicit the mother's approval. Mothers differentially reinforce their children's gender behaviour by rewarding feminine and punishing masculine behaviours in girls, and rewarding masculine and punishing feminine behaviours in boys. When others (e.g., fathers, other adults, peers) reinforce gender-appropriate behaviour in a similar manner, the child learns that the reinforcements forthcoming from one source can generally be anticipated from others; this is known as **stimulus generalization**. Children tend to model the behaviour of same-sex parents and other same-sex adults; this may explain the acquisition of certain subtle aspects of gender behaviour that have not received direct reinforcement (Poulin-Dubois et al., 1994). In an investigation of cognitive and environmental factors in the development of sex typing among 558 Canadian children ages 5 to 13, Serbin et al. (1993) found that the preference for sex-typed activities, occupations, and peers was consistently related to sex typing of the home environment. Children whose mothers modelled non-traditional behaviours were less likely to prefer gender-typed activities; children whose fathers adhered to traditional gender roles were more likely to know what activities and occupations are generally associated with men and women (see also Poulin-Dubois et al., 1998; Powlishta et al., 2001; Schwartzman et al., 1995). Through observation of people in the environment or the media, children incorporate into their repertoire gender behaviours that may be replicated at a later stage of life. A young girl, for example, may observe her mother's reaction to the needs of a younger sibling and store this information for use when she herself is a mother.

Laboratory experiments support learning theory's claim that aggressive behaviour can be promoted or inhibited by the selective application of rewards or punishments. However, the mechanisms underlying the acquisition of gender differences may be more complex. A meta-analytic study by Lytton and Romney (1991) reported that although parents treat their sons and daughters similarly on many dimensions, "one dimension on which some parents ... treat daughters and sons differently ... is [in] the encouragement of gender-typed activities" (Lips, 2001: 312). Evidence indicates that in specific situations, parents differentially reinforce boys and girls for exhibiting the same behaviour (Fagot and Hagan, 1991). Fathers tend to "roughhouse" with boys but treat daughters as if they were more fragile (Lips, 2005: 393). Block (1978) noted that parents emphasize different values for boys and girls, reinforcing achievement and assertiveness in boys but restraining these tendencies in girls, emphasizing interpersonal relationships instead. Parents appear to be most likely to use direct reinforcement in the areas of dress and aggressive behaviour (Losh-Hesselbart, 1987: 545).

Evidence suggests that parents monitor boys' behaviours more closely than girls'. Sons have been found to be rewarded and punished more than daughters (Martin, 1990). Parents also appear to be more concerned about ensuring masculine behaviour in boys than feminine behaviour in girls (McGuffey and Rich, 1999). Cross-sexed "sissy" behaviour in boys elicits a more negative parental response than cross-sexed "tomboy" behaviour in girls— although women tend to be more accepting of their children's cross-sexed behaviour than are men (Martin, 1990; McGuffey and Rich, 1999). Fathers are more likely than mothers to inhibit gender-inappropriate behaviour in their children (Fagot, 1995; Fagot and Hagan, 1991). These findings suggest that mothers are more likely to focus upon gender-appropriate behaviour, while fathers focus mainly upon behaviour that is gender-inappropriate. Pressure on girls to act more feminine does not appear to intensify until around the time of puberty (Harris, 1995).

According to social learning theory, imitation of a same-sex parent is important for the acquisition of gender-appropriate behaviour. However, because fathers are seldom primary caregivers, they are often unavailable to provide imitative role models for their sons; maternal admonitions of "boys don't cry" or "boys don't act like sissies" leave unanswered the question of what boys are *supposed* to do. In contrast, girls receive more reward-type reinforcement from a more available imitative role model. Lynn (1969) suggested that the absence of a male role model accounts for boys' tendency to view masculinity in highly stereotypical terms, as well as for men's tendency to be more anxious and insecure than women about their gender identity and behaviour. These tendencies may be implicated in fathers' greater concern over gender-inappropriate behaviour in their sons.

The claim that children acquire masculinity/femininity by imitating same-sex parents is prized by those who maintain that the lack of "appropriate" gender-role models in single- or homosexual-parent families is damaging to children; however, it appears to be too simplistic (Bos et al., 2007). Maccoby and Jacklin's (1974) early research found that very young children do not consistently imitate same-sex models more than models of the other sex. More recent research, which found that boys were less likely to imitate a female model than girls to imitate a male, suggested that the perceived power of a model may be of more importance than his or her sex (Golombok and Fivush, 1994; McGuffey and Rich, 1999). Harris (1993) argued that unless peer groups support behaviours learned at home, such behaviours will not be displayed within the group. The influence of gender-segregated peer-group cultures may help to explain strongly gendered behaviour among children whose parents have tried to raise them in non-gender-stereotyped ways (Golombok and Fivush, 1994; Serbin et al., 1993). Social learning theory has been unable to identify the qualities (e.g., nurturance, power) that make a model more likely to be imitated, or under what circumstances imitation is most likely to occur. It is possible that children learn equally well from models of either sex, but only perform those behaviours that they see rewarded in others (Martin, 1999).

Perhaps the most persistent criticism of social learning theory has been that it seems to regard the child as a relatively passive object of external rewards and punishments (Davidman, 1995; Lindsey, 1994: 53). Finally, social learning theory does not explicitly address the question of how children learn what femaleness or maleness is, how this knowledge relates to lessons about gender-appropriate or -inappropriate behaviour, and why some behaviours are considered gender-appropriate and others aren't. Social learning theory simply accepts the gendered context for learning and focuses only upon how that learning takes place.

Cognitive Development Theory

Cognitive development theory was formulated by Kohlberg (1966) on the basis of a theoretical framework created by Piaget (1968, 1954, 1950). From empirical research, Piaget concluded that cognitive skills develop in an ordered sequence of qualitatively different stages from infancy to adulthood; in other words, people think, reason, and learn in a distinctly different fashion at each successive stage of development. Kohlberg believed that children's understandings of gender and gender-appropriate roles are based upon their developmentally changing cognitions. Kohlberg's sample was composed of boys only, revealing the common tendency of traditional theorists to generalize male experience to females.

According to Kohlberg, children acquire a rudimentary sense of their own and others' gender some time between 18 months and 3 years of age. However, despite knowing what his/her gender is at the moment, a young child may be uncertain about what it will be in the future and its connection to future behavioural possibilities. Initially, identifications of gender are based upon visible cues such as hair length and clothing styles (Blakemore, 2003;

Leinbach and Fagot, 1993; Poulin-Dubois et al., 1994). According to the logic of this stage of cognitive development, should those visible cues change, so too would gender itself; put a dress on a boy and he becomes a girl, or cut a girl's hair short and she becomes a boy. Kohlberg provides the following example of a child's incomplete conceptualization of gender:

Johnny [age $4^1/_2$]: I'm going to be an airplane builder when I grow up.

Jimmy [just turned 4]: When I grow up I'll be a mommy.

Johnny: No, you can't be a mommy. You have to be a daddy.

Jimmy: No, I'm going to be a mommy.

Johnny: No, you're not a girl, you can't be a mommy.

Jimmy: Yes, I can. (1966: 95)

In asserting that a boy can't become a mommy, Johnny demonstrates a sense of **gender constancy**, the awareness that one's gender is permanent or unchanging. However, Jimmy's sense of gender is still rudimentary, as we see from his insistence that gender can change.

Kohlberg claimed that gender constancy generally develops at around age 5 or 6 and is a crucial motivating factor in the eventual acquisition of gendered behaviour. Gender identity becomes a central part of a child's self-concept and is invested with a positive emotional attachment; thereafter, children are self-motivated to seek out behaviour consistent with their understanding of gender: "I am a boy, therefore I want to do boy things" (Kohlberg, 1966: 89). Thus, cognitive development theory, unlike social learning theory, sees the child as the primary agent in the enterprise of learning how to act as a gendered being. Once gender constancy is acquired, children accumulate stereotypes not only of gender-appropriate behaviours for both sexes but of societal evaluations of each sex. These stereotypes guide the **self-socialization process** and provide content for subsequent gender behaviour. The self-socialization process is supposedly easier for boys because of the more positive evaluations of males in our society. "In the reality of the young child, 'male' is identified with 'big' and synonymous with 'more powerful'" (Kessler and McKenna, 1978: 97). During early childhood, both boys and girls identify to some extent with male role models in their environment. However, girls eventually come to see the female gender role as attractive because of its "niceness" (Kohlberg, 1966: 121–122) and to identify with their mothers as a readily available role model.

Although Kohlberg's theory is based upon examination of boys only, there is some evidence for the existence of the same developmental processes in girls (Gump et al., 2000; Powlishta et al., 2001). However, the timing of these processes has been called into question by research indicating that gender-typed interests appear in children too young to have acquired gender constancy (Gallahan, 2000; Hill and Flom, 2007; Martin et al., 2002). For example, gender-typed patterns of toy play have been observed in children under the age of 2 (Levy, 1999), and, in some studies, as young as 9 months (Campbell et al., 2000, 2002); these findings appear to contradict Kohlberg's hypothesis that such interests should not appear until after the emergence of gender constancy. Martin and Little (1990) concluded that only a rudimentary knowledge of gender need exist before gender stereotypes and preferences are acquired: "Once children can accurately label the sexes, they begin to form gender stereotypes and their behavior is influenced by these gender-associated expectations" (Martin and Little, 1990: 1438). They noted that young children who recognized their own sex and that of others showed greater awareness of gender clothing stereotypes than those who did not, and evinced stronger preferences for gender-typed toys and same-sex peers. Other research has indicated that very young children demonstrate high levels of knowledge on basic measures of gender stereotyping (e.g., "Who usually cooks, boys or girls?") (Martin, 1999; Powlishta et al., 2001). Research examining toddlers' knowledge of the gender stereotyping of household activities revealed that girls as young as 24 months and boys as young as 31 months demonstrated such knowledge (Poulin-Dubois et al., 2002; Serbin et al., 2002).

Consistent with cognitive development theory, it has been noted that young children are more likely than older children or adults to base their predictions about others on the person's sex (Lobel et al., 1993; Zucker et al., 1995). In one study, children heard descriptions of boys and girls with masculine, feminine, or neutral interests; they were then asked how much they would like each child and how much that child would like to play with either masculine or feminine toys (Martin, 1989). While 4- to 6-year-old children focused only on the sex of the target child (predicting, for example, that a boy described as liking to play with kitchen sets and having a girl for a best friend would like masculine but not feminine activities), older children were somewhat more likely to incorporate gender-related information into their judgments. Thus, 8- to 10-year-old children maintained that although a male child described as having feminine interests would "somewhat" like "girls' toys," he would "mainly" enjoy playing with "boys' toys" (Martin, 1989). In a second study, Taylor (1996) asked young children to imagine a young girl raised on an island inhabited only by men (or a young boy raised on an island inhabited only by women), and to predict whether the children would grow up to be male-like or female-like in a number of ways. While children between the ages of 4 and 9 generally believed that a boy would "naturally" want to play football and become a firefighter even when raised in an all-female environment, older children were more likely to recognize the impact of social factors upon behaviour and preferences.

Kohlberg's suggestion that children (i.e., boys) value their gender identity and prefer same-sex peers because they are of the same sex has also found empirical support (Golombok and Fivush, 1994; Levant, 1995). Martin et al. (1995) argued that children develop two simple theories that guide their preference for same-sex individuals: a **within-group similarity theory** (a belief that same-sex children are similar on the basis of a shared "essence") and a **between-group theory** (a belief that children of different sexes are unalike because of distinctive essences). They suggested that a gender-centric pattern of evaluation may stem from a child's perception of within-group similarity (see also Campbell et al., 2004; Martin and Ruble, 2004).

The main focus of Kohlberg's theory is children's internal cognitive processes. Like social learning theory, cognitive development theory does not address the questions of how and why stereotypes and differential standards of gender-appropriate toys, clothes, and behaviours exist. The sociocultural context of sex and gender is simply taken for granted.

Gender Schema Theory

Bem's (1981, 1983/1995) **gender schema theory** blends elements of both social learning and cognitive development theories in its understanding of sex typing: Like the former, it assumes that sex typing is learned; like the latter, it maintains that it is mediated by the individual's cognitive processing. A *schema* is a mental framework or cognitive structure that guides and organizes our perceptual and interpretive processes; schematic information processing "entails a readiness to sort information into categories on the basis of some particular dimension" (Bem, 1983/1995: 87; see also Barbera, 2003). According to Bem (1983/1995: 87), "the developing child invariably learns his or her society's cultural definitions of femaleness and maleness," along with their vast network of sex-linked associations, and gradually learns "to encode and to organize information in terms of an evolving gender schema."

Bem (1983/1995) suggested that a child's gender identity, once acquired within a gendered culture such as our own, provides the foundation for gender-schematic processing (i.e., the spontaneous tendency to organize information about oneself, others, and the world into categories of "feminine" and "masculine"). The readiness to "tag" incoming information in terms of gender categories promotes the acquisition of gendered behaviour by heightening sensitivity to sex-linked information. Bem argued that the gender stereotypes that children learn inform the development of gender-congruent behaviour: "As children learn the contents of their society's gender schema, they learn which attributes are to be linked with their own sex and, hence, with themselves" (Bem, 1983/1995: 88). The gender schema ultimately becomes "a prescriptive standard or guide ... an internalized motivational factor that prompts an individual to regulate his or her behaviour so that it conforms to cultural definitions."

Bem (1983: 154) claimed that "the gendered personality ... has a readiness to superimpose a gender-based classification on every heterogeneous collection of human possibilities that presents itself." A *gender schematic* person, Bem maintained, is more quick than one who is gender aschematic to process information in terms of gender and to make attributions on the basis of gender—for example, blaming bad driving on the operator's gender ("typical woman driver") rather than on poor road conditions. Possession of a gender schema is also believed to heighten one's sensitivity to gender stereotypes; once integrated into a gender schema, these stereotypes gain a tenacious hold because they support and maintain the schema itself. While gender schema are thought to be highly salient in "feminine" women and "masculine" men, even those who do not view themselves as stereotypically masculine or feminine may process information on the basis of gender. For example, a feminist may reject stereotypically feminine behaviour, yet be gender schematic in processing information (e.g., "Did my professor mark my assignment more leniently/harshly because I am a woman?"). It is important to bear in mind that gender schema theory focuses on the process, rather than the content, of sex typing; accordingly, "sex-typed individuals ... differ from other individuals not primarily in the degree of femininity or masculinity they possess, but in the extent to which their self-concepts and behaviours are organized on the basis of gender rather than on the basis of some other dimension" (Bem, 1983/1995: 88).

Some empirical evidence has been generated to support gender schema theory. According to Bem (1983/1995: 87), in cultures such as ours that assert the primacy of the sex dichotomy, even abstract ideas and inanimate objects come to be invested with gender attributes on the basis of a metaphoric connection to sex-linked features; e.g., straight lines and sharp angles are considered "masculine," curves and circles "feminine"; nature and Earth are anointed "Mother," while sky and impersonal time are called "Father." In one study investigating whether children associated non-gender-typed objects more strongly with one sex than with another, children reported that (pointy) fir trees are "for boys" while maple trees are "for girls" (Leinbach et al., 1997). In a second study (Hort and Leinbach, 1993), researchers purposely altered the metaphorical gender cues of a teapot and a pastel "My Little Pony" by painting the teapot brown and the pony black and liberally decorating each with spikes. Confronted with these strong cues, all of the children identified the toys as intended for boys and several boys announced that they wished to receive them as Christmas presents. However, although Bem (1981) reported a consistent pattern of gender bias in information processing, Signorella (1999: 108) noted that "numerous attempts" to replicate Bem's findings in adults have been unsuccessful (see also Katsurada and Sugihara, 2002).

Bem's gender schema theory is attractive in that it suggests that sex typing and gender-based categorization may be mitigated by "gender aschematic" childrearing—that practices such as exposing children to non-traditional female and male models may increase their interest in pursuing non-traditional careers and promote egalitarian attitudes (Nathanson et al., 2002). However, research suggests that the gender schema model is overly simple and that multidimensional models are necessary (Campbell et al., 2004; Spence, 1993). For example, only a weak relationship has been found between the gender knowledge, attitudes, and behaviour of young children (Bigler et al., 1998; Campbell et al., 2004, 2002; Martin et al., 2002; Spence and Hall, 1996). Moreover, Bigler (1999: 142) reported that "changes in an individual's beliefs within a particular domain [e.g., occupations] do not necessarily affect the individual's sex-typed beliefs within other domains or his or her sex-typed behavior." The primary value of Bem's gender schema theory appears to lie in its ability to integrate many of the concepts and principles of social learning and cognitive development theories, and to provide us with a better understanding of how gender-related information is cognitively processed.

SOCIAL-PSYCHOLOGICAL THEORY

Symbolic interactionism is a social-psychological theory whose roots can be traced to sociologist-philosophers, such as Max Weber and George Herbert Mead, and early twentieth-century sociologists, such as Charles Horton Cooley and W.I. Thomas. This theory directs primary attention to the process of becoming gendered and not to the actual content of gender. Interactionists assert that human social behaviour is essentially symbolic behaviour. A **symbol** is something that stands for, or represents, something else; symbols include written and spoken words, non-verbal gestures, and physical signs. Symbols are assigned *meanings* (that is, shared definitions), and come to be responded to in terms of those meanings. In social interaction,

> human beings interpret or "define" each other's actions instead of merely reacting to each other's actions. Their "response" is not made directly to the actions of one another but instead is based on the meaning which they attach to such actions. Thus, human interaction is mediated by the use of symbols, by interpretation, or by ascertaining the meaning of one another's actions. (Blumer, 1969: 79)

Symbolic interactionists focus their analyses upon the symbols exchanged in interactions and the meanings these symbols have for the participants. These meanings may vary according to the particular cultural or subcultural context (e.g., social class, racial/ethnic group) within which they are embedded.

Human symbolic interaction occurs mainly through **role taking**, sometimes referred to as "taking the role of the other." In role taking, each person in an interactive situation attempts to predict or anticipate the actions and reactions of other participants. Symbolic interactionists contend that role taking is the principal mechanism of socialization and the development of a **self**. The self and self-awareness are thought to emerge at about 18 months to 3 years of age, as demonstrated by a child's accurate use of words such as "I," "me," and "mine." According to symbolic interactionists, self development and language development evolve simultaneously (Mackie, 1991: 92). A central element of the self is *gender identity*, an awareness not only of *being* male or female but of the fact that the verbal symbols (i.e., labels) "male" and "female" have certain meanings. Children do not merely recognize that "I," the self, exists as a separate and distinct object; they also label that self as either male or female and incorporate into their self-concept what it means to be a boy or a girl.

The beginnings of self-awareness and gender identity, as well as of the acquisition of language and sex/gender terminology, occur during the early stages of socialization through role-taking encounters between a child and **significant others** (Mead, 1934/1962). Significant others are those individuals with whom one has an important emotional bond (e.g., parents, siblings, teachers, friends). Through interaction with these individuals, children learn to form connections between words (including "male" and "female") and things (including self) in their social and physical environment. They also learn to see themselves as others see them—whether positively or negatively. Cooley's (1902) concept of the **looking-glass self** captures the idea of coming to know oneself in terms of the image reflected back by another person. Accordingly, if a child perceives that others consider him worthwhile because he is male rather than female and does masculine rather than feminine things, he will develop positive feelings about his maleness (and, possibly, negative or disdainful feelings towards females and femininity).

As their world expands with exposure to school and society, children also learn to take the role of the **generalized other** (Mead, 1934/1962); this term stands for the prevailing cultural norms and values that we use as references in evaluating ourselves. This role reflects a greater degree of abstraction: "Instead of a child thinking, 'Dad says I mustn't cry when I don't get my own way,' the more mature youngster can now think, '*They* say boys mustn't cry'" (Mackie, 1991: 94; emphasis in original). The ability to generalize rules, understandings, and meanings beyond one's close circle of significant others allows an individual to adopt the perspective of the larger society and to regulate his/her behaviour in accordance with societal standards and in anticipation of societal reactions.

While emphasizing the importance of social interaction, symbolic interactionists do not suggest that people are passive objects of societal shaping. In the first place, they believe that the self is not entirely socially defined. Mead (1934/1962: 173–178) argued that the self is composed of the "**Me**" (which represents the stable self, developed through interaction with others) and the "**I**" (which represents the spontaneous, autonomous, impulsive self). The oft-heard utterance "I don't know why I did that. It's not at all like me" reflects the fact that our actions are not invariably determined by the imperative to conform to societal expectations. Even though we acquire the social meanings of male and female, masculinity and femininity, our behaviours are not inevitably dictated by those meanings. Symbolic interactionists believe that we are capable of independently seeking out new meanings of "male" and "female" and of masculine, feminine, or non-gendered human behaviours. As West and Zimmerman (1987) stated, "[a] person's gender is not simply an aspect of what one *is*, but, more fundamentally, it is something that one *does*, and does recurrently in interaction with others" (emphasis added). In the second place, role taking, a key component of human social interaction, is an active process, rich with possibilities for new understandings. The more individuals interact with people of other social classes, ethnicities, sexual orientations, and abilities, the greater the likelihood that their self-concepts, definitions, thoughts, and feelings will evolve and expand. Shamara Shantu Riley (1994: 92) has written that as a black lesbian, "I have often simultaneously felt like a 'sistah' and yet still an 'outsider' in the Black, lesbian, and womanist communities.... I am often expected to negate some component of my identity in the name of 'unity' or in order to pass someone's litmus test of acceptance." As humans interact, they negotiate how they will conduct themselves in relation to one another, actively creating their own interpersonal roles (Suh et al., 2004). Finally, meanings that are socially constructed can be socially reconstructed. Since meaning does not inhere in symbols, but is created out of interaction, meaning can change; the meanings—as well as the evaluations—of male and female, masculinity and femininity, are not permanent and can be altered.

THE GENDER PERSPECTIVE

The **gender perspective** arose partly as a reaction against theories such as sociobiology and psychoanalytic theory, which treat gender as a biologically rooted individual characteristic (Thompson, 1993: 557; Zvonkovic et al., 1996: 91). These theories promote the *essentialist* notion that biologically based sex differences are the basis of stable and immutable gender identities; **essentialism** is "the idea that gender differences in behaviour stem from qualities that are resident in, or possessed by, women and men" (Lips, 2001: 457). The gender perspective also reacted against social-psychological theories that stress socialization as the ultimate mechanism of gender acquisition. Like the biologically based theories, socialization-based models tended to view gender as an individual characteristic which retains a fundamental continuity throughout the individual's life. Through the 1970s and 1980s, many feminist and nonfeminist sociologists and psychologists promoted a generic "sex-role" theoretical model to describe the social basis of gender. They understood gender roles (formerly called "sex roles") to be "dichotomous, complementary but unequal, relatively consistent internally, deeply internalized during the process of childhood socialization, and susceptible to only limited change in adulthood" (Potuchek, 1992: 548). As a result, they focused upon identifying the socialization processes leading to our society's patterns of gendered behaviour; alternative patterns of gendered behaviour found in other cultures or eras were simply understood to reflect the different role expectations into which individuals were socialized.

The sex-role socialization model began to receive criticism for its neglect of issues of power and inequality, for contradictions and inconsistencies in social expectations of men and women, and for its inability to adequately explain sex-role changes occurring in adulthood (Connell, 1995). The gender perspective offers in its place a **social construction** approach (Osmond and Thorne, 1993; Thompson and Walker, 1995). "Social constructionists argue that gender differences are not the product of biological properties, whether chromosomal, gonadal, or hormonal. Instead, gender and sexuality are products of social structure and culture" (Lenton, 2004: 126). The gender perspective argues that gender is not a property of the individual, but the product of ongoing, multilevel processes of social construction and reconstruction. Four *levels of social construction* were initially posited: the *individual*, *interactional*, *institutional*, and *sociocultural*. Recently, Connell (1998: 3; Connell, 2005) proposed the addition of a fifth, the *world gender order*, to reflect the realities of an era characterized by economic globalization. Each of these levels exhibits periods of stability and change, as do the social construction processes within each level and the contents of the constructions themselves (Connell and Messerschmidt, 2005).

According to Connell (1998), international relations (particularly in terms of multinational corporations and global economic markets) are inherently imbued with gender politics and have implications for gender formation. "The **world gender order** is unquestionably patriarchal, in the sense that it privileges men over women" (Connell, 1998: 11; see also Connell and Wood, 2005). Historical processes of conquest and settlement, imperialism and post-colonialism have widely disseminated a *hegemonic*, or dominant, ideology of masculinity, along with a concomitant preferred type of femininity. Connell (1998: 16) contended that contemporary economic globalization promotes a **transnational business masculinity**, characterized by "increasing egocentrism, very conditional loyalties (even to the corporation), and a declining sense of responsibility for others (except for purposes of image making)." These preferred masculinities and related femininities, though not embraced worldwide, nonetheless provide points of instability, contention, and debate about gender within individual societies, promoting either change or reinforcement of existing sociocultural gender systems (see also Kimmel, 2003; Neysmith and Chen, 2002).

The *sociocultural level* of social construction involves those symbolic conditions in which men and women live their daily lives within a particular society or culture. Included here are "systems of meaning" (Thompson, 1993: 559), which incorporate values, beliefs, and ideologies that support gender relations and gender-related social arrangements; one example is the belief that only two genders exist and that these may only be experienced and enacted in specific ways. Belief systems change over time; Chapter 3 will examine how industrialization brought about certain changes in Canadian gender beliefs, and how these belief systems were slowly modified over the course of the twentieth century.

The *institutional level* has to do with the structural basis of society. The sociocultural environment informs institutions. According to the gender perspective, each institution in our society (e.g., the economy, the family, the polity, religion) is structured in such a way as to have different consequences for each gender (Kimmel, 2000). Our economy, for example, came increasingly to be defined as a masculine institution as our society became industrialized. The institution of the economy is controlled and shaped by males; what is more, participation in the world of paid work bestows rewards crucial to the construction and confirmation of masculinity. As Canadian women's labour-force participation has increased over the past century, concerns have been expressed that such participation might "masculinize" females. The family, on the other hand, has been defined by our culture as a feminine institution; concerns have been raised about the possibility that intensive participation in family life might "feminize" men.

The *interactional level* has to do with everyday interactions as they shape the gendered thoughts, feelings, and actions of men and women (Thompson, 1993: 562). Many of the concepts of symbolic interactionism are particularly relevant for analyzing and understanding this level of social construction. Maccoby (1998: 9) contended that "[s]ex-linked behaviour turns out to be a pervasive function of the social context in which it occurs." At the interactional level, social expectations combine with situational demands and constraints to shape the presentation of a gendered self. Private, intimate contexts and public, impersonal ones call for different expressions of gender. New situations may bring about unanticipated changes in one's experience and expression of gender. For example, a woman's experience combining motherhood and paid work may differ greatly from the notions of gender instilled by her early socialization, and may dramatically alter her orientation towards breadwinning as an element of her gender role (Potuchek, 1992). Such changes exemplify the power of immediate situations to override general social expectations. In their everyday interactions, individuals negotiate boundaries between gender-appropriate and gender-inappropriate behaviour; they also give meaning to their own and others' actions. Through these activities, interacting individuals confirm or challenge each other's gender and construct/reconstruct their own on a daily basis (Zvonkovic et al., 1996).

The *individual level* involves the form and shape of gender identity, gender consciousness, and gender behaviour (Thompson, 1993: 566). As noted in the last chapter, most research on gender differences has simply noted the "sex" of participants, implying that this information captures an essential, biologically based individual property causally linked to specific social or psychological behaviours. The gender perspective argues that gender (which depends on a person's self-definition) rather than sex (which is a biological contingency) must be the relevant parameter in social and psychological research, and that, moreover, gender is only a relevant domain of concern insofar as a particular individual feels it is relevant to the matter under examination. Individuals' construction of their gender influences their behaviour and should influence how we analyze and interpret the results of our research. What is more, individual women and men vary in the extent to which they are conscious of gender (Beasley, 2005). The higher one's level of gender consciousness, the more likely one is to deliberately try to shape the gender behaviour of self and others. A low level of gender consciousness, in contrast, correlates with an unquestioning attitude towards gender behaviour.

The major contribution of the gender perspective thus far has been to focus attention upon the operation of different levels in the social construction of gender. The gender perspective emphasizes that individual men and women construct their gender through interactions with other gendered beings, in the context of basic institutions within a particular society and culture and at a particular historical time—a time shaped, in our era, by a world gender order. How sociocultural gender meanings shape institutions, and how those institutions, in turn, shape gender interactions and relations is not yet clear; how individuals construct, confirm, and reconstruct gender in relation to each and all of these other levels has yet to be determined. Not only must each level be examined in more detail, but connections between the different levels must be described and analyzed (Thompson, 1993: 567). But most importantly, the gender perspective frees us from the notion that individual gender behaviour is simply a consequence of biology or a matter of conformity to role expectations socialized in childhood. As one of its leading proponents says, "[t]he perspective encourages researchers to ask new questions and discourages us from too-easy answers that blame [biology], society, women, or men for current gender arrangements" (Thompson, 1993: 567).

Key Terms

anal stage	ego	gender perspective
androgens	Electra complex	gender schema theory
Antigone complex	essentialism	generalized other
assigned sex	estrogens	genital stage
between-group theory	Eve first, then Adam principle	gonadal sex
biological sex	evolutionary psychology	gynocentric theorists
brain sex	external genitals	hormonal sex
castration anxiety	external reinforcement	I
chromosomal sex	gender behaviour	id
cognitive development theory	gender constancy	internal reproductive sex
direct imitation	gender identity	Klinefelter's syndrome

latency stage
libido
looking-glass self
Me
metrosexual
modelling
Müllerian duct system
Müllerian inhibiting
    hormone (MIH)
natural selection
observational learning
Oedipal complex
Oedipal male
oral stage

parental investment
penis envy
phallic stage
phallocentric
psychoanalytic feminism
psychoanalytic theory
role taking
self
self-socialization process
sex discordance
significant others
social construction
social learning theory
sociobiology

stimulus generalization
superego
symbol
symbolic interactionism
testosterone
transnational business
    masculinity
Turner's syndrome
within-group similarity
    theory
Wolffian duct system
world gender order
zygote

Chapter Summary

1. Biological sex is not a unitary phenomenon with two simple dichotomous categories of "male" and "female." Rather, it comprises a number of variables that must be considered together: chromosomal, gonadal, hormonal, reproductive, genital, brain, and assigned sex. Of all of these variables, only chromosomal sex, established at conception, is unalterable.

2. Various theories argue that "anatomy is destiny" or that gender behaviour is ultimately the product of our biological nature. These theories include sociobiology, evolutionary psychology, psychoanalytic theory, and psychoanalytic feminism. Critics have charged that the core assumptions of such theories are based on dubious premises, that the theories are essentially untestable, and that theories are often androcentric and/or phallocentric. These theories have also been faulted for genecentrism, i.e., a primary focus on supposedly inherited traits and dispositions.

3. Social learning theory, cognitive developmental theory, and gender schema theory are three psychological theories that have been used to examine the process by which sex typing occurs. According to symbolic interactionism, a social-psychological theory, the meanings of "male" and "female" and of "masculinity" and "femininity" are neither permanent nor fixed.

4. The gender perspective argues that individual gender behaviour is not a consequence of biology, nor a matter of simple conformity to role expectations learned during childhood socialization, but the product of ongoing multilevel social construction and reconstruction processes that occur at the sociocultural, institutional, interactional, individual, and global levels. This perspective maintains that individuals construct their gender through inter-actions with other gendered beings, in the context of basic institutions within a particular society and culture at a particular historical time—a time shaped by a world gender order.

CHAPTER 3

Historical and Structural Perspectives

The structure of a society exerts a major influence on the ways in which gender is experienced and expressed. This chapter begins with a sketch of gender in Canada from pre-industrial times through the mid-1960s, to provide a sense of the historical background of both modern feminist theories and recently developed perspectives on masculinity, and to illustrate how conceptions of femininity and masculinity are constructed relative to time and place.

This chapter focuses primarily on European settlers and their descendants. By the time any systematic study of Aboriginal cultures began, these cultures had already been altered by contact with European explorers, fur traders, missionaries, and settlers. Moreover, accounts of Aboriginal peoples' gender-related practices were often distorted by the blatant or subtle biases of early European observers (Nanda, 2000). It should also be noted that the great diversity of cultural heritages among the Aboriginal peoples in itself limits our ability to generalize about them.

A BRIEF HISTORY OF GENDER IN CANADA

Early Aboriginal Peoples

In the majority of traditional Aboriginal cultures, survival was based on fishing, hunting, and gathering. In the eastern regions of Canada, many groups of Aboriginal peoples practised horticulture (the domestication and cultivation of plants), supplemented by hunting and fishing where possible. Men cleared the land and were responsible for hunting and fishing, while women held primary responsibility for planting, tending, and harvesting the plant crops. Given the unpredictable outcome of the hunt, women's activities supplied a high proportion of a community's sustenance, except among the Inuit (Nett, 1993: 45). The activities of both sexes were

woven into an interdependent social fabric, ensuring tribal or group survival.

While some cultures that depended upon hunting and fishing, such as the Inuit, were **patriarchal** (i.e., controlled by males) and **patrilocal** (wives moved in with their husbands [Peters, 1990: 175]), the social organization of many of the eastern Aboriginal peoples, such as the Iroquois and Huron, was **matrilocal** (husbands moved in with their wives), **matrilineal** (descent was traced through the female line), and **matrifocal** (the central and strongest bonds within the community were those between mothers and their children) (Lynn and Todoroff, 1998). Among the Iroquois, women owned the fields and the crop seeds. However, "even though Iroquois men gained and held power only with female approval, it was males who composed the council of chiefs that led the Iroquois League" (Nett, 1993: 46).

Traditional Aboriginal forms of social organization have undergone significant changes as a consequence of contact with European cultures (see Cassidy et al., 1998 and Peters, 1990 for brief histories). The introduction of European law, which supported patrilineality and patrilocality, forcibly changed the descent rules and residence patterns of many Aboriginal cultures. Ever since the 1850 *Act for the Better Protection of the Lands and Property of Indians in Lower Canada* defined an "Indian," foreign criteria have been imposed on "Indian" status, the determination of band membership, and access to rights tied to status and membership. In 1868, following Confederation, the federal Parliament passed an *Act for the Gradual Civilization of Indian Peoples,* designed with the express intent of assimilating Aboriginal people through the use of three primary tools: "The first was the creation of reservations, which in most cases did not correspond to the traditional territories the tribes had occupied. Secondly, band councils with limited powers were appointed to replace tribal governments. The act also defined who could be classified as Indian and to which band they belonged" (Yates et al., 2000: 57).

Beginning in 1869, Indian women who married non-Indians lost their legal Indian status, and their children were not entitled to be registered as Indians. The 1876 *Indian Act* also took on the task of defining an "Indian," emphasizing male lineage: "An Indian was defined as any male person of Indian blood reputed to belong to a particular band; any child of such a person; and any woman lawfully married to such a person" (Wherrett, 2002: 179). Until 1985, when the *Indian Act* was modified, a female non-Indian who married a Status Indian acquired legal Indian status for both herself and the couples' descendants; however, an Indian woman marrying a non-Indian lost her Indian status, and both she and her descendants lost those benefits to which Status Indians were entitled (Kallen, 2003: 135).

The Pre-industrial Period

During the pre-industrial period (pre-1800s), the economic activity of most European settlers was agrarian, centred in households or on family farms. The family home was thus both a place of residence and a place of work (Gaffield, 1990: 26). Family survival depended upon the interdependent and collective labours of all household members, which might include servants, seasonal labourers, and boarders, in addition to family and kin (Wilson, 1996: 8). Men, women, and children all actively contributed to the family economy (Wilson, 1996: 17); age (as an index of physical capability) was a more important determinant of work contribution than sex. Family structure was hierarchical and patriarchal: Power and authority were vested in the husband/father, wives were subordinate to their husbands, and children were expected to obey their parents.

Given that the economic unit was the family, it is not surprising that the vast majority of people married (and remarried in the event of a spouse's death). Fertility was high (as was infant mortality) and life expectancy was low: Pioneers born in 1700 lived 30 to 35 years on average (Lavoie and Oderkirk, 1993: 3); few women survived to see all of their children grow to adulthood. Division of labour within the family was sex-linked. Mothers had sole responsibility for infant care; later, fathers assumed responsibility for raising their sons by integrating them into farming activities, while mothers continued to raise their daughters and quickly integrated them into household chores (e.g., cooking, clothes-making, laundry), livestock maintenance, gardening, and caring for younger siblings (Wilson, 1996: 18).

Based upon historical examination of middle-class males in the Northern United States, Rotundo (1993: 2) claimed that pre-industrial masculinity was guided by a model of **communal manhood**, according to which a "man's identity was inseparable from the duties he owed to his community." Public usefulness was regarded more highly than economic success. Within an agrarian communal society, status was ascribed at birth on the basis of family standing; accordingly, a man's economic success was deemed less important than whether his family contributed positively to the functioning of his community. Cultural stereotypes credited manhood with greater reason, less passion, and greater virtue than womanhood (Rotundo, 1993: 3); these attributions formed the foundation of the patriarchal society and family. Doyle (1989: 37) suggested that the landowner was the model of colonial masculinity; the "landed aristocrat" epitomized the masculine ideal of "independence, self-confidence, intelligence, and a spirit of individualism."

The Industrializing Period

Industrialization, as well as the urbanization eventually produced by the mechanization of farm labour, began in the early 1800s. The shift from agriculture to factory production brought craftsmen and labourers of all kinds to the cities (Gaffield, 1990: 26–28). Economic production processes were slowly removed from the home and transferred to sites where workers were paid a wage for their labours. The introduction of a wage economy led to the redefinition of "work," which came to refer to paid labour only (Gaffield, 1990: 30); unpaid labour performed in the home was devalued as something less than "real" work, as the appearance in the mid-1800s of the compound term "housework" attests (Wilson, 1996: 64). Paid occupations became valorized and glorified, while **housework** became trivialized (Zaretsky, 1976). Industrialization thus brought about a physical separation of the (private) home place and the (public) "work" place, now generally referred to as the **separate spheres**. This phrase falsely implies a dichotomy; it would be more accurate to think in terms of two overlapping circles: Events in the workplace impact upon the life of the homeplace, while unpaid labour in the home provides crucial support for paid labourers in the workplace and "makes industrial society possible" (Nett, 1993: 51).

Since wages paid to individual workers were initially very low (Nett, 1993: 50), whole families—fathers, mothers, and children—entered the paid-labour force, working together or at different work sites to generate sufficient income to support their family. In this new *family wage* economy, families *pooled wages* rather than productive labour. Under British law, which governed all of the colonies except New France (i.e., Lower Canada [eventually, Quebec]), women were not "persons"; as "non-persons," they had no claim to the rights that legal personhood conferred. Similarly, wives were not recognized as independent beings under the law; accordingly, they had no option but to contribute their wages to the family financial pool. As production of goods and services moved outside of the home, pooled wages were increasingly used to purchase the necessities of family life; the family became essentially a unit not of producers, but of consumers.

Rotundo (1993: 3) suggested that the early stages of industrialization ushered in a new era, in which a man's newly defined work role, not his family role, became central to his personal and social identity. **Self-made manhood** emerged; in this new model of masculinity, "a man took his identity and his social status from his own achievements, not from the accident of his birth" (Rotundo, 1993: 3). The new emphasis upon individualism encouraged men to give free rein to ambition and aggression within business and the professions. Doyle (1989: 38–39) claimed that as the notion of separate spheres developed, and with it a belief that men were best suited to the public sphere of work, the ideal of the landed aristocrat gave way to a new masculine ideal, the **common man**, which dominated between 1820 and 1860. This new masculinity was characterized by "common sense, success in business, personal ingenuity, [and] heightened sexual interests" (Doyle, 1989: 38). Men were expected to channel or sublimate their sexual interests and energies into their work, which was considered more ideally "worthwhile than mere sexual release."

Hochschild (1990) argued that early industrial development probably altered men's lives more than women's. Women's lives still revolved around the familiar tasks and surroundings of home, while men had to negotiate the physical and mental adjustment of moving from the home into a centralized workplace. In the early stages of industrialization, many men still owned land and experienced a double shift, working in some form of manufacturing during the day, then returning home to work their land at night. As well, men had to shift the foundation for their self-concept from possession of land to possession of money. In addition, as Bly (1990) and Pittman (1993) have noted, when fathers began to leave the home to go to work, young sons lost a visible and crucial role model with whom to identify and relate in daily life.

The new ideal of masculinity was one manifestation of the massive societal changes that accompanied continuing urbanization and industrialization. Politicians and public leaders grew concerned about family and societal stability. This led to the promotion of a new ideal of femininity from the 1820s to the mid-1860s. Books—mostly written in Britain and reprinted in Canada and the United States (Fowler, 1993: xvi)—and magazines began to extol the virtues of *true womanhood* (Gaffield, 1990: 37):

> True Women ... were pious, their lives being one long act of devotion to God, husband, children, servants, the poor, humanity. Second, they were passive, without any desire to strive or achieve for themselves. Third, they were "pure." Marriage was their career—spinsters were pitied and regarded as failures—and virginity and total sexual ignorance were crucial.... (Fowler, 1993: xvi)

The **cult of true womanhood** embodied the belief that women could best serve family and society by restricting themselves to the domestic sphere and devoting their energies to the care of others. Love and the satisfaction of interpersonal needs were now slowly becoming important institutionalized elements of the marital relationship (Anderson, 1987: 33–34). During that era, Canadian women—beginning in their mid-20s and continuing through their early 40s—gave birth to an average of 6.6 children (Gee, 1986: 269, 273). New beliefs arose regarding the special emotional needs of children; full-time mothering was now deemed necessary for optimal child development. Mothers were appointed "custodians" (Anderson, 1987: 35) of their children's happiness and well-being. The domestic sphere was now "venerated as a retreat, a place where individuals could truly express their innermost being" (Anderson, 1987: 36), and women were called upon to follow their "natural" vocation of creating an environment conducive to optimal emotional expression, a refuge from the harsh and ruthless ethos of the public/work sphere. The "true woman," the "angel of the hearth" (Hayford, 1987: 7), knew that "domesticity is her honor and glory" (Fowler, 1993: xvii).

"True woman" imagery provided the basis for the stereotype of the "fragile" woman, so pure and delicate that she was only fit to be placed on a pedestal and worshipped. Being fragile, she had to be kept safely at home, "protected" first by her father and later by her husband. Since this ideal was more compatible with the economic circumstances of upper- and middle-class families, the true woman was most often a lady of significant financial refinement as well. Whatsoever her social-class position, the true woman was expected to be the glue that held her family together in the face of the tumultuous social changes wrought by industrialization.

Beginning in the 1840s and 1850s, compulsory formal education came to be viewed as a solution to the problem of youth made idle by the continuing mechanization of the workplace (Gaffield, 1990: 34) and the growing influx of migrants, including young children, from other cultures. Industrialization required a literate, numerate labour force, and schools were seen as the answer. Consequently, school attendance laws, along with laws prohibiting child labour, were gradually enacted over the late nineteenth and early twentieth centuries. Now, mothers were also expected to provide their children with after-school support (supervising homework), in addition to physical care and emotional nurturance. The school curriculum eventually began to include domestic science courses to prepare girls for their future familial role (Gaffield, 1990: 37). The removal of children from the paid-labour force had the additional consequence of transforming children from economic assets into economic liabilities; even as their emotional value increased, their economic value was decreasing. This change was a major contributor to further decline in the Canadian birth rate during the late 1800s.

As we have seen, the sites of unpaid and paid labour had now become firmly gendered. A woman's place was in the home (married to it, as the term **housewife** implies), where she performed unpaid labour; a man's place was on the job, where he performed paid labour. Work—specifically, whether it was paid or unpaid—defined gender and gender defined work. The concept of separate spheres led to the establishment of the male **good provider role** (Bernard, 1981/1995). A good provider was a man who, by dint of his economically productive labour, earned sufficient income to ensure his family the necessities (or better) of life. He was also considered "head" of the household, an entitlement that endured until the late 1970s (Bernard, 1981/1995). In reality, however, only middle- and upper-class Canadian families could survive on the income of one provider. Despite demands (emanating initially from the trade union movement) that business and industry provide men with a family wage (Wilson, 1996: 21), working-class men typically did not earn enough to enable their wives to stay at home. Working-class families continued to depend upon the wage contribution of wives and mothers.

The Industrial Period

By the 1870s, Canada had an industrialized economy (Gaffield, 1990: 27); large factories permitted fully mechanized and centralized economic production. Although a substantial proportion of the population was still involved in agriculture, workers in increasing numbers were leaving farming and moving into the manufacturing and service sectors. This trend would continue for the next hundred years. Females seeking paid-labour-force employment were limited to roles as factory workers, domestics, secretaries, teachers, and nurses. Since the seventeenth century, women's wages had been only one-half to two-thirds as high as men's (Phillips, 1991: 249); as a result, women's chances for attaining financial independence were limited. Women workers were more likely to be single; women were often fired from their jobs when they married, and married women were excluded from most jobs. More and more women became dependent upon the wages of men, with marriage seen as an attractive alternative to living alone at a bare subsistence level, living permanently in one's parental home, or becoming a long-term live-in domestic for another family. In the patriarchal family of the industrial era (from the late 1800s to the 1960s), the new role definitions were men as providers, women as homemakers, and children as dependents. "In the late eighteenth and early nineteenth centuries, women's lives were devoted to motherhood" (Lavoie and Oderkirk, 1993: 4). As in earlier times, the adult lives of most women were devoted mainly to childbearing and childrearing. The average Canadian family size in 1871 was 5.9 persons; an average of four of a woman's six or seven children survived beyond infancy (Anderson, 1987: 28).

Until Britain passed the *Married Women's Property Act* in 1870, wives were required to turn their earnings over to their husbands (Fowler, 1993: 40). In 1872, wives in Ontario were accorded the right to possess their own earnings (Whitla, 1995: 320); wives in Quebec were not granted this right until publication of the Dorion Report in 1929–30 (Krull, 1996: 378). Moreover, until the late 1800s, married women could not control any property inherited from fathers or husbands or acquired by their own efforts. During the last few years of the 1800s and the first two decades of the 1900s, provinces passed legislation granting a married woman the right to own and dispose of her property without her husband's consent (McKie et al., 1983: 33, 42–43). However, these legal changes did not entitle married women to a share of any property acquired by the couple during their marriage (Nett, 1993: 124). It remained encoded in law that women, defined as incapable of caring for themselves, were to be taken care of, first by fathers, then by husbands, and later by sons. Indeed, the Civil Code of Quebec, created in 1866, included married women in the same category as "minors and the feeble minded" (McKie et al., 1983: 34).

During the late 1800s–early 1900s, a new model of masculinity developed: **passionate manhood** (Rotundo, 1993: 5). Competitiveness, aggressiveness, and ambition all became valued in themselves and were no longer attached primarily to the economic sphere. Toughness, physical strength, athletic skill, and personal appearance became vaunted male qualities; tenderness, self-restraint, and self-denial were no longer considered masculine virtues. Play and leisure pursuits were elevated to the status of acceptable areas for masculine self-fulfillment and self-expression, and men were no longer expected to limit themselves to the pursuit of economic success. Doyle (1989: 38) described the male ideal of this time period as **he-man masculinity**, characterized by "strenuous activity, involvement in sports, [and] two-fisted preparedness." Increasing disempowerment in the economic sphere—the monotony of factory work, shrinking opportunities for business success—created a need in men to find new ways to validate their masculinity, leading them to "all-male activities in which they could play at being rough and tough" (Doyle, 1989: 40). This time period was marked by an increase in organized spectator sports and by the proliferation of all-male fraternal organizations (including the Boy Scouts) and men-only clubs and drinking establishments as gathering places for the expression of masculine solidarity (Doyle, 1989: 40–41; Rotundo, 1993: 222–246).

At the same time, middle-class female proponents of "true womanhood" began to claim that its virtues had applicability beyond the domestic sphere (Gaffield, 1990: 38). Later known as **maternal feminists**, these women felt "morally responsible to extend their mothering to society" (Wilson, 1996: 23). Forming groups to address social issues of the day, they initially focused on temperance (abstention from the consumption of alcohol), equality (particularly the abolition of slavery), and poverty, eventually turning their attention to issues affecting them more directly as women, such as child-welfare protections and women's *suffrage* or enfranchisement (i.e., the right to vote). These women saw voting rights as particularly important, partly as a means of exerting more control over their own destinies and partly as a means of taming the aggressive tendencies of men. Most "suffragettes," accepting the prevailing belief that the essential natures of men and women were different, sought to inject feminine values into the public sphere. Concurrently, a different model of femininity arose in response to such writings as John Stuart Mill's *On the Subjugation of Women,* published in 1869. The *New Woman* "demanded the right to have a proper career outside the home, to remain unwed from choice ... to vote and smoke and ride a bicycle.... The New Woman jettisoned piety, submissiveness and domesticity but hung on to her moral purity" (Fowler, 1993: xvii). Middle- and upper-class "new women" challenged existing beliefs about many supposed gender differences and campaigned against the restrictions which they believed that ideologies such as true womanhood had created for women.

Both of these groups, each in their own way, contributed to the **first wave** of feminism that emerged during the late 1800s and lasted into the early 1920s. In Canada, the most prominent victories which this movement won for women were the right to vote and the right (granted in 1929) to be considered *persons*, rather than chattels (i.e., property), under Canadian law. In 1916, women over the age of 21 were granted the right to vote in provincial elections in Alberta, Manitoba, and Saskatchewan; in 1917, in British Columbia and Ontario; in 1918, in Nova Scotia (as well as in Canadian federal elections); in 1919, in New Brunswick; in 1922, in Prince Edward Island; in 1925, in Newfoundland (at first, only women over the age of 25 were granted this right); and in 1940, in Quebec (Whitla, 1995: 320–332). These rights were initially granted to white women only; women (and men) of certain other ethnic groups did not receive the franchise until later years; for example, only in 1948 was the franchise extended to Canadians of Japanese ancestry (Frank, 1994). In addition, as Mossman (1997: 181) pointed out, "prior to 1960, aboriginal women (and men) in Canada were entitled to vote only if they gave up their Indian status."

During the early 1900s, single women continued to form a significant proportion of the Canadian paid-labour force. With the increasing demand for clerical and sales workers, more married women entered and remained in the labour force. Available professions for women were limited primarily to teaching, social work, and nursing—all extensions of the socially defined motherhood role. Social conditions generated by World War I, the Great Depression, and World War II promoted increasing female labour-force participation. During the wars, the shortage of male labour caused by conscription (i.e., compulsory enrolment into the armed forces) resulted in a great demand for female workers. During the Depression—despite the stark economic downturn, the persistent belief that motherhood and paid employment were incompatible, and the notion that every employed woman took a job away from a man—employers hired increasing proportions of married women and mothers because of the lower wages commanded by female employees.

During the war years, the **Warrior** was temporarily added to existing images of ideal masculinity in Canada, as substantial numbers of young men became soldiers, either through conscription or voluntary enlistment. The "Warrior" established only shallow roots in Canadian soil. Canadian men born since the mid-1930s have not faced conscription; their main exposure to warlike images of masculinity has been through documentaries and (mostly American-made) motion pictures. Our experience stands in sharp contrast to that of American men, who, since early in this century until 1969, when the lottery draft system was introduced, were subject between the ages of 19 and 25 to two years of compulsory military service. Although it was possible to obtain an exemption (as it was in Canada during the world wars), draft deferment tended to be granted primarily to men from the "influential, wealthy, and educated classes" (Jones, 1980: 108). America changed over to a voluntary military system, like Canada's, only fairly recently. Still, since at least the time of the Revolutionary War, the Warrior has been and remains an entrenched element of masculinity in the United States.

In Canada, the belief in marriage and motherhood as central to femininity remained strong through the first half of the twentieth century. The wars and the Depression were viewed as exceptional times requiring exceptional alterations to social life; when conditions returned to "normal," women and men were expected to return to their "normal" respective spheres of home and work. In 1921, new rules obliged women working for the peacetime Canadian federal civil service to resign upon marriage (Whitla, 1995: 329). Special services and legislation which had been created to facilitate women's entry into the labour force during World War II were disbanded and repealed after the war (McKie et al., 1983: 49). The *Income Tax Act* had been changed to allow husbands a full tax exemption for working wives, regardless of how much the wives earned; after the war, that exemption was rescinded, and men were only allowed to claim as dependents wives whose incomes fell below a certain level. The structure of the pre- and postwar income-tax laws reinforced the notion of husbands as providers and wives as financial dependents. The Nurseries Agreement, passed during World War II, had seen the federal and provincial governments split costs for nursery, foster, and day care for children from infancy to age 16 in order to allow mothers to work full time; this was rescinded immediately after the war and nurseries and day-care centres created under the agreement were disbanded. These examples all illustrate how gender expectations, founded on essentialist premises, could be conveniently suspended for pragmatic reasons, then reinstated when circumstances changed.

Mid-1940s to Late 1960s

After World War II, Canadian men and women were expected to settle back into their former roles, despite the fact that women had moved beyond the domestic sphere for almost half of the first four decades of the twentieth century. In changing and enlarging their behavioural repertoires, women had demonstrated to themselves and to men that they were capable of holding down jobs while managing a home and family. However, immediately following World War II, extraordinary social pressures were set in motion that eroded this nascent sense of independence and inhibited its resurgence.

The most significant postwar demographic phenomenon was the **baby boom**, which defied the trend of declining fertility that had prevailed in Canada since the mid-nineteenth century. Canada, the United States, Australia, and New Zealand were the only four Western countries to experience a sustained upsurge in the birth rate, lasting far beyond the short-term increase commonly experienced following periods of war. In the United States, the baby boom lasted from 1946 to 1964 (Jones, 1980: 6); in Canada, roughly from 1946 to 1965 (McVey and Kalbach, 1995: 271; Foot, 1996). Unlike many European countries, which had to devote their postwar efforts to rebuilding cities and countrysides ravaged by invasion, Canada could forge ahead immediately with a peacetime economy, buoyed by an optimism or "euphoria" (Kettle, 1980: 34) born of a sense of victory. Government, manufacturers, and advertisers—aided by the increasingly powerful mass media, including the new technology of television—began to promulgate a vision of "the good life." The role allocated to women in this vision emphasized the expression of femininity through wife-and-motherhood. A major mass-circulation magazine of the time, *Look*, offered the following words of praise:

> The wondrous creature marries younger than ever, bears more babies and looks and acts far more feminine than the "emancipated" girl of the twenties or thirties. If she makes an old-fashioned choice and lovingly tends a garden and a bumper crop of children, she rates louder Hosannas than ever before. (quoted in Jones, 1980: 24)

Femininity—in a conception that echoed the previous century's "true womanhood"—was to reside *solely* in being a wife and mother (Friedan, 1963: 11; Jones, 1980: 25).

The power of these messages cannot be underestimated. The generation that produced the baby boom was born during the Depression and grew up during the war years; it was strongly imbued with a sense of duty regarding society's expectations. Not individualism but conformity to societal standards was construed as the way to self-fulfillment. Accordingly, people took to heart the gender messages assailing them from all directions. Bernard (1973: 244) noted that 1950s women "had been convinced that not to get married was indeed a fate worse than death, for without marriage, one could not be completely fulfilled." Friedan (1963: 12) observed that the number of women attending institutions of higher learning declined significantly during this period: "A century earlier, women had fought for higher education; now girls went to college to get a husband. By the mid-fifties, 60 per cent dropped out of college to marry, or because they were afraid too much education would be a marriage bar."

During this time, a variety of factors lead to the development of the **procreation ethic**, a belief system conducive to creating and prolonging the baby boom. The tenets of the procreation ethic were as follows:

1. It was preferable to marry than not to marry. If a person chose to remain single, the onus was on him or her to explain why.

2. It was preferable to be a parent than a nonparent. A couple that did not have children would be considered unconventional and tacitly pressured to make an explanation. The only excuses accepted were medical or financial.

3. It was preferable not to have an "only" child, especially in the suburbs. (Jones, 1980: 31)

Evidence indicates that Canadians complied with the procreation ethic. From 1941 to 1966, the average age at first marriage dropped from 24.4 years for brides and 27.6 for grooms to 22.6 and 25.2 years respectively (McVey and Kalbach, 1995: 225); in the United States, it fell approximately two years lower. During the same time period, the proportion of the Canadian population ages 15 and older who had never been married dropped from 36.5 percent to 28.0 percent, while the married proportion increased from 57.0 to 65.0 percent. Among Canadians ages 20 to 29, the proportion of singles decreased from 59.9 percent to 40.5 percent, while the proportion of marrieds rose from 41.7 percent to 59.0 percent. To put it simply, more Canadians were marrying and were doing so at a younger age. These young marrieds, along with older couples who had deferred childbearing during the war years, all contributed to the baby boom. The number of live births increased from 1941 to 1961, then declined by 1966; the **crude birth rate** (i.e., the annual number of births per 1000 population) rose from 22.4 in 1941 to 28.0 in 1956 and then declined (Statistics Canada, 1967).

One factor that encouraged fertility was Canada's booming economy. Another was the ineffectiveness and limited availability of birth control measures. From 1882 until 1969, Canadian criminal law prohibited the sale or advertisement of contraceptives. In the 1950s, condoms could be purchased at drug stores, where they were usually kept behind the counter; however, asking for these products could be extremely embarrassing: Because manufacturers were prohibited from advertising condoms as contraceptives, "[f]or many years, every tin ... of condoms on the market read 'sold in drug stores only for the prevention of contagious diseases'" (Riedmann et al., 2003: 339). Although the birth control pill became available in Canada during the early 1960s, it was originally restricted to therapeutic uses, such as the regulation of the menstrual cycle. The federal government did not legalize contraception until July of 1969 (Riedmann et al., 2003: 339). Until that time, in keeping with the third tenet of the procreation ethic, Canadian couples tended to have more than one child. From 1946 to 1961, Canadian women gave birth to between 3.4 and 3.9 children, on average (McVey and Kalbach, 1995: 270).

Canadian women were beginning to change their paid-work patterns. During the 1950s and 1960s, following a brief departure after World War II (Statistics Canada, 1983), women began to return in slowly increasing numbers to the paid-labour force. As Table 3.1 indicates, the greatest increases occurred among married women, whose labour-force participation rates increased from 11.2 percent in 1951 to 37 percent by 1971. Single women's participation rates remained steady; a slight drop over the 20-year period was attributable to an increase in the proportions of younger women remaining in school. Men's overall labour-force participation rates generally declined; this was attributable to a combination of earlier retirement and more years spent in school.

Table 3.1 documents notable differences in the sexes' participation in the paid-labour force. In 1961, only the husband worked for pay in 68.3 percent of husband-and-wife families; in 19.5 percent of these families, both husband and wife worked; in 3.2 percent, only the wife; and in 9.0 percent of families, neither husband nor wife was working for pay (not broken down in the table) (McVey and Kalbach, 1995: 253). A single-income marriage and family unit was the statistical and social norm in Canada; men, in keeping with the powerful dictates of the good-provider role, usually generated that income.

Women in the paid-labour force were concentrated in a limited number of occupations. Between 1951 and 1971, approximately 60 percent were clustered in clerical, sales, and service jobs (Kalbach and McVey, 1979: 290); by 1971, more than 70 percent of all clerical workers and 60 percent of all service workers were women (Kalbach and McVey, 1979: 289). During that 20-year period, the proportion of women in professional and technical occupations increased from 10.2 to 17.5 percent; these women were preponderantly concentrated in the teaching and health (especially nursing) professions (Kalbach and McVey, 1979: 290, 294). All of these trends reiterate patterns found in the earlier part of the century.

The general life-course pattern of Canadian women during these times was fairly consistent. Upon completing their education, women who did not go directly from graduation to wedding ceremonies entered the paid-labour force and remained there either until marriage

TABLE 3.1	Percentage of the Population, 15 Years of Age and Over, in the Labour Force, by Marital Status and Sex, Canada: 1951–1971		
Sex and Marital Status	**1951**	**1961**	**1971**
Males			
Single	76.6	63.5	63.5
Married	90.0	86.9	84.4
Widowed and Divorced	46.9	39.2	46.8
Total	84.0	78.1	76.4
Females			
Single	58.4	54.9	53.5
Married	11.2	22.1	37.0
Widowed and Divorced	19.3	23.1	26.6
Total	24.1	29.7	39.9

Source: Statistics Canada (1974). 1971 Census of Canada. Bulletin 3.1–2, Table 3. Ottawa: Information Canada.

TABLE 3.2	Female Labour-force Participation Rates by Age, Canada: 1951 and 1961	
Age Group	1951 (%)	1961 (%)
15–19	37.8	34.2
20–24	46.9	49.5
25–34	24.2	29.6
35–44	21.8	31.1
45–54	20.4	33.4
55–64	14.5	24.4
65+	5.1	6.7
Total	24.1	29.7

Source: Adapted from McVey and Kalbach, 1995: 251. Based upon 1971 Census of Canada, Vol. 3, Part 1, Economic Characteristics, Table 2.

or until motherhood, usually less than two years later. Upon pregnancy or childbirth, the overwhelming majority of these women dropped out of the labour force to concentrate on home management and childrearing. Current social beliefs stressed the crucial importance of a mother's physical presence from the moment of her children's birth to the time they were ready to leave the parental home. Only severe financial hardship was considered legitimate justification for a married woman with children at home to take part in the paid-labour market. A small proportion of married women re-entered the labour force once their children had left the nest. Table 3.2 reveals the bimodal pattern of women's labour-force participation during the period from 1951 to 1961: Participation rates were highest for women ages 15–24, while rates declined markedly for women in the typical childbearing and childrearing years (25–34). Close scrutiny reveals that by 1961, there was a growing trend of women ages 35–54 returning to the labour force; this increase heralded the beginning of changes, accelerating through the 1970s, that saw women balancing the demands of childrearing with expanding social and economic opportunities. Between 1951 and 1961, however, less than one third of all women were in the paid-labour market.

The belief in separate spheres reinforced the related belief in separate gender destinies. Just as femininity was supposed to be realized exclusively in the private sphere through wife-and-motherhood, masculinity was to be demonstrated in the public sphere through paid work and the good-provider role. These rigid roles came to circumscribe and diminish the potential of both men and women. Success as a breadwinner, and the qualities necessary to ensure that success—competitiveness, confidence, ambition, and independence—were the dominant themes of masculinity in postwar Canadian society. It is not surprising that men cited "economic responsibilities" as being among their greatest grievances about marriage as it was constructed at that time (Bernard, 1973: 24).

The impact of marriage and family upon women's lives came under increasing scrutiny during the 1960s. Bernard (1973: 41) suggested that post-wedding life held at least two "shocks" for women. First, many women discovered that their husbands were not as strong and confident as popular stereotypes of masculinity may have suggested, and that a considerable amount of a wife's energies had to be devoted to propping up her husband's self-concept. Second, many women had to adjust to an important shift from being the one catered to prior to marriage, to the one who did the catering forever after. This shift was part of a larger process of "dwindling" into a wife, a person whose range of life was limited to home, children, and husband. The **trapped housewife** became a popular topic in the mass media of the late 1950s and early 1960s. Advice columnists, along with counsellors and therapists, offered women advice on how to adjust to the imperatives of the contemporary wife and mother roles. Implicit within this advice was the assumption that the ideal roles were sacrosanct and not to be challenged. Any difficulties experienced by individual women were considered evidence of their own inadequacies or lack of femininity. However, in *The Feminine Mystique*, Friedan (1963: 7) suggested that the "problem that has no name" resided not within women, but within the gender expectations themselves. "There was a strange discrepancy between the reality of our lives as women and the image to which we were trying to conform, the image that I came to call the feminine mystique" (Friedan, 1963: 7). She asserted that it was no longer possible to ignore the increasing numbers of women who felt "I want something more than my husband and my children and my home" (Friedan, 1963: 27).

The publication of Friedan's work signalled the beginning of intense examination of the conditions that generated female (and male) gender roles and expectations that had been accepted uncritically for most of the postwar period. Contributing to this climate of questioning were an increasing quest for personal freedom, concerns about overpopulation and the contribution of the baby-boom phenomenon to that problem, and a general challenging of social institutions and belief systems. Summarizing the thinking of many social critics writing about women in the 1960s, Bernard wrote the following admonition:

> From the very earliest years, girls will have to learn that however large marriage may loom in their lives, it is not nirvana, that it does not mark the end of their growth, that motherhood is going to be a relatively transient phase of their lives, that they cannot indulge themselves by investing all their emotional and intellectual resources in their children, that they cannot count on being supported all their lives simply because they are wives. They will have to prepare for loving autonomy rather than symbiosis or parasitism in marriage. (Bernard, 1973: 321–322)

Further exploration of these issues was to become central to the women's movement and to the feminist theories that began to be articulated during the mid-1960s.

The **second wave** of the feminist movement in Canada and the United States emerged largely in reaction to events and social beliefs of the mid-1940s to mid-1960s. In terms of the establishment of gender roles, this period saw the culmination of a series of processes that the industrialization of our society had set in motion; at this time, the gendered separate spheres existed in an almost pure form. This was the era that many during the 1990s and early 2000s have cited as a time of "traditional family values." Most of those who sound the call today for a return to such values experienced the 1940s, 1950s, and 1960s in families with homemaker mothers and breadwinner fathers. In essence, they seek to recreate the conditions of their childhood or early adulthood, usually without an awareness of the social and economic climate that made those conditions possible—a climate that no longer exists.

Whether as a focus of nostalgia or of derision, the years from the mid-1940s to the mid-1960s were unique in Canadian history, generating theories and perspectives that have enriched our understanding of the social context of gender.

MAINSTREAM SOCIOLOGICAL THEORIES

Mainstream sociologists concur that social research, like research in the natural sciences, should be value-neutral (i.e., not influenced by the researcher's personal beliefs and judgments) and objective (impersonal, scientifically detached). However, mainstream sociological theories have been accused of focusing primarily on topics of interest to men (particularly the public sphere) and basing their conclusions on male experience; for this reason, much of past sociology has been described as a "malestream" (Eichler, 1984; Marchbank and Letherby, 2007) enterprise. Feminist scholars have claimed that most sociological theorizing has treated women as if they were invisible (Abbott and Wallace, 2005; Delamont, 2003; Wise and Stanley, 2003; Stanley, 2005). Functionalism, however, is one mainstream theory that has extended its analysis to marriage, the family, and gender.

Functionalism

Also known as *structural functionalism*, **functionalism** maintains that human societies are composed of a number of interrelated parts, with each part related to the whole. Functional elements help maintain the equilibrium of a social system, while dysfunctional elements undermine it. "Functionalists seek to identify the basic elements or parts of society, determine the functions these parts play, and then consider how the entire society operates or functions" (Lindsey, 1994: 4). The parts under examination may include basic social institutions, social groups, statuses (positions within society), and roles (either ideal expectations or actual patterns of behaviour). Since functionalism assumes that societies naturally tend towards a state of homeostasis (equilibrium), it offers explanations for how the particular part contributes to stable functioning of the societal whole.

Parsons and Bales (1955), building on an earlier work of Parsons (1942), presented a functionalist analysis of the traditional two-parent nuclear family. They argued that having women and men perform separate specialized and complementary roles contributes to family cohesiveness and stability. Men, filling the **instrumental role**, specialize in providing food and shelter for the family, making "managerial" decisions (Parsons and Bales, 1955: 317), and providing a link between the family and the larger society. Women, filling the **expressive role**, specialize in providing emotional support and nurturance to all family members, cementing relations between family members, and running the family household smoothly and efficiently (Parsons and Bales, 1955: 317–319). Parsons and Bales maintained that such a "division" (a highly contested term in that it implies equality) of labour into these two basic roles is functional for both family and societal equilibrium for two reasons. First, specialization promotes the interdependence of women and men. Each contributes what the other lacks—domestic skills and emotional support in exchange for economic support and protection. Second, well-defined and clearly distinct roles reduce confusion and conflict over marital and gender expectations.

In support of their analysis, Parsons and Bales (1955) adduced anthropological evidence indicating that males in early societies tended to assume the instrumental and females the expressive role. The restrictions that pregnancy, nursing, and infant care placed upon women's mobility led to the concentration of female roles around the home. Males' greater physical mobility led to their assumption of roles outside of the home, such as hunting and warfare; over time, these roles became *institutionalized* (i.e., customarily expected). Parsons and Bales did not merely argue that this division of labour was functional in early societies, but insisted that the sex-linked division of roles is equally applicable to modern-day families and societies. Functionalists further suggested that to depart substantially from these sex-linked roles would be inefficient (or *dysfunctional*), placing women and men in competition with one another, causing confusion, inefficiency, instability, and a lack of family cohesion, and eventually leading to the destabilization of society. Parsons (1949: 268) declared that "it is scarcely conceivable that the main lines of the present situation could be altered without consequences fatal to the total of our unique society."

It is obvious that functionalist theory is inherently conservative. Indeed, Abramovitz (1988) stated that functionalism promotes a "traditional, white middle-class family ethic." Stability, defined as conformity to traditional roles, is presumed to be functional, while change, defined as departure from convention, is presumed to be dysfunctional. Moreover, in claiming that instrumental and expressive roles make "different, but equal" contributions to the operation of the modern family and society, functionalists imply that these roles are also socially rewarded to an equivalent degree in terms of prestige, material benefits, and power—or, if imbalances do exist (e.g., decision-making power within families), they are functionally necessary. Functionalists tend to ignore issues of power, and regard conflict as a wholly negative, destabilizing, and dysfunctional force, rather than a potentially creative and constructive one. It is important to bear in mind that this theory was largely developed in the context of the postwar late 1940s and 1950s, and that the family structure and gender roles characteristic of that period are now considered an historical aberration (Cherlin, 1992; Oppenheimer, 1994).

Conflict Theory

During the 1960s, a new theory emerged to challenge the functionalist point of view. **Conflict theory** has its roots in the early writings of social philosophers Karl Marx (1848/1964; 1867–1894/1967) and Frederich Engels (1884/1902). In sharp contrast to the functionalists, who emphasize consensus and equilibrium, conflict theorists assume that human societies are characterized by fierce competition between social groups for scarce physical and social resources, including power, wealth, and prestige. These struggles are seen as the major engine of social change.

Marx was primarily concerned with *class struggle*, the conflict between the bourgeoisie (the social class that owns and controls the means to produce *capital*, or wealth) and the proletariat (the social class of workers exploited by the bourgeoisie). To him, any apparent stability in the relations between the classes was the product of one group's ability to exert its will over the other by means of legitimized authority and the construction of belief systems (ideologies) that make domination more palatable. Beneath the surface, conflicts between different groups reinforce or change existing power differentials. The dominant group seeks to consolidate ever-greater power and control over the economic system, while the subordinate groups strive to empower themselves.

The application of conflict theory to the study of gender entails redefining "class" to refer to groups identified principally by sex and/or gender and examining their access to and control over scarce resources, such as political and economic power. In the following excerpt, a conflict-theory approach explains women's inequality in structural terms:

> A glance at the Canadian social structure indicates that it is men who own and control the essential resources.... Ownership of the most important resource, the means of production, is mainly

in the hands of a few men who have power over almost all women as well as other men.... Men also have control of the next most important resources, access to the occupational structure and control of policy making in the major areas of social life. (Connelly and Christiansen-Ruffman, 1977/1987: 283)

Modern conflict theorists emphasize power, moving beyond Marx's economic focus to look at other sources of power affecting the relative positions of women and men in Canadian society (Camfield, 2002; Vosko, 2002). They investigate existing social arrangements in an attempt to determine who benefits from them, who suffers, and by what mechanisms these outcomes are distributed. A conflict-theory analysis of the structural positions and socially defined roles of women and men yields a very different picture than a functionalist approach. Functionalism tends to overemphasize social cohesion and stability and essentially ignores conflict and social change; conversely, conflict theory tends to overemphasize the latter and ignore the former.

FEMINIST THEORIES

Feminists challenge sociology's theoretical and research enterprises by questioning whether the social sciences can ever be objective and value-neutral, and, indeed, whether they should be kept separate from policy advocacy and application at the individual or societal level (Eichler, 1984). Feminist theory generally replaces mainstream sociology's pretensions to objectivity and value-neutrality with **value-specification** (Lindsey, 1994: 14; Morawski, 1994): A writer is to explicitly declare her or his values, acknowledging possible biases (this is based on the assumption that individuals can, in fact, be aware of their values and biases). According to Elliot and Mandell (1995: 4), feminist theories aim to "deconstruct errors and myths about women's abilities, add to knowledge about women's empirical realities ... construct theory by and about women ... [and] tend to be explicitly political in their advocacy of social change." The phrase "construct theory *by* and *about* women" (emphasis added) is noteworthy for two reasons: First, it suggests that only theories created by women may qualify as feminist—a contentious point; second, despite the suggestion that feminist theories are only about women, they obviously contain claims about men as well.

The major perspectives within feminist theory presented below draw upon frameworks identified by Jaggar and Rothenberg (1984) and Beasley (2005). Although all feminist theories begin with the same premises—that men and women in all societies are evaluated differently, that women live under conditions of subordination and even oppression, and that these conditions are neither natural nor inevitable—each type of feminist theory has its own analysis of the root causes of oppression and its own vision of how to eliminate inequality. In spite of their differences, "feminist theories ultimately are tools designed for a practical purpose—the purpose of understanding women's subordination in order to end it" (Jaggar and Rothenberg, 1993: xvii).

Liberal Feminism

The "most mainstream and popular" (Elliot and Mandell, 1995: 8) of the theories, **liberal feminism** (also called **egalitarian feminism**), identifies as its goal the creation of "a just and compassionate society in which freedom flourishes" (Wendell in Tong, 1989: 13). Like other liberal discourses on equality, this theory is grounded on the assumption that only *equality of opportunity and individual freedom* can ensure that all members of a society may fulfill their potential. The establishment of a "level playing field" will lead to a **meritocracy**, a society in which social rank is based on merit; liberal feminists accept inequality and hierarchy as inevitable, since individuals possess disparate abilities. Liberal feminism maintains that women have received a lesser share of social rewards because of their unequal participation in institutions outside the domestic sphere—in particular, education and paid work. They assert that women's subordinate status in the economic institution is the consequence of gender discrimination and inferior education. The rational solution to women's subordination, first formulated in 1792 in Mary Wollstonecraft's *Vindication of the Rights of Women* (Code, 1993: 26), is to extend the rights of men to women, assuring equality, defined as equality of opportunity, for both women and men.

Much of the practical agenda for Canadian liberal feminists was established by the 1970 Royal Commission on the Status of Women, whose recommendations were designed to "ensure for women equal opportunities with men in all aspects of Canadian society" (in Wilson, 1996: 10). The Commission's recommendations—which included affirmative-action quotas in business and education, equal-opportunity employment, employment equity, pay equity, parental leave, and subsidized daycare centres—are all congruent with the liberal feminist orientation. Such programs are not only thought necessary to ensure equality of opportunity for women, but considered to be ultimately in the best rational interests of both women and men.

While liberal feminist theory does advocate social change, it does not propose to radically restructure the basic institutions of Canadian society; rather, it stresses the need to restructure the *distribution* of individuals within those slightly modified institutions. Liberal feminists accept a reality in which inequalities of power, prestige, and material benefits are still found between individuals of both sexes. Moreover, while it aims at eliminating gender oppression, it pays little heed to other forms of subordination, such as those stemming from distinctions of class and race/ethnicity.

Evidence suggests that liberal feminism appeals primarily to white middle-class professional women, considered to be the main beneficiaries of the suggested policy interventions (Elliot and Mandell, 1995: 9; Lindsey, 1994: 15). It has been derisively referred to as "assimilationism" (Williams, 1991: 95) for its moderate stance, focus on gaining equal access to traditional male preserves, and emphasis on "sameness." Liberal feminism maintains that gender is not determined by sex. The theory asserts that women are essentially no different than men, and appears to suggest that, with the aid of certain programs, women ultimately will—and should—become "just like men."

Beasley (2005: 32; emphasis added) notes that in recent decades liberal feminism's emphasis on "improving women's legal and political position *as a group*" and subsequent "undercutting [of] the *individualism* characteristic of mainstream Liberalism" has drawn the ire of a "number of usually younger feminists" and, in turn, led to a "third-wave" of liberal feminism. These "third-wave feminists" (sometimes referred to as "post feminists") extol the individualism of mainstream liberalism, maintaining "that women must take individual responsibility and not hide behind a group status as 'victims.'" For example, Naomi Wolf (1990, 1994, 2001) lambastes "victim feminism" for "saddling women with an 'identity of powerlessness'" (Lehrman in Beasley, 2005: 33) and advocates personal empowerment through adoption of the strategies of "power feminism": "I propose specific strategies to make pro-woman action into something that is effective, popularist, inclusive, easy, fun and even lucrative" (Wolf, 1994). Wolf maintains that, should increasing numbers of individual women adopt her pro-capitalist and (rather distinctively American) self-help strategies (e.g., form a "power group" with well-situated women in order to gain a competitive edge; buy a gun to obviate victimhood), women, as a group, will collectively benefit. As Beasley (2005: 33) observes, in Wolf's "traditional reiteration of Liberal conceptions of power and the self, empowered/emancipated individual women can alter power relations. There is virtually no reference to the state or other social institutions in the analysis, but rather a focus on the spreading impact of empowered individuals who take control of their lives." Thus, in contrast to second-wave liberal feminists, who concentrated their energies on legal/political/institutional reforms and advanced a social justice agenda, Wolf's variant of liberal feminism is more obviously focused upon "individual self-realization, self-expression and self-fulfilment as means to alter social hierarchy" (Beasley, 2005: 37),

Marxist Feminism

In contrast to the liberal viewpoint, **Marxist feminism** insists that the entire structure of our society must be changed before true gender equality can be attained. The Marxist approach focuses on the public sphere of formal economic production processes, and argues that the economic institution, as it is organized in a particular society, determines the nature of all other institutions. Furthermore, one's position within the economic institution determines one's relationship to all other aspects of social life. The capitalist economic system, organized as it is around the principles of private ownership of the means of production, the pursuit of profit, and market competition, ensures the unequal distribution of material rewards and is viewed as the primary source of the oppression of women in Canada.

Engels (1884/1902), Marx's collaborator, argued that the subordination of women followed from the institution of private property, which led property-owning men to enforce tight control over women in an attempt to ensure the paternity of potential heirs. Women thus became the property of men and the first oppressed class. Engels further believed that the solution to such oppression required women's equal participation in the economic production process, with an equal share of economic rewards. He called for the creation of collective or communal systems for household labour and childrearing to free more of women's energies for economic production. Unlike Marx, Engels recognized that significant reorganization of the private sphere was a prerequisite to achieving gender equality in the public sphere. However, as the name implies, Marxist feminists have followed the teachings of Marx more closely than those of Engels.

Tong (1989: 51) observed that Marxist feminism has focused overwhelmingly on women's work-related concerns, including "how the institution of the family is related to **capitalism**; how women's domestic work is trivialized as not real work; and, finally, how women are generally given the most boring and low-paying jobs." The family is related to capitalism in critical ways: By their unpaid labour in the home, women not only sustain the adult male worker but raise the next generation of workers as well. Yet women's labour, while supporting and maintaining the capitalist system, is detrimental to the women themselves because it is not regarded as "real work" and receives no formal remuneration. Delphy and Leonard's (1992) *Familiar Exploitation* emphasized the family as an economic institution in which men obtain economic benefits from the labours of their wives both inside and outside the home (and may also—in some countries more than others—derive economic benefits from the labours of their children). According to these authors, it is "the work women do, the uses to which our bodies can be put, which constitutes the reason for our oppression." Marxist feminists, therefore, advocate the development of a system for paying women directly for their household work. Marxist feminists have also adumbrated the utility to the capitalist system of keeping women poorly paid so that they may furnish an exploitable **reserve labour force** (McMullin, 2004: 194; Wilson, 1996: 118)—a pool of workers who can be pulled into and pushed out of the labour force as economic circumstances (such as wars and depressions) warrant. The existence of a pool of cheap labour serves to depress the wages of male workers, who labour under the threat of replacement by lesser-paid females—and to support the capitalist's pursuit of profit. These social arrangements further promote women's economic dependence on men and perpetuate female exploitation and subordination.

According to Marxist feminism, the elimination of women's oppression requires a radical transformation of the economic institution from capitalism to socialism and ultimately to communism. Upon the abolition of private property, the economic production process would belong to society as a whole; every individual would have essentially the same relationship to the process and would receive the same economic rewards. Once the fundamental economic exploitation inherent in capitalism is eliminated, the oppression of women would necessarily disappear of itself. From the Marxist perspective, the unequal status of women is analogous to that of any other disadvantaged group, such as Aboriginal people or the poor. Inequalities of sex, ethnicity, and class are all understood as byproducts of the same underlying cause: the capitalist economic system. Most Marxists do not regard the situation of women as a special case requiring a separate explanation or solution, but as simply another example of how the capitalist economic system works.

Radical Feminism

Unlike Marxist feminism, **radical feminism** does not identify the capitalist economic system as the primary cause of female subordination, but suggests that women live under conditions of inequality in most systems of economic production, be they capitalist, socialist, or communist. According to radical (meaning "root") feminists, the most fundamental oppression—the oldest, most universal, most pervasive, and deepest—is the oppression of women by men.

This oppression is ultimately founded on **patriarchy** (also referred to as "patriarchalism" or "sexism"), a social system in which authority is vested in males. Patriarchy embodies a belief in male superiority that supports and justifies the domination of women by men. In patriarchal societies, as Code (1993: 19) observed,

> men have more power than women and readier access ... to what is valued in the society or in any social sub-group. In consequence of this power and privilege, men ... occupy positions that permit them to shape and control many, if not most, aspects of women's lives.

According to radical feminists, patriarchy pervades not only the economic institution but also, and more oppressively, the family, marriage, sexuality, and biological reproduction. Social change, therefore, is necessary in both the public and private domains. Patriarchal ideology, and all behaviour based upon it, must be eradicated before any meaningful change in women's condition can occur. Since radical feminists suggest that gender is the fundamental form of difference, their theory initially placed little emphasis on differences of ethnicity and social class.

Early radical feminism was deeply influenced by insights derived from women's consciousness-raising (CR) groups formed during the mid-1960s to early 1970s. Eisenstein (1984) noted that "[a] first assumption of consciousness raising was that what women had to say about the details of their daily lives, about their personal experiences and histories, mattered, it had significance, and above all it had validity" (in Wilson, 1996: 8). Certain experiences and concerns, it was found, were common to so many women that they came to be viewed as more than individual problems requiring private solutions. They came to be redefined as public issues (Connelly and Christiansen-Ruffman, 1977/1987) with societal causes that could only be altered by collective political action. This transformation in understanding was reflected in the phrase "the personal is political," an insight that some suggest is the most significant contribution of radical feminism (Jaggar and Rothenberg, 1984: 219). This phrase, initially descriptive, gradually took on a more prescriptive character. As the movement grew, some radical feminists, asserting that "the political is personal," exhorted adherents to transform their private lives to reflect their politics. "Politically correct behavior ... is that which adheres to a movement's morality and hastens its goals" (Dimen, 1984: 139).

Ironically, the notion of "politically correct behaviour" created a fundamental tension within radical feminism and within the feminist movement as a whole. On the one hand lay the values of individualism, freedom of choice, and the validity of personal experience; on the other, the ideals of collectivism, personal sacrifice, and unity in pursuit of political goals (see Prentice, 2000).

Even though radical feminists agree that patriarchy is the fundamental cause of women's subordination, they bring a range of perspectives to the problem. Some radical feminists claim that patriarchy's differential valuation of men and women is founded on a belief that the sexes are inherently different. These feminists take the position that most differences between the sexes are the product of a social-construction process predicated on patriarchy itself; thus, the elimination of patriarchy would lead to the eventual disappearance of these socially created gender differences. In effect, they seek to eradicate gender as a meaningful social category (Echols, 1984) and to replace existing gender roles with androgyny (Decker, 1983: 331, 459). Any remaining differences between women and men would then be considered "human," and not gender, differences.

Some theorists, such as Rich (1980), focus on male control of female sexuality as the basic instrument of female subordination. On the other hand, Firestone (1970) maintained that women must be liberated from the "tyranny of their reproductive biology" that forces them to depend on men to conceive; this, she declared, forms the foundation of patriarchy. As long as women's roles and rewards are tied to reproductive differences, true gender equality cannot be realized. Firestone was optimistic that reliable birth-control measures, technological developments allowing for extra-uterine gestation, and alternative forms of child care (so that the childbearer need not be the childrearer) would ensue in conditions of gender equality. However, faith in the positive power of technology has more recently given way to concern about the possible negative impact of new reproductive technologies upon women (Achilles, 1995; Hartouni, 1995). Radical feminists were among the first to define as feminist issues reproductive and contraceptive rights, abortion, reproductive technologies, the expression and experience of sexuality, and sexual and physical violence against women.

By the early 1980s, another branch of radical feminism became discernible. It originated among feminists who had grown increasingly pessimistic about the likelihood of the kind of radical changes needed to eliminate patriarchy, and who viewed the liberal feminist approach of assimilation into patriarchal culture as unacceptable. The alternative that they proposed was separation from the entire patriarchal system. "Cultural feminism" (West, 1993) is sufficiently different in its focus to merit consideration as a distinct category.

Cultural Feminism

Cultural feminism—sometimes referred to as *integrative feminism* (Miles, 1985), *relational feminism* (after Gilligan, 1982), *difference feminism* (Williams, 1991), *identity politics feminism* (Beasley, 2005) or *separatist feminism* (Cain, 1993)—identifies the suppression of distinctive female qualities, experiences, and values as the primary cause of women's subordination. The solution it proposes is the identification, rehabilitation, and nurturance of women's qualities: "Alleged feminine distinctions are now being proclaimed with pride, rather than denied or minimized" (Mackie, 1991: 34). Some feminists (e.g., Daly, 1978; Squires, 2001) seek to build on women's shared or unique qualities and create an "alternative female consciousness" (Echols, 1984: 53).

Cultural feminists maintain that to achieve an alternative female consciousness, women-centred cultural or subcultural environments must be established to promote women's accomplishments and sense of unity; a hallmark of such "women's cultures" (hence the name "cultural feminism") would be consensual, non-hierarchical decision-making processes (Worell, 1996: 360; see also Ferguson, 1994, Phoca, 2000). Gilligan (1982) claimed that women speak "in a different voice" from men, and that a culture based on "womanly values" would be characterized by responsibility, connection, community, negotiation, altruism, and nurturance, in contrast to the separation, self-interest, combat, autonomy, and hierarchy characteristic of cultures based on male values (see also Ruddick, 1990; Held, 2001). The etiology of these posited gender differences does not appear to be a key concern for the majority of cultural feminists, although they generally seem to subscribe to a belief in a biological or innate basis.

Echols (1984: 51) noted that *eco-feminists* (see Armstrong, 1993; Sturgeon, 1997) and *pacifist feminists* claim that women's "bond with the natural order" (Rich, 1976) uniquely qualifies them to avert ecological disaster and nuclear holocaust. Caldicott (1984: 294, 296) contended that "[o] ne of the reasons women are so allied to the life processes is their hormonal constitution" and that males are "naturally" more fascinated by killing. Russell (1987: 15) claimed that "the nuclear mentality and the masculine mentality are one and the same. To rid ourselves of one, we must rid ourselves of the other." However, Flax (1990: 55) cautioned against asserting the "superiority of the opposite." She suggested that "perhaps women are not any less aggressive than men; we may just express our aggression in different, culturally sanctioned (and partially disguised or denied) ways" (Flax, 1990: 55).

Cultural feminists' belief that male sexuality is "selfish, violent, and woman-hating" (Echols, 1984: 60) is embodied in the axiom "pornography is the theory, rape is the practice" (Morgan in Echols, 1984: 58), which links male sexuality, pornography, and violence against women. Rich (1980/1984), in a provocative analysis of the patriarchal control of heterosexual relations, recommended lesbianism as the paradigm for female-controlled sexual and social life. Lesbianism is described as a personal and political—not biologically determined—choice that expresses the ultimate rejection of patriarchy. According to Martindale's (1995: 75) summary of Rich's argument, "lesbian/feminism is industrial-strength feminism.... If all women became lesbians, the patriarchy would crumble." MacKinnon (1982: 515) declared sexual relations to be the quintessential site of female subordination ("sexuality is to feminism what work is to Marxism"); concurring with that sentiment, lesbian separatists advocate women's separation from men in every way. Non-lesbian cultural feminists, however, only advocate separation from male *values*: "We can choose to dispense with male views and values and we can generate and make explicit our own: and we can make our own views and values authentic and real" (Spender, 1995: 142). Nevertheless, Spender's assertion makes evident why this variant of feminism is sometimes referred to as "**identity politics feminism**": "it claims to speak from and about the identity category of women … [and] advocates a politics that arises from that identity category" (Beasley, 2005: 48).

Cultural feminism has been criticized for **matriarchalism** (an ideology of female dominance) and **essentialism** (i.e., the belief that each sex possesses its own immutable, intrinsic nature, or "essence"). To posit certain traits, such as nurturingness or relatedness, as part of the essential nature of all women supports stereotypes and stereotyping, which are seen by other feminists as a part of women's subordination. Essentialist and romanticized conceptions of women may also rekindle the separate-spheres ideology that historically has functioned to women's disadvantage. Cain (1993: 242), moreover, pointed out that the claim that women speak in a different *voice* is viewed with skepticism by radical feminists who assert that this "voice" has been constructed in response to patriarchy. Radical feminists contend that "[w]oman-identified values, such as caring and connection to others, are suspect because they are values that women have created in response to patriarchy. We value caring because that is what our oppressors have caused us to value" (Cain, 1993: 242; see also Hartsock, 1998: 228–230).

Socialist Feminism

Seeking to address the "gender-blindness of traditional Marxism and the class-blindness of early radical feminism" (Jaggar and Rothenberg, 1993: 122), **socialist feminism** attempts to extend and enrich Marxist analysis by incorporating radical-feminist insights. Socialist feminism argues that a historical combination of capitalist political economy and patriarchal ideology has led to the oppression of women in both the public and the domestic spheres. Gender equality, therefore, requires the elimination of both capitalism and patriarchy.

Mitchell (1973) was one of the first feminists to identify four major focal points for a socialist-feminist inquiry into the problem of women's subordination. According to this analysis, in order to eliminate both class and gender oppression, it is necessary to restructure major societal systems; not only (1) the material systems of production to meet human needs for food, shelter, clothing, etc., but also the socially organized systems of (2) sexuality, (3) childbearing and ministering to family members and the infirm, and (4) childrearing and gender socialization. The traditional sexuality script, which emphasizes male aggressiveness and female passivity, is considered emblematic of gender power relations. MacKinnon (1982: 531) suggested that "gender socialization is the process through which women come to identify themselves as sexual beings, as beings that exist for men." Not only must sexuality roles be restructured to promote gender equality, but also a new female-generated model of sexuality and socialization must be created. Egalitarian solutions must also be examined in relation to one another, to ensure that one system's solutions do not become another system's problems.

Socialist feminists have explored the nature and importance of domestic labour, the nature and location of women's paid-labour experiences, and the interface between women's paid-labour and domestic-labour lives (Luxton and Corman, 2001, 2005; Lynn and Todoroff, 1995). Following Hartmann (1981) and others who view the North American nuclear family as a central site of women's oppression, socialist feminists have examined socialization within the family to investigate how girls and boys are prepared for differential participation in the domestic and paid-labour spheres. However, although socialist feminism explicitly acknowledges class- and gender-based oppression, it has tended to pay less attention to oppression based on ethnicity, sexuality, able-bodiedness, and age.

"Race"/Ethnicity/Imperialism (REI)/Post-colonial Feminisms

REI feminisms (Beasley, 2003) arose in response to expressed concerns that early feminist theory "denied, dismissed, and denigrated the experiences of differently raced, abled, and classed women" (Cassidy et al., 1998; see also Mohanty, 2003a, 2003b). Critics have argued that "white feminists have not only monopolized the [women's] movement with their interests and privileges, but have also carried their equality struggle, in the name of gender, at the expense of aboriginal, black women and women of colour" (Lucas et al., 1991/1995: 534; see also Box 3.1). Thus, as bell hooks (1990: 36) has maintained, "The usurpation of feminism by bourgeois women to support their class interests has been to a very grave extent justified by feminist theory as it has so far been conceived." She has lambasted radical and cultural feminists for suggesting that "'any woman has more in common with any other woman'—regardless of other factors like race—than she has with any man" and for advancing the claim that "all women are [equally] oppressed"; according to hooks, such sweeping generalizations are specious and simply serve to "mask" "white women's monopoly" over the feminist movement (Beasley, 2005: 90–91).

Unlike many feminist writings of the 1970s and 1980s, hooks' analyses (1981, 1984) positioned black women at the centre of theorizing rather than at its peripheries. Employing the language and logic of identity politics, hooks argued that, because of their oppressed position, black women in the United States possess a "special vantage point" (hooks, 1990: 39) that allows them to perceive, with particular clarity, the "truth" of that society. This unique knowledge and expertise, she maintained, infuses their politics with an especial authenticity and authority: "There are white women who had never considered resisting male dominance until the feminist movement created an awareness that they could and should. My awareness of feminist struggle was stimulated by *social circumstance*" (hooks, 1990: 36). Thus, while denouncing "gender essentialism," hooks embraces a "race essentialism" and defines "racism" in a way that make literal the dichotomous construction of "black" versus "white." In her more recent works (e.g., hooks, 1992, 2003), hooks has employed the term "black" inclusively (i.e., to refer to all non-white others) and suggested that her North American–centric accounts are generalizable "across national and cultural boundaries" (Kanneh, 1998: 92). Nevertheless, in directing attention to the insidious consequences of "'white supremacist' culture" and emphasizing the necessity of "uniting black men and women in overthrowing oppression," it is evident that, for hooks, feminism "is not a 'women's movement' alone" (Beasley, 2005: 91–93).

Madeleine Dion Stout (2002) has also pointed out that claims about the universality of male dominance and calls for universal sisterhood have rarely found a receptive audience among Aboriginal women. She observed that "mainstream feminism does not sit easily with Aboriginal women's sense of social reality based upon subsistence and balanced man/woman relationships.... [O]ur feminism differs from that of many of our mainstream counterparts in that we reject the overemphasis upon personal success and achievement.... focusing our

BOX 3.1

A'n't I a Woman?

Sojourner Truth (1797–1883), born into slavery, became well known as a preacher and as an antislavery lecturer after she gained her freedom in 1827. The quotations that follow are from a speech given by Truth extemporaneously at a women's rights convention in Ohio in 1851, in response to audience jeers and arguments that all women, the "universal woman," are by nature delicate creatures who require protection—not the vote. Frances Gage, an abolitionist and feminist activist, recorded Truth's powerful speech as she challenged this elitist and selective depiction of women. Truth's speech reminds us that there is no "universal woman."

Suddenly, Sojourner Truth rose from her seat at the corner of the church. "For God's sake, Mrs. Gage, don't let her speak!" half a dozen women whispered loudly, fearing that their cause would be mixed up with Abolition. Sojourner walked to the podium and slowly took off her sunbonnet. Her six-foot frame towered over the audience. She began to speak in her deep, resonant voice. "Well, children, where there is so much racket, there must be something out of kilter. I think between the Negroes of the South and the women of the North—all talking about rights—the white men will be in a fix pretty soon. But what's all this here talking about?" Sojourner pointed to one of the ministers. "That man over there say that women need to be helped into carriages, and lifted over ditches, and to have the best place everywhere. Nobody helps me any best place. And a'n't I a woman?"

Sojourner raised herself to her full height. "Look at me! Look at my arm!" She bared her right arm and flexed her powerful muscles. "I have ploughed, I have planted and I have gathered into barns. And no man could head me. And a'n't I a woman?"

"I could work as much, and eat as much as a man—when I could get it—and bear the lash as well! And a'n't I a woman? I have born thirteen children and seen most of them sold into slavery, and when I cried out with a mother's grief, none but Jesus heard me. And a'n't I a woman?" The women in the audience began to cheer wildly.

She pointed to another minister. "He talks about this thing in the head. What's that they call it?" ("Intellect," whispered a woman nearby.) "That's it, honey. What's intellect got to do with women's rights or black folks' rights? If my cup won't hold but a pint, and yours holds a quart, wouldn't you be mean not to let me have my little half-measure full?"

"That little man in black there! He says women can't have as much rights as men. 'Cause Christ wasn't a woman." She stood with outstretched arms and eyes of fire. "Where did your Christ come from?"

"Where did your Christ come from?" she thundered again. "From God and a woman! Man had nothing to do with him!"

The entire church now roared with deafening applause. "If the first woman God ever made was strong enough to turn the world upside down all alone, these women together ought to be able to turn it back and get it right-side up again. And now that they are asking to do it the men better let them."

Source: "Sojourner Truth." On the World Wide Web at www.kyphilom.com/www/truth.html.

attention instead upon the ways in which women's oppression is linked to the wider domination of all men and all women."

In stark contrast to feminist approaches which build on the notion of a universalized "Woman," REI feminists disrupt "the political innocence of the category woman" (Beasley, 2005: 79) by pointedly acknowledging the multiple differences that exist among women and by focusing on the intersections between gender and other axes of power. The specific focus may be intranational (e.g., indigenous women's experiences of racism within a specific country) or global (with attention directed, for example, to the delimited "independence" of former colonies and their ongoing political, economic and cultural dominance by imperialist "empires"). Nevertheless, Beasley (2005: 76–77) suggests that REI feminisms are marked by three key features:

> First … recognition of cross-gender commonalities forged by racism/ethnocentrism/imperialism…. REI feminists often note the strategic necessity for solidarity between men and women of culturally marginalised groups. The power divide is no longer simply located between the sexes. Rather, REI feminists highlight the divide between white (or Western) and non-white (or non-Western) in this reappraisal of the position of men…. Secondly … refusal of any straightforward presumption of women's shared subordination…. Thirdly … as a result of their attention to relations *between* women, [REI feminists have] been at the forefront of discussions about the meaning and practice of a feminist political solidarity in the light of women's diversity.

REI feminist writings that direct attention to power relations between "First World" (generally Western) and "Third World" societies are sometimes described as adopting a "post-colonial" approach. **Post-colonial theory** has been described as "a revolt of the margin against the metropolis, the periphery against the centre" (Milner and Browitt, 2002). Gilbert and Tompkins (1996) observed that while the term "post-colonial" is "frequently misunderstood as a temporal concept, meaning the time after colonialism has ceased…. [or] as a naive teleological sequence which supersedes colonialism, postcolonialism is, rather, an engagement with and contestation of colonialism's discourses, power structures and social hierarchies" (p. 2). **Post-colonial feminism** is influenced by the writings of theorists such as Edward Said (1978, 1993), who argued that Western writings cast the Orient as a feminized, irrational "Other," whose culture and peoples are different and inferior to those of the masculine, rational West. Post-colonial feminism seeks to challenge the "arrogantly universal claims and homogenising tendencies in Western thought," expose its "imperialist agenda" and, by doing so, disrupt the **"othering"** principle, which "maintains hierarchical power relations between supposedly dichotomous, discrete, fixed and unitary identity groups and presumes that differences must be regarded differently" (Beasley, 2005: 79).

Although the attention of post-colonial feminists was focused early on upon colonial societies, Gayatri Spivak (1990: 94–95) has argued that, in a world of "planetary capitalism," "post-colonial thinking is no longer even especially about First World/Third World distinctions but about an all-embracing empire of global inequalities." As such, the subject matter of post-colonial feminist theory is broad; it is "concerned with both previous and contemporary 'empires' and involves a rejection not only of the economic and political dominance of these empires but more particularly their (usually racialized) cultural dominance" (Beasley, 2005: 75).

REI feminists retain the dichotomous categories (man/other; West/other) but adopt a strategy which specifically valorizes the marginalized "other"; post-colonial feminists emphasize the "hybrid heterogeneous character of cultures and peoples" and direct attention to the "plural and fluid character of identity, as well as ... the permeability of cultural borders.... [and] the possibilities of borderline/'impure' positioning and mixed cultural ancestry" (Beasley, 2005: 80). For example, in faulting Canadian feminist communities for their silence on the issue of imperialism with respect to transsexualism and transgenderism, Viviane Namaste (2005: xi) argued that it is essential that discussion of these issues be informed by the concerns of post-colonial feminism: "[W]e must understand the ways in which feminist conceptions of the person and of citizenship are marked by specific nationalist and colonialist traditions." Thus, in her examination of how current appeals to transgender rights "are actually bound up with much broader social and economic relations of imperialism," Namaste (2005: xi) begins with the insistent claim that "[w]e cannot take an appeal to 'personhood' or 'citizenship' at face value when these concepts become institutional mechanisms through which imperialism is achieved, denying rights to some humans, according them to others."

REI/post-colonial feminisms may be seen as a subset of ongoing efforts to create a more inclusive feminism that attempts to "challenge ... traditional race-class-sexuality-power arrangements which favour men over women, whites over non-whites ... able-bodiedness over non-able-bodiedness ... and the employed over the non-employed" (Elliot and Mandell, 1998: 5; Bannerji, 2000). The writings of post-colonial and REI feminists make evident that simply including the **voices** of previously ignored (or **silenced**) groups of women as an adjunct to existing theory is inadequate and problematic. The very acknowledgement of "difference" contains the seeds of subordination; "different" may implicitly connote "deficient from" an ideal norm relative to which one is defined. If white, middle-class, heterosexual women are still construed as the "standard" while women of other social categories are defined as "different," the latter are likely to be marginalized—just as all women are when men are defined as the standard and women as "different" and therefore deficient.

Increasingly, representatives of "silenced" groups are claiming the right to reshape feminist theory and feminism itself. Doing so may be difficult; as Stout (2000) pointed out in relation to Aboriginal women, "it is unlikely that the practice of Aboriginal feminism will be free of contradiction and conflict, and indeed Aboriginal women are often told that, by challenging women's oppression, we are betraying our womanhood, and diverting attention away from the larger, and by implication more important, struggle for self-government." Nevertheless, the ultimate goal of REI/post-colonial feminists is to create a theory that explains the multiplicative impacts of the many forms of discrimination. The challenge is to develop an understanding of the commonality of women's subordination, without asserting that subordination on the basis of gender is necessarily more fundamental than other forms which women confront because of their race/ethnicity, class, etc. In some instances, issues of gender supersede issues of race, ethnicity, class, sexuality, or ability; in others, gender is a background issue.

The quest for a more inclusive feminism has created something of a paradox: "[F]eminism seems, still, to require the consciousness-raising that enables women to claim some measure of unity 'as women' even while they concentrate on understanding differences" (Code, 1993: 48). Given the relatively recent emergence of REI/post-colonial discourses, it is not surprising that the voices of ignored and neglected groups are only beginning to be reclaimed (Gray-Rosendale and Harootunian, 2003). The incorporation of these voices into an integrated feminist theory remains a work-in-progress.

Postmodern Feminism

"Postmodern feminists eschew the idea of unitary truth, of objective reality" (Cain, 1993: 242). **Postmodern feminism** exists both as a rebuke to all statements of claim made by other branches of feminist thought and as a perspective in its own right.

Postmodernism challenges the Western tradition of rationalist thought. It rejects basic *modernist* beliefs which, since the Enlightenment, have dominated our way of looking at reality; these include certainty and fixity of meaning, the ability of human reason to arrive at absolute truth, and the notion of scientific objectivity (see Nicholson, 1990: 2–4). Postmodernist criticism attacks the rationalist enterprise for its dogmatic concept of unitary and immutable truth; for its grand theories and ideologies which pursue certainty by repressing or annihilating that which is different or doesn't fit in; for the conceit of scientific detachment (which is untenable, since to observe is to interact), and for its disregard for subjectivity. Modernists believe "that individuals comprise stable, coherent, and rational subjects; that reason, with its scientific laws, provides an objective, reliable, and universal basis for knowledge; that the rational use of knowledge is neutral and socially beneficial" (based on Flax, 1990, in Elliot and Mandell, 1998: 18). Postmodernists, however, have a radically different perspective:

> a conception of the individual as unstable, contradictory, and socially constructed; a conception of what forms of authority or knowledge are legitimate, namely multiple, anti-hierarchical, and participatory forms; a conception of history as non-linear, not necessarily progressive, and as always read through the limited perspective of the present, as well as through particular contexts; and a conception of community as an achievement based on valuing differences without opposition. (Elliot and Mandell, 1998: 19)

Postmodern feminism asserts that the modernist ideals of rationality and scientific objectivity are masculinist conceptions (Nicholson, 1990: 5). These are rejected, along with what postmodern feminists depict as the narrow, white, middle-class feminisms that attempt to universalize the experiences of one "privileged" group to all women. Postmodern feminists argue that the various feminist theories—liberal, Marxist, radical, cultural, and socialist—which postulate a single or even a limited plurality of causes for women's oppression are flawed, inadequate, and typically based upon the suppression of female experiences incompatible with each theory (Flax, 1990: 46–49). Generalization itself is seen as inherently "masculinist"—any theory claiming to be fully explanatory, they maintain, is assuming a dominant and oppressive stance. Postmodern feminists seek to acknowledge the subjective perspectives and experiences of women of all classes, races, ethnicities, abilities, sexualities, and ages, while neither making generalizations about all women nor representing any one or all of these groups as embodying "essential" qualities of womanhood. To postmodern feminists, a feminist theory is impossible because there is no essential "woman"; the category of women is simply "a fiction, a non-determinable identity" (Cain, 1993: 243). Thus, while certain feminist theories (especially cultural feminism) drift towards essentialism, postmodern feminism lurches towards nominalism (i.e., the doctrine that only the particular exists and that general ideas are mere names with no corresponding reality).

Critics have argued that the phrase "postmodern feminism" is itself an oxymoron. As Cain (1993: 242–243) observed, "if postmodernism views the category 'woman' as being so multifarious that it denies unitariness, how can it ever ascribe to be feminist, since feminism is a theory that focuses on the unitary category 'woman'?" It also follows that "[i]f there can be no essential Human and no essential woman/feminine, then there can also be no essential black/ethnic minority/Third World women" (Beasley, 2005: 79). If every woman's experience is unique, as postmodernists claim, then the theoretical enterprise is futile; what is more, any plan of action or advocacy on women's behalf would be unworkable (Di Stefano, 1990: 76; see also Connell, 2000, 2003; Nussbaum, 1999, 2000).

In response to postmodernist entreaties to disaggregate identities and jettison categories such as "woman" or "black" or "Third World," post-colonial feminist Gayatri Spivak (in Darius and Jonsson, 1993) has proposed the adoption of **strategic essentialism**, in which identity categories are employed for the express purpose of addressing issues of power and marginalization. "Essentialism is bad ... but only in its application. Essentialism is like dynamite ... it can be effective in dismantling unwanted structures or alleviating suffering; uncritically employed, however, it is destructive and addictive" (p. 2). Others, however, suggest that Spivak's recommended strategy itself reveals the barrenness of postmodernist theorizing for those who are concerned with political change and committed to advocacy on behalf of the socially marginalized; as Milner and Browitt (2002: 148) have asserted, "what use is a theory that requires, for its effective application, that we pretend not to believe in it?"

Despite such criticisms, postmodern feminism's "anti-generalist, anti-humanist (i.e., antagonistic to the notion of a common core Human nature or agency) and strongly anti-essentialist position" has been influential, inspiring new theorizing in both gender/feminist and, especially, sexuality studies (Beasley, 2005: 24–25). For example, postmodern feminism's opposition to using identity as the basis of politics resonates loudly within Judith Butler's (1990) *Gender Trouble*. According to Butler (1997: 126), "the identity categories often presumed to be foundational in feminist politics ... simultaneously work to limit and constrain in advance the very cultural possibilities that feminism is supposed to open up." Butler maintains that, despite the tendency to view anatomical sex as an external binary that predates culture and creates "gender," it is the other way round—it is "gender" that makes "sex" of import. That is, just as differences in eye colour are not culturally registered as being of profound social import, differences in biological sex need not be. Her conception of the sexed body as, in itself, a "gendered performance" stresses the instability of identity categories.

In asserting that gender is **performative**—a social "fabrication" and "effect of power" that arises from a "decidedly public and social discourse" that, in coercive fashion, insists upon the constant repetition of certain stylized acts—Butler (1997) emphasizes that gender is not biologically impelled but, instead, socially constructed. In enjoining gender performances, such as drag, which create "gender trouble" "by not 'doing gender' as it is supposed to be done" (Hekman, 2000: 292), her aim is "to disrupt categories *per se*, to disrupt the fixity of identity, by showing up its non-natural incoherence.... [and] the artifice ... that is the gendered self" (Beasley, 2005: 102) and to compel a "radical rethinking" of both gender identity and sexuality (Butler, 1993).

Butler's "queer feminism" suggests that gender and sexuality categories of identity can be purposefully displaced by **sexual crossing**—a mixing up of multiple identity pathways; i.e., categories of bodily sex (male/female), gender (feminine/masculine), and sexuality (heterosexual/homosexual). She suggests that these amalgams can challenge the assumption that, for example, the male body is automatically masculine and heterosexual (Beasley, 2005: 108–109). This belief in the political efficacy of identity subversion is even more marked within **queer theory** (a term coined by Teresa de Lauretis in 1991 [Andermahr et al., 2000: 220]).

Queer theory positions sexuality as a central focus of analysis, acknowledges the common history of devaluation that non-heterosexuals share, and challenges the existing power structure that continues to marginalize them (Andermahr et al., 2000; Butler, 1997; Cranny-Francis et al., 2003; Sedgwick, 1985, 2003; Seidman, 2004). Following the writings of Foucault (1980) and, most especially, his concern with "denaturalizing dominant understandings of sexual identity" (Jagose, 1996: 79), *queer theorists* assert that heterosexism continues to shape contemporary society. They maintain that the dominant *discourse* (i.e., a body of ideas or beliefs that have been established as knowledge or become an accepted world view) of sexuality, which has depicted homosexuals as a separate species, is most fundamentally a discourse of *power*. Queer theorists draw upon a combination of theoretical schools, such as feminism, psychoanalysis, and poststructuralism (a theory that emphasizes that "experience" is distinct from "knowledge" and that our identities—our thoughts, meanings, and interpretations—are constituted by language) (see Brookey and Miller, 2001). The aim of queer theory is "to destabilise identity through the construction of a supposedly 'inclusive,' non-normative (almost invariably non-heterosexual) sexuality and a simultaneous dismantling of gender roles. Queer theory sees identity as thoroughly socially constructed and as internally untestable and incoherent" (Beasley, 2005: 255) and "is inclined to reiterate a voluntarist and consumerist **libertarianism** in which we all get to 'choose' from a supermarket of identities … in a 'pick and mix' fashion … in order to assemble a customised, supposedly authentic selfhood beyond socially imposed categories" (Beasley, 2005: 112).

Yet, while queer theory often celebrates **gender outlaws** (Bornstein, 1994)—those whose attributes defy easy placement within gender and sexuality binaries—as exemplars of the "criss-crossing" of identities (Sedgwick, 1985: x), its assertion that transsexualism, for example, involves a "renunciation" and "displacement" of gender as an identity is debatable. As suggested in Chapter 1, others would argue that transsexualism more notably involves an "embrace" of gender and simply the "replacement" of one gendered identity with another (see also Malone, 2001; Prosser, 1998; Whittle, 1996).

PERSPECTIVES ON MEN AND MASCULINITY

Theorizing about men *as* men, and on the nature of masculinity in our society, has a briefer history than feminist thought. It could be argued that such traditional theories as classical liberalism, while purporting to represent generic humanity, actually developed models of men. However, as such theories do not focus on men per se, they do not easily lend themselves to the distillation of specific ideas about men and masculinity. Present-day theorizing has evolved largely in response to feminist theories and social changes initiated by the women's movement. Drawing upon Clatterbaugh (1990, 1997, 2000), six perspectives are presented below.

The Conservative Perspective

According to the **conservative perspective**, the *essential nature* of men and masculinity is different from that of women and femininity. There are two main streams of thought within the conservative perspective. One, following Charles Darwin (1809–1882), locates the roots of essential masculinity in biology, while the other, following Edmund Burke (1729–1797), locates them in the moral order of civilization. Today's biological conservatives generally subscribe to Wilson's (1978) sociobiology argument, discussed in Chapter 2.

Moral conservatives such as Gilder (1973, 1986) and Blankenhorn (1995, 2000) argue that masculinity is a manifestation of society's civilizing force, which harnesses men's unruly nature to produce providers and protectors of women and children. Both these authors suggested that men are by nature antisocial, and that single men especially are prone to drunkenness, criminality, violence, and debt (Blankenhorn, 1995: 35–42; Gilder, 1973: 5, 30, 208). By exercising the power of their sexuality, women supposedly tame and civilize men, bringing out their best and noblest qualities (Gilder, 1973: 38, 98).

Moral conservatives argue in favour of restoring to ascendancy the "traditional" male-dominated nuclear family. Gilder targeted the liberal feminist agenda (e.g., affirmative action, increased availability of contraception, abortion, and day care) as a threat to men's performance of their traditional masculine role. In the face of such a threat, men are likely to flee their responsibilities, abandon their families, and revert to their antisocial tendencies (Gilder, 1973: 265–267). In his defence of the "natural family," William Gairdner, one of Canada's most prominent moral conservatives, grimly warned that

> [u]nless some social pressure is imposed to recruit men and their energies for a purpose higher than themselves and their appetites—in particular, if women are not present, or not willing, or lack confidence, or are afraid to tame errant male proclivities—then "over the whole range of human societies, men are overwhelmingly more prone to masturbation, homosexuality, voyeurism, gratuitous sexual aggression, and other shallow and indiscriminate erotic activity" [Gilder, 1986: 5]. They are also more prone to violent crime. (Gairdner, 1992: 85)

In other words, if masculinity, the family, and society itself are on the brink of moral disaster, it is all the fault of women (especially feminists). When women discard the civilizing role of traditional femininity, men forgo the moral dimensions of traditional masculinity. In the opinion of conservatives, feminist-initiated social reforms are doomed to failure, either because of the irrevocable biological basis of gendered roles or because right-minded men will recognize the importance of the moral order for the survival of civilization.

Clatterbaugh (1997: 31) noted that present-day conservatives have come into positions of power in both Canada (he identified the Reform [later Canadian Alliance, now reconstituted Conservative] Party) and the United States (Republican Party). Like classical conservatives, today's neoconservatives oppose government intervention in economic matters in general, as well as objecting to specific interventions such as affirmative action and sexual-harassment policies. However, unlike classical moral conservatives, they strongly urge government intervention in support of their gender ideology. Many of today's neoconservatives demand interventions to "strengthen the family, teach values in school ... abolish abortions, support church schools, and encourage prayers in public schools" (Clatterbaugh, 1997: 25) in order to bolster men's "natural" provider and women's "natural" childbearing/caregiving roles.

The Profeminist Perspective

According to the **profeminist perspective**, masculinity is socially constructed. In contrast to the conservatives, profeminists argue that the traditional family is not a civilizing institution, but rather an institution "oppressive to women and destructive of men's ability to be caring, loving partners to women" (Clatterbaugh, 1990: 59). They maintain that the removal of the gender restrictions upon masculinity would benefit both women and men. (NOMAS, 1991/2001). Two types of profeminism are discernible, each having developed in response to a different branch of early feminism.

Liberal profeminists tend to find symmetry in the situations of men and women; they see the sexes as being equally, but differently, restricted by existing gender prescriptions (Clatterbaugh, 1997: 48). Arguing that the gender expectations for masculinity prevent men from attaining their full potential as human beings, liberal profeminists focus primarily upon the costs to men created by their gender role in our society. Farrell (1974: 30) early enumerated our society's "10 commandments of masculinity," namely, that men should be unemotional, invulnerable, unresponsive, controlling, condescending, egotistical, non-introspective breadwinners who disdain housework. Other early writers directed attention to the socialized constraints placed upon masculinity in such areas as athletics (Lester, 1976), the provider role (Gould, 1976), and parenting (Fasteau, 1975). While liberal profeminists initially tended to depict a monolithic image of masculinity, they have more recently evinced the influence of feminist, anti-racist, and pro-gay politics, incorporated feminist and postmodernist notions of identity, and emphasized a plurality of "masculinities" (Connell, 2005).

Radical profeminists view contemporary masculinity as the byproduct of a patriarchal society based upon a system of power designed to benefit and privilege men in ways that result in most men being unaware of how privileged they are (Messner, 1997: 4; Messner, 1998). According to this perspective, masculinity is characterized by *misogyny* (hatred of women) and violence towards women, other men, and even self; men are socialized into these characteristics by our patriarchal society. Whereas moral conservatives claim that women hold sexual power over men, radical profeminists argue that men use their greater power to sexually oppress women (Curry, 1991/2001; Messner, 1997: 51). To achieve a new masculinity "beyond patriarchy" (Kaufman, 1987, 1993), radical profeminists advocate the *resocialization* of men to eradicate such socialized features as misogyny, violence against women (e.g., through the White Ribbon campaign in Canada), the assumption of male superiority, men's emotional isolation from one another, and male competitiveness (Beneke, 1997; Pfeil, 1995). They urge the socialization of men into the values of nonviolence, cooperation, and nurturance (Clatterbaugh, 1997: 11; Schoene-Harwood, 2000; Stolenberg, 2000).

Both liberals and radicals employ consciousness-raising group techniques as a means of sensitizing men to their own sexism; these groups also serve as a context for men to provide one another with emotional support. Some profeminists promote the development of men's studies programs as a way of advancing the understanding of masculinity and of combatting sexism (Brod and Kaufman, 1994; Beynon, 2002). Liberal profeminists view androgyny as the optimal alternative to traditional images of masculinity, while radical profeminists are divided on this issue insofar as androgyny still incorporates elements of traditional masculinity. Most radicals would endorse an androgyny that transcends traditional masculinity.

The Men's Rights Perspective

The **men's rights movement** evolved from a liberal profeminist position, incorporating a proliferating number of fathers' rights groups in the 1980s and 1990s. It argues that the current gender system, rather than privileging men, is oppressive and devastating to them (Messner, 1997: 41). "In short, masculinity is riddled with guilt, shaped by guilt, and maintained by guilt" (Clatterbaugh, 1990: 66). Contradictory expectations for masculinity create no-win situations with ultimately lethal consequences for men, in the form of disease, disability, and premature death (Farrell, 1993).

Men's rights advocates deplore the contradictions within contemporary masculine roles:

Men are told to be gentle, while gentle men are told they are wimps. Men are told to be vulnerable, but vulnerable [men] are told they are too needy. Men are told to be less performance oriented, but less successful men are rejected for lack of ambition. This list of contradictions is seemingly endless. (Hayward, 1987: 12)

Since there are no winning choices, failure is a foregone conclusion. When men fail, guilt turns to self-hate, which leads to emotional and physical self-neglect, culminating in higher rates of suicide, alcoholism, disease, drug addiction, and crime (especially violent crime) (Farrell, 1993). Men's rightists, like conservatives, assert that because men are raised to be sexually and emotionally dependent upon women, they seek to base a relationship on the exchange of economic provision and protection for sexual favours. However, whereas conservatives praise women for their civilizing influence, men's rightists emphasize the invidious effects of the feminist movement upon men's lives. According to the men's rights perspective, feminism and "Feminazis" have intensified the contradictions in the masculine gender role by promoting a "new sexism": "[s]exism is discounting the female experience of powerlessness; the new sexism is discounting the male experience of powerlessness" (Farrell, 1986: 196).

"Whereas many in the profeminist movement consider the men's rights perspective to be anti-feminist, men's rights partisans claim to be the *true* antisexist movement" (Clatterbaugh, 1990: 63; emphasis in original); this claim can be found, for example, in the writings of the Movement for the Establishment of Real Gender Equality (MERGE), founded in Edmonton, Alberta. Proponents of the men's rights perspective argue that programs designed to promote women's equality, such as affirmative action, actually further disadvantage and victimize men. Men's rightists are among the most vocal members of the so-called "whitelash" phenomenon (activism on behalf of white, middle-class males, who are identified as the "casualties" of affirmative action). They also draw attention to family- and divorce-law issues, (e.g., child custody decisions) which they believe are based on sexism against men. As part of their exposition of the lethal hazards of being male in our society and the cheapness of men's lives (Farrell, 1993), the men's rights perspective focuses on domestic and societal violence perpetrated against men. Men's rightists also decry negative images of men ("male-bashing"), which they believe are promoted by feminists (Clatterbaugh, 1997: 11).

Every economic, political, and sexual advantage identified by feminists as an example of male privilege is countered by men's rights analysts with an example of the equal or greater oppression of men: the burdens of the provider role that turns men into "success objects," the burdens of leadership, the burdens of sexual initiation and rejection, etc. (see Farrell, 1993). A major stumbling block to the men's rights movement has been the difficulty of generating understanding, empathy, and political action for a social category (i.e., men) perceived as generally privileged. As Richardson (1988: 247) noted, "[men's] privileged position within the system does not give them the structural advantage of challenging their own treatment as unfair. Most of the goals are not easily politicized." Aside from gaining an increasing number of followers, perhaps the most significant political achievement of men's rights advocates thus far has been the institution of changes to Canadian child-custody laws—most notably, the presumption of joint custody (see Chapter 8).

The Spiritual Perspective

Two fairly recent men's movements, the mythopoetic and the Promise Keepers, exemplify the **spiritual perspective** (Messner, 1997). Even though important differences exist in their sources and goals, the two movements are similar in their contention that present-day masculinity suffers from spiritual impoverishment. Both share the desire to provide men with therapeutic means and settings to address this problem.

The mythopoetic men's movement owes an intellectual debt to Carl Jung (1875–1961) (1982). Jung claimed that the psyche—the whole of our being—is innately purposeful or *teleological*, seeking growth, wholeness, and equilibrium. He termed the goal of this process *individuation*, the achievement of a unified Self integrating the many factors of the psyche, both conscious and unconscious. The conscious side of our personality is called the *persona*; this is the mask we wear to face society. Too "perfect" a persona can confine us within a too-narrow spiritual horizon, leading to rigidity, alienation, and neurosis. The *collective unconscious* is a repository of inherited contents, common to all humankind, including the *archetypes*—primordial, unconscious patterns of understanding. The *shadow* is such an archetype: It is our own dark side, characterized by repressed, uncivilized, or unadapted qualities which the ego wishes to keep out of the persona, or public self. Archetypes, such as the shadow, can revitalize life if we honestly face up to them. Symbols and ritual, unlike linear, discursive thought, activate the unconscious; when we engage with them, the *transcendent function* mediates the opposites of unconsciousness and consciousness, allowing us to move from a one-sided attitude to a new and fuller one, thereby restoring the psyche to healthy balance. The *mythopoetic imagination*—the imagination involved in myth-making, fantasy, and dream—partakes of the healing effect of the transcendent function. Building on these concepts, the **mythopoetic men's movement** maintains that masculinity arises out of psychospiritual patterns, and that men may gain access to these ancient archetypes through participation in rituals and exposure to myths and storytelling.

The principal architect of the mythopoetic movement is Bly (1990, 1988, 1987). Bly claimed that modern men have failed to connect with their archetypal masculinity. From his examination of ancient myths, he related this failure to our society's lack of symbolic rituals, conducted by male elders, for the initiation of men into masculinity. "The Industrial Revolution ... pulled fathers away from their sons and, moreover, placed the sons in compulsory schools where the teachers are mostly women" (Bly, 1990: 19). Women cannot properly initiate men into masculinity. "[O]nly men can initiate men, as only women can initiate women.... [B]oys need a second birth, this time a birth from men" (Bly, 1990: 16, 21). The isolated nuclear family compounds the problems of absent fathers by not providing boys with access to male elders who could help initiate them into masculinity. "The ancient societies believed that a boy becomes a man only through ritual and effort—only through the 'active intervention of the older men'" (Bly, 1990: 15).

Bly views feminism as a positive force for women, but only a mixed blessing for men, insofar as it permits men to get in touch with their feminine side but prevents them from finding the deeply masculine within themselves (Bly, 1987: 2–3). Bly's solution is to help men explore the missing elements of their masculinity, primarily by drawing upon the symbolism found in the Grimm brothers' tale of *Iron Hans*, written in the early 1800s, which he renames *Iron John*. "The Iron John story retains memories of initiation ceremonies for men that go back ten or twenty thousand years in northern Europe. The Wild Man's job is to teach the young man how abundant, various, and many-sided his manhood is" (Bly, 1990: 55). The **Wild Man** is an embodiment of the archetypal shadow; the darker, primitive, but also creatively nourishing energies (Bly, 1990: 6) that Bly considers necessary to balance the "softer" masculinity of today. "The aim is not to *be* the Wild Man, but to be *in touch with* the Wild Man" (Bly, 1990: 227; emphasis in original). The agenda of the mythopoetic movement is to provide men with all-male therapeutic settings, in workshops and weekend retreats, for learning ancient myths and stories and gaining exposure to masculinity-initiation rituals. These rituals, led by older men, provide opportunities for younger men to resolve their separation issues with absent fathers, get in touch with their darker spontaneously playful self, and find mentors with whom to identify. The result, they hope, will be stronger, men-defined men, capable of acting with forceful resolve, as opposed to "softer," women-defined men.

Attractive mainly to middle-class, middle-aged, white, heterosexual, professional men (Schwalbe, 1996), the mythopoetic movement takes the essentialist view that the fundamental qualities of masculinity remain unchanged for all time. This movement, more than most of the other perspectives, is concerned mainly with men's relationships with other men rather than with men's relationships with women. It does not advocate social change of a political nature, focusing instead upon the necessity of self-change. The mythopoetic perspective essentially ignores issues related to men's generally more privileged position relative to women within our society.

Promise Keepers is a Christian evangelical men's movement which emerged in the 1990s. The name is taken from the "Seven Promises," a code of responsible and ethical conduct which members swear to uphold upon joining the movement (Clatterbaugh, 1997: 177). Formed in 1990, Promise Keepers follows in the footsteps of relatively short-lived evangelical men's movements that arose in the United States in the early decades of the twentieth century. While those earlier "Muscular Christianity" movements (Messner, 1997: 24) were formed to confront changes in men's roles brought about by industrialization, urbanization, and the first wave of the feminist movement, Promise Keepers developed largely in response to changes occasioned by second-wave feminism.

From very modest beginnings in 1990, Promise Keepers—holding rallies in football stadiums in the United States and hockey arenas in Canada—grew to attract large numbers of men; estimates range from over 600 000 (Messner, 1997: 24) to almost three quarters of a million men in 1995 (Clatterbaugh, 1997: 178) and possibly 1.1 million men in 1996 (Gergen, 1997: 78). By 2007, according to the organization's official website, the group had "directly reached more than five and a half million men" with "[m]ultitudes more ... reached through books, music CDs, multi-media resources, the Internet, satellite and radio broadcasts" (Promise Keepers, 2008). Male athletes often occupy centre stage at rallies, while sports images and metaphors are liberally utilized to help spread Promise Keepers' message (Beal, 1997). Women are usually allowed to participate in "family night" meetings held on the eve of the main rally, and work at concession stands and information booths outside of the main venues, but the rallies themselves are reserved for men only. According to the Promise Keepers' website, the reason for the group's dedication to preserving its men-only focus "is that men ... communicate, learn and relate in substantially different ways than women. One of the most significant relationship differences between men and women is the environment required for open and deep communication.... A male-only context of safety and familiarity ... helps men to achieve that level of intimacy that, in turn, facilitates spiritual growth" (promisekeepers.org, 2004).

Promise Keepers, promoting a Bible-based essentialism, maintains that the major problems facing men in contemporary society stem from blurred gender roles brought about by women taking over and men abdicating traditional male gender responsibilities, all as a consequence of feminism. Late-twentieth-century "moral decline" in Canada and the United States (evinced by rising divorce rates, lone-parent families, fathers' minimal participation in family life, sexual promiscuity, homosexuality, AIDS, and so on) is seen as the result of men having abandoned a Christian, or Christlike, lifestyle. Promise Keepers claims that the solution to societal, familial, and gender ills lies in men reclaiming their rightful and God-given leadership position within families and larger communities (Armato and Marsiglio, 2002).

> The first thing you do is sit down with your wife and say something like this: "Honey, I've made a terrible mistake. I've given you my role. I gave up leading this family, and I forced you to take my place. Now I must reclaim that role." Don't misunderstand what I'm saying here. I'm not suggesting that you *ask* for your role back, I'm urging you to *take it back*. (Evans, 1994: 79; emphasis in original)

Even though this message implies that women should submit to the will of men, Promise Keepers continually asserts that its message is one based upon "respect" (Messner, 1997: 30) and "honour" (Clatterbaugh, 1997: 185) for women. Clearly, however, women are to accept their rightful place under their husband's leadership, a role likely to appeal only to women who share a fundamentalist Christian ideology (Messner, 1997: 32). Basing their vision on a literal interpretation of the Bible, Promise Keepers asserts that families should be hierarchical, with men as leaders, providers, and protectors, women as wives, mothers, and emotional caretakers of their families, and children as subservient and obedient, especially to their fathers (Clatterbaugh, 1997: Messner, 1997: 30).

During the first half of the 1990s, Promise Keepers drew mostly white, heterosexual, middle-aged Protestant males; over the second half of the decade, its message began to attract notable numbers of younger men and men from non-white ethnic groups (Messner, 1997: 26). Despite growing diversity, Promise Keepers' predominant constituency remains white and Christian. Moreover, while its website announces that it "supports" and "welcomes" the inclusion of homosexuals "in all our events," it additionally notes that Promise Keepers "shares the same historic stance taken by Evangelicals and Catholics: that sex is a good gift from God to be enjoyed in the context of heterosexual marriage. We believe that the Bible clearly teaches that homosexuality violates God's creative design for a husband and a wife and that it is a sin" (promisekeepers.org, 2007). While Faludi (1999: 285) observed that "Promise Keepers' appeal began to sag nationally [in the United States] by decade's end," the organization seems to have remained fairly robust in Canada, maintaining "team PK" offices in British Columbia, Alberta, Saskatchewan, Manitoba, and Ontario. In addition, its website reports "a growing international ministry with activity in more than 30 countries in every continent" (promisekeepers.org, 2004).

The Socialist Perspective

The **socialist perspective**, derived from classical Marxism, considers masculinity to be an epiphenomenon of the capitalist economic system, under which a small proportion of the population own and control the means of production, while the mass of men are exploited workers. Furthermore, within each class, men control the labour of women

(Clatterbaugh, 1990: 106). "Masculinity ... is a product of the power relations that exist among men and between men and women in the relations of production" (Clatterbaugh, 1990: 124). A central characteristic of all men in capitalist societies is *alienation*, a sense of estrangement and lack of control over their environment. However, the causes, experiences, and consequences of alienation differ for owners and workers.

The socialist perspective focuses primarily upon workers, but has directed some attention towards the general class of "owners," which includes managers and professionals who represent owners' interests. The working life of owners, while physically safe, is characterized by long hours, intense competition, career insecurity, and the relentless pursuit of money and promotion (Clatterbaugh, 1990: 114). Their relationship to colleagues, competitors, and employees is based on power. Even though owners control the lives of workers, they cannot fully control either the marketplace or their own grasp on power. This lack of control, along with the power-based nature of their work relationships (in which workers are reduced to the status of property or machines and peers to the status of rivals), results in alienation (Clatterbaugh, 1990: 119).

Workers, by definition, cannot control their own labour. Those to whom they sell their labour dictate their productivity and what they produce; workers are alienated from the product of their labour. Working conditions—physical hazards, working hours, pay and benefits scales, employment security—are all beyond the control of workers, especially the large proportion (approximately two thirds in Canada) of blue-collar workers who do not enjoy union protection (Statistics Canada, 2002l). Gray (1987: 219) maintained that a shared sense of masculinity enables men to develop worker solidarity, helping them to resist the power of owners over their lives. Gray (1987: 221–223) further suggested that male workers' efforts to exclude women from full work-force participation represent an attempt to assert masculine control as a defence against the powerlessness they feel in the workplace. Male workers also tend to experience their homes as a respite from the alienation of work, because at home they can exercise at least some measure of control and power over their wives and children (Clatterbaugh, 1990: 111). Working-class masculinity, therefore, reflects a combination of general powerlessness/alienation within the workplace and some degree of power and privilege over women of the same class, at work and (especially) at home (Clatterbaugh, 1990: 118). Thus, the power imbalance in men's relationship to women may be seen as an artifact of a more fundamental power imbalance in the economic system.

Proponents of the socialist perspective argue that masculinity is class-specific. Furthermore, they claim that other perspectives tend to present a monolithic, class-biased image of masculinity:

> Most of the literature on masculinity focuses on men who are owners, managers, and professionals. As the lives of these men are taken as representative, masculinity becomes identified with competitiveness, not solidarity; making ever more money, not getting-by; promotion, not fear of being laid off; learning to live in healthy ways, not being maimed at work; how to spend leisure time, not the exhaustion of compulsory overtime. (Clatterbaugh, 1997: 125)

The socialist perspective not only attempts to redress this class bias, but stresses that any agendas aiming to ameliorate the conditions of masculinity (e.g., alienation) must vary by social class. However, the socialist approach is itself monolithic, focusing solely upon economic determinants of masculinity. According to this perspective, only a radical transformation of the economic system to eliminate the division of workers and owners can bring about equality between men—and between men and women—and an end to alienation.

The Group-Specific Perspective

Like REI feminisms, the **group-specific perspective** sensitizes us to the existence of a range of masculinities within contemporary society. Each of these is situated within a different social location, identified by social class, ethnicity, and/or sexual orientation. This perspective raises numerous challenges to the unitary images of masculinity offered by other perspectives.

Standpoint epistemologies emphasize that knowledge arises out of specific types of social experience. If traditionally the standpoint for much sociological theorizing has been that of white, middle-class heterosexuals, there are many other standpoints (akin to the feminist concept of different "voices") from which to view the world. Thus, theorizing that has positioned homosexuals, rather than heterosexuals, at the centre of analysis has suggested how new insights into masculinity may be gained by listening to non-heterosexual voices (Dowsett, 1998; Plummer, 1994, 2001; Seidman, 1997, 1998, 2004). Kinsman (1987: 104–105) has observed that although gay men "share with straight men the economic benefits of being men ... we do not participate as regularly in the everyday interpersonal subordination of women in the realms of sexuality and violence" (see also Cruz, 2003) The fact that gay men's masculinity is forged without benefit of physical and sexual power over women invites theorists and researchers to consider whether (1) gay masculinity is substantially different from that of heterosexual men; (2) gay masculinity is somehow based upon a latent sexual power of all men over women, regardless of whether that power is ever acted upon; or (3) current explanations of heterosexual masculinity arc incomplete (see also Connell, 2005; Nardi, 2000; Halkitis, 2001).

A second important insight is that heterosexual masculinity is "created and maintained by homophobia" (Clatterbaugh, 1997: 143). A fear of being labelled homosexual promotes hypermasculine behaviour and inhibits close bonding between men; it is also behind the general emotional inexpressiveness of men with women (Kimmel and Mahler, 2003; Larson and Pleck, 1999): "Even the lack of affection between fathers and sons has been attributed to the phobic fear of being seen as homosexual males" (Clatterbaugh, 1997: 145). In his classic article on homophobia, Lehne (1976: 66, 78) argued that the taunt "What are you, a fag?" is used to regulate male behaviour, restricting masculinity within narrow stereotypical parameters. Thompson (1995) reported that male high-school students identified the epithet "fag" as the most humiliating of put-downs. The singular ideal of heterosexual masculinity is also enforced by verbal and physical violence against homosexuals (Swigonski, 2001). The equation of certain behaviours (e.g., the choice of certain occupations, a lack of sexual interest in women) with non-masculinity further promotes heterosexual masculinity as a prescriptive norm. The subordination and devaluation of gay men also reinforces gender inequality: "By devaluing gay men ... heterosexual men devalue the feminine and anything associated with it" (Price and Dalecki, 1998: 155–156). It is not surprising that, as Mooney et al. (2004: 288) pointed out, "individuals with traditional gender role attitudes tend to hold more negative views toward homosexuality."

The group-specific perspective has prompted an examination of how racism and poverty may shape masculinity (Lewis, 2003; Marriott, 2000; Pease, 2000; Ratele, 2003). In an examination of the experiences of black Vietnam-era American soldiers, Graham (2001) found that although black men were targeted by U.S. navy recruitment programs, discrimination prevented them from experiencing "manly fulfillment through rank and status," and resulted in their feeling "emasculated." He argued that the later involvement of these men in both racial militancy (the Black Power Movement) and violent protest can be understood as their attempt to reassert their masculinity. Majors (2001: 209) maintained that black men's domination of organized American sports since World War II (particularly over the last 15 years), as well as the "cool pose" persona that "permeates [these athletes'] lifestyles on and off of the playing field," can be viewed as their attempt to "escape the societal limits imposed upon them by institutionalized racism, poverty, social oppression, and a limited opportunity structure, and to achieve the goals specified by dominant definitions of masculinity outside the traditional channels of U.S. society." The impact of racism upon men's opportunity and ability to perform the provider role, upon the relationship between the provider role and masculinity, and upon the relationship between the provider role, masculinity, and other domains such as family and intimate relations, are all issues that demand exploration.

The group-specific perspective may aid us in answering some key questions. Are the effects of group membership and location within the social structure additive or multiplicative for experienced masculinity? Is there such a thing as a standard masculinity, shared by men located throughout all social categories (e.g., race, ethnicity, social class, sexual orientation) with only minor variations? Does gender transcend those social categories? Or is there a multiplicity of masculinities whose experiences cannot be generalized to each other and must be considered individually? Is there a unique masculinity associated with each socially defined category?

While the group-specific perspective restrains us from conceptualizing masculinity as a singular construct, its unlimited extrapolation may lead us to conclude that as many masculinities exist as individuals. If that conclusion is reached, as Clatterbaugh (1998: 34) pointed out, the value of gender as "explanatory, predictive, or even descriptive" will have been seriously compromised (see also Beynon, 2002: 23–24). The challenge is to find a balance between monolithic masculinity and nominalism.

Key Terms

baby boom

capitalism

common man

communal manhood

conflict theory

conservative perspective on masculinity

crude birth rate

cult of true womanhood

cultural feminism

egalitarian feminism/ assimilationism

essentialism

expressive role

first-wave feminism

functionalism (structural functionalism)

gender outlaws

good provider role

group-specific perspective on masculinity

he-man masculinity

housewife

housework

identity politics feminism

industrialization

instrumental role

liberal feminism

liberal profeminists

libertarianism

Marxist feminism

maternal feminists

matriarchalism

matrifocal

matrilineal

matrilocal

men's rights movement

meritocracy

mythopoetic men's movement

othering

passionate manhood

patriarchy/patriarchalism/ patriarchal

patrilocal

performative

post-colonial feminism

post-colonial theory

postmodern feminism

procreation ethic

profeminist perspective on masculinity

Promise Keepers

queer theory

radical feminism

radical profeminists

REI (race/ethnicity/
   imperialism) feminisms

reserve labour force

second-wave feminism

self-made manhood

separate spheres

sexual crossing

silenced

socialist feminism

socialist perspective on
   masculinity

spiritual perspective on
   masculinity

standpoint epistemologies

strategic essentialism

trapped housewife

value-specification

voice

Warrior model

Wild Man

Chapter Summary

1. Conceptions of masculinity and femininity are constructed in the context of time and place.

2. The industrialization period and the introduction of a wage economy resulted in the sites of unpaid and paid labour becoming firmly gendered. Work defined gender and gender defined work.

3. The early stages of industrialization saw the development of the model of "self-made manhood," which defined the man's work role as central to his personal and social identity. Men were expected to fulfill the "good provider" role. For women, the virtues of "true womanhood" were extolled; women were exhorted to restrict themselves to the domestic sphere and to caregiving activities. Under the law of this time period, a married woman's identity merged with her husband's and she became civilly dead; she could not vote, keep her own earnings, own property, sue, or be sued.

4. The most notable achievements of the "first wave" of Canadian feminism, which began in the late 1880s, were the right to vote and the recognition of the "personhood" of women under Canadian law. These rights were first granted to white women only.

5. The social conditions generated by World War I, the Great Depression, and World War II all promoted increased female labour-force participation in Canada; however, belief in the centrality of marriage/motherhood to femininity and of the "good provider role" to masculinity prevailed through the first half of the twentieth century. The 1960s marked the beginning of intense examination of the generating conditions for women's, and later men's, gender roles and expectations.

6. Structural functionalists maintain that a sex-linked division of labour within the family, with men and women playing "different but equal" roles, is optimal for both families and society. In contrast, conflict theorists ask us to pose the question "Functional for whom?"

7. Although all feminist theories begin with the premise that men and women in all societies are not evaluated similarly, that women live under conditions of subordination and/or oppression, and that these conditions are neither natural nor inevitable, different feminist theories stress different primary causes of women's subordination and advance different solutions for eliminating inequality.

8. While theorizing on men as men, and on the nature of masculinity in our society, is more limited and of more recent origin than feminist thought, six perspectives on men and masculinity were noted: the conservative perspective, the profeminist perspective, the men's rights perspective, the spiritual perspective (the mythopoetic and Promise Keepers), the socialist perspective, and the group-specific perspective.

CHAPTER 4

Development and Socialization in Childhood and Adolescence

Human development has been defined as "any age-related change in body or behavior from conception to death" (Perlmutter and Hall, 1985: 11). All such developmental changes occur in the context of three interacting dimensions: historical time, social time, and individual life time (Clausen, 1986: 2–3; Settersten, 2002: 18–20). The broadest dimension is **historical time**, framed by cultural eras and interspersed with watershed events (e.g., 9/11; the Montreal Massacre) and processes (e.g., the second wave of the woman's movement, changes within the family and economy) (Luciano, 2007; Miller, 2002; Neysmith and Chen, 2002). **Social time** refers to the socially constructed division of the human lifespan into meaningful age categories, such as childhood, adolescence, adulthood, and old age. The number of categories, as well as their boundaries, meanings, and the social expectations attached to them, can vary from one historical epoch to another, both within and across societies. *Gender and age interact:* gender expectations and expressions vary as men and women move through the age categories of social time (Leaper and Friedman, 2007; McMullin, 2005; Russell, 2007). **Individual life time** refers to the movement of individuals through the life course from birth to death. Though life time development is influenced by varying combinations of biological and sociocultural factors (Browne, 2002; Maccoby, 2002; Miller and Costello, 2001), this chapter will focus on the latter.

SOCIALIZATION

The term **socialization** refers to the *lifelong* "process by which people learn the characteristics of their group—the attitudes, values and actions thought appropriate for them" (Henslin and Nelson, 1996: 65).

What is considered "appropriate" may vary significantly across historical time and place and from one society/social group to another. In all cases, however, socialization trains us for our current or future statuses and roles in society. As we age, we become less passive in this process and begin to take a more active part in constructing our own socialization (Heinz, 2002).

Socialization may be direct and intentional or indirect and accidental. Parents may, for example, directly and deliberately tell their children that certain behaviours are "right" and others "wrong." However, they may also indirectly socialize their children by modelling certain kinds of behaviour. Cunningham (2001), using data from a 31-year study of mothers and children, examined which factors predicted how children, upon reaching adulthood, would divide household labour. It was found that although parents'/mothers' explicit transmission of gender-role attitudes was a factor, parental *behaviours* also had enduring effects, especially upon males. Socialization messages may also be either blatant or subtle. The admonition "Big boys don't cry" is a blatant socialization message. Subtle socialization messages may be conveyed by such innocuous vehicles as bedtime stories. For example, such traditional fairy tales as *Sleeping Beauty* may convey the subtle message that a woman can only be "brought to life" by a man (Saltmarsh, 2007). Most socialization takes place indirectly and accidentally, and is conveyed on a subtle level (Bronstein, 2006; Craig and Liberti, 2007; Leaper and Friedman, 2007).

In our society, four major **agencies of socialization** are involved in the socialization process: the *family*, the *school*, the *peer group*, and the *mass media*.

The Family

The **family** is considered the primary agency of socialization for two reasons. First, it is the prototypical example of a **primary group** (i.e., one characterized by intimate relationships). Second, it exerts a **primacy effect**—it is the first world a child ever knows; the family represents society and culture for at least the first three years of a child's life, before other agencies begin to exert influence. However, the family represents the larger society and culture in ways that reflect its own immediate purposes, goals, and desires (Elkin and Handel, 1989: 140).

The family's impact can be profound (McHale et al., 2003). Our family instills our earliest (often enduring) feelings about ourselves as smart or stupid, strong or fragile, worthy or unworthy (Bois et al., 2002; Philpot, 2000). Early family experiences shape our motivations, values, and beliefs (Gecas, 1990). It is within the context of our families that we develop our gender identity and begin to acquire ways to demonstrate masculinity or femininity. Parents' gender-role belief systems may affect their inferences about a child's nature and capabilities, their expectations about the child's future roles and occupations, and the types of opportunities they provide with the aim of developing a child's skills in various domains (Eccles et al., 2000; Maccoby, 2002a; Newman et al., 2007).

"In 2002–2003, 54% of children aged six months to five years were in some form of child care, up from 42% in 1994–1995" (Statistics Canada, 2006a). During that period, our country's youngest children received, on average, 29 hours per week of non-parental care. Considerable debate surrounds the socialization impact of preschool-age day care (Chick et al., 2002; Cole and Cole, 2001; Helburn and Bergmann, 2002). Due to variations between daycare facilities (in terms of size, adult–child ratio, qualifications of personnel, etc.), the short- and long-term socialization consequences of such care are unclear (Clarke-Stewart and Allhusen, 2005; Nelson and Schutz, 2007). However, the overwhelming predominance of female staff within such settings may convey the message that caring for children is fundamentally a woman's role rather than one appropriate for either sex. Some evidence also exists to suggest that preschools may encourage stereotypical gendered behaviour (Chick et al., 2002; Ramsey, 1995; Serbin et al., 1994); gender segregation has been noted to occur as the result of caregiver expectations, the structuring of play activities, and the express interests of young children themselves (Maccoby, 1994; Lips, 2005).

Paley (1984: xi) observed that while a young girl in the "doll corner" may play at being a cartoon superhero, it is the more familiar play scenario of "mother and baby which reign supreme and will continue to do so throughout the kindergarten year." Even at child-care facilities for very young children, "play centres" for girls tend to be furnished with mini-kitchens and "dress-up" paraphernalia such as aprons, adult (female) clothing, high heels, tiaras, and feather boas. These areas are typically enclosed and somewhat removed from the boys' play centres, which often feature a "workman's bench" and an assortment of toy trucks and bulldozers. The structure of the "girls'" area discourages boisterous play—unless a child should borrow the bulldozer and knock down a wall of the "cozy kitchen." Lips (1993: 286) suggested that early childhood teachers would likely discourage such attempts at architectural redesign. Should boys attempt to turn the doll corner into a "Batcave" or "space station" or adapt toy rolling-pins into "pretend" swords, they may be informed that such transformations are inappropriate or that such play belongs "on the playground" rather than in the classroom (Jordan and Cowan, 1995). These messages may establish the domestic sphere as female "turf" and subtly promote gender segregation. Moreover, despite assertions of gender neutrality, early childhood caregivers may subtly reinforce gender-stereotypical behaviour and reward aggressiveness and assertiveness in boys and dependency and passivity in girls. Lips (2001: 328) reported that "a preschool child's compliance with a teacher predicts the teacher's evaluation of the child's intellectual competence—if the child is female.... It appears that female intellectual competence is most likely to be rewarded ... if it is manifested in an 'appropriately feminine' way."

The School

The **school**, in contrast to the family, is an *impersonal* agency of socialization (i.e., one characterized by secondary formal relationships). Although a child may be the apple of parental eyes at home, at school s/he learns that s/he is but one among many. While gender socialization is not part of the school's official mandate, significant socialization messages are transmitted via the **hidden curriculum** (Gillhorn, 1992)—the unwritten rules of behaviour conveyed along with the formal academic curriculum (Dillabough, 2001; Francis and Skelton, 2001; McLeod, 2001). Research indicates that teachers' expectations influence the development, behaviour, and academic success of their students, and that classroom interactions and social curricula construct what it means to be male and female in ways that limit possibilities for both girls and boys (Koch, 2003; O'Reilly, 2001; Orenstein, 2001). Although Canadian society is becoming increasingly diverse, research suggests that Canadian public schools continue to give primacy to the status quo and to white, middle-class, heteronormative perspectives (Canadian Council of Social Development, 1999; Henry et al., 2002).

The Peer Group

The **peer group** consists of people linked by common interests and age (within a range of variation usually limited to less than four years [Santrock, 1981: 242]). In contrast to the family and the school, peer groups provide children with experience of intimate relationships which are **egalitarian** (although power differentials do exist) and, perhaps most importantly, of their own choosing (Elkin and Handel, 1989: 184). Young children can be observed exercising their newfound power of choice as they pronounce themselves "best friends" one day and despised enemies the next (Shiller and Schneider, 2003). Both the family and the school are strongly future-oriented in their socialization intentions, preparing children for adult participation in the larger society (a process known as **anticipatory socialization**); peer groups, on the other hand, are not self-consciously focused upon either socialization or the future. However, they do exert significant longterm influences upon their members (Blakemore, 2003; Updegraff et al., 2000, 2001). Witt's (2000: 1) review of the literature on peer influences on children's gender-role socialization concluded that "[p]eer relationships play an important role in the development of a child's self concept and have a strong impact on how children view the roles of males and females in society."

The Mass Media

Mass media is the collective term for the main vehicles of mass communication, comprising *print* (newspapers, magazines, and books) and *electronic* media (including movies, radio, television, and the Internet). The media are an *impersonal* agency of socialization (Elkin and Handel, 1989: 188), in that messages are transmitted to huge audiences; their impersonality is very different from schools', however, in that mass-media socialization is uni-directional (one-way) rather than interactional or interpersonal. The media educate, entertain, offer role models, and present guidelines for behaviour; however, debate continues over the mass media's socialization potential and actual influence (APA Task Force, 2007). Chapter 5 examines specific types of media and their impact on the social construction of gender.

The Agencies in Relation to One Another

Agencies of socialization do not operate in isolation from one another. No one agency has exclusive responsibility for gender socialization; thus, messages of various agencies may either reinforce or contradict one another. Furthermore, no agency provides socialization for gender exclusively; gender messages are transmitted along with socialization messages for any number of statuses and roles, including those related to religion, social class, ethnicity, and age. Contradictory messages are not uncommon, and socializers may be unaware of the extent to which they are inconsistent as they shift their focus from one status to another.

Obviously, Canada has no master plan for gender socialization. Each family, school system, and media outlet must determine for itself what expectations and skills to impart and promote. This is particularly difficult when "ideal standards" of masculinity and femininity are in a state of transition, as they are in our society (Dennis et al., 2007; Haddock et al., 2003; Miller, 2002; Newman et al., 2007).

Dominant Themes of Gender Socialization

Gender socialization is the process whereby an individual acquires a gender identity and gendered ways of acting, thinking, and feeling. More than 30 years ago, Udry (1971) identified several basic themes of childhood/adolescent gender socialization; these appear to be equally pervasive in present-day Canadian society.

According to Udry (1971: 82), the focal themes of female socialization are "sociability, popularity, and attractiveness." Today, we often speak of *sociability* in terms of "emotional intelligence" or "people skills," which include an interest in relating to others, proficiency at verbal and nonverbal communication, comfort with mutual self-disclosure, and interpersonal sensitivity. Female *popularity* is one of the byproducts of sociability and of being on top of relevant trends. However, the equation of femininity with *physical attractiveness* is perhaps the dominant theme of female gender socialization in our culture. A fourth theme, not identified by Udry, is the equation of femininity with *becoming a wife and mother*; this theme is increasingly emphasized as a girl moves into young adulthood. Male socialization, in contrast, centres around "independence, emotional control, and conquest" (Udry, 1971: 76). *Independence*—being autonomous, self-motivated, and in control of oneself and one's environment—is difficult to develop, given a child's dependency on parents, subordination at school, and often slavish conformity to peer groups. Yet young males are expected to find ways to demonstrate independence even within those limitations. The *emotional control* required of boys is selective: Only those emotions culturally defined as "feminine" (e.g., tenderness, sadness, vulnerability) are to be suppressed; on the other hand, anger and its behavioural counterpart, aggression, are deemed consistent with masculinity. *Conquest*—overcoming all odds and winning—is the desired outcome of being competitive at any- and everything, whether against other males, females, or oneself (as in striving for a "personal best"). To these themes may be added a fourth: the equation of masculinity with *becoming a paid worker and provider*, a theme which, once again, becomes increasingly important as a boy moves into young adulthood.

These themes reflect that which our society deems important and appropriate for women and men. Believing that men and women have different gender destinies, agencies of socialization seek to provide children with repertoires of action, thought, and feeling that will prepare them to function successfully as gendered beings in our society.

THE FAMILY

Family Structure

The family into which we are born or adopted and in which we grow up is known as our **family of orientation**. For most Canadians, this is a two-generational *nuclear family* (a term originally used to denote a couple and their children). Over the past 25 years, the Canadian nuclear family has become increasingly diverse in form and composition. For example, in 2006, only 34.5 percent of Canadian families took the form of the "traditional" nuclear family (i.e., of a married couple and children), compared with 41 percent in 2001, 41.3 percent in 1996, 49.4 in 1986, and 69 percent in 1901 (Statistics Canada, 2007a; Vanier Institute of the Family, 2000). The number of common-law couples with children under the age of 25 has increased from 2.7 percent of all Canadian families in 1986 to 5.5 percent in 2001 and 6.8 percent in 2006. The number of lone-parent families has also grown significantly: In 1966, only 8 percent of families were headed by a lone parent; in 2001, that figure had risen to 15.7 percent and, in 2006, to 15.9 percent. In 2006, the vast majority (80.1 percent) of Canada's lone-parent families were headed by women.

The growth in lone-parent families has alarmed some social commentators, who point to psychoanalytic and social learning theories (see Chapter 2) which claim that gender development requires the presence of, and identification with, a same-sexed parent. Custody battles have been fought on the basis of these theories, as have battles regarding the fitness of gay or lesbian parents. Hopkins (2000: 31) observed that a primary objective of "Big Brothers," an international philanthropic organization that matches boys from female-headed lone-parent families with an adult male friend, is "to instill a masculine culture and nurture a masculine identity in male children by providing an adult male presence, 3–4 hours a week." However, Downey and Powell (1993) found no evidence to support the argument that the absence of a same-sex parent is damaging. Lone parents, after all, are unlikely to populate their children's environment with people of only one sex; as well, lone parents both model and explicitly socialize characteristics stereotypically associated with the other sex. Moreover, although female-headed lone-parent families are often portrayed as the breeding ground for a host of societal ills including delinquency, drug and alcohol abuse, and intergenerational poverty, "research has failed to uncover anything inherently 'pathological' or 'abnormal' in the female-headed family structure" (Renzetti and Curran, 2003: 191; see also Kierkus and Baer, 2003; Perlesz, 2004). In addition, some research has found that parents in non-traditional households are less likely to gender-stereotype their children than parents living in traditional families (Sidanius and Pena, 2003, Slavkin, 2001).

In 2003, the Vatican issued a document, "Considerations Regarding Proposals to Give Legal Recognition to Unions Between Homosexual Persons," which stated, "the absence of sexual complementarity in these [homosexual] unions creates obstacles in the normal development of children who would be placed in the care of such persons. They would be deprived of the experience of either fatherhood or motherhood. Allowing children to be adopted by such persons living in such unions would actually mean doing violence to these children, in the sense that their condition of dependency would be used to place them in an environment that is not conducive to their full human development" (Section III.7). In response to this document, the Canadian Psychological Association issued a press release in August 2003 that explicitly refuted the Vatican's claim, stating, "Psychosocial research into lesbian and gay parenting indicates that there is no basis in the scientific literature for this perception." According to the CPA, the psychosocial research into lesbian and gay parenting indicates that there are "essentially no differences in the psychosocial development, gender identity or sexual orientation between the children of gay or lesbian parents and the children of heterosexual parents." It also emphasized that "[s]tatements that children of gay and lesbian parents have more and significant problems in the areas of psychosocial or gender development and identity than do the children of heterosexual parents have no support from the scientific literature" (Canadian Psychological Association, 2003; see also Malone and Cleary, 2002; Medeiros, 2003).

These assertions are echoed in Bos et al.'s (2007) recent comparison of child adjustment, parental characteristics and childrearing in 100 planned lesbian families (i.e., two-mother families in which the child was born to the lesbian relationship). Their study found that child adjustment was "not associated with family type" and, instead, was predicted by power assertion, parental concern, and satisfaction with the partner as co-parent" (p. 38). Compared with heterosexual fathers, lesbian social (i.e., non-biological) mothers expressed greater satisfaction with their partners and, in relation to child rearing, showed more parental concern and less power assertion. As Lovas (2005: 348) remarked, "There is considerable evidence that children raised in alternative family structures, including those headed by single mothers ... single fathers ... and lesbian and gay parents can thrive. Optimal emotional and social development is dependent upon the quality of parent–child relationships, not upon the gender of the parent or the structure of the family."

One aspect of lone-parent family life that may have an impact on socialization is standard of living. Currently, the single best predictor of family poverty is the sex of the family head. Female-headed lone-parent households are more likely than any other type of family structure to be poor (National Council of Welfare, 2004). Among the main causes of what is often called the **feminization of poverty** are divorce (and the low compliance of non-custodial parents with child-support orders [see Chapter 8]), births to unwed women of limited means, and the lower wages paid to women, particularly those with lower levels of education (see Chapter 6). (Another major cause, the increasing number of elderly widows living on low incomes, will be discussed in Chapter 9.) Poverty affects the ability of parents to parent (Lareau, 2003; Lieb and Thistle, 2005; Nelson and Schutz, 2007). While no socioeconomic group "has a monopoly on strong child-rearing skills—or questionable ones" (Fine, 1999: A4), Canada's National Longitudinal Survey of Children and Youth has reported that the capacity of parents to care for children, and their children's developmental outcomes, improve at each step up the income ladder. Low social support, family dysfunction, and parental depression, all of which have significant negative effects on children, are all more common in low-income households (National Council of Welfare, 1999).

Social-Class Location

One of the statuses we inherit from our parents is social class. Social class has a profound impact upon our mental and physical health, and our chances of dying at younger ages (Health Canada, 1999; Vissandjee et al., 2005; Wilkins et al., 2002); our likelihood of participating in organized sports (Statistics Canada, 2008b), becoming politically active (Gilbert and Kahl, 1993), or being arrested (Hartnagel, 2004); our prospects for social mobility (Corak, 1998); and the kind and content of socialization we receive (Furnham and Kirkcaldy, 2000; Verhoeven et al., 2007). Although the effects of social class on parenting can be subtle, they may be far-reaching (Rank, 2000).

Research indicates that while middle-class parents value self-direction and initiative in their children, parents in working-class families emphasize obedience and conformity (Cancian, 2002; Demo and Cox, 2000). Lareau (2003: 31) described these class-based parenting styles as, respectively, "concerted cultivation" (i.e., an approach that "actively fosters and assesses [the] child's talents, opinions, and skills") and the "accomplishment of natural growth" (i.e., the provision of basic care accompanied with "directives" that command obedience). According to Lareau, the former promotes an "emerging sense of entitlement" in a child and the latter "an emerging sense of constraint." Working-class parents are more likely than upper-middle-class parents to be strict disciplinarians who want children to be neat and clean, obey rules, and stay out of trouble; they are also most likely to use "power-assertive" techniques such as physical punishment (Kohn, 1983; Klute et al., 2002; Kohn and Slomczynski, 2001). Middle-class parents, on the other hand, tend to emphasize self-direction, individuality, ambition, responsibility, curiosity, self-expression, and self-control. These parents prefer "psychological" disciplining techniques, including reasoning with their children and providing or withdrawing privileges, love, and affection (Aries and Seider, 2005; Giroux and Schmidt, 2004; Van Bakel and Riksen-Walraven, 2002). These differences in childrearing practices have been attributed to differences in the work environments the parents experience (Klute et al., 2002). Collins and Coltrane (2000: 235) noted that four decades of research in industrialized countries indicates that working-class jobs cast individuals in the role of "order takers," promoting conformity and obedience, whereas middle-class jobs position individuals as "order givers" and encourage individualism and problem-solving. Expecting their children's lives to be similar to their own, parents of each class strive to socialize their children accordingly. Moreover, Nelson and Schutz (2007) suggest that these class-based messages may be reiterated within child-care facilities. Their research found that a style of "concerted cultivation" was more likely to be on display in centres that served the children of professionals than those that cared for the children of the poor and working class.

Upper-middle-class families are the most likely to endorse relatively egalitarian gender relations and opportunities (De Graaf et al., 2000; Furnham and Kirdcaldy, 2000). In contrast, upper-class, lower-middle-class, working-class, and poor families are all more likely to endorse and express more traditional, less egalitarian gender roles. Ironically, families occupying both the highest and lowest social strata evince a disjunction between beliefs and behaviour. Upper-class families tend to espouse a traditional sex-segregated division of labour and a patriarchal family structure, yet are often headed by a powerful matriarch who is the final authority on the education, occupations, and marriages of children and grandchildren (Cavan, 1969: 88). Lower-middle- and working-class families also endorse a traditional sex-linked division of paid and household labour, yet increasingly rely on the wages of both parents in order to maintain their standard of living (Glossop, 1994: 7). In other words, although parents may strive to uphold the validity of gender distinctions, they may in practice cross important gender boundaries.

Even though families of all social classes engage in differential gender socialization, the *degree* to which gender differences are emphasized increases towards the lower end of the social-class hierarchy. Consistent with Kohn's findings on the relationship between social class and socialization goals/practices, children raised in working-class homes appear more likely to conform to traditional conceptions of masculinity and femininity, while (particularly upper-) middle-class children are likely to embrace more egalitarian models of gender. Tuck et al. (1994) reported that children raised in homes with career-oriented middle-class mothers who model less-stereotypical gender-role choices tend to display more egalitarian attitudes (see also Barrett and Tasker, 2001; Betz, 1993; Bigner, 1999).

Bennedsen et al. (2007: 647–648, 650) observed that "the majority of firms around the world are controlled by their founders or their founders' descendants" and that, even in the United States, "where firm ownership is widely dispersed, founding families own and control at least one-third of large, publicly held firms." Their investigation also found that the sex of the first-born child of a departing Chief Executive Officer was "strongly correlated with the decision to appoint a family CEO: The frequency of family transitions is 29.4 percent when the first-born child is female and increases to 39 percent (a 32.7 percent increase) when the first-born is male."

Social class of origin also has a significant impact upon educational opportunities and attainment, which, in turn, significantly affect occupational opportunities and attainment (Bankston and Caldas, 1998). More well-to-do families are likely to create opportunities for their children (regardless of ability) to be groomed for university, while children from working-class and poor families are more likely to be **streamed** into vocational tracks— each group inheriting life opportunities established by their elders (Call et al., 1997; Vincent and Ball, 2007). Within each social-class domain, parents have also tended to differentially encourage sons and daughters to pursue educational goals. Epstein and Coser (1981) noted that parents have traditionally been more willing to underwrite the education of even academically undistinguished sons than of academically gifted daughters. They also observed a tendency of parents to encourage daughters to set their sights on "gender-appropriate" and lower-status careers (e.g., nurse rather than doctor, elementary-school teacher rather than professor). Women were expected to ascend the social ladder through marriage; too much education might threaten a daughter's marital and social prospects. These parental attitudes reflect the notion of gendered social spheres. As long as women have remained confined to the domestic sphere, families have concentrated on encouraging sons to pursue the education that leads to more prestigious occupations and social mobility. However, as the gender boundaries of the separate spheres have become more permeable, parental attitudes towards educating daughters have evinced a change.

Higginbotham and Weber's (1992) research on 200 female professionals, managers, and administrators from working-class backgrounds found that these women's parents played a significant role in encouraging them to take advantage of their opportunities. Almost uniformly, these parents urged their daughters from an early age to strive towards a better life, stressing that the way to succeed was not only through education but also by postponing marriage. Based on their analysis of National (U.S.) Education Longitudinal Study data on approximately 25 000 8th-grade students, Carter and Wojtkiewicz (2000) reported that daughters experienced more parental involvement with their education than did sons, as measured by discussions about school, parent–school connection, parental expectations, and parental attendance at school events. They suggested that, in response to emergent social trends and new economic realities, parental socialization practices are shifting (see also Domene et al., 2007).

Ethnicity

Being born into a particular family also means being ascribed the ethnicity of one's parents. At some point in adolescence or adulthood, individuals can choose to retain and identify with or to ignore and even conceal selected aspects of their ethnic origins. Distinctive accents or birth names may be altered, or religious membership changed or allowed to lapse. The most enduring of the three basic components of one's ethnic origins ("race," religion, and national origin) is the colour of one's skin.

Although the issue remains highly contested, several researchers (see Bennett et al., 1991; Rowley et al., 2007; Verkuyten and Kinket, 1999) have argued that social-class status and gender exert a greater influence on socialization patterns than do race or ethnicity. However, others have maintained that race overrides social class and that racial (especially black–white) differences are found regardless of social-class location (see Anderson, 2001; Ellis, 2001; Oyserman et al., 2001). Generalizing, even within ethnic groups, is problematic; generalizing across ethnic boundaries is rife with difficulties. For the moment, researchers tend to focus either on describing gender experiences within various ethnic contexts (e.g., Suizzo et al.'s [2008] investigation of childrearing in African American families) or on comparing gender experiences across various ethnic/racial contexts (e.g., Reid and Bing's [2000] examination of the influence of culture, class, and ethnicity on women's sexual development).

Harriet Bradley (1996) asserted that all of us inhabit *fractured identities*—identities that are neither unitary nor essential but plural, variable, and dynamic. She argued that our sense of location in social worlds is determined not by a single variable (e.g., social class) but by the many lived social dimensions we experience as a result of our gender, age, ethnicity, disability, sexuality, etc. (see also Stapleton and Wilson, 2004). Tsang's (2001: 24–25) poignant description of his experience as a gay Asian Canadian male, growing up "with the white world outside, the Asian world at home, and the gay world inside me," reflects this reality. Talbani and Hasanali's (2000) qualitative study of 22 adolescent (age 15 to 17) daughters of Indian, Pakistani, and Bangladeshi immigrants in Montreal also supports the concept of fractured identities. These young women felt that their families and community structure, despite the integration of certain elements of secular European culture, remained male-dominated; traditional gender roles were maintained by means of gender segregation, parental control of girls' social activities, and the practice of arranged marriage. Respondents also voiced the opinion that their communities had "more stringent rules for female socialization that any other community in Canada" and that any attempt to challenge these rules would have a high social cost (see also Dion and Dion, 2001; Kim and Ward, 2007; Longmore et al., 2001).

Maracle (1996: ix), a member of the Sto:lo nation, maintained that to understand the experiences of contemporary First Nations women, it is crucial to examine the impact of colonialism. She wrote that while visiting the elders as a child, she observed "a quiet and deep respect for thinking which extended to men, women and children" and "was shocked as a twenty-year-old by concepts of sexism coming from the mouths of young Native men; no one would have dared doubt the intelligence of women ten years earlier." However, she remarked, "Sexism, racism and the total dismissal of Native women's experience has little to do with who does dishes and who minds babies. These oppressions result from the accumulation of hurt sustained by our people over a long period of time."

Socialization in the Family: A Developmental Perspective

To date, the vast majority of empirical studies on socialization within the family have been conducted with white, heterosexual, middle-class, two-parent families (Peterson et al., 2001; Leaper and Friedman, 2007). Although generalization to other types of families is problematic, these studies do provide a starting point for an exploration of elements in the social construction of gender.

In general, studies conducted in Europe and English-speaking countries find a strong parental preference for children of both sexes, with parents much more likely to have a third or fourth child if existing children are all of the same sex (Jain et al., 2005; Kippen et al., 2007). Although some research suggests an emerging bias towards daughters in at least some European regions (Brockmann, 2001; Hank and Kohler, 2000), studies conducted in the United States since the 1940s have "consistently found a preference among both men and women for a first-born or only son" (Kippen et al., 2007: 583). Marleau and Saucier's (2002: 13) review of 16 studies conducted with first-time-pregnant women found that, especially between 1981 and 1996, women more often expressed a desire for a daughter; expectant fathers preferred a son. A preference for a first-born male child was noted for both non-expectant males and females. When the two sub-periods under review (i.e., pre-1980 and post-1981) were compared, women's preference for a son had decreased and men's had increased slightly. However, the researchers reported that a difference between men and women was evident "whatever the sub-period: men more often prefer a boy than women." Research by Lundberg and Rose (2002, 2003) also seems to suggest the importance that men place on having sons. They found that an unwed mother is 42 percent more likely to marry the father of her child if the child is male rather than female and, that following the birth of a child, fathers of sons are more likely than the fathers of daughters to work longer hours and to strive to find ways of earning additional money.

Before their child is born, parents undergo a form of anticipatory socialization as they and other interested parties speculate on its sex. Folk wisdom concerning "indicators" of fetal sex are often based on gender stereotypes; for example, an "active" fetus who kicks vigorously and often is presumed to be male (Stainton, 1985). Prenatal position is another putative indicator: girls, supposedly, are carried "neatly" in front, boys in a "messy," more "obvious" fashion. Gender-stereotyped expectations are also revealed in parental reactions to ultrasound pictures of the fetus. Sweeney and Bradbard (1988) reported that parents who viewed an ultrasound picture of their child rated fetuses known to be female as "softer, littler, calmer, weaker, more delicate, and more beautiful than male fetuses" (in Lips, 2001: 312). Smith (2005: 51–52) recorded the words that she had used and the feelings she had expressed towards her child *in utero* and noted that her approach changed after she learned the child's sex through an ultrasound in her sixth month of pregnancy. Smith, a Canadian professor of language education, acknowledged that as someone who was "schooled in Women's Studies" and "who lectured on the ill-effects of gender socialization," she was "quite honestly, shocked" by what her field notes recorded:

> Suddenly, there was less tenderness in the way I addressed the baby. He was a boy. He was "stronger" now than the child I had known only one minute before. He did not need to be addressed with such light and fluffy language ... as, "little one".... I lowered my voice to a deeper octave. It lost its tenderness.... I wanted him to be "strong" and "athletic," therefore, I had to speak to him with a stereotypical "strong," "masculine" voice to encourage this "innate strength."

Infancy Gender socialization begins at birth upon the attending medical team's announcement of an infant's genital sex. This is followed almost immediately by the parents' first *ex officio* act, one fraught with gender implications—naming the baby. "First" or "given" names are typically sex-linked and serve as sex identifiers in the absence of other personal information. In Anglo-Saxon Canada, male names usually have a more harsh sound (e.g., Jack, Michael, Derek); female names tend to be more mellifluous, reflecting stereotypical qualities of softness and gentleness (e.g., Sara, Laura, Angela), and often contain more sounds and syllables (Johnson and Scheuble, 2002; Li, 2006; Whissel, 2001; Wright, 2006). In addition, female names are often composed of a male "root" fitted with a diminutive suffix (e.g., Danielle). However, Abel and Kruger (2007) report that the "most distinctive gendered naming characteristic in English speaking countries is the final alphabetic letter: female names are invariably more likely than male names to end in one of three vowels, *a, e,* or *i,* whereas male names generally end in consonants (e.g., Amanda, Jane, Vicki, vs. Mark, Steven and Todd.)" These researchers note that this "gendered phonology" also applies to the names that dog owners select for their pets; "Divet" is more likely to be a male and "Zippy" a female.

Gould (1980/1995) wrote a story about "X," a "fabulous child" whose sex was purposely concealed from everyone outside of "its" family; this tale was designed to draw attention to the significance of names and other elements of gender socialization. Very rarely do real-life parents deliberately create names devoid of sex and gender implications (but see Box 4.1). Lieberson et al. (2000), studying data for all white births from 1916 through 1989 in the state of Illinois, found that a yearly average of less than 3 percent of newborns were given *androgynous* (non-sex-specific) names. Over that time span, the use of androgynous names barely increased. Androgynous names were much more likely to be given to female newborns: "Jordan," "Dakota," and "Shannon" were among recent favourites (see also Lieberson, 2000; Erwin, 2006). Parents appear to be unwilling to hazard the angst that an androgynous name may cause their sons, but hopeful that some advantage may adhere to their daughters. Thus, in Canada in 2006, "Madison" ranked fourth among the five most popular girls' names, whereas for boys, the five most popular names were all unambiguously "masculine": Ethan, Joshua, Matthew, Jacob, and Nathan.

Nicknames, where given, are also linked to gender stereotypes: "[M]ale nicknames related typically to connotations of strength, hardness, and maturity [e.g., Grenade, T-Rex, Dude], while female nicknames related more to beauty, pleasantness, kindness and goodness" (e.g., Bunnikins, Baby) (de Klerk and Bosch, 1996: 526; see also Christopher, 1998). Although males are more likely than females to have nicknames, these are usually coined at a later age by male peers, especially in sports (Kennedy and Zamuner, 2006). Female nicknames are most often endearments bestowed by family members, and tend to be "gentler, more childish and more affectionate than male nicknames" (de Klerk and Bosch, 1996: 540; see also Mehrabian, 2001).

Once names have been chosen, the next significant gender event is the birth announcement, made via newspapers and greeting cards. Prominently displayed near the beginning of the notice will be that all-important datum: the sex of the new arrival. When was the last time you saw a birth notice that simply stated: "It's Alive" or "It's Healthy," neither mentioning the infant's sex nor providing a name clue? Well-wishers, in response, send congratulatory cards that also tend to refer to the child's sex. A study that examined the visual images and verbal messages contained in 122 commercial birth-congratulations cards found that such cards reflect and reinforce gender stereotypes (Bridges, 1993). While cards congratulating parents

BOX 4.1

Naming Babies

University of Waterloo professors Naomi Nishimura and Prabhakar Ragde, both of the Department of Computer Science, intentionally gave their babies first names devoid of gender implications. With the permission of the parent-authors, the first birth announcement, as it appeared on the World Wide Web, follows, along with comments from Professor Ragde on the reactions the proud parents received.

Naomi Nishimura and Prabhakar Ragde would like to announce the birth of Arju Ragde Nishimura, who arrived at 14:37 EDT on 17 September 1992, at Kitchener-Waterloo Hospital, weighing 3080 grams and measuring 51 cm from head to toe. Naomi went through twenty-six hours of pre-labour and seven hours of active labour at home before going to the hospital; after another nine hours of labour there, our natural childbirth was facilitated by the team of Robert Annis (our family doctor), Evelyn Cressman (our midwife), and Set Len Yau (the duty nurse). We left the hospital six hours after the delivery, and we are all resting at home, with all the phones unplugged.

Some answers to questions you may have: Arju (pronounced Are-jew, factually if not grammatically correct, accent on the first syllable) doesn't mean anything. It's a nice sounding pair of syllables, nothing more, and we made it up more than a year ago, after trying lots of different combinations. We wanted a name that was short, sounded good with Nishimura, and didn't lead to any obvious derogatory nicknames. (If you can think of one ... well, it's too late.)

Please don't rush out and buy a gift. We stocked up on the basics before the birth, and it will take us a while to figure out what else we need, or what might prove useful or entertaining. If you still have the gift-giving urge a few weeks from now, we may be able to suggest some possibilities to you. But really, don't feel obligated to do anything more than smile and coo when you first meet Arju (and you don't even have to do that, if you're really in a bad mood).

No, we didn't forget to mention whether Arju was a boy or a girl. We deliberately left it out—another decision made many months ago. We are concerned about early gender stereotyping. Studies have shown (see the bibliography at the end of this announcement) that adult perception of infant behaviour is affected more by the perceived sex of the child than the actual behaviour of the child. There is a difference in the way adults talk to girl babies and boy babies; there is a difference in the way adults hold and play with girl babies and boy babies. We think that the sex of a newborn child who will still be sorting out its senses and perceptions for weeks if not months after birth is the least interesting bit of information about that child. We hope you'll help us in our task of raising our child properly by focusing on Arju as a developing human being, with all the wonder that entails.

No, we don't know when we're going to have a second child. Shame on you for even thinking of asking!

Bibliography

Pomerleau, Bolduc, Malcuit, and Cossetta. "Pink or Blue: Environmental Gender Stereotypes in the First Two Years of Life." *Sex Roles*, v. 22 (1990), nos. 5–6, pp. 359–367.

BOX 4.1

Naming Babies (*Continued*)

Stern and Karraker. "Sex Stereotyping of Infants: A Review of Gender Labeling Studies." *Sex Roles*, v. 20 (1989), nos. 9–10, pp. 501–522.

Sidorowicz and Lunney. Baby X Revisited. *Sex Roles*, v. 6 (1980), no. 1, pp. 67–73.

Approximately three years later, a second birth announcement followed. Not everyone reacted positively to these announcements; as the children's father commented in a letter to the author: "The first one of course caused quite a stir. We got almost no gifts (except from people who could handle the situation) because people couldn't think of what to buy without knowing Arju's sex! Others worried about the effect on Arju of being handled by people ignorant of this crucial fact—even on Arju's sexual orientation.... For months afterwards people would ask us if we'd 'announced it yet.' Strangers would quiz us carefully, hoping to catch a slip. (I slipped four times that I remember—twice for each pronoun 'he' and 'she'!)" Regarding the second child, Ragde observed that "there was much less fuss; everyone was resigned to our eccentricities by then, and Arju would tell anyone who was really curious."

upon the arrival of a son are likely to contain visual images of physical activity (e.g., a rambunctious boy surrounded by toy cars, trucks, and airplanes), cards celebrating the arrival of a girl are more likely to describe the infant as "little," to contain emotionally expressive messages, and to emphasize themes of sweetness and sharing.

In their classic review of empirical research, Maccoby and Jacklin (1974: 338–339) found "surprisingly little differentiation in parent behavior according to the sex of the child" during infancy and early childhood. While Greenglass (1982: 39) suggested that infants' physical and intellectual limitations curtail parental inclinations to differentially socialize, others aver that researchers' measuring instruments may be insensitive to subtle but pervasive forms of gendered socialization (Bronstein, 2006; McHale et al., 2003; Stenberg and Campos, 1990). Most parents believe their interactions with their children to be gender-neutral. Yet, as Lips (2001: 313) has pointed out, "[i]t is quite possible that parents have no idea of the extent to which they are treating boys and girls differently." She pointed to a study which examined the ways in which 11 mothers interacted with a 6-month-old infant who was either dressed in blue pants and called "Adam" or clad in a pink dress and named "Beth." Beth was more likely to be offered a doll and Adam a train set; Beth was more likely to be smiled at and embraced more closely than Adam. Although the infant was, in fact, male, two of the mothers mentioned how Beth's sweetness and soft crying distinguished her as a "real girl." When later interviewed, all of these women—despite their gendered reactions to the young child—maintained that boys and girls of Adam/Beth's age were alike and should not be treated differently, and confidently asserted that they themselves would not do so.

As Golombok and Fivush (1994: 26) emphasized, "Even when we don't think we are behaving in gender-stereotyped ways, or are encouraging gender-typed behaviour in our children, examination of our actual behaviour indicates that we are." Research has found that even parents who avowedly support non-sexist childrearing for their daughters may voice concern if they perceive their young sons to be "too sensitive" or not aggressive or competitive "enough" (Pleck, 1992). Parents who seek advice from parenting magazines may also receive messages that reaffirm gender stereotypes. An examination of 63 articles from the three top-selling parenting magazines of 2000 revealed that roughly 40 percent of the articles were gender-stereotypical and strongly supported traditional gender myths. "The idea that appearance is important for girls was promoted in 54.2%, and the misconception that boys are more athletic/stronger than girls are was endorsed in 41.7% of the stereotypical articles" (Spees and Zimmerman, 2002: 73). Simultaneously, articles on parenting may also reiterate traditional notions of who should or "ought" to be the primary parent and/or concerned with, for example, managing parental guilt or work–family balance issues. Thus, Wall and Arnold's (2007) analysis of a year-long Canadian newspaper series dedicated to family issues found that the series positioned mothers as the primary parent and that "[s]upport for father involvement, to the extent that it exists, occurred within the framework of fathers as part-time, secondary parents whose relationship with children remains less important than mothers" (p. 508). Parents, moreover, model behaviours that may leave lasting impressions upon even the youngest children. Research on the **"stroller effect"** (Mitchell et al., 1992) has found that when both parents are present, fathers are more likely to push a stroller when the child is in it, while the mother pushes when the stroller is empty. Also, when both parents are present, the father is more likely than the mother to carry a child. Such behaviours may convey subtle messages about men's and women's respective dominance, strength, and power within families and society.

During the first year or two following birth, meaningful interaction between parent and infant occurs primarily on a non-verbal level, with the parent most often reacting to the actions of the newborn. Research indicates that parents (and others) differentially interpret an infant's actions depending upon their perception of its sex. Rubin et al. (1974), interviewing parents within 24 hours of their child's birth, found that although infants did not differ in average length, weight, or Apgar scores (a measurement based upon muscle tone, respiratory function, reflexes, and heart rate), parental (especially paternal) depictions of their child were highly stereotypical. Daughters were described as delicate, weak, beautiful, and cute, while sons were characterized as strong, alert, and well coordinated. Efforts to update this investigation have found that although parents' (especially fathers') gender-stereotyped perceptions of newborns have diminished, they have not disappeared (Fagot et al., 2000; Gauvain et al., 2002; Karraker et al., 1995). Reid (1994) reported that parents typically describe their newborn daughters as small and pretty creatures with fine and delicate features, and their sons as tall, large, sturdy, robust, serious, athletic beings with strong hands.

Condry and Condry (1976) showed respondents a videotape of a 9-month-old infant reacting to different stimuli. They reported that the infant's reactions were differently interpreted depending upon its identified sex: the same action was interpreted as anger in boys or fear in girls (see also Martin, 1999). The differential attribution of emotion appears to begin early in life; Leinbach and Hort (1995) reported that 3-year-old children asked to ascribe gender to pictures of animal faces were more likely to label a happy animal face "female" and an angry animal face "male" (see also Becker et al., 2007). Preschoolers in Birnbaum and Croll's (1984) sample held the belief that anger was an emotion more typical of males, whereas such emotions as happiness, sadness, and fear were more characteristic of females. Zahn-Waxler et al. (1991) reported that parents were more tolerant of displays of anger from sons than from daughters, even when children are very young.

Expressions of anger in female infants were more likely to meet with less empathetic and more negative maternal responses (e.g., frowning and anger) than were similar expressions in male infants (see also Brody, 2000).

Research has indicated that during the first 6 months of life, boys generally receive more physical and less non-physical contact (e.g., being looked at or talked to) than do girls (Fagot and Leinbach, 1993; Suizzo and Bornstein, 2006). Fathers in particular are likely to roughhouse with sons but to discourage daughters from engaging in boisterous and rowdy play (Lytton and Romney, 1991; Scott and Panksepp, 2003). It has been suggested that this greater physical contact accounts in part for boys' greater gross motor development and for why, by the age of 24 months, sons are more competent than daughters in active play (Lovas, 2005). However, parents (especially mothers) are more likely to talk with their daughters (Wood, 1994). Clearfield and Nelson's (2006) analysis of mothers' speech and play behaviour with their 6-, 9-, and 14-month-old sons and daughters reported sex differences in mothers' verbal level of engagement with their children. "Mothers of daughters made more interpretations and engaged in more conversation with their daughters, whereas mothers of sons made more comments and attentionals [words or phrases that serve to gain/keep the infants' attention, such as "Look, Jimmy!"], which were typified by instructions rather than conversation. Furthermore, mothers interacted more with their daughters than with their sons across all ages" (Clearfield and Nelson, 2006: 127). Parents' tendency to converse with daughters may account for the fact that, by as early as ages 2 to 4, girls are likely to possess and use a richer vocabulary of emotion words (Cervantes and Callanan, 1998; Lanvers, 2004).

Childhood Researchers have found that despite claims of gender neutrality, parents increasingly gender-differentiate as their sons and daughters develop. Sons are granted more freedoms, yet at the same time are more closely monitored than daughters. Lytton and Romney (1991) noted that sons were allowed more independence and physical freedom to explore their environment. Robinson and Biringen (1995) found that parents tended to regard daughters as more physically fragile and in need of protection than sons and were more restrictive of their physical freedom. Mitchell et al. (1992) observed that parents were more likely to allow male toddlers to walk on their own through public places. Hagan and Kuebli (2007) found differential treatment by parents of preschool-age boys and girls in risk-taking situations (e.g., climbing across a five-foot-high catwalk; walking across a three-foot-high beam). Echoing Block's (1984) contention that while girls develop "roots" that anchor them to the home, boys develop "wings" that allow them to explore vistas beyond it, Lindsey (1997: 64) commented that "[w]hile Dick is allowed to cross the street, use scissors, or go to a friend's house by himself, Jane must wait until she is older."

Fivush and Buckner (2000) suggested that as a result of participation in gender-differentiated activities and interactions, females and males develop different "emotion scripts," coming to understand and integrate emotional experience into their lives in different ways (see also Ferguson and Eyre, 2000; Serbin et al., 2002). In an examination of conversations about past events between mothers and their 2- to 3-year-old children, Fivush (1991) reported that mothers would accept anger and retaliation from sons only; with daughters, they spent more time talking about sadness. She suggested that the lesson conveyed to girls may be that anger is not an acceptable emotional response. More recently, research on 21 white, middle-class 40- to 45-month-old children and their parents examined how each parent discussed with their child four past events during which the child had experienced happiness, anger, sadness, or fear (Fivush et al, 2000). It was found that mothers conversed more overall, talked more about the emotional aspects of the experiences, and used more emotion words in conversations with their children than did fathers. Girls talked more about emotional aspects of their experiences than did boys, and used more emotion words when discussing scary events. Both mothers and fathers made more emotional utterances when discussing sad events with daughters than with sons; parent–daughter dyads also placed emotional experiences in a more interpersonal context than did parent–son dyads (see also Aldrich and Tenenbaum, 2006).

A study which examined 322 young adults' retrospective reports of parental emotional socialization (Garside and Klimes-Dougan, 2002) found gender-based socialization patterns in sadness, anger, and fear. Parents were reported to have modified their ways of socializing sadness and fear according to a child's gender; for example, fathers rewarded daughters for expressing sadness and fear, but punished sons for doing so. Brody (2000) argued that parents' differential reinforcement of emotional expression is shaped by cultural values about gender roles and takes place within a cultural context in which females have less power and status than males. She maintained that differential socialization in emotional expressiveness helps to maintain culturally mandated gender roles, including power and status imbalances.

Using a simulated dispute between puppets, Hay et al. (1992) found in their research on peer conflict that 5-year-old girls were more likely than same-age boys to advance such socialized tactics as "asking nicely." In a study of how children ages $3\frac{1}{2}$ to $5\frac{1}{2}$ attempt to influence their play partners' behaviour, Serbin et al. (1984) found that while girls attempted to use polite suggestion, boys more often used direct demands. Among children ages 9 to 11, boys are more likely than girls to report that they would use confrontational behaviour such as hitting or yelling when angry with a same-sex peer.

In physically active play, boys are encouraged by parents to be tough, fight back, and win—and if they lose, not to whine or "act like a baby." These messages may be reinforced by peer groups: In a year-long study of 3- and 4-year-old children in a preschool setting, Kyratzis (2001) found that the boys evolved norms against the expression of "scaredness," along with norms disparaging "girl" characteristics. Pollack (2000: 17) asserted that the "boy code" strongly discourages the expression of emotion; as one of his young male respondents reflected, "A friend of mine died in the hospital.... I knew that, as a guy, I was supposed to be strong and I wasn't supposed to show any emotion.... I was supposed to be tough." The emphasis placed by both parents and peers on male stoicism and "toughness" may be one reason for sex-correlated differences in pain perception and behaviour; girls and women are more likely to report (and be more voluble in reporting) pain than are boys and men (Myers et al., 2003; Robinson et al., 2003; Wise et al., 2002). This kind of socialization may also help explain why adult males are often loath to seek help, especially mental and physical health care (Addis and Mahalik, 2003; Bowen and John, 2001; Nicholas, 2000), and are more likely to die at a younger age than females (Stillion and McDowell, 2001–2002).

While boys are urged to "tough it out," parents encourage daughters to "talk it out." Because conversation requires parties to align their conduct (i.e., taking turns, not interrupting, responding), parents encourage girls' development of cooperative skills (Fagot et al., 2000; Gauvain et al., 2002; Parke, 2001, 2002). Parental emphasis on cooperative play may explain why girls are more likely to refrain from physical aggression in front of adults (Loeber and Hay, 1997) and to mask their anger, particularly around adults (Underwood, 2003). Girls as young as 2 appear more uncomfortable than boys in an angry environment. They show greater distress at inter-adult anger and are more likely to express a desire for such arguments to stop; boys are more likely to react with aggression (El-Sheikh and Reiter, 1995).

Research by Fagot et al. (1986) indicated that young male and female children were differentially reinforced for attention-seeking behaviour. Parents paid greater attention to boys whose conduct was assertive and aggressive, but were more apt to respond to daughters who requested help in a soft-spoken or gentle tone. Observing these same children nearly a year later, the researchers found that the girls were more talkative than the boys and the boys more aggressive than the girls. Orenstein (1994: 46–47) suggested that some parents, while reminding daughters to be a little quieter and less argumentative, appear to expect sons to interrupt and be rude. Kerig et al. (1993) observed that boys were more likely than girls to be praised for assertiveness; fathers, in particular, were more likely to reward sons for such behaviour while rewarding daughters for compliancy. They also found that both mothers and fathers of $3^{1}/_{2}$-year-old children were more likely to override daughters than sons, especially if daughters attempted to assert themselves. While parents responded to daughters' shyness with warmth and affection, this behaviour in boys elicited disapproval. It is therefore not, perhaps, surprising, that "[g]ender differences in the ability to vary the register, to use cooperative discourse styles, polite forms, [and] direct imperatives ... are well documented from about 4 years onwards" (Lanvers, 2004: 485). Thompson and Moore (2000) reported significant gender differences among their sample of children (ages 2 years 11 months to 5 years 4 months), with girls using more collaborative speech and initiating more verbal turns. Other studies have reported that, from pre-school age onwards, girls demonstrate a more collaborative interactive style and boys, a more controlling style (Nakamura, 2001; Sheldon, 1996).

Many studies find strong differences in the way parents treat their sons and daughters on such dimensions as discipline, warmth, and amount of interaction. For example, Ross and Taylor (1989) observed that with sons, both mothers and fathers were more likely to encourage independent achievement and to discourage demonstrations of emotion. These parents were more likely to identify their relationships with daughters as featuring greater warmth and physical closeness and to perceive their daughters as truthful; they were also more reluctant to discipline them. Research has also found fathers to be more likely to inhibit or punish gender-inappropriate behaviour, particularly in sons (Hardesty et al., 1995; Landolt et al., 2004). Parke (1996), however, reported that although fathers were more likely than mothers to sex-type their children and to favour their sons, shared-parenting fathers appeared to treat sons and daughters similarly. Collins and Coltrane (2000) also noted that when fathers assumed significant responsibility for child care, their interactions with their children came more closely to resemble those of traditional mothers. In addition, McNeill (2007) reports that the parenting of a child with a chronic health condition may serve as a "catalyst for meaningful involvement for many fathers," encouraging them to "transcend traditional male stereotypes and embrace the opportunity for a more intimate and involved style of parenting" (p. 409).

Gendered parental attitudes reveal themselves in many subtle forms. Fiese and Williams (2000) asked 121 sets of parents to tell their 4-year-old children stories about when the parent was growing up; the stories were then coded for themes of affiliation, achievement, and autonomy. Sons were more likely than daughters to be told stories with autonomy themes; fathers told stories with stronger autonomy themes than did mothers. Traditionally gender-typed parents told stories with stronger achievement themes to their sons; non-traditionally gender-typed parents told such stories to their daughters. Research has also found that the household chores assigned to young children reflect parental assumptions about the gender-appropriateness of various tasks: "Patricia will more likely be assigned indoor cooking and laundry tasks; Patrick, outdoor activities, such as painting and mowing" (Riedmann et al., 2003: 74; see also Shiller and Schneider, 2003). Basow (1992: 131) suggested that the allocation to boys of non-routine tasks (e.g., raking leaves) rather than mundane, daily tasks (e.g., making beds, washing dishes) may convey subtle messages about male privilege.

From the time children are born, parents structure their environment by means of room decor, toys, and clothing (Oren and Ruhl, 1997; Pierce, 2000; Yato, 2000). Room decorations, beginning with the mobile suspended over a baby's crib, provide constant yet subtle visual gender messages. Studies of middle-class children's bedrooms in Canada and the United States have found that girls' rooms are apt to be decorated in pink and to feature floral designs, ruffles, and an abundance of dolls. In contrast, boys' rooms are likely to be painted in bold, bright colours and decorated in a more spartan style dominated by animal or sports motifs (Pomerleau et al., 1990; Jones et al., 2007). Boys also tend to have a wider range of toys, as well as more toys, than do girls (Etaugh and Liss, 1992).

Toys Toys entertain, develop skills, and encourage "practising" of roles that may be enacted in adulthood. While boys' toys tend to involve visual and spatial manipulation, emphasize aggressive competition, and reflect an orientation towards the outside world, girls' toys typically involve more placid play, emphasize themes of nurturance and physical attractiveness, and are oriented towards the domestic realm (Alexander, 2003; Leaper, 2002). Within our culture, boys who prefer to play indoors and girls who prefer to play outdoors are likely to be labelled sissies or tomboys (Carr, 1998). Children's toys also lend themselves to use in different settings: Boys' toys are more portable and suitable for outdoor use, while girls' toys are anchored more firmly (by structure, fragility, or cost) to the household. In a study of how parents interact with children playing with masculine-typed, feminine-typed, and neutral toys, Idle et al. (1993) found that parents spent the least amount of time interacting with children playing with feminine-typed toys. A study by Wood et al. (2002) examined the amount of time children and adults played with gender-specific toys, adults' classification of toys into gender categories, and adult desirability-ratings of gender-specific toys. They found that when playing with boys, adults played with "masculine" toys most of the time—although they did not always agree with "expert" classifications (a finding which suggests that gender stereotypes about toys may be shifting somewhat). While playing with girls, however, adults showed greater flexibility in the categories of toys with which they played.

If toys are the building blocks of the future, the blueprint for tomorrow's women is consistent with yesterday's traditional gender messages (Etaugh and Liss, 1992; McAninch et al., 1996). A dollhouse may be of the "starter home" variety, but with the potential to be furnished with an elaborate array of miniature gadgets, such as microwaves, blenders, and candelabras. A young girl can acquire her own miniature domestic world of strollers, stoves, tea sets, and Easy-Bake Ovens. She can shop and cook for a variety of her own toy families including Little Ponies, Bunny Bunny Bunnies, Kitty Kitty Kittens, and Baby Baby Farm Animals—cloyingly diminutive names, suggestive of baby talk. The messages such toys promote about the maternal caregiving role may encourage girls to later assume responsibility for babies (Collins and Coltrane, 2000: 604).

Barbie, a girls' toy rich with implications for anticipatory socialization, warrants special mention, not only because of her extraordinary longevity and popularity but because of her significance as the embodiment of gender stereotypes. In 1959, the year she was first introduced by Mattel at New York City's Toy Fair, 350 000 Barbie dolls were sold; since then, if "placed head to toe, all the Barbie dolls sold ... would circle the earth more than seven times" (Zumhagen, 2004). By 2006, over a billion Barbie dolls had been sold with reportedly "three Barbie dolls sold ... every second" (BBC News, 2006). Marketed in more than 150 countries worldwide, Barbie (so Mattel's website proclaims) is "[m]ore than a doll. For fashion selection to vintage collection, she's everything! From urban teen to fantasy queen, she's every girl! From surf and sand to fairyland, she's everywhere! With more than $3.6 billion at retail, Barbie is the #1 girl's brand worldwide" (Mattel, 2004). Although she may be advertised as "every girl," this icon of feminine beauty was, for the first 21 years of her existence, exclusively white. While "Christie," Barbie's African American friend, was introduced in 1968, it was not until the 1980s that Mattel would launch Black Barbie, Hispanic Barbie, and "Oriental" Barbie; "Native American Barbie" appeared in 1993. Critics continue to charge that Black Barbies are "little more than standard-issue white Barbies dipped in brown paint. The long, straight hair and European facial features are still the same" (Edut, 2003; see also Lam and Leman, 2003). "Becky," Barbie's "differently abled" friend, appeared in 1997; ironically, none of the doors in Barbie's multiple "Dream Houses" are wide enough to accommodate Becky's wheelchair.

Barbie remains the personification of our society's preoccupation with beauty as the *sine qua non* of femininity. Her dimensions also make her characterization as "every girl" dubious at best. Researchers who compared Barbie's gravity-defying proportions (variously reported as 36-20-32 [Renzetti and Curran, 2003: 97], 40-18-32 [Hamilton, 1996: 197] or 38-18-34 [BBC News, 1997]) with the actual measurements of representative groups of young women concluded that the probability of this body shape occurring in nature is less than 1 in 100 000 (Norton et al., 1996); Ken's body dimensions are more realistic (probability: 1 in 50). Presumably, Aerobics Barbie and Rollerblades Barbie exist to help us understand why, when Workout Barbie alights on her Barbie Workout Scale, her inferiority-inducing physique always registers the preset 110 lbs. The physical attributes of Barbie's little sister, Skipper, are even more unusual. "In one version a child can rotate Skipper's arm and she will grow breasts and develop a thinner waist" (Richmond-Abbott, 1992: 73). Doll makers have yet to introduce a comparable technique for an anatomically correct male companion.

In keeping with stereotyped beliefs about women, Barbie is a clotheshorse. "About one billion fashions have been produced for Barbie and her friends during the past four decades. The doll has had over a billion pairs of shoes in that time" (Edut, 2003). Advertisements for the "Barbie Fashion Fever Shopping Boutique" also extol consumerism and enjoin girls to "shop just like grown-up fashionistas: Use a working 'credit card' to shop for the season's must-have Barbie fashions!" Although the Bratz doll franchise (which first appeared in 2001) has challenged Barbie's supremacy in the fashion doll market (and now outsells Barbie in both the United States and the United Kingdom), the 2007 *Report of the American Psychological Association Task Force on the Sexualization of Girls* (APA, 2007: 14) expressed concern over the "objectified sexuality presented by these dolls." Noting that the "Bratz girls ... come dressed in sexualized clothing such as miniskirts, fishnet stockings, and feather boas" and are "marketed in bikinis, sitting in a hot tub, mixing drinks and standing around, while the 'Boyz' play guitar and stand with their surf boards, poised for action," the APA Report concluded that "it is worrisome when dolls designed specifically for 4- to 8-year-olds are associated with an objectified adult sexuality" (APA, 2007: 14; see also Lamb and Brown, 2006).

In the first year of life, Barbie reflected traditional female roles such as bride (Wedding Day Dress Barbie) or Plantation Belle. However, in 1965, Barbie suited up as

"Miss Astronaut" (complete with silver lingerie); since then, she has enjoyed more than 75 careers, including teacher, veterinarian, WNBA player, dentist, rock star, and rapper. In 1976, Barbie was a doctor, surgical nurse, ballerina, and "stewardess" (in the parlance of the day), as well as an Olympic skier, gymnast, and skater. In 1989, she joined the U.S. Army, and, over the next three years, would wear the uniforms of the U.S. Air Force, Navy, and Marine Corps. In the early 1990s, Baywatch Barbie arrived, equipped with all the paraphernalia necessary for success as a lifeguard—a frisbee, hairbrush, and dolphin. In 1999, Working Woman Barbie appeared, with cell phone, lap-top, planner, coffee cup, software, and a copy of *Working Woman* magazine. Barbie For President 2000 came in three versions—Caucasian, Latina, and African American, identically clad in business suits and sensible haircuts—campaigning on a platform that emphasized education, the environment, world peace, equality, and kindness towards animals. Ironically, in the same year, Mattel's Fashion Doll 2000 saw Barbie return to "her ultra-glam fashion doll roots with a 'millennium makeover,' complete with an old-school downward gaze and a heavy coat of runway-friendly face paint" (Zumhagen, 2003). Although most Barbies do not contain soundboxes, those who do utter telling comments; in 1968, when Barbie spoke for the first time, her six phrases included "I have a date tonight!" and "I love being a fashion model!" In 1994, Teen Talk Barbie announced, "Math is hard!"

Although Ken, Barbie's anatomically challenged boyfriend, first appeared in 1960, he has never been advertised as a doll for boys (even though he was re-released in 1969 with bigger muscles and again, in 2006, with a more chiseled physique). Instead, he and Barbie exist to provide young girls with opportunities to "practice the rituals of courtship and romance with the perfect (though certainly not normative) couple" (Uchalik and Livingston, 1980: 92). Although Barbie and Ken broke up in 2004 (with press releases sombrely noting that, "Like other celebrity couples, their Hollywood romance has come to end," and that while the couple felt it necessary "to spend some quality time apart," they would remain "good friends" [BBC News, 2004]), they reunited in 2006; reportedly, Barbie was impressed by the fact that Ken had spent a good portion of his "quality time" buffing up at the gym [CNN.com, 2006]).

Pope et al. (1999: 65) suggested that boys' "action figures" (the preferred name for male dolls)—supermasculine miniature mesomorphs—may provide a "male analog" of fashion dolls such as Barbie. Measuring the waist, chest, and bicep circumferences of the most popular American action figures of the past three decades, they found that these dolls have become more muscular over the years; many contemporary figures far exceed the muscularity of even the largest human bodybuilders. The researchers argued that to the extent that female fashion dolls and male action figures provide an index of cultural ideals of female and male physiques, they may contribute to body-image disorders in both sexes (see also Grieve, 2007; Luciano, 2007; Ricciardelli and McCabe, 2007).

The doll play of Canadian boys is largely defined by American-created action figures that support and promote the "Warrior" theme of masculinity (Goldstein, 1998; Hellendoorn and Harinck, 1995). These action figures—crime fighters, soldiers, and superheroes—are accessorized with weapons (e.g., bows and arrows, guns, grenade and missile launchers), fast cars, spaceships, and activity-oriented equipment such as mountain-climbing gear (Messner, 2000). While it is, of course, possible to construct a fantasy "family" with boys' toys, such as the masculine-sounding Beast Wars Transformers and Primal Rage characters, it is telling that there are no "cozy" kitchen appliances with which to prepare meals in the Batcave, no beds and vanity tables in the Planet Heroes Turbo Shuttle, and no frilly curtains to dot the entranceway of the Slime Pit. G.I. Joe's "action kit" neglects to include a curling iron so that he can style Barbie's hair. Moreover, even though bicycles, in-line skates, and board games may be considered unisex toys, here, too, stylistic details dictate the most likely user. When placed next to a bike emblazoned with "The Boss," the pink or purple "Little Miss Sassy" bicycle—even without the heart-shaped carrier basket— is less likely to be selected as a gift for a boy. The sturdier, more durable in-line skates typically do not sport pink laces.

The majority of parents still actively encourage their children to play with gender-stereotyped toys and discourage play with toys earmarked for the other sex (Campenni, 1999; Leaper et al., 2000). William's (2006: 16, 164) ethnography of American toy stores reported that toy stores are a place where adults "bought what they wanted" with, not unexpectedly, "nostalgia toys" as favoured purchases. Although Idle et al. (1993) suggest that some parents favour gender-neutral toys, most parents appear to succumb to marketing ploys designed to induce them to choose toys presented as gender-specific. Peretti and Sydney (1985) reported that toys stereotyped for boys (e.g., cars, trains, chemistry sets, tool chests, action figures) almost invariably picture boys in ads, catalogues, and on toy packages; similarly, photographs of girls accompany toys stereotyped for female play (see also Blakemore and Centers, 2005). Suggesting that these findings may have equal currency in the new millennium, advertisements in the 2007 Holiday issue of *Toy Wishes* depicted girls gazing rapturously at a Disney Deluxe Princess Castle ("Fully furnished! Play in every room! Ring doorbell for a princess welcome!"); applying their Runway Pink Makeup ("There is nothing like being a girl. A girl can pucker up in front of a mirror and put on the most gorgeous shade of lipstick"); and gyrating to a Barbie "Blossom Player DVD Player" ("girls will love this easy to use front-loading DVD player"). Boys, in contrast, appeared in ads that extolled the merits of "Jack Sparrow's Weapon Gear with Smart Action SFX" ("battle against the most fearsome of pirates") and "Battleground Crossbows & Catapults" ("Prepare your army of warriors to battle the enemy by demolishing their defenses"). Boys were additionally shown pedalling their way through on-screen adventures with Fisher-Price's "Smart Cycle" ["Playing video games. Getting exercise. And learning ... all at the same time.... A really fun way to get smart"); shooting a N-Strike Disk Shot ("Take your blasting skills to the next level with moving targets!"); driving a Nascar Power Wheels car and performing karate moves in the "Spider Man Training Studio." Other ads were even less subtle in the gendered messages they conveyed. Thus, Tonka's "Scoot 'N Scoop 3-in-1 Ride-On" for toddlers is advertised with the caption: "Built for 3 important stages of boyhood": "Smashing!" "Bashing!" "Crashing!" Research on the content of children's letters to Santa (O'Cass and Clarke, 2002; Pine and Nash, 2002) has found that children's toy preferences bear witness to the effectiveness of these gendered marketing techniques.

Up until the age of 2, boys and girls demonstrate strong preferences for gender-typed toys (Alexander, 2003; Caldera and Sciaraffa, 1998). In an examination of the toy choices made by preschool children (ages 4–5 years), Stagnitti et al. (1997) found that girls exhibited less gender typing in their toy choices. In one study, 61 preschoolers (28 girls and 33 boys) were offered a tool set and a dish set, presented either neutrally or as gender-typed (Raag and Rackliff, 1998). Researchers found that preschool boys were as likely to choose the dish set *unless* it was presented as a girl's toy and they thought their fathers would view playing with it as "bad." In a study of 26 male and 24 female 4- and 5-year-olds, Raag (1999) found that the perception that one or more people thought cross-gender-typed play was "bad" predicted the amount of time that boys (but not girls) spent with cross-gender toys; this factor operated independently of an awareness of gender stereotypes.

Children's judgments about a toy's attractiveness are influenced by their observation of same-sex children (Shell and Eisenberg, 1990) and by the toy's gender label. For example, in a study to test the **hot potato effect** (i.e., children's tendency to abandon a toy labelled as "other-sexed"), Martin et al. (1995) showed children six toys, identifying two as toys that girls liked, two as toys that boys liked, and leaving two unlabelled. When the children were asked to rate how much they liked the toys and how much other children would like them, children reported a preference for "same-sex" toys and predicted that other children would demonstrate the same preferences (see also Levy et al., 2000).

The toys that children play with may promote different gender outcomes (Leaper, 2000, 2002; Ruble and Martin, 1998). Giuliano et al. (2000) asked 84 undergraduate women (44 varsity athletes and 44 non-athletes) about their childhood play activities. They found that playing with "masculine" toys and games, playing in predominantly male or mixed-sex groups, and being regarded as a "tomboy" distinguished those women who became university athletes from those who did not. A study of 437 grade 6 students (Jones et al., 2000) revealed that males reported more extracurricular experience with electronic toys and such items as batteries, fuses, microscopes, and pulleys, while females reported more experience with bread-making, knitting, sewing, and planting seeds. Males also indicated greater interest in atomic bombs, atoms, cars, computers, X-rays, and technology, while females expressed more interest in animal communication, rainbows, healthy eating, weather, and AIDS. Boys were more likely than girls to describe science as destructive and dangerous—and more "suitable" for boys; girls were more likely to report that science was difficult to understand. The results of this study, which showed gender differences in science-related experiences and attitudes and in perceptions of science courses and careers, suggest that childhood exposure to different sets of toys and activities may influence the ambitions and career choices of young men and women (see also Blakemore and Centers, 2005; Christophersen and Mortweet, 2003; Upitis, 2001; Ziegler and Heller, 2000). As Marcon and Freeman (1996: 1) observed, "[t]oys typically used by boys and girls develop different cognitive and social skills. Stereotypic toy use may limit children's competencies and restrict opportunities to experiment with future roles, thereby affecting later occupational choice."

Clothing Subtle gender socialization via clothing begins at infancy. Parents go to great lengths to make male and female infants appear different (Coltrane and Adams, 1997). Once a newborn's genital sex has been announced, the infant is typically swathed in colour-coded blankets, toques, and sleepers: pink identifies girls and blue identifies boys (although parents in the early part of the twentieth century tended to dress girls in blue and boys in pink or red [Collins and Coltrane, 2000; Kimmel and Mahler, 2003]). Gifts of clothing also differ; infant girls receive pastel outfits, boys bright, bold-coloured ones (Fagot and Leinbach, 1993). The gender coding of infant clothing operates to guide observers' perceptions along gender-appropriate lines, leading to comments that reinforce gender stereotypes. Passersby seem nonplussed by newborns dressed in non-gender-specific multicoloured outerwear. Denied symbolic cues to direct their responses, they are uncertain whether to remark on a baby girl's beauty ("She's going to be a real heartbreaker!") or a baby boy's strength ("Whoa, look at the muscles on this little guy!"). However, as Shakin et al. (1985) have noted, the colour coding of infant apparel is so pervasive that over 90 percent of the infants they observed in a shopping mall could be readily identified as male or female.

Should colours deceive, there are other cues. Infant clothing styles mimic adult sex-linked fashions. Frills, ribbons, and tiny pierced earrings announce a female, while baseball caps, miniature hockey jerseys, and car and truck motifs mark the infant wearer as male. Sleepwear is also gender coded, with nighties for girls and "astronaut, athlete, or super hero pajamas" for boys (Renzetti and Curran, 1995: 93). Even unisex clothes feature gender-marked insignia and images; sweatsuits featuring male cartoon characters or super-heroes, ribbed in blue or black, are located in the "Boys" section; those displaying Disney "princesses" and Minnie Mouse, ribbed in pink, are located only in "Girls." The nature of sex-typed garments also promotes gender-appropriate behaviour; traditional "little girls" clothing (e.g., dresses, "fancy shoes") tends to be more restrictive, inhibiting boisterous play. Women who self-identified as having been tomboys often recall having disliked feminine attire, especially dresses, which they perceived as making them vulnerable (Carr, 1998: 540).

Perhaps a far more pernicious phenomenon than frills and bows is the current trend of provocative clothing for little girls. For example, "La Senza Girl"-type fashions may be con-strued as an incitement to accelerated sexual precocity, encouraging young girls to think of themselves as sexual objects, and, even more troubling, encouraging others to perceive them as potential sexual partners. Thongs, sometimes adorned with messages such as "eye candy" or "wink wink," are now available at children and "tween" clothing stores (Brooks, 2006; Cook and Kaiser, 2004; Pollett and Hurwitz, 2004). In the first decade of the new millennium, it is common to see girls of early elementary-school age clad in (very) low-rider jeans, with or without "sexy" written across the bum, "short shorts," and off-the-shoulder "crop tops." Meanwhile, boys of the same age may still sport "Franklin the Turtle" sweatsuits or, among the more fashion-conscious, "skate-boarder" pants roomy enough to accommodate a picnic basket. In neither case is the sexuality of the young boy on display.

THE PEER GROUP

Even though a child interacts with children outside of the family from at least the age of 3, early years playmates exert minimal influence on one another. Peer-group influence usually begins at age 7 or 8 and forms a fast-rising curve, peaking between the ages of 14 and 16 (Thornburg, 1982: 124) and only gradually dissipating in early adulthood. Peers constitute an important reference group during the social-time periods of late childhood through mid-adolescence, as young people seek to assert autonomy from their families (Andrews et al., 2002). When asked about their perceived sources of influence, 78 percent of Canadian teens reported that their friends influenced their lives "a great deal" or "quite a bit," with females slightly more likely to report this than males (79 percent versus 77 percent) (Bibby, 2001: 31). Canadian teenagers also report that when faced with a seri-ous problem, they are more likely to turn to friends (35 percent—31 percent of males and 39 percent of females) than to family members (21 percent) (Bibby, 2001: 33). While the 2000 Project Canada survey found that males were somewhat less likely than females to say that friendship was "very important" to them (80 percent of males versus 90 percent of females), "[i]t would be difficult to overstate the role of friends in teenage lives" (Bibby, 2001: 50).

Pioneering research conducted during the 1950s on the leading edge of the baby boom generation (Coleman, 1967) discovered that high school adolescent peer groups espoused and supported values, norms, and styles of conduct noticeably different from those transmit-ted by parents and educators. These values and norms varied for male and female peer groups. Subsequent research (e.g., Adler et al., 1992/1995; Martin, 1994; Martin et al., 1997) has revealed that these important gender differences are also characteristic of pre-adolescent elementary-school-age peer groups.

From Same-Sex to Cross-Sex Peers

Beginning at the age of 2 or 3, young children tend to congregate in loosely structured same-sex play groups; this continues until formal schooling begins (Maccoby, 1998; Martin and Fabes, 1997). For the most part, the more highly structured peer groups which evolve from younger play groups remain restricted to same-sex members until mid-adolescence (Fagot, 1995; Serbin et al., 1994; Smith et al., 2001), at which point they are as likely to contain members of both sexes. Although individual girls and boys may initiate and maintain cross-sex contacts at a younger age, a same-sex peer group remains the most important source of reference and identification from older childhood through early/mid-adolescence. Because acceptance by their peers is so important to young people, peer-group values are enormously influential. These same-sex peer groups create enough of a "world within a world" to warrant their description as **peer gender subcultures** (to modify the term initially used by Udry [1971: 75]). Within these subcultures, relatively distinctive attitudes and perspectives on the world and on the nature and meaning of each gender are disseminated and reinforced. Peer subcultures adapt society's dominant constructs of masculinity and femininity to their own transitional condition between childhood and adulthood (Aydt and Corsaro, 2003).

Several points should be made. First, in keeping with the traditional assumption that the genders are essentially different, researchers have tended to focus more upon the differences than the similarities between male and female gender subcultures. Second, discussions of each subculture have been based mainly on observation of members' same-sex interactions; it is important to note that individuals often exhibit different norms and behaviour in cross-sex contexts. Finally, although researchers have found that the themes and foci of the male subculture have remained relatively unchanged over the past 40 years, slight but important changes have occurred in female subcultures (Adler et al., 1992/1995: 1338), reflecting large-scale societal changes in women's lives.

Boys to Men

Adler et al. (1992/1995) have focused on the role of popularity in gender socialization among elementary-school children. Their research revealed that the determinants of popularity varied greatly between male and female subcultures. *Athletic prowess* was found to be the most important factor affecting boys' rank in the male status hierarchy. *Coolness* (suave self-presentation, possession of socially valued clothing and gear) and *toughness* (defiance towards authority, rule-breaking) also enhanced boys' status, as did *savoir-faire* (sophisticated social acumen, expressed variously as interpersonal grace or as manipulation and control). As well, boys in the higher grades gained status for real or apparent success with girls (see also Becker and Luthar, 2007).

Various studies (Rose, 1995; Walker, 1994, 2002) have indicated that boys tend to develop more extensive networks of same-sex peer friendships than do girls; boys' same-sex friendships tend to be less intense and more superficial. From mid-adolescence on (Korobov, 2004; Muir and Seitz, 2004), males tend to describe their friendships primarily in terms of shared activities, such as sports, athletic events, or drinking together (see also Chapter 7). Recall Udry's (1971: 76) contention that the dominant themes of the male peer group are independence, emotional control, and conquest. Udry has further asserted (1971: 76–81) that males informally teach and reinforce these themes through interactions around three foci—sexuality, sports, and automobiles—that are of paramount interest to males across regions and social classes throughout childhood and adolescence.

The process of gender socialization is fraught with pressures and struggle for most adolescents (Williams, 2002). However, "for young men and women who are moving toward affirmation of an identity as lesbian or gay, dealing with gender-role pressures ... is only part of the task they must face" (Lips, 2001: 327; see also Kimmel, 2001). While concealment of one's homosexual orientation may lead to feelings of isolation, alienation, and worthlessness, disclosure may result in peer rejection and even abuse:

> When Christian Hernandez was 14 and a Grade 9 student at Notre Dame College High School in Niagara Falls, Ont., he screwed up his courage and told his best friend that he was gay.... "He told me he couldn't accept it," recalls Hernandez. "And he began to spread it around." Over the next two years, Hernandez was teased and harassed almost daily. One day, a group of boys waited for him after school. Their leader had a knife, and, says Hernandez, "He told me he didn't accept faggots, that we brought AIDS into the world." The boy then cut Hernandez on the neck, putting him in the hospital for a week. When Hernandez told his parents the reason for the attack, his father ... said he would "rather have a dead son than a queer son." (Fisher, 1999: 4)

A survey of over 3000 high school students found that students who reported having engaged in same-sex relations were more than three times as likely to report avoiding school because they felt unsafe, more than twice as likely to report having been threatened or injured with a weapon at school, and significantly more likely to report having had their property deliberately damaged or stolen at school (Faulkner and Cranston, 1998). Renzetti and Curran (2003: 113) reported that "[b]y some estimates, more than 30 percent of the approximately 5000 suicides committed each year [in the United States] by young women and men between the ages of 15 and 24 are related to emotional trauma resulting from sexual orientation issues and from societal prejudices about same-sex relationships." Fisher (1999: 9) reported that in Canada, gay and bisexual young adults, both white and of colour, are "dramatically overrepresented in attempted suicide statistics"; these findings are evidence of the real human costs of heterosexism and homophobia.

Fisher (1999: 9) observed that a frequently cited precipitant of suicide attempts among gay and lesbian youth is the turmoil that surrounds "coming out" to family and friends. Sadly, a study comparing the attitudes of young adults towards peers who attempted suicide—either after being rejected by parents upon "coming out" or in response to other stressors (including physical illness, relationship loss, or academic failure)—found that "gays and lesbians who engaged in suicidal behaviour following coming out were not viewed in particularly forgiving or empathic ways, as was the case for persons who became suicidal following an incurable illness" (Cato and Canetto, 2003: 201). All suicidal persons were perceived to be "relatively feminine." However, suicidal males were rated as more masculine "if they engaged in suicidal behavior because of an academic failure or a physical illness, while suicidal females were viewed as more masculine only if their suicidal behavior followed an academic failure."

Girls to Women

Girls tend to form less extensive friendship networks than boys. However, girls' same-sex friendships tend to be more exclusive and intimate (Lips, 1999: 145). Whereas early adolescent girls tend to stress the physical similarities between themselves and their friends (e.g., clothing, hairstyles), mid-adolescent females are more likely to stress psychological affinities, such as the ability to "really talk" with one another and share the same hopes and anxieties (Monsour, 2002; Parks and Floyd, 1996).

Whitesell and Harter (1996) suggested that females' expectation of intimacy and deep communication in friendship may deter them from overt aggression for fear of social rejection; Bukowski et al. (1993) reported that direct physical aggression is more strongly associated with peer rejection for girls than for boys. However, girls have consistently been found to demonstrate higher levels of **relational aggression** than boys (Crick and Nelson, 2002; Graham and Wells, 2001; Letendre, 2007). Relational aggression typically has as its goal the damaging of another's peer relationships and reputation (Crick, 1997; Maccoby, 1998: 40). Bjorkqvist et al. (1992) asserted that while direct aggression (physical and verbal) was more common among boys, indirect or relational aggression (e.g., gossiping, spreading injurious rumours, ostracism) was more common among girls (see also Goodwin, 2002; Russell et al., 2003; Shute and Charlton, 2006). During the past decade, several incidents of violent aggression culminating in death perpetrated by female teenagers were widely publicized; nevertheless, such acts remain relatively rare in Canada. Although the *rate* at which female youths were charged with violent crimes more than doubled between 1986 and 2005 (from 60 per 100 000 to 132 per 100 000), this rate is "still quite low compared to male youth"; "[g]enerally, the rate at which females are accused of violations against the person is about one-fifth the rate for males" (AuCoin, 2005: 3; Statistics Canada, 2008a; see also Rosenfeld and Harmon, 2002). While relational aggression is less common among boys, it still takes place, and its consequences can be pernicious. Kimmel and Mahler's (2003: 1439) analysis of the 28 cases of random school shootings that have occurred in American schools since 1982 concluded that (1) "most of the boys who opened fire were mercilessly and routinely teased and bullied"; (2) "the specific content of the teasing and bullying is homophobia"; and (3) the violent acts these young men engaged in were "retaliatory against the threats to their manhood."

In female subcultural peer groups, what Udry (1971: 92) has cited as the dominant themes of female socialization—sociability, popularity, and attractiveness—are elaborated and reinforced through discussions about certain focal issues: other women, men, clothing, and cosmetics (Udry, 1971: 82). Adler et al. (1992/1995) found *physical attractiveness* to be a major determinant of popularity and a major topic of conversation among elementary-school-age girls. Beginning in early grades and throughout high school, girls who are overweight, wear "unfashionable" (i.e., non-designer) clothing, or otherwise do not conform to a stereotypical image of feminine attractiveness (e.g., those with disabilities) may be targeted by other girls for ridicule or rejection (Kenny, 2002; Renzetti and Curran, 2003: 112). Social development is also salient to female popularity: *exclusivity* (the formation of elite social groups) is highly valued, as is *precocity*, including, from the earliest elementary years, a fascination with boys—by "going with" a popular boy, a girl can attain a measure of his prestige. However, girls' subcultures—unlike boys'—do not mandate disdain for academic success. Finally, a girl's popularity is powerfully linked to her parents' *socioeconomic status*. Wealthier parents can afford the fashionable clothing, select extracurricular activities, and other symbols of prestige so crucial to girls' location on the social hierarchy, at least in middle- and upper-class subcultures. Furthermore, affluent parents tend to be more permissive, allowing daughters greater freedom to pursue the adventures vital to popularity.

Adler et al. (1992/1995: 135) concluded that "boys' subculture" is characterized by a "culture of coolness," an "orientation of autonomy," and an "expression of physicality"; on the other hand, "[g]irls' subculture" is characterized by a "culture of compliance and conformity," a "culture of romance," and an "ideology of domesticity"—as well as an "orientation of ascription" (i.e., a sense that the female role is to attract a male who will endow her with his status) (Adler et al., 1992/1995: 136). While the boundaries of female subcultures have been expanding to assimilate stereotypically male dimensions, such as sports, competition, achievement, autonomy, initiative, and perhaps even overt aggression, male subcultures have not evinced a comparable incorporation of values and themes more traditionally associated with females (Adler et al., 1992/1995: 137–138).

Peer Play and Games

Studies on gender differences in play activities and games have yielded somewhat inconsistent findings. Maccoby and Jacklin's (1974) early review concluded that girls tend to play games with few specific rules and little emphasis on competition. However, Hughes' (1988) study of 4th and 5th graders concluded that girls do indeed participate in highly complex and competitive games, often requiring development of conflict-resolution skills; at the same time, girls are more likely to emphasize cooperation and the maintenance of close personal relationships among competitors. Martin (1999: 51) concurred, claiming that "play in girls' groups is marked by cooperation and facilitating interaction." Lerner (1977) found boys' play activities to be generally more complex and rule-bound, tending to involve direct competition between participants; 20 years later, Martin (1999: 51) concluded that "play in boys' groups is marked by concerns with dominance and constriction of interaction." Overall, it appears that boys' play has not changed over the years, whereas girls' play has incorporated some elements traditionally found in boys' play while still retaining an emphasis on cooperation and personal relationships.

Sports: Gender Participation Levels

Gender differences in play activities are carried through into organized sports and strongly reinforced in that realm. Traditionally, sports have been more strongly linked with desirable images of masculinity than of femininity (Biernat and Vescio, 2002). In our society—following a British tradition that credits England's success in business and war to lessons learned on the "playing fields of Eton"—sports has been lauded as the premier mechanism by which boys are transformed into men. Through participation in sports, it is claimed, boys learn to strive for excellence, to value teamwork, to coordinate their actions with others, to subordinate their own impulses to the greater good, and to take directions and orders. These indispensable lessons prepare boys for later success in the public sphere.

Given the centrality of sports in male socialization, it is not surprising that concerns have been expressed about the possibility that sports (particularly competitive full-contact sports) might have a "masculinizing" effect on girls. "The same year women's swimming made its Olympic debut at the 1912 Olympics in Stockholm, Sweden, the *Ladies Home Journal* ran an article under the headline 'Are Athletics Making Girls Masculine?'" (Druzin, 2001: 32). Historically, women's participation was restricted to sports highlighting the grace and beauty of the female form, such as figure skating and gymnastics. Role models of excellence in these sports are typically described in a language of prototypical femininity stressing lithe bodies and graceful movements.

Since the Victorian era, women have gradually been permitted to expand their sport repertoires beyond the gentle arts of archery and croquet. The 1900 Olympics in Paris included women's tennis and golf; women's swimming was introduced at the 1912 Olympics; the 1928 Olympics included five women's track and field events (100-metre dash, 4×100-metre relay, high jump, discus, 800-metre race). In 1932, the 100-metre hurdles and javelin were added, and in 1948, the 200-metre dash, long jump, and shot put. Women were first allowed to compete in rowing at the 1976 Montreal Olympics. Druzin (2001: 20) reported that "[t]here has been a steady increase in the number of female athletes at Olympic games, and in the number of events open to them. In 1900, women represented less than one percent of athletes participating at the Games. One hundred years later, that figure had increased to 38.4 percent." Slightly more than half of our country's representatives at the 1996 Summer Olympic Games and at the 2000 Summer Games were women. At the 2000 Summer Olympics, women were allowed to compete in several events from which they had previously been excluded, including the pentathlon, the pole vault, hammer throw, water polo, and weightlifting. At the 2004 Summer Olympic Games in Athens, 47 percent of the athletes that represented Canada were women.

Clearly, "[t]imes have changed since the days when women's participation in sports was limited to applauding men" (Klotz, 1999). According to the Canadian Hockey Association, women's participation in hockey "has exploded": While in 1988–1989, the association had only 7100 registered female players, the figure soared to over 37 748 in 1998–1999 and, by 2006–2007, it had climbed to 73 791 (Hockey Canada, 2008). Similarly, the 2005 General Social Survey finds that nearly three times as many Canadian girls, ages 5 to 14, played ice hockey in 2005 as in 1998 (Statistics Canada, 2008b). This survey reported that soccer "has become the sport of choice for Canadian boys and girls 5 to 14 years" and that the rate of involvement in soccer was the same for boys and girls in this age cohort. Moreover, while the specific ranking of sports activities for children ages 5 to 14 differed for boys and girls, their choices of sports activities was markedly similar. Among Canadian children ages 5 to 14, the top five most practised sports among girls were, in order, soccer, swimming, basketball, ice hockey, and volleyball; among boys, the most practised sports were soccer, ice hockey, swimming, basketball, and volleyball.

In recent years, Canadian female athletes have won acclaim for their accomplishments in a wide array of non-traditional sports: Catriona Le May Doan (speed skating), Silken Laumann (rowing), Olia Berger (judo), Catherine Dunnette (fencing); Marnie Baizley (squash), Linda Conley (shooting), Charmaine Hooper (soccer), and hockey player Hayley Wickenheiser (the first woman to score a point in a professional men's hockey game) to name just a few. However, while these women could serve as powerful role models for girls, it remains true that women athletes are less visible in the media than their male counterparts (Messner et al., 2003; Pedersen and Whisenant, 2003; Vincent et al., 2003). From 1996 to 1999, for example, only 11 of the 150 issues of *Sports Illustrated* featured a woman athlete on its cover (Klotz, 1999). It is therefore not, perhaps, surprising that Robins (1999) reported that most Canadian girls "have trouble naming even the most successful female athletes." Moreover, evidence suggests that, when female athletes are made visible in the mass media, their appearance is often sexualized, with attention directed to their "sexiness" rather than their athleticism (Hills, 2004). Noting that eight Olympic female athletes were featured in the September 2004 issue of *Playboy* and that swimmer Amanda Beard appeared in the 2005 swimsuit edition of *Sports Illustrated*, the APA Task Force on the Sexualization of Girls (APA, 2007: 9) pointedly observed that "[m]ale athletes are rarely depicted solely as sexual objects in their endorsement work" (see also Fink and Kensicki, 2002; Shugart, 2003). In an attempt to compensate for both the relative invisibility and selective coverage of women athletes in the mainstream media, the website for the Canadian Association for the Advancement of Women and Sport and Physical Activity includes a "Girl-Friendly Shopping" guide which enjoins parents to "buy a ball not a doll" for their daughters, directs them to books for young readers extolling "the fun, health and confidence that comes from playing sports," and furnishes links to websites where posters and collectible items celebrating women athletes are available.

Blinde et al. (2001: 159), recognizing that traditional gender-role socialization has discouraged women from both participating in sports and viewing themselves as strong, competent, and self-determining, have argued that "[b]ecoming empowered at the personal level ... [may] represent a foundation from which women could counteract these limiting self-perceptions as well as gain control over their lives." On the basis of telephone interviews with 24 women athletes in American intercollegiate sports programs, the researchers suggested a link between participation in sports and three empowering qualities in which women are often deficient: bodily competence, perception of a competent self, and a proactive approach to life (see also Hall and Oglesby, 2002). Robins (1999: 2) reported that "it is no coincidence that many senior women executives in Fortune 500 companies have strong athletic backgrounds." However, even though there can be little doubt that women's participation in non-traditional sports is clearly increasing, their doing so is not entirely without challenge. When Courcy et al. (2006) asked 354 Quebec teenagers (180 girls and 174 boys) to write an "opinion letter" on their conception of femininity and of girls who participated in "male sports," they found that girls were far more likely than boys to view this "transgression of the gender sport order" favourably and as a way of contesting the social gender order. In this study, boys were three times more likely than girls to write a letter expressing a negative opinion of girls who participated in male sports.

At the same time, however, it would be myopic to suppose that the traditional "gender sports order" only functions to delimit the opportunities of females. Research by Schmalz and Kerstetter (2006) examined how gender stereotypes impact children's participation in sports. Their research, based on a sample of 444 children ages 8 to 10, found that while the sports participation of the children followed gendered lines, with more girls than boys participating in "feminine" sports and more boys than girls participating in "masculine sports," more girls participated in masculine than feminine sports. Noting that boys' participation in "feminine sports" remained slight, the authors suggested that "[p]articipation in masculine activities by girls and women is more socially accepted than participation in feminine activities by boys and men." Observing that boys who participated in cross-gender sports (dubbed "girlie girl" sports by their respondents) were stigmatized as gay and perceived to "lack aggression, be uncompetitive, gentle and dependent, among other stereotypically feminine characteristics," they concluded that boys "experience greater restriction in their participation [in sports] than girls because of gender stigma." Echoing Henderson and Shaw's (2003) assertion that it is boys who have "become the neglected sex in the realm of sport and gender research," they suggested that "[p]erhaps it is time to increase attention to the social limitations and constraints boys and men experience 'playing their own game.'"

A comparison of findings from the 1998 and 2005 General Social Survey of Canadians age 15 and over indicates that while men are still more likely than women to regularly participate in sports (35.5 percent of men versus 20.7 percent of women), the gap has narrowed since 1998 (43.1 percent of men versus 25.7 percent). Similarly, among children ages 5 to 14, boys remain more actively involved in sports than girls (55 percent vs. 44 percent); while the rate for girls remained stable from 1998, the rate for boys evinced a slight decline.

Some signs of change are apparent. Consider that in 1998, men were more likely to participate in sports through a club or organization than women (19.6 percent versus 18.3 percent), or take part in a sports competition or tournament (17.4 percent versus 7.4 percent). In that year, women and men were equally likely to be involved in an amateur sport as an administrative assistant (7.1 percent of men and 7.0 percent of women), but men were more likely to be involved as coaches (8.1 percent versus 6.2 percent), referees/officials/umpires (4.5 percent versus 3.2 percent), or spectators (33.8 percent versus 29.3 percent). In 2005, however, men were only slightly more likely to participate in sports through a club or organization (17.6 percent versus 17.3 percent) and the gender gap in tournaments and competitions had narrowed (15.1 percent versus 6.8 percent). In 2005, female coaches outnumbered their male counterparts by a slight margin and had also clearly gained ground as referees, officials, or umpires. While in 1992, men outnumbered women as a referees, officials, or umpires in amateur sports by a ratio of 5 to 1, by 2005, this ratio was down to 2 to 1. Similarly, although in 1992 men outnumbered women as administrators or helpers by a ratio of 2 to 1, in 2005, about as many women as men occupied these roles (Statistics Canada, 2004b, 2008c). Nevertheless, as indicated by Figure 4.1, gender differences do persist when it comes to sport.

Data from the 2000–2001 Canadian Community Health Survey indicated that for all age groups combined, more men are physically active (expending more than 1.5 kilocalories per kg per day) than women (50 percent versus 43 percent), with the disparity the greatest in the youngest and oldest groups. The study found that physical inactivity "increases as income adequacy and educational level decrease, and this relation is stronger for women than for men"; it also found that "[p]hysical inactivity varies by ethnicity. Among the least active are Black women (76%) and South Asian women (73%)" (Bryan and Walsh, 2003: 9). Statistics Canada's 2001 Aboriginal Peoples Survey found that while almost two thirds of Aboriginal children participate regularly in sports, with Métis and Inuit children the most involved, Aboriginal boys were more likely to participate in sports than girls (Statistics Canada, 2007b).

Research shows that "girls who are physically active have a reduced risk of developing depression, heart diseases, adult-onset diabetes, osteoporosis, and certain types of cancer" and are also "less likely to smoke, ... to abuse drugs and alcohol, ... [to] wait longer to have sex, ... are more likely to use contraceptives" and "generally do better in school" (Statistics Canada, 2008b). Nevertheless, data from the Canadian Fitness and Lifestyle Research Institute have indicated that male teens devoted more hours per week to physical activities than girls (17 hours compared to less than 12); teenage girls also dropped out of sports at "much higher rates" than boys (Robins, 1999). The 2005 General Social Survey (GSS) also finds that even though sports participation declines with age for both sexes, at all ages, males are more likely to regularly participate in sports than females.

Socialization Lessons of Sports Through sports, boys are expected to learn to control their emotions, and particularly to suppress those culturally labelled as "feminine." Anger and feelings of aggression are to be channelled into purposive effort for the furtherance of individual or team goals. Fear and pain must be concealed behind a mask of stoicism ("tape an aspirin to it and get back out there") lest these vulnerabilities be exploited by the opponent (Nicholas, 2000; Stillion and McDowell, 2001/2002). The image of European-trained athletes writhing on the soccer pitch or arena ice tends to evoke disdain from the

FIGURE 4.1	Active Participation Rates in the Top Ten Sports by Sex, 2005

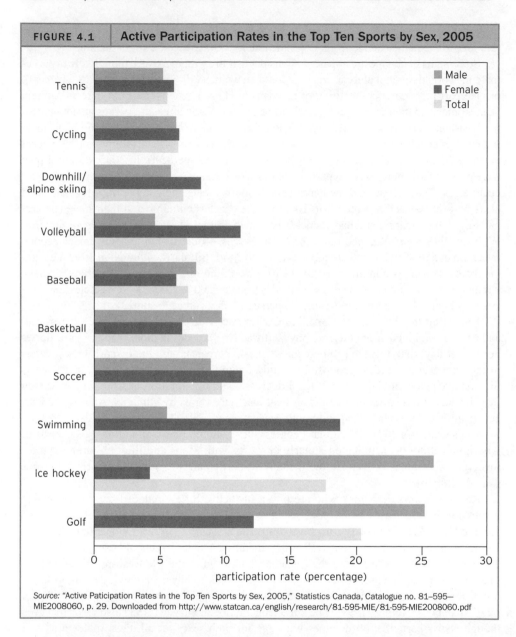

Source: "Active Paticipation Rates in the Top Ten Sports by Sex, 2005," Statistics Canada, Catalogue no. 81–595–MIE2008060, p. 29. Downloaded from http://www.statcan.ca/english/research/81-595-MIE/81-595-MIE2008060.pdf

"truly masculine" Canadian male. Athletes permanently disabled through sport are regarded with admiration and respect, but empathy and compassion for an opponent are generally forbidden (Lance and Ross, 2000). At the thrill of victory, "big boys" may cry, but in the agony of defeat, losers are supposed to weep in private, if at all.

Competitive sports reinforce the conquest theme. Given the low profile of our peacetime armed forces, sports has superseded the army as our society's major vehicle for instilling the "Warrior" image of masculinity. The language of many sports, football in particular, abounds with military analogies. One Canadian professional football team, the Saskatchewan

Roughriders, was named after a famous military fighting unit; the military referent of another, the Hamilton Blue Bombers, is explicit. Football teams are divided into "offensive" and "defensive" "units." Opponents are described as the "enemy." The leader of an offensive team, often referred to as a "general," marches his team down the "battlefield"; by following a "battle plan" and judiciously using the "weapons" in his "arsenal," he may capture some coveted "target objective." The defensive team may attempt to thwart these efforts by "blitzing." The weekend Warrior dons a uniform, usually emblazoned with team names and images connotative of furious aggression channelled into the annihilation of opponents. Boys' teams, modelling themselves after professional sport franchises, typicaly take the names of ferocious beasts: Grizzlies, Raptors, Tiger Cats, etc.; even the Duck has an evil scowl on its face.

Sports imagery and participation teaches boys directly and indirectly that the game is not an end in itself. In theory, Canadian playing fields are governed by the precept, "It doesn't matter whether you win or lose, it's how you play the game." However, an alternative, cynical ethos has entrenched itself in the world of sport, one expressed by such maxims as "Winning isn't everything, it's the only thing," "Nobody remembers who came in second," and "You Don't Win Silver, You Lose Gold" (displayed on a giant billboard in Atlanta during the 1996 Summer Olympic Games). This perspective is founded on the principle that "victory of one party entails loss by the other" (Burstyn, 1999: 43), and is deemed more consonant with contemporary notions of masculinity. Moreover, such attitudes and concomitant strategies are promoted as essential to success in business, politics, relationships, and life. Following immersion in a peer sports subculture, men may treat almost any activity, whether playing a game with a child or relating to a female partner, as a competitive challenge rife with implications for their masculinity.

In adolescent males who strive for status through sports, the craving for the "thrill of victory" may be especially keen. Reporting on a national American study of male high school seniors, Cowart (1990) recorded that approximately 7 percent had at least experimented with anabolic steroids; in the same year, the U.S. Department of Health and Human Services reported that between 5 and 10 percent of male adolescents and between 0.2 and 0.5 percent of female were using steroids. Interviews of a subsample of these adolescents found that four out of five male users believed steroids "made them bigger, stronger, better looking, and, as a result, more popular among their peers" (in Dolan, 1992: 32). Anabolic steroids, which are either derived from or designed to mimic testosterone, enhance performance by hypermasculinizing an athlete's body. Only female gymnasts use hyperfeminizing drugs designed to retard physical growth (Burstyn, 1999: 222).

Lacking opportunities to demonstrate their masculinity in arenas reserved for adults, such as business or breadwinning, young males invest a considerable amount of their masculine identity in success at sports. They are rewarded for doing so by their peers (Adler et al., 1992/1995) and by their parents (Berlage in MacGregor, 1995: 16), particularly their fathers. Nelson (1994) suggested that although a father may decline to bathe, feed, or read a bedtime story to his son, "he will probably at one time or another play catch with his son, take him to a ball game, or quiz him about the current or past feats of male sports heroes" (in MacGregor, 1995: 286). "Sports becomes the bond between many fathers and sons, with games becoming the way in which the male child wins approval from the father" (MacGregor, 1995: 286). A father's approval is often contingent upon a son's demonstration that he is a winner (MacGregor, 1995: 32, 314). Accordingly, a young male may develop a conditional sense of self-worth, hinging upon his performance in the most recent game. Failure in athletics can be devastating to boys in childhood and early adolescence (Pollack, 1998: 273). Messner (1990) maintained that a conditional sense of self-worth encourages young men to construct instrumental (goal-directed rather than emotional) relationships with themselves and others. He further suggested that this tendency may create difficulties for young men in intimate relationships, as they try to relate instrumentally to women, who have been taught to construct their own identities on meaningful relationships, not competitive success.

It is unclear whether fathers' intense zeal for their sons to triumph in sports has to do with sports competition as a kind of rite of initiation into manhood, or with the older men's hunger for vicarious experience as their own active participation in sport declines. On the one hand, there have been notorious incidents of fathers (and more recently, mothers) on the sidelines of various games screaming instructions and insults at their sons and abusing (and in a recent, more disturbing trend, physically attacking) other players, coaches, and referees. On the other hand, there have been incidents of a dramatically different kind, such as one which occurred during a semi-final 400-metre track event at the 1992 Barcelona Olympics, when British runner Derek Redmond tore a hamstring and was dragged and carried to the finish line by his father, who leapt from the stands to come to the aid of his son. MacGregor (1995) describes the senior Redmond's action as a "parent's desperate urge to fix" a hurt suffered by a son, pointing to it as an illustration of the power of sports to forge a bond between males of different generations.

The meaning of success in sports differs by social class (Messner, 1990). For males of lower socioeconomic classes, a career in sports may be perceived as a ticket out of poverty or a meagre future. The gross earnings of professional male athletes have reached astronomical proportions: basketball and baseball superstars earn as much as $28 million per year, hockey superstars $7–10 million (in 2006–2007, the average NHL salary was US$1.8 million); American (though not Canadian) football stars' salaries fall somewhere in between. Because of their high public profiles, top athletes can also supplement their huge salaries with multi-million-dollar product-endorsement deals. Despite the extremely high odds against even moderate athletic success (let alone superstar status), and even though a working-class boy's parents may stress education over sports, an athletically talented boy's experiences in his school, community, and peer group are likely to narrow his occupational aspirations. Potential economic rewards are not the only incentive. MacGregor (1995: 12) describes a working-class value system whereby many Canadian families "would probably rather tell their friends that their boys are NHLers than neurosurgeons." Canadian middle- and upper-middle-class boys, while valuing sports achievement, are more likely to regard sports as only one of a number of paths accessible to them and to find it easier to relinquish dreams of a sports career in favour of more plausible options (Messner, 1990).

Opportunities for financial success are much more limited for aspiring female athletes. For example, while in the 2005 season the maximum salary for a WNBA player was $89 000 and the minimum, $31 200, the maximum salary for an NBA player was over $15.3 million and the minimum, $385 277; in like fashion, the total prize money for the PGA tour during the 2008 season was over five times that of the LPGA tour ($271.1 million versus $58 million) (Women's Sports Foundation, 2008). Although in 2007 Wimbledon announced that its four Grand Slam events would provide equal prize monies to male and female athletes, women athletes are still unlikely to reap financial rewards commensurate with those enjoyed by their male counterparts; in our current cultural climate, women are less likely to be rewarded for what their bodies *do* than for how their bodies *look*.

Physical Attractiveness

Every society constructs ideal standards of physical attractiveness for both women and men. The standards themselves are the product of social and historical circumstances. Abraham and Llewellyn-Jones (1992: 1) observed that for much of recorded history "it was fashionable to be fat": the uncertainty of food supplies made plumpness an enviable symbol of prosperity. However, over the course of the last century, perhaps in response to increased general affluence and a basically stable food supply, our icons of female beauty underwent a transformation. Burstyn (1999: 157) suggested that the "thin aesthetic has become popular because women in industrial societies have had to curtail their childbearing and want models whose bodies imply limited or foregone maternity." Content analyses conducted over a 25-year period on the "vital statistics" of *Playboy* centrefolds and Miss America Pageant contestants have revealed both a decrease in average bust and hip measurements and a significant decline in weight. Whereas in the 1960s the average Miss America stood 5 feet 6 inches tall and weighed 120 pounds, two decades later, while remaining at the same weight, she had grown two inches. *Playboy* "playmates" exhibited the same tendency, dropping in weight by several pounds but gaining several inches in height (Etcoff, 1999: 201). Spitzer et al. (1999) compared the mean body mass indices of Canadians and Americans ages 18 to 24 (using data collected from 11 national health surveys conducted from the 1950s to the 1990s) with those of *Playboy* centrefold models, Miss America Pageant winners, and male *Playgirl* models. They found that the body sizes of Miss America Pageant winners had decreased significantly since the 1950s and that *Playboy* centrefold models remained below normal body weight. In contrast, the body sizes of young adult North American women increased significantly over this time period. While the body sizes of *Playgirl* models also increased, this increase appeared to be a consequence of increased muscularity, whereas in the case of "ordinary" North Americans it was attributable to increased body fat.

As our "Dream Girls" have become thinner, what have become notably fatter are the wallets of those who provide "beauty-enhancing" products and services. In 1999, Canadians spent US$84 million on weight management programs; only six rich countries—all having populations much larger than Canada's—spent more (Ash, 2001: 51). Etcoff (1999: 191) reported that by the mid-1990s, thigh creams alone were "a ninety-million-dollar business, although there is no evidence that they really work." In 2005, more than $11 billion worldwide was spent on "anti-aging" beauty products, with sales "showing the greatest increase in any category of skin-care product" (APA Task Force, 2007: 30). More than 11 million Americans had cosmetic surgery in 2006 and, between 2000 and 2006, the annual rates of various cosmetic procedures soared, with breast augmentations increasing by 55 percent and Botox injections increasing by 449 percent (American Society of Plastic Surgeons, 2007). In Canada, more than 302 000 surgical and non-surgical "cosmetic enhancements" were performed in 2003—up 24.6 percent from 2002—with liposuction (to remove fat around the stomach, hips and thighs) procedures increasing by 16 percent from 2002 and breast augmentations rising by 17 percent (Plastic Surgery Statistics, 2008).

Although the vast majority of cosmetic-surgery consumers are women in both Canada (85.5 percent) and the United States (91 percent) (with the most common procedures obtained by women in both countries the same: liposuction and breast augmentation), the number of Canadian men opting for cosmetic surgery has increased in recent decades, with the most sought-after procedures being lipsosuction, rhinoplasty, and eye lifts). In addition, teenage females are reportedly seeking plastic surgery in record numbers, with nose alterations, ear pinnings, and breast implants the three most commonly performed cosmetic surgeries among this age group. Pearl and Weston (2003) found that two thirds of 16-year-old year females in a suburban American high school knew someone who had had cosmetic surgery and many desired it for themselves, with the most often mentioned procedures being liposuction and breast implants. These expressed desires are also increasingly acted upon: Between 2002 and 2007, the number of American girls 19 and under who received breast implants rose from 3872 to 10 505 (with an additional 1696 "breast lifts" performed on girls in this age group) (American Society of Plastic Surgeons, 2008).

In our culture, a self-fulfilling prophecy exists concerning the relationship between physical attractiveness and social success. It has been found that we impute more appealing personalities to good-looking people than to their less-beautiful peers. Physically attractive infants are more likely to be picked up, held, and embraced, and to have their needs tended to by both mothers and fathers (Etcoff, 1999; Karraker and Stern, 1990). Attractive adults are perceived as more sociable, poised, sophisticated, sexually warm, kind, and genuine (Zebrowitz et al., 2002). The inference of desirable internal qualities from external beauty is known as the **"what is beautiful is good" stereotype** (Dion et al., 1972; see also Ramsey and Langlois, 2002). Beauty operates as a master status; other desirable attributions and social rewards stem from it, a fact that reinforces our equation of beauty and success. Conformity to societal ideals of beauty thus becomes an important personal resource and source of power. Hosoda et al.'s meta analysis (2003) of experimental studies found clear evidence of the employment-related benefits of attractiveness for both women and men. However, women who fall short of ideal standards are described in more negative terms than comparably unattractive men (Snooks and Hall, 2002; Walcott et al., 2003). As well, in a reversal of the "beautiful is good" stereotype, women who belong to socially disapproved-of categories, such as feminists and lesbians, are often stereotyped as physically unattractive (Madson, 2000).

Our socially constructed standards of beauty valorize two qualities above all: youth and thinness. Entire industries invest billions of dollars annually to persuade consumers, especially women, to purchase products or services that promise to help them attain the elusive ideal of physical perfection. Increasing age and weight are linked by advertisers to lonely nights, loss of promotions and status, and social ridicule and scorn. The expression "putting on one's face" (North American slang for the application of makeup) is itself telling; it suggests that a woman's natural face is somehow incomplete on its own. Richardson (1988: 8; emphasis in original) observed that in Western culture, women "frequently report feeling undressed without mascara or lipstick. Although they are literally dressed in their clothing, they feel undressed as women; that is, the process of 'putting on' one's face is a behavior through which some women *achieve* their gender."

In a classic longitudinal study, Elder (1969) illustrated how physical attractiveness could facilitate women's upward mobility through marriage. Comparing the relative impact of physical attractiveness, education, and intelligence on social mobility, Elder found women's opportunities to be "embedded in physical qualities." Women whom a panel of observers rated physically attractive were more likely to be upwardly mobile through marriage than those rated as less attractive. Elder's study suggested that women's physical attractiveness was not merely a factor in sexual or other interpersonal relations, but also correlated with socioeconomic advancement. While increasing numbers of today's women can offer concrete resources to a potential marriage partner, a woman's physical appearance is still important to most men (Miller et al., 2000; Szymanski and Cash, 1995). Research has indicated that men are much more likely than women to openly stress the importance of physical attractiveness in both short- and long-term partners (Davis, 1990; England, 2004). When asked to rate the importance of good looks in a long-term partner on a scale from 3 (indispensable) to 0 (irrelevant or unimportant), American men rated this factor at 2.11 and women at 1.67; across 37 cultures, men on average rated the importance of good looks at 1.86 and women at 1.47 (Etcoff, 1999: 63).

Generally possessing greater status and power, men are less likely to have to use their physical attractiveness as a commodity or "bargaining tool" (Lindsey, 1997: 168) for success. For women, the perceived status of potential partners appears to be more important than physical appearance (Sweeney and Cancian, 2004; England, 2004). Townsend and Levy (1990) showed women pictures of men dressed in either a Burger King uniform and baseball cap or a shirt, tie, blazer, and Rolex watch. Some women viewed Tom and Harry clad in the Burger King regalia and Jim and Dan nattily attired, while others saw Tom and Harry nattily attired and Jim and Dan in Burger King finery. When the men's status was thus made graphically obvious, women's preferences were clear: they were unwilling to date, have sex with, or marry *any* of the men dressed as Burger King employees; however, they were willing to consider *all* of the men whose attire connoted income and success. In a second study, Townsend (1990) showed respondents pictures of men and women who ranged in attractiveness from "great looking" to below-average, and who were represented as training for either low-, medium-, or high-paying professions (waiter, teacher, doctor). When respondents were asked which of the individuals they might like to have a cup of coffee with, date, have sex with, or marry, women's first choice was for the best-looking man with the most money. However, "below him, average-looking or even unattractive doctors received the same ratings as very attractive teachers. Status compensated for looks. This was not true when men evaluated women. Unattractive women were not preferred, no matter what their status" (Etcoff, 1999: 79; see also Townsend, 1998, 1999).

Girls become acquainted early on with our society's emphasis on women's physical appearance through adult comments such as "My, how pretty you look today," "What a lovely dress," or "Doesn't your hair look cute!" (While adults may praise the curls and eyelashes of very small boys, such remarks tend to disappear entirely with the passage of time). Eventually, with the aid of friends and mass media, girls learn to see themselves as "beauty objects." By early adolescence, they also learn to evaluate themselves as "sexual objects" (Slater and Tiggemann, 2002). As a consequence of our relentless focus on female beauty and sexuality, most girls decide that they are inadequate in one way or another (Hall, 2004; Wilkins, 2004). Fredrickson et al. (1998) noted that when female university students were asked to enter a dressing room and try on either a swimsuit or a sweater, those that tried on a swimsuit, regardless of their body size, were more likely to report feelings of "disgust, distaste and revulsion." The authors speculate that, even though the women were alone in the dressing room, the presence of the mirror was sufficient for these women to imagine a critical viewer and, in turn, feel repulsive and ashamed (see also Clark and Tiggemann, 2007).

During girlhood, messages about the importance of physical appearance are reinforced in such activities as gymnastics, figure skating, and ballet, where, despite the necessary athletic ability, coordination, and desire, a girl's success or rejection ultimately hinges on having the "correct" body type. A girl who aspires to enter a prestigious dance school, such as the National Ballet School of Canada, may be distressed to learn, as early as age 6 or 7, that her body appearance is "wrong." Her bone structure may be "too heavy"; she may not possess the preferred delicate face and sharp, distinctive features; her feet may lack a "good arch." For aspiring ballerinas, thinness is as essential a prerequisite as it is for hopeful fashion models. Parents are often cautioned to "watch the baby fat" on 4-year-old daughters. In North American ballet, the "Balanchinian aesthetic" (the "look" demanded by choreographer George Balanchine) remains supreme: fluid, graceful, and super-thin. Mirrors surrounding ballet-studio walls (and figure-skating rinks) promote a preoccupation with the "perfect body." In her examination of exclusive ballet schools, Gordon (1983) observed that students competed with one another not only in terms of technical accomplishment but also in terms of thinness. Teachers amplified this obsessive concern by surprise "weigh-ins," during which they announced each student's weight before everyone in the class. Gains of as little as half a kilogram could prevent advancement into the main dance company (Gordon, 1983: 42). Diets and calories are discussed endlessly within the ballet-school world; from the age of 10 or 11, dancers often take up smoking as a means of weight control. It is, therefore, not surprising that eating disorders such as anorexia nervosa and bulimia are epidemic in the competitive worlds of ballet, gymnastics, and figure skating (Druzin, 2001; CAAWS, 2005). **Anorexia nervosa**, self-imposed starvation practised to achieve a low body weight, is characterized by a morbid fear of becoming fat and by a distorted body image; one is always "too fat" despite objective evidence to the contrary. **Bulimia nervosa** is a pattern of binge-eating and purging, most often by self-induced vomiting, as well as by using laxatives, purgatives, emetics, or diuretics. Unchecked, both anorexia and bulimia can lead to serious health problems and death (Gucciardi et al., 2003; Robert-McComb, 2001).

According to the American College of Sports Medicine, 62 percent of women competing in sports that emphasize appearance (e.g., gymnastics and figure skating) suffer from an eating disorder; 51 percent of the women's gymnastic programs that responded to the 1992 NCAA survey reported eating disorders among their athletes (Starkman, 1994: C3). Among those who aspire to international status, the quest for slimness may be particularly fierce. Druzin (2001: 252) reported that the spectacular success of the 4-foot 11-inch, 86-pound Nadia Comaneci at the 1976 Montreal Games "accelerated a trend in which female gymnasts became smaller and smaller." At the 1956 Melbourne Games, the average height and weight of American female gymnasts was 5 feet 4 inches and 124 pounds; at the 1992 Barcelona Games, it was 4 feet 9 inches and 83 pounds. At the 1992 Olympics, the average size of Canada's female gymnasts—5 feet 1 inch and 107.8 pounds—exceeded the international average of 4 feet 11 inches and 92.18 pounds. At the 2004 Athens Games, the international average for female gymnasts was 5 feet 3 inches and 102.3 pounds; one in five of these young women weighed 90 pounds or less, with the thinnest a meagre 68 pounds. The average height and weight of the American women's gymnastic team at the 2004 Athens Games was 4 feet 11 inches and 102 pounds; the Canadian team of women gymnasts was comparatively "robust" at an average 5 feet 1 inch and 113.6 pounds (calculated from "Athens 2004 Olympics," 2008). A study conducted at a Toronto hospital showed that female athletes are still at risk of eating disorders after they retire. In a sample of about 50 female patients hospitalized with eating disorders during the three-year study, more than half had been professional athletes (Starkman, 1997).

An emphasis upon thinness as critical to physical attractiveness is not, of course, unique to the gymnastics, figure-skating, and ballet subcultures. These worlds magnify a larger cultural view that "thin is beautiful, so the thinner you are, the more beautiful you must be" (Gordon, 1983: 148). Preschoolers prefer thin children over children of average or heavier-than-average weight (Powlishta et al., 1994; Hendy et al., 2001). Girls of 6 and 7 will position themselves in front of mirrors and bemoan the "fact" that they are "too fat" (Gershon et al., 2004; Thompson et al., 2003). Brumberg's (1997) examination of the diaries of American adolescent females over the past century reported that in earlier decades, girls conceptualized self-improvement in terms of becoming more well-mannered and improving in their studies; in more recent decades, however, "self-improvement" was understood to involve changes to the body and "almost exclusively" focused upon improving physical appearance.

Pipher (1994: 190), observing that the social consequences of deviating from the feminine ideal of slenderness may be especially traumatic for young women, claimed that "losing weight is probably the most common goal" of adolescent girls. She noted that approximately half of all teenage girls were currently on diets, while one in five suffered from an eating disorder. "Young women with eating disorders are not all that different from their peers," she remarked. "It's a matter of degree." (pp. 184–185). Recent research based on 2279 girls (ages 10 to 14) in grades 6 to 8 at 42 southern Ontario schools found that 10.5 percent had disturbed eating patterns. Almost one third (31 percent) of girls who were of healthy weight described themselves as "too fat"; 29 percent reported that they were currently dieting. Approximately 4 percent of the girls reported binge-eating regularly, and 1.5 percent admitted practising self-induced vomiting to lose weight (Picard, 2004). In our society, where dieting is a multi-billion-dollar industry and thinness the apex of the definition of female perfection, "Thin Is Perfect," "Thin Is Magic," and "[Only] Thin Is Acceptable" (Crook, 1991: 6–8).

Findings from three *Psychology Today* surveys of predominantly white, highly educated, financially comfortable, heterosexual respondents indicated that dissatisfaction with body weight has increased over the past 25 years. The proportion of women dissatisfied with their body weight rose from 48 percent in 1972, to 55 percent in 1985, to 66 percent in 1997. Rates for men increased from 35 percent to 41 percent to 52 percent over the same time period (Garner, 1997: 42). Fully 89 percent of women in the 1997 *Psychology Today* survey reported wanting to lose weight (Garner, 1997: 36). In contrast to women, men were more likely to want to "bulk up" to achieve a positive body image. Male body builders exemplify the "extreme manly silhouette," with shoulders approximately twice as wide as their waists (Arnold Schwarzenegger, five times Mr. Universe and now governor of California, won renown for his 57-inch chest, 31-inch waist, and roughly equivalent neck, arm, and calf measurements (at 18–20 inches) (Etcoff, 1999: 179; see also Grieve et al., 2006).

Research on male athletes and body builders has uncovered a "reverse form of anorexia nervosa," termed **muscle dysmorphia** and characterized by the distorted perception that one's body is weak and small when, in fact, it is large and muscular. "Just as the anorexic starves herself because of her fears of getting fat, the patient with muscle dysmorphia may abuse steroids and use food supplements for fear of not being big enough" (Etcoff, 1999: 179; see also Farquhar and Wasylkiw, 2007; Hobza et al., 2007; Mills and D'Alfonso, 2007). Regardless of whether the quest is to slim down or bulk up, it must be seen as extremely alarming that, according to the 1997 *Psychology Today* survey (Garner, 1997: 36) 24 percent of women and 17 percent of men reported that they would be willing to give up three years of their lives to achieve their desired weight goals; 15 percent of women and 11 percent of men reported being willing to give up five or more years.

Given the much greater importance of thinness to women's positive body image than to men's (Garner, 1997: 38; Grieve and Bonneau-Kaya, 2007), it is not surprising that approximately 85 to 97 percent of those suffering from anorexia/bulimia are female. The "typical sufferer" is a "white, middle-class woman under the age of 25" (Lips, 2005: 370). The "overwhelming preponderance of female patients confers on eating disorders the distinction of having the most lopsided sex ratio of any known to psychiatry" (Gordon, 1990: 32; see also Richter, 2001). Frank and Thomas (2003) attributed the greater prevalence of disordered eating patterns among females to socialization which teaches females to view themselves in relation to others, to avoid confrontation, and to conform to societal ideals of feminine beauty. They asked 236 undergraduate women, ages 18 to 24, to complete measures related to disturbed eating cognitions and behaviours, body image (bodily dissatisfaction, weight status, perceived importance of shape and weight), and relational variables shaped by differential gender socialization (externalized self-perceptions, self-silencing behaviours and attitudes). They found that externalized self-perceptions and the perceived importance of shape and weight predicted disturbed eating-related cognitions, while self-silencing predicted bulimic behaviours (see also Cash et al., 2004; Lieberman et al., 2001).

THE SCHOOL: FORMAL AND INFORMAL EDUCATION

In all industrialized nations, the school is of fundamental importance in socialization. As a result of Canadian compulsory-education laws and the wide availability of kindergarten, the vast majority of Canadian children ages 5 to 14 attend school. In 2004–2005, just under 5.3 million children were enrolled in Canadian elementary and secondary schools (Blouin and Courchesne, 2007). In its role as a socialization agency, school transmits our culture's values (Henslin and Nelson, 1996: 478–480), which are not gender-neutral. Abbott and Wallace (1990: 49–50) claimed that our education system socializes females into subordinate roles, encourages them to accept dominant ideologies of masculinity and femininity, and channels them into "gender-appropriate" subjects that lead to restricted opportunities in the labour market.

The educational system has come to take over certain functions formerly fulfilled by the family. In addition to providing skills once acquired within the home, school now performs a vital child-care role, especially for families in which a lone parent is, or both parents are, employed. By the time a child has completed secondary school, the public education system has provided almost 13 000 hours of supervised care (Mooney et al., 2004). As the number of years students remain in the education system has increased, so too has the importance of teachers as role models.

Role Models in School

When Martha Hamm Lewis was admitted to a New Brunswick teacher-training school in 1849, the principal cautioned her to "enter the classroom ten minutes before the male students, sit alone at the back of the room, always wear a veil, leave the classroom five minutes before the end of the lesson and leave the building without speaking to any of the young men" (MacLellan, 1972, in Schaefer et al., 1996: 282). Much has changed since then; today, women constitute the overwhelming majority of Canada's 310 000 full-time teachers. While in 1989–1990, 59 percent of Canada's teachers were women, the profession became even more female-dominated in the 1990s with women accounting for 64 percent of Canada's teachers in 1999–2000 (Statistics Canada, 2003b). In 2004–2005, women composed the clear majority of full-time educators in public elementary and secondary schools in all provinces. In Ontario, women accounted for 68.7 percent of teachers; in Saskatchewan,

65.6 percent; in Alberta, 67.2 percent; in B.C., 61.5 percent; in New Brunswick, 72.1 percent; and in Quebec, 71.1 percent (Statistics Canada, 2007c, 2006b). Though Canada's student population is become increasingly multicultural, this is less true of Canada's teachers. According to the Canadian Council on Social Development (1999), "[r]esearch suggests that teachers will continue to be mainly white, middle-aged women." In 2004–2005, a quarter of Canada's primary- and secondary-school educators were age 50 or over, up from 16 percent a decade earlier (Statistics Canada, 2007c, 2006b).

At the start of the new millennium, women represented the vast majority of teachers in Canada's elementary schools (83 percent, as of the 2001 census) (Frenette and Zeman, 2007: 12) and 54 percent of Canadian high school teachers (Frenette and Zeman, 2007: 6, 12). However, they represented only 47 percent of all principals and are more likely to occupy this position within elementary schools (53 percent) than at the secondary-school level (42 percent) (Statistics Canada, 2006b, 2006c).

Women's over-representation as primary-level educators and under-representation at higher levels is not unique to Canada. Renzetti and Curran (2003: 111) reported that in the United States, women represented 87 percent of elementary-school teachers and 90 percent of teacher's aides, but only 45 percent of principals and assistant principals and 40 percent of school administrators and officials. Concern that the "feminization" of primary schooling deprives boys of male role models has prompted several Western European countries to aggressively recruit male primary-school teachers (Skelton, 2003). In research on 56 developed and developing countries, Sivard (1995) found that in both 1980 and 1990, women made up the majority of teachers at the elementary level but less than half at the secondary level, only a quarter at the tertiary level, and a minority of school principals and departmental heads. She remarked that this segregation "can have done little to banish sex stereotypes. Women teachers are clustered in the lower grades and ranks, teach the softer subjects, and in equivalent positions average lower pay than men" (p. 21).

Within institutions of higher learning, this pattern of vertical segregation is equally apparent. While in 2005 women accounted for 54.7 percent of those who taught (full- or part-time) at Canada's colleges and for 40.5 percent of its university instructors, women accounted for less than half (48.2 percent) of full-time college faculty in that year (Lin, 2006). Similarly, men accounted for the majority of Canada's full-time university teachers in tenured positions (72 percent versus 28 percent), tenure-track positions (60 percent versus 40 percent), and non-tenure-track positions (55 percent versus 45 percent) (Drakich and Stewart, 2007: 7). During 2004–2005, women accounted for just 18.1 percent of Canada's full-time full professors (the highest rank), just over a third (34 percent) of full-time associate professors, and 41.3 percent of full-time assistant professors (Drakich and Stewart, 2007: 7). In 2005, "[o]ver half of all full-time female university professors taught in the humanities, education and health domains"—a pattern that "has existed for decades" (Lin, 2006). A 2004–2005 survey conducted by Karen Grant reported that women's growing presence within Canadian universities "has not translated into a surge in the number of women holding leadership positions"; women accounted for less than a third (30 percent) of administrative positions" (in Drakich and Stewart, 2007: 6). As well, research which examined the salaries of full-time Canadian professors between 1970 and 2001 concluded that, while the differences in male–female salaries has narrowed, women professors "still earn less on average than their male counterparts" (Statistics Canada, 2006d).

Community colleges are where women are most likely to be found in full-time, tenured positions (see Conway, 1993; DePalma, 1993). In most of these colleges, teachers are simply referred to as "Instructor." However, even within university settings, females are less likely than males to be addressed by the more prestigious "Professor." A study asking 243 undergraduates how they addressed their professors found that male professors were significantly more likely than females to be addressed by title. The study also found that when 120 students heard a transcript of a class in which either a male or female professor was addressed either by first name or title, they perceived those professors addressed by title as holding higher status, regardless of gender. However, female professors addressed by title were perceived to be less accessible. The researchers noted that an insistence on being addressed by title may reduce female professors' perceived accessibility, even as it enhances their status (Takiff et al., 2001; see also Arbuckle and Williams, 2003). Students may also respond differently to their professors, and to the content of their lectures, based on the professor's sex. Thus, Abel and Meltzer (2007) reported that, when asked to evaluate a lecture on gendered pay disparities in the workplace between men and women, undergraduates— regardless of their sex—rated the male professor and "his lecture" more positively and viewed it as less "sexist" than the female professor's identical lecture. Among male, but not female undergraduates, traditional and gender-stereotypical attitudes towards women were associated with more sexist ratings of the female professor.

The School System and Inclusivity

The need to eliminate sexism in the Canadian educational system was recognized over three decades ago in the 1970 Canadian Royal Commission on the Status of Women. Commission recommendations included "adoption of textbooks that portray both sexes in diversified roles and occupations; provision of career information about the broad field of occupational choice for girls; improved availability of sport programs for both sexes; development of educational programs to meet the special needs of rural and immigrant women and of Indian and Inuit girls and young women; and the continuing education of women with family responsibilities" (as cited in Mackie, 1991: 158). Gaskell et al. (1989/1995) noted a trend, since that time, towards a more integrated curriculum (e.g., industrial arts and cooking classes for both sexes). Many Canadian schools are implementing programs specifically designed to reduce gender stereotyping and streaming. For example, Jensen et al. (2003: 561) reported that a feminist intervention project in Canada which focused on girls' more equitable access to computers "created significant opportunities for girls to develop and experience new identities as technology 'experts' within their school." They noted that "[i]n addition to a significant increase in participants' own technological expertise, there was a marked shift in the ways in which they talked about and negotiated their own gender identities with teachers and other students." The girls who participated in the project became increasingly vocal about what they perceived to be inequitable practices within the school; in turn, this reportedly created, "within the otherwise resilient macroculture of the school, a more supportive climate for the advancement of gender equity well beyond the confines of its computer labs."

Despite such efforts, inclusivity is still a long way off. For example, although textbooks using gender-neutral language and images are being adopted, "[b]ecause of budget constraints, the shelf life of many textbooks is 15 to 20 years ... [and] [e]ven some of the new materials are disappointing" (Gaskell et al., 1989/1995: 114; see also Eichler, 2002; Gaskell and Taylor, 2003; Yanowitz and Weathers, 2004). Moreover, while teachers may claim not to be influenced by students' sex (or race, social class, or sexual orientation), their conduct may belie their words (Alvidrez and Weinstein, 1999; Anderson-Clark et al., 2008).

As Gomme (2004: 373) has noted, some research finds that "socioeconomic status and ethnicity influence teachers' placement of students in ability groups regardless of their past achievement or I.Q. scores," with the result that a disproportionate number of poor or minority-group students are "streamed" into vocational and low-level rather than academic programs. Research conducted by the Toronto Board of Education reported that while 1 in 5 black students was enrolled in a basic program, the ratio for white students was 1 in 10, and for Asians, 1 in 33 (Henry et al., 2002: 239). Livingstone (1999: 743) reported that "[m]any visible minorities, such as native people and Blacks, continue to have much greater school dropout rates." It has been suggested that the existing curriculum and ethnic composition of schools promote alienation among minority students and dampen academic aspirations (Aronson et al., 1998; Saunders et al., 2004). Various studies have suggested that teacher–student interactions may be impacted by race (Chavous et al., 2004; Oyserman et al., 2001) with white students most likely to receive positive reinforcement from their teachers for academic accomplishment and black students more likely to win praise for their social behaviour (AAUW, 1995). Lopez (2002) reported that despite assertions of gender-neutrality and colour-blindness, some teachers perceive young males (particularly from visible-minority groups) as threatening and as potential problem students, while regarding young females more sympathetically. Renzetti and Curran (2003: 108) observed that "[w]hen Black girls perform as well as White boys in school, teachers tend to attribute the Black girls' success to their effort, but at the same time assume that the White boys must not be working up to their full potential."

While race/ethnicity may have an independent effect on students' academic experience (Bankston and Caldas, 1997; Jencks and Phillips, 1998; Watts et al., 2002), the relationship between race/ethnicity and educational achievement is often a result of the association between race/ethnicity and socioeconomic status. Thus, Canadian research has found that while "[v]isible minority status does not adversely impact on academic performance in a systematic way ... Canadian Aboriginals are in a league of their own when it comes to disadvantage" (Gomme, 2004: 371). Although the education gap between the Aboriginal and non-Aboriginal populations decreased between 1996 and 2006, a gap remains. Consider, for example, that in 2006, 8 percent of Aboriginal people in Canada versus 23 percent of non-Aboriginal people had a university degree (Statistics Canada, 2007c).

Fisher (1999: 14) observed that although Canadian teachers, schools, and school boards are taking steps "to ensure that students receive a well-rounded education in an environment welcoming of diversity," gay and lesbian youth are still marginalized. He pointed out that sex-education classes may only consider heterosexual sexuality, and that while diversity-awareness classes may directly address sexism and racism, they often ignore homophobia and heterosexism. A history course may discuss Nazi anti-Semitism and the horrors of the Holocaust, but fail to mention that the symbol of the modern-day gay-rights' movement—the pink triangle—has its origins in the insignia that homosexuals were forced to wear by the Nazis, or that gays and lesbians were exterminated by the thousands in Nazi death camps. Prince (1996) (as cited in Fisher, 1999: 15) reported that the "[t]ypical administrative response ... [to the topic of homosexuality] is to either ignore it or to relegate it to health or sex education class; the implication here is that homosexuality is about sexual activity exclusively and does not involve people who are involved in history, the arts, science, and every other field of study." Although zero-tolerance policies demand that teachers address students' biased and discriminatory comments and behaviours, enforcement of such policies may be neither rigorous nor effective. As Hansman (1998) asserted, "[n]ame-calling rules are only effective when they are put into context within a fairness discussion in which gay/lesbian people are given their humanity and misperceptions challenged. Only then will tolerance be internalized and practiced beyond the classroom" (in Fisher, 1999: 16; see also Avery, 2002). To the extent that social-class bias, racism, sexism, and heterosexism/homophobia prevail, school—to paraphrase Mark Twain—may continue to interfere with an individual's ability to get an education.

Elementary School and Middle School

As children proceed through the school system, they typically become aware that certain subjects (English, art, music, history) are "girls' subjects" while others (math, physics, chemistry, computers) are "boys' subjects" (Kiefer and Sekaquaptewa, 2007; Smith et al., 2007; Steele et al., 2002). Researchers have found that parents evaluate their children's competencies in various areas on the basis of the child's sex (Eccles et al. 1999; 2000; Raty and Kasanen, 2007; Tenenbaum and Leaper, 2002). Stereotypes about one sex's "natural" superiority/inferiority in various areas may also be reinforced, both subtly and blatantly, by teachers (Cousins, 2007; Eccles et al., 2000; Gonzales et al., 2002; Maolin and Lianhua, 2006).

Various scholars have argued that girls' transition to school is easier because of the differential socialization they receive at home. Because girls are raised to be more compliant and sensitive to others' needs, they adapt more easily to the demands of teachers and peers in the classroom setting. Boys, raised to be more independent, assertive, and even aggressive at home, may have greater difficulty adjusting to teachers' demands for compliance and classmates' competing claims for attention. As such, they tend more often than girls to be disruptive in class (Pollack, 1998: 243) and to be identified earlier as having "learning" (frequently a euphemism for "behavioural") problems. Julien and Ertl (1999) reported that, when compared to same-age girls, 10- to 11-year-old boys are less apt to do their schoolwork neatly and carefully (61 percent versus 82 percent), more likely to get into numerous fights (35 percent versus 13 percent), more likely to demonstrate restlessness or hyperactivity (49 percent versus 23 percent) and less likely to show sympathy to a peer who has made a mistake (32 percent versus 49 percent). American data indicated that more than 70 percent of students identified as having learning disabilities (e.g., dyslexia) were male, as were about 75 percent of students identified as having serious emotional problems (Bushweller, 1995; Goldberg, 1999). Similarly, data from Statistics Canada's National Longitudinal Survey of Children and Youth reported that two thirds of children in special education were male and that males represented the "vast majority (83 percent) of children in special education on account of behavioural or emotional problems" (McMullin, 2004: 217). When rated by teachers in various academic subjects and overall, boys ranked "at the top of the class" significantly less often than girls in reading, writing, and overall ability; although they were somewhat more likely to be ranked at the top of the class in mathematics, the difference was minute (Julien and Ertl, 1999). Teachers were also more likely to perceive boys as more physically aggressive, hyperactive, and inattentive than girls—even though "when all behavioural scores were compared, no substantial behavioural differences were found" (McMullin, 2004: 217). Boys are also more likely to be punished for rowdy behaviour, to be "subject to more disciplinary actions in elementary school classrooms, and [to] receive lower marks than girls for deportment (e.g., conduct, effort, paying attention, completing assignments, classroom interest, cooperation, and compliance)" (Renzetti and Curran, 2003: 106; see also Clarke and Kiselica, 2001).

On the basis of participant-observation research in two elementary schools, Thorne (1992, 1993) reported that many cross-sexed interaction rituals, which she referred to as

borderwork, are based upon and reinforce differences and boundaries between girls and boys. She reported that various types of borderwork can be discerned in school play-grounds (e.g., "boys chase the girls") as well as in classrooms; teachers, for example, may pit boys against girls in spelling bees and math contests, assigning these groups such names as "Beastly Boys" and "Gossipy Girls." Although Thorne's research was conducted almost two decades ago in the United States, borderwork seems to persist, transcending national and grade boundaries (Gray and Leith, 2004; Tholander, 2002).

Teachers' attitudes about gender-appropriate behaviour may create self-fulfilling prophecies, fostering independence in boys and dependence in girls. Lips (1999: 112) observed that "many studies in the United States show that teachers, often without realiz-ing it, pay more attention to boys than to girls in the classroom, spend more time outside of class talking with boys than girls, and respond differently to boys' and girls' successes and failures" (see also Duffy et al., 2001; Hopf and Hatzichristou, 1999). While teachers praise boys for successful accomplishment of tasks, they are more likely to congratulate girls on their good behaviour or attractive appearance. Golombek and Fivush (1994) observed that by the time boys are 9 or 10 (grades 4–5), about 90 percent of the praise and a third of the criticism they receive from teachers relates to academic performance, as compared to less than 80 percent of the positive and two thirds of the negative feedback received by girls. The researchers concluded that "[f]rom this pattern of praise and criticism, boys may be learning that they are smart, even if not well behaved. Girls, on the other hand, are learning that they may not be very smart, but that they can get rewards by being 'good'" (in Renzetti and Curran, 2003: 108).

Research has also found that when boys are unable to perform a task, they are exhorted to try harder, assured that they can do it, and given precise instruction on how to tackle it (Sadker and Sadker, 1991). On the other hand, when girls do not succeed, teachers offer rel-atively little feedback and are more likely to perform the task for them than to encourage them to "keep trying." As Lips (1999: 113) remarked, "teachers seem to be guided by the idea that boys do not work hard enough, but that girls (always such well-behaved, good little workers) are already doing the best that they can." As a result, she suggested, girls may define themselves as being of limited ability and feel "that it is no use putting more effort into succeeding at the task." This perception may be reinforced by parental attitudes and behaviours (Bleeker and Jacobs, 2004; Oswald and Harvey, 2003). Casey and Martens (2007) found that, across all grade levels, parents purchase fewer math- and science-related items for their daughters than sons and that paternal attitudes impacted children's expressed interest in mathematics; when fathers expressed more traditional gender stereotypes, sons were apt to express more interest in mathematics and daughters less (in Lips, 2005: 20).

In a study investigating the family as a context for the gender typing of science achievement (Tenenbaum and Leaper, 2003), 52 adolescents of two age levels (mean ages = 11 and 13 years) participated with a parent in four structured teaching activities, including both science- and non-science-related tasks. Although there were no gender or grade-level differences in chil-dren's science-related grades, self-efficacy, or interest, parents were more likely to believe that science was less interesting and more difficult for daughters than for sons. Moreover, parents' beliefs significantly predicted children's interest and self-efficacy in science-related tasks.

Upon examining the style of teaching language used by parents during science tasks, researchers found that fathers tended to use more cognitively demanding speech with sons than with daughters. For high-achieving female students, such gender-differentiated response patterns may have serious consequences. Dweck et al. (1999) reported that when students were given a task too difficult to complete, it was the highest-achieving girls (i.e., the "A students") who evinced the greatest helplessness of any group, tried the fewest approaches, and gave up most quickly. The researchers speculated that girls who in elementary school win praise for being "smart" may come to see themselves as smarter than others. "Smartness" may become an important component of their self-identity. However, they may also assimilate the subtle message that performance is a measure of internal qualities (i.e., intelligence); thus, "[a] diet of early success and praise" may encourage the development of an **entity approach to abilities**—"the notion that each individual has a fixed amount of ability, which is revealed by her or his performance" (Lips, 2001: 332). Dweck's research suggests that high-achieving girls may think of intelligence as a "fixed entity," and, in consequence, perceive failure at any task as "proof" that they are "not smart" after all. Accordingly, they may be reluctant to engage in tasks that require them to master new skills or tackle new challenges, opting instead for "tasks they're sure they'll do well on (so they can keep on feeling intelligent)" (Dweck, 1999: 124). In high school, where "students that are challenge-seeking and persistent and can tolerate periods of confusion have the advantage," these girls may select "easier programs of study, avoiding advanced math and science, because these may feel too risky" (Dweck, 1999: 124). To forestall this situation, she wrote, "an emphasis on challenge, effort, and strategy is absolutely essential for girls.... They should be taught that challenges are exciting ... praised for taking on challenges and sticking with them. They must learn that the hallmark of intelligence is not immediate perfection, but rather the habit of embracing new tasks that stretch your skills and build your knowledge" (Dweck, 1999: 125). LaCampagne et al. (2007) observed that while a large percentage of American girls are now taking advanced placement mathematics courses at the high school level, the majority of extracurricular programs that are designed to enhance mathematics talents and skills are dominated by males "who may then continue their domination throughout their academic and career paths."

Not all social commentators agree that it is girls who are most disadvantaged by the current school system (Martino and Meyenn, 2001). Although a widely cited report commissioned by the American Association of University Women (AAUW, 1995), pointedly titled "How Schools Shortchange Girls," declared gender bias "a major problem at all levels of schooling" and asserted that "girls are plagued by sexual harassment, even at the grade school level, and neglected by sexist teachers," it actually concluded that socioeconomic status—not sex—was "the best predictor of both grades and test scores." Hoff-Sommers (2000: 61) has argued that boys, rather than girls, "are on the weak side of an education gender gap." She pointed out that in the United States, research has found the typical boy to be "a year and a half behind the typical girl in reading and writing"; what is more, boys received poorer grades, were less committed to school, had lower educational aspirations, read fewer books, were less likely to participate in rigorous academic programs, advanced placement programs, student government, honour societies, school newspapers, and debating clubs, and were less likely to go to college or university or to study abroad. Boys, she also noted, continued to "dominate dropout lists, failure lists, and learning-disability lists."

The findings of a recent Canadian study (Frenette and Zeman, 2007: 13) that drew upon Statistics Canada's Youth in Transition Survey (cohort A) paralleled these conclusions, with its authors noting that "[o]n the academic stage, boys trail behind girls on several fronts," including lower overall marks (see Figure 4.2), a greater likelihood of repeating a grade in school (9.9 percent of boys versus 6.5 percent of girls) and poorer performance on standardized reading tests. While almost a third of girls (30.1 percent) scored in the top quartile of the reading distribution, only a fifth (20.4 percent) of boys did so. In complementary

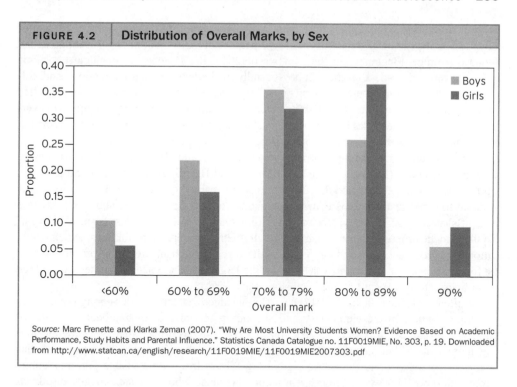

FIGURE 4.2 | Distribution of Overall Marks, by Sex

Source: Marc Frenette and Klarka Zeman (2007). "Why Are Most University Students Women? Evidence Based on Academic Performance, Study Habits and Parental Influence." Statistics Canada Catalogue no. 11F0019MIE, No. 303, p. 19. Downloaded from http://www.statcan.ca/english/research/11F0019MIE/11F0019MIE2007303.pdf

fashion, while almost a third (30.3 percent) scored in the bottom quartile of the reading distribution, only about a fifth (19.5 percent) of girls did so. Compared to girls, boys were more likely to report that they did no homework during an average week (8.5 percent of boys versus 2.5 percent of girls) and less likely to report spending at least 4 hours a week on homework (41.2 percent of girls versus 30.3 percent of boys). Moreover, it was noted that, compared to boys, girls were more likely to report that all of their friends planned to pursue academic education following graduation from high school (36.1 percent versus 26.0 percent) and less likely to report that few or none of their friends intended to do so (15.8 percent versus 24.4 percent). The authors of this study remarked that, in light of the influence that peers may have upon life plans, "boys are once again at a disadvantage" (Frenette and Zeman, 2007: 13). In addition, the study reported that "young men had lower expectations placed upon them. Although as many as 60% had parents who expected them to complete a university degree, this was well behind the 70% of young women in the same situation" (Statistics Canada, 2007d). The authors argued that these combined factors (i.e., lower overall school marks at age 15, poorer performance on standardized reading tests at age 15, lesser amounts of time spent doing homework, and lower parental expectations) account for over three quarters (76.8 percent) of the gender gap in the university participation rate of young Canadian men and women. In 2003, they observed, while "about one-quarter (26 percent) of 19-year-old Canadian men had attended university, almost two in five (39 percent) of 19-year-old Canadian women had done so" (Statistics Canada, 2007d).

After the 1999–2000 Ontario province-wide tests revealed a "cavernous gender gap," with the scores obtained by boys lagging behind those of girls in every board, the district school board in Durham, Ontario, in what is believed to be a Canadian first, directed all schools to develop formal plans for redressing the situation. In Durham, only 39 percent of boys had met provincial standards versus 59 percent of girls—numbers comparable to the Ontario average. Beginning in the summer of 2000, the Durham school board "trained kindergarten and grade 1 teachers in boy-friendly methods of reading instruction" and, following feedback from groups of young boys, "urged teachers to read aloud from books filled with action and adventure." Other strategies, which "mirror the attempt to help girls overcome perceived gender bias in previous years," included bringing male role models (particularly authors) into the classroom, purchasing books and magazines geared toward boys' interests, "scrutinizing reading materials for gender bias," and "finding new, less girl-centred teaching methods" (Fine, 2001; see also Martino and Berrill, 2003; Martino and Meyenn, 2002). Sax (2001) has claimed that over the past 50 years, the shift in the kindergarten curriculum to stress reading preparedness "has had the effect of emphasizing boys' weaknesses and girls' strengths." He urged "reclaim[ing] kindergarten" to make it "less harmful to boys." To this end, he proposed the establishment of alternative kindergartens for boys, which would emphasize group activities and non-verbal skills; a year at such an alternative program would be followed by a year's attendance at a regular kindergarten. If adopted, his strategy would see most boys entering grade 1 at age 7, most girls at age 6.

While McMullin (2004: 216–217) has acknowledged that "the gender-equity issue that is gaining attention in the elementary and secondary school system has been the relative 'underperformance' of boys in comparison to girls," she has argued that "lumping all boys together as 'at-risk' may confuse the issue, because it is more specifically boys from families with low socioeconomic status, Aboriginal boys, boys from some visible-minority ethnic groups, and boys for whom English is a second language who are systematically disadvantaged in the educational system." Pointing to research (Thiessen and Nickerson, 1999) which has found boys' mathematical and problem-solving skills to be "more variable" than girls' and which reveals significant differences among groups of boys in both academic performance and post-secondary participation, McMullin (2004: 217) emphasized the "complexity of identities and the enmeshment of the social relations of class, age, gender, and race and ethnicity, particularly when it comes to social privilege and disadvantage." Unfortunately, recent debate about school performance often has seemed to become mired in battles over which sex is most ill-served by the existing educational system.

Some educational reformers suggest that a return to single-sex schools would be advantageous to both males and females (Daniels et al., 2001; Foster et al., 2001; Martino and Meyenn, 2001; Martino and Berrill, 2003; Martino, 2001). Boys, they argue, would benefit from a "masculine environment" with male teachers serving as positive role models. Dee's (2005) American research, based on the National Educational Longitudinal Survey, suggested that boys and girls benefit from the presence of a same-sex teacher and are disadvantaged by an opposite-sex teacher. Thus, for example, it was estimated that having a male English teacher for simply one year would eradicate almost a third of the gender gap in reading performance among 13-year-olds by causing the performance of boys to improve and, simultaneously, harming the performance of girls. It similarly suggested a closing of the gendered science/mathematics gap could occur after a single year with a female science and/or mathematics instructor. Pollack (1998) contended that in co-educational classrooms, boys from late-elementary through middle school "inhibit" their scholastic performance in order to avoid being accused by other boys of "showing off" for girls; he suggested that all-boy environments would eliminate the teasing and lead to improved academic performance. It has also been suggested that girls placed in same-sex schools would be spared stereotyping by teachers and harassment by male peers. In what seems to be a compromise position, a limited number of Canadian schools have initiated "all-girl" math and science classes to encourage girls to pursue studies in non-traditional areas; the STEM (Science, Technology, English, Mathematics) program at O'Neill Collegiate and Vocational Institute in Oshawa, Ontario, is one example of this. White (1996) reported that girls attending these classes felt more comfortable asking questions and speaking out in class and found the same-sex environment to be "less distracting."

In some Canadian cities, all-girl schools, such as Toronto's Linden and Edmonton's Nellie McClung, have been established with the mandate of offering a "girl-centred school which reflects, responds to and promotes the experience, voice and development of young women in its policies, structures, programmes and curriculum" (Linden School, 2004). Linden School, "Canada's first self-avowedly 'woman-centred' school," (Cannon, 1995) advertises with the claim that its teachers "demonstrate a keen understanding of girls' psycho-social-physiological development, their learning styles, the role of power and relationships within the classroom, and the importance of equity and inclusivity within an educational setting—all of which are essential for girls to find and develop the sense of competence necessary for lifelong success" (Linden School, 2004). Its website boasts that "Linden has produced as many success stories as it has graduates," with 100 percent accepted into university. Like the majority of Canadian private schools, Linden is expensive: tuition for 2007–2008 was $13 350, plus charges for textbooks, field trips, performances, art supplies, work books, speakers, and photocopying. Notwithstanding, these same-sex schools do, assuredly, have their enthusiasts.

In their review of research comparing mixed- and single-sex schools, Hesse-Biber and Carter (2000: 99–100) concluded that girls fare better at girls-only schools: "[F]emale cognitive development is greater; female occupational aspirations and their ultimate attainment are increased; female self-confidence and self-esteem are magnified." They asserted that girls in single-sex schools "receive better treatment in the classroom" and are more likely "to be encouraged to explore—and to have access to—wider curriculum opportunities," as well as to have teachers show respect for their work. Several reasons are offered for these putative benefits: (1) a reduced emphasis on "youth culture," with its focus on "athletics, social life, physical attractiveness, heterosexual popularity, and negative attitudes toward academics"; (2) the forwarding of successful same-sex role models (inasmuch as the top students in all subjects are female); (3) reduced sex-bias in teacher–student interaction; and (4) "elimination of sex stereotypes in peer interaction (generally, cross-sex peer interaction in school involves male dominance, male leadership, and, often, sexual harassment)." However, not all research comparing same- and mixed-sex schools is uniformly glowing (Bornholt, 2001; Jackson and Smith, 2000; Katsurada and Sugihara, 2002).

Kaminer (1999: 6) asserted that although American research tends to suggest that a disproportionate number of high-achieving females attended women-only colleges, such research typically "collapses under scrutiny." She maintained that it is graduates' elite social-class background, rather than their education at single-sex schools, that largely accounts for their success. The results of the most recent international tests of reading, math, and science support this assertion: In 29 countries of the Organization for Economic Co-operation and Development, students from wealthier backgrounds outperformed students from poorer families. While students at private schools out-scored their public-school counterparts in every Canadian province and every country examined, the socioeconomic status of private-school students appears to be more pertinent to their superior performance than the type of school. Students attending private schools are more likely to have parents with greater education and income. Predictably, students with such parents also perform well in the public system (Sokoloff, 2001).

Kaminer (1999: 22) also argued that "the tendency of some affluent parents to choose single-sex schools is not evidence that single-sex education provides advantages to girls. The traditions of the rich, such as coming-out parties, are not necessarily progressive." Moreover, "[s]ince their inception in the nineteenth century, all-girls schools have fostered femininity along with feminism. They are models of equivocation, reinforcing regressive notions of sex difference at the same time that they educate women and help to facilitate their entry into the professions." Although, at their inception, single-sex schools allowed for women's education when co-education was not an option, the case for reinstating them today is dubious. She concluded: "A hundred and fifty years ago, when women were excluded from men's academies, women's academies did indeed represent affirmative action. Today a return to separate single-sex schools may hasten the revival of separate gender roles. Only as the sexes have become less separate have women become more free." Similarly, based on her review of the literature, Maggie Ford (AAUW, 1998) concluded that "separating by sex is not the solution to gender inequity in education. When elements of good education are present, girls and boys succeed" (see also Burrello et al., 2001; Dillabough, 2001).

Future Aspirations

Throughout childhood and adolescence, boys and girls are asked what they plan to be when they "grow up." The question arises out of our achievement-oriented mythos, according to which anyone can be and do whatever s/he wants or dreams of. While young children initially proffer wildly unattainable goals such as fictional heroes ("Superman," "Wonder Woman") or inanimate objects ("a fire truck," "Barbie"), more narrowly defined and plausible outcomes are announced in late childhood ("Supreme Court judge," "Miss Universe") and adolescence ("lawyer," "sociologist"). Gradually, children come to build their plans upon more accurate perceptions of personal and societal realities.

Traditional theories of vocational choice suggested that the process of occupational aspiration and selection unfolds in a series of stages from childhood into adulthood (Hyson, 2002). The individual was understood to make occupational choices in response to evolving internal capabilities and changing environmental opportunities and experiences. However, these androcentric theories tended to examine vocational (and educational) choice in isolation from issues of gender and parenthood (Moen and Orrange, 2002). More recent theorizing that has focused specifically upon women (e.g., Epstein, 1999, Moen, 2001, 2003) has expanded the scope of inquiry, examining vocational choice as part of a more comprehensive context of choices. For example, Larwood and Gutek (1987) maintained early on that women's vocational paths are affected by the following interdependent factors: career preparation, occupational and marital opportunities, whether or not to work after marriage, whether or not to work after childbirth, and the timing of entry or re-entry into the paid-work sphere. These paths depend upon decisions made at various points over the life course regarding education, paid work, marriage, and family (see also Taylor, 2000). Moen and Orrange (2002: 238–240) directed consideration of the relational nature of choice, emphasizing that "[b]ecause women are socialized to consider others' needs and desires in shaping their own lives, their choices tend to be more constrained than those of men." In addition, they stressed the necessity of considering the structural context in which choices are made, emphasizing that "in times of major social upheaval—such as those that we are currently experiencing in gender, work, and family roles—the *society within* (social-ization), and the *society without* (structuration) each signal multiple and contradictory mes-sages, making what might have been men's and women's taken-for-granted work and family career paths in more stable conditions now confusing, complicated and controversial" (Moen and Orrange, 2002: 253).

Hochschild (1990: 15–18) argued that a key element in a woman's vocational decisions is the **gender ideology** she develops during adolescence—her decisions about which sphere she will primarily *identify with* (i.e., home or work) and the *amount of power* she wants to have in her marriage. By implication, this gender ideology also encompasses a woman's attitudes about the primacy of marriage, childbearing, and childrearing in her future. Hochschild claimed that people develop *ideologies* (belief systems) by synthesizing rele-vant cultural ideals with personal feelings about their experiences thus far in life and with opportunities anticipated in the future. Adolescents evaluate their assets (as best they can) against the opportunities they perceive to be available to men or women similar to them-selves, and develop an ideology that makes sense of themselves in the world, both for now and for the foreseeable future. Hochschild's theory, consistent with a gender perspective, embodies the notion that adult women and men are products of the combined interaction of socialization, structural opportunities within a society, and active individual choice.

Hochschild (1990: 15–16) identified three major gender ideologies. **Traditionals** feel that a man should identify with his paid work and a woman with her domestic activities; they believe that a wife should have less power than a husband. **Egalitarians** want husband and wife to identify either with the same sphere or with the same balance of the two spheres; they believe that marital power should be shared. A *transitional* woman wants to identify with both work and home, but feels that her husband should base his identity on work; a *transitional* man is in favour of his wife working, but still expects her to identify primarily with home while he bases his identity on work and participates little at home. The marital-power expectations of transitionals would appear to more closely resemble those of traditionals than of egalitarians, although Hochschild is silent on this point.

Levinson (1996: 39–40) documented the continuing strength of an ideology he dubbed the **traditional marriage enterprise**, according to which femininity is identified with the domestic sphere, masculinity with the public (particularly the work) sphere, and authority in both spheres with men. He claimed that our society has evolved to the point where "it cannot allow women to remain full-time homemakers," and noted that for individual women, that option is becoming less feasible and less attractive (Levinson, 1996: 46). However, an internalized image of femininity that he calls the **Traditional Homemaker Figure** (Levinson, 1996: 49) still exerts a powerful influence over the wishes, dreams, and decision-making processes of North American women, from early adolescence onwards (Greene and DeBacker, 2004). An alternative image, the **Anti-Traditional Figure**, has recently emerged, representing a counterpoint ideology. This figure has a different mes-sage for women: "[Become] more independent, seek more in life than domesticity, acquire occupational skills, [and] defer having a family until you establish yourself as a responsible, competent adult, able to take care of yourself, especially financially" (Levinson, 1996: 55). The anti-traditional woman will invest less of herself and her feminine identity in marriage and family life, seeking additional satisfactions and a meaningful sense of identity in the extradomestic sphere. Levinson argued that for most women in contempo-rary North America, the relative power exerted by these two internalized images waxes and wanes over the course of adolescent and adult life. The Anti-Traditional Figure's appeal appears to be vitiated somewhat by the lack of a consistently positive image of the successful, happy career woman. One of the respondents in Levinson's sample expressed her negative associations:

> My image was that she had to be cold-hearted ... grasping ... cruel ... embittered, frustrated, wishing she had done anything just to be sitting by the fireside knitting in the evening with children. The fear of success isn't the fear of succeeding per se but the fear of what consequences it would have.... total personal disaster. (Levinson, 1996: 54)

Such an image represents marital and family happiness as incompatible with career success. Adler et al. (1992/1995: 136) claimed that today's elementary-school-age girls observe that their career-oriented mothers (employed, for the most part, in traditional "women's jobs") still hold secondary status within the family constellation. This perception may inhibit a young female's aspirations.

Hochschild (1990: 17–18) suggested that once a personal gender ideology crystallizes, the individual creates a **gender strategy** by combining cognitions and deeply felt emotions about gender into a plan of action for achieving her or his goals. The gender strategy guides an active self-socialization process designed to reify a person's chosen ideology. Larwood and Gutek (1987) noted that a young person who does not expect to be self-supporting in later life is less likely to absorb socialization lessons derivable from observation of the paid-work world or from parents' discussion of their jobs, etc. In contrast, a young person who anticipates being self-supporting will attend more carefully to whatever lessons are implicit or explicit in any socialization relevant to the paid-work sphere.

Boys and young adolescent males begin making decisions about their educational and occupational futures without directly considering future marital or familial contingencies. The traditional marriage enterprise (Levinson, 1996) and the traditional or transitional (Hochschild, 1990) ideologies dictate that men not only identify most strongly with the occupational sphere, but also take care of their families, primarily by performing the provider role. Consequently, while most males expect to eventually marry and support a family, they do not expect marital and family life to impinge significantly upon their educational or career development; thus, plans for schooling and work are constructed independently of concerns about marriage and family (DiBenedetto and Tittle, 1990). In other words, men's educational aspirations are directly linked only to their career aspirations (Levinson, 1996: 77). In contrast, girls and adolescent women have traditionally made their educational and vocational choices contingent on anticipated marital and family considerations. School, paid work, marriage, and family are all planned interdependently (DiBenedetto and Tittle, 1990; Greene and DeBacker, 2004).

Research on adolescents during the 1950s, 1960s, and 1970s (e.g., Clausen, 1972: 474, 507; Lowenthal et al., 1975: 16) found that a majority of females claimed that they could not make long-range career plans because they intended to get married; the shape and direction of their lives after marriage would depend primarily upon the needs, wants, and plans of husbands and children. These women's educational aspirations, therefore, were linked primarily to their marital aspirations (Levinson, 1996: 77). More recently, the Michigan Study of Adolescent Life Transitions (MSALT) reported that while female students affirmed the priority of family over career and the desirability of a job in which it would be possible to help others, male students placed more value on fame, high income, and challenging employment, preferably involving math and computers (Jozefowicz et al., 1993). Females were also more likely to mention both family and career in their qualitative descriptions of what a day in their lives might be like at age 25.

Research based on university and college students reflects the orientations of a select group of young adults who have already made the decision to defer both marriage/family life and full-time participation in the labour market. The women interviewed by Machung (1989), while intending to work full time, acknowledged that their career plans would likely be interrupted by the needs and plans of husbands and children. Both male and female students in the Spade and Reese (1991/1995) study expected both work and family life to play important roles in their lives. However, men were much more likely than women to expect that their spouses would not work at some point in the future. Women were much more likely to emphasize their family roles (e.g., housework, marriage and kinship work, child care), and men tended to feel that this was as it should be. When undergraduates (821 women and 535 men) were asked to select the sequence of life-events they preferred, 53 percent of the women but only 6 percent of the men selected "graduation, full-time work, marriage, children, stop working at least until youngest child is in school, then pursue a full-time job" (Schroder et al., 1993). Clearly, more women than men anticipated having to balance paid work and family life (see also Cunningham et al., 2005; Deutsch et al., 2007). Depending on the relative strength of her internal Traditional or Anti-Traditional figures, a woman's educational and occupational aspirations will take different paths. If a girl elects to follow a traditional path, she will be more sensitive to perceived male expectations of women and wives. If she perceives that men disapprove of women who are too intelligent, too competitive, or too ambitious, a girl may "dummy down," become less competitive, or choose a more traditional set of educational and vocational aspirations (Brown and Pinel, 2003; Inzlicht and Ben-Zeev, 2003; Oyserman et al., 2004).

Wilson (1996: 121) noted that young women in Canada generally did not avail themselves of the same types of educational opportunities as men. Adolescent women's avoidance of math and science courses tends to restrict their career opportunities. Sells (1980) referred to mathematics as a "critical filter" for the occupational choices of young people, particularly women. Without a substantial grounding in mathematics, one is virtually excluded from professional careers in medicine, engineering, architecture, accounting, business administration, technology, and the sciences—all highly prestigious, remunerative, and rapidly growing fields (Steele et al., 2002). Computer literacy and proficiency have also come to function as career filters.

Various studies have found that from elementary school onwards, girls rate themselves as having more social and English ability but less athletic and math ability than their male peers (e.g., Eccles et al., 1999; Evans et al., 2002; Kiefer and Sekaquaptewa, 2007; Thomas et al., 2006). Girls are much less likely than boys to feel that math is important, useful, and enjoyable (Eccles and Harold, 1992; Smith et al., 2007; Steele, 2003), an attitude which impairs their occupational possibilities (Breakwell et al., 2003; Eccles et al., 1999). Ziegler and Heller (2000) gave 379 8th-grade boys and girls questionnaires assessing their attitudes towards chemistry. They found that even before receiving instruction in the subject, academically talented girls had significantly lower levels of self-confidence in relation to the subject than boys did (see also Orenstein, 2001). Research also suggests that **stereotype threat**—"awareness that one may be judged by or may self-fulfill negative stereotypes about one's groups" (Lips: 2005: 44)—can have dramatic negative effects on women's math performance (Gonzales et al., 2002; McIntyre et al., 2003; Nosek et al., 2002). Spencer et al. (1999) asked women and men who had demonstrated high math abilities to complete a difficult math test; one group was told that the test results generally revealed gender differences (high stereotype threat); the other was told that the results of the test did not tend to vary by gender. Although the tests used in the two situations were identical, women's performance in the first situation was substantially poorer than men's; in the second situation, it was the same. An individual under stereotype threat may withdraw from the struggle: Rather than battle negative stereotypes and the continued "evaluative threat as one attempts to perform well," one may elect to "disengage or disidentify with the domain ... move away from that domain as a basis for identity or self-esteem" (Lips, 2005: 45–46). Thus, Keller's (2002) study of 75 high school students reported that blatant stereotype threat produced "increased self-handicapping tendencies in women, which in turn led to significantly impaired math performance." The researchers suggest that self-handicapping may represent a "strategic means to cope with obtrusive negative performance expectations" (see also Heilman et al., 2004; Josephs et al., 2003; Keller and Dauenheimer, 2002; Schmader et al., 2004).

Education and training choices depend partially on real and perceived opportunities for employment. As Wilson noted (1996: 120–124), employers have tended to "stream" female applicants into certain jobs on the basis of gender stereotypes. The younger generation of females, noting the occupational distribution of older women, often make educational and vocational selections congruent with existing (as it were, "static") labour market conditions; this may perpetuate a vicious cycle. Breaking the cycle, as the gender perspective would suggest, will require interventions addressing both structural and socialization issues. Further desegregation of the occupational structure will provide a greater range of occupational roles to which young females can aspire. In-school interventions to influence vocational attitudes of adolescent girls and boys may include bringing in female role models in non-traditional careers, revising textbooks and course offerings, and providing vocational counselling. It is crucial to note that programs of change directed only at women will provide at best partial solutions. Only as the attitudes, ideologies, and life-strategies of men as well as women evolve can meaningful change occur in the lives of both.

Post-secondary Education in Canada

Between the end of World War II and 1970, enrolment in Canadian elementary and secondary schools increased significantly, largely as a function of our baby boom. While fertility rates can largely account for exploding enrolment at universities and community colleges during the late 1960s and 1970s, the continuing growth in enrolment since that time is largely attributable to our **credential society** (Collins, 1979)—a society in which diplomas and degrees determine eligibility for jobs, even in cases where those credentials are not directly relevant to the work being performed.

Since the 1970s, one of the most notable changes that has occurred in Canada has been the increase in the number of women obtaining university degrees. Among Canadians over the age of 25, there were four times as many women university graduates in 1996 as in 1971, compared to only twice as many men (Health Canada, 1999). In 1996, women in their 20s were more likely to be college and university graduates than were men of the same age. "In 1991, almost three million [Canadian] women aged 25 to 64, or 41% of the total, had a trade, college, or university education. By 2001, this had jumped to almost 53%" (Statistics Canada, 2003d: 9).

While in 1964–1965 less than one third (31 percent) of full-time undergraduates were female, parity was achieved in 1988. During the 2004–2005 academic year, women accounted for more than half (58 percent) of full-time undergraduates and almost half (49 percent) of graduate students (Drakich and Stewart, 2007: 6). In 2005, women accounted for 61.4 percent of those awarded bachelor's and first professional degrees, 51.8 percent of Master's degree recipients, and 42.9 percent of those who earned doctorates (Statistics Canada, 2006e). However, an examination of the fields in which these men and women received their qualifications is revealing. In 2005, women received the majority of degrees, diplomas, and certificates awarded in Canada in education (75 percent); visual/performing arts and communications technologies (68 percent); social/behavioural sciences and law (66 percent); the humanities (64 percent); physical/life sciences and technologies (58 percent); business, management, and public administration (54 percent); and agriculture, natural resources, and conservation (55 percent). However, they received only the minority of university qualifications awarded in mathematics, computer and information sciences (29 percent) and architecture, engineering and related technologies (24 percent) (Statistics Canada, 2008f). Even though increasing numbers of women are achieving doctoral degrees in non-traditional areas, they remain significantly underrepresented in the fields of engineering and the applied sciences and in mathematics and the physical sciences (Statistics Canada, 2007e).

Gomme (2004: 366) emphasized three reasons why the fields in which men and women receive degrees must be recognized as significant:

> First, some programs offer greater certainty of labour-force entry opportunities. Social sciences, fine art, and humanities, fields in which women are overrepresented, are less directly marketable than others such as engineering and applied science where men predominate. Second, training in some fields leads to jobs with higher levels of remuneration. Engineering and computer science, where women are underrepresented, are examples. Third, sex segregation in the world of work means there is a narrower range of jobs for which women can compete.... Heightened competition in any occupational domain acts to depress wages. Thus, sex segregation in education helps produce and reinforce a sex-segregated labour market and its associated social and economic disadvantages for women.

These issues will be explored at greater length in Chapter 6.

Key Terms

agencies of socialization

anorexia nervosa

anticipatory socialization

Anti-Traditional Figure

borderwork

bulimia nervosa

credential society

egalitarian

egalitarian gender ideology

entity approach to abilities

family

family of orientation

feminization of poverty

gender ideology

gender socialization

gender strategy

hidden curriculum

historical time

hot potato effect

human development

individual life time

mass media

muscle dysmorphia

peer gender subcultures

peer group

primacy effect

primary group

relational aggression

school

social time

socialization

stereotype threat

streaming

stroller effect

traditional gender ideology

Traditional Homemaker Figure

traditional marriage enterprise

transitional gender ideology

"what is beautiful is good" stereotype

Chapter Summary

1. A number of groups, or *agencies of socialization*, are involved in the life-long process of socialization. Each of the four major agencies in our society (the family, the school, the peer group, and the mass media) provides socialization for a number of gender statuses and roles.

2. *Gender socialization* refers to the process whereby an individual acquires a gender identity and gendered ways of acting, thinking, and feeling. In Canada, the current focal themes of female socialization are sociability, popularity, and attractiveness; in contrast, male socialization emphasizes independence, emotional control, and conquest.

3. While socialization practices within the family are affected by family structure, social class, and ethnicity, the vast majority of empirical studies to date have been conducted with white, heterosexual, middle-class, two-parent families. While making generalizations on the basis of such research is difficult, they offer a starting point from which to explore important elements in the social construction of gender.

4. Gender socialization begins at birth upon the announcement of a baby's genital sex. Gender differentiation may be evidenced in the names and nicknames parents give their children, in the toys, room decorations, and clothing they provide, and in their interactions with their children.

5. Same-sex peer groups, which provide an important source of reference and identification throughout childhood and adolescence, reinforce the dominant themes of masculinity and femininity.

6. Gender differences in play activity are carried through and strongly reinforced within organized sports. Sports in general and competitive body-contact sports in particular have traditionally been more strongly linked to desirable images of masculinity than of femininity. Within traditionally feminine sports, the emphasis placed on youth, physical attractiveness, and extreme thinness is noteworthy.

7. While most Canadian schools are no longer segregated by sex, beliefs concerning gender-appropriate roles for girls and boys may create subtly different psychological and social environments. Despite various programs specifically designed to reduce gender stereotyping and streaming, women remain overrepresented in such fields as education and nursing and underrepresented in the traditionally masculine fields of engineering, the applied sciences, and math.

8. *Gender strategies* allow personal *gender ideologies* to be implemented in a practical way, combining thoughts and deeply felt emotions about gender into a plan of action. The strategy chosen will guide an active self-socialization process designed to reify an individual's ideology.

CHAPTER 5

Symbolic Representations of Gender

For some, the June 1993 election that saw Kim Campbell become Conservative Party leader and later, by ascension, Canada's first female prime minister, offered *prima facie* evidence of the equality of Canadian men and women. Yet an examination of newspaper and magazine coverage of these events reveals some curious discrepancies that might challenge that view. Why, one might ask, was Campbell routinely referred to as "Kim" while male candidates were referred to by their surnames? Why did the media emphasize that Campbell was a "divorcee" or direct attention to her "mesmerizing" eye colour (green), but fail to provide such riveting details in their reports on her male competitors? Why did the media widely disseminate a studio photograph in which Campbell posed in a lawyer's robe (but, apparently, nothing else), gush over her "exquisite shoulders" and "overt, flaunting sexuality" (*London Sunday Times*), and dub her "the new Canadian covergirl" (*National Enquirer*)—yet neglect to assess the photogenic qualities and sex appeal of the men campaigning against her? Why was the question of whether Campbell was a "pro-feminist" or an "anti-feminist" a continuing focus of media speculation and debate?

Flash forward to the spring 2004 campaign of Belinda Stronach for leadership of the Conservative Party and similar questions might be asked. Often referred to in the media as "Magna Spice" or "Barbie," Stronach was almost invariably described with two adjectives: "blond" and "attractive." A *Calgary Herald* reporter covering her campaign began his report with the admission that "[o]ne thought immediately crossed my mind when I saw Belinda Stronach's picture on the front page of the *Herald*—she's hot!" (in Campbell, 2004). Not to be outdone, the *Toronto Sun* gave front-page coverage to Stronach's campaign—featuring such headlines as "Blonde Ambition" and "Better than Viagra." Attention was also focused upon Stronach's marital status—"single mother, twice divorced"; a *Globe and Mail* columnist dryly styled her the "young mother who would be prime minister." Not infrequently, journalists made Stronach's marital status—rather than her party platform—the central focus of coverage; in "Blonde Date: Who Should Get Belinda's Rose?" a *Toronto Sun* journalist helpfully offered up a list of eligible bachelors for Stronach's consideration. A fourth descriptor applied to Stronach was "heiress" (or, even more pointedly, "daddy's little rich girl")—typically accompanied by dismissive assessments of her candidacy: "Paris Hilton has as good a chance of becoming prime minister as she has," huffed a *Globe and Mail* columnist. Why, in coverage of Stronach's campaign, were the predominant themes sexuality, marital/parental status, and dependence? And why did media preoccupation with these issues not extend to male candidates as well?

LANGUAGE

Your first reaction to the questions posed above might be to demur at their undue emphasis on "mere words." However, in the 1930s, Edward Sapir and Benjamin Whorf hypothesized that the language we speak predisposes us to make particular interpretations of reality (Sapir, 1949; Whorf, 1956). A "strong version" of their theory postulates that language directly causes certain behaviour in members of a culture; a "moderate" version proposes that "culture and language are intertwined such that the meanings people ascribe to language affect their realities, their self-concepts, and their world view" (Parks and Robertson, 2000: 416). Although the strong version of this theory of *linguistic reflexivity* has not received empirical support (Bing, 1992),

163

there is evidence to support the moderate version and to suggest, for example, that labelling a politician as a "feminist" or an "anti-feminist" shapes our understanding of her (Eagly, 2007; Eagly and Karau, 2002; Smith, 1999). Similarly, directing attention to a female (but not a male) candidate's eye or hair colour or marital status directs our attention away from her platform or abilities (Edwards, 2007 Messner et al., 1993; Herrnson et al., 2003). Thus, when a newspaper serves up a list of a candidate's potential suitors, the implicit message is that we need not take her seriously and that her "blond ambition" would, perhaps, be more properly directed towards the pursuit of a spouse. As Campbell (2004: 2) observed, "How many 'single fathers' are in politics at the moment? Wouldn't know. It never seems to factor in the coverage.... If daddy gives his son a job, money, or connections, it means he learned from the best—a chip off the old block."

The implications of the **Sapir-Whorf hypothesis**, which alerts us to how extensively language and other symbolic representations affect us, are far-reaching. Since most socialization occurs on a verbal level, language is the "inescapable socializer" (Richardson, 1988: 16). Language thus serves as the principal means whereby a society disseminates its ideology on gender. With the acquisition of language, the basis is established for the development of gender schema, identified by Bem (1994) as an integral part of encoding and gendering our social and physical worlds and developing actions, feelings, and thoughts about those worlds. Our images of women and men are an outcome of processes of evaluation and judgment that distinguish appropriate behaviours from inappropriate, acceptable from unacceptable (see also Diekman et al., 2002; Mendoza-Denton et al., 2001; Schmader et al., 2007). These processes and images are all shaped and conveyed by our system of language. A change in our conception of reality involves a change in our language (Liben et al., 2002; Merritt and Kok, 1995; Marchant et al., 2007). Parks and Robertson (1998: 455) defined sexist language as "words, phrases, and expressions that unnecessarily differentiate between females and males *or* exclude, trivialize, or diminish either gender." Encoded in our vocabularies are beliefs about women and men that preserve our patriarchal or "masculinist" (Burstyn, 1999: 9–10) heritage. Sometimes our attitudes and beliefs are articulated explicitly; most often they are expressed subtly and indirectly via the words we use in everyday speech. Individuals may consciously reject sexism, yet remain unaware of the extent to which they convey sexist sentiments in their words. Although sexist language can have deleterious effects on both men and women, empirical research finds that "the preponderance of negative results accrue to women" (Parks and Robertson, 2000: 415). Basow (1986: 129) suggested that our language promotes inequalities between men and women through the processes of *ignoring*, *stereotyping*, and *deprecating*.

Ignoring

To ignore is to exclude, to render invisible. The major difficulty in attempting to grasp hold of the concept of **ignoring** as a mechanism of sexism is that we are trying to focus upon that which is, by definition, not present. The only way to become aware of what is invisible is to concentrate first upon what is visible, then try to discern what is missing. One of the most common linguistic techniques for ignoring women involves the use in English of the so-called generic noun *man* and the related pronouns *he, him,* and *his*. As a generic noun, "man" is used as a synonym for "human being" and intended to include the entire human race. Read the following paragraph and judge whether you feel included or excluded:

> A legislator is often described by men of letters as a "man of the people." Attempting to become a man for all seasons, he hires pollsters to act as middlemen and find out what the common man thinks. As a statesman, he relies on them to devote their manpower and manhours to posing questions, man-to-man, to the man in the street. Pollsters solicit the views of the thinking man, the Renaissance man, the business man, and the working man, as well as the self-made man. To stay in office in a system of one man–one vote, as every schoolboy knows, he must satisfy John Q. Public. In cases where "Big Brother" threatens the interests of the little man, the legislator (as a man of good will who loves his fellow man) speaks up for the forgotten man. Being an elected official is a man-size job, and he is eager to prove himself man enough for the task; as a man of action and a man of his word, he is concerned to demonstrate his commitment to his countrymen, mankind, and the brotherhood of man; after all, all men are created equal.

A generic language is an *exclusionary language*. As Basow (1992) noted, use of the supposedly generic term has the effect of making men the visible norm and women the excluded exception. "Man" (in the sense of "human") becomes interchangeable with "biological male" and woman becomes invisible; this has been documented in empirical research with students from grade 1 through post-secondary education, and with respondents outside of the educational system (see Kortenhaus and Demarest, 1993; Miller, 1994; William, 2001; Turner-Bowker, 1996). Miller and Swift (1993: 73) suggested that upon reading statements such as "man is the highest form of life on earth," a young boy may feel proud and think "wow!" The response of a young girl, however, may be "Who? Does that mean me, too?" Research finds that pseudogeneric terms (e.g., mankind), pronouns (e.g., he) and job titles (e.g., mailman) not only imply the superiority of the masculine over the feminine, but also generate masculine images, cause confusion, and affect the self-concepts of women and men (Gastil, 1990; McConnell and Fazio, 1996; Parks and Robertson, 2000: 416). However, various pseudogeneric terms, such as "fellow" and "brother," are interwoven into our everyday vocabulary. The introductory lyrics of our national anthem, for example, proclaim: "O Canada, our home and native land/True patriot love in all thy sons command." Only "sons" are commanded to be "true patriots." These words might be taken to suggest that women can neither be patriots nor "stand on guard" for our country (Ontario Women's Directorate, 1992: 1). Some women feel that the very fact that the word "woman" contains the generic "man" is itself an instance of ignoring; to them, the "wo" prefix implies that woman is nothing more than a modified man. In an attempt to create a separatist language that supports and promotes a distinct and independent existence, the designations "womon" or "wommon" (singular form), "wimmin" (plural form), or the all-purpose term "womyn" have been suggested as alternatives.

Smith (1985) suggested that woman's historical exclusion from the public sphere resulted in the production of both a language and a culture that effectively ignores her existence. Nilsen (1993) noted that "Who's Who" dictionaries have traditionally listed famous women under their husbands' surnames, even when they were not famous under that name (e.g. Charlotte Brontë as "Mrs. Arthur B. Nicholls"). She commented that the dictionaries' editors seem to have believed that it "was almost indecent to let a respectable woman's name march unaccompanied across the pages of a dictionary" (Nilsen, 1993: 162). Although the practice is changing with the passing of older generations, it is still customary to subsume a woman's identity under that of her husband. It is not uncommon to hear a woman introduced as, for example, "Mrs. Paul Martin"—leaving us to assume that the

Paul Martin with the breasts is the missus. Over the course of the twentieth century, women's total "symbolic annihilation" (Tuchman, 1978) has slowly been replaced by only a partial annihilation (e.g., "Mrs. Sheila Martin").

Married women's retention of their birth surnames is a relatively recent phenomenon which has become more prevalent in Canada since the second wave of the women's movement. European folkways (and sometimes laws) dictated that women drop their family surname upon marriage and adopt their husband's. As pointed out in Box 5.1, the European

---

BOX 5.1

Project Surname: Names and Inuit Culture

In Inuit culture, names ensure the continuity of the lives of individuals, families, and communities. Names are passed from one generation to the next without regard for gender. The same namesake can live through several new people, male or female. The ties are so strong that until puberty, kinship terms, dress and behaviour often follow the namesake relationship, rather than biological sex or conventional gender identification.

> No child is only a child. If I give my grandfather's *atiq* [soul-name], to my baby daughter, she *is* my grandfather. I will call her *ataatassiaq*, grandfather. She is entitled to call me grandson....

"Discovered" by seventeenth-century explorers, the Canadian Arctic has known traders, governments, and European religion since the early 1900s. Since then, visitors have continued to interfere with the ways Inuit define and experience genders and families, and name themselves and their land.... The various missionaries and public officials gave religious or bureaucratic explanations for changing Inuit names. They sought to baptize and bring Inuit into the faith (whichever faith it happened to be). Or they found the absence of surnames "confusing" and the Inuktitut names difficult to pronounce and impossible to accurately record....

Census-taking was filled with inconsistencies and absurdities. Lists followed official standards for "the Canadian family," with no attempt to understand Inuit family structures or traditions. Such understanding would have made it clear that much of the census structure was irrelevant for Inuit. Some of the "standard" categories have no parallels in Inuit culture. There are no titles such as "Dr.," "Mr.," or "Ms." There are no gender-specific pronouns—an "Inuk" is a male or female person. Children who were full family members according to Inuit practice were designated "boarders," "step," or "adopted" by census-takers.... The concept of "head of family" or "head of household," essential to government documentation, is alien. In an Inuit extended family, the "father/husband" is not necessarily the central or most powerful person.... Inuit families feature close ties, grounded in the intricate, intimate naming system. The distinction between a "real" and a "common-law" spouse is meaningful only in non-Inuit terms, for southern law....

In western tradition, a women's renaming at marriage represents the transfer of "property" (the woman) from father to husband. Inuit tradition does not include this kind of marriage tie or reidentification of the woman through the husband's identity.... Inuit in the Northwest Territories were given surnames out of a misguided idea this would give them more power by making them like other Canadians.... In a culture without gender-specific naming, titles, or other status designations, surnaming was absurd. Despite assurances that all was "voluntary," many people had no say in their renaming. In fact, many of them were not even present for the program in which they presumably participated....

Women were renamed in their absence, by men. One Elder remembered her confusion when her husband came home and announced their new name. It made no sense. Women didn't take their husbands' names, yet suddenly, both she and her husband had his father's last name. The new name was not just a confusion or an inconvenience, it undercut the relationship between name, name avoidance, and respect in the family. In many communities, a woman may not speak the name of her husband's father. To follow traditional practice, a woman surnamed for her husband's family would now have to avoid speaking her own last name.

Source: Abridged from Valerie Alia, "Inuit Women and the Politics of Naming in Nunavut," *Canadian Woman Studies/les cahiers de la femme, 14* (4), 1994: 11-14.

name-change custom symbolized the exchange of property (a woman) from the home of her father and his family to that of her husband and his family. While a series of legal changes in the nineteenth and early twentieth centuries eventually granted women the status of independent beings, the tradition of adopting a husband's surname helps perpetuate the ignoring of women's independent existence. In most Canadian provinces and territories, name-changing upon marriage is a social custom, not a legal requirement. Since 1981, women in Quebec have been legally required to retain their birth names for legal documentation purposes throughout their entire lifetimes. A woman in Quebec may use whatever name she chooses for social purposes, but in legal matters such as wills, contracts, or lawsuits, she must be identified by the name registered for her at birth.

From a sociological perspective, it is unfortunate that departments of vital statistics do not tally the frequency with which Canadian women either retain or change their surnames upon marriage. Observation suggests that the vast majority of Canadian women still adopt their husband's surname, thus symbolically ignoring their own (or, at least their father's) family history. Some unknown but smaller number choose either to retain their birth surname, to retain it as a penultimate surname (placing their husband's surname last), or to hyphenate their birth and husband's surnames to form a new composite (inviting the question of what happens when the future daughter of Mr. and Mrs. Silverstein-Utumchandandi marries the son of Mr. and Mrs. Zawadowski-Papadopoulis?). Men rarely, if ever, drop their family surname and adopt the surname of their wife. Few also incorporate their wife's surname as a new "middle" name. The vast majority of men appear to simply carry on post-marriage without any symbolic changes to their identity.

Kaplan and Bernays (1997: 139) reported that women who retain their birth names "tend to be achievers and individualists who have already established their names professionally, or wish to, and see no reason to surrender them." They observed that the likelihood of a woman retaining her birth name is positively correlated with her level of education, and noted that according to a 1994 survey, "[f]ewer than 5 percent of wives who do not have a college education use something other than their husband's name, compared with 15 percent of those with bachelor's degrees and more than 20 percent of those with postgraduate degrees" (in Kaplan and Bernays, 1997: 139). Nevertheless, Suter (2004: 58) observed that "only an estimated 10 percent of U.S. women have departed from tradition." When 153 young female intro-psychology students (overwhelmingly middle- or upper-middle class, heterosexual, and unmarried) were asked to choose one of seven options for their own surnames after marriage and one of six options for their future children's, approximately 60 percent indicated that they would take their husband's name and almost 80 percent said that they expected their children to have their husband's name. Similar percentages have been reported in other studies (e.g., Johnson and Scheuble, 2002; see also Table 5.1).

When asked to explain the reasons for their choice, those who had opted to take a husband's surname typically stressed the role of tradition ("Traditionally, that's the way it is supposed to be") and the importance of symbolic bonding ("The same last name would symbolize this 'two becoming one' idea" [Twenge, 1997: 424]). Those who opted to do otherwise emphasized their desire to retain a sense of personal identity ("It makes no sense to give up my identity just because I marry. It is sexist, archaic and illogical" [p. 424]) or the importance of retaining ties to their ethnic culture ("I want to keep my last name because it reflects my culture" [p. 424]). In accounting for why their children would be given their husband's surname, respondents were most likely to stress that it was "traditional" to do so and that it would avoid confusion. A common sentiment among those who wished their children

TABLE 5.1	Young Women's Preferred Name Choice at Marriage (N=153)
Choices for Own Last Name	**%**
Take husband's name	59.5
Keep own name for all purposes	9.8
Use my name for professional purposes, husband's for social	13.7
Hyphenate my name, but not expect him to hyphenate his	9.2
Hyphenate my name, and he will hyphenate his	3.9
Husband and I will choose new name and both use	0.7
Other	3.3
Choices for Children's Last Name	**%**
Husband's name	79.6
My name	0.7
Hyphenated name	12.1
Daughters will have my name, sons my husband's	0.7
New name	0.7
Other	3.9

Source: Jean M. Twenge. 1997. "'Mrs. His Name': Women's Preferences for Married Names." *Psychology of Women Quarterly*, 21: Table 1, p. 422.

to use a hyphenated combination was that "[t]heir names should be a combination of our last names, since that is what they are, a combination of both of us" (p. 425).

In Canada, it may be noted, the legal surname of children depends on the laws of the particular province in which the children are born. In Ontario, for example, if both parents consent, a child can be given the surname of either parent, or a hyphenated or combined surname. If the parents disagree about what the child's surname should be, the child must be given a surname that consists of both parent's surnames, hyphenated or combined in alphabetical order. Nevertheless, research indicates that "[i]n western societies, patronymic naming conventions (whereby children are given their father's surname) still form the dominant pattern of choice of surnames for children born to heterosexual couples, particularly when the couple is married" (Almack, 2005: 239; see also Johnson and Scheuble, 2002). Lundberg et al. (2007: 83) found that, among unmarried parents, boys are approximately 20 percent more likely to be given their fathers' last name than are girls and that this effect is even larger when the child is the first child born to its mother. Among same-sex families, the patronymic naming pattern is less slavishly adhered to. Suter et al. (2008: 30) found that, in an attempt to symbolically construct a legitimate parental identity for the non-biological parent in lesbian families, the surnames given to children could incorporate the last names of both the biological and non-biological mother (see also Bergen et al., 2006). Almack's (2005) research on 20 lesbian couples reported considerable variation in the choice of a child's surname. While some couples opted to use the birth mother's surname or the social mother's surname or a combination of both mothers' names as the child's surname, others adopted the surname of one of the mothers as the "family surname" for all family members or, alternatively, elected to adopt an alternative surname for all family members which was different from either of the mothers' surnames.

Although research on name-changing in same-sex unions is sparse, Suter and Oswald's (2003) investigation of last name practices in committed lesbian relationships found that name-changing was viewed as a strategy for securing external recognition and acceptance of family status by outsiders; retaining birth names was identified as a strategy designed to preserve each partner's individual identity. Among this small sample of 16 respondents, age 25 to 52 years of age, name-change was not associated with having had a commitment ceremony. However, "name-changing was ritualized on other occasions, special to the individual couple, such as an anniversary, a partner's birthday, or an intimate dinner party among friends" (p. 71).

A study of 258 American-born students attending a small college in the Midwest United States (Scheuble and Johnson, 1993) reported that while the majority of women (91.8 percent) felt that it was all right for a married woman to keep her "maiden" name, only a slight majority (57 percent) of the men agreed. When asked to select (from a limited list) acceptable reasons for a woman to retain her maiden name, both men and women chose (and similarly ranked) the same top three: a woman's being in a profession, her liking her maiden name, and her desire to keep her family name alive. Nevertheless, the vast majority of women in this study (about 80 percent) planned to symbolically merge their identity with their husband's. It may be, as Kaplan and Bernays (1997: 138) argued, that "[t]he woman who refuses to submit to the conventional practice of taking her husband's name risks having her loyalties questioned and, except in relatively sophisticated communities, being viewed as a subversive." It is evident that in terms of marital naming, language reform remains controversial.

Recent efforts to develop an inclusive language are based on the recognition of how our language currently either excludes women or gives unequal prominence to men. Thus, when the intention is to refer to the entirety of the human species, speakers are reminded that words such as "humankind," "humanity," or the "human race" all "count women in." Similarly, job titles should reflect the work role rather than the gender of the person assumed to occupy it (e.g., fire fighter versus fireman, worker versus workman, police officer versus policeman, postal worker versus postman). There have been some notable successes in the establishment of gender-inclusive language: In 1978, the federal Manpower and Immigration and Unemployment Commission was renamed Employment and Immigration Canada; in 1981, feminists were successful in having the word "person" replace the generic "man" within the *Canadian Charter of Rights and Freedoms*; and in 1986, the National Museum of Man was renamed the National Museum of Civilization (later, the Canadian Museum of Civilization). Yet resistance remains. A study of undergraduates found that more than half (53 percent) opposed some aspects of inclusive language, while 21 percent resisted inclusive language in any form (Parks and Robertson, 1998). It should be noted, however, that at least one study has demonstrated that people's attitudes towards sexist language are not always linked to their use of it (Rubin et al., 1994).

There are, to be sure, difficulties in constructing a neutral yet inclusive language. First of all, apart from the unacceptable "it," the English language lacks a gender-neutral pronoun. Although there are a variety of ways to avoid the use of gendered pronouns, such as combining the masculine and feminine pronouns ("he/she" or "s/he"), using the first person (e.g., I, me, we, ours), or using the plural form (they, them, their) (Kennison and Trofe, 2003; Shears, 1985), some find such strategies unwieldy and unappealing. There are additional difficulties; over two decades ago, Kramarae (1980: 64) found evidence that some supposedly "gender-neutral" words had already become gendered. She reported, for example, that when the term "chairperson" was used, it was likely to be in reference to a woman, while the term "chairman" continued in use to refer to a man. Moreover, for some, the campaign for inclusive language is simply a misguided "assault" upon the English language in the name of "political correctness."

Stereotyping

Language is the principal means by which stereotypes are conveyed and maintained. Words highlight boundaries between women and men by selectively drawing attention to supposed gender characteristics. Some words or phrases do this directly; consider, for example, the expression "woman driver," the import of which is that one sole fact accounts for the (objectionable) driving behaviour of the person behind the wheel: her femaleness. Thus women are **stereotyped** as egregious drivers and singled out as unique among all other varieties; men drivers are not, since we never hear specific reference to them—even though recent Canadian research has found that male drivers are more likely than female drivers to engage in acts of "road rage" and driver violence (Hennessy and Wiesenthal, 2001). The phrase "career girl" makes a twofold distinction: first, as one never hears of career "boys," the patronizing term "girl" deprecates females who pursue a career as being—unlike their male counterparts—childlike in some way; second, the phrase distinguishes the referent from both all men and all other types of women. This phrase reflects our society's attitude that some women are atypical from the norm and must be identified with a special label.

Other words or phrases are more complex and reverberate throughout many dimensions of gendered social life. Graham (1977: 1) asserted that the word "woman" has "been defined as something less than a lady and something more than a girl." In the English language, the words "lady" and "woman" are neither semantic nor symbolic equivalents. The word "lady" is classist in its origins, and, like "gentlewoman" (and "gentleman"), originally referred to a person who was "well-bred" and thus deemed of superior moral and/or social character. While the word "lady" is no longer used strictly to signify a woman's social rank, it remains an evaluative term that measures conformity to a narrow definition of femininity and to its stereotypical, stylized enactments. Some examples may help illuminate this word's connotations: The admonition to "act like a lady" suggests that ladylike behaviour is of a much higher standard than normally observed by women. Imagine your reaction were you to be asked to join the Ladies Liberation Movement. The term "little old lady" conveys fragility and childlike dependency yet refinement. "Lady of the evening" is a glamorous euphemism for "prostitute." The condescending term "little lady," when addressed to an adult woman, infantilizes her, suggesting that she is being viewed as a child.

For men, what our society considers most important is professional/occupational status and financial success; for women, physical attractiveness and marriage. This distinction is reinforced in language that defines men by occupational role or title, and women in terms of appearance and/or relationships; an example might be "Dr. Smith and his lovely wife Stella" (Foreit et al., 1980). We are given no clue as to Dr. Smith's appearance; it is significant that descriptors such as "balding, fat, and knock-kneed" or "a Brad Pitt look-alike" seem unnecessary. The achieved occupational status of "Dr."—not his loveliness—is considered primary to the definition of the male Smith (identified formally by his surname). Stella (identified familiarly by her given name) is apparently most to be admired for getting married and looking lovely.

The *Toronto Star* announced the 1992 space flight of Canadian astronaut Dr. Roberta Bondar with the headlines "Canadian in space does 'housework'" and "Bondar spends hour tidying up shuttle" (in Ontario Women's Directorate, 1992: 9). On April 6, 1997, radio commentators congratulating Canada's national team for winning the Women's World Hockey Championship referred to them as the "Maple Leafettes" and described Lesley Reddon and Danielle Dubé as having looked "fetching" in goal. The professional attainments of these women were clearly of secondary importance. Bondar's housekeeping skills were, apparently, so impressive that she was dispatched by Molly Maid to tidy up the space shuttle. Reddon's and Dubé's singular accomplishment appears to have been that they—unlike any male goaltenders anywhere in the world who helped their team to a championship—looked "fetching." The depiction of these women should not be considered anomalous; sports-reporting commonly emphasizes the appearance of female athletes—and the strength and power of males (e.g., "he's a Laker; she's a 'looker'" [Knight and Giuliano, 2001; Duncan and Messner, 2000; Tuggle and Owen, 1999]). "In effect, the media tend to represent female athletes as women first (i.e., through focusing on their hair, nails, clothing, and attractiveness) and athletes second; however, male athletes for the most part are portrayed solely in terms of their athleticism" (Knight and Giuliano, 2001: 219). An analysis of broadcast commentary on the 2000 men's and women's National Collegiate Athletic Association Final Four Tournament basketball championship revealed that male athletic performance was categorically evaluated in terms of physicality and athleticism, while female athletes were categorically evaluated in terms of positive consonance, personality, looks and appearance, and background. Men's games generated more lines of broadcast commentary than women's; comments made about women's performance were often gendered (e.g., "Man, that was a pretty shot!") (Billings et al., 2002). Eastman and Billings's (2001) examination of 1156 descriptors in sportscaster commentary during 66 televised men's and women's college basketball games noted that while black men players tended to be stereotyped as naturally athletic, quick, and powerful, white men were touted for their hard work, effort, and mental skills; the same racial stereotypes appeared in the commentary about women basketball players.

One may also consider that while the term "Mr." does not denote a man's marital status, the titles "Miss," "Mrs.," and "Ms." announce important symbolic boundaries that signify different socially meaningful "types" of women. The transformative wedding ceremony that traditionally turned a woman into a wife—but left the man unchanged ("I now pronounce you man and wife")—also granted her the right (and often the obligation) to adopt the prefix "Mrs."—a title she was expected to retain even upon widowhood. In this way, our society made an important linguistic division between never-married and at-least-once-married women.

The title "Ms." arose in an attempt to avoid or cease defining and differentiating women through their relationships to men. "Ms." "established 'women' as a linguistic category in its own right.... [and] symbolically elevated women to personhood from their previous commodity status in the marriage market where 'Miss' meant 'for sale,' and 'Mrs.' meant 'sold'" (Davy, 1978: 47; see also Fuertes-Olivera, 2007). However, Stewart et al. (1990) noted that only since 1987 would major North American newspapers such as the *New York Times* print "Ms." if a woman expressed this as her preference. Nor do all women prefer to be thus identified. Some resist the title "Ms.," believing that it invites inferences of "feminism"—unwelcome among many young women today (Rosell and Hartman, 2001; Williams and Wittig, 1997)—or signifies being uninterested in (or unappealing to) men. The adoption of "Ms." can be consequential: Research has indicated that women distinguished by the titles "Miss" or "Mrs." are perceived as more likeable, stronger in expressive traits (e.g., tact, gentleness), and lower in instrumental traits (e.g., leadership, competence) than identically described women differentiated only by the title "Ms." (Dion and Cota, 1991; Malcolmson and Sinclair, 2007). "Ms." women tend to be categorized as unlikeable, tough, roughshod, strong, independent women capable of making their own way, who either do not need or do not want relationships with men. Apparently, marital-status semantics stereotype women one way or another.

Marital-status stereotypes linger even after divorce; a formerly married woman is still customarily referred to as "Mrs.," especially if she has children (Ehrlich and King, 1993). In general, divorced women in Canada can resume their maiden names without formal court order. However, although it may rankle to be tied, through the conventions of language, to her former spouse, a woman may feel that resuming her birth name will create a linguistic discontinuity between herself and her children ("My name is Mary Smith and these are my children, Harvey and Myrtle Brown"). If she is the custodial parent, a woman may apply to court to formally change her child's surname; the court, however, will generally require the consent of the child's father. Even though non-custodial parents do not have absolute right to forbid surname changes, and Canadian courts have allowed such changes to be made over a non-custodial parent's objections (especially in cases where the non-custodial parent has not contributed to the child's support or has disappeared from the child's life), the anticipation of legal wrangles may discourage some women. A woman may also opt to retain her married name and title in order to avoid raising speculations as to her child's legitimacy. All of these factors make it likely that divorced women will continue to use their married surnames and the title "Mrs." prefixed to it. This fact, combined with the fact that divorced men are more likely to remarry, may result in multiple "Mrs. Nelsons," all linked by a common surname to a singular "Mr. Nelson."

Stereotyping in language also favours an active/passive dichotomization of men and women. Men are more often described in the active voice ("he seduced her; "he swept her off her feet"; "he took her hand in marriage") and women in the passive voice ("she was wed on June 4 in a candlelit ceremony"; "she was swept off her feet"; "she got laid"). The phrase "lost one's virginity," seldom used in reference to a male, conveys the impression of there being something accidental or unintentional about the process—as if a woman had inadvertently misplaced her virginity among the debris at the bottom of her handbag ("I could swear I had it with me this morning when I left the house"). The phrase also suggests that while a woman may be chided for an act of omission (i.e., failing to keep her virginity in a safe place), she is not to be faulted for a deliberate act of commission (i.e., setting out purposefully to rid herself of her virginity). Thus the phrase simultaneously conveys the ideas that virginity for females is important and should be safeguarded lest it be lost, and, secondly, that women who do lose it should not be held fully culpable. The man is understood to be the active agent, the conqueror, as it were, who has prevailed in the amorous struggle over the woman and "won" her virginity.

Basow (1992: 142) offered another example of the active/passive distinction by noting that "when a newspaper reports, 'Blonde found murdered,' the reader knows that the corpse is a female (men rarely are referred to solely by their hair color)." Such headlines implicitly suggest that victimization is somehow congruent with femininity. In contrast, the subject of a headline reading "Teenager Arrested for Arson" is understood to be male. The construction of passive female (victim) and active male (offender) is evident. Exceptions to the passivity-stereotyping of women are "Lady Luck" or "Dame Fortune"—however, luck's feminine characterization may be based less upon woman's power than on her stereotypical unpredictability and emotional volatility. In a study of media reports of violent offences by young women in Britain, Muncer et al. (2001) noted that the press has branded these women "laddettes" or "yobettes," suggesting that women who contravene cultural expectations of female passivity may become symbolically transsexed.

A solution to the problem of linguistic gender stereotyping requires the breaking down of stereotypes by (1) exposing their limited generalizeability, and (2) using gender-neutral terms to emphasize actions/thoughts/feelings rather than the gender of the subject. As has been the case with inclusive language, the search for a non-stereotyped language has yielded some attempts that ridicule and trivialize the process. Hurricanes are renamed "himmicanes," humans become "hufems," testimony becomes "ovarimony," seminal becomes "ovarian," a seminar is turned into an "ovular," and the classic phallocentric distinction between the "hard" (masculine) and "soft" (feminine) sciences becomes a vaginocentric distinction between the "dry" and "wet" sciences. Politically correct dictionaries and fairy tales swap one set of stereotypes for another and, somewhat depressingly, manage to become international best sellers.

Nevertheless, some hopeful signs have appeared. An analysis of obituaries of business leaders in daily newspapers in 1974, 1980, and 1986 found that the qualities ascribed to females and males were highly dissimilar. Success-related and task-oriented descriptions (e.g., intelligent, knowledgeable, experienced, outstanding instructors, enviable entrepreneurial spirit) were consistently used in reference to male managers, while females were described in terms such as "venerable" and "likeable" (Kirchler, 1992). However, an update of this research (Rodher et al., 2001), examining similar obituaries published in 1974, 1980, 1986, 1992, and 1998, found that while male stereotypes have remained relatively constant, female images have changed considerably. Whereas in the 1970s, deceased female leaders were praised for qualities of warmth, loyalty, and expressiveness, in the 1990s, the terms of approbation tended to be much more obviously work-related (e.g., "committed," "professional"). And while in male leaders' obituaries, task-oriented terms remained a constant through the years, the 1990s revealed a new emphasis on such person-oriented attributes as "humane" and "open-minded." The authors suggested that as the roles of men and women approach one another, descriptors based on rigid stereotypes may become less common (see also Eagly and Karau, 2002).

Deprecating

Deprecating occurs when a term in our language carries a derogatory connotation. How often have you heard "woman driver" used in a congratulatory fashion? Deprecations can be explicit; for example, "all men are pigs" or "dumb broad." Most often, however, deprecations are expressed in an indirect form that subtly promotes sexism. The disparaging term "sissy," a diminutive form of the word "sister," not only condemns males for being unmasculine, but also implies that sisters are of a lesser status than brothers. The prioritizing of male over female in such word-pairs as "man (or husband) and wife," "Mr. and Mrs.," "males and females," "brothers and sisters," "king and queen," "Adam and Eve," "boys and girls" reflects the historical primacy of men in our society (Miller, 1994: 268). Henley et al. (1985: 171) remarked that "this order is not coincidental, but was urged in the sixteenth century as the proper way of putting the worthier party first." Exceptions to this pattern (e.g., "ladies and gentlemen") are relatively few. Amare's (2007) recent examination of seven university-affiliated online grammar guides found that all seven of these websites revealed linguistic sexism, with the positioning of men first and the male-heavy male-to-female ratio as far more common problems than the use of the generic "he" and "man."

Stouffer (1949) reported that during World War II, officers used accusations of femininity to motivate soldiers. To exhibit inferior courage or endurance was to risk the charge of not being a man: "Whatsa matter, bud—got lace on your drawers?" A generation later, similar jibes were still being used to prepare American soldiers to fight in Vietnam: drill sergeants would mock troops, sneering, "Can't hack it, little girls?" (Eisenhart, 1975). Gilham (1989) found that the worst insult to a male recruit in the United States Marines is likening his performance to a woman's. Foley (1997) noted that football coaches accuse boys who don't play well of "wearing skirts"; Stockard and Johnson (1980), observing basketball, reported that boys who missed a basket were called a "woman." Coaches in all sports at all age levels regularly attempt to motivate male players with a sarcastic "come on, ladies." The slang term "wuss" (a polite form of "puss," as in "pussy") is always used to demote a male to female status. All of this name-calling reflects the generalized devaluation of women in our society: "There is no comparable phenomenon among women, for young girls do not insult each other by calling each other 'man'" (Stockard and Johnson, 1980: 12).

Deprecation also occurs through the intentional or unintentional use of words that condescend to or infantilize adult women (e.g., "Now dear/little lady/girls, you're overreacting"; "c'mon, baby"; "women and children will be evacuated first"). Secretaries of all ages are commonly referred to as the "girls in the office." Over the past 30 years, efforts have been made to educate people to use the term "woman" instead of "girl" when referring to adult females. However, a particular usage of "girl" has entered white culture from the black culture, where it has long been acceptable; the term "girl" has been rehabilitated for special use (as in the encouraging "You go, girl!" and congratulatory "Looking good, girl!") (Emerson, 2002; Suitor and Pillemer, 2007; Vogels, 2002).

Deprecatory words often identify women with animals (Nelson and Robinson, 1994: 29). Whether a woman is praised as a "chick," "fox," or "Mother Bear," or condemned as a "bitch," "bowser," "dog," "pig," "sow," "heifer," "old hen," or "old nag," the imagery is all animal-reductionist. A man dominated by his wife is described as "henpecked" or "pussy-whipped." A woman may also be likened to food items (sugar, honey, tomato, hot tamale, sweetie pie, cupcake)—the implication being that she "looks good enough to eat" or is a "toothsome morsel." However complimentary at first, such endearments reduce women to commodities intended for male consumption and sustenance. They also remind women that they have only a short shelf life before turning stale and unappealing.

The verbs and adjectives applied to women and men often have different connotations. For example, women perceived as powerful are often deprecated with words connoting sexual threat to men (ballbreaker, castrator, emasculator). No comparable words are used to deprecate men. A "breast beater" conjures up an archetypal Tarzan, mighty and virile, while "stud-muffin" and "hunk" evoke sexual prowess and desirability. Women conversing together are described as "gossiping," "chattering," "nattering," "cackling away," or engaging in "girl talk." Tebbutt (1995) reported that historically, women's gossiping or "self-indulgent gadding" was believed to promote a preoccupation with "sexual conduct and scandal" and lead to "lax sexual behaviour among women." Lochrie (1999) observed that during the Middle Ages, gossip was considered a female vice of extraordinary power, affording women voyeuristic and even erotic pleasure; as such, it was strongly condemned and numbered among the Seven Deadly Sins. She wrote, "Just as women's bodies and sexuality were commonly associated with secrecy (and deception) ... so their speech was conceived as occult and transgressive" (in Vogels, 2002: 15). Today, gossip is rarely considered sinful; however, referring to women's talk as "gossip" not only pre-emptively discounts its importance for female bonding (Crnkowich, 1990; Regnier-Bohler, 1993) but trivializes its content. In contrast, men talking among themselves are more likely to be "brainstorming"; consider the semantic divide between a (male) "power lunch" and a (female) "hen party." Even the phrase "pissing contests" (occasionally used to describe male conversations characterized by exhibitions of power) pays subtle positive homage to male competitiveness.

The positive–negative dichotomy between characterizations of men and women pervades the language: He is described as "persistent," while she "nags"; he is "cautious," she is "hesitant"; he is "choosy," she is "picky"; he is "forceful," she is "bitchy" and "opinionated"; his "character lines" make his face look "distinguished"; she is "wrinkled" and has "let herself go"; he is a "carefree bachelor" or "playboy," while she is an "old maid/spinster," or has "been around" and become "used goods." Adams and Ware (1996) reported that our culture has many more terms to describe stupid/superficial women (e.g., bimbo, ditz, airhead, dumb blond, Valley girl) than stupid/superficial men. Generally, the more terms a culture or subculture creates to refer to something, the more significant and prevalent that phenomenon is thought to be.

Sex-inflected suffixes, such as "-ess" (e.g., waitress, actress, stewardess), "-(en)ne" (e.g., comedienne, heroine) and "-ette" (e.g., jockette, suffragette, Leafette), distinguish the occupational descriptions of women. Such suffixes imply diminution—as though, despite the equivalency of male and female versions of these roles, a woman's performance of the role were of lesser value than a man's. An inclusive language either replaces "masculine" and "feminine" forms with gender-neutral terms (e.g., server, flight attendant, comic) or "de-sexes" the noun, making it neutral (thus an "actor" is simply any person, male or female, who acts).

Even when confronted with the most blatant forms of **linguistic sexism** (the devaluation of members of one sex through language), people may fail to object. Research finds that, in general, individuals are far more likely to contemplate than to actually assertively confront those whose conduct/comments suggest prejudice and/or discrimination. For example, Hyers (2007) reports that when women were asked to keep diaries that recorded the incidents (if any) of sexism, heterosexism, anti-Semitism, and racism they encountered and how they responded, participants were far more likely to contemplate making an assertive response than to actually make one (75 percent versus 40 percent). In a two-part study, Swimm and Hyers (1999) asked a sample of women how they would react to a sexist remark, then placed them in a situation in which they were exposed to one in order to observe whether their responses were consistent with their earlier assertions. The majority of women had indicated that they would confront a sexist speaker; yet, when faced with such a speaker, most did not do so. The overwhelming majority of women recalled feeling upset at the sexist remark and not liking the speaker; however, although they described themselves as angry and resentful, they did not challenge the speaker for fear of being seen in a negative light. An experiment conducted by Dodd et al. (2001) suggested that the fear of being viewed negatively—at least by men—is somewhat justified. A sample of undergraduates (60 women and 60 men) were asked to read a transcript of a fictive conversation between friends (two men and one woman), in which one of the male characters made a sexist or ambiguous remark and the female character either ignored or confronted him. The results indicated that while female participants both liked and respected the target woman more when she challenged the sexist speaker, male respondents liked her less when she did so (although their respect for her was not affected).

LANGUAGE AND SPEECH PATTERNS

Language is a very powerful tool in the gender-construction toolbox. Words create images and understandings of gender, yet *what* we say can be either reinforced or undermined by *how* we say it. Women and men tend to use different styles of verbal communication. These speaking styles reflect and help to maintain gender imbalances in social power (Strand, 1999).

While some researchers (e.g., Cameron et al., 1993; Hopper, 2003; Ridgeway and Smith-Lovin, 1999) found few gender differences in speaking styles, others maintain that men and women use language in a different manner. For example, Adams and Ware (1996: 415) reported that "one of the most consistent findings of those who have studied sex-based variations in English has been that women, no matter what their socio-economic level, race, or age, use more grammatically correct forms than men and pronounce words in more acceptable ways" (see also Holmes, 1995). Holtgraves and Yang (1992) found that female students were significantly more polite than male students when making requests. A study of communication styles in chat rooms also has reported that in all-female chatrooms, "there were more overt expressions of politeness, thanks, and appreciation, as well as expressions of support of others" (in Vogels, 2002: 9).

Research has also found that girls and women are less likely than boys or men to use contentious language or to swear, and that they show greater restraint in "verbal dueling" situations (Adams and Ware, 1996; Jay, 1992; Ribeau et al., 1994).

Various explanations have been advanced for gender differences in grammatical patterns. On the one hand, Trudgill (1972) maintained that the traditional primacy of appearance as a vehicle of female social mobility has made women, as a group, "status conscious." He argued that where presentation is central to the achievement of recognition and reward, women carefully monitor their language as part of their general striving to create a positive impression. On the other hand, Adams and Ware (1996) suggested that whereas women may worry about losing status by speaking in a "low-status" way, men may perceive the use of non-standard English as accentuating their male "toughness" and deliberately adopt a cruder style as a result.

Slang

Carl Sandburg once defined **slang** as "language that rolls up its sleeves, spits on its hands and goes to work." Thorne (1990: iii–iv) observed that slang typically involves "the substitution of more forceful, emotive or humorous forms for standard words" (p. v). On the "spectrum of formality," he remarks, "[s]lang is at the end of the line ... where language is considered too racy, raffish, novel, or unsavoury for use in conversation with strangers" (Thorne, 1990: iii). According to Kramarae (1975), slang reflects societal change and is of critical importance in the evolution of language. She contended that the bulk of slang in North American society is created and adopted by men. Adams and Ware (1983: 484) noted that "[n]ot only is [slang's] usage more frequent in the speech of males, but also many of the terms used for swearing, such as *son of a bitch*, vilify women" (emphasis in original). They reported that women were more likely to define swearing as objectionable and to limit themselves to milder expletives, such as "hell and damn" (see also Crawford, 1995).

It can be argued that the avoidance of slang and swearing leaves a speaker at a distinct disadvantage in the expression of strong emotions, especially when the conversational other is not bound by similar constraints. When women do use expletives, they are more likely to use them in such a way as to "maintain a degree of politeness" (Lindsey, 1997: 79)—hence the euphemistic "Oh sugar/shoot/shucks/fudge/darn!" Bear in mind that the gender slang gap is based upon relative, not absolute, measures. According to Danesi's (2003) research on Canadian teens, gender slang parity may, for better or worse, be fast approaching.

Conversation Patterns

The conversations of men are more likely to focus upon external events (sports, politics, sexuality, paid work, and other men) than are the conversations of women (Shields, 1995; Walker, 2002; West, 1994). Men are more likely to speak more loudly, to use more forceful statements ("You tell that guy to take a hike"), and to impose their viewpoints on others ("This is how you handle it") (Lawson, 2003; Leaper and Ayre, 2007). According to Wood (1997: 173), giving advice functions on two levels: First, it establishes the speaker as the expert who "knows" what should and should not be done; second, it directs attention to instrumental activity. Women are more likely than men to speak about feelings, to make personal disclosures, to relay anecdotes, to reveal their psychological or physical state ("I'm so mad I could just scream!"), and to show support for others ("I know just how you feel. I've done the same thing myself a hundred times") (Filardo, 1996; Manthorpe, 2003). For example, Vogels (2002: 132, 157) maintains that

> "fat talk"—repeatedly using expressions like "I'm so fat"—is a way of being part of a group, since it requires the listeners to jump in and say, "No you're not." It's a way of saying, Hey girls, we may feel competitive, but it's not our fault. We are all victims of the same cultural pressures and messages.... We know exactly what another woman means when she says she's feeling bloated or frustrated because she had to get out her "fat pants" because she's put on ten pounds. Although a guy may just roll his eyes to tell us to get over it when we say we're feeling fat, a girlfriend will know this is merely a call for reassurance.

In contrast, Hargreaves and Tiggemann's (2006) research on 14- to 16-year-old boys found that while boys were also concerned about their physical appearance, they were notably reluctant to concede that they were. For these young men, the topic of body image was "a feminine or gay issue" and, as such, best avoided in conversations with their male peers. A recent study which examined the linguistic behaviour of 102 men and 66 women in unscripted, televised interviews found that, compared to men, women were more likely to use language that focused on social and sensory processes and to express themselves with simpler language and more self-referent nouns. Compared to women, men were more likely to use less common language, larger words, and more passive, third-person, and depersonalized speech (Brownlaw et al., 2003).

Tannen (1990: 77) referred to men's preferred speaking style as "report-talk" and to women's as "rapport-talk." **Report-talk** is a language of hierarchy, separation, independence, and action. **Rapport-talk** is a language of connection, compromise, mediation, and emotion. "Each sex finds the other's style of speech uncomfortable. Men see women's speech as consisting of illogical recitals of feelings and women see men's speech as wearing and competitive" (Richmond-Abbott, 1992: 94). When men employ the emotional language associated with femininity, they are likely to be perceived as effeminate; when women adopt the assertive language associated with masculinity, they are likely to be perceived as arrogant, haughty, and uncaring (Kelly and Huston-Comeau, 1999).

Men and women also differ in how they manage conversations and in the amount they speak within mixed-sex groups; according to Schmid Mast (2001: 538), "[t]ime talked is a widely used and validated indicator of dominance" with the association between dominance and speaker time greatest in all-male versus mixed-sex groups (Schmid Mast, 2002). Billings et al. (2002) reported that male sportscasters significantly monopolized airtime, even in the presence of female sportscasters and even when the coverage was of women's championship events. Although the stereotype of woman-as-chatterbox suggests that it is the woman's voice (and not her "strong but silent" partner's) that dominates conversation, the reverse may actually be more accurate (LeFrance, 1992). An examination of 56 studies of the amount talked by males and females found some evidence that men speak more than women, not only in public but in all settings (James and Drakich, 1993; see also Rosenthal et al., 2001). Of 24 studies that examined talking in formal task activities, 13 found that men talked more than women overall, three found that men talked more than women in certain circumstances, and only one reported that women talked more than men overall. Of the 16 studies which focused on male–female talk in non-task situations, nine found that men talked more than women overall, three reported that men talked more than women in certain circumstances, and one found that women talked more than men overall.

DeFrancisco (1991) observed that within mixed-sex groups, men often interrupted women to make a point and were more likely than women to answer questions directed to other people. "Interruption is an intrusion, a trampling on someone else's right to the floor, an attempt to dominate" (Tannen, 1994: 189). However, when a woman interrupts a man, she may be negatively evaluated as disrespectful, abrasive, or "too assertive," particularly if she is a white woman interrupting a white man (LeFrance, 1992). Noting that men are more likely to interrupt as well as to control changes of topic, some have suggested that conversations between men and women are more likely to resemble those that take place between employers and employees than between social equals (Tannen, 1990). Edelsky (1981) noted that in "overlaps" (i.e., situations in which two people start to speak at the same time), it is customary for the man to continue speaking and the woman to fall silent. This female deference would appear to be silent acknowledgement of the power imbalance between men and women. Yet tentativeness is not an invariant quality of female talk; in her study of women and men interacting in same-sex and mixed-sex pairs, Carli (1990) discovered that women who speak tentatively are more influential with men (but less influential with women) than women who speak assertively. Even as interviewers posing "tough" questions, females employ more indirect requests for information than do males (Macaulay, 2001).

According to Lipman-Blumen (1984), the stereotype of the pushy, loud female functions as a mechanism of informal social control, directing women to be solicitous of male speakers and to be deferential and unassuming within mixed-sex groups. Within mixed-sex dyads or larger groups, women do most, if not all, of the **conversation-work**—work designed to maintain a conversation and move it along smoothly (Rose, 2002). For example, women are more likely than men to engage in a continuous stream of what Tannen (1990) referred to as **listening noises** (e.g., "mm-hmm," "uh-huh," etc.), cajoling male speakers into continuing through the use of compliments ("That's incredible. I didn't know breeding iguanas was so fascinating"), verbal prompts ("You must have a hundred amazing stories to tell us"), head nods (even when a woman docs not agree with the speaker's remarks), verbal reinforcements ("right!"; "awesome!"; "really?"), and "spontaneous" laughter (Hopper, 2003: 227; Ridgeway and Smith Lovin, 1999). Generally, women nurture conversation and direct their energies towards its maintenance.

In contrast, men have been found to be more likely than women to monopolize a conversation and to dispute or disparage another's argument—on- or off-line (Spender, 1995)—or to employ techniques that discourage others in the group, particularly women, from speaking. The **delayed response** is perhaps the best known of these. "The woman says something like 'You'll never guess what happened to me today.' Only after a long pause does her male companion say, 'Oh, what?' At other times the only response to the woman is silence" (Richmond-Abbott, 1992: 95).

Predating Tannen's (1990) identification of report-talk and rapport-talk, Lakoff (1975) argued that the speech of men and women is motivated by contrasting goals. Based on introspection ("I have examined my own speech and that of my acquaintances, and have used my own intuitions in analyzing it" [Lakoff, 1975: 4]) rather than a formal research design, Lakoff's investigations suggested that while men's speech is motivated by a desire for the "pure transmission of factual knowledge" (p. 71), women's speech is motivated by the goal of "politeness" (p. 51). These contrasting goals, she suggested, result in distinct verbal styles. The first style embodies the desire to impart information to the listener "by the least circuitous route" (p. 71), and is characterized by short, succinct, unambiguous sentences. Within this mode of speech, information is conveyed as a series of unqualified propositions of fact, which are ordered in accordance with a linear logic. These features, Lakoff argued, convey the authority and autonomy of the speaker.

In contrast, the "polite" style, typical of the speech patterns of women, is crafted to sustain connection with the listener. Polite speech does not announce the authority of the speaker to make definitive statements about the world; rather, it is characterized by a deferential and tentative quality. Even while speaking, the speaker tries to discern the listener's feelings towards both the speaker and the statements being uttered. In so doing, the speaker cedes power to the listener to determine the message that the speaker actually conveys (Lakoff, 1975: 70). Polite speakers employ various "hedges," including an interrogative inflection that ends a sentence on a rising note, "tag questions" ("Dinner at five, OK?" versus "Dinner at five"), hyper-fastidious circumlocutions ("While I've really enjoyed the time we've spent together, I was thinking that it might, perhaps, be best if we didn't see each other any more"), semantically ambiguous qualifiers ("Well, I guess that might be sorta OK with me"), and empty adjectives ("What a divine darling little dress!"). Hedges effectively allow listeners "great linguistic latitude to determine" what has been communicated and "undercut the claim to authority that is implicit in declarative syntax" (White, 1991: 406). Although Lakoff acknowledged that social rather than linguistic change is necessary to improve women's position in society, she suggested that women's adoption of the speech forms typically associated with men would help advance their quest for equal treatment.

Kramarae (1975, 1981), however, contended that **women's language** embodies alternative values that should be reassessed, recognized as positive, and embraced. For Kramarae, the "polite" form of speech typically associated with women should be the preferred model of communication. Human social life, she suggested, is not concrete and uni-dimensional, nor can any one perspective capture all of its multi-dimensionality. As no single speaker can lay claim to absolute truth, no opinion should be delivered from a stance of arrogant authority. She argued that because women's language incorporates ambiguity, it allows for the adoption of multiple perspectives; moreover, its tentative style is ideal for promoting negotiation between interlocutors. Kramarae contended that feminists should analyze the norms, values, and ideals embodied in "women's language" and translate these into feminist campaigns for social change. Gilligan (1982), maintaining that men speak in the voice of public rationality and women in the voice of relational sensitivity, also argued that it is women's voice which is transformative.

Gender Differences or Power Differences?

Since the 1980s, researchers who have studied the speech patterns of economically and racially subordinate groups in North America have challenged the construction of "polite speech" as "women's language." They have observed that the typical features of this language pattern (extreme politeness, tentativeness, deference, etc.) are common among those who hold little power (including inexperienced court witnesses, unemployed persons, assembly line workers, and the uneducated), and that "polite speech" might more accurately be reconceptualized as **powerless speech** (Conley and O'Barr, 1990; Hopper, 2003; Popp et al., 2003). The early research of Thorne and Henley (1975) anticipated this view: They claimed that women's tendency to utilize proper "standard English" and men's tendency to break grammatical rules may be more a function of power than of gender. Aries (2006: 28) notes that those who hold power demonstrate less politeness than those who do not and that people are predictably more polite when addressing a superior. Similarly, Hopper (2003: 183, 184) has argued that women's greater tendency to "clutter their speech with qualifying particles and disclaimers" (e.g., I'm no expert, I may be wrong") and to use hedges "reflects social position more than gender. It is not too surprising that there are more powerless women than men; but powerless men use the same features. The features do not seem to be specifically gendered."

O'Barr's (1983) research on courtroom testimony found that minority men, working-class men, and others who occupy "relatively powerless social positions" (O'Barr, 1983: 104) all adopted the same linguistic patterns characteristic of women. Those lacking in social power cannot afford to speak in a manner that might be perceived as dogmatic, opinionated, or confrontational. Rather, they anticipate and seek to defuse potential antagonism and retaliation by conveying meekness—a readiness to have their assertions challenged or rejected. And this outcome is a strong possibility: O'Barr reported that jurors in simulated trials evaluated speakers who used powerless language as "less credible, competent, intelligent, or trustworthy than speakers who use typically 'male' speech patterns" (in White, 1991: 406). While analysts agree that the speech patterns of women and men reflect and reinforce unequal gender status, there has been less agreement on solutions, which have ranged from women becoming more like men (endorsed by liberal feminists) to men becoming more like women (espoused by cultural feminists). A third strategy is to "provide a more level playing field for men and women" (Hopper, 2003: 208). The location of the phenomena of language and speech patterns within a power hierarchy reminds us that gender differences in verbal communication are more situational than essential (De Welde, 2003).

NON-VERBAL COMMUNICATION

Language, of course, is not the only means by which we communicate. We also communicate through our bodies. Posture and bearing; spatial behaviour; hand, arm, and leg gestures; facial expressions; eye movements such as gaze, contact, and avoidance; touch—all of these are imbued with culturally shared meanings. Even though much of body language is learned, most of us remain unaware that we are engaging in it. Body language, therefore, provides an important source of information, subtly corroborating or contradicting verbal communication. Gender differences in **non-verbal communication** not only reinforce presentations of gender in everyday life, but also undergird the unequal status of women and men in our society (Hall et al., 2002, 2002a, 2002b; LaFrance, 2000).

Guess which sex is more likely to have sore facial muscles from smiling throughout an evening of socializing? Which sex is more likely to raise one or both hands to their mouth immediately following an outburst of emotion (swearing, crying, screaming for joy), or to prevent themselves, out of fear or embarrassment, from giving utterance to some feeling? Who is more likely to gaze intently into another person's eyes or face during conversation, yet to break off eye contact first if an approaching person is a stranger? Which sex is more likely to bow their head slightly and look up at another person through their eyelashes? Who controls more space—men or women—and how do they accomplish this feat?

A central question in the study of gendered non-verbal communication is whether observed differences reflect essential gender characteristics or situational status and power differentials. In our society, women are more likely to find themselves in subordinate positions; accordingly, they adopt non-verbal communication patterns common to members of other subordinate groups. For example, research has indicated that women smile more often than men (Dodd et al., 1999; Hall, 2006; LaFrance and Hecht, 2000). Henley et al. (1984) suggested that the act of smiling is "women's badge of appeasement," a means of placating or appearing non-threatening to others. Hochschild (2003: 85) reported that whereas men mask fear, women mask anger; women are more likely than men to smile when experiencing feelings of anger or frustration. Other research has noted that increased smiling may stem from the motive to ingratiate (Hall et al., 2001: 688). In their meta-analysis of moderator variables, Hall and Halberstadt (1997) found that women's tendency to smile more than men increased in tense or anxious situations.

Ekman et al. (1980) opined that crying may also function as a culturally acceptable way for women to mask anger, especially in situations where an expression of anger might be disruptive or seen as inappropriate for one of subordinate status. The relatively low frequency and intensity of crying among men may reflect not only male "socialization-for-inhibition" of emotions (Williams and Morris, 1996), but also their relatively advantaged social position. In research on male undergraduates, Lombardo et al. (2001: 543) observed a negative correlation between education and the socialized inhibition against crying as an expression of sadness: "Men with more education were less traditional in their gender role orientation and, therefore, more likely to cry. Nevertheless, men with more education were less likely to be sad and, therefore, less likely to cry."

Table 5.2 highlights the similarities between characteristics of the powerful/less powerful and males/females as documented in scholarly research from 1995 through 2004.

TABLE 5.2	Behaviour Comparison between More and Less Powerful Communicators and Male and Female Communicators			
	Power		Sex	
Behaviour	High	Low	Male	Female
1. Approach	+	–	+	–
2. Inhibition	–	+	–	+
3. Interrupt more	+	–	+	–
4. Give directives	+	–	+	–
5. Talk more in groups	+	–	+	–
6. Other directed	–	+	–	+
7. Show anger more	+	–	+	–
8. Elevated mood	+	–	+	–
9. Sadness or depression	–	+	–	+
10. Stereotype more	+	–	+	–
11. Display more non-verbal cues	+	–	+	–
12. Better at interpreting non-verbal cues	–	+	–	+
13. Aware of potential loss of status and resources	–	+	–	+
14. Engage in self-censorship	–	+	–	+

Source: Pamela J. Kalbfleisch and Anita J. Herold 2006 "Sex, Power and Communication." In Kathryn Dindia and Daniel J. Canary (eds.) *Sex Differences and Similarities in Communication*, 2nd Edition. Mahwah, NJ: Lawrence Erlbanum Associates, p. 303.

Building on the hypothesis that gender status differences underlie non-verbal gender behaviours (i.e., that high-status individuals behave as men do, while low-status individuals behave as women do), Hall et al. (2001) photographed dyads of faculty or staff members at a university. Of each set of photographs, four were candid shots, taken as participants conversed about work; a fifth was taken with the participants deliberately facing the camera. Subsequently, each member of every dyad was asked about his/her status relative to the other. The non-verbal behaviour of the respondents was found to be congruent with their status: The higher-status person tended to tilt his/her head down more, literally "looking down on" the lower-status person, who "looked up to" the superior. Higher-status individuals were also more likely to adopt a relaxed body posture, resting elbows on a leg or on furniture, while low-status individuals showed greater tenseness and more of a forward lean. The researchers noted that "[s]tatus effects were not always constant across gender, and gender differences were not always constant across candid/posed photographs" (p. 690). However, in general, women were more likely than men to demonstrate more erect body posture, to lean forward more, and to raise their eyebrows more often.

Research has also found that both men and women can adopt similar styles when circumstances require it. Our cultural folklore bestows unique status upon what is commonly referred to as "women's intuition." Intuition is generally understood to refer to an immediate perception and accurate interpretation of available cues. As such, intuition is related to empathy, the ability to feel for another. Despite cultural-feminist claims that women are "naturally" more empathetic than men, no evidence exists to suggest that differences in empathy are the result of innate or biological predispositions (Tavris, 1992: 64). For example, research has found that men training for or working in occupations requiring heightened interpersonal sensitivity are "as good as women at decoding nonverbally expressed emotions" (Ickes et al., 2000); "[w]hether this finding can be attributed to the effects of practice or to the self-selection of unusually sensitive men for such occupations is difficult to know" (Lips, 2001: 132). In a series of laboratory experiments in which both males and females were assigned into either superordinate or subordinate roles, Snodgrass (1985, 1992) found that people in subordinate positions, regardless of sex, were more sensitive to the non-verbal signals provided by superordinates than the reverse. Snodgrass concluded that the phrase "women's intuition" might more fittingly be termed **subordinate's intuition**.

Tavris (1992) stressed that empathy should be considered not a "female trait" but a learned "self-protective" skill, characteristic of those who have lesser amounts of power. Puka (1990) noted that prisoners, slaves, and members of other oppressed groups all demonstrate an interpersonal sensitivity considered "typical" of women. Lips (2001: 132) reported that "[o]f interest in this regard are findings of greater nonverbal sensitivity among Blacks than Whites in the United States." Power relations, in combination with socialization, appear to account for women's greater sensitivity to non-verbal cues. A great amount of information about others' thoughts and feelings is derived from visual cues. Women are more likely than men to engage in a great degree of eye contact with conversational partners or to gaze fixedly at them (Hall et al., 2000, 2002). In everyday interactions, women more often "read" other individuals' facial expressions, and are more accurate in interpreting them (Hall and Halberstadt, 1997).

Feminists since the 1970s have drawn attention to the sexist meanings implicit in many of the non-verbal acts subsumed under the heading of *chivalry*. The chivalrous act of opening a door for a woman, for example, embodies an assumption about female weakness (despite the fact that modern doors are substantially lighter than in days of yore). Such acts as lighting a woman's cigarette, taking her arm when crossing a street, walking between her and the curb, etc., all cast men into active roles and women into passive, protected roles. Traditionalists argue that such acts are simple courtesies that should not be discarded, and ask: "What's wrong with men acting like gentlemen?" There is, of course, nothing inherently wrong with being helpful or courteous; however, it has been argued that the gendered nature of such rituals, along with their underlying assumptions, may reinforce the unequal gender statuses of men and women.

Space

In our society, men command more *personal space*—that protective "bubble" that surrounds each of us—than women do. When seated, women typically keep their feet flat on the floor and their knees firmly together, or cross their legs at the ankles or thighs, covering the genital area. Elbows are usually tucked in towards the body, with arms folded, or hands may rest on their laps (Spain, 1992; Weisman, 1992). In contrast, men tend to "sprawl" with knees wide apart; or, if cross-legged, resting one ankle on the opposite knee or thigh, genital region exposed. (A serpentine intertwining of the legs, with one foot tucked behind the calf or ankle of the other leg, is not considered masculine in our culture.) Hands may rest apart on each thigh with elbows pointing away from the body, or may be clasped behind the head; or the arms may be spread out to either side, resting on the backs of chairs. Men are likely to stand "at ease," military fashion, with feet planted (firmly) apart. Women are more apt to stand with legs close together or crossed at the ankle. Richmond-Abbott (1992: 96) suggested that women's restricted use of space attests most fundamentally to their relative lack of power and dominance. The "dainty," "truly feminine" woman takes up a minimum of space.

A summary of experimental research has indicated that

> (1) women have more tolerance for invasion of their personal space than men have; (2) women stand closer to other women than men stand to other men, and when women get as close to men as they do to other women, the men retreat; (3) when men get as close to other men as they normally do to women, the male subjects "fight" (accuse the experimenter of being pushy or homosexual); and (4) both men and women stand closer to women than they do to men. (Richmond-Abbott, 1992: 96–97)

Despite folkways prescribing that a man move aside to "let a lady pass," women are the more likely to take evasive measures and move to one side to allow a man to pass should they approach each other in a narrow hall or passageway (Richmond-Abbott, 1992: 97).

Touch

Generally, high-status individuals initiate touch more frequently and touch subordinates more often than the reverse (Spain, 1992); it is generally considered inappropriate for subordinates to put their hands on superiors. Touching behaviour in interpersonal gender relations follows the same general principle: Males are more likely than females to initiate touch. Females are more likely to be touched than males and are likely to be touched on more areas of the body by strangers, friends, acquaintances, and intimates than are males (Henley, 1995).

How we interpret a touch involves not only such incident-specific factors as duration, intensity, frequency, and site, but also the meanings of touching learned through gender socialization. One experiment (Thayer, 1988) found that brief touching of patients by a female nurse during pre-surgery information sessions lowered the blood pressure and anxiety levels of females, both before the surgery and for more than an hour afterwards. Women patients experienced being touched as therapeutic and reassuring. In contrast, male patients in identical circumstances responded with rising blood pressure and anxiety levels both before and following surgery. Instead of finding it comforting to be touched, men in this situation appeared to experience it as a threatening reminder of their vulnerability and dependence. Perhaps this is why men tend to be more likely to use the disdainful label "touchy-feely" to refer to any real or potential touching they themselves neither initiate nor control.

Non-verbal communication is linked to a complex web of assumptions about women and men and their "right" to choreograph how interaction will proceed in various social settings (Diekman et al., 2004; Dollar et al., 2004). Many observers have suggested that in our essentially no-touch culture, interpersonal tactile contact is permeated with sexual meanings. Even if a specific touch is not directed towards an intimate portion of a man's or a woman's anatomy, non-intimate touching will often either precipitate sexual touching or signal a desire for more intimate contact. In consequence, a hand placed upon another's knee and left to remain there may be interpreted as a welcome indicator of sexual interest, an innocuous event, or an anxiety-provoking act of sexual harassment. Berdhal et al.'s (1996: 109–110) research on 138 male and female undergraduates found that while both sexes had experienced **sexual harassment** (i.e., unwanted behaviours aimed at coercing compliance with the harasser's sexual desires), male undergraduates generally identified sexual attentions from women (including instructors and professors) as non-threatening, very often defining such attentions as entertaining, satisfying to their egos, or validating of their masculinity. The research of Struckman-Johnson and Struckman-Johnson (1997) also found that a "beauty bias" may influence a man's perception of sexually coercive acts committed by a female. They found that 142 male undergraduates who viewed a series of vignettes depicting such acts were more apt to react positively if the perpetrator was very attractive, regardless of the specific acts and whether or not (low or moderate) force was involved. Commitment to another person could also affect subjects' responses to hypothetical coercive sexual advances and their tendency to label such conduct as sexual harassment. Men instructed to imagine they had a girlfriend evinced a slightly negative to neutral reaction to the perpetrator's behaviour; men told to assume that they had no romantic partner had a slightly positive response.

Katz et al. (1996) reported that in order to be seen as sexual harassment, conduct must be perceived by the target as "repetitive, unwelcome and inherently coercive." In a study of 197 undergraduates, they found that when the behaviour was perpetrated by a man against a woman, males and females held very similar views about what constitutes sexual harassment. However, in the case of actions perpetrated by a woman against a man, females rated such interactions as more harassing and negative than did males. Research has indicated that behaviour that women defined as unacceptable or offensive, especially in the workplace, was viewed by men as normal and appropriate (Pollack, 1990; Childers, 1993). Pryor and Whalen (1997) pointed out that numerous studies have detected a gender bias in perception: Men demonstrated a greater tendency to misinterpret certain non-verbal behaviours, such as sustained eye contact or close physical proximity, as indicators of sexual interest or receptiveness to sexual overtures. Norton (2002: 91) reported that "a number of gender-related stereotypes may dramatically affect how 'acceptable' behaviour is defined" by perpetrators, victims, and outsiders; for example, the stereotype that defines men as "naturally" more sexual than women may lead to the perception that "you can't blame a guy for trying"—after all, "boys will be boys." This stereotype is likely to militate against a man's consciousness of moral trespass when he engages in actions that his target defines as unwelcome; as well, it may encourage others to discount the seriousness of his actions. Similarly, the stereotype of woman-as-seductress promotes a belief that the female target of harassment must somehow have "provoked" it. De Judicibus and McCabe (2001: 414) reported that while gender is an important predictor of the tendency to "blame the victim" of sexual harassment, "[m]ales and females with more sexist attitudes were more likely than those with egalitarian views to attribute blame to the victim."

Wood (1997: 196) suggested that "[b]ecause masculine socialization encourages men to enter the private spaces of others, particularly women, and to use touch to establish power, they may engage in touching that women co-workers will perceive as harassing." She remarked, "Women's training to be nice to others may make them reluctant to speak forcefully to a boss or co-worker," especially if the offending party is intimidating by virtue of their height, weight, or apparent confidence that they can do just as they please.

"Sexual harassment generally involves a power differential" (Hambright and Decker, 2002: 129); targets are likely to be subordinate to the harasser in terms of their organizational, educational, or socioeconomic rank, in-group/out-group status, or access to valued resources. This dynamic helps to explain why heterosexual women are more likely to experience sexual harassment than heterosexual men, why lesbians are more likely to experience it than heterosexual women, and why gay men may be "targets of sexual harassment significantly more often than lesbians" (Hambright and Decker, 2002: 129; see also Street et al., 2007). Subordinates may perceive that they are ill-positioned to confront or publicly rebuke their harassers, especially when the organizational environment tolerates or encourages a high level of sexualized behaviour (Dellinger and Williams, 2002). As De Judicibus and McCabe (2001: 416) pointed out, even where formal policies prohibit it, sexual harassment may be "okay" according to the informal norms regulating day-to-day life in the workplace; attempts to challenge these may meet with great resistance and antagonism. Thus, harassers may escape censure; instead, targets of harassment may be urged to revise their definition of the experience, to "alter their perceptions and behaviour, and interpret potentially harassing behaviours as normal interactions." This course of action may also be encouraged by messages emanating from the broader social environment. In an exploration of our society's attitude towards sexual harassment, Montemurro (2003) analyzed the themes and content of 56 episodes of five workplace-based television sitcoms. Montemurro concluded that although these programs rarely discussed sexual harassment, their predilection for making jokes at women's expense and their depiction of sexual harassment as a laughing matter has contributed to the problem's persistence. "Trivialization of sexual harassment has been a major means through which its invisibility has been enforced. Humour, which may reflect unconscious hostility, has been a major form of that trivialization" (MacKinnon, 1979: 52).

THE MEDIA

Symbolic representations of gender in the media are salient sources of gender socialization. Contemporary media depictions of gender are considerably more diverse than they once were; however, research suggests that men and women continue to be represented in stereotypical ways (Fleras, 2003: 314).

Books and Magazines

Children's Books In a now classic study, Weitzman et al. (1972) examined children's books that had won the American Library Association's prestigious Caldecott Medal for best illustrations. Selection of a book for a Caldecott Medal is significant in that all children's libraries in both the United States and Canada almost always order winning books. Despite the fact that females accounted for more than half the population in both countries, female characters were all but invisible in the books examined. Almost all of the books told stories about male adventures and featured boys, men, and even male animals. For every one female animal, 95 male animals were depicted. Girls were portrayed in passive and doll-like ornamental roles, while boys were portrayed as active and adventurous. The majority of the girls were depicted as trying to please brothers or fathers; the boys, in contrast, were depicted as engaging in tasks requiring independence and self-confidence. Later replications of the Weitzman et al. study (e.g., Clark et al., 2003; Kortenhaus and Demarest, 1993; Tepper and Cassidy, 1999) found that while female characters now appear in about the same numbers as male, depictions of females have remained essentially unchanged. Males are still portrayed as active and independent, while females are still shown as essentially passive, dependent, and intent upon pleasing others.

Crabb and Bielawski (1994) examined material culture as portrayed in Caldecott Award–winning books between 1937 and 1989. They discovered that household-labour artifacts were consistently presented as intended primarily for female use, while non-domestic artifacts were presented as intended primarily for males. They also found no change over the years in the proportion of female characters portrayed with household artifacts. In an examination of differential language in children's books, Turner-Bowker (1996) focused on the words used to describe males and females in Caldecott Award–winning and runner-up books between 1984 and 1994. The 20 adjectives most commonly employed to describe female characters differed in stereotypical ways from the 20 adjectives most commonly used to describe male characters. While male characters were *big, horrible, fierce, great, terrible, furious,* and *proud,* female characters were *beautiful, frightened, worthy, sweet, weak,* and *scared.*

Recognition of the harmful effects of gender stereotyping in children's books has prompted some publishers (e.g., McGraw-Hill; Scott Foresman and Company) to develop guidelines for eliminating sexist roles in children's books and textbooks. Feminists have also encouraged the publication of non-sexist books that allow "Dick ... [to] speak of his feelings of tenderness without embarrassment and Jane ... [to] reveal her career ambitions without shame or guilt" (Williams et al., 1987: 154). In the 1980s and 1990s, females became more visible within both award-winning and non-award-winning children's print books (Tepper and Cassidy, 1999). Gooden and Gooden (2001) examined gender representations in 83 picture books designated by the American Library Association as "Notable Books" for the period 1995–1999. Noting that "[t]he ALA Notable Children's Books List provides parents, librarians, and teachers with outstanding quality books for use by young children" (p. 93), they reported that "steps toward equity have advanced based on the increase in females represented as the main character" (p. 89). In 40 percent of the books analyzed, the main character was female while the main character was male in 39 percent; in the remaining 21 percent, the books had neither a female nor a male character. However, the authors noted that gender stereotypes remained prevalent within children's literature. While male adults tended to be portrayed in a variety of roles, the majority of women's roles were traditional (e.g., mother, grandmother). In addition, while males and females were described with some non-traditional characteristics and portrayed in some non-traditional roles, males were seldom portrayed as caregivers and "never shown doing household chores" (p. 96).

Hamilton et al.'s (2006) exploration of top-selling children's books published in 2001 and a seven-year sample of Caldecott Award–winning books (which yielded a combined sample of 200 books) reported nearly twice as many male as female titles and main characters. Male characters were featured in more illustrations than female characters and more often depicted in outdoor than indoor settings. Compared to male main characters, female main characters were frequently depicted in nurturing roles. The occupations that these storybook characters held were gender-stereotyped and more women than men appeared to have no paid work role. The authors concluded that there were few differences between the best-selling and Caldecott Award–winning books and that, compared to children's books from the 1980s and 1990s, the more recently published books "did not reveal reduced sexism" (p. 757).

Children's storybooks offer behavioural blueprints that may either promote or challenge gender-role stereotypes (Diekman and Murnen, 2004). Research has noted that children as young as nursery-school age showed greater diligence in completing a task after hearing a story in which a same-sex character was depicted performing that task; they were also more apt to select a non-stereotypical toy to play with after being read a non-stereotypical picture book (Lips, 2001). However, since most children are exposed only to conventional storybooks, conformity to, rather than challenge of, traditional gender expectations is more often the outcome.

For the past two decades, such books as *The Paper Bag Princess* by Robert Munsch, *Princess Prunella and the Purple Peanut* by Margaret Atwood, *Petronella* by Jay Williams, and *The King's Equal* by Katherine Patterson have purposefully attempted to rectify biased images by using a tactic known as **fairy tale fracturing** (Gooden and Gooden, 2001: 91)— changing the gender of characters in well-known fairy tales in order to counteract gender stereotypes, or offering new endings for familiar tales that suggest a wider range of possibilities for males and females. For example, Munsch's *The Paper Bag Princess* sees the female protagonist embark on a mission to save her fiancé, Prince Ronald, after a fire-breathing dragon abducts him. Demonstrating ingenuity and cunning, the princess bests the dragon and rescues the prince. Prince Ronald, however, shows little appreciation and chides her for having "messy hair" and tattered clothes. Rather than be mortified by Ronald's criticisms, the princess replies, "You, Prince Ronald, are a bum." Eschewing the usual fairy-tale "happily ever after" ending, the tale concludes by noting that the prince and princess do not get married after all. Series such as *The Berenstain Bears* by Stan and Jan Berenstain, Joanna Cole's *The Magic School Bus,* and Phoebe Gilman's *Jillian Jiggs to the Rescue* also portray males and females in a wide variety of roles that implicitly convey the message that heroic qualities are not exclusively "masculine," nor nurturant behaviours solely "feminine" (see also Purcell and Stewart, 1990).

Some books targeted for young readers attempt to combine a non-sexist and non-heterosexist message. For example, in *Asha's Mum*, by Rosamund Elwin and Michelle Paulse, one of the story's characters informs her classmate that it is not wrong to have two mothers "if they're nice to you and you like them"; other books, such as Johnny Valentine's *One Dad, Two Dads, Brown Dads, Blue Dads* and Lesléa Newman's *Belinda's Bouquet* deliberately acknowledge that some children are raised within two-father or two-mother households. However, stories such as these not only form a very small proportion of books for young readers but have been attacked by some parents—generally on religious grounds—as "subversive." Although none of the above-mentioned books explicitly define the relationship between the two parental figures or use the terms "gay," "lesbian," "homosexual," or "sex," their presence in a Surrey, B.C., elementary-school classroom led to heated parental protests and a school-board ban of the books from classroom settings; this ban was later overturned by the B.C. Supreme Court in a 1998 landmark ruling (EGALE, 1999a).

A variety of non-sexist books are now available for pre-teenagers; examples include Latoya Hunter's *The Diary of Latoya Hunter*, a non-fictional account of a young Jamaican immigrant's life; Marie Lee's *Finding My Voice*, a story of a young Chinese girl dealing with prejudice, parental pressure, and the search for self-identity; and Scott O'Dell's *Black Star, Bright Dawn*, a story of a young Inuit girl competing in the thousand-mile Iditarod sled dog race. Unfortunately, a jarring discontinuity exists between the new non-sexist material designed for a very young audience and reading materials that purposefully target somewhat older readers.

Comics Robbins (1996: 2) observed that since the 1933 introduction of Superman in *Action Comics* No. 1, "superheroes [have] entered the world's consciousness" through syndicated comic strips and comic books. "The success of the Superman character naturally led to imitation, and new superheroes popped up almost faster than a speeding bullet" (Robbins, 1996: 2): Batman left the Batcave in 1939 to embark on the quest to avenge his murdered parents, and Flash ("the "fastest man alive"), Hawkman, the Human Torch, and Captain Marvel all appeared in 1940. Superheroes both past and present have overwhelmingly been white and male; men of colour, when they have appeared, have usually been depicted as evil "foreigners" and "arch enemies." In superhero comics of the 1950s, for example, "[t]here were no African Americans anywhere in Metropolis or Gotham City— not as heroes, villains, or even passers-by" (Wright, 2001: 65).

Although the first female superhero (Peggy Allen, aka "The Woman in Red") entered the scene in 1940, she shared the fate of the majority of female comic-book action characters: "None ... ever appeared in her own book, and they were invariably short-lived, rarely lasting for more than three appearances before fading into permanent obscurity" (Robbins, 1996: 3). Wright (2001) argued that the subordinate status of female characters both reflected and reinforced traditional gender expectations. He remarked that "[t]he primary function served by women was to resist the romantic advances of the superhero's alter-ego, pine for the superhero, scheme to get close to him, screw things up, get captured by the bad guy, and await rescue by the hero, who usually scolded her for being so bold in the first place" (Wright, 2001: 184–185).

The creation of Wonder Woman (initially known as "Amazon Princess Diana") in 1941 represented a purposive attempt by her creator, psychologist William Marston, to provide female readers with a same-sex superhero. Marston reasoned that "the comics' worst offence was their blood-curdling masculinity.... It's smart to be strong. It's big to be generous, but it's sissified, according to exclusively male rules, to be tender, loving, affectionate, and alluring. 'Aw, that's girl stuff!' snorts our young comics reader, 'Who wants to be a girl?' And that's the point: not even girls want to be girls so long as our feminine archetype lacks force, strength ... " (in Robbins, 1996: 7). In her original incarnation, Wonder Woman was a muscular, flat-chested young woman with a strong chin, who made villains (the majority of whom were other women) see the error of their ways—not by the exercise of super powers, but through "the message of love and humanitarianism" (Robbins, 1996: 10).

Robbins (1996: 10) claimed that "[t]he most powerful humanistic message in Wonder Woman, and the one most consistently repeated, is that super powers are not necessary for a girl to become a superheroine"; she noted that this message was re-emphasized in a feature box which appeared in every issue of the comic book and directed attention to such real-life heroes as Florence Nightingale.

While Wonder Woman, along with other female American superpatriots such as America's Joan of Arc and Yankee Girl, "fought Germans and Japanese on land, on sea, in the air, and on the pages of America's comics" (Robbins, 1996: 37), these androgynous role models faced a formidable new challenge in 1947 with the emergence of *Young Romance*, which pioneered the genre of the "romance comic." Adopting the formula of "true-confessions" magazines, romance comics sought to capture the attention of females who largely disdained to purchase comic books. They succeeded; the half-million copies of the comic's first edition quickly sold out and prompted the publisher to double its monthly circulation. "By 1949 romance comic books ... outsold all other genres and cut deeply into the market for confessional magazines" (Wright, 2001: 128). Like confessional magazines, romance comics such as *My Date, Teen-Age Romance,* and *Teen-Age Brides* featured "true love stories" about adolescent characters and offered their readers "cautionary morality tales told from the perspective of a female protagonist (though generally written by men) [which] illustrated the perils of female independence and celebrated the virtues of domesticity.... [They] seldom strayed from the central premise that women were incomplete without a man" (Wright, 2001: 129). Some of these comic books also provided advice pages, which extolled female sexual restraint and chaste devotion to boyfriends in committed relationships. "Man-chasers" were disparaged and readers admonished that "decent boys" would avoid women who aggressively pursued them or who allowed themselves to be kissed in public. In general, "[r]omance comic books encouraged women to marry young and grow up quickly from schoolgirl to devoted housewife" (Wright, 2001: 130) and discouraged them from entering the paid labour force. Young female readers were warned that women who worked were destined to live unhappy and unfulfilled lives, inasmuch as men disliked "ambitious" women.

While the 1960s saw the introduction of comic books featuring "superhero groups" that included females, these female superheroes were rarely presented as heroic. Sue Storm (aka the "Invisible Girl of the Fantastic Four") was the quintessential "wimp," with a behavioural repertoire that consisted of fainting, bursting into tears, and becoming hysterical. Jean Gray (aka "Marvel Girl" of the first incarnation of the X-Men) also demonstrated a marked tendency to faint whenever she attempted to telekinetically budge any large object; perhaps in consequence, she was largely portrayed serving meals. While "[f]eminism, in a slightly addled form," had an impact upon the comic-book world of the 1970s, with characters such as Jungle Queen Shanna: the She-Devil and Ms. Marvel, "by the eighties ... with the original feminist influence weakened or forgotten, [female superheroes] were getting sillier" (Robbins, 1996: 138). The She-Hulk attempted to charge after her opponents while carrying 650 pounds on a six-foot-seven-inch frame; the Dazzler, a disco diva, was a crime fighter on roller skates, whose singular power was the ability to blind and bemuse villains with a psychedelic light show. "By the nineties," Robbins (1996: 166–167) remarked, "comic books had become not merely a boy's club, but a Playboy Club," with female characters depicted as "pinup material" with alarmingly large breasts (invariably bursting out of their outfits), long, slender legs, and "bedroom hair."

While the observation that "chick books don't sell" has become the comic-book industry's standard explanation for its preponderance of male heroes, Robbins (1996: 166) diagnosed a circular logic: "Of course, as long as female comic characters are insulting to the average woman, she won't read comics." Female readers may, of course, opt for such traditional "girl" comics as *Archie, Betty and Veronica*, and *Betty*, which—like romance comics since the 1940s—continue to emphasize and privilege love, romance, and marriage over alternative pursuits. While Archie will celebrate his 70th birthday in 2009 (the series first appeared in 1939), the comic-book series remain popular with both young readers and their parents. Reportedly, these comics are especially popular in Canada, where "[t]he various Archie titles sell a total of between 850 000 and 900 000 copies per month, down considerably from the pre-television days of the '40s and '50s, when they sold millions, but still an impressive number in these supposedly post-literate days" (*Toronto Star*, 2001). In the mythical land of Riverdale (which is overwhelmingly white and middle-to upper-middle class), reference may be made to contemporary pop idols or other celebrities (albeit with slightly altered names), but the message remains highly traditional. Love, romance, and dating are the province of heterosexuals (gays and lesbians are conspicuous by their absence) and intraracial couples (Chuck dates Nancy—but never Midge or Cheryl Blossom—and Archie, despite his compulsive philandering, has yet to swoon over a woman of colour). While the "zany mishaps" of Archie are a constant feature of the series, emphasis is placed on the contrasting dating strategies employed by good girl Betty (e.g., baking a cake to win Archie's heart via his stomach, being sweet and virtuous) and rich, scheming Veronica (e.g., dazzling Archie with her beauty, wardrobe, and "feminine wiles"). For both, the quest is to capture and sustain Archie's interest and affection; without their "dream man," they sigh, life is incomplete and profoundly unsatisfying. This theme also pervades reading materials intended for older female audiences.

Teen Romance Novels Girls who find the comic-book world unappealing or "childish" often gravitate towards the Juvenile–Young Adult section of local bookstores. Once saturated with Nancy Drew and Hardy Boys mysteries and the everyday adventures of the Bobbsey Twins and Cherry Ames, bookshelves began changing by the 1980s to accommodate a greater variety of reading fare for young, predominantly female, readers. The old standards are still available, but are increasingly being outsold by novels focusing upon apparently more enthralling themes of love and romance.

While romance novels for adolescents date back to the 1940s and 1950s, "[w]hat is new ... is the transposing of adult romance formats from Harlequin Romances to young adult publishing ... big-budget marketing campaigns ... and the use of the series format in which several books each month are issued" (Christian-Smith, 1988: 78). Teen romance novels now consistently rank in the top three types of books read and purchased by girls age 9 to 15.

Christian-Smith, analyzing 34 American adolescent romance novels written between 1942 and 1982, discovered consistent themes and messages: that femininity is "devotion to home, heart, and hearth, that a woman is incomplete without a man, that motherhood is women's destiny, and women's rightful place is at home" (Christian-Smith, 1988: 78). Utilizing central characters whom readers can easily identify with as peers, the essential message of these primers-for-future-women is that romance shapes sexuality and femininity. In asserting that romance is "the only proper context for sexuality" and that adolescent sexuality should be non-genital (Christian-Smith, 1991/1998: 102), teen romance novels exert informal social control over young women's sexual experience and expression. The teenage reader is taught to know she is in love by the presence of various physical sensations, such as a throbbing head and fluttery feelings in her stomach (somewhat akin to the flu), sensations that are awakened and released only by boys and always with a kiss (Christian-Smith, 1991/1998: 103–105). "Romance ultimately involves the construction of feminine identity in terms of others, with boys in the powerful position of giving girls' lives meaning.... While teen romances run counter to the realities of many women's and girls' actual lives, they nevertheless serve to maintain traditional views of what should constitute those lives" (Christian-Smith, 1988: 92–93).

In a study which examined the extent and nature of children's voluntary reading and the effect of gender on reading choices, Coles and Hall (2002) asked 7976 students (age 10, 12, and 14) to complete a questionnaire on the types of books they had read. They found that females favoured romance/relationship stories, along with animal-related, horror/ghost, and adventure stories. In contrast, male subjects read more science fiction, fantasy, sports-related, war, and spy stories. However, periodicals were the most popular type of reading among all subjects (see also Nippold et al., 2005).

Teen Magazines The overwhelming majority of general magazines published for pre-adolescent or adolescent audiences, such as the American-produced *Teen Beat, 'Teen, Sassy, Seventeen, CosmoGirl, ElleGirl,* and *Teen Vogue,* are aimed towards female purchasers and readers. Commercially available teen magazines featuring non-stereotypical images of the female role appear to be the exception rather than the rule. Examples of these include the socially conscious *Teen Voices* (advertised as "[w]ritten by and for teen women since 1990," which "encourages girls to feel better about themselves, [and] to challenge media images of girls and women"), the American *New Moon: The Magazine for Girls and Their Dreams* (advertised as "For every girl who wants her voice heard and her dreams taken seriously"), and the Canadian *Reluctant Hero* (advertised as "written by girls for girls 13 to 16"), which features such avowedly feminist messages as "Fun things to do on your period," "As good as the guys," and "The Look: wear your self-esteem" (*Reluctant Hero*, vol. 1, issue 2, n.d.). Unquestionably more familiar to the vast majority of Canadian teenagers are the celebrity-laden magazines dominated by a plethora of information about young male stars of American television and movies, along with the standard beauty, diet, lifestyle, and relationship tips reflecting conventionally narrow definitions of femininity. Although "[a]t least 38 experiments, 32 surveys and 2 interview studies" (APA, 2007: 23) have reported that exposure to sexualizing words and idealized women's bodies increase self-objectification, appearance anxiety, and body dissatisfaction among preadolescents, adolescents and young women (e.g., Monro and Huon, 2005; Roberts and Gettman, 2004; Slater and Tiggemann, 2002), these types of words and images abound in magazines that target young females.

The May 2004 cover of *Seventeen* tantalized readers with such features as "Flatter Abs in 10 Days!" "The Hottest Celebrity Cuts," and "Love Talk: What Makes Him Open Up?" The cover of the May 2004 issue of *Cosmo Girl!* alerted readers to "Your Top 6 Beauty Mistakes" and "Lines Guys Use to Make You Say Yes"; it also promised advice on how to "Turn Your Guy Friend Into Your Boyfriend!" and offered a test-yourself quiz to determine "What's Your Perfect Date?" Among its other enticements: "Eye Candy: A brand-new sexy-guy centrefold!" and "Secrets: Confessions that will make you gasp!" Adjacent magazines invited readers to feast their eyes on "gorgeous guys"—invariably pop singers and actors; on occasion, "interactive" features invite readers to code such pictures with symbols, such as an eyeball (to indicate "bedroom eyes"), a mouth ("luscious lips"), or a flexed arm ("bodacious bods"). The Winter 2008 issue of *Teen* enticed with featured articles on "What do guys notice first?" "Bad hair is, like, so over," "Boys, bffs and your body" and, as well, promised a definite answer to that veritable brain-teaser, "How many doughnuts can the Jonas boys eat?" Female celebrities, when featured, are likely to be found rhapsodizing about their current object of desire or revealing diet secrets.

Like magazines designed for adult females, teen magazines abound with articles on makeup, for those who are coupled ("Post-make-out Maintenance: Hide the evidence of your latest lovefest with these foolproof cover-up tips") and those who are not ("Breakup makeup: eye gels, concealers and zit zappers: What you need to beat post-relationship beauty blahs").

Advertisements within these magazines reflect the same preoccupations as the articles. An ad introducing a "new airbrush makeup made just for legs" directs girls to "Spray-on Perfect Legs in an Instant!" Or, using slogans that parody and trivialize the message of feminism, ads exhort girls to "Express Your Cell!" (i.e., buy a cell phone); "Stand Up and Shout" (for ultra-thin panty liners); be "Strong & Beautiful" (i.e., by wearing a deodorant which "protects, soothes and nourishes underarm skin"); or "Ban Self Doubt; Ban Peer Pressure, Ban Fear, Ban Stereotypes, Ban Inhibition, Ban Broken Hearts, Ban Conformity, Ban Ignorance, Ban Hate (i.e., by—you guessed it—using Ban deodorant ["We'll take care of sweat & odour. The rest is up to you"]). One advertisement commands, "Women of the World, Raise Your Right Hand" (and slip on "the new diamond right hand ring"—available in "vintage, romantic, floral and contemporary styles").

Magazines targeting adolescent females commonly include a "Real Life True Story"—contemporary morality tales that chronicle the disasters faced by young women who stray from the "good girl" role. "I'm a College Freshman—and a Mom: Can Chelsea, 18, take care of her baby *and* keep her scholarship?" (*Seventeen*, May 2004), offers what is purportedly a first-person account of "a straight-A high school student who believed in abstinence until marriage," from a very religious family ("My family was very involved in our church, and my grandparents owned a Christian bookstore"), who became pregnant at age 16. Exactly how this occurred is never explained; indeed, the article makes no reference whatsoever to the child's father. Instead, "Chelsea" expresses gratitude to her parents for not rejecting her (a reaction very common, she reports, among her former friends), and glumly recounts the hardships she has experienced in attempting to combine life as a single young mother with school and paid employment. "Summer of my STD" (*Seventeen*, Summer 2000) begins, "I never dreamed that a ... girl from a good home could get a sexually transmitted disease. Then I was diagnosed with one." Perhaps not unexpectedly, the same issue of this magazine features an article entitled "Worth the Wait," in which a young woman itemizes the reasons why she has opted to remain a virgin until she meets the "right guy" (*Seventeen*, Summer 2000). Consider here the schizoid split these magazines embody and reflect: on the one hand, images and articles which titillate, entice, endorse, and exhort to sexual preoccupation and activity, and glorify sexuality as if it were the zenith of all human endeavour; and simultaneously, on the other, the pious messages that continue to emphasize a sober chastity!

Based on a content analysis of three years of *Seventeen*, Peirce (1990) concluded that the non-fiction articles teach a girl "that her job is to look good, find a boyfriend, and take care of home and hearth" (p. 61). Peirce's (1993) later analysis of five years of fiction from *Seventeen* and *'Teen* found that characters generally hold stereotypical occupations and that heroines typically rely on someone else, generally a male, to solve their problems. Garner et al.'s (1998) analysis of the advice provided by five magazines that target girls, adolescents, and young women (*YM, Teen, Seventeen, Glamour,* and *Mademoiselle*) found that the messages they proffered encouraged self-objectification as a sex object, reaffirmed traditional gender stereotypes, and conveyed the message that women were incomplete without a man. Thus, for example, women were advised that men found "innocence" appealing but disliked women who were assertive ("demanding," "bossy," "pushy").

The content of magazines which target young men is also problematic. For example, exposure to fitness magazines has been linked to body dissatisfaction and a **drive for muscularity** (McCreary and Sasse, 2000; see also Ricciardelli and McCabe, 2007) among adolescents and young men (Botta, 2003; Halliwell et al., 2007; Smolak and Stein, 2006). Arbour and Martin Ginis (2006) found that exposure to less realistic and hypermasculine images are more likely to result in greater levels of body dissatisfaction than exposure to more realistic images. The extreme popularity of gaming magazines such as *Game Informer Magazine* (which boasts a circulation approaching 2 million) and *Electronic Gaming Monthly* (which is listed as one of the highest-circulation teen magazines in *Marketer's Guide to Media* and is, reportedly, especially popular with prepubescent boys [Adweek Incorporated, 2006]) has prompted concern that these magazines may encourage their readers to model themselves on a hypermuscular adult male body ideal and, in so doing, contribute to body dissatisfaction and low self-esteem (Jung and Peterson, 2007; Tylka et al., 2005). Harrison and Bond (2007: 275–276) argued that the popularity of gaming magazines among young male readers should be of especial concern for at least two reasons. First, they emphasized that "developmental research on media message processing shows that the distinction between reality and fantasy can be blurry for children in the preadolescent years, particular those under the age of 8." Noting that "perceived realism does not appear to affect the extent to which children wish to be like their favorite media characters," they suggested that the characters depicted in gaming magazines may inspire both "idealization and emulation." Second, while they acknowledged that fitness, fashion, and sports magazines all promote images of the "ideal" male body, they maintained that the extremely muscular male images contained in gaming magazines may be particularly influential among young readers inasmuch as the characters they portray "are frequently cast as superheroes, thereby promoting an association between hypermuscularity and the power, control, and agency that superheroes symbolize to children (see also Bickham et al., 2003; Scharrer, 2004).

While it has been noted that magazines are an important source of sex information for both young women and young men (Treise and Gotthoffer, 2002), the messages these young people are getting may be gendered. Articles which ask "Can you tame Justin Timberlake?" or purport to furnish details on what "hottie" Zac Efron is "really like," along with contests which dangle the prospect of meeting a young male celebrity, may all be promoting the ultimate form of "safe sex"—fantasy relationships with inaccessible men (see McCutcheon et al., 2002). These parasocial, or one-sided relationships, in which "fans" feel a spurious intimacy with celebrities (derived through watching them on television, listening to their music, reading about them in gossip columns, etc.), are, of course, highly unlikely to lead to actual contact and even less so to sexual consummation (Cohen, 2003; Karniol, 2001, McCutcheon et al., 2002).

An analysis of 244 articles on sexuality and romance that appeared in *Seventeen* from 1974 to 1994 found that while the variety of sexual scripts discussed did expand to recognize female desire, homosexuality, masturbation, oral sex, and recreational sexuality, the traditional sexual scripts that reinforced dominant gender and sexual norms were favoured (Carpenter, 1998; see also McCracken, 1993; Treise and Gotthoffer, 2002). Batchelor et al.'s (2004) examination of how sexuality is represented in magazines targeted at young people found a "vast range of useful discussion including information about health concerns and in-depth exploration of issues such as consent and examples of couples exploring whether or not they were 'ready' for sex," with "the right of girls to 'say no' ... vividly foregrounded" (p. 669). At the same time, however, they found that both contraception and managing "how far to go" were depicted as the responsibility of the female. Moreover, they report "a limited range of representations for young men, a lack of positive images of lesbian and gay teenagers, and a failure to represent diversity" (see also Jackson, 2005).

On the other hand, young men who turn to magazines such as *Playboy* are likely to receive quite a disparate message. A study based on self-reports of 22 men found that these men viewed their first exposure to *Playboy* as a very memorable event; they identified the magazine as serving as an important source of their sex-related knowledge and contributing to the development of their sexual self-concept (Beggan and Allison, 2003). However, some researchers have suggested that the message embodied in such magazines promotes what Levant (1995: 10) termed "non-relational sex"—"sex as lust without any requirements for relational intimacy, or even for more than a minimal connection with the object of one's desires"—what Brooks (1997: 28) has dubbed the **centrefold syndrome** (see also Bridges et al., 2003; Krassas et al., 2001).

Romance Novels Upon graduating from teen magazines and the Juvenile–Young Adult section, many women gravitate towards what has been described as "a pornography just for women" (Stoller, 1985: 37): romance novels. In male erotica, the predominant formula involves "women who are sexually insatiable and are thus incapable of resisting any type of male sexual advance" (Reiss, 1986: 193). The female fantasy-story counterpart features a male who is "romantically obsessed.... He must pursue her, give her what she desires, and treat her properly" (Reiss, 1986: 195). Not only can he not be rejecting but, in keeping with masculine stereotypes, must also be relentless in pursuit of the object of his desire. Readers of this genre are almost exclusively female (Grescoe, 1996).

Harlequin Enterprises Limited, a Canadian company founded in 1949, dominates the production and sales of romance novels worldwide. Since 1970, Harlequin's annual sales of romance novels have soared from 3 million to "more than 160 million worldwide"; in 1998, the company's operating revenue was over $1.3 billion (eHarlequin.com, 2004). Harlequin novels are now available in 23 languages in more than 100 international markets, and are read by over 50 million women worldwide. According to the company's website, about "one in every six mass-market paperbacks sold in North America is a Harlequin or a Silhouette [owned by the same parent company] novel" (eHarlequin.com, 2004). Grescoe (1996: 16) reported that "the average romance reader" spends approximately $1200 a year on Harlequin novels and consumes from 3 to 20 books a month.

Since their beginnings in the late 1940s, contemporary North American romance novels have undergone a number of transformations. Initially, Harlequin Romances were avowedly "clean, easy to read love stories about contemporary people, set in exciting foreign places"

(Jensen, 1984, in Kaplan, 1991: 324). These stories followed a formula well known to even the most casual reader: "[G]irl meets boy, girl and boy resist each other's allure, boy finally meets girl's expectations, and by the final page they either wed or bed—all told from the heroine's point of view" (Grescoe, 1996: 2). From an original focus on contemporary white, middle-class characters, the range of romantic fantasies captured in print has expanded to include historicals (set in the 1800s—often referred to as "bodice-rippers" because of their provocative cover images), Westerns, medieval and ancient fantasies, supernaturals, gothics, contemporary mysteries, New Age tales, time travels, speculative fictions, New Reality stories dealing with chemical addictions and sexual abuse, and multiculturals featuring non-white and explicitly gay themes and characters (Grescoe, 1996: 7–8). Harlequin's *Flipside* series provides "a romantic comedy for women who appreciate that if love makes the world go round, there's more fun with a few laughs along the way"; *American Romance* offers "upbeat, lively romances about the pursuit of love in the backyards, big cities, and wide-open-spaces of America; *Blaze* promises "Harlequin's sexiest series yet! Red-hot reads that you will want to get your hands on"; the *Present* series entices readers with the promise that they will "meet sophisticated men of the world and captivating women in glamourous, international settings. Seduction and passion guaranteed"; while the *Temptation* series promises a steady stream of stories that are "Sexy, sassy and just a little bit naughty" (eHarlequin.com, 2004).

One of the most noticeable changes in the romance genre—in addition to the presentation of diversity in temporal and geographical settings, ethnicities, and sexual orientations—is an increasingly explicit eroticism. While the traditional romance novel—featuring essentially chaste characters locked in passionately romantic but euphemistically described sexual embraces—still exists, more and more "romantic fiction is for women who move their hips when they read" (Grescoe, 1996: 6). Even though love still conquers all, today's romance novels tend to explicitly depict women as sexual conquests and men as conquerors from the beginning of a tale to its end. According to Laframboise (1996), the consumption of sexually explicit romance novels by a female audience demonstrates "that the female erotic imagination is as varied as the male one" (p. 267), and that women are "capable of feeling desire as powerfully as any man" (p. 264).

A second notable change in romance novels since the 1980s has been a general trend towards the depiction of more balanced gender-power alignments and more self-motivated and autonomous female protagonists. Increasingly, these characters are portrayed as successfully asserting their needs and desires economically, erotically, and romantically. No longer are they solely defined by (more-powerful) males. However, one important imbalance remains. In a twist on the formula typical to male-oriented erotica, in which his masculinity unleashes her sexuality, female-oriented novels are now characterized by a theme of her femininity taming his masculinity and releasing his previously dormant "desperate need for romance" (Grescoe, 1996: 7). Romance novels offer female readers the opportunity "to fantasize about what it would be like to be so attractive that men view you as a 'prize' to be sought after, fought over and worth breaking laws to get their hands on" (Laframboise, 1996: 262). At the end of the story, most Harlequin and other erotic romances provide the central female character with a husband. Supported by plot and dominant imagery, these novels' central message to women—namely, that an intimate relationship is a necessity—remains a constant.

As romance novels have increased in popularity over the years, the reactions of analysts have varied. Some have argued that such escapist fare may foster inaction and acceptance of the status quo by offering women a fantasy refuge from the dissatisfactions of their everyday lives. Shore (2000: 132), asserting that these novels are read "not as mere fantasy or enter-tainment but as a road map for life," denounces their aggressive marketing as symptomatic of a "girl-poisoning culture." Others have offered grudging approval, insofar as the novels bestow some dignity on the experience of surviving under oppressive circumstances. Radway (1984) maintained that romance novels may represent a paradoxical "escapist protest" against conditions that result in unfulfilled lives, and may in fact be the first, imaginative movement towards a nascent independence. Lovgren's (1992: 34) textual analysis of romance novels reported that the contemporary heroines of these novels "exhibit greater independence and that feminine values win out in the plots." Parameswaren's (2002: 832–851) ethnography of young, single, middle- and upper-middle-class women between the ages of 17 and 21 in one urban setting in South India suggested that romance novels serve these women "as mod-ern manuals on sexuality that afford them escape from the burdens of preserving the honor of family and community." Today's romance novels may provide a blueprint for a realignment of gender and gender relations; however, consuming 10 to 20 romance novels a month would seem to provide little time for praxis.

Television

Watching television is the most time-consuming leisure activity of Canadian men and women; indeed, "free time" often becomes "prime time." On average, Canadian men and women spend more time each day watching television than socializing (at home or in other settings), playing sports, or enjoying a meal in a restaurant (*Canadian Global Almanac 2000*: 75). In 2004, Canadians devoted an average of 21.4 hours per week to watching television (Statistics Canada, 2006g).

Recognizing its primary importance in advancing role models and behavioural guide-lines, Marshall McLuhan identified television as the "first curriculum" for young people in contemporary society (in Chidley, 1996: 40). Regarding the content of that curriculum, television has traditionally perpetuated and reinforced traditional stereotypes of men and women. Research conducted in the 1980s found that children's television shows over-whelmingly featured more males than females, and males outnumbered females by four or five to one in the world of animated cartoons (Morgan, 1982, 1987). This pattern was also found in prime time, where male characters outnumbered females by two to one; male characters were also more likely to be portrayed in high-status positions (Davis, 1990; Vande Berg and Streckfuss, 1992). Content analysis conducted by Davis (1990) revealed that men represented 65.4 percent of all prime-time television characters and were more likely to be cast in dramatic roles. Women, in contrast, were not only less visible but were primarily to be found in comedies (suggesting, perhaps, that they need not be taken very seriously). In an examination of an 11-week-long sample of prime-time (9–11 p.m.) televi-sion dramas broadcast between 1990 and 1998, Signorielli and Kahlenberg (2001) found that although television improved its portrayals of the occupations of women and people of colour, the prime-time world still contained stereotypical depictions of gender, race, mari-tal status, and work.

The content of situation comedies, like dramas, may reinforce stereotypes of men and women. In a content analysis of 18 prime-time situation comedies, Fout and Burggraf (2000) examined the body weights of 37 central female characters (92 percent white, 8 percent black), the negative comments these characters received from male characters about their weights and bodies, and audience reaction (e.g., laughter) to such comments. They reported that females of below-average weight were over-represented in these comedies. As well, the heavier the female character, the greater the number of negative comments that were made about or to her, and the more such jibes were reinforced by laughter. The researchers suggested that this combination of thinness-modelling and vicarious reinforcement may contribute to viewers' internalization of gender and weight stereotypes (see also Lampman et al., 2002; Montemurro, 2003). By examining interactions between female and male characters during the 1999–2000 prime-time season, Lauzen and Dozier (2002) attempted to discern whether the hiring of women writers had produced a mitigating effect on appearance-related comments. They found, somewhat ironically, that the employment of women writers was associated with a significant *increase* in the overall number of appearance-related comments; however, it was also associated with a significant decrease in the number of insults. Their research finds that while female and male characters were equally likely to make appearance-related comments, female characters were twice as likely to be the object of those comments. As well, the sex of the character influenced the type of appearance-comment made. Male characters were more likely to insult males than females and more likely to compliment females than males; female characters, however, insulted and complimented both male and female characters with equal frequency. Sexual comments are also pervasive on television and their target is most frequently female, with the speaker being male (Lampman et al., 2002; Ward, 2003).

Role Models The early research of Sternglanz and Serbin (1974) noted the pervasiveness of gender stereotyping in programming directed at children. They found that males were typically cast as adventurous, aggressive, and heroic figures who rescued others from danger, whereas females were likely to be depicted as submissive and passive. Similarly, while male characters engaged in a wide variety of behaviours and were rewarded for their accomplishments, the behavioural repertoire of females was more limited and their endeavours less likely to eventuate in success. More recently, various researchers (Gerber, 1993; Kahan and Norris, 1994) have commented on the continuing relative scarcity of female characters in children's and family programs, and the narrowness of the roles in which female characters are cast. Signorielli (1991), for example, reported that in the world of cartoons, males (including anthropomorphized animals) outnumbered females at a ratio of approximately five to one, while Pollitt (1991: 22) observed that female cartoon characters were usually invisible or cast in token roles, such as the "little sister" (see also Thompson and Zerbinos, 1995). Leaper et al. (2002) examined the gender-stereotyped content of children's TV cartoons across four genres: traditional adventure (e.g., *Spiderman*), non-traditional adventure (e.g., *Reboot*); educational/family (e.g., *Magic School Bus*), and comedy (*Animaniacs*). They found that male characters were still significantly more likely than female characters to be featured in the traditional-adventure and comedy genres. Males in the traditional-adventure genre were more likely than females to use physical aggression. Across all genres, the behaviours that female characters were relatively more likely to exhibit included showing fear, acting romantic, being polite, and acting supportive.

Meehan (1993) found that male and female television characters tended to be gender-typed from an early age. Boy characters were portrayed as significantly more active, assertive, rational, and sarcastic (especially towards parents); they also engaged in more diverse activities than girl characters. Young female characters were more likely to be presented talking on the telephone, reading books and magazines, and helping out with household chores. Descheneau-Guay's (2006) analysis of four television shows preferred by

Quebec children age 7 to 12 (N=398) argued that these programs served to promote apolitical and stereotypical images of females.

Children as young as 2 years old have been found to model their behaviour on what they see on television (Comstock and Paik, 1991; Wood et al., 1991), especially behaviours exhibited by same-sex characters (Evans, 1993). These findings have stimulated concern about the stereotyped gender roles presented in children's programming (Davies et al., 2002). Signorielli (1991) reported that children who spent the greatest amount of time watching television were likely to hold the most gender-typed and stereotypical values. The impact of television, however, is not restricted to children. A sample of undergraduates (96 male, 106 female) completed a questionnaire investigating sexual expectations in relationships. After controlling for several key variables (including characteristics of respondents' romantic relationships, perceptions of the reality of television, and motivation to watch television to learn about the world), researchers found that, in males, exposure to sexually oriented television was related to the expectation of a broad range of sexual activities; in females, it was related to the expectation of earlier sex (Aubrey et al., 2003; see also Ward et al., 2002).

American prime-time television shows from the 1950s through the 1990s most often presented viewers with main characters who embodied familiar male and female stereotypes (Lindsey, 1997: 71). Glascock (2001), in an examination of characters featured on prime-time TV since the 1970s, found the under-representation of females to be less pronounced than in the past; in comedies, the proportion of female major characters has remained consistent over time. Female characters, when portrayed as employed, are still generally depicted in lower-paying and less-prestigious occupations; males are twice as likely to be portrayed as bosses. Male characters' occupational status is still more likely to be identified than females'; however, more females are depicted as holding a job. In terms of physical appearance, female characters have remained young, provocatively dressed, and predominantly blond or red-haired. Depictions of gender appear to be unrelated to race; in general, however, whites are over-represented at the expense of people of colour (see also Darling-Wolf, 2004; Eschholz et al., 2002; Lauzen and Dozier, 2002; Mahtani, 2001). Schooler's (2008) longitudinal research on 52 young Latina girls (age 11 to 17) reported that while frequent viewing of mainstream television was associated with decreased body satisfaction; frequent viewing of black-oriented television was associated with greater body satisfaction.

Armstrong (2007) reports that in a two-week monitoring of prime-time television programming in the United Kingdom, homosexuals were "woefully underrepresented across all national television channels" and that "there were just six minutes that portrayed lesbian and gay lives in a positive manner, as opposed to 32 minutes involving negative terms or comments" (see also Chung, 2007; Clarke and Kitzinger, 2005). Raley and Lucas' (2006) content analysis of prime-time network television during fall 2001 examined the representation of gay male, lesbian, and bisexual characters in shows that contained at least one non-heterosexual character in a reoccurring role. Building on past research that suggested four stages of media representation for minority groups—non-representation, ridicule, regulation, and respect—they suggested that gay males and lesbians have "progressed" into the stage of ridicule with only some movement into the later stages of regulation and respect (see also Bonds-Raacke et al., 2007; Castiglia and Reed, 2007; Fouts and Inch, 2005).

Noting the increasing presence of gay men as designers and participants on lifestyle television, particularly on shows dedicated to homemaking and interior decorating, Gorman-Murray (2006) argued that these programs may challenge the hetero-normalization of "home" and "family" through their presentation of "gay domesticity." However, Westerfelhaus and Lacrois (2006) maintained that shows such as *Queer Eye for the Straight Guy* (cancelled in 2007) function "as a mediated ritual of rebellion that domesticates queers, contains queer sexuality,... [and] places straight men at the sociosexual center" (Westerfelhaus and Lacrois, 2006). Others have directed attention to the stereotypical gay images that these types of shows may reproduce and perpetuate (e.g., Meyer and Kelley, 2004; Weiss, 2005). Diamond's (2005) analysis of American media representations of female–female sexuality argued that while these images may counter stereotypes of lesbians as "unattractive, masculine and hostile ... they also implicitly convey that the most desirable and acceptable form of female–female sexuality is that which pleases and plays to the heterosexual male gaze, titillating male viewers while reassuring them that the participants remain sexually available in the conventional heterosexual market-place" (p. 104). She noted that female–female sexuality is often presented as simply "experimental" behaviour with pains taken "to clarify that the participants are not, in fact, lesbians" (see also Keegan, 2006).

Although contemporary "reality-TV" shows feature strong, aggressive, and independent women (notably *Judge Judy* and contestants on such series as *Survivor* and *The Apprentice*), a jarring number of these programs continue to depict women as obsessed with their appearance and with snaring a (preferably rich) man (e.g., *The Swan, Blind Date, Elimidate, Extreme Dating, Extreme Makeover, What Not to Wear, The Bachelor, America's Top Model, Joe Millionaire, Buff Brides,* etc.). Zurbriggen and Morgan (2006) found that among undergraduate women, there is a positive correlation between frequency of reality dating program viewing and both acceptance of a sexual double standard and the belief that dating is a "game" in which men and women are adversaries. In addition, compared to those young women who were not frequent viewers of reality TV, frequent viewers were more likely to express strong belief in the importance of appearance. In non-reality shows, females are still more likely to be portrayed as passive and indecisive, dominated by men, and enmeshed in non-egalitarian intimate relationships. While female characters may be presented as dominant within their families (e.g., *Everybody Loves Raymond, King of Queens*), they remain less likely than male characters to be shown in leadership and decision-making positions outside the home; women occupying leadership positions are often portrayed as relying heavily upon advice provided by male co-workers, mentors, and intimates. In general, female characters are more likely than males to be shown pursuing altruistic goals in service of home and family, or to be cast as victims needing rescue from homicidal stalkers (Davis, 1990; Wood, 1994). Signorielli (1991: 89, 94) observed that women of colour, older women, and foreign women are especially likely to be depicted as the victims of violent crime (see also Walz, 2002).

However, television stereotypes men just as it does women. Scharrer (2001) analyzed 321 male characters from American police and detective dramas televised in November of 1997, focusing on the relationship between hypermasculinity and three dimensions of antisocial behaviour: callousness towards women or sex, thrill-seeking, and toughness. A strong association was found between hypermasculinity and antisocial behaviour/physical aggression. Aggression and criminal behaviour (in "bad guys") correlated with both callous attitudes towards females/sex and thrill-seeking; "good guys" exhibited a correlation between thrill-seeking and toughness (see also Scharrer, 2001a).

While female television characters are often located within the home and occasionally presented as "Domestic Divas," house-husbands and single fathers have been a rarity. The location of such anomalous males in comedies serves to reinforce their fish-out-of-water condition (Scharrer, 2001b; Douglas, 2003). *Two and a Half Men*, for example, a comedy about a divorced father living with his young son in the house of his sex-obsessed playboy brother, directs primary focus to the playboy's constant amorous adventures; housekeeping chores, in this show, are handled by a hired (female) domestic. Nurturant males are more likely to be located in comedies (*Frazier, Friends, Will & Grace*) than in dramas; in both genres, such men are typically portrayed as having high-status occupations (e.g., physicians, lawyers, psychiatrists). Working-class men, whether in cartoons, comedies, or dramas, are more apt to be depicted as sexist Neanderthals or loutish buffoons than as "sensitive New Age men." In television as in real life, the evolution of gender representations away from stereotypes has been more noticeable in female characters than in male. Meehan (1993) found that androgyne characters (i.e., characters who combine masculine instrumental and feminine expressive traits and behaviours) were much more likely to be female than male (e.g., Captain Janeway of *Star Trek: Voyager*, Buffy of *Vampire Slayer* fame, and the various and interchangeable assistant district attorneys found on the multiple *Law and Order* series).

In both past and present, daytime soap operas—kindred spirits of the romance novel— have provided a notable exception to television's limited and limiting portrayals of women (Larson, 1996). In soap operas, women are hardly under-represented, nor are their lives confined primarily to the private spheres of homemaking and parenting. On the contrary, in the world inhabited by soap opera characters, houses only need cleaning when a murder or an affair has been committed and a cover-up is taking place. While parents may dramatically proclaim their children to be the centre of their lives, only rarely are they seen engaging in active parenting roles, schlepping their children to hockey practice or orthodontist appointments. Even pregnancy requires less energy—but is more absorbing, especially when paternity is uncertain. Female characters afflicted with the common soap opera problem of amnesia often forget where, and who, their children are. Parents of any soap-opera child are also likely to be divorced, to maintain separate residences with their latest true loves, to be perpetually fearful of having their child kidnapped (especially by rejected fathers or deranged women who cannot conceive), and to employ a retinue of housekeepers and nannies to deal with such mundane matters as child care, meal preparation, and housecleaning. In soap-opera families, young children are usually seen as extensions of adults, are mentioned more often than shown (except at occasional birthday parties that provide convenient excuses for the adults to converse and connive), and only become prominent as the subject of custody battles. When the dust settles, children are sent back to their bedrooms to play until they become adolescents and can resurface, all grown up, during the summer months when students are more likely to be watching.

Soap-opera women may be powerful in the business world, but generally in gender-appropriate or gender-linked areas, becoming doyennes of the fashion, cosmetics, and hospitality industries. Women are often depicted as acquiring their power through personal ties to powerful men or by exercising their devious "feminine wiles." A frequently occurring storyline involves a man rescuing the company of a weaker female; this theme reinforces the stereotype of women's unsuitability for the high-pressure world of business. Moreover, soap-opera women who demonstrate stereotypical femininity are often presented as morally superior to those who are more masculine or androgynous. Strong women who are successful, assertive, and highly determined to survive without men are most often portrayed as hydras and "villains" (Benokraitis and Feagin, 1995).

Advertising and Commercials By the time an adolescent reaches the age of 18, he or she has watched approximately 360 000 television commercials (Garst and Bodenhausen, 1997). Stereotypical "ideal" images of women and men are reinforced through advertising (Edens and McCormick, 2000; Wolin, 2003). An early study of gender in advertising noted that women were typically portrayed either as demented housewives, pathologically obsessed with cleanliness and cleaning products, or as wannabe sex objects, driven to purchase a never-ending array of cosmetics (Courtney and Lockeretz, 1971). By the mid-1970s, Venkatesan and Losco (1975) reported a decline in the "most obnoxious" types of gendered advertising, although they noted that the messages being conveyed remained consistent. Three years later, Tuchman et al. (1978) reported that more than three quarters of the television ads featuring women still were for products employed in the bathroom or kitchen. Women continue to be significantly over-represented in commercials for domestic products. Bartsch et al. (2000), examining 757 commercials aired on major American networks, reported that the proportion of advertisements featuring female representatives increased from 50 percent to 59 percent from 1976 to 1998; over the same time period, the proportion of advertisements with female voice-overs also increased from approximately 10 percent to 30 percent. However, females remained over-represented in domestic-product advertisements, while males remained over-represented in advertisements for non-domestic products (see also Monk-Turner et al., 2007).

It appears that even today, a "wrong"-sexed voice may be considered less effective in selling gender-imaged products. Whipple and McManamon's (2002) research, based on 472 undergraduates, found that while men and women were judged equally effective as presenters for gender-neutral products, the sex of the spokesperson and of the announcer significantly affected evaluations of commercials for a female-gender-imaged product; for male-gender-imaged products, the sex of the presenters had no impact on evaluations. Peirce (2001) was curious about what might happen if, for example, the Energizer Bunny were female; to this end, undergraduates were shown three versions of commercials created for each of three products (golf clubs, vacuum cleaners, and coffee), using either a male, female, or gender-neutral spokes-"character." Participants indicated that the perceived congruence between gender and product type affected their perceptions about the product. A male spokes-character was seen as more appropriate for a male-oriented product, whereas a female spokes-character promoted the perception that the product was less male-oriented. Morrison and Shaffer (2003) asked men and women with various gender-role orientations (e.g., masculine, feminine, androgynous) to evaluate gender-stereotyped and non-stereotyped advertisements for supposedly "gendered" products that are, in reality, used by both sexes. They found that men and women with traditional gender-role orientations (i.e., masculine men, feminine women) responded more favourably to traditional (i.e., gender-stereotyped) advertisements; non-traditional ("androgynous") participants reacted somewhat more favourably to the non-traditional advertisements.

Although the rigidity of gender stereotypes has declined over the past 15 to 20 years, women's lives as depicted in commercials continue to bear only a nodding acquaintanceship with the breadth and depth of women's lives outside of television (Garst and Bodenhausen, 1997; Lusk, 2000). A content analysis of 1337 prime-time commercials shown on the three major American networks (ABC, CBS, and NBC) in 1998 found that female and male characters were cast in much the same way that they had been in the 1980s (Ganahl et al., 2003), and concluded that television commercials continue to perpetuate traditional stereotypes about men and women. Women remained under-represented in primary roles, except in commercials for health and beauty products; older women were the most under-represented group of all. In the main, women's role in commercials was to serve as younger, supportive adjuncts to men (see also Grant and Hundley, 2007). A positive relationship between extensive television viewing and the maintenance of rigid gender stereotypes has been reported in studies conducted on children, adolescents, and adults (e.g., Edens and McCormick, 2000; Lanis and Covell, 1995; Milkie, 1994; St. Lawrence and Joyner, 1991).

Coltraine and Messineo (2000) reported that advertising imagery may contribute to the perpetuation of subtle prejudice by exaggerating cultural differences. Their findings, based on an examination of 1699 television commercials aired on programs with high ratings from 1992 to 1994, indicated that white or male characters in television commercials enjoyed more prominence and exercised more authority. "In general, 1990s television commercials tend to portray White men as powerful, White women as sex objects, African American men as aggressive, and African American women as inconsequential" (Coltraine and Messineo, 2000: 363; see also McLaughlin and Goulet, 1999). Feldstein and Feldstein (1982) observed that male dominance is also modelled in commercials intended to influence young children; except in advertisements for dolls, male characters are numerically over-represented in children's commercials, and girls are presented as being more passive than boys. Sobieraj (1998) reported that children's toy advertisements have continued to reveal rigid gender dichotomies: Girls and girls only are depicted as fawning over physical appearance, while boys and boys only are shown exhibiting aggressive behaviour (see also Larson, 2003). Larson's (2001) content analysis of 595 commercials featuring children (aired during children's programming) found that although nearly equal numbers of girls and boys were portrayed in cooperative activity, single-gender commercials continued to portray girls in stereotypical domestic settings.

Commercials aimed at children use presentation style as well as explicit content to target the intended purchaser by gender. Welch et al. (1979) noted that commercials targeting boys are distinguished by such features as "rapid action, frequent cuts, loud music, sound effects, and many scene changes," while those for girls feature "background music, fades and dissolves, and female narrations" (in Lips, 1993: 273). Research has found girls to be particularly susceptible to advertising's promotion of name-brand products (Kwak et al., 2002; Ragas and Kozlowski, 1998; Underhill, 1999). Pine and Nash (2003) reported that when preschool children (age 4 to 5 years) were asked to identify the drink, snack, toy, breakfast cereal, and sportswear that most children of their own gender preferred, 78 percent of girls chose the brand-name, advertised product in preference to the non-brand product; "only" 58 percent of boys did so.

The impact of advertising, however, goes beyond the inculcation of a preference for brand-name products. Twitchell (2003) has argued that our society has been profoundly and invidiously affected by the messages and pervasiveness of advertising. He has charged the advertising industry with engendering "AdCult"—a culture permeated with the values and beliefs promulgated by advertising; the "AdCult" mentality expresses itself in an obsessive desire to live the lifestyle presented in commercials and advertisements. In particular, he has accused the anti-acne and makeup industries of continuing to exploit and mislead women by defining "beauty" in narrow and stereotypical ways (see also Blaine and McElroy, 2002; Kacen, 2000; Kinsella, 2001; Oderkerken-Schorder et al., 2002).

Men and their roles, both within and outside the home, are also presented stereotypically in television commercials. Hirschman (2003) reported that advertisements featuring men continue to exalt the ethos of rugged individualism and personal power, depicting males amidst dogs, guns, and cars. When portrayed in a home or family setting, men are unlikely to be shown performing housework (e.g., cleaning, doing dishes) or household-related tasks (e.g., shopping) (Kaufman, 1999). When depicted with children (but no visible spouse), the children are much more likely to be boys. "Commercial" dads are rarely shown physically caring for children; most often, they are portrayed reading to, teaching, eating with, or playing with them. In general, men "appearing alone with children are more likely to be shown outside the home than women alone with children" (Kaufman, 1999: 439).

In Canadian and American advertising, the increase in nudity and near-nudity perpetuates a stereotype of women as decorative sexual objects (Davies et al., 2002; Johnson and Young, 2003; Thompson, 2000). Gill (2008) suggested that in recent years, there appears to have been a significant shift in advertising representations of women, "such that rather than being presented as passive objects of the male gaze, young women in adverts are now frequently depicted as active, independent and sexually powerful." However, Gill argued that the stock figures of these "new representations"—for example, "the vengeful woman set on punishing her partner or ex-partner for his transgressions, and the hot lesbian almost always entwined with her beautiful Other or double" (p. 35)—are equally prescriptive in their demand that "young women should not only be beautiful but sexy, sexually knowledgeable/practised and always 'up for it.'" While the faces of men are shown more often than their bodies ("face-isms"), women's bodies ("body-isms") or body parts ("partial-isms") appear prominently. Thus, a late 1990s advertisement for White Label PC CD-ROM Games featured a portion of a woman's body (from mid-rib to upper-thigh) clad only in a small white thong bikini. The caption read: "It's the quality in the box that counts."

Davies et al.'s (2002) experimental research reported that when university-age women are exposed to highly feminine-stereotyped television commercials (i.e., that lay emphasis upon the desirability of women's physical beauty and sexual attractiveness), they expressed less interest in vocations that emphasize quantitative reasoning (e.g., math and science) and voiced lower leadership aspirations that did their counterparts who viewed gender-neutral or counter-stereotypical ads. The findings of this study suggest that gendered and sexualized ads may not only encourage women to think of their value as defined by their looks but, as well, "'prime' lower achievement orientation among young women" (APA, 2007: 33).

Belknap and Leonard (1991: 105) observed that the "selling [of] products that depict more traditional cultural patterns has been slow to change." Only since the obsession with abdominal muscles ("abs") began in the mid-1990s have men's bodies been more prominent in advertising, often reduced to a six-pack partial-ism (Reichert and Lambiase, 2003; Rohlinger, 2002; Stern, 2003). The depiction of minority women has been particularly resistant to change; minority women have primarily figured as "exotic" ornaments—when they have appeared at all (Fleras, 2003: 316). As measured by number of appearances in advertisements and articles over a 30-year period, women of colour have been largely invisible in Canada's national newsmagazine, *Maclean's* (MacGregor, 1995). Millard and Grant's (2006) examination of women in magazine advertisements and fashion spreads in *Cosmopolitan, Glamour,* and *Vogue* (N=226) found that, compared to white models, black models were portrayed significantly less often in explicitly sexual poses but significantly more often in submissive poses. Bailey's (2006) examination of the portrayal of African American men in advertising found that while their representation was high, they were far more likely to appear in ads for clothes, shoes, and accessories and seldom portrayed in occupational roles or in business and work-related settings. Advertising is also rife with ageism; older women are also relatively invisible, confined to appearances in ads for adult diapers, hair dyes, dentures, and wrinkle creams (Jamieson, 1995; Maas and Hasbrook, 2001).

There can be little doubt that advertising's images of men and women stress differences rather than similarities. Consider, for example, "feminine protection products" advertisements and the significant cultural meanings they convey. Such ads are particularly interesting for the manner in which they promote products for a bodily function that has typically been treated as "taboo" within our own and other societies (Frost, 2001; Houppert, 1999). Implicit in the advertising are messages reinforcing stereotypical conceptions about women.

The idea that women—menstruating women in particular—are unclean, contaminated, or cosmically dangerous is neither new nor unique to North American society (Forbes et al., 2003; Matlin, 2003; Rempel and Baumgartner, 2003). Many cultures have created normative prohibitions regulating women's behaviour during menses, ranging from being secluded in a "menstrual hut," avoidance of contact with weapons for hunting and warfare, and avoidance of sexual activity, to restriction of hair-washing or swimming, curtailment of strenuous physical activity, and temporary suspension of aircraft-flying privileges. The idea of menstruation as both an experience and a topic to be avoided is captured in our language; menstruation may be directly anathematized as "the curse" (a monthly reminder of women's responsibility, according to Christian religious beliefs, for the human fall from grace), or acknowledged indirectly via a panoply of euphemisms. The expression favoured by marketers, "feminine hygiene products," is itself significant for its double message. In a spectacular stroke of advertising illogic, menstruation—a sex-linked irreducible difference—is characterized as both unhygienic *and* unfeminine; however, as these ads quickly inform us, their product can restore both a woman's hygiene and her femininity (Kissling, 2002; Park, 1996).

Advertisers expound the virtues of a bewildering array of products designed for that famous "time of month"; there are napkins for "heavy days," "medium days," and "light days," tampons ("slim line," "satin," and/or with environmentally friendly disposable wrappers), maxipads (including the oxymoronic "ultra-thin maxis"), minipads (scented and unscented varieties), and panty liners. It would seem that the aim of advertisers is to keep all women padded, tamponed, and panty-lined for all 28 days of each and every (theoretically constructed) menstrual cycle for approximately 40 years of menses (give or take a pregnancy or two).

Over the past 20 years, advertising has become somewhat more direct. Friday (1996: 190) wrote: "When I was growing up, the only references to feminine hygiene were the full-page ads of beautiful women in elegant gowns and in a corner the discreet message, 'Modess Because.' Because what?" In 2001, in an attempt to break away from "the tired clichés used to sell most feminine hygiene products" (e.g., "a woman on a horse, wearing white pants"), the ad agency Ogilvy and Mather unveiled an ad for Kotex's "Security Tampon" that opted to use direct language and the verboten "p" word to sell the brand (Littman, 2001). However, they hit a snag when "[v]irtually every network in the United States and Canada balked at the idea, saying the spots would offend viewers" (Littman, 2001). Although the ad agency eventually persuaded at least some of the networks to air the ads—and the sales figures indicated that women appreciated the frank talk—such ads remain the exception rather than the rule.

A 2004 television ad for "mini-tampons" featured a young woman in a high school classroom attempting to pass a tampon to another woman seated in the next row; she is caught in the act by a male teacher who asks her to hand over the object, saying, "I trust you have enough for everyone in the class?"—to which the young woman replies, "Well, enough for the girls." At this witticism, the girls laugh uproariously while the teacher and male students look bemused. Other ads for "feminine protection" remain similarly oblique, avoiding direct mention of what, exactly, the product is to be used for. Thus, rather than assert that a product is to be used for the collection of menstrual blood, the product is advertised with vague mutterings and promises that the product will bring about "freedom." Ads for the Stay-Free line of products are a distinguished example: They invariably depict women (assumedly using their product) romping in wide-open spaces and engaging heartily in vigorous exercise. On occasion, the veiled language and imagery within such ads can become truly absurd. One example: A 2004 magazine advertisement for Tampax "Satin Teen" featured cartoon drawings of two tampons—one a large, ominous tampon with shark-like teeth, and the other, a slim and smiling tampon, adorned with blue eyes and long eyelashes, one "hand" poised on its "hip" and the other waving. The caption under the first reads: "Big scary tampon"; under the second: "Nice friendly tampon."

Advertisers marketing other products "for women" also display a penchant for euphemism. Perhaps the most egregious examples may be found in ads promoting "feminine hygiene sprays" or "feminine deodorant sprays." Throughout the 1980s and 1990s, such ads often featured women, typically mothers and daughters, dressed in white, diaphanous garments, having intimate conversations on the decks of boats, or while walking along a beach or through fields of daisies, and discussing how to feel "really clean inside." Or a young woman would hesitantly approach an older woman who was happily gardening and timidly say, "Sometimes I don't feel fresh enough. Did you ever have this problem?" The older woman would invariably reply, "Of course," in a gentle all-knowing voice. The two women would hug and the brand name of the product would appear discreetly across the bottom of the television screen. Precisely what problem both women suffered from was never clearly identified. Such ads, then and now, implicitly convey that to be female is to suffer biological afflictions too unspeakable to address in a straightforward fashion. In addition, these ads suggest that in order to be sexually desirable, women must douse themselves vigorously with a variety of proprietary products. Apparently, during moments of sexual ecstasy, nothing excites a man like a woman whose genitals smell like a Glad Plug-in.

Men, evidently, do not suffer from such problems. Only one serious attempt was made to cajole men into trying a "masculine deodorant spray." In the early 1980s, Brut came out with a product designed to make men feel really clean outside—PUB: Below the Belt. However, Pub's high alcohol content irritated men's sensitive scrotal skin. In response to numerous complaints, the product was taken off the market in less than a year. In stark contrast, feminine protection sprays—"when you want to feel like a woman"—are still being strongly promoted despite suspected links to vaginal cancer.

Popular Music

As Frith (1981) pointed out, prior to the 1950s, young people adopted the musical preferences of their parents. "There were adult records and children's records, and nothing in between" (Palmer, 1995: 17). In the late 1950s, as part of a new trend towards segmented marketing (i.e., the targeting of specific sectors of the market), business began targeting the emerging and large teen population of war babies and baby boomers. The economic prosperity of the postwar years had also put more money into the hands of these nascent adults. Before long, the television, movie, advertising, and marketing industries joined forces with the music industry to tap the potential of the adolescent market. Canadian youth were soon exposed not only to American "rock 'n' roll" stars such as Elvis Presley but to Canadian performers such as the Crew Cuts, the Diamonds, and Paul Anka (Melhuish, 1996: 62; Palmer, 1995: 30).

From the outset, the rock 'n' roll industry was male-dominated. Music writers, arrangers, producers, performers, concert promoters, and radio-station managers, along with disc jockeys and the play-list programmers who determined which music got played, were overwhelmingly male (Dickerson, 1998). Sexism and racism both influenced rock's early form and content. Although the roots of rock 'n' roll were in the rhythm-and-blues music of black musicians, the 1950s music industry deliberately produced "bland, well-crafted songs" for the teenage market, purposefully grooming chosen performers as **teenage entertainers** (Frith, 1981). White "boys next door" from the new middle-class suburbs or the old working-class neighbourhoods were strategically cast as the new teen idols (Palmer, 1995); such "squeaky clean" young white men as Bobby Curtola, Frankie Avalon, and Cliff Richards were considered "perfect for the whitebread market" (Szatmary, 1996: 67) and "safe" fantasy objects for young white girls.

Technological innovations played a part in the burgeoning of rock 'n' roll. The growing popularity and affordability of television sets (and programs such as *American Bandstand, Canadian Bandstand, Rock 'n' Roll Dance Party*, and *Soul Train*), the increasing availability of both AM and FM radio, and the introduction of car radios, portable transistor radios, and inexpensive 45-rpm records (manufactured almost exclusively for teenagers) all made rock 'n' roll easily accessible to a young generation living in comparatively prosperous times. Adolescence was romanticized in the song lyrics of the day; "[t]he music of the Dick Clark era, the Brill Building songwriters, the Beach Boys, the Motown artists, and the early Beatles showed a preoccupation with dating, cars, high school and teen love" (Szatmary, 1996: xii). Songs by early all-female (then referred to as "all-girl") groups, such as the Ronettes, the Supremes, the Marvelettes, and the Shirelles, were especially likely to feature the "limited language of sentiment, in the rhyming simplicities of moon and June" (Frith, 1981: 35). The meteoric rise of young female rock stars to fame and a lifestyle of inconceivable wealth and glamour turned them into role models and served "to create the fantasy among many young girls that they too could become famous ... [and] the fantasies of teenage girls helped ... establish a music-publishing empire" (Szatmary, 1996: 74, 77–78).

Over time, the "wholesome" whitebread image of rock 'n' roll gave way to grittier alternatives, created partly by the musicians themselves and partly by the music marketers. Elvis Presley had broken the mould, introducing an electric and dangerous sexuality that scandalized parents and irrevocably changed the insipid popular music scene. Later, the Rolling Stones became the original "bad boys of rock"; promoting this image, a 1964 headline in *Melody Maker* asked, "Would You Let Your Daughter Go Out With A Rolling Stone?" (Szatmary, 1996: 137). While the Beatles chastely announced, "I Wanna Hold Your Hand," the Stones flaunted a more overtly sexual and frequently misogynistic message in songs such as "Just Make Love to Me," "Under My Thumb," and "Stupid Girl." If "cock-rock performers" (Frith, 1981: 227) offered "a masturbatory celebration of penis power," the association between "sex, drugs, and rock 'n' roll" (rapidly becoming youth's pledge of allegiance) was furthered by acid psychedelic rockers and tunes such as "Dirty Old Man," "Touch Me," "Love Me Two Times," and "Light My Fire."

The splitting of rock into a host of subgenres was partly a reflection of marketing attempts to identify and target more specific adolescent as well as older audiences on the basis of ethnicity and lifestyle. Soul music—which black disc jockey Magnificent Montague described in the 1960s as expressing that "last to be hired, the first to be fired, brown all-year-round, sit-in-the-back-of-the-bus feeling"—and songs such as Aretha Franklin's "Respect" and "Think" (which ends with the repetition of the word "freedom") were to attract greater mainstream interest following the Detroit inner-city riots and renewed civil-rights activism of the late 1960s. Other young people, embittered and disillusioned with American society and the Vietnam War, responded to the pronounced pessimism and anti-war sentiment of heavy-metal groups such as Led Zeppelin and Black Sabbath. The emergent gay-liberation movement of the 1970s led to a greater openness about bisexuality and homosexuality and encouraged a variety of rock performers to publicly experiment with a gender-bending style. From the pink boas of Elton John and the changing personas of David Bowie, to the sexual ambiguity of Boy George in the 1980s and of Marilyn Manson in the 1990s, theatrical androgyny became an accepted convention of popular music. The industry also began to manufacture and deliberately package musical acts (such as the Monkees in the 1960s and the Backstreet Boys and Spice Girls in the 1990s) to appeal to specific demographic groups in the marketplace.

Frith (1981: 227) observed that the world of popular music at the end of the 1970s was strongly gendered. Female fans were overwhelmingly attracted to **teeny-bop music** and its performers, who plaintively expressed vulnerability and need. Female audiences attended mainly to the lyrics of songs and less to their rhythms; in this genre, sexuality was sublimated into "a kind of spiritual yearning, carrying only vague hints of physical desire. The singer wants someone to love—not as a bedmate, but as a soul mate" (Frith, 1981: 227; see also Rothbaum and Tsang, 1998). In sharp contrast, males were overwhelmingly attracted to **cock-rock music** and its performers, who expressed a raw, aggressive, unabashedly physical sexuality. "Their bodies are on display (plunging shirts and tight trousers, chest hair and genitals), mikes and guitars are phallic symbols (or else caressed like female bodies), the music is loud, rhythmically insistent, built around techniques of arousal and release" (Frith, 1981: 227). The teeny-bop/cock-rock distinction persists today. However, the continuing proliferation of popular music forms makes classification more complicated and cock-rock strutting rarely moves today's jaded audiences to more than raised eyebrows—unless, as does happen, performers expose breasts/genitals onstage (Wenner, 2008).

Although women have always been fairly well-represented in the country, soul, and light-pop music genres, only a few, such as Janis Joplin, Pat Benatar, Joan Jett, and Tina Turner, broke through into the higher echelons of rock music in the 1970s and 1980s. In the 1970s, Helen Reddy's soft-rock tune "I Am Woman" became the unofficial anthem of the women's movement. However, by the mid-1980s women accounted for less then 10 percent of rock performers (Groce and Cooper, 1990) and less than a quarter of the performers in music videos (Vincent et al., 1987). Female stars were exceptions to the male-ruled rock-music scene; frequently, their fame was enhanced by some unique quality of their public persona or private lifestyle. Janis Joplin was controversial as much for her alcohol-fuelled performances as for her jagged lyrics about womanhood and raw sexual sound. Madonna—an average singer and protean entertainer—shrewdly recognized the profitability of notoriety and has exploited it with spectacular success since her appearance in the 1980s (Faith, 1993).

From an examination of the "Top 20" charts in *Billboard* magazine (considered the bible of the recording industry), Dickerson (1998) reported that 1996 was a watershed year for women in rock music. In that year, for the first time since rock became acknowledged as a distinct musical form in 1954, the majority of Top 20 charting artists (drawn from all genres of music) were female. Suggestive of women's growing presence within the music industry, 11 of the 15 winners of the "New Artist" Grammy from 1994 to 2008 were women. These award-winning women, who include Amy Winehouse, Carrie Underwood, Norah Jones, Alicia Keys, Sheryl Crow, and Lauryn Hill, represent a wide variety of musical genres. In 2002, Canadian Avril Lavigne's *Let Go* was ranked North America's top-selling debut CD; the singer, who early on eschewed spandex and belly tops for jeans, neckties, and a Napanee Home Hardware T-shirt, also "set a whole new standard for chic among female rock stars" (*Canadian Global Almanac 2004*: 626).

Awards to honour achievement in the recording industry, such as the Grammys, the Junos, the MTV Video Music Awards, the Canadian Country Music Awards, the East Coast Music Awards (for artists performing, recording, or rooted in Atlantic Canada), and the ADISQ or "Felix" Awards (for achievement in Canada's French-language music and performance scene), still routinely feature distinct categories for "Best Female Artist/Vocalist" or "Best Male Pop Vocal" or "Best Male Country Vocal Performance." These sex-based awards are curious, given that in many other award categories the sex of the performer is ostensibly irrelevant (e.g., "Best Rap Album," "Best Alternative Album," "Best R&B/Soul Recording," "Best Reggae/Calypso Recording," "Best Vocal Jazz Album"). A focus on musical excellence rather than sex would help advance what Sarah McLachlan identified as her goal in establishing the Lilith Fair tours of 1997–1999: "a time when we're not referred to as women musicians, [but] we're called musicians [period]" (as quoted in the *Edmonton Journal*, 4 December 1997: C7).

Music-label executives carefully control and monitor the careers and material of their recording artists; accordingly, the predominant theme of mainstream female singers, following a well-established formula, has been the pains and joys of heterosexual love. The birth of "underground" music in the 1970s, however, posed a challenge to the industry. Since that time, a new pattern has emerged: First, alternative styles arise out of protest against the mainstream; eventually, the industry co-opts those styles, assimilating them into the commercial music machine. An iteration of this pattern (which has also occurred in punk, hip-hop, and rap) occurred in the 1990s with what has been referred to as **women's music**. Lont (1997: 127) observed that "[w]omen's music was originally defined as music by women, for women, about women, and financially controlled by women. By this definition, a song written by women, about women, and for women would not be considered a part of women's music if it were recorded on a major label."

Lont (1997: 126–127) noted that knowledgeability about women's music served in earlier decades as "a key into the lesbian community": "If a woman mentioned certain performers such as Cris Williamson or Meg Christian, it identified her as a lesbian." Sport (2007: 343) argued that women's music has "contributed to societal understanding of issues centering on women, sexuality and alternative sexuality, feminism, sexism, and those outside of the mainstream." Some performers, such as Melissa Etheridge and Tracy Chapman, who originally performed before primarily female audiences, have sought and achieved broader renown. Others, including some punk rock and Riot Grrl bands, have preferred to resist commercial success so they can continue to "broach issues formerly untouched, such as rape, abuse, assault and other intensely personal themes" (Blofson and Aron, 1997: 15). Blofson and Aron (1997: 16) noted that while the fashion industry was quick to turn "that 'grrl thang' into a commodity [complete with plastic barrettes and "Girls Rock" T-shirts] ... Riot Grrl was virtually split between those who wanted to keep it underground and those who were willing to talk in the press and sacrifice secrecy to reach out to other girls." As with symbolic representations in other media, traditional gender images are transmitted by mass distribution while alternative images receive only limited distribution. The price to be paid for increased access to mainstream audiences is frequently the dilution of the original visionary message.

At present, it is the lyrical content of popular rock music which is the primary focus of social scrutiny and expressed concern. Bretthauer et al.'s (2007) content analysis study of the lyrics contained within *Billboard*'s "Hot 100" list of songs suggested that these songs commonly extolled power over, objectification of, and violence against women. Their analysis identified six focal themes: "men and power; sex as top priority for males; objectification of women; sexual violence; women defined by having a man; and women as not valuing themselves" (p. 29). While accusations that pop-music lyrics promote violence against women are not new, these charges are now levelled most vehemently against rap. Rap—"gangsta" rap in particular—has been criticized for its characterization of women as "bitches" and "hos" (whores), and "for graphic lyrics boasting about the abuse, rape, and murder of women" (Burk and Shaw, 1995: 437; Peterson et al., 2007). Cobb et al. (2002: 3) reported that "[f]ew recent pop-cultural issues have generated as much media attention as when the rapper Eminem was nominated for a Grammy. Almost immediately following the nomination, women's groups (and lesbian groups) mobilized to protest." In a November 14, 2000, newspaper article, the music critic for the *Vancouver Sun* emphasized the overt misogyny of Eminem's lyrics, noting that in the song "Bonnie and Clyde," "Slim Shady" (Eminem's persona/alter ego) "stalks his ex-wife then murders her in front of their child. On 'Kim' he murders his wife all over again, except he puts her name to it. Where's the satire here? Where's the lesson that 'bitch-slapping' is a bad thing, not a right of manhood?" (in Cobb et al., 2002: 3). Martino et al's (2006) content analysis of 164 songs sung by 16 artists who are especially popular with teens reported that while only 15 percent contained lyrics that were sexually degrading, the majority of songs that did were by rap and rap metal artists. Their national longitudinal survey of 1461 American adolescents additionally found that "the more youths listened to degrading sexual music content, the more likely they were to subsequently initiate intercourse and progress in their noncoital activity" (p. e435). Johnson et al.'s (1995) research on black adolescent girls found that those who were exposed to sexualized rap videos evinced greater acceptance of teen dating violence than those who were not. However, while the lyrics of Ja Rule's "Living It Up" smugly announce, "Half the ho's hate me, half them love me/The ones that hate me/Only hate me 'cause they ain't f***ed me/.../Do you think I've got time/To f*** all these ho's?" it is assuredly true that the song lyrics of non-rappers can be equally vexatious. One might consider, for example, Kid Rock's tender ditty, "F*** off" which directs "So blow me bitch I don't rock for cancer/I rock for the cash and the topless dancers" or the provocative question that is coyly posed by the burlesque-inspired Pussycat Dolls, "Don'tcha wish your girlfriend was hot like me?" As Christenson and Roberts (1998) observed, references to sexual behaviour, sometimes coupled with love/romance and sometimes not, are rife in the music preferred by North American adolescents; indeed, Pardun et al.'s (2005) analysis of the content of television programs, movies, magazines, newspapers, and music that is popular with teens reported that sexual content was more common in teen music than in any other medium.

While some feminist cultural critics have charged that "rape and rap just go together a little too well" (Brownsworth, 2001), rap has been heralded by others as an inherently political "vehicle for trenchant social protest," which addresses serious themes and gives voice to unpalatable social truths (Palmer, 1995: 284; Santoro, 1994: 112–124; Richardson, 2007). Both Moore's (2007) investigation of the punk subculture and Mullaney's (2007) examination of the third wave of the straight-edge hardcore music scene have issued similar cautions against presuming that certain forms of music are necessarily more gender-regressive/progressive than others. Munoz-Laboy et al.'s (2007) three-year ethnographic study of hip-hop culture, which included in-depth interviews with young women and men ages 15 to 21 years, emphasized that the hip-hop club scene represents a setting in which gender relations are not static but negotiated, and in which "young men's masculinities are contested by the social environment, where women challenge hypermasculine privilege and where young people can set the stage for what happens next in their sexual and emotional interactions" (see also Gaunt [2006]). In like fashion, while concern has been expressed that women in rap videos are often depicted in ways that emphasize their body parts and sexual readiness while men are portrayed as sexually insatiable (Ward and Rivadeneyra, 2002), it should be noted that these patterns are hardly restricted to videos within this genre of music (see Andsager and Roe, 1999, 2003; Sommers-Flanagan et al., 1993).

Regardless of which genre of music they accompany, however, these highly sexualized images may be consequential. Gan et al.'s (1997) experimental research found that while exposure to sexualized images of black women in R&B music videos did not impact raters' assessments of white women, "the Black women encountered later were judged least good, most bad, and furthest from the 'ideal' (APA, 2007: 32; see also Peterson et al., 2007). Other experimental research has reported that exposure to sexualized music videos is associated with acceptance of sex-role stereotyping and of rape myths among male and female students in middle school (Kaestle et al., 2007), high school (Ward et al., 2006), and university (Kalof, 1999; MacKay and Covell, 1997).

Computers and the Internet

Since the first personal computer was introduced in 1975 (the MITS Altair 8800), the use of computers has grown exponentially. Computer industry estimates put the number of computers in the world at 98 million in 1990, 222 million in 1995, and 579 million in 2000 (Ash, 2001: 213). In 2000, Canada, with 17.2 million computers, ranked seventh among countries with the most computers, seventh among countries with the most Internet users (15.4 million), and first among countries in money spent on console and computer games, with sales totalling $1.732 billion (Ash, 2002: 210, 215, 278). In 2003, Canada ranked fifth among OECD countries in terms of the at-home availability of computers to 15-year-old students (with 89 percent of these students having a home Internet connection) and second in terms of access to computers at schools (Statistics Canada, 2007f, 2008d). While young Canadian woman ages 15 to 19 are slightly more likely than their male counterparts to report using a computer, in other age categories men are more likely to do so (Normand, 2000: 91). Even though, as Fenna (1999: 1182) observed, most Internet statistics become "obsolete almost at the moment [they are] calculated," Veenhof's (2006) analysis of 2005 General Social Survey data found that Canadian females were more likely than males to be non-users of the Internet (51.6 percent versus 48.4 percent) while males were more likely to be moderate users (5 minutes to 1 hour per day) (50.4 percent versus 49.6 percent) or heavy users (over an hour daily) (58.9 percent versus 41.1 percent) (see also Bernier and LaFlamme, 2005).

Research also finds evidence of the gendering of computing artifacts and applications. For example, when Selwyn (2007) asked 406 undergraduates to rate 26 different features of computers and computer-based applications using a seven-point Likert scale (that ranged from "very feminine" to "very masculine"), his sample of university students in this study identified "arcade-style" computer games as the most "masculine" aspect of computers and computing. Additionally, they identified gaming applications, high-tech peripherals (e.g., digital music players, personal digital assistants), online banking, online auctions, using spreadsheets, and downloading music from the Internet as being "relatively masculine." Conversely, using the computer for the purposes of studying or e-learning, art and design, or communicating via chat rooms and emails were rated as "feminine" aspects of computing. Cooper's (2006) overview of research published in the last two decades on the gendered "digital divide" concluded that "females are at a disadvantage relative to men when learning about computers" and suggested that this divide "is fundamentally a problem of computer anxiety whose roots are deep in socialization patterns of boys and girls and that interact with the stereotype of computers as toys for boys."

While computer technology is theoretically gender-neutral, computer and Internet usage seem to reflect our society's existing gender roles and rules. In an attempt to investigate whether computer clipart would embody new, egalitarian goals for gender and racial equality or depict more traditional, differentiated images, Milburn et al. (2001) examined 2713 images of human beings in two computer clipart packages (Microsoft Office 97 and Print Shop Ensemble III). They found that computer clipart—like television and picture books—depicted Caucasian males more frequently and in more active/non-nurturant and desirable roles than any other group. Wajcman (1991: 153) pointed out that advertisements for home computers "are aimed at a male market and often feature pictures of boys looking raptly at the screen." She noted that the first video game designed by MIT in the 1960s, "Space War," along with its more recent descendants, "are simply programmed versions of traditionally male non-computer games, involving shooting, blowing up, speeding, or zapping in some way or another" (p. 154) (see also Cassell and Jenkins, 1998; Daiches, 2004). Although the majority of children of both sexes play video games (70 percent of adolescents and 87 percent of pre-adolescents [Paik, 2001]), boys are more likely than girls to play these games for over an hour a day (41 percent of boys versus 18 percent of girls) (Roberts et al. 2005) and almost twice as frequently as girls (Rideout et al., 2005).

Vogt (1997) reported that of the over 3500 available video games, only 10 are designed exclusively for girls. Sheldon's (2004) content analysis of educational software for preschoolers found "significantly more" male than female characters with male characters more likely than female characters to exhibit stereotypical traits. In addition, while female characters were more likely to exhibit counter-stereotypical behaviours than male characters, they were more gender-stereotyped in their appearance. Jansz and Martis' (2007) investigation of the "Lara phenomenon" (the appearance of powerful women characters such as "Lara Croft" in a dominant position) in video games reported that these supposedly heroic characters were portrayed with a sexualized emphasis and were overwhelmingly white (see also Ivory, 2006). Beasley and Standley's (2002) examination of the portrayal of women in 47 randomly selected games for Nintendo 64 and Sony PlayStation reported a significant sex bias in both the number of male versus female characters in these games and in the way in which the male and female characters were dressed. Of the 597 game characters coded, only 82 (13.74 percent) were female, with the Nintendo 64 games containing the fewest female characters. When compared to male characters, the majority of female characters wore more revealing clothing. Similarly, examination of the 10 top-selling video games for each of the three major systems (Sony PlayStation, Dreamcast, and Nintendo) revealed that 54 percent contained female characters, whereas 92 percent contained male characters. Of the female characters displayed, over one third had significantly exposed breasts, thighs, stomachs, midriffs, or bottoms, and 46 percent had "unusually small" waists.

Ironically, research has shown that among children ages 9 to 12, heavier girls play more video games (this finding does not hold true for heavier boys) (Vandewater et al., 2004). Moreover, although evidence suggests that girls, in contrast to boys, prefer non-violent video games, more than half of the female characters were portrayed engaging in violent behaviour (Children Now, 2000; Hartman and Klimmt, 2006). Brenick et al.'s (2007) research on late adolescents' evaluation of and reasoning about gender stereotypes in video games reported that females were less likely than males to view these stereotypes as acceptable and more likely than males to believe that video games had a negative impact upon players' behaviour and attitudes.

Over the past decade, video-game manufacturers started to recognize the potential profitability of targeting products to a hitherto-untapped demographic: girls 8 to 17 years old. However, many of the computer games that have been produced for girls convey highly traditional messages. Toy manufacturer Mattel came under fire in 2000 after producing a pink, flowered Barbie computer "Designed Just for Girls!" and a blue Hot Wheels computer for boys. The social significance of the gender-specific computers became apparent (and public criticism began) when it was revealed that the accompanying software packages were different: The boys' software had more educational titles (Bannon, 2000). Nevertheless, the games targeted to girls continue to reiterate the importance of appearance and caregiving behaviour for women. Mattel's computer version of *Clueless*, for example, allows players to select outfits for their game characters from capacious clothes closets, do their makeup, and change their hair. Mattel's "Barbie" CD-ROMs (which include Barbie Magic Hair Styler, Barbie Fashion Designer, Adventures with Barbie Ocean Discovery, and Barbie Storymaker) allow users to "play dolls" and to change Barbie's outfits and hairstyles on a computer screen. Mattel's "Talk With Me Barbie" doll comes with her own CD-ROM and allows Barbie to sit at her own (pink) toy computer which, in turn, can be plugged into an actual home computer.

Computers, like the video arcades, pinball arcades, and pool halls before them, remain the turf of male hobbyists (Breidenbach, 1997; Brown et al., 1997; Children Now, 2001); the popular hand-held computer game was not named "Game Boy" by accident. Wajcman (1991: 154) maintained that the gendered experience of leisure time—with boys exempted from and girls expected to participate in housework—means that boys may have more leisure to surf the Net or play computer games. Turkle (1984: 216) described the world of **computer hackers** as a "macho culture" and suggested that "the preoccupation with winning and of subjecting oneself to increasingly violent tests make their world peculiarly male in spirit, peculiarly unfriendly to women." Jordan and Taylor's (1998) research on computer hackers and the hacking community amplified the profile of hacking as a "male activity." They also noted, recounting an incident of sexual harassment, that "the collective identity hackers share and construct ... is in part misogynist" (p. 768).

There is debate about whether males and females relate differently to computers. Based on observations of young children, Turkle (1984) contended that young boys preferred a "hard" style of mastering programming, characterized by attempts to "control" the computer in a structured linear manner. In contrast, girls preferred a "soft," more "interactive" and "relational" programming style. "While the hard master thinks in terms of global abstractions, the soft master works on a problem by arranging and rearranging these elements, working through new combinations" (Turkle, 1984: 103). Even though Turkle maintained that neither style is inherently superior or inferior, teachers may evaluate female efforts as "getting the right results by the wrong method" and hence inferior (Wajcman, 1991: 157).

Tannen (1994a: 53) hypothesized that males would be more likely than females to become enamoured of computer technology: "Boys are typically motivated by a social structure that says if you don't dominate you will be dominated. Computers, by their nature, balk: you type a perfectly appropriate command and it refuses to do what it should." According to Tannen, while males will view this as an occasion to demonstrate mastery ("I'm going to whip this into line and teach it who's boss!"), "[g]irls and women are more likely to respond: 'This thing won't cooperate. Get it away from me!'" Although Tannen acknowledged that there are undoubtedly "plenty of exceptions," she contended that women would be less likely to become "excited by tinkering with the technology, grappling with the challenge of eliminating bugs or getting the biggest and best computer" and suggested that her own relationship to her computer "is—gulp—fairly typical for a woman.... E-mail appeals to my view of life as a contest for connections to others. When I see that I have 15 messages I feel loved." Research (Odell et al., 2000) which examined Internet use among 843 American undergraduates found some support for Tannen's hypothesis. Although little difference was found between the amounts of time male and female subjects spent online, there was a significant difference in their purposes. Female subjects tended to use the Internet for email and for school research, while significantly more male subjects visited sex sites, researched purchases, checked news, played games, and listened to and copied music. Weiser (2000) reported similar findings in his study of Internet-use patterns among 506 undergraduate psychology students: Males used the Internet primarily for entertainment and leisure purposes, whereas women used it mainly for interpersonal communication and research. A third study (Jackson et al, 2001: 363) described the pattern of Internet behaviour demonstrated by their sample of 630 Anglo American undergraduates as "women communicating and men searching."

Kantrowitz (1994: 50) claimed that men were more likely than women "to be seduced by the technology itself" and to become absorbed by the **faster-race-car syndrome**—"bragging about the size of their discs or the speed of their microprocessors." Noting that computers were more likely to be purchased and used by men, Kantrowitz further suggested that "[i]t may be new technology, but the old rules still apply. It's that male–machine bonding thing, reincarnated in the digital age." Hackett (1994: 54) reported that men were more likely than women to use their computers to talk to others about the capacities of their software and computers and/or to purchase the very latest versions of the programs they use "even if the update does nothing new besides correcting the faulty handling of annotated footnotes on certain Korean color inkjet printers." "What do women want? Who knows. What do men want? Something bigger, faster and cooler than yours" (Hackett, 1994: 54).

Skeptical of the claim that males and females have distinctive computing styles, Wajcman (1991: 157) suggested that a self-fulfilling prophecy may be operating in young women's relationships to computers. The social construction of computers as a "male domain" may mean "that girls approach the computer less often and with less confidence than boys" (Wajcman, 1991: 158). Ironically, the first computer programmers were women, and programming was initially viewed as "tedious clerical work of low status." Ada Lovelace, who worked with Charles Babbage in the 1880s on his mechanical computing machines, is considered to be "the very first computer programmer" (Kantrowitz, 1994: 51). However, as the complexity and value of programming became recognized, "it came to be considered creative, intellectual and demanding 'men's work'" (Wajcman, 1991: 158). As in so many other areas of social life, the sex of the worker eventually dictates the power and prestige of the work itself and sets another self-fulfilling prophecy in motion.

Spender (1995: 193) claimed that both access to and navigation on the Internet are influenced by gender, contending that the same patterns of male dominance that apply within real-world mixed-sex conversations apply, with a vengeance, in cyberspace. She noted the research of Herrig et al. (1992), which found that men contributed between 70 and 80 percent of the postings on various discussion lists. When a "feminist topic" was raised, "[a]ccusations came from the men that they were being silenced"; some threatened to unsubscribe from the list, and one man wrote a 1098-word protest (in Spender, 1995: 193–194). Spender noted that a 1993 study of the newsgroup alt.feminism similarly found that men dominated the conversational space, contributing 74 percent of the postings. Wylie (1995: 197) also observed that "[w]hen men attack women's posts (by flaming, intellectualizing, or posting lengthy line-by-line rebuttals of women's messages), women retreat into silence." Online patterns of mixed-gender interaction appear to replicate patterns observed in face-to-face mixed-sex exchanges. Wylie found that women's ideas online are more apt to be received with silence, that female-initiated subjects generate less than one third as many responses as those initiated by males, that male postings are typically lengthier than female postings, and that female-initiated postings tend to be usurped by male voices online (see also Guiller and Durndell, 2007). However, Postmes and Spears (2002) found that although men dominate online conversations when the topic is "masculine," they do not do so when the topic is "feminine."

Wylie (1995) reported that professional women hosting online discussions may find their expertise ignored and themselves inundated with irrelevant queries as to their looks, their marital status, and whether or not they are menstruating. The anonymity of the Net may encourage some individuals to behave in more offensive and intimidating ways than they would dare to in face-to-face interaction (Maas et al., 2003). An exploratory study of 339 American undergraduates found that approximately 10 to 15 percent of students reported receiving repeated email or Instant Messenger messages that "threatened, insulted or harassed," and that over half had received unwanted pornography; gays and lesbians were especially likely to receive online harassment from strangers (Finn, 2004; see also Griffiths, 2000; Schneider, 2000). Kramarae and Taylor (1993: 56) reported that "[s]exual harassment on the networks is a problem being reported by many women at many sites"; Spender (1995: 202–211) provided numerous examples, including messages sent to a female user that informed her that she "would have ... [her] throat cut and be gangbanged." However, Sinclair (1997: 71) argued that women should not be fearful of going online: "You're not going to get on the Internet and end up attacked in some dark alley." Some women have sought to avoid male Internet dominance, gender harassment, and stalking by establishing or logging on to networks run by or exclusively for women. However, in contrast to those who would adopt a woman-only separatist response, techno-feminists, such as Cherny and Weise (1996), have urged women to "turn the tables and hold their ground," or even to reconceptualize hostile cybersex websites "as an opportunity to assert themselves by creating a woman-friendly climate that provides a more accurate representation of women's sexuality and humanity" (in Michals, 1997: 72; see also Hawthorne and Klein, 1999; Kirkup et al., 2000; Wolmark, 1999).

Kacen (2000) praised the "ethereality of the Internet, where existence is ephemeral," as in itself constituting a challenge to traditional notions of gender, and suggested that in the "utopian cyber future that awaits us," gender will be transformed into a rich "pastiche of possibilities." Similarly, Ketchum's (2000) analysis of "Internet Relay Chat" and other chatroom-dominated computer environments pointed to the ambiguity of identities on the Internet: "How do we know whom it is we are talking to? Is it a boy or is it a girl? Does it matter?" However, Cornetto and Nowak (2006) report that even though gender markers are not always obvious in usernames (e.g., "foxygirl" versus "weasel"), "questions about gender are the first to be asked in online interactions and sex categorization has maintained [its] salience." Similarly, in directing attention to the widespread popularity of sites such as MySpace.com that encourage sexualized self-descriptions and provocatively posed photographs, Kornblum (2006) warned of the dangers that inhere within such sites, particularly for the young.

Key Terms

centrefold syndrome	ignoring	slang
cock-rock music	linguistic sexism	stereotyping
computer hackers	listening noises	subordinate's intuition
conversation-work	non-verbal communication	teenage entertainers
delayed response	powerless speech	teeny-bop music
deprecating	rapport-talk	women's language
drive for muscularity	report-talk	women's music
fairy tale fracturing	Sapir-Whorf hypothesis	
faster-race-car syndrome	sexual harassment	

Chapter Summary

1. Language, as the "inescapable socializer," may be seen as the principal means of disseminating a society's ideology on gender. It has been suggested that the English language promotes inequalities between men and women through the processes of ignoring, stereotyping, and deprecating.

2. Recent efforts to build an inclusive language are based on the recognition that our language often excludes women or confers unequal prominence on men.

3. While some researchers report few gender differences in speaking styles, others argue that men and women use language differently. For example, various researchers have concluded that women use more grammatically correct forms than men, pronounce words in more acceptable ways, are significantly more polite, and are less likely to use contentious language or to swear.

4. The conversation patterns of men are more likely to focus upon external events (e.g., sports, politics, paid work) than are the conversations of women. One researcher has described the preferred speaking style of men as "report-talk," and that of women as "rapport-talk."

5. Within mixed-sex dyads or larger groups, women do most of the "conversation-work," employing a host of techniques designed to maintain a conversation and move it along smoothly.

6. While some researchers have argued that the speech of men and women is motivated by contrasting goals (i.e., "the pure transmission of factual knowledge" versus "politeness"), others suggest that "women's language" would be better reconceptualized as "powerless speech" (i.e., the speech patterns characteristic of those who occupy relatively powerless social positions).

7. Gender differences in non-verbal communication undergird the unequal status of men and women in our society and reinforce presentations of gender in everyday life.

8. Symbolic representations of gender in the media have traditionally reinforced stereotypical images of women and men. However, some evidence suggests that these images are slowly being challenged and transformed.

9. While computer technology is, in theory, gender-neutral, existing rules and roles pertaining to gender in our society continue to influence men's and women's use of computers and the Internet.

CHAPTER 6

Work

Gender in our society is inextricably intertwined with work and the family. These social institutions create and sustain gender as much as they are created and sustained by it. This chapter focuses upon both paid and unpaid work.

THE WORK-ROLE MODEL

Pleck and Corfman (1979: 409) maintained that men in our society are strongly influenced by a pervasive male work-role model, which is inculcated subtly via socialization and comprises a set of three interrelated beliefs: "The male work-role model in our society calls for full-time, continuous work from graduation to retirement, subordination of other roles to work, and actualization of one's potential through it."

The first principle of the male work-role model is that men are to work in paid employment from graduation until retirement or death; only then have they permission to cease labouring for pay. Most members of our society share this belief. According to social tradition, paid labour ("honest labour") bestows worth and dignity upon the labourer. The notion of an adult lifestyle based upon permanent non-participation in the labour force is completely foreign to most men. Unless severely physically or psychologically disabled, men work; even in such cases, most men feel they should perform some form of paid work. Our society looks with disfavour on male financial dependency, especially long-term; men are expected to support themselves and usually others.

> Men are neither supposed nor allowed to be dependent. They are expected to take care of both others *and* themselves. And when they cannot do it, or "will not" do it, the built-in assumption at the heart of the culture is that they are *less than men* and therefore unworthy of help. (Marin, 1991/1995: 490; emphasis in original)

In these comments, Marin was attempting to identify the attitudes underlying our society's hostility towards homeless men. While homeless women and children may be seen as victims of unjust circumstance, homeless (usually unemployed) men more often evoke contempt and even violence. A society that grants agency (i.e., the power to act and to be self-determining) to men also demands agency *from* them. The predominant attitude of most Canadians towards the (male) unemployed can be summed up in three words: Get a job. However, not just any job will do; a lifetime of seasonal, part-time, or intermittent work will not satisfy the male work-role model. A young man considering a career as a summer lifeguard will find that prospective spouses, in-laws, the Employment Insurance Commission, and Social Assistance (welfare) are highly unlikely to support the plan. In the absence of suitable work, men are expected to take on a less-desirable "McJob," but only as a temporary expedient; a "proper job" is one that is permanent, continuous, and full-time.

In accordance with the second tenet of the work-role model, a man is to make his job the central focus of his adult life and to subordinate all other roles to it. Our society holds it true that if a man performs his paid-work role well, everyone benefits: the worker himself, his dependents, and society as a whole. The work-role model is linked to the notion of gendered separate spheres; the male breadwinner-provider must give priority to his role in the public paid-work sphere in order to successfully fulfill his private-sphere familial duties. Men are often accused of focusing upon work to the neglect of family life; yet, according to the logic of the male work-role model, it is through paid labour that a man best serves his family. In consequence, a man's family role may be reduced to moneymaking machine and financial-success object.

The charge that men care more about their jobs and making money than about their families may be a sad misattribution. Men, successfully socialized into the work-role model, do indeed care about their families; it is their jobs that do not. The male work-role model works well for business, industry, and government; work as an institution is not family-friendly. The workplace is no respecter of the worker's personal wishes: "The family is controlled not by the male but by his job" (Pleck and Corfman, 1979: 394). Work only accommodates the needs of families when it is in its own interests to do so; accommodations are rarely made, and then usually only for female employees. By and large, it is the institution of the family that must make all necessary accommodations. Paid work is more likely to have a negative impact upon family life than the other way around; the demands of work leave little time or energy for family at the end of each working day (Deutsch, 2007; Small and Riley, 1990).

It is important to recognize that attitudes and behaviours often attributed to gender may in fact be a function of the nature of the institution of work. Work exerts an independent influence on gender, and is at the root of many tensions in gender relations. Beyond a doubt, work organizations are responsible for many outcomes that are often blamed solely, and improperly, on male gendered behaviour. However, it must also be noted that work places equal demands upon female workers, yet available data clearly indicate that full-time employed women do find the time and energy to take care of homes, relationships, and child rearing to a much greater extent than do men (Grzywacz and Carlson, 2007; Sussman and Bonnell, 2006). Despite evidence of growing gender convergence in the division of domestic labour (Marshall, 2006), men may still govern themselves by the work-role model and act as if private-sphere activities are the responsibilities of women (Bittman et al., 2003; Mannino and Deutsch, 2007). Research on self-employed women and men tellingly finds that when "freed from the time demands of employers, men who work for themselves are much more likely than their female counterparts to use their flexibility to establish the primacy of work, whereas women are more likely to use it to accommodate family or personal lives" (Loscocco and Spitze, 2007: 938). Clearly, socialized gender roles are operating along with the work-role model.

The third tenet of the male work-role model is expressed in the language of the human-potential movement that dominated the 1970s. *Self-actualization* (Maslow, 1970) refers to the maximization of one's human potential. The male work-role model exalts paid labour as the optimal context for men's self-actualization. When the question "What are you going to be when you grow up?" is posed to a young male, it is in expectation of hearing what kind of paid work he intends to do. For males, you *are* what you *do*, and what you do is work for a living. Men in our society are socialized to invest a great deal of their social, personal, and masculine identity in their paid work, and derive from it, in turn, much of their sense of personal and masculine worth. Harris (1995) noted that men who earn higher incomes feel more "masculine" than those with lower incomes. Women, on the other hand, are socialized to believe that wife-and-motherhood is the ideal context for female self-actualization. Since World War II, one of the major social trends in Canada has been the increasing labour-force participation of adult women of every age group, social class, and marital/family status. Yet despite their growing tendency to follow a male pattern of employment, women generally have neither been socialized into nor adopted a work-role model identical to men's (Cunningham et al., 2005; Roxburgh, 2005; Sayer, 2005). In our society, breadwinning has constituted a "critical gender boundary" (Potuchek, 1992, 1997: 549; Loscocco and Spitze, 2007: 935), not only differentiating men's behaviour from women's but having important implications for gender identity. While the increase in female labour-force participation might be expected to pose a challenge to the gender boundary of the provider–breadwinner role, the rate of change has been slow (Cooke, 2004; Gordon and Whelan-Berry, 2005; Singley and Hynes, 2005).

The employment conditions most women experience make participation in the workplace less appealing and less rewarding for them than for men. What is more, internalized social expectations regarding marriage and children curtail women's desire to be breadwinners or primary providers. Few women in our society anticipate full-time, continuous, permanent employment from graduation until retirement; few expect to place their paid-work role ahead of all other roles (Blair-Loy, 2003; Deutsch et al., 2007). In addition, few women believe that employment will provide the optimum context for their self-actualization (Kerpelman and Schvaneveldt, 1999; Novack and Novack, 1996). Never-married women express ambivalence, questioning whether the costs of employment (usually defined in terms of lost marital and parenting opportunities) outweigh its considerable benefits (Wong, 2003). While female lone parents often find themselves compelled to adopt tenets of the male work-role model in order to provide for their families, assumption of the breadwinner role is typically not something they had planned for (Bailey, 2007). Employed women in dual-earner marital or cohabiting relationships tend not to define themselves as breadwinners (Brennan et al., 2001; Loscocco, 1997; Zuo, 2004).

From her late-1980s study of predominantly white American dual-earner couples, Potuchek (1992: 552–553, see also Potuchek, 1997) derived an eightfold taxonomy of employed women's orientations towards breadwinning. *Employed homemakers*, the largest group (21 percent), viewed their husbands' jobs as more important than their own, which they regarded as furnishing money for "extras." Nineteen percent defined themselves as *helpers*, working to help their husbands meet family needs. Fifteen percent considered themselves *co-breadwinners*, contributing to family income to the same degree as their husbands. Fourteen percent were *reluctant providers*, "behaving like breadwinners not because they want to or think that they should, but because they have no choice." Twelve percent were *supplementary providers*, who thought of themselves as performing an important provider function, but defined their husbands as primary provider and considered his job more important than their own. Another 12 percent were *reluctant traditionals*, who, despite their feeling that the provider role should not be based on gender, were rarely employed full-time and put their income towards "extras." Resembling co-breadwinners in ideology, these women resembled employed homemakers in behaviour. The remainder were either *family-centred workers* (five percent), who believed providers should be male and reserved the right to quit their jobs if needed at home; or *committed workers* (three percent) who derived enormous non-material satisfaction from being in the labour force, were committed to particular jobs, and (almost incidentally) found that their families relied on the income they brought in.

Of these eight categories of working wives, only the co-breadwinners (15 percent) actively challenged the traditional gender boundary of the provider role. Some groups may have wished to do so, but did not; others challenged it by their actions, but not by their ideology. This latter group, constituting the majority of the sample, still thought that, ideally, the man should be the family breadwinner. Yet there are signs of change: When Potuchek (1997; see also Potuchek 1992) interviewed the same couples five years later (i.e., in the early 1990s), 28 percent of the women and 40 percent of the men (up from 15 percent and 36 percent in the earlier study) viewed themselves as co-providers. Change is also evident in Willinger's (1993) study on the attitudes of male university students in

1980, 1985, and 1990: Progressively fewer men reported feeling uncomfortable about being out-earned by their wives. As Deutsch (2003: 292) has emphasized, "[a]s we enter the 21st century, the sheer force of women's increasing contributions to family income should debunk the myth that women's earnings are peripheral to families' economic well-being." Nevertheless, her own research on 102 men and 112 women in dual-earner couples (with children living at home) found that "the responsibility for family earnings, rather than the earnings themselves, is what women want from their husbands. In contrast, men want their wives to make money, but are not especially grateful if wives' incomes threaten to usurp men's provider role. Breadwinning still appears to be an important component in men's family roles and a critical component of doing gender."

Research conducted on dual-earner couples in which the wives are the primary breadwinners suggests the validity of Deutsch's observation. In both Canada and the United States, the proportion of wives who are primary wage-earners has risen in recent decades and particularly dramatically since the 1990s. Commuri and Gentry (2005: 185) observed that, at the end of the last millennium, wives outearned husbands in almost a third of all American families. Similarly, while only 11 percent of wives in Canadian dual-earner couples were primary breadwinners in 1967, this rose to 18 percent in 1982 and jumped to 25 percent during the recession of the early 1990s; in 2003, wives were the primary-earners in 29 percent of Canada's dual-earner couples (Sussman and Bonnell, 2006: 10). Nevertheless, inasmuch as "providing is such an important way that men accomplish gender ... earning income often means something different depending on whether it is done by a man or a woman. Both men and women are more likely to see women's income as helping, and providing as men's responsibility, irrespective of what women earn" (Loscocco and Spitze, 2007: 935).

The longitudinal research of Commuri and Gentry (2005: 190) on 20 heterosexual couples found that even though all of the wives earned at least $10 000 a year more than their husbands, these couples tended to organize their monies in strategic ways that sought "to recognize the wife's economic contributions while at the same time not undermining the husband's good provision role." For example, in order to allow the men to maintain the fiction that they, and not their wives, were the primary provider, a couple who maintained separate bank accounts as well as a joint account could agree that it would be the husband who would pay for such "critical expenses" as the house mortgage and utilities from his separate account. Even when this division of resources required, on occasion, that a wife transfer some of her earnings into her husband's separate account, the "symbolic value of demonstrating command over certain expenditures" (p. 192)—specifically, those that were defined as "critical expenses" rather than "luxuries"—was thought important: it functioned to direct attention away from income differences and "to celebrate the husband as the good provider against the reality that he is not the primary economic provider" (p. 193). This strategy obviously required the wife to forgo recognition that, in reality, she, rather than her husband, was the principal economic actor in the household and "embrace the burden of underplaying [her] role and status of primary provider" (p. 193).

Tichenor's (2005) examination of how husbands and wives negotiated identity and power when wives earned substantially more than their husbands also suggested how men's status as primary breadwinner is preserved, even in the absence of their traditional economic dominance, and how "gendered practices and ideology can act as 'micro-level discount factors' that diminish the value of a wife's income" (p. 192). Rather than suggesting "gender disruption," Tichenor found that her sample of husbands and wives engaged in a "team effort to construct appropriate gender identities" with both attempting to present themselves and their spouses "as conforming to the identities of homemaker and bread-winner." In order to preserve the man's identity as breadwinner, for example, couples creatively redefined the term in ways that allowed the husband to fulfill it. By expanding the definition of a breadwinner in ways that placed greater emphasis on managing, rather than earning, the family income, or placing unusual emphasis on a breadwinner's ability to meet the emotional, rather than strictly financial, needs of family members, a stay-at-home husband married to a high-earning attorney could be accorded status as a good provider and his identity as a breadwinner preserved (see also Warren, 2007).

A longitudinal study by Zvonkovic et al. (1996) illuminated how decisions involving work and family are based upon gender understandings, and how those decisions, in turn, reaffirm or "cement" gender. Data was collected on work decisions made by 61 predomi-nantly middle-class couples over a period of one and a half years. Thirty-six of the couples made decisions concerning a wife's job. In all cases, discussion focused on whether she should increase or decrease her paid-work hours; the idea of her becoming a breadwinner or co-provider, even temporarily, was not discussed. Nineteen of the couples made decisions about whether the husband should change jobs, but never about whether he should increase or decrease his work hours; the husband's role as sole breadwinner was not subject to debate. All decisions firmly supported existing constructions of gender, both in the workplace and at home. In most cases (15 out of 36), decisions about a wife's work-hours were based on family circumstances beyond her control (specifically, the ages of children); neither ages of children nor other family circumstances played a part in decisions about husbands' employment.

Couples gave higher priority to decisions affecting a husband's job. As well, husbands involved themselves more actively in decisions related to themselves personally, taking more of a "bystander" stance in decisions pertaining to their wives' changing circum-stances. While a husband commented: "She went to work. It was her choice. She arranged daycare," his wife stated: "My job *had* to be part-time. The hours *had* to coincide with the children's school and daycare.... I pay so much money out just to be able to work" (in Zvonkovic et al., 1996: 95; emphasis in original). These statements illustrate how wives construct and organize their working lives around the needs of other family members. A wife's paycheque, not her husband's, is most often applied to the purchase of child-care and housecleaning services to make her employment possible; this reflects a construction of gender according to which the woman retains primary responsibility for home and chil-dren. As earlier noted, allocating a husband's paycheque to family "essentials" is congruent with the construction of male as breadwinner; on the other hand, earmarking a wife's earn-ings for "extras" may, as Deutsch (2003: 301) has noted, represent a strategy that couples use to downplay the importance of these earnings. She noted research in which a wife's income that was "clearly defined as secondary, 'only' went towards mortgage payments."

Most couples in Zvonkovic et al.'s study emphasized that their decisions were based upon consensus and mutual support. Consensus, however, was more apparent than real; although husbands enjoyed support from their wives, the converse was not always true (Zvonkovic et al., 1996: 96–97). Wives' attempts to alter gender constructions were usually met with passivity or opposition on the part of their husbands, who failed to recognize how much their wives needed but did not receive support. Decision-making processes similar to these preserve male and female gender boundaries. In consequence, some women may feel that they can only construct an alternative gender model for themselves outside of the traditional confines of marriage and family.

PAID WORK

"Over the twentieth century, male labour force participation rates gradually dropped, while rates for women soared" (Vanier Institute of the Family, 2000: 80). The decline in male employment has been a consequence of a number of factors, foremost being the growing tendency of men in their mid- to late fifties to take early retirement (Krahn and Lowe, 1993: 63) or accept buy-outs from employers—sometimes voluntarily, but of late more often involuntarily as a result of business and government downsizing (Sussman and Bonnell, 2006). In addition, young men in the 15–24 age bracket have been delaying their entry into the labour market by staying in school longer to attain higher credentials (Beaujot, 2003). The change in women's **labour-force participation rates** is attributable to a combination of factors: changing opportunities in Canada's occupational structure (particularly expansion of the service sector in the 1960s and 1970s), inflationary pressures necessitating higher family incomes, and changing gender expectations and beliefs about employment, marriage, parenthood, and parenting. Social gender expectations that once constrained married women (especially those with dependent children) from seeking paid employment no longer have the same potency (Ghalam, 2000); thus, at the beginning of the last century, women represented less than 15 percent of the labour force, whereas in 2006 they constituted nearly half (47.1 percent) (see Table 6.1).

As Table 6.2 indicates, at the beginning of the 1960s, female participation in the Canadian labour force exhibited a bimodal pattern. The participation rate of women of typical early childrearing age (25–34) dropped off dramatically from that of the next-youngest (20–24) group. The next-highest participation level was found among women 45 to 54 years old, at which age most had completed active childrearing. A scan of subsequent census years reveals that the bimodal pattern has disappeared. Rates remain high throughout the childbearing and childrearing years and only begin to drop off significantly (as they have done every census year) among women 55 to 64 years of age. However, while the gap between the employment levels of men and women has narrowed, women between the ages of 25 and 64 are still considerably less likely than their male counterparts to be employed. In 2006, among people ages 25 to 44, 77.2 percent of women and 86.8 percent of men had jobs; for those ages 45 to 54, the respective figures are 76.8 percent and 85.1 percent; and for those ages 55 to 64, 48.7 percent versus 62.8 percent (Statistics Canada, 2007g).

Over the course of the last century, the marital status of the female labour force also changed dramatically. "Until the 1960s, the modal, or typical, female labour-force worker was a never-married (single) woman" (Boyd, 2004: 221). Since then, however, the most significant increases in labour-force participation have occurred among married women. "In the female labour force today, it is married women who make up the majority of the workers (63 percent), with single women representing only one-quarter (25 percent) of female workers" (Boyd, 2004: 221).

In addition, "[t]here has been particularly sharp growth in the employment rate of women with children in the past quarter century" (Statistics Canada, 2004c: 7; see Table 6.3). Between 1976 and 2006, the employment rate of Canadian women with children under 16 years old increased from 38.3 percent to 73.6 percent. There have also been especially dramatic increases in the employment levels of women with very young children. Indeed, by 2006, "64.3% of women with children under age 3 were employed, more than double the figure in 1976 when only 27.6% of these women were employed outside of the home. Similarly, 69.4% of women whose youngest child was aged 3–5 worked for pay or profit in 2006, up

TABLE 6.1	Labour-force Participation Rates for Females and Males (Age 15 and Over) in Canada, 1901–2006		
	Labour-force Participation Rates (%)		Females as Percentage of the Total Labour-force Population
Year	Females	Males	
1901	14.4	78.3	14.8
1911	16.6	82.0	14.9
1921	17.2	80.3	17.0
1931	19.4	78.4	18.6
1941	22.9	85.6	20.2
1951	24.4	84.4	22.3
1961	29.3	81.1	26.4
1971	39.4	77.3	34.4
1981	47.7	72.8	40.6
1991	52.8	66.9	45.0
1996	52.1	65.0	45.9
1998	53.7	65.9	45.4
1999	54.6	66.7	45.7
2000	55.4	67.3	45.9
2001	55.6	66.8	46.0
2002	56.6	67.1	46.1
2003	57.4	67.6	46.4
2004	57.8	67.8	46.8
2005	57.8	67.7	46.8
2006	58.3	67.7	47.1

Source: Adapted from Boyd (2004: 221) and Statistics Canada, 2007g.

from 36.8% in 1976" (Statistics Canada, 2007g). However, the age of children continues to have a significant effect on mothers' paid employment; while more than three quarters (78.2 percent) of women whose youngest child was between the ages of 6 and 15 worked outside the home in 2006, only two thirds (66.4 percent) of women with children under the age of 6 did so.

In the late 1970s, female lone parents were more likely than mothers with partners to be employed; however, this situation has reversed: "In 2006, 69.9 percent of female lone parents with children under age 16 living at home were employed, compared with 73.6 percent of their counterparts in two-parent families" (Statistics Canada, 2007g, 2006h). As Table 6.3 indicates, while the employment rate of mothers with partners has grown steadily since the 1970s, surpassing that of lone mothers by the mid-1980s, the proportion of employed lone mothers has increased substantially since the mid-1990s. Nevertheless, the presence of very young children continues to have a greater dampening effect on employment for lone

TABLE 6.2	Female Labour-force Participation Rates by Age, Canada 1961–2003					
Age Group	1961	1971	1981	1991	1996	2003
15–19	34.2	36.9	44.3	47.5	45.9	54.9
20–24	49.5	62.5	77.1	81.1	71.8	76.6
25–34	29.6	44.5	65.7	78.5	77.7	81.0
35–44	31.1	43.9	64.1	79.6	78.8	82.2
45–54	33.4	44.5	55.7	71.9	72.4	79.3
55–64	24.4	34.4	35.4	39.2	36.5	47.7
65+	6.7	8.2	5.5	5.6	3.5	4.1
Total	29.7	39.9	51.0	59.9	57.4	61.6

Source: 1961–1991: Adapted from McVey and Kalbach (1995: 251); 1996: Statistics Canada, 1998; 2003: Statistics Canada, 2004.

mothers than for partnered mothers. In 2006, 66.4 percent of partnered mothers with children under the age of 3 were employed, compared to 48.3 percent of lone mothers; among those whose youngest child was age 3 to 5, the respective figures were 70.1 percent and 66.2 percent.

Overall, these changes attest to the changing face of the paid labour force in Canada. However, it would be presumptuous to suppose that gender no longer impacts upon the

TABLE 6.3	Employment of Women with Children, by Family Status and Age of Youngest Child, 1976–2006						
	Female Lone Parents				Women with Partners		
	Youngest child under age 3	Youngest child age 3–5	Youngest child age 6–15	Total with children under age 16	Youngest child under age 3	Youngest child age 3–5	Youngest child age 6–15	Total with children under age 16
1976	27.6	45.1	54.0	48.3	27.6	36.0	45.5	38.3
1981	32.5	51.8	61.5	54.5	39.7	46.0	55.4	48.7
1986	29.7	47.0	60.0	51.5	51.0	55.5	62.1	57.3
1991	30.9	47.5	62.3	52.1	57.0	62.3	70.3	64.5
1996	32.9	46.2	62.6	53.1	61.0	63.3	71.4	66.6
2001	45.5	61.0	73.7	66.5	63.2	68.3	75.7	70.9
2003	46.5	61.1	75.2	68.3	64.5	69.9	77.1	72.3
2006	48.3	66.2	76.6	69.9	66.4	70.1	78.6	73.6

Source: Adapted from the Statistics Canada Publication "Women in Canada: Work Chapter Updates, 2006," Catalogue 89F0133XIE, April, 2007, Table 6.

work experience. In various ways, the current paid- and unpaid-work roles of contemporary men and women continue to reflect the gendered "breadwinner" and "homemaker" roles. The Vanier Institute of the Family (2000: 86) noted that, at the end of the 1990s, (1) fathers with children under 15 were still more likely than mothers to be employed in the paid-labour force (approximately 95 percent of fathers); (2) even though the majority of mothers (both lone and partnered) were employed, they were still "less likely to be in the work force than fathers, particularly those with pre-school children"; and (3) while lone parents were the least likely to be in the paid workforce at the end of the twentieth century, "84% of lone fathers with children under age six and 86% of those with school-aged children were labour force participants [compared to] 55% of lone mothers with pre-schoolers and 75% with school-aged children." Moreover, although labour-force participation rates of men and women became roughly equivalent by the end of the century, this was not synonymous with "equal earnings or responsibilities. On average, women's earnings were not equal to men's, more women worked part-time, and they carried the main load of household duties and child rearing" (Vanier Institute of the Family, 2000: 80).

Boyd (2004) asserted that, despite the growing presence of women in the public sphere of paid work, gender inequality persists and is evidenced by occupational sex-segregation and sex typing, the wage gap, and the over-representation of women in part-time and non-standard work. She also emphasized that women's participation in paid labour has not resulted in their "liberation from unpaid work." Let us examine these issues in turn.

Occupational Distributions and Segregations

Paid work is highly gendered. As a group, women tend to be employed in jobs with little prestige and low pay, where no product is produced, and where they serve as facilitators for others. Women are also more likely to hold positions of little or no authority within the work environment. This situation is not unique to Canada. Investigating the gender gap in organizational authority in seven countries (Australia, Canada, Japan, Norway, Sweden, the United Kingdom, and the United States), Wright et al. (1995: 419) concluded that, in every country, "women are less likely than men to be in the formal authority hierarchy, to have sanctioning power over subordinates, or to participate in organizational policy decisions." Smith's (2002: 509) summary of the literature on workplace authority elaborates upon this finding, concluding that (1) "men are more likely than women to have authority, and employer behaviors and organizational policies are more important than women's attitudes and behaviors in explaining the gender gap in authority"; (2) "[e]ducation and job tenure exert a stronger effect on the authority attainment of men than women—especially at higher levels of authority"; (3) "[f]amily ties improve men's, but not women's, chances to gain authority, and to the extent that women occupy managerial positions, they tend to be located at the bottom of the command chain—largely supervising other women and receiving lower earnings than men who occupy similar positions"; and (4) "gender differences in authority attainment account for much of the pay differences between men and women at high levels of authority ... but have a modest effect at lower levels (i.e., supervisory authority)."

The concentration of women within certain occupations and men in others is referred to as **occupational sex segregation**. Although the proportion of Canadian women employed in traditionally female-dominated occupations has declined over the past decades, the most common occupations of women in 2006 were "retail salespersons and sales clerks" followed, in turn, by "cashiers" and "nurses." In 2006, "67% of all employed women [versus 30% of employed men] were working in one of teaching, nursing and related health occupations, clerical or other administrative positions or sales and service occupations" (Statistics Canada, 2007g: 9); in 1987, 74 percent of employed Canadian women worked in these occupations. The modest decline in the proportions of women in these traditionally female occupations is largely attributable to the decreasing proportions of women working in clerical and related administrative jobs (24.1 percent in 2006, compared to 30 percent in 1987). In 2006, "retail salespersons and sales clerks" were also the most common occupation for men followed closely by "truck drivers" (Statistics Canada, 2008e, 2008f)

As Table 6.4 indicates, in 2006, women continued to account for the majority of Canada's nurses and health-care workers, clerical and administrative workers, teachers, and sales-and-service personnel. However, it is also evident that women were "making inroads in many 'nontraditional' areas, particularly in highly skilled occupations [i.e., occupations which normally require a university degree]" (Statistics Canada, 2003a: 8). Between 1991 and 2002,

TABLE 6.4	**Women as a Percentage of Total Employed, by Occupation, 1987, 1994, 1999, and 2006**				
	1987	1994	1999	2003	2006
Managerial					
Senior management	16.9	19.8	26.8	24.2	26.3
Other management	30.6	36.9	35.7	36.1	36.9
Total management	28.9	35.1	35.1	35.4	36.3
Professional					
Business and finance	40.7	44.6	49.4	48.4	51.6
Natural sciences/engineering/ mathematics	16.7	17.0	19.6	22.0	22.0
Social sciences/religion	47.8	56.5	58.2	63.8	71.3
Teaching	57.3	59.4	62.1	62.9	63.9
Doctors/dentists/other health	44.1	48.7	47.1	52.1	55.3
Nursing/therapy/other health-related	87.3	87.1	86.5	87.7	87.4
Artistic/literary/recreational	50.4	53.6	54.6	53.4	54.1
Total professional	49.8	52.2	51.8	53.4	55.9
Clerical and administrative	74.4	74.9	75.3	75.1	75.0
Sales and service	55.7	56.4	58.7	58.7	56.8
Primary	20.0	21.3	21.6	19.7	20.5
Trades, transport, and construction	5.3	5.4	6.2	6.6	6.5
Processing, manufacturing, and utilities	30.2	29.2	29.8	28.9	31.1
Total*	43.0	45.3	45.9	46.6	47.1

* Includes occupations that are not classified.

Source: Adapted from Statistics Canada, Labour Force Surveys.

women accounted for more than one half of the growth in these professions; "their numbers doubled in information technology occupations and more than doubled in professional occupations in business and finance" (Statistics Canada, 2003a: 3). In 2006, women accounted for over half (51.6 percent) of business and financial professionals, 55.3 percent of doctors and dentists, and 71.3 percent of professionals in the social sciences and religion (Statistics Canada, 2007g). Women's share of total employment in managerial positions also increased, although they were better represented among low- rather than high-level managers. Yet women continued to account for only a minority of professionals in the natural sciences, engineering, and mathematics. Given that they accounted for only a minority of undergraduate and graduate students in these areas in 2005 (see Chapter 4), it is unlikely that the near future will see a dramatic increase in women's representation in these fields. In addition, relatively few women were employed in the traditionally male-dominated goods-producing occupations. Although the representation of women in trades, transport, and construction increased marginally from 5.3 percent in 1987 to 6.5 percent in 2006, women accounted for less than a third (31.1 percent) of workers in manufacturing and roughly a fifth (20.5 percent) in primary industries.

Boyd (2004: 224) pointed out that, in Canada, the decline in occupational sex segregation has been largely attributable to the movement of women into previously male-dominated occupations, rather than of men into traditionally female-dominated ones. This should not seem surprising, given that, "[i]n general, jobs in male-dominated fields offer better pay and benefits, authority, and independence than jobs in female-dominated fields" (Furr, 2002: 55). Jobs traditionally dominated by women generally offer fewer monetary and social rewards. What is more, men who seek employment in "women's" fields may find that there is a "prestige penalty" to pay: their masculinity may be called into question (Jacobs, 1993). McCormick (2002: 161) maintained that workplaces are not only gendered but heterosexualized; women's traditional occupations are "imbued with the behavioural expectations associated with traditional feminine heterosexuality, becoming 'feminine heterosexualized' occupations." Consider secretaries, for example—often referred to as "office wives," and stereotyped as young women with "large breasts, long legs and short skirts" (Pringle, 1997: 360). Pringle argued that the common assumption that male secretaries are gay reflects "a conventional way of interpreting a male sexuality that is perceived as lacking power and a statement about the place of sexuality in people's perceptions of the boss/secretary relation."

Furr (2002: 57–58) reported that men who enter female-dominated occupations often encounter "role entrapment," finding themselves cast into one (or more) of four stereotypical roles: *ladderclimbers*, *troublemakers*, *he-men*, and *homosexuals*. The role of "ladderclimber" builds upon the expectation that men will enact the stereotype of male aggressiveness by ambitiously pursuing advancement even in non-traditional careers; in consequence, women may regard men in cross-gender careers as posing an especial threat to their own occupational aspirations. The "troublemaker" role is a projection of employers' expectation that male employees will be less compliant and docile, more autonomous, and more likely to "rock the boat" by questioning workplace policies and forcefully asserting opposing opinions. The "he-man" stereotype casts men into the role of on-the-job handyman—or, in the field of childhood education, of strong and stern disciplinarian. The "homosexual" tag stems from the assumption that a man who deviates from traditional expectations in his choice of occupation must not be "fully masculine." Furr (2002: 58) observed that "[a]lthough males in female-dominated occupations do not attempt to fight the first three stereotypical roles, the role of 'homosexual' elicits strong reactions due to the stigmatizing nature of the label," and that "[f]ear of this label keeps some males from pursuing non-traditional career interests, leaving the field to those who are either confident about or unconcerned with their gender identity."

Men and women who enter fields in which they are a gender minority may share certain difficulties arising from their status as *tokens*. Kanter (1977) defined "tokens" as members of a minority population who are treated as exemplars or symbols of a specific category (e.g., "women," "blacks," "gays") rather than as individuals. She suggested that three dynamics structure the experience of tokens in the workplace: visibility, polarization, and stereotyping. Because of their numeric rarity, tokens have high *visibility* within a work-place and are therefore likely to experience heightened pressure to perform (see also Sekaquaptewa and Thompson, 2003). Adding to this pressure is the token's uncomfortable awareness that his/her failure may be construed by others as evidence of the essential unworthiness of all members of the category (e.g., women, blacks, gays). *Polarization* refers to the creation of a division between tokens and dominants via social isolation (as occurs when female nurses exclude a male colleague from informal social gatherings and conversations) or heightened differentiation (as occurs when male construction workers inform female co-workers that they "should be at home having babies," or jeer at their "inferior" strength). By directing attention to a preconceived set of qualities, *stereotyping* may in fact interfere with optimal job performance. Furr (2002: 57) found that male elementary-school teachers reported refraining "from demonstrating caring qualities because they did not want to invite suspicions of abuse. Behavior that was considered natural to women was often off-limits to men." Simultaneously, however, "[a] paradox is created if ... male teachers emphasize their masculinity too much because it contradicts their image as an emotionally sensitive teacher."

While both men and women who enter cross-gender fields may confront challenges related to token status, the status differential between males and females in the larger society may condition their experience. Heightened differentiation, for example, may operate differently for male and female tokens: Male tokens may pointedly draw attention to their difference from (female) dominants, while female tokens are more likely to be the objects of such distancing efforts. Thus, male nurses, to distinguish themselves from female colleagues, will often direct attention to their area of specialization (e.g., psychiatric nurs-ing, anesthesiology) and emphasize their interest in the scientific/technical (rather than the nurturing) aspects of their profession (Heikes, 1991). Similarly, male elementary-school teachers may coach school sports teams or run science and computer clubs as a way of dif-ferentiating themselves from female counterparts (Allan, 1993). A degree of elasticity within job titles may also allow men to eschew status devaluation: The "male secretary" may be semantically recast as a "junior" manager or "managerial assistant."

Kanter (1977) suggested that a token's heightened visibility, compounded by performance pressure, could lead to under- or overachievement. Research on male nurses and elementary-school teachers suggests that overachievement is the more common response (Furr, 2002: 56). This may partly account for the fact that males in traditionally female fields often enjoy considerable occupational success; for example, although men constitute only a minority of teachers in elementary schools, they hold the majority of principalships and upper administrative positions (see Chapter 4). Another explanation is that men entering female-dominated professions may have the advantage of their status as males. On the basis of interviews conducted with 76 men and 23 women in four traditionally female-dominated professions (elementary-school teacher, librarian, nurse, and social worker), Williams (1995) found that men working in traditionally female-dominated fields often received preferential treatment in hiring and promotion and gained accelerated access to desirable work assignments and higher salaries. She concluded that men in female-dominated occupations may ride a "**glass escalator**" (Williams, 1992/2001) to career success. According to Henslin et al. (2004: 181), "[t]he motor that drives the glass escalator is gender, the stereotype that because someone is male he is more capable."

In contrast, women who pursue careers in traditionally male-dominated fields are more likely to experience a **glass ceiling**—an invisible socially created barrier that prevents women (and other minorities) from moving into the highest echelons of the workplace. According to the International Labour Organization, "the higher the position, the more glaring the gender gap" (in Dranoff, 2001: 59). There is some evidence that the glass ceiling may be cracking. For example, statistics prepared by the Law Society of Upper Canada indicate that, in Ontario, women represented 57 percent of those called to the bar in 2005 (Law Society of Upper Canada, 2006). Similarly, a recent report by the Canadian Bar Association (2005: 14) points out that in 1990–1991, "female law students outnumbered males for the first time" in Canada and, that in 2003, 60 percent of law school enrollees were women. In addition, this report notes that while "in 1970, only one in 20 lawyers in Canada was female ... [t]oday, one of every three lawyers is a woman, with the majority under age 35." (Bearing witness to the dynamics of past practices, it can be noted that, in Canada, only one in ten lawyers over the age of 50 is female).

Nevertheless, other research tells a different story. A recent longitudinal study of women lawyers in Ontario (Kay et al., 2004) found that "more women lawyers than ever are working part-time; that male lawyers are still more highly represented in partnership positions and are more likely to be solo practitioners; ... that women are under-represented in the over $200,000 income bracket and most highly represented in the under $40,000 bracket; that, of solo practitioners, male lawyers earn on average $126,000 annually compared to $86,000 for women; that women lawyers are more likely to have several legal positions over the course of their careers, and more likely to make lateral professional moves; and that there are very high attrition rates for women" (in Canadian Bar Association, 2005: 14).

Cooper et al. (2004) similarly find that women "remain under-represented in authority and leadership positions in large law firms, perhaps out of choice, but perhaps not" (in Canadian Bar Association, 2005: 14). Women lawyers in Canadian law firms continue to be under-represented in partnerships, advance to partnerships more slowly than men, and exit law practice at a much higher rate than their male colleagues (Kay, 1997; see also Brockman, 2001). Research also found that women held less than 11 percent of all seats on the boards of Fortune 500 companies (Klein 1998) and held only 14 percent of corporate officer positions within Canada's 500 largest companies (Macionis and Gerber, 2005: 244).

Smith (2002: 509) emphasizes that, "Despite significant advancements in the overall socioeconomic status of minorities and working women, race and gender remain important impediments to their attainment of authority." While research that examined Fortune 500 companies focusing on the experience of visible-minority employees suggested that gender is more of a factor in "organizational treatment" than "race" (Cianni and Romberger, 1997), such conclusions invite the false assumption that race and gender may be separated into independent categories of experience and analysis. As Crenshaw (1993: 389) observed more generally of analyses and policies that failed to acknowledge the cross-currents of racism and sexism, "the failure to embrace the complexities of compoundedness is not simply a matter of political will, but is also due to the influence of a way of thinking about discrimination which structures policies so that struggles are categorized as singular issues." She contended that to conceptualize disadvantage along a single axis "marginalizes those who are multiply burdened" and creates "a distorted analysis of racism and sexism because the operative conceptions of race and sex become grounded in experiences that actually represent only a subset of a much more complex phenomenon" (pp. 383–384).

Multiple Jeopardies

The Canadian government has identified four groups as "disadvantaged because of their labour force participation and unemployment rates, their income levels, and their persistent occupational segregation" (Moreau, 1991: 26): women, Aboriginal people, visible minorities (i.e., people of colour and non-Caucasians/non-Aboriginals), and people with disabilities. There is little dispute that Aboriginal people have higher rates of unemployment and lower rates of labour-force participation than non-Aboriginal Canadians (Luffman and Sussman, 2007). "In 2001, 47% of Aboriginal women aged 15 and over were employed, compared with 56% of non-Aboriginal women. Aboriginal women were also less likely than their male counterparts, 47% versus 53%, to be employed that year" (Statistics Canada, 2006e). While Métis women were as likely as non-Aboriginal females to be employed, only 48 percent of Inuit women, and 43 percent of Aboriginal women were employed in 2001. Although the gap between the employment rates of Aboriginal and non-Aboriginal women in that year was especially large in women 15 to 24 years of age, (35 percent versus 57 percent), at all ages Aboriginal women were less likely to be employed than either Aboriginal men or non-Aboriginal women. Moreover, a large proportion of Aboriginal women with jobs in that year worked part-time or part-year (57 percent of Aboriginal women versus 54 percent of Aboriginal men and 49 percent of non-Aboriginal women). Findings from the 2006 Canadian Census indicate that even though "unemployment rates dropped and employment rates rose for people who identified as an Aboriginal person between 2001 and 2006, substantial gaps remained between Aboriginal and non-Aboriginal persons" (Statistics Canada, 2008f). For example, the employment rate for Aboriginal people age 25 to 54 was 65.8 percent in 2006, compared to 81.6 percent among non-Aboriginal people. Similarly, while the unemployment rate among core working-age Aboriginal people was 13.2 percent in 2006, among non-Aboriginal peoples it was 5.2 percent. "As with other women, Aboriginal women are heavily concentrated in low-paying occupations traditionally held by women" (Statistics Canada, 2006e: 198).

Of all Aboriginal women who were employed at some time during 2000, six in ten worked in either sales or service (37.1 percent) or business, finance, or administration jobs (22.9 percent); among non-Aboriginal women, these occupations accounted for 57 percent of employed women. Employed Aboriginal men are concentrated in manual occupations; in 2001, more than one in three (34.5 percent) were employed in trades or as transport and equipment operators (versus one in four, or 25.5 percent, of non-Aboriginal men). "The most common occupational category for Aboriginal men in 2001 was construction trades—7.4% compared with only 4.1% of non-Aboriginal men. Such jobs include plumbers, carpenters, painters, and shinglers" (Luffman and Sussman, 2007: 23). In that year, the most common occupations among Aboriginal women were clerical (e.g., general office clerks, data entry clerks, letter carriers, bank/financial/office clerks). Both Aboriginal men and women, however, earn yearly incomes well below Canadian averages; in 2000, "[t]he average employment income for Aboriginal women ages 15 and over was $16,979, more than $6,500 less than that of non-Aboriginal females and $6,800 less than that of Aboriginal males" (Macionis and Gerber, 2005: 251). Findings from the 2005 Labour Force Survey conducted by Statistics Canada indicate that while one in four Aboriginal employees earned less than $10 per hour in 2005, this was true for one in six non-Aboriginal workers; conversely, while four in ten non-Aboriginal employees earned at least $20 per hour, less than three in ten Aboriginal employees earned this amount (see Table 6.5).

Visible-minority women are also generally more likely to be unemployed (8.7 percent) than non-visible-minority women (5.6 percent) and visible-minority men (7.4 percent) (Statistics Canada, 2006e: 249). Akin to findings for Aboriginal women, while unemployment rates are especially high among female visible-minority women in the 15 to 24 age group, at all ages, visible-minority women are more likely to be unemployed than their non-visible-minority counterparts. There is, however, considerable variation among women in different visible-minority groups. Thus, for example, among those ages 25 to 64 in 2001, "16% of both West Asians and Arabs were unemployed, while the figure in the remaining groups ranged from 11% among Latin Americans to around 5% for Japanese women and Filipinas" (Statistics Canada, 2006e: 249).

As with non-visible-minority women, visible-minority women in Canada are most likely to work in either sales or service jobs or in business, clerical, and related administration occupations (in 2001, 51 percent of all employed visible-minority women, 52 percent of all non-visible-minority women). Visible-minority men were also more likely to be employed in these types of jobs than other men (31 percent versus 24 percent). Visible-minority women were also about as likely as other women to occupy management positions (7 percent of employed visible-minority women and 8 percent of non-visible-minority women). However, "visible minority women made up a disproportionate share of women employed in occupations in the natural and applied sciences" (Statistics Canada, 2006e); while visibility-minority women represented 13 percent of all women who were in the paid workforce in 2001, they accounted for almost one in five (19 percent) of the women employed in these sectors. Conversely, visible-minority women were somewhat less likely than other women to be employed within other professional occupations (23 percent versus 28 percent). Compared to other Canadian women, visible minorities were also three times

TABLE 6.5	Average Hourly Earnings of Employees, Aboriginal and Non-Aboriginal Men and Women, 2005					
	Aboriginal			Non-Aboriginal		
	Both Sexes	Men	Women	Both Sexes	Men	Women
Overall ($ per hour)	14.20	14.80	13.60	15.60	16.10	14.80
$0.01 to $9.99	24.8%	20.7%	28.6%	16.5%	12.1%	21.1%
$10.00 to $15.99	32.8	30.6	34.8	28.3	24.6	32.1
$16.00 to $19.99	13.8	13.6	14.0	15.2	14.5	16.0
$20.00 and over	28.6	35.1	22.6	40.0	48.8	30.8

Source: Luffman and Sussman (2007: 24).

more likely to be employed in manufacturing and related jobs in 2001 (12 percent versus 4 percent); approximately one in four South Asian women was employed in a manufacturing job in that year. Compared to other women in Canada, visible minorities generally earn less. "Among those employed on a full-time, full-year basis in 2000, for example, visible minority women earned an average of $32,100. This was just over $3,000, or about 10%, less than the employment earnings of their non-visible counterparts" (see Figure 6.1).

The Participation and Activity Limitation Survey (PALS), a post-censal survey conducted by Statistics Canada, was based on a sample of 43 000 persons who answered "Yes" to the 2001 Census disability filter question; within this study, "persons with disabilities" refers to those "who reported difficulties with daily living activities, or who indicated that a physical or mental condition or health problem reduced the kind or amount of activities they could do" (Statistics Canada, 2002a). According to this survey, persons of both sexes with disabilities were less likely than Canadians without disabilities to be employed in 2001.

| FIGURE 6.1 | Average Earnings of Women in a Visible Minority Employed Full-time, Full-year, by Group, 2000 |

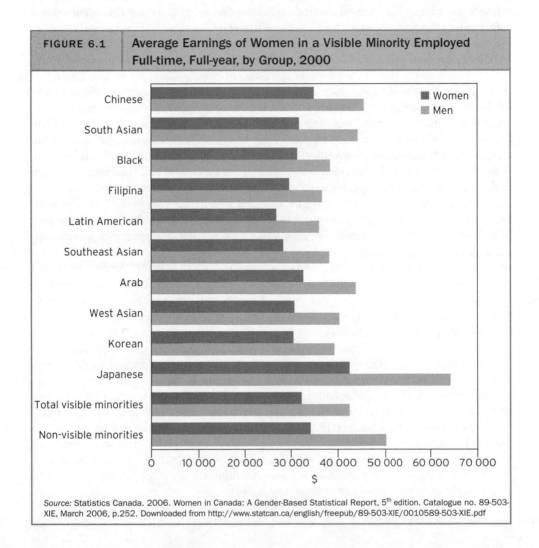

Source: Statistics Canada. 2006. Women in Canada: A Gender-Based Statistical Report, 5th edition. Catalogue no. 89-503-XIE, March 2006, p.252. Downloaded from http://www.statcan.ca/english/freepub/89-503-XIE/0010589-503-XIE.pdf

Among Canadians ages 15 to 64 with disabilities in 2001, women were less likely than men to be employed (38.5 percent versus 44.9 percent) (Statistics Canada, 2002b, 2002c).

Both the degree (i.e., severe, moderate, or mild) and type of disability (e.g., chronic health problems, hearing impairment, learning disabilities, mental disorders, mobility impairments, psychiatric disorders) may affect individuals' ability to obtain and keep a job. Men and women with disabilities are more likely than other Canadians to experience disruptions to their employment; this is partly a result of the nature of certain disabilities, which may necessitate absence from the workplace for varying lengths of time (Statistics Canada, 2007h). However, employment discontinuities also reflect the fact that persons with disabilities are often the last hired and the first fired. Dranoff (2001: 54) noted that "[t]he largest number of new complaints to the Canadian Human Rights Commission in recent years has been claims of discrimination based on disability."

Across Canada, human-rights codes prohibit employers from discriminating on the basis of physical or mental handicap or disability; however, important caveats exist. An employer may refuse to hire or may fire a person who lacks an ability deemed to be a **bona fide occupational requirement** (i.e., one necessary for proper or efficient performance of job duties). For example, the ability to see would constitute a bona fide occupational requirement for a job as a pilot. In other cases, such refusal may be a matter of discrimination; for example, a person with partial deafness might be denied a job even though acuity of hearing would not be necessary for its performance. Proving discrimination before a human-rights board of inquiry or tribunal (be it on the basis of disability or any other prohibited ground) is a long, drawn-out process. Even when discrimination can be proven, an employer may successfully argue that accommodating the special needs of an employee with a disability would cause "undue hardship" (i.e., entail modifications that would adversely affect the economic viability of the business). Although the Supreme Court of Canada has ruled that employers have a legal duty to accommodate such needs, the employer is not expected to incur "undue hardship" in order to do so.

A further bar to the employment of Canadians with disabilities is the fact that while many income-support programs (including social assistance and disability pensions) provide support for disability-related expenses (e.g., medication, transportation), such supports disappear when an individual becomes employed. Accordingly, if one's employment income is insufficient to cover such expenses, one cannot "afford to work." As Fawcett (1999) pointed out, "persons with disabilities who look for work face a dilemma: in their attempts to convince potential employers that they are capable of working, they may disqualify themselves from the social assistance and disability supports they need in order to survive" (see also Statistics Canada, 2002d).

Fawcett (1999) reported that the earnings of women with disabilities employed in full-year, full-time employment were typically lower than those of both men with disabilities and persons of both sexes without disabilities. According to the 2001 PALS, the median income among employed Canadians ages 15 to 64 with disabilities was $21 981 for men and $12 152 for women. In the same year, the incomes of men and women of comparable age without disabilities were $31 133 and $19 504 respectively (Statistics Canada, 2002b, 2002c). Put somewhat differently, in 2000, almost half (47.2 percent) of men with disabilities and almost seven out of ten women with disabilities (68 percent) had a yearly income of less than $20 000; among Canadians without disabilities, only 32.6 percent of men and 50.6 percent of women subsisted at this income level.

Fine and Asch (1988) have referred to the experience of women with disabilities as **"sexism without the pedestal"** (see also Traustadottir, 1997). Women with disabilities are more likely than their male counterparts to be discouraged from seeking/holding a job and to be cast into the "handicapped role" (i.e., viewed and treated as helpless, dependent, and passive) (Lonsdale, 1990). According to the DisAbled Women's Network Ontario (DAWN) (2004), "Regardless of country or culture, from the least developed to the most highly developed nations, disabled women are employed at rates far lower than disabled men. The pattern is established early on and is similar from country to country: as girls they have less access to education; as adolescents, they have fewer chances to socialize or receive guidance about planning their futures; and as adults they have fewer chances to receive rehabilitation services, enter training programs or the labour market." Mobility-impaired mothers of young children may be discouraged by the lack of accessible transport to and from work and child-care facilities. One Canadian mother with disabilities reported to Fawcett (1999) that in order to take her pre-schooler to daycare and then proceed to her workplace she had to book two separate accessible buses "with up to an hour of waiting in between." While noting the significant challenges faced by women with disabilities, it is important to emphasize that, given the centrality of the "good provider" role to our society's construction of masculinity, men with disabilities who are unable to work may face a severe threat to their sense of self.

Earnings Differentials

In 1967, when data on Canadian female-to-male earnings were first collected, the earnings-differential ratio stood at 58.4 percent. Since then, it has increased notably (see Table 6.6). "Earnings have ... evolved very differently by gender over the last two decades. They have been stagnant for men, increasing in 2000 for the first time since

TABLE 6.6	Earnings Ratio among Full-year, Full-time Workers, Canada, 1993–2003		
	$ Constant 2003		Earnings Ratio
Year	Women	Men	(%)
1993	34 300	48 100	71.3
1994	33 500	48 900	68.5
1995	34 900	48 200	72.4
1996	34 300	47 400	72.3
1997	34 000	49 700	68.3
1998	36 500	50 700	71.9
1999	35 000	51 300	68.4
2000	36 200	51 200	70.6
2001	36 500	52 300	69.9
2002	36 800	52 400	70.2
2003	36 500	51 700	70.5

Source: Adapted from the Statistics Canada, Women in Canada 2005, Catalogue no 89-504-XIE, Table 6.9, p. 152.

1980. In contrast, earnings have increased steadily in each decade for women" (Statistics Canada, 2003a). However, "[d]espite substantial gains in earnings during the past two decades, women still earn less than men" (Statistics Canada, 2003a). In 2003, women working in full-year, full-time jobs earned an average of $36 500, while comparably employed men earned $51 700—producing an earnings ratio of 71.3 (Statistics Canada, 2003c). The **gender wage gap** is widespread and exists in all occupational categories (see Table 6.7).

Boyd (2004: 229) noted that four explanations are commonly offered for the wage gap between men and women: "(1) gender differences in the characteristics that influence pay rates; (2) gender differences in the type of work performed; (3) discrimination; and (4) societal devaluation of women's work." The first of these explanations, sometimes referred to as the **human capital hypothesis**, asserts that female–male pay differences are a function of differences in women's and men's levels of education, skills, training, and work experience. The argument is "that earnings reflect the productivity of workers and that productivity is increased by factors such as higher education, longer labour-force experience, and length of time on the job" (Boyd, 2004: 229). Those who favour this explanation maintain that the wage gap reflects women's putative inferior productivity, a result of inferior educational attainment and the greater likelihood of family-related interruptions to their employment. The second explanation focuses on organizational variables, particularly

TABLE 6.7	Average Annual Earnings of Women and Men, by Occupation, 2003, Full-time Workers		
Occupation	Women ($)	Men ($)	Earnings Ratio*
Managerial	46 600	69 900	67.4
Administrative	35 500	55 700	63.7
Professionals			
Business/finance	55 800	80 400	69.3
Natural sciences	55 300	66 500	83.1
Social sciences/religion	63 900	91 200	70.0
Teaching	47 500	63 300	75.0
Medicine/health+	61 100	116.30	52.5
Artistic/recreational	33 600	41 900	80.0
Clerical	33 300	41 800	79.7
Sales/service	24 100	43 300	55.7
Trades/transportation	24 800	43 500	57.1
Primary	19 200	31 500	60.8
Manufacturing	26 200	45 100	58.1
All occupations	36 500	51 700	70.5

* Represents women's earnings as a percentage of those of men.
+ Includes registered nurses and nurse supervisors.

Source: Women in Canada 2005, Catalogue no. 89-503-XIE, Table 6.11., p. 153.

women's occupational segregation in the *pink-collar ghetto*—low-status, low-wage, low-benefits jobs in the clerical, sales, and service fields—as well as their over-representation in part-time and non-standard forms of work.

Discrimination, the third explanation, may be either "personal and deliberate" or "impersonal"—"produced by the standard, unquestioned practices of assigning women to certain jobs and men to others, and of paying men and women different wages even when they hold the same jobs" (Boyd, 2004: 229). Boyd also observed that "[m]uch of this impersonal discrimination is called **statistical discrimination**, the process whereby employers make decisions about whether to hire and how much to pay any given woman on the basis of the employers' perception of the average characteristics of *all* women" (emphasis in original). Thus, an employer's generalized beliefs about women (e.g., that they are less productive and committed workers, are apt to balk at overtime or business-related travel, will absent themselves for long stretches of time to raise their children) may influence the type of work a woman is given and the pay she receives. The fourth explanation, referred to as the **devaluation hypothesis**, suggests that women are paid less because the work they perform is socially defined as less valuable than the work performed by men.

Each of these explanations has both enthusiasts and critics. Testing the devaluation and human capital hypotheses in the United States, Tam (1997) concluded that the latter is a more important determinant of the income gender gap. Marini et al. (1997) also found support for the human capital hypothesis, but their research supported the second and third explanations as well. They found organizational variables (i.e., characteristics of the business, corporation, or industry) to be important in the gender income gap; they also reported that employers channel new hires into sex-specific jobs that carry different wage rates. Tomaskovic-Devey (1993) found the percentage of females in an occupation to be the best predictor of an income gender gap: The higher the percentage of females, the lower the pay. An analysis of National Longitudinal Survey data on over 5000 men and over 5000 women supported this observation; Kilbourne et al. (1994: 708) concluded that occupational pay is gendered and that "occupations lose pay if they have a higher percentage of female workers or require nurturant skills."

The narrowing of the wage gap in Canada might be explained with reference to the facts that more women are working and more are working longer hours. In addition, they are more highly qualified; since 1980, the proportion of women workers with a university degree has almost tripled, and the proportion of women earners with a university degree now exceeds the proportion of men (Statistics Canada, 2003d). Worldwide, income differences between men and women tend to decrease as educational differences decrease (Wootton, 1997; Educational Indicators, 1998); in general, the higher one's education, the higher one's income. Yet, contrary to what the human capital hypothesis would suggest, research finds that even when women and men have identical levels of educational achievement and work full-time, women, on average, earn less than men (Statistics Canada, 2006e; Table 6.8). Although women with a university degree earn substantially more than women with lower levels of education, women university graduates employed full-time, full-year, in 2003 earned just 69 percent as much as their male counterparts.

The persistent wage gap between these highly educated young women and men may be partially explained by their career choices. Consider, for example, that despite the dramatic increase in the proportion of young Canadian women who possess a university degree (rising from 21 percent in 1991 to 34 percent in 2001), the earnings gap between 25- to 29-year-old Canadian men and women witnessed only a modest decline during this period; while in

TABLE 6.8	Average Annual Earnings of Women and Men Employed Full-time, Full-year, by Educational Attainment, 2003		
Educational attainment	Women	Men	Women's Income as % of Men's
Less than grade 9	21 700	31 200	69.4
Some secondary school	22 900	40 000	57.3
Secondary-school graduate	30 500	43 000	71.0
Some post-secondary	31 500	41 600	75.6
Post-secondary certificate			
or diploma	34 200	49 800	68.6
University degree	53 400	77 500	68.9
Total	38 500	51 700	70.5

Source: Statistics Canada, Women in Canada 2005, Catalogue no. 89-503-XIE, Table 6.10, p. 153.

1991, women ages 25 to 29 earned 20 percent less than their male counterparts in 1991, this gap narrowed slightly and stood at 18 percent in 2001. One reason for this modest decline was that, during this time period, the earnings gap between male and female university graduates increased (rising from 12 percent to 18 percent)—largely as the result of "real wage declines in female-dominated disciplines, such as health and education, and real wage increases in male-dominated disciplines, such as engineering, mathematics, computer sciences and physical sciences" (Frenette and Coulombe, 2007). However, while the wage gap narrows when women pursue occupations most commonly chosen by men, it still exists. In 2000, university-educated women ages 25 to 29 who worked in the 10 occupations most commonly chosen by men of the same age group and qualifications earned about 89 cents for every dollar earned by their male counterparts (Statistics Canada, 2004d).

A Canadian study based on data obtained from the Survey of Labour and Income Dynamics reported that women's lower levels of work experience appear to have a significant bearing on the persistent gender wage gap. According to this study, about 18 percent (almost one fifth) of the wage gap "reflects the fact that women generally have less experience than their male counterparts, supervise other employees less often and are involved in administrative decisions less frequently" (Statistics Canada, 1999a). This relative lack of work experience helps explain why the gender wage gap is smallest among young workers and widens with age. In this study, women ages 45 to 54 had 6.4 fewer years of work experience than did comparable men. The study noted several other factors, including differences in job tenure and the fact that men are more likely to graduate from programs such as engineering and commerce, while women are more likely to graduate from education and social-science programs. However, while acknowledging that "wages differ by field of study," they reported that differences in the educational choices of men and women accounted "for at most six percent of the wage-disparity between the two sexes in 1997" (Statistics Canada, 1999a). Differential job status and women's greater likelihood of working part-time are calculated to account for seven percent of the wage gap. The study concluded that "[m]uch of the wage gap remains a puzzle, leaving at least one half of the discrepancy unaccounted for" (Statistics Canada, 1999a).

Boyd (2004: 230) reported that "[m]ost sociologists emphasize discrimination and the devaluation of work performed by women as the main explanations for gender inequalities in earnings." Yet it remains true that the gender earnings gap is partly attributable to occupational distributions, attained education, and differential gender employment histories. Age is another important contributing factor, in that younger people benefit from social and legal expectations that promote greater equality in wage and pay scales. Efforts have been made to eliminate sex discrimination in pay scales by legislative means. The first legislation requiring Canadian employers to pay women the same wages as men for equal work was enacted in Ontario in 1951; however, as Dranoff (2001: 49) observed, this obligation existed "only on paper": "[T]hese laws stated lofty principles but did not have the programs and enforcement to give them teeth and bite. Nor did these laws result in fair wages, because many women were segregated into female occupations, such as nursing and secretarial jobs, and few men were doing precisely the same work." In the 1970s, some provinces enacted laws ordering employers to pay equal wages to women performing "substantially the same" work as men; once again, however, these laws could easily be circumvented by employers claiming that disparate wages were based on grounds other than sex.

Since 1978, the *Canadian Human Rights Act* has specifically prohibited employers from discriminating between male and female employees who perform work of equal value. However, it was only in the mid-1980s that some provincial governments amended their laws to explicitly state that "work of equal value" must be equally compensated. In 1985, Manitoba became the first Canadian province "to require its public sector to be pro-active and develop plans to secure for provincial government employees what 'equal pay for work of equal value' came to be called—'**pay equity**'" (Dranoff, 2001: 49; emphasis added). Three years later, Ontario took an even bolder step with its *Pay Equity Act*, becoming the only Canadian jurisdiction to require not only public-sector employers but private-sector employers with 10 or more employees to adjust their pay scales in accordance with the principle of equal pay for work of equal value, and to establish and maintain compensation practices that would result in pay equity. Employers were required to determine the proportion of male and female employees in various jobs, to compare the jobs usually performed by women with those usually performed by men, and to group similar jobs together into a job class. This term refers to positions marked by similar duties, responsibilities, and qualifications, filled by similar recruiting procedures, and compensated according to the same wage schedule, salary grade, or range of salaries; "[f]or example, in an assessment of municipal government jobs, the work of nurses (female) would be compared with that of police constables (male)" (Lowe, 1995: 10–16). The Pay Equity Commission of Ontario uses the following analogy to explain the logic underlying pay equity: "Comparing female and male job classes is similar to comparing apples and oranges to assess how they are similar or comparable, rather than how they are different. Apples and oranges are both fruits, are both round and colourful, produce juice, and contain vitamins and fibre. The characteristics are different in each fruit, but the total value of each fruit is about the same" (Government of Ontario, nd: 3). In 1997, proactive pay-equity legislation directed at employers with 10 or more employees took effect in Quebec. Since then, most provinces have adopted such legislation.

Pay-equity legislation was designed to address the fact that, historically and into the present, women have been employed in undervalued jobs and have therefore received lower wages than men. Nevertheless, it is not without its problems. As observers have noted, pay equity as a policy cannot be applied to firms in which the labour force is exclusively female; also, the method of evaluating the comparative worth of two jobs "does not correct for the a priori understandings of certain skills" (Boyd, 1995: 3–24). Lowe (1995: 10–16) noted that pay-equity legislation covers a limited pool of workers, largely situated in relatively good public-sector jobs, and that its highly technical procedures are cumbersome to apply. Even when pay-equity legislation is in place, enforcing compliance and achieving financial redress for past and present inequities is typically an arduous and protracted process. Employers (including federal and provincial governments) have demonstrated a willingness to tie up equity cases in the courts for years and even decades, all the while still paying workers inequitable wages. In the meantime, they continue to reap benefits in the form of lower costs from differential pay scales, viewing final court judgments as simply a "cost of doing business."

The Chilly Climate: Gender Bias and Sexual Harassment The term **chilly climate** reflects the fact that even in workplaces in which men and women are officially "equal," some people may (to quote George Orwell's *Animal Farm*) be "more equal than others." Despite the growth in cross-gender labour-force participation, persistent cultural beliefs about the gender-appropriateness of certain jobs may create an inhospitable work environment for those who are the "wrong sex."

Acker (1990: 152) noted that women have historically been viewed as a disruptive influence in the workplace: "Women's bodies—female sexuality, their ability to procreate and their pregnancy, breast-feeding, and child care, menstruation and mythic 'emotionality'.... [were viewed as] suspect, [and were] stigmatized, and used as grounds for control and exclusion." McCormick (2002: 160) observed that these notions are still used to "justify the relegation of women in the workforce to low-status, low-income occupations." Martin (1992: 200) reported that women may be excluded by male employers who fear that the admittance of women may diminish the prestige of their profession or believe that "the ideal worker is normatively masculine." Similar attitudes have been observed among business students. In a study of 194 Canadian business students (71 female and 123 male undergraduate and graduate students), Burke (1994) found that, compared to female students, male students exhibited significantly more negative attitudes towards women as managers. He suggested that this "augers badly" for women, because these men (1) would be unlikely, as colleagues, to support initiatives to develop women's careers and might even endorse "backlash" strategies; (2) would be unlikely to provide women with mentorship and may act as poor role models for other men; and (3) would be unlikely, as intimate partners, to support women's career aspirations.

Marquat (1990) found that, during medical-school interviews, while male applicants were more frequently asked about their reasons for pursuing a career in medicine and their envisaged specialty, female applicants were more frequently queried about their plans for marriage and children. Komaromy et al. (1993) observed that female medical students were more likely to report being physically harassed by trainers of higher professional status; Schulte and Kay (1994) noted that patients were more likely to direct inappropriate sexual behaviour towards female medical students (71 percent) than towards male medical students (29 percent), and that female medical students were more likely to be subjected to such behaviour repeatedly. As practitioners, women are over-represented within certain fields (e.g., pediatrics, obstetrics/gynecology, internal medicine, family practice, and psychiatry) and notably under-represented in others (e.g., sports medicine, research and administration, surgery) (Furr, 2002: 50). Riska and Wegar (1993) observed that women physicians reported less opportunity to acquire surgical experience. Lorber (1993) found that the perception of women physicians with children as being less committed to their careers has limited their access to positions of authority. Finally, a meta-analytic review of seven observational studies that investigated the relation between patient–physician communication and physician's sex found that although patients spoke more to female physicians, disclosed more biomedical and psychosocial information, and made more positive statements to them, they were also more assertive in their dealings with female physicians and tended to interrupt them more (Hall and Roter, 2002; see also Roter et al., 2002).

Research reveals that women in science generally hold lower-level positions than males with comparable levels of expertise, and that women's representation steadily declines at higher rungs of the career ladder (Pattucci, 1998). This disparity abides despite the fact that "the majority of women in science choose to ... postpone childbearing until their careers are established and a substantial minority choose not to have children" (Furr, 2002: 51). Research on the career experiences of women engineers has yielded similar findings (Robinson and McIlwee, 1991). Furr (2002: 51) noted that although male engineers commonly asserted that male and female engineers were treated alike, there were significant differences between the sexes in terms of job assignments, travel, and promotion; she concluded that "[t]he more strongly the culture of an engineering office is identified with the male gender, the more difficulty a woman engineer will encounter with occupational status and mobility."

Sexism in the workplace may also take the form of **sexual harassment**, which "may be an expression of power or desire or both" (Aggarwal, 1987: 1). Sexual harassment is a multifaceted phenomenon that may include sexual assault; unwanted touching or patting; leering; sexually suggestive gestures; demands for sexual favours; derogatory or degrading remarks directed towards members of one sex or sexual orientation; repeated offensive sexual flirtations/advances/propositions; verbal threats or abuse; questions or comments about an individual's sex life; the use of sexually degrading words to describe a person; sexist jokes that cause embarrassment; and the display of sexually offensive material. In identifying this non-exhaustive list of behaviours held by the courts to constitute sexual harassment, the Law Society of Upper Canada acknowledged that "[w]hether a particular type of conduct constitutes sexual harassment is sometimes difficult to determine," and asserted that although "the severity of the conduct may be the most conclusive factor ... what is determinative is a combination of frequency, severity and persistence" (in Mossman, 1997: 244).

Two general types of sexual harassment can be distinguished. The more obvious of the two, **quid pro quo**, describes instances in which a victim is threatened with adverse employment repercussions for non-compliance with demands for sexual favours. The second, a **poisoned work environment**, is more subtle. It "describes situations in which the conduct creates a working environment that is intimidating, uncomfortable or offensive to any employee," even though the offensive behaviour may not necessarily be directed against a specific person (Law Society of Upper Canada, 1991). The Supreme Court of Canada in *Janzen v. Platy Enterprises et al.* (1989) established as a point of law that sexual harassment can constitute discrimination on the basis of sex. In his judgment on the Janzen case, Chief Justice Dickson averred that although quid pro quo tends to be regarded as a more serious form of sexual harassment than a "poisoned work environment," the distinction is specious: "The main point in allegations of sexual harassment is that unwelcome sexual conduct has invaded the workplace, irrespective of whether the consequences of the harassment included a denial of concrete employment rewards for refusing to participate in sexual activity" (in Mossman, 1997: 246). Sexual harassment occurs at all occupational levels; some research suggests that the incidence of sexual harassment is inversely proportional to the number of women in an occupational category (Fitzgerald and Shullman, 1993; Schneider and Phillips, 1997). However, as emphasized in Chapter 5, sexual harassment is not exclusively a "women's problem."

In the case of *Robichaud v. Canada (Treasury Board)*, (1987), the Supreme Court of Canada ruled that "[a]n employer can be held responsible for the unauthorized acts of its employees, in the course of their employment." Under the *Canadian Human Rights Act* and/or provincial human-rights codes, businesses may be held liable for acts of sexual harassment committed by their employees. The *Canadian Human Rights Act* obliges employers to give evidence of their attentiveness to the possibility that sexual harassment may occur within their workplace. Employers are to do so by creating policies that define prohibited conduct and assert a commitment to ensuring a workplace free of harassment and discrimination, by demonstrating that procedures exist to deal with these types of complaints, and by imposing penalties upon anyone contravening these policies. Provincial human-rights codes also contain provisions aimed at curtailing sexual harassment. For example, Ontario's Human Rights Code (R.S.O., 1990, c. H.19) asserts that "[e]very person who is an employee has a right to freedom from harassment in the workplace because of sex by his or her employer or agent of the employer or by another employee"; moreover, sexual harassment is defined as "a compensable injury under the provisions of the Ontario Worker's Compensation Act" (DeKeseredy and Hinch, 1991: 127). Nevertheless, some continue to discount the perniciousness of sexual harassment and jeer at efforts to mitigate its impact. Thus, Fekete (1994) argued that the "flat and flatulent formula of zero tolerance" (p. 198), along with other "politically correct" measures, stem from a "bio-feminist" conspiracy. For Fekete (1994: 207), the "real victims" are those who have stood accused of acting or speaking in a sexist, "racist," ablist, or homophobic manner, or who have made "innocent remarks that happened to cause displeasure." From this perspective, those who are injured or offended are the problem, not those who injured or gave offence.

Affirmative Action: Solution or Problem? Affirmative action has been defined as "a program of temporary measures designed to eliminate systemic factors that prevent members of minority or other groups from competing equally with members of the majority in terms of opportunities, usually in employment" (Hill and Schiff, 1988: 35). Section 15 of the *Canadian Charter of Rights and Freedoms* states that every individual is considered equal and that government cannot discriminate in its laws or programs. However, subsection 15(2) specifically guarantees that programs, such as affirmative action, that have been set up by government to ameliorate the conditions of certain disadvantaged groups are permissible even if perceived as discriminatory to the majority. Kallen (2003: 231) observed that "[t]he constitutional sanction for affirmative action, given by its incorporation under section 15 of the Charter, makes Canada one of the few countries in the world where programs of affirmative action, including special measures, have gained status recognition under the provisions of the supreme law of the land."

The origins of affirmative action in Canada can be traced to the attempts of the Royal Commission on Bilingualism and Biculturalism to increase francophone participation in the federal public service. "At the time, underrepresentation of francophones in the federal public service was acknowledged to be a manifestation of systemic discrimination ... [and] it was deemed necessary by government authorities to introduce affirmative action programs ... to recruit, place and promote francophones" (Kallen, 2003: 226). In 1977, the passage of the *Canadian Human Rights Act* (CHRA) provided the legal foundation for such policies at the federal government level. In relation to employment, the CHRA asserted that it was not a discriminatory practice to adopt or carry out a special program, plan, or arrangement designed to prevent, eliminate, or reduce disadvantages suffered by persons or groups because of race, national or ethnic origin, skin colour, religion, age, sex, family status, marital status, or disability by improving their opportunities; thus, the *Act* explicitly stated that "employment equity" did not constitute "reverse discrimination." Indeed, under the terms of reference of the Canadian Human Rights Commission (charged with administering the *Act*), an affirmative-action program may in fact be required as part of the settlement of a complaint of discrimination "when a case of discrimination against an individual is found to be indicative of categorical discrimination against the minority s/he represents" (Kallen, 2003: 226).

The 1984 Royal Commission on Equality in Employment (aka the "Abella Commission") inquired into "the most efficient, effective, and equitable means of promoting employment opportunities, eliminating systemic discrimination and assisting all individuals to compete for employment," with a directed focus on women, Aboriginals, visible minorities, and persons with disabilities. Following its recommendations, the federal government instituted two mandatory affirmative actions—or, as they came to be known, **employment equity** programs. The first, the *Employment Equity Act* (1985), was designed to redress discrimination against four target groups: women, Aboriginals, visible minorities, and people with disabilities. It required all sizeable employers (i.e., those with 100 or more employees) in the federal sector to ensure that their procedures for hiring, firing, promoting, and training were equitable to all groups. The second, the Federal Contractors Program, was directed at sizeable contractors (with at least 100 employees) who bid on federal contracts for goods and services worth a minimum of $200 000. These contractors were obliged to sign an agreement indicating their willingness to develop and carry out an employment-equity program that would identify and eliminate barriers to the employment, training, and promotion of the four target groups. However, critics observed that both programs, "though garbed in mandatory trappings were de facto voluntary because they lacked mandatory implementation of plans with special goals and timetables, systematic monitoring mechanisms, and effective sanctions for non-compliance" (Kallen, 2003: 232); they were also limited in scope (neither policy, for example, extended to the Armed Forces or the RCMP). Moreover, although employers were required to implement employment equity and to file progress reports documenting their efforts, the only violation for which they could be penalized was failure to file the reports.

In response to such criticisms, a new *Employment Equity Act* and related *Regulations*, governing both private- and public-sector employers under federal jurisdiction, came into being in 1996. Under the *Employment Equity Act* (1996), employers are required to identify and eliminate employment barriers, institute positive policies and practices, and develop a plan defining both short-term (i.e., less than three years) and long-term goals. All employees within the federal public sector (including the RCMP, the Canadian Armed Forces, and the Canadian Security Intelligence Service) are covered under this legislation. As well, any private-sector employer with a minimum of 100 employees who is involved with a "federal work, undertaking or business" must comply with the *Act*. This legislation is enforced by the Canadian Human Rights Commission, which has authority to conduct compliance audits to ensure that "numerical goals" (not quotas) are met and to levy fines of up to $50 000 for non-compliance. Nevertheless, it has been noted that although Canada's federal employment-equity policies and programs "rank among the most advanced in the world," progress in achieving the aims they were designed for "has been very modest, especially in the case of visible minorities, whose current representation is less than 60 percent of their workplace visibility"; unfortunately, "this seemingly sluggish rate of progress, given the high cost of maintaining the employment equity system, feeds the sharp edge of criticism levied by opponents" (Kallen, 2003: 237–238).

Elsewhere in Canada, the status of employment equity is uneven. The territories are covered by federal law; however, of the seven Canadian provinces with employment-equity policies (British Columbia, Manitoba, Saskatchewan, Quebec, Nova Scotia, New Brunswick, and Prince Edward Island), only British Columbia has employment-equity legislation, and only Quebec has extended its mandate beyond the public sphere (Kallen, 2003: 232). The employment-equity legislation that Ontario had enacted in 1993 was repealed by the Conservatives after they came to power in 1995—however, in response to specific complaints, the Ontario Human Rights Commission (like other provincial human-rights commissions) may order an organization found to engage in systemic discrimination to adopt equity-type programs. Analysis of provincial employment-equity policies reveals that progress has been substantial in the case of women but more limited among the other target groups.

The topic of employment equity continues to provoke intense debate. Proponents insist that "equality does not necessarily mean that everyone should be treated the same" (Blair et al., 2003: 99), maintaining that intervention is necessary to ensure full equality of opportunity for targeted groups. Opponents generally advance three counter-arguments. First, they maintain that this strategy will not bring about equality or attenuate discrimination and may, contrary to its aim, rekindle the degrading colour/race/gender-consciousness of times past. Second, they claim that affirmative-action policies "have served to reinforce and 'justify' stereotypes of minority inferiority" (Kallen, 2003: 230). Certain findings seem to support this claim: The Canadian Bar Association Task Force on Gender Equality in the Legal Profession (1993) reported that "even when admitted under the regular admission policy, minority [law] students frequently felt forced to defend affirmative action policies, given the ever present assumption that such students have inferior abilities and, therefore, do not deserve to be attending law school" (in Mossman, 1997: 25). Third, they argue that such policies are underwritten by a simplistic view of the nature of minority-group membership in society. For example, when Wilfred Laurier University, in 1999, posted a job advertisement for a psychology professor specifying that only women would be considered, numerous protests were lodged with the Ontario Human Rights Commission. Although the chairperson of Laurier's psychology department defended the sex-specific posting as an attempt to "address a gender imbalance" (at the time, the department had 18 male and 4 female professors), critics maintained that women academics were "hardly a disadvantaged group" (*National Post*, August 6, 1999: A4; see also Hyde et al., 2002).

Part-time and Non-standard Work

Between 1976 and 2000, the proportion of **part-time** workers in the Canadian labour force increased more than 100 percent. In 2000, almost one fifth of all Canadians in the labour force worked part-time (i.e., fewer than 30 hours per week) (Pold, 2001: 13). Women have consistently represented approximately 70 percent of all part-time workers. "In 2006, more than 2 million employed women, 26% of all women in the paid labour force, worked less than 30 hours per week at their main job, compared with just 11% of employed men" (Statistics Canada, 2007g). While young women are more likely than older women to work part-time (52 percent of women ages 15 to 24 versus 20 percent of those ages 25 to 54 and 30 percent of those ages 55 to 64), "[w]omen in all age groups ... are far more likely than their male counterparts to work part-time" (Statistics Canada, 2004c: 8).

The rising rates of part-time employment are largely a consequence of "the increased globalization of the Canadian economy and the downsizing and restructuring of businesses and industry in the face of a persistent recession and increasing international competition for markets" (McVey and Kalbach, 1995: 319), and of cutbacks in the public service due to cost-saving measures adopted by provincial and federal governments. A recent labour-force survey reflected the effects of these large-scale changes in our economy. Respondents were asked to select the single best reason for their participation in part-time work (see Table 6.9). Among men, 41.7 percent identified "going to school" as their primary reason for working part-time, while 25.4 percent cited "personal preference." Approximately 26 percent indicated that working part time was involuntarily—a result of their inability to find full-time work. Only 1.3 percent of men identified "caring for children" as their primary reason for working part time, while another 1.3 percent cited "other personal/family responsibilities." On the other hand, roughly one in five women (21.3 percent) reported working part time because of personal/family responsibilities, including caring for children. Among respondents ages 25 to 44, this disparity was particularly noticeable: 42.9 percent of women, compared to 11.1 percent of men, identified personal/family responsibilities/child care as their primary reason for working part time. Women were slightly more likely than men to report working part time due to personal preference (28.1 percent), and slightly less likely

TABLE 6.9	Reasons for Part-time Work, by Age and Sex, 2006 (Percentages)						
	Women ages				Men ages		
	Total	15–24	25–44	45 and over	Total	15–24	25–44	45 and over
Own illness	0.4	2.9	5.7	3.0	0.6	5.1	6.0	3.1
Caring for children	1.6	35.5	5.8	14.6	F	4.0	1.4	1.3
Other personal/family responsibilities	0.6	4.5	5.7	3.7	0.6	2.0	2.1	1.3
Going to school	74.1	8.0	0.9	26.7	76.2	18.9	0.7	41.7
Personal preference	5.9	19.8	57.3	28.1	5.6	20.9	60.4	25.4
Other voluntary	0.3	1.1	0.7	0.7	0.4	2.5	1.3	1.1
Other*	17.1	28.2	23.8	23.2	16.4	46.8	28.2	26.1
Total employed part-time (thousands)	648.4	690.1	690.0	2028.5	467.7	189.7	288.7	946.1
% employed part time**	51.5	19.3	23.6	26.1	36.6	4.7	8.4	10.8

F Too unreliable to include.

* Includes business conditions and inability to find full-time work.

** Expressed as a percentage of total employed.

Source: Statistics Canada, Women in Canada, Work Chapter Updates, 2006, Table 9.

to report resorting to part-time work involuntarily (23.2 percent) (Statistics Canada, 2007g). However, Brym et al. (2003: 296) have noted that Canadian surveys indicate that "about one-third of women officially classified as voluntary part-time workers would work more hours if good child care or elder care was available."

Whatever their reasons, men and women who work part time are likely to be working at or below minimum wage: "[P]art-time workers make up about two-thirds of the people working at or below minimum wage" (Brym et al., 2003: 296). According to data from the 1999 Workplace and Employee Survey (WES) conducted by Statistics Canada (2003e), "[a]bout 30 percent of women working part time earned less than $9 an hour, almost twice the proportion of 16 percent among women who worked full time. Women in part-time work were 50 percent less likely than those who worked full time to report access to non-wage benefits." The lack of benefits is a second major disadvantage of part-time work; full-time workers are far more likely to receive benefits, such as dental plans, employee insurance plans (which cover at least part of the cost of eyeglasses or contact lenses), prescription drug plans, or supplemental health care. Part-time jobs also provide little opportunity for advancement. Moreover, part-time workers are typically offered little in the way of job security since the majority of part-time work is non-unionized: The rate of unionization among Canadian men who worked part-time in 2006 was 17.4 percent compared to 30.4 percent among their full-time counterparts; among women, the unionization rate for full and part-time women was 31.1 percent versus 25.4 percent respectively (Statistics Canada, 2007g: 6). In consequence, of all classes of the employed, part-time workers are the most vulnerable to exploitation. In light of the disadvantages experienced by part-time workers, and noting women's over-representation in the category, Boyd (2004: 228) has referred to part-time work as "an employment ghetto for women."

Self-employment

According to Statistics Canada's Labour Force Survey, almost 2.5 million individuals were **self-employed** in 2006. "Self-employment has expanded dramatically in Canada, account-ing for over one-quarter of all new jobs since the mid-1970s and roughly three-quarters of all new jobs in the 1990s" (Hughes, 2003: 1). While much of the growth in men's self-employment occurred during the recessions of the early 1980s and 1990s, the 1990s wit-nessed a rapid growth in women's self-employment: "The number of women who reported earnings from self-employment grew 6.9% from 1997 to 2001, more than the increase in the female working-age population (+6.4%)" (Statistics Canada, 2002e). Nevertheless, women are still less likely than men to be self-employed: In 2006, 1 621 400 Canadian males were self-employed, compared to 876 600 women (Statistics Canada, 2007g). In 2006, men accounted for almost two thirds (65 percent) of self-employed Canadians; in that year, 18.6 percent of employed men and 11.3 percent of employed women were self-employed (Statistics Canada, 2007g).

The self-employed can be divided into two categories: those who employ other workers (employers) and those who work alone (own-account workers). The self-employment of both male and female own-account workers has risen steadily since the mid-1970s and increased sharply in the 1990s. There has been moderate growth in the number of female employers and a slight decline among males. Women account for approximately 40 percent of own-account workers and approximately one quarter of employers. The majority of the self-employed (approximately three quarters of women and three fifths of men) are own-account workers. Traditionally, self-employed females—both own-account workers and employers—have been concentrated in the sales and service sectors; male own-account workers have been concentrated in sales, construction, and transport, while male employers have worked in a more diverse array of industries. Over time, as women have entered previously male-dominated domains, the occupational profiles of men and women employers have become more similar (Hughes, 2003: 1). Nevertheless, while self-employed women now work in a broader array of sectors than in the past, significant numbers of women (particularly own-account workers) are still concentrated in such traditional areas as trade, food/accommodation, and services.

According to the Canadian Survey of Self-Employment, about 80 percent of those who were self-employed in 2000 had voluntarily chosen self-employment; the remainder reported becoming self-employed because of a lack of opportunities for suitable paid employment (Statistics Canada, 2002e). Those who expressed an intention to remain self-employed were more likely to be employers, to possess a university degree, and to have been self-employed longer. Both self-employed women and men reported that the aspect of self-employment that they liked best was "entrepreneurial values"; "[h]owever, a close second for women was the flexible hours or the ability to work from home" (Statistics Canada, 2002e). Arai's (2000) analysis of data from Statistics Canada's Survey of Work Arrangements (N=11 828 female and 13 766 male respondents) also found that for women (but not men), self-employment may represent one way of coping with family and work pressures. Hundley (2001) reported that for married women, the self-employment experience is associated with less negative job-to-home spillover, greater job satisfaction, and less job burnout. Self-employment offers other advantages, including being one's own boss, experiencing a sense of independence, and having the opportunity to increase work-related knowledge by formal or informal means. The Canadian Survey of Self-Employment found that nearly four in five of the self-employed reported having taken part in some type of informal learning activity (e.g., reading manuals or books) in the past year; over a quarter reported having taken formal training. A study examining self-employment among Canadian college and university graduates (Finnie et al., 2002) suggested that self-employment was perceived as a "relatively attractive job status on average"; self-employment was more common among male postsecondary graduates (6.5 to 11.1 percent for different age cohorts) than among female (from 3.2 to 6.7 percent) (see also Statistics Canada, 2002g, 2002h).

Nevertheless, self-employment has its disadvantages. The Survey of Self-Employment found that the most-disliked aspects of self-employment were "uncertainty and insecurity (reported by 22% of respondents); long hours and no time off work (15%); income and cash flow fluctuations (12%); and lack of benefits (7%)" (Statistics Canada, 2002e). This survey also reported that 60 percent of the self-employed did not have supplemental health insurance or disability insurance, and two thirds lacked dental insurance; "[t]he rates of health and dental insurance coverage were lower for self-employed individuals than for employees, a majority of whom have these benefits" (Statistics Canada, 2002e). Moreover, while self-employed orthodontists and other professionals may earn lofty salaries, for most of the self-employed, material success is hardly guaranteed. "In 2001, on average in Canada, men earned $18 327 from self-employment, while women earned $10 523" (Statistics Canada, 2003e). Although women's net income from self-employment remained low and was lower than men's, women's average net self-employment income rose 16.8 percent (after adjusting for inflation) between 1997 and 2001, while males' average net self-employment income increased by only 11.8 percent (Statistics Canada, 2003e). In addition,

Hundley (2001) has observed that "[where] pre-school children are present, the earnings of self-employed women are much less than the earnings of the organizationally employed." His earlier analysis of the gender earnings gap among the self-employed (Hundley, 2000) reported that self-employed women's earnings declined with marriage, family size, and hours of housework, whereas self-employed men's earnings increased with marriage and family size.

Another disadvantage of self-employment stems from the fact that Canada's tax laws have yet to catch up with the changing composition of the Canadian workforce. In 1993, the Supreme Court of Canada ruled that mothers who are also self-employed businesspersons cannot claim child-care expenses as a tax deduction, even if these expenses were incurred in order to earn income. This ruling stemmed from a court challenge by Elizabeth Symes, a self-employed Toronto lawyer, who had hired a nanny to provide in-home care for her two young children on weekdays while she and her spouse pursued their respective careers. For the taxation years 1982 to 1985, Symes attempted to deduct the nanny's salary as a business expense. To understand her rationale in doing so, it is crucial to note that under section 18 of Canada's federal *Income Tax Act*, self-employed persons are allowed to deduct any reasonable expense incurred in order to produce income. Certain expenses, such as leased office space and equipment, office telephone bills, and employee salaries are specifically mentioned within the *Act* as deductible or partially deductible; in other cases, the rules may be ambiguous or fail to explicitly address a particular type of expense. In cases where the tax department challenges a self-employed person's claim, as it did in Symes' case, it may fall to the courts to rule on whether or not the expense is a "business expense."

The Minister of National Revenue disallowed Symes's child-care deductions, maintaining that the nanny's salary was a living or personal expense rather than a business one, and that Symes could only claim the standard child-care deduction. In turn, Symes appealed to the Federal Court, Trial Division. She argued that the Minister's interpretation of section 18 constituted discrimination on the basis of sex, contrary to the equality guarantee in section 15 of the *Charter*, and won. However, the Minister of National Revenue appealed the ruling and the Federal Court of Appeal sided with the tax department. Symes then appealed to the Supreme Court of Canada, which gave short shrift to her argument that preventing her from deducting child-care expenses infringed on her right to equality. Relying on customary accounting practice, which does not accept the costs of child care as a business expense, the Supreme Court ruled against her, with both women members dissenting. The dissenting opinion, delivered by Madam Justice L'Heureux-Dubé, recommended that the tax laws be modified—as they have in the past to adapt to evolving business realities—to reflect the changing role of women in the workplace, emphasizing that women tend to bear the costs of child care and that women's ability to pursue employment, unlike men's, often rests upon it. Concurring, Macklin (1992: 512) observed that

[a]s long as business has been the exclusive domain of men, the commercial needs of business have been dictated by what men [think they] need to spend in order to produce income.... [T]he courts have in the past permitted businessmen to deduct club fees because men like to conduct business with each other over golf.... Because some men believe expensive cars enhance their professional image, driving a Rolls Royce has been held to be an incident of a professional expense. Similarly, it is difficult to sustain the claim that making charitable contributions to enhance one's reputation in a community inheres in the business of manufacturing boxes. It seems closer to the truth to suggest that these practices inhere in the way men, or some men, engage in business. Of course, since men have (until very recently) been the only people engaging in business, it is easy

enough to confuse the needs of businessmen and the needs of business.... [O]ne might reasonably demand a reconceptualization of "business expenses" that reflects the changing composition of the business class.

Canada's tax laws, however, do not recognize child-care expenses as a business expense; in effect, child care is officially regarded as one of the personal costs of parenting—of mothering, in particular.

Paid Work and the Costs of Parenting

In the early twentieth century, first-wave feminists seeking to establish women's rights to participation in the public sphere confronted an entrenched "separate spheres" ideology, which maintained that women's role within the family disqualified them for the world of paid work. In 1873, in a now-notorious decision, Mr. Justice Barker of the U.S. Supreme Court wrote that "[t]he natural and proper timidity and delicacy that belongs to the female sex evidently unfits it for many of the occupations of civil life.... The paramount destiny and mission of women are to fulfil the noble and benign offices of wife and mother. This is the law of the Creator" (Stevens, 1983: 82). When, in 1905, Mabel Penery French petitioned to be admitted to the New Brunswick legal profession after completing all the necessary training, the Canadian judge quoted approvingly from this decision and declared that "if I dare to express my own views I would say that I have no sympathy with the opinion that women should in all branches of life come into competition with men. Better let them attend to their own legitimate business." The "legitimate business" of married women and/or mothers was understood to be located in the home, and even such liberals as John Stuart Mill "considered that equal rights of education, political life, and the professions should be granted only to single women without the responsibilities of family" (Mossman, 1997: 50; see also Albisetti, 2000: 825).

Although it is obvious that such attitudes have abated (although see Browne, 2002, 2006 for an evolutionarily based argument on why efforts to increase women's participation in the workforce are, supposedly, doomed to failure), women and men continue to experience a "differential permeability of work and family boundaries" (Pleck, 1977, in Mortimer and London, 1984: 28). While women are expected to disrupt their paid-work roles to accommodate their families, men are expected to subordinate their family role to their paid-work role. Moreover, insofar as mothers usually fill the role of primary child-care provider, women who seek to combine paid employment with those responsibilities are compelled to grapple with the tension between parenting and work in a way that men are not (Roberts, 2004). Consider the fact that until 1983, under the old *Unemployment Insurance Act*, most women were denied the right to claim pregnancy benefits (Atcheson et al., 1984: 20–21); furthermore, it was only in 1989 that the Supreme Court of Canada ruled that employment discrimination against pregnant women was an instance of discrimination on the basis of sex, and, as such, a violation of human-rights protections under Canadian law.

The challenge of combining paid work with parenthood is exacerbated by a lack of affordable, quality child care. Although "[c]hild care is a fact of life for Canadian children and their families, very little regulated child care even exists in Canada" (National Council of Welfare, 1999a: 17). In addition, while the costs of child care, especially for preschoolers, are high and rising, federal, provincial, and territorial governments have cut funding for social programs, cut or frozen fee subsidies to low-income families, and made eligibility criteria for subsidies more restrictive (Doherty et al., 1998). Parents of children with special needs, as well as those who work irregular hours or shift work, may find it impossible to obtain child care. However, not all Canadian provinces and territories have shown equal commitment to providing Canada's working parents with access to safe, affordable, and accessible child care.

In 1997, the province of Quebec introduced a comprehensive new family policy in an attempt to integrate family benefits, paid parental leave, child care, and kindergarten. Its child-care component brought universally available, affordable child care to that province. In September 1997, all 5-year-olds in Quebec became entitled to free full-time kindergarten, with after-school care available for $5 per day. Similarly, all 4-year-olds became entitled to full-time junior kindergarten or child care for $5 a day; additional early intervention services are available at no cost to children whose parents receive welfare. In September 1998, all 3-year-olds became eligible for $5-a-day child care; care for younger children and infants as well as for school-age children was also phased in and, by September 2000, all children in that province, ages 0 to 4, were eligible. In that same year, Quebec launched 10 pilot projects offering evening, weekend, and even overnight child care—all available at the same rate of $5 a day (Dougherty and Jelowicki, 2000). In November of 2003, the cost to parents was increased to a modest $7 per day. While the costs of providing such a comprehensive child-care system are substantial, Quebec's family policy has been lauded as "a pioneering approach to family supports in North America" (National Council of Welfare, 1999b: 44). According to Statistics Canada's Survey of Household Spending, "[f]amilies in Quebec stood out with the lowest average per reporting household expenditure on daycare centres in 2002 ($1,400) which represented a significant drop from amounts reported in 2000 and 1998" (Bushnik, 2006: 22). For purposes of comparison, one might consider that, in 2002, the average annual household expenditures on day-care centres in Canada was $2500 and, in some provinces, even higher. For example, in the Atlantic provinces it was $2900, in B.C., $3100, and in Ontario, $3600 (Bushnik, 2006: 22).

Responsibility for home and family continues to impinge upon the employment of mothers to a degree rarely seen among fathers. Familial obligations contribute substantially to women's higher rates of employee absenteeism (Akyeampong, 2007). The presence of preschool-age children, in particular, "exerts a strong influence on work absences for personal or family responsibilities, especially for women. In families with preschoolers, women lost 3.4 days for this reason [in 1998], about double that for men (1.6) in similar circumstances" (Statistics Canada, 1999b: 8; see also Statistics Canada, 2007i). In cases where work absences result in lost wages, the lower wage-earner in a dual-earner family, typically the mother, is generally designated to stay home and meet child-care needs (Akyeampong, 2001; Akyeampong and Nadwodny, 2001).

Absenteeism is disruptive to employers' expectations of worker productivity and to workers' own self-expectations. Family-related absenteeism and other behaviours (such as a refusal to work overtime because of family priorities) can also have a deleterious impact upon a worker's chances for raises and promotion. Concerned with businesses' need to find an efficient way to deal with the "inconvenience" posed by women's maternal responsibilities, management consultant Felice Schwartz (1989) proposed the creation of two "streams" of career mobility for women: a fast track for career-primary women who would not allow motherhood to interfere with career, and a **mommy track** (a term coined by journalists, not Schwartz)—a lower-paid, less-demanding career path for women balancing career and family roles. The fast track would be comparable to the male career pattern upon which all business and industry is modelled, while the "mommy track" would offer a solution for both female employees and employers wishing to accommodate women's dual sets of responsibilities. How employers and the employees themselves were to determine who should be assigned to which track, and under what circumstances, remained unclear.

If some saw the "mommy track" as an admirable and sensible solution allowing women to have the best of both spheres, others were less enthusiastic. Ehrenreich and English (1989/1995: 215) argued that "[b]umping women—or just fertile women, or married women, or whomever—off the fast track may sound smart.... [but] it is the corporate culture itself that needs to slow down to a human pace.... Work loads that are incompatible with family life are ... a kind of toxin—to men as well as women, and ultimately to businesses as well as families." In a more recent book, Schwartz (1992) called for what may be termed a **parent track**, supportive of both mothers and fathers, maintaining that "the business world must enlarge its infrastructure to support the family needs of employees" and warning that failure to do so will ensue in "unacceptable rates of turnover, terrible losses in productivity, and exclusion from the leadership pool of high-potential, high-performing women (and increasingly, men) who want to be involved in their children's lives."

According to research conducted by the Canadian Centre of Management Development, when asked what employers could do to support work and family, 23 percent of employed mothers mentioned flexible work schedules, 20 percent identified increased family leave, and 19 percent mentioned on-site child care (Lee et al., 1994; see also Bachmann, 2000; Cappelli et al., 2000). Flexible work arrangements include flextime, a compressed work week, telework or telecommuting, and job sharing. Such arrangements, along with part-time work, have been described as family-friendly practices and portrayed as "'win-win' arrangements that can help today's employees obtain a better blend between their work and non-work lives while providing organizations with a means of recruiting, retaining, and motivating their workforce" (Comfort et al., 2003: 30; see also Higgins et al., 2000). **Flextime** refers to a work arrangement that allows workers to begin and end the workday at different times, as long as a certain number of hours per week (typically 40) are maintained. A **compressed work week** allows employees to compress a week's worth of work-hours into three or four longer days. **Telework** is a "work-at-home arrangement wherein employees work at least some of their regularly scheduled hours at home and for pay" (Comfort et al., 2003: 32); similarly, **telecommuting** refers to a work arrangement that allows employees to work full- or part-time at home or at a satellite office. With **job sharing**, two workers share the hours and responsibilities of one job.

On the basis of data obtained by the 1999 Workplace and Employee Survey, Comfort et al. (2003) concluded that the majority of Canadian companies "do not foster climates that promote the integration of work and family through formal workplace practices" (Statistics Canada, 2003e; emphasis added). While slightly more than a third of Canadian employees reported access to flextime, "access to other family-friendly work arrangements was extremely low ... linked to establishment characteristics such as industry and company size, and ... virtually unrelated to employees' personal or family characteristics" (Comfort et al., 2003: 61). They reported pronounced gender differences in access to flextime, but "in the direction opposite to that which might have been expected" (Comfort et al., 2003: 34)— a greater proportion of men than women reported flextime participation (44 percent versus 36 percent). They also pointed out that access to flextime was highest among women and men ages 15 to 24 rather than among those of childrearing age—a finding which suggests that flexible schedules may be most common at entry-level positions. Access to child-care services also was curiously skewed: they were found to be most widely available to people in the 45-to-64 age bracket. As Comfort et al. (2003: 34) stoically observed, "[t]his pattern indicates that childcare services may be most available to employees in age ranges least likely to have need for them." Access also varied by education; university or college graduates had "considerably greater access" to family-friendly practices than did those with vocational/trade certification or less. Managers and professionals were more likely to have access to family-friendly arrangements; yet, even within these ranks, women's rate of access to flextime was lower than men's. Observing that women's rate of participation in flexible work arrangements was lower than men's, the researchers suggested that "even within occupations, women may perform tasks that are less amenable to flexible time or place" (Comfort et al., 2003: 60).

Marshall (2006: 5) observes that although "[e]mployers may be well over the idea that women's earnings are simply pin money for the family ... accepting that men's work schedules are increasingly affected by home responsibilities, such as picking up children from daycare, staying home with a sick child, or taking parental leave, is relatively new." Moreover, she notes that while "WLB (work–life balance) has emerged as a critical public policy issue in Canada" and resulted in changed labour legislation (e.g., parental, maternity, and compassionate care leave) and workplace practices (e.g., on-site daycare, flexible workplace practices), "[t]he increasing number of dual-earner families and a heavier overall workload make balancing a job and home life that much more difficult."

Hochschild (1997) conducted a three-year study of an American company that prided itself on its family-friendly work provisions. She discovered an unevenness in the accessibility of such provisions to different kinds of workers and a notable reluctance on the part of workers to take advantage of family-friendly policies. The most common reason workers gave for not doing so was that they preferred to be at work. She reported that workers perceived their "second shift" of housekeeping and child-care responsibilities as onerous and a source of ongoing conflict with their partners. Soothing aggrieved family members who resented the worker's absence from the home could also necessitate a "third shift" of emotion work. In addition to long hours on the job, many workers brought work home with them; as a result, "family time" could become scheduled, abbreviated, and tense. "Quality time" with family members was often punctuated by work-related tasks—checking voicemail, returning calls, or "tying up loose ends" ("Just give me a couple of minutes and I'll be right back"). Hochschild (1997: 217) reported that "[p]art of modern parenthood now includes coping with children's resistance to the tight-fitting temporal uniforms required when home becomes work and work becomes home."

In contrast, workers were likely to perceive the workplace as offering many attractive advantages. Compared to the home, where family relationships evoked feelings of uncertainty and self-doubt, the job supported feelings of competence and success. Supportive friendships with co-workers, "office teams," and superiors promoted "a sense of being cared for" (Hochschild, 1997: 208). Workers also felt comparatively relaxed at work, where it was possible to comfortably take a coffee-break or go for lunch with colleagues and enjoy adult conversation. At home, multi-tasking was common (e.g., putting a load of laundry in the washing machine and feeding the baby while waiting for a document to print) and often stressful.

Having multiple roles (e.g., employed spouse and parent) can enhance personal happiness—provided that one has enough time to perform them (Hughes et al. 1992). However, time is an often-scarce resource. According to the 2005 General Social Survey (GSS), the average total workday (including both paid and unpaid work) of Canadians ages 25 to 54 was

8.6. hours, up from 8.2 hours in 1986. More specifically, "[b]etween 1986 and 2005, the workday became longer for both men and women—0.6 hours for men and 0.7 hours for women" (Statistics Canada, 2006i). Among men, although the bulk of the increase stemmed from doing unpaid work in the home (on average, 2.5 hours per day, up from 2.1 hours in 1986), time devoted to paid employment also increased (from 6.1 to 6.3 hours). Among women, the increased length of the workday came solely from paid work; in 2005, women spent, on average, 4.4 hours at the office (up from 3.3 hours in 1986); this additional investment of time offset the half-hour decrease in the time they allotted to unpaid labour (from 4.8 to 4.3 hours).

For employed parents, especially those with young children, juggling paid and unpaid work can be very stressful. The 2005 General Social Survey indicated that 42 percent of fathers and 55 percent of mothers felt time-stressed. "[A]mong couples with the longest workday and children at home, two-thirds of the women felt time-stressed compared with one-half of the men" (Marshall, 2006: 15). Riley and Keith (2003) pointed out that the stress of combining full-time employment with homemaking may be more arduous for some employed women than others. Researching married women's subjective evaluations of their work, they reported that professional women reported fewer symptoms of depression than did sales/clerical workers, service/blue-collar workers, or housewives (see also Barnett and Gareis, 2002).

UNPAID WORK

The Vanier Institute of the Family (2000: 140) has pointed out that "Canadian family members spend 20 billion hours doing housework each year" and that two thirds of this unpaid labour is performed by women. The unpaid labour of Canadian men and women has been valued at no less than $197 billion, "even when estimated at the (admittedly low) wage rates of personal service occupations in the labour market.... In terms of hours they devote to housework, family members are doing the equivalent of 10 million full-time jobs when working around the home" (Vanier Institute of the Family, 2000: 140). Yet it was not until 1996 that the Canadian census, by including questions on unpaid work, implicitly recognized unpaid child care, elder care, and home maintenance as "work." Our society has resisted attaching a dollar value to **housework** and dependent care, constructing them as a woman's voluntary and selflessly performed "labour of love" (Luxton, 1980). To be sure, much of this work is performed out of love and may be described by those who perform it as personally rewarding (Ahlander and Bahr, 1995; Kroska, 2003; Spitze and Loscocco, 2000). However, the contribution of this unpaid labour to the economy tends to be overlooked and its value and importance dismissed in our materialistic culture where "value" is generally denoted with a dollar sign.

The 2001 census reported that women "still had the lion's share of the number of hours devoted to unpaid housework" (Statistics Canada, 2003f: 17). More recently, the 2006 census found that while men have increased "their unpaid hours spent in caring for family members or friends, or performing housework or maintenance during the past decade ... they still lagged behind women in the time they allocated to these activities" (Statistics Canada, 2008f: 31). While the share of men participating in unpaid housework increased by 3.5 percentage points between 1996 and 2006, rising from 84.4 percent to 87.9 percent, "the corresponding rate among women held relatively steady at 92.6% in 2006" (Statistics Canada, 2008f: 31). Similarly, while in 2001, "about 16 percent of women aged 15 and over reported spending 30 hours or more on [unpaid] childcare, more than twice the proportion of 7 percent among men" (Statistics Canada, 2003f: 12); in 2006, 47.3 percent of women and 21.8 percent of men reported doing so. "In 2006, 86% of women living in a private household with at least one child under 15 years, reported spending some time in unpaid child care activities—this share remained relatively constant over 10 years.... At the same time, the proportion of men who spent any unpaid time caring for children rose from 77.1% [in 1996] to 79.5%" (Statistics Canada, 2008f: 31).

Marshall (2006: 10) observes that, "The increase in husbands' participation is a logical reaction to the reality that most wives are now engaged in paid labour and for longer hours, and therefore have less time to do housework." Yet, she notes that even though the overall difference in the time allotted to housework has lessened, "married women, particularly those with children, continue to do significantly more housework than married men." In like fashion, despite significant increases in men's participation in "primary child care" (e.g., feeding, helping, teaching, reading to, talking or playing with, medical care, chauffeuring them to activities), women are still more likely to provide this type of care. Among those in dual-earner families with pre-school aged children, 90 percent of wives, versus 73 percent of husbands, reported providing primary child care in 2005. Moreover, as Daly (2004: 12) has noted, despite a trend towards convergence in the amount of time that men and women spend with their children, "women continue to carry most of the responsibility dimension that involves the planning, scheduling, orchestrating and coordination of family activities."

Housework

As discussed in Chapter 3, the industrialization process that began in the 1800s led to the development of gendered work spheres. A woman's work site was the home, where her role was to perform unpaid labour for her husband and children. These labours were believed to benefit the woman, her family, and society at large. Only rarely were the consequences of these cultural beliefs questioned and challenged.

Material feminists (Hayden, 1981) in the latter part of the 1800s argued that women benefited least from existing social arrangements, identifying the isolation of housework in individual homes as a major factor in women's subordination. Their proposed solution lay in collectivizing housework through the establishment of women-controlled and -operated communal kitchens, dining halls, nurseries, and laundry facilities. Not only would women's isolation be alleviated, but individual household maintenance would be reduced, freeing women to benefit from recreational activities with their families on an equitable basis. New models of house-design were conceived; for example, "kitchenless houses," linked by covered walkways, were suggested as a way to release women from their bondage to meal-preparation. By providing a communal alternative, material feminists hoped to create utopian communities. Their ideas were perfectly in keeping with the times; during the 1800s, a large number of religious-based communes were established in the Midwestern and Northeastern United States. Practising variations upon the theme of "Biblical Communism," groups such as the Shakers (Roberts, 1971) and the Oneida community (Robertson, 1970) created communal kitchens and other facilities. While the Shakers practised a strict sex-linked division of labour, the Oneidans promoted "mingling of the sexes" (Robertson, 1970: 58) and a sharing of all forms of work. Only a small number of women attempted to put the non-religious-based material-feminist theory into practice

(Wilson, 1996: 66) and a communal solution to the isolating oppression of housework was abandoned by the turn of the twentieth century. One reason this "lost feminist tradition" floundered was the difficulty of overcoming sex and class divisions. Hayden (1981: 201) noted that "[f]eminists with capital who could afford the new physical environment for collective domestic work never thought of voluntarily sharing that domestic work themselves"; thus, the liberation of middle-class women from the drudgery of undervalued domestic labour often meant the exploitation of lower-class women (see Box 6.1).

Liberal feminists in the 1960s and 1970s assumed that the creation of equal economic opportunity outside the home was key to improving the status of women. To that end, they proposed significant changes to public economic, educational, and political institutions; however, they paid little attention to the private institutions of home and family, or to domestic labour. Marxist and socialist feminists initially regarded domestic labour as an important support system, sustaining workers in the formal economy and developing the next generation of labourers. However, they came to recognize that domestic labour, because it is not socially rewarded, is a major source of women's social inequality. Feminists now acknowledge that the organization of housework exerts a crucial influence upon women's participation in the world of paid labour, on gender equality in both the public and private spheres, and on the continued construction of gender (Jackson, 1992; Leonard, 2001).

Housework has been transformed in many ways over the course of the past century. Bradbury's (1994) analysis of the impact of technological changes on working-class women in nineteenth-century Montreal shows how such innovations (including running water, cast-iron stoves, improved lighting fuels, steam laundries, and store-bought bread) lightened the load of those who could afford them. While the provision of running water and toilet facilities eased the burdens of women married to skilled workers, much of the working-class wife's day was still consumed in onerous domestic labour. "Chickens were usually bought unplucked, fish unscaled.... Wood or coal ... had to be carried inside, and ... [w]hile men may have chopped the wood, lack of storage space within houses meant that carrying the wood or coal, often up one or two flights of stairs, usually fell to the wife or children" (Bradbury, 1994: 38–39). As a consequence of technology, many kinds of work once done in the home (e.g., food production and processing, clothing manufacture and repair) have shifted to outside sources, and the household has become more a site of consumption than of production (Cowan, 1984).

New appliances are continually being invented, altering the way housework is performed. The first modern appliances (following World War I) were hailed as "liberating" the homemaker from domestic labour (Fox, 1993: 154). Henthorn (2000: 153) chronicled how, "in the wake of WWII and the battle for military dominance between the US and the USSR, household technology became a fresh battlefield for social dominance between communism and 'commercialized' democracy." During this time period, mass media advertisements presented the North American middle-class housewife "as an emblem of glamour and leisure, attesting to the superiority of US technology and a revolutionized and liberated domesticity." Today, appliances and other household products are marketed as a means to help the homemaker meet modern-day standards of hygiene, sanitation, nutrition, and appearance.

Early in the twentieth century, "[t]he phrase 'Cleanliness is next to godliness,' which had originally referred to moral cleanliness, was applied to housework contexts" (Ahlander and Bahr, 1995: 55). Keeping a clean and tidy house became a woman's moral duty and the state of her home an outward indicator of her inner moral purity. The development of the domestic science movement, the germ theory of disease, and the idea of "scientific mother-hood" in the early years of the 1900s remodelled the ideology of housewifery. Standards of cleanliness and appearance have constantly been "inflated" (Fox, 1993: 151) over the course of the past century. It is estimated that the actual amount of labour required to maintain a middle-class home has not changed significantly since the latter part of the eighteenth century (Levold and Aune, 2003). What is more, analysis of American time-use studies conducted between the 1920s and 1960s has revealed that the introduction of electricity and "labour-saving devices" into farm homes did not result in a reduction of rural women's homemaking hours, which remained constant at about 54 hours per week (Kline, 1997).

The introduction of new appliances appears at times to be a mixed blessing. Rocks and washboards used down by the river and clotheslines strung outside the home were replaced first by the single-cycle washing machine (usually filled with stove-boiled water), complete with hand-cranked wringer, and eventually by the automatic washer and dryer. While only one in six Canadian households had these appliances in 1961, four out of five did by 1992 (Statistics Canada, 1998). In the first half of the twentieth century, Canadian houseworkers commonly devoted one full day a week to washing and another to ironing (Luxton, 1980: 152–158); today, appliances allow these tasks to be performed at variable times over the course of days or weeks (VanEvery, 1995). Modern appliances afford the scheduling autonomy which is one of housework's few prized qualities (Stokvis, 2001). However, income is needed to acquire these devices (Armstrong, 1990: 72). This need, in conjunction with greater freedom over chore-scheduling, promotes the movement of women out of the home and into the labour force (in order to go to work to earn the money to buy the appliances to save the time to go to work ... and on the cycle goes).

Research Findings In their study of household labour in 10 Western countries, Bittman and Wajcman (2000: 173) concluded that "women continue to be responsible for the majority of hours of unpaid labour," with women's share ranging from a low of 70 percent in Sweden to a high of 88 percent in Italy (see also Apparala et al., 2003). Research in Canada (Gazso-Windle and McMullin, 2003; McFarlane et al., 2000), the United States (Artis and Pavalko, 2003; Bianchi and Mattingly, 2004), Australia (Baxter, 2002; Bittman et al., 2003) and Britain (Sullivan, 2000; Windebank, 2001) has found that, despite couples' changing attitudes, women consistently devote more absolute and proportional time than their male partners to household duties. Brayfield (1992) found that French-Canadian couples generally allocated housework more equitably than either English-Canadian or recently arrived immigrant couples. A more recent comparison of men's participation in domestic work in France, Italy, and Quebec (Des Rivieres-Pigeon et al., 2002: 397) also reported that for "nearly all the child care and housework tasks studies, answers indicating an unequal division were more frequent in Italy than in France, and more frequent in France than in Quebec."

At the beginning of the new millennium, a gender-based division of household labour still endures despite growing gender convergence; findings from the 2005 General Social Survey indicate that, in dual-earner couples, women performed 62 percent of housework (Marshall, 2006: 12). Women are typically assigned or assume primary responsibility for in-home tasks, with the notable exception of household repairs. Of all indoor household tasks (e.g., cooking, dish washing, vacuuming, bed-making, diapering children), men are most likely to get involved with dish washing (Twiggs et al., 1999). Men are typically assigned or assume responsibility for tasks outside the home. An exception appears to occur in relation to "chauffeuring"—now an essential component of childrearing among the middle- and upper-middle classes. Chauffeuring appears to be one of the few outdoor duties where women have the greatest proportional responsibility. Demo and Acock's (1993: 325) analysis of an American national sample finds that, among mothers with at least one under-18-year-old child still at home, divorced and never-married mothers are responsible for driving other household members to work, school, or other activities at least 90 percent of the time, while first-married and stepfamily mothers are responsible for driving at least 67 percent of the time.

The differential use of technologies also reflects the gendered division of household labour (Silva, 2002).Various researchers have noted that technology enters the home with gendered meanings; thus, Keightley (2003) noted that items in the domain of domestic leisure (e.g., VCRs, audio systems) are more likely to be defined as "his" than are dishwashers and pasta-makers. Vincent (2003: 171) declared that "Tupperware projects a quintessentially gendered image" of "middle-class white domestic femininity," and suggested that the "enduring success of Tupperware as a company associated with a specific image is thus a useful barometer indicating how women are contending with the combined pressures of home and work."

Most of men's household tasks are seasonal (e.g., cleaning out the eavestroughs, hanging up the Christmas lights) or non-routine (shovelling snow, cutting the grass), are performed intermittently rather than daily, and allow considerable scheduling autonomy. Men's tasks also tend to be more discrete (in the sense of having a definite beginning and end), in contrast to women's tasks, which tend to flow into one another without much of a sense of completion or accomplishment. Women's tasks tend to be routine, repetitive, monotonous, and invisible (i.e., not noticed unless undone) (Luxton and Corman, 2001). Research in Canada (Marshall, 2006), the United States (Ruitjer et al., 2005), and Australia (Dempsey, 2001) found that—true to the epithet "housewife"—women devoted more hours per week to house care than to child care.

Among married and cohabiting women, full-time employment is associated with a lesser likelihood of primary responsibility for domestic chores. However, only minimal differences exist between part-time-employed and non-employed women, suggesting that part-time-employed women structure their time in such a way as to accommodate household responsibilities. As Shelton (1990: 132) noted, "women, rather than men, continue to adjust their time to accomplish both paid and unpaid work." Reporting on the unpaid labour time-use patterns of husbands/male cohabitors ages 25 to 44, Frederick (1995: 28) found that male partners of employed women spent about 18 minutes less per day on overall unpaid work than did males whose partners were not employed. This research also reported that men with full-time-employed partners devoted significantly more time to "deadline" chores (i.e., those which cannot be put off until later). Apparently, when these men spent more time in the kitchen, they compensated by reducing their time in non-kitchen chores to such an extent that their overall time contribution fell below that of men whose partners were not employed.

A man's modification of his housework role to include chores typically performed by his wife increases her satisfaction about the fairness of the division of household labour (Benin and Agostinelli, 1988). A husband who increases his participation in "her" tasks impresses his wife much more than one who increases participation in "his" tasks; he is more likely to enhance her perception of fairness by cleaning the toilet than by cleaning the sidewalk. Such participation not only lightens her workload but demonstrates that he values the tasks that she performs. However, his contribution must be somewhat substantial.

Blair and Johnson (1992: 578) found that employed wives whose husbands contributed only a few hours per week to tasks defined as "female" viewed the division of labour as being less fair. From a wife's perspective, it was apparently better for a husband to contribute nothing at all than to make only a "token" contribution of one to four hours a week to household labour. Moreover, men's increased participation in "feminine" tasks may have ramifications beyond marital satisfaction. Noting that research has consistently found that the negative relationship between housework and wages is stronger for women than for men, Noonan (2001) focused her research on the different types of household chores performed by men and women. Using longitudinal data from the U.S. National Survey of Families and Households, she reported that "a more equitable distribution of not only the amount, but also the type, of housework performed by men and women ... may lead to narrowing of the gender gap in wages."

Shifting Responsibilities Over Relationship Time Moving in together in a heterosexual marital relationship appears to promote adoption of a gendered division of household labour. Bridal-shower, wedding, and housewarming gifts rarely include executive briefcases and snowblowers for her, and a set of cookware and subscription to *Martha Stewart Living* for him. Regardless of the skills either partner possesses prior to establishing a common household, being the "woman of the house" carries a gender imperative of primary housework responsibility in a way that becoming the "man of the house" does not. Upon formation of a couple household, men decrease the amount of time they devote to housework; upon its dissolution, they increase it. In contrast, women increase their housework activities upon entering a couple household and decrease them upon leaving (Ciabattari, 2004; Gupta, 1999). Following the semantic logic: since a "housewife" does "housework," it follows that "housework" is an integral part of "wifework."

While household labour is more equitably "shared" among spouses without children, the arrival of the first child brings about a gendered shift both in the assignment of housekeeping chores and in time expended on housework (Nomaguchi and Milkie, 2003; Helms-Erikson, 2001). Becoming a mother involves more than the assumption of primary responsibility for child care and childrearing; it also signals the acquisition of additional responsibility for housekeeping. Substantial housework inequities persist between husbands and wives until the children leave home, when, once again, participation in domestic chores becomes almost as equitably distributed as in the pre-child phase (Binstock and George, 1996). Understandably, wives' satisfaction with the division of household labour demonstrates a pronounced "U"-shaped curve over the marital life course, with the lowest point occurring when children are of preschool age (Suitor, 1991).

Research has consistently found that marital satisfaction is greater when wives feel that their husbands share equitably in housework (Ahlander and Bahr, 1995; Donaghue and Fallon, 2003). Perceived unfairness of the division of labour leads to psychological distress, which, in turn, leads to a perception of lowered marital quality (Roxburgh, 1997; Voydanoff and Donnelly, 1999). Based on data from two national American surveys (from 1980 and 2000) of married individuals, Amato et al. (2003: 1) found that increasing husbands' share of housework "appeared to depress marital quality among husbands but to improve marital quality among wives." A second American study, based on a nationally representative sample of individuals in dual-earner marriages, reported that perceived inequity in the division of household labour was negatively associated with both husbands' and wives' reported marital happiness but positively associated with the likelihood that wives would seek divorce

(Frisco and Williams, 2003). The researchers suggested that "unfair perceptions of the division of household labour not only decrease women's marital quality but also lead to role strain that makes them more likely to end unsatisfying marriages" (p. 51).

While some researchers have found that men's level of participation in housework does not differ significantly between cohabiting and married couples (e.g., Gupta, 1999), others have reported the following: Cohabiting women spend less time performing household labour than their married counterparts (Shelton and John, 1993); those who hold egalitarian attitudes are more likely to cohabit than to marry (Clarkberg et al., 1995); and, in comparison to marriage, the experience of cohabitation is associated with higher levels of gender egalitarianism (Moors, 2003). Drawing on panel data from a sample of 586 young adults spanning 31 years, Cunningham (2005: 1057) suggested that gendered power relations may operate differently for cohabiting and married couples. Observing that while "cohabiting women's relative participation in routine housework was reflective of their attitudes about gender,... this was not true for married women," he speculated that some women may choose cohabitation rather than marriage in the belief that the former type of relationship provides for less gendered family practices: "Although most cohabiting unions ... are short lived, it seems that a segment of the population may choose cohabitation because it is perceived to minimize gender-related obligations relative to marriage" (p. 1057). In addition, he suggested that factors and processes associated with the gendered division of labour differ for married and cohabiting couples and that these differences "appear to provide cohabiting women with relatively greater voice in the negotiation of gendered behavioral displays relative to their married peers." For example, he reported that while married men's attitudes about gender in early adulthood were more influential upon housework patterns than married women's attitudes, this was not the case among cohabiting couples.

In complementary fashion, other researchers have argued that the meaning of "gender" may differ among those who opt for cohabitation rather than marriage. Thus, Brines and Joyner (1999: 234) have argued that, in contrast to those who elect to marry, cohabitors "tend to embrace individualism, as well as ideals of personal autonomy and equity" and, as a result, are less likely to endorse a sex-linked division of labour within the household. According to their research, while a specialized division of labour was positively associated with marital duration, a division of labour associated with equality was positively associated with cohabitation duration.

Wives' Changing Strategies Marital and cohabitation partners use a variety of techniques— from persuasion and joking or playing dumb to intimidation or violence—in their attempts to influence the division of household labour (Dempsey, 2000; Leonard, 2001; Luxton and Corman, 2001; Van der Lippe et al., 2004). Hochschild (1990: 258–259) identified three basic strategies used by women. The majority of full-time-employed married women with children initially attempt to live up to the media-created image of the **supermom**, the woman who can do and be all things for all people. In trying to scale the heights of supermom-dom, these employed mothers substantially reduce the amount of time they devote to leisure activities, such as gardening, visiting with friends and relatives, watching television, eating, sleeping, and, perhaps most frequently, being alone. "Nearly 50 percent of full-time employed [Canadian] boomer mothers reported they would like to spend more time alone. The proportion for men never rises much above 25 percent" (Frederick, 1995: 58). Since husbands do not reduce their leisure-time expenditures to any significant degree, the result is a substantial gender leisure gap (Hochschild, 1990: 4). Supermoms are often depicted as if naturally endowed with boundless energy and enthusiasm, an innate sense of time-management, and a drive to "have it all" in the realms of paid employment, marriage, motherhood, and homemaking (Nelton and Berney, 1987). It is rarely recognized that supermom-ing is a forced adaptation to a highly demanding set of traditional and modern gender beliefs about what women "should" want in today's society.

Hochschild (1990: 127) suggested that the arrival of a second child provokes a real crisis in the marital division of labour. Supermoms realize that they do indeed "have it all"—all of the responsibility. The realization that the demands upon them exceed their ability to cope impels women to find a different strategy. **Cutting back at work**, or "scaling back" (Becker and Moen, 1999)—either shifting from full- to part-time or scaling down aspirations and productivity levels—is one strategy adopted where family economics permit. This adaptation to the supermom time-crunch demonstrates how family and household responsibilities can constrain women's ability to attain equality in the paid workforce and even jeopardize their economic futures. Where cutting back at work is not feasible (and since women's frequent cry, "I need a wife," does not point to a viable option), some women adopt a third strategy of cutting back on housework, marriage, and children, typically in that order.

Cutting back on marriage is a phenomenon commonly associated with the shift from a marital to a family relationship. Studies in both Canada and the United States have found that marital satisfaction is lowest during the years when children are present in the home (e.g., Bird, 1997; Somers, 1993; White and Edwards, 1990). In large part, the decline in satisfaction is due to partners' spending less time together as a couple, frequently as a consequence of physical and emotional exhaustion. Cutting back on child care involves reducing the physical care provided to children (e.g., fewer baths, less-frequent changes of clothing). It may also take the form of spending less time with children or paying less attention to their emotional needs (Hochschild, 1990: 197–198). The shift in the focus of parenting from "quantity time" to "quality time" is partially a reflection of adaptive strategies to the phenomenal time-crunch experienced by Canadians over the past few decades. However, the most frequently adopted strategy is cutting back on household labour, usually by lowering standards (cleaning less frequently), buying help (e.g., housekeeping or laundry services), or obtaining assistance from family, friends, or neighbours. Couples are rewriting the Canada Food Guide to include five new basic food groups: take-out, delivery, frozen, meals-in-a-cup, and restaurant. Coltrane and Ishii-Kuntz (1992: 54) suggested that a wife's willingness to lower her housecleaning standards may be influenced by how long she delays childbearing. Postponing childbearing allows a woman to establish a more independent, usually work-related, identity. Less likely to derive her sense of identity and self-worth from her wife–homemaker role, she is also less likely to view a messy house as reflecting badly on her essential femininity. While acknowledging that this theory might be correct, Pittman and Blanchard (1996) argued that the fact that women who delay childbearing have fewer children and therefore less cleaning to do may have more to do with it.

When mothers cut back on housework, neither fathers nor children fill the entirety of the gap. Demo and Acock (1993: 327–328) found that all mothers in the full-time labour force, irrespective of marital status, devoted significantly less time to housework per week than did unemployed mothers. Furthermore, even though children of divorced mothers participated more in household labour than did children in other types of families (especially first-marriage families), children still contributed only minimally to running a household. Age was not a factor in the amount children contributed, but gender was. As noted in Chapter 4, daughters are more likely than sons to perform assigned housework duties and to do more than sons even when both participate in housework. The disparities are most noticeable in families in which both parents are employed full-time (Benin and Edwards, 1990), in larger families, and in lone-parent families (Dodson and Dickert, 2004). Even by the teenage years, a gendered leisure gap is firmly in place (Stokowski, 2000).

When an employed married mother adopts the strategy of cutting back on housework, the overall amount of time her dual-income family expends on housework decreases. However, it is important to understand that as the wife's proportional contribution to housework declines, the husband's proportional contribution rises significantly as a result, even if his absolute housework participation remains constant or increases only marginally. For this reason, researchers' use of proportional measures can foster a false impression of an egalitarian distribution of housework. In terms of gender social trends, the tendency towards convergence in male and female labour-force participation levels is due primarily to women's increased labour-force activity; the trend towards convergence in unpaid labour distributions is due primarily to women's decreased housework activity. In both cases, the most significant agents of change are not men, but women.

Why Don't Men Do More? A number of social-structural and social-psychological reasons have been advanced to explain why men generally resist increasing their participation in household labour. First, men receive little social and public support for expanding their repertoire of domestic skills or for employing such skills at home. While a wife may brag to her friends about how much her husband "helps out" around the house, or praise his cooking or cleaning skills, her husband is unlikely to brag to his friends about his own prowess with a breadmaker or a vacuum cleaner. Should he do so, it is doubtful that he would get much in the way of affirmation from his male peers. For many men, a certain stigma attaches to "women's work"; just as in the military, where assignment to K.P. ("kitchen patrol") or lavatory-cleaning is intended—and understood—to be punitive and humiliating, a man may construe participation in housework as demeaning and unmanly (Hollows, 2003). Also, men obtain little moral or logistical support from their peer networks with child-care and house-hold tasks. While wives may turn to other women for help and information, husbands are less likely to call up a buddy for advice on choosing a fabric softener.

Men are unlikely to perceive any intrinsic personal gain in increased participation in household tasks. By being situated outside of the market economy, housework is trivialized and denied equal status with paid work. Linguistic devices such as "professional homemaker" notwithstanding, the low-status "just-a-housewife" image persists. Although the "job" of houseworker may provide some economic fringe benefits, it comes with "no job security, no retirement, and no pension" (Wilson, 1991: 57). A sense that to participate more in housework will diminish their prestige gives men little incentive to do so. Hochschild (1990: 215) suggested that "one way to reverse this devaluation is for men to share in that devalued work, and thereby help to revalue it." This leads to an intriguing question: If men were to increase their participation in housework, would the prestige of housework rise, or would their own prestige fall? In our patriarchal culture, one might expect the work to gain lustre from the sex of the worker. However, since we live in a period of cultural transition in which "men's work" is no longer automatically accorded higher prestige, the outcome is not easy to predict. When men, by choice or necessity, become "househusbands," taking on the tasks typically associated with wives, the social response is rarely positive (Marshall, 1998). When Swearinghen-Hilker and Yoder (2002) asked 90 male and 90 female undergraduates to evaluate vignettes in which one member of a dual-employed married couple was presented as doing two thirds of the weekly housework, respondents indicated feeling that men were more entitled to undercontribute than women; raters holding sexist attitudes were especially likely to view men's undercontributing as acceptable.

Our cultural beliefs about gender define different work agendas for men (public and paid) and women (private and unpaid). These beliefs also promote structural conditions that militate against men's participation in housework. Climbing the career ladder involves working long, hard hours that leave little time or energy for helping out at home. What is more, the paid-work world offers little structural support for such involvement. Male workers are not rewarded for taking paternity leave or rearranging their work schedules to accommodate child care or housework. Neither government nor major corporations appear to be willing to institutionalize a "daddy track."

Explanatory Models for Housework Participation A number of models have emerged to explain the current gendered division of household labour (Shelton, 2000). The **time availability model** focuses upon structural or situational constraints; simply put, whoever has more time does the housework (see McFarlane et al., 2000). The **rational investment perspective**, expanding on this view, asserts that "couples attempt to maximize the family economy by trading off between time and energy investments in paid market work and unpaid household labour" (Riedmann et al., 2003: 433). In other words, spouses agree that each will concentrate on those tasks at which s/he is the most efficient. However, these explanations set up a chicken-and-egg type of question: Do husbands perform less housework because they have less available time/are less efficient at it, or do they devote more time to their jobs/display greater inefficiency at housework in order to avoid an increased share of household labour? Given research showing that stay-at-home dads devoted less hours per day on average to housework and child care than did stay-at-home moms— although they did spend more hours at these tasks than single-earner mothers or single-earner fathers (Marshall, 1998), these models would seem to provide only a partial explanation for the gendered division of household labour.

The **resource power model** argues that the greater a partner's power in the relationship, the less housework that partner performs. According to this model, power is determined primarily by the economic resources a partner brings into the relationship. Although many studies confirm a general relationship between power resources and housework participation levels (e.g., Blair and Lichter, 1991; Brayfield, 1992; Pittman and Blanchard, 1996; Kenney, 2006), findings are inconsistent, ambiguous and, at times, difficult to interpret because of methodological variations. Thus, the resources examined may be employment status (full-time, part-time, unemployed) or employment correlates (income, level of education); correlates may be measured in absolute or in relative terms (i.e., as a proportional difference between the partners); research may focus upon the impact of resources upon one's own or one's partner's housework participation.

While Blair and Lichter (1991: 94) claimed that wives with greater resources are "better able to 'extract' labor from their husbands as well as influence the types of family work these men do," other research has found that wives' employment has no effect upon the time husbands allot to household chores (Frederick, 1995); this might mean that a wife's employment is not in itself a sufficiently powerful resource to "extract" any housework. Even though the influence of one's own resources upon another person's behaviour is somewhat uncertain, increased resource power does appear to result in a decrease of one's own participation in housework. Data from the 2005 General Social Survey suggests that a wife's sole responsibility for housework and a husband's propensity for doing housework both decline as each individual's income level rise. Marshall (2006: 14) reports that "a wife's income is likely to influence the husband's time spent on housework as well as her own. For him, time spent doing housework rises along with her income, while for her, the time falls."

Absolute income appears to be a resource that permits the "'buying out' of household tasks" (Brayfield, 1992: 28; Bianchi et al., 2000) by reducing one's own participation levels, hiring someone else to perform certain tasks, or both. For example, Palameta (2003) notes that high-income households are twice as likely to have hired domestic help when the primary earner is female rather than male. However, as Deutsch et al. (2007) have argued, while outsourcing domestic labour may provide women with a means to pursue employment, it may not provide them with true equality within their families. Their research, which examined the preferences for different life scenarios and attitudes about work and family life among 143 heterosexual undergraduate women, noted that those who expected to out-source "did not have an assertive conflict resolution style, nor did they expect their work to bring in equal money or to be accorded equal treatment in their families" (p. 106). They suggest that, among these women, the plan to outsource may be best understood as a "strategy for contending with their pessimism about getting husbands to share"; as Novak and Novak (1996) have observed, even highly achieving women who aspire to high-powered careers in the workplace may not expect equality in the home. The research of Blair-Loy (2003) among young female executives additionally notes that the majority of women who adopted an outsourcing strategy remained "responsible for hiring, scheduling, supervising, and, if necessary, firing their childcare workers" (p. 93)—duties which reiterate the notion that child-care management is the responsibility of wives, rather than husbands and wives equally. It is also evident that outsourcing domestic labour does not require a man to adopt an unconventional orientation towards masculinity nor de-emphasize or disrupt the tenets of the male work model (Cooper, 2002). In addition, it is evident that outsourcing arrangements may result in the racialized exploitation of hired domestic workers (see Box 6.1).

Consistent with research that finds that "increases in [the] wife's education, as a proxy for wage rate, tend to be associated with an increased share of housework for the husband" (Anxo and Carlin, 2004: 30), findings from the 2005 General Social Survey indicate that women with higher educational levels were less likely to have sole responsibility for housework (Marshall, 2006: 12). The 2005 GSS also suggested parity in housework labour when wives had high incomes, noting that "[w]hen wives have an income of $100,000 or more, the division of paid labour and housework between partners is more likely to be split equally" (Marshall, 2006: 13). However, income differentials appear to interact with other factors, such as gender ideologies, to influence a couple's negotiation of housework participation levels.

In sum, research provides partial but inconsistent support for the resource power hypothesis. A reason for this lack of consistency may be researchers' failure to control for the differential impact resources may have at different stages of a couple's relationship. On the basis of their own findings, Coltrane and Ishii-Kuntz (1992: 54) suggested that a wife's income resources may exert a greater influence at an early stage, when family income levels are generally low and her proportional contribution comparatively high. Her income resources may not exert as significant an influence over the division of labour later on, when her proportional economic contribution is lower.

While the general pattern of gendered income inequality outside of the home may account for the general pattern of gendered housework inequality within, it should be noted that

BOX 6.1

Live-in Nannies Face Exploitation in Canada

When Jennifer Wasike entered Canada under the Live-In Caregiver Program, it wasn't because she really wanted a career as a nanny—she was overqualified for that. But the program was the only way Wasike, who had worked in Canada as a high school teacher, could begin the process of getting permanent residence here, after her application for a standard immigration visa was turned down. Although joining the two-year program meant a long separation from her two children in Kenya, she saw it as a viable way to fulfill her dream of living in Canada. After the two-year period, she would be eligible for permanent resident status and could sponsor her family to join her. "If you're living in absolute poverty and you're given an opportunity to go to a place which is going to elevate you out of that poverty, you will do anything possible," explains Wasike. But Wasike wasn't prepared for the "nightmare" of a bureaucracy that moves at a snail's pace, coupled with exploitation by various employers who expected her to work a 14-hour day even though she was paid for only eight.... "They think that because you're a live-in caregiver you must be dumb. I have a degree in education and a degree in psychology and have been a high school teacher for years, but after I got here ... I was treated like crap."

Under the program, the caregiver is given three years to fulfill the required 24 months of full-time employment. During that time, the caregiver must live in the home of the employer and may only work for the person whose name is on the work permit. If the caregiver's services are no longer needed or she wants to change employers, there's a wait of at least three months, while Citizenship and Immigration Canada (CIC) issues a new work permit. During that time, the caregiver, who is prohibited from receiving social assistance or taking any kind of training course, is without an income if she doesn't qualify for employment insurance.

The Live-In Caregiver Program was started in 1992 to fulfill a shortage of nannies in Canada, which occurred mainly because Canadians were unwilling to do the job. Over 100,000 Filipinos—70 to 80 percent of whom are women—have come to Canada as caregivers, making the Philippines the main supplier of nannies to Canada. Many of them are trained nurses. According to Deanna Okun-Nakoff, a lawyer with the Vancouver-based West Coast Domestic Workers Association (WCDWA), the Live-In Caregiver Program has been rife with problems since it began. Okun-Nakoff says it typically takes three years to complete the program, and an additional two-plus years for CIC to process a permanent residence application. This means that women who enter Canada under the program— many of whom have left children in their home country—are separated from their family for at least five years.... Because of the processing delays at CIC, in many cases the caregivers can't finish the program in the time allotted and choose to return home or are deported. They may re-apply to enter the program, but the time they have already put in isn't taken into account, so they have to begin again from scratch. "The limitations of the program are very clear," says Glecy Duran, chair

---

BOX 6.1

Live-in Nannies Face Exploitation in Canada (*Continued*)

of Siklab, a national organization that advocates for Filipino migrant workers in Canada. "The program promises that families can come together in 24 months, but the processing time takes so long that the nannies and their children have become strangers to one another."... Duran says about one employer in 10 treats the caregiver well, while "the majority are taken advantage of.... There are so many cases that we have been handling here at Siklab ... women being treated like slaves, some have been raped, some are working overtime without pay...."

Caregivers in the program are paid minimum wage, minus $325 for room and board as well as other deductions. With many having to support a family back home, the $400 they're left with doesn't go very far, which is why some nannies, according to Okun-Nakoff, have been turning to prostitution to make ends meet. Wasike recalls that one employer she worked for allowed only one measured serving of foods at mealtime. She was constantly hungry, she says, but was unable to go out at night to purchase more food due to a restrictive 8:30 pm curfew. In another instance, her employer—ironically a taxation lawyer—neglected to deduct enough taxes from her pay, resulting in a surprise bill from Revenue Canada for $2,758. Both CIC and her employer refused to pay it, so she had to scramble to take out a bank loan.

Duran says that because of changes to the *Employment Standards Act* in B.C., if caregivers in the program want to file a complaint they have to do it through a "self help kit," which requires informing their employer that they're filing a complaint—an option most shy away from. But on the whole, mistreated nannies are reluctant to complain, fearing their already precarious position will be jeopardized further.

Source: Abridged from Joan Delaney. 2007. "Live-in Nannies Face Exploitation in Canada," *Epoch Times Victoria*, February 23. Available on the World Wide Web at http://en.epochtimes.com/tools/printer.asp?id=52014.

---

almost all of the existing research to date has been conducted on heterosexual couples. The motto "whoever brings home the most bacon doesn't have to cook it" (Brayfield, 1992: 20) appears to be equally applicable to gay—but not to lesbian—households (Blumstein and Schwartz, 1983; Schwartz, 1994; Schwartz et al., 1994; Halez-Banez and Garrett, 2002). Research indicates that lesbian couples make a concerted effort to ensure that the values of the marketplace, with its equation of worth with income, do not intrude into the equitable context of the home (Schwartz, 1994; Laird, 2003; Peplau and Spalding, 2003; Matthews et al., 2003). This finding shows that the resource model of relationships is not inevitable and is subject to subcultural modification or even neutralization. It also points to one of the shortcomings of resource theory: it ignores the fact that the differential resources of husbands and wives are an epiphenomenon of the more fundamental power imbalance that comes of being born male or female in our society (Lero, 1996: 42; Natalier, 2003).

Greenstein (2000) observed that a breadwinner wife and a dependent husband may perceive that they are regarded as "deviant." In an attempt to forestall possible labelling, the wife may purposefully increase and the husband decrease participation in housework. This is congruent with Hochschild's "balance theory." Hochschild (1990: 218, 221) described a principle of **balancing**, whereby men who lose power over women in one area make up for it in another. Men who earn much more than their wives hold power and have no need to compensate for power lost elsewhere; as a result, they are more willing to contribute to housework. However, the more a man's sense of power is threatened by his wife's greater financial resources, the less he can afford to have his basic power base—founded not on control of economic resources but on his status as a male in a patriarchal society— threatened by engaging in what has traditionally been defined as "women's work." According to Hochschild, these men's refusal to do housework is an assertion of male power by which they attempt to balance a lack of economic power.

While Hochschild's balance hypothesis is founded primarily upon resource theory, it incorporates features of existing gender ideologies with its references to the distinction between men's and women's work and the patriarchal foundation of men's power. The balance hypothesis is compatible with the notion that, because of the gendered work spheres, housework has come to represent an important "gender boundary" (Gerson and Peiss, 1985), which may become more important when the "provider" boundary becomes blurred. Arrighi and Maume (2000: 464) found that there was a link between the challenges men faced to their identities in the workplace and their behaviour within the home: "[T]he extent of men's workplace subordination was negatively related to their performance of 'feminine' tasks in the home. Moreover, this relationship was stronger in families in which wives' earnings approached those of their husbands." Men who feel they are losing some gender distinctiveness as a result of not fulfilling the provider role may draw the boundary line of housework even more firmly in order to maintain their sense of masculinity; in other words, having lost some "gender points," they may be anxious to avoid further losses that crossing the housework gender boundary would entail.

The "balance" or "boundary" hypothesis may help to explain why unemployed Canadian husbands of employed wives have been found to perform only 40 percent of the household tasks traditionally assigned to women (Brayfield, 1992: 29; Marshall, 1998). Research conducted in Sweden (Stro, 2002: 89) also concluded that although unemployment was linked to alterations in the gendered division of housework, gender remained "the best predictor of levels of domestic labour activity." The balance hypothesis may also provide insight into the results of a study based on data from Australia and the United States: Bittman et al. (2003: 186) found that wives engaged in less housework as their earnings increased, up to the point where they and their husbands contributed equally to household income; however, when the wives' income exceeded their husbands', "the change in housework [was] opposite to what exchange theory predicts: couples that deviate from the normative income standard (men make more money than women) seem to compensate with a more traditional division of household work."

Men's perceptions of powerfulness and powerlessness—grounded not merely in economics but also in a sense of maleness reinforced by maintaining gender boundaries— appear to be important variables mediating the extent of their participation in housework. However, attempts to maintain gender boundaries within the home are not all one-sided. Mederer (1993: 143) noted that although women may find the allocation of housework tasks and responsibility unfair, they are more likely to demand a redistribution of tasks than a re-allocation of management responsibility. Based on this, Mederer suggested that household and family management may be a firmly "embedded" element of women's gender definition, and that women may resist sharing management responsibilities for fear of losing an important source of power. Housework, therefore, may be an important component in our society's construction of gender. Beliefs about the gender-appropriateness of housework are part of the third model that has been used to explain housework distribution: gender ideology.

Gender Ideology Two ideal-typical **gender ideologies** are dominant in Canadian society today: the traditional and the egalitarian. The **traditional** belief system divides the social world into two discrete gendered spheres: Men, working in the public, paid sphere, are breadwinners; women, working in the private, unpaid sphere, are homemakers. However, despite the functionalist claim (Parsons and Bales, 1955) that husbands and wives coexist in equal and complementary worlds, our society values and rewards men's instrumental work as breadwinners much more highly than women's work as homemakers. Both the functionalist and traditional paradigms place women's crucial homemaking services outside of the market economy, framing what are in fact instrumental activities as expressive gestures devoid of economic meaning. For women, "[i]t starts when you sink into his arms and ends with your arms in his sink" (Jackson and Scott, 1996: 13). One consequence of a traditional ideology is that "it seems more acceptable to do without certain amounts of/kinds of unpaid labor than to have it done by the person of the 'wrong' gender" (Ferree, 1990: 876).

The newer **egalitarian ideology** maintains that work, both inside and outside the home, should be allocated not on the basis of sex but on "desirability, availability, capability, and turntaking" (Mandell, 1989: 239). The **principle of equity** dictates that all responsibilities—work and family management, income provision, domestic chores, child care, and emotional intimacy—be equally divided between partners. The emotional interdependence of a couple is expected to support and promote flexibility and sharing. While the traditional ideology maintains (despite all evidence to the contrary) that the domains of men and women are separate but equal, the egalitarian ideology stresses that they must be integrated and equitable, regarding the concept of gendered "spheres" as meaningless. Cunningham (2005: 1040) reports a "growing consensus that egalitarian attitudes about gender are positively related to patterns of participation in routine housework, especially when housework is assessed in relative rather than absolute terms" and notes that empirical work in this area finds that "couple members who are generally supportive of egalitarian roles for women and men are more likely to share routine housework." However, Greenstein (1995) directs especial attention to men's attitudes, suggesting that men and women may possess a differential ability to put their attitudes about an "appropriate" division of labour in the family into practice. That is, "although women's egalitarian attitudes constitute a sufficient condition for the sharing of domestic labor, men's attitudes constitute a necessary condition for such sharing.... To the extent that the division of family work is reflective of gendered power relations in families, men's attitudes may be more likely to influence housework allocation" (Cunningham, 2005: 1043).

Mandell (1989: 241) argued that "most Canadian marriages do not fit neatly into either the traditional or the egalitarian model." She suggested that most could best be described as neotraditional or pseudoegalitarian. These relationships are still essentially asymmetrical and male-dominated; the husband's work still dictates the patterns of family life, and his perceptions of himself as breadwinner and his wife as homemaker still prevail despite any assertions of equality. In other words, their gender ideology is something of a blend of the dominant two—what Hochschild (1990: 15) calls a transitional ideology. Research conducted in Israel that compared three ethnic-religious groups exemplifying traditional, transitional, and egalitarian ideologies found that, for both men and women, perceived fairness mediated the relationship between the division of household labour and marital quality; in other words, if the participants felt an unequal arrangement to be fair, it had no negative impact on their marital satisfaction. It was also found that for women (but not for men), gender ideology mediated the perceived fairness of the division of housework. Women with a traditional ideology did not perceive an unequal distribution of household labour as unfair; women with an egalitarian ideology did. For the latter group, unequal division of household labour was directly linked to lower marital quality (Lavee and Katz, 2002).

Weiss (1990: 121–122) identified three principles shaping men's involvement in housework: the traditional principle, the principle of helping out, and the principle of equity. The traditional principle divides household chores into "men's work" and "women's work," essentially confining male participation to maintenance and repair tasks. According to the principle of helping out, a husband may participate in some daily household tasks to "help his wife out" if needed; in effect, this principle reinforces the traditional principle, since "helping out" does not mean assuming primary responsibility for a task or altering the fundamental allocation of gender responsibilities. The principle of equity poses a direct challenge to the first two principles. Equity requires that all the work of a marriage and family, both in- and outside the home, be divided fairly and evenly between partners. The "transitional" gender ideology prevalent today could be said to reflect a shift from the "traditional" principle to "helping out," with the "principle of equity" as yet unattained.

The influence of the "traditional" and "helping out" principles may help explain not only why men are slow to increase their participation in housework, but also why 75 percent of Canadian dual-earner wives with sole responsibility for almost all housework reported being satisfied with the arrangement (Marshall, 1993/1995: 306), as well as why American "mothers typically respond[ed] that the work is 'fair to both'" (Demo and Acock, 1993: 328). Himsel and Goldberg (2003: 843) maintained that, in the absence of "clear guidelines for the fair and equitable allocation of family work," individuals commonly compare themselves with others to gain a sense of what is "normal." They found that women who did less housework than their female friends reported higher levels of satisfaction with the division of housework; those whose husbands did more than other male comparison-referents also reported greater satisfaction and less role strain. Men in this study reported more satisfaction with the division of labour when their wives did more housework than their own mothers had; men also commonly invoked a "generalized other" to "make their own contribution to housework seem more noteworthy." This research suggests that, under conditions of uncertainty, conformity to a comfortable set of "traditional expectations" can produce an overall sense of satisfaction. Research has indicated that older, lesser-educated, and lower-income couples are more likely to endorse a traditional/ helping-out pattern (Apparala et al., 2003), while support for a truly egalitarian ideology is most likely to come from "younger, better educated, and employed women" (Mandell, 1989: 243). Men with higher levels of education are also likely to endorse a more equitable arrangement; Coltrane and Ishii-Kuntz (1992: 54–55) found that among better-educated, more affluent couples who had their first child later in life, the husband's ideology contributed to a more equitable division of labour (see also Zuo and Tang, 2000).

To the extent that the inequitable distribution of housework found in most Canadian families is a social and not just an individual-couple problem, solutions will have to address many factors, including the distribution of available time, the balance of power between men and women, and underlying gender ideologies (Wilkinson, 1999). These solutions will have to be sought not only within the private sphere of the household, but also within the public sphere of paid work.

Key Terms

absenteeism

balancing

bona fide occupational
requirement

chilly climate

compressed work week

cutting back at work

devaluation hypothesis

egalitarian ideology

employment equity

flextime

gender ideology model

gender wage gap

glass ceiling

glass escalator

housework

human capital hypothesis

job sharing

labour-force participation
rates

mommy track

occupational sex segregation

parent track

part-time work

pay equity

poisoned work environment

principle of equity

quid pro quo harassment

rational investment
perspective

resource power model

self-employment

sexism without the pedestal

sexual harassment

statistical discrimination

supermom

telecommuting

telework

time availability model

traditional ideology

Chapter Summary

1. Gender in our society is inextricably intertwined with work and the family. These social institutions create and sustain gender as much as they are created and sustained by it.

2. In our society, men are strongly influenced by the "male work-role model," an accumulation of messages that stress the centrality of paid work to ideal stereotypical masculinity. Theoretically, the significant increase in female labour-force participation could pose a challenge to the gender boundary of the provider–breadwinner role; however, this has not occurred.

3. The single greatest change to the face of the Canadian labour force since 1961 has been the increased participation of women, especially mothers of young children.

4. "Occupational sex segregation" refers to the concentration of women in certain occupations and men in others. Although in some occupations, such as medicine and dentistry, sex segregation has decreased in recent years, women are still over-represented in low-status, low-wage "pink-collar" jobs that offer few benefits. Women in higher-paying jobs may face a "glass ceiling"—an invisible barrier that prevents them and other minorities from moving into top positions.

5. As a result of the gendered division of labour within the family, women who seek to combine a career with motherhood are compelled to grapple with the tension between parenting and work in a way that men are not.

6. Research in both Canada and the United States has shown that wives and women cohabitors, whether employed full- or part-time or not at all, consistently devote more absolute and proportional time to household duties, performing approximately 75 to 80 percent of all housework. Several models have been offered in explanation of this gendered division of labour, including time availability, resource power, and gender ideology.

CHAPTER 7

Intimate Relations

FRIENDSHIP

Rubin (1985: 59) noted that in our society, male same-sex friendship has been held up as the model of friendship. Male bonding has been exalted as a necessary precondition of individual and social survival (e.g., Tiger, 1969; Oliker, 1998); current laments about men's inability to sustain emotionally rich relationships with other men (e.g., Burleson and Kunkel, 2006; Cox, 2006) reflect more modern times and concerns. Women's same-sex friendships, however, have largely been ignored. Only recently have these friendships been extolled as an ideal relationship form (e.g., Goodman and O'Brien, 2000; Vogels, 2002).

In childhood, females tend to have less extensive but more intensive friendship networks than males; this pattern carries through into adulthood. Partly because they use more criteria to define friendship (Rubin, 1985: 61), women usually list fewer friends than do men (Bunkers, 1993). Men tend to found friendships on a narrower basis, often having different friends with whom they pursue different activities (Connell, 2002; Walker, 1994). Wright and Scanlon (1991) observed that men's friendships generally revolve around a specific focus of interaction; a man's "drinking buddies" may be distinct from the "guys" he plays basketball with on Tuesday nights. The basis and content of same-sex friendships appear to differ for each gender: Following patterns formed in adolescence, adult "women's friendships are based primarily on emotional sharing and men's friendships on engaging in common activities" (Brehm, 1992: 365). All friendships probably partake of both dimensions, but women and men tend to stress different ones (Monsour, 1992, 2002).

Women friends are more likely to spend time talking about themselves, their feelings for each other, and other people (Fehr, 2004). These discussions may consist of **deep talk** (about powerful feelings and worries), **small talk** (about daily life), or both (Tavris, 1992: 252). Rubin (1985: 61) stated that women's same-sex friendships rest upon "shared intimacies, self-revelation, nurturance and emotional support." Wright (1982), noting men's tendency to engage only rarely in deep talk, characterized their friendships as **side-to-side**, whereas women tend to have **face-to-face** friendships (see also Wright and Scanlon, 1991). The key gender difference appears to have to do with levels of self-disclosure (Sullins, 1992; Martin 1997; see Box 7.1). Women tend to be more self-disclosing with other women than men are with men, and both genders are more comfortable confiding in a woman (Derlaga et al., 1994, 1997; Dindia et al., 1997).

Wright and Scanlon (1991) noted that friendships among women tend to feature breadth of knowledge: Women invite each other to learn in detail about most aspects of their lives. In contrast, men's friendships are founded on shared activities, particularly sports, rather than verbal intimacies (Bischoping, 1993; Wood and Inman, 1993). Swain (1989) suggested that male friendships are based on "closeness in the doing." More than two thirds of his male respondents reported that their most meaningful times with friends were spent in activities other than conversation; as well, their friendships emphasized the give-and-take of help and expertise. He contended that men's friendships are as intimate as women's, even though "men generally do not express intimacy through self-disclosure" (p. 168)—a difference partly attributable to the injunction against emotional expression, which forms part of boys' socialization (Kyratzis, 2001; Walker, 2002; Zarbatany et al., 2000) and which disparages emotional volubility as "feminine" (Burleson et al., 2005). Thus, men tend to downplay the role of emotions in their friendships with other men. Confronted with a troubled male friend, men are more likely to offer a diversionary activity than a shoulder to cry on.

Communicating with Friends and Intimates

In the following extract, Pulitzer prize–winning journalist Dave Barry offers a whimsical commentary on male and female friendships.

Today's Topic for Guys Is: Communicating with Women.

If there's one thing that women find unsatisfactory about guys—and I base this conclusion on an extensive scientific study of the pile of *Cosmopolitan* magazines where I get my hair cut—it is that guys do not communicate enough.

The problem has arisen in my own personal relationship with my wife, Beth. I'll be reading the newspaper and the phone will ring; I'll answer it, listen for 10 minutes, hang up, and resume reading. Finally Beth will say: "Who was that?"

And I'll say, "Phil Wonkerman's mom."

Phil is an old friend we haven't heard from in 17 years.

And Beth will say, "Well?"

And I'll say, "Well what?"

And Beth will say, "What did she SAY?"

And I'll say, "She said Phil is fine," making it clear by my tone of voice that, although I do not wish to be rude, I AM trying to read the newspaper here, and I happen to be right in the middle of an important panel of "Calvin and Hobbes."

But Beth, ignoring this, will say, "That's ALL she said?"

And she will not let up. She will continue to ask district attorney–style questions, forcing me to recount the conversation until she's satisfied that she has the entire story, which is that Phil just got out of prison after serving a sentence for a murder he committed when he became a drug addict because of the guilt he felt when his wife died in a freak submarine accident while Phil was having an affair with a nun, but now he's straightened out and has a good job as a trapeze artist and is almost through with the surgical part of his sex change and just became happily engaged to marry a prominent member of New Kids on the Block, so in other words he is fine, which is EXACTLY what I told Beth in the first place, but is that enough? No. She wants to hear *every single detail*.

We have some good friends, Buzz and Libby, whom we see about twice a year. When we get together, Beth and Libby always wind up in a conversation, lasting several days, during which they discuss virtually every significant event that has occurred in their lives and the lives of those they care about, sharing their innermost feelings, analyzing and probing, inevitably coming to a deeper understanding of each other, and a strengthening of a cherished friendship. Whereas Buzz and I watch the playoffs.

This is not to say Buzz and I don't share our feelings. Sometimes we get quite emotional.

"That's not a FOUL??" one of us will say.

Or: "YOU'RE TELLING ME THAT'S NOT A FOUL???"

I don't mean to suggest that all we talk about is sports. We also discuss, openly and without shame, what kind of pizza we need to order. We have a fine time together, but we don't have heavy conversations, and sometimes, after the visit is over, I'm surprised to learn — from Beth, who learned it from Libby— that there has recently been some new wrinkle in Buzz's life, such as that he now has an artificial leg.

BOX 7.1

Communicating with Friends and Intimates (*Continued*)

(For the record, Buzz does NOT have an artificial leg. At least he didn't mention anything about it to me.)

I have another good friend, Gene, who's going through major developments in his life. Our families recently spent a weekend together, during which Gene and I talked a lot and enjoyed each other's company immensely. In that entire time, the most intimate personal statement he made to me is that he has reached Level 24 of a video game called Arkanoid. He has even seen the Evil Presence, although he refused to tell me what it looks like. We're very close, but there is a limit.

I know what some of you are saying. You're saying my friends and I are Neanderthals, and a lot of guys are different. This is true. A lot of guys don't use words at *all*. They communicate entirely by non-verbal methods, such as sharing bait.

But my point, guys, is that you must communicate on a deeper level with a woman, particularly if you are married to her. Open up. Don't assume that she knows what you're thinking. This will be difficult for guys at first, so it would help if you women would try to "read between the lines" in determining what the guy is trying to communicate:

GUY STATEMENT: "Do we have any peanut butter?"

INNER GUY MEANING: "I hate my job."

GUY STATEMENT: "Is this all we have? Crunchy?"

INNER GUY MEANING: "I'm not sure I want to stay married."

If both genders work together, you can have a happier, healthier relationship, but the responsibility rests with you guys, who must sincerely.... Hey, guys, I'm TALKING to you here. Put down the sports section, OK? HEY! GUYS!

Source: Dave Barry. 1994. *Dave Barry Is Not Making This Up*. New York: The Ballantine Publishing Group, a division of Random House, Inc., pp. 224–227.

Riessman (1990) suggested that for men, this technique may be more effective in relieving stress and promoting feelings of closeness than talking about a problem.

Rohlfing (1995) argued that the instrumental, activity-based emphasis of male friendships explains why women's friendships are more likely to survive geographic barriers whereas men's tend to dissolve (see also Wada, 2001). While mutual self-disclosure may continue via letters, phone calls, and email, "[i]t's more difficult to shoot hoops or go to concerts with someone who lives miles away" (Wood, 1997: 225). Moreover, research comparing the style and content of men's and women's emails to friends found that men's were more impersonal and less likely to contain features associated with the maintenance of rapport and intimacy (Colley and Todd, 2002; see also Jackson et al., 2001).

Research has indicated that apparent gender differences in self-disclosure and emotionality may be as much a function of social expectations as of the actual quality of gender friendships. Derlaga et al. (1994) concluded that men are as capable as women of forming intimate same-sex friendships but choose not to relax learned social expectations and inhibitions. Our heterosexist social climate pressures men to de-emphasize the emotional component of their same-sex friendships lest they be suspected of homosexual attachment; accordingly, men stress the more superficial (but valued) activities they share (Monroe et al., 1997). Within the male subculture, joking, teasing, and acts of mock aggression (Swain, 1989) become means of expressing affection. For explicit verbal and emotional intimacy, especially during times of crisis, men most often turn to the women in their lives (Voss et al., 1999), if to anyone at all.

Rubin (1985: 62–64, 170) found that out of a multi-class sample of straight and homosexual singles ages 25 to 55, more than three quarters of the women had no difficulty naming a best friend (almost always another female), but more than two thirds of the men could not do so; those who could usually named a woman. "About two thirds of the women who were named by a man as a close friend disavowed that definition of the relationship" (Rubin, 1985: 159); this finding may indicate that women apply more stringent criteria in their definitions of friendship. Tannen (1990) reported that men have fewer close friends than women, discussed more impersonal topics (e.g., work, politics, school) with their close friends than did women, and responded differently to their close friends' problems. However, these findings have been questioned by others. In a survey of 168 students (ages 18 to 57) designed to test Tannen's findings, Oxley et al. (2002) did conclude that, compared to women, men discussed more impersonal topics with their five closest friends and were less likely to listen to their friends' problems or comfort them. However, in contrast to both Rubin (1985) and Tannen (1990), Oxley et al. found that men and women did not differ in either their number of reported close friends or their likelihood of offering advice when a friend turned to them.

Davis (1985) reported that when asked to identify the sex of their close friends, 56 percent of male respondents and 44 percent of female respondents identified at least one person of the other sex. Gender-role orientation appeared to affect both the inclination for, and the relative frequency of, cross-sex friendships. Drawing upon a sample of 278 adults who completed a version of the Bem Sex Role Inventory, Reeder (2003) found that "feminine" men and "masculine" women had significantly higher proportions of cross-sex friendships than did "masculine" men and "feminine" women. Evidence has suggested that cross-sex friendships are less intimate and stable and offer less emotional support than same-sex friendships (Diamond and Dube, 2002; McWilliams and Howard, 1993; Rawlins, 1993). Baumgarte (2002) cited obstacles to the longevity of cross-sex friendships (including negotiating the line between a platonic and a romantic relationship) but suggested that these friendships can be rewarding despite the difficulties. They reported that cross-sex friendships provided each member with insight into the psychological and social orientations of the other sex and offered an "insider's perspective" helpful in dealing with dating partners. Women provided their male friends with emotional and expressive support, while men provided their female friends with activity-based companionship. Women also reported receiving protection from their male friends and perceived this protection as highly beneficial (Bleske and Buss, 2000). Kalmijn's (2002: 101) research on young adults indicated that highly socially skilled women whose social settings afford them the opportunity to interact with people of both sexes are more likely to have cross-sex friendships; men with egalitarian sex-role attitudes and a high degree of loneliness are more likely to have such friendships. However, for both women and men, the "chance of having opposite-sex friendships declines sharply over the early life course."

Riessman (1990) suggested that most women consider marriage just one of their close relationship ties; most men, however, consider marriage an exclusive primary relationship with one who is simultaneously mate and best friend. In Rubin's (1985) sample, married men were even less likely than single men to be able to name a best friend; those who could usually named their wives. In contrast, married women, whether or not employed outside of the home, had no difficulty naming one or more best friends, and rarely numbered their husbands among them. "While men usually choose their wife as their confidante, women generally turn to each other to confide their innermost thoughts, their joys, miseries, and problems. More than men, women lead separate emotional lives after marriage" (Etaugh and Bridges, 2001: 56). Rubin (1985: 60, 140) concluded that women are more likely to "make time" for the creation and maintenance of friendships, largely because they value friendship more highly than do men; furthermore, women prize their conversations with women friends precisely because of a lack of verbal engagement with the men in their lives. Diamond's (2002: 5) examination of intimate friendships among 80 adolescent and young-adult sexual-minority females (ages 18 to 25) revealed that many subjects reported having a same-sex best friendship that they considered "as committed, passionate, and intense as a romantic relationship." Although these passionate friendships contained components of both the normative heterosexual friendship script and the normative romantic relationship script and frequently involved such forms of physical intimacy as cuddling and hand-holding, they rarely involved sexual contact.

A number of observers (e.g., Vogels, 2002: 110–118; Tavris, 1992: 252) have remarked on men's tendency—whether with women or with other men—to talk about impersonal topics such as work, sports, or world events; or to intellectualize if discussing feelings (e.g., "Like most people, I think I feel ..." rather than "I feel ..."). As well, men's problem-solving orientation tends to be non-congruent with women's preference for simply *sharing* problems (Etaugh and Bridges, 2001). Levinson (1996: 42) noted men's extreme reluctance to talk (especially with a woman) about their experiences of failure, disappointment, anxiety, or confusion—subjects which evoke feelings of having failed in some way to live up to cultural notions of masculinity. Men may fear that opening up such topics could lead to being judged less of a man (Tavris, 1992: 267); as a result, most men choose reticence.

COURTSHIP AND MATE-SELECTION PRACTICES

During the sixteenth and seventeenth centuries, relationships within the home were most often characterized by "respect, deference, obligation, and fear rather than by sentiment and attachment" (Anderson, 1987: 33). Over the course of the next two centuries, with the shift from the extended to the nuclear family, domestic relations became more a personal and private matter. The concepts of romantic love and marriage gradually intertwined; during the nineteenth century, the idea of love as a basis for marriage (rather than a desired outcome) became accepted in Europe and North America (Rotundo, 1993: 110). With the ascendancy of the creed of individualism, older adolescents and young adults began to assert greater independence from their parents. **Courtship** and the mate selection process came out from under parental control and greater power of choice devolved to the individuals seeking mates.

Within North America, the degree of personal choice now exercised by young people varies significantly by social class (Baca Zinn and Eitzen, 1993: 227–228). Generally, the higher the social class, the greater the amount of parental influence and control over the intimate relationships of their children (Knox and Schacht, 1997: 224). Working- and lower-class parents apply the least amount of control and supervision over their children's intimate activities. In Canada, parents in some ethnic groups exert considerable influence over their children's selection of a spouse (Kalbach, 2000; Peters, 1990), in some cases arranging marriages between their children and mates living in Canada or abroad (Riedmann et al., 2003: 179–182).

Bride wealth and *dowry* (see Collins and Coltrane, 2000: 51) are two customs that were common in pre-industrial Europe (and still prevalent in much of Africa and parts of Asia), vestiges of which persist in contemporary North America. **Bride wealth** is a negotiated amount of money or valued goods which a groom must pay to a bride's family to cement an alliance between the two households; a **dowry**, on the other hand, is the money/goods which the groom receives from the bride's family. Which custom prevails appears to be partially determined by cultural beliefs about the value of a woman; in a bride-wealth system, a woman is deemed more valuable than in a dowry system. In European societies, the dowry system predominated; a marriageable maiden's value was enhanced by the amount of material possessions her family could bestow. With the growing emphasis upon individualism and romantic love, the dowry system gradually declined, although traces may still be found in customs such as the *trousseau* and in the folkway etiquette that the bride's parents finance the wedding gala (see Driscoll, 2002: 171–200 for a discussion of "bridal culture"). The trousseau, comprising mainly items such as linen, china, and kitchenware, was devised to defray the costs of establishing an independent household; the bridal shower, similarly, is an opportunity for guests to equip the bride-to-be with household items. In contrast, "stag" parties for grooms-to-be rarely feature gift-giving, and even more rarely gifts of houseware.

A formal bride-price system has never existed in Canada, although the social expectation that a prospective husband possess the financial stability to support a wife and children might be said to imply an informal one. The engagement ring does more than reify an intangible emotional commitment; it signifies a man's ability to support a certain standard of living. Jewellery-store advertisements with a spend-money-to-prove-your-love theme also reinforce the role of men as success-objects (Farrell, 1986: 27–30).

Courtship Practices

Courtship is an archaic term still used by family sociologists to refer to the entire system of "dating" (itself another archaic term that contemporary adolescents and young adults have replaced with such phrases as "hanging out," "going with," "dealing with," "seeing," and "getting nice") and heterosexual mate selection. Norms developed during the late nineteenth and early twentieth centuries established a script familiar to most Canadians today. Men were expected to be the initiators of all phases of a relationship's development (Asmussen and Shehan, 1992; de Weerth and Kalma, 1995). It was up to the man to initiate contact with women of his choosing. Men were expected to dominate and channel conversation, initiate touching and sexual contact, determine the level of emotional commitment, and make any formal proposal for marriage. Men were also expected to assume all financial responsibility for the couple's activities.

In contrast, women were expected to observe a decorous passivity—to be the pursued, not the pursuers. A woman's chief power lay in the exercise of her right to pick and choose among her suitors (Carpenter, 1998); ostensibly, her most formidable weapon was the power of refusal; the right to say "no." However, ambiguities in communication could occur; the traditional script, which discouraged women from explicitly expressing a desire for sexual intimacy, encouraged them "to initially resist men's sexual advances even when they find them desirable and plan on reciprocating," (Harnish et al., 1990: 1334). "This traditional female script, which precludes the explicit communication of sexual interests ... may lead women to send out ambiguous messages as to their sexual intentions, and it may encourage men to think that a woman's rejection of their sexual advances indicates token resistance rather than genuine resistance" (Krahe et al., 2000: 314). What is more, the conquest theme of male socialization, coupled with a culturally sanctioned belief that men should dominate women, could encourage men to regard "no" as an invitation to persuade or coerce women into shifting their response from "no" to "maybe" and from "maybe" to "yes" (Krahe et al., 2000; O'Sullivan and Allgeier, 1998).

While maintaining the outward semblance of passivity, women were still able to employ subtle means (disparagingly referred to as "feminine wiles") to pursue a desirable mate (Cashden, 1993, 1997; de Weerth and Kalma, 1995). However, courtship and mate selection were (and to a large extent still are) embedded in the notion of "separate spheres." Men sought a woman who exhibited the potential to run a household efficiently, bear and rear children, and serve as an appealing sexual partner and affable companion; women—denied equal access to well-paying occupations, power, and prestige—evaluated a potential mate primarily in terms of what kind of provider he would be. A woman's husband would "determine where she lived, what level of wealth and status she attained, and how she might structure her life" (Rotundo, 1993: 113).

Most of the qualities sought in a mate remain the same today; however, there have been some additions to the job descriptions. South (1991) found that men were unwilling to marry a woman who did not have, or at least show promise of obtaining, steady employment. Strassberg and Holty (2004) noted that when they placed four "female seeking male" ads on two large Internet bulletin boards specializing in such notices, the most popular ad was one in which the woman described herself as "financially independent ... successful [and] ambitious"; this ad produced over 50 percent more responses than the next most popular ad, in which the woman described herself as "lovely ... very attractive and slim." These findings appear to reflect current economic realities and the increasing difficulty of being sole breadwinner. For their part, women seek mates who are capable of providing emotional support and exhibit interpersonal warmth (Sprecher and Regan, 2002). Jensen-Campbell et al. (1995) reported that—contrary to the old saying "nice guys finish last"—men described as considerate, kind, cooperative, and sympathetic were more likely than others to be rated by women as physically and sexually attractive and as desirable dating partners. When 96 female undergraduates were asked what type of man they were most attracted to, personality criteria preceded economic considerations. According to this study, "[f]eminine males were preferred as friends and romantic partners over masculine males" (Desrochers, 1995: 375).

Whether the quest be for a marital or a cohabitation partner, most mate-selection takes place within the set of people who share a similar ethnic background, age, and social class (as measured by occupational ranking and educational achievement). The phenomenon of "like selecting like," known as **endogamy** or **homogamy**, still remains prevalent despite a declining emphasis upon national origins and religion (Blackwell and Lichter, 2000; Kalbach, 2000; Qian, 1998). However, some important variations do occur. These can be illuminated with reference to the **marriage gradient** (Riedmann et al., 2003: 205–206), a concept that has also been applied to dating relationships and referred to as the **dating differential** (Saxton, 1990: 191). The marriage gradient involves a rank ordering, from low to high, of all objectively and subjectively measured qualities considered desirable in a mate or intimate partner. Both men and women rank themselves and others on the gradient according to possession of these attributes. The practice of selecting a partner more highly ranked than oneself is known as **hypergamy**; choosing a lower-ranking partner exemplifies **hypogamy**. In our society, the most common scenario involves female hypergamy, in which a woman enters into a relationship with a man of slightly superior social characteristics (Murstein, 1991; O'Brien and Foley, 1999). In accordance with our relationship-formation norms, women tend to mate "up," selecting intimate partners who possess, for example, a better education, greater occupational prestige, and a higher income (real or potential), and are larger, taller, and older. An "older and wiser" man to literally "look up" to, one who offers physical, social, and monetary protection, is held up to women in our culture as a kind of matrimonial jackpot from their earliest exposure to fairy tales (Etcoff, 1999). These cultural ideals emerged out of the model of the breadwinner–homemaker separate-spheres marital arrangement, within which a woman's social status depended (and to a large extent still does) on that of her male partner, rather than on her own accomplishments, abilities, or even family history. Women, therefore, have a lot to gain by hypergamy, i.e., marrying "upwards."

A study of the expectations of undergraduates revealed that most of the women expected their husbands to be "superior in intelligence, ability, success, income, and education. Less than 10 percent of the women in this sample expected to exceed their marriage partner on any of the variables measured" (Ganong and Coleman, 1992: 61). Surveys of female medical students have found that these highly educated and potentially high-earning women wished to marry men of social status and earning power at least as great as, and preferably greater than, their own (Townsend, 1998). Analysis of personal advertisements placed in newspapers and on the Internet has revealed that whereas men continue to stipulate that potential partners be physically attractive, thin, and sexy—a finding consistent across racial and class lines—women's ads frequently emphasize the desire for a partner who is "secure," "professional," "successful," and "ambitious" (e.g., Jagger, 2001; Koziel and Pawloski, 2003; Phua, 2002). Regan et al. (2000) observed that women have continued to emphasize characteristics pertaining to social status, while men still place substantial emphasis on the physical attractiveness and sexual desirability of prospective mates. The social status of men is less strongly affected by that of their female partners, although upper-class men are more carefully monitored by parents and kin to prevent their being "dragged down" by an "inappropriate" marriage; men in other social classes can afford to be hypogamous.

Hypergamy and hypogamy have historically resulted in two different pools of undated and unmated men and women. Women occupying the upper echelons of the gradient or differential have found few men to look "up" to as prospective partners; conversely, the most lowly ranked men have found few women to look "down" on. Writing in the mid-1970s, Bernard (1973: 36) reported that "cream-of-the-crop" women and "bottom-of-the-barrel" men were disproportionately likely to be involuntarily single. More recently, Etcoff (1999: 74) has pointed out that men with low-status, low-income jobs are less likely to be married than men with higher-status jobs and higher permanent incomes; what is more, "for the already married, the possibility of separation and divorce increases if a man's relative earnings decline (relative to his past earnings, or relative to his peers)." Various researchers have also reported that high-income women and women at the top of their professions are less likely to marry (Riedmann et al., 2003). The study of medical students referred to earlier, for example, found that 60 percent of male students, in contrast to their female peers, voiced a preference for a lower-earning mate; 40 percent said they preferred a spouse of lower occupational status than their own (Townsend, 1998).

Nevertheless, recent research has suggested that women of higher education and socioeconomic status are now more likely to marry than those not university-educated/of low socioeconomic status (Goldstein and Kenney, 2001). According to Renzetti and Curran (2003: 195), "[t]his may be because both women and men who are employed and financially secure are seen as more attractive marriage partners because of the resources they can bring to the household." In addition, the conquest theme of masculinity may impel some men to pursue women of higher status than their own. Goode's (1996) analysis of responses to fictive ads placed in four personal columns found that although some males preferred women of lower socioeconomic status, "[m]en are more likely to see dates with more desirable partners as their courtship entitlement." He suggested that even where such a sense of entitlement is unfounded, men may act on it, advancing themselves as suitable partners for higher-status women. One factor involved in such behaviour may be men's "blitzer" or "minimalist" style of personals-generated courtship (i.e., answering multiple ads and putting little time and effort into any single response).

LOVE AND INTIMATE RELATIONSHIP STYLES

Prior to industrialization, relationships in the combined home/workplace were simultaneously personal and impersonal. As the boundary between home and workplace became more entrenched, relationships within these places became more differentiated. The workplace and other public spheres assumed an ever-more-sternly reason-dominated, impersonal character, while the world of the home grew increasingly private and intimate. The nature of the harsh Industrial Revolution workplace reinforced an existing stereotype that men themselves were rational, tough-minded, and unemotional. These characteristics were believed to be ideally suited to survival and success in business and industry; however, the qualities considered exemplary in men's orientation to the world were ill-suited to the day-to-day running of the family home. Women were assigned the role of guardians of the hearth, whose primary responsibility was to see to the physical and emotional well-being of all members of the household. This role involved monitoring and anticipating family members' feelings and needs; this reinforced an existing stereotype of women as interpersonally gifted, sensitive, and emotional.

As the "survival of the fittest" ethos of the outside world grew more ruthless, personal (what are now known as "intimate") relationships within the home became, compensatorily, all the more important. Women were called upon to provide a "haven" in an increasingly impersonal and "heartless" world (Lasch, 1977). The ideal woman was to be "attentive, compassionate, comforting, and cooperative [whereas the] ideal man was ambitious, independent and self-made" (Thompson, 1993: 559). Women's qualities were deemed to be ideally suited for survival and success in love, marriage, and intimate family relationships. One outcome of the processes associated with industrialization is that love became "feminized" during the nineteenth century (Cancian, 1987). Women's preferred expressions of love were established as the accepted norm (Tavris, 1992: 248). Women also became the "love experts" (Safilios-Rothschild, 1977: 3).

Love

Throughout most of the twentieth century, love has been one of the most important preconditions for marriage in industrialized societies (Riedmann et al., 2003: 182). Although homogamy and considerations of hypergamy/hypogamy play important roles, a dominant expectation in North America is that the selection of an intimate partner should be based first and foremost upon "being in love" (Levine et al., 1995). Although the definitions of what sociology refers to as **romantic love** and psychology as **passionate love** differ slightly in emphasis, they both refer to the same phenomenon. A classic definition of romantic love is: "(1) a strong emotional attachment toward a person of the opposite [*sic*] sex; (2) the tendency to think of this person in an idealized manner; and (3) a marked physical attraction the fulfillment of which is reckoned in terms of touch" (Kephart, 1966: 311; see also Hendrick and Hendrick, 2000).

Empirical research on love began in earnest during the 1950s and reached a peak in the late 1970s–1980s. It is important to note that most studies have assumed that observed differences between male and female experiences and expressions of love are a function of the essential properties of gender, and not an artifact of other factors. The vast majority of empirical studies on love have been conducted on middle-class, predominantly Caucasian, Canadianized or Americanized college/university students. In their focus on sex-related differences, researchers have largely neglected to explore other sources of variability, including social class, ethnicity, sexual orientation, and educational qualifications; as a result, there has been a tendency to overlook similarities between the sexes and variabilities within each sex. Bearing this caveat in mind, let us look at the findings.

Studies in both the United States and Canada have found that males tend to be more idealistic about love than are females (e.g., Brehm, 1992; Sprecher and Toro-Morn, 2002). Males are more likely to believe in love "at first sight," to believe that love has the power to overcome all obstacles, that love cannot be rationalized, and that an ideal mate exists somewhere for everyone. Interpreters of existing research have tended to conclude that males are generally naive and idealistic about love, and females more realistic, pragmatic, or practical (Hendrick and Hendrick, 2000). Males typically identify themselves as being "in love" earlier in a relationship than women do (Knox and Schacht, 1997); research conducted on university undergraduates found that men were also significantly more likely to report saying "I love you" earlier in a relationship (Brantley et al., 2002). Women, however, "fall out of love" more readily (Bradsher, 1990). Harris (in Walster and Walster, 1978: xi) summarized the findings of these studies by suggesting that women tend to be the "last in and the first out" (**LIFO**) of relationships, whereas men are the "first in and the last out" (**FILO**).

In general, women appear to discriminate more finely between liking, love, and romance than men do (Silliman and Schumm, 1995). Once having acknowledged being in love, however, women report experiencing the emotions of the relationship more intensely than do men (Walsh, 1991). Furthermore, women tend to feel that they give more than they receive in love relationships with men (Hochschild, 2003). Nolen-Hoecksema and Girgus (1994) found that men tended to suffer more severely than women in the event of a breakup and took longer to get over a relationship. Money (1980) maintained that men tend to suffer more "love sickness" after a relationship is over than do women.

Structural Explanations Explanations for most of the findings on love focus upon the different structural locations of women and men within our society. As previously noted, women have a greater vested interest in the rewards to be gained from intimate partnerships. A man looks for a wife, mother for his future children, companion, and housekeeper. A woman looks for a husband, father for her children, companion, breadwinner, source of standing in the community, and guarantor of a standard of living (Eichler, 1981). "As long as most women still must depend on their husbands for income, economic security, and social status, they cannot afford to rely primarily on love as the basis for marriage" (Safilios-Rothschild, 1977: 3). For most women, therefore, economic and social-status considerations condition intimacy. Only upper-class women, it would seem, can (quite literally) afford to marry strictly for love; however, these women may find their marital options circumscribed by familial preoccupation with the sharing of wealth and position (Collins and Coltrane, 2000).

Being less dependent upon the financial and social contributions of an intimate partner, men can better afford to ignore the implications of being carried away by romantic feelings; this may explain why they tend to be more idealistic about love, to fall in love more quickly, and to be less likely to recognize a problematic future. Generally, women must harness their emotions to practical concerns. Only when circumstances portend a good "match" can women permit themselves the luxury of indulging their feelings (Angier, 2000: 363–368). Not surprisingly, one of women's principal romantic fantasies involves being "swept away" by love, without any consideration of practicalities (Masters, Johnson, and Kolodny, 1985: 346).

Emotion Work Another important explanation for gender differences in love involves what has been labelled **emotion work**, or **feeling work** (Hochschild, 1983, 2003). Emotion work involves monitoring one's emotional state, identifying current feelings, and ensuring that these feelings are appropriate for objective circumstances. Ensuring appropriateness may involve either manufacturing new feelings or suppressing existing ones.

As a consequence of their socialization experiences, women tend to pay closer attention to their own emotional state and are better able to identify and analyze their ongoing feelings. Men are less likely to be able to tune in to and identify their emotional states:

> Stop a woman in mid-sentence with the question, "What are you feeling right now?" and you might have to wait a bit while she reruns the mental tape to capture the moment just passed. But, more than likely, she'll be able to do it successfully.... The same is not true of a man. For him, a similar question usually will bring a sense of wonderment that one would even ask it, followed quickly by an uncomprehending and puzzled response. "What do you mean?" he'll ask. "I was just talking." (Rubin, 1983: 69)

Men tend to possess less extensive emotional vocabularies, and, perhaps for that reason, to make less refined discriminations between emotions, than women do (Christensen and Heavey, 1993; Wood and Inman, 1993). In response to a "What are you feeling now?" question from a female intimate partner, a male may run through a short mental checklist of general feeling states ("Am I hungry? Angry? Anxious? Depressed?") and, if none readily apply, answer with the all-purpose "nothing." Men appear to make fewer distinctions than women do between love and liking; accordingly, they are more likely to define their feeling state as "love" earlier in a relationship and to retain that definition even after the relationship is over. Greater proficiency at emotion work accounts for women's tendency to be more slow to acknowledge feelings as "love" early on and more quick to discount such emotions in a relationship deemed unsuitable. If a woman realizes that her feelings for a man are inappropriate because the relationship has no future (e.g., he can't hold a job, he is married), she will likely "work" to suppress the positive feelings, create appropriate feelings of indifference, and attempt to end the relationship (Silliman and Schumm, 1995). As long as women need marriage for economic reasons more than men do, emotion work will remain of particular importance for women. Emotion work for men traditionally takes the form of learning not to express emotions that may make them seem vulnerable (Lombardo et al., 2001). Appearing emotionally needy or dependent violates our culture's stereotype of the strong, stoic, independent male.

Intimate Relationship Styles

In keeping with their roles in the separate social spheres, women and men demonstrate different relationship styles in heterosexual intimate partnerships. Women's relationship style emphasizes emotional closeness, verbal expression of feelings, and sharing of mutual vulnerability (Dindia and Allen, 1992; Tavris, 1992). "The image of feminine love gives women responsibility for love and defines love as self-sacrifice, emotional warmth, expressiveness, vulnerability, and sensitivity" (Thompson, 1993: 559). Men's relationship style reflects "work-world" (Levinson, 1996: 42) or "action" values (Tavris, 1992: 250); expressions of this style include providing instrumental aid (money, practical help, or problem solving), spending time together, and having sex. By projecting responsibility for a relationship's emotional dimension onto women, men can better preserve an image of strength, control, and power.

In lesbian relationships, both partners tend to assume responsibility for nurturing the relationship and providing emotional support. This is thought to reflect both women's having absorbed the socialization message that females are responsible for the nurturing of intimate relationships (Griffin, 2002; Kurdek, 2003, 2000a; Wood, 2002). An examination of lesbian dating and courtship patterns from young adulthood to midlife among 38 predominantly white lesbians (ages 22 to 63) found that "friendship was the most widely used courtship script across all age groups" (Rose and Zand, 2002: 85). Among the "unique aspects of lesbian dating" reported were "freedom from gender roles, heightened intimacy/friendship, the rapid pace of lesbian relationship development"; as well, these women directly addressed the effects of prejudice. Moreover, this study found that "few subjects adhered to traditional gender roles in dating, and those who reported assuming the feminine reactive role rejected the traditional notion that females should limit sexual contact." A second study of 301 lesbian couples (Beals et al., 2002) reported that lesbian partners demonstrated relatively high levels of investment in their relationships, with 40 percent maintaining a joint chequing account and 47 percent maintaining a joint savings account. In addition, 80 percent reported that over half of their friends were also friends of their partners; 24 percent indicated that all of their friends were also friends of their partners. Julien et al. (1999) noted that lesbian couples tended to have fewer separate friends and to rely less on separate kin for support, and, as a result, tended to embrace greater joint responsibility for their relationships.

Shumsky (2001) reported that the closeness between lesbian partners endures even after the breakup of the romantic relationship, and that within the lesbian community, it is common for ex-lovers to remain "vitally important in each other's lives" as best friends, "soul mates," companions, and surrogate family members. Lesbian relationships are also reported as having the highest level of equality of all types of intimate relationships (Eldridge and Gilbert, 1990; Kurdek, 1998, 2002; Patterson, 2000). Huston and Schwartz (2002) reported that among gay couples there is the lowest likelihood of one relational partner taking care of the relationship and cultivating the development of the couple as a unit. While both lesbian and gay relationships resemble the relationships of "best friends" with the added dimension of sexuality and romance, the relationships of gay men rank lower than those of lesbians and heterosexuals in terms of expressiveness and nurturance. Ambert (2003: 4) reported that "[a]s is the case among heterosexuals, saying 'I love you,' showing physical affection, gift-giving, and cooking for the other are frequently mentioned expressions of love among same-sex partners.... [However] [g]ift-giving is more often mentioned among males than females, perhaps as a substitute for verbal expressions of affection."

One consequence of gendered lovestyle preferences is that both women and men in heterosexual relationships fail to fully appreciate the contributions flowing from the other gender's relationship style. Measuring men's behaviour by a "feminine ruler" (Cancian, 1987: 74) has led scholars to unwittingly create a **deficit model of manhood** (Doherty, 1991). Intimate partners, therapists, and family-studies scholars—lamenting, "Why can't a man be more like a woman?"—have often depicted men as "deficient" in intimacy skills, "threatened by intimacy," or "stunted [in] emotional development" (Balswick, 1988; Doherty, 2001; Mazur and Olver, 1987: 533). Dressel and Clark (1990) found that women defined anticipating another's needs as an important element of caring behaviour. The wives in their study believed themselves to be more likely than men to do things to please or serve their spouses, including things that the men could do for themselves. Although the authors concluded that women's solicitousness reflected deference to men's power in marriage, the study did not actually assess power. An equally plausible explanation is that women are more aware of the social expectation that they anticipate and meet an intimate partner's needs, especially within the domestic context. Clearly, the propensity to do things to please another is not the monopoly of one gender. Some caring gestures, however, may become so taken for granted that they may not be recognized as expressions of love. As Pedersen observed (1991: 188),

> [a] man's expectations of himself as a loving partner may strongly rest on the traditional idea of "providing for," so that he feels he is being loving by fulfilling those expectations. He is surprised, as well as hurt, when his partner expresses disappointment in his providence as well as his performance. A man typically counters his wife's accusations that he doesn't love her with reference to all the things he's done to make her happy ... he bought her a new car ... he makes a good salary ... he sends the kids to private school, and so on, but none of these satisfies his wife's sense of what it means to feel loved by him.

Hochschild (2003: 111) maintained that, thanks to a combination of new economic realities and old gender codes, the likelihood has increased of a "gender gap in the economy of gratitude." She asserted that "[t]he most common form of 'mis-giving' occurs when the man offers a traditional gift—hard work at the office—but the woman wants to receive a modern one—sharing the work at home. Similarly, the woman offers a modern gift—more money—while the man hopes for a traditional gift—a happily home-cooked meal. As external conditions create a gender gap in the economy of gratitude, they disrupt the ordinary ways men and women express love."

Men are, at best, ambivalent about women's relationship styles. They may perceive women's requests for greater self-disclosure as unwelcome and threatening (Guerrero and Afifi, 1997; Parks and Floyd, 1996). "Wives push for more attention, responsiveness, communication, and closeness; husbands withdraw and withhold. This scenario renders women unhappy with husbands who are silent and insensitive and men unhappy with wives who do not recognize their best efforts at care" (Thompson, 1993: 560). This "female-demand-male-withdrawal" (Vogel and Karney, 2002) or "pursuer-distancer" (James, 1989) pattern *may* reflect each gender's preferred levels of autonomy and connection. Wood (1997: 236) argued that although all individuals seek both, strongly masculine individuals typically desire more autonomy and less connection than do more feminine persons, "whose relative priorities are generally reversed." As she observed regarding heterosexual intimate relationships, "[t]he irony is that the very thing that creates closeness for one partner impedes it for the other." The pattern of "demand-withdrawal" is less likely to surface in gay and lesbian relationships, since "both partners tend to have congruent desires for autonomy and connection" (Wood, 1997: 237). However, autonomy and connection are not the only factors that can account for the **demand–withdrawal pattern**.

Men's Silence The "strong silent type" has been an icon of masculinity revered in our folklore and mass media for over a century. This type supposedly embodies key masculine qualities admired by women and men alike. Yet, as is often the case, the very qualities that initially attract us may frustrate or even repel us later on. "Women may be attracted to men's independent, self-contained ways because it reassures them of strength. Yet as relationships develop, women often resent men for being distant and invulnerable" (Baca Zinn and Eitzen, 1993: 253). Many theorists trace male inexpressiveness to a socialization stressing the centrality of emotional control (e.g., Real, 1997). According to this analysis, men are taught to believe that most emotions are unmasculine and therefore not worth analyzing or discussing but best ignored. Women, on the other hand, tend to believe that talking about feelings is a sound strategy for forestalling relationship problems. One man expresses his frustration with this strategy:

> We can have a minor problem—like an issue between us, and it's really not serious stuff. But can we let it go? No way.... She wants "to talk about it." And I mean talk and talk and talk and talk. There's no end to how long she can talk about stuff that really doesn't matter. I tell her that she's analyzing the relationship to death and I don't want to do that. She insists that we need "to talk things through." That may work for her, but, honestly, it makes no sense to me. Why can't we just have a relationship, instead of always having to talk about it? (in Wood, 1997: 215)

On the basis of more than 10 years of research on heterosexual couples interacting in controlled laboratory experiments, Gottman (1994) concluded that men are likely to be the ones who "stonewall" their partners (i.e., withdraw into silence) during intense moments in a relationship. Using videotaped observations and physiological measurements, he discovered that withdrawal is precipitated by being "flooded" (Gottman, 1994: 110) with stressful emotions, which elevate both blood pressure and heart rates to higher levels in men than in women. Retreating into silence is a defensive technique men use to protect themselves from being overwhelmed by the emotions of the moment. "Talking about the relationship as she wants to do will feel to him like taking a test that she has made up and he will fail ... he is likely to react with withdrawal" (Cancian, 1987: 93).

Gottman (1994: 95, 116, 138–140) vaguely attributed men's withdrawal response to some combination of a biological, evolution-based "fight or flight" response with a socialization that renders men inexperienced and uncomfortable with emotions. Others propose alternative explanations for male withdrawal into silence. Sattell (1976) suggested that men withhold their emotions as a means of both controlling the emotional intensity of a relationship and retaining power over their female partners. To lose one's cool is to risk giving up control to another. Silence is not only less risky, but also tends to force one's partner to work harder to find out what lies under the silent veneer. While Sattell envisioned silence as a deliberate power strategy used by men, Tavris (1992: 271) noted that a silent partner may neither wish to be nor actually feel powerful. Rather than signify power and control, men's silence can reflect limited coping mechanisms in the face of out-of-control feelings. Some support for this view is suggested by research which examined the behaviour of 59 dating couples randomly assigned to discussions involving high or low degrees of emotional vulnerability (Vogel et al., 2003). When the degree of emotional vulnerability was high, men, but not women, acted in ways that confirmed gender stereotypes. The researchers speculated that for men, emotional vulnerability (i.e., a state of being open to emotional hurt or rejection) "leads to stereotype confirmation, as normative expectations are less risky and easier to enact than nonnormative behaviour" (p. 519; see also Vogel et al., 2007).

Essential or Situational Differences? The **feminization of love** reflects the belief that the private sphere is not only a woman's appropriate domain, but one for which she is pre-eminently gifted. The feminization of love and the deficit model of manhood might suggest that women have more power in the private sphere than men. However, that impression is misleading: Though some may impugn men's styles of loving as "deficient," this putative deficiency does not result in any loss of male power (Hochschild, 2003: 85). Moreover, our dominant cultural ideals discourage men from altering their relationship style: "[M]ost men who weep, speak their feelings, and reveal fears and passions are denigrated as being too weak, shrill, feminine, and emotional. The male norm of emotional suppression continues to be held up as the public ideal of adult behavior" (Tavris, 1992: 270).

In reaction against the deficit model of manhood, some have called for greater recognition of men's traditional ways of loving (Levant, 1996; West, 1994). This response is founded on a belief that existing relationship styles reflect essential gender differences that cannot, and should not, be changed. It is important to stress, however, that researchers' conclusions about gender differences in romantic love—idealism, the timing of "falling in love," emotion work, the withdrawal into silence, etc.—are all based on average scores and tendencies; in other words, observed differences are neither absolute nor essential. Both genders are capable of responding in alternative ways depending upon the characteristics of the social situation. Laboratory experiments have revealed that when confronted with men's demands for change, women are as likely to withdraw into silence as are men (Christensen and Heavey, 1993; Klinetob and Smith, 1996). The fact that men are more often the ones who withdraw is a consequence of the fact that women, charged with the responsibility for maintaining relationships, are most often in the position of asking men to address some aspect of the relationship. Demand–withdrawal is thus seen to be a function of the power dynamics of intimate relationships, wherein the "spouse with the most to gain by maintaining the status quo is likely to withdraw" (Klinetob and Smith, 1996: 945), and not a gender-specific tendency. As the gender perspective would predict, situational factors appear to account for many of the differences often attributed to "essential" gender characteristics. What men and women tend to do in intimate relationships does not necessarily reveal what they are capable of doing (Ickes et al., 2000).

POWER IN INTIMATE RELATIONSHIPS

Power is a multifaceted phenomenon. It refers to the ability to exert one's will and translate one's wishes into meaningful action; it also refers to one's ability to influence or resist the influence of another. Relationships vary in terms of how explicitly power is expressed, but a power dimension is always present.

According to the principles of **exchange theory** (also referred to as *resource theory*), an individual's power is determined by a number of factors operating simultaneously (Foa and Foa, 1980). The first major factor involves the amount of actual or perceived control a person has over resources. The general principle is that the more resources one possesses or is seen to possess, the more power one has in a relationship. The second factor is the extent to which one's partner values those resources. If the other person has no interest in the resources one controls, they will not be relevant to power. Only valued and desired resources confer power. The third factor is the availability of alternative sources. The fewer the available alternatives (i.e., the scarcer the valued resources), the greater the partner's power. The fourth, enunciated by Waller (1938) as the **principle of least interest**, is related to the fact that dependence and power are inversely related. The scarcer the alternatives, the greater one's *dependence* upon the person who controls the resources; the greater one's dependence, the lesser one's power. According to this principle, the person with the least interest in maintaining a relationship holds the most power. Having less interest in a relationship is related to the real or perceived availability of alternative sources of satisfaction. The person who feels that their needs could be better met in an alternative relationship will be less willing to make sacrifices or concessions to maintain the current one. Conversely, the person who greatly values their current partner and sees few alternative sources of satisfaction is dependent and not powerful. Making a partner believe that one is essential to their well-being is one way of attempting to keep him or her dependent. Of course, the harder one works to make oneself indispensable, the more one is faced with the truth of one's own powerlessness (Richeson and Ambady, 2001). Studies of both marital and heterosexual dating relationships have found that women who report loving their partners less than they are loved in return perceive themselves as having more power in those relationships (Sprecher and Felmlee, 1997).

Eichler (1981) argued that "frontier families" were probably relatively egalitarian, as they were based upon a mutual or symmetrical dependency of husband and wife. However, with the evolution of the breadwinner–housewife family, dependency became asymmetrical. The housewife's access to food, shelter, and other necessities of life depended upon the income provided by the breadwinner. In contrast, the breadwinner could simply purchase "wifely" services from an increasing variety of sources. This system of asymmetrical dependency resulted in men having greater power than women in marital and family relationships. "Second-wave" feminists championed the goals of decreasing women's dependence upon men, increasing women's access to resources external to the home, and promoting greater symmetry in the distribution of power within intimate relationships.

In response to the growing influence of the women's movement in the late 1960s and early 1970s, a counterwave of anti-feminist publications (e.g., Andelin, 1974) and seminars swept North America. Their basic message was "(a) that men should lead, women should obey, (b) that women benefit from patriarchy, and (c) that it's a woman's job to keep her marriage happy and it is mainly her fault if it's unhappy" (Hochschild, 2003: 19). These authors and speakers claimed that the secret to women's happiness was not to be found in political, economic, or educational equality. Rather, women were advised to exercise domestic power, to "accumulate domestic capital and invest at home" (Hochschild, 2003: 22). Women were enjoined to make themselves indispensable to their husbands in the family home, to bolster men's egos, and, in various ways, to reaffirm the traditional notion that the male sex was superior. Towards this end, Morgan (1973: 114–115) recommended that the "total woman" greet her husband at the door "in a cloud of powder and cologne," dressed, if need be, in costume: "Never let him know what to expect when he opens the front door, make it a surprise package. You may be a smoldering sexpot or an All American Fresh beauty. Be a pixie or a pirate, a cowgirl or a showgirl. Keep him off guard" (Morgan, 1973: 117). Alternatively, she advised wives to welcome their husbands swathed only in plastic wrap. These choreographed bits of marital theatre would supposedly guarantee a husband who was "breathless" with "romance," sexually intrigued, and eager to fulfill his wife's every non-sexual wish and demand.

This form of anti-feminist flurry receded into the background by the early 1980s. However, a new variation surfaced in the mid-1990s in the form of *The Rules: Time-tested Secrets for Capturing the Heart of Mr. Right,* a best-selling book (Fein and Schneider, 1995), with related workshops, that paid homage to the message of an earlier era. Subsequent books by these authors, including *The Rules 2: More Rules to Live and Love By* (1997); *The Rules Dating Journal* (1997); *The Little Book of Rules* (1998); *The Rules for Marriage: Time-tested Secrets for Making Your Marriage Work* (2001); *The Rules for Online Dating: Capturing the Heart of Mr. Right in Cyberspace* (2002); and *The Complete Book of Rules* (2003) also became bestsellers. These manuals represent a revival of the old-fashioned manipulative technique known as "playing hard-to-get" ("make Mr. Right obsessed with having you as his by making yourself seem unattainable" [Fein and Schneider, 1995: 5]). It is not surprising their message has found a receptive audience in a society that designates women the "love experts" and blames them if they make foolish romantic choices. Power relations exist within a sociocultural context, which conditions both what is considered a valuable resource (e.g., the "hard-to-get" woman) and the strategies whereby individuals can access resources (e.g., the "Rules").

According to exchange theory, the fifth factor which determines an individual's power is the fact that in patriarchal societies, males hold greater power simply by virtue of their being male. The basic institutions of patriarchal societies are so structured as to allow males greater access to positions that yield a greater share of socially valued rewards and resources. As a consequence of being more highly positioned in the structures of our economic, political, and legal institutions, males in general have greater **structural power** (Guttentag and Secord, 1983: 26). This is apparent in our courtship norms, which have traditionally granted men the power to initiate all phases of intimate relationships. Even today, "[g]irls are often considered to be more reserved when it comes to asking a boy out on a date and are conventionally viewed as having a passive role in the initiation of dating" (Council of Ministers of Education Canada, 2003). Research based on the self-reports of American undergraduates (de Weerth and Kalma, 1995) and Canadian secondary-school students (Council of Ministers of Education Canada, 2003: 108) has found that most students of both sexes feel that it is now acceptable for a girl to make the first move. Nevertheless, "female dominance in a heterosexual relationship is less acceptable *to both parties* than is male dominance" (Brehm, 1992: 244; emphasis in original).

Types of Resources

Many types of resources are relevant to power within relationships. The simplest list would include money and material possessions, social status, love, and sexuality (Foa and Foa, 1980). These resources differ in more than the obvious ways. Money is a **concrete resource** (Johnson, 1976); it is *quantifiable* (i.e., measured or counted) and amounts can be compared. It can also be transferred from one person or relationship to another. Social status can also be conferred or vicariously achieved; for example, "[a]ccording to the traditional [gender] code, a man's success at work reflects glory on his wife" (Hochschild, 2003: 107). In addition, both money and status can be used to provide access to other valuable resources (e.g., higher education, a political career) which are in themselves sources of power.

Love, on the other hand, is a **personal resource** (Johnson, 1976). It cannot be quantified; it is also particularized and cannot readily be transferred to other persons or relationships. Finally, love cannot as easily provide access to other forms of power (although this does occur). Sexuality, which intersects with love, may serve as a means of access to other forms of power, particularly when it is deemed a valuable, scarce resource. Nevertheless, while many might desire our money or social status, not everyone wants our love. Similarly, while it is relatively easy to assess whether a new partner represents more money or social status than a current one, it is not as easy to evaluate whether they represent more love or better sexual experiences.

Traditionally, males have controlled resources of money and social status; females, resources of love and sexuality. Even though this distribution is slowly transforming, current conditions still favour an exchange of resources within intimate relationships. Unfortunately, the parties to such an exchange do not necessarily have equal bargaining power. Lipman-Blumen (1976: 16–17) noted that "in relationships between the sexes, males have a disproportionate amount of resources under their control. They could bargain their power, status, money, land, political influence, legal power, and educational and occupational resources (all usually greater than women's) against women's more limited range of resources consisting of sexuality, youth, beauty, and the promise of paternity." In our materialistic society, personal resources are not valued as highly as concrete ones; for this reason, relationships are unlikely to be egalitarian. Characteristics of the heterosexual mating gradient also promote the pairing of unequal partners (Cooney and Uhlenberg, 1991; Schwartz, 1994).

An underlying principle of exchange/resource theory—that monetary resources derived from the outside world will determine the nature of relationships within a couple's home—appears to apply equally to gay and heterosexual couples. Blumstein and Schwartz's large-scale empirical study of heterosexual, gay, and lesbian married and cohabiting couples found that "[m]oney establishes the balance of power in relationships, except among lesbians" (Blumstein and Schwartz, 1983: 53). The fact that money does not determine the balance of power in lesbian relationships demonstrates that resource theory does not offer a full explanation of power. Schwartz et al. (1994) argued that women in our society are not used to judging their own self-worth in monetary terms and therefore do not measure the worth of an intimate female partner (but will measure a male partner's worth) according to that standard. Men, however, measure their own worth, that of other men, and (increasingly) that of their intimate female partners by a monetary-resource yardstick. The lesbian experience illustrates the second precept of exchange theory: If one's partner does not value a particular resource, that resource is of no consequence to power. "By noting that even gay male couples gain advantage over one another when one partner has a high income, we see that money may create inequality even when there is no gender difference. But we also see, by looking at lesbian couples, that money need not have that effect" (Blumstein and Schwartz, 1983: 55; for similar findings see Kurdek, 1993, 2003; Huston and Schwartz, 2002). Clearly, belief systems, or ideologies, can modulate the influence of resources.

Power Techniques

Men and women differ not only in the amount of resource power they control but in their techniques of using the power they have. "When the dominant group controls the major institutions of society it relies on **macromanipulation** through law, social policy, and military might when necessary, to impose its will and ensure its rule. The less powerful become adept at **micromanipulation** using intelligence, canniness, intuition, interpersonal charm, sexuality, deception, and avoidance to offset the control of the powerful" (Lipman-Blumen, 1984: 8).

Macromanipulation is a more direct and forceful set of techniques, whereas micromanipulation techniques tend to be more indirect and subtle. Their differential use typically reflects the extent to which the user has access to structural power.

Men generally tend to use the macro, women the micro means of influencing others. However, these are typical tendencies only. Men are not averse to using micromanipulation techniques and may, for example, "play dumb" to avoid performing housework. Thus, men who boast of their technological savvy may feign incompetence when it comes to operating toaster ovens or multistage washers. Similarly, women can engage in macromanipulation when they have the opportunity to do so. For example, women's groups have successfully marshalled the force of law to promote or prohibit various actions within our society. The differential use of manipulation or power techniques is as much a function of opportunity or necessity as it is of preference.

In societies where men possess greater structural power and women lack access to the means for establishing their independent social standing, sexuality becomes one of the few resources that women can exchange for social status and upward mobility (Safilios-Rothschild, 1977: 2). Since the 1970s, however, with the rise in premarital sexuality for both men and women, sexuality no longer has the same value as a "bargaining chip." Women's possession of other resources such as education, employment, and increased income allows them to become less dependent upon marriage and sexuality as means of physical and social survival.

Resources, Control, and Ideologies

Chapter 6 noted that housework responsibilities are redistributed when women's occupational and monetary resources increase (Stohs, 1995, 2000). Wives' employment promotes greater equalization of the balance of power in most marriages and cohabitation relationships, for at least three interrelated reasons (Blumstein and Schwartz, 1983). First, by providing greater financial independence, money increases women's bargaining power in a relationship. Second, both money and employment enhance the sense of self-worth and confidence a woman brings to a relationship. Third, husbands understand and respect the stresses and achievements of paid employment, and therefore give employed wives credit for their additional resources. Increased resources also permit women to purchase more services (e.g., restaurant meals, cleaning/nanny services). However, it does not appear from the existing research that an increase in a wife's resources leads to a meaningful increase in her husband's participation in household tasks. "The relationship between macro and microlevel power dynamics indicates that as women's income and education levels increase, the disparities between spouses on time and tasks are decreased, but not eliminated" (Stohs, 2000: 356; see also Tichenor, 1999, 2005).

Structural power, while important, is not necessarily the determining factor in power in dyadic (Guttentag and Secord, 1983: 26) or intimate relationships; possession of resources is only part of the picture. On the basis of the first precept of resource theory, it might be expected that men would attempt to control a relationship only when possession of greater concrete resources endowed them with power to do so. However, unemployed married men typically refuse to shoulder the greater load of housework and child care (Marshall, 1998). Stets (1993) claimed that individuals will attempt to assert/reassert control over a partner if they perceive that current conditions may reduce their control below a desired level. It may be that men may perceive that to assume an increased share of the domestic burden would threaten their desired level of control. Hochschild (2003: 113–114) described one husband who refused to help his high-earning wife with housework and child care, yet nonetheless insisted that he was "'a one in a hundred' kind of man. For, as he said with great feeling, 'Most men couldn't take it if their wives out-earned them this much!'" Issues of real or perceived control can exert as much influence in a relationship as differential possession of resources.

Ideology is another factor that can influence power relations between men and women. Research conducted in Canada and the United States found that a majority of couples now endorse an egalitarian ideology and declare that their relationships are egalitarian (i.e., that power is distributed equally between the partners) (e.g., Blaisure and Allen, 1995; Zvonkovic et al., 1996). However, such assertions are often found to be at odds with actual practice.

Egalitarian Relationships Researchers have found that most so-called **egalitarian relationships** are, in fact, male-dominated (Blaisure and Allen, 1995; Hochschild, 2003; Schwartz, 1994). Kompter (1989) argued that many instances of "apparent consensus" in intimate relationships in fact reflect males' "hidden" power and prestige. Ostensibly consensual decisions are often based on a woman's anticipation of the man's negative reaction should she disagree, or on her feeling of resignation ("the outcome is a foregone conclusion anyway, so why bother arguing?"). In both cases, the appearance of egalitarian mutuality disguises what is really going on: women deferring to men's power. What is more, women often construe their compliance as a sign of their love rather than of their lesser power. Marriage has been referred to as a "tangle of love and domination" (Thorne, 1982: 12); the two are often not easily disentangled.

Power may be exercised in everything from the most momentous work- and family-related concerns to such trivial matters as who controls the "remote" for the television set (Walker, 1996). Who actually holds power, however, is not always easy to discern. Consider the following exchange, commonplace among intimate partners: Question: "What do you want to do tonight?" Answer: "I don't know. You decide." Who has the power here—the person who manifestly gets to "decide," or the one who appointed the other decision-maker? A clue may lie in whether the person who seems to have relinquished power usually exercises veto rights until the "designated decider" comes up with the decision the designator wants. More often than not, veto power remains in male hands despite the semblance of equality.

Blaisure and Allen's (1995) small purposive-sample study of white, mid-30s couples illuminates not only the disparity between ideology and practice but also the characteristics of couples who successfully translate beliefs into behaviour. Husbands and wives in this sample possessed comparable educational, occupational, and monetary resources; 90 percent had children. All respondents' avowed commitment to feminism and the principle of gender equality pre-dated their marriage, and they remained committed to egalitarianism in their marriages of a 10-year median duration; in all cases, partners remained in their marriages by choice.

It was found that in 60 percent of the marriages, there were discrepancies between couples' egalitarian ideologies and their actual housekeeping, child-care, and marital relationship practices. Forty percent of the couples essentially practised what they believed. All of the couples engaged in what the researchers term **vigilance**, defined as "an attending to and a monitoring of equality, within and outside of their relationship" (Blaisure and Allen, 1995: 10). For both men and women, vigilance began with the selection of a partner whose principles and practices appeared to be congruent with their own, with whom they intended to create a relationship "superior" to traditional marriage, one in which women would preserve their own separate identities and men would be emotionally connected to their wives and children (Blaisure and Allen, 1995: 11). The researchers found that vigilance comprises five different processes. All of the couples practised three of these: critique of gender injustice, public acts of equality, and support of wives' activities. *Critique of gender injustices* involved both partners freely pointing out and discussing experiences of sexism, harassment, and rigid gender expectations. In doing so and working together to negate the influence of these injustices in their own lives, couples maintained a commitment to their ideology. Women noted that one of the benefits of feminism was the provision of a "language to help them clarify their experiences of injustice, and [to] make sense of their world and define themselves" (Blaisure and Allen, 1995: 11); men found themselves better able to empathize with their wives and to express their own frustrations with the restrictiveness of the traditional male role. *Public acts of equality* included such items as wives retaining their birth surnames, spouses maintaining separate bank accounts and credit ratings, and public joint decision-making. As one husband remarked, "people ... expect me to make any decision that is confronting what we should do. They talk to me, and I don't like that. I don't want them to talk to me. I want them to talk to both of us" (in Blaisure and Allen, 1995: 120). Husbands' *support of wives' activities* included giving priority to wives' employment opportunities (including residential location), arranging work schedules to accommodate their wives', and practical support of wives' involvement in feminist organizations.

However, only couples whose beliefs and behaviours were congruent practised two additional kinds of vigilance: reflective assessment and emotional involvement. *Reflective assessment* involves the constant monitoring of each partner's contributions to the relationship in order to identify and correct any imbalances. This differs from traditional and feminist-discrepant marriages, in which any such monitoring is usually done only by wives and may result in demand–withdrawal syndrome. In discrepant marriages, the unit of comparison individuals use to gauge their own contribution is other members of their gender (i.e., partners ask themselves what other wives or other husbands would do); in congruent marriages, the unit of comparison is one's marital partner. *Emotional involvement* has to do with verbally communicating emotions, even in the face of disagreement or outright conflict. Continued emotional involvement maintained a couple's feelings of closeness. Wives whose marriages were not characterized by expression of emotions reported turning to their friends to fill this important need. Others noted that emotional inexpressiveness created more relationship-work for themselves. As one wife states: "we'll go through this, 'Well, how are you feeling?' and I try to drag things out of him at times when I know he should be depressed and he should be upset" (in Blaisure and Allen, 1995: 16). Feminist-congruent couples, in contrast, made emotional expressiveness a responsibility of both partners. Married couples who put their feminist beliefs into practice appear to adopt a "feminized" conception of love that stressed the importance of shared feelings for maintaining an intimate relationship.

SEXUALITY

Sex, gender, and sexuality are profoundly interconnected. However, the interconnections between these variables are neither wholly natural nor inevitable. Regardless of sex or sexual orientation, every individual's interest in the entire range of manifestations of sexuality varies along an erotophile (strong positive)–erotophobe (strong negative) continuum (see Saxton, 1996: 130–131). This inventory includes everything from dominance–submissiveness to fetishism. Consequently, generalizations about "male sexuality" or "female sexuality" must be tempered by an acknowledgment that sexuality is not the direct result of biological sex, but the product of a complex constellation of factors.

Part of our socialization involves exposure to social definitions that distinguish the sexual from the non-sexual, label some forms of sexuality as acceptable and others abhorrent, and construct sexuality scripts for women and men. These social definitions are all shaped, conveyed, and reinforced via language.

Languages of Sexuality

Thinking and communicating about sexuality are constrained by our understandings of what sexuality is. Whether or not a sexual meaning is imputed to a particular thing depends upon the language a culture uses to define it. For example, in our society, an erect penis is not invariably defined as an indicator of sexual interest (e.g., erections that occur in infancy or upon waking from REM sleep). Erect nipples may be defined as an indicator of sexual arousal—or as a response to cold weather. Although breastfeeding can produce feelings of sexual stimulation, that aspect is typically ignored, and attention directed to breastfeeding's non-sexual nurturant dimension.

In this culture, what is defined as "real" sexuality largely reflects male standards expressed in a heterosexist language system. In our historically *pronatalist* society (i.e., one oriented towards promoting a high birth rate), heterosexuality is privileged, whereas homosexuality is marginalized and stigmatized. The defining characteristic of "real sexuality" is held to be penile penetration of the vagina. Although this act could be described differently (e.g., "vaginal envelopment of the penis"), our most common description of coitus implicitly reinforces active male–passive female stereotypes. Coitus is also portrayed as bracketed by two subordinate categories of activity: foreplay and afterplay.

Foreplay refers to activities engaged in prior to intercourse (e.g., kissing, manual and oral stimulation of erogenous zones). Over the course of the twentieth century, definers of "normal sexuality" in the medical and therapeutic communities have acknowledged oral-genital sexuality as an increasingly common part of the sexual repertoires of women and men (Michael et al., 1994). However, pronouncements on its acceptability—reflecting a pronatalist bias—still hinge on whether it is practised as an adjunct to, or substitute for, reproductive sexuality. Creith (1996: 6) remarked that authors of best-selling sex manuals have often presented oral sex as "not as good as real heterosexual sex" or as simply "a warm-up exercise for action with the boys." By implication, acts of oral-genital sex engaged in by same-sex partners, especially lesbians, are something other than "real sex." **Afterplay** is usually defined as post-intercourse activities (e.g., talking and hugging) that take place after ejaculation has occurred. Once again, the androcentric terminology defines lesbian sexuality into non-existence; as Creith (1996: 65) sardonically asks, "[W]hen does lesbian sex officially 'begin' and 'end'? How can we be sure we've had 'it'?" Consider, in this context, Blumstein and Schwartz's (1983) oft-cited research which found that lesbian couples were less sexual and "had sex" less frequently than male homosexual and heterosexual couples. According to this research, 47 percent of lesbian couples, compared to merely 15 percent of heterosexual married couples, had sex once a month or less. Marilyn Frye (1992) challenged the veracity of that statistic:

> Do lesbian couples really "have sex" any less frequently than heterosexual couples? My own view is that lesbian couples "have sex" a great deal less frequently than heterosexual couples. I think, in fact, we don't "have sex" at all. By the criteria that I'm betting most of the heterosexual people

used in reporting the frequency with which they have sex, lesbians don't have sex. There is no male partner whose orgasm and ejaculation can be the criterion for counting "times."

The equation of sexuality with heterosexual penetration was reinforced by Freud's notion that "a clitoral orgasm is an 'infantile' orgasm, a vaginal one a 'mature' orgasm, and that only by shifting her focus from her vestigial phallus to her unmistakably feminine vagina would a woman find psychosexual fulfillment" (Angier, 2000: 67). Freud's claim was eventually discredited by empirical research, which revealed that all female orgasm originates with the clitoris (Angier, 2000). Intercourse typically fails to provide women with sufficient orgasm-inducing stimulation; reportedly 50 to 75 percent of women (exact figures vary by researchers) require direct manual or oral clitoral stimulation to reach orgasm (Reinisch, 1990: 201). In one study, 64 percent of women who did not experience orgasm during intercourse reported the primary reason to be lack of non-coital clitoral stimulation (Darling et al., 1991). Among women who do attain orgasm during penile thrusting, the majority typically prefer other forms of clitoral manipulation (Masters et al., 1994). According to Angier (2000: 67), "Freud's proposal was an anomaly, a blot on history's understanding of female sexuality. For thousands of years, experts and amateurs alike recognized the centrality of the clitoris to a woman's pleasure and climactic faculty."

During the second wave of the feminist movement, activists "rediscovered" the clitoris and emphasized its significance for women's sensual pleasure. Amidst assertions of women's right to control all aspects of their bodies, and a growing concern about overpopulation, the strong pronatalist orientation of the past shifted towards an emphasis on erotic enjoyment and women's right to sexual pleasure (Laqueur, 1990). "Think clitoris" was one of the catchphrases of this era (Angier, 2000: 66). Yet our definition of "real sexuality" continues to emphasize a penetrative method of stimulation—one guaranteed to provide men, but not necessarily women, with orgasmic satisfaction. It is, therefore, not surprising that in feminist circles, penetrative sexuality has often been equated with an oppressive, exploitative sexuality, and seen as a metaphor for all aspects of male–female relations in the context of a male-dominated society.

Comparative Images of Male and Female Sexuality

Western understandings of male sexuality have been shaped by the "belief in a sometimes overpowering male sex drive and the belief that men have immutable sexual needs that are manifested over and above individual attempts at repression" (Blumstein and Schwartz, 1990, in Bird and Melville, 1994: 139). According to our folklore, a "real man is someone who's always interested in sex and ready for it" (Zilbergeld, 1992: 46). This notion of a powerful, often uncontrollable, male sexuality has remained unchanged for centuries. In contrast, our cultural images of female sexuality have undergone a number of significant transformations over time (Leiblum, 2002).

Some of our earliest images of female sexuality were developed within a religious framework devised to establish social and sexual morality. The Christian Church propagated a dualistic view of woman, as personified in the non-sexual Virgin Mary and the sexual temptress Eve (Laws and Schwartz, 1977: 13–14). Female sexuality was evaluated in terms of its outcomes for men: The good, non-sexual woman, epitomized by the Virgin Mary, did not tempt man to lustful preoccupations, but helped him focus his attentions and energies on his immortal soul. The bad, sexual woman, epitomized by Eve, turned man away from the spirit towards the flesh, precipitating his fall from grace. Women's sexuality was thus implicated in men's salvation or damnation. Implicit in these icons is a vision of female sexuality as a powerful force that must be curbed lest men succumb to evil.

Religious injunctions against an active female sexuality were reinforced in the latter half of the nineteenth century by an almost exclusively male medical profession which coined the terms *heterosexuality* and *homosexuality* (Blumstein and Schwartz, 1983: 41). Members of the medical profession provided politicians, lawyers, and judges with "scientific" evidence to justify the regulation of homosexual (Kinsman, 1996) and various pleasure-motivated heterosexual (Katz, 1995) practices. The norms of "healthy" female sexuality were defined as chastity before marriage and fidelity within marriage. Women who deviated from this sexual script were diagnosed as physically or mentally ill (Everaerd et al., 2000). Beliefs began to change over the first half of the twentieth century. Yet "marriage manuals" (written largely by men with medical training) continued to define and shape women's sexuality. According to experts of the day, two characteristics defined female sexuality: **monogamy** and **dormancy** (Gordon and Shankweiler, 1971). Females were pronounced monogamous by nature; men, "naturally" polygamous. As a monogamous being, a woman "saved" her sexuality for one man and one alone—her husband. Female sexuality was also held to be essentially dormant, quietly residing under a surface of asexuality until awakened in true Sleeping Beauty fashion by a man—a husband. Men were cast into the role of "sexpert" and charged with the task of teaching women about female sexuality. A "good woman" was now permitted to demonstrate erotic interest, desire, and activity—so long as these were confined to her marital bed. Nevertheless, the norms of female chastity and fidelity remained firmly in place until challenges began to arise in the 1960s.

Residues of earlier attitudes, however, can still be found (Christopher and Sprecher, 2000). For example, a study based on 97 male and 192 female undergraduate virgins found that although the fear of AIDS and STDs is an increasingly influential factor in the decision to remain chaste, women reported more social pressure to remain virgin and were also more likely to retain this status longer than men (Sprecher and Regan, 1996; see also Lammers et al., 2000). Holland et al. (2000: 221) found that for young men, the first experience of heterosexual sex is an empowering moment through which agency and identity are confirmed; however, for young women, the experience is often more complicated: "[T]heir ambivalent responses to it are primarily concerned with managing loss" (see also Carpenter, 2001, 2002). Similarly, despite the fact that some researchers proclaimed that the 1960s "sexual revolution" had sounded the death knell of the "double standard" (i.e., a societal attitude that condoned premarital sex for men but not for women) (e.g., Gentry, 1998), reports of its death may have been premature. A recent ethnography of women ages 16 to 18 indicated that the double standard still dominated young women's negotiations of heterosexuality (Jackson and Cram, 2003). A survey of 413 young Canadian men and women (ages 18 to 28) also revealed that although participants were likely to reject the double standard personally, the majority nevertheless perceived it as existing at the societal level; women were especially likely to report this perception (Milhausen and Herold, 2001: 63; see also Milhausen and Herold, 1999). In addition, two studies of young American women, Leora Tanenbaum's (2001) *Slut! Growing Up Female with a Bad Reputation* and Emily White's (2002) *Fast Girls: Teenage Girls and the Myth of the Slut,* found evidence that the double standard (as well as "slut bashing," as Tanenbaum calls it) is still thriving in the new millennium.

Common terms used to refer to sexually active men and women reveal the continuing legacy of earlier attitudes. As Sloane (1993: 154) observed, "Everyone knows that a nymphomaniac is a woman with an excessive sex drive. Why is it that hardly anyone knows the same condition in males is satyriasis?" In response to this rhetorical query, Angier (2000: 54) poses a second: "Is it because in women excessive lust is considered a disease worthy of a name tag, while in men the same drive is considered mandatory?" Danesi's (2003: 73) recent research on the spontaneous conversations of Canadian teenagers noted the persistence of a double standard; as one of his female respondents remarked, "I change boyfriends a lot; everyone at school calls me a whore, a slut. But guys get away with it. They're called players or studs instead. You know what I mean?" (p. 73). While a vast number of terms continue to encode society's disapproval of "promiscuous" women (e.g., bimbo, bitch, fallen woman, floozy, harlot, ho, hooker, hussy, piece, slut, tail, tramp), the comparatively few terms used to describe promiscuous men (e.g., Casanova, Don Juan, ladykiller) almost always register societal approval or admiration (Hopper, 2003; Orenstein, 2001). (Reflective of this: When the author asked one of her undergraduate classes, "What terms are currently used to refer to men who engage frequently in sex?" a student shouted out, "Lucky!")

Women's sexuality continues to be defined in terms which relate it to men's. A woman who wants sex more frequently than her partner or who engages in non-monogamous sex may be derisively called a "skank" or a "nympho." She may be identified as suffering from the recently discovered "condition" known as "persistent sexual arousal syndrome" (Leiblum and Nathan, 2001; see also Cacchioni, 2007; Fishman and Mamo, 2001; Radner, 2008). A female who wants sex less frequently than her male partner or who rejects a man's request for sex may be labelled "frigid" or a "dyke." Alternatively, she may be diagnosed as suffering from "female sexual arousal disorder" (Derogatis et al., 2002). In contrast, men's sexuality is rarely evaluated in terms of women's. A man who desires to be sexually active more often than his female partner may simply be described as "normal."

For most of the twentieth century, it was assumed that women did not possess an active and self-determined sexuality (Leiblum, 2002). Our socially constructed model portrayed female sexuality as essentially reactive. The dictum that sexuality is a less important part of female than of male consciousness may have turned into a self-fulfilling prophecy, discouraging women from learning about their bodies, tending to their sexual desires, and writing their own sexual story (Bryant and Schofield, 2007; Foley et al., 2002). As Rubin (1983: 108) observed, "For most women, the 'essence of womanhood' would not lie in their genitals or in their experience of their sexual powers." Over the past 30 years, a key issue of debate has been whether female sexuality has been either *repressed* or *socially constructed* (Jackson and Scott, 1996: 6; Blumstein and Schwartz, 1999; Baumeister and Twenge, 2002). The notion of a repressed sexuality implies the existence of an internal "authentic" sexuality or sexual potential not permitted full expression. According to this viewpoint, external social forces deny women the opportunity to gratify their desires or translate them into reality. However, female sexual repression can only be ascertained by comparing it with the putative freedom of male sexual expression. Not only is male sexuality under constraints of its own, but such comparison implies that the meaning and nature of female sexuality are still to be derived via comparison to male. Once again, male sexuality becomes normative, and efforts to remove constraints upon female sexuality become designs to bring it into conformity with male sexuality. Thus, the repression argument ultimately becomes phallocentric. The social construction argument, on the other hand, contends that because of the prevailing language of sexuality, women are unaware that certain sexual wants, desires, or expressions are possible. The androcentric language of sexuality prevents women from experiencing and articulating desires for anything other than what is encompassed within the prevailing sexuality script.

The Sexual Script

As mentioned in Chapter 1, "sexuality scripts" consist of culturally created guidelines defining appropriate sexuality and the roles to be performed by participants in a sexual encounter. These scripts typically involve variations upon the same underlying themes. For example,

> In one [script] ... he is expected to get an erection from her naked beauty, keep his erection, arouse her passions, and hold off his orgasm until she reaches hers. He's required to do all this without any information about what really turns her on. The woman is passive, beautiful, and graceful while she waits for this incredible experience called orgasm, and when nothing happens, she concentrates on the romance. In another [script], the poor woman is responsible for the man's erection. She does oralsex [*sic*] to get him hard and remains focused exclusively on his pleasure. He gets on top and does what feels good for him and she accommodates him, going into her act of passionate sounds to excite him all the more. He comes, she fakes it, and he dozes off holding her in his arms. She's happy because she has pleased him, and she loves the closeness. He's happy because her response has proved he's a good lover, and he loves her loving him. (Dodson, 1996: 16)

This description portrays two variations on the central heterosexual script. Unlike same-sex couples, for whom there is no institutionalized script prescribing "who does what to whom," heterosexual partners have definite roles: "Among heterosexual couples, the content of sexual behavior in the relationship is guided by gender. Men direct the couple's sexual life and women modify what happens by what they choose to accept" (Blumstein and Schwartz, 1983: 244; see also Kiefer and Sanchez, 2007).

Our traditional sexuality script assigns men the role of teachers and women the role of naive but willing students. Men are expected to be more knowledgeable and—as the ones with the more powerful sexuality—ever ready. Our culture's presumption that a woman's sexual drive is less compelling contributes to her being assigned the role of "gatekeeper"—regulator of the progression of intimacies; this role dictates that she "engage in sexual behavior only to the extent necessary to satisfy her boyfriend's needs, not her own" (Lott, 1994: 120).

Our predominant sexual script is not only a set of guidelines for shaping and attaining sexual pleasure, but also a "testing ground" for masculinity and femininity. Success or failure in the sexual encounter affirms or threatens one's own and one's partner's sense of gender in a particularly significant way. Our culture decrees that to be masculine is to be sexual; to fail at sex, therefore, is to fail as a man. In consequence, men have a considerable ego and gender investment in successfully performing their sexual role—a fact well known to women, who begin to surmise in adolescence that there is more at stake in males' vehement pursuit of sex than simple sexual pleasure. Using a sample of 638 male and 1021 female heterosexual undergraduates, Sprecher et al. (1995) investigated gender differences in emotional reactions to first intercourse. It was found that regardless of the stage and length of the relationship in which the event occurred, men reported having experienced less guilt, but more pleasure *and* anxiety, than women did.

One of the man's scripted tasks is to (attain and) maintain an erection for the duration of a sexual encounter. The contemporary script has added the expectation that he take responsibility for the woman's orgasm. "You can't consider yourself a good lover unless you give your partner an earthshaking experience" (Zilbergeld, 1992: 53). Failure to attain/maintain an erection (known as "impotence" or "erectile dysfunction disorder") or "premature" ejaculation (i.e., ejaculation which occurs prior to the woman's orgasm) constitute "failures" ("dysfunctions," in the language of sexual therapy) on his part. A man's worry over one or both of these possibilities, known as **performance anxiety**, may lead to diminished desire for interpersonal sexual encounters (rarely does a man complain about erection problems when masturbating). Viagra, a drug used for the treatment of erectile dysfunction disorder, was approved for sale in Canada in March 1999; by November 2000, Canadian doctors had written one million—and almost half a million men had filled—prescriptions for this drug (*Canadian Press*, 16 November 2000). By 2003, over 20 million Viagra pills had been dispensed in this country; the dollar value of those sales amounted to about $100 million a year (Taylor, 2003). The extreme profitability of this product attests to men's investment in their erections for their sexuality and sense of masculinity (Castro-Vazquez, 2006; Fishman and Mamo, 2001; Pridal, 2001; Watson, 2000).

Women are also "tested" upon their sexual performance and are expected to meet certain requirements (Cohen and Shotland, 1996; Maass, 2007). For example, a woman's "failure" to achieve orgasm can lead to her being labelled "frigid" ("preorgasmic," in the language of sexual therapy)—or it may be perceived as casting doubt upon the expertise (and masculinity) of her "sexpert" male partner. Women may fake orgasm to avoid negative labelling and gratify male egos. Although research on this phenomenon is spare, a study of 161 young adult women (ages 18 to 27) found that over half reported having faked orgasm during sexual intercourse. Compared to non-pretenders, pretenders were significantly older, had been younger at first intercourse, reported having had a higher number of (lifetime) sexual partners, and scored higher on measures of sexual esteem and erotophilia (Wiederman, 1997).

At times of sexual intimacy, body-image issues are intensified for both men and women. For men, a common preoccupation is penis length: "In most surveys men seem to feel that theirs are not large enough" (Etcoff, 1999: 181). In 1999, over 10 thousand American men underwent surgery to lengthen or widen their penises; "penis exposure" procedures are now commonly performed on men in Canada, Japan, Australia, Germany, Britain, and other countries (Etcoff, 1999: 181). In addition, the image of the muscular male body, displayed more and more prominently in films and men's magazines, has heightened men's concern with achieving this masculine ideal and led to an increase in reports of body dissatisfaction and related body-image concerns (Ricciardelli and McCabe, 2001: 190; see also Henword et al., 2002; McCreary et al., 2004). Indeed, Tantleff-Dunn and Thompson (2000) reported that satisfaction with chest size is now a more important aspect of body image and self-esteem for men than satisfaction with breast size is for women (see also Tantleff-Dunn, 2002). The covers of magazines such as *Muscle and Fitness* (read by six million people each month) and *Men's Health* typically feature an oiled male mesomorph being admired by a beautiful young woman (Rohlinger, 2002). The implicit message of such images was succinctly articulated by one gym's billboard ad that read: "NO PECS, NO SEX" (in Etcoff, 1999: 177). Among gay males as well, being "buff"—well-muscled and perfectly toned—is an important attribute of desirability (Martins et al., 2007; Yelland and Tiggemann, 2003). To enhance sexual desirability and achieve the requisite chest-of-armour look, some men undergo surgical procedures such as liposuction (to remove flab from stomachs and chests) and pectoral implants (to make the chest seem broader and more muscular).

Researchers have documented women's concern with conforming to a largely unattainable standard of physical attractiveness and sexual desirability (e.g., Barnett et al., 2001; Bransford, 1997; Sanchez and Kiefer, 2007) and found that "[w]omen, as a group, are more dissatisfied with their bodies than are men" (Forbes et al., 2001: 462). Women who are dissatisfied with their bodies report a later onset of masturbation (Wiederman and Pryor, 1997) and are less likely to receive (although not less likely to perform) oral sex

(Wiederman and Hurst, 1998). Higher levels of body self-consciousness also predict lower levels of sexual assertiveness, experience, and condom use self-efficacy and higher levels of sexual risk-taking (Sanchez et al., 2006; Schooler et al., 2005). While women with disabilities, regardless of their sexual orientation, may experience particular challenges in developing and maintaining a positive identity of themselves as sexually desirable (APA, 2007: 27), lesbians generally evince less concern than heterosexual women about their weight and general appearance (Krakauer and Rose, 2002). Yancey et al. (2003) reported that "lesbians who were obese and overweight were less likely than other women to define themselves as such" (Ambert, 2003: 3). Owens et al. (2003: 15) concluded that "belonging to a lesbian subculture may provide some protection against the societal imperative toward thinness," but emphasized that "it likely does not counter the larger societal preference that women be thin." Share and Mintz (2002) investigated differences between lesbian and heterosexual women (ages 24 to 52) on three dimensions: (1) disordered eating; (2) awareness and internalization of cultural attitudes about thinness; and (3) body esteem in relation to weight, physical condition, and sexual attractiveness. Although they found no differences between the two groups in awareness of cultural standards, lesbians "exhibited higher levels of body esteem in relation to sexual attractiveness, and lower levels of internalization of cultural standards." An analysis of personal ads written by heterosexual and homosexual men and women also reported that whereas gay men were the group most likely to emphasize physical characteristics, lesbians were the least likely to do so (Gonzales and Meyers, 1993).

Both heterosexual and lesbian women contemplating sexual intimacy must confront strong negative stereotypes about their genitals. These stereotypes are reiterated daily via advertisements for douches and "feminine hygiene sprays" and "a lot of big fish stories" (Angier, 2000: 57). Since most women, in childhood, do not receive a positive introductory orientation towards their own genitals (Angier, 2000: 71–76), exposing their bodies to a new sexual partner may be more intimidating for women than for men.

Gender and Experienced Sexuality

From a physiological standpoint, males and females respond in similar ways as they proceed through the four phases of the human sexual response cycle (excitement, plateau, orgasm, resolution). The bodies of both sexes undergo similar changes in localized blood flow (vasocongestion), muscle tension (myotonia), heightened blood pressure, and heart, pulse, and respiration rates (Masters et al., 1994). Furthermore, male and female bodies are capable of proceeding through all four phases at the same speed (Riedmann et al., 2003). Some gender differences exist in body-based experiences at certain times during the first two phases of the sexual response cycles, such as "ballooning" of the vagina (which creates a sensation of an inner "void"), greater awareness of vaginal (as opposed to penile) lubrication, or of penile (as opposed to clitoral) erection. However, the subjective experience of orgasm is the same for men and women (Mah and Binik, 2002).

In males, orgasm typically coincides with ejaculation. Once ejaculation occurs, male bodies enter a refractory phase of variable duration, during which they are essentially insensate to further stimulation and incapable of another ejaculation. During this time, vasocongestion and myotonia subside relatively quickly. Should orgasm (and, in males, ejaculation) not occur, tissues remain engorged (swollen) with blood and muscles remain tense for a longer period of time, producing feelings of discomfort for both males and females. Cultural myths about male sexuality allow men to invoke this discomfort (colloquially referred to as "blue balls") as grounds for pleading for orgasmic relief lest they suffer permanent damage. While it may be noted that no analogous argument has been accorded women with which to justify their own sexual demands, no tissue damage in fact is incurred by either sex should orgasmic release not be forthcoming, and both male and female bodies eventually return to their pre-excitement states.

Females typically do not ejaculate, although Ladas et al. (1982) contended that some unknown proportion of the female population possess a "G-spot" (named after German gynecologist Ernst Grafenberg, who supposedly discovered it). The G-spot is reputedly "a sort of second, internalized clitoris" (Angier, 2000: 82) located on the front wall of the vagina that, if properly stimulated, can induce orgasm and ejaculation. Its existence is accepted by some (Levin, 2001; Whipple, 2000) and disputed or mocked by others (Angier, 1999; Lancaster, 2003; Tavris, 1992). Without ejaculation, female bodies do not enter into a refractory phase; therefore, they are capable of responding continuously to further sexual stimulation. Estimates suggest that about 15 percent of women regularly have multiple orgasms and that approximately one quarter to one third of all North American women have been multiorgasmic with a partner (Lamanna and Riedmann, 2000: 562; Masters et al., 1994: 68).

This difference in orgasmic potential may not be sex-irreducible. Sexuality therapists claim to have succeeded in training men to become "multiorgasmic" by delaying ejaculation until a final desired orgasm (Hartmann, 1991, in Rice, 1996: 166), although these claims have been questioned (Masters et al., 1994: 68). Nevertheless, sex researchers have found that the only "training" women need to become multiorgasmic is experimentation via self-exploration and a readiness to take responsibility for their own sexual pleasure. According to Angier (2000: 76), sex researchers have found that this readiness is a trait shared by women who are easily and multiply orgasmic. "They don't depend on the skillfulness or mind-reading abilities of their lovers to get what they want. They know which positions and angles work best for them, and they negotiate said postures verbally or kinesthetically." Women's capacity to be multiorgasmic challenges our traditional assumption that females are "naturally less sexual" than males. However, although women *can be* multiorgasmic, whether they *actually are* at any moment in their lives or over their life course is another matter (Everaerd et al., 2000: 115–116).

Vance (1984) argued that for women, sexuality involves a powerful "tension" between *pleasure* and *danger*:

> For some [women], the dangers of sexuality—violence, brutality, and coercion, in the form of rape, forcible incest, and exploitation, as well as everyday cruelty and humiliation—make the pleasures pale by comparison. For others, the positive possibilities of sexuality—exploration of the body, curiosity, intimacy, sensuality, adventure, excitement, human connection, basking in the infantile and non-rational—are not only worthwhile, but provide sustaining energy. (Vance, 1984: 1)

Although sexuality does pose dangers for men, its dangers appear to be greater for women (Casteneda and Burns-Glover, 2004; Russell and Oswald, 2001; Spitzberg, 1999). Ambivalence towards sexuality is greater and more pronounced for women. For women, sexuality may be associated with such things as loss of reputation, exploitation or coercion, unplanned or unwanted pregnancy, and discomfort or even death from sexually transmitted diseases (a danger shared with men). Some feminists argue that it is not sexuality per se but heterosexuality that holds dangers for women (Jackson and Scott, 1996: 17); sexuality with men poses dangers insofar as power is typically distributed unequally in heterosexual relationships. However, the connection between gender, sexuality, and power is neither simple nor straightforward.

Sexuality and Power For both men and women, sexual behaviour often springs from non-sexual motives and satisfies non-sexual objectives. Sexuality and power appear to be configured into different pathways for each gender: For men, power begets sexuality; for women, sexuality generates power. Men's social, political, and economic power can act as a potent symbolic aphrodisiac. Consider, for example, the marriage of sexagenarian billionaire Donald Trump to a model decades younger. As David Buss remarked, when asked to comment on the frequent pairing of aging male movie stars and much-younger women, "There is a point where men cease to embody the qualities that women desire, but it's not much shy of a wheelchair and the need for total medical care" (in Etcoff, 1999: 67). In a patriarchal society, some men may feel that being members of the "superior" sex entitles them to impose their sexuality upon women. Feminists maintain that confronting and challenging this male sense of entitlement, which is anchored in gendered social power, is of critical importance in combatting both sexual harassment and sexual assault (e.g., Pollock, 2000; Senn et al., 2000).

As noted earlier, sexuality has historically served women as a means of gaining power. Where women have little direct access to power, money, or prestige, sexuality can be strategically employed to gain both tangible (money, material goods, marriage) and intangible rewards. Although the need to rely on their sexuality for non-sexual gain has declined as women have gained greater access to power through education, occupational opportunity, and independent income, older messages still reverberate. "Girls and women learn that sex[uality] can be exchanged not only for commodities, but also for intimacy or commitment" (Lott, 1994: 118). Females may be encouraged to think of their sexuality as a powerful force that may be used to advantage at the intimate-relationships bargaining table. Especially during adolescence, when females have few other resources (e.g., meaningful occupation or income), the awareness that one is sexually desired and that this desirability can translate into other positive outcomes (e.g., popularity, gifts or pledges of love, "promise rings") may produce a heady sense of power. However, women may also experience a sense of disillusionment and disappointment about a process which reduces them to sexual commodities ("sex objects").

It is not always easy to determine who has the power and what motives are being served in any specific sexual encounter. Men sometimes use power to obtain sex, and sometimes use sexuality to express power. However, sexuality is also one of the principal means by which men communicate love, affection, and caring for their intimate partner (Lamanna and Riedmann, 2000: 88). In the sexual experience, power, vulnerability, pleasure, and danger may coexist in an uneasy admixture. One of Rubin's (1983) students expressed her feelings of exposure and vulnerability:

> ... there's ... that instant when he's about to enter me when I get this tiny flash of fear. It comes and goes in a second, but it's almost always there.... I guess it's like being invaded, and I want to protect myself against it for that instant. Then he's in and it's gone, and I can get lost in the sexual excitement. (Rubin, 1983: 10)

Danger and power are frequently juxtaposed; the same respondent, for example, reported a "moment in sex when I know I'm in control, that he really couldn't stop anymore because his drive is so great, that I feel wonderful. I feel like the most powerful person in that instant" (Rubin, 1983: 109). Both women and men feel powerful when they have stimulated a partner to the point where the drive to orgasm is inexorable. Both can experience feelings of vulnerability to various dangers as well as intense physical, psychological, and emotional pleasure during a sexual experience. That women more often than men experience and emphasize the dangers is partly attributable to their differential histories of sexuality socialization (Craig, 2003; Kiefer et al., 2006; Stephan et al., 2000).

Contemporary Gender-Sexuality Socialization and Development

Our society has both a history of believing that sexuality is "natural" (instinctive or biologically determined) and a strong antisexual heritage (Saxton, 1986: 110–113). Our sexuality socialization tends to direct a prosexual message at boys and men and a more antisexual one at girls and women. While male sexuality scripts continue to emphasize that "sex is a good thing," female scripts generally stress the relational components of sexuality and fuse it with love and intimacy. The 2000 Project Canada survey on teenagers ages 15 to 19 found that although 82 percent of young people (85 percent of males and 80 percent of females) either strongly approved or approved of sex before marriage when people "love each other," young males were significantly more likely than young women to endorse premarital sex for those who simply "like each other" (68 percent versus 48 percent) (Bibby, 2001: 90; see also Marston and King, 2006). Even though "waiting until marriage" has been replaced with waiting until a stable, affectionate, respectful relationship comes along, women's initial socialization emphasizes sexuality as an intimacy-driven, not orgasm-driven, activity. Rubin (1983: 103) claimed that "for men, the erotic aspect of any relationship remains forever the most compelling, while, for women, the emotional component will always be the more salient." Over time, however, most women do acquire a more genital focus for their sexuality (Kaplan, 1974: 110–111).

For men, sexual experience is crucial to a series of important "rites of passage" symbolizing the transition from boyhood into manhood, culminating in the first experience of heterosexual intercourse. Like gender itself, sexual manhood, once attained, must constantly be demonstrated and reaffirmed. Since most males first learn sexuality through masturbation, success and satisfaction tend initially to be measured in orgasms, not intimacy. With input from female partners and changing social expectations, most men learn, by middle age or sooner, to acquire a greater sensate (versus genital) focus and enhanced sensitivity towards the interpersonal components of sexual intimacy (LeVay and Valente, 2003).

Families Simon and Gagnon (1970) maintained that the most important processes of childhood sexuality socialization (which occur in the context of the family) involve the acquisition of gender identity and the learning of gendered behaviour patterns. One aspect of this socialization that has important implications for men's and women's experiences of sexuality has to do with *naming genitals*.

Gartrell and Mosbacher (1984) gathered introspective data from a sample of college students, physicians, and mental health professionals on the earliest names they, as children, had been taught for the genitalia of both sexes. Responses collected from this highly educated group were classified according to whether they had been taught anatomically correct names, anatomical names incorrectly applied (e.g., vagina instead of vulva for the entire female genital region), non-anatomical names (i.e., euphemisms), or no names at all. Males typically had been taught either anatomically correct names (39.9 percent) or euphemisms (41.6 percent) for their own genitals. These euphemisms typically reflected the penis' urinary function (e.g., Piddler, Pipi, Wee-wee), or were common derivations (e.g., Dick, Dink, Peter). No male had been taught an incorrectly applied anatomical name, and less than one fifth of the sample (18.5 percent) had never been taught a name for their genitals at all.

In contrast, the largest group of women (44.3 percent) had never been given a name for their genitals; 41.7 percent had been given euphemistic names. Parents were remarkably creative when naming a daughter's genitalia, employing a variety of terms whose meanings were idiosyncratic and obscure (e.g., Dee-dee, Christmas), explicit and negative (e.g., Nasty, Shame), or extremely vague (e.g., Yourself, Down Under). Less than 10 percent of the female respondents had been given either anatomically correct (6.1 percent) or anatomically incorrect (7.8 percent) names. Females were likely to have learned either no name (36.4 percent) or a euphemism (30.9 percent) for male genitalia, although almost one third (29 percent) had been taught anatomically correct names; males were most likely (56.1 percent) to have been provided with no name for female genitalia at all.

The acquisition of unique, euphemistic, or negative names for genitalia is likely to make subsequent communication about sexuality difficult or embarrassing. Negative names may lead to negative feelings about genitalia and ultimately about sexuality; leaving an entire region of the body unnamed clearly implies that there is something terribly negative about it. On average, both male and female respondents learned correct anatomical names for their own and the opposite sex's genitalia at between 10 and 15 years of age. Both males and females acquired names for male genitalia earlier than for female genitalia, and males learned anatomically correct names for female genitalia earlier than did most females (Gartrell and Mosbacher, 1984: 872). This finding suggests that men's bodies and sexuality are privileged over women's.

The hallmark of biological maturity is the ability to reproduce (Perlmutter and Hall, 1985: 5). In females, this is signalled by the onset of menses (even though the ability to conceive typically does not occur until approximately two years later), and in males by the ability to ejaculate (although orgasm can occur among boys of earlier age) (Masters et al., 1994; Reinisch, 1990). Over the course of the past century, the onset of menses in Western women has been occurring at an ever-younger age. "In 1860, the average girl first menstruated when she was 16 or 17 years old. By 1920, this age was 14.5 years, and now it is about age 12.5, about two years earlier than when boys reach puberty" (Baca Zinn and Eitzen, 1993: 235–236). Cesario and Hughes (2007) observed that "precocious puberty" (the appearance of secondary sex characteristics before 8 years of age or the onset of menarche before age 9) is also on the rise and 10 times more common among girls than boys. Maticka-Tyndale (2001: 1) reported that "[y]oung men have seen the same decline in spermarche (when they first produce viable sperm)"; boys' genitals begin pubertal growth at around age 11–12 and typically attain adult size and shape around 14–15 (Masters et al., 1994). Although the mechanisms controlling the pubertal clock are still unclear, body fat/lean ratios, influenced by nutritional levels, appear to be the most important (Finley, 2003).

The sexuality of sons is relatively easy for parents to ignore; evidence of ejaculatory capability is easily hidden from prying eyes, and even if discovered, is unlikely to trigger discussions about masturbation or the reproductive consequences of coital ejaculation (Nolin and Petersen, 1992). The myth of the father-son chat about "the birds and the bees" is exactly that. However, the advent of menstruation cannot be ignored. Evidence indicates that the onset of a menstrual cycle forces parents (usually mothers) to acknowledge the incipient sexuality of their daughters and to initiate limited discussions about the topic

(Nolin and Petersen, 1992). However, these initial discussions are typically framed in terms of reproductive rather than erotic sexuality (Council of Ministers of Education Canada, 2003).

Socialization messages aimed at early adolescent females are typically negative, focusing on the risk of pregnancy from (penetrative) sexual activity. The message conveyed is often one of males as dangerous sexual predators. Women in their thirties commonly express the wish that their mothers had been more explicit in discussing sex, and, in particular, had presented them with more positive messages about sexuality (Brock and Jennings, 1993; Yowell, 1997). Parents who present positive messages about sexuality may still find themselves unprepared for the early age at which their children become sexually active, and may react negatively to their children's sexual interest and activities (Rubin, 1990: 80–83).

The media and peer groups are additional sources of information (and misinformation), role models, and depictions of the prevailing sexuality scripts for men and women (Furnham et al., 2001; Moore and Davidson, 1990; Barrett et al., 1999: 246). An empirical investigation of how 175 male and female university students obtained their knowledge found that, contrary to stereotypes, pornography does not play an important role in the dissemination of sexual information; peers appear to be the primary source (Trostle, 2003). Peer groups also provide young men and women with expanded sexual vocabularies (Vogels, 2002). If findings from an extremely limited-sample survey of college students (Cameron, 1992) can be generalized, males tend towards a more eloquent language for discussing the penis than do females. Under competitive conditions, males recalled or created 144 penis terms compared to the 50 generated by females. Males characterized the penis as (in descending order of frequency) a person (e.g., his Excellency, Mr. Happy), a tool (e.g., garden hose, jackhammer), an animal (e.g., King Kong, snake), a weapon of conquest (e.g., passion rifle, heat-seeking moisture missile), a foodstuff (e.g., love popsicle, Whopper), or "miscellaneous" (e.g., pussy pleaser).

Although women's responses were not as easy to categorize, conspicuous by their absence were terms depicting the penis as a symbol of authority, tool, ferocious animal, or weapon. "One might generalize by saying that women find the penis endearing, ridiculous, and occasionally disgusting, but not awe-inspiring or dangerous" (Cameron, 1992: 374). Many of the terms on the females' list also appeared on the males'; however, some distinctive terms evidenced familiarity with romance novels (e.g., throbbing manhood, swelling hardness). Others were classified by the researcher as "nonsense" (e.g., prickola, doodad), or under "miscellaneous" (e.g., God's gift to women). Though men often invest the penis with positive-association masculine qualities, it seems that a penis by any other name is still just a penis for most women. Brown and Kitzinger's (2001) examination of slang terms for female and male genitalia, based on questionnaires completed by 156 18- to 50-year-old women and 125 16- to 36-year-old men, reported that more female terms were coded as standard slang, euphemism, space, receptacle, abjection, hair, animal, or money and more male terms were coded as personification, gender identity, edibility, danger, or nonsense.

Attitudes towards and practices of **masturbation** are key indicators of societal and individual orientations towards erotic, pleasure-oriented, non-reproductive sexuality (Saxton, 1986: 113). Although infants and young children often engage in exploring their genitals or rubbing them against inanimate objects (Kinsey et al., 1953, 1948), their motives are most likely to be pleasure-seeking, not sexual. Only once the individual has acquired an awareness of the meaning of sexuality in our society and of which actions are or are not considered sexual, can his/her activity be accurately labelled masturbation—an activity stemming from a sexual motive and designed intentionally and explicitly to provide sexual pleasure (Gagnon, 1977).

Whereas females typically learn to masturbate through their own experimentation (Saxton, 1996: 117), most males learn to masturbate from another boy (Saxton, 1996: 111). Girls tend to masturbate alone, whereas boys, in early adolescence, often gather in groups (Elkin and Handel, 1989: 294) to validate one another's right to be sexual and to express their sexuality in masturbation. It is not uncommon for boys to engage in contests ("circle jerks") in which each contestant demonstrates his masturbation prowess in terms of knowledge, technique, and frequency. The competitive nature of these games may be an influence in men's use of sports metaphors (particularly from baseball) to chart the progress of a sexual relationship, the emphasis on "scoring," and the tendency to broadcast "batting average" to presumably appreciative peers. Although men may boast of the nature and frequency of their casual sexual experiences, they are less likely to share sexual details of an emotionally intimate relationship.

Males' early introduction to their own sexuality through masturbation promotes "a capacity for detached sexual activity—activity whose only sustaining motive is sexual. This may be the hallmark of male sexuality in our society" (Simon and Gagnon, 1970: 32). This capacity establishes a model for male sexuality of "conquest with orgasm, but with as little tenderness, intimacy, and emotionality as possible" (Baca Zinn and Eitzen, 1993: 252); it promotes the compartmentalization of physical sexuality and emotional intimacy.

Most males establish a consistent pattern of masturbation during early adolescence, whereas females typically do not begin to masturbate until their dating or married years (Reinisch, 1990); even then, the incidence patterns of masturbation are more variable for females than for males. As part of the movement of women towards taking greater control of their bodies, some early second-wave feminists created a vaginal art form designed to acquaint women with the variability in female genitalia and to desensitize them to the negative imagery they had received. Others (e.g., Dodson, 1996, 1974) not only advocated masturbation, but created "self-love" workshops to help women become more comfortable with their genital sexuality. However, researchers have continued to document significantly lower rates of masturbation among females than males during childhood and adolescence (e.g., Michael et al., 1994; Dekker and Schmidt, 2002). A meta-analysis (surveying 177 sources reporting gender-difference data on 21 different measures of sexual attitudes and behaviours) found that the largest gender difference was in incidence of masturbation (Oliver and Hyde, 1993; see also Halpern et al., 2002). The 2002 Canadian Youth, Sexual Health and HIV/AIDS Study also reported that although grade 11 students were more likely than grade 9 students to agree/strongly agree with the statement "It's alright to masturbate," males in both grades were considerably more likely to agree with the statement than were females. Whereas about 6 out of 10 males at both grade levels endorsed masturbation (59 percent of males in grade 9 and 63 percent of males in grade 11), roughly 3 in 10 girls did so (31 percent of females in grade 9 and 35 percent in grade 11) (Council of Ministers of Education Canada, 2003: 72). Girls and young women do not receive from their peers the validating messages about genital sexuality and masturbation that boys do from theirs (Kelly and Bazzini, 2001).

In childhood and early adolescence, female peer groups preserve the continuity of the socialization girls receive at home and from the media by reinforcing the emphasis on love and the importance of establishing intimate relationships prior to sexual involvement. As a result of this emphasis, "girls appear to be well-trained precisely in that area in which boys are poorly trained—that is, a belief in and a capacity for intense, emotionally-charged [*sic*] relationships and the language of romantic love" (Simon and Gagnon, 1970: 36). Whereas a typical male relationship script reads "sexuality first, love later, whenever," a typical female relationship script reads "love first, sexuality later." "It is not that men are not attracted by romance, but, for them, they often say, romance is a means to an end and the end they are striving towards is sexual intercourse. Women, in contrast, often say that what is arousing about the sexual ending is the romantic beginning" (Michael et al., 1994: 150). This female script applies to premarital, marital, and extramarital sexual relationships (Cameron, 1997; Riedmann et al., 2004). A recent study which explored gender differences in the sexual fantasies of university students also found that "love, affection, and romance were involved in women's fantasies far more than in those of men" (Kimmel and Plante, 2002: 55).

Contemporary Sexual Behaviour A claim propagated by the media and in everyday conversation has to do with the age at which men and women attain their sexual "peaks." Women supposedly reach the peak of their sexuality in their mid-30s; men, in their mid- to late teens. This belief originated in research by Kinsey et al. (1953, 1948) identifying the average age at which the frequency of orgasm is highest for either sex. However, what the Kinsey researchers actually documented was not an immutable feature of male and female sexuality; in fact, they reflected the double standard of sexuality that prevailed during the first half of the twentieth century (Barr et al., 2002).

Because of the greater sexual freedom men have historically enjoyed, males have typically become sexually active in late childhood or early adolescence. During adolescence, males establish a regular pattern of orgasm and ejaculation that is maintained, relatively undiminished, into old age (Reinisch, 1990). Until late adolescence, ejaculation occurs almost exclusively from masturbation; thereafter, from varying combinations of self- and with-partner stimulation. Howsoever brought about, the frequency of orgasm follows a highly consistent pattern over a man's lifetime. As a result, the notion of a "peaking" of male sexual expression is almost useless, unless we focus only upon orgasms obtained by a specific method of stimulation (e.g., intercourse).

Female orgasmic patterns, however, are more subject to situational contingencies. During the first half of the twentieth century, females were severely restricted from engaging in premarital sexual activity. Once married, most women had to be resocialized to think of themselves as sexual beings and to express their sexuality freely and comfortably; in consequence, orgasm frequency tended to rise significantly among older married women. The putative "peaking" of women's sexuality documented by Kinsey was in fact an artifact of socially constructed opportunity, not a function of biology. Orgasmic frequency and sexual response do, however, change over a woman's lifetime (Reinisch, 1990; Barr et al., 2002).

According to Darling et al. (1989: 238), one of the twentieth century's major sexual trends has been an increase in premarital coitus among both sexes; since 1970, the increase has been particularly dramatic among women. The result has been a general trend towards convergence in the sexual behaviour of women and men. A summary of surveys conducted in Canada over the past three decades determined that the proportions of sexually experienced adolescent and young adult men and women had doubled in Canada since the 1970s (Hobart, 1996: 150; see also Mesten et al., 1996; Bibby, 2001: 186). Not only are a higher number of teenagers participating in oral, anal, and coital sex, but young people are becoming sexually active at a younger and younger age, resulting in a notable increase in the average number of lifetime sexual partners. It would appear, then, that cultural rather than biological forces are the prime determinants of "peaking"; as females as well as males become sexually active earlier, the gender difference in peak sexual activity has been converging towards a norm previously identified with males.

In the late 1990s, the Global Sex Survey (commissioned by SSL International Plc, the world's leading condom manufacturer) interviewed 4200 teenagers and young adults (ages 15 to 21) in 14 countries. This survey found that Canadian youth were first having sex almost a year earlier than the global average of 15.9 years of age, and reported that "the age of first intercourse in Canada is decreasing at an alarming rate. Among the 21-year-old Canadian respondents, 16.7 was the average age for loss of virginity, while among the 16-year-olds in the study, 14.3 was the average—'a staggering 2.4 drop'" (Cherney, 1999). These results, based on a small sample of 300 Canadian youth, conflict with several larger Canadian studies that suggest that first vaginal-intercourse experiences tend to occur between the ages of 16 and 18 (Maticka-Tyndale et al., 2000). The 1996 National Population Health Survey, based on a nationally representative sample of 4447 Canadian youth ages 15 to 19, found that about half of the females (55 percent) and males (47 percent) had experienced vaginal intercourse; only 24 percent of girls and 18 percent of boys had experienced sexual intercourse by age 15. According to this data, Canadian 15-year-olds were less likely than their counterparts in countries such as the United States, France, and Finland to have experienced sexual intercourse (see Figure 7.1). Nevertheless, it remains true that in Canada, "more young people are initiating vaginal intercourse at young ages with each new birth cohort and ... this trend toward decreasing age is greater among women than men" (Maticka-Tyndale, 2001: 9).

Most recently, the 2002 Canadian Youth, Sexual Health and HIV/AIDS Survey (CYSHHAS) (Council of Ministers of Education Canada, 2003) asked students in grades 9 (N=3841) and 11 (N=3697) to report on the type and frequency of their sexual activities. This study found that about a third of grade 9 students (32 percent of males and 28 percent of females) and over half of grade 11 students (53 percent of males and 52 percent of females) reported having engaged in oral sex at least once. Fewer students reported having experienced vaginal sexual intercourse. Among grade 9 students, 23 percent of boys and 19 percent of girls reported engaging in sexual intercourse at least once. Among grade 11 students, 40 percent of boys and 46 percent of girls claimed to have experienced vaginal sexual intercourse (Council of Ministers of Education Canada, 2003: 75). This study also found that of those who had experienced vaginal intercourse, about half reported having had only one sexual partner; boys were more likely than girls to report a greater number of sexual partners. For example, among sexually active grade 9 boys, 22 percent claimed to have had sexual intercourse with 4 to 10 partners, and 7 percent with 11 or more; the respective figures for girls were 14 percent and less than 1 percent (Council of Ministers of Education Canada, 2003: 83). This discrepancy is consistent with other research that has found men more likely than women to report a large lifetime number of sexual partners (Alexander and Fisher, 2003). For example, one Canadian survey, based on telephone interviews with 1400 adult Canadians (randomly selected from all 10 provinces) reported that 36 percent of Canadian men (as compared to 13 percent of Canadian women) reported having had six or more sexual partners in their lifetimes (*Maclean's*, 2000: 52). Yet such differences in self-reportage may be at least partially attributable to respondents' awareness

FIGURE 7.1	**Percentage of 15-Year-Olds Who Reported Having Had Sexual Intercourse (1997/1998)**

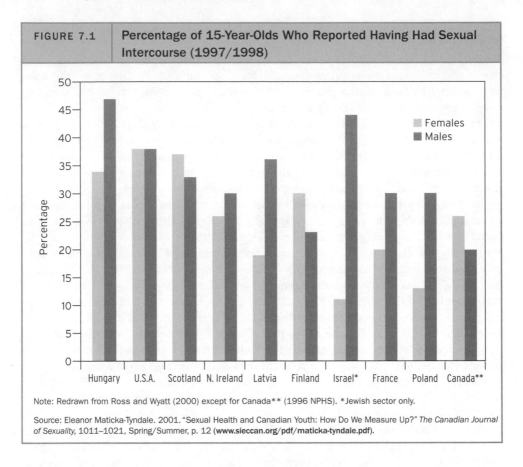

Note: Redrawn from Ross and Wyatt (2000) except for Canada** (1996 NPHS). *Jewish sector only.

Source: Eleanor Maticka-Tyndale. 2001. "Sexual Health and Canadian Youth: How Do We Measure Up?" *The Canadian Journal of Sexuality,* 1011–1021, Spring/Summer, p. 12 (**www.sieccan.org/pdf/maticka-tyndale.pdf**).

of normative expectations for men and women (Alexander and Fisher, 2003; Brown and Sinclair, 1999; Wiederman, 1997, 2001). If masculinity is a quality that must be continuously proven or asserted, one arena for doing so is sexual congress. One may consider here Messner's (1992) finding that a "Big Man on Campus" was expected to demonstrate considerable heterosexual activity and that among high school students, being a "real" guy meant "you get 'em into bed" (p. 96).

When the CYSHHAS asked sexually active grade 9 and 11 students to select one of seven possible reasons for having had their *first* experience of sexual intercourse, the most common responses cited were "love for the person," "curiosity/experimentation" and "influence of alcohol/drugs." However, as Figures 7.2a and 7.2b indicate, girls in both grades were more likely than boys to select "love for the person," and boys more likely than girls to select "curiosity/experimentation" (Council of Ministers of Education Canada, 2003: 81–83; see also Shulman and Seiffge-Krenke, 2001; Wyndol, 2002). Across grades, 10 percent of boys cited "losing [their] virginity" as their motive for having sex; only 3 percent of girls chose this reason. It was also found that when students who had not had sex were asked to choose one of 10 possible reasons for their abstinence, "[m]ore boys than girls in both grades selected 'Have not had the opportunity' as their main reason" (Council of Ministers of Education Canada, 2003: 79; see also Hyde and Jaffee, 2000; Little and Rankin, 2001). Among grade 11 students, 42 percent of males, compared to 11 percent of

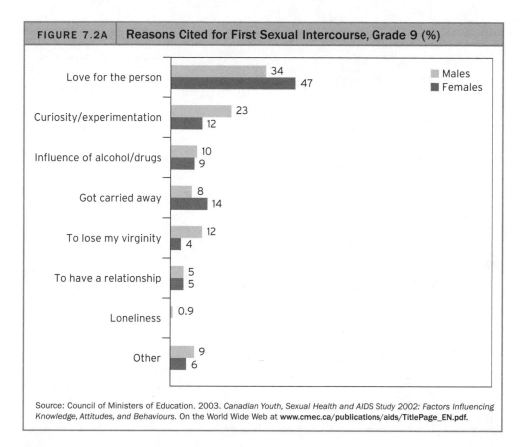

| FIGURE 7.2A | Reasons Cited for First Sexual Intercourse, Grade 9 (%) |

Source: Council of Ministers of Education. 2003. *Canadian Youth, Sexual Health and AIDS Study 2002: Factors Influencing Knowledge, Attitudes, and Behaviours.* On the World Wide Web at **www.cmec.ca/publications/aids/TitlePage_EN.pdf.**

females, choose this as their primary reason (Council of Ministers of Education Canada, 2003: 81). A large-scale American survey (Michael et al., 1994: 90) also reported that among adults of all ages, the largest group of women (48 percent) cited "affection for partner" as the major reason they first had intercourse, followed by 24 percent who cited "curiosity/readiness for sex"; on the other hand, 51 percent of males cited "curiosity" and only 25 percent identified "affection" as their primary reason (Michael et al., 1994: 93). "Virtually *no* women said that they wanted or went along with sex for physical pleasure" (Michael et al., 1994: 94; emphasis in original).

The traditional sexual script is definitely being challenged, but the revised version remains a work-in-progress (Hyde and Oliver, 2000). Based on interviews with 1267 female and 793 male French-speaking undergraduates throughout the province of Quebec, Otis et al. (1997) reported that changes affecting the sociosexual life of teenagers have led to increased equality in a number of contraceptive and sexual behaviours, as well as greater sexual autonomy for women. However, they stressed that the full acceptance of gender equality has yet to be achieved and that the behaviour and attitudes of their student sample reflected a transitional phase in sociosexual norms. As evidence of this, one may consider the results of experimental research examining women's attitudes about female use of contraceptives and their assumptions about men's attitudes towards female contraceptive users (Hynie and Lydon, 1995). In this study, female participants (ages 17 to 30) read a fictitious

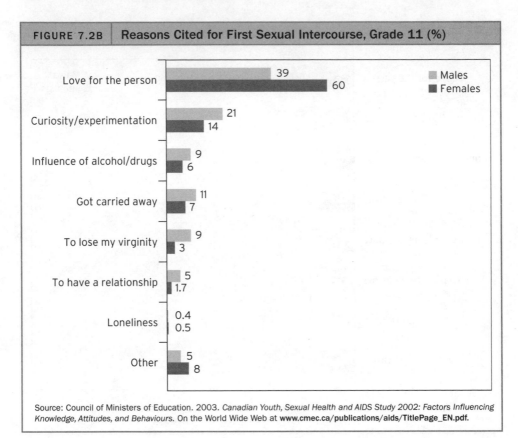

| FIGURE 7.2B | Reasons Cited for First Sexual Intercourse, Grade 11 (%) |

Source: Council of Ministers of Education. 2003. *Canadian Youth, Sexual Health and AIDS Study 2002: Factors Influencing Knowledge, Attitudes, and Behaviours*. On the World Wide Web at **www.cmec.ca/publications/aids/TitlePage_EN.pdf**.

woman's diary describing a sexual encounter in which either the woman or the man provided a condom or the couple had unprotected intercourse. Respondents rated the target's behaviour more negatively, and as more inappropriate, when she provided a condom than when her partner did so, and also assumed that her partner would feel less positive towards her when she was the condom-provider (see also Kelly and Bazzini, 2001). It is also noteworthy that even though three quarters of the teenage girls surveyed by the CYSHHAS claimed that they would ask their partners about using condoms prior to having intercourse, almost one quarter of girls in both grades 9 and 11 reported being too embarrassed to buy condoms themselves (Council of Ministers of Education Canada, 2003: 91; see also Penman-Aguilar et al., 2002). Grade 9 girls who had experienced sexual intercourse were also more likely than virgins to agree with the statement "I am often sorry for the things I do," "indicating a sense of guilt" (p. 117); grade 7 girls who had engaged in the preliminary sexual activity of touching below the waist were "more likely to have negative self-esteem" (p. 120). Among grade 11 girls, those who had engaged in risky sexual behaviours (e.g., multiple sexual partners, inconsistent use of contraception, lack of protection against sexually transmitted diseases) were less likely than non-risk-takers to agree with the statement "I have confidence in myself" (59 percent and 78 percent respectively) (p. 123).

The CYSHHAS findings underscore the fact that sexual intercourse can occur out of *compliance* rather than pleasure. The traditional sexual script, which encourages women to behave unassertively with men, promotes compliance (i.e., agreeing to sexual activity without actually wanting it) (Byers and O'Sullivan, 1996: 21). Compliance has been linked to the experience of sexual aggression (Krahe et al., 2001). Girls in both grades 9 and 11 were more likely than boys to report having had sex unwillingly (see also Shortland and Hunter, 1995). This finding suggests that acts of compliance are linked to gendered power imbalances within dating relationships. "Of girls in grades 9 and 11 whose boyfriends usually decide how to spend their time together, one-third report being pressured to have sex when they did not want to. Similarly, of girls in grades 9 and 11 whose boyfriends usually decide how to spend their time together, one-fifth report having had sex when they did not want to" (Council of Ministers of Education Canada, 2003: 107).

Research has also found that some ethnic groups in Canada are more likely than others to demonstrate allegiance to traditional sexual scripts. In a study examining differences in sexual behaviour between 356 Asian and 346 non-Asian Canadian undergraduates, Meston et al. (1996) found Asians to be more conservative than non-Asians on measures of interpersonal sexual behaviour (e.g., petting and intercourse) and sociosexual restrictiveness (e.g., lifetime number of partners and number of "one-night stands"). Riedmann et al. (2003: 121) asserted that "certain cultures still place considerable emphasis upon women remaining virgins until marriage." According to Oh (2001: 44), sanctions for contravening traditional sexual scripts can be severe; in some cases, "[a] woman's future can hang, literally, by a membrane." Without evidence of an intact hymen, she reports, Canadian women from Middle Eastern Muslim cultures may be "shunned as whores," or, "in extreme cases, even murdered by male relatives to restore family honour" (p. 44). In illustration, she describes the desperate quest of a Muslim woman in Toronto to find a plastic surgeon who would perform plastic surgery to reconstruct her hymen—an emerging specialty among some Canadian plastic surgeons. The woman, whose hymen had been damaged in an erotic encounter with a boyfriend, told Oh (2000: 43) that "My first thought was that I'd have to kill myself to avoid hardship and shame for myself and my family."

As Reiss (1986: 212) noted, "the greater the power of one gender, the greater that gender's sexual rights in that society." As women challenge power alignments in politics, education, employment, and the family, they also continue to challenge conventional wisdom about their sexuality. Part of this challenge involves rewriting the sexual script in the context of a new sexual revolution brought about by the nexus of computers, the Internet, and sexuality itself. The configuration of "access, affordability, and anonymity" (Cooper et al., 2000: 520) is fostering the construction of a new script that provides for a wide range of erotic fantasies for both sexes (Fisher and Barak, 2001; Hicks and Leitenberg, 2001), a more candid exchange of information earlier in relationships, and a greater willingness to experiment with alternatives (Kibby and Costello, 2001; Schneider, 2000). Leiblum (2001: 389) declared that the Internet "has become 'home' to tens of millions of women who sign on for connection, education and titillation," furnishing women of any age, appearance, and physical condition with a democratization of sexual access, enhanced "educational opportunities and support,... opportunities for developing and exploring romantic and sexual relationships and an entree into new erotic worlds and marketplaces." Brym and Lenton (2001) reported that Canadians are increasingly trying "love online" and "digital dating" (see also Strassberg and Holty, 2003). A survey of 760 Canadian university students (Boies, 2002) found that half reported having used the Internet to obtain sexual information and having benefited from doing so. Although men were more likely to report engaging in sexual entertainment activities both on- and offline, approximately 40 percent of the students reported going online to meet new people and to view sexually explicit materials (see also Goodson et al., 2001). Mooney et al. (2004: 293) noted that the World Wide Web has also helped gays, lesbians, and bisexuals "create safe places for support and information" and find intimate partners (see Alexander, 2003).

From the 1960s through the 1980s, feminists waged war against pornography, guided in part by Steinem's (1978) distinction between **erotica** (depictions of sexuality involving mutually consenting adults participating in egalitarian sexual encounters) and **pornography** (depictions of sexual relations characterized by dominance, exploitation, and violence). This definition differentiated between "good" and "bad" sexuality on the basis of the distribution of power between participants: In pornography, male participants and viewers possessed power, whereas the females being exhibited were understood to be powerless. Fuelled by a strong belief that pornography, broadly and vaguely defined, incites men to commit sexual and non-sexual violence against women, feminists, led by Dworkin (1981) and MacKinnon (1987), fought to ban virtually all explicit depictions of sexuality. Although evidence for a causal link between exposure to/use of pornography and sexual violence remains inconclusive (Boyle, 2000; Millburn et al., 2000; Oddone-Paolucci et al., 2000; Shope, 2004), the movement to ban pornography has intensified in reaction to cyberporn (Fabi, 2004; Lillie, 2002)—and in particular, to the advent of Internet rape sites in which "the pain caused to the victim is a primary selling point" (Gossett and Byrne, 2002: 689; see also Itzin, 2002; Mehta, 2001). As a result, as Luff (2001: 78) has noted, an odd "alliance" links the anti-pornography activities of feminists and various pro-family organizations— "even where such alliance is neither sought or desired."

Although pornography entails the objectification and commodification of women depicted in positions of unequal power, the anti-pornography movement has met with resistance not only from without but from within feminist ranks. Norton (1999: 113) accused anti-pornography feminists of advancing a model of male dominance and female subordination that "reduces the indefinite complexity of power dynamics within heterosexual and homosexual relations to a mechanical binary system that explains little more than the most abusive situations." Norton, speaking from the vantage point of queer theory, pointed out that "[t]o maintain their position that sexuality amounts to male abuse of women and that pornography represents the essence of sexuality, MacKinnon et al. must make men in pornography invisible (and incomprehensible) except as the occupants of a monolithic position as perpetrators of sexual violence" (see also Segal, 1998). In addition, concern has been expressed about the issue of censorship, in particular the censorship of sexuality. Some feminists are anti-censorship but not necessarily pro-pornography (see Burstyn, 1985; Heider and Harp, 2002); others are pro-pornography (see Beggan and Allison, 2002; Cornell, 2000; Smith, 2002; Sonnet, 1999). The latter use the term "pornography" to refer to any explicit depictions of sexuality, and do not consider power to be either a central or a contentious issue. Any objections they raise against existing pornography pertain to poor production values and an orientation solely to male tastes. Pro-pornography feminists advocate support for a better-quality pornography—written, produced, and directed by women for women, designed to appeal to, explore, and extend female sexual fantasies and to promote discussion and debate about female sexuality—what amounts, in other words, to females literally writing, performing, and disseminating their own sexuality scripts.

There is some evidence that women are doing so. Podlas's (2000) investigation of 71 cyberporn sites found that 35 sites were female-owned, 32 were male-owned, and 4 were of mixed-sex ownership. A significant portion of cyberporn operators were female; of the 35 female-owned sites, all were owner-operated, and 34 sites featured the owner as performer.

Asked why they maintained cyberporn sites, female owner-operators cited the perceived opportunity for artistic expression, personal erotic pleasure, control of work environment, and increased salary. Aguilera (2000) reported that "countless Internet websites, many run by women" produce pornography that is aimed specifically at "devotees"—individuals sexually aroused by people with disabilities. Though some researchers have charged that disabled females inherit ascriptions of passivity and weakness and are often portrayed by both male and female pornographers as the "ultimate compliant sex object" (Elman, 2001), others claim that these Internet sites challenge the prevailing stereotypes of disabled persons as "asexual" and may be especially empowering for women with disabilities (Waxman-Fiduccia, 1999).

The pro-pornography movement stresses the importance of women gaining power and control over their sexuality and their roles in sexual scripts. Without the freedom to explore their own sexuality, they argue, women will remain bound by limitations created and enforced by men—and, through socialization conditioning, by women themselves. The "feminist sexuality wars"—between feminists who insist that only egalitarian, consensual, non-directive sexuality constitutes an acceptable sexuality for women, and others who reject so-called "vanilla" sexuality and argue that women should be encouraged and permitted to pursue any and all forms of sexual pleasure, including sadomasochism (e.g., Califia, 1997, 1996; Sheff, 2005)—have persisted for more than two decades and promise to continue. Moreover, the degree of success women will have in renegotiating existing heterosexuality scripts or in getting new scripts accepted remains to be seen. "The reality of heterosexual relationships, however, works against women redefining sexual practices" (Jackson and Scott, 1996: 19). Clearly, issues surrounding sexuality, gender, and power have yet to be resolved.

VIOLENCE IN INTIMATE RELATIONSHIPS

It has long been a central tenet of family sociologists that one of the major functions of the family is to provide members with protection from bodily harm by outsiders (Ogburn, 1922). Until relatively recently, sociologists assumed that intimate partners did not require protection from one another. Between the years 1939 and 1969, the *Journal of Marriage and the Family*—the principal journal for the sociological study of the family—did not contain a single article on husband–wife violence (O'Brien, 1971). Things were much the same in the popular press. Killoran's (1984) analysis of the content of *Chatelaine* magazine between 1939 and 1980 found that whereas 245 articles dealt with family conflict, a mere 11 addressed the issue of violence, and these attributed its incidence to individual pathology. Even though violence against intimate partners is hardly a new phenomenon, "the terms 'battered wife' and 'wife abuse' were not available as ways to think about the experience" prior to the 1970s (Walker, 1990: 97). These terms, along with "battered husbands," "husband abuse," and "partner abuse," have now been added to our intimacy lexicon and direct our attention to the phenomenon of **intimate violence**: actual or threatened acts of violence committed against persons by their current or former spouses, common-law partners, girlfriends, or boyfriends.

Defining Intimate Violence

Intimate violence is a complex phenomenon; finding a concept capable of capturing its essence and extent is a highly contentious task (Duffy and Momirov, 1997). Gender-neutral terms (e.g., *family violence, domestic violence, marital violence, conjugal assault, spousal abuse*) and gender-specific terms (e.g., *violence against women, woman abuse, wife abuse, wife battering, husband battering, husband abuse*) all reflect the theoretical, empirical, or ideological orientations of their creators and/or users. Existing definitions and their meanings may become even less precise when some writers insist on forging metaphysical links between real-life violence against women and the "symbolic annihilation" (Tuchman, 1978) of women on television and movie screens (Krassas et al., 2001; Monk-Turner and Purcell, 1999) or video games (Badique et al., 2002; Children Now, 2000).

A number of writers protest the use of gender-neutral terms as misleading. Based upon "historical and political justifications," Neidig and Friedman (1984: 3) urged the adoption of a "male-as-perpetrator view of spousal abuse"; Freedman (1985: 44) further argued that terms such as "marital violence" should be rejected, as they ignore "the direction [male to female] in which most of this violence flows" (see also Kimmel, 2002). Straus (1993: 76), on the other hand, maintained that research "does not support the hypothesis that assaults by wives are primarily acts of self-defense or retaliation" and strongly discouraged the use of terms that would pre-emptively deny the possibility of female violence. Moreover, Straus and Gelles (1988: 25) asserted that recognition of violent acts committed by women must be considered "a critically important issue for the safety and well-being *of women*" (emphasis in original). They elaborated as follows:

> Let us assume that most of the assaults by women are of the "slap the cad" genre and are not intended to and do not physically injure the husband. The danger to women of such behaviour is that it sets the stage for the husband to assault her. Sometimes this is immediate and severe retaliation. But regardless of whether that occurs, the fact that she slapped him provides the precedent and justification for him to hit her when she is being obstinate, "bitchy," or "not listening to reason" as he sees it. Unless women also forsake violence in their relationships with male partners and children, they cannot expect to be free of assault. Women must insist as much on non-violence by their sisters as they rightfully insist on it by men. (Straus and Gelles, 1988: 25–26)

Adopting this vantage point, Wallace (1996: 164–165) advocated gender-neutral terms, such as "spousal abuse" and "partner abuse."

At present, sociologists apply both narrow and broad definitions to concepts such as "abuse" and "violence." While early writers focused attention on physical abuse, it became increasingly evident that emotional and psychological abuse can also have devastating effects (Kirkwood, 1993; Schmidt, 1995), and that family members could experience a "continuum of unsafety" (Stanko, 1993). Accordingly, Straus and Gelles (1990: 23) recommended the extension of the term "abuse" to cover a variety of acts, including "verbal abuse or verbal battering, physical abuse, sexual abuse, and fiscal abuse." Similarly, Alvi et al. (2000: 219) argued that the "continuum" of family violence "ranges from non-physical acts such as insults to acts such as beatings and rapes" and maintained that "[n]one is automatically more injurious than another." Others, however, favour a far more delimited definition of abuse (Fekete, 1994; Pearson, 1997).

Rather than focusing on specific *acts*, Johnson and Ferraro (2001) directed attention to four *patterns* of violence within intimate partnerships: Situational couple violence, intimate terrorism, violent resistance, and mutual violent control. **Situational couple violence** or *common couple violence* refers to mutual violence that usually has its origins in arguments in a noncontrolling relationship that "get out of hand" but do not generally escalate to a serious or life-threatening level. **Intimate terrorism** or *patriarchal terrorism* is defined as violence motivated by a wish to control one's partner and involving the systematic use not only of physical violence but of economic subordination, threats, isolation, verbal and emotional abuse, and other control tactics. "Intimate terrorism is almost entirely perpetrated by men and is more likely to escalate over time and to result in serious injury" (Mooney et al., 2004: 145). **Violent resistance** refers to acts of violence committed in self-defence against a violent controlling partner and "is almost exclusively perpetrated by women against a male partner" (Mooney et al., 2004: 145). **Mutual violent control** is a reportedly rare form of abuse "that could be viewed as two intimate terrorists battling for control" (Johnson and Ferraro, 2001: 169).

The Incidence of Intimate Violence

Violence against women within intimate relationships has been transformed from a "private trouble" into a "public issue" (Mills, 1959) commanding the attention of academics, the media, the public, and collective action groups. Over the past four decades, there has been an explosion of knowledge about intimate violence. In Canada, social scientists and others wishing to understand the nature and extent of this phenomenon commonly draw upon two sources of data: official statistics (based on incidents reported to police, hospitals, or social service agencies) and victimization surveys (which ask respondents whether they have been victims of intimate violence). Analysis of police incident reports has consistently found that women are significantly more likely than men to be the victims of police-reported spousal violence (defined here as "cases of murder, attempted murder, sexual and physical assault, threats, criminal harassment and other violent offences in which the accused person is a spouse, ex-spouse or common-law partner of the victim" [Statistics Canada, 2003i]). Although rates of (police-reported) spousal violence against both men and women increased from 1995 to 2001, the rates of such violence against men were much lower than the rates against women: "In 2001, there were 344 incidents for every 100 000 women aged 15 and older in the population, compared with 302 in 1995. For men, there were 62 incidents for every 100 000 men in the population, up from only 37 six years ago" (Statistics Canada, 2003i). From 1998 to 2004, women represented 87 percent of the victims of partner abuse reported to Canadian police agencies (Johnson, 2006). "Visible minority women were more likely than other women to report spousal violence to the police: 45% compared with 35%. For immigrant women, reporting rates were very similar to non-immigrant women (39% compared with 37%) (Johnson, 2006: 57).

Under zero-tolerance policies now in place in Canadian police departments, police are obliged to lay a charge whenever there are "reasonable grounds" to believe that a domestic assault has occurred, regardless of the victim's stated preference, the presence/absence of visible injuries, or the availability of independent witnesses. However, Comack (2004: 184) has found that although this policy has resulted in "increasing numbers of men—and women—being charged," a "large proportion of charges" result in either a dismissal or stay of proceedings. Her analysis of spousal assault cases in Winnipeg revealed that 80 percent of charges against women and about half (51 percent) of those against men were subsequently stayed by the Crown. Johnson's (2006: 48) summary of research on sentencing in Canadian spousal violence cases reported the following: 80 percent of convictions were for common assault; women were more likely than men to be convicted of major assault; women convicted of spousal violence were more likely than men to be sentenced to probation while men were more likely to receive prison sentences; regardless of the specific violent offence committed, ex-spouses were more likely than current spouses to receive a prison sentence; among those who received a prison sentence, "more than one half of prison terms ordered ... were one month or less in duration in all offences, with the exception of major assault"; compared to others who commit major assaults, spouses receive prison sentences that are shorter on average.

The 2004 General Social Survey (GSS), using a large, representative Canada-wide sample, investigated both male and female experiences of violence at the hands of current/former legal or common-law spouses or same-sex partners. Respondents were asked to indicate if, "in the past 5 years, your spouse/partner has (1) threatened to hit you with his/her fist or anything else that could have hurt you; (2) thrown anything at you that could have hurt you; (3) pushed, grabbed, or shoved you in a way that could have hurt you; (4) slapped you; (5) kicked, bit, or hit you with his/her fist; (6) hit you with something that could have hurt you; (7) beaten you; (8) choked you; (9) used or threatened to use a gun or knife on you; (10) forced you into any unwanted sexual activity by threatening you, holding you down, or hurting you in some way." (Although this survey included questions about emotional abuse, the findings that follow reflect only physical abuse.)

Estimates derived from this survey suggested that 7 percent of Canadian women and 6 percent of Canadian men had experienced some form of violence at the hands of a current or former spouse over the preceding five years (Statistics Canada, 2005). Compared to men, women were more likely to have experienced severe forms of violence. Women were more likely than men to report having been beaten, choked, or threatened with a knife or gun (23 percent versus 15 percent) or sexually assaulted (16 percent versus 0 percent). Men were more likely to report having been pushed, shoved or slapped (40 percent versus 34 percent), or kicked, bitten, or hit (34 percent versus 10 percent). Aboriginal people were three times more likely than other Canadians to report having been assaulted by a spouse (21 percent of Aboriginal people [or, more specifically, 24 percent of Aboriginal women and 18 percent of Aboriginal men] compared with 7 percent of the non-Aboriginal population) (Statistics Canada, 2005; see also Statistics Canada, 2006j, 2007j).

Data from the 2004 GSS also indicated that, compared to male victims, female victims were more than twice as likely to have been injured, twice as likely to have been the target of violence on more than 10 occasions, five times more likely to have received medical attention, and three times more likely to report that the violence they experienced had caused them to fear for their lives. Women were also more likely than men to report multiple incidents of spousal violence. These findings are similar to those obtained from surveys conducted in the United States and Britain (Archer, 2000; Graham and Wells, 2001). The GSS data also revealed that women and men of all ages, incomes, and educational levels experienced violence within common-law and marital relationships. However, it found that rates of spousal violence were highest among "those aged 15 to 24; those in relationships of three years or less; those who had separated; and those in common-law unions" (Statistics Canada, 2005; see also Statistics Canada, 2006j, 2007j). In contrast to findings derived from reports to police agencies, the 2004 GSS found that rates of spousal violence were lower, rather than higher, for visible-minority women compared to non-visible-minority women (with a five-year rate of 4 percent versus 8 percent).

Intimate violence does not always end when a relationship breaks up—a fact addressed in the 1993 enactment of a law against "criminal harassment." Criminal harassment or "stalking" includes repeatedly following, communicating (via cards, letters, telephone, faxes, emails, or gifts), watching a person's home or workplace, and/or uttering direct or indirect threats or promises of violence or forcible intimacy. Stalking may stem from a variety of motives, including one partner's adamant refusal "to believe that the relationship has ended" (Kong, 1997; see also Mechanic et al., 2002; Sheridan et al., 2003). This criminal offence carries a maximum penalty of 10 years' imprisonment. Findings from the 2004 GSS indicate that female victims were more likely than male victims to report being stalked by a current or former spouse/dating partner (21 percent versus 10 percent); male victims were more likely than females to report being stalked by an acquaintance (e.g., neighbour, co-worker). Those who were stalked by a former intimate partner (spouse or boyfriend/girlfriend) were more likely than other victims of stalking to experience violence or threats, to fear that their life was in danger, and to be stalked for a longer period of time than those who were stalked by a stranger/acquaintance (with 60 percent of those who were stalked by former spouses harassed for more than a year). They were also more likely to report being stalked to the police and to seek a restraining order (Johnson, 2006; Statistics Canada, 2005; AuCoin, 2005, Rosenfeld and Harmon, 2002). Although criminal harassment does not typically culminate in murder, "between 1997 and 1999, it was identified as a precipitating factor in 12 percent of homicides committed by male ex-partners" (Johnson, 2007: 33).

Despite research proclaiming lesbian relationships to be the most egalitarian of all forms of intimate partnership (Blumstein and Schwartz, 1983; Eldridge and Gilbert, 1990), these relationships are not immune to violence (Ristock, 2003). West (2002: 121) concluded that "[i]ntimate partner violence may be as prevalent in intimate lesbian relationships as among heterosexuals" and noted that the "full range" of spousal violence may be evidenced within these relationships, including verbal, psychological, physical, and sexual abuse. Many of the dynamics characteristic of abusive heterosexual relationships are also found in abusive same-sex partnerships (Kurdek, 1994; Renzetti and Milley, 1996; Stanley et al., 2006). Like heterosexual abusers, the same-sex abuser is generally jealously possessive and uses violence or the threat of it to control his/her partner (Island and Letellier, 1991). As in heterosexual relationships, intimate violence in same-sex relationships often results from conflicts over relational commitment, autonomy, or dependency (Kurdek, 2000, 2000a; Ristock, 2003). Violence in lesbian relationships, paralleling the patterns found in heterosexual relationships, tends to increase in both frequency and severity over time (Renzetti, 1992; Renzetti and Milley, 1996), and to be associated with the use of alcohol or other drugs (Lockhart et al., 1994; Schilt, Lie, and Montagne, 1990; Fortunata and Kohn, 2003). As with individuals involved in heterosexual relationships, people involved in same-sex relationships are likely to deny or minimize intimate partner violence and to believe that such violence is at least partly the victim's fault (Renzetti and Curran, 2003).

Some differences have been observed between intimate violence in same- and opposite-sex relationships. Riedmann et al. (2004: 306) reported that "[l]esbians as well as gay men may fight back more often than do heterosexual women, a situation that leads to confusion about who is the battered and who is the batterer. Furthermore, some lesbians and gay men who are battered in one relationship may become batterers in another relationship." However, they noted that compared to heterosexual men who batter, lesbians who batter their intimate partners are less likely to feel that they have a right to do so and more likely to enter treatment voluntarily. Research suggests that intimate violence in same- and opposite-sex relationships may also differ in terms of the reactions it evokes from outsiders (Kuehnle and Sullivan, 2003; Rose, 2003). Poorman et al. (2003) asked 171 male and female university students to read scenarios describing a domestic abuse incident; the scenarios systematically varied the sexes of victim and perpetrator to produce four different conditions. Respondents perceived male-against-female abuse as more serious than same-sex abuse; they were also more likely to recommend that the victim press charges in male-against-female abuse than in same-sex abuse situations. As well, they perceived same-sex victims as less believable than heterosexual victims. A correlation was found between respondents' perceptions of a victim's believability and their sentencing recommendations—a finding that suggests that those who engage in violence in same-sex relationships may be accorded greater leniency.

Violence and sexual exploitation have been called the "darkside" (Lloyd, 1991) of courtship and dating. Although figures vary from one study to another, generally 15 to 40 percent of university students sampled report having either inflicted or suffered dating violence (e.g., DeKeseredy and Schwartz, 1998; Simons et al., 1998). According to one national survey of Canadian university and college students, about 14 percent of male students reported abusing a dating partner during the previous year, while almost 23 percent of female students reported having been victims of dating violence (DeKeseredy and Schwartz, 1998). Barnes et al. (1991) found that almost 43 percent of their all-male University of Manitoba sample had committed some form of physical abuse in their dating relationships. Pushing, slapping, and threats of violence were much more common than assault with a weapon or an object, and emotional abuse was more common than physical abuse. Some research has suggested that women are at least as likely as men to physically aggress in dating relationships (Stets, 1993; Stets and Henderson, 1991). However, a study which sought to investigate the "sexual symmetry thesis" using a national representative sample of Canadian university/college students found that "only a small number of women initiated such assaults" and "[a] large amount of the total violence reported by women was in self-defense" (DeKeseredy et al., 1997). Drinking alcohol prior to a conflict is associated with physical aggression among both men and women (Abbey et al., 2004; Gross et al., 2001; Lloyd and Emery, 2000; White and Chen, 2002).

An exploratory study using discussion groups with 24 Canadian teens ages 14 to 19 (Lavoie et al., 2000) found that teen dating relationships are often marred by violence. Other Canadian research has found males to be the most common perpetrators and females the most common targets of teen dating violence (Totten, 2003). Investigating the dating violence experienced by 521 adolescents (gay, lesbian, bisexual, and heterosexual) who attended a gay/lesbian/bisexual youth rally, Freedner et al. (2002) found that reports of dating violence were common across all sexual orientation groups. Although there were few statistically significant differences, bisexual males (controlling for age) were more likely than heterosexuals to report any type of dating violence, and bisexual females were more likely to report sexual abuse. Controlling for age, lesbians were more likely than heterosexual females to report fearing for their safety, and bisexual males and females were more likely than gays and lesbians to have faced threats of "outing."

In the case of **date rape**, the definition of intimate violence must be expanded to encompass the acts of acquaintances and even first-date "strangers" as well as of intimates (Kanin, 2003; Senn et al., 2000; Wilson and Leith, 2001). University women report a higher incidence of rape by a steady date than by an acquaintance or a stranger (Martin and Hummer, 2003). A Canadian survey (DeKeseredy and Kelly, 1993) found that 20.2 percent of female university students said they had engaged in unwanted sexual intercourse because they felt overwhelmed by a man's continued arguments and pressure; 6.6 percent reported having had unwanted sexual intercourse because a man threatened or used some degree of physical force against them; and 13.6 percent stated that while they were drunk or high on drugs, a man had attempted to engage them in unwanted acts of sexual intercourse. Ward et al. (1991) found that when their sample of American female university students was asked about their dating experiences in the past year, 34 percent reported experiencing some form of forced sexual contact, 20 percent had had a partner forcibly attempt intercourse, and 10 percent had experienced complete forcible vaginal, oral, or anal intercourse.

An all-female study conducted at an Ontario university revealed that while less than 1 percent of the sample acknowledged having been "raped" on a date during the previous year, 22 percent acknowledged having had intercourse when they did not want to because they felt "it was useless to attempt to stop him," and an additional 9 percent had had unwanted intercourse because they "felt pressured by his continual arguments" (DeKeseredy et al., 1993: 267). However, rape by a stranger is more likely to be defined as a criminal act and reported to authorities than rape by an acquaintance or, especially, by a partner in an ongoing intimate relationship (Geiger et al., 2004; Buddie and Miller, 2001; Frese et al., 2004). Because women are socially held responsible for the mainte-nance and regulation of intimate relationships (Osman, 2003) and are still likely to be blamed when an encounter exceeds acceptable boundaries, many women are reluctant to acknowledge to others or to themselves that the unacceptable has happened (Frese et al., 2004; Van Wie and Gross, 2001). Allison and Wrightsman (1993) reported that while women will frequently answer "yes" to the question "Have you ever had sex with a man when you did not want to, because he used physical force against you?" they will simul-taneously reply "no" when asked if they have ever been raped. Although men may also be the targets of coercive sexuality, they may be deterred from identifying themselves as victims of date rape by stereotypes that portray "real men" as being always eager for sex. When men do attempt to disclose being date-raped, others, including the police, may insist on alternative labels, suggesting that their experience of unwanted sexual acts may be "more correctly" viewed as "seduction" or "initiation" (Nelson, 1994).

Struckman-Johnson and Struckman-Johnson (2003) found that 43 percent of their sample of college men reported having had at least one incident of "pressured or forced sexual contact" with a woman since the age of 16 (see also Simono, 2002; Anderson and Struckman-Johnson, 1998). Research by Russell and Oswald (2001) on 285 undergraduate women found that 18 percent reported engaging in sexually coercive behaviour; overall, women reported using more verbal than physical tactics. Of the 52 respondents who had engaged in sexual coercion, 20 reported saying things that they did not mean, 12 reported obtaining sexual intercourse through continual arguments, but only 3 said that they had used physical force to obtain sex play (e.g., kissing, petting). Compared to those who did not report engaging in sexually coercive behaviours, coercive women exhibited higher tol-erance of sexual harassment and a *ludic* (manipulative, game-playing approach towards love) lovestyle. Regression analyses also found that women who were high in femininity were more likely to be sexually coercive—a finding that caused the researchers to specu-late that "women who have exaggerated femininity may use femininity in a manipulative manner" and to suggest that "[p]erhaps excessively feminine coercive women perceive their strategies as being "seductive" rather than "coercive" (p. 112). In addition, a signifi-cant difference was found between coercive and non-coercive women with respect to self-reported victimization; 81 percent of women who reported using coercive strategies identified themselves as having been sexually victimized at some point in the past.

Although Canadian sexual assault laws recognize both males and females as potential offenders *and* victims, conventional thinking may continue to construct date rape in gendered ways. For example, an analysis of questionnaires completed by 170 Canadian adults indi-cated that although the majority of respondents defined date rape in gender-neutral terms and included concepts of consent and force in their definitions, females "most often described a gender-specific understanding of rape as most of their scenarios described females as victims and males as perpetrators" (Verberg et al., 2000). In consequence, the figures provided above are likely to underestimate the full extent of date rape (see also Calder, 2004; Martin and Hummer, 2003).

Prior to the introduction of Canada's sexual assault laws in 1983, it was legally impossible for a man in this country to "rape" his wife, because the rape law contained a marital exemption. This legal exemption stemmed from the belief, encoded in law, that marriage gave a husband the right of sexual access to his wife. In consequence, a husband could only be charged with the rape of his wife if he was complicit in someone else's rape of her (e.g., if he forcibly restrained his wife while another man raped her), or upon the legal dissolution of the marriage. Since 1983, Canadian spouses can be charged for acts of sexual assault; however, such charges are extremely rare. Although an estimated 7 to 13 percent of married women have been raped by their husbands (Monson et al., 1996), victims, offenders, and the general public may resist labelling such acts as crimes. An American nationally representative telephone survey which examined attitudes towards wife-rape found that older, non-white respondents were less likely than others to believe that wife-rape occurs; older and less-educated respondents were less likely to believe that forced-sex scenarios between a husband and wife constituted "rape." Males, in general, and the more highly educated among both men and women, were less likely to believe that wife-rape occurs frequently. Among women, those who had never experienced forced sex were also significantly less likely than those who had to believe that wife-rape can occur (Basile, 2002).

Explanations

Researchers and theorists have attempted to find explanations for the violent victimization of women by men more than for any other form of intimate violence. Straus (1979) identified three factors which helped direct academic attention to violence against women. First, the social protest, political assassinations, and rise in violent crime that marked the 1960s and 1970s heightened sensitivity to the issue of violence in general. Second, during that same period, conflict theorists began to challenge functionalism's idealized view of the family, which had suggested that women and men led harmonious and complementary lives. Third, the second wave of the women's movement began. Feminists increasingly rejected traditional societal and academic understandings of violence against women, maintaining that there was "more to the story of 'battered women' than their experiences with violence and the relationship in which violence is enacted" (Kirkwood, 1993: 1). The women's movement raised the consciousness of our entire society about the extent of violence against women.

Feminist scholarship has been credited with directing the greatest amount of attention to the issue of intimate violence against women (Duffy and Momirov, 1997; DeKeseredy and Macleod, 1997; Godenzi et al., 2001; DeKeseredy and Dragiewicz, 2007). Feminism "explains and articulates the ways in which violence against women in the home is a critical component of the system of male power" (Yllo, 1993: 54). Defining a patriarchal system as one that affirms male control and promotes the suppression of women, feminists argue that, in a patriarchal society, violence against women is employed as a tool of social control at both the personal and institutional levels (Brownmiller, 1975). Restrictions placed upon women's personal and physical freedom are enforced by the fear and the threat of male-orchestrated violence (Schecter and Gary, 1989). Different feminist groups propose different ways to address the problem according to their particular perspectives. As Duffy and Momirov (1997: 136) observed, while radical feminists direct attention to the role of patriarchy and assert that ending violence requires a social transformation, socialist feminists "emphasize the role of economic forces (notably capitalism) in disempowering women." Ecofeminists, who "link violence against women with the general patterns of exploitation and destruction of the natural order endemic to the military industrial complex that currently dominates the world order," also feel that systemic change is essential. However, for liberal feminists, institutional changes (e.g., more shelters) will suffice.

"By the 1980s feminists, particularly radical feminists in the shelter movement, had developed their major theoretical initiative: the power and control approach to family violence and the wider society" (Duffy and Momirov, 1999: 136). Their basic message is that violence is a mechanism by which an individual male exerts or maintains his control over an individual female; the collective accretion of these individual acts manifests the reality that violence is a tool used by men to preserve male privilege. Dworkin (1974) coined the term **gynocide** to refer to the "systematic crippling, raping, and/or killing of women by men ... the relentless violence perpetrated by the gender class men on the gender class women"; she argued that "under patriarchy, gynocide is the ongoing reality of life lived by women" (Dworkin, 1974: 16, 19). In contrast, Thompson (1991), in a study of 336 undergraduates, reported that both men and women who abused their intimate partners had strong masculine gender orientations (i.e., valued control and dominance) and weak feminine gender orientations (i.e., placed lesser value on interpersonal harmony). This research suggested that gender orientation is a more salient factor in violence than the biological sex of the offender.

The sociologically oriented family-violence perspective accepts the importance of sexism and patriarchalism, but "emphasizes the family as a system embedded within the larger society" (Coates and Leong, 1988: 177). From this perspective, wife abuse "is only one aspect of the general pattern of family violence, which includes parent–child violence, child-to-child violence, and wife-to-husband violence" (Straus et al., 1980: 44). Proponents of this perspective claim that violence in intimate relationships stems from our society's acceptance of violence as a legitimate means of enforcing compliance and solving conflicts at the personal, national, and international levels (Viano, 1992). They maintain that violence and abuse within intimate relationships may be linked to cultural factors such as violence in the media, acceptance of corporal punishment, gender-role socialization, and the view of women and children as property. For example, drawing upon their five-year longitudinal study of the relationship between childhood victimization experiences and sexually coercive behaviours during adolescence and university, White and Smith (2004) reported that men who were physically punished or sexually abused or who witnessed domestic violence in childhood were more likely to perpetrate sexually coercive acts during their high school years. Men who engaged in these acts during high school were also at greater risk of engaging in sexually coercive behaviour while at university.

According to Gelles (1993: 35), it is the nature of family or intimate relationships, rather than the gendered relationship between men and women, that is the central violence-generating condition. Gelles identified a large number of factors that contribute to making the family (and any intimate relationship) a "violence-prone institution." These include (1) a high frequency of interaction between partners, which serves to increase a "time risk" for conflict and violence; (2) the participation by intimates in a wide array of activities together, increasing the likelihood that disagreements and tensions will surface; (3) intensity of involvement; the combination of (4) "built-in structural conflicts" and (5) the hierarchical structure of the family, according to which interactions between family members are founded upon power and dependence; and (6) the privacy and social isolation that surrounds intimate relations in our society and which decreases the likelihood of intervention by third parties.

The phenomenon of violence in lesbian relationships poses a challenge to those feminists who argue that the abuse of power and the use of violence is uniquely and essentially "male" (Schilit et al., 1990). Ristock (1991) stated that in the past, lesbians have been averse to breaking the silence surrounding violence in lesbian relationships out of fear of promoting and exacerbating negative stereotypes. She has suggested that violence in lesbian relationships may be understood as part of "a continuum of violence against women, the roots of which are in the hierarchical, oppressive nature of our society," and claims that through the mechanism of socialization, lesbians learn to hate women and to "accept violence as a form of power and control" (Ristock, 1991: 75; see also Corteen, 2002; Giorgio, 2002). According to this paradigm, lesbian violence represents internalized misogyny that results from "institutionalized and internalized homophobia and heterosexism" (Ristock, 1991: 75). A complementary viewpoint is put forward by Renzetti (1992): Observing that intimate abuse among lesbians is associated with the dynamics of power and dependency, Renzetti suggested that lesbians, like heterosexuals, are raised to recognize families as hierarchical social units and to appreciate that the person who has the greater amount of resources holds the greater amount of power. As White and Kowalski (1994: 485) remarked, "to the extent that power corrupts men, it may also corrupt women."

Explanations for courtship violence and date rape focus upon a combination of gender expectations and the sociosexual norms embodied in our dominant courtship and sexuality scripts. Traditional male gender roles encourage men to be aggressive and dominant in male–female relationships (Stets and Pirog-Good, 1990). Accordingly, Russell (1975: 206) has argued, rape may be not so much a deviant act as an instance of **overconforming**. From this perspective, rape can be viewed as an exaggerated form of "normal" gender relations in sexual situations. However, Messerschmidt (1993) contended that the relationship between masculinity and violence—whether in the form of physical assault, sexual assault, or sexual harassment—is far more complex. He emphasized that not all men engage in violent or abusive behaviour and that "masculinity" is not a "fixed entity," but "socially constructed and reconstructed." In consequence, a number of "masculinities" exist.

Messerschmidt stated that "[i]n contemporary Western industrialized societies, **hegemonic masculinity** is defined through work in the paid-labour market, the subordination of women, heterosexism, and the driven and uncontrollable sexuality of men" (1993: 82; see also Connell and Messerschmidt, 2005). Yet a number of different "masculinities" are also possible and "are constructed relative to an individual man's position in society, the resources at hand, and the constraints of specific circumstances" (Johnson, 1996: 22–23). He suggested that sexual assault can be seen as a "gendered response" and as "the product of a specific type of constructed masculinity that represents the desire to dominate, control and humiliate women" (in Johnson, 1996). From this vantage point, sexual assault and battering represent attempts on the part of some men who are denied masculine status in other ways (e.g., economic success) to construct masculinity through physical and sexual demonstrations of power. According to Messerschmidt, the "fewer the resources for proving maleness legitimately, the greater is the need to dominate women physically" (in Johnson, 1996).

Support of this position is provided by Anderson (1997), who noted that men who earn less money than their partners are more likely to be violent towards them. The researcher offers the following explanation of such behaviour: "Disenfranchised men ... must rely on other social practices to construct a masculine image. Because it is so clearly associated with masculinity in ... [our] culture, violence is a social practice that enables men to express a masculine identity" (Anderson, 1997: 667).

Key Terms

afterplay	face-to-face friendships	micromanipulation
bride wealth	feeling work	monogamy
concrete resource	feminization of love	mutual violent control
courtship	FILO	overconforming
date rape	foreplay	passionate love
dating differential	gynocide	performance anxiety
deep talk	hegemonic masculinity	personal resource
deficit model of manhood	homogamy	pornography
demand–withdrawal pattern	hypergamy	principle of least interest
dormancy	hypogamy	romantic love
dowry	intimate terrorism	side-to-side friendships
egalitarian relationships	intimate violence	situational couple violence
emotion work	LIFO	small talk
endogamy	macromanipulation	structural power
erotica	marriage gradient	vigilance
exchange theory	masturbation	violent resistance

Chapter Summary

1. Although we might prefer to think of our quest for an intimate partner as an intensely unique and personal odyssey, mating gradients and changing gender expectations and behaviours all place different, yet interrelated, constraints on our options.

2. Women and men exhibit distinct styles of relating to others. These styles are partly the product of changing historical circumstances and partly the product of differential socialization.

3. Although relationships differ in terms of how explicitly or obviously power is manifested, a power dimension is always present. As has been the case historically, males generally control the resources of money and social status, whereas females generally control the resources of love and sexuality. Even though this distribution is slowly being transformed, current conditions promote "bargaining" or an exchange of resources within intimate relationships. However, this is not necessarily an exchange between equals, and the resulting relationships are unlikely to be egalitarian.

4. Observable differences in human sexuality are not biologically driven; rather, they are socially constructed through lifelong participation in differential socialization processes within variable sociocultural contexts. Part of socialization involves exposure to social definitions, which construct distinctive sexuality scripts for men and women and also privilege some forms of sexuality and censure others.

5. Only recently have family sociologists acknowledged the problem of violence in intimate relationships. Attempts to name and frame the problem of intimate violence, to define its parameters, measure its incidence, and explain it remain steeped in controversy.

CHAPTER 8

Marriage and Parenting

Marriage, while indisputably an "intimate relationship," is also governed by laws and unique informal conventions. As recently as two decades ago, Canadian law "took little notice of a union known as 'common-law marriage'" (Dranoff, 2001: 99). Since then, in response to the increased social acceptance of **cohabitation** for both opposite- and same-sex couples, Canadian courts have gradually broadened the legal definition of "spouse" and extended many of the rights and obligations that were once associated exclusively with marriage (e.g., spousal support, spousal Canada Pension Plan benefits) to partners in "marriage-like" relationships (Bailey, 2000: 3). In 2000, for example, the federal government enacted the *Modernization of Benefits and Obligations Act*, which equalized the treatment of same-sex and opposite-sex common-law couples under 68 federal laws (EGALE, 2001). Perhaps the most noteworthy change, however, has occurred in relation to the definition of **marriage** itself.

In July 2002, three Ontario Superior Court judges made Canadian legal history when they ruled that the opposite-sex limitation in common law (which restricted marriage to the union of one man and one woman) was unconstitutional. This decision was echoed in 2003 in British Columbia, and, in 2004, in Manitoba, Nova Scotia, Saskatchewan, Quebec, and Newfoundland and Labrador. In the fall of 2004, the federal government presented a "Reference re Same-Sex Marriage" to the Supreme Court of Canada, requesting that the Court clarify whether the opposite-sex requirement for marriage was consistent with the guarantees of equality enshrined in the *Canadian Charter of Rights and Freedoms*. In response, the Supreme Court stated that the federal government had the power to change the definition of marriage to include same-sex couples and that their doing so would be constitutional. The Supreme Court of Canada likened our system of laws to a "living tree which by way of progressive interpretation, accommodates and addresses the realities of modern life," noting that the definition of marriage in Canada's constitution "does not exclude same-sex marriage." The Court also observed that the clergy could, as an expression of freedom of religion, refuse to conduct marriage ceremonies involving same-sex couples. With the passage of Bill C-38, Parliament changed the definition of marriage to comply with the *Charter* and, on July 20, 2005, the *Civil Marriage Act* received royal assent.

MARRIAGE

An overwhelming majority of the populations of Canada and the United States have participated in legal marriage for a substantial portion of their adult lives. Ninety percent of the adult American population eventually marry (with recent surveys reporting that "generations X and Y are even more enthusiastic about marriage than their predecessors" [Skolick, 2006: 85]), while close to 95 percent of the population born in Canada between the mid-1800s and the mid-1900s married at least once before reaching the age of 50 (Le Boudrais et al., 2000). In 2006, of the total population of Canada age 15 and older, just over one third had never been married (38.2 percent of the males and 31.7 percent of the females); almost half (47.9 percent) were currently married (49.4 percent of the males and 46.5 percent of the females); about 3 percent had been married at least once but were currently separated (2.7 percent of the males and 3.2 percent of the females); roughly 8 percent were divorced (7.2 percent of the males and 8.8 percent of the females); and just over 6 percent were widowed (2.5 percent of the males and 9.7 percent of the females) (Statistics Canada, 2008g, 2007a). To put it another way, at the start of the new millennium, roughly two thirds of Canadians (62 percent of males and 68 percent of females) were, or had been, involved in a legal marital relationship. The 2006 Canadian census, reflecting the 2005 legalization of same-sex marriages across Canada as of July 2005, was the first to enumerate same-sex married couples. It reported that of Canada's 45 300 same-sex couples, about 16.5 percent (7500) were married; "[o]ver half (53.7%) of same-sex married spouses were men in 2006, compared with 48.3% who were women (Milan et al., 2007: 12).

Orientations towards, and experiences of, marriage vary significantly for men and women. Marriage represents a much more important "stamp," as it were, in the passport to adult femininity than it does in the passport to adult masculinity. At least since the time of the "cult of true womanhood" in the 1800s, the Traditional Marriage Enterprise (Levinson, 1996) has stressed the centrality of marriage to women's lives. Marriage still is emphasized in today's Modified Marriage Enterprise (Levinson, 1996; Humble et al., 2008) although it shares centre stage with paid employment. For women, one of the chief motives for entering into heterosexual marriage used to be to gain economic security or advancement (Saxton, 1996: 239). Socialized to the belief that only men should engage in paid labour, and denied opportunities for employment, women were forced to rely upon marriage for survival. Nowadays, women are less likely to perceive marriage as an economic necessity. Nevertheless, given the persistence of the wage gap, marriage still offers significant financial incentives; indeed, for most women, marriage still promises a higher standard of living than singlehood.

In the past, men derived direct economic benefits from marriage in the form of the **dowry** (transfer of money or property that accompanied a bride). Today, men can anticipate an improvement to their own standard of living if they marry an employed woman *or* man. Sweeney and Cancian (2004) report that men today, in comparison to decades past, are more likely to take into consideration the earning power of their potential matrimonial partners (see also England, 2004). Men also obtain indirect economic benefits from marriage in the form of housework and child care. In general, marriage continues to furnish men with more physical comforts than singlehood. Women may also be motivated to marry by the prospect of protection for themselves and their children (although enhanced security does not always ensue). As well, women (to a greater extent than men) may see marriage as a socially acceptable way of gaining independence from parents and restrictive parental supervision.

While the proportion of young Canadian adults (both married and unmarried) who live in their parents' homes has been rising over the past two decades, smaller proportions of women do so than men (Riedmann et al., 2004: 158; Statistics Canada, 2006k, 2007k). The finding that young men ages 20 to 34 are more likely than their female counterparts to remain in the parental nests has "led to speculation about male domestic dependency that is not always flattering" (Riedmann et al., 2004: 159): "There is hot food on the table and clean socks in the drawers. Mom nags a little and dad scowls a lot, but mostly they don't get in the way" (Gross, 1991: 1). However, "[p]arents do 'get in the way' of women who live at home. They are more likely to try to limit daughters' freedom to come and go or to be suspicious of suspected sexual activity" (Riedmann et al., 2004: 160). Living under more constraints as adolescents and young adults, women may view marriage as a visa to independence and sexual freedom.

For both women and men, marriage may be an act of social conformity. A study of 26 gay or bisexual men (mean age 47.5 years) who were married to women reported that "internalized homophobia is a factor that leads men into mixed-orientation marriages," and noted that the two most frequent reasons for heterosexual marriage cited by respondents were that "it seemed natural, and a desire for children and family life" (Higgins, 2002: 29).

Moreover, even though a growing proportion of Canadians are opting (at least temporarily) for cohabitation (with the number of common-law-couple families rising 18.9 percent between 2001 and 2006 [Statistics Canada, 2007a]), legal marriage remains a commonly accepted indicator of adult status in our society. Family and friends may encourage courting couples to "settle down." Socialization messages also encourage women to see marriage as an essential means of fulfilling their gender destiny. According to our heterosexist cultural folklore, for every woman, there exists a "Mr. Right"—the ideal man who will marry and live with her in happily-ever-after fashion; furthermore, the three most important days in a woman's life are held to be the day she gets engaged, the day she gets married, and the day she gives birth.

These cultural messages, however, are increasingly being challenged. When asked to rate the importance of marriage to happiness in life, just over 70 percent of Canadian women in 1984 and 67 percent in 1995 rated marriage as "very important" or "important" (Wu, 2000: 65–66). In 1995, Canadian women rated marriage as less important than did Canadian men (although the difference is slight): In Quebec, for example, just over 53 percent of women and 59 percent of men rated marriage as "very important" or "important" (Wu, 2000: 65–66; see also Laplante, 2006). Observing a similar trend in the United States, Goldscheider (1997) has called women's growing lack of interest in marriage a "revolution."

Ehrenreich (1983) claimed that whereas in the 1940s men sought to demonstrate their masculinity through marriage and the "good provider" role, from the 1950s through the 1980s a "breadwinner revolt" occurred, with singlehood increasingly legitimated as a viable option. More recently, Gerson (1993) suggested that changes in our economy have made the role of family breadwinner more difficult and less appealing to a growing number of men. Nevertheless, despite "clear evidence that people now place less emphasis on marriage than they did a decade ago ... we should not lose sight of the broader picture: A majority of Canadians feel that it is very important, or important, to be married.... Marriage is not going out of style soon" (Wu, 2000: 66; see also Clark and Compton, 2006; Skolnick, 2006).

Marital Roles

Outside of Quebec, Canadian family law (the body of law that governs relations between spouses and their children) derives from the English common law system. **Common law** is a system of dispute resolution that evolved out of decisions arrived at by the English courts of justice from the time of the Norman Conquest (1066). This body of law is derived from custom and judicial precedent. In contrast, the legal system of Quebec is based on **civil law** and has its origins in the French and Roman codification of law tradition; family law in that province has also been heavily influenced by the teachings of the Catholic Church. Both systems of law have historically upheld a vision of the family in which the husband/father was paramount and the labour and services of the wife belonged to her husband as a right.

Under common law, wives did not exist as independent beings: "By marriage, the husband and wife are one person in law; the very being or legal existence of the woman is suspended during the marriage, or at least is incorporated and consolidated in that of the husband, under whose wing, protection and cover, she performs everything" (Blackstone, 1805: 442). A man, upon marriage, automatically became head of the household, and in that capacity was expected to provide protection, security, and financial maintenance (food, shelter, and clothing) for his wife and their children. A woman, upon marriage, was expected to assume domestic responsibility for household and child care, and to make herself sexually available to her husband. Early matrimonial law decreed that a husband assumed control or ownership of his wife's personal property and that a wife was not entitled to compensation for her labour. Similarly, the Quebec Civil Code "consecrated a notion of 'paternal authority,' which made the husband the head of the family and gave him considerable powers over his wife and children" (Grey, 1999: 816).

The concept of wife as property was evident in legal provisions allowing husbands to receive compensation for loss of **consortium**. English common law decreed that a husband had a right to his wife's company and services (including sex) and could sue a third party who interfered with his enjoyment of this right. The underlying assumption here was that "since wifely services could easily be equated with those of any servant, legal liabilities for interference with the master–servant relationship was easily extended to cases of injury to the husband–wife relationship" (Steel, 1987: 159). In such actions, compensation commensurate with the presumed value of the woman as a wife and mother (as demonstrated by her conduct and social character) would be awarded. In some Canadian provinces, such as British Columbia, Alberta, Saskatchewan, and Quebec, a husband did not have to prove that he had lost the totality of his wife's company and services, but merely that he had sustained a partial or temporary loss of one aspect of the marital relationship, such as sexual relations. Until 1952, the House of Lords in Britain recognized no such rights for wives. Whereas an attack on a man's wife was legally construed as an attack upon the husband and his estate, "an attack on the man ... did not interfere with any right the woman had, unless the man could no longer provide her with support and protection" (Rozovsky and Rozovsky, 1982: 62).

Old English Common Law additionally recognized the wrongful act of **criminal conversation**, defined as a man having sex with another man's wife without the husband's consent. This **heartbalm tort** (Brode, 2002) gave a cuckolded husband the right to sue his wife's lover in civil court and claim financial compensation for "injury to his feelings, the blow to his marital honour and his loss of honour and the hurt to his matrimonial and family life." A husband's right to sue his wife's paramour was not nullified by the wife's consent to the act(s) of extramarital sex, nor was the husband required to prove that the adulterous conduct had resulted in the separation of the spouses. Although the right to sue for criminal conversation was abolished in England in 1857, it persisted in Ontario until 1978 and even longer in the Atlantic and Prairie provinces (Rozovsky and Rozovsky, 1982: 62).

Following the passage of the *Married Women's Property Act of 1882* in England, similar acts, permitting wives to hold property separately from their husbands, were passed in common-law jurisdictions in both Canada and the United States. Since then, and with growing momentum since the 1970s, reforms have altered the formerly harsh legal situation of married women. In general, "[t]he thrust of legal reform has been on ensuring that both men and women have equality of opportunity. Legal rules have been made gender neutral, so much so that there are no more wives or husbands in family law, only spouses" (Steel, 1987: 160). Quebec's revised Civil Code (1980) insisted on the absolute equality of spouses; both spouses possess the same rights and obligations and "owe each other respect, fidelity, succour and assistance." The married couple "are bound to live together ... [and] together take in hand the moral and material direction of the family, exercise parental authority and assume the tasks resulting therefrom."

Such legal pronouncements notwithstanding, gender remains an organizing principle in heterosexual marriages. Blumstein and Schwartz (1983: 324) noted that "gender provides a shortcut and avoids the decision-making process" when it comes to assigning roles, such as who takes out the garbage, initiates sexual contact, or does housework (see also Kaufman and Taniguchi, 2006; Waller, 2005). Gays and lesbians, however, are less likely to adopt traditional masculine and feminine roles in their relationships (Kurdak, 2003; Shumsky, 2001). In his discussion of gay male relationships, Blachford (1981/1995: 68) argued that homosexual men are "more able to ignore the so-called 'natural connection between sexual position (inserter, insertee, for example) and gender role. In other words, if one partner gets fucked, he is not necessarily expected to make the breakfast the next morning or act effeminately." A recent study compared the division of household labour among three groups of people—212 lesbians and 123 gay men who had gotten civil unions in Vermont (during the first year that this option was available), 166 lesbians and 72 gay men (in the first group's friendship network) who had not sought civil unions, and 219 heterosexual married women and 193 heterosexual married men (consisting of the first group's siblings and their spouses). Married heterosexual couples were found to have a more traditional division of labour and child care than did lesbians and gay men in both types of couples (Solomon et al., 2004). In general, research has found same-sex unions to be characterized by greater equality and role-sharing than heterosexual marriages (Golden, 2004). One factor promoting this pattern may be that "pairings of two men and two women generally provide members of the couple with similar incomes, whereas a heterosexual couple tends to be characterized by higher income, and therefore more power, for males" (Riedmann et al., 2003: 164; see also Burgoyne, 2004; Goddard, 2003). According to Shehan and Kammeyer (1997: 154), "gay and lesbian relationships rarely pattern themselves after heterosexual husband-and-wife roles. They are more likely to follow a best friends or roommates model that emphasizes similarity of experiences and equal sharing of resources and responsibility" (see also Peplau and Fingerhut, 2007).

Nye and Berardo (1973) have distinguished six adult roles within marriage and the family: *provider, housekeeper, sexual, therapeutic, child-care,* and *child-socialization*. These **marital roles**, along with a seventh, *kinkeeper*, will be discussed in turn.

Provider, Housekeeper, and Sexual Roles Previous chapters have discussed the gendered **provider**, **housekeeper**, and **sexual roles** in depth; therefore, it will suffice at this point to note that the majority of marriages in the early 2000s feature two providers rather than a solitary male "breadwinner." However, the housekeeper role is still performed primarily by wives. The husband is still most likely to be the prime initiator of marital sexual contact; as a result, the sexual rhythms of a marriage are mostly likely to conform to his preferences.

Therapeutic Role The **therapeutic role** comprises a bundle of activities oriented towards the care and maintenance of the marital relationship and of the spouse's physical and emotional health. "The therapeutic role for women appears to be clearly recognized.... Women should listen to their husbands' frustrations, serve as a 'sounding board' for their novel ideas, build them up when they are discouraged, and reassure them when they feel insecure" (Nye and Berardo, 1973: 258). Although in theory either spouse could perform it, social expectations dictate that the therapeutic role be assigned to the wife (Minnotte et al., 2007; Strazdins and Broom, 2004; Zipp et al., 2004). This has to do, in part, with the traditional hierarchical structure of marriage; the inferior partner is expected to minister to the superior partner (Baker and Jacobsen, 2007; Heyn, 1997: 173). However, it also has to do with the presumption that women are better qualified than men, either innately or via specialized socialization, to perform the part. In the words of one respondent, "I understood that I was the relationship pro. That it was 'our' marriage, but my emotional responsibility. I was the one who would end the fight, manage the emotional stuff, keep the marriage on an even keel.... I was the one who was better at relationships, so my new position sort of codified that responsibility" (Heyn, 1997: 37). It has been consistently found that whereas husbands' negative emotions are directed towards and absorbed by their wives, the reverse does not occur (Larson and Almeida, 1999: 6); this fact offers indirect evidence of the allocation of the therapeutic role to the wife.

The therapeutic role embodies the quality of "selflessness" long attributed to the "good woman." The "good wife" (Heyn, 1997: 89) and/or "good mother" is encouraged to fashion a career out of these roles, to identify her husband and children as parts of her "extended self" (Belk, 1988) and to perform unpaid labour on their behalf. Activities not related to the better provision of service to husband and children may be viewed as "selfishness" and a violation of the good wife role. Whether such selfishness is a vice or a virtue is a focal point of debate between champions of "traditional family values" (of which the good wife role is one) and proponents of an alternative vision. While the debates continue, contemporary wives often feel that they have a right to some selfishness, yet experience guilt over asserting that right.

In addition to emotional nurturance, wives are expected to provide their husbands with physical care and therapy. Upon marriage, a wife is to commence monitoring her husband's lifestyle (particularly his diet) as "proof" of her love and concern for his well-being (Ross, 1995). Such monitoring may also extend to his wardrobe ("Are you going out wearing that?"), on the principle that a devoted wife ought not to allow her husband to incur public derision because of his taste in apparel. Most husbands—except for those with a high possessiveness–jealousy quotient—do not usually monitor or try to change their wives to such a degree. Comments about their wives' appearance are more likely to be general than specific (e.g., "You look nice" versus "You look much better in bold colours than in pastels"), and prompted (i.e., as a response to queries such as "Do I look fat in these pants?") rather than spontaneous (e.g, "Wow! With that perm, you look uncannily like Sponge Bob!"). What is more, wives monitor themselves: their own voices, "their dress, their mannerisms, [and] their entire self presentation" to become "less playful, less flirtatious, less ambitious, less assertive, less sexual, less open, and less honest with their partners, their families, their friends, and themselves" (Heyn, 1997: 26). In the name of protecting the images of her marriage, husband, and self, a woman may wear a mask with practically everyone.

Another function of the therapeutic role is to create and maintain marital and family rituals. Dyck and Daly (2006) report that while fathers play an important role in instigating "couple time," mothers play a significant role in its implementation. In addition, wives are usually the family social coordinators, keeping track of important dates and organizing birthdays, anniversaries, quiet evenings at home, holidays, meal times, as well as celebrations of career moves and promotions, school recitals and graduations. Possible exceptions are Valentine's and Mother's days, in which cases advertisers provide the reminders, offer suggestions for expressing love and appreciation in material form, and hint that such efforts will be amply rewarded (see Phipps et al., 2001; Such, 2006).

Kinkeeper The **kinkeeper** (Rosenthal, 1995) maintains formal and informal ties with relatives or friends, all regarded as members of an extended family. The kinkeeper, typically the wife, is in charge of acknowledging special occasions and buying, expressing appropriate sentiments in, and sending cards and suitable gifts. If the kinkeeper does not perform these tasks directly, she usually is in charge of prompting other family members to perform them (Salari and Zhang, 2006). Failing that, husbands and children usually turn to her to learn what cards, gifts, and appropriate sentiments were sent on their behalf. Kinkeepers also maintain informal ties via phone calls and email, shared meals or coffees, shopping, etc. Kinkeeping may also involve providing physical care and emotional sustenance to aging, ill, or infirm members of the extended family.

Viewed from one standpoint, therapy and kinkeeping fall under "companionship"; viewed from another, they fall under "community service." Wives provide the familial counterpart of governmental social services; as federal, provincial, and municipal governments cut back on crucial services in the politically expedient name of fiscal responsibility, it is wives and mothers who are called upon to assume an increasing share of the burden. The new fiscal and social conservatism places a number of additional burdens upon wives. The majority of employees in the education, social-services, and health-care fields are women; what is more, it is women who tend to access these services the most, either for themselves or on behalf of family members. Thus, women are hit with a triple whammy: They are not only the most likely to lose their jobs, but also the most likely to suffer from cutbacks to subsidized child care, children's special-needs programs, nursing homes, caregiver respite, home care for the sick/elderly, mental-health services, and hospital beds—and, to top it off, they are required to replace those missing services as part of their own unpaid labour.

Armstrong (1996: 223) argued that "cutbacks in health care are accompanied by [an] attempt to resurrect 'the family' and make into family responsibilities many of the services that have, for years, been provided by paid female workers in the public sector." Such expectations conveniently ignore the fact that a large percentage of wives and mothers are still employed, despite the cutbacks, and are already performing a "double shift." The call to return the care of family members into the hands of women acknowledges neither the increasing length of time such care may be required (especially in the case of elder care), nor the increased sophistication of the kinds of home medical care demanded today. Women no longer learn many skills needed to perform various kinds of homecare (how many women today can change surgical dressings or confidently administer intravenous medications?). Nevertheless, if present trends continue, the ideal kinkeeper role will expand substantially.

Marital Interaction

Despite the fact that all marriages are unique in some respects, research has consistently found certain gendered patterns of **marital interaction**.

Epstein et al. (1994) concluded that during marital arguments, wives are more likely than husbands to engage in direct negative communication patterns, which include complaining, fault-finding, and making belittling or derogatory comments; participants often refer to these behaviours as "nagging." Part of this gender difference is attributable to men's greater likelihood of either retreating into silence or leaving the scene of a conflict, especially when a discussion focuses upon emotional issues (Dunbar and Burgoon, 2005; Vogel et al., 2007). Husbands' physical and emotional withdrawal constitutes indirect negative communication. While more likely to engage in direct negative communication, wives also more effectively and more frequently communicate positive, complimentary, or loving messages. As noted in the previous chapter, husbands typically attempt to convey positive messages indirectly, via activities whose intentions and meanings are subject to misinterpretation (e.g., offering advice, washing the car, initiating sexual contact). Wives perform instrumental activities as well, but typically also extend unambiguously soothing words to bridge disrupted harmony or (re)establish emotional intimacy (Weigel et al., 2006).

During the exchange of traditional wedding vows, wives promise to "obey" their husbands and husbands promise to "cherish" their wives, a difference that establishes a basis for patriarchal marital relationships. Since the 1947 wedding of then-Princess Elizabeth to Prince Philip, women in our society have been released from automatically taking a vow of obedience, and few women today incorporate the traditional wording into their wedding ceremonies. However, despite the deletion of that symbolic affirmation of inequality, the vast majority of marriages today are still characterized by an imbalance of power stemming from other sources. The "bride and groom" are transformed into "husband and wife" and "Mr. and Mrs. (insert his family last name here)," linguistic constructions which signal male precedence.

Resource power derived from income and benefits, pensions, occupational prestige, age, height, weight, body mass, and strength are unequally distributed in favour of husbands in most marriages. In accordance with social expectations and limited alternatives, wives typically have more of a social, psychological, and economic stake in marriage than do husbands; this imbalance grants husbands, according to the "principle of least interest," an additional source of power.

As discussed in Chapter 7, husbands usually hold the balance of coercive physical power within marriage and even beyond the boundaries of a legally dissolved marriage (Rogers et al., 2005; Stets and Burke, 2005). Wives typically hold the balance of sexual power in marriage and are much more likely than husbands to use sexuality as a bargaining chip in non-sexual realms of marital relations (Blumstein and Schwartz, 1983; Bryant and Schofield, 2007; Radner, 2008; van de Rijt, 2006). Udry's (1968) early research reported that relationship satisfaction precedes sexual satisfaction for wives, but the converse is true for husbands. This pattern, reported more recently by Oggins et al. (1993), Maass (2007), and Castaneda and Burns-Glover (2004), is congruent with the typical sexuality socialization experienced by men and women in our society. Unless a marital relationship provides a desired level of stability and security, wives are less likely to commit themselves sexually in a wholehearted fashion. The statement, "I can't fight with you all day and want to have sex with you at night" is more likely to be voiced by a woman than a man (Beck and Bozman, 1995; Knox and Schacht, 1997: 292; Weigel et al., 2006). To husbands, however, sexual satisfaction is a most important barometer of overall marital satisfaction (Betchen, 2006).

Over the past three decades, research has consistently found that the arrival of children and parenting responsibilities result in a noticeable decline in marital quality; this occurs earlier and more precipitously for wives than for husbands (e.g., Bird, 1997; Collins and Coltrane, 2000; Roxburgh, 1997). Mothers assume the lion's share of children's care and socialization. Wives/mothers also do most of the housework, and the majority hold jobs as well. These tremendous demands upon their time and energies typically leave wives/mothers with depleted resources to devote to the care and maintenance of their husbands. Husbands' evaluations of marital quality deteriorate following the birth of each child, partly as a consequence of feeling rejected and no longer the sole focus of wifely attention (Cowan and Cowan, 1992). Even though young couples today claim to favour a more equitable distribution of labour in their homes, empirical evidence indicates that they actually replicate and perpetuate traditional patterns of inequality (Brewster and Padavic, 2000; Van Willigen and Drentea, 2001).

His and Hers Marriages Bernard (1973) was one of the first sociologists to argue that marriage has such different meanings and consequences for women and men that generalizations about marriage *per se,* which ignore gender differences, are almost meaningless. The notion of **his and hers marriage** suggests that in each legal union, "his marriage" differs anywhere from a little to a lot from "her marriage" (see also Waller, 2005).

Research has found that various health benefits are associated with marriage (Collins and Coltrane, 2000; Waite and Gallagher, 2000); the mental and physical well-being of cohabitants has been found to be midway between that of singles and marrieds (Kurdek, 1991). White (1992) cautioned Canadians not to accept the results of these largely American studies uncritically, emphasizing that in the United States, where health care is not a universal right "but a commodity to be sold at the highest price" (Henslin and Nelson, 1996: 567), being married may simply increase the likelihood of being able to afford superior care or obtain medical coverage through a spouse's employer. Thus, it may be the increased accessibility of health care, rather than marriage, that accounts for some of the health advantages enjoyed by married couples in that country. This caveat should be borne in mind as we continue our discussion.

Research has indicated that married men are generally healthier than are never-married, widowed, and divorced men, while married women are less healthy than never-married, widowed, and divorced women (Lips, 2005). Married men are also generally healthier than married women. Rates of physical, emotional, and mental illness among never-married, widowed, and divorced men have been found to be either comparable or slightly higher than rates among women (Graham et al., 2006; Murphy et al., 1997; Wickrama et al., 1997). The most striking mental-health differences have been found between married men and stay-at-home housewives, between housewives and women not currently married, and between housewives and employed wives (Riedmann et al., 2003: 170; Whisman et al., 2006).

Two major types of explanations have been offered for these findings. The **selectivity hypothesis** holds that only certain kinds of people are selected to become or remain marriage partners, while other kinds are found wanting and rejected (Angier, 1998). While this hypothesis might explain the male health–gender connection, it fails to explain the connection between marriage and women's health. An alternative explanation is that the institution of marriage, as traditionally and presently constituted, causes the observed outcomes. Specifically, while men benefit from wives' performance of a therapeutic role in marriage, no such benefits accrue to wives themselves (Renzetti and Curran, 2003: 397).

It has been suggested that the disadvantages of marriage for women are built into the transformative process of becoming a wife. Bernard, who initially (1942) proposed the **shock theory of marriage** for women, cited research indicating the presence of an almost **reverse Pygmalion effect**, whereby traditional housewives gradually lose their sense of independence, become more submissive and accommodating, and slowly become much like their husbands. Eventually, in keeping with the words often intoned during wedding ceremonies, the "two shall become as one," and that "one" is the husband. Problems experienced by many women are exacerbated by the isolating nature of the wife/mother role, where meaningful contact with other living beings is most often limited to young children and one's spouse (Baca Zinn and Eitzen, 1993: 271–272). Despite role-strain pressures that employed "'double shift' wives and mothers" experience (Moen, 1992), evidence indicates that having a role beyond "housewife" is a source of satisfaction for women, manifesting in improved scores on indicators of physical, emotional, and mental health (Barnett, 1994; Lee, 2002: 234). Such benefits do not ensue automatically, but depend on the development of effective role-balancing techniques (Stohs, 2000).

Despite a socially constructed wife role that may be hazardous to their health, wives generally evaluate their marriages as being very to mainly satisfying overall, even during the pressure-filled childrearing years. Bernard (1973: 54–58) argued that this apparent paradox may be explicable in terms of the high value our society places upon conformity. Marriage is held to be part of women's gender destiny; having conformed by getting married, women evaluate themselves as successful and their marriages as satisfying. After all, our societal norms tell us, it is only women who never marry who are "failures." Moreover, even though the marital division of labour tends to be heavily skewed against wives, accepting this imbalance as simply part of women's lot in life tends to influence women's perceptions of fairness and their evaluations of marital relationships (Hobart, 1996: 167–169; Stohs, 2000).

Bernard offers an additional possible explanation:

> For to be happy in a relationship which imposes so many impediments on her, as traditional marriage does, a woman must be slightly ill mentally. Women accustomed to expressing themselves freely could not be happy in such a relationship; it would be too confining and too punitive. We therefore "deform" the minds of girls, as traditional Chinese used to deform their feet, in order to shape them for happiness in marriage. It may therefore be that married women say they are happy because they are sick rather than sick because they are married. (Bernard, 1973: 56–57)

Changing Demographics of Marriage In 1972, the **marriage rate** in Canada per 1000 population reached 9.2 (Milan, 2000: 6)—a level previously attained only immediately following World War II—and the actual number of marriages performed exceeded 200 000 for the only time in Canadian history (Nault, 1996: 39). Demographers anticipated that baby boomers, upon reaching marriageable age, would continue this trend of growth. Such expectations proved groundless; the tendency from 1972 on has been in the opposite direction, with decreases in both annual marriage rates and the numbers of marriages performed (with a slight exception in the later 1980s). The number of marriages rose slightly between 1993 and 1995, held steady at 5.1 in the late 1990s, and then declined sharply in 2001, sinking to 4.7, "its lowest level ever" (Statistics Canada, 2003j) and, in 2003, remained at this record low (Statistics Canada, 2007l). Although Canada's marriage rate is lower than that of its closest neighbour, the United States (7.5), it is markedly similar to that of many European countries, most notably that of France, Austria, and Germany, which all had a marriage rate of 4.6 in 2003 (Statistics Canada, 2007l).

In 1972, the average age at first marriage in Canada reached an all-time low of 22.2 years for brides and 24.7 years for grooms (Nault, 1996); by 2001, it had risen to 28.2 for brides and 30.2 for grooms (Statistics Canada, 2003j) (average-age differentials between brides and grooms reflect the operation of the marriage gradient). In 2003, the average age of persons marrying for the first time was approximately five years higher than in the early 1970s. "In 2003, in Canada (excluding Ontario), the average age of persons marrying for the first time (to someone of the opposite sex) was 30.6 years for men and 28.5 years for women" (Statistics Canada, 2007l). Among same-sex couples who married in the province of British Columbia in that year, the average age at first marriage for same-sex couples between men was 43.9 years and, among women, 41.6 years (Statistics Canada, 2007l).

From a strictly demographic perspective, one reason for the decline in marriage rates is that the marriageable population (especially the younger cohort typically marrying for the first time) was smaller in the 1990s. Other reasons include "changing values that made divorce and nonmarital childbearing more acceptable; widespread access to and use of contraception; women's growing participation in higher education and the workforce and their resulting financial independence; an unpredictable job market; and a genera-tion pursuing self-fulfillment and avoiding long-term commitments" (Nault, 1996: 40; see Box 8.1). Single women's earnings are increasing, while high levels of unemployment and underemployment mean that single men's are either remaining stable or declining.

BOX 8.1

Hearing the Beat of a Different Drummer: People Who Don't Expect to Marry

Using 2001 General Social Survey data, the following abridged article focuses on "mature singles" (i.e,. men and women who are older than the average age at which people first marry [28 for women, 30 for men] but not yet past prime working age [under 55]) and examines some of the differences between those who do and do not expect to marry.

There are socio-economic differences between *wills* and *won't-marrys* that may play into their respective suitability as marriage partners. But it seems the real sticking point is that love (being part of a couple), marriage and family are simply not as important to *won't-marrys* as they are to other mature singles.

As one might expect, men who do not have good employment prospects more frequently believe they will never marry. Compared with employed mature singles, men with a long-term illness (8.1) have significantly higher odds of being *won't-marrys*. Being unemployed or out of the labour force for other rea-sons does not seem to affect the proba-bility of being a *won't-marry*, perhaps because these men expect the duration of their non-employment to be short. While employment status is not a predictor of marital expectation among women, edu-cation is, and those mature single women with less than a high school education have odds 5.2 times higher than univer-sity graduates of being *won't-marrys*, all

other factors being held constant. Having a child or children also increases the odds that a woman is a *won't-marry* (1.7) but has no impact on men.

Some cultural factors affected the probability of being a *won't-marry*. Odds are 4.6 times higher for a male francoph-one than a male anglophone. A woman living in Quebec has much higher odds (3.7) compared with a woman living elsewhere in Canada, when all other variables were held constant. In contrast, a mature single who was in an intimate relationship has a significantly lower odds (0.6) of being a *won't-marry*....

...Single people who do not expect to marry represent a small but distinct group of adults. For the most part, they are quite similar to mature singles who plan to marry, but they differ in some key ways: for instance, many are single par-ents, their incomes tend to be lower, and they are less likely to be well-educated.... But it seems that the key distinction between mature singles who do not expect to marry and those who do are attitudinal: they have decidedly less con-ventional views about the importance of love, marriage and family. These charac-teristics have undoubtedly presented *won't-marrys* with different life options than other mature singles. But it is impossible to say whether their opinions have shaped their behaviour and thus their life choices, or whether their views have grown out of their life experiences.

BOX 8.1

Hearing the Beat of a Different Drummer: People Who Don't Expect to Marry (*Continued*)

Age and attitudes are the main predictors of being a won't-marry

Odds ratio that a mature single would not expect to marry	Men (Model 1)	Women (Model 2)
Love and marriage		
Not at all or not very important to be part of a couple	4.8*	3.0*
Important or very important to be part of a couple	1.0	1.0
Not at all or not very important to be married	7.4*	8.8*
Important or very important to be married	1.0	1.0
Not currently in an intimate relationship with someone	...	1.0
Currently in an intimate relationship	...	0.3*
Age group		
29 to 34	0.5*	1.0
35 to 39	1.0	1.0
40 to 44	1.7	5.4*
45 to 49	1.3	5.0*
50 to 54	2.6*	13.1*
Highest level of schooling completed		
University	...	1.0
College or trade/technical diploma	...	1.3
Some postsecondary	...	1.4
High school	...	2.0
Less than high school	...	5.2*
Children		
Have one or more children	...	1.7*
Have no children	...	1.0
Region		
Quebec	...	3.7*
Rest of Canada	...	1.0
Main activity during the year		
Working	1.0	...
Looking for work	1.8	...
Family-related (includes child care, household work, paternity leave)	1.5	...
Long-term illness	8.1*	...
Other (includes going to school and retired)	0.5	...
Main language spoken at home		
English	1.0	...
French	4.6*	...
Other	0.4	...

Note: This table presents the odds that a respondent would not expect to marry in the future, relative to the odds of a benchmark group when all other variables in the model are held constant. Age range for males is 31 to 54 years of age.

... Not applicable.

* Statistically significant difference from benchmark group ($p < 0.05$).

Source: Statistics Canada, General Social Survey, 2001.

Source: Abridged from Susan Crompton. 2005. "Always the Bridesmaid: People Who Don't Expect to Marry." *Canadian Social Trends*, vol. 77. On the World Wide Web at www.statcan.ca/english/freepub/11-008-XIE/2005001/articles/7961.pdf

Oppenheimer (1994) concluded that women are therefore less dependent than they once were upon men's financial support—and that men are less able to provide such support. These conditions reduce the proportions of women marrying, or at least increase the amount of time they are prepared to postpone marriage. The change over the years in average marrying age demonstrates that younger people are less eager to rush into marriage; one factor contributing to this trend is the increasing acceptability of permanent singlehood and cohabitation. In addition to these oft-cited reasons, however, some of the decline in marriage rates must also be attributed to a decreased willingness on the part of Canadian women to commit themselves to an institution that, upon increased scrutiny, appears not to be an attractive bargain for their gender.

Standing on the outside looking in, 88 percent of Canadian teens say they expect to marry (Bibby, 2001: 143). However, statistical projections suggest that only 63 percent of men and 67 percent of women born in Canada in the last decades of the twentieth century will marry before the age of 50—down from the 85 to 95 percent characteristic of Canadians in the early 1900s (Oderkirk, 1994: 5). Projected marriage rates for males and females respectively are 44 percent and 48 percent in Quebec, 70 percent and 74 percent in the rest of Canada (Le Boudrais and Marcil-Gratton, 1996: 422). The lower projections for Quebec reflect the greater acceptability of cohabitation in that province than in other parts of Canada (Bélanger, 1999: 33–34), with the possible exception of the territories.

DIVORCE

Almost all the explanations offered earlier for Canadians not getting married serve just as well for Canadians not staying married. Lewis and Spanier (1979) theorized that whether or not a marriage remains intact depends upon an array of factors, some pertaining to the quality of the marital relationship itself, others to conditions external to the marriage. Marital quality is influenced by factors such as "marital adjustment, satisfaction, happiness, conflict and role strain, communication, and integration" (Lewis and Spanier, 1979: 287; see also Edwards, 2004; Mackey et al., 2004); the balance of attraction and tension internal to a marriage determines its judged quality (Amato and Previti, 2003).

One factor occurring outside family boundaries which exerts an important influence within the contemporary family is the significant increase in the labour-force participation of married women since the mid-1960s. In general, employed women, particularly those who work more hours (Greenstein, 1995), have higher divorce rates than non-employed women (Amato et al., 2003; Heckert et al., 1998). A woman's income—even as it contributes to the financial survival of her family—cannot help but stimulate her awareness of her capacity for economic self-sufficiency. Employment may also contribute to divorce by giving unhappily married women the economic power, independence, and self-confidence to seek divorce (Hiedermann et al., 1998). "[A]s more women participate in the labour force and all women have access to social assistance, they are partly freed from their former dependency on their husbands and now have an alternative not available to women in the past.... [A] relatively low income or even poverty is often preferable to living in an unhappy or violent relationship" (Richardson, 1996: 216; see also Coontz, 2000; Phillips-Miller et al., 2000). While income leads some women to the awareness that divorce is possible, it is more often the case that awareness of a possible divorce leads women to a decision to find employment (Rogers, 1999). Skolnick (1996: 270) argued that "a woman who enters marriage assuming she will be supported for life, and with no thought for how she might support herself, is much more foolhardy in a statistical sense than someone who smokes three packs of cigarettes a day."

Hobart (1996: 171) claimed that

> paid employment has greatly reduced the time available to wives for domestic work, and having paycheques has empowered them, giving them increased influence and independence. Conflict has resulted over (1) husband's reluctance to share the domestic work fairly, and (2) wives' refusal to be traditionally subservient.

Waite (1995: 499) asserted that "employed wives have less time and energy to focus on their husbands, and are less financially and emotionally dependent on marriage, than wives who work only in the home." Employed wives appear to find that the benefits of being married decrease while the emotional, psychological, and physical costs increase—a calculus that amplifies any disposition to divorce (Amato et al., 2003; Diefenbach and Opp, 2007). A wife's employment can also lead to her husband's greater willingness to end an unhappy marriage, in the knowledge that she is no longer dependent upon his income for survival.

Important factors external to the marital dyad include the influence of religious doctrines (which tend to positively evaluate intact marriages), the availability and evaluation of non-marital alternatives, the strength of the stigma attached to divorce and divorced persons, and legal accessibility of divorce (Riedmann et al., 2003: 482–487). Over the past three decades, both singlehood and cohabitation have become more socially acceptable and positively evaluated alternatives to marriage. Divorce traditionally carried a strong stigma, connoting "failure" on the part of one or both marital partners. This stigma was more readily applied to wives than to husbands, as women were considered responsible for the maintenance of marital relationships. A wife was held more culpable in the dissolution of a marriage than a husband: Even if a marriage broke apart as a consequence of his overt drinking, gambling, or infidelity, family, friends, and the general community were likely to maintain that if only she had been a better wife, he would not have needed to drink, gamble, or seek out the affections of other women. Over the past three decades, the stigma attached to divorce has interacted with the incidence of divorce in such a way that as divorce has become more common, the stigma attached to both partners, but especially to wives, has lessened. A more negative stigma is still attached to those who divorce more than once.

Prior to the liberating reform of our *Divorce Act* in 1968, Canada had one of the lowest **divorce rates** of all industrialized societies. Marriages that remain intact are not necessarily happier than marriages that dissolve via separation or divorce, since many can be characterized as "empty shell" relationships (Goode, 1982: 149), held together for appearance rather than for their intrinsic qualities (Hyden, 2005; Previti and Amato, 2002, 2004). Until the 1980s, more marriages ended with the death of one of the partners than with divorce; the situation is now reversed (Milan, 2000: 8). This change is attributable not only to the trend towards greater longevity, but to changes made to Canadian divorce law in 1985 in the effort to make divorce more accessible.

Divorce Law in Canada

In matters of family law, Canada has a divided jurisdiction. Under the *Constitution Act, 1867,* the provinces and federal government share jurisdiction over marriage and marriage-like relationships. While provincial laws govern such matters as marriage licensing, adoption, guardianship, and matrimonial-property disputes, divorce falls under federal jurisdiction. This means that after Confederation, Canadian provinces and territories could no longer independently enact any new divorce legislation; however, due to the opposition of Roman Catholic Quebec to divorce in any form, the federal government was extremely reluctant to attempt to enact a national divorce act or to establish divorce courts. In the absence of these, individual provinces had to ask the federal government to pass divorce acts that would apply exclusively to themselves. In consequence, divorce was available only in certain Canadian provinces until 1968. In Quebec, for example, provincial courts could not grant divorce; residents seeking divorce were forced to apply to Parliament to dissolve their marriage. In order to obtain a "parliamentary" divorce, "a private member's bill had to pass first reading in both the Commons and the Senate; after second reading in the House of Commons, it could be heard by a special divorce committee" (Boyd, 1998: 229).

In provinces that did allow divorce, the law was based primarily upon the *British Divorce and Matrimonial Causes Act of 1857*. This act contained a sex-linked double standard. Whereas a husband was entitled to petition for divorce on the grounds that his wife had committed adultery, a wife could only petition for divorce if she could prove that her husband's adultery was coupled with incest, bigamy, rape, sodomy, bestiality, cruelty, or desertion for at least two years. Encoded in law was the notion that her adultery constituted a major violation against the marriage, whereas his was but a minor transgression unless coupled with some more unacceptable offence. In 1925, this double standard was removed from Canadian divorce law by the deletion of the additional requirements on wives. Thereafter, either spouse could petition for divorce on the same grounds.

Between 1867 and 1968, adultery was the only legally recognized ground for divorce in most of Canada; Nova Scotia also recognized cruelty as grounds, and New Brunswick recognized frigidity, impotence, and consanguinity. New Brunswick was the only province to ever acknowledge sexual and reproductive "failure" on the part of either spouse as a "fault" or "offence" against the marriage. The *1968 Divorce Act*, the first Canada-wide divorce act, expanded the list of fault-grounds that entitled a petitioner to an immediate divorce; these included mental or physical cruelty, addiction to alcohol or other drugs, sodomy, bestiality, or homosexual acts. This act also took a first step towards **no-fault divorce**: Divorce was permitted on the grounds of unspecified "marital breakdown," if the couple had lived "separate and apart" for a three-year period and jointly consented to being divorced. In the event that one party did not wish to be divorced, the court required that five years pass from the time of separation before application be made for divorce. However, this act continued to place strong emphasis on the virtues of marriage; lawyers for each spouse were legally obliged to discuss reconciliation with their clients. Divorce-trial judges were also required to determine whether reconciliation was possible, and a judge who felt there was insufficient evidence of matrimonial fault or of marital breakdown could deny a divorce. In one 1976 case, for example, divorce was denied to a woman whose husband refused to let her work outside of the home; in a 1980 case, divorce was denied to a husband whose wife had undergone an abortion without his knowledge. In both of these cases, the presiding judged ruled that the actions of the offending spouse were insufficient to warrant a divorce on the fault-ground of "mental cruelty" (Dranoff, 2001: 249–250).

The *1985 Divorce Act* (effective in 1986) simplified the divorce process. Under this act, only one ground is available for divorce: marital breakdown. This simplification of divorce procedures was intended to reflect our society's endorsement of individualism and gender egalitarianism (Peters, 1987). Essentially, the power to decide if a marriage should be terminated has been placed in the hands of the spouses themselves, with the courts relegated mainly to an administrative role, ensuring that proper form is followed in legally dissolving the relationship, as well as an adjudicative role in cases where there are contested issues. For purposes of divorce, a couple having lived separate and apart for a period not less than one year, or one partner having committed adultery, or one partner having treated the other with mental or physical cruelty, are viewed as sufficient evidence of marital breakdown. At the start of the new millennium, over 80 percent of Canadian divorces were based on evidence of a one-year separation (Rogerson, 2002).

The new divorce law was intended to be gender-neutral. Regardless of the gendered nature of a former marriage, gender was no longer to be a major basis for dividing financial assets, for awarding financial support, or for determining custody of any dependent children. Because division of marital property falls under provincial jurisdiction (under the *Constitution Act*), there is no federal property law that applies throughout Canada. While all Canadian provinces and territories have laws requiring spouses to share assets in the event of marital breakdown, the precise definition of what constitutes "property" or a "family asset" varies and creates inconsistencies across jurisdictions (Dranoff, 2001: 276). In theory, the "family assets" that spouses are to share on marital breakdown are those used and enjoyed by both spouses and/or their children, including, for example, the family home and its contents, any other real estate (e.g., cottages), Canadian or Quebec Pension Plan credits, RRSPs, investments, cars and other recreational vehicles, bank accounts normally used for family purposes, and other tangible assets accumulated jointly over the course of a marriage. However, given the variation from province to province in the division of "non-family" or business assets, gifts, inheritances, employment-related benefits, lottery winnings, and private pensions, it would be misleading to suggest that "sharing" always results in a 50–50 split. Moreover, arguably the most valuable "new property" (Glendon, 1981) for most couples is the enhanced earning power accruing from professional degrees, work experience, or other investments in "human capital." "When property is legally divided in divorce, the wife may get an equal share of tangible property, such as a house or savings, but that usually does not put her on an equal footing with her former husband" (Riedmann et al., 2003: 466; see also Goode, 2007).

Spousal Support Alimony (from a Latin verb meaning "to nourish") has its roots in English common law and a traditional division of labour whereby married women could not seek paid employment. Upon marriage, a husband gained control of his wife's assets and typically reaped financial benefits from that control. The husband, therefore, was expected to assume responsibility for his wife's financial support during their marriage and to continue providing such support in the event of its dissolution (Weitzman, 1985). In Canada prior to 1968, a husband would commonly be ordered to pay a monthly sum of alimony to his wife, either in perpetuity (i.e., until the death of either spouse) or until she remarried, at which time the obligation of financial provision would be legally transferred to her new husband. Although it was theoretically possible for a husband to be awarded alimony from a former wife, this situation was extremely rare. Moreover (consistent with the fault-finding ethos of pre-1968 divorce proceedings), wives who had committed adultery were generally denied alimony; spurned wives were awarded more, by way of compensation for their pain. The concept of alimony thus reaffirmed traditional gender roles (provider husband/dependent wife) beyond the lifespan of the marriage.

With the introduction of **maintenance** in 1968 and **support** in 1985, the concept of alimony was replaced with a supposedly egalitarian, gender-neutral legal premise: Both spouses were presumed to have, or to be able quickly to achieve, economic self-sufficiency. Specific reasons why a marriage had ended were no longer of relevance in establishing post-marital financial obligations, nor would the court consider spousal misconduct in its deter-mination of support. "Spousal support" was redefined as **rehabilitative alimony**, an interim measure designed to provide a spouse with support for a limited period of time (typically four to five years), during which s/he was to initiate significant steps (through education, training, or retraining) towards economic self-sufficiency. This system was to create signif-icant hardship for **displaced homemakers** (Coontz, 2000)—full-time, often older home-makers who, upon divorce, found themselves without a provider, adequate support, or the educational qualifications or work experience to become self-supporting (Machum, 2002).

In their 1992 landmark decision in *Moge v. Moge*, the Supreme Court of Canada rec-ognized the precarious position of displaced homemakers when it held that it was unrea-sonable to expect total self-sufficiency from a long-term homemaker (generally the wife), and that in cases in which marital responsibilities have eroded a spouse's earning ability, **compensatory spousal support** (in the form of either periodic or lump-sum payment) may be awarded. The compensatory support model directs attention to the roles that each spouse assumed within marriage and their effect on a spouse's earning potential upon divorce, as well as to such factors as career sacrifice, contribution to a spouse's career, and duration of the marriage. In the 1999 case of *Bracklow v. Bracklow*, the court held that the duration of a relationship was to be considered an important factor in determining the term of support to be awarded on the basis of hardship or need. In the case of a long-lasting relationship, a spouse with a disability, for example, might be granted indefinite support, whereas a more limited period of support would be awarded if the relationship had been of short duration.

Nevertheless, available research suggests that spousal support is granted "in only a small percentage of divorce cases—ranging from the low twenties at best, to the low teens at worst" (Rogerson, 2002: 59). An analysis using data from the ongoing Maintenance Enforcement Survey (which provides data on the collection and enforcement of both spousal and child-support payments in Canada), and extrapolated from spousal-support orders registered in British Columbia and Saskatchewan as of March 31, 2000, found spousal support to be even more rare:

> With respect to Saskatchewan, spousal support only was found in 4.1% of Divorce Act orders registered in the program and combined spousal and child support orders represented 7.4% of Divorce Act support orders (for a total of 11.5% of all support orders). For British Columbia, spousal support only was found in 4.1% of Divorce Act orders registered in the program and combined spousal and child support orders represented 4.8% of Divorce Act support orders (for a total of 8.9% of Divorce Act support orders). (Rogerson, 2002: 60)

Similarly, Martin and Robinson (2008: 10) pointedly report that "[m]ost divorces or sep-arations do not involve support arrangements." They note that while there were two mil-lion cases of divorce or separation in Canada's 10 provinces (including those involving common-law unions) between 2001 and 2006, only a third of the cases involved an arrangement for support payments and, that when these arrangements existed, the "vast majority" (85 percent) involved support payments with a child as the intended benefici-ary. Their analysis of 2006 General Social Survey data finds that while "almost two-thirds

(64 percent) of cases of divorce or separation involving children had support arrangements in place ... very few separating couples without children had an arrangement for paying support (8 percent)."

There are a number of possible explanations for the low incidence of spousal support. One possibility is that the data sources used by researchers are inadequate, leading to underestimates of its actual incidence. If, as some have suggested, spousal support is a "higher-income phenomenon" (Rogerson, 2002: 61) that tends to be arranged via private settlements rather than court proceedings, research that relies on court-based data may be of limited utility. Although welfare recipients are obligated to register their orders for enforcement, not all Canadians are bound by such edicts. Another possibility is that "uncertainty about the spousal support obligation prevents claims from being made" (Rogerson, 2002: 61). Additional reasons why individuals may elect to forego spousal support include feelings of self-sufficiency or awareness of alternative sources of support; a desire for a clean break; and doubt that spousal support would be granted or, if granted, paid. Some research also suggests that younger women are less likely to pursue spousal support than older women or those who have been married for longer periods of time (Skolnick, 1996: 316).

Incidence of Divorce

It is possible to measure the impact on the incidence of divorce on social changes—such as the diminished influence of religious ideologies concerning the sanctity of marriage vows; the lessening stigma attached to divorce and divorced persons; the greater ease of access to formal divorce procedures; the growing acceptance of singlehood and cohabitation as alternatives to marriage; and the significant rise of women's labour-force participation, enabling greater economic self-sufficiency. More difficult to quantify are the contributions over the past three decades of two ideologies: the ideology of rising expectations, which places great demands upon marriage and marital partners to become major sources of personal satisfaction and growth; and the ideology of feminism, which demands a restructuring of the marital bargain to produce a more equitable interpersonal arrangement. Although the impact of these two ideologies cannot be ascertained in any simple cause-and-effect way, they (along with the other social changes mentioned above) have undoubtedly contributed to the significant increase in divorce since the mid-1960s.

The number of divorces per 100 000 population in Canada, known as the *crude divorce rate*, rose from 36.0 in 1961 to 271.0 in 1981, reached a peak of 362.3 in 1987, then declined to 282.0 by 1991 and, by 2002, to 223.7 (Ambert, 2002; Statistics Canada, 2004e). The decline in divorce rates since the late 1980s is linked, in large part, to a declining marriage rate, which (obviously) places fewer couples at risk for divorce. It is cautiously estimated that if recent patterns remain constant, 33 to 40 percent of marriages contracted recently in Canada will end in divorce (Ambert, 2002; see also Statistics Canada, 2006l), even though 88 percent of Canadian adolescents idealistically anticipate that they will stay with the same marital partner for life (Bibby, 2001: 144).

The Decision to Divorce and Post-divorce Adjustments

The fact that women file the majority of divorce petitions (Collins and Coltrane, 2000; Kitson, 1992) has been interpreted by some as evidence that women find marriage, as it is presently constituted, inherently oppressive (Heyn, 1997). "[T]he family," McMullin thundered (2004: 140), "is a primary site of oppression of and violence against women, children, and the elderly." Others, however, point out that the issue of who actually instigates a divorce is far from obvious (Amato and Previti, 2003; Hopper, 1993). The spouse who files the formal petition is not always the spouse who feels especially aggrieved or who most contributes to the conditions that precipitate the action. Most often, the matter of who files the formal petition simply has to do with convenience.

Research suggests that women who initiate the decision to divorce are likely to experience the period prior to separation as the most stressful time, whereas men are more likely to experience the immediate post-divorce period as the most stressful (Amato, 2001; Rahav and Baum, 2002; Waite and Gallagher, 2000). Women tend to meet the period following divorce with a sense of relief and freedom (Bailey, 2003; Madden-Derdich and Leonard, 2002). Kitson (1992) found that approximately half of former husbands claimed to have had no warning that their marriages had deteriorated to a point where their wives not only wanted out, but were willing to take the legal steps necessary to terminate the relationship. These men, who were the last to know their marriages were over, were the most likely to experience negative effects, such as depression, loneliness, and other emotional or physical disturbances, following the divorce. "Men have much more difficulty replacing what a wife and family provided. Divorce creates expressive hardships for men that it does not create for women" (Riessman, 1990: 209; see also Lehr and MacMillan, 2001). A recent study, based on longitudinal data from the National Population Health Survey (Statistics Canada, 2007m), found that both men and women, ages 20 to 60, who had divorced or separated, were more likely to report an episode of depression than their still-married counterparts. Men who experienced the end of a marriage or a common-law relationship were six times more likely to report an episode of depression than their still-married counterparts; women who experienced a marital breakup were 3.5 times as likely as their married counterparts to have experienced a bout of depression. This increased risk of depression may be attributable to various disruptive life changes that accompany divorce; 19 percent of men and 15 percent of women who separated/divorced reported a decline in their level of social support; 43 percent of women and 15 percent of men encountered financial difficulties following the dissolution of their relationship; and 34 percent of men and 3 percent of women experienced the departure of children from their household (see also Walzer, 2008).

Some rejected husbands who fail to accept the finality of separation or divorce stalk, harass, or even kill their former partners (Mechanic et al., 2002; Sheridan et al., 2003). Although this response is by no means exclusively male, it is more common among men than women (Statistics Canada, 2007j). Other men launch into a frenzied social and sexual life immediately after divorce while also trying to cope with a disorganized household and, in some cases, the loss of daily contact with their children (Kalmijn and Van Groenou, 2005; Knox, 1998; Pasley and Minton, 2001). Divorced wives may reduce their contact with friends, but typically have a more extensive support network to call upon should they wish (Arendell, 1995). Research which compared four categories of men and women—marrieds, cohabitors, those who were dating, and those with no partner—found that divorced men had the lowest levels of emotional support of any group, while divorced women experienced a level of emotional support "not that much lower than married women's" (Ross, 1995: 138). Gender differences were slightest among child-free spouses, who appeared to cope the best with the emotional turbulence, altered standard of living, and establishment of a new household.

REMARRIAGE

In 1971, approximately 10 percent of Canadian marriages involved at least one previously married partner (Richardson, 1996: 243). A decade later, this figure had risen to 23.6 percent, and in 2001, to 32.6 percent—almost one third of marriages (Statistics Canada, 2003j). In 2000, "more than one half [55.1%] of previously divorced brides or grooms were getting married to a partner for whom this was a first marriage.... Both partners were previously divorced in 37.5% of these marriages in 2000" (Statistics Canada, 2003j). Marriages between a previously divorced person and a widow/widower were relatively uncommon, accounting for merely 7.5 percent of all marriages involving a divorced person. Based on their examination of 2001 General Social Survey data, Clark and Crompton (2006) report that "about 43% of Canadian adults whose first marriage had ended in divorce had married again by the time of the GSS, as had about 16% of those whose first spouse had died." While more than 16.6 million Canadians age 25 and over had been legally married at some point in their lives in 2001, 89 percent had been married once, 10 percent had been married twice and less than 1 percent had walked down the aisle more than twice (almost always three times).

Overall, remarriage rates for all marital statuses have declined. Among all Canadians age 15 and over, the marriage rate per 1000 population declined from 148.0 in 1975 to 40.5 in 1995 for the previously divorced, and from 13.5 to 6.0 for the previously widowed (Statistics Canada, 1998). During the early 1970s, about 85 percent of divorced men and 79 percent of divorced women remarried. These proportions decreased to 76 percent for men and 64 percent for women by the mid-1980s (Adams and Nagnur, 1990, in Richardson, 1996: 243), and continued to decline into the 1990s. Ambert (2002) reported the incidence of remarriage for divorced men and women as 45 and 35 percent respectively in Quebec, and 70 and 58 percent respectively in the rest of Canada. As with first marriages, some unknown proportion of the overall decline in remarriage is accounted for by the increase in the numbers of divorced people who choose to remain single or cohabit rather than marry (see Wu, 2000; Clark and Crompton, 2006). Nevertheless, for divorced people of both sexes, remarriage is still the most frequent outcome everywhere in Canada except Quebec (Kelley, 2003/2004).

As a consequence both of mortality differentials that favour aging women and of the mating gradient, the pool of eligible men available for women interested in remarriage declines with age. However, the pool of eligible women expands in both age directions for men interested in finding a new mate. Men's emotional dependence on women's therapeutic/companionship skills and physical dependence on women's housekeeping skills increases their motivation to remarry (Coleman et al., 2000). Thus, a combination of motivation and opportunity appear to account for the consistent findings over the years that men are more likely to remarry than women, in both the United States (Teachman et al., 2000) and Canada (Milan, 2000: 9; McCloskey, 2003/2004), and to do so sooner after a divorce than women (Preece, 2003/2004; see also Chapter 9).

Younger divorced women are more likely to remarry than older divorced women. "[A]ge discriminates against women the older they are; the older they are, the lower their chances of remarrying. But this is not the case for men. Such is the double standard" (Ambert, 1998: 7). Among divorced people ages 25 to 34, the probability of remarriage is 66 percent for women and approximately 80 percent for men; for those between the ages of 35 and 50, the respective figures are 48 percent and 61 percent (Ambert, 2002: 5). As with first marriages, very high income level is associated with high probability of remarriage for men; however, for women, that same factor, along with very high education level, is associated with low probability of remarriage. This disparity between "cream of the crop" men and women may be due to the availability of a more limited pool of eligibles for high-status women to choose from, in combination with the fact that such women have little financial incentive to remarry. Remarriage appears to lose much of its lustre for women when financial security is not an issue (Renzetti and Curran, 2003: 193).

The presence of children also reduces the likelihood of remarriage for women, but not for men; the greatest impact is noticeable among divorced women with three or more children (Buckle et al., 1996; Goldscheider and Sassler, 2006). These women will, on average, be older than women with fewer children and thus will have fewer eligibles to choose from. What is more, a divorced man may be reluctant to take on the role of **dual-provider father**—providing or co-providing for both his former wife and their children (via support payments) and his current wife and hers/theirs. The financial responsibilities associated with an "instant family" might deter a man from pursuing a long-term relationship with a woman who has many children (Hetherington and Stanley-Hagan, 2002; Kheshgi-Genovese and Genovese, 1997). As well, the children of a divorced custodial mother may not want any man, or a particular man, to become emotionally and physically involved with their mother (Bray, 1999; Gamache, 1997). Courtship is a more complicated process for the formerly married, especially those with children (Riedmann et al., 2003: 490–491).

Remarriage Dynamics and Stability

In a follow-up study of divorced individuals who remarried, Furstenberg and Spanier (1984: 71–77) found that remarried women described themselves as less submissive and more willing to assert themselves than they had been in their previous marriage, even if this meant more discussion, debate, or conflict than had characterized their first marriage. This assertiveness arises partly from reflection on the earlier marriage: having realized that they should have asserted their rights more strongly, women may vow to do so in any future relationships. Increased assertiveness may also result from a woman's having been head of a solo-parent household in the interim. Remarried women are also more likely to be employed and to have a lengthier employment history, which increases their resource power in marital relationships. Remarried men described themselves as being less assertive and more accommodating than they had been in their previous marriage. Couples generally agreed that decision-making processes and participation levels were more egalitarian in their remarriages. Similar findings have been reported in more recent studies, both American (Coleman et al., 2000, 2006; Ganong and Coleman, 1994) and Canadian (Hobart, 1991). However, even though these remarried husbands claimed greater involvement in housework, their wives disagreed. According to Demo and Acock's (1993) research, remarriages are not more egalitarian; wives still bear the brunt of housework and childrearing.

Cherlin (1992: 86) argued that remarriage is still an "incomplete institution," with insufficient normative guidelines and shared meanings about how men and women should function as spouses and step-parents in remarried families. As a consequence, remarriages may flounder as partners attempt to construct a new married unity all on their own (Mason, 1998). Research indicates that most remarried individuals, having already survived one divorce, are more accepting of divorce and more likely to divorce than remain in an unsatisfying second or subsequent remarriage (Booth and Edwards, 1992). Ambert (2002: 5) reported that while "[r]emarriages without children from previous unions or with children born to the union have a rate of divorce equivalent to that of first marriages ... remarriages after a divorce have an approximately 10 percent higher rate of dissolution or a projected rate of redivorce of around 41 percent." Remarriage is less common now than in previous years because of the increased tendency to cohabit, particularly among younger divorced persons and among divorced men. Estimates suggest that Canadian divorced women in their 30s and 40s are now twice as likely to live common-law as to remarry (Le Boudrais et al., 2000).

PARENTING

Chapter 5 noted that language itself plays a role in reinforcing a differentiated and oppressive pattern of gender relations. The terms "good mother" and "unfit mother" are common evaluative descriptors of women who have children; "mothering" is also understood to encompass a wide range of nurturing behaviours. In contrast, the phrase "good father" is most often narrowly associated with fulfillment of the provider role; the term "unfit father" seems contrived and lacking any immediately discernible referent. As David (1985: 22) maintained, "[m]otherhood is a social concept, fatherhood barely recognised. To father a child refers only to the act of procreation."

The biological mother's assumption of responsibility for the care of her child, especially during the child's early years, is central to the **ideology of motherhood**, and has been translated into the **tender years doctrine** in child-custody law. However, the assumptions underlying this doctrine impact on a broader constituency than petitioners in child-custody cases. The sex-irreducible fact that women "menstruate, gestate, and lactate" encourages a belief that motherhood is simply a biological fact, decreed by "Nature" (or "Mother Nature"), and, as such, is not amenable to any fundamental reorganization. However, as Virginia Woolf (1978: 203) cynically remarked in another context, "[n]ature is now known to vary greatly in her commands and to be largely under control."

The *naturalistic* theory of heterosexual motherhood contains four interrelated assumptions: (1) all "normal" women desire to be mothers; (2) mothering takes place within a heterosexual family; (3) women and men play complementary rather than functionally equivalent roles within the family; (4) motherhood takes its shape as a response to a biological imperative and, as such, is largely a biological rather than a social role. Women who are child-free by choice or who opt to limit the number of children they bear are often portrayed as "unnatural" (Gairdner, 1992; Faludi, 1991: 55).

The second wave of feminism has been accompanied by the reconceptualization of motherhood within a social-conflict framework. McMahon (1995: 9) noted that feminist analysis during the 1960s and 1970s set out to debunk "'the feminine mystique'; the motherhood 'myth'; [and to expose] the real work of housework and childrearing; the compulsory nature of childbearing; the lack of access to abortion, contraception, and reproductive health information women faced; and so on." She remarked that in consequence, "the 'demon texts' of this period of feminism are falsely read as antimotherhood. The target ... was patriarchy, not mothers" (p. 9). She emphasized that feminist analysis has "validated women, and their work, qualities, and experiences" by examining women's experiences of birth and "maternal thinking" in a "revalorization of maternity that was both radical and feminist.... The challenge facing feminist analysis became one of valuing women's social capacity to care and/or their biological capacity to give birth while resisting having these capacities considered definitive or 'essential' or best in what it is to be a woman" (pp. 9–10).

In Canada, birth rates have been falling since the middle of the nineteenth century, except during the baby-boom years that followed World War II. One of the most notable changes has been the decline of the large families that resulted from continuous pregnancy and birthing by women of the 1800s. While at one time families with 8 to 13 or more children were not at all uncommon, by the year 2001 less than 1 percent (0.6 percent) of all families in Canada had 5 or more (*Canadian Global Almanac,* 2004, 2003: 69). This decline in family size reflects the rising cost of raising a child, lower child mortality rates, the reduced need for children as labourers and as insurance for their parents' old age, the increased availability of effective contraception, and women's increased participation in the paid-labour force. The average number of children born to the average woman (known as the **total fertility rate** or **TFR**) declined from 3.54 in 1921 to 2.83 in 1941, increased during the "baby boom" years to 3.84 in 1961, and fell to a record low of 1.49 in 2000 (*Canadian Global Almanac,* 2004, 2003: 55). While "Canada recorded its highest numbers of births—and its highest total fertility rate—in seven years in 2005, thanks mostly to women in their 30s ... the total fertility rate [at 1.54] is still far below the replacement level fertility" (Statistics Canada, 2007n).

Women are not only having fewer children but are having them at a later age. Since the 1970s, most Canadian women have been delaying first childbirth until their late twenties and early thirties (Grindstaff, 1995: 14); in 2002, the average age at first childbirth was 27.7 (Statistics Canada, 2004h). Overall, the proportion of births to women in their twenties has declined while the proportion of births to mothers in their thirties has grown: While women in their twenties gave birth to 66.2 percent of babies in 1982, "[o]nly 47.9% of births were to mothers in this age group in 2002.... By 2002, 44.8% of births were to mothers aged 30 to 39, up from only 23.0% of births in 1982" (Statistics Canada, 2004h). In 2005, women ages 30 to 34 had the highest proportion of births (31.4 percent of total births), followed by women ages 25 to 29 (30.9 percent), and women 35 to 39 (14.5 percent) (Statistics Canada, 2007n). In 2006, 9 percent of Canadian children age 4 and under had a mother who was between the ages of 40 and 49 (up from 7.8 percent in 2001) (Milan et al., 2007: 6). Although research suggests that the numbers and proportions of women who choose to remain child-free are increasing, a large majority of women do become mothers at some point. Having children adds still another stamp in the adult passport to both masculinity and femininity (Marsiglio et al., 2000). The 2000 Project Canada Survey found that almost all (96 percent) of those Canadian teens who plan to marry desire children, as well as over six in ten (62 percent) of those who do not plan to marry (Bibby, 2001: 146).

Inventing Motherhood

Social expectations of motherhood vary markedly across cultures and historical eras. Summarizing cross-cultural research, Ambert (1994: 530–531) stated that "the Western focus on individual mothers at the core of children's development is not universal," pointing out that in many agrarian and gathering societies, for example, practices such as multiple mothering, multiple parenting, and sibling parenting are common. Basow (1992: 236) reminded us that in times past (and present), women have been expected to abandon or murder a child who was of the "wrong" sex, possessed a physical or mental disability, or was perceived as a financial liability.

In some tribal societies, childrearing is considered everyone's responsibility, and the role of "mother" occupies only a peripheral part of women's social identity. However, in the West, the identities of "women" and "mothers" have come to overlap considerably since the eighteenth and nineteenth centuries (Moore, 1994), as a result of changes to both our societal organization and our cultural conceptions of children and childhood. Generally, the culturally emphasized importance of mothers for child development has waxed and waned over history in response to general economic conditions: When a mother's labour outside the home is required, the mother–child bond is de-emphasized; when a mother's labour outside the home is not required, mothers and mothering are glorified and deemed essential for optimal child development (Coontz, 2000). Prior to the eighteenth century, parenting efforts were devoted primarily to breaking a child's will and inherent selfishness. By the age of 6 or 7, a child was expected to behave like a little adult in family relations; thus parenting, as conceived by people of that time, was limited to only the first few years of a child's life.

The concept of an indulgent and extended childhood did not emerge and become part of the North American cultural ethos until sometime during the industrializing eighteenth and nineteenth centuries (Coontz, 2000). As women were presumed to have no place in an industrial labour force, the role of women as mothers changed. While fathers had once assumed responsibility for socializing their sons and integrating them into adult life almost as soon as the boys were weaned, now, with industrialization taking men out of the home, parenting became almost exclusively the responsibility of women. Women also came to be defined solely as keepers of the hearth and heart. Over time, as children became economically useless, they—at least on a symbolic level—came to be defined as socio-emotionally priceless and "gradually acquired a culturally sacred value" (McMahon, 1995: 27); accordingly, they were deemed to require more intensive care and nurturing.

It is noteworthy that the developing images of ideal childhood, as well as those of womanhood and motherhood, were both classist and racist. Valverde (1991), for example, has noted that the historical representations of motherhood and gender within Canadian social-purity movements were robustly racist and relied upon symbols that were both white and Protestant. Then, as now (Woldequiorguis, 2003), only children of certain racial or socioeconomic groups were viewed as "priceless" beings, to be cherished and protected by their devoted mothers and by society.

As early as the 1820s in the United States, the maternal role began to be seen as "somewhat other-worldly and sublime" (Light and Prentice, 1980: 134). The **motherhood mystique** (Hoffnung, 1989), which emerged in the eighteenth century, forwarded a romanticized vision of the "all-loving, kind, gentle, and selfless" mother (Anderson, 1997: 163). It suggested that "only by having a child can a woman actualize her full potential and achieve the ultimate meaning of her life" (Lips, 1993: 314); motherhood was seen as the culmination of feminine fulfillment for all "normal" women (Cowdery and Knudson-Martin, 2005). A "want of maternal feeling" was thought to characterize only "unnatural" or criminal women who "psychologically and anthropologically ... belong more to the male than to the female sex" (Lombroso and Ferrero, 1895: 153). This **Motherhood Mandate** (Basow, 1992: 234), with its premise that all "normal" women possess a deep-rooted "maternal instinct" that motherhood alone can fulfill, ignores the labour that mothering entails. As Graham (1984: 153–154) observed, the work involved in mothering "is most in evidence when it is not done, when clothes and faces are left unwashed, rooms and hair are untidy, and children are ill-disciplined and noisy. When a mother works successfully to maintain the standards of dress, decor and decorum her labour is at its most invisible." Nevertheless, the Motherhood Mandate remains a powerful part of many secular and religious ideologies, and "[w]omen who cannot bear children tend to be pitied, and women who are voluntarily child-free are viewed by others as misguided, maladjusted, or selfish" (Basow, 1992: 234).

As noted in Chapter 4, an important element of girls' socialization is "playing house" and performing the role of mothers. Given the consistency of messages which reiterate that caring for children is a "feminine" role, it is not surprising that babysitting is one of the first jobs suggested to preadolescent and early adolescent girls (but not boys). Nor is it surprising that 98 percent of those who provide "surrogate" mothering as daycare workers are women (Ontario Women's Directorate, 1995: 19; see also Statistics Canada, 2006a). In addition, cultural models of "good girl" sexuality, which link love and romance to married intercourse and procreation, implicitly refurbish the Motherhood Mandate. Although birth-control measures have been legal in Canada since 1969, cultural inhibitors persist that discourage women from frankly facing their sexuality and taking responsibility for contraception (Chiappori and Oreffice, 2008). The mystique—propagated by romance novels—of the unpremeditated encounter that bursts into sexual spontaneous combustion is another factor. In the romantic scenario of being swept away by passion, contraception is not an encoded part of the script. One may here consider a novel study that reports a relationship between women's reading of romance novels (which commonly present women being "swept away" by passion) and their attitudes towards condom use. Diekman et al. (2000) found that among female undergraduates, high levels of romance reading were associated with negative attitudes towards condoms and reduced intent to use them.

Motherhood as Institution

Rich (1986: 58) suggested that women's experience of motherhood has been co-opted by "motherhood as institution"—an interlocking power structure of legal, medical, and cultural expertise which has functioned to create an "invisible institution" of male control. For example, it had long been the custom, in Canada and elsewhere, for midwives to deliver babies; assisting with pregnancy and childbirth was viewed as something to which women were "naturally" best suited. Indeed, it was considered indecent for men to know much about pregnancy (let alone participate in the birthing process), and even after physicians gained admittance to the rooms in which women were "confined," decency required that the physician fumble "blindly under a sheet in a dark room, his head decorously turned aside" (Henslin and Nelson, 1996: 547).

Over the course of the eighteenth century, certain factors encouraged (male) physicians in Canada and elsewhere to assert their control over childbirth; these included (1) the professionalization of medicine; (2) the movement of childbirth from home into newly established hospitals; (3) the increasing power vested in the medical establishment; and (4) the development of obstetric forceps, which allowed their user to shorten the duration of labour and deliver live infants in circumstances in which mother and/or child would otherwise have died (Ehrenreich and English, 1979). Physicians maintained that pregnancy and childbirth were not normal events but "medical conditions"—potentially pathological events that required the assistance of an able professional (man), not a "dirty, ignorant and incompetent" midwife. In Canada, the Victorian Order of Nurses, founded in 1897 by the National Council of Women to assist rural women who lacked access to medical care, originally included midwifery in their work. However, as Mitchinson (1993: 396) observed, "the opposition of the medical establishment in Canada was so great to what it saw as an infringement of its prerogatives that the idea was to die."

During the twentieth century, childbirth became increasingly medicalized and managed through the use of new technologies and practices, such as anaesthesia, forceps delivery, episiotomies, artificial inductions, as well as increased use of Caesarian sections—all to be performed in hospital settings and not at home. While medicalization has reduced the dangers of childbirth for mothers and newborns, it has also decreased women's autonomy over their reproductive lives and increased the degree to which childbirth is managed and regulated by professionals, the majority of whom are men. Martin (1989) argued that the terms employed in obstetrical discourse reflect the logic of **Fordism**—a post-war form of industrial economy based on mass production. She claimed that childbirth is regulated as if it were commensurable with factory labour, with only a certain amount of time allotted to each stage; as a result, the role of the shop steward (obstetrician) is elevated and the role of the worker (mother) devalued. In addition, pregnancy and childbirth are increasingly viewed according to a "risk factor ideology," which directs attention to the dangers posed to a fetus by "not just the mother's genetic background, but other variables such as age, weight, blood pressure, overall health, etc., as well as ... personal habits and lifestyle" (e.g., consumption of drugs or alcohol during pregnancy, smoking, etc.) (Queniart 1992: 164–165). This ideology, coupled with technological advances that allow for fetal monitoring and surgery, reinforces the belief that "the mother's interests and personal needs should automatically be second to those of her offspring.... Being pregnant (and then giving birth) is increasingly becoming a private matter that takes place between a woman and her physician, in a relationship increasingly mediated by technology" (Queniart, 1992: 170).

Since the 1978 birth of "test-tube baby" Louise Brown (the first child to be conceived from *in vitro* fertilization techniques), conception no longer need involve heterosexual intercourse. The growth of infertility clinics and sperm banks seems to simply offer reproductive choice to women who would otherwise be unable to become pregnant. However, feminists are notably divided as to whether the **new reproductive technologies** are, as radical feminists had originally hoped, a liberating force. For example, Maier (1992: 149–150) cautioned that these technologies and the concepts of "the best interests of the child" and "fetal rights" may lead to "reproductive wrongs" in which a woman's "right to bodily integrity, that is, her security of the person," may be denied and her basic human rights coercively violated "under the guise of child protection." She emphasized that, in both Canada and the United States, "[w]omen with the least power and who are the most oppressed by virtue of their socioeconomic or racial status are the most vulnerable to having their fetuses apprehended or their pregnancies policed" (p. 153; see also Dershowitz, 1994). It should also be noted that the costs involved in the new reproductive technologies are considerable, which makes it unlikely that they will be an equally viable option for all women (Chabot and Ames, 2004; Rothman, 1999). Some feminists have voiced concern that arrangements such as surrogate mothering can be classist, resulting in the exploitation of poor women to serve as "baby farms" for those who are affluent—or seek to be. French (1992: 149) observed that "[t]he mothers ... are paid a small fee; the lawyers, doctors, and middlemen who arrange the implantation are paid a large fee."

In 2006, a Spanish woman, who had received *in vitro* fertilization using donor eggs, became the oldest known birth mother in the world when, one week prior to her 67th birthday, she delivered twins. Controversy erupted around a variety of different issues. Some opined that the woman would be too old to provide effective parenting for a teenager; others pointed out that many grandparents raise their grandchildren through adolescence and do so effectively. Outcry over the "unnaturalness" of a woman in her sixties mothering a child typically overlooked the fact that men between the ages of 60 and 80 not infrequently father children, both biologically and socially. Nevertheless, it is evident that the "reproductive revolution" (Eichler, 1989, 1996) has led to an explosion of new questions about motherhood and fatherhood: "[W]hat does parenthood mean when artificial wombs are being developed by which men can be pregnant through the implantation of an embryo in the male abdomen? When women are impregnated from semen that combines donations from their husbands and strangers? When babies conceived through artificial insemination from the husband are carried by surrogate mothers?" (Mackie, 1991: 118). These questions raise issues about the nature and meaning of the concepts "mother" and "father," in both their biological and social senses. It is currently possible for a person to have at least three mothers (an egg mother, a womb and birth mother, and a parenting mother), as well as at least two fathers (a sperm father and a parenting father). Both gay and heterosexual men may some day be able to undergo artificial insemination themselves. In September 2000, newspaper headlines reported that gay male couples may, in the near future, be able to sire "motherless" children through cell nuclear replacement, a technique originally seen as a way to treat infertility and metabolic disorders. "Under cell nuclear replacement, scientists replace the nucleus from the egg of a female donor with the nucleus from a sperm cell. The resulting 'male egg,' containing only male DNA, is then fertilized in vitro by sperm from another man" (Honore, 2000). Issues of real or fictive kinship links pale beside the new questions these developments raise about the "natural" or "unnatural" connections between sex, gender, sexual orientation, and parenting.

The Good Mother

The promotion of motherhood since the 1800s has been accomplished both by exhortation and by prescription. In an analysis of advice offered to mothers from the time of Rousseau onwards, Badinter (1981) observed how practical advice (e.g., do not swaddle your baby, do breastfeed your baby) has been interspersed with inculcation of the creed that motherhood should generate deep and powerful feelings in a woman. The development of "scientific motherhood" (Ehrenreich and English, 1979: 4) saw "experts" pontificating on "woman's true nature ... to prescribe the 'natural' life plan for women" and using their authority "to define women's domestic activities down to the smallest details of housework and child raising." "Parental" responsibility became a misnomer, as a gendered division of parenting roles led to the "privatization of motherhood"—the allocation of the responsibility for child care into maternal hands. Done correctly, motherwork is to produce a "marketable product ... an adjusted and achieving child" (Epstein, 1988: 197; Johnston and Swanson, 2006).

As the "good mother" evolved from supplier of a child's physical needs to ideal role model and creator of an optimal physical, social, and emotional environment for her child, the likelihood increased that a mother would be found wanting in some way and held accountable in the production of a less-than-perfect child (Gorman and Fritzsche, 2002). As Tavris (1992: 275) has noted, "[m]others are held responsible for almost any disorder that their offspring might develop, including bedwetting, schizophrenia, aggression, learning problems, and homicidal transsexualism. The concepts of competent motherhood and incompetent fatherhood are almost nowhere to be seen in the clinical literature" (see also Douglas and Michael, 2004).

Employed mothers are often faulted for spending "insufficient" time with their children (e.g., Gairdner, 1992), even though research now suggests that children of employed mothers are not, on the whole, neglected or adversely affected by their mother's employment (Bryant and Zick, 1996; Chira, 1994). Studies comparing the children of employed and unemployed mothers have found that where differences do emerge, children of employed mothers generally seem to be at an advantage (Muller, 1995; Youngblut et al., 2001). These children are likely to be more independent, to have higher career goals and motivation to achieve, to evaluate female competence more highly, and to hold less rigid and traditional conceptions of gender roles (Riedmann et al., 2003: 426). While daughters are particularly likely to benefit from the positive model of female achievement, research also suggests that sons of employed middle-class mothers are likely to hold less stereotyped gender-role perceptions and to exhibit better social adjustment than sons of unemployed middle-class women.

In a study of 205 mother–child dyads, Makri-Botsari and Makri (2003) found that a mother's unemployment had a direct negative effect on her own mental health and on her child's scholastic competence. In a study of 145 mothers and their first-born children, Harrison and Ungerer (2002) reported that mothers who expressed more commitment to work and less anxiety about the use of non-family child care and who returned to work earlier were more likely to have secure infants. Fuller et al. (2002) reported that maternal employment was significantly associated with a lower incidence of aggressive behaviour and inattentiveness among girls ages 24 to 42 months. Despite conservative social commentators' claim that delinquency is a result of maternal employment, research based on 707 American adolescents found that maternal employment patterns (e.g., whether or not mothers worked currently or when their children were preschoolers) had relatively little or no influence on delinquency (Vander Ven et al., 2001).

However, not all research findings on the effects of maternal employment on children have been positive. Youngblade (2003) conducted research on 171 third- and fourth-grade children from two-parent families, controlling for gender, maternal ethnicity, social class, and current maternal employment status. He found that children (especially boys) whose mothers had been employed during their first year of life exhibited more acting-out and less frustration-tolerance, and were more often complained of by peers for "hitting" and "being mean" than children whose mothers were not employed. Various researchers have also reported negative associations between maternal employment during the first year of life and children's cognitive outcomes (Brooks-Gunn et al., 2002; Burchinal and Clarke-Stewart, 2007; Han et al., 2001).

In general, children appear to benefit from having mothers who have positive attitudes towards their multiple roles (Harrison and Ungerer, 2002). A mother's being employed is not, in and of itself, harmful to her children; rather, the impact upon children is influenced by such variables as her attitude towards her job, the characteristics of her job (e.g., working conditions, remuneration), the family environment, and the quality of child care secured (Newcombe, 2003; Nomaguchi and Milkie, 2006). However, whether employed or not, mothers are often the targets of criticism: Mothers who work outside the home are criticized as inadequate and negligent parents, while stay-at-home mothers are disparaged as "overprotective" or accused of "smother love."

Parton (1990: 48) observed that "[t]he reality of mothering is frequently very different from the romantic ideal of feminine fulfilment." A new mother typically has little or no previous experience of responding to a newborn, preparing bottles, giving baths—or of breastfeeding. Indeed, Blum and Vandewater (1993: 5) identified as one reason for the La Leche League's remarkable success the fact of their being "the major source of practical breastfeeding advice." Although breastfeeding is currently advocated by medical practitioners "and popular among the white middle-class, [it] remains outside the expertise of most physicians." While breastfeeding is undeniably a most "natural" act, the fact that more than two million copies of the La Leche League's manual, *The Womanly Art of Breastfeeding,* have been sold might suggest otherwise.

The privatization of motherhood contributes to the plight of women whose feelings about motherhood do not accord with the romanticized ideal. A belief in the existence of a "maternal instinct" may deter a woman not only from admitting her own ambiguous or negative feelings about being a mother but also from acknowledging to others that she requires assistance; the structural conditions of the nuclear family (as compared to the extended family) decrease the likelihood that she will obtain support (Vandell et al., 2003). Goldberg and Perry-Jenkins (2004) asked women about the division of household and child-care tasks before the birth of their first child and upon their returning to work. They found that for women with a traditional gender ideology, who expected that they themselves—and not their husbands—should be the primary givers of child care, the violation of this expectation was associated with increased post-natal distress. Thus, despite the stresses of caring for an infant, a mother with a traditional gender ideology may resist a partner's attempt to share child-care duties or may feel distressed when he undertakes more child care than she expects of him.

Anderson and Leslie (1991) reported that the mother of a young child is likely to be under greater stress than her husband, regardless of whether or not she participates in the labour force. Isolation and lack of support may be particularly acute for single mothers and mothers of children with disabilities (Avison et al., 2007). Various authors have suggested that addictions to cigarettes and alcohol represent the aftermath of attempts to cope with the stresses of caring for preschool-age children (Coxhead and Rhodes, 2006; DeKoninck et al., 2003; Dunlap et al., 2006; Golden, 2005; Litzke, 2004); the description of gin as "mother's helper" has a long history.

Rosenberg (1987/1995: 311–312) argued that because childbirth and childrearing are seen as "natural," we fail to recognize the structural origins of women's emotional problems (e.g., depression) following childbirth or adoption. She noted that although between 60 and 90 percent of women in Western societies experience emotional problems following the birth of a child, and depression and anxiety are also reported by men and women who adopt, "the psychiatric literature still characterizes women with postpartum depression as infantile, immature, having unresolved conflicts with their mothers, failing to adjust to the feminine role, and having penis envy" (p. 314). Rosenberg likened motherhood to the highly stressful, low-control, high-demand jobs performed by industrial workers. She observed that although the ways in which motherhood is organized within contemporary society produce psychological and physical symptoms of "burnout," dominant explanations of "postpartum depression" and infanticide are "explicitly asocial" (see also Meersand and Turchin, 2003). Little notice, for example, is given to the fact that new mothers are now sent home far more quickly after delivery (typically within 24 hours of a vaginal birth or 48 hours after a Caesarean section), or to the fact that because of the greater survival rate of premature infants, newborns may be smaller, more fragile, and in need of more care.

Boulton (1983) reported that nearly one third of her sample of new mothers neither enjoyed the daily tasks of child care nor derived much sense of meaning or purpose from their children. An additional 30 percent noted the tiring, repetitive, and irksome nature of child care and domestic work, and the social isolation and loss of financial independence that motherhood entailed. She observed that these problems were particularly acute for working-class and single mothers, who often cared for their children in inhospitable environments, simultaneously coping with the challenges of poverty, unshared parenting, and inadequate housing. Berardo (1998) argued that isolation within the home is a major factor in mothers' physical abuse of their children; child physical abuse is more common in cases where mothers have been unable to develop or maintain links with supportive friends or family because of the costs of travel, telephone, or babysitting (see also Rodriquez and Green, 1997).

Okin (1989: 4) observed that "an equal sharing between the sexes of family responsibilities, especially childcare, is 'the great revolution that never happened.'" In Canada, responsibility for child care continues to fall disproportionately on women (see Chapter 6).

Homemaker Mothers Though predominant in Canada during the 1940s and 1950s, the husband/provider–housewife/mother family celebrated by the New Right as the traditional and ideal family form is increasingly becoming the exception rather than the rule. By 1976, only 6 in 10 Canadian families (59 percent) were of the single-earner husband–wife form with children at home; by 2002, less than one in three (28 percent) (Statistics Canada, 2003c). Although in the past, much of a woman's adult life was occupied in rearing dependent children, "[t]oday ... a couple might spend two thirds of their married life free of the responsibility for young children, and a third without any children at home" (Robertson, 1980: 269). Greater longevity and the trend towards fewer children per family account for the significant reduction in the proportion of adult lives devoted to child care today.

Research conducted on undergraduates has found that homemaker mothers, as compared to employed mothers, are viewed as more family-oriented and less professionally competent and are ranked less highly on instrumental qualities (Etaugh and Nekolny, 1990). Yet—despite the apparent inference that homemaker and employed mothers constitute distinct "types"—circumstances rather than personality characteristics may determine whether a mother becomes one or the other. Canadian research has revealed that as a result of financial constraints, the role of "homemaker mother" is, for the majority of Canadian women, of extremely brief duration—not atypically only that period of time allowed under maternity leave. Results from the longitudinal Survey of Labour and Income Dynamics have indicated that self-employment and the absence of maternity leave are linked to a quick return to the paid workplace. "The odds of the mother's returning to work by the end of the first month [following a child's birth] were almost six times higher when she did not receive maternity leave benefits. Also, the odds of returning early were almost eight times higher for the self-employed than for employees" (Marshall, 1999: 22). A Statistics Canada Survey of Labour and Income Dynamics found that new mothers took an average of 6.4 months off work (Statistics Canada, 1999a).

Only 7 percent of all Canadian women who gave birth in the early 1990s did not return to paid work; non-returnees were more likely to have been employed part-time, and less likely to have held a unionized or professional job. In addition, non-returnees had, on average, spent less time in their last job and earned lower median salaries than those who returned. Non-returnees were also younger and more unlikely to be married. "Some 30 percent of non-returnees were on their own (living without a partner), compared with just four percent of the women who returned to work" (Marshall, 1999: 23). These data suggest that mothers who return to paid employment quickly after childbirth perceive that they have more to gain and more to lose than those who do not. However, the return to work, regardless of its timing, may be experienced as stressful, especially among women. Findings of the 2006 General Social Survey indicate that women who return to work following the birth or adoption of a child undergo far more stress than men who take advantage of parental leave time. "In fact, 6 out of every 10 mothers (62%) reported that the transition ... was stressful. One-fifth described it as very stressful. On the other hand, most fathers (65%) rated the transition as not too stressful, or even not stressful at all" (Statistics Canada, 2007o).

In 2001, Canada's Employment Insurance (EI) program doubled the length of paid maternity/parental leave from six months to one year for eligible claimants. EI allows 15 weeks (the first two of which are unpaid) of maternity benefits, providing the woman has worked at least 600 hours during the previous year. These benefits provide women with 55 percent of their normal weekly pay, to a maximum of $435 dollars per week (gross). Fathers or mothers may also apply for parental benefits for an additional 35 weeks following the birth or adoption of a child. Evidence suggests that this provision has resulted in significant change: Results from the first full year of the new program "showed a 24% increase in the number of people taking time off. The most dramatic change was among men: 12 010 fathers took time off to be with their baby in 2000 compared with 21 530 in 2001, an 80% increase" (Smyth, 2003). Whereas in 2000, a mere 3 percent of fathers claimed paid parental benefits, in 2001, "this proportion had more than tripled to 10 percent" (Statistics Canada, 2003l). Findings from the 2006 General Social Survey indicate that the proportion of Canadian fathers who took any kind of leave for the birth or adoption of a child (including parental leave) rose from 38 percent in 2001 to 55 percent in 2006 (Statistics Canada, 2007o).

These recent changes represent an undeniable improvement. However, according to an international study that compared maternity/parental-leave benefits in 33 countries, Canada ranks fifteenth in the generosity of its maternity-leave benefits (Smyth, 2003). Overall, the Scandinavian countries are the most generous in terms of both leave and maternity pay, with Norway providing the highest statutory maternity benefits. In that country, a mother or father earning $38 000 per year receives $19 000 during his/her first six months home with a newborn; in Canada, a person earning an equivalent salary would receive about half that amount ($9500). Norway also provides parents with 52 weeks of leave at 80 percent of the parent's pay, and allows parents to take an additional two years, paid at a flat rate, to care for their child. In Sweden, the birth of a child entitles parents to 360 days of parental leave at 80 percent of the parent's salary and an additional 90 days at a flat rate; fathers are allowed to take an additional 10 days of paid leave when the child is born. Sweden also offers a variety of other benefits; for example, parents are entitled to free consultations at "well baby clinics," parents of a sick child under the age of 12 can obtain temporary parental benefits, and one parent may take up to 60 days off work per sick child per year at 80 percent of salary. In addition, Sweden maintains a heavily government-subsidized, high-quality daycare system and provides families with generous direct cash payments based on number of children (Brym et al., 2003: 383; see also Chronholm, 2002).

Employed Mothers As Chapter 6 pointed out, Canadian mothers have been entering the workforce in increasing numbers since the 1960s; also, the boundary between paid work and family is more permeable for employed mothers than for employed fathers. Primary providers of child care are more likely to have higher work-absentee rates, to scale back career aspirations, to refuse promotions that entail increased work responsibilities, and to resist transfers that might unsettle stable family life; as a result, their career trajectories are characteristically flatter. At the same time, paid employment alters the organization of mothering. Upon entering or re-entering the labour force, mothers face the task of securing child care (just as they must see to the reorganization of housework), and typically pay for child care out of their own earnings.

Cellphone ads notwithstanding, technological "fixes" allowing women to be accessible to their kids in an emergency are unlikely to assuage the ambivalence which mothers of very young children feel towards paid employment or towards their own childrearing practices. Worry about a child's well-being may detract from optimal job performance. Certain feelings are common: fear—at the thought of something bad befalling a child in one's absence; wistfulness—about missing such developmental milestones as the first word or first unaided steps; and guilt—because scientific research maintains that the constant presence of *someone* is a vital component of early child development, and in our culture, that "someone" is usually understood to mean "mother." For women, therefore, balancing employment and childrearing involves learning how to manage what Eyer (1996) has termed **motherguilt**.

Hochschild (1997: 220–238) found that employed mothers, confronting the major "time binds" that result from shouldering both employment and child-care responsibilities, develop a number of strategies. Perhaps the most common is "downsizing" what both parents and children consider indispensable in their daily lives. If needs can be pared down and prioritized, guilt can be held at bay and the belief salvaged that quality time is superior to quantity time. If hot noon-time meals are available to workers (at a restaurant) and children (at daycare or school), then evening meals can be cold. The necessity for daily baths and wardrobe changes can be re-evaluated. Instead of lavishing time and attention upon children, employed parents may now emphasize a child's need for "independence." Allowing a child to stay home alone after school may be declared a life-enhancing experience of early autonomy.

Another strategy practised by growing numbers of employed mothers is "outsourcing" many aspects of parenting (Van der Lippe et al., 2004). "Instead of trying to meet these needs themselves, they paid others to do it for them and detached their own identities from acts they might previously have defined as part of being 'a good parent'" (Hochschild, 1997: 221). Instead of planning a child's birthday party, some well-heeled professional women can hire a service (typically staffed by women) to provide a full birthday party experience, complete with cake, goody bags, and even gifts. "As the idea of the 'good mother' retreats before the time pressures of work and the expansion of 'motherly services,' actual mothers must continually reinvent themselves" (Hochschild, 1997: 233). Hiring sitters, enrolling children in a wide variety of lessons, and buying videotapes and videogames to keep children occupied and entertained are all acceptable under the revised definition of a "good mother." Children's needs are acknowledged; only the means of meeting them have changed.

A third strategy involves mothers (and fathers) splitting themselves into "potential" and "real" parental selves (Hochschild, 1997: 235–238). The potential parent is the ideal, filled with ideas about what she or he will do with a child when time constraints are not an issue. Ideal parents promise their children (and themselves) future camping trips, outings to the zoo, and entire evenings or weekends devoted to child-centred activities. In the meantime, however, real selves continue to make do with less by downsizing, outsourcing, and devoting what limited energies they have to hands-on parenting.

Lone-Parent Mothers In 2006, 15.9 percent of Canadian families were lone-parent families. In the first half of the twentieth century, death of a spouse was the major cause of lone parenthood (Oderkirk and Lochhead, 1992). Currently, however, the main causes are divorce, separation, and births outside of marriage. In 2006, 19.0 percent of Canada's lone-parent families involved a widowed parent (compared to 66.5 percent in 1951) and 29.5 percent involved a parent who had never been married (compared to 1.5 percent in 1951) and the remainder involved a parent who was either divorced (29.9 percent) or separated (21.6 percent) (Milan et al., 2007: 14). Although it is evident that increasing numbers of women have chosen to give birth and raise children without marriage, single parenting is most often the result of marital dissolution (either by separation or divorce); in the overwhelming majority of cases, it is the mother with whom the children remain, either by formal award of sole custody or by informal arrangement. In 2006, the vast majority (80.1 percent) of Canada's lone-parent families were headed by females. However, while "[f]or at least the past 20 years, there has been a fairly consistent pattern of about four lone-parent families headed by women for every one lone-parent family headed by a man ... families headed by men have been growing at a faster pace. Between 2001 and 2006, lone-father families rose 14.6%, more than twice the pace of 6.3% for lone-mother families" (Milan et al., 2006: 15).

Although child poverty in Canada is not restricted to families headed by lone parents, a far higher proportion of children of single parents (especially lone-parent mothers) live in low-income circumstances (National Council of Welfare, 2002; Statistics Canada, 2006e). Lone-parent mothers are more likely to be younger and less well educated than lone-parent fathers, and to have less income; typically they bear greater responsibility for younger-aged children than do lone-parent fathers (National Council of Welfare, 2000). In general, the younger the age of children at the time of the dissolution of their parents' marriage or common-law relationship, the more likely they are to be living in a low-income situation (Ambert, 2002).

Child Custody

Examination of annual divorce statistics reveals that at least half of all divorces awarded each year in Canada involve married couples with dependent children. In addition to deciding who gets to keep the house, car, and cat, partners must also come to an agreement on custody of their children. Canadian law is, in many ways, less clear on matters of child custody than on the division of material assets. In the majority of cases, parents themselves, rather than the courts, decide the issue of custody (Statistics Canada, 2007p). Although judges may overturn a couple's mutually agreed-upon arrangements if they believe these to be detrimental to the child or children, it appears that they seldom do so.

Until the mid- to late 1800s, custody decisions in Canada were based on the English common-law rule that a father was sole legal guardian of children. In the event of their father's death, a mother could only become the legal guardian of her children if he had appointed her testamentary guardian. Following a separation, a mother had no legal right, under common law, of either custody or visitation. Even in cases where a father gave his former wife a signed form consenting to her retaining custody of their children, such documents were held to be unenforceable and "contrary to public policy" (McBean, 1987: 184). Mothers, opined legal scholar William Blackstone, were entitled only to "reverence and respect," whereas the power of a father "continues even after his death for he may by his will appoint a guardian to his children" (in Lowe, 1982: 27). Children were held to be the "natural property" of their fathers; this status reflected the fact that women were not considered independent persons before the law and could not take legal action on their own before the court. Only in cases of gross paternal neglect, or where a child over the "age of discretion" (generally set at 16 years for girls and 14 for boys) indicated a strong desire to do so, would a court allow a child to remain with its mother.

Dissatisfaction with fathers' **absolute privilege** later prompted a slight shift in child-custody determinations, which came to be governed by the principle of **paternal preference**. Both principles, however, were based on the assumption that fathers needed the labours of their children (especially older children) for family survival, as well as the belief that children needed to be raised and guided with a firm hand. Since fathers were stereotyped as strong and mothers as weak, fathers were deemed to be best suited for preparing children for adult life.

Towards the end of the nineteenth century, two influences—psychoanalytic theory and the increasing recognition of women's and children's rights—led to a gradual replacement of the concept of paternal preference with a supposedly child-oriented principle known as the tender years doctrine. With the evolution of child-development theories that recognized the critical importance of emotional development and stressed the importance of nurturance from the "emotional" sex, judicial opinion shifted towards a belief that children during their early years should be raised by their mothers. The logic underlying the tender years doctrine was well articulated in the judge's ruling from the 1955 case of *Bell v. Bell*:

> No father, no matter how well intentioned or how solicitous ... can take the full place of the mother. Instinctively, a little child, particularly a little girl, turns to her mother in her troubles, her doubts and her fears.... The feminine touch means so much to a little girl; the frills and flounces and the ribbons in the matter of dress; the whispered consultations and confidences on matters which to the child's mind should only be discussed with Mother, the tender care, the soothing voice; all these things have a tremendous effect on the emotions of the child. (in McBean, 1987: 186)

In effect, the tender years doctrine was a euphemism for **maternal preference**. The "tender years" themselves were never precisely defined, but ranged approximately from birth up to the age of 7 to 12. It was also held to be true that adolescents' needs would best be served by placement of older children with the same-sex parent.

In the *Divorce Act of 1985*, the tender years doctrine was supplanted by a principle known as the **best interests of the child**. Section 16, subsection 8, of this act states: "In making an order under this section, the court shall take into consideration only the best interests of the child of the marriage as determined by reference to the condition, means, needs, and other circumstances of the child." The subsection does not define what the best interests of a child actually are; accordingly, considerable discretion is permitted to the judiciary. Dranoff (2001) suggested that in making this determination, the court may consider a number of factors including, but not limited to, the following: both parents' proposals for the children's upbringing and daily patterns of living; the child's emotional relationship with each parent; the extent and nature of each parent's previous involvement in child care; the physical and mental capacity of the parents to meet their children's needs; whether the custodial parent will facilitate access by the non-custodial parent; and the career commitment of both parents and the amount of time each parent will have available for the children. Although, legally speaking, the right of custody is a child's right, and the child's express wishes should therefore be taken into account, only rarely are they given precedence (Wallace and Koemer, 2003).

Parental conduct is another important factor in determinations of child custody, but only if that conduct is believed to be directly relevant to the best interests of the child. Accordingly, adultery is no longer considered a relevant factor in child-custody determinations, but substance addiction is—as, of course, is child abuse. What is or is not deemed relevant may at times seem questionable; Canadian courts have ruled, for example, that a husband's commission of assault upon his wife does not invalidate his application for custody or his claim to be a "good father" (Mechanic et al., 2002).

In awarding custody, the alternatives available to the courts are **sole custody** (one parent is awarded custody), **joint custody** (parents share custody), **split custody** (the children are divided between the parents, generally along gender lines), or custody to a third party (most often a grandparent or other relative). Since the 1990s, men's rights groups in Canada have promoted a "presumption" of joint custody (i.e., that the court "presume," or automatically prefer, joint custody unless compelling evidence dictates otherwise). This campaign has met with apparent success. Whereas in 1997 joint custody was awarded in only 28 percent of Canadian divorce proceedings, in 2002 it was awarded in 41.8 percent of cases and, in 2003, in 43.8 percent of cases (Milan et al., 2007: 15), "continuing a 16-year trend of steady increases in joint custody arrangements" (Statistics Canada, 2004e). The proportion of cases in which sole custody was awarded to the wife has declined steadily since 1988, when wives were awarded custody of 75.8 percent of dependents; that figure dropped to 49.5 percent in 2002—"the first time ever that custody was awarded to the wife for less than half of dependents" (Statistics Canada, 2004e) and 47.7 percent in 2003 (Milan et al., 2007: 15).

It should be borne in mind, however, that these statistics reflect only judicial decisions and not necessarily the actual living relationships that exist between parents and children. A parent with sole custody may still involve the other parent in almost all dimensions of a child's life. On the other hand, children may not spend equal amounts of time with both parents despite a joint-custody arrangement, as illustrated by a study examining the impact on fathers of the presumption of joint-custody law that has been in place in several American states for over two decades. By examining days and nights of father–child contact per month as well as paternal attendance at children's activities, participation in decision-making, and payment of child-support orders, this researcher determined that the presumption law had not resulted in more post-divorce paternal involvement (Douglas, 2003).

Concern has been voiced that judgments based on the "best interests of a child" may embody a subtle bias against some women by reinforcing the ideology of "good" motherhood. Boyd (1987: 172) argued that "[t]he ideology is a double-edged sword for women in custody battles because the bias it creates in favour of mothers only operates where the mother's conduct or life-style accords with the assumptions and expectations of the ideology of motherhood. If they do not, the chances are good for a father who wishes to challenge the 'unfit' mother for custody." Chesler (1991) offered numerous examples, drawn from American custody cases, of women who lost custody because they were employed (too ambitious), not employed (too lazy), involved with a man (immoral), or with a woman (even more immoral), or not involved with any partner at all (unable to provide a stable family). A father's ability to offer a "mother substitute" is often viewed more favourably by the court than a mother's ability to offer a "father substitute," especially if the biological father convincingly argues that he can provide the child with "a family set-up which most closely resembles the traditional nuclear family, including 'female care' ... [in the shape of] a new female partner, a grandmother or other female relative who ... [is] willing to perform the stay-at-home motherly functions which accord with the ideology of motherhood" (Boyd, 1987: 179).

It appears that to the minds of judges, a child's best interests are ensured when the custodial parent does not veer very far from traditional gendered expectations. Accordingly, although the working father who takes an "interest" in caregiving may be successful in his claim for child custody, the "househusband" is likely to meet with disappointment. For example, in the 1987 case of *Peterson v. Peterson*, the presiding judge ruled that "he would never award custody of a boy to a house-husband because with such a role model the child would be 'socially crippled when he is an adult'" (in Wikler, 1993: 49). Although dated, this judgment is a useful reminder of the subjective reasoning and biases that can underlie judicial determinations of a child's "best interests" (see also Boyd, 2000; Tye, 2003; Walter, 2003).

Financial Support   Canadian divorce law distinguishes between spousal- and child-support court orders. Prior to 1997, child-support payments were negotiated between parents and/or their lawyers and then ratified or altered by the courts. Even though amendments to the *Divorce Act of 1985* stipulated that spouses had a joint financial obligation to maintain their children, and that this obligation should be apportioned between them according to their relative abilities to contribute, the payments awarded by court order varied greatly from one case to another. While this was to some extent a reflection of each divorcing pair's unique economic circumstances, it also reflected power imbalances between either the partners (with the more powerful partner coercing the other into accepting inequitable terms) or their lawyers. Payments typically flowed from the non-custodial father to the custodial mother. Yet research has consistently found that a woman's (but not necessarily a man's) economic status is inversely related to the length of time she has been divorced, i.e., "the longer the period of divorce (or widowhood) of a woman, the more she is likely to be poor" (Ambert, 2002; see also Demo et al., 2000).

Bill C-41 received royal assent in February 1997, becoming law in May of that year. This legislation, designed in part to reduce the risk of poverty to divorced women and their children, included a number of measures to help enforce spousal- and child-support payment orders: (1) amendments to the Family Orders and Agreements Enforcement Assistance (FOAEA); (2) the addition of Revenue Canada to the list of federal departments whose databanks could be searched for the purpose of locating individuals in breach of family-support orders; (3) a new federal licence-denial scheme, authorizing suspension of passports and certain federal transport licences to persons who persistently breach child-support obligations; and (4) expanded access to the pension benefits of federal public-service employees in order to satisfy support orders. As a result of this federal legislation, persons in all Canadian provinces enjoy protection against the non-payment of child support, even though registration of support orders and agreements is mandatory only in certain provinces (e.g., Ontario and Quebec) and voluntary in others (e.g., British Columbia, Alberta, Saskatchewan, and Prince Edward Island).

Despite such measures, "deadbeat" parents and ex-spouses remain a serious problem. According to the 2006–2007 Child and Spousal Support Maintenance Enforcement Survey, which included data for 10 provinces and territories, non-compliance with support orders is still a significant problem. As of March 2007, "just over two-thirds of cases (67%) were in compliance in the 10 reporting jurisdictions" with compliance rates ranging from 56% of cases in Nova Scotia and the Northwest Territories to 77% of cases in Quebec" (Martin and Robinson, 2008: 12).

Some maintain that non-custodial parents' non-compliance with support orders is closely related to custodial parents' non-compliance with access awards. Thus, non-compliance may be "justified" with reference to the actions of hostile custodial ex-spouses who encourage children to hate the other parent. Indeed, the suggestion has been made that support should be terminated when a custodial parent has caused a child to experience **parental alienation syndrome** (PAS), defined as "an emotional and psychological disturbance in which children engage in exaggerated and unjustified denigration and criticism of a parent" (Mooney et al., 2004: 161) and/or that the criminal law be amended to recognize PAS as a form of child abuse (Gardner, 2002; Vassilious and Cartwright, 2003).

Although access to visitation and financial support are technically separate and independent dimensions of post-divorce childrearing, there are undoubtedly linkages between the two. An analysis of data derived from the National Longitudinal Survey of Children and Youth found a strong positive relationship between the frequency of visits of a non-resident father with his children and the likelihood that he would make regular support payments (Statistics Canada, 2007q). Unfortunately, this study found that while approximately one half of children saw their non-resident fathers frequently (with 27 percent seeing their fathers at least weekly and 22 percent seeing their fathers every two weeks), "[a]lmost one-third saw their father monthly, for holidays only or irregularly. The remainder (19%) had no paternal visits at all, though some had contact by phone or mail" (Statistics Canada, 2007q). The Canadian National Child Survey also reported that after parents separate, about one third of children have very little contact with their fathers (i.e., either irregular visits or none at all); children of common-law unions are even less likely to see their fathers than are children born to married parents (National Council of Welfare, 1999: 51; see also Bailey, 2003; Emmers-Sommer et al., 2003). "Since fathers who have low levels of contact with their children are less likely to pay child support, these findings indicate that many, many Canadian children are at high risk for losing both the personal and financial support of their fathers when their parents separate" (National Council of Welfare, 1999: 51). However, although there is little doubt that "[d]ivorce is a direct cause of poverty for a large proportion of women and their children" (Ambert, 1998: 9), some research has suggested that the principal reason for non-compliance with support orders is unemployment or underemployment (Kelly and Rinaman, 2003; Meyer and Bartfield, 1996; Henry, 1999). In view of this, Braver et al. (1991: 184–185) have suggested that coercive enforcement strategies may be less successful than has been hoped, pointing out that the real key to reducing post-divorce poverty "appears to be the old and unglamorous one, of solving un- and underemployment, both for the fathers and the mothers."

Fatherhood

It has been cynically observed that "[f]atherhood has a long history, but virtually no historians" (Demos et al., 1982: 425). Popular and scholarly interest in the topics of fathering and fatherhood has fluctuated throughout the twentieth century. In their examination of popular magazine articles published from 1900 to 1989, Atkinson and Blackwelder (1993) found that prior to the 1940s, fathers were more likely to be portrayed as providers than as nurturers. Such portrayals may have been more reflective of belief in the desirability of a rigid gender-based division of family roles than of an actual absence of paternal nurturing behaviour (LaRossa and Reitzes, 1995). Since the 1940s, depictions of fathers have alternated between these two images (Alkinson and Blackwelder, 1993). It is arguably only since the mid-1960s that, as Fein (1978: 242) observed, discussions of fatherhood have become "fashionable" within academic literature. With the significant increase in mothers' labour-force participation came a shift of emphasis from "mothering" to "parenting," accompanied by the discovery, by society and academics alike, of fathers and fatherhood (see Marsiglio 1995; Marsiglio et al., 2000, 2000a, 2001).

McKee and O'Brien (1982: 4–7) attributed this focusing of academic attention upon fathers to a combination of social and structural changes, including (1) second-wave feminism and its questioning of women's domestic and maternal roles; (2) increased numbers of single-parent families; (3) increases in male unemployment; (4) decreases in average family size; (5) the shortening of the work week and concomitant rise in leisure time; (6) the nascent men's movement; and (7) the continuance of a child-centred ideology emphasizing the provision of child care by the nuclear family. Blum and Vandewater (1993: 4) noted that "because gender is always relationally constructed,... ideologies of motherhood that have powerfully shaped women's subordination must be seen in relation to equally powerful ideologies of masculinity, fatherhood, and dominance." LaRossa (1988/1995: 365; emphasis in original) has additionally suggested that to fully understand fatherhood, we must recognize the distinction between what he terms the "*culture of fatherhood* (the shared norms, values, and beliefs surrounding men's parenting) ... and the '*conduct of fatherhood* (what fathers do, their parental behaviors).'" LaRossa contended that "**the culture of fatherhood** has changed more rapidly than the conduct" (p. 365; see also LaRossa et al., 2001).

Prior to modern times, concluded McKee and O'Brien (1982: 17), paternal authority was "uncontested" and absolute, and "reflected the social reality that itself was characterized by hierarchical social relations and by the governance of the father, the husband, the master, and the lord" (even though the way in which this absolute power was exercised varied by class, occupation, and geographical region). Roberts (1978), examining the memoirs of 168 Victorians born between 1800 and 1850, suggested that the development of a "self-conscious" and "admonitory" form of fathering stemmed from both increased urbanization and the rise of Puritanism and evangelism. During the eighteenth and early nineteenth centuries, fathers were viewed as playing a vital role in the moral and vocational education of their children, particularly their sons. Among the "well-born," the concept and code of the gentleman required that a man's behaviour be governed by an essential integrity towards his obligations and duties; accordingly, the **paterfamilias** (i.e., male head of a household)—if not out of native generosity than at least from consciousness of proper form—could be expected to look to the well-being of his dependents.

More complex images of fathering emerge from Thomson's (1977) analysis of 500 men and women selected from England's 1911 census. He noted, for example, that in textile districts, where female employment was high, male participation in housework and child care was much greater than in those areas of heavy industry where men were employed in physically exhausting labour. Further, Medick (1976) noted that in families dependent on a cottage-industry form of economy, the roles of husbands/fathers and wives/mothers became considerably more blurred. However, it was not until after World War II that the employment-dictated absence of fathers from the family home was re-evaluated and criticized by scholars and social critics who decried the unavailability of a gender role model (Basow, 1992: 246). A new model of the "nurturant father" (Lamb, 1987) or "androgynous father" (Pruett, 1987) emerged during the mid-1970s. This new father was expected to become intimately involved from the moment his partner's pregnancy was announced and to perform an active and nurturant role in his children's lives from birth onwards. Whereas, in 1945, childrearing guru Dr. Benjamin Spock had advised fathers to get involved and "prepare a formula on Sundays," by 1985, his recommendations had changed with the times and he was directing fathers to do half the work of baby care (Shehan and Kammeyer, 1997: 220). In sum, historical analysis reveals the socially constructed nature of "father," illuminating how, at various times, fathers have been viewed as providers, moral guides, sex-role models, and nurturers, and how these images have been affected by such factors as race, class, religious affiliation, and rates of women's participation in the labour force (Marsiglio, 1995; Mintz, 1998). At present, however, no singular ideology governs the culture of fatherhood; instead, we witness an uneasy blending of new models and old.

Research suggests that a high proportion of men attach importance to becoming fathers. The 2000 Project Canada survey of Canadian teens found that "a surprising number of males, as well as females—around 45% in both instances—say they expect to eventually stay home and raise their children" (Bibby, 2001: 146). Males view fatherhood as a means of building family ties, expressing love for their partners, and growing as human beings; however, they are more likely than women to perceive the multiple roles of parent, spouse, and worker as being in conflict with one another, to view having children as a leading cause of adults' diminished life satisfaction, and to doubt their own ability to interact effectively with their children (Gerson, 1997; Lips, 2001: 261–262). Men are also less likely to view parenthood as an important vehicle for achieving adult status (Knox and Schacht, 1997: 426); this perception is likely attributable to the historically greater access of men to a wider variety of options in the public sphere. Research has also suggested that despite any ambivalence towards parenthood, a man is likely to view his own infertility as a major disruption to his envisaged "natural" adult career plan and a threat to his self-definition as masculine and virile (Marsiglio, 1998; Marsiglio et al., 2001). An infertile man may also feel himself a failure in the eyes of his wife if he is unable to provide her with a motherhood career (evidence shows that a woman may experience analogous and even more severe feelings about her own infertility; see Abbey, 2000).

Experiencing Fatherhood

Although fathers, particularly in the middle class, are now increasingly likely to attend birth classes with their partners and to be present at the birth of their children, assignment of responsibilities—even in supposedly egalitarian marriages—tends to become markedly more traditional upon the birth of a child (Collins and Coltrane, 2000). Pedersen (1987) reported that fathers of infants devote less time to caretaking activities than do mothers. Entwhistle and Doering (1988) found that many fathers felt unskilled in infant care and, by way of compensation, tended instead to emphasize their abilities as protectors and providers. These roles, Harris and Morgan (1991: 532) pointed out, require men to assume "some paternal responsibilities for training and discipline" but do not require that the father–child relationship be especially close.

Basow (1992: 251) noted that a number of factors favour the likelihood of a father experiencing a satisfying involvement with his infant child; these include (1) his satisfaction with the marital relationship and with marital decision-making; (2) the birth order and sex of the child, with first-born sons commanding greater attention than first-born daughters or subsequent children; (3) his possession of child-centred parenting attitudes and anticipation of involvement in the provision of child care; (4) positive relations in his family of origin; (5) good self-esteem; and (6) specific instruction in traditionally female-assigned tasks such as feeding and diapering a child. However, Basow found that paternal involvement is "best predicted by the wife's encouragement of such involvement," noting that "[a] father's participation is greatest when an employed mother works long hours, earns more than the father, and supports the father's involvement in child care" (pp. 251, 254). A longitudinal study exploring factors associated with the involvement of fathers (in intact families) with their children found that although paternal involvement was predicted by different factors with children of different ages, it generally was continuous, multidimensional, and strongly associated with maternal involvement. With children 7 years of age, low parental socioeconomic status was related to low father involvement; with older children (ages 11 and 16), low father involvement was related to family size and poor school performance (Flouri and Buchanan, 2003; see also Marsiglio and Cohan, 2000).

According to conventional wisdom, children "need their mothers" during infancy and toddlerhood; but as they grow older, they increasingly need paternal involvement. However, a father's actual involvement with older children depends upon such factors as his work constraints, his gender ideology, the support he receives from a child's mother and his friends, and his own motivation, self-confidence, and skill (McBride and Rane, 1998). The best predictors of paternal involvement have been found to be a wife/mother's employment and a father's flexible definition of the masculine role (Basow, 1992: 251–252). Research has found that although the proportion of child care provided by fathers did increase with maternal employment, the actual time fathers with employed wives spent directly caring for an under-5-year-old child increased by less than half an hour per week and occurred primarily on weekends (Marsiglio, 1995). Husbands of professionally employed women have been found the most likely to share equally in young children's physical care (Darling-Fisher and Tiedje, 1990), and more highly educated, high-status fathers to offer more "assistance" in general child care (Booth and Crouter, 1998; Seward et al., 1996).

LaRossa (1988/1995: 370), cautioning that estimates of the actual amount of time fathers spend with their children may be inflated by both fathers and researchers, posed a rhetorical question:

> If we took ... the time to scrutinize the behavior of fathers and mothers in public would we find that ... the division of childcare is still fairly traditional? When a family with small children goes out to eat, for example, who in the family—mom or dad—is more accessible to the children; that is to say, whose dinner is more likely to be interrupted by the constant demands to "put ketchup on my hamburger, pour my soda, cut my meat"?

Paternal child-care activities most often reflect the father as recreational specialist—reading to or playing with children, taking them to the park, movie theatre, or sports events—while mothers continue to be charged with the bulk of such mundane, repetitive, physical-care tasks as feeding, dressing, and bathing (Ehrensaft, 1990). Thompson and Walker's (1991) review of research on parental roles summarized this division by terming fathers "playmates" and mothers "caregivers and comfort givers." Harris and Morgan (1991) have also noted that although fathers' involvement is typically greater with sons than with daughters from infancy onwards, the father–son relationship may become particularly thorny because of issues of competition and dominance (Basow, 1992: 252). However, some research finds evidence of change. Hall's (2005) cohort analysis of American fathers from two nationally representative data sets and from two time periods (1977 and 1997) reports that, compared to their counterparts in 1977, fathers in 1997 reported spending more time with their children on both workdays and non-workdays. Other research, however, echoes LaRossa's contention that the "culture of fatherhood" has changed more notably than the "conduct of fatherhood" (see, for example, Mormon and Floyd, 2002, 2006).

LaRossa (1988/1995: 370), noting that upper-middle-class professionals write the majority of books and articles heralding the arrival of "new and improved" fathers, observed that such authors cannot be considered in any way representative of North American fathers. He suggested that even when "putting in time" with their children, many fathers may be characterized as being "'there' in body, [but] ... someplace else in spirit" (LaRossa, 1988/1995: 371). Further, he remarked, "[t]oday ... the culture and conduct of fatherhood appear to be out of sync.... Fatherhood is different today than it was in prior times but, for the most part, the changes that have occurred are centered in the culture rather than the conduct of fatherhood" (La Rossa, 1988/1995: 373, 375).

Basow (1992: 252) suggested that given fathers' limited involvement with their children, "it is not surprising that most children and teenagers report a closer and better relationship with their mother than with their father." Based on his nationally representative survey of Canadian teens, Bibby (2001: 55) reported that "[t]he proportion of teens who say they receive high levels of enjoyment from their mothers (71%) is somewhat higher than the proportion who say the same things for dads (62%)"; he suggested that one reason "may be the limited time many fathers spend 'doing things' with their sons and daughters." He pointed to a recent Statistics Canada survey which found that whereas full-time working mothers spent 6.4 hours per day with their under-5-year-old children, similarly employed fathers spent 4.3 hours per day; "[b]y the time kids hit their teens, dads were giving an average of one hour a day to leisure activities with their teenagers— and three hours to such activities without them. Moms working full-time outside the home were finding about one hour of leisure time a day for their teens, and about two hours for themselves." An earlier Canadian survey found that "when something big goes wrong," 61 percent of Canadian teenagers wanted to tell their friends and 22 percent wanted to tell someone in their family. Ten percent wanted to tell their mothers, ten percent a sibling or grandparents, but only two percent wanted to share the news with dad. When "something great happens," 15 percent of teenagers wanted to share the news with family; 9 percent with "other" family members, 5 percent with mom, and only 1 percent with dad (Bibby and Posterski, 1992: 11). Whether with good news or bad, for support or advice, fathers are the least likely to be approached and appear to be perceived as the least approachable members of Canadian families.

Lamb (1987 in LaRossa, 1988/1995: 368) divided the concept of "parental involvement" into three components: **engagement**, in which a parent engages in one-to-one interaction with the child, be it play, helping with homework, or feeding; **accessibility**, in which a parent is occupied with one task but is available to tend to the child if needed; and **responsibility**, the most demanding form of involvement, which entails decision-making, planning, and carrying out tasks necessary to a child's well-being, from making sure the child has winter boots that fit to organizing the semi-annual visit to the dentist. Based upon a review of existing research, Lamb concluded that in dual-parent families where only fathers were employed, fathers spent only one fifth to one quarter as much time as mothers in "engagement," and two thirds as much in "accessibility." Regardless of whether mothers were employed or not, fathers did not assume the "responsibility" component of parental involvement. Only in the absence of a mother did fathers take on the responsibility role.

Solo Fathers Much of the research on solo parenting has focused on families headed by women; to date, research on single-father families remains limited (Meyer and

Garasky, 1993: 74). The available research suggests that **solo fathers** are neither incompetent nor superdads. Conway (1990: 20) observed that "studies of single parent fathers suggest they are quite successful at parenting, and they express more satisfaction than single-parent mothers." As he noted, their success may reflect the fact that solo fathers, as compared with **solo mothers**, tend to be older, better off financially, and (due to vestiges of the tender years doctrine) more likely to be raising older children. The finding that solo fathers tend to be more authoritarian than solo mothers may be explained with reference to men's familiarity with traditional parenting roles (Thomson et al., 1992) that assign fathers the responsibility for discipline and control. However, Hetherington et al. (1982), comparing the behaviour of mothers immediately after divorce to their behaviour two years later, found that mothers tended to assume "paternal behaviours," exerting greater control over time. For both male and female solo parents faced with the imperative of filling "all roles in one," parental-role performances tend towards eventual congruency (Emmers-Sommer et al., 2003).

Stepfathers In 1995, 10 percent of Canadian families (approximately 430 500 families) were stepfamilies; by 2001, the figure had risen to 12 percent (503 100). The configuration of these families reflects the most common child-custody arrangements: 50 percent of stepfamilies comprised a mother, her children, and a stepfather; only 10 percent consisted of a father, his children, and a stepmother. The other 40 percent were classified as "blended" families, comprising the children of one or both spouses' previous unions, along with any children born of the current union (*Canadian Global Almanac 2004*: 67). Although it is beyond the scope of this text to fully discuss the experience of stepfathers, one matter that has obvious relevance for the study of gender is the finding that various forms of child abuse appear to occur more frequently in stepfather families (Riedmann et al., 2003: 312; Margolin, 1992).

Research has indicated that even though only a low percentage of stepchildren are physically or sexually abused, the incidence of child abuse, especially sexual abuse, by stepfathers is higher than by biological fathers (Giles-Sim, 1997; Popenoe, 1998). In accounting for this finding, some theorize that stepfathers may feel less bound than biological fathers by culturally normative injunctions against incest (Popenoe, 1996). They invoke the "relative stranger" (Beer, 1988) explanation, especially for sexual abuse that occurs during the early stages of new stepfamily formation. Thomson et al. (1992) found that compared to biological parents, stepmothers, stepfathers, and cohabiting male partners (informal stepfathers) reported having significantly less to do with the children and responding to them less positively. Herman (1991) argued that as a result of their absence during a child's early years, stepfathers are less likely to perceive their stepchildren as "children" and more likely to regard them as sexual beings and therefore to react to them in a sexual way. Noting that the rate of sexual abuse by stepmothers is very low (as it is with mothers), she argued further that the gender gap in intrafamilial child sexual abuse is at least partly attributable to women's typical assumption of the child-nurturer role within the family. She maintained that the long-term routine of washing and diapering infants' bottoms disinclines most women from viewing a child's genitalia as "alluring" or "sexual" (see also Marsiglio, 2004), and contended that the greater participation of fathers and stepfathers in the physical care and nurturing of children would reduce their likelihood to abuse.

ULTIMATE VIOLENCE

This chapter concludes by noting that coercive and brutal behaviour between intimates, discussed in the previous chapter, sometimes culminates in **ultimate violence**: violence that results in death. Even though the circumstances that surround each act may be unique in many ways, homicides involving intimates commonly reveal gendered characteristics.

Spousal Homicide

In Canada, rates of spousal homicide have generally declined since the mid-1970s for both women and men (Statistics Canada, 2007j). Fedorowycz (1999) suggested that this decline "may primarily be the result of reduced exposure to abusive or violent relationships as a consequence of the changing living arrangements of men and women, improvements in the economic status of women, and increases in the availability of domestic violence services (e.g., safe houses or shelters, counselling, financial aid)." While a slight increase in spousal homicides occurred between 2005 and 2006 (marking the first increase in five years), and this increase was attributable to the increase in men killed by their wives (from 12 in 2005 to 26 in 2006), women remain the most likely victims of lethal violence in spousal relations. "Between 1975 and 2005, the rate of spousal homicide against females has been 3 to 5 times higher than against males (Ogrodnik, 2007). Aboriginal people in Canada suffer dispropor-tionately from spousal homicide, with the rate for Aboriginal women eight times the rate for non-Aboriginal women and for Aboriginal men, 38 times higher than for non-Aboriginal men (Ogrodnik, 2007: 67).

Canada's annual Homicide Survey (which provides national, police-reported data on the characteristics of all homicides that become known in a given year) has indicated that although males are more than twice as likely to be murdered than females (Dauvergne, 2003), "female homicide victims are far more likely than male victims to be killed by an intimate partner" (Koenig and Linden, 2004: 415). Between 1996 and 2005, 39 percent of spousal homicides involved victims living in a common-law relationship, 35 percent involved married persons, 24 percent involved those who were separated and 2 percent involved those who were divorced (Ogrodnik, 2007: 10). Of the 78 spousal homicides committed in 2006, 62 involved a current spouse (legally married or common-law) and 16 involved a former spouse (Statistics Canada, 2007j). Following marital separation, Canadian women (but not men) face a heightened risk of homicide victimization. Between 1997 and 2005, one third of spousal homicides involved couples that had separated or were in the process of separating, with the majority (57 percent) occurring during the separation process (e.g., following one partner's announcing an intent to leave, during the process of moving, while going through divorce proceedings) (Aston, 2007). In addition, "between 1961 and 2003, 1 in 10 solved homicides were cases in which the sus-pect took his/her own life following the homicide. Over one-half (57%) of family homicide-suicides involved spouses, and of these incidents, virtually all (97%) involved female victims killed by a male spouse" (Statistics Canada, 2005). Of the spousal homicide-suicides that have occurred in Canada since 1991, 42 percent of spousal homicide-suicide victims were killed by a legally married spouse, 30 percent were killed by a spouse from whom they were separated (30 percent) or divorced (3 percent), and 23 percent were killed by a common-law spouse. Approximately 2 percent of spousal homicide-suicide victims involved males killed by a female spouse. For the last three decades, men have also committed over 90 percent of all familicides in Canada. **Familicide** refers to a form of spousal homicide in which the offender kills not only a spouse but one or more of the couple's children at the same time (Barraclough and Harris, 2002; Fishbein, 2003).

Silverman and Kennedy (1993) noted that most spousal homicides are not sudden anomalous events but the culmination of escalating sequences of spousal violence. In cases where the partners are still living together, one of the most common legal defences offered by men charged with spousal homicide is "provocation." This defence may procure the reduction of charges from "murder" to "manslaughter" if the defendant is found to have killed "in the heat of passion caused by sudden provocation." Men who have found their wives in bed with another man have long employed this defence successfully. A relatively new defence has been offered in the case of wives charged with murdering their husbands: the **battered woman syndrome.**

The term "battered woman syndrome" was originally popularized by Walker (1979) to describe a pattern of **learned helplessness** in which a battered women, because of the persistent abuse she has experienced at the hands of her male partner, feels incapable of making any change in her way of living. In the precedent-setting case of *Regina v. Lavallee*, a trial court in Manitoba allowed expert testimony on this syndrome in support of a self-defence claim by Angelique Lavallee in her trial for second-degree murder. Historically, the law has required that force used in self-defence be no greater than one might expect a "reasonable man" to employ to defend himself when there are "reasonable and probable grounds" to believe that his life is in danger. However, expecting battered women to behave like "reasonable men" may itself be unreasonable.

At trial, Lavallee testified that she had shot her abusive male partner in the back of the head as he was leaving her room after having physically assaulted her and threatened her with death. The trial judge allowed expert testimony on Lavallee's behalf and a psychiatrist testified that Lavallee "had been terrorized [by her partner] to the point of feeling trapped, vulnerable, worthless and unable to escape the relationship despite the violence" (in Verdun-Jones, 2004: 81). The jury acquitted Lavallee, a decision that would later be upheld by the Supreme Court of Canada, which ruled that the trial judge had been correct in allowing the psychiatrist to testify and that his expert opinion had been useful in clarifying for the jury whether or not Lavallee's beliefs and actions were reasonable. As a result of a later Supreme Court decision in *R. v. Malott* (1998), testimony on the battered woman syndrome may now be presented to Canadian juries in order to assist their understanding of "(i) why an abused woman might remain in an abusive relationship; (ii) the nature and extent of the violence that may exist in an abusive relationship; (iii) the woman's ability to perceive when her partner was dangerous; and (iv) whether she believed on reasonable grounds that she could not otherwise preserve herself from death or grievous bodily harm."

Although acknowledgment of the battered woman syndrome may undoubtedly be of value to battered women in pleas of self-defence, certain concerns have been raised. First, it has been suggested that the term "syndrome" may refurbish the notion that women who kill abusive partners are deeply pathological individuals rather than normal people who have been forced to live in abnormal circumstances for a prolonged time. Schneider (in Faith, 1993: 104) remarked that "to successfully plead a Battered Woman Syndrome defense, a defendant must be presented as a defeated woman, a passive helpless victim whose irrational behaviour was the desperate act of a trapped animal." Second, the introduction of yet another "syndrome" to explain why women act the way they do ignores the ways in which society, including the criminal justice system, may fail to protect women and men from acts of lethal violence.

Key Terms

absolute privilege
accessibility
alimony
battered woman syndrome
best interests of the child
civil law
cohabitation
common law
compensatory spousal
    support
consortium
criminal conversation
culture of fatherhood
displaced homemakers
divorce rates
dowry
dual-provider father
engagement
familicide
Fordism
heartbalm tort

his and hers marriages
housekeeper role
ideology of motherhood
joint custody
kinkeeper role
learned helplessness
maintenance
marital interaction
marital roles
marriage
marriage rate
maternal preference
motherguilt
Motherhood Mandate
motherhood mystique
new reproductive
    technologies
no-fault divorce
parental alienation
    syndrome
paterfamilias

paternal preference
provider role
rehabilitative alimony
resource power
responsibility
reverse Pygmalion effect
selectivity hypothesis
sexual role
shock theory of marriage
sole custody
solo fathers
solo mothers
split custody
support
tender years doctrine
therapeutic role
total fertility rate (TFR)
ultimate violence

Chapter Summary

1. This chapter highlights how marriage and gender create and recreate one another in a continually interacting fashion.

2. In our society, marriage has traditionally served as an important rite of passage for adult femininity and, to a lesser degree, for adult masculinity.

3. Gender and gender inequality often become organizing principles in heterosexual marriages; external as well as internal cultural expectations about the roles of husband and wife dictate gender performance.

4. Assignment of the *therapeutic role* to women would seem to be based upon the traditional hierarchical structure of marriage, whereby the inferior partner is expected to nurture the superior partner. The role of *kinkeeper* represents an additional invisible strand of women's unpaid labour within the home. Research has noted that mothers assume the vast majority of responsibilities and duties associated with children's care and socialization, as well as perform most household chores.

5. Statistical projections suggest that the proportion of the Canadian population who marry will continue to decline, as will the proportion who will stay married. Despite changes to laws governing divorce, spousal support, and child custody, the economic

aftermath of divorce is often gendered, with solo mothers and their children at heightened risk of poverty.

6. Social constructions of "motherhood" and "fatherhood" result in gendered patterns of parenting. While some have suggested that we are witnessing the advent of a "new and improved" type of highly involved father, others suggest that the changes are more noticeable in the "culture of fatherhood" than in the "conduct of fatherhood."

7. Ultimate violence includes spousal homicide and familicide. Although every act of lethal violence is in many ways unique, homicides involving intimates nevertheless reveal gendered patterns.

CHAPTER 9

Gender and Aging

Although members of our youth-oriented society might prefer not to think in such terms, the processes of aging begin at birth. While the precipitants, processes, and outcomes of physical aging are more similar than they are different for women and men, the *social* processes of aging are more different than they are similar (Bedford, 2003). This chapter will focus on selected aspects of aging, and, more importantly, the social meanings of the aging process for each gender.

SEX-RATIO AND LIFE-EXPECTANCY DIFFERENTIALS

Sex-Ratio Differentials

The **sex ratio** of chromosomal male (XY) conceptions to chromosomal female (XX) conceptions is approximately 140 to 100 (Money and Tucker, 1975). In other words, at the moment of conception (and in the absence of technological intervention), 140 male embryos are created for every 100 female embryos. From conception onwards, as a consequence of gestation-period misfortunes such as miscarriages, spontaneous abortions, and stillbirths, that ratio begins to decline. The ratio of male to female births is generally around 106 (McVey and Kalbach, 1995: 56) or 105 (Saxton, 1990: 26) to 100. However, research on sex trends in Canadian live births from 1930 to 1990 reveals that there has been "a cumulative loss of 2.2 male births per 1000 live births from 1970 to the 1990s" (Allan et al., 1997: 37). Davis et al. (1998) also found a "statistically significant decline in the ratio of male to female births in several industrialized countries, including Denmark, the Netherlands, Canada, and the United States, that cannot be attributed to known factors." Pointing to parallel declines in Sweden, Germany, and Norway, and to reported increases both in birth defects of the male reproductive tract and in diseases such as testicular cancer, they suggested that this trend "may be a sentinel health indicator that some, as yet, unrecognized environmental health hazards are affecting both sex ratio and the other unexplained defects in male reproduction" (see also Grech et al., 2003).

Following birth, male and female survivorship and resulting sex ratios at different stages of the human life span vary from one society to another and within each society at different periods in history and across ethnic groups and social classes (Guttentag and Secord, 1983). Sen (2001) has emphasized that "[i]n some regions of the world, inequality between women and men directly involves matters of life and death, and takes the brutal form of unusually high mortality rates of women and a consequent preponderance of men in the total population, as opposed to the preponderance of women found in societies with little or no gender bias in health care and nutrition." He observed that this form of inequality has been "observed extensively" in North Africa and Asia.

One of the causes of mortality inequality is female infanticide, a practice primarily associated with South Asian countries but which has also periodically been reported in the Canadian Punjabi community (Marleau and Laporte, 1999; Stephen, 1991). In Tamil Nadu, India, the incidence of female infanticide has increased in recent years; this has been attributed to various factors, including "the low status of women, decreasing fertility and consequent intensification of son preference, spread of the practice of dowry across all caste groups, the green revolution and the resulting marginalization of women in agriculture, and a shift to cash cropping" (George, 2002: 190). The government of Tamil Nadu has undertaken various initiatives to combat female infanticide. In 1992, it launched the "Cradle Babies Scheme," which encouraged families to place unwanted baby girls in government-provided cradles, to be raised by primary health centres. Later that year, the "Jayalalitha Protection Scheme for the Girl Child" was introduced for poor families with no sons and one or two daughters. This program, designed to cover 20 000 families annually, offered financial incentives (in the form of a fixed account to be held in the name of the infant girl until her 21st birthday) if one parent agreed to be sterilized. The program aimed, unsuccessfully, to totally eradicate female infanticide by the year 2000. (In 1997, the Prime Minister of India announced a similar scheme—without the coercive sterilization stipulation—for the entire country).

Sex ratios may also be impacted by **natality inequality**. Sen (2001) reported that "with the availability of modern techniques to determine the gender of the fetus, sex-selective abortion has become common in many countries." He observed that this practice of "high-tech sexism" is "particularly prevalent in East Asia, in China and South Korea ... but also in Singapore and Taiwan, and is beginning to emerge as a statistically significant phenomenon in India and South Asia as well" (see Box 9.1). **Prenatal diagnosis (PND)** of sex through ultrasound or amniocentesis, followed by female **feticide** (i.e., killing of a fetus), has been "the most common method of sex selection practiced around the world for the last three decades" (Bhatia et al., 2003). However, several new genetic and asexual reproductive technologies also have the potential to alter sex ratios. Gene splicing is one; another is artificial insemination with "washed" sperm, in a sophisticated sex-preselection technique known as **Preimplantational Genetic Diagnosis (PGD)** or *Ericsson's technique* (Rajalakshmi, 2000). In this technique, a special solution is used to separate sperm bearing X-chromosomes from those bearing the sex-preferred Y-chromosomes, which are then collected and implanted into the fallopian tubes.

In North America, various "sex-sorting" methodologies are currently being touted as user-friendly techniques for achieving "family balancing" or "gender variety." Advertisements bearing such boldface headlines as "Do You Want to Choose the Gender [*sic*] of Your Next Baby?" have appeared in the *Sunday Styles* section of *The New York Times*, as well as in Canadian and American newspapers targeting South Asians living abroad (e.g., *Indian Express* and *India Abroad*) (Darnovsky, 2003). The cost of these "family-balancing" techniques is very high. For example, MicroSort (the trademarked name for one method of sperm-sorting originally developed for use in livestock production) carries a $3200 (US) price tag; in 2001, most American couples using this technique did so three times, at a reported cost of nearly $10 000 (US) (Bhatia et al., 2003: 2). *Fortune* magazine has estimated the U.S. market for this single method of sperm-sorting at between $200 million and $400 million per year "if aggressively marketed" (Darnovsky, 2003). Various companies are already turning huge profits marketing sex-selection devices in South Asian countries; General Electric leads the pack with "the largest market share for ultrasound scanners in India," including a "disproportionate number of these machines in Northwest India where the female to male child sex ratio is the lowest." In India, the use of PND, PGD, and pre-conception techniques remains "rampant" despite India's *Pre-Conception and Pre-Natal Sex Selection/Determination (Prohibition and Regulation) Act, 2001*, which specifically prohibits their use (Bhatia et al., 2003: 1; see also Park Ridge Centre, 2002). The legal status of prenatal sex-selection elsewhere is uneven.

In March 2003, China passed a law banning PND for sex-selection; in response to sex-selective abortions, Mainland China has made it illegal for physicians to reveal a fetus' sex. Article 4 of the Council of Europe's *Convention on Human Rights and Biomedicine* stipulates that "[t]he use of techniques of medically assisted procreation shall not be allowed for the purpose of choosing a future child's sex except where serious hereditary sex-related disease is to be avoided." "Although Vietnam in 2003 banned fetal sex-selection, many

Missing Women—Revisited

In the 1990s, Amartya Sen, 1998 Nobel Laureate in Economics, called attention to the phenomenon of "missing women." In his early writings, he emphasized how, in societies that devalue women, gender bias in health care and nutrition could result in unusually high female-mortality rates and a consequent preponderance of men in the population's sex-structure (see Sen, 2001). In the excerpt below, he suggests how the preference for boys over girls in male-dominated societies may lead to natality inequality.

The concept of "missing women" ... refers to the terrible deficit of women in substantial parts of Asia and north Africa, which arises from sex bias in relative care. The numbers are very large indeed. For example, using as the standard for comparison the [female-to-male] ratio of 1.022 observed in sub-Saharan Africa (since women in that region receive less biased treatment), I found the number of missing women in China to be 44 m[illion], in India 37 m[illion], and so on, with a total that easily exceeded 100 m[illion] worldwide, a decade or so ago. Others used different methods and got somewhat different numbers—but all very large (for example, Stephan Klasen's sophisticated demographic model yielded 89 m[illion] for the countries in question).

How have things moved more recently? At one level they have not changed much. The ratio of women to men in the total population, while changing slowly (getting a little worse in China and a little better in India, Bangladesh, Pakistan, and west Asia), has not altered radically in any of these countries. Even though the total numbers of missing women have continued to grow (Klasen's 89 m[illion] is now 93 m[illion] for the

same countries and 101 m[illion] for the world as a whole), this has resulted mainly from the absolute growth in population.

But another more important and radical change has occurred over the past decade. There have been two opposite movements: female disadvantage in mortality has typically been reduced substantially, but this has been counterbalanced by a new female disadvantage—that in natality—through sex-specific abortions aimed against the female fetus. The availability of modern techniques to determine the sex of the fetus has made such sex-selective abortion possible and easy, and it is being widely used in many societies. Compared with the normal ratio of about 95 girls being born per 100 boys (which is what we observe in Europe and North America), Singapore and Taiwan have 92, South Korea 88, and China a mere 86 girls born per 100 boys. Given the incompleteness of birth registration in India, that ratio is difficult to calculate, but going by the closely related ratio of girls to boys among young children (below 6) we find that the [female-to-male] ratio has fallen from 94.5 girls per 100 boys in the census of 1991 (almost in line with the ratio in Europe and North America) to 92.7 girls per 100 boys in the census of 2001.

The drop may not look particularly high (especially in comparison with China or Korea), but further grounds for concern exist. Firstly, these could be "early days," and it is possible that, as sex determination of the fetus becomes more standard, the Indian ratio will continue to fall. This is quite possible despite the fact that the Indian parliament has outlawed sex determination of the fetus (except when it is medically required) precisely to prevent its abuse

BOX 9.1

Missing Women—Revisited (*Continued*)

for sex-selective abortion. Secondly, variations within India are gigantic, and the all-India average hides the fact that in several states—in the north and west of India—the [female-to-male] ratio for children is very much lower than the Indian average and lower even than the Chinese and Korean numbers.

More interestingly, a remarkable division seems to run right across India, splitting the country into two nearly contiguous halves. Using the European [female-to-male] ratios of children (the German figure of 94.8 per 100 was used as the dividing line), all the states in the north and west have ratios that are very substantially below the benchmark figure, led by Punjab, Haryana, Delhi, and Gujarat (between 79.3 and 87.8 girls per 100 boys). On the other side of the divide, the states in the east and south of India tend to have [female-to-male] ratios that equal or exceed the benchmark line of 94.8, with Kerala, Andhra Pradesh, West Bengal, and Assam leading the pack with 96.3 to 96.6 girls per 100 boys. The solitary exception in this half is Tamil Nadu, with a figure just below 94, but that too is close to the European dividing line of 94.8 and well above the numbers for every northern and western state.

The higher incidence of sex-specific abortions in the north and the west cannot be explained by the availability of medical resources (Kerala or West Bengal do not have fewer of these than Bihar or Madhya Pradesh). The difference does not lie in religious background either, since Hindus and Muslims are divided across the country, and the behaviour of both groups conforms to the local pattern of the region. Nor can it be explained by the income level (since the list of deficit

states includes the richest, such as Punjab and Haryana, as well as the poorest, like Madhya Pradesh and Uttar Pradesh). Nor can it be explained by variations in economic growth (it includes fast-growing Gujarat as well as stagnating Bihar). Even female education, which is so effective in cutting down sex bias in mortality does not seem to have a similar effect in reducing sex bias in natality....

The remarkable division of India (splitting the country into disparate halves) is particularly puzzling. Are there differences in traditional cultural values that are hidden away? Is there any cultural or deep political significance in the fact that religion-based parties have been able to make much bigger inroads precisely in the north and the west and not in the east and the south? A simple but imperfect indication of this can be seen in the fact that in the last general election (held in 1999), 169 of the 197 parliamentary members of the Hindu right-wing parties were elected precisely from northern and western states. Or is all this purely coincidental, especially since the rise of religion-centred politics and the emergence of female feticide are both quite new in the parts of India where they have suddenly become common? We do not know the answer to any of these questions, nor to a great many others that can be sensibly asked. Sex bias in natality calls for intensive research today in the same way that sex bias in mortality—the earlier source of "missing women"—did more than a decade ago....

Source: Abridged from Amartya Sen. 2003. Editorial: Missing Women–Revisited: Reduction in Female Mortality Has been Counterbalanced by Sex Selective Abortions. BMJ, 327: 1297-1298, 8 December, http://bmj.bmjjournals.com/cgi/content/full/327/7427/1297. Amended and reproduced with permission from the BMJ Publishing Group.

doctors tell parents-to-be if they are expecting a boy or girl in ultrasound practices that have mushroomed in increasingly affluent Vietnam" (AFP, 2007). The Canadian government has wrestled with the legal and ethical challenges posed by the new reproductive technologies for almost two decades. In 1989, a Royal Commission on New Reproductive Technologies was established, issuing its final report (tellingly entitled *Proceed with Care*) in 1993; among its findings were that some commercial clinics in Canada were offering parents the service of treating sperm for sex-selection purposes. The federal government reacted by placing a voluntary moratorium on nine controversial practices, one of which was sex-selection of fetuses. The introduction of Bill C-47, the *Reproductive and Genetic Technologies Act* (which proposed criminalizing sex-selection) followed but died after first reading in the House of Commons when a federal election was called in the spring of 1997. After three more failed attempts to create a law to govern reproductive technologies, the *Assisted Human Reproduction Act* (Bill C-13) received royal assent on March 26, 2004. Among its provisions, this act makes sex-selection a crime if used for purposes other than the prevention, diagnosis, and treatment of a sex-linked disorder or defect (i.e., unless used to screen against an X- or Y-linked condition). In the United States, however, free enterprise reigns supreme; while the American Society of Reproductive Medicine, a trade association, discourages the use of PGD for sex-selection, clinics are not bound by its recommendations; thus, at present, there are "no legislative limits on the applications of PGD or sperm sorting in the United States" (Darnovsky, 2003).

It is evident that, where not prohibited, reproductive technologies have the potential to let couples custom-make an "ideal" family to please their tastes, not only in terms of sex composition (e.g., all boys, all girls, one of each) but of sex birth order (e.g., a first-born son, a second-born daughter). The potential impact of such decisions upon the overall sex ratio and the longer-term consequences for society as a whole have lead to serious discussions about the ethical use of reproductive technologies. As Bhatia et al. (2003) noted, "Screening out embryos of 'the wrong sex' underlies how the method is already used without reflection about its impact on how people are valued (or devalued) in society.... The issues of sex selection are strongly related to forms of oppression based not only on gender, but also on race, ability and class."

In their recent book, *Bare Branches: Security Implications of Asia's Surplus Male Population*, political scientists Hudson and den Boer (2004) argued that sex-selection technologies that skew sex ratios in favour of males may create imbalances unprecedented in human history and lead to ominous consequences. Extrapolating from historical case studies that suggest heightened social instability within countries with sex-ratio imbalances (i.e., "surplus" males), they predicted an enhanced likelihood of domestic instability and interstate war in many East and South Asia countries, particularly China and India, in the future. According to these researchers, sex-ratio imbalances often trigger both domestic and international violence. In countries with unbalanced sex ratios, they claimed, disproportionate numbers of restless, low-status young men (*guanggun*—a Chinese word for "bare branches" or "sticks"), thwarted in their efforts to find mates and lacking stable social bonds, generate high levels of crime and social disorder. Citing news reports of recent spikes in drinking, gambling, and violent crime among young men in certain rural villages in India, the authors forecasted that "[a]s their ranks grow, these unmarried young men are likely to be attracted to militant organizations" (in Glenn, 2004). In an attempt to cope with the social strains caused by these surplus men and provide a "safety valve" for their aggressive energies, governments may enlist them into military campaigns and high-risk public-works projects. The outcome favours increased militarism and ultranationalism: "The security logic of high-sex-ratio societies," the authors maintained, "predisposes nations to see some utility in interstate conflict. In addition to stimulating a steadier allegiance from bare branches, who are especially motivated by issues which involve national pride and martial prowess, conflict is often an effective mechanism by which governments can send bare branches away from national population centers, possibly never to return"(in Glenn, 2004).

The "bare branches" argument echoes a theory advanced in the late 1990s by two Canadian evolutionary psychologists. Mesquida and Wiener (1996) argued that "male coalitional aggression" is a reproductive fitness-enhancing social behaviour which, although unlikely to enhance the welfare of the general population, promotes the fitness of coalition participants. Their analyses of interstate and intrastate episodes of collective aggression since the 1960s revealed a "consistent correlation between the ratio of males 15 to 29 years of age per 100 males 30 years of age and older, and the level of coalitional aggression as measured by the number of reported conflict-related deaths." They argued that "the age composition of the male population should be regarded as the critical ecological/demographic factor affecting a population's tendency toward peace or violent conflict" (Mesquida and Wiener, 1996: 247; see also Kimmel, 2003). However, other scholars have scoffed at this argument, declaring the concept of "surplus males" offensive in itself for *a priori* casting low-status men as potential criminals and militants. They have accused the researchers of selectively using examples that bolster their claims while ignoring those that do not, and of failing to examine "how sex ratios interact with other variables that are believed to be linked to instability and war: rapid population growth, ethnic tension, poverty, and unstable availability of resources" (Glenn, 2004; see also Hall, 2002).

In Canada, male-to-female sex ratios of the overall population slowly (and somewhat erratically) declined over the twentieth century, from 106 in 1921 to parity (100) in 1971 (Statistics Canada, 1972), falling to 97.2 in 1991, 96.1 in 2001, and 95.9 in 2006 (Statistics Canada, 1997, 2007r). In 2006, women outnumbered men in all provinces with the exception of Alberta, where the sex ratio was 100.2 (Statistics Canada, 2007r). In all three territories, however, as well as in the northern region of most provinces, men outnumbered women—a situation which reflects the nature of employment opportunities in these areas as well as the relative youthfulness of the population.

Our declining sex ratio is primarily a consequence of three factors. First, with the notable exception of the post–World War II baby boom, our fertility levels have been gradually declining since the middle of the nineteenth century and are currently below the replacement level (Statistics Canada, 2007r: 7). Second, proportionately more men die at all ages than do women (Wilkins, 1996). Third, significantly more women live to older ages than do men. The ratio of men to women in our society declines rapidly among older age groups. In 2006, for example, "nearly two out of three persons aged 80 years and over were women" (Statistics Canada, 2007r: 4). Of the 4635 Canadian centenarians at the time of the 2006 Canadian census, 3825 (82.5 percent) were women (Statistics Canada, 2007r: 11).

TABLE 9.1	Sex Ratio*, Select Years, Canada, Provinces and Territories													
	Canada	N.L	P.E.I.	N.S	N.B.	Que.	Ont.	Man.	Sask.	Alta.	B.C.	Y.T.	N.W.T.	Nvt.
1956	102.8	106.3	103.5	103.4	101.7	100.3	101.4	103.6	108.6	109.1	106.3	130.2	138.3	-
1966	100.9	104.5	102.6	101.3	101.1	99.7	99.9	101.1	104.9	104.1	102.5	118.7	118.2	-
1976	99.2	103.3	100.7	99.9	100.4	97.9	98.3	98.9	101.8	102.9	99.9	115.5	111.3	-
1986	97.4	100.1	98.7	97.3	97.8	96.1	96.4	97.1	99.8	101.6	98.1	110.3	110.4	-
1996	96.5	97.6	96.4	94.7	96.7	95.8	95.7	96.7	97.7	100.0	97.7	106.7	106.2	109.9
2006	95.9	94.6	93.4	92.9	94.9	95.6	95.2	96.3	96.4	100.2	95.9	101.3	104.9	105.2

* Number of males for 100 females.

Note: In this table, Nunavut is included in the Northwest Territories until 1986.

Source: Adapted from Statistics Canada, 2007: 25.

Life-Expectancy Differentials

The age limit of human longevity, or **life expectancy**, was established with the evolution of modern-day humans more than 100 000 years ago. The maximum human **life span** is approximately 120 years (Perlmutter and Hall, 1985: 61). Examination of successive editions of the *Guinness Book of Records* reveals that those who have held the title of "world's oldest living human being" have usually been women. According to this source, the world record for longevity (as fully authenticated by official documents) was attained by France's Jeanne-Louise Calment, who died in 1997 at the age of 122 years and 164 days. Upon Calment's death, French Canadian Marie-Louise Meilleur became the oldest individual in the world; in 1998, when she died, Meilleur was 117 years, 230 days old. At the time of writing (April, 2008), American Edna Parker was the world's oldest living woman (at 114 years, 341 days), and Tomoji Tanabe of Japan (at 112 years, 190 days), the world's oldest man (guinnessworldrecords.com, 2008). In Canada, "[a]ccording to the latest population projections, the number of centenarians could triple to more than 14,000 by 2031" (Statistics Canada, 2007r: 10). Nevertheless, the proportion of those who will reach the upper limits of the human life span is small.

Based upon known **mortality** rates for males and females at various ages and assuming that these rates remain constant (i.e., barring major catastrophes and miracle cures), it is possible to calculate average life expectancies. In pre-Confederation Canada, the average life expectancy of early European pioneers was 30 to 35 years (Lavoie and Oderkirk, 1993: 3). Canadians born in the twentieth century, however, have benefited enormously from rapidly improving conditions. For the past several decades, the life expectancy of Canadians "has consistently ranked among the top 10 of all OECD (Organization for Economic Co-operation and Development) countries" (DesMeules et al., 2003: 1). In Canada, life expectancy at birth "increased slightly to new record highs for both sexes in 2001. A woman born in 2001 could expect to live 82.2 years, up 0.2 years from 2000. A man's life expectancy at birth reached 77.1 years in 2001, up 0.3 years" (Statistics Canada, 2003g). In 2002, the life expectancy at birth for Canadian men, but not women, increased; "[m]en who were born in 2002 could expect to live to the record high age of 77.2." The life expectancy of women at birth remained unchanged at 82.1 years (Statistics Canada, 2004g).

It should be emphasized, however, that not all Canadians have benefited equally from these increases. Research has been undertaken to examine the impact of income on mortality by comparing life expectancy at birth of residents of the poorest and richest neighbourhoods of Canada's urban areas. It was found that although the gap in life expectancy narrowed substantially between 1971 and 1996, in 1996 there was still a five-year gap between the life expectancies of men in the lowest- and highest-income neighbourhoods, and a smaller but still significant gap (less than two years) for women. Similarly, while only 53 percent of men and 73 percent of women in the poorest neighbourhoods were expected to survive to age 75, the comparable figures for those in the richest group were 69 and 80 percent respectively (Statistics Canada, 2002i). Differences were also evident in infant mortality, with 6.4 deaths per 1000 live births in Canada's poorest neighbourhoods, compared to 4.0 in the richest. In addition, the life expectancy of Aboriginal people is seven to eight years lower than that of non-Aboriginal Canadians, and the infant-mortality rate double that among the non-Aboriginal population (Health Canada, 1999; Trovato, 2001). In 2001, life expectancy in "Inuit-inhabited areas" (i.e., the Inuvialuit region of the Northwest Territories, Nunavut, Nunatsiavut [Labrador], and Nunvik [northern Quebec]) was more than 12 years less than for Canada as a whole and the infant mortality rate was approximately four times higher than elsewhere in Canada (Statistics Canada, 2008h).

Table 9.2 shows increases in life expectancy for men and women born in Canada during the twentieth century. A few preliminary comments are necessary before proceeding to gender-specific issues. Each column in the table indicates *the number of additional years an individual can be expected to live upon achieving a particular age* (assuming that existing death rates remain constant). Up to a point, the longer a person lives, the longer that person can be expected to live. If a person survives the hazards associated with a specific stage of life in a specific historical period, his/her chances of living even longer increase.

During the early part of the twentieth century—an historical period of high infant mortality—the first birthday represented a major survival milestone for Canadian infants (King et al., 1991). Males and females born in 1926 (not shown in table) could expect to live about 57 and 59 years respectively. However, for boys who succeeded in reaching their first birthday, life expectancy rose to approximately 64 years; for girls, to between 64 and 65 years. Thus, surviving that first perilous year increased the life expectancy of Canadians by five or six years. Between 1921 and 2001, significant improvements in diet, nutrition, and sanitation, as well as new medical technologies and the greater availability of health-care delivery systems, led to at-birth life expectancy increasing 21.6 and 18.2 years for women and men respectively. The first year of life is not as hazardous as it once was, even though the infant mortality rate in Canada (5.4 per 1000 live births in 2005) is still relatively high compared to the rate in Japan (2.8) and Sweden (2.4) (Statistics Canada, 2008i). According to DesMeules et al. (2003: 1), "approximately half of the increase in life expectancy before the 1980s can be attributed to a decline in infant mortality, whereas more recent increases are due to a decline in the mortality rate of older people."

TABLE 9.2	Life Expectancy by Age and Sex, Canada, Selected Years: 1921–2001							
	At birth		At age 20		At age 40		At age 65	
Year	Women	Men	Women	Men	Women	Men	Women	Men
1921	60.6	58.8	49.1	48.9	32.7	32.1	13.6	13.0
1931	62.1	60.0	49.8	49.1	33.0	32.0	13.7	13.0
1941	66.3	63.0	51.8	49.6	34.0	31.9	14.1	12.8
1951	70.9	66.4	54.4	50.8	35.7	32.4	15.0	13.3
1961	74.3	68.4	56.7	51.5	37.4	33.0	16.1	13.6
1971	76.4	69.4	58.3	51.8	39.1	33.3	17.6	13.8
1981	79.1	71.9	60.2	53.4	40.8	34.7	18.9	14.6
1991	80.9	74.6	61.7	55.6	42.2	36.8	19.9	15.7
1996	81.2	75.4	61.9	56.3	42.4	37.4	19.9	16.0
2001	82.2	77.0	62.8	57.9	43.3	38.8	20.6	17.1

Source: Lindsay and Almey, 2006: 76.

The gap in the life expectancies of Canadian men and women increased over much of the last century, peaking in the early 1980s at more than seven years and diminishing since then. While the **gender life-expectancy gap** has narrowed over the past two decades, a gap (of 4.8 years in 2004) remains. A major factor in women's increased life expectancy over the course of the last century has been the reduction in the health hazards associated with pregnancy and childbirth. Until the 1940s, the mortality rates of Canadian women of childbearing age (i.e., age 20 to 49) were higher than those of same-aged men; today, however, the mortality rates of Canadian women are lower than those of men across all age groups: "Over the latter half of the twentieth century, a 52% reduction in the female age-adjusted mortality rate from all causes combined has been observed, as compared with a 39% decrease for males" (DesMeules et al., 2003: 1). Canadian women also enjoy a longer "health-adjusted life expectancy" than Canadian men, "although the sex gap is less pronounced than that of life expectancy" (DesMeules et al., 2003: 2).

In economically developed countries such as Canada and the United States, the lack of commensurate life-expectancy gains for men is linked to the fact that, at all ages, men are more likely to die than women. This phenomenon appears to be attributable to the more hazardous lifestyle associated with masculinity in our society. Former radical profeminist and now leading men's rights activist Warren Farrell (1993, 1986) is appalled that this has become an acceptable fact of life in our society, claiming that men have become the marginalized "disposable" sex. He has questioned our society's priorities and commitment to equality, pondering what might happen if "we cared as much about saving males as saving whales" (Farrell, 1993: 229). Farrell (1993) explored the stresses of masculinity, the health and safety hazards of many male-dominated occupations and work environments (including the military), the causes and consequences of men's greater likelihood of becoming victims of violence, and the connection between precepts of masculinity and suicide. Many leading causes of mortality, including motor-vehicle accidents, suicide, lung and other smoking-related cancers, and HIV/AIDS, account for significantly more deaths among men than among women in Canada. Good et al. (2000) focused attention on the adverse health effects of cultural messages directed at men, such as "be tough and restrict emotions," "be competitive and successful," "be aggressive, fearless, and invulnerable," "be independent," and "be a stud."

In his discussion of the "fragile male," Kraemer (2000) concurred with many of these arguments, but emphasized that male vulnerability may stem in part from biology. Writing that "[t]he human male is, on most measures, more vulnerable than the female," he pointed out that from the time of conception, a male fetus faces greater risk of damage or death and that stillbirths, premature births, congenital deformities of the genitals and limbs, cerebral palsy, and perinatal brain damage are all more common among males than females; he also noted that this pattern of disadvantage continues throughout life. He maintained that the "excess of non-fatal and fatal accidents among boys seems to be part of a pattern of poor motor and cognitive regulation in the developing male, leading to misjudgment of risk" and suggested that "[a]ndrogens could be implicated in the earlier death of males." He believed that men's lesser longevity may result from an interaction of biology and environment. Although, as he observed, "a typical attitude to boys is that they are, or must be made, more resilient than girls," this stance simply adds "social insult to biological injury" (p. 1609).

The facts of life and death for men, however, are not unremittingly grim. "[S]ince 1981, gains in life expectancy among females have only been about half those experienced by males. Indeed, between 1981 and 2001, the life expectancy of newborn females increased by over three years, whereas the figure among males was up 5 years in the same period" (Lindsay and Almey, 2006d: 55). Similarly, while life expectancy in Canada rose in 2004 for both sexes, "the growth was stronger among men. For men, life expectancy increased by 0.4 years to 77.8 years, while for women, it went up by only 0.2 years to 82.6 (Statistics Canada, 2006m). The recent decrease in the life-expectancy gap appears to be attributable to a growing similarity between the lifestyles of the sexes, with a greater increase in health among males and a slight increase in ill-health among females. The increase in women's ill-health appears to be a consequence of their increased participation in life-threatening activities (including certain formerly male-dominated occupations) and use of unhealthy coping methods, such as alcohol and tobacco (Stillion and McDowell, 2001/2002; Stillion and Noviello, 2001).

Gender Mortality Differentials

The leading causes of death for both men and women are the same: cardiovascular disease and cancer. While the proportion of deaths caused by cardiovascular disease has declined over the past quarter century (with deaths among males declining at a slightly faster rate than female deaths [-5.5 percent versus -4.3 percent]) and the proportion of deaths caused by cancer has increased (with female deaths increasing at a slightly faster rate [8.5 percent versus 5.4 percent]), these two causes combined accounted for approximately 60 percent of all deaths in 2004.

"From 1979 to 2004, the sex ratio for deaths due to cardiovascular diseases decreased sharply, from 125 to 101 males per 100 females. During the same period, the sex ratio for deaths due to cancer declined gradually, from 126 to 111 males per 100 females" (Statistics Canada, 2007s, 2007t; Figure 9.1). In 2004, heart disease was responsible for 30 percent of all deaths in Canada, while cancer was responsible for 23 percent (Statistics Canada, 2007s). The death rate due to heart disease among Canadian women is currently about half that of men. There are also some notable differences in the characteristics of heart disease in the male and female population. Among them: "[w]omen tend to experience a wider range of symptoms; they are less likely than men to be investigated and treated for the disease with medication, surgery and other interventions; and they generally have poorer health outcomes" (Lindsay and Almey, 2006d: 58). Moreover, some of the risk factors for heart disease, such as hypertension, diabetes, and depression, appear to pose greater risks among females than males.

Although "the cancer death rate among women is currently 50% lower than that of males" (Lindsay and Almey, 2006d: 58), some ominous changes have occurred. For example, while the age-standardized lung cancer death rate declined by 10 percent between 1979 and 2001, the death rate due to lung cancer for females doubled. From 2000 to 2004, female deaths due to cancer of the trachea, bronchus, and lung increased three times faster than male deaths (16 percent versus 5 percent). While the incidence of new cases of cancer remains lower among Canadian women than men, the number of cases of cancer detected for every 100 000 females in 2004 was 3 percent higher than in 1994; the incidence of new cases of cancer among men declined by 8 percent over this period (p. 58). While breast cancer accounts for the largest share of new cases of cancer among Canadian women, "[b]etween 1994 and 2004 the age-standardized incidence rate of new cases of lung cancer among women was 22% higher, while the figure declined 17% among men" (p. 61).

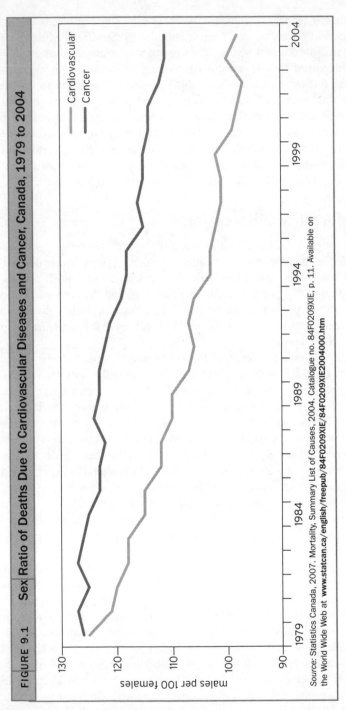

FIGURE 9.1   Sex Ratio of Deaths Due to Cardiovascular Diseases and Cancer, Canada, 1979 to 2004

Source: Statistics Canada, 2007. Mortality, Summary List of Causes, 2004. Catalogue no. 84F0209XIE, p. 11. Available on the World Wide Web at **www.statcan.ca/english/freepub/84F0209XIE/84F0209XIE2004000.htm**

An examination of mortality in Canada by DesMeules et al. (2003: 4) distinguished "external" or *exogenous* causes of death (e.g., accidents, smoking-related causes, and other causes that could be forestalled through primary prevention) from "internal"(i.e., sex/biology-related) or *endogenous* causes of death. Among women, endogenous causes include breast cancer, gynecologic tumours (e.g., cancers of the endometrium, ovaries, vulva, vagina, placenta, adnexa, and cervix), and complications of pregnancy; among men, endogenous causes include prostate disease and cancers of the genital organs. They reported that "[o]verall, internal causes of death are more common among women ... than among men." External causes—especially related to HIV/AIDS—are a much greater factor in the mortality rates of Canadian men. Deaths due to another external cause—suicide—are also notably higher among Canadian males than females. Based on their analysis of suicides among Canadians 10 years of age and older between 1979 and 1998, Langelois and Morrison (2003) reported that while the Canadian suicide death rate remained fairly stable during this period, the suicide rate of males was approximately four times that of females. "[I]n 2002, there were 5 suicides for every 100,000 women, compared with 18 per 100,000 men" (Lindsay and Almey, 2006d: 68).

Morbidity Differentials

Morbidity has been defined as "acute and chronic illnesses and diseases and the symptoms and impairments they produce" (Mooney et al., 2003: 32) or, more succinctly, as "departure from an overall state of health" (DesMeules et al., 2003a: 19). In 2003, Canadian men were only slightly more likely than women to self-rate their health as either "excellent" (23.2 percent of men versus 21.5 percent of women) or "very good" (36.3 percent of men versus 35.8 percent of women) (Statistics Canada, 2003h). In Canada, as elsewhere, self-reported health is positively associated with social class as measured by household income; for example, while roughly three quarters (73 percent) of Canadian men and women in the highest-income households defined their health as either "excellent" or "very good," only 61 percent of those in middle-income households and 47 percent in the lowest-income households did so (Health Canada, 1999: 15). According to the 2000–2001 Canadian Community Health Survey, wealthier women are almost twice as likely as lower-income women to report excellent/very good health (Maclean et al., 2003a: 5). Health benefits also accrue to well-educated Canadians: University graduates are more likely than those with less than a high-school education to rate their health as excellent (Health Canada, 1999: 42). The 2000–2001 Canadian Community Health Survey also found that highly educated women are more likely than their less-educated counterparts to engage in health-promoting practices (e.g., physical activity, health-improvement measures), about twice as likely to rate their health as excellent/very good, and less likely to engage in risky health practices (e.g., smoking, unprotected sex) (Maclean et al., 2003a).

While Canadian women enjoy a higher life expectancy than men, "they do not appear to have a similar advantage when morbidity is defined in a variety of ways (e.g., hospitalization rates, prevalence of chronic conditions, or disability)" (DesMeules, 2003a: 19). Thus, while hospitalization rates for both women and men have steadily declined over the past several decades, women are hospitalized about four times more frequently than men, especially during the young-adult years. Data on hospital emergency-room visits reveal a similar pattern (DesMeules et al., 2003a: 1). Differential hospitalization rates are partially explicable with reference to pregnancy: More than half of all hospitalizations among women ages 20 to 44 are related to pregnancy and childbirth (DesMeules et al., 2003: 19). Whereas men are more likely than women to be hospitalized for circulatory and respiratory diseases and for injury/poisoning, women are more likely than men to be hospitalized for cancer, mental disorders, and musculoskeletal diseases. As well, chronic conditions are generally more prevalent among women; "[i]n 2003, 74% of the female population aged 15 and over living in a private household had at least one ... chronic health condition, compared with 65% of their male counterparts" (Lindsay and Almey, 2006d: 54). Prevalence rates of such chronic conditions as allergies, bronchitis, emphysema, back ailments, arthritis and rheumatism, and high blood pressure are higher among women; women are also more likely than men to report a multiplicity of chronic conditions. "The higher prevalence of disability ... among women as compared with men is also fairly well established ... and is at least in part accounted for by the higher prevalence of disabling chronic conditions, such as arthritis, among women" (DesMeules et al., 2003a: 2).

According to the Canadian Mental Health Association (2002), one in five Canadians will be affected by a mental illness at some time in their lives. The Canadian Community Health Survey on Mental Health and Well-Being, conducted in 2002, reported that women of all ages, but particularly young women age 15 to 24, are more likely than men to perceive their mental health to be simply "fair" or "good" (Lindsay and Almey, 2006d: 67). The most common mental disorder, depression, is estimated to affect one in four Canadian women and one in ten Canadian men at some point in their lives (Canadian Psychiatric Association, 2002). The National Population Health Survey found that the self-reported incidence of depression in Canada in 1999 was 5.7 percent among women and 2.9 percent among men, with the highest rates of depression occurring among women of reproductive age (Stewart et al., 2003: 39). Women who were lone parents were more likely than other women to experience depression (15 percent versus 7 percent). Being overweight and daily smoking are associated with depression in women; predictive factors for depression include previous depression, chronic health problems, traumatic events in childhood/young adulthood, a lack of emotional support, and a low sense of mastery (Stewart et al., 2003: 39). Although depression may be treated with medication, this survey indicates that more than two thirds (67.6 percent) of women experiencing depression were not taking antidepressants and that "[o]nly 43% of those reporting a major depressive episode had consulted a health professional about the problem" (Stewart et al., 2003: 39). However, women are still more likely to be diagnosed and treated for depression than are men (Kessler, 2000; Lips, 2001: 287); proposed explanations for these differences include underreporting by men, mood amplification in women, gender roles, and biological influences (Frank, 2000; Rosenfeld, 2000).

While the rate of mood disorders (e.g., depression, anxiety) is higher among women, the rate of personality disorders (e.g., antisocial personality disorder) is higher among men; men are also more likely to suffer from alcoholism (Flanagan and Blashfield, 2003; Health Canada, 1999: 171–172; Lewis-Hall et al., 2002). *Dementia*, characterized by "severe losses of cognitive and emotional abilities" (Burke et al., 1997: 24) that eventually interfere with the ability to function in daily life, may strike both men and women as a result of Alzheimer's disease, Huntington's chorea, or other conditions. Lindsay and Anderson (2003: 41) reported that "while prevalence and incidence rates of dementia do not differ markedly between women and men, women live longer on average, so the number of women with dementia is greater than that of men"; for both sexes, the prevalence of dementia increases with age, "approximately doubling every five years from ages 65 to 84."

According to the 2000–2001 Canadian Community Health Survey, "[w]omen are more likely than men to use prescribed psychoactive drugs of all categories" (e.g., pain relievers: 24 percent versus 20 percent; sleeping pills: 21.2 percent versus 1.7 percent; tranquilizers: 1.1 percent versus 0.8 percent) (Cormier et al., 2003: 13). National Population

Health data also revealed that Canadian women were more likely than men (87 percent compared to 70 percent) to have taken at least one prescription or over-the-counter drug in the previous two days: "Across all age groups, women were more likely than men to be taking one or two medications, but less likely to be taking three at the same time" (Health Canada, 1999: 151). Our knowledge of the greater incidence of physical-health problems among women is due, at least in part, to the fact that women are more likely than men to report having consulted a physician (87 percent versus 73 percent). While Health Survey findings revealed no noticeable differences between men's and women's reported contacts with dentists, eye doctors, or chiropractors, women were more likely than men to use alternative health-care providers (e.g., chiropractors, acupuncturists, homeopaths, massage therapists): In 2003, 17 percent of Canadian women age 15 and over, compared to 9 percent of their male counterparts, reported that they had used some form of alternative health care.

One factor contributing to women's greater contact with physicians is pregnancy; another is a growing responsiveness to widespread campaigns exhorting women over the age of 40 to get regular examinations for early detection of cancer—particularly breast cancer, the most common invasive cancer among Canadian women (Bryant, 2003). Mothers are also typically the ones responsible for taking children to the doctor; as such, they may have greater opportunity to consult with physicians. However, this heightened opportunity does not guarantee that care will be sought or superior care obtained. In relation to cardiovascular disease (CVD), for example, Grace et al. (2003: 31) observed that although women "present with a wider range of symptoms," they are "more likely to delay seeking medical care, and are less likely to be investigated and treated for CVD with evidence-based medications, angioplasty, or coronary artery bypass graft than are men." The fact that men report less contact with physicians appears to be largely attributable to socialization messages dictating that men "tough it out." Researchers have also found that the sexes "respond differently to minor illnesses," with women more likely to respond quickly to cold or flu symptoms with some type of self-treatment or by consulting a physician, and men more likely to ignore symptoms altogether (Statistics Canada, 2001). Men may also fail to benefit from early diagnosis and treatment for potentially serious maladies; for example, despite the wide availability of detection tests and successful treatments for prostate cancer, 3708 Canadian men died from this disease in 2002 (Statistics Canada, 2004g).

However, it is assuredly true that factors other than gender impact upon the likelihood that Canadians will consult with health-care professionals. For example, data from the 2003 and 2005 Canadian Community Health Survey indicates that "[g]ay men, lesbians and bisexuals were more likely than heterosexuals to report having had an unmet health care need in the past year". Compared to heterosexual women, "[l]esbian and bisexual women had higher odds of not having a regular doctor". Women's use of preventive screening for cancer also varied by sexual identity with, for example, "[f]ewer than two-thirds of lesbians ... [reporting] having had a Pap test within the past three years, well below the figures for heterosexual (77.1%) and bisexual women (76.2%)" (Statistics Canada, 2008j).

Smoking rates have dropped substantially among Canadians 15 years of age and over. However, "the decline in smoking prevalence among men has been much more pronounced than it has for women over the last few decades" (Kirkland et al., 2003: 11): down from 61 percent to 25 percent among men from 1965 to 2003, as compared with a reduction from 38 percent to 21 percent over this period among women (Lindsay and Almey, 2006d: 61). While smoking rates are highest among francophone and Aboriginal peoples in Canada, smoking behaviour also varies by age. Anti-smoking campaigns and school/workplace bans on smoking behaviour have been somewhat less effective on young women than on young men; smoking rates among teenage girls now slightly exceed rates among their male counterparts. In 2003, 3.9 percent of females ages 12 to 14 smoked daily or occasionally, compared to 2.9 percent of males; at ages 15 to 19, 22.2 percent of females, compared to 21.8 percent of males, did so (Lindsay and Almey, 2006d: 78). The likelihood of smoking also varies by social class: According to the 1998–1999 National Population Health Survey (NPHS), 29.2 percent of Canadian men and 26.4 percent of Canadian women were current smokers; however, among the highest-income group, 21.2 percent of women and 22.1 of men were smokers, compared to 33.7 percent of women and 44.5 percent of men among the lowest-income group (Kirkland et al., 2003: 11).

In general, males are more likely than females to use or abuse alcohol. In 2003, among Canadians 12 and over, 51 percent of females and 69 percent of males reported that they drank an alcoholic beverage at least once a month. At all ages, men are also more likely to be heavy drinkers. "[I]n 2003, 12% of females aged 12 and over who were current drinkers, versus 29% of their male counterparts, reported they had had five or more drinks at one sitting at least once a month" (Lindsay and Almey, 2006d: 70). Among those Canadians who were "regular" drinkers (i.e., consuming one to six drinks each week), men were more likely to report a higher average weekly consumption than women and to drink more frequently (Cormier et al., 2003; Mooney et al., 2003). The 2000 Project Canada survey on youth found that while one in five Canadian teens drank beer, wine, or other forms of alcohol at least once a week, the weekly level for males was almost twice that of females (Bibby, 2001: 97). Binge drinking (the consumption of five or more alcoholic beverages on at least one occasion) is most common among the young, but more common among young men (Health Canada, 1999: 171). Women are also much less likely to report driving after drinking (5 percent versus 15 percent).

Using the Body Mass Index (BMI), a measure of weight relative to height, researchers have found that men are more likely than women to be overweight (a BMI of 25 to 29) or obese (BMI higher than 30). "Between 1985 and 2000–2001, the prevalence of overweight ... increased from 19% to 26 % among women" (Bryant and Walsh, 2003: 9). While overweight also increased among men, it decreased between 1994 and 2001 (from 44 percent to 40 percent). The prevalence of obesity among both sexes also increased over this time (from 7 to 14 percent among women and 6 to 19 percent among men). In 2003 in Canada, "39% of the female population aged 18 and over were considered to be either overweight or obese, whereas this was the case for 57% of males" (Lindsay and Almey, 2006d: 72). Among Canadians ages 20 to 64 years old, a higher percentage of women than men are underweight (BMI under 20)—12.3 percent versus 3.9 percent— with the problem of low body weight particularly pronounced among young Canadian women; in the 20–24 age group, one in four (25.2 percent) are below the healthy weight range.

Overall, available data indicate that in our society, adult women have higher rates than adult men of most forms of morbidity (with the exception of sex-specific forms), a pattern that has consistently been found in previous decades of Canadian and American research. A number of hypotheses have been offered in explanation of gender morbidity differentials. Each has its supporters and critics, but no wholly satisfactory theory has yet emerged, a fact that hints at the complexity of the issue. The **social acceptability hypothesis** (Gee and Kimball, 1987: 34) contends that as a consequence of gender socialization and existing gender expectations, women are more likely than men to report symptoms of illness and also to take action by seeking medical help. While some researchers have argued that measures of health which rely on self-ratings may simply reflect women's greater propensity to *report* ill-health (Walters et al., 2002), other research has suggested otherwise (see McMullin, 2004: 255). The **role compatibility hypothesis** (Gee and Kimball, 1987: 34) holds that because women's roles are less onerous than men's (a dubious contention, clearly based on the premise that "women's work" is not really "work"), women can more easily find more time both to be "sick" and to seek out treatment. The somewhat related **fixed role obligations hypothesis** (Gee and Kimball, 1987: 34) argues that women face fewer time constraints and are less likely to be locked into a fixed schedule, which gives them more freedom to define themselves as "sick" or to engage in the "sick-role" (Parsons, 1953). All three of these hypotheses imply that women's higher morbidity rates do not really mean that they are more likely to experience genuine ill-health.

In contrast, the *nurturant* (Gee and Kimball, 1987: 34) or **differential exposure hypothesis** (McMullin, 2004: 255) suggests that the stresses and strains associated with nurturing or caring for others, in both familial and non-familial contexts, contributes to greater ill-health among women. This hypothesis argues that as a consequence of their social assignment into the role of "caregiver," women actually *do* suffer more ill-health than men. Antonucci (2001: 433) observed that the intensity of women's friendships and their greater tendency to feel personally responsible for solving the problems of their spouses, family members, and friends may be hazardous to their health: "Women have been shown to reflect this concern through lower levels of happiness and higher levels of depressive symptomatology." While men's more distal relationships and relative lack of a support network may produce feelings of loneliness or estrangement, women's more intense relationships may also prove hazardous to their well-being. Antonucci noted that "evidence suggests that, in fact, women have both more positive and more negative relationships with others, often the same people." Although women are more likely than men to "feel strong, positive feelings of affection towards their spouse, children, family, and friends," they are also more likely to report "higher levels of conflict, disagreement, and frustration with these same relationships" (p. 450).

The complementary **differential vulnerability hypothesis** maintains that "women are more affected by stressors than men on account of a 'generalized female disadvantage in social roles and coping resources'" (McDonough and Walters, 2001: 549, in McMullin, 2004: 255). Since no one hypothesis can account for all reported and actual differences in men's and women's health, certain hypotheses might best be applied to limited areas (e.g., frequency of medical appointments).

Baruch et al. (1983) identified two crucial components of women's mental health: **mastery** (the degree of control a woman feels she has over her life) and **pleasure** (the degree to which she enjoys her life). Their research discovered that the best single predictor of mastery was participation in a challenging and well-paid job that allowed a woman to use her skills and make decisions; the best single predictor of pleasure was a positive relationship with a husband (including an active and satisfying sexual life) and children. The highest scores of overall well-being were found among employed married women with children in the home, while the lowest scores occurred among unemployed, child-free married women. Maclean et al. (2003: 1) noted that most studies have found that "women employed outside the home tend to experience better mental health outcomes than those who are not employed outside the home, depending upon the specific characteristics of the job and the level of social support" (see also Arber, 1997; Waldron, 1991).

Based on a large national sample of respondents, Russo and Zierk (1992) found the mental well-being of mothers to be positively related to employment and negatively related to number of children. Shields (2000, 2000a), however, reported an association between certain employment characteristics (e.g., shift work, long hours) and an elevated risk of depression or psychological distress in women. Studies of specific groups of women have also indicated variability in women's susceptibility to and experience of stress, depression, and anxiety. Research on immigrant women, for example, has revealed that the "competing demands of family and work are exacerbated by the larger challenge of balancing traditional and Canadian values" and that the "changing roles of immigrants have been shown to affect their mental health, and in particular to put them at greater risk of depression" (Maclean et al., 2003: 2).

An analysis of data obtained in the 1998–1999 National Population Health Survey directed attention to the effects of different role-combinations and socioeconomic factors on women's mental health. Maclean et al. (2003: 3) investigated eight different role-combinations: (1) single mothers, employed and unemployed; (2) partnered mothers, employed and unemployed; (3) women without children, partnered and single; and (4) women without children, employed and unemployed. To measure distress, these researchers used a six-item scale that assessed feelings of sadness, anxiety, hopelessness, worthlessness, and "the feeling that everything had been an effort within the past month." Scores on this scale could range from 0 (no distress) to 24 (highly distressed). Two measures of stress were assessed; *personal stress* was signalled by the presence of role stressors: "trying to take on too much at once, feeling pressure to be like other people, feeling that others expect too much, feeling that work around the home is not appreciated, and feeling that others are too critical." *General chronic stress* was assessed using the same five items plus several others: "experiencing financial stress; having friends that are a bad influence, having a desire to move but being unable to do so; living in a neighbourhood or community that is too noisy or polluted; having an ill parent, partner or child; and having a family member with an alcohol or drug problem" (Maclean et al., 2003: 3). Women who scored at or above the 75th percentile on these measures were defined as experiencing a high degree of stress.

The researchers reported that regardless of employment status, single mothers were significantly more likely than partnered mothers to be poor, to experience financial stress and food insecurity, and to report feelings of high personal and chronic stress. While employment had a "significant effect on the stress and distress levels of single mothers" (Maclean et al., 2003: 3), this was not the case for partnered women. Unemployed single mothers were more than twice as likely as all other groups of women to experience a high level of distress. Women with children reported a higher level of personal stress than women without children; this effect was particularly pronounced among single mothers. This research attests to the need to consider the impact of myriad factors, including socio-economic status, family structure, and labour-force participation, in analyses of morbidity.

ADULT DEVELOPMENT

Adulthood, arbitrarily defined in chronological terms, spans the years from 18 to 65. For two reasons, developmental research largely neglected this vast period of human life until the late 1960s. First, the predominant biological model of development posited only three major phases of human development—growth, stability, and decline; this conception promoted a belief that not much of developmental significance occurred during adulthood. "An adult ... is an individual who has *completed his* [sic] *growth*" (Hurlock, 1968, in Troll, 1975: 1; emphasis added). Second, influenced by Freud's psychoanalytic theory, many psychologists asserted that basic personality structures were firmly established by the age of 5. Since these structures were thought to be highly resistant to change, any developments transpiring during "normal" adulthood were assumed to be of no significance. However, research in the fields known as *life span development* (in psychology) or **life course development** (in sociology) has challenged these simplistic beliefs.

Adulthood is now viewed as comprising a number of sequential stages of development. Periods of instability (also called *transition, passages,* etc.) alternate with periods of stability and interact with them in a dialectical fashion. Towards the end of each period of stability, dissatisfactions or a lack of fulfillment prompt the individual to examine the external and internal dimensions of his/her life. This process precipitates the transition stage, during which the individual makes crucial life decisions and commits to a future course of action; this may take the form of rededication to old goals or the pursuit of new ones. Time, energy, and personal capacities are adapted to these commitments, which are actualized during the ensuing stage of stability; and so the cycle of growth and development continues.

It should be noted that the age markers used in the following sections are offered for illustrative purposes only. It is also important to acknowledge the presence of an implicit heterosexist bias in the existing literature (Allen and Demo, 1995: 121).

Young Adulthood

Men Research findings about male young adulthood are highly consistent, and male patterns of development comparatively simple. Perhaps not surprisingly, male adult development is closely linked with occupational development. During late adolescence, occupation begins to form the central component of nascent masculinity (see Chapter 4). From early adulthood and through middle age, the most significant events shaping men's lives are those pertaining to the progress of their paid-work careers. It has been found that the timing and nature of periods of stability and change in men's lives are most strongly influenced by what does or does not occur on the job front.

A number of researchers have noted the existence within men of certain mental representations that have been referred to as the **Dream** (Levinson et al., 1978: 91–97) and the **career clock** (Kimmel 1980: 303) or **work clock** (Newman and Newman, 1975: 317). The Dream encompasses a set of images of what one's adult life will be like. These images may include an intimate relationship, children, a general lifestyle, and various material possessions. However, a central component of a man's Dream is his career or work "clock." This clock "contains" not only the image of a particular career, but a picture of progress over time towards a specific occupational goal, such as owning a business, becoming shop steward, or being elected to Parliament. Embedded within this picture is a timetable of milestones, such as promotions, income levels, or amounts of power, the achievement of which will mark his progress towards that ultimate goal.

At various points during their adult years, men pause to assess their progress and determine if they are on, behind, or ahead of schedule. Clausen (1972: 477) suggested that men in managerial positions and the professions make a first assessment during their early forties. Researchers (studying primarily middle- and upper-middle-class men) have suggested that sometime between the ages of 28 and 32, an initial (and somewhat superficial) review takes place, the most typical result of which is rededication to the original career choice and occupational Dream (Gould, 1978; Levinson et al., 1978). According to these researchers, the majority of men undertake a more intensive occupational life review in their late thirties and early forties, impelled by an increasingly urgent sense of time running out. Most men, at this time, must confront the disparity between their Dreams and their reality (Levinson et al., 1977: 288).

As relatively few men achieve their Dreams, let alone exceed them, most find they must come to some sort of terms with their unsuccess (Drebing and Gooden, 1991). Their options typically include scaling down their aspirations and learning to settle for what they have, devoting themselves to a period of fervid career activity before time completely runs out (after all, they are still relatively young), or changing jobs in the hopes of finding another occupational venue in which to capture either an old or a newly revised Dream (what Brim [1968: 204] referred to as **repotting**). According to the available research, the options are usually chosen in the order listed above. It should be borne in mind that most of the research on male adults and occupational development occurred prior to the downsizing frenzy of the middle 1990s, when large numbers of workers were fired in the name of debt-reduction and greater profit-making. That research found the processes of assessment and choice delineated above to be voluntary and self-initiated; today, however, many men find that the decision to search for a new line of work has been made for them, thanks to corporate cutbacks.

Men who choose to scale back their occupational Dreams typically hope to involve themselves more deeply in family life. Partly out of a desire to seek a fulfillment no longer found in work, and partly out of a desire to make up for missed opportunities, they may seek to establish or re-establish intimate connections with their spouses and children. However, by the time these men turn to their families, other family members have often begun moving away from partners/fathers and family life and seeking their own satisfactions elsewhere.

For some adult men (and women), the process of reflection may result in "coming out" as homosexual and attempting to construct a new identity. Johnston and Jenkins' (2004: 19) exploratory study examined psychosocial issues faced by adult gays and lesbians who had "come out" during mid-adulthood. They identified six common themes: "[C]oming out in mid-adulthood disrupts relationships; the loss of everything is feared; self-destructive behaviors are used to cope with heterosexism and oppression; the loss of a 'normal' adolescence is grieved; religion is the most oppressive force encountered; and coming out in mid-adulthood requires great courage and strength."

Women Women's adult development has not been charted as extensively as that of men; most research has tended to focus upon either one portion of the life course (e.g., middle age or menopause) or one dimension of women's lives (e.g., adapting to motherhood) (Smith, 2001). Based upon findings from his (admittedly small) female sample, Levinson (1996) concluded that although the processes of sequential stage development from early to late adulthood are very similar for women and men, the content and central issues are quite different.

Research conducted during the late 1960s and early 1970s concluded that female adult development closely paralleled developments in marriage and family. The key turning points in adult women's lives were found to occur within the context of the family and were linked, in particular, to the development of their children. Children's birth, their beginning school, puberty, graduation, and "launching" from the family home all had greater impact on the lives of women than of men. A pioneer in the study of middle age made this observation:

> Women, but not men, tend to define their age status in terms of timing of events within the family cycle. For married women, middle age is closely tied to the launching of children into the adult world, and even unmarried career women often discuss middle age in terms of the family they might have had. (Neugarten, 1968a: 95)

In contrast to men, who are expected to break away from their families of origin and establish identities independent of marital and family ties, women have been traditionally expected to "find themselves" within the context of marriage and family (Hays, 1996; Levinson, 1996). Given the power of the social mandates that assign primary family responsibilities to women, it is not surprising that research has confirmed the centrality of family-life events to women's lives. For most women (but not for most men), identity issues and intimacy issues are conflated. The marked increase in women's paid labour-force participation since the mid-1970s and the resulting influence of employment conditions have complicated the lives of Canadian women, most of whom are strongly influenced by their family responsibilities.

Employment conditions interact with marriage and family patterns in a number of ways. As noted in previous chapters, pay scales, the presence or absence of maternity-leave programs, employers' attitudes towards female workers with children and their willingness to accommodate family needs, and opportunities for promotion and pensions can either push or pull women into or out of the labour force. Family conditions, such as children's health and stage of development, also influence women's occupational paths. Varying numbers of women return to the labour force when their children are launched or ready to enter high school, elementary school, or daycare. The general trend since the mid-1970s, however, has been for women to re-enter the labour force at younger ages. Women who are separated, divorced, or widowed typically must participate in the paid labour force without the luxury of choice. The diverse ways in which women combine family life and paid work and the stronger impact of family life upon women create a more complex picture of adult development for females than for males.

Research has indicated that during the years between young- and middle-adulthood, the lives of child-free women follow a pattern very similar to those of most men, closely paralleling occupational development (Levinson, 1996; Somers, 1993). However, married women's career decisions appear to be more influenced by their husbands' careers than the other way around. The Traditional Homemaker Figure still exerts an influence over many of women's career decisions, from whether or not to accept increased responsibilities and promotions to whether or not to remain in a certain career. For some women today, choosing a full-time career may feel like being compelled to choose not to have children or even a marital relationship (Moen, 2003, 2005).

Middle Adulthood

In the scientific and popular literature, this portion of the adult life course has been referred to as *middle age, mid-life, midolescence, middlescence, the menopausal years,* and *second adulthood.* The chronological-age markers for this stage of life are a matter of debate. Suggested age ranges have varied from 31–50 (Newman and Newman, 1975) or 30–54 (Beaujot et al., 1995) to 40–65 (Levinson, 1996); the vast majority of writers focus upon the years from the late 40s to early 60s. The existence of disagreement suggests that middle age is influenced more by a social than by a biological calendar.

The age of entry into the middle years appears to vary by social class; lower classes tend to identify an earlier age, and higher classes a later one (Neugarten, 1968b: 144–145). Sheehy (1995) suggested that baby boomers approaching their fifties during the 1990s have attempted to push the entry-age marker even farther. The self-perception of boomers leads them to reject parallels between themselves and their parents at a comparable age. Some of the indicators of middle age (e.g., changes in appearance, reduced strength and stamina, the "empty nest," peaking of careers, intimations of mortality) are more amenable to personal control than ever before and can to various degrees be forestalled. Only in certain cases, such as menopause, is timing biologically determined and essentially unalterable. Generally, the greater the extent of real or apparent control, the greater the tendency of individuals today to attempt to defer the inevitable and to deny that they have entered middle age.

The Empty Nest Prior to the mid-1960s, clinicians claimed that many middle-adulthood women in our society suffered from **empty nest syndrome** (Rubin, 1981: 13). This term referred to a period of depression occasioned by the departure of their children and the loss of an active parenting role. For women who had dedicated themselves to the Traditional Marriage Enterprise (Levinson, 1996), confronting an empty nest was thought to be analogous to men's confrontation of retirement: The major source of life's meaning and social rewards had been removed. The problem was what to do with oneself. Since role expectations for adult life were forged in an earlier historical context in which many women died before their last child left home, few social guidelines were provided for a life after children, except, perhaps, in roles such as "meddlesome mother-in-law" (Leslie, 1967: 670) or "doting grandmother."

Women adjusting to the loss of their primary role were often advised to take up charity work. Paid employment was not considered a viable option for most middle-aged women, because of a lack of training or rusty occupational skills and ageism in the labour market. For those women whose husbands' incomes could sustain both partners, volunteer work was seen as the best solution for filling the empty hours. However, research from the late 1960s onward revealed that middle-aged women were describing the empty nest period not as a time of loss, but as one of increased options and freedom. An early study which focused on white, black, and Mexican American women concluded that "*if* the empty-nest syndrome occurs, it may occur to a greater degree in a particular cohort of White middle-class women because of a unique set of social circumstances in which they live and a unique set of family values and social norms concerning women's 'proper' norms" (Borland, 1982: 117; emphasis added). Better-educated women in particular reported experiencing this phase of their lives as rich with opportunities to explore various options, including paid employment, that could not easily be pursued during their peak childrearing years (Defey et al., 1996; Guttman, 1994; Weinstein, 1996). In contrast to the stereotype of women devastated by this "syndrome," it was more often fathers, anxious to make up for lost time, who were "pained by the children's imminent or actual departure" (Rubin, 1981: 31).

Associated with many middle-adult women's desire to explore new directions is a growing awareness of the necessity of preparing for a life on their own. Women in their late forties, typically married to men in their fifties, become aware of a husband's increasing concerns about his physical health. As men become sensitized to the reality of their own mortality, wives confront the prospect of their husbands' eventual deaths. Concern for a husband's health and awareness of the demographic reality of life-expectancy differentials become part of a "rehearsal for widowhood" (Neugarten, 1968b) that for many women begins in middle adulthood. Lest this appear unduly morbid, we must bear in mind that until age 40, Canadian "women are more likely than men to be married; afterwards it is men who are more likely to be married" (Beaujot et al., 1995: 39) and women who are more likely to be widowed and living alone.

Women's mid-life search for sources of fulfillment outside the home may also be instigated by the fact that marital satisfaction tends to be at its lowest ebb around the time that children are about to be launched (Lavee et al., 1996; White and Edwards, 1990). Marital satisfaction generally increases among couples in the post-parental phase of the marital career (Orbuch et al., 1996; Binstock and George, 1996). For those marital partners who survive the childrearing years, a return to couple-only status appears to improve the relationship. Reduced child-care responsibilities for wives and provider responsibilities for husbands, along with wives' heightened satisfaction from participation in the public sphere, all contribute to enhanced marital quality for those couples who remain together.

While the empty nest is no longer a negative experience for most women, it now appears that an unwillingness or inability of children to leave home "on schedule" is creating a problem for parents of both sexes (Weinstein, 1996). Rising educational requirements, an unstable job market, or the return of adult children (known as **boomerang children**) to the parental home following job loss or a dissolved marriage may result in a "cluttered nest" (Beaujot, 2004; Boyd and Norris, 2000). This is increasingly becoming a source of stress for parents (particularly mothers) impatient to get on with their child-free lives (Riedmann et al., 2003).

Gender Depolarization Theories of "life span gender development" attempt to describe "how behavior is connected to the stereotypic gender-related role behavior of men and women, which changes developmentally over time" (Sinnott and Shifren, 2001: 466). Relatively recent research (mostly conducted in the 1970s and 1980s) has suggested an intriguing phenomenon in adult development: At some point during the middle-adult years, polarized gender roles are "reversed or ... combined into a complex role" and ultimately "transcended to the point that sex roles matter relatively little to the individual or the construction of the individual's identity" (p. 467). This significant decline of previously polarized sex-linked personality and behavioural characteristics is referred to as **gender depolarization** (Sinnott, 1998; Sinnott et al., 1996; Hyde et al., 1991; Moen, 2003; Moen and Spencer, 2006).

Neugarten's (1968b: 140) early research observed that with increasing age, "[m]en seem to become more receptive to affiliative and nurturant promptings; women, more responsive towards and less guilty about aggressive and egocentric impulses." Based upon a comparison of self-administered Adjective Ratings Lists for different age groups, Lowenthal et al. (1975: 71) found men in their late fifties and sixties to be characteristically more "mellow," less hostile and driven, and more reasonable than any of the younger men in their sample; older women, in contrast to younger women, saw themselves as "less dependent and helpless and as more assertive." Other researchers have reported that men develop more traditionally "feminine" attitudes and interests as they age (Barrows and Zuckerman, 1976); that masculinity scores decline with age (Douglas and Arenberg, 1978); and that when evaluated on the Bem Sex Role Inventory (see Chapter 1), older subjects (both men and women) are much more likely to be classified as "androgynous" than traditionally masculine, feminine, or undifferentiated (Sinnott and Shifren, 2001). Drawing inspiration from Jung (1982), who suggested that cross-sex behaviour would start to emerge during the later half of life, Gutman (1987) gathered data from various cultures and found evidence that a gender "role reversal" occurred during later life: In terms of their "younger" definitions, older men adopted a more "feminine" and older women a more "masculine" stance towards life. Sheehy (1995: 318, 341; 1976: 286, 287) noticed a tendency for women in their forties to integrate aggressive and achievement-oriented characteristics, while men become more comfortable with emotional expressiveness (especially tearfulness) and more willing to show vulnerability. Turner and Turner (1991) reported that middle-aged and older men were viewed as being less assertive, less autonomous, and consequently less masculine. Overall, this body of research seems to indicate that individuals become more androgynous with advancing age—or, perhaps, that those with androgynous characteristics are more likely to survive to old age (Greenwood, 1999).

Various theorists have sought to explain the depolarization phenomenon. Biological reductionists claim that women and men are "hard-wired" (i.e., genetically or hormonally programmed) to develop in two different directions over the first half of the life course. As depolarization demands an explanation of how this programming might be rewired at some point during middle age, these researchers search for hormonal changes that could account for changes in the balance of (for example) aggressive and nurturant qualities in women and men. Others, however, conceptualize the process differently. Hefner et al. (1975) have advanced a **life span hierarchical stage progression model** that proceeds from "global undifferentiated" to "polarized traditional" to "combined or transcendent roles." According to this model, "[a]lthough the young child most likely has not defined a role, and the adolescent most likely has over-defined it, the adult synthesizes the masculine and feminine roles. But rather than stopping at this androgyny-like stage, adults may go beyond traditional roles. At that final point, adjustment is no longer tied to roles at all; roles just do not matter as much as organizers of identity" (Sinnott and Shifren, 2001: 468).

Sinnott (1995, 1998) has proposed a **postformal theory** that marries cognitive theory (see Chapter 2) with postmodernism (see Chapter 3). She hypothesized that as cognitive skills become more sophisticated, social roles can be thought about and enacted in more complex ways. According to this theory, *postformal operations* "subsume and organize several formal operational logical systems, and they have a quality of necessary subjectivity (that is, the knower realizes that truth is partly created by the way he or she conceptualizes things)" (Sinnott and Shifren, 2001: 469). By extension, "complex adult sex roles, viewed postformally, are roles that are not absolute but that are consciously created to some degree by the actor selecting a view of truth." Sinnott maintained that as individuals attempt to resolve "ill-structured everyday problems about identity and how to behave ... [p]ostformal thought-based roles in adulthood and older age might permit greater creativity in using strategies to solve problems" (p. 469).

A **general systems theory of sex roles** builds on the premise that all "living systems" (individuals, societies, or cells) appear to proceed through a similar set of stages: "They begin in disorder, with few parts concretely defined; they gradually become more orderly; they end when they are too rigid to face challenges successfully" (Sinnott and Shifren, 2001: 469–470). This theory maintains that gender-role development over the life span may be explained by considering the individual and society as living systems which seek both continuity and survival. According to this theory, the earliest stages of life are "disorderly" (i.e., there are no clear-cut gender roles); over time, life becomes more orderly (i.e., more clearly defined masculine and feminine gender roles develop). However, because too-rigid roles would not permit the individual to respond flexibly to the new challenges of advancing age, "the post-parental imperative results in the need to change structured roles or risk foundering on dysfunctional rigid roles" (Sinnott and Shifren, 2001: 470).

For social constructionists, polarization and depolarization reflect different age-related, situationally normative gender scripts to which the individual is constrained to adjust. Levinson (1996: 38–39) argued that rigid gender divisions reflect what he termed **gender splitting**. This operates on many levels: the domestic sphere is split from the extradomestic sphere, the provider role from the homemaker role, "women's work" from "men's work," and masculinity from femininity. Social forces operate to reinforce gender splitting in all domains from earliest childhood through middle adulthood; however, it is possible that from middle adulthood on, they may permit a process of **gender splicing**. Cameron's early study (1976) emphasized that age-sex norms vary over the life course; adult respondents in this study perceived that the social pressure to display gender differences increased during young adulthood and decreased during middle- and older adulthood. During early adulthood, compliance with social expectations is strongly emphasized; much energy is directed towards demonstrating conformity with gendered personal, work, and family roles. However, when people reach a stage in life at which they have discharged the bulk of their gender duties, they may be socially granted the freedom to explore inner qualities that have been repressed or left dormant; the result is depolarization.

In addition, the changing situations of men and women in the second half of life may call for the development of new qualities. For women, paid employment may promote greater assertiveness and more of an achievement orientation. A woman's increasing likelihood of being alone also necessitates that she focus more on meeting her own needs. Among men, an increasing desire to find fulfillment in intimate relationships requires the cultivation of affiliative and nurturant qualities. As noted in Chapter 6, basic social institutions create gender as much as gender creates institutions; presumably, the earlier in life that men participate in the domestic sphere and women in the extradomestic, the earlier depolarization will occur.

As yet, researchers have not been able to identify at what point the gender depolarization process begins and whether, within our society, depolarization is a constant element in adult development ("the normal unisex of later life," [Brim, 1974]) or only characteristic of certain historically shaped age cohorts (Greenwood, 1999: 129). Existing studies focus upon women and men born between the late 1920s and the early 1940s. These individuals moved through young adulthood during the 1950s and the early 1960s, when social norms strongly endorsed strict gender divisions in personal qualities and behaviours. They reached middle adulthood during the 1970s and 1980s, when the women's and men's movements, along with the human potential and therapeutic movements (Rubin, 1990: 6–7), all proclaimed the desirability and necessity of breaking down rigid gender roles (Rubin, 1990: 6–7; Adams and Blieszner, 1998). The question is whether or not members of younger age cohorts, raised in a context of less rigid gender constraints, will demonstrate the same patterns of early adulthood polarization followed by mid-life depolarization. Some journalists (e.g., Sheehy, 1995: 329) have gone so far as to announce that in the middle years a gender "crossover crisis" occurs, in which men become like women and women become like men. However, based upon the findings of gender-depolarization research among respondents in the Baltimore Longitudinal Study, Costa et al. (1983) claimed that it would take an "average" 75-year-old man 136 years to reach the average femininity scores of a 75-year-old woman. In other words, the overall trend is *towards* greater gender convergence; neither actual convergence nor gender "reversal" is actually achieved.

Menopause and Men's Pause Biological changes occurring during middle adulthood, particularly those associated with changes in hormone production from the ovaries, testes, pituitary gland, and hypothalamus, are generically referred to as the **climacteric**. While the term "climacteric" is often incorrectly used as a synonym for "menopause," the latter term is properly applied only to changes associated with reduced production of hormones from the ovaries. As noted in Chapter 2, women's menstrual periods result from the ovaries' cyclical production of hormones (*estrogen* and *progesterone*) which are linked into a feed-back loop with the pituitary gland and the hypothalamus. At some time during women's forties or early fifties, the production of estrogen significantly decreases, precipitating a series of physiological changes (Masters et al., 1994). Short-term consequences of declining estrogen production include changes to menstrual periods, which over time become shorter and more infrequent and eventually cease. As well, many women experience "hot flashes" (sudden rushes of heat, often accompanied by reddening of the skin and drenching perspiration), "night sweats," insomnia, weight gain, vaginal dryness, and "stress incontinence" (occasional involuntary release of urine). Long-term effects can include bladder infections, rising cholesterol levels, and bone-density loss leading to osteoporosis.

The time period during which estrogen production declines and menstruation becomes more irregular is **perimenopause**. The World Health Organization has defined perimenopause as "the two to eight years preceding menopause and one year following menopause" (Cheung et al., 2003: 2). The term **menopause** refers specifically to the cessation of menses. However, "[t]here is currently no single biological marker to identify when a woman has reached menopause" (Cheung et al., 2003: 2), and it is confirmed only in retrospect after an adult woman, who is neither pregnant nor lactating, has gone one full year without a menstrual period—a somewhat arbitrary but convenient convention, which allows menopause to be declared without extensive testing and measurement of estrogen levels or ova viability. "The average age of natural menopause in Western societies is estimated to be 51 years; women in Canada can therefore expect to live, on average, a third of their lives in post-menopausal years" (Cheung et al., 2003: 1).

The experience and meaning of menopause for women appears to be strongly influenced by the social context in which this series of events occurs. Few "symptoms" of a disruptive nature have been observed among women in China, a finding that has been attributed to the fact that Chinese society accords women greater respect as they age and does not equate menopause with a critical loss of social significance (Chou and Chi, 2002). In contrast, in Canada and the United States, a variety of negative stereotypes have existed and continue to circulate. In the early part of the twentieth century, medical doctors referred to menopause as the "death of the woman in women" (Ehrenreich and English, 1979); the terms "castrate" and "post-menopausal" were often used interchangeably. During the first few decades following World War II, perimenopause and menopause were thought to provoke a "crisis" in women as they tried to cope with the loss of their ability to conceive children (Gee and Kimball, 1987: 49). Images of irrational post-menopausal women abound and are perpetuated in posters and greeting cards that feature crazed-looking females and the inevitable caption, "I'm Out of Estrogen and I've Got a Gun" (see also Sheehy, 1995: 202).

Empirical evidence belies these images. Cheung et al. (2003: 3) have found that "[c]ontrary to widely held beliefs, menopause is not associated with an increase in psychiatric disorders," although some research has found a higher prevalence of certain psychiatric symptoms (notably depression, anxiety, and psychosomatic symptoms) during perimenopause (Burt et al., 1998; Novaes and Almeida, 1999). Depression during perimenopause may be a result of psychosocial stressors (e.g., fears of diminished sexual attractiveness, anticipated changes in family roles) and/or the result of "alterations in the levels of reproductive hormones [that] may directly affect central neurotransmitter activity and contribute to a deregulation of the hypothalamic-pituitary-adrenal axes, leading to the onset of depression in vulnerable women" (Cheung et al., 2003: 3). A prior history of depression, as well as smoking and stress, seem to be linked to the appearance of depression in perimenopausal women (Harlow et al., 1999; Stewart and Boydell, 1993). Moreover, despite the stereotype of the menopausal woman as sexually "past it," many women report heightened sexual interest, responsiveness, and orgasmic frequency after menopause (Lips, 2001); many also report feeling less inhibited in their sexuality thanks to freedom from the risk of pregnancy. On the other hand, women may experience some discomfort or pain during intercourse (Masters et al., 1994: 468–479) as a result of reduced vaginal lubrication or thinning of the vaginal lining caused by lower estrogen levels. More rarely, women report reduced responsiveness to clitoral stimulation or a less intense experience of orgasm.

Seizing the opportunity presented by the large demographic of 40- to 55-year-old baby-boomers, the pharmaceutical industry has leapt into action. "Marketing menopause" has become big business for drug manufacturers and advertisers who extol the virtues of calcium supplements, vaginal lubricants, adult diapers, and both prescription and non-prescription drugs. Of the available products, those containing replacement hormones are the most controversial. Hormone replacement therapy (HRT or HT) medicalizes a natural process, treating perimenopause, menopause, and (particularly) post-menopause as conditions of "deficiency" that require long-term medical intervention. Replacement therapy is designed to counteract a loss of ovarian-produced estrogens by supplying synthetic estrogens, via injections or pills, to prevent calcium loss and reduce the likelihood of osteoporosis, restore vaginal lubrication and vaginal wall elasticity, eliminate hot flashes, and reduce the risk of heart disease from elevated cholesterol levels. *Estrogen replacement therapy* (ERT), when used alone (mainly for women whose uterus has been removed), has been linked to breast cancer, gall bladder problems, fluid retention, blood clots, ovarian and endometrium cancers, and migraines. While debate continues over whether ERT is responsible for these outcomes, new questions have been raised by the addition of synthetic progesterone to the therapeutic arsenal. Progesterone may counteract the negative effects of ERT, but it can also lead to a resumption of menstrual periods (Masters et al., 1994: 470–472). At present, for women who have a uterus, a combination of estrogen plus progestin is favoured (Cheung et al. 2003).

As one part of the Women's Health Initiative (WHI)—a major multi-centre American study—a randomized, double-blind controlled experiment involving 16 608 women was conducted to compare the effects of a placebo with an orally administered daily dose of combined estrogen plus progestin. The study was aborted when it became clear that the risks of the HT outweighed its benefits. "After an average of 5.2 years of follow-up, there was a 26% increase in breast cancer, a 29% increase in coronary heart disease and a 41% increase in stroke among hormone users. There was, however, a 34% decrease in hip fractures and a 37% decrease in colorectal cancers" (Cheung et al., 2003: 4). A later study, also based on WHI data, reported that HT may increase the risk of dementia in women age 65 and older (Shumaker et al., 2003). As a result of these and similar findings, various medical bodies in both Canada and the United States, including the Society of Obstetricians and Gynaecologists of Canada and the Canadian Task Force on Preventive Health Care, now recommend that "use of HT in post-menopausal women should be limited to the treatment of perimenopausal symptoms, the dose should be as low as possible, the duration should be as short as possible, and the use of HT should be periodically evaluated by the woman and her health care provider" (Cheung et al., 2003: 5).

Although the term "male menopause" is bandied about in everyday speech and in the popular press, no biologically based event of this kind exists (Knox and Schacht, 1997: 299). While men do experience aging-related biological changes in their reproductive and sexual capacities, these changes are highly variable across all men and very gradual within individual men. In contrast to the precipitous decline in estrogen production experienced by women, testosterone production decreases only gradually among men in their mid-forties/mid-fifties, eventually (typically when men are in their seventies) reaching a plateau only slightly lower than its former level (Consumer Reports on Health, 1993/1995). Similarly, whereas women's ovaries eventually cease releasing ova (eggs), men's testes continue to produce viable sperm throughout the post-pubertal lifespan. Although total sperm counts do decline over time, the degree of decline is highly variable, and many men, subject to interest and opportunity, can contribute their needed share to the conception process when they are well into their seventies and beyond. Men do lose a small amount of muscle mass and bone density between the ages of 40 and 70, but the amounts lost typically do not place men at high risk, compared to women, for osteoporosis-related bone injuries during older adulthood. These physiological changes bear only a slight relationship to gradually declining testosterone levels (Consumer Reports on Health, 1993/1995: 164).

During late-middle and older adulthood, erectile tissue in the penis may be slower to engorge with blood upon stimulation and may not maintain its swollen state for as long a time (Masters et al., 1994: 409); penile sensitivity may also decline. In some men, the prostate gland may become enlarged, pressing more firmly upon surrounding tissues, slowing down urination and weakening ejaculation. Older men also typically experience a more generalized and diffuse sense of sexual pleasure and become less genital- and orgasm-focused in their sexual expression (Masters et al., 1994). In response, drug companies have come to the rescue once again with an HRT for men, in the form of testosterone booster shots and patches which, according to the ads, can "rejuvenate" aging men in the throes of "male menopause," "andropause," or "viropause" (as it is known in Europe). Such therapies primarily benefit the drug manufacturers, marketers, and health practitioners involved. Any benefits to recipients appear to be far outweighed by the risks: Synthetically increased testosterone has been found to exacerbate or initiate prostate cancer (*Consumer Health Reports*, 1993/1995: 163–164).

Accounts of "male menopause" are apocryphal, perpetuated by mass-media depictions of the mild-mannered man who, upon hitting a certain age, abandons job, wife, and children and runs away to Tahiti with a much-younger paramour. Other stereotypes paint middle-aged men as being mired in depression. However, the male mid-life crisis is not confirmed by empirical research, and most clinical studies do not find evidence of an increase in depression among men during this life phase (Consumer Reports on Health, 1993/1995: 164). As mentioned earlier, some adult-development research has found evidence that during middle adulthood, many men go through a period of reflection as they assess their life's progress to that point and decide whether to rededicate themselves to or revise their youthful Dreams. This period of contemplation and stock-taking, sort of a **men's pause**, most often leads only to minor changes. Trying to posit an analogy between this portion of men's lives and women's peri- and post-menopausal experience is both unwarranted and misleading.

The Double Standard of Aging While it is our physical bodies that age, our experience of that process and the meanings we attach to it are interwoven with social interpretations. Our society is characterized by a **double standard of aging** (Sontag, 1972), whereby aging women are judged by a much narrower and more youth-obsessed standard than men. According to the popular adages, "women grow old; men become distinguished," or "women grow age lines; men develop character lines." While "[m]en may find their sexual attractiveness actually increasing with age ... [t]he commonest image of a middle-aged woman is someone who is lumpy, dumpy, and frumpy" (Greer, 1991: 295; see also Tunley et al., 1999). Based on in-depth interviews with 42 women and men, Halliwell and Dittmar (2003: 11) found distinctive gender differences in attitudes towards body aging. Women viewed aging "most negatively in terms of its impact on appearance," whereas men felt that aging had a "neutral or even positive impact on appearance." They noted that men and women commonly conceptualized and construed their bodies differently, with men viewing the body holistically and focusing on its functionality, and women holding "compartmentalized conceptualizations" of the body, tending to focus "on its display."

Observable departures from beauty standards may prompt some men and women to engage in efforts to forestall the "ravages of time." These may include exercise, ranging from aerobics to weight-training to yoga; less strenuous approaches involve a host of products that promise to "banish grey," "vanish" wrinkles, or "keep him guessing" about one's age. Other measures are more drastic: Cosmetic surgery is one option that may appeal to the more affluent. According to Stephen Mulholland, a Toronto plastic surgeon, aging baby boomers are "the fastest-growing group of men and women seeking cosmetic surgery.... They created jogging, the tennis club, the cult of youth, and vitality. And now they're finding that genetics is not allowing them to maintain that edge" (in Underwood, 2000: 39). Women "swamp men when it comes to fixing up aging skin"; 91 percent of face lifts and 85 percent of eyelid lifts are performed on women. While these procedures also rank among the five most popular cosmetic surgeries performed on males, men appear to be most vexed by hair loss, with hair transplants "the most common plastic surgery for men" (Etcoff, 1999: 111, 125). For those of modest means, the problem of thinning hair may be tackled with the standard comb-overs, cover-ups (i.e., wigs and toupees), and a plethora of hair-growing lotions and potions. The current trend among men of shaving their heads has arguably made baldness desirable (though not in women). While head-shaving may be a "pre-emptive strike, a bold move to erase a sign of aging," it may also serve "to exaggerate signals of strength. The smaller the head, the bigger the look of the neck and the body" (Etcoff, 1999: 127); it is noteworthy that professional body builders commonly crop their hair to exaggerate the dimensions of their shoulders/chest. Baldness is also interpreted by some as a symbol of virility and potency.

While one segment of the middle-adulthood population seeks to steal beauty back from time, another strives to push back the upper age limit of our society's standards of beauty, literally "advancing beauty into a new time period" (Friday, 1996: 493). To appeal to this large consumer group, advertisers are incorporating an increasing proportion of "older" (i.e., over 40) models and spokespersons. However, these poster-children for aging baby boomers still conform closely to the slender, physically fit youthful ideal. Drawing upon their own experiences and enhanced awareness of the double standard, several icons of the second wave of the feminist movement have mocked the idiocy of exalting beauty as the ultimate measure of a woman's worth and have pointed to other qualities that should be more highly valued with increasing age, such as knowledge, wisdom, experience, and power (Friday, 1996; Friedan, 1993; Greer, 1991). As part of this movement to "banish beauty," some have also sought to rehabilitate and positively value the image and role of the crone, the witch, and the wrinkled, old, wise, and powerful woman. Complementing this perspective, Holstein (2001/2002) has decried "anti-aging medicine" and allied procedures, arguing that these will "reinforce stereotypes ... medicalize women's bodies and ... strengthen existing divisions along social class, racial, and ethnic lines."

Adult-Elder Caregiving During middle adulthood, many Canadians find that in addition to providing some degree of care for their own children, they must also give care to one or both of their parents or parents-in-law. Journalists have described these individuals as the **sandwich generation** (or, in the case of four-generation families in which adults provide care for children, parents, and grandparents, the "clubhouse sandwich generation"). The word "generation" is in fact inaccurate here, as it implies a unique cohort of people whose experiences will never be repeated (e.g., the "baby-boom generation"). Given the **greying of Canada** (i.e., the aging of the Canadian population), it is unlikely that the "sandwich" phenomenon will be limited to only one generation (Beaujot, 2003). Projections by the Vanier Institute of the Family have indicated that by 2016, the number of seniors over 65 will approach six million (an increase of 64 percent over 1991), and the numbers of Canadians older than 85, close to one million (Immen, 2004). In 2006, the 65-and-over population "made up a record 13.7% of the total population in Canada" (Statistics Canada, 2007r). As well, during 2001 and 2006, the number of Canadians age 80 and over topped the one million mark for the first time ever.

In the 2006 Canadian census, 18.4 percent of Canadians 15 years of age and over reported devoting some time to providing unpaid care or assistance to seniors, with women more likely to do so than men (20.9 percent versus 15.7 percent). Most spent only a limited amount of time doing so; only 3.9 percent of women and 2.2 percent of men reported spending over 10 hours a week caring for seniors. Within this census, "unpaid care" was defined as "personal care to a senior family member, visiting seniors, talking with them on the telephone, and helping them with shopping, baking, or with taking medication" (Statistics Canada, 2007d). Although definitions of "caregiving" vary, most research focuses upon **instrumental activities**, such as meal preparation, housecleaning, shopping, yard work, transporting, bill-payment, and banking; and **personal care activities**, such as bathing, dressing, and toileting. Only some, such as the 1996 General Social Survey (GSS) (Cranswick, 1997), augment this list with **caring-about activities** (e.g., providing emotional support, reassurance, and encouragement) even though American research has identified such activities as important components of adult caregiving (Piercy, 1998).

Research has consistently found that primary elder-caregivers are most likely to be women, in their roles as wives, daughters, or daughters-in-law (e.g., Choi, 2003; Lawrence et al., 2002); however, "living nearby and being without siblings may 'default' men into being more involved" in elder caregiving (Campbell and Martin-Matthews, 2000: 57). As noted in Chapter 8, women are the designated "kinkeepers" in our culture, whose job it is to keep in touch with and, if necessary, care for adult relatives (Rosenthal, 1995; see also Brewer, 2001).

Findings of the Canadian Study of Health and Aging reflect this fact: Women represented three quarters of all caregivers of people suffering from dementia in the community and just over seven in ten (71 percent) of the caregivers of those institutionalized with dementia; "[d]aughters represented 45% of the informal caregivers of institutionalized dementia patients" (Lindsay and Anderson, 2003: 41). In conformity with prevailing gender stereotypes which emphasize different skills for each gender, female caregivers are more likely to assume responsibility for a cognitively/behaviourally impaired elder than are men, who are more likely to provide instrumental aid for one who is physically impaired (Starrels et al., 1997).

Davidson et al. (2002: 536) noted that "[m]ost care of older, ailing, or disabled people within the home is carried out by a spouse." Tomiak et al.'s (2000) examination of a representative sample of Manitobans, 65 years of age and over, found that, besides age, marital status was an important factor for nursing-home entry among men; unpartnered men—or women—may experience difficulty accessing necessary assistance outside of such settings. Sinnott and Shifren (2001: 465) reported that "[w]hen it comes to providing self-care rather than care to others, women over 70 perform more instrumental activities for longer durations than men when they are widowed women, even after controlling analyses for age, long-term-care residence, income and education" (Sinnott and Shifren, 2001: 465). Research by Carriere and Martel (2003: 139) found that the likelihood of receiving assistance from adult children was the same for older widowed males and females; however, whereas older separated or divorced women were as likely as those who were widowed to receive assistance from their children, older separated or divorced men were about 11 times less likely to receive such assistance.

Although the number of hours working Canadians devote to child care still exceeds those devoted to elder care, the gap is narrowing among people 45 years of age and over. A 2003 Statistics Canada report, *Caring for an Aging Society*, found that 20 percent of women and 13 percent of men age 45 to 54 reported having to reduce their work-hours in order to meet elder-care demands. Of Canadians providing care to one or more over-65 adults living in a separate residence, approximately one third of the men (32 percent) and one quarter of the women were also caring for children under the age of 15. A reanalysis of data from the 1996 GSS also found that women with children who were also caring for elders were approximately 30 percent more likely than their childless counterparts to change their hours of work, and about 25 percent more likely to decline a job or promotion because of their double-duty caregiving responsibilities (Immen, 2004). The 1996 GSS found that just over half (55 percent) of female caregivers and just under half (45 percent) of male caregivers reported that their caregiving responsibilities had affected their employment, necessitating their coming in late, leaving early or taking days off (Cranswick, 1997: 5). Starrels et al. (1997: 869) found that taking time off from paid work is more stressful for male caregivers than for female; they attributed this finding to a combination of two factors: men "having a larger social investment than women in their employment roles," and employers being less sympathetic and tolerant towards male family-related absenteeism.

Although only a small minority of caregivers find their responsibilities onerous (Cranswick, 1997: 4), elder care is increasingly likely to be experienced as a burden as the time it demands escalates (Frederick and Fast, 1999: 29). While gender differences revealed by the 1996 GSS research are modest, they indicate that women are more likely than men to feel taxed by their caregiving responsibilities, a finding which may be attributable to the differential distribution of the caregiving burden; research has indicated, for example, that caregivers find it more stressful to cope with an elder suffering from dementia-related cognitive/behavioural problems than with one suffering from physical impairments only (see Dunn and Strain, 2001; Kelly et al., 2002). Finally, even though Canadian male and female caregivers were about equally likely to find that caregiving affected their holiday plans, sleep patterns, and financial situation, women (27 percent) were more than twice as likely as men (12 percent) to report that caregiving had had a negative affect upon their health (Cranswick, 1997: 6). This finding would seem to provide support for the "nurturant role" hypothesis of morbidity differentials.

Marital Status in Late Middle-Adulthood and Older Adulthood Table 9.3 presents marital-status data for Canadian adults in five-year age groups, from age 50 through to age 90 and above. Between the ages of 50 and the late 80s, the percentage of people who fall into the "single" (i.e., never-married) category declines; for the oldest age group, it increases. To a large extent, variations in the marital status of today's older adults reflect economic conditions in the historical eras in which they reached adulthood—a time when males could more-or-less easily afford to marry and support a spouse and family. Given that in those days it was generally "up to the man" to take the initiative in the decision to marry, female marriage statistics are partly a reflection of marital opportunities which were themselves a function of male circumstances. An indeterminate proportion of the never-married population chose to remain single for personal reasons. Some unknown portion of this population are gay or lesbian individuals who, in times past, never had the opportunity to marry legally in our society.

Clearly, the younger the age cohort, the higher the percentage of males and females who fall into the "divorced" category. This fact reflects changing social mores and the

TABLE 9.3	Marital Status by Selected Five-year Age Groups, in Percentages, Canada, 2006							
	Single		Married*		Widowed		Divorced	
Age	Male	Female	Male	Female	Male	Female	Male	Female
50–54	15.5	12.1	65.4	63.3	1.1	3.5	13.8	16.5
55–59	10.7	8.8	69.5	64.3	1.8	6.4	14.2	16.8
60–64	8.0	6.9	72.4	63.3	3.1	11.5	13.1	15.7
65–69	6.7	5.8	74.7	60.1	5.1	19.8	10.6	11.7
70–74	6.0	5.6	74.9	52.6	8.6	31.2	7.8	8.6
75–79	6.1	5.8	72.2	41.0	13.9	45.5	5.5	6.0
80–84	5.9	6.7	66.6	27.6	21.7	61.1	3.7	3.9
85–89	5.6	6.9	58.3	15.6	31.7	74.4	2.5	2.4
90+	6.9	8.8	43.9	6.6	45.7	82.8	1.8	1.5

* Includes same-sex marriages.

Source: Calculated from Statistics Canada. 2008k. Topic-Based Tabulations, Legal Marital Status, Age Groups and Sex for the Population 15 Years and Over of Canada, 2006 Census—100% Data.

increasing availability of separation and divorce; younger men and women had recourse to these options if relationships became unsatisfying or unworkable. Older men and women, however, faced greater social and personal pressures to remain together "until death us do part."

The most striking gender differences are found in the "married" and "widowed" categories. Between the ages of 50 and 89, the majority of men are still legally married and living with a spouse. With increasing age, the proportion of married men declines gradually, except for a steep drop in the 85–89 age group and in the oldest (age 90 and over) group. This precipitous drop is attributable to the fact that the oldest age-grouping has no upper limit (i.e., is not limited to a five-year age span). Only among men age 90 and over are less than 50 percent currently married. In contrast, the proportion of females currently married declines dramatically over the age groups considered.

As we look at increasingly old age groups, the declining percentages of currently married Canadians are largely accounted for by increases in the "widowed" category. The "widowed" column manifests the gender mortality differences described at the beginning of the chapter. The proportions of men who are currently widowed are very small among the younger age groups; only in the 75–79 age group do more than 10 percent of men have that status. These low figures reflect two factors: greater female longevity and the greater likelihood of men remarrying after widowhood. At ages 85 to 89, just under one third (31.7 percent) of the men are currently widowed, and not until ages 90 and over do more than 40 percent of men identify themselves as widowed. In sharp contrast, almost a third of women (31.2 percent) between the ages of 70 to 74 are widowed; this reflects the combined effects of lower male longevity and the lesser likelihood of female remarriage after a spouse's death. By the ages of 85 to 89, almost three-quarters (74.4 percent) of women are widowed.

Older Adulthood

According to the United Nations, a society can be classified as "aged" if 8 percent or more of its population is 65 years of age or older (McVey and Kalbach, 1995: 75). In terms of that index, Canada was officially classified as an "aged" society in 1971. In 2006, Canada had the oldest population of the Americas; while the elderly represented 13.7 percent of Canada's population in that year, they accounted for 12.4 percent of the population in the United States and only 5 percent of Mexico's population (Statistics Canada, 2007r).

At present, older adulthood is still an emergent stage in the life course of Canadians, with few specific age-related gender norms; it is quite literally a "work in progress." It remains to be seen whether this stage will be divided into two or three subphases, demarcated roughly by chronological age, such as "young olds" (age 65–80) and "old olds" (over 80); or "young olds" (age 65–75), "middle olds" (75–85), and "old olds" (over 85). For now, let us examine three major experiences common to many Canadians age 65 and over: retirement, poverty, and widowhood.

Retirement In earlier eras characterized by shorter life expectancies, the concept of **retirement** from the paid labour force did not exist in our society. Prior to industrialization, women and men laboured to provide for their own and their families' survival until they were physically unable to continue. Industrialization may have altered the meaning of "work" itself and the nature of the tasks performed, but paid workers still strove to remain employed until incapable of going on, since neither government nor business nor industry provided any kind of financial compensation for older Canadians. "Most North Americans prior to the Second World War worked until disability or death, or depended upon their children for assistance" (Baker, 1988: 78). Even though old-age and post-retirement programs had long been a feature of many European countries and had begun to emerge in our society during the late 1920s, it was not until the postwar prosperity of the 1950s and 1960s that national social safety-net programs for older citizens came fully into being in Canada. These programs helped establish the now entrenched notion that workers, upon completing a certain number of years of service or reaching a defined age, should still receive some form of income. However, "retirement can be difficult in that 'worth' is often equated with 'work.' A job structures one's life and provides an identity; the end of a job culturally signifies the end of one's productivity" (Mooney et al., 2003: 196).

Retirement has also become a major rite of passage, denoting the transition from middle into older adulthood, particularly for men. Initially, Canada arbitrarily set the age of eligibility for retirement at 70, but in 1966 gradually began lowering it (Oderkirk, 1996: 3); since then, 65 has become the expected age of retirement. In 1946, prior to the establishment of universal social security and old-age pensions, nearly half of Canada's male population over the age of 65 were still in the labour force; 40 years later, that figure had dropped to 11 percent (McDonald and Wanner, 1990: 42). Since the mid-1970s, the actual age of retirement in Canada has become more variable, particularly among men. The corporate and government restructuring/downsizing frenzy that swept the Canadian economy during the early to mid-1990s resulted in large numbers of men being laid off, fired, "outsourced," or induced to take early retirement. Many of these were **displaced providers**, men born between the mid-1930s and mid-1940s who were socialized into the "good provider" role but prevented from continuing on the path of their perceived gender destiny. While some displaced providers re-entered the work force through part-time, contract, or self-employment, not all were successful; generally, the higher a man's credentials, the more likely he was to seek and find subsequent employment. Ageism (including negative stereotypes of the elderly), lower levels of education, and fewer marketable skills adversely affect the employment chances of older Canadians, who are likely to remain unemployed for almost twice as long as those ages 15 to 24 (Statistics Canada, 1998; see also Statistics Canada, 2006o, 2007w).

Since the 1990s, the average age of retirement has risen from a low of 60.9 in 1998 to 61.5 in 2006 (Marshall and Ferrao, 2007: 5). Similarly, even though labour force participation falls dramatically for those 65 years of age and over, in 2006 "a record proportion of 60- to 64-year-olds"—45 percent—were in the labour force (Marshall and Ferrao, 2007: 5). Moreover, according to a Labour Force Survey, approximately 320 000 Canadians 65 years of age and over participated in the labour force in 2005; the vast majority (308 000) were employed, while 11 000 were actively looking for work. In 2005, seniors with a university degree were over four times as likely to participate in the labour force than those with eight years or less of formal schooling (Statistics Canada, 2007w).

Although Canadian women are less likely than men to have an employer pension plan, they are more likely to opt for early retirement (Lowe, 1992). Moreover, while both men and women cite health-related reasons as important in their decision to retire, women are more likely than men to identify marriage and/or family responsibilities as important factors. In 2002, 12 percent of Canadian women, compared with 6 percent of Canadian men, retired to take care of a family member (Statistics Canada, 2006o).

Research conducted on 228 American couples (Smith and Moen, 1998) indicated that a wife's decision to retire was significantly more likely to be influenced by a husband's employed/retired status than the other way around. While in 2002, 48 percent of Canadian women and 46 percent of Canadian men reported that they expected to retire at the same time as their partner, "[t]he proportion jumped to 60% among women who were the same age as their husbands, and fell to 39% among women who were five to nine years younger" (Statistics Canada, 2006o). Compared to women in their forties, women in their late fifties are less likely to anticipate retiring at the same time as their partner, and "this may be explained in part by the higher percentages of persons already retired among those in their late 50s" (Statistics Canada, 2006o). The expectation of joint retirement also varies between salaried and self-employed workers, occupational groups, and on the wife's economic dependency upon her spouse. Thus, while just over two-thirds (68 percent) of self-employed workers expected joint retirement, this was true of less than half (44 percent) of salaried workers. In general, however, the odds are higher that a woman will view the timing of her retirement independently of her spouse if: she is in a managerial/professional occupation; has her own pension coverage; and contributes the majority of the household income.

In general, research has found the concept of retirement to be more complex among older women. Predictive models based upon male experience appear to be less effective when applied to women's decisions to retire. Monette (1996a: 10) reported that while many older women share with men a definition of retirement as a permanent exit from the paid labour force, some women define themselves as "retired" even though they actually left the paid labour force for the birth of their first child years, even decades, in the past and never returned. Within this latter group, some women did not label themselves as "retired" until their husbands began collecting a pension cheque (in other words, their self-definition was not self-determined, but dependent on the situation of their spouse). In addition, women are far more likely than men to view retirement "as involving more than just getting a pension or stopping paid work. Women tend to include in their concept the time they spend doing unpaid work, such as care giving, volunteering and so on" (Statistics Canada, 2006o).

Early writings on the experience of retirement promoted the belief that because paid employment, for men, is a paramount source of accomplishment, identity, and income, and also plays a crucial role in structuring time, its cessation would precipitate a "crisis" for men (Friedmann and Havighurst, 1954). This crisis was thought to parallel the "empty nest crisis" supposedly triggered in women by their children's departure from the family home and the attendant loss of their meaningful role and identity as childrearer. Inconsistent research findings have led to the conclusion that while some men initially find retirement a difficult experience, many, if not most, do not (Timmer et al., 2003). Health, finances, anticipatory socialization, actual preparedness, and attitudes towards retirement all influence how the event and the transition into post-retirement life are experienced (Ballantyne and Marshall, 2001; McDonald and Wanner, 1990).

Social relationships, particularly meaningful ones, are positively correlated to satisfaction with retirement (McDonald and Wanner, 1990: 90–91). Men's social relationships in adulthood, being connected primarily to their careers, appear to decline in number following retirement, while women's social relationships, particularly those developed through involvement in religious and volunteer activities, tend to increase (Atchley, 1997). To the extent that social relationships furnish an alterative source of life satisfaction after retirement, women appear to adjust more satisfactorily than men. Contact with relatives and neighbourhood friends remains essentially the same for both men and women following retirement (Riedmann et al., 2003).

Retirement is more likely to bring about a sense of discontinuity or disjuncture in the lives of men than in the lives of women. This disjuncture is experienced as a major break from the past, with few continuities from a life dominated by employment. The central task facing men upon retirement is to find alternative activities that not only provide meaning and satisfaction, but fill in the substantial amounts of free time suddenly available. While retiring women must confront similar issues, their lives are characterized by underlying continuities not shared by men. Women's role as caregiver, especially towards husbands, continues after retirement and may intensify as husbands age and typically experience an increase in health problems (Townsend and Franks, 1997). As well, because men tend to drift away from friendships with former co-workers, wives often find their husbands to be even more emotionally dependent upon them following retirement. Thus, wives' marriage-maintenance role continues, possibly becoming even more important.

Men's greater dependency can become a source of either greater closeness or increased irritation (Brubaker, 1991). As they do in the pre-retirement years, women continue to perform the great majority of household tasks after retirement, although men's participation levels do increase somewhat (Szinovacz, 2000). Even if such labour holds little in the way of intrinsic satisfactions, the continuity that it ensures helps prevent, for older women, the development of an acute sense of dislocation or disjuncture from earlier stages of adult life. Ironically, housework, once the scourge of life, becomes a stabilizing factor in the transition to the post-retirement years—although retired men's sudden fascination with either doing or supervising housework as a means of filling in the time may become a source of dissatisfaction for wives or conflict between spouses.

Although retirement is often thought of as an abrupt event, many people ease into retirement by gradually reducing their work hours (Atchley, 1997; Bowlby, 2007). A study of well-educated men over the age of 65 reported that many of them left and returned to the labour force several times before retiring permanently (Elder and Pavlko, 1993). A study based on data from the Survey of Labour and Income Dynamics concluded that "easing into retirement is a real phenomenon" (Statistics Canada, 2002j). This research reported that almost two in five older workers (age 50 to 67) who terminated a full-time career job (i.e., one held for at least eight years) between 1993 and 1997 began another job within two years; the majority obtained a new full-time job while a smaller portion opted for part-time employment. Freedom of choice seems to play a role in the likelihood of a worker re-entering the workforce: Of those who voluntarily left a career job, 62 percent did not work again during the following two years and only 21 percent started a new full-time job; however, the situation was reversed among those who had left involuntarily, with 61 percent starting a new full-time job and 21 percent not working again during the two-year follow-up period. Age also figures in the likelihood of re-employment. Among those age 50 to 54, more than half (58 percent) began a new full-time job within two years; after two years, only 26 percent did not have a job. This finding suggests that these relatively young men may have envisaged leaving their former job as part of a career progression. In contrast, less than a third of those ages 55 to 69 started another full-time job within two years and more than half (54 percent) had no job after two years; this finding may indicate the impact of ageism or the desire of these somewhat older workers to become "early retirees." Sex differences also affect the likelihood of re-entering the labour force: Almost 60 percent of older women who ended a full-time job remained jobless for the following 24 months, compared to about one half of their male counterparts (Statistics Canada, 2002j). Compared to Canadian men, Canadian women have a greater likelihood of experiencing involuntary retirement and are more likely than men to retire from the paid labour force when they experience an involuntary job change (Statistics Canada, 2006o).

An earlier study (Monette, 1996b) reported that those individuals who retired because they were offered early retirement incentives were the most likely to return to paid work at a later time, followed by those who had lost their previous job, those who felt old enough to retire, and those who retired simply out of personal choice. People who retired for reasons of health, family care, spouse's retirement, or mandatory retirement were the least likely to return to the workforce. Additional factors prompting a return to work included financial need (particularly for those with larger households), the perception of work as a way of keeping busy, the feeling of being too young to retire, having a partner in the labour force, and awareness of new paid-work opportunities. Higher education was positively correlated to the decision to return to the labour force, as was past background in professional or managerial occupations. This research found that women were more likely than men to take on part-time employment following an earlier decision to retire, and also more likely to take on contract (temporary) employment.

Men's greater likelihood of returning to the paid labour force appears to reflect both their historically greater attachment to paid work and their greater difficulty in finding satisfying alternatives. After an initial flurry of travel, new hobbies, wandering around shopping malls, or having coffee with old workmates, some men feel dissatisfied and unfulfilled. The identity of "retiree" may seem less gratifying than their previous work-related one. In contrast to men, most women who are of retirement age today did not acquire a socialization that emphasized that the paid-work role should form the crux of their identity. Some of these women remain in the labour force as long as possible or return to it after a tentative departure out of financial necessity rather than choice. For others, however, the prospect of resuming their labour-force role may be far from compelling. These women may perceive that the roles of wife, mother, grandmother, kinkeeper, caregiver, and housewife provide ample alternative bases for their social identity.

Whether younger generations of men and women will follow in their elders' footsteps upon retirement is difficult to predict. Although their behaviour is not necessarily consistent with what they espouse, today's young men increasingly claim to derive their sense of identity and masculinity less from paid work and more from marriage, family, and non-employment activities. Should this indeed be the case, the retirement experiences of these men may well be different and perhaps will come to resemble the experiences of retired women. Today's young women, including those in middle adulthood, have a stronger attachment to the labour force than have any cohort of women since the end of World War II. Employment has become integrated into their conceptions of femininity. It is reasonable to hypothesize that women currently in professional and managerial occupations will be less likely to retire simply because their husbands do. As well, women today (especially those under 65) are distributed more variably across all marital statuses than in the past. Widowed and never-married women typically face fewer financial constraints on their decision to retire than do divorced and separated women. These women are all more likely to make retirement decisions independently than are married women, who have a relationship partner to consider. However, given the changes of the past 30 years, married women are also less likely to base their decisions solely upon a husband's needs or desires. To what extent the retirement experiences of men and women will converge in the future remains to be seen.

Poverty For many Canadians, even the near-elderly, financial security during retirement seems to be only a remote concern. As Townson (1995: 6) remarked, "[s]urveys indicate a wide gap between the optimistic expectations of Canadians for retirement and the reality of inadequate final resources that most will face." In the 2002 tax year, 5 991 440 Canadian tax-filers contributed just under $27.1 billion to a registered retirement saving plan (RRSP), with a median contribution of $2500; women accounted for 46 percent of contributors and made a median contribution of $2100. However, both the number of Canadians contributing to an RRSP and the amount of their contributions has declined since 2000. In addition, "[t]he contributions in 2002 represented only about 9% of the total room available to those who filed taxes in 2002, and less than half of the new room that was generated in 2002" (Statistics Canada, 2002k). Still, "Canadians are saving for retirement as never before," with about two thirds of Canadians doing so. However, those with limited income are unlikely to have anything left over to "save" after paying for basic necessities.

For some Canadians, financial security during retirement is anchored to improbable fantasies of winning a jackpot; according to one 1999 survey, 11 percent of Canadians are hoping to use lottery winnings to support themselves during later life. However, "[s]ince the odds of winning the 6/49 lottery are about 14 million to one, this is not really a sound financial plan" (Kendall et al., 2000: 380). A Statistics Canada study also reported that in 2001, "an estimated 390 000 full-time permanent employees in the private sector, or 4% of the total, thought they had a retirement plan, but in reality did not. They were working in firms that offered neither a registered pension plan (RPP) nor a group registered retirement savings plan (RRSP)" (Statistics Canada, 2004f). Among immigrants who arrived in 1991 or more recently, 9 percent believed that they had at least one retirement plan when in fact they did not. This lack of knowledge is only partially attributable to their under-representation in unionized jobs and in jobs in large companies, where information tends to be more reliable. In contrast, misinformation was minimal among university graduates, unionized employees, workers in large establishments, and those employed in finance, insurance, communications, and other utilities.

Earlier in this chapter it was noted that at older ages, women are less likely than men to be married. This demographic fact becomes important because marital status has a significant impact on the likelihood of **poverty** in old age. "Almost one in five of all seniors who are living on their own live on low income. Almost half (49 percent) of single, widowed, and divorced women 65 or over and 60 percent of those 75 and older are poor" (Henslin et al., 2004: 229). An important reason why this occurs is the fact that although federal income-security programs effectively protect most senior couples from poverty, they are less effective in safeguarding seniors who live alone.

At present, Canada's retirement income system comprises three tiers: (1) governmental benefits such as Old Age Security (OAS) and the Guaranteed Income Supplement (GIS), designed to forestall the likelihood of poverty by furnishing all seniors with a taxable, flat-rate benefit (adjusted every three months as the Consumer Price Index increases), which is paid monthly regardless of work history or life circumstances; (2) government-sponsored pension plans, CPP (Canada)/QPP (Quebec), which are designed to provide workers with a retirement income based upon their pre-retirement earnings from age 18 to 65; and (3) private savings, which include employer-sponsored private pension plans, private investments, and Registered Retirement Savings Plans (RRSPs) (Townson, 1995: 27).

OAS pension benefits are based on age and residency. A person qualifies for a full OAS pension after having resided in Canada for 40 years after age 18. Those who are ineligible for a full pension may receive a pro-rated partial pension after a minimum of 10 years residency in Canada. For the April–June 2008 period (amounts are adjusted quarterly), the maximum monthly OAS pension was $502.31. While OAS pension is payable at age 65, some exemptions do exist. For example, in 2008, those Canadian seniors whose net incomes exceeded $64 718 yearly were required to repay some or all of their OAS benefits. The full OAS pension was clawed back when an individual's net income exceeded $104 903.

The GIS was introduced in 1966 to assist those seniors with little or no income other than their OAS pension. The amount given depends upon the pensioner's income, conjugal relationship status, and whether the recipient's partner also receives an OAS pension or Old Age Allowance income. For example, for a single pensioner or married/common-law person whose partner did not receive such benefits, the April–June 2008 rate for the maximum monthly GIS payment was $634.02. In addition, married or common-law spouses of pensioners (opposite- or same-sex), as well as the conjugal survivors of deceased pensioners, may also qualify for an Old Age Allowance provided that they are between the ages of 60 and 64 and qualify under an income test. Although GIS and OAS benefits are unrelated to an individual's prior income history, CPP/QPP benefits are directly based on a person's income earned between the age of 18 and the time they claim retirement (between the ages of 60 and 70), and proportionately reflect their prior income patterns. Although full benefits do not begin until age 65, partial CPP/QPP payments can be received by retired persons, under certain circumstances, as early as age 60. In April–June of 2008, the maximum monthly pension payable at age 65 under the CPP was $884.58.

A study examining the incomes of younger retired women (ages 65 to 69) in Canada over the past three decades reported that women in this age group "have higher incomes than women their age have ever had" (Statistics Canada, 2002a). Yet although their incomes have grown 10 times faster than men's since 1971, their financial situation remains precarious inasmuch as "women are earning only 61 percent as much as men in their early retirement years, and Old Age Security is still their principal source of income." In 1997, the average after-tax income of women in their early retirement years was $14 200, compared with $23 300 for men. In that year, OAS/GIS was the principal source of income for women ages 67 to 69, accounting for just over one third (34 percent) of their total income—down from 1971, when it accounted for more than half (51 percent). For men, the most important sources of income were private pensions (accounting for 26 percent of total income), followed by the CPP/QPP and employment income; less than one fifth (19 percent) of their income was derived from OAS/GIS (down one percentage point since 1971). While the retirement-income gap between men and women narrowed over the past three decades, "[t]he average amounts women received from public and private pensions, and their total income, also remained considerably lower than those of men."

This study reported that the recent gains in women's retirement income reflected their increased labour-force participation rates. The women in this study—born between 1935 and 1939—were more likely to evince the bimodal pattern of female labour-force participation described in Chapter 6 (i.e., with women dropping out of the paid labour force during their early childrearing years and returning when their children began to leave home). In contrast, women today demonstrate higher rates of labour-force participation across all ages and are much less likely to interrupt their careers after childbirth—a fact which suggests that women's CPP/QPP and private pension benefits should improve in the decades to come. In the interim, however, the risk of poverty for elderly women remains significant, as relatively few have access to additional private-sector (i.e., non-government) pensions, such as those provided by employers. "Currently only 51 percent of Canadian female employees aged 35 to 54 and 67 percent of their male counterparts have some form of pension coverage" (Henslin et al., 2004: 223). Certain groups, such as low-wage workers, part-time workers, service workers, First Nations women, and women with disabilities, are particularly unlikely to be covered by a private pension plan (Morissette and Drolet, 2001: 54).

To a large extent, women's lack of company-sponsored pension coverage reflects their limited representation in sectors where pension coverage is quite high, such as manufacturing, construction, transportation, communications, and government services; and their over-representation in such areas as retail trade, where coverage is low. A woman employed as a secretary or as a salesperson for a small business is unlikely to receive a benefits package; if she does, it is unlikely to be as comprehensive as those won for workers whose pension plans are negotiated by trade unions on their behalf. Moreover, Asian, Caribbean, and South European women immigrants who are self-employed as seamstresses, as domestics, or in other poorly paid roles in the "invisible economy" receive no benefits for their years of underground employment. A recent Statistics Canada report has noted the particular vulnerability of immigrants, observing that, for older immigrants, employment was the major source of income from 1980 to 2002, and that this group "has not benefitted as much as the Canadian-born from the maturation of public and private pension systems. Workplace pension income for immigrants 65 and over was 21% lower than for the entire elderly population" (Statistics Canada, 2006o). Moreover, insofar as "housework brings no work-related benefits, no disability or unemployment insurance, no health benefits, and, most importantly, no pension coverage" (Wilson, 1996: 54), women will continue to be penalized for their pattern of interrupted labour-force participation.

The majority of women who are 65 and over today did not anticipate it becoming their responsibility to provide for themselves or their children financially. Some of these women are **displaced homemakers**—women who devoted their adult lives to being full-time wives, mothers, and kinkeepers, but (usually as a result of divorce) suddenly found themselves with neither job nor money. Like displaced providers, they had followed an earlier model, which assigned men the provider role and enjoined women to invest in their marriages rather than in careers or RRSPs; their assumption was that their husbands would always provide for them. Many of these women are now finding that their husbands did not or could not.

Widowhood One of the most stressful life events a person can experience is the death of a spouse (Martin Matthews, 1991; Miller et al., 1998). The vast majority of research conducted to date on the experience of widowhood has focused primarily on women for several reasons. First, gender differences in life expectancy, in combination with the mating gradient, increase the likelihood that a husband will predecease his wife. As a result, there is a gender **widowhood** gap. "After 30 years of marriage a woman, compared with a man, runs three times the risk of widowhood" (Novak, 1997: 267). Among couples age 65 or older whose marriages had ended at the death of one partner, it was the husband who had died in 72 percent of the cases (Norland, 1994: 25). Given their greater longevity, women today can expect to be widows for longer. A woman widowed at 65 can expect to live for almost two more decades, while a woman widowed at the age of 80 may expect to live for an additional nine years (Novak, 1997: 267–268).

Second, from the mid-1870s through the mid-1990s, the widowed have had the lowest marriage rates in Canada, and those rates have declined substantially over time, especially in Quebec (Nault, 1996: 42–44). Male remarriage rates are generally higher than female remarriage rates at any given age, and the rates for widowed older adults are no exception. Wu (1995) noted that five years following the death of a spouse, 12 percent of widowed men had remarried, compared to less than 4 percent of widowed women. Ten years after being widowed, 35 percent of men versus 11 percent of women had remarried. Using figures obtained from the National Advisory Council, Novak (1997: 267) reported that among Canadian seniors 70 years of age and over, the remarriage rate of men was nine times that of women.

Since widowhood now tends to occur at older ages, it is not surprising that the mean age at remarriage for widowed men and women has been on the rise: In 1997, the mean age was 62.1 years for grooms and 55.5 years for brides; in 2001, it rose to 62.9 and 56.4 (Statistics Canada, 1996: 24; Statistics Canada, 2003m). As Canadian women move into their senior years, our double standard of aging may have a particularly harsh impact upon their probability of remarrying. Available data indicate that the age gap between intimate partners in Canada increases with age, as older men select from a wider and younger range of women (Wu and Balakrishnan, 1992); this leads to a smaller pool of "older" men for senior women to marry.

As a result of a combination of women's greater longevity and the effects of the mating gradient, Canadian women are not only more likely than Canadian men to become widowed, but are also more likely to remain in that status for the rest of their lives. For at least some, however, this status is preferred. Based on interviews with 25 widows and 26 widowers over the age of 65, Davidson (2001) reported that while none of her male respondents used the term "freedom" to describe their current situation, women commonly did and associated this freedom "with not having to look after someone all the time." Similarly, while women commonly used the term "selfish" to describe their situation, few men did so. Davidson argued that the desire for re-partnering after widowhood may be gender-specific, maintaining that "widows are more likely to choose to remain without a partner for intrinsic factors—the reluctance to relinquish a new-found freedom—while for widowers, extrinsic factors of older age and poor health are more salient issues in new partnership formation choices and constraints" (p. 297; see also Davidson, 2002).

In 2006 in Canada, elderly women were more likely than men to be divorced/widowed and living on their own. While 65.7 percent of men age 80 and above lived in a private household with a spouse or common-law partner, this was true for only 22.3 percent of women (Statistics Canada, 2007r). Despite the onus placed upon men in our society to continue providing for their wives "after you're gone" via life insurance benefits and savings accounts, the death of a husband and encroaching poverty often compel women to sell the family home and move to rental or institutional settings (National Council of Welfare, 2002; Statistics Canada, 2006p). A recent study which evaluated the economic consequences of widowhood for Canadian men and women found that senior men suffered economically from widowhood to a much larger degree than senior men. Following the loss of their husbands, "[s]enior widows saw their median family adjusted income decline continuously in the five years following the loss of their husband. Five years after the death of the spouse, senior women saw their adjusted income decline by more than 15%.... Widowers walked a much different path.... After five years of widowhood ... [the adjusted median income] was 5.8% higher than in the year before widowhood" (Statistics Canada, 2006p).

In 2004/2005, merely 1 out of every 30 seniors age 50 and over resided in one of Canada's 1952 homes for the aged (Statistics Canada, 2007x). However, senior women were almost twice as likely as their male counterparts to do so; of those who resided in homes for the aged in 2004–2005, 70.4 percent were women. Among those age 85 and over, almost 18 percent of women, versus 12 percent of men, lived in a home for the aged—a finding that is partly explained by the fact that older men are almost twice as likely as women to be married or living in a common-law relationship. Moreover, research suggests that movement of women into homes for the elderly and/or health care institutions is necessitated less often by failing health than by a lack of funds to keep up with the inexhaustible expenses of home ownership (repair, maintenance, taxes, etc.). However, moving away from long-time neighbours and friends—who provide emotional support and frequently fill a "family comforter" role (Bess, 1999: 3; Yeh et al., 2004)—often leads to increased social isolation, which may partially explain the finding that older women tend to have less stable mental health than older men (Nett, 1993; Byles et al., 1999). While most older men "have built-in housekeepers and nurses—their wives" (National Council of Welfare, 1990/1995: 214)—elderly widowed women may, because of a lack of money, be unable to partake of the comfort that visiting nurses and home-help could provide. Insofar as older individuals are apt to identify living independently as an important measure of personal autonomy (Bess, 1999; Mutchler, 1992), having the financial ability to continue doing so may be as important to their well-being as physical health.

Although women in Canada are statistically more likely to face widowhood, Canadian men also experience widowhood as a markedly stressful life event. McPherson (1994: 249) reported that although widowed men "are not often faced with economic burdens, they apparently have more difficulty in adapting to their new role, as evidenced by higher suicide rates, higher rates of remarriage, and higher rates of mortality following bereavement." An early study by Benjamin and Wallis (1963) found that in the months following a wife's death, men's mortality rate increased sharply; some of their deaths were due to suicide. Datan (1989: 16) reported that "if a man is widowed, his mortality rises by 67 percent in the first year after the death of his spouse, while if a woman is widowed, her mortality rises by only about 3 percent." More recently, a Canadian study which examined mortality among individuals age 65 and older over the period from 1994–1995 to 2000–2001 concluded that "[t]he social support that seniors get through marriage is associated with a lower risk of dying—but only for men" (Statistics Canada, 2003o). This study, which used longitudinal data from the National Population Health Survey, found that although being married did not have a "protective" impact upon women's mortality, "[m]arried men had a 40% lower risk of death, compared with men who were single, widowed, divorced or separated" (Statistics Canada, 2003o, 2006q; see also Manor and Eisenbach, 2003).

Loneliness and intense feelings of isolation following widowhood are associated with a relative lack of social supports (Lee et al., 1998; Pinquart, 2003). Men's greater likelihood of identifying their spouse as their "best friend" often means that "[w]idowed men are doubly bereft—they have lost both a helpmate and confidante.... Conversely, the widowed woman is unlikely to be entirely devoid of close friends" (Hess and Soldo, 1985 cited in

Novak, 1997: 269). The desire for companionship, a sexual partner, and a housekeeper may partially explain the fact that widowed men are more likely to remarry and to do so relatively promptly (Gierveld, 2002). In contrast, women's kinship network—kept vital through their performance of the kinkeeper role—as well as their more intensive friendship network—helps buffer the loss of spousal companionship (Atchley, 1997: 324–333).

For both men and women, the death of a spouse involves a wrenching-away of identities that have merged over the years (DiGiulio, 1992). McPherson (1994: 249) suggested that widowed men and women typically go through a series of stages, beginning with a period of mourning that may last up to two years, in which the bereaved person attempts to build a network of others for social support. He reported that the process of adjustment is easier if the person has a group of same-age friends who themselves have experienced widowhood. Although social supports may ease the transition (Connidis and Davies, 1992), those women survivors whose primary identity for much of their lives has been "Mrs. John Smith" must come to grips with the question "Who am I?" now that Mr. Smith has gone (Bennett and Vidall-Hall, 2000; Lopata, 2000; van den Hoonaard, 2001). Research based on 297 individuals from the Changing Lives of Older Couples (CLOC) study, a prospective study of widowhood among adults age 65 and older, found that widowed men and women "who were once highly dependent upon their spouses" may, despite their former dependency, "reap psychological rewards from the recognition that they are capable of managing on their own" (Carr, 2004: 220). This research reported that widowed women "who were most emotionally dependent on their spouses had the poorest self-esteem while still married ... [but] evidence the highest levels of self-esteem following loss"; widowed men "who were most dependent on their wives for home maintenance and financial management tasks experience the greatest personal growth following loss."

Due to the comparative rarity of death among young people, younger women experience a greater degree of anguish and a more difficult adjustment upon a husband's death than do older women (Novak, 1997: 270). The sudden death of a young spouse may be experienced as a tragedy for which one is totally unprepared, while the death of an elderly spouse tends to be experienced as a sad but predictable event. Older survivors, knowing that a spouse's death is impending and having the experiences of age-mates to draw upon, may make preparations that smooth the transition from married to widowed status (e.g., arranging finances, pre-planning funerals, preparing themselves psychologically). Saying goodbye and cultivating treasured last memories become important parts of adjusting to imminent widowhood.

Key Terms

boomerang children

caring-about activities

climacteric

differential exposure hypothesis

differential vulnerability hypothesis

displaced homemakers

displaced providers

double standard of aging

Dream (career clock/work clock)

empty nest syndrome

feticide

fixed role obligations hypothesis

gender depolarization

gender life-expectancy gap

gender splicing

gender splitting

general systems theory of sex roles

greying of Canada

instrumental activities

life course development

life expectancy

life span

life span hierarchical stage progression model

mastery

menopause

men's pause

morbidity

mortality

natality inequality

perimenopause

personal care activities

pleasure

postformal theory

poverty

Preimplantational Genetic Diagnosis (PGD)

Prenatal Diagnosis (PND)

repotting

retirement

role compatibility hypothesis

sandwich generation

sex ratio

social acceptability hypothesis

widowhood

Chapter Summary

1. This chapter has focused upon selected events associated with aging and upon the social meanings of aging for both women and men.

2. The persistence of a gender life-expectancy gap which favours women appears to be largely attributable to the more hazardous lifestyle associated with masculinity in our society.

3. Available data indicate that adult women have higher rates of most forms of morbidity than adult men in our society. Explanations for the gender morbidity gap include the *social acceptability, role compatibility, fixed role obligations, differential exposure (nurturant),* and *differential vulnerability* hypotheses.

4. Research has revealed the intriguing phenomenon of *gender depolarization,* a significant decline in previously polarized sex-linked personality and behavioural characteristics during the middle-adult years.

5. In our youth-oriented society, aging women confront a "double standard" of physical attractiveness and sexual desirability.

6. Among Canadians currently in the late phase of middle adulthood are *displaced homemakers* and *displaced providers*.

7. Three major experiences common to many Canadians age 64 and over are retirement, poverty, and widowhood; there are gender-based differences in these experiences.

CHAPTER 10

Gender, Equality, and Social Change

An underlying theme of this text has been that over the course of the past century, societal changes have resulted in greater equality for Canadian men and women. Comparing and contrasting Canada with other societies may help us to both appreciate these changes more fully and identify areas where further change may be needed.

THE UNFINISHED JOURNEY: HOW DOES CANADA COMPARE?

In 1990, the United Nations began seeking analytical tools and methods that would make it possible to compare how well nations promote "long, healthy and creative lives" (United Nations Development Programme, 1995: 11) for all their citizens. Up until that time, most researchers and research organizations had focused upon such measures as national economic growth or per-capita Gross National Product (GNP). The GNP is usually calculated by dividing the total dollar value (expressed in U.S. currency equivalents) of all goods and services produced by a nation in one year by the total number of its inhabitants. Such measures lend themselves to cross-national comparisons, but take no account of the crucial issue of the actual *distribution* of national wealth; in many countries, economic growth or per-capita GNP may be high, but actual wealth is concentrated in the hands of a small proportion of the population, while the vast majority eke out a bare subsistence. What is more, a comparison based solely on economic factors fails to acknowledge many essential elements of social life.

In 1990, the United Nations Development Programme adopted the composite **Human Development Index** (HDI). This method of measuring national development uses indicators of longevity (life expectancy), knowledge (based upon adult literacy rates and [at first] mean years of schooling), and

income or *purchasing-power parity* (PPP)—the per-capita GNP adjusted for local cost of living. These specific indicators were selected primarily on pragmatic grounds; data for each were readily available and in a form that permitted cross-national comparisons. The United Nations Development Programme acknowledged that the use of national averages in the derivation of such measures as mean years of schooling and per-capita GNP could, by concealing ranges of variation, obscure inequalities among segments of a nation's population. "Mean years of schooling" was eventually replaced by a more comprehensive measure representing the proportion of a population enrolled in primary, secondary, and tertiary levels of education. The composite HDI does not measure the well-being or happiness of a country's residents, but it does provide an indication of a nation's progress towards promoting long life, good health, and informed choices among its citizenry (United Nations Development Programme, 1995: 12).

The United Nations Development Programme further sought to evaluate how nations promote the human development of significant societal groups. This information could then be used to compare the treatment of different groups within a nation and of similar groups in other nations. In 1995, the Human Development Report introduced two new measures designed to highlight the status of women within nations (United Nations Development Programme, 1995: 72–86). The **Gender-related Development Index** (GDI) uses the same measures as the HDI, but applies them to assess the extent of inequality between men and women within a nation: "In other words, the GDI is the HDI adjusted for gender inequality" (United Nations Development Programme, 1995: 73). Disparities between women and men in terms of life expectancy, adult literacy, or purchasing-power parity lower a country's GDI ranking. In the case of most countries, the GDI ranking is lower than the overall HDI, indicating that the distribution of development-growth factors in that country favours men over women. A third device, the **Gender Empowerment Measure** (GEM), focuses upon women's political, economic, and professional advancement. The GEM assesses the extent to which women are able to participate in political and economic decision-making so as to take advantage of a nation's opportunities. Three indicators are used to construct this measure: (1) women's share of seats in parliament or in parliamentary caucus; (2) women's share of administrative/managerial and professional/technical jobs; and (3) women's earning power, reflecting their access to jobs and wages. Taken together, these indicators provide information about the extent to which a nation's women are able to use their capabilities. As with HDI parameters, GEM parameters were selected primarily because relevant data are more readily available than data on such matters as women's power within households. For most nations, GEM rankings are dramatically lower than HDI rankings, a fact that attests to the underutilization of women's capabilities.

Scores for each of the HDI, GDI, and GEM can range from a low of 0.0 to a high of 1.0; no society has attained a "perfect" score of 1.0, which indicates that room for improvement exists even within the "best" countries. "The HDI value for each country indicates how far that country has to go to attain certain defined goals: an average life span [*sic*] of 85 years, access to education for all and a decent level of income. The closer a country's HDI is to 1, the less the remaining distance that country has to travel" (United Nations Development Programme, 1995: 18). The GDI value indicates how far a country has yet to go to achieve gender equality in those three areas; the GEM value indicates how far it still must go to empower women to participate meaningfully in economic and political decision-making in the public sphere. HDI, GDI, and GEM rankings are calculated by plugging weighted indicators into certain statistical formulae to produce a score or "value." Since both the indicators and formulae are constantly being refined, no meaningful comparisons can be made of a nation's scores over time. However, within any given year, comparisons can be made among nations.

On HDI comparisons, Canada has fared well, ranking first among 174 or 175 nations every year from 1995 through 2000. However, our status has typically declined on ratings of GDI and GEM. Thus, in 1995, Canada ranked first on HDI, but ninth of 130 countries on GDI, and fifth of 116 countries on GEM (United Nations Development Programme, 1995); in 2000, Canada ranked first of 174 countries on HDI, first of 143 on GDI, but eighth of 70 on GEM (United Nations Development Programme, 2000). In 2007, Canada was fourth of 177 countries on HDI, fourth of 157 on GDI, and tenth of 93 countries on GEM (United Nations Development Programme, 2007: 326, 330). Table 10.1 provides HDI, GDI, and GEM rankings for various countries, based upon information contained in the *Human Development Report* of 2007.

Data available to the United Nations Development Programme permitted GDI comparisons of 79 countries from 1970 to 1992. Over that time period, GDI values in all countries increased (United Nations Development Programme, 1995: 80); however, international comparisons reveal that both Canada and the United States dropped in their comparative rankings, Canada from second to ninth, and the United States from first to fifth. While gender equality did improve in both countries over the 1970s and 1980s, many other societies outstripped them in the rate of progress. In particular, Scandinavian countries (e.g., Sweden, Finland, and Norway) made great strides in promoting and implementing gender equality in those areas measured by the GDI, especially earned income. Canada's ninth-place ranking in 1992 was due primarily to its low score on the measure of women's

TABLE 10.1	Selected Countries*, Ranked According to HDI, GDI, and GEM**, 2007		
Country	HDI Rank	GDI Rank	GEM Rank
Iceland	1	1	5
Norway	2	3	1
Australia	3	2	8
Canada	**4**	**4**	**10**
Ireland	5	15	19
Sweden	6	5	2
Switzerland	7	9	27
Japan	8	13	54
Netherlands	9	6	6
France	10	7	18
Finland	11	8	3
United States	12	16	15
Spain	13	12	12
Denmark	14	11	4
United Kingdom	18	10	14
Italy	20	17	21
Germany	22	20	9
Israel	23	21	28
Greece	24	24	37
United Arab Emirates	39	43	29
Chile	40	40	60
Mexico	51	51	46
Philippines	90	77	45
Iran	94	84	87
Sri Lanka	99	89	85
Pakistan	136	125	82
Yemen	153	136	93

* Inclusion in this table was based partly upon availability of complete data for all three measures.

** HDI refers to Human Development Index; GDI refers to Gender Development Index; GEM refers to Gender Empowerment Measure. HDI rank order is based upon 177 reporting countries; GDI rank order is based upon 157 reporting countries; GEM rank order is based upon 93 reporting countries.

Source: Adapted from United Nations Development Programme. 2007. *Human Development Report 2007/2008.* New York: Oxford University Press, Appendix Tables 28, (pp. 326–329); 29 (pp. 330–333).

earning power relative to men's (United Nations Development Programme, 1995: 79). The fact that GDI values for all 79 countries increased during these two decades suggests that even though the pace of change may be uneven, once normative policies, programs, and general expectations are established, societal movement towards greater gender equality is difficult to reverse. Regressive social movements may attempt to return a society to "the good old days"; however, perhaps nothing short of fundamentalist revolution in the name of religious purity and hegemony (such as occurred in late-1990s Afghanistan with the Taliban) can reverse societal trends.

Nevertheless, rank-orderings of countries conceal as much as they reveal. An examination of more recent United Nations findings yields further insight. Table 10.2 provides a summary of HDI, GDI, and GEM values for 25 countries (United Nations Development Programme, 2007). A quick inspection of GDI values reveals why the UN has repeatedly observed that "no society treats its women as well as its men" (United Nations Development Programme, 1997: 39, 1995: 75). Even though Iceland garnered the highest HDI and GDI scores in 2007, that country's GDI still falls short of its HDI, and its GEM is even lower. In Canada, the situation is similar. As the tables show, the countries with the highest HDI and GDI rankings and values tend to be found in Northern and Western Europe and the "Anglo-Saxon overseas" (Trovato and Lalu, 1996) societies of Australia, Canada, New Zealand, and the United States, as well as in Japan. However, examination reveals considerable variation in terms of HDI and GDI ranks and values. A high HDI ranking and value does not predict equally high GDI and GEM rankings and values. Disparities demonstrate that "gender equality does not depend on the income level of a society" (United Nations Development Programme, 1995: 75). Other factors, such as a society's commitment to ensuring gender equality of access to these systems, are at least as important. Commitment to gender equality can itself have a meaningful impact, independent of the state of a country's economy.

GEM is a nation's most telling index of gender equality. The "GEM" columns in Tables 10.1 and 10.2 indicate how far away women of various nations still are from holding an equitable share of power in important areas of public-sphere decision-making. Table 10.2 reveals that GEM values are typically much lower than either HDI or GDI values for all countries being compared, although the drop is more precipitous in some countries (e.g., Japan, Switzerland) than in others (e.g., Norway, Sweden, Denmark). The fact that the gender equality tends to be greater in richer countries would seem to suggest that gender equality is a function of economic development. However, notable exceptions to the pattern belie such a conclusion. For example, while the Philippines and the Dominican Republic rank 90th and 79th on HDI, both have higher GEM rankings (45th and 53rd) than Japan, which ranks 8th on HDI but 54th on GEM. Furthermore, in some of the formerly communist countries of Eastern Europe, GEM is higher than might be expected given low levels of economic development: e.g., Slovakia (33), Poland (39), Czech Republic (34), and Latvia (38). Meanwhile, in some of the Islamic countries, gender equality is notably lower than one would expect given high levels of economic development (e.g., the United Arab Emirates, Egypt). It is evident from these findings that gender equality (particularly women's empowerment) is not a function of standard of living. As the 2003 *Human Development Report* observed, "In the Arab states high incomes have improved many aspects of human development since 1970. Yet of all regions the Arab states have the widest gap between incomes and other aspects of human development" (United Nations Development Programme, 2003: 38). For example, in Arab states with parliaments, women hold merely 5 percent of seats (p. 38). The greatest commitment to women's empowerment has been

TABLE 10.2	Selected Countries*, HDI, GDI, and GEM Values, 2007**		
Country	HDI Value	GDI Value	GEM Value
Iceland	.968	.962	.862
Norway	.968	.957	.910
Australia	.962	.960	.847
Canada	**.961**	**.956**	**.820**
Ireland	.959	.940	.699
Sweden	.956	.955	.906
Switzerland	.955	.946	.660
Japan	.953	.942	.557
Netherlands	.953	.951	.859
France	.952	.950	.718
Finland	.952	.947	.887
United States	.951	.937	.762
Denmark	.949	.944	.875
United Kingdom	.946	.944	.783
Italy	.941	.936	.693
Germany	.935	.931	.831
Greece	.926	.922	.622
Barbados	.892	.887	.649
Czech Republic	.891	.887	.627
Poland	.870	.867	.614
United Arab Emirates	.868	.855	.652
Latvia	.855	.861	.619
Saudi Arabia	.812	.783	.254
Iran	.759	.750	.347
Pakistan	.551	.525	.377
Yemen	.508	.472	.129

* Countries are listed according to their HDI rank, not index or measure, order.

** HDI refers to Human Development Index; GDI refers to Gender Development Index; GEM refers to Gender Empowerment Measure.

Source: Adapted from United Nations Development Programme. 2007. *Human Development Report 2007/2008.* New York: Oxford University Press, Appendix Tables 1 (pp. 229–232), 28 (pp. 326–329), and 29 (pp. 330–333).

demonstrated by the Nordic countries of Iceland, Norway, Sweden, and Denmark. Their GEM values, which range from .910 to .862, indicate that women in these countries are more than 86 percent of the way to equality with men on the three pertinent dimensions (i.e., women's share of seats in parliament; women's share of administrative, managerial, professional, and technical jobs; and women's earning power).

A better understanding of where we stand in Canada today in terms of gender empowerment measures can be obtained from examination of Table 10.3. Because of the limitations of data currently available to the United Nations, women's access to political power

TABLE 10.3	Comparison of Selected Countries, Ranked According to Gender Empowerment Measures, 2007				
Country	Gender Empowerment Measure (GEM) Rank	GEM Value	Seats in Parliament (as % of total)	Female Professional and Technical Workers (as % of total)	Ratio of Estimated Female to Male Earned Income
Norway	1	.910	37.9	50	0.77
Sweden	2	.906	47.3	51	0.81
Finland	3	.887	42.0	55	0.71
Denmark	4	.875	36.9	53	0.73
Iceland	5	.862	31.7	56	0.72
Netherlands	6	.859	36.0	50	0.64
Belgium	7	.850	35.7	49	0.55
Australia	8	.847	28.3	56	0.70
Germany	9	.831	30.6	50	0.58
Canada	**10**	**.820**	**24.4**	**56**	**0.64**
New Zealand	11	.811	32.2	53	0.70
Spain	12	.794	30.5	48	0.50
Austria	13	.788	31.0	49	0.46
United Kingdom	14	.783	19.3	47	0.66
United States	15	.762	16.3	56	0.63
Ireland	19	.699	14.2	52	0.53
Bahamas	20	.696	22.2	60	0.70
Costa Rica	24	.680	38.6	40	0.53
Lithuania	25	.669	24.8	67	0.69
Israel	28	.660	14.2	54	0.65
United Arab Emirates	29	.652	22.5	25	0.25
Barbados	30	.649	17.6	52	0.63
Tanzania	44	.597	30.4	32	0.73
Dominican Republic	54	.559	17.1	51	0.43
Malaysia	65	.504	13.1	40	0.36
Romania	68	.497	10.7	57	0.69
Brazil	70	.490	9.3	52	0.58
Turkey	90	.298	4.4	32	0.35
Saudi Arabia	92	.254	0.0	6	0.16

Source: United Nations Development Programme. 2007. *Human Development Report 2007/2008.* New York: Oxford University Press, Appendix, Table 29 (pp. 330–333).

can only be measured at national (but not local) levels of government. Generally, the representation of women in Canadian politics tends to be greater at municipal and provincial rather than federal levels of government (Wilson, 1996: 144–145).

The United Nations Development Programme has formulated a five-point strategy for "accelerating progress" towards gender equality. Point three states the following: "A critical 30 percent threshold should be regarded as a minimum share of decision-making positions held by women at the national level" (United Nations Development Programme, 1995: 9); this threshold is not to be construed as a final objective, but rather as an exigent minimum on the road to gender equality. This point, initially recommended in 1990, pertains to representation in parliament (and, where applicable, in caucus or cabinet) and at the administrative and managerial levels of government and economic institutions. While the employment of women in professional and technical jobs is also important, the decision-making power wielded in parliamentary or administrative/managerial roles is likely to have a greater bearing upon women's lives. It should be emphasized that women who attain such roles do not necessarily employ their power in ways that benefit all women, and that women outside the official corridors of power (such as the numerous female philanthropists in our country) may exert an influence beneficial to both sexes (Nowell, 1996). However, the number of women occupying positions of power does reflect the extent to which various avenues to power are open or closed to women in our society.

"No gender-specific training is required to be a parliamentarian. Neither public speaking, nor the ability to represent the opinions of the electorate, nor the art of winning public confidence requires exclusively masculine traits. But politics remains an obstacle course for women" (United Nations Development Programme, 1995: 83). Out of 177 nations providing information as of 31 May 2007 (United Nations Development Programme, 2007: 343–346), in only 19 did women occupy the UN's recommended minimum of 30 percent of decision-making roles in the political arena. These countries included the seven with the highest GEM rankings (see Table 10.3), plus Rwanda (45.3 percent), Cuba (at 36.0 percent), Costa Rica (38.6 percent), Argentina (36.8 percent), Mozambique (34.8 percent), South Africa (32.8 percent), New Zealand (32.2 percent), Burundi (31.7 percent), Germany (30.8 percent), Spain (30.5 percent), and Tanzania (30.4 percent). At 24.3 percent, Canada ranked 38th among 177 nations, behind countries such as Uganda (29.8 percent), Peru (29.2 percent), Guyana (29.0 percent), Namibia (26.9 percent), and Vietnam (25.8 percent). However, the United States (16.3 percent), United Kingdom (19.3 percent), and Japan (11.1 percent) all ranked lower than Canada. The lowest-ranking nations (most not shown in Table 10.3) were Saint Kitts and Nevis, Saudi Arabia, Solomon Islands (all at 0.0 percent), Yemen (0.7 percent), Papua New Guinea (0.9), and Kuwait (3.1). In response to the under-representation of women in the political arena, some countries have instituted quotas. In India, for example, an amendment passed in 1993 reserves one third of all seats in local contests for women. In Britain, a law passed in 1996 stipulates that a minimum of 20 percent of each party's candidates be women. Countries with similar policies include Finland, Germany, Mexico, South Africa, and Spain (Sheehan, 2000).

As Table 10.4 indicates, Canada has certainly come a long way since 1921, the year of the first federal election in which women were allowed to vote and run for office. In the 1921 federal election, in which only four women ran for office, a Canadian first was achieved when Agnes Campbell McPhail was elected to the House of Commons. "Between 1921 and 2006, 3402 women candidates stood in the 39 general elections and won on 426 occasions" (Heard, 2007). In 1989, the election of Audrey MacLaughlin as leader of the New Democratic Party marked the first time that a woman had been elected

TABLE 10.4	Women Candidates in Canadian Federal Elections, 1921–2006			
Year	Candidates	Elected	% Elected	% of MPs
1921	4	1	25	0.4 (of 235)
1925	4	1	25	0.4 (of 245)
1926	2	1	50	0.4 (of 245)
1930	10	1	10	0.4 (of 245)
1935	6	2	12.5	0.8 (of 245)
1940	9	1	11.1	0.4 (of 245)
1945	19	1	5.26	0.4 (of 245)
1949	11	0	0	0 (of 262)
1953	47	4	8.51	1.5 (of 265)
1957	29	2	6.89	0.8 (of 265)
1958	21	2	9.52	0.8 (of 265)
1962	26	5	19.23	1.9 (of 265)
1963	40	4	10	1.5 (of 265)
1965	37	4	10.81	1.5 (of 265)
1968	36	1	2.77	0.4 (of 264)
1972	71	5	7.04	1.9 (of 264)
1974	137	9	6.56	2.9 (of 301)
1979	195	10	5.12	3.5 (of 282)
1980	218	14	6.42	5.0 (of 282)
1984	214	27	12.61	9.6 (of 282)
1988	302	39	12.91	13.2 (of 295)
1993	476	53	11.13	18.0 (of 295)
1997	408	62	15.19	20.6 (of 301)
2000	373	62	16.62	20.6 (of 301)
2004	391	65	16.62	21.1 (of 308)
2006	380	64	16.8	20.8 (of 308)

Source: Based on data provided in Heard. 2008. "Elections." Available on the World Wide Web at www.sfu.ca/~aheard/elections/women.html.

leader of a national Canadian political party. And Conservative Party leader Kim Campbell became Canada's first female prime minister (albeit by ascension and for a term of less than six months) in 1993.

In general, however, the more important the political office, the lower the probability that a woman will hold it (Bedard and Tremblay, 2000). Successful political campaigns require large sums of money, the backing of powerful individuals and interest groups, and a willingness on the part of the voting public to elect women. Writing in the 1980s, Hunter and Denton (1984) observed that Canadian political parties evinced a marked tendency to nominate women only after suffering losses at the polls, or in "lost cause" ridings where other parties enjoyed overwhelming voter support. Stark (1992) concluded that party elites obstruct women "in securing nominations in the first place and, beyond this, in gaining nominations which carry a reasonable prospect of victory" (see also Fox and Oxley, 2003). Given that minority women face even greater structural barriers to election, it is not surprising that these women have represented an even smaller percentage of our elected officials. Thus, while Mary Ellen Smith became, in 1918, the first woman elected to the British Columbia Legislative Assembly and the first woman in the British Empire to serve as a cabinet minister, it was not until 1972 that a black woman, Rosemary Brown, won a seat in that province. Brown was the first black woman elected to any Canadian legislature. In 1991, Zanana Akande became the first black woman elected to the Ontario legislature, and also the first black woman to become a cabinet minister in that province (Mandell, 1995: 347).

Table 10.5 presents 2005 data on female economic activity and employment in various economic sectors in selected countries. The higher rates of economic activity among women in countries of the former Soviet Bloc reflects the communist policy, enunciated by Engels and Marx, of promoting female employment in a wide range of occupations. In sharp contrast, the lowest rates of female economic activity are found in Muslim countries, where religious beliefs either preclude or severely restrict women's participation in the paid labour force.

Participation rates furnish only a partial glimpse into the gender structure of a nation's or society's labour force. The distribution of men and women within that labour force has a much greater impact upon each gender's life events and opportunities. Table 10.5 indicates that women are most likely to be employed within the service sector: "Approximately 50 percent of the world's working women are employed in the service sector: wholesale and retail trades, restaurants, hotels, communications, insurance, real estate, business services, and social and personal services" (Neft and Levine, 1997: 62). One hundred nations provided information to the UN on their percentages of female professional and technical workers; included under this rubric are "teachers, nurses, scientists, laboratory workers, medical and dental technicians" (Neft and Levine, 1997: 66). Canada, with 56 percent, ranked 20th, tying with Iceland, Australia, and the United States (based upon figures contained in the United Nations Development Programme, 2007: Appendix Table 29, pp. 330–333). Ranked ahead of Canada were nations such as Estonia (70 percent), Lithuania and Kazakhstan (67 percent), Moldova (66 percent), the Russian Federation (65 percent), Cuba (62 percent), the Ukraine (64 percent), Georgia (62 percent), the Philippines (61 percent), and Bulgaria (60 percent). The lowest percentages were found in Saudi Arabia (6 percent), Bangladesh (12 percent), and Yemen (15 percent).

Generally, women are more likely to be found in professional and technical occupations than in administrative and managerial positions. The "glass-ceiling" phenomenon is not limited to Canada and the United States, but appears to be a feature of the occupational structures of almost all societies. Out of 98 nations providing information to the United Nations in 2007, there were only three in which women constituted 50 percent or more of the legislators, senior officials, and managers: the Philippines (58 percent), Saint Lucia (55 percent), and Mongolia (50 percent). Canada, along with New Zealand and Bolivia, tied for 23rd place on this measure (with 36 percent), well behind such countries as the Bahamas (46 percent), the Barbados and Lithuania (both at 43 percent), Panama, Trinidad and Tobago (all at 43 percent), and the United States (42 percent), but well ahead of others,

TABLE 10.5	Gender Inequality in Economic Activity, Selected Countries*, 2005

| | Female Economic Activity Rate (age 15 and above) | | Employment by Economic Activity (%) | | | | | |
| | Rate (%) | As % of Male rate | Agriculture | | Industry | | Services | |
			Female	Male	Female	Male	Female	Male
Iceland	70.5	86	4	11	11	34	85	55
Norway	63.3	87	2	5	8	32	90	63
Australia	56.4	80	3	5	9	31	88	65
Canada	**60.5**	**84**	**2**	**4**	**11**	**32**	**88**	**64**
Sweden	58.7	87	1	3	9	34	90	63
Japan	48.3	66	5	4	18	35	77	59
Netherlands	56.2	77	2	4	8	30	86	62
United States	59.6	82	1	2	10	30	90	68
Denmark	59.3	84	2	4	12	34	86	62
Slovenia	53.6	80	9	9	25	47	65	43
Czech Republic	51.9	77	3	5	27	49	71	46
Poland	47.7	78	17	28	17	39	66	43
Slovakia	51.8	76	3	6	25	50	72	44
Estonia	52.3	80	4	7	24	44	72	49
Latvia	49.0	77	8	15	16	35	75	49
Saudi Arabia	17.6	22	1	5	1	24	98	71
Russian Fed'n	54.3	80	8	12	21	38	71	50
Egypt	20.1	27	39	28	6	23	55	49
Pakistan	32.7	39	65	38	16	22	20	40
Kenya	69.1	78	16	20	10	23	75	57
Nigeria	45.4	53	2	4	11	30	87	67

* Countries are listed according to their HDI rank; inclusion in this table was based partly upon availability of complete data for all measures.

Source: Adapted from United Nations Development Programme, 2007. *Human Development Report 2007/2008* Table 31, pp. 338–341.

such as Japan (10 percent), Switzerland, Korea, and the United Arab Emirates (all at 8 percent), Egypt (9 percent), and the lowest-ranked Pakistan (2 percent) and Yemen (4 percent). Once again, it is obvious that sex distribution within occupational structures and the resulting distributions of power are not simply a function of a nation's overall economic development. Some less-developed countries have a higher percentage of female administrators and managers than do most developed countries. Gender ideology appears to be a more influential factor than economic development.

One major factor that tends to keep women's share of the paid labour force at or below the 50 percent level is the sex ratio. As noted in Chapter 9, between birth and age 50, men tend to outnumber women. In consequence, men are more likely to outnumber women in the labour force, especially between the ages of 15 and 50. In any society, women typically begin to outnumber men after the age of 50, and may or may not outnumber them in the labour force, depending upon the societal level of support for women's employment (Neft and Levine, 1997: 55–56). A second factor limiting women's participation in the paid labour force, especially in more highly skilled occupations, is unequal access to education. According to the 2003 *Human Development Report*, immense gender gaps remain in women's access to education: "three-fifths of the 115 million children out of school are girls, and two-thirds of the 876 million illiterate adults are women" (United Nations Development Programme 2003: 6). The report stresses that giving women greater access to education is "more than social justice—it promotes development" (p. 18): "Better-educated girls tend to marry later. They have fewer, better-educated, healthier children. And they earn higher incomes in the workforce. If girls are kept out of school or educated women are not allowed to fully participate in the labour market, these potential gains are squandered" (United Nations Development Programme, 2003: 18; see also Figure 10.1 and Box 10.1).

In sum, Canada's performance on the measures created and presented by the United Nations makes it clear that compared to many countries around the world, Canada has done

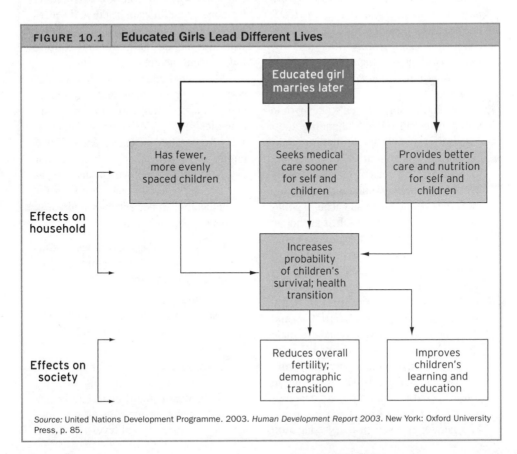

FIGURE 10.1 | **Educated Girls Lead Different Lives**

Source: United Nations Development Programme. 2003. *Human Development Report 2003*. New York: Oxford University Press, p. 85.

BOX 10.1

Promoting Capabilities and Agency: An International Agenda for Change

The following extract is abridged from the United Nations Human Development Report (2003: 86). It emphasizes that while the goal of eliminating gender disparity in all levels of education by 2015 is, in itself, an official Millennium Development Goal, "[u]nless women's capabilities are improved and gender equality increased, the other Millennium Development Goals [which include: eradicate extreme poverty and hunger; achieve universal primary education; promote gender equality and empower women; reduce child mortality; improve maternal health; combat HIV/AIDS, malaria, and other disease; ensure environmental sustainability: land and air; and strengthening partnerships between rich and poor countries] will not be achieved."

Strengthening women's agency and voice is essential to enhancing their capabilities—and strengthening their capabilities is essential to enhancing their agency and voice.... Gender equality in education helps women secure employment outside the home and acquire political power, contributing to their agency in the public sphere. But gender equality must also extend to the private domain.

Today gender inequality undermines women's capabilities in education and health. Still, some progress is being made. For example, between 1990 and 2001 the ratio of literate female to male 15- to 24-year-olds in countries with low human development increased from 70 to 81 women per 100 men, though in countries with medium human development it increased only from 91 to 93. The gender ratio in primary education

also made limited progress, rising from 86 to 92 girls per 100 boys in developing countries between 1999 [and] 2000. At current rates gender equality in education will not be achieved until 2025—20 years after the target set by the Millennium Development Goals. Among young girls (15-to-24-year-olds) in developing countries literacy is 60%, compared with 80% for young men. In addition, more women suffer from HIV/AIDS. Maternal mortality is another dimension of women's additional burdens.... Without action to increase women's capabilities in health and education, they will have limited prospects for working outside the home and earning independent incomes....

Many challenges undermine gender equality in employment and community and political participation. In developing countries most poor female workers outside of agriculture are engaged in informal employment and receive low, irregular pay.... Although employment and education are considered basic strategies for strengthening women's agency and voice, stronger agency also requires not just:

Recognizing the importance of education, but also improving its content, provision and returns.

Creating more jobs for women, but also improving their nature and terms—including sustainable livelihoods.

Increasing the number of women in parliaments, but also raising women's visibility in positions of authority and decision-making—from the local to the national levels.

> Thus, empowering women requires policies that address both practical needs (supporting the basic capabilities required to function, such as by improving living conditions and increasing employment, health care and safe water supplies) and strategic needs (strengthening women's voice and agency to renegotiate their roles at home and in society, such as through legal rights to assets and laws ensuring equal wages, reproductive rights and freedom from violence). Moreover, these policies must be backed by laws guaranteeing equal rights—for both women and men in the private and public spheres.
>
> Source: United Nations Development Programme. 2003. *Human Development Report 2003*. New York: Oxford University Press, p. 28.

much to promote the equality of its male and female citizens. However, evidence of inequality remains.

RESISTANCE TO FEMINISM

Aside from such changes in gender roles as have been occasioned by economic developments (e.g., industrialization), most gender-role change in Canada has resulted, directly or indirectly, from the impetus provided by feminist movements. Even though the various branches of feminist activism have disagreed about the preferred direction of change, they have remained in agreement about its desirability.

"Success" is an outcome not easily measured. The more general and multifaceted a movement's goals and aspirations, the more difficult it is, for insiders and outsiders alike, to agree upon what constitutes success and to determine whether it has been achieved. Some elements of the movement may feel satisfied with accomplishments thus far, while others may not; splinter groups may develop who accuse satisfied leaders and members of the larger movement of having "sold out." Success also begets both legitimacy and opposition. Legitimacy—official recognition and validation—is reflected in new laws, policies, and circumstances that arise in response to the movement's efforts. Another aspect of legitimacy involves the transformation of the movement into a mainstream social institution, complete with formal organization and hierarchical structure. The first-wave and second-wave women's movements have been successful in bringing about the passage and implementation of new laws and social policies. The present-day women's movement is represented at an official level by the National Organization of Women (NOW) in the United States and by the National Action Committee (NAC) on the Status of Women in Canada. As a social movement gains adherents and experiences success, two kinds of counter-movements may emerge: **resistance movements**, which seek to forestall further change to existing social conditions; or **regressive movements**, whose goal is to restore social conditions and structures to their pre-change state. Both the first- and second-wave feminist movements engendered a series of counter-movements of both kinds (Durham, 2003; Steuter, 1992/1995; Faraut, 2003). In Canada, a number of self-styled "pro-family" organizations exemplify the **anti-feminist regressive movement** (Anderson and Langford, 2001; Steuter, 1992/1995). R.E.A.L. (Realistic, Equal, Active, and for Life) Women is the most visible and well known.

Erwin's (1988, 1993) Canadian survey of 1200 members of R.E.A.L. Women and other avowedly pro-family women's organizations revealed that most active members were over-40 Catholic or Protestant fundamentalists with a high degree of religious commitment, who had achieved a relatively high degree of financial success, although they may have come from poorer families. Various studies have reported that anti-feminists in general are disproportionately likely to be married, to be religiously and politically conservative, to support a fundamentalist view of Biblical truth, and to deny that poverty is caused by structural (as opposed to individual) factors (Morgan and Wilcox, 1992; Salecl, 1992). Of pivotal importance to R.E.A.L. Women is "reprivatizing" the family by limiting forms of government assistance. R.E.A.L. Women and the Christian Heritage and Family Coalition political parties state as their goal the restoration of "traditional family values," upon which, they argue, Canada as a nation and as a society was founded and to which Canada must return if it is to regain its former greatness.

R.E.A.L. Women explicitly blames feminism (as the aforementioned political parties do implicitly) for a decline in "family values" and consequent moral and social degeneration of our society. Using the same arguments as male biological and moral conservatives (see Chapter 3), these regressive opposition groups clamour for the return of the "natural" heterosexual, breadwinner–homemaker family. Other "pro-family, anti-feminist" federal and provincial political parties and political pressure groups informally share these basic tenets. Accordingly, conservative opposition groups in Canada and the United States favour such policies as paying men a "family wage" ample to release wives from the necessity of sharing provider responsibilities, increasing tax exemptions for dependent spouses, withdrawing government financial support for daycare centres, increasing tax credits and deductions for dependent children to encourage more mothers to stay at home, abolishing school sexuality-education classes, promoting chastity and fidelity, severely restricting access to contraception and abortion, and reducing or even eliminating access to divorce. In general, groups which have adopted this banner have expressed vigorous opposition to extending the right to marry to same-sex couples (see Vescio and Biernat, 2003).

A STALLED REVOLUTION

Noting the differential rates of change of male and female gender roles and of the North American institutional contexts in which these players perform their parts, Hochschild (1990: 12) has introduced the concept of a **stalled revolution**. She noted that during the early years of the Industrial Revolution, men's roles changed more dramatically than women's. The institution of the economy was simultaneously changed by mechanization and by men's induction into the role of paid worker. However, since the second wave of the feminist movement in the mid- to late 1960s, women's roles have changed much more dramatically and rapidly than men's. Substantial increases in the number of female paid workers have changed the gender balance of the economic institution. However, women have adapted to fit the economic institution more than it has adapted to fit them. Even though some changes have occurred in the institution of the family, women still bear primary responsibility for housework, parenting, and relationship/family maintenance. The differential pace of gender and institutional changes produces strain, which affects both women and men and the relationships between them: "This strain between the change in women and the absence of change in much else leads me to speak of a 'stalled revolution'" (Hochschild, 1990: 12).

Although not couched in the language of a "stalled revolution," the research findings and analyses of Chafetz and Hagan (1996) provided evidence that Hochschild's insights are applicable beyond the United States. They compared 21 nations (including Canada), nearly all of which were industrialized prior to World War II, examining them for changes in economic and family institutions between 1960 and 1990. During those three decades, the same general patterns were found to have occurred in all nations examined: (1) women's labour-force participation expanded dramatically; (2) women's post-secondary enrolment rates increased; (3) first-marriage rates decreased, particularly among young women; (4) divorce rates increased; (5) total fertility fell to below replacement levels (2.1 children per woman); and (6) women increasingly deferred first childbirth until their late 20s and beyond (Chafetz and Hagan, 1996: 197).

Chafetz and Hagan used a **modified rational choice** approach (Marini, 1992, in Chafetz and Hagan, 1996: 200) to explain these patterns: "We argue that women increasingly behave as economically rational actors to the same extent as do men, yet are unwilling to abandon the socioemotional rewards of romantic relationships and children" (Chafetz and Hagan, 1996: 200). Women operate within social contexts which, while providing increased access to education and economic participation, maintain relatively unchanged expectations regarding women's familial and domestic obligations. These conditions, along with well-developed feminist ideologies, have interacted to produce an increasingly popular gender strategy: Women are striving to maximize self-realization and monetary rewards in paid employment, while reducing (but not foregoing) their participation in marriage, housekeeping, and childrearing. A modified-rational model for "having it all" involves the acquisition of educational credentials with the potential to secure satisfying employment that does not demand extra commitment in terms of overtime, geographic relocation, or promotions that come with heavy workloads. On the personal front, sexual relationships and cohabitation-style romantic commitments are possible, but marriage and childrearing (and the acceptance of primary responsibility for both) may not be seen as rational alternatives. Rationally modified adaptations in these areas may include remaining child-free, having fewer children, purchasing domestic and childrearing services, and (re)negotiating a new division of marriage, household, and childrearing labours. A more equal balance of power resources between partners, coupled with the increased availability of divorce, makes breaking up a more common option in the event of an intimate partner's refusal to (re)negotiate. Chafetz and Hagan (1996: 212) argued that although younger and more affluent women may be the trendsetters, these new patterns "diffuse" through a society to reach both older and less affluent women and even men, eventually becoming "legitimated as normative changes."

The observations and findings of Hochschild and of Chafetz and Hagan suggest the uneven pace of gender change. In Canada and other industrial societies, women have changed much more than men and have gone perhaps as far as they can on their own. And yet, that statement is on the one hand an oversimplification which overlooks both the lack of change in some women and the change experienced or instigated by men; on the other, it captures an important truth about the state of gender in Canada today. We are, at best, still in the middle of a gender "revolution" or transformation process; until men initiate substantial changes in their roles and in the institutions they formally or informally control, the gender revolution will remain stalled.

Postgender Marriages

Contributing to a stalled revolution are situations in which the appearance of gender equality masks an underlying reality of gender inequality. To paraphrase LaRossa's (1988/1995) comment about fatherhood, our culture of gender equality, as expressed by language, has changed faster than our behaviour, particularly at the level of intimate relationships. Previous chapters noted that while many heterosexual couples claim to have an egalitarian relationship, most actually fall short of that ideal (Blaisure and Allen, 1995; Hochschild, 1990; Zvonkovic et al., 1996; see also Zvonkovic et al., 2005). Knudson-Martin and Mahoney (1998) suggested that more couples speak a **myth of equality** than live out the reality of an egalitarian relationship.

According to these researchers, couples maintain their "myth" through the use of one or more types of **equality talk** (Knudson-Martin and Mahoney, 1998: 86). **Give-and-take talk** emphasizes mutuality (e.g., "she's going to be there for me and vice versa") without acknowledging which partner is most often "there" for the other. **Free-choice talk** obliterates inequalities under a guise of freedom of choice (e.g., "she chooses to do all the housework because she's better at it than I am"). **Oneness talk** emphasizes a couple's unity, asserting that what is good for one is good for the other and good for the relationship (e.g. "we all benefit when I stay late at work"), without admitting which one of the partners more frequently speaks for "the relationship." **Partnership talk** implies mutual decision-making (e.g., "she can be assertive when I don't feel like being assertive, and I can be assertive when she doesn't feel like being assertive") without recognizing whose assertiveness most often carries the day.

The rhetoric of equality is only one of the means by which couples maintain a facade of equality. A variety of other strategies may be used to avoid confronting actual relationship inequalities (Knudson-Martin and Mahoney, 1998: 86–87). **Benign framing/rationalization** involves labelling a condition of inequality as something else ("She has better judgment about the house," "It doesn't bother me to clean the house," "We each know our roles as mother and father"). **Not examining the consequences** is a strategy that focuses only upon the immediate present, ignoring an arrangement's long-term consequences for individual partners ("We never discussed living any place else—my business is here"). **Settling for less** is a strategy in which one partner draws an artificial "line in the sand," as if current conditions and what is being defined as "intolerable" represent poles of equality and inequality, when in fact both conditions represent various degrees of inequality ("I will not dust his books! I really can't deal with that!"). **Hiding the issues** requires a high degree of cooperation and coordination in order to ensure that the reality of a couple's inequality never intrudes upon their fantasy. Hochschild (1990) describes a couple who managed to publicly insist that they shared housekeeping duties "50–50," even though the "half" he was responsible for represented less than one quarter of the house's actual size. Finally, **placing responsibility on the wife** is a commonly adopted strategy in which she is made responsible for maintaining the illusion of equality by becoming more accommodating ("If I have decent arguments, he will listen," "If I'm not getting what I should from her, then I'm not going to give it myself").

Inequality stems from an imbalance of power in cross-gender relationships. However, not all power is overt: "**Invisible power** is the power to prevent issues from being raised. **Latent power** derives from the operation of dominant values and institutional procedures which shape a person's perceptions and preferences in such a way that they can see or imagine no alternative to the status quo or they see it as natural or unchangeable" (Knudson-Martin and Mahoney, 1998: 82). A language of equality and the aforementioned strategies all conceal the extent to which invisible and latent power imbalances continue to promote male dominance and female subordination in intimate relationships. Relationships in which women continually accommodate themselves to men's wishes only perpetuate those inequalities, even when the accommodations are made in the name of "love."

Empirical evidence obtained from a longitudinal study of marital relationships has found that love for their husbands is a major motivating factor in new mothers' renunciation of their own preferences regarding child-care responsibility in favour of their husbands' (Johnson and Huston, 1998). Whether or not wives possessed personal resources (e.g., income, education) that could influence the balance of power and the decision-making process, "the more wives loved their husbands, the more their preferences changed toward their husbands' preferences, regardless of whether their husbands were more patriarchal or more egalitarian in preferences about the performance of child-care tasks" (Johnson and Huston, 1998: 200). Husbands' love for their wives, in contrast, did not lead them to alter their preferences to conform to or better accord with their wives'. These findings suggest that the unequal distribution of child-care responsibilities may be less a unilateral patriarchal imposition, supported by a husband's possession of a greater share of personal resources, than the product of an active choice made by wives who, by dint of their resources, might have altered the outcome but chose not to. This active choice substantiates the existence of an invisible power dimension to the gendered relationships of husbands and wives. Johnson and Huston (1998: 202) argued that women, out of love for their husbands and children, may decide to perform relationship work designed to minimize conflict and enhance harmony, hoping that this will benefit all family members. To this end, "keeping the peace may be more important to wives than husbands doing their fair share" (Johnson and Huston, 1998: 202). Thus, even though such decisions may result in women's assumption of an inequitable share of domestic, relationship, and child-care burdens, they are chosen as a means of furthering women's own goals (i.e., a harmonious family environment). Still, even should these decisions achieve the hoped-for outcome, they serve to reinforce men's power in marital and family relationships, as husbands and fathers are rarely aware of the extent to which their own wishes and desires are anticipated and provided for without negotiation. Inequality remains unchallenged.

Gottman and his colleagues (Gottman et al., 1998) presented an impressive array of empirical evidence, obtained from detailed observations of newly married couples over a six-year period, which suggested that conflict-resolution style is a critical factor in marital happiness or unhappiness. Although it is too soon to predict whether these findings can be generalized to all heterosexual couple-relationships, two key elements clearly differentiated marriages that ended in divorce from happy, stable marriages and from unhappy, but still stable, marriages: **female "start-up,"** and male willingness to accept influence from a female. In both laboratory and everyday life situations, women typically initiate conflict discussions (see Chapter 7): "Usually the wife brings marital issues to the table for discussion, and she usually brings a detailed analysis of the conditions in which this problem occurs, its history, and suggestions for a solution" (Gottman et al., 1998: 18). How a wife starts a conflict discussion appears to dictate its ensuing tone. A "soft" start-up, characterized by gentleness and neutral affect, portends well for both partners. A "hard" start-up, in which her initial neutral affect quickly dissolves into a negative affective tone (e.g., contempt, belligerence, defensiveness), almost always leads to a negative outcome for both partners.

Following this initial stage, whether a husband will respond with hard, high-intensity negative affect (including withdrawal) or in a temperate, receptive manner, depends in large part upon his willingness to be influenced by a woman. Men whose marriages end up stable and happy are willing to be influenced by their wives; men whose marriages end either in divorce or in unhappy stasis are not. Preliminary analysis of data suggests that "unwilling" husbands do not differ from willing ones in terms of age, income, occupation, or educational level, but do tend to be "rated by observers as dominating their wives ... [and also] make the major decisions in the family, have suffered financial or emotional hardships in the marriage, are physically shorter ... and are more physically active in one-on-one competitive sports than men who accept influence from their wives" (Gottman et al., 1998: 19). Power appears to be the thread linking these characteristics, and the threat of a shift in existing power relations appears to underlie these men's rejection of their wives' influence. Although power based upon educational, occupational, and financial resources has become more equalized among heterosexual couples, power held by virtue of being male has not. Many men reject a woman's influence simply because she is a woman, irrespective of any power resources she may possess; one power resource she can never possess is the biological status of being male. Still, the fact that other men have overcome this sexist attitude indicates that it is not immutable.

Risman and Johnson-Sumerford (1998) collected data from a small sample of 15 couples with marriages characterized by equitable, shared responsibilities for housework and child care. The data reveal a number of different "paths" towards creation of a **postgender marriage** (one in which gender does not operate as a major organizing principle for the distribution of household labour). **Dual-career couples** (the majority in the sample) are equally interested in career success and in co-parenting their children. **Dual-nurturer couples** place greater emphasis upon family and children than upon careers. **Posttraditional couples** had once experienced "traditional" gendered partnerships but changed to an equitable relationship. Finally, some couples are "pushed" into forming equitable relationships by circumstances perceived as being beyond their control (e.g., a partner's chronic illness; a partner's highly demanding, inflexible, high-paying job).

Among postgender dual-career couples, traditional gender manifests itself in the general tendency of wives to hold higher housekeeping standards. In addition to learning at a very young age to notice other people's feelings, girls also learn to place a high value on household cleanliness. Boys do not. "Men can't see dust. Men don't know what dust is. I still don't see it. I don't know it's there. I know that the nirvana of non-sexist male development is dust. If I get to the dust stage, I'll know that I've really made it" (male respondent, in Risman and Johnson-Sumerford, 1998: 31). However, even though dual-career wives were more likely to see dust, this aptitude did not translate into a greater share of housecleaning responsibilities. The couples negotiated acceptable standards of cleanliness and of equitable participation in cleaning chores. Traditional gender also manifests itself in the area of emotions. Of the 15 couples, 6 exhibited a woman-as-emotion-expert pattern, 5 couples shared emotion work, and 4 couples were described as **parallel emotion workers** (Risman and Johnson-Sumerford, 1998: 36), continuously attending to both their own emotions and those of others in the family. In all of these couples, each partner described the other as an irreplaceable best friend. As well, both partners in all couples devoted approximately equal amounts of time in parenting activities and assumed equal responsibility for child care and emotion-monitoring. Only in the "women-as-emotion-expert" group was a mother described as having a more intense emotional connection with the children and as being more likely to monitor the emotional health of the marital relationship. This propensity was described by both partners as an idiosyncratic personality trait and was not considered grounds for delegating an inequitable share of emotion-responsibilities to wives. The findings of Risman and Johnson-Sumerford demonstrate that participation in a gendered world need not inevitably result in differential, gendered conduct within a family.

Various researchers (e.g., Blaisure and Allen, 1995; Risman and Johnson-Sumerford, 1998; Schwartz, 1994) have argued that the chances of organizing an intimate partnership on principles other than sex and gender are heightened by certain conditions. Risman and Johnson-Sumerford (1998: 27) contended that "women in our society don't have the clout or self-assurance to seek a postgender marriage unless they are highly educated, income-producing professionals." The statistical rarity of postgender marriages indicates that high levels of education and income by no means guarantee such an outcome. In our society, most well-educated, comfortably incomed women and men establish relationships that by and large follow traditional gendered patterns. However, superior education and income specifications do appear to be prerequisites for women who successfully achieve postgender arrangements. Higher education enables women and men to conceive of alternative possibilities and may help them overcome the latent power limitations of our existing gender system. Income equality removes one important basis for an inequitable distribution of power in couple relationships. As well, financial and material survival are not the foremost issues governing the daily lives of high-earning, dual-income couples. Does this mean that a postgender life will be available only to a highly educated, comfortably incomed, elite few? Not necessarily. As Chafetz and Hagan (1996) pointed out, although social change typically originates within these groups, such change reverberates throughout society.

THE UNFINISHED JOURNEY: WHERE DO WE GO FROM HERE?

As Canadians, we can be proud but not complacent about the progress our country has made towards gender equality. However, the journey is not complete. The persistence of a wage gap between men and women, substantial inequalities in the areas of housework and child care, occupational segregation, the dearth of family-friendly benefits, and the social problems of intimate and ultimate violence all attest to the difficulty of achieving equality or eliminating inequality.

The question "Where do we go from here?" is difficult to answer. A fundamental issue, which may never be resolved, is whether gender should or should not remain a central organizing principle for the allocation of economic, political, and marital roles. For some, the obvious response is that it should not. Recall, for example, that radical feminists once demanded the abolition of gender as an organizing principle of social life; their perspective seems to be echoed by researchers such as Risman and Johnson-Sumerford (1998) in their discussion of postgender marriages. Others consider the opposite conclusion equally obvious: Both right-wing conservatives, who believe that God and nature ordain gender, and cultural feminists, who promote "feminine" values, share the opinion that gender must remain central. As advocates on both sides are likely to remain convinced of their truth, the issue may not be resolved anytime soon. But while feminist and anti-feminist voices struggle to shape public debate and policy, it should be emphasized that gender is acted out, shaped, and reshaped on the stage of everyday life. Most Canadians "do gender" (West and Zimmerman, 1987), not in the halls of government nor in public forums established to debate the future of gender, but (with varying degrees of self-consciousness) simply in their day-to-day lives. Some Canadians guide their gender presentations in accordance with or as a reaction against various gender philosophies. However, since the mid-1990s, a growing number of people are participating in what is now referred to as transgenderism.

The term "transgender" was coined in the late 1980s by non-traditionally gendered individuals who perceived that existing terms were inadequate to capture their experience (Prosser, 1997). The term "transsexual" was perceived as problematic, for these individuals did not always perceive the need to "reconfigure their bodies surgically and hormonally" nor did they desire to "'pass' or to fit into normative gender categories of male and female" (Carroll et al., 2002: 3). The term "transvestite" was also rejected because of its "psychiatric, clinical, and fetishistic connotations" (Carroll et al., 2002: 13). The term that was subsequently adopted—**transgender**—refers to the crossing of gender boundaries and to a transcending or rising above traditional gender forms and expressions (Bolin, 1996). Transgender is an umbrella term that refers to a broad "range of behaviors, expressions, and identifications that challenge the pervasive bipolar gender system in a given culture" (Carroll et al., 2002: 13). This inclusive term covers a broad spectrum of differing identity categories including but not limited to transsexual (see Chapter 1), intersex (see chapters 1 and 2), drag queen and drag king (gay men and lesbians, respectively, who cross-dress for entertainment purposes in gay and/or lesbian bars), cross-dresser (heterosexuals who cross-dress on a part-time basis for pleasure, stress relief, or to express "opposite" sex feelings), and transgenderist, a term coined by Virginia Prince and used to refer to individuals who "dis-identify" with the sex they were assigned at birth and "live full time in congruence with their gender identity. This may include a regime of hormone therapy, but usually transgenderists do not seek or want sex reassignment surgery (Carroll et al., 2002: 13). Other terms which are used interchangeably with transgender include gender-variant persons, a term which "refers to individuals who stray from socially accepted gender roles in a given culture" and which "may be used in tandem with other group labels, such as gender-variant gay men and lesbian," and "trans persons." "Trans," like "transgender," is an umbrella term that is used to refer to "cross-dressers, transsexuals, transgenderists and others who permanently or periodically dis-identify with the sex they were assigned at birth," and preferred by some over "transgender" in that it "does not minimize the experiential specificities of transsexuals" (Carroll et al., 2002: 3, 13).

In an attempt to provide a framework for the multiplicity of gender identifications that exist within the transgendered community, Eyler and Wright (1997) proposed a **nine-point gender continuum**. This continuum encompasses gender identities ranging from female-based to male-based, with bigendered identities (i.e., those that alternate between feeling/behaving like a woman and feeling/behaving like a man) located in the centre (see also Winter and Udomsak, 2002). However, as Nanda (2000: 99) has observed, though "[t]rans-gender identities vary widely ... the philosophy of transgenderism is well summarized in the words of one transperson who says: ' ... you no longer have to fit into a box ... it is okay to be transgendered'" (Bolin, 1996: 475). She noted that transgenderism derives from the "ancient tradition of androgny ... which both validates a range of gender roles and identities within society and even within an individual." As both an individual and a collective phenomenon, transgenderism rejects the dichotomous sex/gender categories of "male" and "female," "masculine" or "feminine," as simply "boxes" which unnecessarily and illegitimately imprison individuals. "Unlike transsexuals, transpeople (transgenderists) do not consider themselves limited to a choice of one of two genders"; rather, they perceive a "continuum of options, from ... undergo[ing] sex reassignment surgery to ... liv[ing] their lives androgynously" (Nanda, 2000: 98). As a way of life, transgenderism may be full-time or occasional, public or strictly private. "Some [transgendereds] are attracted to males, some to females, some to both, some are asexual, and some are attracted to other transgenders" (Cole et al., 2000: 161; see also Winter and Udomsak, 2002).

Over the past two decades, many other terms have emerged to describe this community of individuals whose "lives are proof that sex and gender are much more complex than a delivery room doctor's glance at genitals can determine, more variegated than pink or blue birth caps" (Feinberg, 1998: 5). The considerable diversity that exists within transgender communities is suggested by the rich lexicon of terms that have been created by their constituents. While stressing that these terms and their definitions are not universally accepted and that "[v]ariations exist both within and outside trans communities" in their usage and interpretation, Carroll et al. (2002: 12–13) reported that the term "gender-bender" is used to refer to an individual who "brazenly and flamboyantly flaunts society's gender conventions by mixing elements of "masculinity" and "femininity." "Gender outlaw," "popularized by trans activists such as Kate Bornstein [1994, 1998] and Leslie Feinberg [1996, 1998]," is used to connote a person "who transgresses or violates the 'law' of gender (i.e., one who challenges the rigidly enforced gender roles) in a transphobic, heterosexist, and patriarchal society." "Gender queer" "refers to individuals who 'queer' the notions of gender in a given society" and "may also refer to people who identify as both transgendered and queer (i.e., individuals who challenge both gender and sexuality regimes and see gender identity and sexual orientation as overlapping and interconnected)." Carroll et al. (2002: 12) observed that while the term "queer" is "often an abusive epithet when used by heterosexuals, many queer-identified people have taken back the word to use it as a symbol of pride and affirmation of difference and diversity." The term "gender trash" "calls attention to the way that differently gendered individuals are often treated like 'trash' in a transphobic society"; the term "transphobia" is used to refer to the "irrational fear and hatred of all those individuals who transgress, violate, or blur the dominant gender categories in a given society" (Carroll et al., 2002: 3, 12–13).

Social constructionists have pointed to these "gender rule breakers as the very proof that gender is a variable and not a constant, that one can change one's gender, construct one's sex, or maintain a status not directly identifiable as one or the other classic gender" (Gilbert, 2000; see also White et al., 2000). Roen (2002) noted that some applaud transgenderism as a "subversive crossing" that may eventually lead to the disruption and abandonment of such labels as "man," "woman," and "transsexual." Others, however, are skeptical. Raymond (1996: 215) maintained that while transgenderism may be "personally provocative, it never moves beyond the issue of personal gender expression to define a more concerted political rebellion against the patriarchal system." Raymond contends that while "the largely one-way flow of men who dress up or otherwise take on the appearance of women ... may flout gender conventions, transgenderists do not fundamentally contradict the political reality of patriarchy, favouring instead an androgynous humanism over a feminist politics." She argued that the "assimilationist mentality of androgynous humanists cannot fulfil political goals" and that "gender-bending" represents no more than a "gender identity disconnected from feminist or lesbian politics." Hausman (2001) charged that a proliferation of new gender variants as basic ontological categories "will mire radical gender politics in an ill-defined coalition sensibility" (see also Sweeney, 2004). For yet others, such as Bureau (1994: 164), who insist that the binarism characteristic of Western gender systems is both universal and innate, the expansion of labels under the rubric of transgenderism merely represents a strategic attempt "to invent new categories of sexual identity in order to euphemize and condone perversions."

Given the diversity of the transgendered population, it is not surprising that researchers have been stymied in their attempts to ascertain with any exactitude the prevalence of transgenderism in the general population; estimates range from 3 to 10 percent (Ettner, 1999). Regardless of their exact number, Carroll et al. (2002: 3) reported that "the emerging political activism and organization of the transgender community is both the cause and consequence of several recent sociocultural events." These include the following developments: (1) the closing of American university gender clinics affiliated with hospitals, which perform sex-reassignment surgery, and the subsequent opening of private, more "client-centred" sites for sex-reassignment surgery that are "less subject to professional 'gatekeeper' decisions about who is psychologically appropriate for such surgery" (Nanda, 2000: 100); (2) the 1992 International Conference on Transgender Law and Employment Policy; (3) in 1995, the First International Conference on Gender, Cross-Dressing, and Sex Issues; (4) a demonstration at the 1996 meeting of the American Academy of Pediatrics by the Intersex Society of North America (ISNA) to protest the "corrective" surgery performed on infants with ambiguous genitalia; (5) in 1997, lobbying of the U.S. Congress by the ISNA to extend the federal ban on genital cutting—originally "aimed mainly at African cultural practices of cliterodectomy"—to pediatric surgeries which "reduce or remove infant clitorises deemed 'abnormally' large, a practice affecting about 2000 babies a year" (Nanda, 2000: 99). In doing so, the ISNA directed attention to several issues which continue to be debated, including "who has the right to decide what are aesthetically acceptable genitalia, whose interests are served by surgical intervention, and whether sex/gender identity is so intertwined with the appearance of the genitals that it is worth subjecting infants or children to this operation" (Nanda, 2000: 99–100).

In addition, in October of 2002, the Northwest Territories became the first Canadian jurisdiction to explicitly prohibit discrimination on the ground of gender identity, thus providing trans-identified people with explicit protection from discrimination. Elsewhere in Canada, however, such provisions are lacking. EGALE Canada, founded in 1986, is a national organization with over 3300 members which seeks to advance equality for **LGBT** (lesbian, gay, bisexual, and transgendered) persons across Canada, "carrying out political action to lobby for more equitable laws for LGBT people; intervening in legal cases that have an impact on human rights and equality; increasing public education and awareness by providing information to individuals, groups and media" (EGALE, 2004c). Among its campaigns is the proposal that the *Canadian Human Rights Act* and provincial human-rights acts be amended along the lines of the Northwest Territories' new legislation (EGALE 2004d). In 2004, EGALE launched the first-ever "Canadian Trans Awareness Week," "to inspire, inform, and educate" Canadians about the lives of transgendered persons and the challenges they face, with a host of events scheduled in St. John's, Toronto, Edmonton, and Vancouver (EGALE, 2003, 2004b).

Transgendered persons have also formed support groups and information clearinghouses and created magazines such as *Gendertrash, Transgender Tapestry,* and *Chrysalic Quarterly*. Various researchers have reported that cyberspace has furnished a particularly hospitable environment for transgender activism (Gagne et al., 1997; Whittle, 1998), with a wide range of easily accessible websites and chat rooms now available (Carroll et al., 2002; Cole et al., 2000). The visibility of transgenderism has also increased, and media offerings have drawn attention to and challenged the intolerance and violence directed against transgendered persons. The tragic true story of Teena Brandon, a young woman who attempted to live as a man (Brandon Teena) and who was brutally raped and murdered by two men when her biological sex became known, has been the subject of two films, *The Brandon Teena Story* and *Boys Don't Cry* (see Sloop, 2000). In 1999, a "Trans Day of Remembrance" was held in San Francisco to commemorate those "who have died as a result of violent attacks caused by fear and hatred of transgendered and transsexual persons"; since then, an international day of remembrance has been observed annually to publicly mourn those who have died as a result of violence and to raise awareness of hate crimes. On November 20, 2007, this day was commemorated in Canada with services in Vancouver, Victoria, Edmonton, London, Ottawa, and Toronto.

Obviously, the question "Where do we go from here?" defies an easy answer. However, it should be evident that gender does not exist in isolation, but as part of a complex set of interactive processes with our society's basic institutions. Thus, marriage and gender create and recreate each other, as do gender and work (Chapter 6) and gender and parenting (Chapter 8). At present, we can only reflect on how these institutions might be reconstructed, given the kaleidoscope of images and visions of gender that exist, and ponder what the future may hold.

Key Terms

anti-feminist regressive movement

benign framing/ rationalization

dual-career couples

dual-nurturer couples

equality talk

female "start-up"

free-choice talk

Gender Empowerment Measure (GEM)

Gender-related Development Index (GDI)

give-and-take talk

hiding the issues

Human Development Index (HDI)

invisible power

latent power

LGBT (lesbian, gay, bisexual, transgendered)

modified rational choice

myth of equality

nine-point gender continuum

not examining the consequences

oneness talk

parallel emotion workers

partnership talk

placing responsibility on the wife

postgender marriage

posttraditional couples

regressive movements

resistance movements

settling for less

stalled revolution

transgender

Chapter Summary

1. Throughout most of the 1990s and through the year 2000, Canada was ranked by the United Nations as the "number one" nation in which to live. However, when measures designed to highlight the status of women were applied—specifically, the Gender Empowerment Measure (GEM) and the Gender-related Development Index (GDI)—Canada's ranking fell. Although Canada has made marked progress in eliminating gender inequality, much work remains.

2. Gender equality does not depend solely on a country's standard of living. In general, the Nordic countries have evinced the greatest commitment to women's empowerment.

3. Although most of the gender change in North America has flowed from the feminist movement, both the first- and second-wave feminist movements have engendered counter-movements, including a number of self-styled "pro-family" regressive movements. Opposition can also be found among individuals who feel alienated from the mainstream organizational women's movement.

4. A "stalled revolution" is the term that sociologist Arlie Hochschild coined to describe the differential rates and speed of change for men and women, and their respective roles. The gender revolution may remain stalled until men initiate substantial changes in their roles and in the institutions they formally or informally control.

5. Empirical research suggests that at the present time, more couples speak a "myth of equality" than live in relationships in which equality actually prevails. At present, post-gender arrangements remain a statistical rarity among intimate relationships.

6. A greater range of expressions of transgenderism and transgender identities have emerged since the 1990s than in previous decades or even centuries. This suggests that gender is neither inevitable nor immutable, but can be transformed as all of us "do gender."

References

AAUW. 1995. *How Schools Short-change Girls.* Washington, D.C.: American Association of University Women.

Abbey, A. 2000. "Adjusting to Infertility." In *Loss and Trauma*, eds. J.H. Harvey and E.D. Miller: 331–344. New York: Brunner-Routledge.

Abbey, A., T. Zawacki, P.O. Buck, A.M. Clinton, and P. McAuslan. 2004. "Sexual Assault and Alcohol Consumption: What Do We Know About Their Relationship and What Types of Research Are Still Needed?" *Aggression and Violent Behavior* 9(3): 271–303.

Abbott, P., and C. Wallace. 1990. *An Introduction to Sociology.* London: Routledge and Kegan Paul. 2005. *An Introduction to Sociology,* 3rd. ed. London: Routledge.

Abel, E.L. and M.L. Kruger. 2007. "Gender Related Naming Practices: Similarities and Differences Between People and Their Dogs." *Sex Roles* 57(1–2): 15–19.

Abel, M.H. and A.L. Meltzer. 2007. "Student Ratings of a Male and Female Professor's Lecture on Sex Discrimination in the Workforce." *Sex Roles* 57(3–4): 173–180.

Abraham, S., and D. Llewellyn-Jones. 1992. *Eating Disorders,* 2nd ed. Oxford, UK: Oxford University Press.

Abramovitz, M. 1988. *Regulating the Lives of Women.* Boston: South End.

Abu-Laban, S.M., A. McDaniel, and R.A. Sydie. 1994. "Gender." In *Sociology*, eds. W. Meloff and D. Pierce: 225–252. Toronto: Nelson.

Achilles, R. 1995. "Assisted Reproduction: The Social Issues." In *Gender in the 1990s*, eds. E.D. Nelson and B.W. Robinson: 346–364. Toronto: Nelson.

Acker, J. 1990. "Hierarchies, Jobs, Bodies: A Theory of Gendered Organizations." *Gender & Society* 4: 139–158.

Acoose, J. 1995. *Neither Indian Princesses nor Easy Squaws.* Toronto: Women's Press.

Adams, H. and L. Phillips. 2006. "Experiences of Two-Spirit Lesbian and Gay Native Americans: An Argument for Standpoint Theory in Identity Research." *Identity* 6(3): 273–291.

Adams, K.L., and N.C. Ware. 1996. "Sexism and the English Language: The Linguistic Implications of Being a Woman." In *Women,* 5th ed., ed. J. Freeman: 331–346. Palo Alto, CA: Mayfield; 1983. "Sexism and the English Language: "The Linguistic Implications of Being a Woman." In *Women,* 3rd ed., ed. J. Freeman: 478–491. Palo Alto, CA: Mayfield.

Adams, R.G., and R. Blieszner. 1998. "Baby Boomer Friendships." *Generations* 22(1) Spring: 70–75.

Addis, M.E., and J.R. Mahalik. 2003. "Men, Masculinity and the Contexts of Help Seeking." *American Psychologist* 58(1): 5–14.

Adler, P.A., S.J. Kless, and P. Adler. 1992/1995. "Socialization to Gender Roles: Popularity among Elementary School Boys and Girls." *Sociology of Education*, 65: 169–187. Reprinted in *Gender in the 1990s*, eds. E.D. Nelson and B.W. Robinson: 119–141. Toronto: Nelson Canada.

Adweek Incorporated. 2006. *Marketer's Guide to Media* (Vol. 29). New York: Adweek.

AFP. 2007. "Alarm over 'Missing Daughters' Trend in Vietnam." November 1.

Aggarwal, A.B. 1987. *Sexual Harassment in the Workplace.* Toronto: Butterworths.

Aguilera, R.J. 2000. "Disability and Delight: Staring Back at the Devotee Community." *Sexuality & Disability,* Special Issue: Disability, Sexuality, and Culture: Societal and Experiential Perspectives on Multiple Identities Part II, 18(4): 255–261.

Ahlander, N.R., and K.S. Bahr. 1995. "Beyond Drudgery, Power and Equity: Toward an Expanded Discourse on the Moral Dimensions of Housework in Families." *Journal of Marriage and the Family* 57: 54–58.

Akyeampong, E. 2007. "Trends and Seasonality in Absenteeism." *Perspectives on Labour and Income*, Catalogue no. 75-001-XIE, June. Ottawa: Statistics Canada 13–15; 2001. "Fact

Sheet on Work Absences." *Perspectives on Labour and Income*, Catalogue No. 75-001-XPE, Winter. Ottawa: Statistics Canada: 47–54.

Akyeampong, E., and R. Nadwodny. 2001. "Evolution of the Canadian Workplace: Work from Home." *Perspectives on Labour and Income* Catalogue No. 75-001-XPE, Winter. Ottawa: Statistics Canada: 30–36.

Albisetti, J.C. 2000. "Portia Ante Portas: Women and the Legal Profession in Europe, ca. 1870–1925." *Journal of Social History* 33(4): 825–857.

Aldrich, N.J. and H.R. Tenenbaum. 2006. "Sadness, Anger, and Frustration: Gendered Patterns in Early Adolescents' and Their Parents' Emotion Talk." *Sex Roles* 55(11–12): 774–785.

Alexander, G.M. 2003. "An Evolutionary Perspective of Sex-Typed Toy Preferences: Pink, Blue and the Brain." *Archives of Sexual Behavior* 32(1): 7–14.

Alexander, J. 2003. "Queer Webs: Representations of LGBT People and Communities on the World Wide Web." *International Journal of Sexuality & Gender Studies* 7(2–3): 77–84.

Alexander, J. and K. Yescavage. 2005. "Gay Genes and Moral Panics: Science Fact and Science Fiction." *Culture Health & Sexuality* 7: S4–S5.

Alexander, M.C., and T.D. Fisher. 2003. "Truth and Consequences: Using the Bogus Pipeline to Examine Sex Differences in Self-Reported Sexuality." *Journal of Sex Research*, Special Issue: Gender and Sexuality, 40(1): 27–35.

Alia, V. 1994. "Inuit Women and the Politics of Naming in Nunavut." *Canadian Woman Studies* 14: 411–414.

Allan, B.B., R. Brant, J.E. Seidel, and J.F. Jarrell. 1997. "Declining Sex Ratios in Canada." *Canadian Medical Association Journal* 156(1): 37–41.

Allan, J. 1993. "Male Elementary Teachers: Experiences and Perspectives." In *Doing Women's Work*, ed. C.L. Williams: 113–127. Newbury Park, CA: Sage.

Allen, K.R. and D.H. Demo. 1995. "The Families of Lesbians and Gay Men: A New Frontier in Family Research." *Journal of Marriage and the Family* 57(1): 111–127.

Allison, J.A., and L.S. Wrightsman. 1993. *Rape*. Newbury Park, CA: Sage.

Almack, K. 2005. "What's in a Name? The Significance of the Choice of Surnames Given to Children Born Within Lesbian-Parent Families." *Sexualities* 8(2): 239–254.

Alvi, S., W. DeKeseredy, and D. Ellis. 2000. *Contemporary Social Problems in North American Society*. Don Mills, ON: Addison-Wesley.

Alvidrez, J. and R. Weinstein. 1999. "Teacher Perceptions and Later Student Academic Achievement." *Journal of Educational Psychology* 91(4): 731–746.

Amare, N. 2007. "Where Is She? Gender Occurrences in Online Grammar Guides." *Research in the Teaching of English* 42(2): 165–189.

Amarto, M., and W. Marsiglio. 2002. "Self-Structure, Identity and Commitment: Promise Keepers' Godly Man Project." *Symbolic Interaction* 25(1): 41–65.

Amato, P.R. 2001. "The Consequences of Divorce for Adults and Children." In *Understanding Families into the New Millennium*, ed. R.M. Milardo: 488–506. Minneapolis, MN: National Council on Family Relations.

Amato, P.R., and D. Previti. 2003. "People's Reasons for Divorcing: Gender, Social Class, the Life Course and Adjustment." *Journal of Family Issues* 24(5): 602–626.

Amato, P.R., D.R. Johnson, A. Booth, and S.J. Rogers. 2003. "Continuity and Change in Marital Quality Between 1980 and 2000." *Journal of Marriage and the Family* 65(1): 1–22.

Ambert, A.M. 2003. Same-Sex Couples and Same-Sex-Parent Families: Relationships, Parenting, and Issue of Marriage. **www.vifamily.ca/library/cft/samesex.html**; 2002. Divorce: Facts, Figures and Consequences. Rev. ed. **www.vifamily.ca/library/cft/divorce.html**; 1998. Divorce: Facts, Figures and Consequences. **www.vifamily.ca/cft/divorce/divorce.html**; 1994. "An International Perspective on Parenting: Social Change and Social Constructs." *Journal of Marriage and the Family* 56: 529–543.

American Society of Plastic Surgeons. 2007. "Procedural Statistics Trends 2000–2007." **www.plasticsurgery.org/mediastatistics/index.cfm**

Andelin, H.B. 1974. *Fascinating Womanhood*. Rev. ed. New York: Bantam.

Andermahr, S., T. Lovell, and C. Wolkowitz. 2000. *A Concise Glossary of Feminist Theory*. London: Arnold.

Anderson, E.A., and L.A. Leslie. 1991. "Coping with Employment and Family Stress: Employment Arrangements and Gender Differences." *Sex Roles* 24: 223–237.

Anderson, G., and T. Langford. 2001. "Pro-Family Organizations in Calgary, 1998: Beliefs, Interconnections and Allies." *Canadian Review of Sociology and Anthropology* 38(1): 37–56.

Anderson, K.L. 1987. "Historical Perspectives on the Family." In *Family Matters*, eds. K.L. Anderson et al.: 21–39. Toronto: Methuen; 1997. "Gender, Status and Domestic Violence: An Integration of Feminist and Family Violence Approaches." *Journal of Marriage and the Family* 59: 655–659.

Anderson, M.L. 1997. *Thinking About Women*. 4th ed. Boston: Allyn & Bacon.

Anderson, N. 2001. "Towards a Theory of Socialization Impact: Selection as a Pre-Entry Socialization." *International Journal of Selection & Assessment* 9(1–2): 84–91.

Anderson, P.B., and C. Struckman-Johnson (eds.). 1998. *Sexually Aggressive Women*. New York: Guilford Press.

Anderson-Clark, T.N., R.J. Green, and T.B. Henley. 2008. "The Relationship Between First Names and Teacher Expectations for Achievement Motivation." *Journal of Language and Social Psychology* 27(1): 94–99.

Andrews, J.A., E. Tildesley, H. Hops, and F. Li. 2002. "The Influence of Peers on Young Adult Substance Use." *Health Psychology* 21(4): 349–357.

Andsager, J. and K. Roe. 2003. "What's Your Definition of Dirty Baby?: Sex in Music Videos." *Sexuality & Culture: An Interdisciplinary Journal* 7(3): 79–97.

Angier, N. 2000. *Woman*. New York: Anchor Books.

Antonucci, T.C. 2001. "Social Relations: An Examination of Social Networks, Social Support and Sense of Control." In *Handbook of the Psychology of Aging*, 5th ed., eds. J.E. Birren and K. Warner Schaie: 427–453. San Diego: Academic Press.

Anxo, D. and P. Carlin. 2004. "Intra-Family Time Allocation to Housework: French Evidence." *International Journal of Time Use Research* 1(1): 14–36.

APA Task Force on the Sexuality of Girls (E.L. Zurbriggen, R.L. Collins, S. Lamb, T. Roberts, D.L. Tolman, L.M. Ward and J. Blake). 2007. *Report of the APA Task Force on the Sexualization of Girls*. Washington, DC: American Psychological Association.

Apparala, M.L., A. Reifman, and J. Munsch. 2003. "Cross-National Comparison of Attitudes Towards Fathers' and Mothers' Participation in Household Tasks and Childcare." *Sex Roles* 48(5–6): 189–203.

Arai, A.B. 2000. "Self-Employment as a Response to the Double Day for Women and Men in Canada." *Canadian Review of Sociology and Anthropology* 37(2): 125–142.

Arber, S. 1997. "Comparing Inequalities in Women's and Men's Health: Britain in the 1990s." *Social Science Medicine* 44: 773–787.

Arbour, K.P. and K.A. Martin Ginis. 2006. "Effects of Exposure to Muscular and Hypermuscular Media Images on Young Men's Muscularity Dissatisfaction and Body Dissatisfaction." *Body Image* 3: 153–161.

Arbuckle, J., and B.D. Williams. 2003. "Students' Perceptions of Expressiveness: Age and Gender Effects on Teacher Evaluations." *Sex Roles* 49(9–10): 507–516.

Archer, J. 2004. "Sex Differences in Aggression in Real-World Settings: A Meta-Analytic Review." *Review of General Psychology* 8(4): 291–322; 2000. "Sex Differences in Aggression Between Heterosexual Partners: A Meta-Analytic Review." *Psychological Bulletin* 126(5): 651–680.

Arendell, T. 1995. *Fathers and Divorce*. Thousand Oaks, CA: Sage.

Aries, E. 2006. "Sex Differences in Interaction: A Reexamination." In *Sex Differences and Similarities in Communication*, eds. K. Dindia and D.K. Canary: 21–36. Mahwah, NJ: Lawrence Erlbaum Associates.

Aries, E. and M. Seider. 2005. "The Interactive Relationship Between Class Identity and the College Experience: The Case of Lower Income Students." *Qualitative Sociology* 28(4): 419–443.

Armstrong, L. 1993. "Connecting the Circles: Race, Gender, and Nature." *Canadian Woman Studies* 13(3): 6–10.

Armstrong, P. 1996. "Resurrecting 'The Family': Interring 'The State.'" *Journal of Comparative Family Studies* 27: 221–247; 1990. "Economic Conditions and Family Structures." In *Families*, 2nd ed., ed. M. Baker: 67–92. Toronto: McGraw-Hill Ryerson.

Armstrong, S. 2007. "Disappearing Act." *New Statemen* 136: 40–42.

Aronson, J., D.M. Quinn, and S.J. Spencer. 1998. "Stereotype Threat and the Academic Underperformance of Minorities and Women." In *Prejudice*, eds. J.K. Swim and C. Stangor: 83–103. San Diego, CA: Academic Press.

Arrighi, B.A., and D.J. Maume Jr. 2000. "Workplace Subordination and Men's Avoidance of Housework." *Journal of Family Issues* 21(4): 464–487.

Artis, J.E., and E.K. Pavalko. 2003. "Explaining the Decline in Women's Household Labor: Individual Change and Cohort Change." *Journal of Marriage and the Family* 65(3): 746–761.

Ash, R. 2002. *The Top 10 of Everything 2003*, Canadian Edition. Toronto: Dorling Kindersley; 2001. *The Top 10 of Everything 2002*, Canadian Edition. Toronto: Dorling Kindersley.

Ashmore, R.D., and F.K. Del Boca. 1979. "Sex Stereotypes and Implicit Personality Theory: Toward a Cognitive-Social Psychological Conceptualization." *Sex Roles* 5: 219–248.

Asmussen, L., and C.L. Shehan. 1992. "Gendered Expectations and Behaviors in Dating Relationships." *Proceedings: Family and Work* 2: 32. Orlando, FL: National Council on Family Relations.

Aspin, C., and J. Hutchings. 2007. "Reclaiming the Past to Inform the Future: Contemporary View of Maori Sexuality." *Culture, Health & Sexuality* 9(4): 415–427.

Aston, C. 2007. "Spousal Homicide Narratives, 1997 to 2005." In *Family Violence in Canada: A Statistical Profile 2007*, Statistics Canada, Catalogue no. 85-224: 16–17.

Atcheson, E., M. Eberts, E. Symes, and J. Stoddart. 1984. *Women and Legal Action*. Ottawa: Canadian Advisory Council on the Status of Women.

Atchley, R. 1997. *Social Forces and Aging*. Belmont, CA: Wadsworth.

Athens 2004 Olympics. 2008. "Athletes." **www.sports.yahoo.com/olympics/ athens2004/athletes?sport+gymastics**

Atkinson, M. 2002. "Pretty in Ink: Conformity, Resistance, and Negotiation in Women's Tattooing." *Sex Roles* 47(5–6): 219–235.

Atkinson, M., and S. Blackwelder. 1993. "Fathering in the 20th Century." *Journal of Marriage and the Family* 55: 975–986.

Aubrey, J.S., K. Harrison, L. Kramer, and J. Yellin. 2003. "Variety versus Timing: Gender Differences in College Students' Sexual Expectation as Predicted by Exposure to Sexually Oriented Television." *Communication Research* 30(4): 432–460.

AuCoin, K. 2005. "Stalking-Criminal Harassment." In *Family Violence in Canada: A Statistical Profile*. Catalogue no. 85-002-XIE. Canadian Centre for Justice Statistics. Ottawa: Statistics Canada.

Auster, C.K., and S.C. Ohm. 2000. "Masculinity and Femininity in Contemporary American Society: A Reevaluation Using the Bem Sex-Role Inventory." *Sex Roles* 43(7–8): 719–750.

Avery, P.G. 2002. "Political Socialization, Tolerance, and Sexual Identity." *Theory & Research in Social Education* 30(2): 190–197.

Avison, W.R., J. Ali, and D. Walters. 2007. "Family Structure, Stress and Psychological Distress: A Demonstration of the Impact of Differential Exposure." *Journal of Health and Social Behavior* 48(3): 301–317.

Aydt, H., and W.A. Corsaro. 2003. "Differences in Children's Construction of Gender Across Culture: An Interpretive Approach." *American Behavioral Scientist* 46(1): 1306–1325.

Baca Zinn, M., and D. Stanley Eitzen. 1993. *Diversity in Families*. 3rd ed. New York: Harper Collins College.

Bachman, K. 2000. *Work–Life Balance: Are Employers Listening?* Ottawa: Conference Board of Canada.

Baciagalupo, A.M. 2004. "The Mapuche Man Who Became a Woman Shaman: Selfhood, Gender Transgression, and Competing Cultural Norms." *American Ethnologist* 31(3): 440–457.

Badinter, E. 1981. *Mother Love*. New York: Macmillan.

Badique, E., M. Cavazza, G. Klinker, G. Mair, T. Sweeney, D. Thalmann, and N.M. Tahlman. 2002. "Entertainment Applications of Virtual Environments." In *Handbook of Virtual Environments*, ed. K.M. Stanney: 1143–1164. Mahwah, NJ: Lawrence Erlbaum Associates.

Bailey, A.A. 2006. "A Year in the Life of the African-American Male in Advertising—A Content Analysis." *Journal of Advertising* 35(1): 83–104.

Bailey, M. 2000. *Marriage and Marriage-Like Relationships*. **www.lcc.gc/ca/cgi-bin/ repee_en.c...y%2C+Martha&;language =en&;range=1&;numdoc**

Bailey, S.J. 2003. "Challenges and Strengths in Nonresidential Parenting Following Divorce." *Marriage & Family Review* 35(1–2): 29–44; 2007. "Family and Work-Role Identities of Divorced Parents: The Relationships of Role Balance to Well-Being." *Journal of Divorce and Remarriage* 46(3–4): 63–82; 2007a. "Unraveling the Meaning of Family: Voices of Divorced Nonresidential Parents." *Marriage & Family Review* 42(1): 81–102.

Baker, M. 1988. *Aging in Canadian Society: A Survey*. Toronto: McGraw-Hill Ryerson.

Baker, M.J. and J.P. Jacobsen. 2007. "Marriage, Specialization, and the Gender Division of Labor." *Journal of Labor Economics* 25(4): 763–793.

Baldus, B., and V. Tribe. 1995. "Children's Perceptions of Social Inequality." In *Everyday Life*, 2nd ed., eds. L. Tepperman and J.E. Curtis: 161–169. Toronto: McGraw- Hill.

Ballantyne, P., and V.M. Marshall. 2001. "Subjective Income Security of (Middle) Aging and Elderly Canadians." *Canadian Journal on Aging* 20(2): 151–173.

Balswick, J. 1988. *The Inexpressive Male*. Lexington, MA: Lexington Books.

Bandura, A. 1986. *The Social Foundations of Thought and Action*. Englewood Cliffs, NJ: Prentice-Hall.

Bankston, C.L., and S.J. Caldas. 1998. "Family Structure, Schoolmates, and Racial Inequalities in School Achievement." *Journal of Marriage and the Family* 60(3): 715–723.

Bannerji, H. 2000. "The Paradox of Diversity: The Construction of a Multicultural Canada and Women of Colour." *Women's Studies International Forum* 23(5): 537–560.

Bannon, L. 2000. "Why Girls and Boys Get Different Toys." *Wall Street Journal*, February 14: B1.

Barash, D. 1979. *The Whisperings Within*. New York: Harper & Row.

Barbera, E. 2003. "Gender Schemas: Configuration and Activation Processes." *Canadian Journal of Behavioral Sciences* 35(3): 176–184.

Barnes, G.E., L. Greenwood, and R. Sommer. 1991. "Courtship Violence in a Canadian Sample of Male College Students." *Family Relations* 40: 37–44.

Barnett, H.L., P.K. Keel, and L.M. Conoscneti. 2001. "Body Type Preferences in Asian and Caucasian College Students." *Sex Roles* 45(11–12): 869–878.

Barnett, R.C. 1994. "Home-to-Work Spillover Revisited: A Study of Full-Time Employed Women in Dual-Earner Couples." *Journal of Marriage and the Family* 56: 647–656.

Barnett, R.C., and K.C. Gareis. 2002. "Full-Time and Reduced-Hours Work Schedules and Marital Quality: A Study of Female Physicians with Young Children." *Work and Occupations* 29(3): 364–379.

Baron-Cohen, S. 2003. *The Essential Difference*. New York: Basic Books.

Baron-Cohen, S., R.C. Knickmeyer, and M.K. Belmonte. 2005. "Sex Differences in the Brain: Implications for Explaining Autism." *Science* 310(5749): 819–823.

Barr, A., A. Bryan, and D.T. Kenrick. 2002. "Sexual Peak: Socially Shared Cognitions About Desire, Frequency, and Satisfaction in Men and Women." *Personal Relationships* 9(3): 287–299.

Barraclough, B. and C. Harris. 2002. "Suicide Preceded by Murder: The Epidemiology of Homicide-Suicide in England and Wales 1988–92." *Psychological Medicine* 32(4): 577–584.

Barrett, H., and F. Tasker. 2001. "Growing Up with a Gay Parent: Views of 101 Gay Fathers on Their Sons' and Daughters' Experiences." *Educational & Child Psychology* 18(1): 62–77.

Barrett, M., A. King, J. Levy, E. Maticka-Tyndale, and A. McKay. 1999. "Canada." In *The International Encyclopedia of Sexuality*, ed. R. T. Francoeur: 221–343. New York: Continuum.

Barrows, G.W., and M. Zuckerman. 1976. "Construct Validity of Three Masculinity-Femininity Traits." *Journal of Consulting Clinical Psychology* 34: 1–7.

Bartsch, R.A., T. Burnett, T.R. Diller, and E. Rankin-Williams. 2000. "Gender Representing in Television Commercials: Updating an Update." *Sex Roles* 43(9–10): 735–743.

Baruch, G.K., R.C. Barnett, and C. Rivers. 1983. *Lifepoints*. New York: McGraw-Hill.

Basile, K.G. 2002. "Attitudes Towards Wife Rape: Effects of Social Background and Victim Status." *Violence & Victims* 17(3): 341–354.

Basow, S.A. 1992. *Gender,* 3rd ed. Pacific Grove, CA: Brooks/Cole; 1986. *Gender Stereotypes,* 2nd ed. Monterey, CA: Brooks/Cole.

Basu, Jayanti. 2001. "Some Social and Legal Difficulties of Treatment of Transsexuals in India." *Social Science International* 17(1): 74–81.

Batchelor, S.A., J. Kitzinger, and E. Burtney. 2004. "Representing Young People's Sexuality in the 'Youth' Media." *Health Education Research* 19(6): 669–676.

Baumeister, R.F., and J.M. Twenge. 2002. "Cultural Suppression of Female Sexuality." *Review of General Psychology* 6(2): 166–203.

Baumgarte, R. 2002. "Cross-Gender Friendship: The Troublesome Relationship." In *Inappropriate Relationships*, ed. R. Goodwin: 103–124. Mahwah, NJ: Lawrence Erlbaum Associates.

Baxter, J. 2002. "Patterns of Change and Stability in the Gender Division of Household Labour in Australia, 1986–1997." *Journal of Sociology* 38(4): 399–424.

BBC News. 1997. "Barbie Undergoes Plastic Surgery." November 18; 2004. "Passion Over for Barbie & Ken." February 13; 2006. "Vintage Barbie Struts Her Stuff." September 22.

Beal, B. 1997. "The Promise Keepers' Use of Sport in Defining 'Christlike' Masculinity." *Journal of Sport and Social Issues* 21(3): 274–284.

Beals, K.P., E.A. Impett, and L.A. Peplau. 2002. "Lesbians in Love: Why Some Relationships Endure and Others End." *Journal of Lesbian Studies* 6(1): 53–63.

Beasley, B.. and T.C. Standley. 2002. "Shirts Vs. Skins: Clothing as an Indicator of Gender Role Stereotyping in Video Games." *Mass Communication & Society* 5(3): 279–293.

Beasley, C. 2005. *Gender & Sexuality*. London: Sage Publications.

Beaujot, R. 2004. "Delayed Life Transitions: Trends and Implications." **http: //222. vifamily.ca/ library/cft/delayed_life.html**; 2003. "Projecting the Future of Canada's Population: Assumptions, Implications and Policy." *Canadian Studies in Population* 30(1): 28.

Beaujot, R., E.M. Gee, F. Rajulton, and Z.R. Ravanera. 1995. "Family Over the Life Course." *Current Demographic Analysis Series*: 37–75. Ottawa: Statistics Canada.

Beck, E.T. 1992. "From 'Kike' to 'Jap': How Misogyny, Anti-Semitism, and Racism Construct the 'Jewish American Princess.'" In *Race, Class and Gender*, eds. M.L. Anderson and P. Hill Collins: 88–95. Belmont, CA: Wadsworth.

Beck, J.G., and A.W. Bozman. 1995. "Gender Differences in Sexual Desire: The Effects of Anger and Anxiety." *Archives of Sexual Behavior* 24(6): 595–612.

Becker, B.E., and S.S. Luthar. 2007. "Peer-Perceived Admiration and Social Preference: Contextual Correlates of Positive Peer Regard Among Suburban and Urban Adolescents." *Journal of Research on Adolescence* 17(1): 117–144.

Becker, D.V., D.T. Kenrick, S.L. Neuberg, K.C. Blackwell, and D.M. Smith. 2007. "The Confounded Nature of Angry Men and Happy Women." *Journal of Personality and Social Psychology* 92(2): 179–190.

Becker, P.E., and P. Moen. 1999. "Scaling Back: Dual-Earner Couples' Work-Family Strategies." *Journal of Marriage and the Family* 61: 995–1007.

Bedard, G., and M. Tremblay. 2000. "Perception of the Role of Women in Politics in Canada: The Case of Municipal Counselors in Quebec in 1997." *Canadian Journal of Political Science* 33(1): 101–131.

Bedford, V.H. 2003. "Men and Women in Old Age: Incorporating Aging into Psychology of Gender Courses." In *Integrating Aging Topics into Psychology*, eds. S.K. Whitbourne and J.C. Cavanaugh: 159–172. Washington, DC: American Psychological Association.

Beegan, J.K., and S.T. Allison. 2003. "What Sort of Man Reads *Playboy*? The Self-Reported Influence of *Playboy* on the Construction of Masculinity." *Journal of Men's Studies* 11(2): 189–206.

Beer, W.R. (ed.). 1988. *Relative Strangers*. Totawa, NJ: Rowman & Littlefield.

Beggan, J.K., and S.T. Allison. 2002. "The Playbox Playmate Paradox: The Case Against the Objectification of Women." *Advances in Gender Research* 6: 103–156.

Bélanger, A.1999. *Report on the Demographic Situation in Canada 1998–1999*. Ottawa: Statistics Canada.

Belk, R.W. 1988. "Possessions and the Extended Self." *Journal of Consumer Research* 15: 139–168.

Belknap, P., and W.M. Leonard II. 1991. "A Conceptual Replication of Erving Goffman's Study of Gender Advertisements." *Sex Roles* 25(3–4): 103–118.

Bem, S.L. 1994. *The Lenses of Gender*. New Haven: Yale University Press; 1983/1995. "Gender Schema Theory and Its Implications for Child Development: Raising Gender-Aschematic Children in a Gender-Schematic Society." *Signs* 8: 598–616. Reprinted in *Gender in the 1990s*, eds. E.D. Nelson and B.W. Robinson: 83–99. Toronto: Nelson Canada; 1981. "Gender Schema Theory: A Cognitive Account of Sex-Typing." *Psychological Review* 88: 354–364; 1974. "The Measurement of Psychological Androgyny." *Journal of Consulting and Clinical Psychology* 42: 155–162.

Beneke, T. 1997. *Reflections on Men and Sexism*. Berkeley, CA: University of California Press.

Benin, E.H., and E. Edwards. 1990. "Adolescents' Chores: The Difference Between Dual and Single Earner Families." *Journal of Marriage and the Family* 52(2): 349–361.

Benin, M.H., and J. Agostinelli. 1988. "Husbands' and Wives' Satisfaction with the Division of Labor." *Journal of Marriage and the Family* 50(2): 349–361.

Benjamin, B. and C. Wallis. 1963. "The Mortality of Widowers." *The Lancet* 2: 454–456.

Bennedsen, M., K.M. Nielsen, F. Perez-Gonzales, and D. Wolfenzon. 2007. "Inside the Family Firm: The Role of Families in Succession Decisions and Performance." *The Quarterly Journal of Economics*: 647–691.

Bennett, K.M., and S. Vidal-Hall. 2000. "Narratives of Death: A Qualitative Study of Widowhood in Later Life." *Aging & Society* 20(4): 413–428.

Bennett, M., C. Dewberry, and C. Yeeles. 1991. "A Reassessment of the Role of Ethnicity in Children's Social Perceptions." *Journal of Child Psychology & Psychiatry & Allied Disciplines* 32(6): 969–982.

Benokraitis, N.V., and J.R. Feagin. 1995. *Modern Sexism,* 2nd ed. Englewood Cliffs, NJ: Prentice-Hall.

Berardo, F. 1998. "Family Privacy." *Journal of Family Issues* 19(1): 4–19.

Berdhal, J.L., V.J. Magley, and C.R. Waldo. 1996. "The Sexual Harassment of Men? Exploring the Concept with Theory and Data." *Psychology of Women Quarterly* 20: 527–547.

Berenbaum, S.A., and J.M. Bailey. 2003. "Effects on Gender Identity of Prenatal Androgens and Genital Appearance: Evidence from Girls with Congenital Adrenal Hyperplasia." *Journal of Clinical Endocrinology and Metabolism* 88: 1102–1106.

Bergen, K.M., E.A. Suter, and K.L. Daas. 2006. "'About as Solid as a Fish Net': Symbolic Constructions of a Legitimate Parental Identity for Nonbiological Lesbian Mothers." *Journal of Family Communication* 6(3): 201–220.

Bernard, J. 1981/1995. "The Good-Provider Role: Its Rise and Fall." *American Psychologist* 36(1): 1–12. Reprinted in *Gender in the 1990s*, eds. E.D. Nelson and B.W. Robinson: 156–171. Toronto: Nelson Canada; 1973. *The Future of Marriage*. New York: Bantam; 1942. *American Family Behavior*. New York: Harper.

Bernhardt-House, P.A. 2003. "'So, Which One Is the Opposite Sex?' The Sometimes Spiritual Journey of a Metagender." In *Finding the Real Me*, eds. T. O'Keefe and K. Fox: 46–59. San Francisco, CA: Jossey-Bass.

Bernier, C., and S. LaFlamme. 2005. "Uses of the Internet According to Genre and Age: A Double Differentiation." *Canadian Review of Sociology and Anthropology* 42(3): 301–323.

Bess, I. 1999. "Widows Living Alone." *Canadian Social Trends* 63: 2–5.

Best, D.L. 2001. "Gender Concepts: Convergence in Cross-Cultural Research and Methodologies." *Cross-Cultural Research: The Journal of Comparative Social Science*, Special Issue in Honor of Ruth H. Munroe: Part 2, 35(1) : 23–43.

Best, D.L., and J.E. Williams. 1998. "Masculinity and Femininity in the Self and Ideal Self Descriptions of University Students in 14 Countries." In *Masculinity and Femininity*, eds. G. Hofstede et al.: 106–116. Thousand Oaks, CA: Sage.

Betchen, S.J. 2006. "Husbands Who Use Sexual Dissatisfaction to Balance the Scales of Power in their Dual-Career Marriages." *Journal of Family Psychotherapy* 17(2): 19–35.

Betz, N. 1993. "Career Development." In *Handbook on the Psychology of Women*, eds. F.L. Denmark and M.A. Paludi. Westport, CT: Greenwood.

Beynon, J. 2002. *Masculinities and Culture*. Buckingham: Open University Press.

Bhatia, R., R. Mallik, and S. Das Gupta. 2003. *Sex Selection*. Center for Genetics and Society. **www.genetics-and-society.org/ resources/background/factsheet.html**

Bianchi, S.M., and M.J. Mattingly. 2004. "Time, Work, and Family in the United States." *Advances in Life Course Research* 8: 95–118.

Bianchi, S.M., M.A. Milie, L.C. Sayer, and J. Robinson. 2000. "Is Anyone Doing the Housework? Trends in the Gender Division of Household Labor." *Social Forces* 79: 191–228.

Bibby. R.W. 2001. *Canada's Teens*. Toronto: Stoddart.

Bibby, R.W., and D.G. Posterski. 1992. *Teen Trends*. Toronto: Stoddart.

Bickman, D.S., E.A. Vandewater, A.C. Huston, J. Lee, A.G. Caplovitz, and J.C. Wright. 2003. "Predictors of Children's Electronic Media Use: An Examination of Three Ethnic Groups." *Media Psychology* 5: 107–137.

Biernat, M., and T.K. Vescio. 2002. "She Swings, She Hits, She's Great, She's Benched: Implications of Gender-Based Shifting Standards for Judgment and Behavior." *Personality & Social Psychology Bulletin* 28(1): 66–77.

Biernat, M., and D. Kobrynowicz. 1999. "A Shifting Standards Perspective on the Complexity of Gender Stereotypes and Gender Stereotyping." In *Sexism and Stereotypes in Modern Society*, eds. W.B. Swann, Jr., J.H. Langlois, and L.A. Gilbert: 75–106. Washington, DC: American Psychological Association.

Biernat, M., and M. Manis. 1994. "Shifting Standards and Stereotype-Based Judgements." *Journal of Personality and Social Psychology* 66: 5–20.

Bigler, R.S. 1999. "Psychological Interventions Designed to Counter Sexism in Children: Empirical Limitations and Theoretical Foundations." In *Sexism and Stereotypes in Modern Society*, eds. W.B. Swann, Jr., J.H. Langlois, and L.A. Gilbert: 129–152. Washington, DC: American Psychological Association.

Bigler, R.S., L.C. Jones, and D.B. Lobliner, 1998. "Social Categorization and the Formation of Intergroup Attitudes in Children." *Child Development* 68: 530–543.

Bigner, J.J. 1999. "Raising Our Sons: Gay Men as Fathers." *Journal of Gay & Lesbian Social Services* 10(1): 61–77.

Billings, A.C., K.K. Halone, and B. Benham. 2002. "'Man! That Was a Pretty Shot!' An Analysis of Gendered Broadcast Commentary Surrounding the 2000 Men's and Women's NCAA Final Four Basketball Championships." *Mass Communication & Society* 5(3): 295–315.

Bing, J. 1992. "Penguins Can't Fly and Women Don't Count: Language and Thought." *Women and Language* 15(2): 11–14.

Binstock, R.H., and L.K. George. 1996. *Handbook of Aging and the Social Sciences*. 4th edition. San Diego, CA: Academy Press.

Bird, C. 1997. "Gender Differences in the Social and Economic Burdens of Parenting and Psychological Distress." *Journal of Marriage and the Family* 59: 809–823.

Bird, G., and K. Mellville. 1994. *Families and Intimate Relationships*. New York: McGraw-Hill.

Birnbaum, P., and W. Croll. 1984. "The Etiology of Children's Stereotypes about Sex Differences in Emotionality." *Sex Roles* 10: 677–691.

Bischoping, K. 1993. "Gender Differences in Conversation Topics, 1922–1990." *Sex Roles* 28(1–2): 1–18.

Bishop, K.M., and D. Wahlsten. 1997. "Sex Differences in the Human Corpus Callosum: Myth or Reality?" *Neuroscience & Behavioral Reviews* 21(5): 581–601.

Bittman, M., and J. Wajcman. 2000. "The Rush Hour: The Character of Leisure Time and Gender Equity." *Social Forces* 79: 165–189.

Bittman, M., P. England, L. Sayer, N. Folbre, and G. Matheson. 2003. "When Does Gender Trump Money? Bargaining and Time in Household Work." *American Journal of Sociology* 109(1): 186–214.

Bjorkqvist, K., K. Lagerspetz, and A. Kaukiainen. 1992. "Do Girls Manipulate and Boys Fight? Development Trends in Regard to Direct and Indirect Aggression." *Aggressive Behavior* 18: 117–127.

Blachford, G. 1981/1995. "Male Dominance and the Gay World." In *The Making of the Modern Homosexual*, ed. K. Plummer: 184–204. London: Century Hutchinson. Reprinted in *Gender in the 1990s*, eds. E.D. Nelson and B.W. Robinson: 58–72. Toronto: Nelson Canada.

Black, P. 2004. *The Beauty Industry*. New York: Routledge.

Blackless, M., A. Charuvastra, A. Derryck, A. Fausto-Sterling, K. Lauzanne, and E. Lee. 2000. "How Sexually Dimorphic Are We? Review and Synthesis." *American Journal of Human Biology* 12: 151–166. **www3.interscience.wiley.com/cgi-bin/ issuetoc?ID=69504032**

Blackwell, D.L., and D.T. Lichter. 2000. "Mate Selection Among Married and Cohabiting Couples." *Journal of Family Issues* 21(3): 275–302.

Blaine, B., and J. McElroy. 2002. "Selling Stereotypes: Weight Loss Infomercials, Sexism and Weightism." *Sex Roles* 46(9–10): 351–357.

Blair, A., W. Costiniuk, L. O'Malley, and A. Wasserman. 2003. *Law in Action*. Toronto: Pearson/Prentice Hall.

Blair, S.L., and M.P. Johnson. 1992. "Wives' Perceptions of the Fairness of the Division of Household Labor: The Intersection of Housework and Ideology." *Journal of Marriage and the Family* 54: 570–581.

Blair, S.L., and D.T. Lichter. 1991. "Measuring the Division of Household Labour." *Journal of Family Issues* 12(1): 91–113.

Blair-Loy, M. 2003. *Competing Devotions*. Cambridge, MA: Harvard University Press.

Blaisure, K.R., and K.R. Allen. 1995. "Feminists and the Ideology and Practice of Marital Equality." *Journal of Marriage and the Family* 57: 5–19.

Blakemore, J.E.O. 2003. "Children's Beliefs About Violating Gender Norms: Boys Shouldn't Look Like Girls, and Girls Shouldn't Act Like Boys." *Sex Roles* 48(9–10): 411–419.

Blakemore, J.E.O., and R.E. Centers. 2005. "Characteristics of Boys' and Girls' Toys." *Sex Roles* 53(9–10): 619–634.

Blankenhorn, D. 1996. *Fatherless America*. New York: HarperCollins.

Bleeker, M.M., and J.E. Jacobs. 2004. "Achievement in Math and Science: Do Mothers' Beliefs Matter 12 Years Later?" *Journal of Educational Psychology* 91(1): 97–109.

Bleske, A.L., and D.M. Buss. 2000. "Can Men and Women Be Just Friends?" *Personal Relationships* 7(2): 131–151.

Blinde, E.M., D.E. Taub, and L. Han. 2001. "Sport Participation and Women's Personal Empowerment: Experiences of the College Athlete." In *Contemporary Issues in the Sociology of Sport*, eds. A. Yiannakis and M.J. Melnick: 159–168. Champaign, IL: Human Kinetics.

Block, J.H. 1984. *Sex Role Identity and Ego Development*. San Francisco: Jossey-Bass; 1978. "Another Look at Sex Differentiation in the Socialization Behaviors of Mothers and Fathers." In *The Psychology of Women*, eds. J.A. Sherman and F.L. Denmark: 29–87. New York: Psychological Dimensions.

Blofson, B., and N. Aron. 1997. "Riot Grrls." *Reluctant Hero*, n.d., 1(1): 14–17.

Bloom, D. 2002. *Normal*. New York: Random House.

Blouin, P., and M. Courchesne. 2007. *Education Indicators in Canada: Report of the Pan-Canadian Education Indicator Program*. Statistics Canada, Catalogue no. 81-582-XIE, no. 5. December 12.

Blum, D. 1997. *Sex on the Brain*. New York: Viking Press.

Blum, L., and E. Vanderwater. 1993. "Mothers Construct Fathers: Destablized Patriarchy in Le Leche League." *Qualitative Sociology* 16(2): 3–22.

Blumer, H. 1969. *Symbolic Interactionism*. Englewood Cliffs, NJ: Prentice-Hall.

Blumstein, P., and P. Schwartz. 1999. "The Creation of Sexuality." In *Gender, Culture and Ethnicity*, eds. L.A. Peplau and S.C. DeBro: 228–240. Mountain View, CA: Mayfield Publishing; 1983. *American Couples*. New York: William Morrow.

Bly, R. 1990. *Iron John*. Reading, MA: Addison-Wesley; 1988. *When a Hair Turns Gold*. St. Paul, MN: Ally Press;1987. *The Pillow and the Key*. St. Paul, MN: Ally Press.

Boies, S.C. 2002. "University Students' Uses of and Reactions to Online Sexual Information: Links to Online and Offline Sexual Behavior." *Canadian Journal of Human Sexuality* 11(3): 77–89.

Bois, J.E., P.G. Sarrazin, R.J. Brustad, D.O. Trouilloud, and F. Cury. 2002. "Mothers' Expectancies and Young Adolescents' Perceived Physical Competence: A Year-long Study." *Journal of Early Adolescence* 22(4): 384–406.

Bolin, A. 1996. "Transcending and Transgendering: Male-to-Female Transsexuals, Dichotomy and Diversity." In *Third Sex, Third Gender*, ed. G. Herdt: 447–486. New York: Zone.

Bonds-Raacke, J.M., E.T. Cady, R. Schlegel, R.J. Harris, and L. Firebaugh 2007. "Remembering Gay/Lesbian Media Characters: Can Ellen and Will Improve Attitudes Towards Homosexuals?" *Journal of Homosexuality* 53(3): 19–34.

Booth, A., and A.C. Crouter. 1998. *Men in Families*. Mahwah, NJ: Lawrence Erlbaum Associates.

Booth, A., and J. Edwards. 1992. "Starting Over: Why Remarriages Are More Unstable." *Journal of Family Issues* 13(2): 179–194.

Borland, D.C. 1982. "A Cohort Analysis Approach to the Empty-Nest Syndrome Among Three Ethnic Groups of Women: A Theoretical Position." *Journal of Marriage and the Family* 44: 117–28.

Bornholt, B. 2001. "Self-Concepts, Usefulness and Behavioral Intentions on the Social Context of Schooling." *Educational Psychology* 21(1): 69–78.

Bornstein, K. 1994. *Gender Outlaw*. New York: Random House. 1998. *My Gender Workbook*. New York: Routledge.

Borsel, J.V., G. DeCuypere, and H. Van den Berghe. 2001. "Physical Appearance and Voice in Male-to-Female Transsexuals." *Journal of Voice*, 15(4): 570–575.

Bos, H.M.W., F. van Balen, and D.C. van den Boom. 2007. "Child Adjustment and Parenting in Planned Lesbian-Parent Families." *American Journal of Orthopsychiatry* 77(1): 38–48.

Botta, R.A. 2003. "For Your Health? The Relationship Between Magazine Reading and Adolescents' Body Image and Eating Disturbances." *Sex Roles* 48: 389–399.

Boulton, M. 1983. *On Being a Mother*. London: Tavistock.

Bowen, A., and A.M. John. 2001. "Gender Differences in Presentation and Conceptualization of Adolescent Self-Injurious Behaviour: Implications for Therapeutic Practice." *Counseling Psychology Quarterly* 14(4): 357–379.

Bowlby, G. 2007. "Defining Retirement." *Perspectives on Labour and Income*, Statistics Canada Catalogue no. 75-001-XIE, February: 15–19.

Boyd, M. 2004. "Gender Inequality: Economic and Political Aspects." In *New Society*, 4th ed., ed. R.J. Brym: 214–243. Toronto: Nelson

Boyd, M., and D. Norris. 2000. "Crowded Nest? Young Adults at Home." In *Canadian Social Trends,* 3: 157–160. Toronto: Thompson Educational Publishing.

Boyd, N. 1998. *Canadian Law*. Toronto: Harcourt Brace Canada.

Boyd, S.E. 2000. "Custody, Access, and Relocation in a Mobile Society: (En)Gendering the Best Interests Principle." In *Law as a Gendering Practice*, eds.

D.E. Chunn and D. Lacombe: 158–180. Don Mills, ON: Oxford University Press.

Boyle, K. 2000. "The Pornography Debate: Beyond Cause and Effect." *Women's Studies International Forum* 23(2): 187–195.

Boysen, G.A., D.L. Vogel, S. Madon, and S.R. Wester. 2006. "Mental Health Stereotypes About Gay Men." *Sex Roles* 54(1–2): 69–82.

Bradbury, B. 1994. "Women's Workplaces: The Impact of Technological Change on Working-Class Women in the Home and in the Workplace in Nineteenth-Century Montreal." In *Women, Work, and Place*, ed. A. Kobayashi: 27–44. Montreal: McGill-Queen's University Press.

Bradley, H. 1996. *Fractured Identities*. Cambridge: Polity Press.

Bradsher, K. 1990. "Modern Tale of Woe: Being Left at the Altar." *New York Times*, March 7.

Bransford, H. 1997. *Welcome to Your Facelift*. New York: Doubleday.

Brantley, A., D. Knox, and M.E. Zusman. 2002. "When and Why Gender Differences in Saying 'I Love You' Among College Students." *College Student Journal* 36(4): 614–615.

Braun, V., and C. Kitzinger. 2001. "'Snatch,' 'Hole' or "Honey-Pot'? Semantic Categories and the Problem of Nonspecificity in Female Genital Slang." *Journal of Sex Research* 38(2): 146–158.

Braver. S.L., P.J. Fitzpatrick, and R.C. Bay. 1991. "Noncustodial Parent's Report of Child Support Payments." *Family Relations* 40(2): 180–185.

Bray, J.H. 1999. "From Marriage to Remarriage and Beyond." In *Coping with Divorce*, ed. E. Mavis Hetherington: 253–271. Mahwah, NJ: Lawrence Erlbaum Associates.

Brayfield, A.A. 1992. "Employment Resources and Housework in Canada." *Journal of Marriage and the Family* 54: 19–30.

Breakwell, G.M., V.L. Vignoles, and T. Robertson. 2003. "Stereotypes and Crossed-Category Evaluations: The Case of Gender and Science Education." *British Journal of Psychology* 94(4): 437–455.

Brehm, S.S. 1992. *Intimate Relationships*. 2nd ed. New York: McGraw-Hill.

Breidenbach, S. 1997. "Where Are All the Women?" *Network World* 14(41): 68–69.

Brenick, A., AA. Henning, M. Killen, A. O'Connor, and M. Collins. 2007. "Social Evaluations of Stereotyping Images in Video Games: Unfair, Legitimate, or 'Just Entertainment'?" *Youth & Society* 38(4): 395–419.

Brennan, R.T., R.C. Barnett, and K.C. Gareis. 2001. "When She Earns More Than He Does: A Longitudinal Study of Dual-Earner Couples." *Journal of Marriage & the Family* 63(1): 168–182.

Brescoll, V., and M. LaFrance. 2004. "The Correlates and Consequences of Newspaper Reports of Research on Sex Differences." *Psychological Science* 15: 515–520.

Bretthauer, B., T.S. Zimmerman, and J. H. Banning. 2007. "A Feminist Analysis of Popular Music: Power Over, Objectification of, and Violence Against Women." *Journal of Feminist Family Therapy* 18(4): 29–51.

Brewer, L. 2001. "Gender Socialization and the Cultural Construction of Elder Caregivers." *Journal of Aging Studies* 15(3): 217–235.

Brewer, P.R. 2003. "The Shifting Foundations of Public Opinions About Gay Rights." *Journal of Politics* 65(4): 1208–1220.

Brewster, K.L., and I. Padavic. 2000. "Changes in Gender-Ideology, 1977–1996. The Contributions of Intracohort Change and Population Turnover." *Journal of Marriage and the Family* 62(2): 477–487.

Bridges, A.J., R.M. Bergner, and M. Hesson-McInnis. 2003. "Romantic Partners' Use of Pornography: Its Significance for Women." *Journal of Sex & Marital Therapy* 29(1): 1–14.

Bridges, J.S. 1993. "Pink or Blue: Gender-Stereotypic Perceptions of Infants as Conveyed by Birth Congratulations Cards." *Psychology of Women Quarterly* 17(2): 193–205.

Brim, J.A. 1974. "Social Network Correlates of Avowed Happiness." *Journal of Nervous and Mental Disease* 158(6): 432–489.

Brim, O.G. Jr. 1968. "Adult Socialization." In *Socialization and Society*, ed. J.A. Clausen: 182–226. Boston: Little, Brown.

Brines, J., and K. Joyner. 1999. "The Ties That Bind: Commitment and Stability in the Modern Union." *American Sociological Review* 64: 333–356.

Brizendrine, L. 2006. *The Female Brain*. New York: Morgan Road Books.

Broad, K.L. 2002. "GLB+T?: Gender/Sexuality Movements and Transgender Collective Identity (De)Constructions." *International Journal of Sexuality & Gender Studies* 7(4): 241–264.

Brock, L.J., and G.H. Jennings. 1993. "Sexuality Education: What Daughters in Their 30s Wish Their Mothers Had Told Them." *Family Relations* 42: 61–65.

Brockman, J. 2001. *Gender in the Legal Profession*. University of British Columbia Press.

Brockmann, H. 2001. "Girls Preferred: Changing Patterns of Sex Preferences in the Two German States." *European Sociological Review* 17: 189–202.

Brod, H., and M. Kaufman (ed.). 1994. *Theorizing Masculinities*. Thousand Oaks, CA: Sage.

Brode, P. 2002. *Courted and Abandoned*. Toronto: University of Toronto Press.

Brody, L.R. 2000. "The Socialization of Gender Differences in Emotional Expression: Display Rules, Infant Temperament and Differentiation." In *Studies in Emotion and Social Interaction*, ed. A.H. Rischer: 24–47. New York: Cambridge University Press.

Bronstein, P. 2006. "The Family Environment: Where Gender Role Socialization Begins. In *Handbook of Girls' and Women's Psychological Health*, eds. J. Worell and C.D. Goodheart: 262–271. New York: Oxford University Press.

Brookey, R.A., and D.H. Miller. 2001. "Changing Signs: The Political Pragmatism of Poststructuralism." *International Journal of Sexuality & Gender Studies* 6(1–2): 139–153.

Brooks, G.R. 1997. "The Centerfold Syndrome." In *Men and Sex*, eds. R.F. Levant and G.R. Brooks: 28–57. New York: Wiley.

Brooks, R. 2006. "No Escaping Sexualization of Girls." *Los Angeles Times*, August 25: 12.

Brooks-Gunn, J., W. Han, and J. Waldfogel. 2002. "Maternal Employment and Child Cognitive Outcomes in the First Three Years of Life: The NICHD Study of Early Child Care." *Child Development* 73(4): 1052–1072.

Brotman, S., B. Ryan, Y. Jalbert, and B. Rowe. 2002. "Reclaiming Space-Regaining Health: The Health Care Experiences of Two-Spirit People in Canada." *Journal of Gay & Lesbian Social Services: Issues in Practice, Policy & Research* 14(1): 67–87.

Brown, N.R., and R.C. Sinclair. 1999. "Estimating Number of Lifetime Sexual Partners: Men and Women Do It Differently." *Journal of Sex Research* 36(3): 292–297.

Brown, R.B., and E.C. Pinel. 2003. "Stigma on My Mind: Individual Differences in the Experience of Stereotype Threat." *Journal of Experimental Social Psychology* 39(6): 626–633.

Brown, R.M., L.R. Hall, R. Holtzer, S.L. Brown, and N.L. Brown. 1997. "Gender and Video Game Performance." *Sex Roles* 36(11–12): 793–812.

Browne, K.R. 2006. "Evolved Sex Differences and Occupational Segregation." *Journal of Organizational Behavior* 27(2): 143–162; 2002. *Biology at Work*. New Brunswick, NJ: Rutgers University Press.

Brownlaw, S., J.A. Rosamond, and J.A. Parker. 2003. "Gender-Linked Linguistic Behavior in Television Interviews." *Sex Roles* 49(3–4): 121–132.

Brownmiller, S. 1975. *Against Our Will*. New York: Simon and Schuster.

Brownworth, V.A. 2001. "Less Than Lyrical." *Curve* 11: 53–54.

Brubacher, T.H. 1991. "Families in Later Life: A Burgeoning Research Area." In *Contemporary Families*, ed. A. Booth: 226–248. Minneapolis, MN: National Council on Family Relations.

Brumberg, J.J. 1997. *The Body Project*. New York: Vintage.

Bryan, S., and P. Walsh. 2003. "Physical Activity and Obesity." In *Women's Health Surveillance Report*: 9–10. Ottawa: Institute for Canadian Health Information.

Bryant, H. 2003. "Breast Cancer in Canadian Women." In *Women's Health Surveillance Report*: 25–26. Ottawa: Canadian Institute for Health Information.

Bryant, J., and T. Schofield. 2007. "Feminine Sexual Subjectivities: Bodies, Agency and Life History." *Sexualities* 10(3): 321–340.

Bryant, W.K., and C.D. Zick. 1996. "An Examination of Parent-Child Shared Time." *Journal of Marriage and the Family* 58(1): 227–237.

Brym, R.J., and J. Lie. 2003. *Sociology*. Belmont, CA: Wadsworth.

Brym, R.J., J. Lie, A. Nelson, N. Guppy, and C. McCormick. 2003. *Sociology,* Canadian Edition. Toronto: Nelson Thomson.

Brym, R.J., and R. Lenton. 2001. *Love Online: A Report on Digital Dating in Canada.* **www.nelson.com/nelson/harcourt/ sociology/ newsociety3e/loveonline.pdf**

Buckle, L., G.G. Gallup Jr., and Z.A. Rodd. 1996. "Marriage as a Reproductive Contract: Patterns of Marriage, Divorce, and Remarriage." *Ethology and Sociobiology* 17: 363–377.

Buddie, A.M., and A.G. Miller. 2001. "Beyond Rape Myths: A More Complex View of Perceptions of Rape." *Sex Roles* 45(3–4): 139–160.

Bukowski, W., C. Gauze, B. Hoza, and A. Newcomb. 1993. "Differences and Consistency in Relations with Same-Sex and Other-Sex Peers During Early Adolescence." *Developmental Psychology* 29: 255–263.

Bunkers, S.L. 1993. "Faithful Friends: Diaries and the Dynamics of Women's Friendships." In *Communication and Women's Friendships*, eds. J. Ward and A. Mink. Bowling Green: Bowling Green State University Popular Press.

Burchinal, M.R., and K.A. Clarke-Stewart. 2007. "Maternal Employment and Child Cognitive Outcomes: The Importance of an Analytic Approach." *Developmental Psychology* 43(5): 1140–1155.

Bureau, J. 1994. "Transgenderism? A New Label for an Old Reality: The Misery of Being a Man." *Revue Sexologique* 2(2): 164–173.

Burgess, D., and E. Borgida. 1999. "Who Women Are, Who Women Should Be: Descriptive and Prescriptive Gender Stereotyping in Sex Discrimination." *Psychology, Public Policy & Law* 5(3): 665–692.

Burgoyne, C. 2004. "Heart-Strings and Purse-Strings: Money in Heterosexual Marriage." *Feminism & Psychology* 14(1): 165–172.

Burk, M., and K. Shaw. 1995. "How the Entertainment Industry Demeans, Degrades, and Dehumanizes Women." In *Issues in Feminism*, 3rd ed., ed. S. Ruth: 436–438. Mountain View, CA: Mayfield.

Burke, M., J. Lindsay, I. McDowell, and G. Hill. 1997. "Dementia Among Seniors." *Canadian Social Trends* 45: 24–27.

Burke, R.J. 1994. "Canadian Business Students' Attitudes Towards Women as Managers." *Psychological Reports* 75: 1123–1129.

Burleson, B.R., A.J. Holmstrom, and C.M. Gilstrap. 2005. "'Guys Can't Say That to Guys': Four Experiments Assessing the Normative Motivation Account for Differences in the Emotional Support Provided by Men." *Communication Monographs* 72(4): 468–501.

Burleson, B.R., and A. Kunkel. 2006. "Revisiting the Different Cultures Thesis: An Assessment of Sex Differences and Similarities in Supportive Communication." In *Sex Differences and Similarities in Communication*, 2nd edition, eds. K. Dindia and D.J. Canary : 137–194. Mahwah, NJ: Lawrence Erlbaum Associates.

Burr, V. 2002. "Judging Gender from Samples of Adult Handwriting: Accuracy and Use of Cues." *Journal of Social Psychology* 142(6): 691–700.

Burrello, L.C., C. Lashley, and E.E. Beatty. 2001. *Educating All Students Together*. Thousand Oaks, CA: Corwin Press.

Burstyn, V. 1999. *The Rites of Men*. Toronto: University of Toronto Press; 1985. *Women Against Censorship*. Vancouver: Douglas & McIntyre.

Burt, V.K., L.L. Altschuler, and N. Rasgon. 1998. "Depressive Symptoms in the Perimenopause: Prevalence, Assessment and Guideline for Treatment." *Harvard Review of Psychiatry* 6(3): 121–132.

Bushnik, T. 2006. *Child Care in Canada*. Statistics Canada Children and Youth Research Paper Series, Catalogue no. 89-599-MIE, No. 003, April. Ottawa: Minister of Industry.

Bushweller, K. 1995. "Turning Our Backs on Boys." *Education Digest* January: 9–12.

Buss, D.M. 1996. "The Evolutionary Psychology of Human Social Strategies." In *Social Psychology*, eds. E.T. Higgins and A.K. Kruglanski: 3–38. New York: Guilford; 1995. "Psychological Sex Differences: Origins through Sexual Selection. *American Psychologist* 50, 164–168; 1994. *The Evolution of Desire*. New York: BasicBooks.

Butler, A.C. 2000. "Trends in Same-Sex Gender Partnering, 1988–1998." *The Journal of Sex Research* 37(4): 333–343.

Butler, J. 1997. *Excitable Speech*. New York: Routledge; 1997a. "Performative Acts and Gender Constitution" in *Writing on the Body*, eds. K. Conboy et al: 404–417. New York: Columbia University Press; 1993. *Bodies That Matter*. New York: Routledge; 1990. *Gender Trouble*. New York: Routledge.

Byers, E.S., and L.F. O'Sullivan. 1996. *Sexual Coercion in Dating Relationships*. New York: Haworth Press.

Byles, J.E., S. Feldman, and G. Mishra. 1999. "For Richer, for Poorer, in Sickness and in Health: Older Widowed Women's Health, Relationships and Financial Security." *Women & Health* 29(1): 15–30.

CAAWS (Canadian Association for the Advancement of Women and Sport and Physical Activity). 2005. *Success Stories*. Ottawa: CAAWS.

Cacchioni, T. 2007. "Heterosexuality and 'the Labour of Love': A Contribution to Recent Debates on Female Sexual Dysfunction." *Sexualities* 10(3): 299–320.

Cain, P.A. 1993. "Feminism and the Limits of Equality." In *Feminist Legal Theory*, ed. D.K. Weisberg: 237–247. Philadelphia: Temple University Press.

Calder, C. 2004. "The Language of Refusal: Sexual Consent and the Limits of Post-Structuralism." In *Making Sense of Sexual Consent*, eds. M. Cowling and R. Reynolds: 51–57. Aldershot England: Ashgate.

Caldera, Y.M., and M.A. Sciaraffa. 1998. "Parent–Toddler Play with Feminine Toys: Are All Dolls the Same?" *Sex Roles* 39(9–10): 657–668.

Caldicott, H. 1984. *Missile Envy*. New York: William Morrow.

Calhoun, A., M. Goeman, and M. Tsethlikai. 2007. "Achieving Gender Equity for American Indians." In *Handbook for Achieving Gender Equity Through Education*, 2nd ed., eds. S.S. Klein, B. Richardson, D.A. Grayson, L.H. Fox, C. Kramarae: 525–551. Mahwah, NJ: Lawrence Erlbaum Associates Publishers.

Califia, P. 1997. "Dildo Envy and Other Phallic Adventures." In *Dick for a Day*, ed. F. Giles: 90–109. New York: Villard; 1996. "Femininism and Sadomasochism." In *Feminism and Sexuality*, eds. S. Jackson and S. Scott: 230–237. New York: Columbia University Press.

Call, K., L. Grabowski, J. Mortimer, K. Nash, and C. Lee. 1997. *Impoverished Youth and the Attainment Process*. Presented at the Annual Meeting of the American Sociological Association, Toronto, Ontario. August.

Cameron, D. 1992. "Naming of Parts: Gender, Culture and Terms for the Penis Among American College Students." *American Speech* 67(4): 367–382; 2005. "Language, Gender, and Sexuality: Current Issues and New Directions." *Applied Linguistics* 26(4): 482–502.

Cameron, D., McAlinden, F., and K. O'Leary. 1993. "Lakoff in Context: The Social and Linguistic Functions of Tag Questions." In *Women's Studies*, ed. S. Jackson: 421–426. New York: New York University Press.

Cameron, E. 1997. *No Previous Experience*. Toronto: Viking.

Cameron, P. 1976. "Masculinity/Femininity of the Generations: As Self-Reported and as Stereotypically Appraised." *International Journal of Aging and Human Development* 7(2): 143–151.

Camfield, D. 2002. "Beyond Adding on Gender and Class: Revisiting Feminism and Marxism." *Studies in Political Economy* 69: 37–54.

Campbell, A., L. Shirley, and J. Candy. 2004. "A Longitudinal Study of Gender-Related Cognition and Behaviour." *Developmental Science* 7(1): 1–9.

Campbell, A., L. Shirley, and L. Caygill. 2002. "Sex-Typed Preferences in Three Domains: Do Two-Year-Olds Need Cognitive Variables?" *British Journal of Psychology* 93(2): 203–217.

Campbell, A., L. Shirley, C. Heywood, and C. Crook. 2000. "Infants' Visual Preferences for Sex-Congruent Babies, Children, Toys and Activities: A

Longitudinal Study." *British Journal of Developmental Psychology* 18(4): 479–498.

Campbell, D. 2004. "Stronach Grouped by Sexist Crum." *The Tyee,* February 3. **www.thetyee.ca/NR/exeres/18F13115-A15F-49C3-89E6-A86C6988B3C1,0871939**

Campbell, L.D., and A. Martin-Matthews. 2000. "Caring Sons: Exploring Men's Involvement in Filial Care." *Canadian Journal on Aging* 19(1): 57–97.

Campenni, C.E. 1999. "Gender Stereotyping of Children's Toys: A Comparison of Parents and Nonparents." *Sex Roles* 40(1–2): 121–138.

Campo, J., and M. Zorggroep. 2003. "Psychiatric Comorbidity of Gender Identity Disorders: A Survey." *American Journal of Psychiatry* 160(7): 1332–1336.

Canadian Bar Association. 2005. *Crystal Clear.* Report of the CBA Futures Committee.

Canadian Council on Social Development. 2001. *The Progress of Canada's Children 2001—Highlights.* **www.ccsd.ca/pubs/2=1/pcc2–1.hl.htm**; 1999. *Thinking Ahead.* **www.ccsd.ca/pubs/gordon/toc.htm**

Canadian Global Almanac 2004. (Nicole Langlois, editor-in-chief). 2003. Toronto: John Wiley and Sons Canada.

Canadian Global Almanac 2000. (Susan A. Girvin, editor-in-chief). 1999. Toronto: Macmillan/CDG Books Canada Inc.

Canadian Mental Health Association. 2002. *Depression and Manic Depression.* **www.cmha.ca/ english/info_centre/ mh_pamphlets/ mh_pamphlet_15.htm**

Canadian Press. 2000. Viagra Prescriptions Top One-Million in Canada. November 16. **www.canoe.ca/Health0011/16_viagra-cp.html**

Canadian Psychiatric Association. 2002. Anxiety, Depression, and Manic Depression. **http://cpa-apc.org/MIAW/pamphlets/Anxiety.asp**

Canadian Psychological Association. 2003. "'Gays And Lesbians Make Bad Parents': There Is No Basis in the Scientific Literature for this Perception." August 6. **www.cpa.ca/documents/GayParenting-CPA.pdf**

Canary, D.J., and K. Dindia. 1998. *Sex Differences and Similarities in Communication.* Mahwah, NJ: Lawrence Erlbaum Associates.

Cancian. F.M. 2002. "Defining 'Good' Child Care: Hegemonic and Democratic Standards." In *Child Care and Inequality,* eds. F.M. Cancian, D. Kurz, A.S. London; R. Reviere, and M.C. Tuominen: 65–78. New York: Routledge; 1987. *Love in America.* New York: Cambridge University Press.

Cannon, M. 1995. "No Boys Allowed." *Saturday Night,* February: 19, 20, 22, 24.

Cantor, C. 2002. "Transsexualism—Need It Always Be a DSM-IV Disorder?" *Australian & New Zealand Journal of Psychiatry* 36(1): 141–142.

Caporael, L.R. 1997. "The Evolution of Truly Social Cognition: The Core Configurations Model." *Personality and Social Psychology Review* 1: 276–298.

Cappelli, P., J. Constantine, and C. Chadwick. 2000. "It Pays to Value Family: Work and Family Tradeoffs Reconsidered." *Industrial Relations* 39(2): 175–198.

Carli, L.L. 1990. "Gender, Language and Influence." *Journal of Personality and Social Psychology* 59(5): 941–951.

Carpenter, L.M. 2002. "Gender and the Meaning and Experience of Virginity Loss in the Contemporary United States." *Gender & Society* 16(3): 345–365; 2001. "The Ambiguity of 'Having Sex': The Subjective Experience of Virginity Loss in the United States." *Journal of Sex Research* 38(2): 127–139; 1998. "From Girls into Women: Scripts for Sexuality and Romance in *Seventeen* Magazine, 1974–1994." *Journal of Sex Research* 35(2): 158–168.

Carpenter, S., and S. Trentham. 2001. "Should We Take 'Gender' Out of Gender Subtypes? The Effects of Gender, Evaluative Valence, and Context on the Organization of Person Subtypes." *Sex Roles* 45(7–8): 455–480.

Carr, C.L. 1998. "Tomboy Resistance and Conformity: Agency in Social Psychological Gender Theory." *Gender & Society* 12: 528–53.

Carr, D. 2004. "Gender, Preloss Marital Dependence and Older Adults' Adjustment to Widowhood." *Journal of Marriage and the Family* 66(1): 220–235.

Carriere, Y., and L. Martel. 2003. "Can Widowed or Divorced Older Persons in Canada Rely on Their Children for Assistance?" *Cahiers Quebecois de Demographie* 32(1): 139–153.

Carroll, L., P.J. Gilroy, and J. Ryan. 2002. "Counseling Transgendered, Transsexual, and Gender-Variant Clients." *Journal of Counseling & Development* 80(2): 1–15.

Carter, R.S., and R.A. Wojtkiewicz. 2000. "Parental Involvement with Adolescents' Education: Do Daughters or Sons Get More Help?" *Adolescence* 35(137): 29–44.

Casey, E., and L. Marten. 2007. *Gender and Consumption: Domestic Cultures and the Commercialization of Everyday Life*. Aldershot, England: Ashgate.

Cash, T.F., S.R. Melnyk, and J.I. Hrabosky. 2004. "The Assessment of Body Image Investment: An Extensive Revision of the Appearance Schemas Inventory." *International Journal of Eating Disorders* 35(3): 305–316.

Cashdan, E. 1997. "Women's Mating Strategies." *Evolutionary Anthropology* 4: 134–142; 1993. "Attracting Mates: Effects of Paternal Investment on Mate Attraction Strategies." *Ethology & Sociobiology* 14(1): 1–23.

Cassell, J., and H. Jenkins. 1998. *From Barbie to Mortal Kombat*. Cambridge: MIT Press.

Cassidy, B., R. Lord, and N. Mandell. 1998. "Silenced and Forgotten Women: Race, Poverty and Disability." In *Feminist Issues*, 2nd ed., ed. N. Mandell: 26–54. Scarborough: Prentice Hall Allyn and Bacon Canada.

Castaneda, D., and A. Burns-Glover. 2004. "Gender, Sexuality and Intimate Relationships." In *Praeger Guide to the Psychology of Gender*, ed. M.A. Paludi: 69–91. Westport, CT: Praeger.

Castiglia, C., and C. Reed. 2007. "'Ah, Yes, I Remember It Well': Memory and Queer Culture in *Will and Grace*." In *Sexualities & Communication in Everyday Life*, eds. K.E. Lovaas and M.M. Jenkins: 217–231. Thousand Oaks, CA: Sage.

Castro-Vazquez, G. 2006. "The Politics of Viagra: Gender, Dysfunction and Reproduction in Japan." *Body & Society* 12(2): 109–129.

Cato, J.E., and S.S. Canetto. 2003. "Young Adults' Reactions to Gay and Lesbian Peers Who Became Suicidal Following 'Coming Out' to Their Parents." *Suicide & Life-Threatening Behavior* 33(2): 201–210.

Cavan, R.S. 1969. *The American Family*. 4th ed. New York: Thomas Y. Crowell.

CBC. 2001. Beauty by Design: Cosmetic Surgery in Canada. **www.cbc.ca/programs/sites/features/hm.cosmeticsurgery/overview.html**

Cervantes, C.A., and M.A. Callanan. 1998. "Labels and Explanations in Mother-Child Emotion Talk: Age and Gender Differentiation." *Developmental Psychology* 34(1): 88–98.

Cesario, S.K., and L.A. Hughes. 2007. "Precocious Puberty: A Comprehensive Review of Literature." *Journal of Obstetric, Gynecologic & Neonatal Nursing* 36(3): 263–274.

Chabot, J.M., and B.D. Ames. 2004. "It Wasn't 'Let's Get Pregnant and Go Do It': Decision-Making in Lesbian Couples Planning Motherhood via Donor Insemination." *Family Relations* 53(4): 348–356.

Chafetz, J.S., and J. Hagan. 1996. "The Gender Division of Labor and Family Change in Industrial Societies: A Theoretical Accounting." *Journal of Comparative Family Studies* 27(2): 187–219.

Chanter, T. 2000. "Gender Aporias." *Signs* 25: 1237–1241.

Chavous, T.M., A. Harris, D. Rivas, L. Helaire, and L. Green. 2004. "Racial Stereotypes and Gender in Context: African Americans at Predominantly Black and Predominantly White Colleges." *Sex Roles* 51(1–2): 1–16.

Cherlin, A.J. 1992. *Marriage, Divorce, Remarriage*. Rev. and enlarged ed. Cambridge, MA: Harvard University Press.

Cherney, E. 1999. "Sex Experts Dispute Condom Maker's Claims on Virginity." *National Post*, September 22: A1.

Cherny, L., and E.R. Weise. 1996. *Wired Women*. New York: Seal Press.

Chesler, P. 1991. *Mothers on Trial*. New York: Harcourt Brace Jovanovich.

Cheung, A.M., R. Chaudhry, M. Kapral, C. Jackevicius, and G. Robinson. 2003. "Perimenopausal and Postmenopausal Health." In *Women's Health Surveillance Report*: 47–48. Ottawa: Canadian Institute for Health Information.

Chiappori, P.A., and S. Oreffice. 2008. "Birth Control and Female Empowerment: An Equilibrium Analysis." *Journal of Political Economy* 116(1): 113–140.

Chick, K.A., R.A. Heilman-Houser, and M.W. Hunter. 2002. "The Impact of Child Care on Gender Role Development and Gender Stereotypes." *Early Childhood Education Journal* 29(3): 149–154.

Childers, J. 1993. "Is There a Place for a Reasonable Woman in the Law? A Discussion of Recent Developments in Hostile Environment Sexual Harassment." *Duke Law Journal* 42: 854–904.

Chidley, J. 1996. "Toxic TV." *Maclean's* 109(25): 36.

Children Now. 2001. "Girls and Gaming: Gender and Video Game Marketing." *Media Now* (Winter). **www.childrennow.org/media/ medianow**; 2000. Top-Selling Video Games "Unhealthy" for Girls Research Shows. News Release, February 12. **www.childrennow.org/ newsroom**

Chira, S. 1996. "Study Says Babies in Child Care Keep Secure Bonds to Mothers: Federal Research Counters Some Earlier Reports." *New York Times*, April 21.

Chodorow, N. 2003. "'Too Late': Ambivalence About Motherhood, Choice, and Time." *Journal of the American Psychoanalytic Association* 54(1): 1181–1198; 2002. "Born into a World at War: Listening for Affect and Personal Meaning." *American Imago* 59(3): 297–315; 2002a. "Response and Afterword." *Feminism & Psychology* 12(1): 49–53; 1999. *The Power of Feelings*. New Haven, CT: Yale University Press; 1996. "Theoretical Gender and Clinical Gender: Epistemological Reflections on the Psychology of Women." *Journal of the American Psychoanalytic Association* (44) Suppl: 215–238; 1978. *The Reproduction of Mothering*. Berkeley: University of California Press.

Choi, N.G. 2003. "Coresidence Between Unmarried Aging Parents and their Adult Children: Who Moved in with Whom and Why?" *Research on Aging* 25(4): 384–404.

Chopra, R. 2006. "Invisible Men: Masculinity, Sexuality, and Male Domestic Labour." *Men and Masculinities* 9(2): 152–167.

Chou, K., and I. Chi. 2002. "Successful Aging Among the Young-Old, Old-Old and Oldest-Old Chinese." *International Journal of Aging and Human Development* 54(1): 1–14.

Chrisler, J.C. 2007. "The Subtleties of Meaning: Still Arguing After All These Years." *Feminism & Psychology* 17(4): 442–446.

Christensen, A., and C.L. Heavey. 1993. "Gender Differences in Marital Conflict: The Demand-Withdraw Interaction Pattern." In *Gender Issues in Contemporary Society*, eds. S. Oskamp and M. Constanzo: 113–141. Newbury Park, CA: Sage.

Christiansen, P.G., and D.F. Roberts. 1998. *It's Not Only Rock & Roll*. Cresskill, NJ: Hampton Press.

Christian-Smith, L.K. 1991/1998. "Young Women and Their Dream Lovers: Sexuality in Adolescent Fiction." In *Sexual Cultures and the Construction of Adolescent Identities*, ed. J.M. Irvine: 206–225. Philadelphia, PA: Temple University Press. Reprinted in *The Politics of Women's Bodies*, ed. R. Weitz: 100–111. New York: Oxford University Press; 1988. "Romancing the Girl: Adolescent Romance Novels and the Construction of Femininity." In *Becoming Feminine*, eds. L.G. Roman, L.K. Christian-Smith, and E. Ellsworth: 76–101. London: Falmer Press.

Christopher, A.N. 1998. "The Psychology of Names: An Empirical Examination." *Journal of Applied Social Psychology* 28(13): 1173–1195.

Christopher, F.S., and S. Sprecher. 2000. "Sexuality in Marriage, Dating, and Other Relationships: A Decade Review." *Journal of Marriage & the Family* 62(4): 999–1017.

Christophersen, E.R., and S.L. Mortweet. 2003. "Getting the Most Out of Toys, Games and Sports." In *Parenting That Works*, eds. E.R. Christophersen and S.L. Mortweet: 131–162. Washington, DC: American Psychological Association.

Chronholm, A. 2002. "Which Fathers Use Their Rights? Swedish Fathers Who Take Parental Leave." *Community, Work & Family* 5(3): 365–370.

Chung, S.K. 2007. "Media Literacy Art Education: Deconstructing Lesbian and Gay Stereotypes in the Media." *International Journal of Art & Design Education* 26(1): 98–107.

Ciabattari, T. 2004. "Cohabitation and Housework: The Effects of Marital Intentions." *Journal of Marriage and the Family* 66(1): 118–125.

Cianni, M., and B. Romberger. 1997. "Life in the Corporation: A Multi-Method Study of the Experiences of Male and Female Asian,

Black, Hispanic and White Employees." *Gender, Work and Organization* 4(2): 116–129.

Clark, L., and M. Tiggemann. 2007. "Sociocultural Influences and Body Image in 9- to 12-Year-Old Girls: The Role of Appearance Schemas." *Journal of Clinical Child and Adolescent Psychology* 36(1): 76–86.

Clark, R., J. Guilmain, P.K. Saucier, and J. Tavarez. 2003. "Two Steps Forward, One Step Back: The Presence of Female Characters and Gender Stereotyping in Award-Winning Picture Books Between the 1930s and the 1960s." *Sex Roles* 49(9–10): 439–449.

Clark, V., and C. Kitzinger. 2005. "'We're Not Living on Planet Lesbian': Constructions of Male Role Models in Debates About Lesbian Families." *Sexualities* 8(2): 137–152; 2004. "Lesbian and Gay Parents on Talk Shows: Resistance or Collusion in Heterosexism." *Qualitative Research in Psychology* 1(3): 195–217.

Clark, W., and S. Crompton. 2006. "Till Death Do Us Part? The Risk of First and Second Marriage Dissolution." In *Canadian Social Trends* Summer 2006(81).

Clarkberg, M.E., R.M. Stolzenberg, and L.K Waite. 1995. "Attitudes, Values and Entrance into Cohabitational Versus Marital Unions." *Social Forces* 74: 609–634.

Clarke, E., and M.S. Kiselica. 2001. "A Remedy for Boys Who Bully: A Gender-Equal School Environment." In *Elementary School Counseling in the New Millennium*, ed. D.S. Sandhu: 145–158. Alexandria, VA: American Counseling Association.

Clarke-Stewart, A., and V.D. Allhusen. 2005. *What We Know About Childcare*. Cambridge, MA: Harvard University Press.

Clatterbaugh, K. 2000. "Literature of the U.S. Men's Movements." *Signs* 25(3): 883–894; 1997. *Contemporary Perspectives on Masculinity,* 2nd ed. Boulder, CO: Westview; 1990. *Contemporary Perspectives on Masculinity*. Boulder, CO: Westview.

Clausen, J.A. 1986. *The Life Course*. Englewood Cliffs, NJ: Prentice-Hall; 1972. "The Life Course of Individuals." In *Aging and Society*, Vol. 3, eds. M.W. Riley, M. Johnson, and A. Foner: 457–514. New York: Russell Sage.

Clearfield, M.W., and N.M. Nelson. 2006. "Sex Differences in Mothers' Speech and Play Behavior with 6-, 9-, and 14-Month Old Infants." *Sex Roles* 54(1–2): 127–137.

CNN.com. 2006. "Madeover Ken Hopes to Win Back Barbie." February 10.

Coates, C.J., and D.J. Leong. 1988. "A Psychosocial Approach to Family Violence: Application of Conceptual Systems Theory. In *Violence in Intimate Relationships*, ed. G.W. Russell: 177–201. Costa, Mese, CA: PMA Publishing Corporation.

Cobb, M.D., W. Boettcher, and A.J. Taylor. 2002. "Exposure to Misogynistic Rape Music and Hostile and Benevolent Sexism: Does Eminem Really Promote Gender Stereotyping?" Department of Political Science and Public Administration, North Carolina State University.

Cockburn, C. 1997. "Domestic Technologies: Cinderella and the Engineers." *Women's Studies International Forum* 20(3): 361–371.

Code, L. 1993. "Feminist Theory." In *Changing Patterns*, 2nd ed., eds. S. Burt, L. Code, and L. Dorney: 19–57. Toronto: McClelland & Stewart.

Cohen, J. 2003. "Parasocial Breakups: Measuring Individual Differences in Responses to the Dissolution of Parasocial Relationships." *Mass Communication & Society* 6(2): 191–202.

Cohen, L.L., and R.L. Shotland. 1996. "Timing of First Sexual Intercourse in a Relationship: Expectations, Experiences and Perceptions of Others." *Journal of Sex Research* 33(4): 291–299.

Colapinto, J. 2000. *As Nature Made Him*. Toronto: HarperCollins.

Cole, E.R., and A.N. Zucker. 2007. "Black and White Women's Perspectives on Femininity." *Cultural Diversity & Ethnic Minority Psychology* 13(1): 1–9.

Cole, M., and S.R. Cole. 2001. *The Development of Children*. New York: Worth.

Cole, S., D. Denny, A.E. Eyler, and S.L. Samons. 2000. "Issues of Transgender." In *Psychological Perspectives on Human Sexuality*, eds. L.T. Szuchman and F. Mascarella: 149–195. New York: John Wiley & Sons.

Coleman, M., L. Ganong, and M. Fine. 2000. "Reinvestigating Remarriage: Another Decade of Progress." *Journal of Marriage and the Family* 62(4): 1288–1307.

Coleman, M., L. Ganong, and K. Leon. 2006. "Divorce and Postdivorce Relationships." In *The Cambridge Handbook of Personal Relationships*, eds. A.L. Vangelisti and D. Perlman: 157–173. New York: Cambridge University Press.

Coles, M., and C. Hall. 2002. "Gendered Readings: Learning from Children's Reading Choices." *Journal of Research in Reading* 25(1): 96–108.

Colley, A., and Z. Todd. 2002. "Gender-Linked Differences in the Style and Content of E-Mails to Friends." *Journal of Language and Social Psychology* 21(4): 380–392.

Collins, P.H. 2004. *Black Sexual Politics*. New York: Routledge; 2001. "Black Mother–Daughter Relationships." In *Gender and Social Life*, ed. R. Satow: 44–48. Needham Heights, MA: Allyn & Bacon.

Collins, R. 1979. *The Credential Society*. New York: Academic Press.

Collins, R., and S. Coltrane. 2000. *Sociology of Marriage and the Family*, 2nd ed. Chicago: Nelson-Hall.

Coltrane, S., and M. Adams. 1997. "Work-Family Imagery and Gender Stereotypes: Television and the Reproduction of Difference." *Journal of Vocational Behavior* 50(2): 323–347.

Coltrane, S., and M. Ishii-Kuntz. 1992. "Men's Housework: A Life Course Perspective." *Journal of Marriage and the Family* 54: 43–57.

Coltrane, S., and M. Messineo. 2000. "The Perpetuation of Subtle Prejudice: Race and Gender Imagery in 1990s Television Advertising." *Sex Roles* 42(5–6): 363–389.

Comack, E. 2004. "Women and Crime." In *Criminology*, ed. R. Linden: 164–195. Toronto: Nelson Thomson.

Comfort, D., K. Johnson, and D. Wallace. 2003. Part-Time Work and Family-Friendly Practices in Canadian Workplaces. Statistics Canada, the Evolving Workplace Series, No. 71-584-MIE, no. 6, June. **www.statcan.ca/ english/ freepub/71-584-MIE/ 71-584-MIEO3006.pdf**

Commuri, S., and J.W. Gentry. 2005. "Resource Allocation in Households with Women as Chief Wage Earners." *Journal of Consumer Research* 32(2): 185–195.

Comstock, G., and H. Paik. 1991. *Television and the American Child*. San Diego, CA: Academic Press.

Condry, J., and S. Condry. 1976. "Sex Differences: A Study of the Eye of the Beholder." *Child Development* 47: 812–819.

Conley, J., and W. O'Barr. 1990. *Rules versus Relationships*. Chicago: University of Chicago Press.

Connell, R.W. 2005. "Change Among the Gatekeepers: Men, Masculinities, and Gender Equality in the Global Arena." *Signs* 30(3): 1801–1825; 2003. "Masculinities, Change and Conflict in Global Society: Thinking About the Future of Men's Studies." *The Journal of Men's Studies* 11(3): 249–266; 2001/2002. "Studying Men and Masculinity." *RFR/DRF* 29(1–2): 43–56; 2000. *The Men and the Boys*. Cambridge: Polity Press; 1998. "Masculinities and Globalization." *Men and Masculinities* 1: 3–23; 1995. "Politics of Changing Men Revisited." *Socialist Review* 25(1): 135–159.

Connell, R.W., and J. Messerschmidt. 2005. "Hegemonic Masculinity: Rethinking the Concept." *Gender & Society* 19(6): 829–859.

Connell, R.W., and J. Wood. 2005. "Globalization and Business Masculinities." *Men and Masculinities* 7(4): 347–364.

Connelly, P., and L. Christiansen-Ruffman. 1977/1987. "Women's Problems: Private Troubles or Public Issues?" *Canadian Journal of Sociology* 2: 167–178. Reprinted in *Gender Roles,* eds. E.D. Salamon and B.W. Robinson: 283–295. Toronto: Methuen.

Connidis, I.A., and L. Davies. 1992. "Confidants and Companions: Choices in Later Life." *Journal of Gerontology: Social Sciences* 47(3): S115–S122.

Consumer Reports on Health. 1993/1995. "Do Men Go Through Menopause?" In *Human Sexuality 95/96*, ed. S.J. Bunting: 163–66. Guilford, CT: Dushkin.

Conway, J.F. 1993. *The Canadian Family in Crisis*. Rev. ed. Toronto: James Lorimer; 1990. *The Canadian Family in Crisis*. Toronto: James Lorimer.

Cook, D.T., and S.B. Kaiser. 2004. "Betwixt and Between: Age Ambiguity and the Sexualization of the Female Consuming Subject." *Journal of Consumer Culture* 4: 203–227.

Cooke, L.P. 2004. "The Gendered Division of Labour and Family Outcomes in Germany." *Journal of Marriage and Family* 66: 1246–1259.

Cooley, C.H. 1902. *Human Nature and the Social Order*. New York: Scriber's.

Cooney, T.M., and P. Uhlenberg. 1991. "Changes in Work-Family Connections Among Highly Educated Men and Women: 1970 to 1980." *Journal of Family Issues* 12: 69–90.

Coontz, S. 2000. "Marriage: Then and Now." *Phi Kappi Phi Journal* 80: 10–15.

Cooper, A., S. Bois, M. Mahe, and D. Greenfield. 2000. "Sexuality and the Internet: The Next Sexual Revolution." In *Psychological Perspectives on Human Sexuality*, eds. L.T. Szuchman and F. Muscarella: 519–545. New York: John Wiley & Sons.

Cooper, J. 2006. "The Digital Divide: The Special Case of Gender." *Journal of Computer Assisted Learning* 22(5): 320–334.

Cooper, M. 2002. "Being the 'Go-To Guy': Masculinity and the Organization of Work in Silicon Valley." In *Families At Work*, eds. N. Gerstel, D. Clawson, and R. Zumman: 5–31. Nashville, TN: Vanderbilt University Press.

Corak, M. 1998. "Getting Ahead in Life: Does Your Parents' Income Count?" *Canadian Social Trends* 49: 6–15.

Cormier, R.A., C.A. Dell, and N. Poole Dip. 2003. "Women and Substance Abuse Problems." In *Women's Health Surveillance Report*: 13–15. Ottawa: Canadian Institute for Health Information.

Cornell, D. (ed.) 2000. *Feminism and Pornography*. Oxford, England: Oxford University Press.

Cornetto, K.M., and K.L. Nowak. 2006. "Utilizing Usernames for Sex Categorization in Computer-Mediated Communication: Examining Perceptions and Accuracy." *Cyberpsychology & Behavior* 9(4): 377–387.

Corteen, K. 2002. "Lesbian Safety Talk: Problematic Definitions and Experiences of Violence, Sexuality and Space." *Sexualities* 5(3): 259–280.

Costa, L., and A. Matzner. 2007. *Male Bodies, Women's Souls*. New York: Haworth Press.

Costa, P.T. Jr., R.R. McCrae, and D. Arenberg. 1983. "Recent Longitudinal Research on Personality and Aging." In *Longitudinal Studies of Adult Psychological Development*, ed. K.W. Schaie: 222–265. New York: Guilford.

Council of Ministers of Education Canada. 2003. Canadian Youth, Sexual Health, and HIV/AIDS Study: Factors Influencing Knowledge, Attitudes and Behaviours. **www.cmec.ca/publications/aids/ TitlePage_EN.pdf**

Courcy, I., S. Laberge, C. Erard, and C. Louveau. 2006. "Sport as a Site of Reproduction and Contestation of Stereotyped Representations of Femininity." *Recherches Feministes* 19(2): 29–61.

Courtney, A.E., and S.W. Lockeretz. 1971. "A Woman's Place: An Analysis of the Roles Portrayed by Women in Magazine Advertisements." *Journal of Marketing Research* 8: 92.

Cousins, A. 2007. "Gender Inclusivity in Secondary Chemistry: A Study of Male and Female Participation in Secondary School Chemistry." *International Journal of Science Education* 29(6): 711–730.

Cowan, C.P., and P.A. Cowan. 1992. *When Partners Become Parents*. New York: Basic Books.

Cowan, R.S. 1984. *More Work for Mother*. New York: Basic Books.

Cowart, V.S. 1990. "Teenage Steroid Use Surveyed" *Facts on File* 14 September: 684.1.

Cowdery, R.S., and C. Knudson-Martin. 2005. "The Construction of Motherhood: Relational Connection and Gender Equality." *Family Relations* 54(3): 335–345.

Cox, A.J. 2006. *Boys of Few Words*. New York: Guilford Publications.

Coxhead, L., and T. Rhodes. 2006. "Accounting for Risk and Responsibility Associated with Smoking Among Mothers of Children with Respiratory Illness." *Sociology of Health and Illness* 28(1): 98–121.

Cozzarelli, C., M.J. Tagler, and A.V. Wilkinson. 2002. "Do Middle-Class Students Perceive Poor Women and Poor Men Differently?" *Sex Roles* 47(11–12): 519–529.

Crabb, P.B., and D. Bielawski. 1994. "The Social Representations of Material Culture and Gender in Children's Books." *Sex Roles* 30: 69–79.

Craig, A. 2003. "My Dangerous Desires: A Queer Girl Dreaming Her Way Home." *Archives of Sexual Behavior* 32(5): 487–488.

Craig, M.L., and R. Liberti. 2007. "'Cause That's What Girls Do': The Making of a Feminized Gym." *Gender & Society* 21(5): 676–699.

Cranny-Francis, A., W. Waring, P. Stavropoulos, and J. Kirby. 2003. *Gender Studies.* Basingstoke: Palgrave Macmillan.

Cranswick, K. 1997. "Canada's Caregivers." *Canadian Social Trends* 47: 2–6.

Crawford, M. 1995. *Talking Difference.* London: Sage.

Crawford, M., and E. Kimmel. 1999. "Promoting Methodological Diversity in Feminist Research." *Psychology of Women Quarterly* 23(1): 1–6.

Creed, W., E. Douglas, M.A. Scully, and J.R. Austin. 2002. "Clothes Makes the Person? The Tailoring of Legitimate Accounts and the Social Construction of Identity." *Organization Science* 13(5): 475–496.

Creighton, S., and C. Mihto. 2001. "Managing Intersex." *BMJ: British Medical Journal* 323(7324): 1264–1265.

Creighton, S.M., C.L. Minto, and S.J. Steele. 2001. "Objective Cosmetic and Anatomical Outcomes at Adolescence of Feminising Surgery for Ambiguous Genitalia Done in Childhood." *Lancet* 358: 124–125.

Creith, E. 1996. *Undressing Lesbian Sex.* London: Cassell.

Crenshaw, K. 1993. "Demarginalizing the Intersection of Race and Sex: A Black Feminist Critique of Antidiscrimintion Doctrine, Feminist Theory and Antiracist Politics." In *Feminist Legal Theory: Foundations,* ed. D.K. Weisberg: 383–398. Philadelphia: Temple University Press.

Crick, N. 1997. "Engagement in Gender Normative versus Nonnormative Forms of Aggression: Links to Social-psychological Adjustment." *Developmental Psychology* 33: 610–617.

Crick, N., and D.A. Nelson. 2002. "Relational and Physical Victimization within Friendships: Nobody Told Me There'd Be Friends Like These." *Journal of Abnormal Child Psychology* 30(6): 599–607.

Crnkovich, M. (Ed.) 1990. *Gossip.* Ottawa: Canadian Arctic Resources Committee, 1990.

Crompton, S. 2005. "Always the Bridesmaid: People Who Don't Expect to Marry." *Canadian Social Trends* 77.

Crook, M. 1991. *The Body Image Trap.* North Vancouver: Self-Counsel Press.

Cruz, J.M. 2003. "'Why Doesn't He Just Leave?' Gay Male Domestic Violence and the Reasons Victims Stay." *The Journal of Men's Studies* 11(3): 309–323.

Cunningham, M. 2005. "Gender in Cohabitation and Marriage: The Influence of Gender Ideology on Housework Allocation Over the Life Course." *Journal of Family Issues* 26(8): 1047–1061; 2001. "Parental Influences on the Gendered Division of Housework." *American Sociological Review* 66(2): 184–203.

Curry, T.J. 1991/2001. "Fraternal Bonding in the Locker Room: A Profeminist Analysis of Talk About Competition and Women." *Sociology of Sport Journal* 8(2): 119–135. Reprinted in *Men's Lives,* 5th ed., eds. M.S. Kimmel and M.A. Messner: 188–201. Boston: Allyn and Bacon.

Daiches, A. 2004. "Boys Will Be Boys: Breaking the Link Between Masculinity and Violence." *Clinical Child Psychology & Psychiatry* 9: 156–157.

Daly, K. 2004. *Exploring Process and Control in Families Working Nonstandard Schedules.* Mahwah, NJ: Lawrence Erlbaum Associates.

Daly, M. 1978. *Gyn/Ecology.* Boston: Beacon Press.

Danesi, M. 2003. *Forever Young.* Toronto: University of Toronto Press.

Daniels, H., A. Creese, V. Hey, D. Leonard, and M. Smith. 2001. "Gender and Learning: Equity, Equality and Pedagogy." *Support for Learning* 16(3): 112–116.

Darius, S., and S. Jonsson. 1993. "Interview with Gayatri Spivak." *Boundary* 2(2): 2.

Darling, C.A., J.K. Davidson, and R.P. Cox. 1991. "Female Sexual Response and the Timing of Partner Orgasm." *Journal of Sex and Marital Therapy* 17: 3–21.

Darling, C.A., D.J. Kallen, and J. Van Dusen. 1989. "Sex in Transition, 1900–1980." In *Family in Transition,* 6th ed., eds. A.S. Skolnick and J.H. Skolnick: 236–244. Glenview, IL: Scott, Foresman.

Darling-Fisher, C., and L.B. Tiedje. 1990. "The Impact of Maternal Employment Characteristics on Fathers' Participation in Child Care." *Family Relations* 39: 20–26.

Darling-Wolf, F. 2004. "Sites of Attractiveness: Japanese Women and Westernized Representations of Feminine Beauty." *Critical Studies in Media Communication* 21(4): 325–345.

Dar-Nimrod, I., and S.J. Heine. 2006. "Exposure to Scientific Theories Affects Women's Math Performance." *Science* 314(5798): 435.

Darnovsky, N. 2003. Sex Selection Goes Mainstream. **www.alternet.org/story/16837**

Darwin, C. 1859. *The Origin of Species*. Chicago: Conley.

Datan, N. 1989. "Aging Women: The Silent Majority." *Women's Studies Quarterly* 17(1–2): 12–19.

Dauvergne, M. 2003. "Homicide in Canada, 2001." *Juristat* 22(7). Statistics Canada Catalogue no. 85-002-XPE.

David, M. 1985. "Motherhood and Social Policy—A Matter of Education?" *Critical Social Policy* 12: 28–43.

Davidman, L. 1995. "Gender Play." *Qualitative Sociology* 18(1): 105–107.

Davidson, K. 2002. "Gender Differences in New Partnership Choices and Constraints for Older Widows and Widowers." *Aging International* 27(4): 43–60; 2001. "Late Life Widowhood, Selfishness and New Partnership Choices: A Gendered Perspective." *Aging & Society* 21(3): 297–317.

Davidson, K, S. Arber, and J. Ginn. 2002. "Gendered Meanings of Care Work Within Late Life Marital Relationships." *Canadian Journal on Aging* 19(4): 536–553.

Davidson, K.S., and G. Fennell. 2002. "New Intimate Relationships in Later Life." *Aging International* 27(4): 3–10.

Davies, P., S.J. Spencer, D.M. Quinn, and R. Gerhardstein. 2002. "Consuming Images: How Television Commercials That Elicit Stereotype Threat Can Restrain Women Academically and Professionally." *Personality & Social Psychology Bulletin* 28(12): 1615–1628.

Davies, W., and L.S. Wilkinson. 2006. "It Is Not All Hormones: Alternative Explanations for Sexual Differentiation of the Brain." *Brain Research* 1126(1): 36–45.

Davis, D. 1990. "Portrayals of Women in Prime-Time Network Television: Some Demographic Characteristics." *Sex Roles* 23(5–6): 325–332.

Davis, D.L., M.B. Gottlieb, and J.R. Stampritzky. 1998. "Reduced Ratio of Male to Female Births in Several Industrialized Countries: A Sentinel Health Indicator?" *JAMA* 279: 1016–1023.

Davis, K.E. 1985. "Near and Dear: Friendship and Love Compared." *Psychology Today* 19: 22–30.

Davis, S. 1990. "Men as Success Objects and Women as Sex Objects: A Study of Personal Advertisements." *Sex Roles* 23: 43–50.

Davy, S. 1978. "Miss to Mrs: Going, Going, Gone!" *Canadian Woman Studies* 1: 47–48.

Dawkins, R. 1976. *The Selfish Gene*. London: Oxford University Press.

DAWN (DisAbled Women's Network). 2004. Factsheets on Women with Disabilities. **www.dawn.thot.net/fact.html**

Deaux, K. 1999. "An Overview of Research on Gender: Four Themes from 3 Decades." In *Sexism and Stereotypes in Modern Society*, eds. W.B. Swann, Jr., J.H. Langlis, and L. Albino Gilbert: 11–34. Washington, DC: American Psychological Association.

Deaux, K., and L. Lewis. 1984. "Structure of Gender Stereotypes: Interrelationships among Components and Gender Label." *Journal of Personality and Social Psychology* 46: 991–1004.

de Beauvoir, S. 1961. *The Second Sex*. Trans. and ed. H.M. Parshely. New York: Bantam.

Decker, B.S. 1983. *The Women's Movement*. 3rd ed. New York: Harper & Row.

Dee, T.S. 2005. *Teachers and the Gender Gaps in Student Achievement*. National Bureau of Economic Research Working Paper No. 11660. Cambridge, MA: National Bureau of Economic Research.

Defey, D., E. Storch, S. Cardozo, and O. Diaz. 1996. "The Menopause: Women's Psychology and Health Care." *Social Science & Medicine* 42(10): 1447–1456.

DeFrancisco, V. 1991. "The Sounds of Silence: How Men Silence Women in Marital Relations." *Discourse and Society* 2: 413–423.

DeFrancisco, V.F., and C.H. Palczewski. 2007. *Communicating Gender Diversity*. Thousand Oaks, CA: Sage Publications.

De Graaf, N.D., P.M. de Graaf, and G. Kraaykamp. 2000. "Parental Cultural Capital and Educational Attainment in the Netherlands: A Refinement of the Cultural Capital Perspective." *Sociology of Education* 73: 92–111.

De Judicibus, M., and M.P. McCabe. 2001. "Blaming the Target of Sexual Harassment: Impact of Gender Role, Sexist Attitudes, and Work Role." *Sex Roles* 44(7–8): 401–418.

DeKeseredy, W.S., and M. Dragiewicz. 2007. "Understanding the Complexities of Feminist Perspectives on Woman Abuse." *Violence Against Women* 13(8): 874–884.

DeKeseredy, W., and R. Hinch. 1991. *Woman Abuse*. Toronto: Thompson Educational Publishing.

DeKeseredy, W.S., and K. Kelly. 1993. "The Incidence and Prevalence of Woman Abuse in Canadian University and College Dating Relationships." *Canadian Journal of Sociology* 18: 137–159.

DeKeseredy, W.S., and L. Macleod. 1997. *Woman Abuse: A Sociology Story*. Toronto: Harcourt Brace.

DeKeseredy, W.S., D.G. Saunders, M.D. Schwartz, and S. Alvi. 1997. "The Meanings and Motives of Women's Use of Violence in Canadian College Dating Relationships: Results from a National Survey." *Sociological Spectrum* 17: 199–222.

DeKeseredy, W.S., and M.D. Schwartz. 1998. *Woman Abuse on Campus*. Thousand Oaks, CA: Sage.

de Klerk, V., and B. Bosch. 1996. "Nicknames and Sex-Role Stereotypes." *Sex Roles* 35(9–10): 525–541.

Dekker, A., and G. Schmidt. 2002. "Patterns of Masturbatory Behaviour: Changes Between the Sixties and the Nineties." *Journal of Psychology & Human Sexuality* 14(2–3): 35–48.

De Konick, M. L. Guyon, and P. Morissette. 2003. "The Experience of Motherhood and Substance Abuse." *Recherches Feministes* 16(2): 107–137.

Delamont, S. 2003. *Feminist Sociology*. London: Sage.

DeLisi, R., and L. Soundranayagam. 1990. "The Conceptual Structure of Sex Role Stereotypes in College Students." *Sex Roles* 23(11–12): 593–611.

Dellinger, K., and C.L. Williams. 2002. "The Locker Room and the Dorm Room: Workplace Norms and the Boundaries of Sexual Harassment in Magazine Editing." *Social Problems* 49(2): 242–257.

Delphy, C., and D. Leonard. 1992. *Familiar Exploitation*. Cambridge: Polity Press.

Demo, D.J., and A.C. Acock. 1993. "Family Diversity and the Division of Domestic Work: How Much Have Things Really Changed?" *Family Relations* 42: 321–331.

Demo, D.J., and M.J. Cox. 2000. "Families with Young Children: A Review of Research in the 1990s." *Journal of Marriage and the Family* 62(4): 878–900.

Demo, D.J., M.A. Fine, and L.H. Ganong. 2000. "Divorce as a Family Stressor." In *Families & Change*, 2nd ed., eds. P.C. McKenry and S.J. Price: 279–302. Thousand Oaks, CA: Sage Publications.

Demos, D.J., M.A. Fine, and L.H. Ganong. 1982. "The Changing Face of Fatherhood: A New Exploration in American Family History." In *Father and Child*, eds. S.H. Cath, A.R. Gurwitt, and J.M. Ross: 425–445. Boston: Little, Brown.

Dempsey, K.C. 2001. "Feelings About Housework: Understanding Gender Differences." *Journal of Family Studies* 7(2): 141–159; 2000. "Men and Women's Power Relationships and the Persisting Inequitable Division of Housework." *Journal of Family Studies* 6(1): 7–24.

Denner, J., and N. Dunbar. 2004. "Negotiating Femininity: Power and Strategies of Mexican American Girls." *Sex Roles* 50(5–6): 301–314.

Dennis, T.A., M. Talih, P.M. Cole, C. Zahn-Waxler, and I. Mzuta. 2007. "The Socialization of Autonomy and Relatedness: Sequential Verbal Exchanges in Japanese and U.S. Mother–Preschooler Dyads." *Journal of Cross-Cultural Psychology* 38(6): 729–749.

DePalma, A. 1993. "Rare in Ivy League: Women Who Work as Full Professors." *New York Times*. 24 January 1993: 1, 13.

Derlaga, V.J., A.P. Barbee, and B.A. Winstead. 1994. "Friendship, Gender and Social Support: Laboratory Studies of Supportive Interactions." In *Communication of Social Support*, eds. B.R. Burleson and T.K. Albrecht: 136–151. Thousand Oaks, CA: Sage.

Derogatis, L.R., R. Rosen, S. Leiblum, A. Burnett, and J. Heiman. 2002. "The Female Sexual Distress Scale (FSDS): Initial Validation of a Standardized Scale for Assessment of Sexually Related Personal Distress in Women." *Journal of Sex & Marital Therapy* 28(4): 317–330.

Dershowitz, A. 1994. *Contrary to Popular Opinion*. Berkeley, CA: Berkeley Publishing Group.

Descheneau-Guay, A. 2006. "Gender Role Stereotypes in Television Shows: Recuperation of a Feminist Idea of Collective Emancipation and Emergence of Culture of Consensus." *Recherches Feministes* 19(2): 143–154.

Desert, M., and J. Leyens. 2006. "Social Comparisons Across Culture: Gender Stereotypes in High and Low Power Distance Cultures." In *Social Comparison and Social Psychology*, ed. M. Desert: 303–317. New York: Cambridge University Press.

DesMeules, M., D. Manuel, and R. Cho. 2003. "Mortality: Life and Health Expectancy of Canadian Women." In *Women's Health Surveillance Report*: 17–18. Ottawa: Canadian Centre for Health Information.

DesMeules, M., L. Turner, and R. Cho. 2003a. "Morbidity Experiences and Disability Among Canadian Women." In *Women's Health Surveillance Report*: 19–20. Ottawa: Canadian Centre for Health Information.

DesRivieres-Pigeon, C., M. Saurel-Cubizolles, and P. Romito. 2002. "Division of Domestic Work and Psychological Distress One Year After Childbirth: A Comparison Between France, Quebec and Italy." *Journal of Community & Applied Social Psychology* 12(6): 397–409.

Desrochers, S. 1995. "What Types of Men Are Most Attractive and Most Repulsive to Women?" *Sex Roles* 32(5–6): 375–391.

DeSteno, D.A., and P. Salovey. 1996. "Evolutionary Origins of Sex Differences in Jealousy? Questioning the 'Fitness' of the Model." *Psychological Science* 7: 367–372.

Deutsch, F.M. 2007. "Undoing Gender." *Gender & Society* 21(1): 106–127; 2003. "How Gender Counts When Couples Count Their Money." *Sex Roles* 48(7–8): 291–304.

Deutsch, F.M., A.P. Kokot, and K.S. Binder. 2007. "College Women's Plans for Different Types of Egalitarian Marriages." *Journal of Marriage and Family* 69(4): 916–929.

DeWall, C.N., T.W. Altermatt, and H. Thompson. 2005. "Understanding the Structure of Stereotypes of Women: Virtue and Agency as Dimensions Distinguishing Female Subgroups." *Psychology of Women Quarterly* 29(4): 396–405.

DeWeerth, C., and A. Kalma. 1995. "Gender Differences in Awareness of Courtship Initiation Tactics." *Sex Roles* 32(11–12): 717–734.

DeWelde, K. 2003. "Getting Physical: Subverting Gender Through Self-Defense." *Journal of Contemporary Ethnography* 32(3): 247–278.

Diamond, L.M. 2005. "'I'm Straight, But I Kissed a Girl': The Trouble with American Media Representations of Female-Female Sexuality." *Feminism & Psychology* 15(1): 104–110; 2002. "'Having a Girlfriend without Knowing It': Intimate Friendships Among Adolescent Sexual Minority Women." *Journal of Lesbian Studies* 6(1): 5–16.

Diamond, L.M., and E.M. Dube. 2002. "Friendship and Attachment Among Heterosexual and Sexual-Minority Youths: Does the Gender of Your Friend Matter?" *Journal of Youth & Adolescence* 31(2): 155–166.

Diamond, M. 1998. "Pediatric Management of Ambiguous and Traumatized Genitalia." Paper Presented at the meeting of the American Academy of Pediatrics, Urology Section. Mosconi Center, San Francisco, California, 17 October; 1982. "Sexual Identity: Monozygotic Twins Reared in Discordant Sex Roles and a BBC Follow-up." *Archives of Sexual Behavior* 11: 181–186.

Diamond, M., and H.K. Sigmundson. 1999. "Sex Reassignment at Birth." In *The Nature-Nurture Debate*, eds. S.J. Ceci and W.W. Williams: 55–75. Maldan, MA: Blackwell.

DiBenedetto, B., and C.K. Tittle. 1990. "Gender and Adult Roles; Role Commitment of Women and Men in a Job-Family Trade-off Context." *Journal of Counseling Psychology* 37: 41–48.

Dickerson, J. 1998. *Women on Top*. New York: Billboard Books.

Diefenbach, H., and K. Opp. 2007. "When and Why Do People Think There Should Be a Divorce? An Application of the Factorial Survey." *Rationality and Society* 19(4): 485–517.

Diekman, A.B., A.H. Eagly, and P. Kulesa. 2002. "Accuracy and Bias in Stereotypes About the Social and Political Attitudes of Women and Men." *Journal of Experimental Social Psychology* 38(3): 268–282.

Diekman, A.B., W. Goodfriend, and S. Goodwin. 2004. "Dynamic Stereotypes of Power: Perceived Change and Stability in Gender Hierarchies." *Sex Roles* 50(3–4): 201–215.

Diekman, A.B., M. McDonald, and W.L. Gardner. 2000. "Love Means Never Having to Be Careful: The Relationship Between Reading Romance Novels and Safe Sex Behavior." *Psychology of Women Quarterly* 24(2): 179–188.

Diekman, A.B., and S.K. Murnen. 2004. "Learning to be Little Women and Little Men: The Inequitable Gender Equality of Nonsexist Children's Literature." *Sex Roles* 50(5–6): 373–385.

DiGiulio, R.C. 1992. "Beyond Widowhood." In *Marriage and Family in a Changing Society,* 4th ed., ed. J.M. Henslin: 457–469. New York: Free Press.

DiLeonardo, M. 1998. *Exotics at Home.* Chicago: University of Chicago Press.

Dillabough, J. 2001. "Gender Theory and Research in Education: Modernist Traditions and Emerging Contemporary Themes." In *Investigating Gender*, eds. B. Francis and C. Skelton: 11–26. Buckingham, England: Open University Press.

Dimen, M. 1984. "Politically Correct? Politically Incorrect?" In *Pleasure and Danger*, ed. C.S. Vance: 138–148. Boston: Routledge & Kegan Paul.

Dindia, K., and M. Allen. 1992. "Sex Differences in Self-Disclosure: A Meta-Analysis." *Psychological Bulletin* 112(1): 106–124.

Dindia, K., M.A. Fitzpatrick, and D.A. Kenny. 1997. "Self-Disclosure in Spouse and Stranger Interaction: A Social Relations Analysis." *Human Communication Research* 23(3): 388–412.

Dinnerstein, D. 1976. *The Mermaid and the Minotaur*. New York: Harper & Row.

Dion, K., E. Berscheid, and E. Walster. 1972. "What Is Beautiful Is Good." *Journal of Personality and Social Psychology* 24: 285–290.

Dion, K.L., and A.A. Cota. 1991. "The Ms. Stereotype: Its Domain and the Role of Explicitness in Title Preference." *Psychology of Women Quarterly* 15: 403–410.

Dion, K.K., and K.L. Dion. 2001. "Gender and Cultural Adaptation in Immigrant Families." *Journal of Social Issues* 57(3): 511–521.

Di Stefano, C. 1990. "Dilemmas of Difference: Feminism, Modernity, and Postmodernism." In *Feminism/Postmodernism,* ed. L.J. Nicholson: 63–82. New York: Routledge.

Dodd, E.H., T.A. Giuliano, J.M. Boutell, and B.E. Moran. 2001. "Respected or Rejected: Perceptions of Women Who Confront Sexist Remarks." *Sex Roles* 45(7–8): 567–577.

Dodd, D.K., B.L. Russell, and C. Jenkins. 1999. "Smiling in School Yearbook Photos: Gender Differences from Kindergarten to Adulthood." *Psychological Record* 49: 543–554.

Dodson, B. 1996. *Sex for One*. New York: Crown Trade Paperbacks.

Dodson, L., and J. Dickert. 2004. "Girls' Family Labor in Low-Income Households: A Decade of Qualitative Research." *Journal of Marriage and the Family* 66(2): 318–332.

Doherty, G., M. Friendly, and M. Oloman. 1998. *Women's Support, Women's Work*. Ottawa: Status of Women Canada.

Doherty, W.J. 1991. "Beyond Reactivity and the Deficit Model of Manhood: A Commentary on Articles by Napier, Pittman, and Gottman." *Journal of Marital and Family Therapy* 17: 29–32.

Dolan, E.F. 1992. *Drugs in Sports*. Rev. ed. New York: Franklin Watts.

Dollar, K.M., A.R. Perry, M.E. Fromuth, and A.R. Holt. 2004. "Influence of Gender Roles on Perceptions of Teacher/Adolescent Student Sexual Relations." *Sex Roles* 50(1–2): 91–101.

Domene, J.F., R.G. Arim, and R.A. Young. 2007. "Gender and Career Development Projects in Early Adolescence: Similarities and Differences Between Mother-Daughter and Mother-Son Dyads." *Qualitative Research in Psychology* 4(1–2): 107–126.

Donaghue, N., and B.J. Fallon. 2003. "Gender-Role Self-Stereotyping and the Relationship Between Equity and Satisfaction in Close Relationships." *Sex Roles* 48(5–6): 217–230.

Dougherty, K., and A. Jelowicki. 2000. "Night Daycare to Make Debut." *The Montreal Gazette*, August 31. **www.childcarecanada.org/ccin/2000/ccin8_31_00.html**

Douglas, E.M. 2003. "The Impact of a Presumption for Joint Legal Custody on Father Involvement." *Journal of Divorce & Remarriage* 39(1–2): 1–10.

Douglas, K., and D. Arenberg. 1978. "Age Changes, Cohort Differences and Cultural Change on the Guilford-Zimmerman Temperament Survey." *Journal of Gerontology* 33: 286–293.

Douglas, S.J., and M.W. Michaels. 2004. *The Mommy Myth*. New York: Free Press.

Downey, D.B., and B. Powell. 1993. "Do Children in Single-Parent Households Fare Better Living with Same-Sex Parents?" *Journal of Marriage and the Family* 55: 55–71.

Dowsett, G. 1998. "Wusses and Willies: Masculinity and Contemporary Sexual Politics." *Journal of Interdisciplinary Gender Studies* 3(2).

Doyle, J.A. 1989. *The Male Experience*. 2nd ed. Dubuque, IA: Wm C. Brown.

Doyle, J.A., and M.A. Paludi. 1995. *Sex and Gender*, 3rd ed. Madison: WCB Brown & Benchmark.

Drakich, J., and P. Stewart. 2007. "After 40 Years of Feminism, How Are University Women Doing?" *The Journal of High Education Academic Matters*, February: 6–9.

Dranoff, L.S. 2001. *Everyone's Guide to the Law*. Toronto: Harper-Collins Publishers Ltd.

Drebing, C.E., and W.F. Gooden. 1991. "The Impact of the Dream on Mental Health Functioning in the Male Midlife Transition." *International Journal of Aging and Human Development* 32: 277–287.

Dreger, A. 1998. "Ambiguous Sex—or Ambivalent Medicine? Ethical Issues in the Treatment of Intersexuality." *Hastings Center Report* 28(3): 24–35.

Dreifus, C. 2001. "A Conversation with Anne Fausto-Sterling: Exploring What Makes Us Male or Female." *The New York Times*, January 2: F3.

Dressel, P.L., and A. Clark. 1990. "A Critical Look at Family Care." *Journal of Marriage and the Family* 52: 769–792.

Driscoll, C. 2002. *Girls*. New York: Columbia University Press.

Druzin, R. 2004. "Are Women Reclaiming Gymnastics From the Pixies." CBC Sports Online, June 11; 2001. *Women in Sports*. Toronto: Prentice Hall Canada.

Duffy, A., and J. Momirov. 1997. *Family Violence*. Toronto: James Lorimer & Company.

Duffy, J., K. Warren, and M. Walsh. 2001. "Classroom Interactions: Gender of Teacher, Gender of Student, and Classroom Subject." *Sex Roles* 45(9–10): 579–593.

Dunbar, N.E., and J.K. Burgoon. 2005. "Perceptions of Power and Interactional Dominance in Interpersonal Relationships." *Journal of Social and Personal Relationships* 22(2): 207–233.

Duncan, M.C., and M.A. Messner. 2000. *Gender Stereotyping in Televised Sports: 1989, 1993, and 1999*. Los Angeles, CA: Amateur Athletic Foundation of Los Angeles.

Dunkle, J.H., and P.L. Francis. 1990. "The Role of Facial Masculinity/Femininity in the Attribution of Homosexuality." *Sex Roles* 23(3–4): 157–167; 1996. "'Physical Attractive Stereotype' and the Attribution of Homosexuality Revisited." *Journal of Homosexuality* 30(3): 13–26.

Dunlap, E., G. Sturzenhofecker, and B. Johnson. 2006. "The Elusive Romance of Motherhood: Drugs, Gender and Reproduction in Inner-City Distressed Households." *Journal of Ethnicity in Substance Abuse* 5(3): 1–27.

Dunn, N.J., and L.A. Strain. 2001. "Caregivers at Risk? Changes in Leisure Participation." *Journal of Leisure Research* 33(1): 32–55.

Durham, M. 2003. "The Home and the Homeland: Gender and the British Extreme Right." *Contemporary British History* 17(1): 67–80.

Durik, A.M., J.S. Hyde, A.C. Marks, A.L. Roy, D. Anaya, and G. Schultz. 2006. "Ethnicity and Gender Stereotypes of Emotion." *Sex Roles* 54(7–8): 429–445.

Duverger, S. 2007. "Who's Afraid of Gay Parents?" *Radical Philosophy* 146: 2–8.

Dweck, C.A. 1999. *Self-Theories*. Philadelphia, PA: Psychology Press.

Dworkin, A. 1981. *Pornography*. New York: Penguin; 1974. *Woman Hating*. New York: Dutton.

Dyck, V., and K. Daly. 2006. "Rising to the Challenge: Fathers' Role in the Negotiation of Couple Time." *Leisure Studies* 25(2): 201–217.

Eagly, A.H. 2007. "Female Leadership Advantage and Disadvantage: Resolving the Contradictions." *Psychology of Women Quarterly* 31(1): 1–12.

Eagly, A.H., M.C. Johannesen-Schmidt, and M.L. van Engen. 2003. "Transformational, Transactional and Laissez-Faire Leadership Styles: A Meta-Analysis Comparing Women and Men." *Psychological Bulletin* 129(4): 569–591.

Eagly, A.H., and S.J. Karau. 2002. "Role Congruity Theory of Prejudice Toward Female Leaders." *Psychological Review* 109(3): 573–698.

Eastman, S.T., and A.C. Billings. 2001. "Biased Voices of Sports: Racial and Gender Stereotyping in College Basketball Announcing." *Howard Journal of Communications* 12(4): 183–201.

Eccles, J.S., C. Freedman-Doan, P. Frome, J. Jacobs, and K.S. Yoon. 2000. "Gender-Role Socialization in the Family: A Longitudinal Approach." In *The Developmental Social Psychology of Gender*, eds. T. Eckes and H.M. Trautner: 333–360. Mahwah, NJ: Lawrence Erlbaum Associates.

Eccles, J.S., and R.D. Harold. 1992. "Parent School Involvement During the Early Adolescent Years." *Teachers College Record* 94(3): 568–587.

Eccles, J.S., R. Roeser, A. Wigfield, and C. Freedman-Doen. 1999. "Academic and Motivational Pathways Through Middle Childhood." In *Child Psychology*, ed. L. Balter: 287–377. Philadelphia: Psychology Press.

Eccles, J.S., A. Wigfield, C. Midgley, and D. Reuman. 2000. "Negative Effects of Traditional Middle Schools on Students' Motivation." *Elementary School Journal* 93(5): 553–574.

Echols, A. 1984. "The Taming of the Id: Feminist Sexual Politics, 1968–83." In *Pleasure and Danger*, ed. C.S. Vance: 50–72. Boston: Routledge & Kegan Paul.

Eckes, T. 1994. "Explorations in Gender Cognition: Content and Structure of Female and Male Subtypes." *Social Cognition* 12: 37–60.

Edelsky, C. 1981. "Who's Got the Floor?" *Language in Society* 10: 383–421.

Edens, K.M., and C.B. McCormick. 2000. "How Do Adolescents Process Advertisements? The Influence of Ad Characteristics, Processing Objective and Gender." *Contemporary Educational Psychology* 25(4): 450–453.

Educational Indicators, 1998. "Indicator 18: Gender Differences in Earnings." National Center for Educational Statistics. Washington, DC: U.S. Department of Education.

Edut, O. 2004. Eastern Exposure? Asian American Barbie Is a No-Show. **www.adiosbarbie. com/bology/bology_asian.html**

Edwards, J.L. 2007. "Drawing Politics in Pink and Blue." *Political Science & Politics* 40(2): 249–253.

Edwards, R. 2004. "Present and Absent in Troubling Ways: Families and Social Capital Debates." *The Sociological Review* 52(1): 1–21.

EGALE. 2007. "Frequently Asked Questions: Age of Consent to Sexual Activity." **www.egale.ca/ index.asp?lang-E&menu=1&item=1329**; 2007a. "Events for Transgender Day of Remembrance, 2007." **www.egale.ca/ index.asp?lang-E&menu=34&itme=1373**; 2004. "Egale Fact Sheet: Who We Are and What We Do"; 2001. "2001 Census to Recognize Same-Sex Couples" [press release]. May 10; 1999. "Press Release."

eHarlequin.com. 2004. "About Harlequin." **http://store.eharlequin.com/cms/about/ aboutArticle.jhtml?pageID=021101cu05001**

Ehrenreich, B. 1983. "On Feminism, Family & Community." *Dissent* 30(1): 103–106.

Ehrenreich, B., and D. English. 1989/1995. "Blowing the Whistle on the 'Mommy Track.'" *Ms* 18(1–2). Reprinted in *Gender in the 1990s*, eds. E.D. Nelson and B.W. Robinson: 211–215. Toronto: Nelson Canada; 1979. *For Her Own Good*. Garden City, NY: Anchor Press.

Ehrensaft, D. 1990. "Feminists Fight for Fathers." *Socialist Review* 20(4): 57–80.

Ehrlich, S., and R. King. 1993. "Gender-Based Language Reform and the Social Construction of Meaning." In *Women's Studies Essential Readings*, 2nd ed., ed. S. Jackson. New York: New York University.

Eichler, M. 2002. "The Impact of Feminism on Canadian Sociology." *The American Sociologist* 33(1): 27–41; 1996. "The Impact of the New Reproductive and Genetic Technologies on Families." In *Families*, 3rd ed., ed. M. Baker: 104–118. Toronto: McGraw-Hill Ryerson; 1989. "Reflections on Motherhood, Apple Pie, the New Reproductive Technologies and the Role of Sociologists in Society." *Society/Société* 13: 1–5; 1984. "Sexism in Research and Its Policy Implications." In *Taking Sex into Account,* ed. J. McCalla Vickers: 17–39. Ottawa: Carleton University Press; 1981. "Power, Dependency, Love and the Sexual Division of Labour." *Women's Studies International Quarterly* 4(2): 201–219; 1980/1995. "Sex Change Operations: The Last Bulwark of the Double Standard." In *The Double Standard*, ed. M. Eichler: 72–88. London: Croom Helm. Reprinted in *Gender in the 1990s*, eds. E.D. Nelson and B.W. Robinson: 29–37. Toronto: Nelson Canada.

Einstein, G. 2007. *Sex and the Brain*. Cambridge, MA: MIT Press.

Eisenhart, R.W. 1975. "You Can't Hack It, Little Girl: A Discussion of the Covert Psychological Agenda of Modern Combat Training." *Journal of Social Issues* 31: 13–23.

Eisenstein, H. 1984. *Contemporary Feminist Thought*. London: Unwin.

Eitzen, D.S., and M. Baca Zinn. 1994. *Social Problems*. 6th ed. Boston: Allyn and Bacon.

Ekman, P., W.V. Friesen, and S. Ancoli. 1980. "Facial Signs of Emotional Experience." *Journal of Personality and Social Psychology* 39: 1125–1134.

Elder, G. 1969. "Appearance and Education in Marriage Mobility." *American Sociological Review* 34: 519–533.

Elder, G.H., and E.K. Pavalko. 1993. "Work Careers in Men's Later Years: Transitions, Trajectories, and Historical Change." *Journal of Gerontology: Social Sciences* 48(4): 180–191.

Eldridge, N.S., and L.A. Gilbert. 1990. "Correlates of Relationship Satisfaction in Lesbian Couples." *Psychology of Women Quarterly* 14(1): 43–62.

Elkin, F., and G. Handel. 1989. *The Child and Society*, 5th ed. New York: Random House.

Elliott, J.L., and A. Fleras. 1992. *Unequal Relations*. Scarborough, ON: Prentice-Hall.

Elliot, P., and N. Mandell. 1995. "Feminist Theories." In *Feminist Issues*, ed. N. Mandell: 3–31. Scarborough, ON: Prentice Hall Canada.

Ellis, A.L., and R.W. Mitchell. 2000. "Sexual Orientation." In *Psychological Perspectives on Human Sexuality*, eds. L.T. Szuchman and F. Muscarella: 196–231. New York: John Wiley & Sons.

Ellis, E.M. 2001. "The Impact of Race and Gender on Graduate School Socialization, Satisfaction with Doctoral Study and Commitment to Degree Completion." *Western Journal of Black Studies* 25(1): 30–45.

Ellis, K.M., and K. Eriksen. 2002. "Transsexual and Transgenderist Experiences and Treatment Options." *Family Journal— Counseling & Therapy for Couples & Families* 10(3) : 289–299.

Ellis, L., B. Robb, and D. Burke. 2005. "Sexual Orientation in United States and Canadian College Students." *Archives of Sexual Behavior* 34(5): 569–581.

Elliston, D.A. 1999. "Negotiating Transitional Sexual Economies: Female Mahu and Same-Sex Sexuality in Tahiti and Her Islands." In *Female Desires*, eds. E. Blackwood and S.E. Wieringa: 230–252. New York: Columbia University Press.

Elman, R.A. 2001. "Mainstreaming Immobility: Disability Pornography and Its Challenge to Two Movements." In *Sourcebook on

Violence Against Women, eds. C.M. Renzetti and J.L. Edelson: 193–207. Thousand Oaks, CA: Sage.

El-Shiekh, M., and S. Reiter. 1995. "Children's Responding to Live Angry Interactions: The Role of Form of Anger Expression." Poster presented at the biennial meeting of the Society for Research in Child Development, Indianapolis: Indiana, 30 March–2 April.

Emerson, R.A. 2002. "'Where My Girls At?' Negotiating Black Womanhood in Music Videos." *Gender & Society* 16(1): 15–135.

Emmers-Sommer, T.M., R. David, L. Triplett, and B. O'Neill. 2003. "Accounts of Single Fatherhood: A Qualitative Study." *Marriage & Family Review* 35(1–2): 99–115.

Engels, F. 1884/1902. *The Origin of the Family, Private Property, and the State*. Chicago: C.H. Kerr.

England, P. 2004. "More Mercenary Mate Selection? Comment on Sweeney and Cancian (2004) and Press (2004)." *Journal of Marriage and Family* 66(4): 1034–1037.

Entwistle, D.R., and S. Doering. 1988. "The Emergent Father Role." *Sex Roles* 18: 119–141.

Epstein, C.F. 2007. "Great Divides: The Cultural, Cognitive and Social Bases of the Global Subordination of Women." *American Sociological Review* 72(1): 1–22; 1988. *Deceptive Distinctions*. New York: Russell Sage Foundation and Yale University Press; 1986. "Inevitabilities of Prejudice." *Society* September–October: 7–15.

Epstein, C.F., and R.L. Coser. 1981. *Access to Power*. London: George Allen & Unwin.

Epstein, N., L. Evans, and J. Evans. 1994. "Marriage." In *Encyclopedia of Human Behavior*, ed. V.S. Ramachandran, Vol. 3: 115–125. New York: Academic Press.

Epstein, S. 2003. "Sexualizing Governance and Medicalizing Identities: The Emergence of 'State-Centered' LGBT Health Politics in the United States." *Sexualities* 6(2): 131–171.

Erikson, E. 1963. *Childhood and Society*, 2nd ed. New York: W.W. Norton.

Erwin, L.K. 1993. "Neo-Conservatism and the Canadian Pro-Family Movement." *Canadian Review of Sociology and Anthropology* 30(3): 401–420; 1988. "REAL Women, Anti-Feminism, and the

Welfare State." *Resources for Feminist Research* 17(3): 147–149.

Erwin, P.G. 2006. "Children's Evaluative Stereotypes of Masculine, Feminine and Androgynous Names." *Psychological Record* 56(4): 513–519.

Eschholz, S., J. Bufkin, and J. Long. 2002. "Symbolic Reality Bites: Women and Racial/Ethnic Minorities in Modern Film." *Sociological Spectrum* 22(3): 299–334.

Esgate, A., and M. Flynn. 2005. "The Brain-Sex Theory of Occupational Choice: A Counterexample." *Perceptual and Motor Skills* 100(1): 25–37.

Etaugh, C.A., and J.S. Bridges. 2001. *The Psychology of Women*. Boston: Allyn and Bacon.

Etaugh, C., and M.B. Liss. 1992. "Home, School, and Playroom: Training Grounds for Adult Gender Roles." *Sex Roles* 26: 129–147.

Etaugh, C., and K. Nekolny. 1990. "Effects of Employment Status and Marital Status on Perceptions of Mothers." *Sex Roles* 23: 273–280.

Etcoff, N. 1999. *Survival of the Prettiest*. New York: Anchor Books.

Ettner, R. 1999. *Gender Loving Care*. New York: Norton.

Evans, D. 1993. *Beauty and the Best*. Colorado Springs, CO: Focus on the Family Publishing.

Evans, E.M., H. Schweingruber, and H.W. Stevenson. 2002. "Gender Differences in Interest and Knowledge Acquisitions: The United States, Taiwan and Japan." *Sex Roles* 47(3–4): 153–167.

Evans, T. 1994. "Spiritual Purity." In *Seven Promises of a Promise Keeper*: 73–81. Colorado Springs, CO: Focus on the Family Publishing.

Everaerd, W., E.T.M. Laan, S. Both, and J. Van Der Velde. 2000. "Female Sexuality." In *Psychological Perspectives on Human Sexuality*, eds. L.T. Szuchman and F. Muscarella: 101–146. New York: John Wiley & Sons.

Ewing, V.L., A.A. Stukas, and E.P. Sheehan. 2003. "Student Prejudice Against Gay Male and Lesbian Lecturers." *Journal of Social Psychology* 143(5): 569–579.

Eyer, D.E. 1996. *Mother-Infant Bonding*. New Haven, CT: Yale University Press.

Eyler, A.E., and K. Wright. 1997. "Gender Identification and Sexual Orientation Among Genetic Females with Gender-Blended Self-Perception in Childhood and Adolescence." *International Journal of Transgenderism*, 1(1) **www.syjposium.com/ ihtc0101.htm**

Fabi, M. 2004. "Cybersex: The Dark Side of the Force." *International Journal of Applied Psychoanalytic Studies* 1(2): 208–209.

Fagot, B.I. 1995. "Parenting Boys and Girls." In *Handbook of Parenting*, Vol. 1, ed. M.H. Bornstein: 163–183. Mahwah, NJ: Erlbaum; 1986. "Beyond the Reinforcement Principle: Another Step Toward Understanding Sex Role Development." *Developmental Psychology* 21: 1097–1104.

Fagot, B.I., and Hagan, R. 1991. "Observations of Parent Reactions to Sex-Stereotypic Behaviors: Age and Sex Effects." *Child Development* 62: 617–628.

Fagot, B., and M.D. Leinbach. 1993. "Gender-Role Development in Young Children: From Discrimination to Labeling." *Developmental Review* 13: 205–224; 1995. "Gender Knowledge in Egalitarian and Traditional Families." *Sex Roles* 32(7–8): 513–526.

Fagot, B.I., C.S. Rodgers, and M.D. Leinbach. 2000. "Theories of Gender Socialization." In *The Developmental Social Psychology of Gender*, eds. T. Eckes and H.M. Trautner: 65–89. Mahwah, NJ: Lawrence Erlbum Associates.

Faith, K. 1993. *Unruly Women*. Vancouver: Press Gang Publishers.

Faludi, S. 1999. *Stiffed*. New York: William Morrow; 1991. *Backlash*. New York: Crown.

Faraut, M. 2003. "Women Resisting the Vote: A Case of Anti-Feminism?" *Women's History Review* 12(4): 605–621.

Farquhar, J.C., and L. Wasylkiw. 2007. "Media Images of Men: Trends and Consequences of Body Conceptualization." *Psychology of Men & Masculinity* 8(3): 145–160.

Farrell, W. 1993. *The Myth of Male Power*. New York: Simon & Schuster; 1986. *Why Men Are the Way They Are*. New York: McGraw-Hill; 1974. *The Liberated Man*. New York: Bantam.

Fasteau, M.F. 1975. *The Male Machine*. New York: Delta.

Faulkner, A.H., and K. Cranston. 1998. "Correlates of Same-Sex Sexual Behavior in a Random Sample of Massachusetts High School Students." *Journal of Public Health* 88: 262–266.

Fausto-Sterling, A. 2000. *Sexing the Body*. New York: Basic Books; 1993. "The Five Sexes: Why Male and Female Are Not Enough." *The Sciences* 33(2): 20–25.

Favreau, O.E. 1993. "Do the Ns Justify the Means? Null Hypothesis Testing Applied to Sex and Other Differences." *Canadian Psychology* 34(1): 64–78.

Fawcett, D. 1999. "Disability in the Labour Market: Barriers and Solutions." *Perception* 23(3) December. Canadian Council on Social Development. **www.ccsd.ca/perception/233/ disab.htm**

Fedorowycz, O. 1999. "Homicide in Canada, 1998." *Juristat*, 19(1) Cat. 85-002-XIE.

Fehr, B. 2004. "Intimacy Expectations in Same-Sex Friendships: A Prototype Interaction-Pattern Model." *Journal of Personality & Social Psychology* 86(2): 265–284.

Fein, E., and S. Schneider. 1995. *The Rules*. New York: Warner Books.

Fein, R.A. 1978. "Research on Fathering: Social Policy and an Emergent Perspective." *Journal of Social Issues* 31(1): 122–135.

Feinberg, L. 1998. *Trans Liberation*. Boston, MA: Beacon Press; 1996. *Transgender Warriors*. Boston: Beacon Press.

Feingold, A. 1995. "Cognitive Gender Differences: What Are They and Why Are They There?" *Learning and Individual Differences* 8(1): 25–32.

Fekete, J. 1994. *Moral Panic*. Toronto: Robert Davies.

Feldstein, J.H., and S. Feldstein. 1982. "Sex Differences on Televised Toy Commercials." *Sex Roles* 8: 581–587.

Fenna, D. 1999. "Internet." In *The Canadian Encyclopedia*, ed. James H. Marsh. Toronto: McClelland and Stewart, Inc: 1181—1182.

Ferguson, A. 1994. "Twenty Years of Feminist Philosophy." *Hypatia* 9(3): 197.

Ferguson, T.J., and H.L. Eyre. 2000. "Engendering Gender Differences in Shame and Guilt: Stereotypes, Socialization and

Situational Pressures." In *Gender and Emotion*, ed. A.H. Fischer: 254–276. New York: Cambridge University Press.

Ferree, M.M. 1990. "Beyond Separate Spheres: Feminism and Family Research." *Journal of Marriage and the Family* 52: 866–884.

Fieland, K.C., K.L. Walters, and J.M. Simoni. 2007. "Determinants of Health Among Two-Spirit American Indians and Alaska Natives." In *The Health of Sexual Minorities*, ed. I.L. Meyer and M.E. Northridge: 268–300. New York: Springer Science and Business Media.

Fiese, B.H., and G. Williams. 2000. "Gender Differences in Family Stories: Moderating Influence of Parent Gender Role and Child Gender." *Sex Roles* 44(5–6): 267–283.

Filardo, E.K. 1996. "Gender Patterns in African American and White Adolescents' Social Interactions in Same-Race, Mixed-Gender Groups." *Journal of Personality and Social Psychology* 71(1): 71–81.

Fine, M., and A. Asch. 1988. *Women with Disabilities*. Philadelphia, PA: Temple University Press.

Fine, S. 2001. "Schools Told to Fix Boys' Low Grades." *Globe and Mail*, August 27. **www. theglobeand mail.com/series/school/fix. html**; 1999. "Child Development More Affected by Parenting than Social Class." *Globe and Mail,* October 4: A4.

Fingerhut, A.W., and L.A. Peplau. 2006. "The Impact of Social Roles on Stereotypes of Gay Men." *Sex Roles* 55(3–4): 273–278.

Fink, J.S., and L.J. Kensicki. 2002. "An Imperceptible Difference: Visual and Textual Constructions of Femininity in Sports Illustrated and Sports Illustrated for Women." *Mass Communication & Society* 5: 317–339.

Finley, H. 2003. Average Age of Menarche in Various Cultures. **www.mum.org/ menarage.htm**

Finn, J. 2004. "A Survey of Online Harassment at a University Campus." *Journal of Interpersonal Violence* 19(4): 468–483.

Finnie, R., C. Laporte, R. Morissette, and M. Rivard. 2002. *Setting Up Shop: Self-Employment Amongst Canadian College and University Graduates*. Analytic Studies Branch Research Paper Series, no. 183, Statistics Canada, Catalogue no. 11F0019ME2002183, March 21.

Firestone, S. 1970. *The Dialectic of Sex*. New York: William Morrow.

Fishbein, D.A. 2003. "Suicide Preceded by Murder: The Epidemiology of Homicide-Suicide in England and Wales 1988–92: Comment." *Psychological Medicine* 33(2): 375.

Fisher, J. 1999. *Reaching Out: A Report on Lesbian, Gay & Bisexual Youth Issues in Canada.* **www.egale.ca/index/ asp?lang+E&menu=33&item+305**

Fisher, W., and A. Barak. 2001. "Internet Pornography: A Social Psychological Perspective on Internet Sexuality." *Journal of Sex Research* 38(4): 312–323.

Fishman, J.R., and L. Mamo. 2001. "What's in a Disorder: A Cultural Analysis of Medical and Pharmaceutical Constructions of Male and Female Sexual Dysfunction." *Women & Therapy* 24(1–2): 179–193.

Fiske, S.T. 1998. "Stereotyping, Prejudice, and Discrimination." In *The Handbook of Social Psychology*, eds. D.T. Gilbert, S.T. Fiske, and G. Lindsey: 357–411. New York: McGraw-Hill.

Fitzgerald, L.R., and S.L. Shullman. 1993. "Sexual Harassment: A Research Analysis of Agenda for the '90s." *Journal of Vocational Behavior* 40: 5–27.

Fivush, R. 1991. "Gender and Emotion in Mother–Child Conversations about the Past." *Journal of Narrative and Life History* 1: 325–341.

Fivush, R., M.A. Brotman, J.P. Buckner, and S.H. Goodman. 2000. "Gender Differences in Parent–Child Emotion Narratives." *Sex Roles* 42(3–4): 233–253.

Fivush, R., and J.P. Buckner. 2000. "Gender, Sadness, and Depression: The Development of Emotional Focus Through Gendered Discourse." In *Gender and Emotion*, ed. A.H. Fischer: 232–253. New York: Cambridge University Press.

Flanagan, E.H., and R.K. Blashfield. 2003. "Gender Bias in the Diagnosis of Personality Disorders: The Roles of Base Rates and Social Stereotypes." *Journal of Personality Disorders* 17(5): 431–446.

Flax, J. 1990. "Postmodernism and Gender Relations in Feminist Theory." In *Feminism/ Postmodernism*, ed. L.J. Nicholson: 39–62. New York: Routledge.

Fleras, A. 2003. *Mass Media Communication in Canada*. Toronto: Nelson Thomson.

Flouri, E., and A. Buchanan. 2003. "What Predicts Fathers' Involvement with Their Children? A Prospective Study of Intact Families." *British Journal of Developmental Psychology* 21(1): 81–97.

Foa, E.B., and U.G. Foa. 1980. "Resource Theory: Interpersonal Behavior as Exchange." In *Social Exchange*, eds. K.J. Gergen, M.S. Greenber, and R.H. Willis: 79–94. New York: Plenum.

Foley, D.E. 1993. "The Great American Football Ritual." In *Down to Earth Sociology*, 7th ed., ed. J.M. Henslin: 418–431. New York: Free Press.

Foley, S., K.A. Kope, and D.P. Sugrue. 2002. *Sex Matters for Women*. New York: Guilford Press.

Foot, D., with D. Stoffman. 1996. *Boom, Bust, and Echo*. Toronto: Macfarlane, Walter and Ross.

Forbes, G.B., L.E. Adams-Curtis, B. Rade, and P. Jaberg. 2001. "Body Dissatisfaction in Women and Men: The Role of Gender-Typing and Self-Esteem." *Sex Roles* 44(7–8): 461–484.

Forbes, G.B., L.E. Adams-Curtis, K.B. White, and K.M. Holmgren. 2003. "The Role of Hostile and Benevolent Sexism in Women's and Men's Perceptions of the Menstruating Woman." *Psychology of Women Quarterly* 27(1): 58–63.

Foreit, K.G., T. Agor, J. Byers, J. Larue, H. Lokey, M. Palazzini, M. Patterson, and L. Smith. 1980. "Sex Bias in the Newspaper Treatment of Male-Centered and Female-Centered News Stories." *Sex Roles* 6: 475–480.

Fortunata, B., and C.S. Kohn. 2003. "Demographic, Psychosocial, and Personality Characteristics of Lesbian Batterers." *Violence and Victims* 18(5): 557–568.

Foschi, M. 2000. "Double Standards for Competence: Theory and Research." *Annual Review of Sociology* 26: 21–42.

Foster, V., M. Kimmel, and C. Skelton. 2001. "What About the Boys? An Overview of the Debates." In *What About the Boys?*, eds. W. Martino and B. Meyenn: 1–23. Buckingham, England: Open University Press.

Foucault, M. 1980. *The History of Sexuality*, Vol. 1. New York: Vintage.

Fouts, G., and K. Burggraf. 2000. "Television Situation Comedies: Female Weight, Male Negative Comments and Audience Reactions." *Sex Roles* 42(9–10): 925–932.

Fouts, G., and R. Inch. 2005. "Homosexuality in TV Situation Comedies: Characters and Verbal Comments." *Journal of Homosexuality* 49(1): 35–45.

Fowler, M. 1993. *In A Gilded Cage*. Toronto: Vintage.

Fox, B.J. 1993. "The Rise and Fall of the Breadwinner–Homemaker Family." In *Family Patterns, Gender Relations*, ed. B.J. Fox: 147–157. Toronto: Oxford University Press.

Fox, R.L., and Z.M. Oxley. 2003. "Gender Stereotyping in State Executive Elections: Candidate Selection and Success." *Journal of Politics* 65(3): 833–850.

Francis, B., and C. Skelton. 2001. *Investigating Gender*. Buckingham, England: Open University Press.

Frank, E. 2000. *Gender and Its Effects on Psychopathology*. Washington, DC: American Psychiatric Publishing.

Frank, J. 1994. "Voting and Contributing: Political Participation in Canada." In *Canadian Social Trends* 2: 333–337. Toronto: Thompson Educational Publishing.

Frank, J.B., and C.D. Thomas. 2003. "Externalized Self-Perceptions, Self-Silencing, and the Prediction of Eating Pathology." *Canadian Journal of Behavioural Science* 35(3): 219–228.

Frederick, J.A. 1995. *As Time Goes By…; Time Use of Canadians*. Cat. 89–544E. Ottawa: Minister of Industry.

Frederick, J.A., and J.E. Fast. 1999. "Eldercare in Canada: Who Does How Much?" *Canadian Social Trends* 54: 26–30.

Fredericks, J., and J.S. Eccles. 2002. "Children's Competence and Value Beliefs From Childhood Through Adolescence: Growth Trajectories in Two Male-Sex-Typed Domains." *Developmental Psychology* 38(4): 510–533.

Fredrickson, B.L., T. Roberts, S.M. Noll, D.M. Quinn, and J.M. Twenge. 1998. "That Swimsuit Becomes You: Sex Differences in Self-Objectification, Restrained Eating and Math Performance." *Journal of Personality and Social Psychology* 75: 269–284.

Freedman, J. 1985. *The Politics of Women's Liberation*. New York: Doubleday.

Freedner, N., L.H. Freed, Y.W. Yang, and S.B. Austin. 2002. "Dating Violence Among Gay, Lesbian, and Bisexual Adolescents: Results from a Community Survey." *Journal of Adolescent Health* 31(6): 469–474.

French, M. 1992. *The War Against Women*. New York: Ballantine Books.

Frenette, M., and S. Coulombe. 2007. *Has Higher Education Among Young Women Substantially Reduced the Gender Gap in Employment and Earnings?* Statistics Canada, Catalogue 11F0019 No. 301, June.

Frenette, M., and K. Zeman. 2007. *Why Are Most University Students Women? Evidence Based on Academic Performance, Study Habits and Parental Influences.* Analytic Studies Branch Research Paper Series, Catalogue No. 11F0019, No. 303, September. Ottawa: Statistics Canada.

Frese, B., M. Moya, and J.L. Megias. 2004. "Social Perception of Rape: How Rape Myth Acceptance Modulates the Influence of Situational Factors." *Journal of Interpersonal Violence* 19(2): 143–161.

Freud, S. 1933/1964. "Femininity." In *New Introductory Lectures on Psychoanalysis:* 112–135. New York: Norton; 1925/1974. "Some Psychical Consequences of the Anatomical Distinction Between the Sexes." In *The Standard Edition of the Complete Works of Sigmund Freud*, ed. J. Strachey: 241–260. London: Hogarth.

Friday, N. 1996. *The Power of Beauty*. New York: Harper Collins.

Friedan, B. 1993. *The Fountain of Age*. New York: Simon & Schuster; 1963. *The Feminine Mystique*. New York: Dell.

Friedmann, E.A., and R.J. Havighurst. 1954. *The Meaning of Work and Retirement*. Chicago: University of Chicago Press.

Frisco, M.L., and K. Williams. 2003. "Perceived Housework Equity, Marital Happiness, and Divorce in Dual-Earner Households." *Journal of Family Issues* 24(1): 51–73.

Frith, S. 1981. *Sound Effects*. New York: Pantheon Books.

Frost, L. 2001. *Young Women and the Body*. New York: Palgrave.

Frye, M. 1992. "Lesbian Sex." In *Essays in Feminism 1976–1992*, ed. M. Frye: 109–119. Freedom, CA: Crossing Press.

Fuertes-Olivera, P.A. 2007. "A Corpus-Based View of Lexical Gender in Written Business English." *English for Specific Purposes* 26(2): 219–234.

Fuller, B., G. Caspary, S.L. Kagan, C. Gauthier, D. Huang, J. Carroll, and J. McCarthy. 2002. "Does Maternal Employment Influence Poor Children's Social Development?" *Early Childhood Research Quarterly* 17(4): 470–497.

Furnham, A. 2001. "Parental Attitudes to Pocket Money/Allowances for Children." *Journal of Economic Psychology* 22(3): 397–422.

Furnham, A., and B. Kirkcaldy. 2000. "Economic Socialization: German Parents' Perceptions and Implementations of Allowances to Educate Children." *European Psychologist* 5(3): 202–215.

Furr, S.R. 2002. "Men and Women in Cross-Gender Careers." In *The Psychology of Sex, Gender, and Jobs*, eds. L. Diamant and J.A. Lee: 47–68. Westport, CT: Praeger.

Furstenberg, F.F., and G.B. Spanier. 1984. *Recycling the Family*. Beverly Hills, CA: Sage.

Gaffield, C. 1990. "The Social and Economic Origins of Contemporary Families." In *Families,* 2nd ed., ed. M. Baker: 23–40. Toronto: McGraw-Hill Ryerson.

Gagne, P., R. Tewksbury, and D. McGaughey. 1997. "Coming Out and Crossing Over: Identity Formation and Proclamation in a Transgender Community." *Gender & Society* 11: 478–508.

Gagnon, J.H. 1977. *Human Sexualities*. Glenview, IL: Scott, Foresman.

Gairdner, W.D. 1992. *The War Against the Family*. Toronto: Stoddart.

Gallahan, L.B. 2000. "Research and Conceptual Approaches to the Understanding of Gender." In *Issues in the Psychology of Women*, eds. M. Biaggio and M. Hersen: 33–52. Dordrecht, Netherlands: Kluwer Academic Publishers.

Gallup Organization. 2000. *Gallup Poll Topics: A–Z.* **www.gallup.com/poll/indicators/indhomo sexual.asp**

Gamache, S.J. 1997. "Confronting Nuclear Family Bias in Stepfamily Research." *Marriage and Family Review* 26(1–2): 41–50.

Gan, S., D. Zilmann, and M. Mitrook. 1997. "Stereotyping Effect of Black Women's Sexual Rap on White Audiences." *Basic and Applied Social Psychology* 19: 381–399.

Ganahl, D.K., T.J. Prinsen, and S.B. Netzley. 2003. "A Content Analysis of Prime Time Commercials: A Contextual Framework of Gender Representation." *Sex Roles* 49(9–10) : 545–551.

Ganong, L.H., and M. Coleman. 1994. *Remarried Family Relationships.* Thousand Oaks, CA: Sage; 1992. "Gender Differences in Expectations of Self and Future Partner." *Journal of Family Issues* 13(1): 55–64.

Gardner, R.A. 2002. "Parental Alienation Syndrome vs. Parental Alienation: Which Diagnosis Should Evaluators Use in Child-Custody Disputes?" *American Journal of Family Therapy* 30(2): 93–115.

Garner, A., H.M. Sterk, and S. Adams. 1998. "Narrative Analysis of Sexual Etiquette in Teenage Magazines." *Journal of Communication* 49: 59–78.

Garner, D.M. 1997. "The 1997 Body Image Survey Results." *Psychology Today* 30: 30–44, 74–80, 84.

Garnets, L.D., G.M. Herek, and B. Levy. 2003. "Violence and Victimization of Lesbians and Gay Men: Mental Health Consequences." In *Psychological Perspectives on Lesbian, Gay, and Bisexual Experiences*, 2nd ed., eds. L.D. Garnets and D.C. Kimmel: 188–206. New York: Columbia University Press.

Garrett, M.T., and B. Barret. 2003. "Two Spirit: Counseling Native American Gay, Lesbian, and Bisexual People." *Journal of Multicultural Counseling and Development* 31(2): 131–142.

Garside, R.B., and B. Klimes-Dougan. 2002. "Socialization of Discrete Negative Emotions: Gender Differences and Links with Psychological Distress." *Sex Roles* 47(3–4): 115–128.

Garst, J., and G.V. Bodenhausen. 1997. "Advertising Effects on Men's Gender Roles." *Sex Roles* 16 (9–10): 551–583.

Gartrell, N., and D. Mosbacher. 1984. "Sex Differences in the Naming of Children's Genitalia." *Sex Roles* 10(11–12): 869–876.

Gaskell, J., A. McLaren, and M. Novogrodsky. 1989/1995. "What's Worth Knowing? Defining the Feminist Curriculum. Claiming an Education: Feminism and Canadian Schools." Toronto: Our Schools/Our Selves Education Foundation. Reprinted in *Gender in the 1990s*, eds. E.D. Nelson and B.W. Robinson, 100–118. Toronto: Nelson Canada.

Gaskell, J., and S. Taylor. 2003. "The Women's Movement in Canadian and Australian Education: From Liberation and Sexism to Boys and Social Justice." *Gender and Education* 15(2): 151–168.

Gastil, J. 1990. "Generic Pronouns and Sexist Language: The Oxymoronic Character of Masculine Generics." *Sex Roles* 23: 629–643.

Gaunt, K.D. 2006. *The Games Black Girls Play.* New York: New York University Press.

Gauvain, M., B.L. Fagot, C. Leve, and K. Kavanagh. 2002. "Instruction by Mothers and Fathers During Problem Solving with Their Young Children." *Journal of Family Psychology* 6(1): 81–90.

Gavigan, S.A. 2000. "Mothers, Other Mothers, and Others: The Legal Challenges and Contradictions of Lesbian Parents." In *Law as a Gendering Practice*, eds. D.E. Chunn and D. Lacombe: 100–118. Don Mills, ON: Oxford University Books.

Gazso-Windle, A., and J. McMullin. 2003. "Doing Domestic Labour: Strategising in a Gendered Domain." *Canadian Journal of Sociology* 28(3): 341–366.

Gecas, V. 1990. "Families and Adolescents: A Review of the 1980s." *Journal of Marriage and the Family* 52: 941–958.

Gee, E.M. 1986. "The Life Course of Canadian Women: An Historical and Demographic Analysis." *Social Indicators Research* 18: 263–283.

Gee, E.M., and M.M. Kimball. 1987. *Women and Aging*. Toronto: Butterworths.

Geiger, B., M. Fischer, and Y. Eshet. 2004. "Date-Rape-Supporting and Victim-Blaming

Among High School Students in a Multi-Ethnic Society." *Journal of Interpersonal Violence* 19(4): 406–426.

Geiger, W., J. Harwood, and M.L. Hummert. 2006. "College Students' Multiple Stereotypes of Lesbians: A Cognitive Perspective." *Journal of Homosexuality* 51(3): 165–182.

Gelles, R. 1993. "Family Violence." In *Family Violence*, eds. R.L. Hampton, T.P. Gullotta, G.R. Adams, E.H. Potter III, and R.P. Weissberg: 1–24. Newbury Park, CA: Sage Publications.

Gentry, M. 1998. "The Sexual Double Standard: The Influence of Number of Relationships and Level of Sexual Activity in Judgments of Women and Men." *Psychology of Women Quarterly* 22(3): 505–511.

George, S. 2002. Female Infanticide in Tamil Nadu, India: From Recognition Back to Denial? **www.hsph.harvard.edu/ Organizations/healthnet/SAsia/suchana/ 0225/george.html**

George, S.M. 2002. "Sex Selection/ Determination in India." *Reproductive Health Matters* 10(19): 190–192.

Gerber, G. 1993. *Women and Minorities on Television*. A Report to the Screen Actors Guild and the American Federation of Radio and Television Artists. Philadelphia: University of Philadelphia.

Gergen, D. 1997. "Promises Worth Keeping." *U.S. News & World Report*, September 20: 78.

Gerrard, N., and N. Javed. 1995. "The Psychology of Women." In *Feminist Issues*, ed. N. Mandell: 123–151. Scarborough, ON: Prentice Hall Canada.

Gershon, A., L.K. Gowen, L. Compian, and C. Hayward. 2004. "Gender-Stereotyped Imagined Dates and Weight Concerns in Sixth-Grade Girls." *Sex Roles* 50(7–8) 515–523.

Gerson, J.M., and K. Peiss. 1985. "Boundaries, Negotiation, Consciousness: Reconceptualizing Gender Relations." *Social Problems* 32: 317–331.

Gerson, K. 1997. "The Social Construction of Fatherhood." In *Contemporary Parenting: Challenges and Issues*, ed. T. Arendell: 119–153. Thousand Oaks, CA: Sage; 1993. *No Man's Land*. New York: Basic Books.

Ghalam, N.Z. 2000. "Paid and Unpaid Work." In Statistics Canada, *Women in Canada 2000: A Gender-Based Statistical Report*: 97–134. Ottawa: Statistics Canada.

Gierveld, J. 2002. "The Dilemma of Repartnering: Considerations of Older Men and Women Entering New Intimate Relationships at Later Life." *Ageing International* 27(4): 61–78.

Gilbert, D., and J.A. Kahl. 1993. *The American Class Structure*, 4th ed. Homewood, IL: Dorsey Press.

Gilbert, H., and J. Tompkins. 1996. *Post-Colonial Drama*. New York: Routledge.

Gilbert, M. 2000. "The Transgendered Philosopher." *International Journal of Transsexualism* 4(3): 13–29.

Gilder, G. 1986. *Men and Marriage*. Gretna, LA: Pelican; 1973. *Sexual Suicide*. New York: Bantam.

Giles-Sims, J. 1997. "Current Knowledge About Child Abuse in Stepfamilies." In *Stepfamilies*, eds. I. Levin and M.B. Sussman: 215–230. New York: Haworth.

Gilham, S.A. 1989. "The Marines Build Men: Resocialization in Recruit Training." In *The Sociological Outlook*, 2nd ed., ed. R. Luhman: 232–244. San Diego: Collegiate Press.

Gillhorn, D. 1992. "Citizenship, 'Race' and the Hidden Curriculum." *International Studies in the Sociology of Education* 2(1): 57–73.

Gill, R. 2008. "Empowerment/Sexism: Figuring Female Sexual Agency in Contemporary Advertising." *Feminism & Psychology* 18(1): 35–60.

Gilligan, C. 1982. *In a Different Voice*. Cambridge, MA: Harvard University Press.

Giorgio, G. 2002. "Speaking Silence: Definitional Dialogues in Abusive Lesbian Relationships." *Violence Against Women* 8(1): 1233–1259.

Giroux, H.A., and M. Schmidt. 2004. "Closing the Achievement Gap: A Metaphor for Children Left Behind." *Journal of Educational Change* 5(3): 213–218.

Giuliano, T.A., K.E. Popp, and J.L. Knight. 2000. "Footballs versus Barbies: Childhood Play Activities as Predictors of Sport Participation by Women." *Sex Roles* 42(3–4): 159–181.

Glascock, J. 2001. "Gender Roles on Prime-Time Network Television: Demographics and Behaviors." *Journal of Broadcasting & Electronic Media* 45(4): 656–669.

Glendon, M.A. 1981. *The New Family and the New Property*. Toronto: Butterworths.

Glenn, D. 2004. "A Dangerous Surplus of Sons?" *The Chronicle of Higher Education* 50 April 30. **www.chronicle/com/free/v50/i34/34a/01401.htm**

Glick, P., J. Diebold, B. Bailey-Werner, and L. Zhu. 1997. "The Two Faces of Adam: Ambivalent Sexism and Polarized Attitudes Toward Women." *Personality and Social Psychology Bulletin* 12: 1323–1334.

Glick, P., and S.T. Fiske. 1999. "Sexism and Other 'Isms': Independence, Status, and the Ambivalent Content of Stereotypes." In *Sexism and Stereotypes in Modern Society*, eds. W.B. Swann, Jr., J.H. Langlois, and L.A. Gilbert: 193–222. Washington, DC: American Psychological Association.

Glossop, R. 1994. "Robert Glossop on the Canadian Family." *Canadian Social Trends* 35: 2–10.

Goddard, A.J. 2003. "Lesbian Love and Relationships." *Journal of Sex & Marital Therapy* 29(4): 323–327.

Goddard, J.C., R.M. Vickery, and T.R. Terry. 2007. "Development of Feminizing Genitoplasty for Gender Dysphoria." *Journal of Sexual Medicine* 4(4): 981–989.

Godenzi, A., M.D. Schwartz, and W.S. DeKeseredy. 2001. "Toward a Gendered Social Bond/Male Peer Support Theory of University Woman Abuse." *Critical Criminology* 10(1): 1–16.

Goldberg, A.E., and M. Perry-Jenkins. 2004. "Division of Labor and Working-Class Women's Well-Being Across the Transition to Parenthood." *Journal of Family Psychology* 18(1): 225–236.

Goldberg, C. 1999. "After Girls Get Attention, Focus is on Boys' Woes." In *Themes of the Times*. Upper Saddle River, N.J.: Prentice-Hall.

Goldberg, S. 1993. *Why Men Rule*. Chicago, IL: University of Chicago Press; 1989. "The Theory of Patriarchy: A Final Summation, Including Responses to Fifteen Years of Criticism." *The International Journal of Sociology and Social Policy* 9(1): 15–62; 1974. *The Inevitability of Patriarchy*. New York: Morrow.

Golden, C. 2004. "Exploring Lesbian Relationships from the Inside." *Psychology of Women Quarterly* 29(2) : 183–184.

Golden, J. 2005. *Message in a Bottle*. Cambridge, MA: Harvard University Press.

Goldie, T. 2001. *In a Queer Country*. Vancouver: Arsenal Pulp Press.

Goldscheider, F., and S. Sassler. 2006. "Creating Stepfamilies: Integrating Children into the Study of Union Formation." *Journal of Marriage and Family* 68(2): 275–291.

Goldscheider, F.K. 1997. "Recent Changes in U.S. Young Adult Living Arrangements in Comparative Perspective." *Journal of Family Issues* 18(6): 708–724.

Goldstein, J. 1998. "Immortal Kombat: War Toys and Violent Video Games." In *Why We Watch*, ed. J.H. Goldstein: 53–68. London: Oxford University Press.

Goldstein, J.R., and C.T. Kenney. 2001. "Marriage Delayed or Marriage Foregone? New Cohort Forecasts of First Marriage for U.S. Women." *American Sociological Review* 66: 506–519.

Golombok, S., and R. Fivush. 1994. *Gender Development*. Cambridge: Cambridge University Press.

Gomme, I. 2004. "Education." In *New Society*, 4th ed., ed. R.J. Brym: 359–381. Scarborough: Nelson Thomson.

Gonzales, M.H., and S.A. Meyers. 1993. "'Your Mother Would Like Me': Self-Presentations in the Personals Ads of Heterosexual and Homosexual Men and Women." *Personality & Social Psychology Bulletin* 19(2): 131–142.

Gonzales, P.M., H. Blanton, and K.J. Williams. 2002. "The Effects of Stereotype Threat and Double-Minority Status on the Test Performance of Latino Women." *Personality & Social Psychology Bulletin* 28(5): 659–670.

Good, G.E., N.B. Sherrod, and M.G. Dillon. 2000. "Masculine Gender Role Stressors and Men's Health." In *Handbook of Gender, Culture and Health*, eds. R.M. Eisler and M. Hersen: 63–81. Mahwah, NJ: Lawrence Erlbaum Associates.

Goode, E. 1996. "Gender and Courtship Entitlement: Responses to Personal Ads." *Sex Roles* 34(3–4): 141–169.

Goode, J. 2007. "Whose Collection Is It Anyway? An Autoethnographic Account of 'Dividing the Spoils' Upon Divorce." *Cultural Sociology* 1(3): 365–382.

Goode, W.J. 1982. "Why Men Resist." In *Rethinking the Family*, eds. B. Thorne and N. Yalom: 287–310. New York: Longmann.

Gooden, A.M., and M.A. Gooden. 2001. "Gender Representation in Notable Children's Picture Books: 1995–1999." *Sex Roles* 45(1–2): 89–102.

Goodman, E., and P. O'Brien. 2000. *I Know Just What You Mean*. New York: Simon and Schuster.

Goodson, P., D. McCormick, and A. Evans. 2001. "Searching for Sexually Explicit Materials on the Internet: An Exploratory Study of College Students' Behavior and Attitudes." *Archives of Sexual Behavior* 30(2): 101–118.

Goodwin, M.H. 2002. "Building Power Asymmetries in Girls' Interaction." *Discourse Society* 13(6): 715–730.

Gordon, J.R., and K.S. Whelan-Berry. 2005. "Contributions to Family and Household Activities by the Husbands of Midlife Professional Women." *Journal of Family Issues* 26(7): 899–923.

Gordon, M., and P.J. Shankweiler. 1971. "Different Equals Less: Female Sexuality in Recent Marriage Manuals." *Journal of Marriage and the Family* 33: 459–466.

Gordon, S. 1990. 1983. *Off Balance*. New York: McGraw-Hill.

Gorman, C. 1997. "A Boy Without a Penis." *Time*, 24, March: 83.

Gorman, K.A., and B.A. Fritzsche. 2002. "The Good-Mother Stereotype: Stay at Home (Or Wish That You Did)." *Journal of Applied Social Psychology* 32(1): 2190–2201.

Gorman-Murray, A. 2006. "Queering Home or Domesticating Deviance: Interrogating Gay Domesticity Through Lifestyle Television." *International Journal of Cultural Studies* 9(2): 227–247.

Gossett, J.L., and S. Byrne. 2002. "'Click Here': A Content Analysis of Internet Rape Sites." *Gender & Society* 16(5): 689–709.

Gottman, J.M. 1993. "The Roles of Conflict Engagement, Escalation, or Avoidance in Marital Interaction: A Longitudinal View of Five Types of Couples." *Journal of Consulting and Clinical Psychology* 61: 6–15.

Gottman, J.M., J. Coan, S. Carrere, and C. Swanson. 1998. "Predicting Marital Happiness and Stability from Newlywed Interactions." *Journal of Marriage and the Family* 60: 5–22.

Gottman, J., with N. Silver. 1994. *Why Marriages Succeed or Fail*. New York: Simon & Schuster.

Gottschalk, L. 2003. "Same-Sex Sexuality and Child Gender Non-Conformity: A Spurious Connection." *Journal of Gender Studies* 12(1): 35–50.

Gough, B. 2002. "'I've Always Tolerated It But...': Heterosexual Masculinity and the Discursive Reproduction of Homophobia." In *Lesbian and Gay Psychology*, eds. A. Coyle and C. Kitzinger: 219–238. Malden, MA: Blackwell Publishers.

Gould, L. 1980/1995. "X: A Fabulous Child's Story." *Ms.*, May: 61–64. Reprinted in *Gender in the 1990s*, eds. E.D. Nelson and B.W. Robinson: 75–82. Toronto: Nelson Canada.

Gould, R. 1976. "Measuring Masculinity by the Size of a Paycheck." In *The Forty-Nine Percent Majority*, eds. D.S. David and R. Brannon: 113–118. Reading, MA: Addison-Wesley.

Gould, R.L. 1978. *Transformations*. New York: Simon & Schuster.

Goulding, W. 2001. *Just Another Indian*. Calgary: Fifth House Ltd.

Government of Ontario. n.d. "Pay Equity: It's a Matter of Fairness." **www.bsa.cbse.org/gol/ bsa/ interface..nsf/engdoc/9.11.2.2.html**

Grace, S.L., R. Fry, A. Cheung, and D.E. Stewart. 2003. "Cardiovascular Disease." In *Women's Health Surveillance Report*: 15–17. Ottawa: Canadian Health Institute.

Graham, A. 1977. "Words That Make Women Disappear." *Redbook*, March: 21.

Graham, H. 1984. *Women, Health and the Family*. Brighton: Wheatsheaf.

Graham, H. III. 2001. "Black, and Navy Too: How Vietnam-Era African-American Sailors Asserted Manhood Through Black Power Militancy." *Journal of Men's Studies* 9(2): 227–241.

Graham, J.E., L.M. Christian, and J.K. Kiecolt-Glaser. 2006. "Marriage, Health and Immune Function." In *Relational Processes and DSM-V*, eds. S.R. Beach, M.Z. Wamboldt, N.J. Kaslow et al.: 61–76. Washington, DC: American Psychiatric Association.

Graham, K., and S. Wells. 2001. "The Two Worlds of Aggression for Men and Women." *Sex Roles* 45(9–10): 595–622.

Grant, J.A., and H.L. Hundley. 2007. "Myths of Sex, Love, and Romance of Older Women in Golden Girls." In *Critical Thinking About Sex, Love, and Romance in the Mass Media*, eds. M. Galician and D.L. Merskin: 121–139. Mahwah, NJ: Lawrence Erlbaum Associates.

Gray, C., and H. Leith. 2004. "Perpetuating Gender Stereotypes in the Classroom: A Teacher Perspective." *Educational Studies* 30(1): 3–17.

Gray, J. 1992. *Men Are From Mars, Women Are From Venus*. New York: HarperCollins.

Gray, S. 1987. "Sharing the Shop Floor." In *Beyond Patriarchy*, ed. M. Kaufman: 216–234. Toronto: Oxford University Press.

Gray-Rosendale, L., and G. Harootunian (eds.) 2003. *Fractured Feminisms*. Albany, NY: State University of New York Press.

Grech, V., P. Vassalio-Agius, and C. Savona-Ventura. 2003. "Secular Trends in Sex Ratios at Birth in North America and Europe over the Second Half of the 20th Century." *Journal of Epidemiology & Community Health* 56(8): 612–615.

Green, B. 1994. "African American Women." In *Women of Color*, eds. L. Comas-Diaz and B. Greene: 10–29. New York: Guilford Press.

Green, R. 1992. *Sexual Science and the Law*. Cambridge, MA: Harvard University Press.

Green, R., and R. Young. 2001. "Hand Preference, Sexual Preference and Transsexualism." *Archives of Sexual Behavior* 30(6): 565–574.

Greene, B.A., and T.K. DeBacker. 2004. "Gender and Orientations Toward the Future: Links to Motivation." *Educational Psychology Review* 16(2): 91–120.

Greenglass, E.R. 1982. *A World of Difference*. Toronto: Wiley.

Greenstein, T.E. 2000. "Economic Dependence, Gender, and the Division of Labor in the Home: A Replication and Extension." *Journal of Marriage and the Family* 62: 322–335.

Greenstein, T.N. 1995. "Gender Ideology, Marital Disruption, and the Employment of Married Women." *Journal of Marriage and the Family* 57(1): 31–42.

Greenwood, N.A. 1999. "Androgyny and Adjustment in Later Life: Living in a Veteran's Home." *Journal of Clinical Geropsychology* 5(2): 127–137.

Greer, G. 1991. *The Change*. New York: Fawcet Columbine.

Grescoe, P. 1996. *The Merchants of Venus*. Vancouver: Raincoast.

Grey, J. 1999. "Family Law." In *Canadian Encyclopedia*, ed. J. Marsh: 816. Toronto: McClelland & Stewart Inc.

Grieve, F.G. 2007. "A Conceptual Model of Factors Contributing to the Development of Muscle Dysmorphia." *Eating Disorders* 15(1): 63–80.

Grieve, F.G., and C.M. Bonneau-Kaya. 2007. "Weight Loss and Muscle Building Content in Popular Magazines Oriented Toward Women and Men." *North American Journal of Psychology* 9(1): 97–102.

Grieve, F.G., D. Wann, C.T. Henson, and P. Ford. 2006. "Healthy and Unhealthy Weight Management Practices in Collegiate Men and Women." *Journal of Sport Behavior* 29(3): 229–241.

Griffin, C. 2002. "Girls' Friendships and the Formation of Sexual Identities." In *Lesbian and Gay Psychology*, eds. A. Coyle and C. Kitzinger: 45–62. Malden, MA: Blackwell Publishers.

Griffiths, C.T., and J.C. Yerbury. 1995. "Understanding Aboriginal Crime and Criminality: A Case Study." In *Canadian Criminology*, eds. M.A. Jackson and C.T. Griffiths: 383–398. Toronto: Harcourt, Brace Canada.

Griffiths, M. 2002. "Invisibility: The Major Obstacle in Understanding and Diagnosing Transsexualism." *Clinical Child Psychology & Psychiatry* 7(3): 493–496; 2000. "Excessive Internet Use: Implications for Sexual Behavior." *CyberPsychology & Behavior* 3(4): 537–552.

Grindstaff, C.F. 1995. "Canadian Fertility, 1951 to 1993." *Canadian Social Trends* 39: 12–16.

Groce, S.B., and M. Cooper. 1990. "Just Me and the Boys? Women in Local-Level Rock and Roll." *Gender & Society* 2: 220–228.

Gross, A.M., T. Bennett, L. Sloan, B.P. Marx, and J. Juergens. 2001. "The Impact of Alcohol and Alcohol Expectations on Male Perception of Female Sexual Arousal in a Data Rape Analog." *Experimental & Clinical Psychopharmacology* 9(4): 380–388.

Gross, J. 1991. "More Young Single Men Still Clinging to Apron Strings." *New York Times*, June 16.

Grossman, A.L., and J.S. Tucker. 1997. "Gender Differences and Sexism in the Knowledge and Use of Slang." *Sex Roles* 37(1–2): 101–110.

Grossman, F.L., L. Kruger, and R.P. Moore. 1999. "Reflections on a Feminist Research Project: Subjectivity and the Wish for Intimacy and Equality." *Psychology of Woman Quarterly* 23(1): 117–135.

Grzywacz, J.G., and D.S. Carlson. 2007. "Conceptualizing Work–Family Balance: Implications for Practice and Research." *Advances in Developing Human Resources* 9(4): 455–471.

Gucciardi, E., N. Celassun, F. Ahmad, and D.E. Stewart. 2003. "Eating Disorders." In *Women's Health Surveillance Report*: 43–44. Ottawa: Canadian Institute for Health Information.

Gudgeon, C. 2003. *The Naked Truth*. Vanvcouver, BC: Greystone Books.

Guerrero, L.K., and W.A. Afifi. 1999. "Toward a Goal-Oriented Approach for Understanding Communicative Responses to Jealousy." *Western Journal of Communication* 63(2): 216–248.

Guiller, J., and A. Durndell. 2007. "Students' Linguistic Behavior in Online Discussion Groups: Does Gender Matter?" *Computers in Human Behavior* 23(5): 2240–2255.

Guimond, S., N.R. Branscombe, S. Brunot, A. Buunk, A. Chatard, M. Desert, D. Garcia, S. Haque, D. Martinot, and V. Yzerbyt. 2007. "Culture, Gender and the Self: Variations and Impact of Social Comparison Processes." *Journal of Personality and Social Psychology* 92(6): 1118–1134.

Gump, L.S., R.C. Baker, and S. Roll. 2000. "Cultural and Gender Differences in Moral Judgment: A Study of Mexican Americans and Anglo-Americans." *Hispanic Journal of Behavioral Sciences* 22(1): 78–103.

Gupta, S. 1999. "The Effects of Transitions in Marital Status on Men's Performance of Housework." *Journal of Marriage and the Family* 61: 700–711.

Gutman, D. 1994. *Reclaimed Powers*. Evanston, IL: Northwestern University Press. 1987. *Reclaimed Powers*. New York: Basic Books.

Guttentag, M., and P.F. Secord. 1983. *Too Many Women?* Beverly Hills: Sage.

Habermeyer, Elmar, Ingrid Kamps, and Wolfram Kawohl. 2003. "A Case of Bipolar Psychosis and Transsexualism." *Psychopathology* 36(3): 168–170.

Hackett, G. 1994. "Online: alt.men.waste-time." *Newsweek*. May 16: 54.

Haddock, G., and M.P. Zanna. 1994. "Preferring 'Housewives' to 'Feminists': Categorization and the Favorability of Attitudes Toward Women." *Psychology of Women* Quarterly 18: 25–52.

Haddock, S.A., T.S. Zimmerman, and K.P. Lyness. 2003. "Changing Gender Norms: Transitional Dilemmas." In *Normal Family Processes*, 3rd ed., ed. F. Walsh: 301–336. New York: Guilford Press.

Hagan, L.K., and J. Kuebli. 2007. "Mothers' and Fathers' Socialization of Preschoolers' Physical Risk Taking." *Journal of Applied Developmental Psychology* 28(1): 2–14.

Haig, D. 2004. "The Inexorable Rise of Gender and the Decline of Sex: Social Change in Academic Titles, 1945–2001." *Archives of Sexual Behavior* 33: 87–96.

Hales, D. 1998/1999. "The Female Brain." In *Ladies' Home Journal*, May: 128, 173, 176, 184. Reprinted in *Marriage and Family: 99/00*, ed. K.R. Gilbert: 36–39. Sluice Dock, Guilford, Con.: Dushkin/McGraw-Hill.

Haley-Banez, L., and J. Garrett. 2002. *Lesbians in Committed Relationships*. New York: Haworth Press.

Halkitis, P. 2001. "An Exploration of Perceptions of Masculinity Among Gay Men Living with HIV." *The Journal of Men's Studies* 9(3): 413–429.

Hall, C.C. 2004. "Mixed-Race Women: One More Mountain to Climb." *Women Therapy* 27(1–2): 237–246.

Hall, J.A., D.R. Carney, and N.A. Murphy. 2002. "Gender Differences in Smiling." In *An Empirical Reflection on the Smile*, ed. M.H. Abel: 155–185. Lewiston, NY: Edwin Mellen Press.

Hall, J.A., J.D. Carter, and T.G. Horgan. 2000. "Gender Differences in Nonverbal Communication of Emotion." In *Gender and Emotion*, ed. A.H. Fischer: 97–117. Cambridge, UK: Cambridge University Press.

Hall, J.A., J.D Carter, M.C. Jimenez, and N.A. Frost. 2002. "Smiling and Relative Status in News Photographs." *Journal of Social Psychology* 142(4): 500–510.

Hall, J.A., E.J. Coats, and L.S. LeBeau. 2005. "Nonverbal Behavior and the Vertical Dimension of Social Relations: A Meta-Analysis." *Psychological Bulletin* 131(6): 898–924.

Hall, J.A., and A.G. Halberstadt. 1997. "Subordination and Nonverbal Sensitivity: A Hypothesis in Search of Support." In *Women, Men, and Gender*, ed. M.R. Walsh: 120–133. New Haven: Yale University Press.

Hall, J.A., T.G. Hogan, and J.D. Carter. 2002. "Assigned and Felt Status in Relation to Observer-Coded and Participant-Reported Smiling." *Journal of Nonverbal Behavior* 26(2): 63–81.

Hall, J.A., N.A. Murphy, and M.S. Mast. 2006. "Recall of Nonverbal Cues: Exploring a Definition of Interpersonal Sensitivity." *Journal of Nonverbal Behavior* 30(4): 141–155.

Hall, J.A., and D.L. Roter. 2002. "Do Patients Talk Differently to Male and Female Physicians? A Meta-Analytic Review." *Patient Education & Counseling* 48(3): 217–224.

Hall, J.A., L.B. Smith LeBeau, J. Gordon, and F. Thayer. 2001. "Status, Gender, and Nonverbal Behavior in Candid and Posed Photographs: A Study of Conversations Between University Employees." *Sex Roles* 44(11–12): 677–692.

Hall, K. 2002. "'Unnatural' Gender in Hindi." In *Gender Across Languages*, Vol. 2, eds. M. Hellinger and H. Bussman: 133–162. Amsterdam, Netherlands: John Benjamin Publishing Company.

Hall, R.L., and C.A. Oglesby. 2002. *Exercise and Sport in Feminist Therapy*. New York: Haworth Press.

Hall, S. 2005. "Change in Paternal Involvement from 1977 to 1997: A Cohort Analysis." *Family and Consumer Sciences Research Journal* 34(2): 127–139; 2002. "Daubing the Drudges of Fury: Men, Violence and the Piety of the 'Hegemonic Masculinity' Thesis." *Theoretical Criminology* 6(1): 35–61.

Halliwell, E., and H. Dittmar. 2003. "A Qualitative Investigation of Women's and Men's Body Image Concerns and Their Attitudes Towards Aging." *Sex Roles* 49(11–12): 675–684.

Halliwell, E., J. Dittmar, and A. Orsborn. 2007. "The Effects of Exposure to Muscular Male Models Among Men: Exploring the Moderating Role of Gym Use and Exercise Motivation." *Body Image* 4(3): 278–287.

Halpern, C.J.T., J.R. Udry, C. Suchindran, and B. Campbell. 2000. "Adolescent Males' Willingness to Report Masturbation." *Journal of Sex Research* 37(4): 327–332.

Hambright, M.K., and J.D. Decker. 2002. "The Unprotected: Sexual Harassment of Lesbians and Gays." In *The Psychology of Sex, Gender and Jobs*, eds. L. Diamant and J.A. Lee: 121–144. Westport, CT: Praeger.

Hamer, D., and P.F. Copeland. 1996. *The Science of Desire*. New York: Touchstone Books.

Hamer, D., P.F. Copeland, S. Hu, V.L. Magnuson, N. Hu, and A.M.L. Pattatucci. 1993. "A Linkage Between DNA Markers on the X Chromosome and Male Sexual Orientation." *Science* 261: 321–327.

Hamilton, M.C., D. Anderson, M. Broaddus, and K. Young. 2006. "Gender Stereotyping and Under-Representation of Female Characters in 200 Popular Children's Picture Books: A Twenty-First Century Update." *Sex Roles* 55(11–12): 757–765.

Hamilton, R. 1996. *Gendering the Vertical Mosaic*. Toronto: Copp Clark.

Han, W., J. Waldfogel, and J. Brooks-Gunn. 2001. "The Effects of Early Maternal Employment on Later Cognitive and Behavioral Outcomes." *Journal of Marriage & the Family* 63(2): 336–354.

Hank, K., and H. Kohler. 2000. "Gender Preferences for Children in Europe: Empirical Results From 17 FFS Countries." *Demographic Research* 2(1).

Hardesty, C., D. Wenk, and C.S. Morgan. 1995. "Paternal Involvement and the Development of Gender Expectations in Sons and Daughters." *Youth and Society* 267(3): 283–297.

Hare-Mustin, R.T., and J. Maracek. 1990. "Gender and the Meaning of Difference." In *Making a Difference*, eds. R.T. Hare-Mustin and J. Maracek: 22–64. New Haven, CT: Yale University Press; 1994. "Asking the Right Questions: Feminist Psychology and Sex Differences." *Feminism & Psychology* 4(4): 531–537.

Hargreaves, D.A., and M. Tiggemann. 2006. "'Body Image Is For Girls': A Qualitative Study of Boys' Body Image." *Journal of Health Psychology* 11(4): 567–576.

Harlow, B.L., L.E. Cohen, and M.W. Otto. 1999. "Prevalence and Predictors of Depressive Symptoms in Older Premenopausal Women." *Archives of General Psychiatry* 56: 418–424.

Harnish, R.J., A. Abbey, and K.G. DeBono. 1990. "Toward an Understanding of 'The Sex Game': The Effects of Gender and Self-Monitoring on Perceptions of Sexuality and Likability in Initial Interactions." *Journal of Applied Social Psychology* 20(16): 1333–1344.

Harper, G.W., and M. Schneider. 2003. "Oppression and Discrimination Among Lesbian, Gay, Bisexual, and Transgendered People and Communities: A Challenge for Community Psychology." *American Journal of Community Psychology* 31(3–4): 243–252.

Harris, I. 1995. *Gender, Change and Society*. Philadelphia, PA: Taylor & Francis.

Harris, K.M., and S.P. Morgan. 1991. "Fathers, Sons, and Daughters: Differential Paternal Involvement in Parenting." *Journal of Marriage and the Family* 53 (3): 531–544. Harrison, K. and B.J. Bond; 2007. "Gaming Magazines and the Drive for Muscularity in Preadolescent Boys: A Longitudinal Examination." *Body Image* 4(3): 269–277.

Harrison, L.J., and J.A. Ungerer. 2002. "Maternal Employment and Infant-Mother Attachment Security at 12 Months Postpartum." *Developmental Psychology* 38(5): 758–773.

Harstock, N. 1998. *The Feminist Standpoint Revisited & Other Essays*. Boulder, CO: Westview Press.

Hartmann, H. 1981. "The Unhappy Marriage of Marxism and Feminism: Towards a More Progressive Union." In *Women and Revolution*, ed. L. Sargent: 1–41. Boston: South End Press.

Hartmann, T., and C. Klimmt. 2006. "Gender and Computer Games: Exploring Females' Dislikes." *Journal of Computer-Mediated Communication* 11(4): 31–55.

Hartnagel. T. 2004. "Correlates of Criminal Behaviour." In *Criminology*, 5th ed., ed. R. Linden: 120–163. Toronto: Harcourt Brace and Company.

Hartouni, V. 1995. "Reproductive Technologies and the Negotiation of Public Meanings: The Case of Baby M." In *Provoking Agents*, ed. J. Kegan Gardiner: 115–132. Chicago: University of Chicago Press.

Hausman, B.L. 2001. "Recent Transgender Theory." *Feminist Studies* 27(2): 465–490.

Hawthorne, S., and R. Klein (eds.) 1999. *Cyberfeminism*. Melbourne: Spinifex.

Hay, D., C. Zahn-Waxler, M. Cummings, and R. Iannotti. 1992. "Young Children's Views about Conflict with Peers: A Comparison of the Daughters and Sons of Depressed and Well Women." *Journal of Child Psychology and Psychiatry* 33: 669–683.

Hayden, D. 1981. *The Grand Domestic Revolution*. Cambridge, MA: MIT Press.

Hayford, A. 1987. "Outlines of the Family." In *Family Matters*, ed. K.L. Anderson et al.: 1–19. Toronto: Methuen.

Hays, S. 1996. *The Cultural Contradictions of Motherhood*. New Haven, CT: Yale University Press.

Hayward, F. 1987. "A Shortage ... of Good Women." *Single Scene Magazine* September: 12.

Health Canada. 2003. *Women's Health Surveillance Report*. Ottawa: Health Canada and the Canadian Population Health Institute; 1999. *Toward a Healthy Future*.

Prepared by the Federal, Provincial, and Territorial Advisory Committee on Population Health for the Meeting of Ministers of Health, Charlottetown, PEI, September.

Heard, A. 2008. "Women & Canadian Elections." **www.sfu.ca/~aheard/elections/women.html**

Heckert, D.A., T.C. Cowak, and K.A. Snyder. 1998. "The Impact of Husbands' and Wives' Relative Earnings on Marital Disruption." *Journal of Marriage and the Family* 60(3): 690–703.

Hefner, R., M. Rebecca, and B. Oleshansky. 1975. "Development of Sex Role Transcendence." *Human Development* 18: 143–158.

Hegarty, P. 2002. "'It's Not a Choice, It's the Way We're Built': Symbolic Beliefs About Sexual Orientation in the U.S. and Britain." *Journal of Community & Applied Social Psychology* 12(3): 153–166.

Hegarty, P., and C. Buechel. 2006. "Androcentric Reporting of Gender Differences in APA Journals: 1965–2004." *Review of General Psychology* 10(4): 377–389.

Hegarty, P., and F. Pratto. 2004. "The Difference That Norms Make: Empricism, Social Constructionism, and the Interpretation of Group Differences." *Sex Roles* 50(7–8): 445–453.

Heider, D., and D. Harp. 2002. "New Hope or Old Power: Democracy, Pornography and the Internet." *Howard Journal of Communications* 13(4): 285–259.

Heikes, E.J. 1991. "When Men Are the Minority: The Case of Men in Nursing." *Sociological Quarterly* 32: 389–401.

Heilbrun, C. 1973. *Reinventing Womanhood*. New York: W.W. Norton & Company.

Heilman, M.E., A.S. Wallen, D. Fuchs, M.M. Tamkins, and M.E. Heilman. 2004. "Penalties for Success: Reactions to Women Who Succeed at Male Gender-Typed Tasks." *Journal of Applied Psychology* 89(3): 416–427.

Heinz, W.R. 2002. "Self-Socialization and Post-Traditional Society." In *New Frontiers in Socialization*, eds. R.A. Settersten and T.J. Owens: 41–64. Kidlington, Oxford: Elsevier Science Ltd.

Hekman, S. 2000. "Beyond Identity: Feminism, Identity and Identity Politics." *Feminist Theory* 1(3): 289–308.

Helburn, S.W., and B.R. Bergmann. 2002. *America's Childcare Problem*. New York: Palgrave.

Held, V. 2001. "Caring Relations and Principles of Justice." In *Controversies in Feminism*, ed. by J. Sterba. Lanham, MD: Rowman & Littlefield.

Hellendoorn, J., and F.J.H. Harinck. 1995. "War Toy Play and Aggression in Kindergarteners." *Kind en Adolescent* 16(4): 228–243.

Helms-Erikson, H. 2001. "Marital Quality Ten Years After the Transition to Parenthood: Implications of the Timing of Parenthood and the Division of Housework." *Journal of Marriage and the Family* 63(4): 1099–1110.

Hendrick, S.S., and C. Hendrick. 2000. "Romantic Love." In *Close Relationships*, eds. C. Hendrick and S.S. Hendrick: 203–215. Thousand Oaks, CA: Sage Publications.

Hendy, H.M., C. Gustitus, and J. Leitzel-Schwalm. 2001. "Social Cognitive Predictors of Body Image in Preschool Children." *Sex Roles* 44(9–10): 557–570.

Henley, N.M. 1995. "Gender Politics Revisited: What Do We Know Today?" In *Gender, Power, and Communication in Human Relationships*, eds. P.J. Kalbfleisch and M.J. Cody: 27–61. Hillsdale, NJ: Erlbaum.

Henley, N.M., B. Gruber, and L. Lerner. 1985. "Studies on the Detrimental Effects of 'Generic' Masculine Usage." Paper presented at the Eastern Psychological Association, Boston, March.

Henley, N., M. Hamilton, and B. Thorne. 1984. *Womanspeak and Manspeak*. St. Paul, MN: West.

Hennessy, D.A., and D.L. Wiesenthal. 2001. "Gender, Driver Aggression, and Driver Violence: An Applied Evaluation." *Sex Roles* 44(11–12): 661–676.

Henry, F., C. Tator, W. Mattis, and T. Rees. 2002. *The Colour of Democracy*. Toronto: Harcourt Brace & Company.

Henry, R.K. 1999. "Child Support at the Crossroads: When the Real World Intrudes

Upon Academics and Advocates." *Family Law Quarterly* 33(1): 235–264.

Henslin, J., D. Glenday, A. Duffy, and N. Pupo. 2004. *Sociology*, 3rd ed. Toronto: Pearson.

Henslin, J., and A. Nelson. 1996. *Sociology*. Scarborough, ON: Allyn & Bacon.

Henthorn, C.L. 2000. "The Emblematic Kitchen: Labor-Saving Technology as National Propaganda, the United States, 1939–1959." *Knowledge and Society* 12: 153–187.

Henwood, K., R. Gill, and C. McLean. 2002. "The Changing Man." *Psychologist*, 15(4): 182–186.

Herman, J.L. 1991. "Sex Offenders: A Feminist Perspective." In *Sexual Assault Issues*, eds. W.I. Marshall, D.R. Laws, and H.E. Barabee: 177–194. New York: Plenum Press.

Herman-Jeglinska, A., A. Grabowska, and S. Dulko. 2002. "Masculinity, Femininity, and Transsexualism." *Archives of Sexual Behavior* 31(6): 527–534.

Herold, E.S., and R.R. Milhausen. 1999. "Dating Preferences of University Women: An Analysis of the Nice Guy Stereotype." *Journal of Sex & Marital Therapy* 25(4): 333–343.

Herrig, S., D. Johnson, and T. Dibenedetto. 1992. "Participation in Electronic Discourse in a Feminist Field." In *Proceedings of the Second Berkeley Women and Language Conference*, eds. K. Hall, M. Bucholz, and B. Moonwoman. Berkeley: University of California.

Herrnson, P.S., J.C. Lay, and A. K. Stokes. 2003. "Women Running 'As Women': Candidate Gender, Campaign Issues, and Voter-Targeting Strategies." *Journal of Politics* 65(1): 244–255.

Hess, B.B., and M.M. Ferree. 1987. "Introduction." In *Analyzing Gender*, eds. B.B. Hess and M.M. Ferree: 9–30. Newbury Park, CA: Sage.

Hesse-Biber, S., and G.L. Carter. 2000. *Working Women in America*. New York: Oxford University Press.

Hetherington, E.M., and R. Cox. 1982. "Effects of Divorce on Parents and Children." In *Nontraditional Families*, ed. M. Lamb. Hillsdale, NJ: Lawrence Erlbaum Associates.

Hetherington, E.M., and M. Stanley-Hagan. 2002. "Parenting in Divorced and Remarried Families." In *Handbook of Parenting*, ed. M.H. Bornstein: 287–315. Mahwah, NJ: Erlbaum Associates.

Heyn, D. 1997. *Marriage Shock*. New York: Villard.

Hicks, T.V., and H. Leitenberg. 2001. "Sexual Fantasies About One's Partner Versus Someone Else: Gender Differences in Intimacy and Frequency." *Journal of Sex Research* 38(1): 43–50.

Hiedermann, B., O. Suhomlinova, and A.M. O'Rand. 1998. "Economic Independence, Economic Status, and Empty Nest in Midlife Marital Disruption." *Journal of Marriage and the Family* 60(1): 219–231.

Higginbotham, E., and L. Weber. 1992. "Moving with Kin and Community: Upward Social Mobility for Black and White Women." *Gender & Society* 6(3): 416–440.

Higgins, C., L. Duxbury, and K. Johnson. 2000. "Part-Time Work for Women: Does It Really Help Balance Work and Family?" *Human Resources Management* 39(1): 17–32.

Higgins, D.J. 2002. "Gay Men from Heterosexual Marriages: Attitudes, Behaviors, Childhood Experiences, and Reasons for Marriage." *Journal of Homosexuality* 42(4): 15–34.

Hill, D.G., and M. Schiff. 1988. *Human Rights in Canada*, 3rd ed. Ottawa: Human Rights and Education Centre, University of Ottawa.

Hill, S.A. 2001. "Class, Race, and Gender Dimensions of Child Rearing in African American Families." *Journal of Black Studies* 31(4): 494–508.

Hill, S.E., and R. Flom. 2007. "18- and 24-Month-Olds' Discrimination of Gender-Consistent and Inconsistent Activities." *Infant Behavior & Development* 30(1): 168–173.

Hillyer, B. 1993. *Feminism and Disability*. Norman, OK: University of Oklahoma Press.

Himsel, A.J., and W. A. Goldberg. 2003. "Social Comparisons and Satisfaction with the Division of Housework: Implications for Men's and Women's Role Strain." *Journal of Family Issues* 24(7): 843–866.

Hines, M. 2004. *Brain Gender*. New York: Oxford University Press.

Hines, M. 1982. "Prenatal Gonadal Hormones and Sex Differences in Human Behavior." *Psychological Bulletin* 92: 56–80.

Hinz, A. 2003. "The Pictures of Women and Men in Jokes: A Qualitative Analysis." *Zeitschrift fuer Sozialpsychologie* 34(1): 37–45.

Hinze, S.W. 2000. "Inside Medical Marriages: The Effect of Gender on Income." *Work and Occupations* 27(4): 464–499.

Hirschman, E.C. 2003. "Men, Dogs, Guns and Cars." *Journal of Advertising* 32(1): 9–22.

Hobart, C. 1996. "Intimacy and Family Life: Sexuality, Cohabitation and Marriage." In *Families*, 3rd ed., ed. M. Baker: 143–173. Toronto: McGraw-Hill Ryerson;1991. "Conflict in Remarriages." *Journal of Divorce and Remarriage* 15: 69–86.

Hobza, C.L., K.E. Walker, O. Yakushko, and J.L. Peugh. 2007. "What About Men? Social Comparison and the Effects of Media Images on Body and Self-Esteem." *Psychology of Men & Masculinity* 8(3): 161–172.

Hochschild, A.R. 2003. *The Commercialization of Intimate Life*. Berkeley: University of California Press; 1997. *The Time Bind*. New York: Metropolitan Books.

Hochschild, A.R., with A. Machung. 1990. *The Second Shift*. New York: Avon.

Hoffnung, M. 1989. "Motherhood: Contemporary Conflict For Women." In *Women*, 4th ed., ed. J. Freeman: 157–175. Palo Alto, CA: Mayfield.

Hoff-Sommers, C. 2000. *The War Against Boys*. New York: Simon & Schuster.

Hogan, C.C. 2003. "Applying Multicultural Competences in the School Setting: Sexual Identity of an African American Adolescent." In *Multicultural Competencies*, ed. G. Roysircar: 173–183. Alexandria, VA: Association for Multicultural Counseling & Development.

Holland, J., C. Ramazanoglu, S. Sharpe, and R. Thomson. 2000. "Deconstructing Virginity: Young People's Accounts of First Sex." *Sexual & Relationship Therapy* 15(3): 221–232.

Hollows, J. 2003. "Oliver's Twist: Leisure, Labour and Domestic Masculinity in the Naked Chief." *International Journal of Cultural Studies* 6(2): 229–248.

Holmes, J. 1998. *Language and Gender*. Walden, MA: Blackwell; 1995. *Women, Men, and Politeness*. London: Longman.

Holmes, V.M. 1995. "A Crosslinguistic Comparison of the Production of Utterances in Discourse." *Cognition* 54(2): 169–207.

Holstein, M.B. 2001–2002. "A Feminist Perspective on Anti-Aging Medicine." *Generations* 25(4): 38–43.

Holt, C.L., and J.B. Ellis. 1998. "Assessing the Current Validity of the Bem Sex Role Inventory." *Sex Roles* 39: 929–931.

Holtgraves, T., and J.N. Yang. 1992. "Interpersonal Underpinnings of Request Strategies: General Principles and Differences Due to Culture and Gender." *Journal of Personality and Social Psychology* 62(2): 246–256.

Honore, C. 2000. "'Male Egg' Could Enable Two Men to Conceive a Child." *National Post*, September 26: A1, A12.

hooks, b. 2003. *Rock My Soul*. New York: Atria Books; 1992. *Black Looks*. Boston, MA: South End Press; 1990. *Yearning*. Boston, MA: South End Press; 1984. *Feminist Theory*. Boston, MA: South End Press; 1981. *Ain't I A Woman*. Boston, MA: South End Press.

Hopf, D., and C. Hatzichristou. 1999. "Teacher Gender-Related Influences in Greek Schools." *British Journal of Educational Psychology* 69(1): 1–18.

Hopkins, J. 2000. "Signs of Masculinism in an 'Uneasy' Place: Advertising for 'Big Brothers.'" *Gender, Place and Culture* 7(1): 31–55.

Hopper, J. 1993. "The Rhetoric of Motives in Divorce." *Journal of Marriage and the Family* 55: 801–813.

Hopper, R. 2003. *Gendering Talk*. East Lansing, MI: Michigan State University Press.

Horney, K. 1967. *Feminine Psychology*. New York: W.W. Norton; 1926/1973. "The Flight from Womanhood." In *Psychoanalysis and Women*, ed. J.B. Miller: 5–20. Baltimore, MD: Penguin Books.

Hort, B.E., and Leinbach, M.D. 1993. "Children's Use of Metaphorical Cues in Gender-Typing of Objects." Paper presented at the meetings of the Society for

Research in Child Development, New Orleans, LA, April.

Hosada, M., E.E. Stone-Romero, and G. Coats. 2003. "The Effects of Physical Attractiveness on Job-Related Outcomes: A Meta-Analysis of Experimental Studies." *Personnel Psychology* 56: 431–462.

Houppert, K; 1999. *The Curse*. New York: Farrar, Straus and Giroux.

Hubbard, R. 1994. "Race and Sex as Biological Categories." In *Challenging Racism and Sexism*, ed. E. Tobach and B. Rosoff. New York: Feminist Press at City University of New York.

Hudson, V.M., and A.M. Den Boer. 2004. *Bare Branches*. Boston, MA: MIT Press.

Hughes, D., E. Galinsky, and A. Morris. 1992. "The Effects of Job Characteristics on Marital Quality: Specifying Linking Mechanisms." *Journal of Marriage and the Family* 54(1): 31–42.

Hughes, K.D. 2003. Gender and Self-Employment in Canada: Assessing Trends and Policy Implications. **www.cprn.com/Release/Back/bgse_e.htm**

Hughes, L.A. 1988. "But That's Not Really Mean: Competing in a Cooperative Mode." *Sex Roles* 19: 669–687.

Humble, A., A.M. Zvonkovic, and A.J. Walker. 2008. "'The Royal We': Gender Ideology, Display and Assessment in Wedding Work." *Journal of Family Issues* 29(1): 3–25.

Hundley, G. 2001. "Domestic Division of Labour and Self: Organizationally Employed Differences in Job Attitudes and Earnings." *Journal of Family and Economic Issues* 22(2): 121–139; 2000. "Male/Female Earnings Differences in Self-Employment: The Effects of Marriage, Children, and the Household Division of Labour." *Industrial and Labor Relations Review* 54(1): 95–114.

Hunter, A.A., and M.A. Denton. 1984. "Do Female Candidates 'Lose Votes'? The Experience of Female Candidates in the 1979 and 1980 Canadian General Elections." *Canadian Review of Sociology and Anthropology* 21(4): 395–406.

Huston, M., and P. Schwartz. 2002. "Gendered Dynamics in the Romantic Relationships of Lesbians and Gay Men." In *Readings in the Psychology of Gender*, eds. A.E. Hunter and C. Forden: 167–178. Needham, MA: Allyn & Bacon.

Hutson-Comeaux, S.L., and J.R. Kelly. 2002. "Gender Stereotypes of Emotional Reactions: How We Judge an Emotion as Valid." *Sex Roles* 47(2–3): 1–10.

Hyde, J.S. 2005. "The Gender Similarities Hypothesis." *The American Psychologist* 60(6): 581–592; 2001. "The Next Decade of Sexual Science: Synergy from Advances in Related Sciences." *Journal of Sex Research* 38(2): 97–101; 2001a. "Reporting Effect Sizes: The Roles of Editors, Textbook Authors, and Publication Manuals." *Educational & Psychological Measurement* 61(2): 225–228; 1985. *Half the Human Experience*. 2nd ed. Toronto: D. C. Heath.

Hyde, J.S., C. I. Hall, N.A. Fouad, G.P. Keita, M.E. Kite, N.F. Russo, and S.S. Brehm. 2002. "Women in Academe: Is the Glass Completely Full?" *American Psychologist* 57(12): 1133–1134.

Hyde, J.S., and S.R. Jaffee. 2000. "Becoming a Heterosexual Adult: The Experiences of Young Women." *Journal of Social Issues* 56(2): 283–296.

Hyde, J.S., M. Krajnik, and K.S. Kuldt-Niederberger. 1991. "Androgyny Across the Life Span: A Replication and Longitudinal Follow-up." *Developmental Psychology* 27: 516–519.

Hyde, J.S., and M.B. Oliver. 2000. "Gender Differences in Sexuality: Results from Meta-Analysis." In *Sexuality, Society, and Feminism*, eds. C.B. Travis and J.W. White: 57–77. Washington, DC: American Psychological Association.

Hyden, M. 2005. "'I Must Have Been an Idiot to Let it Go On': Agency and Positioning in Battered Women's Narratives of Leaving." *Feminism & Psychology* 15(2): 169–188.

Hyers, L.L. 2007. "Resisting Prejudice Everyday: Exploring Women's Assertive Responses to Anti-Black Racism, Anti-Semitism, Heterosexism, and Sexism." *Sex Roles* 56(1–2): 1–12.

Hynie, M., and J.E. Lydon. 1995. "Women's Perceptions of Female Contraceptive Behavior: Experimental Evidence of the Sexual Double Standard." *Psychology of Women Quarterly* 19(4): 563–581.

Hyson, D. 2002. "Understanding Adaptation to Work in Adulthood: A Contextual Development Approach." *Advances in Life Course Research* 7: 93–110.

Ickes, W., P.R. Gesn, and T. Graham. 2000. "Gender Differences in Empathic Accuracy: Differential Ability or Differential Motivation." *Personal Relationships* 7: 95–109.

Idle, T., E. Wood, and S. Desmarais. 1993. "Gender Role Socialization in Toy Play Situations: Mothers and Fathers with Their Sons and Daughters." *Sex Roles* 28: 679–692.

Immen, W. 2004. "Caught in the 'Sandwich.'" *The Globe and Mail*, March 17: C1–C2.

Intons-Peterson, M.J. 1988. *Children's Concepts of Gender*. Norwood, NJ: Ablex.

Inzlicht, M., and T. Ben-Zeiv. 2003. "Do High-Achieving Female Students Underperform in Private? The Implications of Threatening Environments on Intellectual Processing." *Journal of Educational Psychology* 95(4): 796–805.

Island, D., and P. Letellier. 1991. *Men Who Beat the Men Who Love Them*. New York: Haworth.

Itzin, C. 2002. "Pornography and the Construction of Misogyny." *Journal of Sexual Aggression* 8(3): 4–42.

Ivory, J.D. 2006. "Still a Man's Game: Gender Representation in Online Review of Video Games." *Mass Communication and Society* 9(1): 204–114.

Jackson, C., and I.D. Smith. 2000. "Poles Apart? An Exploration of Single-Sex and Mixed-Sexual Educational Environments in Australia and England." *Educational Studies* 26(4): 409–422.

Jackson, L.A., K.S. Ervin, P.D. Gardner, and N. Schmitt. 2001. "The Racial Digital Divide: Motivational, Affective, and Cognitive Correlates of Internet Use." *Journal of Applied Social Psychology* 31(1): 2019–2046; 2001. "Gender and the Internet: Women Communicating and Men Searching." *Sex Roles* 44(5–6): 363–380.

Jackson, S. 2005. "'I'm 15 and Desperate for Sex': 'Doing' and "Undoing' Desire in Letters to a Teenage Magazine." *Feminism & Psychology* 15(3): 295–313; 1992.

"Towards a Historical Sociology of Housework: A Materialist Feminist Analysis." *Women's Studies International Forum* 15(2): 153–172.

Jackson, S., and S. Scott. 1996. "Sexual Skirmishes and Feminist Factions: Twenty-Five Years of Debate on Women and Sexuality." In *Feminism and Sexuality*, eds. S. Jackson and S. Scott: 1–31. New York: Columbia University Press.

Jackson, S.M., and F. Cram. 2003. "Disrupting the Sexual Double Standard: Young Women's Talk About Heterosexuality." *British Journal of Social Psychology* 42(1): 113–127.

Jacobs, J.A. 1993. "Men in Female-Dominated Fields: Trends and Turnover." In *Doing "Women's Work,"* ed. C.L. Williams: 49–63. Thousand Oaks, CA: Sage.

Jaggar, A.M., and P.S. Rothenberg. (eds.) 1993. *Feminist Frameworks*. 3rd ed. New York: McGraw-Hill. 1984. *Feminist Frameworks*. 2nd ed. New York: McGraw-Hill.

Jagger, E. 2001. "Marketing Molly and Melville: Dating in a Postmodern, Consumer Society." *Sociology* 35(1): 39–57.

Jagose, A. 1996. *Queer Theory*. New York: New York University Press.

Jain, T., S.A. Missmer, R.S. Gupta, and M.D. Hornstein. 2005. "Preimplantation Sex Selection Demand and Preferences in an Infertility Population." *Fertility and Sterility* 83: 649–658.

James, D., and J. Drakich. 1993. "Gender Differences in Amount of Talk: Critical Review of Research." In *Gender and Conversational Interaction*, ed. D. Tannen: 276–293. New York: Oxford.

James, N.N. 1989. "Emotional Labor: Skill and Work in the Social Regulation of Feelings." *The Sociological Review* 37(1): 15–42.

James, W.H. 2000. "Secular Movements in Sex Ratios of Adults and of Births in Populations During the Past Half-Century." *Human Reproduction* 15(5): 1178–1183.

James, W.H., and I. Banks. 2001. "The Fragile Male." *British Medical Journal* 322(7285): 617a–617.

James, W.H., P.A. Lancaster, P.L. Day, B. Greenfield, D.L. Davis, M. Gottlieb, and J. Stampnitzky. 1998. "Declines in Population Sex Ratios at Birth." *Journal of the American Medical Association* 280(13): 1139–1141.

Jamieson, K.H. 1995. *Beyond the Double Bind.* New York: Oxford University Press.

Jansz, J., and R.C. Martis. 2007. "The Lara Phenomenon: Powerful Female Characters in Video Games." *Sex Roles* 56(3–4): 141–148.

Jay, T. 1992. *Cursing in America.* Philadelphia: John Benjamins.

Jencks, C., and M. Phillips. 1998. "America's Next Achievement Test: Closing the Black-White Test Score Gap." *The American Prospect* September/October: 44–53.

Jensen, J., S. De Castell, and M. Bryson. 2003. "'Girl Talk': Gender, Equity, and Identity Discourses in a School-Based Computer Culture." *Women's Studies International Forum* 26(6): 561–573.

Jensen, M.A. 1984. *Love's Sweet Return.* Toronto: Women's Educational Press.

Jensen-Campbell, L.A., W.G. Graziano, and S.G. West. 1995. "Dominance, Prosocial Orientation, and Female Preferences: Do Nice Guys Really Finish Last?" *Journal of Personality & Social Psychology* 68(3): 427–440.

Johnson, D.R., and L.K. Scheuble. 2002. "What Should We Call Our Kids? Choosing Children's Surnames When Parents' Last Names Differ." *Social Science Journal* 39(39): 419–429.

Johnson, E.M., and T.L. Huston. 1998. "The Perils of Love, or Why Wives Adapt to Husbands During the Transition to Parenthood." *Journal of Marriage and the Family* 60: 195–204.

Johnson, H. 2007. "Measuring Violence Against Women: Statistical Trends 2006." Statistics Canada, Catalogue no. 85-570. Ottawa: Minister of Industry; 1996. *Dangerous Domains.* Scarborough, ON: Nelson Canada.

Johnson, J.D., M.S. Adams, L. Ashburn, and W. Reed. 1995. "Differential Gender Effects of Exposure to Rap Music on African American Adolescents' Acceptance of Teen Dating Violence." *Sex Roles* 33: 597–605.

Johnson, K. 2007. "Psychology." In *Introduction to Gender*, eds. J. Marchbank and G. Letherby: 111–129. Harlow, England: Pearson Longman.

Johnson, M.D., and B.M. Young. 2003. "Advertising History of Televisual Media." In *The Faces of Televisual Media*, ed. E.L. Palmer: 265–285. Mahwah, NJ: Lawrence Erlbaum Associates.

Johnson, M.P., and K. Ferrero. 2001. "Research on Domestic Violence in the 1990s: Making Distinctions." In *Understanding Families into the New Millennium*, ed. R.M. Milardo: 167–182. Minneapolis, MN: National Council on Family Relations.

Johnson, P. 1976. "Women and Interpersonal Power: Toward a Theory of Effectiveness." *The Journal of Social Issues* 32: 99–110.

Johnston, D.D., and D.H. Swanson. 2006. "Constructing the 'Good Mother': The Experience of Mothering Ideologies by Work Status." *Sex Roles* 54(7–8): 509–519.

Johnston, L., and D. Jenkins. 2004. "Coming Out in Mid-Adulthood: Building a New Identity." *Journal of Gay and Lesbian Social Services* 16(2): 19–42.

Jones, B. E. 2001. "Is Having the Luck of Growing Old in the Gay, Lesbian, Bisexual, Transgender Community Good or Bad Luck?" *Journal of Gay & Lesbian Social Services* 13(4): 13–14.

Jones, L.Y. 1980. *Great Expectations.* New York: Ballantine.

Jones, M.G., A. Howe, and M.J. Rua. 2000. "Gender Differences in Students' Experiences, Interests, and Attitudes Toward Science and Scientists." *Science Education* 84(2): 180–192.

Jones, R.M., D.E. Taylor, A.J. Dick, A. Singh, and J.L. Cook. 2007. "Bedroom Design and Decoration: Gender Differences in Preference and Activity." *Adolescence* 42(167): 539–553.

Jordan, E., and A. Cowan. 1995. "Warrior Narratives in the Kindergarten Classroom: Renegotiating the Social Contract?" *Gender & Society* 9(6): 727–743.

Jordan, T., and P. Taylor. 1998. "A Sociology of Hackers." *Sociological Review* (November): 757–778.

Josephs, R.A., M.A. Newman, R.P. Brown, and J.M. Beer. 2003. "Status, Testosterone, and Human Intellectual Performance. Stereotype Threat as Status Concern." *Psychological Science* 14(2): 158–163.

Jozefowicz, D.M., B.L. Barber, and J.S. Eccles. 1993. (March). "Adolescent Work-Related Values and Beliefs: Gender Differences and Relation to Occupational Aspirations." Paper presented at the biennial meeting of the Society for Research on Child Development, New Orleans, LA.

Julien, A., and H. Ertl. 1999. "Children's School Experiences in the NLSCY, 1994–1995." *Education Quarterly Review* 6(2): 20–34. Statistics Canada Catalogue 81-003.

Julien, D., E. Chartrand, and J. Begin. 1999. "Social Networks, Structural Interdependence, and Conjugal Adjustment in Heterosexual, Gay, and Lesbian Couples." *Journal of Marriage and the Family* 61: 516–530.

Jung, C.G. 1982. *The Complete Works*. London: Routledge & Kegan Paul.

Jung, J., and M. Peterson. 2007. "Body Dissatisfaction and Patterns of Media Use Among Preadolescent Children." *Family and Consumer Sciences Research Journal* 36(1): 40–54.

Jurgensen, M., O. Hiort, P. Holterhus, and U. Thyen. 2007. "Gender Role Behavior in Children with XY Karyotype and Disorders of Sex Development." *Hormones and Behavior* 51(3): 443–453.

Kacen, J.J. 2000. "Girrrl Power and Boyyy Nature: The Past, Present, and Paradisal Future of Consumer Gender Identity." *Marketing Intelligence & Planning* 18(6–7): 345–355.

Kaestle, C.E., C.T. Halpern, and J.D. Brown. 2007. "Music Videos, Pro Wrestling, and Acceptance of Date Rape among Middle School Males and Females: An Exploratory Analysis." *Journal of Adolescent Health* 40(2): 185–187.

Kahan, N., and N. Norris. 1994. "Creating Gender Expectations Through Children's Advertising." In *Images of the Child*, ed. H. Eiss. Bowling Green, OH: Bowling Green State University Press.

Kalbach, M.A. 2000. "Ethnicity and the Altar." In *Perspectives on Ethnicity in Canada*, eds. M.A. Kalbach and W.E. Kalbach; 111–121. Toronto: Harcourt Canada.

Kalbach, W.E., and W.W. McVey. 1979. *The Demographic Bases of Canadian Society*. 2nd ed. Toronto: McGraw-Hill Ryerson.

Kalbfleisch, P.J., and A.L. Herold. 2006. "Sex, Power and Communication." In *Sex Differences and Similarities in Communication*, 2nd edition, eds. K. Dindia and D.J. Canary: 299–313. Mahwah, NJ: Lawrence Erlbaum Associates.

Kallen, E. 2003. *Ethnicity and Human Rights in Canada*. 3rd ed. Don Mills, ON: Oxford University Press.

Kalof, L. 1999. "The Effects of Gender and Music Video Imagery on Sexual Attitudes." *Journal of Social Psychology* 139: 378–385.

Kalmijn, M. 2002. "Sex Determinants of Friendship Networks: Individual and Structural Determinations of Having Cross-Sex Friends." *European Sociological Review* 18(1): 101–117.

Kalmijn, M., and M.B. Van Groenou. 2005. "Differential Effects of Divorce on Social Integration." *Journal of Social and Personal Relationships* 22(4): 455–476.

Kamin, L.J. 1985. "Genes and Behavior: The Missing Link." *Psychology Today* 19(10): 76–78.

Kaminer, W. 1999. "The Trouble with Single-Sex Schools." *The Atlantic Monthly* April 28 1(4): 22–36. **www.theatlantic.com/issues/98apri/singsex.htm**

Kanin, E.J. 2003. "Date Rapists: Differential Sexual Socialization and Relative Deprivation." In *Violence and Society*, ed. M. Silberman: 207–224. Upper Saddle River, NJ: Prentice Hall.

Kanneh, K. 1998. "Black Feminisms" in *Contemporary Feminist Theories*, eds. S. Jackson and J. Jones. New York: New York University Press.

Kanter, R. 1977. "Some Effects of Proportions on Group Life: Skewed Sex Ratios and Responses to Token Women." *American Journal of Sociology* 82: 965–990.

Kantrowitz, B. 1994. "Men, Women & Computers." *Newsweek*, May 16: 48–55.

Kaplan, H.S. 1974. *The New Sex Therapy*. New York: Brunner/Mazel.

Kaplan, J., and A. Bernays. 1997. *The Language of Names*. New York: Simon & Schuster.

Kaplan, L.J. 1991. *Female Perversions*. New York: Anchor Books.

Karniol, R. 2001. "Adolescent Females' Idolization of Male Media Stars as a Transition into Sexuality." *Sex Roles* 44(1–2): 61–77.

Karraker, K.H., and M. Stern. 1990. "Infant Physical Attractiveness and Facial Expression: Effects of Adult Perceptions." *Basic and Applied Social Psychology* 11(4): 371–385.

Karraker, K.H., D.A. Vogel, and M.A. Luke. 1995. "Parents' Gender-Stereotyped Perceptions of Newborns: The Eye of the Beholder Revisited." *Sex Roles* 33(9–10): 687–701.

Kashak, E. 1992. *Engendered Lives*. New York: Basic Books.

Katsurada, E., and Y. Sugihara. 2002. "Gender-Role Identity, Attitudes Toward Marriage, and Gender-Segregated School Backgrounds." *Sex Roles* 45(5–6): 249–258.

Katz, J.N. 1995. *The Invention of Heterosexuality*. New York: Dutton.

Katz, R.C., R. Hannon, and L. Whitten. 1996. "Effects of Gender and Situation on the Perception of Sexual Harassment." *Sex Roles* 34(1–2): 35–43.

Kaufman, G. 1999. "The Portrayal of Men's Family Roles in Television Commercials." *Sex Roles* 41(5–6): 349–358.

Kaufman, G., and H. Taniguchi. 2006. "Gender and Marital Happiness in Later Life." *Journal of Family Issues* 27(6): 735–757.

Kaufman, M. 1993. *Cracking the Armour*. Toronto: Penguin; 1987. *Beyond Patriarchy*. Toronto: Oxford University Press.

Kay, F.M. 1997. "Flight from Law: A Competing Risks Model of Departures from Law Firms." *Law and Society Review* 31(2): 301–333.

Kay, F.M., C. Masuch, and P. Curry. 2004. *Diversity and Change*. Report to the Law Society of Upper Canada.

Keegan, C. 2006. "Household Remedies of Queer Containment in the Television Movie." *Journal of Lesbian Studies* 10(1–2): 107–123.

Keightley, K. 2003. "Low Television, High Fidelity: Taste and the Gendering of Home Entertainment Technologies." *Journal of Broadcasting & Electronic Media* 47(2): 236–259.

Keller, J. 2002. "Blatant Stereotype Threat and Women's Math Performance: Self-Handicapping as a Strategic Means to Cope with Obtrusive Negative Performance Expectations." *Sex Roles* 47(3–4): 193–198.

Keller, J., and D. Dauenheimer. 2003. "Stereotype Threat in the Classroom: Dejection Mediates the Disrupting Threat Effect on Women's Math Performance." *Personality & Social Psychology Bulletin* 29(3): 371–381.

Kelley, P. 2003–2004. "Suddenly Siblings: Helping Children Adapt to Life in a Stepfamily." *Transition Magazine* 33(4): 8–11.

Kelly, A.W., K.C. Buckwalter, G. Hall, A.L. Weaver, and H.K. Butcher. 2002. "The Caregivers' Story: Home Caregiving for Persons with Dementia." *Home Health Care Management & Practice* 14(2): 99–109.

Kelly, J., and D.G. Bazzini. 2001. "Gender, Sexual Experience, and the Sexual Double Standard: Evaluations of Female Contraceptive Behavior." *Sex Roles* 45(11–12): 785–799.

Kelly, J.R., and S.L. Huston-Comeau. 1999. "Gender-Emotion Stereotypes Are Context Specific." Sex Roles 40(1–2): 107–120.

Kelly, R.F., and R.C. Rinaman. 2003. "The Structure and Prediction of Classes of Divorce Settlements Involving Dependent Children in a National Sample." *Journal of Divorce & Remarriage* 38(3–4): 1–29.

Kendall, D.J., L. Murray, and R. Linden. 2000. *Sociology in Our Times*. 2nd Canadian ed. Toronto: Nelson Thomson Learning.

Kennedy, R., and T. Zamuner. 2006. "Nicknames and the Lexicon of Sports." *American Speech* 81(4): 387–422.

Kennelly, I., S.N. Merz, and J. Lorber. 2001. "What Is Gender?" *American Sociological Review* 66(4): 598–605.

Kenney, C.T. 2006. "The Power of the Purse: Allocative Systems and Inequality in Couple Households." *Gender & Society* 20(3): 354–381.

Kennison, R. 2002. "Clothes Make the (Wo)man: Marlene Dietrich and 'Double Drag.'" *Journal of Lesbian Studies* 6(2): 147–156.

Kennison, S.M., and J.L. Trofe. 2003. "Comprehending Pronouns: A Role for Work-Specific Gender Stereotype Information." *Journal of Psycholinguistic Research* 32(3): 355–378.

Kenny, L.D. 2002. "Daughters of Suburbia: Growing Up White, Middle Class, and Female." *Adolescence* 37(147): 651–652.

Kephart, W.M. 1966. *The Family, Society and the Individual*. 2nd ed. Boston: Houghton Mifflin.

Kerig, P., P. Cowan, and C. Cowan. 1993. "Marital Quality and Gender Differences in Parent–Child Interaction." *Developmental Psychology* 29: 931–939.

Kerpelman, J.L., and P.L. Schvaneveldt. 1999. "Young Adults' Anticipated Identity Importance of Career, Marital and Parental Roles: Comparisons of Men and Women with Different Role Balance Orientations." *Sex Roles* 41: 189–217.

Kersting, A., M. Reutemann, U. Gast, P. Ohrmann, T. Suslow, N. Michael, and V. Arolt. 2003. "Dissociative Disorders and Traumatic Childhood Experiences in Transsexuals." *Journal of Nervous & Mental Disease* 191(3): 182–189.

Kessler, R.C. 2000. "Gender Differences in Major Depression: Epidemiological Findings." In *Gender and Its Effects on Psychopathology*, ed. E. Frank: 61–84. Washington, DC: American Psychiatric Publishing.

Kessler, S.J. 1990/1995. "The Medical Construction of Gender: Case Management of Intersexed Infants." In *Signs* 16(2): 3–26. Reprinted in *Gender in the 1990s*, eds. E.D. Nelson and B.W. Robinson: 8–28. Toronto: Nelson Canada.

Kessler, S., and W. McKenna. 2000. "Who Put the 'Trans' in Transgender? Gender Theory and Everyday Life." *International Journal of Transgenderism* 4(3): 31–59; 1978. *Gender*. New York: John Wiley and Sons.

Ketchum, M.D. 2000. "Disembodied Plastic Sexuality: The Internet and Sexual Discourse—How Do We Study It?" Paper presented at the meetings of the Southern Sociological Society.

Kettle, J. 1980. *The Big Generation*. Toronto: McClelland and Stewart.

Kheshgi-Genovese, Z., and T.A. Genovese. 1997. "Developing the Spousal Relationship within Stepfamilies." *Families in Society* 78(3): 255–264.

Kibby, M., and B. Costello. 2001. "Between the Images and the Act: Interactive Sex Entertainment on the Internet." *Sexualities* 4(3): 353–369.

Kiefer, A.K., and D.T. Sanchez. 2007. "Scripting Sexual Passivity: A Gender Role Perspective." *Personal Relationships* 14(2): 269–290.

Kiefer, A.K., D.T. Sanchez, and C.J. Kalinka. 2006. "How Women's Nonconscious Association of Sex with Submission Relates to their Subjective Sexual Arousability and Ability to Reach Orgasm." *Sex Roles* 55(1): 83–94.

Kiefer, A.K., and D. Sekaquaptewa. 2007. "Implicit Stereotypes, Gender Identification, and Math-Related Outcomes: A Prospective Study of Female College Students." *Psychological Science* 18(1): 13–18.

Kierkus, C.A., and D. Baer. 2003. "Does the Relationship Between Family Structure and Delinquency Vary According to Circumstances? An Investigation of Interaction Effects." *Canadian Journal of Criminology* 45(4): 405–429.

Kilbourne, B.S., G. Farkas, K. Beron, D. Weir, and P. England. 1994. "Return to Skill, Compensating Differentials and Gender Bias: Effects of Occupational Characteristics on the Wages of White Women and Men." *American Journal of Sociology* 100: 689–719.

Killoran, M.M. 1984. "The Management of Tension: A Case Study of Chatelaine Magazine 1939–1980." *Journal of Comparative Family Studies* XV: 3: 407–426.

Kim, J.L., and L.M. Ward. 2007. "Silence Speaks Volumes: Parental Sexual Communication Among Asian American Emerging Adults." *Journal of Adolescent Research* 22(1): 3–31.

Kimball, M.M. 2007. "Adding Gender to the Mix: A Commentary on 'Toward a Redefinition of Sex and Gender.'" *Feminism & Psychology* 17(4): 453–458.

Kimmel, D.C. 1980. *Adulthood and Aging*, 3rd ed. New York: John Wiley and Sons.

Kimmel, M.S. 2003. "Globalization and Its Mal(e)contents: The Gendered Moral and Political Economy of Terrorism." *International Sociology* 18(3): 603–620; 2002. "'Gender Symmetry' in Domestic Violence: A Substantive and Methodological Research Review."

Violence Against Women 8(11): 1332–1363; 2001. "Masculinity as Homophobia: Fear, Shame and Silence in the Construction of Gender Identity." In *The Masculinities Reader*, eds. S.M. Whitehead and F.J. Barrett: 266–287. Cambridge: Polity; 2000. *The Gendered Society*. New York: Oxford University Press.

Kimmel, M.S., and M. Mahler. 2003. "Adolescent Masculinity, Homophobia, and Violence: Random School Shootings, 1982–2001." *American Behavioral Scientist* 46(10): 1439–1458.

Kimmel, M.S., and R.F. Plante. 2002. "The Gender of Desire: The Sexual Fantasies of Women and Men." *Advances in Gender Research* 6: 55–77.

Kimura, D. 2002. "Sex Differences in the Brain." Scientific American, Special Edition: 32–37.

King, D. 2003. "Gender Migration: A Sociological Analysis (or the Leaving of Liverpool)." *Sexualities* 6(2): 173–194.

King, M., J. Gartrell, and F. Travato. 1991. "Early Childhood Mortality, 1926–1986." *Canadian Social Trends* 21: 6–10.

Kinsella, S. 2001. *Confessions of a Shopaholic*. New York: Bantam Dell.

Kinsey, A., C. Pomeroy, W. Gebhard, and C. Martin. 1953. *Sexual Behavior in the Human Female*. Philadelphia: W.B. Saunders.

Kinsey, A., C. Pomeroy, and C. Martin. 1948. *Sexual Behavior in the Human Male*. Philadelphia: W.B. Saunders.

Kinsman, G. 1996. *The Regulation of Desire: Homo and Hetero Sexualities*. 2nd ed. Montreal: Black Rose; 1987. *The Regulation of Desire: Sexuality in Canada*. Montreal: Black Rose.

Kippen, R., A. Evans, and E. Gray. 2007. "Parental Preference for Sons and Daughters in a Western Industrial Setting: Evidence and Implications." *Journal of Biosocial Science* 39: 583–597.

Kirchler, E. 1992. "Adorable Women, Expert Man: Changing Gender Images of Women and Men in Management." *European Journal of Social Psychology* 22: 363–373.

Kirkland, G., with G. Lawrence. 1986. *Dancing on My Grave*. Garden City, NY: Doubleday.

Kirkland, S., L. Greaves, and P. Devichand. 2003. "Gender Differences in Smoking and Self-Reported Indicators of Health." In *Women's Health Surveillance Report* 11–12. Ottawa: Canadian Institute for Health Information.

Kirkup, G., L. Janes, K. Woodward, and F. Hovenden (eds.) 2000. *The Gendered Cyborg* London: Routledge.

Kirkwood, C. 1993. *Leaving Abusive Partners*. Newbury Park, CA: Sage.

Kissling, E.A. 2002. "On the Rag on Screen: Menarche in Film and Television." *Sex Roles* 46(1–2): 5–12.

Kitson, G.C. 1992. *Portrait of Divorce*. New York: Guilford.

Kitzinger, C. 2005. "'Speaking as a Heterosexual': (How) Does Sexuality Matter for Talk-in-Interaction?" *Research on Language and Social Interaction* 38(3): 221–265.

Klein, M. 1957. *Envy and Gratitude*. London: Tavistock; 1998. "Women's Trip to the Top." *American Demographics*, February: 22.

Kline, R.R. 1997. "Ideology and Social Surveys: Reinterpeting the Effects of 'Laboursaving' Technology on American Farm Women." *Technology and Culture* 38(2): 355–385.

Klinetob, N.A., and D.A. Smith. 1996. "Demand-Withdraw Communication in Marital Interaction: Tests of Interspousal Contingency and Gender Role Hypotheses." *Journal of Marriage and the Family* 58: 945–957.

Klotz, H. 1999. "Real Girls Do Play Sports." *Ottawa Citizen*, June 16. **www.caaws.ca/ Girls/ottcitz_jun16.htm**

Klute, M.M., A.C. Crouter, A.G. Sayer, and S.M. McHale. 2002. "Occupational Self-Direction, Values, and Egalitarian Relationships: A Study of Dual-Earner Couples." *Journal of Marriage and the Family* 64(1): 139–151.

Knight, G.P., I.K. Guthrie, M.C. Page, and R.A. Fabes. 2002. "Emotional Arousal and Gender Differences in Aggression: A Meta-Analysis." *Aggressive Behavior* 28(5): 366–393.

Knight, J.L., and T.A. Giuliano. 2001. "He's A Laker; She's a 'Looker': The Consequences of Gender-Stereotypical Portrayals of Male and Female Athletes by the Print Media." *Sex Roles* 45(3–4): 217–230.

Knox, D. 1998. *The Divorced Dad's Survival Book*. New York: Insight Books.

Knox, D., and C. Schacht. 1997. *Choices in Relationships*, 5th ed. Belmont, CA: Wadsworth.

Knudson-Martin, C., and A.R. Mahoney. 1998. "Language and Processes in the Construction of Equality in New Marriages." *Family Relations* 47: 81–91.

Koch, J. 2003. "Gender Issues in the Classroom." In *Handbook of Psychology: Educational Psychology*, eds. W.M. Reynolds and G.E. Miller: 259–281. New York: John Wiley & Sons.

Koenig, D., and R. Linden. 2004. "Conventional or 'Street' Crime." In *Criminology*, 5th ed., ed. R. Linden: 408–443. Toronto: Nelson Thomson.

Koenig, S. 2002. "Walk Like a Man: Enactments and Embodiments of Masculinity and the Potential for Multiple Genders." *Journal of Homosexuality* 43(3–4): 145–159.

Kohlberg, L. 1966. "A Cognitive-Developmental Analysis of Children's Sex Role Concepts and Attitudes." In *The Development of Sex Differences*, ed. E. Maccoby: 82–172. Stanford, CA: Stanford University Press.

Kohn, M.L. 1983. "On the Transmission of Values in the Family: A Preliminary Formulation." *Research in Sociology of Education and Socialization* 4: 3–12.

Kohn, M.L., and K.M. Slomczynski. 2001. "Social Structure and Self-Direction." In *Self in Society*, ed. A. Branaman: 210–217. Malden, MA: Blackwell.

Kojima, Y., Y. Hayashi, K. Mizuno, S. Sasaki, Y. Fukui, P. Koopman, K. Morohashi, and K. Kohri. 2007. "Up-Regulation of S0X9 in Human Sex-Determining Region on the Y Chromosome (SRY)-Negative XX Males." *Clinical Endocrinology* 68(5): 791–799.

Komaromy, M., A. Bindman, R. Haber, and M. Sande. 1993. " Sexual Harassment in Medical Training." *New England Journal of Medicine* 328: 322–326.

Komarovsky, M. 1988. "The New Feminist Scholarship: Some Precursors and Polemics." *Journal of Marriage and the Family* 50: 585–593.

Kompter, A. 1989. "Hidden Power in Marriage." *Gender & Society* 3: 187–216.

Kong, R. 1997. "Criminal Harassment in Canada." *Canadian Social Trends* 45: 29–33.

Kornblum, J. 2006. "Adults Question MYSpace's Safety." *USA Today*, January 8.

Korobov, N. 2004. "Inoculating Against Prejudice: A Discursive Approach to Homophobia and Sexism in Adolescent Male Talk." *Psychology of Men & Masculinity* 5(2): 178–189.

Kortenhaus, C.M., and J. Demarest. 1993. "Gender Role Stereotyping in Children's Literature: An Update." *Sex Roles* 28: 219–232.

Koziel, S., and B. Pawloski. 2003. "Comparison Between Primary and Secondary Mate Markets: An Analysis of Data from Lonely Hearts Columns." *Personality & Individual Differences* 35(8): 1849–1857.

Krahe, B., R. Scheinberger-Olwig, and S. Kolpin. 2000. "Ambiguous Communication of Sexual Intentions as a Risk Marker of Sexual Aggression." *Sex Roles* 42(5–6): 313–338.

Krahe, B., R. Scheinberger-Olwig, and S. Schuetze. 2001. "Risk Factors of Sexual Aggression and Victimization Among Homosexual Men." *Journal of Applied Social Psychology* 31(7): 1385–1408.

Krahn, H.K., and G.S. Lowe. 1993. *Women, Industry and Canadian Society*. 2nd ed. Scarborough, ON: Nelson Canada.

Krakauer, I.D., and S.M. Rose. 2002. "The Impact of Group Membership on Lesbians' Physical Appearance." *Journal of Lesbian Studies* 6(1): 31–43.

Kramarae, C. 1981. *Women and Men Speaking*. Rowley, MA: Newbury; 1980. "Proprietors of Language." In *Women and Language in Literature and Society*, eds. S. McConnell-Ginet, R. Borker, and N. Furman: 58–68. New York: Praeger; 1975. "Women's Speech: Separate but Unequal?" In *Language and Sex*, eds. B. Thorne and N. Henley: 43–56. Rowley, MA: Newbury House Publishers.

Kramarae, C., and H.J. Taylor. 1993. "Women and Men on Electronic Networks: A Conversation or a Monologue?" In *Women, Information Technology, and Scholarship*, eds. H.J. Taylor, C. Kramarae, and M. Ebben. Urbana-Champaign, IL: Center for Advanced Studies, University of Illinois.

Kraemer, S. 2000. "The Fragile Male." *BMJ* 321: 1609–1612. **http://bmj.bmjjournals.com/ cgi/content/full/321/7276/1609?ikey= aaa137b6128593b9e87**

Krane, V., P.Y. Choi, S.M. Baird, C.M. Aimar, and K.J. Kauer. 2004. "Living the Paradox: Female Athletes Negotiate Femininity and Muscularity." *Sex Roles* 50(5–6): 315–329.

Krassas, N.R., J.M. Blauwkamp, and P. Wesselink. 2001. "Boxing Helena and Corseting Eunice: Sexual Rhetoric in Cosmopolitan and Playboy Magazines." *Sex Roles* 44(11–12): 751–772.

Kroska, A. 2003. "Investigating Gender Differences in the Meaning of Household Chores and Child Care." *Journal of Marriage and the Family* 65(2): 456–473.

Krull, C.D. 1996. "From the King's Daughters to the Quiet Revolution: A Historical Overview of Family Structures and the Role of Women in Quebec." In *Voices*, ed. M. Lynn: 370–396. Toronto: Nelson Canada.

Kuebli, J., S.A. Butler, and R. Fivush. 1995. "Mother–Child Talk About Past Emotions: Relations of Maternal Language and Child Gender Over Time." *Cognition and Emotion* 9: 265–283.

Kuehnle, K., and A. Sullivan. 2003. "Gay and Lesbian Victimization: Reporting Factors in Domestic Violence and Bias Incidents." *Criminal Justice & Behavior* 30(1): 85–96.

Kurdek, L.A. 2003. "Differences Between Gay and Lesbian Cohabiting Couples." *Journal of Social & Personal Relationships* 20(4): 411–436; 2002. "Predicting the Timing of Separation and Marital Satisfaction: An Eight-Year Prospective Longitudinal Study." *Journal of Marriage & Family* 64(1): 163–179; 2000. "Attractions and Constraints as Determinants of Relationship Commitment: Longitudinal Evidence from Gay, Lesbian and Heterosexual Couples." *Personal Relationships* 7(3): 245–262; 2000a. "The Link Between Sociotropy/Autonomy and Dimensions of Relationship Commitment: Evidence From Gay and Lesbian Couples." *Personal Relationships* 7(2): 153–164; 1998. "Relationship Outcomes and Their Predictors: Longitudinal Evidence from Heterosexual Married, Gay Cohabiting Couples." *Journal of Marriage and the Family* 60: 553–568; 1994. "Areas of Conflict for Gay, Lesbian and Heterosexual Couples: What Couples Argue About Influences Relationship Satisfaction." *Journal of Marriage and the Family* 56(4): 923–934; 1993. "The Allocation of Household Labor in Gay, Lesbian, and Heterosexual Married Couples." *Journal of Social Issues* 49(3): 127–139; 1991. "The Relations Between Reported Well-Being and Divorce History, Availability of a Proximate Adult, and Gender." *Journal of Marriage and the Family* 53(1): 71–78.

Kwak, H., G.M. Zinkhan, and J.R. Dominick. 2002. "The Moderating Role of Gender and Compulsive Buying Tendencies in the Cultivation Effects of TV shows and TV Advertising: A Cross-Cultural Study Between the United States and South Korea." *Media Psychology* 4(1): 77–111.

Kyratzis, A. 2001. "Emotion Talk in Preschool Same-Sex Friendship Groups: Fluidity Over Time and Context." *Early Education & Development* 12(3): 359–392.

LaCampagne, C., P.B. Campbell, S. Damarin, A.H. Herzig, and C.M. Vogt. 2007. "Gender Equity in Mathematics." In *Handbook for Achieving Gender Equity Through Education*, eds. S.S. Klein, B. Richardson, D.A. Grayson, L. Fox, C. Kramarae et al.: 235–253. Mahwah, NJ: Lawrence Erlbaum Associates.

Ladas, A.K., B. Whipple, and J.D. Perry. 1982. *The G Spot and Other Recent Discoveries About Human Sexuality*. New York: Holt, Rinehart and Winston.

Laframboise, D. 1996. *Princess at the Window*. Toronto: Penguin.

LaFrance, M. 1992. "Gender and Interruptions: Individual Infraction or Violation of the Social Order." *Psychology of Women Quarterly* 16(4): 497–512.

LaFrance, M., and M.A. Hecht. 2000. "Gender and Smiling: A Meta-Analysis." In *Gender and Emotion*, ed. A.H. Fischer: 118–142. New York: Cambridge University Press.

Laird, J. 2003. "Lesbian and Gay Families." In *Normal Family Processes*, 3rd ed., ed. F. Walsh: 176–209. New York: Guilford.

Lakoff, R. 1975. *Language and Woman's Place*. New York: Harper Colophon.

Lam, V.L., and P.J. Leman. 2003. "The Influence of Gender and Ethnicity on Children's Inferences About Toy Choice." *Social Development* 12(2): 269–287.

Lamanna, M.A., and A. Riedmann. 2000. *Marriages and Families*. Belmont, CA: Wadsworth.

Lamb, M.E. (ed.). 1987. *The Father's Role*. Hillsdale, NJ: Lawrence Erlbaum.

Lamb, S. and L.M. Brown. 2006. *Packaging Girlhood*. New York: St. Martin's Press.

Lammers, C., M. Ireland, M. Resnick, and R. Blum. 2000. "Influences on Adolescents' Decision to Postpone Onset of Sexual Intercourse: A Survival Analysis of Virginity Among Youths Aged 13 to 18 Years." *Journal of Adolescent Health* 26(1): 42–48.

Lampman, C., B. Rolfe-Maloney, E. K. David, M. Yan, N. McCermott, S. Winters et al. 2002. "Messages About Sex in the Workplace: A Content Analysis of Prime-Time Television." *Sexuality & Culture* 6: 3–21.

Lancaster, R.N. 2003. *The Trouble with Nature*. Berkeley, CA.: University of California Press; 1997. "Guto's Performance: Notes on the Transvestism of Everyday Life." In *Sex and Sexuality in Latin America*, ed. D. Balderston and D. Guy: 559–574. New York: New York University Press.

Lance, L.M., and C.E. Ross. 2000. "View of Violence in American Sports: A Study of College Students." *College Student Journal* 34(2): 191–199.

Land, V., and C. Kitzinger. 2005. "Speaking as a Lesbian: Correcting the Heterosexist Presumption." *Research on Language and Social Interaction* 38(4): 371–416.

Landolt, M.A., K. Bartholomew, C. Saffrey, D. Oram, and D. Perlamn. 2004. "Gender Nonconformity, Childhood Rejection and Adult Attachment: A Study of Gay Men." *Archives of Sexual Behavior* 33(2): 117–128.

Landrine, H. 1999. "Race 3 Class Stereotypes of Women." In *Gender, Culture and Ethnicity*, ed. L.A. Peplau and S.C. DeBro: 38–61. Mountain View, CA: Mayfield Publishing Company.

Langlois, S., and P. Morrison. 2004. "Suicide Deaths and Suicide Attempts." *Health Reports* 13(2): 9–22. Catalogue 82-003-XPE.

Lanis, K., and K. Covell. 1995. "Images of Women in Advertisements: Effects on Attitudes Related to Sexual Aggression." *Sex Roles* 22(9–10): 639–649.

Lanvers, U. 2004. "Gender in Discourse Behavior in Parent-Child Dyads: A Literature Review." *Child Care Health and Development* 30(5): 481–493.

Laqueur, T.W. 2003. *Solitary Sex*. New York: Zone Books; 1990. *Making Sex*. Cambridge, MA: Harvard University Press.

Laplante, B. 2006. "The Rise of Cohabitation in Quebec: Power of Religion and Power Over Religion." *Canadian Journal of Sociology* 31(1): 1–24.

Lareau, A. 2003. *Unequal Childhoods*. Berkeley, CA: University of California Press.

LaRossa, R. 1988/1995. "Fatherhood and Social Change." *Family Relations* 37 October 1988: 451–457. Reprinted in *Gender in the 1990s*, eds. E.D. Nelson and B.W. Robinson: 365–379. Toronto: Nelson Canada.

LaRossa, R., and D.C. Reitzes. 1995. "Gendered Perceptions of Father Involvement in Early 20th Century America." *Journal of Marriage and the Family* 57: 223–229.

LaRossa, R., C. Jaret, M. Gadgil, and G.R. Wynn. 2001. "Gender Disparities in Mother's Day and Father's Day Comic Strips: A 54-Year History." *Sex Roles* 44(11–12): 693–718.

Larson, M.S. 2003. "Gender, Race and Aggression in Television Commercials That Feature Children." *Sex Roles* 48(1–2): 67–75; 2001. "Interactions, Activities and Gender in Children's Television Commercials: A Content Analysis." *Journal of Broadcasting & Electronic Media* 45(1) : 41–56; 1996. "Sex Roles and Soap Operas: What Adolescents Learn About Single Motherhood." *Sex Roles* 35(1–2): 97–110.

Larson, R., and J. Pleck. 1999. "Hidden Feelings: Emotionality in Boys and Men." In *Gender and Motivation*, ed. D. Bernstein, Vol. 45: 25–74. Lincoln, NE: University of Nebraska Press.

Larson, R.W., and D.M. Almeida. 1999. "Emotional Transmission in the Daily Lives of Families: A New Paradigm for Studying Family Process." *Journal of Marriage and the Family* 61: 5–20.

Larwood, L., and B.A. Gutek (eds.). 1987. "Working Toward a Theory of Women's

Career Development." In *Women's Career Development*: 170–183. Newbury Park, CA: Sage.

Lasch, C. 1977. *Haven in a Heartless World*. New York: Basic Books.

Lauzen, M.M., and D.M. Dozier. 2002. "Equal Time in Prime Time? Scheduling Favoritism and Gender on the Broadcast Networks." *Journal of Broadcasting & Electronic Media* 46(1): 137–153; 2002a. "You Look Mahvelous: An Examination of Gender and Appearance Comments in the 1999–2000 Prime-Time Season." *Sex Roles* 46(11–12): 429–437.

Lauzen, M.M., D.M. Dozier, and M.V. Hicks. 2001. "Prime-Time Players and Powerful Prose: The Role of Women in the 1997–1998 Television Season." *Mass Communication & Society* 4(1): 39–59.

Lavee, Y., and R. Katz. 2002. "Division of Labor, Perceived Fairness, and Marital Quality: The Effect of Gender Ideology." *Journal of Marriage and the Family* 64(1): 27–39.

Lavee, Y., S. Sharlin, and R. Katz. 1996. "The Effect of Parenting Stress on Marital Quality: An Integrated Mother–Father Model." *Journal of Family Issues* 17(1): 114–135.

Lavoie, F., L. Robitaille, and M. Hebert. 2000. "Teen Dating Relationships and Aggression." *Violence Against Women* 6(1): 6–36.

Lavoie, Y., and J. Oderkirk. 1993. "Social Consequences of Demographic Change." *Canadian Social Trends* 31: 2–5.

Law Society of Upper Canada. 2006. *The Changing Face of the Legal Profession*. **www.lsuc.on.ca/news/a/fact/changing**

Lawrence, A. 2003. "Factors Associated with Satisfaction or Regret Following Male-to-Female Sex Reassignment Surgery." *Archives of Sexual Behavior* 32(4): 299–315.

Lawrence, J.A., J.J. Goodnow, K. Woods, and G. Karantzas. 2002. "Distributions of Caregiving Tasks Among Family Members: The Place of Gender and Availability." *Journal of Family Psychology* 16(4): 493–509.

Laws, J.L., and P. Schwartz. 1977. *Sexual Scripts*. Hinsdale, IL: Drysden Press.

Lawson, H.M. 2003. "Gender and Selling Cars: Attacking Nicely." In *Down to Earth Sociology*, 12th ed., ed. J. M. Henslin: 187–201. New York: Free Press.

Leaper, C. 2002. "Parenting Boys and Girls." In *Handbook of Parenting*: Volume 1, 2nd ed., ed. M.H. Bornstein: 189–225. Mahwah, NJ: Lawrence Erlbaum Associates; 2000. "The Social Construction and Socialization of Gender During Development." In *Toward a Feminist Developmental Psychology*, eds. P.H. Miller and E. Kofsky Scholnick: 127–152. Florence, KY: Taylor & Frances/ Routledge.

Leaper, C., and M.M. Ayres. 2007. "A Meta-Analytic Review of Gender Variations in Adults' Language Use: Talkativeness, Affilliative Speech and Assertive Speech." *Personality and Social Psychology Review* 11(4); 328–363.

Leaper, C., K. Breed, L. Hoffman, and C.A. Perlman. 2002. "Variations in the Gender-Stereotyped Content of Children's Television Cartoons Across Genres." *Journal of Applied Social Psychology* 32(8): 1653–1662.

Leaper, C., and C.K. Friedman. 2007. "The Socialization of Gender." In *Handbook of Socialization*, eds. J.E. Grusec and P.D. Hastings: 561–587. New York: Guilford Press.

Le Bourdais, C., G. Neill, and P. Turcotte. 2000. "The Changing Face of Conjugal Relationship." *Canadian Social Trends* 56: 14–17.

Le Bourdais, C., G. Neill, and N. Vachon. 2000. "Family Disruption in Canada: Impact of the Changing Patterns of Family Formation and of Female Employment." *Canadian Studies in Population* 27(1): 85–105.

Le Bourdais, C., and N. Marcil-Gratton. 1996. "Family Transformations Across the Canadian-America Border: When the Laggard Becomes the Leader." *Journal of Comparative Family Studies* 27(2): 415–436.

Lee, C., L. Duxbury, and C. Higgins. 1994. *Employed Mothers*. Ottawa: Canadian Centre for Management Development.

Lee, G.R., M.C. Willetts, and K. Seccombe. 1998. "Widowhood and Depression: Gender Differences." *Research on Aging* 20(5): 611–630.

Lee, J. 2002. "Role Conflicts: Family Life, Work, and Gender." In *The Psychology of*

Sex, Gender, and Jobs, eds. L. Diamant and J.A. Lee: 233–248. Westport, CT: Praeger.

Lee, J.W., and L.K. Guerrero. 2001. "Types of Touch in Cross-Sex Relationships Between Coworkers: Perceptions of Relational and Emotional Messages, Inappropriateness, and Sexual Harassment." *Journal of Applied Communication Research* 29(3): 197–220.

LaFrance, M., and M. Banaji. 1992. "Toward a Reconsideration of the Gender-Emotion Relationship." In *Review of Personality and Social Psychology*, ed. M. Clark. Beverley Hills, CA: Sage.

Lehne, G. 1976. "Homophobia Among Men." In *The Forty-Nine Percent Majority*, eds. D. Brannon and R. Brannon: 66–88. Reading, MA: Addison-Wesley.

Lehr, R., and P. MacMillan. 2001. "The Psychological and Emotional Impact of Divorce: The Noncustodial Fathers' Perspective." *Families in Society* 82(4): 373–382.

Leiberson, S. 2000. *A Matter of Taste*. New Haven, CT: Yale University Press.

Leiblum, S.R. 2002. "Reconsidering Gender Differences in Sexual Desire: An Update." *Sexual & Relationship Therapy* 17(1) February: 57–68; 2001. "Women, Sex and the Internet." *Sexual & Relationship Therapy* 16(4): 389–405.

Leiblum, S.R., and S.G. Nathan. 2001. "Persistent Sexual Arousal Syndrome: A Newly Discovered Pattern of Female Sexuality." *Journal of Sex & Marital Therapy* 27(4): 365–380.

Leinbach, M.D., and Fagot, B.I. 1993. "Categorical Habituation to Male and Female Faces: Gender Schematic Processing in Infancy." *Infant Behavior and Development* 16: 317–332.

Leinbach, M., and B. Hort. 1995. "Do Young Children Sex-Type Emotions?" Poster presented at the biennial meeting of the Society for Research in Child Development, Indianapolis, Indiana. 30 March to 2 April.

Leinbach, M.D., B.E. Hort, and B.I. Fagot. 1997. "Bears Are for Boys: Metaphorical Associations in Young Children's Gender Stereotypes." *Cognitive Development* 12: 107–130.

Leonard, M. 2001. "Old Wine in New Bottles? Women Working Inside and Outside the Household." *Women's Studies International Forum* 24(1): 67–78.

Lerner, G. 1977. *The Female Experience*. Indianapolis: Bobbs-Merrill.

Lero, D.S. 1996. "Dual-Earner Families." In *Voices*, ed. M. Lynn: 19–53. Toronto: Nelson.

Leslie, G.R. 1967. *The Family in Social Context*. New York: Oxford.

Lester, J. 1976. "Being a Boy." In *The Forty-Nine Percent Majority*, eds. D.S. David and R. Brannon: 270–273. Reading, MA: Addison-Wesley.

Letendre, J. 2007. "'Sugar and Spice But Not Always Nice': Gender Socialization and its Impact on Development and Maintenance of Aggression in Adolescent Girls." *Child and Adolescent Social Work* 24(4): 353–368.

Levant, R.F. 1996. "The New Psychology of Men." *Professional Psychology, Research and Practice* 27(3): 259–265; 1995. "Toward the Reconstruction of Masculinity." In *A New Psychology of Men*, ed. W.S. Pollack: 229–251. New York: Basic Books; 1995a. "Nonrelational Sexuality in Men." In *Conceiving Sexuality*, eds. R.G. Parker and J.H. Gagnon: 9–27. New York: Routledge.

Levay, S., and S.M. Valente. 2003. *Human Sexuality*. Sunderland, MA: Sinauer Associates.

Lever, J. 1994. "The 1994 Advocate Survey of Sexuality and Relationships: The Men." *Advocate*, August 23: 16–24.

Levin, R.J. 2001. "Sexual Desire and the Deconstruction and Reconstruction of the Human Female Sexual Response Model of Masters and Johnson." In *Sexual Appetite, Desire and Motivation*, eds. W. Everaerd and E. Laan: 63–93. Amsterdam, Netherlands: Koninklijke Nederlandse Akademie van Wetenschappen.

Levine, R., S. Sato, T. Hashimoto, and J. Verma. 1995. "Love and Marriage in Eleven Cultures." *Journal of Cross-Cultural Psychology* 26(5): 554–571.

Levinson, D.J. 1996. *The Seasons of a Woman's Life*. New York: Alfred A. Knopf; 1977. "Periods in the Adult Development of Men:

Ages 18 to 45." In *Beyond Sex Roles*, ed. A.G. Sargent: 279–291. St. Paul: West.

Levinson, D.J., et al. 1978. *The Seasons of a Man's Life*. New York: Alfred A. Knopf.

Levold, N., and M. Aune. 2003. "'Cooking Gender': Home, Gender and Technology." *Sosiologisk Tidsskrift* 11(3): 273–299.

Levy, G.D. 1999. "Gender-Typed and Non-Gender-Typed Category Awareness in Toddlers." *Sex Roles* 41(11–12): 851–873; 1989. "Relations Among Aspects of Children's Social Environments, Gender Schematization, Gender Role Knowledge and Flexibility." *Sex Roles* 21: 803–811.

Levy, G.D., A.L. Sadovsky, and G.L. Troseth. 2000. "Aspects of Young Children's Perceptions of Gender-Typed Occupations." *Sex Roles* 42(11–12): 993–1006.

Levy, M.J. Jr. 1989. *Our Mother-Tempers*. Berkeley, CA: University of California Press.

Lewis, G. 2003. "Black-White Differences in Attitudes Toward Homosexuality and Gay Rights." *Public Opinion Quarterly* 67(1): 59–78.

Lewis, R.A., and G.B. Spanier. 1979. "Theorizing About the Quality and Stability of Marriage." In *Contemporary Theories About the Family*, eds. W.R. Burr, R. Hill, F.I. Nye, and I.L. Reiss: 268–294. New York: Free Press.

Lewis-Hall, F., T.S. Williams, J.A. Panetta, and J.M. Herrera. 2002. *Psychiatric Illness in Women*. Washington, DC: American Psychiatric Publishing.

Li, K. 2006. "Zhi-Ming and Chun-Jiau: Why Are Men's Names and Women's Names Always Different?" *Taiwanese Sociology* 12: 1–67.

Liben, L.S., R.S. Bigler, and H.R. Krugh. 2002. "Language at Work: Children's Gendered Interpretations of Occupational Titles." *Child Development* 73(3) May: 810–828.

Liberman, M. 2006. "Sex on the Brain." *The Boston Globe*, September 24.

Lieb, H., and S. Thistle. 2005. "The Changing Impact of Marriage, Motherhood and Work on Women's Poverty." *Journal of Women Politics & Policy* 27(3–4): 5–22.

Lieberman, M., L. Gauvin, W.M. Bukowski, and D.R. White. 2001. "Interpersonal Influence and Disordered Eating Behaviors in Adolescent Girls: The Role of Peer Modeling, Social Reinforcement and Body-Related Teasing." *Eating Behaviors* 2(3): 215–236.

Lieberson, S., S. Dumain, and S. Baumann, 2000. "The Instability of Androgynous Names: The Symbolic Maintenance of Gender Boundaries." *American Journal of Sociology* 105: 1249–1287.

Light, B., and A. Prentice. 1980. *Pioneer and Gentlewomen of British North America, 1713–1867*. Toronto: New Hogtown Press.

Lightfoot-Klein, H., C. Chase, T. Hammond, and R. Goldman. 2000. "Genital Surgery on Children Below the Age of Consent." In *Psychological Perspectives on Human Sexuality*, eds. L.T. Szuchman and F. Muscarella: 440–479. New York: John Wiley & Sons.

Lillie, J.J.M. 2002. "Sexuality and Cyberporn: Toward a New Agenda for Research." *Sexuality & Culture* 6(2) Spring: 25–47.

Lin, J. 2006. *The Teaching Profession: Trends from 1999 to 2005*. Statistics Canada, Catalogue 81-004-XIE.

Linden School. 2004. *Mission Statement*. **www.lindenschool.ca/Who Are We/ Mission.html**

Lindsay, C. and M. Almey. 2006a. "Income and Earnings." In *Women in Canada,* 5th edition. Statistics Canada, Catalogue no. 89-503-XIE: 133–158; 2006b. "Women in a Visible Minority." In *Women in Canada,* 5th edition. Statistics Canada, Catalogue no. 89-503-XIE: 239–263; 2006c. "Family Status." In *Women in Canada*, 5th edition. Statistics Canada, Catalogue no. 89-503-XIE: 33–52; 2006d. "Health." In *Women in Canada*, 5th edition. Statistics Canada, Catalogue no. 89-503-XIE: 53–87; 2006e. "The Female Population in Canada." In *Women in Canada*, 5th edition. Statistics Canada, Catalogue no. 89-503-XIE: 19–32; 2006f. "Paid and Unpaid Work." In *Women in Canada*, 5th edition. Statistics Canada, Catalogue no. 89-503-XIE: 133–158.

Lindsay, J., and L. Anderson. 2003. "Dementia and Alzheimer's Disease." In *Women's Health Surveillance Report*: 41–42. Ottawa: Canadian Institute for Health Information.

Lindsey, L.L. 1997. *Gender Roles*. 3rd ed. Englewood Cliffs, NJ: Prentice Hall; 1994.

Gender Roles. 2nd ed. Englewood Cliffs, NJ: Prentice Hall.

Linstead, S., and A. Pullen. 2006. "Gender as Multiplicity: Desire, Displacement, Difference and Dispersion." *Human Relations* 59(8): 1287–1310.

Linton, R. 1945. *The Cultural Background of Personality*. New York: Appleton-Century-Crofts.

Lipman-Blumen, J. 1984. *Gender Roles and Power*. Englewood Cliffs, NJ: Prentice-Hall; 1976. "A Homosocial Theory of Sex Roles: An Examination of the Sex Segregation of Social Institutions." In *Women and the Workplace*, eds. M. Blaxall and B. Reagan. Reading, MA: Addison-Wesley.

Lippa, R.A. 2005. *Gender, Nature and Nurture*, 2nd edition. Mahwah, NJ: Lawrence Erlbaum Associates; 2001. "Gender-Related Traits in Transsexuals and Nontranssexuals." *Archives of Sexual Behavior* 30(6): 603–614.

Lips, H.M. 2005. *Sex & Gender*, 5th edition. Boston: McGraw-Hill; 2001. *Sex & Gender*. Toronto: Mayfield; 1999. *A New Psychology of Women*. Mountain View, CA: Mayfield Publishing Company;1993. *Sex & Gender*, 2nd ed. Mountain View, CA: Mayfield.

Little, C.B., and A. Rankin. 2001. "Why Do They Start It? Explaining Reported Early-Teen Sexual Activity." *Sociological Forum* 16(4): 703–729.

Littlewood, R. 2002. "Three Into Two: The Third Sex in Northern Albania." *Anthropology & Medicine* 9(1): 37–50.

Littman, M. 2001. What Women Want? Ogilvy & Mather Breaks New Ground with Frank Ads. *Business*, 2.0, November 26. **www.business2.com/ b2/web/articles/ 0,17863,514257,00.html**

Litzke, C.H. 2004. "Social Constructions of Motherhood and Mothers on Drugs: Implications for Treatment, Policy and Practice." *Journal of Feminist Family Therapy* 16(4): 43–59.

Livingstone, D.W. 1999. *The Education-Jobs Gap*. Toronto: Garamond Press.

Lloyd, S.A. 1991. "The Darkside of Courtship: Violence and Sexual Exploitation." *Family Relations*. 40: 14–20.

Lloyd, S.A., and B.C. Emery. 2000. *The Dark Side of Courtship*. Thousand Oaks, CA: Sage Puiblications.

Lobel, T.E., Bempechat, J., Gerwirtz, J., Shoken-Topaz, T., and Bashe, E., 1993. "The Role of Gender-Related Information and Self-Endorsement of Traits in Preadolescents' Inferences and Judgements." *Child Development* 64, 1285–1294.

Lochrie, K.1999. *Covert Operations*. Philadelphia: The University of Pennsylvania Press.

Locke, W.S., and M.M. Gibbons. 2008. "On Her Own Again: The Use of Narrative Therapy in Career Counseling with Displaced New Traditionalists." *The Family Journal* 16(2): 132–138.

Lockhart, L.L., B.W. White, V. Causby, and A. Issac. 1994. "Letting Out the Secret: Violence in Lesbian Relationships." *Journal of Interpersonal Violence* 9(4): 469–492.

Loeber, R., and D. Hay. 1997. "Key Issues in the Development of Aggression and Violence from Childhood to Early Adulthood." *Annual Review of Psychology* 48: 371–410.

Lombardo, W.K., G.A. Cretser, and S.C. Roesch. 2001. "For Crying Out Loud—The Differences Persist into the '90s." *Sex Roles* 45(7–8): 529–548.

Lombroso, C., and E. Ferrero, 1895. *The Female Offender*. New York: D. Appleton.

Long, R.E. 2004. *Men, Homosexuality and the Gods*. Binghamton, NY: Harrington Park Press/The Haworth Press.

Longmore, M.A., W.D. Manning, and P.C. Giordano. 2001. "Preadolescent Parenting Strategies and Teens' Dating and Sexual Initiation: A Longitudinal Analysis." *Journal of Marriage & the Family* 63(2): 322–335.

Lonsdale, S. 1990. *Women and Disability*. New York: St. Martin's Press.

Lont, C.M. 1997. "Women's Music: No Longer a Small Private Party." In *Feminist Frontiers IV*, eds. L. Richardson, V. Taylor, and N. Whittier: 126–134. New York: McGraw-Hill.

Lopata, H.Z. 2000. "Widowhood: Reconstruction of Self-Concept and Identities." *Studies in Symbolic Interaction* 23: 261–275.

Lopez, N. 2002. "Rewriting Race and Gender High School Lessons." *Teachers College Record* 104(6): 1187–1203.

Lorber, J. 1993. "Why Women Physicians Will Never Be True Equals in the American Medical Profession." In *Gender, Work and Medicine*, eds. E. Riska and K. Wager: 62–76. London: Sage.

Loscocco, K. 1997. "Work–Family Linkages Among Self-Employed Women and Men." *Journal of Vocational Behavior* 50: 204–226.

Loscocco, K., and G. Spitze. 2007. "Gender Patterns in Provider Role Attitudes and Behavior." *Journal of Family Issues* 28(7): 945–954.

Losh-Hesselbart, S. 1987. "Development of Gender Roles." In *Handbook of Marriage and the Family*, eds. M.B. Susman and S.K. Steinmetz: 535–563. New York: Plenum.

Lott, B. 2002. "Cognitive and Behavioral Distancing from the Poor." *American Psychologist* 57(2): 100–110; 1994. *Women's Lives*, 2nd ed. Pacific Grove, CA: Brooks/Cole.

Lowe, G.S. 1995. "Work." In *New Society*, ed. R.J. Brym: 10.1–10.25. Toronto: Harcourt Brace & Company; 1992. "Canadians and Retirement." *Canadian Social Trends* 26: 18–21.

Lowe, N.V. 1982. "The Legal Status of Fathers: Past and Present." In *The Father Figure*, eds. L. McKee and M. O'Brien: 26–42. London: Tavistock.

Lowenthal, M.F., M. Thurnher, and C. Chiriboga. 1975. *Four Stages of Life*. San Francisco: Jossey-Bass.

Lovas, G.S. 2005. "Gender and Patterns of Emotional Availability in Mother-Toddler and Father-Toddler Dyads." *Infant Mental Health Journal* 26(4): 327–353.

Lovgren, K. 1992. "Dangerous Attraction." *Nord Nytt* 47 November: 34–37.

Lucas, S., J.V. Persad, G. Morton, S. Albuquerque, and N. El Yassir. 1991/1995. "Changing the Politics of the Women's Movement." *RFR/DRF* 20(1–2): 3–4. Reprinted in *Gender in the 1990s*, eds. E.D. Nelson and B.W. Robinson: 534–536. Toronto: Nelson Canada.

Luciano, L. 2007. "Muscularity and Masculinity in the United States: A Historical Overview." in *The Muscular Ideal*, eds. J.K. Thompson and G. Cafri: 41–65.

Washington, DC: American Psychological Association.

Lueptow, L.B., L. Garovich-Szabo, and M.B. Lueptow. 2001. "Social Change and the Persistence of Sex Typing: 1974–1997." *Social Forces* 80(1): 1–36.

Luff, D. 2001. "'The Downright Torture of Women': Moral Lobby Women, Feminists and Pornography." *The Sociological Review* 49(1): 78–99.

Luffman, J., and D. Sussman. 2007. "The Aboriginal Labour Force in Western Canada." Perspectives on Labour and Income, Statistics Canada, Catalogue no. 75-001-XIE, January, 13–27.

Lundberg, S., S. McLanahan, and E. Rose. 2007. "Child Gender and Father Involvement in Fragile Families." *Demography* 44(1): 79–92.

Lundberg, S., and E. Rose. 2002. "The Effects of Sons and Daughters on Men's Labor Supply and Wages." *Review of Economics and Statistics* 84(2): 251–268; 2003. "Child Gender and the Transition to Marriage." *Demography* 40(2): 333–349.

Lusk, B. 2000. "Pretty and Powerless: Nurses in Advertisements, 1930–1950." *Research in Nursing & Health* 23(3): 229–236.

Luxen, M.F. 2007. "Sex Differences, Evolutionary Psychology and Biosocial Theory: Biosocial Theory Is No Alternative." *Theory & Psychology* 17(3): 383–394.

Luxton, M. 1980. *More Than a Labour of Love*. Toronto: Women's Press.

Luxton, M., and J. Corman. 2001. *Getting By in Hard Times*. Toronto: University of Toronto Press; 2005. "Families at Work: Making a Living." In *Canadian Families*, 3rd ed., eds. N. Mandell and A. Duffy: 346–371. Toronto: Nelson Thomson.

Lynn, D.B. 1969. *Parental and Sex Role Identification*. Berkeley, CA: McCutchan.

Lynn, M., and M. Todoroff. 1998. "Women's Work and Family Lives." In *Feminist Issues*, ed. N. Mandell: 244–271. Scarborough, ON: Prentice Hall Canada.

Lytton, H., and D. Romney. 1991. "Parents' Differential Socialization of Boys and Girls: A Meta-Analysis. *Psychological Bulletin* 109: 267–296.

Maas, A., M. Cadinu, G. Guarnieri, and A. Grasselli. 2003. "Sexual Harassment Under

Social Identity Threat: The Computer Harassment Paradigm." *Journal of Personality & Social Psychology* 85(5): 853–870.

Maas, K.W., and C.A. Hasbrook. 2001. "Media Promotion of the Paradigm Citizen/Golfer: An Analysis of Golf Magazines' Representations of Disability, Gender and Age." *Sociology of Sport Journal* 18(1): 21–36.

Maass, V.S. 2007. *Facing the Complexities of Women's Sexual Desire*. New York: Springer Science.

Macaulay, M. 2001. "Tough Talk: Indirectness and Gender in Requests for Information." *Journal of Pragmatics* 33(2): 293–316.

Maccoby, E.E. 2002. "The Interaction of Nature and Socialization in Childhood Gender Development." In *Psychology at the Turn of the Millennium*, eds. C. Von Fosten and L. Backman: 37–52. Florence, KY: Taylor & Frances/Routledge; 2002. "Perspectives on Gender Development." In *Growing Points in Developmental Science*, eds. W.W. Hartup and R.K. Silbereisen: 202–222. Philadelphia, PA: Psychology Press; 1998. *The Two Sexes*. Cambridge, MA: Harvard University Press.

Maccoby, E.E., and C.N. Jacklin. 1974. *The Psychology of Sex Differences*. Stanford, CA: Stanford University Press.

MacGregor, R. 1995. *The Home Team*. Toronto: Viking.

Machum, S.T. 2002. "The Farmer Takes a Wife and the Wife Takes the Farm: Marriage and Farming." In *Social Context & Social Location in the Sociology of Law*, ed. G.M. MacDonald: 133–158.

Machung, A. 1989. "Talking Career, Thinking Jobs: Gender Differences in Career and Family Expectations of Berkeley Seniors." *Feminist Studies* 15: 35–58.

Macionis, J.J., and L.M. Gerber. 2005. *Sociology*, 5th edition. Toronto: Pearson.

MacKay, N.L., and K. Covell. 1997. "The Impact of Women in Advertisements on Attitudes Toward Women." *Sex Roles* 36: 573–583.

Mackey, R.A., M.A. Diemer, and B.A. O'Brien. 2004. "Relational Factors in Understanding Satisfaction in the Lasting Relationships of Same-Sex and Heterosexual Couples."

Journal of Homosexuality 47(1): 111–136; 2000. "Conflict-Management Styles of Spouses in Lasting Marriages." *Psychotherapy* 37(2): 134–148.

Mackie, M. 1991. *Gender Relations in Canada*. Toronto: Butterworths; 1987. *Constructing Women and Men*. Toronto: Holt, Rinehart and Winston of Canada.

MacKinnon, C.A. 1987. *Feminism Unmodified*. Cambridge, MA: Harvard University Press; 1982. "Feminism, Marxism, Method, and the State: An Agenda for Theory." *Signs* 7: 515–544; 1979. *Sexual Harassment of Working Women*. New Haven: Yale University Press.

Macklin, A. 1992. "Symes v. M.N.R.: Where Sex Meets Class." *Canadian Journal of Women and the Law* 5(2): 498–517.

Maclean, H.K., K. Glynn, and D. Ansara. 2003a. "Multiple Roles and Women's Health in Canada." In *Women's Health Surveillance Report*: 3–4. Ottawa: Canadian Institute for Health Information.

Maclean, H.K., K. Glynn, Z. Cao, and D. Ansara. 2003. "Personal Health Practices." In *Women's Health Surveillance Report*: 5–6. Ottawa: Canadian Institute for Health Information.

Maclean's. 2000. "Politics, Society and Sex." December 25–January 1: 52–54.

Madden-Derdich, D.A., and S.A. Leonard. 2002. "Shared Experiences, Unique Realities: Formerly Married Mothers' and Fathers' Perceptions of Parenting and Custody After Divorce." *Family Relations* 51(1): 37–45.

Madon, S. 1997. "What Do People Believe About Gay Males? A Study of Stereotype Content and Strength." *Sex Roles* 37(9–10): 663–685.

Madon, S., L. Jussim, S. Keiper, J. Eccles, A. Smith, and P. Palumbo. 1998. "The Accuracy and Power of Sex, Social Class and Ethnic Stereotypes: A Naturalistic Study in Person Perception." *Personality & Social Psychology Bulletin* 24(12): 1304–1318.

Madon, S., A. Smith, L. Jussim, D.W. Russell, J. Eccles, P. Palumbo, and M. Walkiewicz. 2001. "Am I as You See Me or Do You See Me as I Am? Self-Fulfilling Prophecies and Self-Verification." *Personality & Social Psychology Bulletin* 27(9): 1214–1224.

Madson, L. 2000. "Infererences Regarding the Personality Traits and Sexual Orientation of Physically Androgynous People." *Psychology of Women Quarterly* 24: 148–160.

Mah, K., and Y.M. Binik. 2002. "Do All Orgasms Feel Alike? Evaluating a Two-Dimensional Model of the Orgasm Experience Across Gender and Sexual Context." *Journal of Sex Research* 39(2): 104–113.

Mahtani, M. 2001. "Mapping the Meanings of 'Racism' and 'Feminism' Among Women Television Broadcast Journalists in Canada." In *Feminism and Antiracism*, eds. F.W. Twine and K.M. Blee: 349–366. New York: New York University Press.

Maier, K.E. 1992. "Assessing Reproductive Wrongs." In *Anatomy of Gender*, eds. D.H. Currie and V. Raoul: 147–160. Ottawa: Carleton University Press.

Majors, R. 2001. "Cool Pose: Black Masculinity and Sports." In *The Masculinities Reader*, eds. S.M. Whitehead and F. J. Barrett: 209–217. Cambridge: Polity.

Makri-Botsari, E., and E. Makri. 2003. "Maternal Employment: Effects on Her Mental Health and Children's Functional Status." *Psychological Studies* 48(1): 36–46.

Malcolmson, K.A., and L. Sinclair. 2007. "The Ms. Stereotype Revisited: Implicit and Explicit Facets." *Psychology of Women Quarterly* 31(3): 305–310.

Malone, K. 2001. "Review of Who's That Girl? Who's That Boy? Clinical Practice Meets Postmodern Gender Theory." *Signs* 27(1): 286–290.

Malone, K., and R. Cleary. 2002. "(De)Sexing the Family: Theorizing the Social Science of Lesbian Families." *Feminist Theory* 3(3): 271–293.

Maltry, M., and K. Tucker. 2002. "Female Fem(me)ininities: New Articulations in Queer Gender Identities and Subversion." *Journal of Lesbian Studies* 6(2): 89–102.

Mandell, N. (ed.). 1995. *Feminist Issues*. Scarborough: Prentice Hall Canada; 1989. "Marital Roles in Transition." In *Family and Marriage*, ed. K. Ishwaran: 239–252. Toronto: Wall and Thompson.

Mannino, C.A., and F.M. Deutsch. 2007. "Changing the Division of Household Labor: A Negotiated Process Between Partners." *Sex Roles* 56(5–6): 309–324.

Manor, O., and Z. Eisenbach. 2003. "Mortality After Spousal Loss: Are There Socio-Demographic Differences?" *Social Science and Medicine* 56(2): 405–413.

Manthorpe, J. 2003. "Speaking from the Heart: Gender and the Social Meaning of Emotion." *Journal of Gender Studies* 12(2): 150–151.

Maolin, Y., and Y. Lianhua. 2006. "An Experimental Study on the Stereotyping of High School Students Expecting to Major in Liberal Arts or Sciences." *Psychological Science* 29(4): 991–993.

Maracle, L. 1996. *I Am Woman*. Vancouver: Press Gang Publishers.

Marchant, A., A. Bhattacharya, and M. Carnes. 2007. "Can the Language of Tenure Criteria Influence Women's Academic Advancement?" *Journal of Women's Health* 16(7): 998–1003.

Marchbank, J., and G. Letherby. 2007. *Introduction to Gender*. Harlow, England: Pearson Longman.

Marcon, R.A., and G. Freeman. 1996. "Linking Gender-Related Toy Preferences to Social Structure: Changes in Children's Letters to Santa Since 1978." *Journal of Psychological Practice* 2(1): 1–10.

Margolin, L. 1992. "Child Abuse by Mothers' Boyfriends: Why the Overrepresentation?" *Child Abuse & Neglect* 16: 541–551.

Marin, P. 1991/1995. "The Prejudice Against Men." *The Nation*, 8 July. Reprinted in *Gender in the 1990s*, eds. E.D. Nelson and B.W. Robinson: 490–498. Scarborough: Nelson Canada.

Marini, M. Mooney, and P. Fan. 1997. "The Gender Gap in Earnings at Career Entry." *American Sociological Review* 62: 588–608.

Marleau, J.D., and L. Laporte. 1999. "Gender of Victims and Motivation of Filicidal Parents: Is There a Relationship?" *Canadian Journal of Psychiatry* 44(9): 924–925.

Marleau, J.D., and J.F. Saucier. 2002. "Preference for a First-Born Boy in Western Societies." *Journal of Biosocial Science* 34(1): 13–27.

Marquat, J.A. 1990. "The Influence of Applicants' Gender on Medical School Interviews." *Academic Medicine* 65: 410–411.

Marriott, D. 2000. *On Black Men*. Edinburgh: Edinburgh University Press.

Marshall, K. 2006. "Converging Gender Roles." *Perspectives on Labour and Income* 18(3): 7–19; 1999. "Employment After Childbirth." *Perspectives on Labour and Income*: 15–25. Catalogue 75-001-XPE; 1998. "Stay-at-Home-Dads." *Perspectives on Labour and Income*: 9–15. Catalogue 75-001-XPE; 1993/1995. "Dual Earners: Who's Responsible for Housework?" *Canadian Social Trends*. Cat. 11–008E, 11–14. Reprinted in *Gender in the 1990s*, eds. E.D. Nelson and B.W. Robinson: 302–310. Toronto: Nelson Canada.

Marshall, K., and V. Ferrao. 2007."Participation of Older Workers." *Perspectives on Labour and Income* 8(8), Statistics Canada, Catalogue no. 75-9910XIE, 5–11.

Marsiglio, W. 2004. "When Stepfathers Claim Stepchildren: A Conceptual Analysis." *Journal of Marriage and the Family* 66(1): 22–39; 1998. "In Search of a Theory: Men's Fertility and Parental Investment in Modern Economics." In *Men in Families*, eds. A. Booth and A.C. Crouter: 123–131. Mahwah, NJ: Lawrence Erkabum Associates; 1995. *Fatherhood*. Thousand Oaks, CA: Sage Publications.

Marsiglio, W., P. Amato, R.D. Day, and M.E. Lamb. 2000. "Scholarship on Fatherhood in the 1990s and Beyond." *Journal of Marriage and the Family* 62(4): 1173–1191.

Marsiglio, W.S., and M. Cohan. 2000. "Contextualizing Father Involvement and Paternal Influence: Sociological and Qualitative Themes." *Marriage & Family Review* 29(2–3): 75–95.

Marsiglio, W., S. Hutchinson, and M. Cohen. 2001. "Young Men's Procreative Identity: Becoming Aware, Being Aware and Being Responsible." *Journal of Marriage and the Family* 63(1): 123–135; 2000. "Envisioning Fatherhood: A Social Psychological Perspective on Young Men without Kids." *Family Relations* 49(2): 133–142.

Marston, C., and E. King. 2006. "Factors That Shape Young People's Sexual Behavior: A Systematic Review." *Lancet* 368(9547): 1581–1586.

Martin, C., and P. Robinson. 2008. *Child and Spousal Support: Maintenance Enforcement Survey Statistics, 2006/2007*. Statistics Canada, Catalogue no. 85-228-XIE, March. Ottawa: Minister of Industry.

Martin, C.L. 1999. "A Developmental Perspective on Gender Effects and Gender Concepts." In *Sexism and Stereotypes in Modern Society*, eds. W.B. Swann, Jr., J.H. Langlois, and L.A. Gilberts: 45–74. Washington, DC: American Psychological Association; 1990. "Attitudes and Expectations about Children with Nontraditional and Traditional Gender Roles." *Sex Roles* 22: 151–165; 1989. "Children's Use of Gender-Related Information in Making Social Judgements." *Developmental Psychology* 25: 80–88.

Martin, C.L., Eisenbud, L., and Rose, H. 1995. "Children's Gender-Based Reasoning About Toys." *Child Development*, 66: 1453–1471.

Martin, C.L., and R.A. Fabes. 1997. "Building Gender Stereotypes in the Preschool Years." Paper presented at the meetings of the Society for Research on Child Development, Washington, DC.

Martin, C.L., and J.K. Little. 1990. "The Relation of Gender Understanding to Children's Sex-Typed Preferences and Gender Stereotypes." *Child Development* 61: 1427–1439.

Martin, C.L., and D. Ruble. 2004. "Children's Search for Gender Cues: Cognitive Perspectives on Gender Development." *Current Directions in Psychological Science* 13(2): 67–70.

Martin, C.L., D.N. Ruble, and J. Szkrybalo. 2002. "Cognitive Theories of Early Gender Development." *Psychological Bulletin* 128(6): 903–933.

Martin, E. 2003. "Science and Fairy Tales: The Romance Between the Egg and the Sperm." In *Down to Earth Sociology*, 12th ed., ed. J.M. Henslin: 411–420. New York: Free Press; 1989. *The Woman in the Body*. Boston: Beacon Press.

Martin, J. I., and W. Meezan. 2003. "Applying Ethical Standards to Research and Evaluations Involving Lesbian, Gay, Bisexual and Transgender Populations." *Journal of Gay & Lesbian Social Services* 15(1–2): 181–201.

Martin, P.Y. 1992. "Gender, Interaction, and Inequality in Organizations." In *Gender, Interaction and Inequality*, ed. C. Ridgeway: 208–31. New York: Springer-Verlag.

Martin, P.Y., and R.A. Hummer. 2003. "Gender Oppression: Fraternities and Rape on Campus." In *Down to Earth Sociology*, 12th ed., ed. J.M. Henslin: 321–330. New York: Free Press.

Martin, R. 1997. "'Girls Don't Talk About Garages!' Perceptions of Conversation in Same- and Cross-Sex Friendships." *Personal Relationships* 4(2): 115–130.

Martindale, R. 1997. "What Makes Lesbianism Thinkable? Theorizing Lesbianism from Adrienne Rich to Queer Theory." In *Feminist Issues*, ed. N. Mandell: 67–94. Scarborough: Prentice Hall Canada.

Martin Matthews, A. 1991. *Widowhood*. Toronto: Butterworths.

Martino, S.C., R.L. Collins, M.N. Elliott, A. Strachman, D.E. Kanouse, and S.H. Berry. 2006. "Exposure to Degrading Versus Nondegrading Music Lyrics and Sexual Behavior Among Youth." *Pediatrics* 118(2): e430–e441.

Martino, W. 2001. "'Dickheads, Wusses, and Faggots': Addressing Issues of Masculinity and Homophobia in the Critical Literacy Classroom." In *Negotiating Critical Literacies in Classrooms*, eds. B. Comber and A. Simpson: 171–187. Mahwah, NJ: Lawrence Erlbaum Associates.

Martino, W., and D. Berrill. 2003. "Boys, Schooling and Masculinities: Interrogating The 'Right' Way to Educate Boys." *Educational Review* 55(2): 99–117; 2002. *What About the Boys?* Buckingham, England: Open University Press.

Martino, W., and B. Meyenn. 2002. "War, Guns and Cool, Tough Things: Interrogating Single-Sex Classes as a Strategy for Engaging Boys in English." *Cambridge Journal of Education* 32(3): 303–324; 2001. *What About the Boys?* Buckingham, England: Open University Press.

Martins, Y., M. Tiggemann, and A. Kirkbride. 2007. "Those Speedos Become Them: The Role of Self-Objectification in Gay and Heterosexual Men's Body Image." *Personality and Social Psychology Bulletin* 33(5): 634–647.

Marx, K. 1848/1964. *Selected Writings in Sociology and Social Philosophy*, eds. T.B. Bottomore and M. Rubel. Baltimore: Penguin; 1867–1894/1967. *Das Capital*. New York: International.

Maslow, A.H. 1970. *Motivation and Personality*. New York: Harper & Row.

Mason, M.A. 1998. *The Modern American Stepfamily*, eds. M.A. Mason, A. Skolnick, and S.D. Sugarman: 95–116. New York: Oxford University Press.

Masson, J.M. 1985. *The Assault on Truth*. New York: Penguin.

Masters, W.H., V.E. Johnson, and R.C. Kolodny. 1994. *Heterosexuality*. New York: Harper Perennial; 1986. *Masters and Johnson on Sex and Human Loving*. Boston: Little, Brown; 1985. *Human Sexuality*. 2nd ed. Boston: Little, Brown and Company.

Matthews, A.K., J. Tartaro, and T.L. Hughes. 2003. "A Comparative Study of Lesbian and Heterosexual Women in Committed Relationships." *Journal of Lesbian Studies* 7(1): 101–114.

Maticka-Tyndale. 2001. "Sexual Health and Canadian Youth: How Do We Measure Up?" *The Canadian Journal of Human Sexuality* 10(1–2): 1–16.

Maticka-Tyndale, E., M. Barrett, and A. McKay. 2000. "Adolescent Sexual and Reproductive Health in Canada: A Review of National Data Sources and Their Limitations." *Canadian Journal of Human Sexuality* 9(1): 41–65.

Matlin, M.W. 2003. "From Menarche to Menopause: Misconceptions About Women's Reproductive Lives." *Psychology Science* 45(Supp. 12): 106–122.

Mattel. 2004. "More Than a Doll." **www.mattel. com/our_toys/ot_barb.asp**

May, K. 2002. "Becoming Women: Transgendered Identities, Psychosexual

Therapy and the Challenge of Metamorphosis." *Sexualities* 5(4): 449–464.

Mazur, E., and R.R. Olver. 1987. "Intimacy and Structure: Sex Differences in Imagery of Same-Sex Relationships." *Sex Roles* 16(11–12): 539–558.

McAninch, C.B., R. Milich, G.B. Crumbo, and M.N. Funtowicz. 1996. "Children's Perception of Gender-Role-Congruent and -Incongruent Behavior in Peers: Fisher-Price Meets Price Waterhouse." *Sex Roles* 35(9–10): 619–638.

McBean, J. 1987. "The Myth of Maternal Preference in Child Custody Cases." In *Equality and Judicial Neutrality*, eds. S.L. Martin and K.E. Mahoney: 184–192. Toronto: Carswell.

McBride, B.A., and T.R. Rane. 1998. "Parenting Alliance as a Predictor of Fatherhood Involvement: An Exploratory Study. " *Family Relations* 47: 229–236.

McCloskey, D. 2003–2004. "Canada's Stepfamilies." *Transition Magazine* 33(4). **www.vifamily. ca/library/transition/ 334-334.html**

McConnell, A.R., and R.H., Fazio. 1996. "Women as Men and People: Effects of Gender-Marked Language." *Personality & Social Psychology Bulletin* 22(1): 1004–1013.

McCormick, M.J. 2002. "The Search for the Ideal Heterosexual Role Player." In *The Psychology of Sex, Gender and Jobs*, eds. L. Diamant and J.A. Lee: 155–170. Westport, CT: Praeger.

McCracken, E. 1993. *Decoding Women's Magazines*. London: Macmillan.

McCreary, D.R., and N.D. Rhodes. 2001. "On the Gender-Typed Nature of Dominant and Submissive Acts." *Sex Roles* 44(5–6): 339–350.

McCreary, D.R., and D.K. Sasse. 2000. "An Exploration of the Drive for Muscularity in Adolescent Boys and Girls." *Journal of American College Health* 49: 297–304.

McCreary, D.R., D.K. Sasse, D.M. Saucier, and K.D. Dorsch. 2004. "Measuring the Drive for Muscularity: Factorial Validity of the Drive for Muscularity Scale in Men and Women." *Psychology of Men & Masculinity* 5(1): 49–58.

McCutcheon, L.E., R. Lange, and J. Houran. 2002. "Conceptualization and Measurement of Celebrity Worship." *British Journal of Psychology* 93(1): 67–87.

McDonald, P.L., and R.A. Wanner. 1990. *Retirement in Canada*. Toronto: Butterworths.

McDonough, P., and V. Walter. 2001. "Gender and Health: Reassessing Patterns and Explanations." *Social Science and Medicine* 52(4): 547–559.

McFarlane, S., R. Beaujot, and T. Haddad. 2000. "Time Constraints and Relative Resources as Determinants of the Sexual Division of Domestic Work." *Canadian Journal of Sociology* 25(1): 61–82.

McGuffy, C.S., and B.L. Rich. 1999. "Playing in the Gender Transgression Zone: Race, Class, and Hegemonic Masculinity in Middle Childhood." *Gender & Society* 13(5): 608–627.

McHale, S., A.C. Crouter, and S.D. Whiteman. 2003. "The Family Contexts of Gender Development in Childhood and Adolescence." *Social Development* 12(1): 125–148.

McInerney, J.D. 2000. "'How the Gay Gene(s) Might Work' in Question." *American Biology Teacher* 62(7): 469–470.

McIntyre, R.B., R.M. Paulson, and C.G. Lord. 2003. "Alleviating Women's Mathematics Stereotype Threat Through Salience of Group Achievements." *Journal of Experimental Social Psychology* 39(1) January: 83–90.

McKee, L., and M. O'Brien (eds.). 1982. *The Father Figure*. London: Tavistock.

McKie, D.C., B. Prentice, and P. Reed. 1983. *Divorce*. Ottawa: Minister of Supply and Services Canada.

McLaughlin, T.L., and N. Goulet. 1999. "Gender Advertisements in Magazines Aimed at African Americans: A Comparison to their Occurrence in Magazines Aimed at Caucasians." *Sex Roles* 40(1–2): 61–71.

McLean, R., I. Marini, and M. Pope. 2003. "Racial Identity and Relationship Satisfaction in African American Gay Men." *Family Journal-Counseling & Therapy for Couples & Families* 11(1): 13–22.

McLelland, M. 2002. "The Newhalf Net: Japan's 'Intermediate Sex' On-Line."

International Journal of Sexuality & Gender Studies 7(2–3): 163–175.

McLeod, J. 2001. *"*When Poststructuralism Meets Gender.*"* In *Governing the Child in the New Millennium*, eds. K. Hultqvist and G. Dahlberg: 259–289. New York: Routledge.

McMahon, M. 1995. *Engendering Motherhood*. New York: The Guilford Press.

McMullin, J.A. 2005. "Patterns of Paid and Unpaid Work: The Influence of Power, Social Context, and Family Background." *Canadian Journal on Aging* 24(3): 225–236; 2004. *Understanding Social Inequality*. Don Mills, ON: Oxford University Press.

McNeill, T. 2007. "Fathers of Children with a Chronic Health Condition: Beyond Gender Stereotypes." *Men and Masculinities* 9(4) April: 409–424.

McPherson, B.D. 1994. "Aging: The Middle and Later Years." In *Sociology*, eds. L. Tepperman, J. Curtis, and J. Richardson: 230–266. Toronto: McGraw-Hill Primus.

McVey, Jr., W.W., and W.E. Kalbach. 1995. *Canadian Population*. Toronto: Nelson Canada.

McWilliams, S., and J.A. Howard. 1993. "Solidarity and Hierarchy in Cross-Sex Friendships." *Journal of Social Issues* 49(3): 191–202.

Mead, G.H. 1934/1962. *Mind, Self, and Society*, ed. C.W. Morris. Chicago: Phoenix.

Mechanic, M.B., M.H. Uhmansiek, T.L. Weaver, and P.A. Resick. 2002. "The Impact of Severe Stalking Experienced by Acutely Battered Women: An Examination of Violence, Psychological Symptoms and Strategic Responding." In *Stalking*, eds. K.E. Davis and I.H. Frieze: 89–111. New York: Springer Publishing Company.

Medeiros, D.M. 2003. "Get Used to It! Children of Gay and Lesbian Parents." *Archives of Sexual Behavior* 32(5): 490–491.

Mederer, H.J. 1993. "Division of Labor in Two-Earner Homes: Task Accomplishment versus Household Management as Critical Variables in Perceptions About Family Work." *Journal of Marriage and the Family* 55: 133–145.

Medick, H. 1976. "The Proto-Industrial Family Economy: The Structural Function of Household and Family During the Transition from Peasant Society to Industrial Capitalism." *Social History:* 1–2: 291–315.

Meehan, D.M. 1993. "The Strong-Soft Woman: Manifestations of the Androgyne in Popular Media." In *Taking Sides*, 2nd ed., eds. A. Alexander and J. Hanson: 48–54. Guilford, CT: Dushkin.

Meersand, P., and W. Turchin. 2003. "The Mother-Infant Relationship: From Normality to Pathology." In *Infanticide*, ed. M.G. Spinelli: 209–233. Washington, DC: American Psychiatric Publishing.

Mehrabian, A. 2001. "Characteristics Attributed to Individuals on the Basis of their First Names." *Genetic, Social & General Psychology Monographs* 127: 59–89.

Mehta, M.D. 2001. "Pornography in Usenet: A Study of 98,000 Randomly Selected Images." *CyberPsychology & Behavior* 4(6): 695–703.

Melhuish, M. 1996. *Oh What a Feeling*. Kingston, ON: Quarry Press.

Mendoza-Denton, R., G. Downey, V.J. Purdie, A. Davis, and J. Pietrzak. 2002. "Sensitivity to Status-Based Rejection: Implications for African American Students' College Experience." *Journal of Personality & Social Psychology* 83(4): 896–918.

Merritt, R.D., and C.J. Kob. 1995. "Attribution of Gender to a Gender-Unspecified Individual: An Evaluation of the People=Male Hypothesis." *Sex Roles* 33: 145–157.

Merton, R.K. 1968. *Social Theory and Social Structure*. New York: Free Press.

Mesner, M.A., M.C. Duncan, and C. Cooky. 2003. "Silence, Sports Bras and Wrestling Porn." *Journal of Sport & Social Issues* 27: 38–51.

Mesquida, C.G., and N.I. Wiener. 1996. "Human Collective Aggression: A Behavioral Ecology Perspective." *Ethology & Sociobiology* 17(4): 247–262.

Messerschmidt, J.W. 1993. *Masculinities and Crime*. Lanham, MD: Roman and Littlefield.

Messner, M.A. 2000. "Barbie Girls Versus Sea Monsters: Children Constructing Gender." *Gender & Society* 14(6): 765–784; 1998. "The Limits of 'The Male Role': An Analysis of the Men's Liberation and Men's

Rights Movement." *Gender & Society* 12(3): 255–276; 1997. *Politics of Masculinities*. Thousand Oaks, CA: Sage; 1992. "Like Family: Power, Intimacy, and Sexuality in Male Athletes' Friendships." In *Men's Friendships*, ed. P.M. Nardi: 215–237. Thousand Oaks, CA: Sage; 1990. "Boyhood, Organized Sports, and the Construction of Masculinities." *Journal of Contemporary Ethnography* 18(4): 416–444.

Messner, M.A., M.C. Duncan, and K. Jensen. 1993. "Separating the Men from the Girls: The Gendered Language of Televised Sports." *Gender & Society* 7: 121–137.

Meston, C.M., P.D. Trapnell, and B.B. Gorzalka. 1996. "Ethnic and Gender Differences in Sexual Behavior Between Asian and Non-Asian University Students." *Archives of Sexual Behavior* 25: 33–72.

Meyer, D.R., and J. Bartfield. 1996. "Compliance with Child Support Orders in Divorce Cases." *Journal of Marriage and the Family* 58(1): 201–212.

Meyer, D.R., and S. Garasky. 1993. "Custodial Fathers: Myths, Realities and Child Support Policy." *Journal of Marriage and the Family* 55: 73–89.

Meyer, M.D., and J.M. Kelley. 2004. "Queering the Eye? The Politics of Gay White Men and Gender (In)visibility." *Feminist Media Studies* 4(2): 214–217.

Meyer-Cook, F., and D. Labelle. 2004. "Namaji: Two-Spirit Organizing in Montreal, Canada." *Journal of Gay & Lesbian Social Services* 16(1): 29–51.

Michael, R.T., J.H. Gagnon, E.O. Laumann, and G. Kolata. 1994. *Sex in America*. Boston: Little, Brown.

Michals, D. 1997. "Cyber-Rape: How Virtual Is It?" *Ms.* March–April: 68–72.

Michel, A., M. Ansseau, J.J. Legros, W. Pitchot, and C. Mormont. 2002. "The Transsexual: What About the Future?" *European Psychiatry* 17(6) October: 353–362.

Milan, A. 2000. "One Hundred Years of Families." *Canadian Social Trends* 56: 2–12.

Milan, A., M. Vezina, and C. Wells. 2007. *Family Portrait: Continuity and Change in Canadian Families and Households in 2006, 2006 Census*. Catalogue no. 97-552-XIE, September. Ottawa: Minister of Industry.

Milburn, A.S., D.R. Carney, and A.M. Ramirez. 2001. "Even in Modern Media, the Picture is Still the Same: A Content Analysis of Clipart Images." *Sex Roles* 44(5–6): 277–294.

Miles, A. 1985. *Feminist Radicalism in the 1980s*. Montreal: CultureTexts.

Milhausen, R.R., and E.S. Herold. 2001. "Reconceptualizing the Sexual Double Standard." *Journal of Psychology & Human Sexuality* 13(2): 63–83; 1999. "Does the Sexual Double Standard Still Exist? Perceptions of University Women." *Journal of Sex Research* 36(4): 361–368.

Milkie, M.A. 1994. "Social World Approach to Cultural Studies." *Journal of Contemporary Ethnography* 23(3): 354–380.

Millard, J.E., and J.R. Grant. 2006. "The Stereotypes of Black and White Women in Fashion Magazine Photographs: The Pose of the Model and the Impression She Creates." *Sex Roles* 54(9–10): 659–673.

Millburn, M.A., R. Mather, and S.D. Conrad. 2000. "The Effects of Viewing R-Rated Movie Scenes That Objectify Women on Perceptions of Date Rape." *Sex Roles* 43(9–10): 645–664.

Miller, A. 1990. *Banished Knowledge*. Trans. L. Vennewitz. New York: Doubleday.

Miller, C. 1994. "Who Says What to Whom?" In *The Women and Language Debate*, eds. C. Roman, S. Jubasz, and C. Miller. New Brunswick, NJ: Rutgers University.

Miller, C., and K. Swift. 1993. "Who Is Man?" In *Gender Basics*, ed. A. Minas. Belmont, CA: Wadsworth.

Miller, E.J., J.E. Smith, and D.L. Tremblath. 2000. "The 'Skinny' on Body Size Requests in Personal Ads." *Sex Roles* 43(1–2): 129–141.

Miller, E.M., and C.Y. Costello. 2001. "The Limits of Biological Determinism." *American Sociological Review* 66(4): 592–598.

Miller, J.B. 1974. *Psychoanalysis and Women*. London: Penguin.

Miller, M.L. 2002. "Male and Female Civility: Toward Gender Justice." *Sociological Inquiry* 72(3): 456–466.

Miller, N.B., V.L.L. Smerglia, D.S. Gaudet, and G.C. Kitson. 1998. "Stressful Life Events, Social Support, and the Distress of Widowed and Divorced Women: A Counteractive Model." *Journal of Family Issues* 19(2): 181–203.

Miller, S., and T.E. Malloy. 2003. "Interpersonal Behavior, Perception, and Affect in Status-Discrepant Dyads: Social Interaction of Gay and Heterosexual Men." *Psychology of Men & Masculinity* 4(2): 121–135.

Mills, C.W. 1959. *The Sociological Imagination*. New York: Oxford University Press.

Mills, J.S., and S.R. D'Alfonso. 2007. "Competition and Male Body Image: Increased Drive for Muscularity Following Failure to a Female." *Journal of Social & Clinical Psychology* 26(40): 505–518.

Milner, A., and J. Browitt. 2002. *Contemporary Cultural Theory*, 3rd edition. Sydney, Australia: Allen & Unwin.

Minnotte, K.L., D. Pedersen Stevens, M.C. Minnotte, and G. Kiger. 2007. "Emotion-Work Performance Among Dual-Earner Couples: Testing Four Theoretical Perspectives." *Journal of Family Issues* 28(6): 773–793.

Mintz, S. 1998. "From Patriarchy to Androgyny and Other Myths: Placing Men's Family Roles in Historical Perspective." In *Men in Families*, eds. A. Booth and A.C. Crouter: 3–30. Mahwah, NJ: Lawrence Erlbaum Associates.

Mitchell, G., S. Obradovich, F. Harring, C. Tromborg, and A.L. Burnes. 1992. "Reproducing Gender in Public Places: Adults' Attention to Toddlers in Three Public Locales." *Sex Roles* 26(7–8): 323–330.

Mitchell, J.J. 1973. *Women's Estate*. Toronto: Random House.

Mitchinson, W. 1993. "The Medical Treatment of Women." In *Changing Patterns*, 2nd ed., eds. S. Burt, L. Code, and L. Dorney: 391–421. Toronto: McClelland & Stewart.

Moen, P. 2005. "Beyond the Career Mystique: 'Time In,' 'Time Out,' and 'Second Acts.'" *Sociological Forum* 20(2): 189–208; 2003. "Unscripted: Continuity and Change in the Gendered Life Course." In *Our Studies*, ed. P. Moen: 105–114. New York: Oxford University Press; 2003. *It's About Time*. Ithaca, NY: Cornell University Press; 2001. "Constructing a Life Course." *Marriage & Family Review* 30(4): 97–106; 1992.

Women's Two Roles. New York: Auburn House.

Moen, P., and R.M. Orrange. 2002. "Careers and Lives: Socialization, Structural Lag and Gendered Ambivalence." In *New Frontiers in Socialization*, eds. R.A. Setterson and T.J. Owens: 231–262. Kidlington, Oxford: Elsevier Science Ltd.

Moen, P., and D. Spencer. 2006. "Converging Divergences in Age, Gender, Health and Well-Being: Strategic Selection in the Third Age." In *Handbook of Aging and the Social Sciences*, eds. R.H. Binstock and L.K. George: 127–144. Amsterdam, Netherlads: Elsevier.

Mohanty, C. 2003. "'Under Western Eyes' Revisited: Feminist Solidarity Through Anticapitalist Struggles." *Signs* 28(2): 499–535; 2003. *Feminism Without Borders*. Durham, NC: Duke University Press.

Monette, M. 1996a. "Retirement in the '90s: Retired Men in Canada." *Canadian Social Trends* 42: 8–11; 1996b. "Retirement in the '90s: Going Back to Work." *Canadian Social Trends* 41: 12–14.

Money, J. 1993. *The Adam Principle*. Amherst, NY: Prometheus Books; 1988. *Gay, Straight, and In-Between*. New York: Oxford University Press; 1980. *Love and Love Sickness*. Baltimore: Johns Hopkins University Press.

Money, J., and A.E. Ehrhardt. 1972. *Man and Woman, Boy and Girl*. Baltimore: Johns Hopkins University Press.

Money, J., and P. Tucker. 1975. *Sexual Signatures*. Boston: Little Brown.

Monk-Turner, E., and H.C. Purcell. 1999. "Sexual Violence In Pornography: How Prevalent Is It? *Gender Issues* 17(2): 58–67.

Monk-Turner, E., T. Kouts, K. Parris, and C. Webb. 2007. "Gender Role Stereotyping in Advertisements on Three Radio Stations: Does Musical Genre Make a Difference?" *Journal of Gender Studies* 16(2); 173–182.

Monro, F. and G. Huon. 2005. "Media-Portrayed Idealized Images, Body Shame and Appearance Anxiety." *International Journal of Eating Disorders* 38: 85–90.

Monroe, M., R.C. Baker, and S. Roll. 1997. "The Relationship of Homophobia to

Intimacy in Heterosexual Men." *Journal of Homosexuality* 33(2): 23–37.

Monson, C.M., G.R. Burd, and J. Langhinrichsen-Rohling. 1996. "To Have and to Hold: Perceptions of Marital Rape." *Journal of Interpersonal Violence* 11: 410–424.

Monsour, M. 2002. *Women and Men as Friends*. Mahwah, NJ: Lawrence Erlbaum Associates; 1992. "Meanings of Intimacy in Cross- and Same-sex Friendships." *Journal of Social and Personal Relationships* 9: 277–295.

Montemurro, B. 2003. "Not a Laughing Matter: Sexual Harassment as 'Material' on Workplace-Based Situation Comedies." *Sex Roles* 48(9–10): 433–445.

Mooney, L. A., D. Knox, C. Schacht, and A. Nelson. 2004. *Understanding Social Problems*, 2nd ed. Scarborough: Nelson Thomson Learning.

Moore, M. 1994. "Female Lone Parenting." *The Canadian Journal of Sociology* 14(3): 335–352.

Moore, N.B., and J.K. Davidson, Sr. 1990. "Sex Information Sources: Do They Make a Difference in Sexual Decisions." Paper presented at the Annual Meeting of the National Council on Family Relations, November, Seattle.

Moore, R. 2007. "Friends Don't Let Friends Listen to Corporate Rock: Punk as Field of Cultural Production."*Journal of Contemporary Ethnography* 36(4): 438–474.

Moors, G. 2003. "Estimating the Reciprocal Effect of Gender Role Attitudes and Family Formation: A Log-Linear Path Model with Latent Variables." *European Journal of Population* 19: 199–221.

Morawski, J.G. 2001. "Feminist Research Methods: Bringing Culture to Science." In *From Subjects to Subjectivities*, eds. D.L. Tolman and M. Brydon-Miller: 57–75. New York: New York University Press; 1994. *Practicing Feminisms, Reconstructing Psychology*. Ann Arbor: University of Michigan Press.

Moreau, J. 1991. "Employment Equity." *Canadian Social Trends* 22: 26–28.

Morgan, A., and C. Wilcox. 1992. "Anti-Feminism in Western Europe, 1975–1987." *Western European Politics* 15(4): 151–169.

Morgan, M. 1987. "Television, Sex-Role Attitudes and Sex-Role Behavior." *Journal of Early Adolescence* 7(3): 269–282; 1982. "Television and Adolescents' Sex Role Stereotypes: A Longitudinal Study." *Journal of Personality and Social Psychology* 43: 947–955.

Morgan, M. 1973. *The Total Woman*. London: Hodder and Stoughton.

Morissette, R. and M. Drolet. 2001. "Pension Coverage and Retirement Savings." *Perspectives on Labour and Income* 13(2): 39–46.

Morman, M.T., and K. Floyd. 2006. "Good Fathering: Father and Son Perceptions of What It Means to Be a Good Father." *Fathering* 4(2): 113–136; 2002. "A 'Changing Culture of Fatherhood': Effects on Affectionate Communication, Closeness, and Satisfaction in Men's Relationships with their Fathers and their Sons." *Western Journal of Communication* 66(4): 395–411.

Morrison, M.M., and D.R. Shaffer. 2003. "Gender-Role Congruence and Self-Referencing as Determinants of Advertising Effectiveness." *Sex Roles* 49(5–6): 265–175.

Mortimer, J.T., and J. London. 1984. "The Varying Linkages of Work and Family." In *Work and Family*, ed. P. Voydanoff: 20–35. Palo Alto, Ca.: Mayfield.

Mossman, M.J. 1997. *Readings on Law, Gender, Equality*. Materials prepared for the study use of students at Osgoode Hall School of Law of York University.

Muir, K., and T. Seitz. 2004. "Machismo, Misogyny and Homophobia in a Male Athletic Subculture: A Participant-Observation Study of Deviant Rituals in Collegiate Rugby." *Deviant Behavior* 25(4): 303–327.

Mullaney, J.L. 2007. "'Unity Admirable But Not Necessarily Needed': Going Rates and Gender Boundaries in the Straight Edge Hardcore Music Scene." *Gender & Society* 21(3): 384–408.

Muller, C. 1995. "Maternal Employment, Parent Involvement, and Mathematics Achievement Among Adolescents." *Journal of Marriage and the Family* 57(1): 85–100.

Muncer, S., A. Campbell, V. Jervis, and R. Lewis. 2001. "'Ladettes,' Social Representations, and Aggression." *Sex Roles* 44(1–2): 33–44.

Munoz-Laboy, M., H. Weinstein, and R. Parker. 2007. "The Hip-Hop Club Scene: Gender, Grinding and Sex." *Culture, Health & Sexuality* 9(6): 615–628.

Murphy, M., K. Glaser, and E. Grundy. 1997. "Marital Status and Long-Term Illness in Great Britain." *Journal of Marriage and the Family* 59: 156–164.

Murstein, B. 1991. "Dating: Attracting and Meeting." In *Marriage and Family in Transition*, eds. J.N. Edwards and D.H. Demo. Boston: Allyn and Bacon.

Mutchler, J.E. 1992. "Living Arrangements and Household Transitions among the Unmarried in Later Life." *Social Science Quarterly* 73(3): 565–580.

Myers, C.D., J.L. Riley, and M.E. Robinson. 2003. "Psychosocial Contributions to Sex-Correlated Differences in Pain." *Clinical Journal of Pain* 19(4): 225–232.

Myers, D.G. 2007. *Psychology*, 8th edition. New York: Worth.

Nakamura, K. 2001. "Gender and Language in Japanese Preschool Children." *Research on Language and Social Interaction* 34(1): 15–43.

Namaste. V. 2000. *Invisible Lives*. Chicago: University of Chicago Press.

Nanda, S. 2000. *Gender Diversity*. Illinois: Waveland Press Inc.; 1990. *Neither Man nor Woman*. Belmont, CA: Wadsworth.

Nardi, P. 2000. *Gay Masculinities*. Thousand Oaks, CA: Sage.

Natalier, K. 2003. "'I'm Not His Wife': Doing Gender and Doing Housework in the Absence of Women." *Journal of Sociology* 39(3): 253–269.

Nath, J.K., and V.R. Nayar. 1997. "India." In *The International Encyclopedia of Sexuality*, Vol. 2, ed. R.T. Francoeur: 557–606. New York: Continuum.

Nathanson, A.I., B.J. Wilson, J. McGee, and M. Sebastian. 2002. "Countering the Effects of Female Stereotypes on Television via Active Mediation." *Journal of Communication* 52(4): 922–937.

National Council of Welfare. 2004. *Welfare Incomes, 2003* (Spring 2004). **www.ncwcnbes. net/htmdocument/principales/ onlinepub_e.htm**; 2002. *Poverty Profile, 1999* (Spring 2002). **www.ncwcnbes.net/ htmdocument/principales/ onlinepub_e.htm**; 2000. *Proverty Profile 1998*. Ottawa: Ministry of Public Works; 1999. *Preschool Children*. **www.ncwcnbes.net.htm document/ reportpromise/firstpag.html**; 1999. *Children First: A Pre-Budget Report* (Autumn 1999). **www.ncwcnbes.net. htmdocument/reportchildfirst.htm**

National Post. "Job Ad Seeking Only Women Draws Criticism." August 7, 1999, A4.

Nault, F. 1996. "Twenty Years of Marriages." *Health Reports* 8(2): 39–46.

Neft, N., and A.D. Levine. 1997. *Where Women Stand*. New York: Random House.

Neidig, P.H., and S.H. Friedman. 1984. *Spouse Abuse*. Champaign, IL: Research Press.

Nelson, E.D. 1994. "Females Who Sexually Abuse Children: A Discussion of Gender Stereotypes and Symbolic Assailants." *Qualitative Sociology* 17(1): 63–88.

Nelson, M. B. 1994. *The Stronger Women Get, the More Men Love Football*. New York: Harcourt.

Nelson, M.K., and R. Schutz. 2007. "Day Care Differences and the Reproduction of Social Class." *Journal of Contemporary Ethnography* 36(3): 281–317.

Nelson, T., M. Biernat, and M. Manis. 1990. "Everyday Base Rates (Sex Stereotypes): Potent and Reliable." *Journal of Personality and Social Psychology* 59: 664–675.

Nelton, S., and K. Berney 1987. "Women: The Second Wave." *National Business* May: 18–27.

Nett, E.M. 1993. *Canadian Families*, 2nd ed. Toronto: Butterworths.

Neugarten, B.L. 1968a. "The Awareness of Middle Age." In *Middle Age and Aging*: 93–98. Chicago: University of Chicago Press; 1968b. "Adult Personality: Toward a Psychology of the Life Cycle." In *Middle Age and Aging*: 137–147. Chicago: University of Chicago Press.

Newcombe, N.S. 2003. "Some Controls Control Too Much." *Child Development* 74(4): 1050–1052.

Newman, B.M., and P.R. Newman. 1975. *Development Through Life*. Homewood, IL: Dorsey.

Newman, B.S. 2007. "College Students' Attitudes About Lesbians: What Difference Does 16 Years Make? *Journal of Homosexuality* 52(3–4): 249–265.

Newman, J., T. Bidjerano, A. Ali Ozdogru, C. Kao, C. Ozkose, and J. Johnson. 2007. "What Do They Usually Do After School? A Comparative Analysis of Fourth-Grade Children in Bulgaria, Taiwan and the United States." *Journal of Early Adolescence* 27(4): 431–456.

Newman, L.K. 2002. "Sex, Gender and Culture: Issues in the Definition Assessment and Treatment of Gender Identity Disorder." *Clinical Child Psychology and Psychiatry* 7(3): 352–359.

Neysmith, S., and X. Chen. 2002. "Understanding How Globalization and Restructuring Affect Women's Lives: Implications for Comparative Policy Analysis." *International Journal of Social Welfare* 11(3): 243–253.

Ng, S., and J. Bradac. 1993. *Power in Language*. Newbury Park, CA: Sage.

Nicholas, D.R. 2000. "Men, Masculinity and Cancer: Risk-Factor Behaviors, Early Detection, and Psychosocial Adaptation." *Journal of American College Health* 49(1): 27–33.

Nicholson, L.J. (ed.). 1990. *Introduction to Feminism/Postmodernism*. New York: Routledge.

Niemann, Y.F., L. Jennings, and R.M. Rozelle. 1994. "Use of Free Response and Cluster Analysis to Determine Stereotypes of Eight Groups." *Personality and Social Psychology Bulletin* 20: 379–390.

Nilsen, A.P. 1993. "Sexism in English: A 1990s Update." In *Experiencing Race, Class and Gender in the United States*, ed. V. Cyrus. Mountain View, CA: Mayfield.

Nippold, M.A., J.K. Duthie, and J. Larsen. 2005. "Literacy as a Leisure Activity: Free-Time Preferences of Older Children and Young Adolescents." *Language, Speech and Hearing Services in Schools* 36(2): 93–102.

Nolen-Hoecksmema, L.S., and J.S. Girgus. 1994. "The Emergence of Gender Differences in Depression During Adolescence." *Psychological Bulletin* 115(3): 424–443.

Nolin, M.J., and K.K. Petersen. 1992. "Gender Differences in Parent–Child Communication About Sexuality: An Exploratory Study." *Journal of Adolescent Research* 7: 59–79.

Nomaguchi, K.M., and M.A. Milkie. 2006. "Maternal Employment in Childhood and Adults' Retrospective Reports of Parenting Practices." *Journal of Marriage and Family* 68(3): 573–594. 2003. "Costs and Rewards of Children: The Effects of Becoming a Parent on Adults' Lives." *Journal of Marriage and the Family* 65(2): 356–374.

NOMAS. 1991/2001. "Statement of Principles. The National Organization for Men Against Sexism." Reprinted in *Men's Lives*, 5th ed., eds. M.S. Kimmel and M.A. Messner: 539. Boston: Allyn and Bacon.

Noonan, M.C. 2001. "The Impact of Domestic Work on Men's and Women's Wages." *Journal of Marriage and the Family* 63(4): 1134–1145.

Norland, J.A. 1994. *Profile of Canada's Seniors.* Scarborough, ON: Statistics Canada and Prentice Hall.

Normand, J. 2000. "Education." In *Women in Canada 2000: A Gender-Based Statistical Report*: 85–96. Ottawa: Statistics Canada. Catalogue 89-503-XPE.

Norton, J. 1999. "Invisible Man: A Queer Critique of Feminist Anti-Pornography Theory." In *Sexwork and Sex Workers*, eds. B.M. Dank and R. Refinetti: 113–124. New Brunswick, NJ: Transaction.

Norton, K.I., T.S. Olds, S. Olive, and S. Dank. 1996. "Ken and Barbie at Life Size." *Sex Roles* 34(3–4): 287–294.

Norton, S. 2002. "Women Exposed: Sexual Harassment and Female Vulnerability." In *The Psychology of Sex, Gender and Jobs*, eds. L. Diamant and J.A. Lee: 83–102. Westport, CT: Praeger.

Nosek, B.A., M.R. Banaji, and A.G. Greenwald. 2002. "Math=Male, Me=Female, Therefore Math Not=Me." *Journal of Personality & Social Psychology* 83(1): 44–59.

Novaes, C., and O. Almedia. 1999. "Premenstrual Syndrome and Psychiatric Morbidity at the Menopause." *Psychosomatic Obstetric Gynecology* 20: 56–57.

Novak, L.L., and D.R. Novack. 1996. "Being Female in the Eighties and Nineties: Conflicts Between New Opportunities and Traditional Expectations Among White, Middle-Class, Heterosexual Women." *Sex Roles* 35: 57–77.

Novak, M. 1997. *Aging and Society*, 3rd ed. Scarborough, ON: Nelson.

Nowell, I. 1996. *Women Who Give Away Millions*. Toronto: Hounslow.

Nussbaum, M. 2000. *Women and Human Development*. Cambridge: Cambridge University Press; 1999. *Sex and Social Justice*. Oxford: Oxford University Press.

Nye, F. I., and F.M. Berardo. 1973. *The Family*. New York: Macmillan.

O'Barr, W. 1983. "The Study of Language in Institutional Contexts." *Journal of Language & Social Psychology* 2: 241–251; 1983. *Linguistic Evidence*. New York: Academic Press.

O'Brien, E., and L. Foley. 1999. "Homogamy, Hetereogamy, Hypergamy, and Hypogamy." *Teaching Sociology* 27(2): 145–149.

O'Brien, J.E.. 1971. "Violence in Divorce-Prone Families." *Journal of Marriage and the Family* 33: 692–698.

O'Brien, M. 1981. *The Politics of Reproduction*. London: Routledge & Kegan Paul.

O'Cass, A., and P. Clarke. 2002. "Dear Santa, Do You Have My Brand? A Study of the Brand Requests, Awareness and Request Styles at Christmas Time." *Journal of Consumer Behavior* 2(1): 37–56.

Odell, P.M., K.O. Korgen, P. Schumacher, and M. Delucchi. 2000. "Internet Use Among Female and Male College Students." *CyberPsychology & Behavior* 3(5): 855–862.

Oderkirk, J. 1996. "Government Sponsored Income Security Programs for Seniors: Old Age Security." *Canadian Social Trends* 40: 3–7; 1994. "Marriage in Canada: Changing Beliefs and Behaviours 1600–1900." *Canadian Social Trends*: 2–7.

Oderkirk, J., and C. Lochhead. 1992. "Lone Parenthood: Gender Differences." *Canadian Social Trends* 32: 19–25.

Oddone-Paolucci, E., M. Genuis, and C. Violato. 2000. "A Meta-Analysis of the Published Research on the Effects of Pornography." In *The Changing Family and Child Development*, eds. C. Violato and E. Oddone-Paolucci: 48–59. Aldershot, England: Ashgate Publishing Limited.

Oderkerken-Schroder, G., K. De Wulf, and N. Hofstee. 2002. "Is Gender Stereotyping in Advertising More Prevalent in Masculine Countries? A Cross-National Analysis." *International Marketing Review* 19(4): 408–419.

O'Donnell, V. 2006. "Aboriginal Women in Canada." In *Women in Canada*, 5th edition. Statistics Canada, Catalogue no. 89-503-XIE: 181–209.

Ogburn, W.F. 1922. *Social Change*. New York: Viking Press.

Oggins, J., J. Veroff, and D. Leber. 1993. "Perceptions of Marital Interaction Among Black and White Newlyweds." *Journal of Personality & Social Psychology* 65(3): 494–511.

Ogrodnik, L. 2007. "Spousal Homicide or Attempts and Prior Police Contact for Spousal Abuse." In *Family Violence in Canada: A Statistical Profile 2007*: 9–15. Statistics Canada, Catalogue no. 85-224. Ottawa: Minister of Industry.

Oh, S. 2000. "Just Like a Virgin." *Maclean's*, June 12: 44.

Okazaki, S. 2002. "Influence of Culture on Asian Americans' Sexuality." *Journal of Sex Research* 39: 34–41.

O'Keefe, T., and K. Fox, eds. 2003. *Finding the Real Me*. San Francisco, CA: Jossey-Bass.

Okin, S.M. 1989. *Justice, Gender and the Family*. New York: Basic Books.

Oliker, S.J. 1998. "The Modernization of Friendship: Individualism, Intimacy, and Gender in the Nineteenth Century." In *Placing Friendship in Context*, eds. R.G. Adams and G. Allan: 18–42. New York: Cambridge University Press.

Oliver, M.B., and J.S. Hyde. 1993. "Gender Differences in Sexuality: A Meta-Analysis." *Psychological Bulletin* 114(1): 29–51.

Ontario Women's Directorate. 1995. *Sex-Role Stereotyping*. Toronto: Ontario Women's Directorate; 1992. *Words That Count Women In*. Toronto: Ontario Women's Directorate.

Oppenheimer, V.K. 1994. "Women's Rising Employment and the Future of the Family in Industrial Societies." *Population and Development Review* 20(2): 293–342.

Orbuch, T.L., J.S. House, R.P. Mero, and P.S. Webster. 1996. "Marital Quality Over the Life Course." *Social Psychology Quarterly* 59(2): 162–171.

O'Reilly, P. 2001. "Learning to Be a Girl." In *Educating Young Adolescent Girls*, eds. P. O'Reilly and E.M. Penn: 11–27. Mahwah, NJ: Lawrence Erlbaum Associates.

Oren, T., and K.L. Ruhl. 1997. "Assessing Infant Environments." *Infant-Toddler Intervention* 7(3): 141–160.

Orenstein, P. 2001. "Unbalanced Equations: Girls, Math and the Confidence Gap." In *Gender and Social Life*, ed. R. Satow: 149–152. Needham Heights, MA: Allyn & Bacon; 2001b. "Sluts and Studs." In *Self and Society*, ed. A. Branaman: 36–37. Malden, MA: Blackwell; 1994. *School Girls*. New York: Doubleday.

Osman, S.L. 2003. "Predicting Men's Rape Perceptions Based on the Belief that 'No' Really Means 'Yes.'" *Journal of Applied Social Psychology* 33(4): 683–692.

Osmond, M.W., and B. Thorne. 1993. "Feminist Theories: The Social Construction of Gender in Families and Society." In *Sourcebook of Family Theories and Methods*, eds. PG. Boss, W.J. Doherty, R. LaRossa, W.R. Schumm, and S.K. Steinmetz: 591–622. New York: Plenum.

O'Sullivan, L.F., and E.R. Allgeier. 1998. "Feigning Sexual Desire: Consenting to Unwanted Sexual Activity in Heterosexual Dating Relationships." *Journal of Sex Research* 35(3): 234–243.

Oswald, D.L., and R.D. Harvey. 2003. "A Q-Methodological Study of Women's Subjective Perspectives on Mathematics." *Sex Roles* 49(3–4): 133–142.

Otis, J., J. Levy, J. Samson, F. Pilote, and A. Fugere. 1997. "Gender Differences in Sexuality and Interpersonal Power Relations Among French-Speaking Young Adults from Quebec." *Canadian Journal of Human Sexuality* 6(1): 17–28.

Owens, L.K., T.L. Hughes, and D. Owens-Nicholson. 2003. "The Effects of Sexual Orientation on Body Image and Attitudes About Eating and Weight." *Journal of Lesbian Studies* 7(1): 15–33.

Oyserman, D., K. Harrison, and D. Bybee. 2001. "Can Racial Identity Be Promotive of Academic Efficacy?" *International Journal of Behavioral Development* 25(4): 379–385.

Oyserman, D., D. Rybee, K. Terry, and T. Hart-Johnson. 2004. "Possible Selves as Roadmaps." *Journal of Research in Personality* 38(2): 130–149.

Oxley, N.L., M.T. Dzindolet, and J.L. Miller. 2002. "Sex Differences in Communication with Close Friends: Testing Tannen's Claims." *Psychological Reports* 91(2): 537–544.

Paglia, C. 1990. 1991. *Sex, Art and American Culture*. New York: Vintage Books.

Paik, H. 2001. "The History of Children's Use of Electronic Media." In *Handbook of Children and the Media*, eds. D.G. Singer and J.L. Singer: 7–27. Thousand Oaks, CA: Sage.

Palameta, B. 2003. "Who Pays For Domestic Help?" *Perspectives on Labour and Income*, Statistics Canada, Catalogue no. 75-001-XIE, August.

Paley, V.G. 1984. *Boys and Girls*. Chicago: University of Chicago.

Palmer, R. 1995. *Rock & Roll*. New York: Harmony Books.

Papoulias, C. 2006. "Transgender." *Theory, Culture & Society* 23(2–3): 231–233.

Parameswaren, R. 2002. "Reading Fictions of Romance: Gender, Sexuality and Nationalism in Postcolonial India." *Journal of Communication* 52(4): 832–851.

Pardun, C.K., K.L. L'Engle, and J.D. Brown. 2005. "Linking Exposure to Outcomes: Early Adolescents' Consumption of Sexual Content in Six Media." *Mass Consumption & Society* 8(2): 75–91.

Park Ridge Center for Health, Faith and Ethics. 2002. Sex-Selective Abortion: Social, Cultural and Religious Considerations. **www.parkridge center.org/ ethics_may02.html**

Park, S.M. 1996. "From Sanitation to Liberation? The Modern and Postmodern Marketing of Menstrual Products." *Journal of Popular Culture* 20(2): 149–167.

Parke, R.D. 2002. "Fathers and Families." In *Handbook of Parenting*, Vol. 3, 2nd ed., ed.

M.H. Bornstein: 27–73. Mahwah, NJ: Lawrence Erlbaum Associates; 2002. "Parenting in the New Millennium: Prospects, Promises and Pitfalls." In *Retrospect and Prospect in the Psychological Study of Families*, eds. J.P. McHale and W.S. Grolnick: 656–693. Mahwah, NJ: Lawrence Erlbaum Associates; 1996. *Fatherhood*. Cambridge: Harvard University Press.

Parke, R.D., M. Kin, M. Flyr, D.J. McDowell, S.D. Simpkins, C.H. Killian, and M. Wild. 2001. "Managing Marital Conflict: Links with Children's Peer Relationships." In *Interparental Conflict and Child Development*, eds. J.H. Grych and F.D. Fincham: 291–314. New York: Cambridge University Press.

Parke, R.D., S.D. Simpkins, D.J. McDowell, M. Kim, C. Killian, J. Dennis, M.L. Flyr, M. Wild, and Y. Rah. 2002. "Fatherhood." In *Blackwell Handbook of Childhood Social Development*, eds. P.K. Smith and C.H. Hart: 156–177. Malden, MA: Blackwell Publishers.

Parks, J.B., and M.A. Robertson. 2000. "Development and Validation of an Instrument to Measure Attitudes Toward Sexist/Nonsexist Language." *Sex Roles* 42(5–6): 415–438; 1998. "Influence of Age, Gender, and Context on Attitudes Toward Sexist/Nonsexist Language: Is Sport a Special Case?" *Sex Roles* 38(5–6): 477–494.

Parks, M.R., and K. Floyd. 1996. "Meanings for Closeness and Intimacy in Friendship." *Journal of Social & Personal Relationships* 13(1): 85–107.

Parsons, T. 1953. "Illness and the Role of the Physician: A Sociological Perspective." In *Personality in Nature, Society and Culture*, 2nd ed., eds. C. Kluckhorn and H.A. Murray: 609–617. New York: Knopf; 1949. "The Social Structure of the Family." In *The Family*, ed. R. Anshen: 173–201. New York: Harper and Brothers; 1942. "Age and Sex in the Social Structure." *American Sociological Review* 7: 601–616.

Parsons, T., and R.F. Bales. 1955. *Family, Socialization and Interaction Process*. New York: Free Press.

Parton, N. 1990. "Taking Child Abuse Seriously." In *Taking Violence Against Children Seriously*, ed. The Violence Against Children Study Group: 7–24. London: Unwin Hyman.

Pasley, K., and C. Minton. 2001. "Generative Fathering After Divorce and Remarriage: Beyond the 'Disappearing Dad.'" In *Men and Masculinity*, ed. T.F. Cohen: 239–248. Belmont, CA: Wadsworth.

Patterson, C.J. 2000. "Family Relationships of Lesbians and Gay Men." *Journal of Marriage and the Family* 62: 1052–1069.

Pattinson, J. 2006. "'Playing the Daft Lassie with Them': Gender, Captivity and the Special Operations Executive During the Second World War." *European Review of History* 13(2): 271–292.

Pattucci, A. 1998. "Trespassers on Private Property." In *Women in Science*, ed. A. Pattatucci: 1–14. Thousand Oaks, CA: Sage.

Pearl, A. and J. Weston. 2003. "Attitudes of Adolescents About Cosmetic Surgery." *Annals of Plastic Surgery* 50(6): 628–630.

Pearson, P. 1997. *When She Was Bad*. Toronto: Random House.

Pease, A., and B. Pease. 2006. *Why Men Don't Have a Clue and Women Always Need More Shoes*. New York: HarperCollins; 2001. *Why Men Don't Listen and Women Can't Read Maps*. New York: Random House.

Pease, B. 2000. *Recreating Men*. Politics. London: Sage.

Pedersen, F.A. 1987. *Men's Transition to Parenthood*: Hillsdale, NJ: Lawrence Erlbaum Associates.

Pedersen, P.M., and W.A. Whisenant. 2003. "Examining Stereotypical Written and Photographic Reporting on the Sports Page: An Analysis of Newspaper Coverage of Inter-Scholastic Athletics." *Women in Sport and Physical Activity* 12: 67–86.

Pederson, L.E. 1991. *Dark Hearts*. Boston, MA: Shambhala Press.

Peele, S., and R. DeGrandpre. 1995. "My Genes Made Me Do It." *Psychology Today* 28(4): 50–53, 62–68.

Peirce, K. 2001. "What if the Energizer Bunny Were Female?: Importance of Gender in Perceptions of Advertising Spokes-Character Effectiveness." *Sex Roles*

45(11–12): 845–858; 1997. "Women's Magazine Fiction: A Content Analysis of the Roles, Attributes and Occupations of Main Characters." *Sex Roles* 37(7–8): 581–593; 1993. "Socialization of Teenage Girls Through Teen-Magazine Fiction: The Making of a New Woman or an Old Lady?" *Sex Roles* 29(1–2): 59–68; 1990. "A Feminist Theoretical Perspective on the Socialization of Teenage Girls Through Seventeen Magazine." *Sex Roles* 23: 491–500.

Peletz, M.G. 2006. "Transgenderism and Gender Pluralism in Southeast Asia Since Early Modern Times." *Current Anthropology* 47(2): 309–340.

Penman-Aguilar, A., J. Hall, L. Artz, M.R. Crawford, N. Peacock, J. Van Olphen, L. Peters, and M. Macaluso. 2002. "Presenting the Female Condom to Men: A Dyadic Analysis of Effect of the Woman's Approach." *Women & Health* 35(1): 37–51.

Peplau, L.A., and A.W. Fingerhut. 2007. "The Close Relationships of Lesbians and Gay Men." *Annual Review of Psychology* 58: 405–424.

Peplau, L.A., and L.R. Spalding. 2003. "The Close Relationships of Lesbians, Gay Men, and Bisexuals." In *Psychological Perspectives on Lesbian, Gay, and Bisexual Experiences*, eds. L.D. Garnets and D.C. Kimmel: 449–474. New York: Columbia University Press.

Peretti, P.O., and T.M. Sydney. 1985. "Parental Toy Stereotyping and Its Effect on Child Toy Preference." *Social Behavior and Personality* 12: 213–216.

Perlesz, A. 2004. "Deconstructing the Fear of Father Absence." *Journal of Feminist Family Therapy* 16(3): 1–29.

Perlmutter, M., and E. Hall. 1985. *Adult Development and Aging*. New York: John Wiley & Sons.

Peters, J. 1990. "Cultural Variations: Past and Present." In *Families*, 2nd ed., ed. M. Baker: 166–191. Toronto: McGraw-Hill Ryerson; 1987. "Changing Perspectives on Divorce." In *Family Matters*, eds. K.L. Anderson et al.: 141–162. Toronto: Methuen.

Peterson, G.W., D.A. Bodman, K.R. Bush, and D. Madden-Derdich. 2001. "Gender and Parent-Child Relationships." In *Handbook*

of Family Diversity, eds. D.H. Demo and K.R. Allen: 82–104. London: Oxford University Press.

Peterson, S.H., G.M. Wingood, R.J. DiClemente, K. Harrington, and S. Davies. 2007. "Images of Sexual Stereotypes in Rap Videos and the Health of American American Female Adolescents." *Journal of Women's Health* 16(8): 1157–1164.

Pfeil, F. 1995. *White Guys*. London: Verso.

Phillips, B. 1990. "Nicknames and Sex Role Stereotypes." *Sex Roles* 23: 281–289.

Phillips, R. 1991. *Untying The Knot*. Cambridge: Cambridge University Press.

Philpot, C.L. 2000. "Socialization of Gender Roles." In *Handbook of Family Development and Intervention*, eds. W.C. Nichols and M.A. Pace-Nichols: 85–108. New York: John Wiley & Sons.

Phillips-Miller, D.L., N.J. Campbell, and C.R. Morrison. 2000. "Work and Family: Satisfaction, Stress and Spousal Support." *Journal of Employment Counseling* 37(1): 16–30.

Phipps, S., P. Burton, and L. Osberg. 2001. "Time as a Source of Inequality Within Marriage: Are Husbands More Satisfied with Time for Themselves Than Wives?" *Feminist Economics* 7(2): 1–21.

Phoca, S. 2000. "Feminism and Gender." In *The Routledge Critical Dictionary of Feminism and Postfeminism*, ed. S. Gamble. New York: Routledge.

Phua, V.C. 2002. "Sex and Sexuality in Men's Personal Advertisements." *Men & Masculinities* 5(2): 178–191.

Piaget, J. 1968. *Six Psychological Studies*. Trans. A. Tenzer, ed. D. Elkind. New York: Vintage; 1954. *The Construction of Reality in the Child*. New York: Basic Books; 1950. *The Psychology of Intelligence*. London: Routledge & Kegan Paul.

Picard, A. 2004. "Dieting Commonplace Among Preteen Girls." *Globe and Mail*, May 11: A21.

Pierce, D. 2000. "Maternal Management of the Home as a Developmental Play Space for Infants and Toddlers." *American Journal of Occupational Therapy* 54(3): 290–299.

Piercy, K.W. 1998. "Theorizing About Family Caregiving: The Role of Responsibility."

Journal of Marriage and the Family 60: 109–118.

Pillard, R. C., and J. M. Bailey. 1998. "Human Sexuality Has a Heritable Component." *Human Biology* 70: 347–365.

Pine, K.J., and A. Nash. 2003. "Barbie or Betty? Preschool Children's Preference for Branded Products and Evidence for Gender-Linked Differences." *Journal of Developmental & Behavioral Pediatrics* 24(4): 219–224; 2002. "Dear Santa: The Effects of Television Advertising on Young Children." *International Journal of Behavioral Development* 26(6): 529–539.

Pinker, S. 1997. *How the Mind Works*. New York: W.W. Norton.

Pinquart, M. 2003. "Loneliness in Married, Widowed, Divorced, and Never-Married Older Adults." *Journal of Social and Personal Relationships* 20(1): 31–53.

Pipher, M. 1994. *Reviving Ophelia*. New York: Ballantine.

Pittman, F.S. 1993. *Man Enough*. New York: Perigee.

Pittman, J.F., and D. Blanchard. 1996. "The Effects of Work History and Timing of Marriage on the Division of Household Labor: A Life-Course Perspective." *Journal of Marriage and the Family* 58: 78–90.

Plastic Surgery Statistics. 2008. "Plastic Surgery Information Canada."

Pleck, J.H. 1992. "Prisoners of Manliness." In *Men's Lives*, eds. M.S. Kimmel and M.A. Messner: 98–107. New York: Macmillan; 1977. "The Work–Family Role Systems." *Social Problems* 24: 417–427.

Pleck, J.H., and E. Corfman. 1979. "Married Men: Work and Family." In *Families Today*, ed. E. Corfman, vol. 1: 387–411.

Plummer, K. 2001. *Documents of Life-2*. London: Sage; 1994. *Telling Sexual Stories*. New York: Routledge.

Podlas, K. 2000. "Mistresses of their Domain: How Female Entrepreneurs in Cyberporn are Initiating a Gender Power Shift." *CyberPsychology & Behavior* 3(5): 847–854.

Pold, H. 2001. "Trends in Part-Time Work." *Perspectives on Labour and Income* 13 (1): 13–15. **www.dsp-psd.pwgsc.gc.ca/ dsp-psd/Pilot/Statcan/75-001-XIE/ 75-001-XIE.html**

Pollack W. 2000. *Real Boys' Voices*. New York: Random House.1998. *Real Boys*. New York: Random House.

Pollack, W.S. 1990. "Men's Development and Psychotherapy: A Psychoanalytic Perspective." *Psychotherapy* 27(3): 316–321.

Pollett, A., and P. Hurwitz. 2004. "Strip Til You Drop." *The Nation*, January 12: 24–25.

Pollitt, K. 1991. "The Smurfette Principle." *New York Times Magazine*, April 7: 22–23.

Pomerleau, A., D. Bolduc, G. Malcuit, and L. Cossette. 1990. "Pink or Blue: Gender Stereotypes in the First Two Years of Life." *Sex Roles* 22(5–6): 359–367.

Pomerantz, E.M., J.L. Saxon, and G.A. Kenney. 2001. "Self-Evaluation: The Development of Sex Differences." In *Cognitive Social Psychology*, ed. G.B. Moskowitz: 59–73. Mahwah, NJ: Lawrence Erlbaum Associates.

Poorman, P.B., E.P. Seelau, and S.M. Seelau. 2003. "Perception of Domestic Abuse in Same-Sex Relationships and Implications for Criminal Justice and Mental Health Responses." *Violence & Victims* 18(6): 659–669.

Pope, H.G. Jr., R. Olivardia, and A. Gruber. 1999. "Evolving Images of Male Body Image as Seen Through Action Toys." *International Journal of Eating Disorders* 26(1): 65–72.

Popenoe, D. 1998. "The Decline of Marriage and Fatherhood." In *Seeing Ourselves*, 4th ed., eds. J.J. Macionis and N.V. Benokraitis: 312–319. Upper Saddle River, NJ: Prentice Hall; 1996. *Life without Father*. New York: Martin Kessler Books.

Popp, D., R.A. Donovan, M. Crawford, K.L. Marsh, and M. Pcele. 2003. "Gender, Race and Speech Style Stereotypes." *Sex Roles* 48(7–8): 317–325.

Postmes, T., and R. Spears. 2002. "Behavior Online: Does Anonymous Computer Communication Reduce Gender Inequality?" *Personality and Social Psychology Bulletin* 28(8): 1073–1083.

Potuchek, J.L. 1997. *Who Supports the Family?* Stanford, CA: Stanford University Press; 1992. "Employed Wives' Orientations to Breadwinning: A Gender Theory

Analysis." *Journal of Marriage and the Family* 54: 548–558.

Powlishta, K.K., M.G. Sen, L.A. Serbin, D. Poulin-Dubois, and J.A. Eichstedt. 2001. "From Infancy Through Middle Childhood: The Role of Cognitive and Social Factors in Becoming Gendered." In *Handbook of the Psychology of Women and Gender*, ed. R.K. Unger: 116–1232. New York: John Wiley & Sons.

Poulin-Dubois, D., L.A. Serbin, and A. Derbyshire. 1998. "Toddler's Intermodal and Verbal Knowledge About Gender." *Merrill-Palmer Quarterly* 44(3): 338–354.

Powlishta, K.K., L.A. Serbin, A. Doyle, and D.R. White. 1994. "Gender, Ethnic and Body Type Biases: The Generality of Prejudice in Childhood." *Developmental Psychology* 30(4): 526–536.

Poulin-Dubois, D., L.A. Serbin, J.A. Eichstedt, M.G. Sen, and C.F. Beissel. 2002. "Men Don't Put on Make-Up: Toddlers' Knowledge of the Gender Stereotyping of Household Activities." *Social Development* 11(2): 166–181.

Poulin-Dubois, D., L.A. Serbin, B. Kenyon, and A. Derbyshire. 1994. "Infants' Intermodal Knowledge About Gender." *Developmental Psychology* 30: 436–442.

Preece, M. 2003–2004. "When Lone Parents Marry: The Challenge of Stepfamily Relationships." *Transition Magazine* 33(4): 5–8.

Prentice, D.A., and E. Carranza. 2002. "What Women Should Be, Shouldn't Be, Are Allowed to Be and Don't Have to Be: The Contents of Prescriptive Gender Stereotypes." *Psychology of Women Quarterly* 26(4): 269–281.

Prentice, S. 2000. "The Conceptual Politics of Chilly Climate Controversies." *Gender and Education* 12(2): 195–207.

Press, J.E. 2004. "Cute Butts and Housework: A Gynocentric Theory of Assortive Mating." *Journal of Marriage and the Family* 66(4): 1029–1033.

Previti, D., and P.R. Amato. 2004. "Is Infidelity a Cause or a Consequence of Poor Marital Quality?" *Journal of Social and Personal Relationships* 21(2); 217–220; 2002. "Why Stay Married? Rewards, Barriers and Marital Stability."

Journal of Marriage and the Family 65(3): 561–573.

Price, J., and M.G. Dalecki. 1998. "The Social Basis of Homophobia: An Empirical Illustration." *Sociological Spectrum* 18: 143–159.

Pridal, C.G. 2001. "Male Gender Role Issues in the Treatment of Sexual Dysfunction." In *The New Handbook of Psychotherapy and Counseling with Men*: 309–334. San Francisco, CA: Jossey-Bass.

Priest, L. 1990. *Conspiracy of Silence*. Toronto: McClelland and Stewart.

Pringle, R. 1993. "Male Secretaries." In *Doing Women's Work*, ed. C.L. Williams: 128–151. Newbury Park, CA: Sage.

Promise Keepers. 2008. "About Us." **www.promisekeepers.org/about**

Promise Keepers Canada. 2004. Promise Keepers Canada. **www.promisekeepers.ca/content/faq**

Prosser, J. 1998. *Second Skins*. New York: Columbia University Press.

Prossner, J. 1997. "Transgender." In *Lesbian and Gay Studies*, eds. A. Medhurst and S.R. Munt: 309–326. Herndon, VA: Cassell.

Pruett, K.D. 1987. *The Nurturing Father*. New York: Warner Books.

Pryor, J.B., and N.J. Whalen. 1997. "A Typology of Sexual Harassment: Characteristics of Harassers and the Social Circumstances Under Which Sexual Harassment Occurs." In *Sexual Harassment*, ed. W. O'Donohue: 129–151. Boston: Allyn & Bacon.

Pryzgoda, J., and J.C. Chrisler. 2000. "Definitions of Gender and Sex: The Subtleties of Meaning." *Sex Roles* 43: 553–569.

Puka, B. 1990. "The Liberation of Caring: A Different Voice for Gilligan's Different Voice." *Hypatia* 5: 59–82.

Purcell, P., and L. Stewart. 1990. "Dick and Jane in 1989." *Sex Roles* 22(3–4): 177–185.

Queniart, A. 1992. "Risky Business: Medical Definitions of Pregnancy." In *Anatomy of Gender* eds. D.H. Currie and V. Raoul: 161–174. Ottawa: Carleton University Press.

Qian, Z. 1999. "Who Intermarries? Education, Nativity, Region, and Interracial Marriage, 1980 and 1990." *Journal of Comparative Family Studies* 30(4): 579–597.

Raag, T. 1999. "Influences of Social Expectations of Gender, Gender Stereotypes, and Situational Constraints on Children's Toy Choices." *Sex Roles* 41(1–2): 809–831.

Raag, T., and C.L. Rackliff. 1998. "Preschoolers' Awareness of Social Expectations of Gender: Relationships to Toy Choices." *Sex Roles* 39(9–10): 685–700.

Radner, H. 2008. "Compulsory Sexuality and the Desiring Woman." *Sexualities* 11(1–2) February: 94–100.

Radway, J. 1984. *Reading the Romance*. Chapel Hill: University of North Carolina Press.

Ragas, M.C., and K. Kozlowski. 1998. *Read My Lips*. San Francisco: Chronicle Books.

Rahav, G., and N. Baum. 2002. "Divorced Women: Factors Contributing to Self-Identity Change." *Journal of Divorce & Remarriage* 37(3–4): 41–59.

Rajalakshmi, T.K. 2000. "Sex Selection and Questions of Law. *Frontline* 17(21) 14–27.

Raley, A.B., and J.L. Lucas. 2006. "Stereotype or Success? Prime-Time Television's Portrayals of Gay Male, Lesbian, and Bisexual Characters." *Journal of Homosexuality* 51(2): 19–38.

Ramsey, J.L., and J.H. Langlois. 2002. "Effects of the 'Beauty is Good' Stereotype on Children's Information Processing." *Journal of Experimental Child Psychology* 81(3): 320–340.

Ramsey, P.G. 1995. "Changing Social Dynamics in Early Childhood Classrooms." *Child Development* 66(3): 764–773.

Rank, M.R. 2000. "Socialization of Socioeconomic Status." In *Handbook of Family Development and Intervention*, eds. W.C. Nichols and M.A. Pace-Nichols: 129–142. New York: John Wiley and Sons.

Ratele, K. 2003. "We Black Men." *International Journal of Intercultural Relations* 27(2): 237–249.

Raty, H., and K. Kasanen. 2007. "Gendered Views of Ability in Parents' Perceptions of their Children's Academic Competencies." *Sex Roles* 56(1–2): 117–124.

Rawlins, W.K. 1993. "Communication in Cross-Sex Friendships." In *Women and Men Communicating*, eds. L. Arliss and D. Borisoff. Fort Worth, TX: Harcourt Brace Jovanovich.

Raymond, J. 1996. "The Politics of Transgenderism." In *Blending Genders*, eds. R.Ekins and D. King: 215–223.

London: Routledge; 1982. *The Transsexual Empire*. London: The Women's Press Ltd.

Razack, S. 1993. "Exploring the Omissions and Silence in Law Around Race." In *Investigating Gender Bias*, eds. J. Brockman and D.E. Chunn: 37–48. Toronto: Thompson Educational Publishing.

Real, T. 1997. *I Don't Want To Talk About It*. New York: Scribner.

Reddy, G. 2005. "Geographies of Contagion: Hijras, Kolthis and the Politics of Sexual Marginality in Hyderabad." *Anthropology & Medicine* 12(3): 255–270.

Reeder, H.M. 2003. "The Effect of Gender Role Orientation on Same- and Cross-Sex Friendship Formation." *Sex Roles* 49(3–4): 143–152.

Regan, P.C., L. Levin, S. Sprecher, F.S. Christopher, and R. Cate. 2000. "Partner Preferences: What Characteristics Do Men and Women Desire in Their Short-Term Sexual and Long-Term Romantic Partners?" *Journal of Psychology & Human Sexuality* 12(3): 1–21.

Regnier-Bohler, D. 1993. "Literary and Mystical Voices." In *Silences of the Middle Ages*, ed.M. Klapisch-Zuber: 251–259. Cambridge: The Belknap Press of Harvard University Press.

Reichert, T., and J. Lambiase, eds. 2003. *Sex in Advertising*. Mahwah, NJ: Lawrence Erlbaum Associates.

Reid, G.M. 1994. "Maternal Sex-Stereotyping of Newborns." *Psychological Reports* 75: 1443–1450.

Reid, P.T., and V.M. Bing. 2000. "Sexual Roles of Girls and Women: An Ethnocultural Lifespan Perspective." In *Sexuality, Society and Feminism*, eds. C.B. Travis and J.B. White: 141–166. Washington, DC: American Psychological Association.

Reiner, W.G., and J.P. Gearhart. 2004. "Discordant Sexual Identity in Some Genetic Males with Cloacal Exstrophy Assigned to Female Sex at Birth." *New England Journal of Medicine* 350: 333–341.

Reinisch, J.M. 1990. *The Kinsey Institute New Report on Sex*. New York: St. Martin's Press.

Reiss, I. 1986. *Journey into Sexuality*. Englewood Cliffs, NJ: Prentice-Hall.

Rempel, J.K., and B. Baumgartner. 2003. "The Relationship Between Attitudes Towards Menstruation and Sexual Attitudes, Desires, and Behavior in Women." *Archives of Sexual Behavior* 32(2): 155–163.

Renzetti, C.M. 1992. *Violent Betrayal.* Newbury Park, CA: Sage.

Renzetti, C.M., and D.J. Curran. 2003. *Women, Men, and Society.* 5th ed. Boston: Allyn and Bacon; 1995. *Women, Men, and Society.* 3rd ed. Boston: Allyn and Bacon.

Renzetti, C.M., and C.H. Milley, 1996. *Violence in Gay and Lesbian Domestic Partnerships.* Newbury Park, CA: Sage Publications.

Ribeau, S.A., Baldwin, J.R., and M.L. Hecht. 1994. "An African-American Communication Perspective." In *International Communication*, 7th ed., eds. J. Samovar and R. Porter: 140–147. Belmont, CA: Wadsworth.

Ricciardelli, L.A., and M.P. McCabe. 2007. "Pursuit of Muscularity Among Adolescents." In *The Muscular Ideal*, eds. J.K. Thompson and G. Cafri: 199–216. Washington, DC: American Psychological Association; 2001. "Dietary Restraint and Negative Affect as Mediators of Body Dissatisfaction and Bulimic Behavior in Adolescent Girls and Boys." *Behaviour Research & Therapy* 39(11): 1317–1328.

Rice, F.P. 1996. *Intimate Relationships*, 3rd ed. Mountain View, CA: Mayfield.

Rice, G., C. Anderson, N. Risch, and G. Ebers. 1999. "Male Homosexuality: Absence of Linkage to Microsatellite Markers at Xq28." *Science* 23 284(5415): 665–667.

Rich, A. 1986. *Of Woman Born.* New York: W.W. Norton; 1980/1984. "Compulsory Heterosexuality and Lesbian Existence." *Signs* 5: 631–660. Reprinted in *Desire*, eds. A. Snitow, C. Stansell, and S. Thompson. London: Virago; 1976. *Of Woman Born.* New York: Norton.

Richardson, C. J. 1996. "Divorce and Remarriage." In *Families*, ed. M. Baker: 215–248. Toronto: McGraw-Hill Ryerson.

Richardson, E. 2007. "'She Was Working like Foreal': Critical Literacy and Discourse Practices of African American Females in the Age of Hip Hop." *Discourse & Society* 18(6): 789–809.

Richardson, L. 1988. *The Dynamics of Sex and Gender*, 3rd ed. New York: Harper & Row.

Richeson, J.A., and N. Ambady. 2001. "Who's in Charge: Effects of Situational Roles on Automatic Gender Bias." *Sex Roles* 44(9–10): 493–512.

Richmond-Abbott, M. 1992. *Masculine & Feminine.* 2nd ed. Toronto: McGraw-Hill Inc.

Richter, J.S. 2001. "Eating Disorders and Sexuality." In *Eating Disorders in Women and Children*, ed. J.J. Robert-McComb: 201–208. Boca Raton, FL: CRC Press.

Ricks, K.L., and S.F. Dziegielewski. 2005. "Perceptions of Evil and Lesbians." *Journal of Human Behavior in the Social Environment* 11(2): 61–75.

Rideout, V.L., D.F. Roberts, and U.G. Foehr. 2005. *Generation M.* Menlo Park, CA: Henry J. Kaiser Family Foundation.

Ridgeway, C.L., and L. Smith Lovin, 1999. "The Gender System and Interaction." *Annual Review of Sociology* 25: 191–216.

Riedmann, A., M.A. Lamanna, and A. Nelson. 2003. *Marriages and Families.* Toronto: Thomson Nelson.

Riessman, C.K. 1990. *Divorce Talk.* New Brunswick, NJ: Rutgers University Press.

Riley, A.L., and V.M. Keith. 2003. "Work and Housework Conditions and Depressive Symptoms Among Married Women: The Importance of Occupational Status." *Women & Health* 38(4): 1–17.

Riley, S.S. 1994. "Sistah Outsider." In *Life Notes*, ed. P. Bell-Scott: 92–108. New York: Norton.

Riska, E., and J. Wegar. 1993. "Women Physicians: A New Force in Medicine?" In *Gender, Work and Medicine*, ed. E. Riska and K. Wegar: 77–93. London: Sage.

Risman, B.J., and D. Johnson-Sumerford. 1998. "Doing It Fairly: A Study of Postgender Marriages." *Journal of Marriage and the Family* 60: 23–40.

Ristock, J.L. 2003. "Exploring Dynamics of Abusive Lesbian Relationships: Preliminary Analysis of a Multisite Qualitative Study." *American Journal of Community Psychology* 31(3–4): 329–341; 1991. "Beyond Ideologies: Understanding Violence in Lesbian Relationships." *Canadian Woman Studies* 12(1): 74–79.

Robbins, T. 1996. *The Great Woman Super Heroes*. Northampton, MA: Kitchen Sink Press.

Robert-McComb, J.J. 2001. *Eating Disorders in Women and Children*. Boca Raton, FL: CRC Press.

Roberts, C. 2002. "'A Matter of Embodied Fact': Sex Hormones and the Historiy of Bodies." *Feminist Theory* 3(1): 7–26.

Roberts, D. 1978. "The Paterfamilias of the Victorian Ruling Classes." In *The Victorian Family*, ed. A.S. Wohl. London: Croom Helm.

Roberts, J. 2004. "Involved Fathering and Men's Adult Development, Provisional Balance." *Family Relations* 53(1): 116–117.

Roberts, R.E. 1971. *The New Communes*. Englewood Cliffs, NJ: Prentice-Hall, Spectrum.

Roberts, T.A., and J. Gettman. 2004. "'Mere Exposure': Gender Differences in the Negative Effects of Priming a State of Self-Objectification." *Sex Roles* 51: 17–27.

Robertson, C.N. 1970. *Oneida Community*. Syracuse, NY: Syracuse University Press.

Robertson, I. 1987. *Sociology*. 3rd ed. New York: Worth; 1980. *Social Problems*. 3rd ed. New York: Worth Publishing.

Robins, S. 1999. "Sports Help Girls Make the Grade." *Ottawa Citizen*, June 14. **www.caaws.ca/Girls/ottcitz_jun14.htm**

Robinson, J., and K. McIlwee. 1991. "Men, Women, and the Culture of Engineering." *Sociological Quarterly*, 32: 403–421.

Robinson, J.L., and Z. Biringen. 1995. "Gender and Emerging Autonomy in Development." *Psychoanalytic Inquiry* 15(1): 60–74.

Robinson, M.E., C.M. Gagnon, E.A. Dannecker, J.L. Brown, R.L. Jump, and D. D. Price. 2003. "Sex Differences in Common Pain Events: Expectations and Anchors." *Journal of Pain* 4(1): 40–45.

Rochelin, M. 1982 "The Language of Sex: The Heterosexual Questionnaire." *Changing Men* (Spring). Waterloo, ON: University of Waterloo.

Rodher, C., E. Kirchler, and E. Holzl. 2001. "Gender Stereotypes of Leaders: An Analysis of the Contents of Obituaries from 1974 to 1998." *Sex Roles* 45(11–12): 827–844.

Rodriguez, C.M., and A.J. Green. 1997. "Parenting Stress and Anger Expression as Predictors of Child Abuse Potential." *Child Abuse & Neglect* 21(4): 367–377.

Roen, K. 2002. "'Either/Or' and 'Both/Neither': Discursive Tensions in Transgender Politics." *Signs* 27(2): 501–522.

Rogers, L. 2002. *Sexing the Brain*. New York: Columbia University Press.

Rogers, S.J. 1999. "Wives' Income and Marital Quality: Are There Reciprocal Effects? *Journal of Marriage and the Family* 61: 123–132.

Rogers, W.S., J. Bidwell, and L. Wilson. 2005. "Perception of and Satisfaction with Relationship Power, Sex and Attachment Styles: A Couples Level Analysis." *Journal of Family Violence* 20(4): 241–251.

Rogerson, C. 2002. "Developing Spousal Support Guidelines in Canada: Beginning The Discussion: Background Paper." Paper prepared for the Department of Justice Canada. **www.canada.justice.ca/en/dept/pub/spousal/**

Rohlfing, M.E. 1995. "'Doesn't Anybody Stay in One Place Anymore?': An Exploration of the Understudied Pheneomenon of Long-Distance Friendships." In *Understudied Relations*, eds. J.T. Wood and S. Duck, vol. 6: 173–196. Thousand Oaks, CA: Sage.

Rohlinger, D.A. 2002. "Eroticizing Men: Cultural Influences on Advertising and Male Objectification." *Sex Roles* 46(3–4): 61–74.

Rose, C. 2002. "Talking Gender in the Group." *Group Analysis* 35(4): 525–539.

Rose, S. 1995. "Women's Friendships." In *Variations on a Theme*, eds. J.C. Chrisler and A.H. Hemstreet: 79–105. Albany: State University of New York Press.

Rose, S.M. 2003. "Community Interventions Concerning Homophobic Violence and Partner Violence Against Lesbians." *Journal of Lesbian Studies* 7(4): 125–139.

Rose, S.M., and D. Zand. 2002. "Lesbian Dating and Courtship from Young Adulthood to Midlife." *Journal of Lesbian Studies* 6(1): 85–109.

Rosell, M.C., and S.L. Hartman. 2001. "Self-Presentation of Beliefs About Gender Harassment and Feminism." *Sex Roles* 44(11–12) June: 647–660.

Rosenberg, H. 1987/1995. "Motherwork, Stress, and Depression: The Costs of Privatized Social Reproduction." Originally in

Feminism and Political Economy, eds. H.J. Maroney and M. Luxton: 181–196. Toronto: Methuen. Reprinted in *Gender in the 1990*, eds. E.D. Nelson and B.W. Robinson: 311–329. Toronto: Nelson.

Rosenfeld, B., and R. Harmon. 2002. "Factors Associated with Violence in Stalking and Obsessional Harassment Cases." *Criminal Justice & Behavior* 29(6): 671–691.

Rosenfeld, R.A. 2002. "What Do We Learn About Difference from the Scholarship on Gender?" *Social Forces* 81(1): 1–24.

Rosenfield, S. 2000. "Gender and Dimensions of the Self: Implications for Internalizing and Externalizing Behavior." In *Gender and Its Effects on Psychopathology*, ed. F. Ellen: 23–36. Washington, DC: American Psychiatric Publishing.

Rosenthal, C.J. 1995. "The Comforter: Providing Personal Advice and Emotional Support to Generations in the Family." In *Aging & Society*, ed. M. Novak: 342–351. Scarborough: Nelson Canada.

Rosenthal, C.S., J.A. Ronsethal, and J. Jones. 2001. "Preparing for Elite Participation Simulations and the Political Socialization of Adolescents." *Social Science Quarterly* 82(3): 633–646.

Ross, C.E. 1995. "Reconceptualizing Marital Status as a Continuum of Social Attachment." *Journal of Marriage and the Family* 57: 129–140.

Ross, H., and H. Taylor. 1989. "Do Boys Prefer Daddy or His Physical Style of Play?" *Sex Roles* 20(1–2): 23–31.

Ross, J.M. 2000. "What Do Men Want?" *Issues in Psychoanalytic Psychology* 22(1): 53–68.

Roter, D.L., J.A. Hall, and Y. Aoki. 2002. "Physician Gender Effects in Medical Communication: A Meta-Analytic Review." *JAMA* 288(6): 756–764.

Rothbaum, F., and B.U. Tsang. 1998. "Lovesongs in the United States and China: On the Nature of Romantic Love." *Journal of Cross-Cultural Psychology* 29(2): 306–319.

Rothman, B.K. 1999. "Comment on Harrison: The Commodification of Motherhood." In *American Families*, ed. S. Coontz: 435–438. New York: Routledge.

Rotundo, E.A. 1993. *American Manhood*. New York: BasicBooks.

Rowley, S.J., B. Kurtz-Costes, R. Mistry, and L. Feagans. 2007. "Social Status as a Predictor of Race and Gender Stereotypes in Late Childhood and Early Adolescence." *Social Development* 16(1): 150–168.

Roxburgh, S. 2005. "Parenting Strains, Distress and Family Paid Labor: A Modification of the Cost-of-Caring Hypothesis." *Journal of Family Issues* 26(8): 1062–1081; 2002. "Racing Through Life: The Distribution of Time Pressures by Roles and Role Resources Among Full-Time Workers." *Journal of Family and Economic Issues* 23(2): 121–145; 1997. "The Effect of Children on the Mental Health of Women in the Paid Labour Force." *Journal of Family Issues* 18(3): 270–289.

Rozovsky, L.F., and F.A. Rozovsky. 1998. *Legal Sex*. Toronto: Doubleday Canada.

Rubin, D.L., K. Greene, and D. Schneider. 1994. "Adopting Gender-Inclusive Language Reforms: Diachronic and Synchronic Variation." *Journal of Language and Social Psychology* 13(2): 91–114.

Rubin, J.Z., F. J. Provenzano, and Z. Lurra. 1974. "The Eye of the Beholder." *American Journal of Orthopsychiatry* 44: 512–519.

Rubin, L.B. 1990. *Erotic Wars*. New York: Farrar. Straus & Giroux; 1985. *Just Friends*. New York: Harper & Row Perennial; 1983. *Intimate Strangers*. New York: Harper & Row; 1981. *Women of a Certain Age*. New York: Harper Colophon.

Rubin, L.R., C.J. Nemeroff, and N.F. Russo. 2004. "Exploring Feminist Women's Body Consciousness." *Psychology of Women Quarterly* 28: 27–37.

Ruble, D., and C.L. Martin. 1998. "Gender Development." In *Handbook of Child Psychology*, Vol. 3, 5th ed., eds. W. Damon and N. Eisenberg: 933–1016. New York: Wiley.

Ruddick, S. 1990. *Maternal Thinking*. London: The Women's Press.

Rudman, L.A., and P. Glick. 1999. "Feminized Management and Backlash Toward Agentic

Women: The Hidden Costs to Women of a Kinder, Gentler Image of Middle Managers." *Journal of Personality & Social Psychology* 77(5): 1004–1010.

Ruijter, E. de, J.K. Treas, and P.N. Cohen. 2005. "Outsourcing the Gender Factory: Living Arrangements and Service Expenditures on Female and Male Tasks." *Social Forces* 84(1): 305–322.

Russell, A., C.H. Hart, C.C. Robinson, and S.F. Olsen. 2003. "Children's Sociable and Aggressive Behavior with Peers: A Comparison of the US and Australian, and Contributions of Temperament and Parenting Styles." *International Journal of Behavioral Development* 27(1): 74–86.

Russell, B.L., and D.L. Oswald. 2002. "Sexual Coercion and Victimization of College Men: The Role of Love Styles." *Journal of Interpersonal Violence* 17(3): 273–285; 2001. "Strategies and Dispositional Correlates of Sexual Coercion Perpetrated by Women: An Exploratory Investigation." *Sex Roles* 45(1–2): 103–115.

Russell, D.E.H. 1987. "The Nuclear Mentality: An Outgrowth of the Masculine Mentality." *Atlantis* 12: 10–15; 1975. *The Politics Of Rape*. New York: Stein and Day.

Russell, R. 2007. "The Work of Elderly Male Caregivers: From Public Careers to an Unseen World." *Men and Masculinities* 9(3): 298–314.

Russell, S.T. 2002. "Queer in America: Citizenship for Sexual Minority Youth." *Applied Developmental Science* 6(4): 258–263.

Russo, N.P., and K.L. Zierk. 1992. "Abortion, Childrearing and Women's Well-Being." *Professional Psychological Research Practice* 23: 269–280.

Ryan, C., and I. Rivers. 2003. "Lesbian, Gay, Bisexual and Transgender Youth: Victimization and Its Correlates in the USA and UK." *Culture, Health & Sexuality* 5(2): 103–119.

Saad, L. 2007. "Tolerance for Gay Rights at High-Water Mark." *Gallup* May 29.

Sadeghi, M., and A. Fakhrai. 2000. "Transsexualism in Female Monozygotic Twins: A Case Report." *Australian & New Zealand Journal of Psychiatry* 34(5): 862–864.

Sadker, M.P., and D.M. Sadker. 1991. *Teachers, Schools and Society*. New York: McGraw-Hill.

Safilios-Rothschild, C. 1977. *Love, Sex & Sex Roles*. Englewood Cliffs, NJ: Prentice-Hall.

Said, E. 1993. *Culture and Imperialism*. London: Chatto & Windus; 1978. *Orientalism*. Harmondsworth: Penguin.

Salari, S., and W. Zhang. 2006. "Kin Keepers and Good Providers: Influence of Gender Socialization on Well-Being Among USA Birth Cohorts." *Aging & Mental Health* 10(5): 485–496.

Salecl, R. 1992. "Nationalism, Anti-Semitism, and Anti-Feminism in Eastern Europe." *New German Critique* 57: 51–65.

Saltmarsh, S. 2007. "Picturing Economic Childhoods: Agency, Inevitability and Social Class in Children's Picture Books." *Journal of Early Childhood Literacy* 7 (1)l: 95–113.

Sanchez, D.T., and A. K. Kiefer. 2007. "Body Concerns in and Out of the Bedroom: Implications for Sexual Pleasure and Problems." *Archives of Sexual Behavior* 36(6): 808–820.

Sanchez, D.T., A.M. Kiefer, and O. Ybarra. 2006. "Sexual Submissiveness in Women: Costs for Sexual Autonomy and Arousal." *Personality and Social Psychology Bulletin* 32(4): 512–524.

Santoro, G. 1994. *Dancing in Your Head*. New York: Oxford Unversity Press.

Santrock, J.W. 1981. *Adolescence*. Dubuque, IL: Wm. C. Brown.

Sapir, E. 1949. *Selected Writings of Edward Sapir on Language, Culture and Personality*, ed. D.G. Mandelbaum. Berkeley, CA: University of California Press.

Satell, J.W. 1976. "The Inexpressive Male: Tragedy or Sexual Politics?" *Social Problems* 23: 469–477.

Saunders, J., L. Davis, T. Williams, and J.H. Williams. 2004. "Gender Differences in Self-Perceptions and Academic Outcomes: A Study of African American High School Students." *Journal of Youth & Adolescence* 33(1): 81–90.

Sax, L. 2002. "How Common Is Intersex? A Response to Anne Fausto-Sterling." *Journal of Sex Research* **www.findarticles.com/ cf_0/m2372/3_39/94130313/print.jhtml**; 2001a. "Reclaiming Kindergarten: Making

Kindergarten Less Harmful to Boys." *Psychology of Men & Masculinity* 2(1): 3–12; 2001b. "Reclaiming Kindergarten: Making Kindergarten Less Harmful to Boys: Erratum." *Psychology of Men & Masculinity* 2(2): 49.

Saxton, L. 1996. *The Individual, Marriage, and the Family*. 9th ed. Belmont, CA: Wadsworth; 1990. *The Individual, Marriage and the Family*. 7th ed. Belmont, CA: Wadsworth; 1986. *The Individual Marriage and the Family*. 6th ed. Belmont, CA: Wadsworth.

Sayer, L.C. 2005. "Gender, Time and Inequality: Trends in Women's and Men's Paid Work, Unpaid Work and Free Time." *Social Forces* 84(1): 285–303.

Scarbrough, J.W. 2001. "Welfare Mothers' Reflections on Personal Responsibility." *Journal of Social Issues* 57(2): 261–276.

Schaefer, R.T., R.P. Lamm, P. Biles, and S.J. Wilson. 1996. *Sociology*. Toronto: McGraw-Hill Ryerson.

Scharrer, E. 2004. "Virtual Violence: Gender and Aggression in Video Game Advertisements." *Mass Communication & Society* 7: 393–412; 2001. "Men, Muscles, and Machismo: The Relationship Between Television Violence Exposure and Aggression and Hostility in the Presence of Hypermasculinity." *Media Psychology* 3(2): 159–188; 2001a. "Tough Guys: The Portrayal of Hypermasculinity and Aggression in Televised Police Dramas." *Journal of Broadcasting & Electronic Media* 45(4): 615–634; 2001b. "From Wise to Foolish: The Portrayal of the Sitcom Father, 1950s–1990s." *Journal of Broadcasting & Electronic Media* 45(1): 23–40.

Schecter, S., and L. Gary. 1989. "A Framework for Understanding and Empowering Battered Women." In *Abuse and Victimization Across the Life Span*, ed. M. Strauss: 240–253. Baltimore: John Hopkins University Press.

Scheuble, L., and D.R. Johnson. 1993. "Marital Name Change: Plans and Attitudes of College Students." *Journal of Marriage and the Family* 55: 747–754.

Schiappa, E., P.B. Gregg, and D.E. Hewes. 2006. "Can One TV Show Make a Difference? Will & Grace and the Parasocial Contact Hypothesis." *Journal of Homosexuality* 51(4); 15–37.

Schilit, R., G. Lie, and M. Montagne. 1990. "Substance Use as a Correlate of Violence in Intimate Lesbian Relationships." *Journal of Homosexuality* 9: 51–65.

Schmader, T., J. Whitehead, and V.H. Wysocki. 2007. "A Linguistic Comparison of Letters of Recommendation for Male and Female Chemistry and Biochemistry Job Applicants." *Sex Roles* 57(7–8): 509–514.

Schmalz, D.L., and D.K. Kerstetter. 2006. "Girlie Girls and Manly Men: Children's Stigma Consciousness of Gender in Sports and Physical Activities." *Journal of Leisure Research* 38(4): 536–557.

Schmidt, K. L. 1995. *Transforming Abuse*. Gabriola Island, British Columbia: New Society Publishers.

Schmid Mast, M. 2001. "Gender Differences and Similarities in Dominance Hierarchies in Same-Gender Groups Based on Speaking Time." *Sex Roles* 44(9–10): 537–556.

Schneider, J.P. 2000. "A Qualitative Study of Cybersex Participants: Gender Differences, Recovery Issues, and Implications for Therapists." *Sexual Addiction & Compulsivity* 7(4): 249–278.

Schneider, M., and S. Phillips. 1997. "A Qualitative Study of Sexual Harassment of Female Doctors By Patients." *Social Science and Medicine* 45: 669–676.

Schoene-Harwood, B. 2000. *Writing Men*. Edinburgh: Edinburgh University Press.

Schooler, D. 2008. "Real Women Have Curves: A Longitudinal Investigation of TV and the Body Image Development of Latina Adolescents." *Journal of Adolescent Research* 23(2); 132–153.

Schooler, D., L.M. Ward, A. Merriwether, and A. Caruthers. 2005. "Cycles of Shame: Menstrual Shame, Body Shame, and Sexual Decision-Making." *Journal of Sex Research* 42: 324–334.

Schope, R.D., and M.J. Eliason. 2004. "Sissies and Tomboys: Gender Role Behaviors and Homophobia." *Journal of Gay and Lesbian Social Services* 16(2): 73–97.

Schroeder, K.A., L.L. Blood, and D. Maluso. 1993. "Gender Differences and Similarities Between Female and Male Undergraduates Regarding

Expectancies for Career and Family Roles." *College Student Journal* 27(2): 237–249.

Schulte, H.M., and J. Kay. 1994. "Medical Students' Perceptions of Patient-Initiated Sexual Behavior." *Academic Medicine* 69: 383–394.

Scott, E., and J. Panksepp. 2003. "Rough and Tumble Play in Children." *Aggressive Behavior* 29(6): 539–551.

Schwalbe, M. 1996. *Unlocking the Iron Cage.* New York: Oxford University Press.

Schwartz, F. 1989. "Management Women and the New Facts of Life." *Harvard Business Review* 67: 65–76; 1992. *Breaking With Tradition.* New York: Warner.

Schwartz, P. 1994. *Love Between Equals.* New York: Free Press.

Schwartz, P., and V. Rutter. 1998. *The Gender of Sexuality.* Thousand Oaks, CA: Pine Forge Press.

Schwartzman, A.E., P. Verlaan, P. Peters, and L.A. Serbin. 1995. "Sex Roles as Coercion." In *Coercion and Punishment in Long-Term Perspectives*, ed. J. McCord: 362–375. New York: Cambridge University Press.

Sczesny, S., S. Spreeman, and D. Stahlberg. 2006. "Masculine=Competent? Physical Appearance and Sex as Sources of Gender-Stereotypic Attributions." *Swiss Journal of Psychology* 65(1): 15–23.

Sedgwick, E.K. 2003. *Touching Feeling.* Durham, N.C.: Duke University Press; 1985. *Between Men.* New York: Columbia University Press.

Segal, L. 1998. "Only the Literal: The Contradictions of Anti-Porn Feminism." *Sexualities* 1(1): 43–62.

Seidman, S. 2004. *Contested Knowledge.* Malden, MA: Blackwell; 2004. *Beyond the Closet.* New York: Routledge; 1998. *Contested Knowledge*, 2nd edition. Oxford: Blackwell.

Sekaquaptewa, D., and M. Thompson. 2003. "Solo Status, Stereotype Threat and Performance Expectancies: Their Effects on Women's Performance." *Journal of Experimental Social Psychology* 39(1): 68–74.

Sekayi, D. 2003. "Aesthetic Resistance to Commercial Influences: The Impact of the Eurocentric Beauty Standard on Black College Women." *The Journal of Negro Education* 72: 467–477.

Sell, I. 2004. "Third Gender: A Qualitative Study of the Experience of Individuals Who Identify as Being Neither Man nor Woman." In *Saints and Rogues*, eds. R. Marchesani and M. Stern: 131–145. New York: Haworth Press.

Sells, L.W. 1980. "The Mathematics Filter and the Education of Women and Minorities." In *Women and the Mathematical Mystique*, eds. L.H. Fox, L. Brody, and D. Tobin. Baltimore: Johns Hopkins University Press.

Selwyn. 2007. "e-Learning or she-Learning? Exploring Students' Gendered Perceptions of Education Technology." *British Journal of Educational Technology* 38(4): 744–746.

Sen, A. 2003. "Missing Women-Revisited." *British Medical Journal* 327: 1297–1298. 2001. "Many Faces of Gender Inequality." *Frontline* 10(22) October 27–November 9.

Senn, C.Y., S. Desmarais, N. Verberg, and E. Wood. 2000. "Predicting Coercive Sexual Behavior Across the Lifespan in a Random Sample of Canadian Men." *Journal of Social & Personal Relationships* 17(1): 95–113.

Serbin, L.A., L.C. Moller, J. Gulko, K.K. Powlishta, and K.A. Colburne. 1994. "The Emergence of Gender Segregation in Toddler Playgroups." In *Childhood Gender Segregation*, ed. C. Leaper. San Francisco: Jossey-Bass.

Serbin, L.A., D. Poulin, and J.A. Eichstedt. 2002. "Infants' Response to Gender-Inconsistent Events." *Infancy* 3(4): 531–542.

Serbin, L.A., D. Poulin-Dubois, K.A. Colburne, M. G. Sen, and J.A. Eichstedt. 2001. "Gender Stereotyping in Infancy: Visual Preferences for and Knowledge of Gender-Stereotyped Toys in the Second Year." *International Journal of Behavioral Development* 25(1): 7–15.

Serbin, L.A., K.K. Powlishta, and J. Gulko. 1993. "Sex Roles, Status and the Need for Social Change." *Monographs of the Society for Research in Child Development* 58(2) : 93–95.

Serbin, L.A., D.M. Stack, A.E. Schwartzman, J. Cooperman, V. Bentley, C. Saltaris, and J.E. Ledingham. 2002. "A Longitudinal

Study of Aggressive and Withdrawn Children into Adulthood: Patterns of Parenting and Risk to Offspring." In *The Effects of Parental Dysfunction on Children*, eds. R.J. McMahon and R.D. Peters: 43–69. New York: Kluwer Academic/Plenum.

Setterson, R.A. 2002. *New Frontiers in Socialization*. London: JAI.

Seward, R.R., D.E. Yeatts, and L. Stanley-Stevens. 1996. "Fathers' Changing Performance of Housework: A Bigger Slice of a Smaller Pie." *Free Inquiry in Creative Sociology* 24(1): 28–36.

Shakin, M., D. Shakin, and S.J. Sternglanz. 1985. "Infant Clothing: Sex Labeling for Strangers." *Sex Roles* 12: 955–964.

Share, T.L., and L.B. Mintz. 2002. "Differences Between Lesbian and Heterosexual Women in Disordered Eating and Related Attitudes." *Journal of Homosexuality* 42(4): 89–106.

Shears, M. 1985. "Solving the Great Pronoun Debate: 14 Ways to Avoid the Sexist Singular." *Ms.* October: 106–109.

Sheehan, M. 2000. "Women Slowly Gain Ground in Politics." In *Vital Signs*, ed. L. Starke: 152–153. New York: W.W. Norton Company.

Sheehy, G. 1995. *New Passages*. New York: G. Merritt Corporation.

Shehan, C.L., and K.C.W. Kammeyer. 1997. *Marriages and Families*. Boston: Allyn and Bacon.

Sheldon, A. 1996. "Constituting Gender Through Talk in Childhood: Conversations in Parent-Child, Peer and Sibling Relationships." *Research on Language and Social Interaction* 29(1): 1–5.

Sheldon, J.P. 2004. "Gender Stereotypes in Educational Software for Young Children." *Sex Roles* 51(7–8): 433–444.

Shell, R., and N. Eisenberg. 1990. "The Role of Peers' Gender in Children's Naturally Occurring Interest in Children." *International Journal of Behavioral Development* 13(3): 373–388.

Shelton, B.A. 2000. "Understanding the Distribution of Housework of Housework Between Husbands and Wives." In *The Ties That Bind*, eds. L.J. Waite, C. Bachrarch, M.Hindin, E. Thomson, and A. Thorton: 344–355. New York: Aldine de Gruyter;

1990. "The Distribution of Household Tasks: Does Wife's Employment Status Make a Difference?" *Journal of Family Issues* 11(2): 115–135.

Shelton, B.A., and D. John. 1993. "Does Marital Status Make a Difference? Housework Among Married and Cohabiting Men and Women." *Journal of Social Issues* 14(3): 401–420.

Sheridan, L., R. Gillett, G.M. Davies, E. Blaauw, and D. Patel. 2003. "There's No Smoke Without Fire: Are Male Ex-Partners Perceived as More 'Entitled' to Stalk Than Acquaintance or Stranger Stalkers?" *British Journal of Psychology* 94(1): 87–98.

Shields, M. 2000. "Long Working Hours and Health." *Perspectives on Labour and Income*, Statistics Canada." Catalogue 75-001-XPE; 2000. "Shift Workers and Health." *Health Reports*, 13(4): 11–33.

Shields, S. 1995. "The Role of Emotion, Beliefs and Values in Gender Development." In *Social Development* (edited by N. Eisenberg): 212–232. Thousand Oaks, CA: Sage.

Shiller, V.M., and M.F. Schneider. 2003. "You're Not My Friend Anymore!": Getting Along with Others." In *Rewards for Kids!* eds. V.M. Schiller and M.F. Schneider: 47–55. Washington, DC: American Psychological Association.

Shin, Y., D. Kim, T. Ha, H.Park, W. Moon, E. Chung, J. Lee, I. Kim, S. Kim, and J. Kwon. 2005. "Sex Differences in the Human Corpus Callosum: Diffusion Tensor Imaging Study." *Neuroreport* 16(8): 795–798.

Shope, J.H. 2004. "When Words Are Not Enough: The Search for the Effect of Pornography on Abused Women." *Violence Against Women* 10(1): 56–72.

Shore, Z.L. 2000. "Girls Learning, Women Teaching: Dancing to Different Drummers." *Educational Studies* 31(2): 132–145.

Shotland, R.L., and B.A. Hunter. 1995. "Women's 'Token Resistance' and Compliant Sexual Behaviors Are Related to Uncertain Sexual Intentions and Rape." *Personality & Social Psychology Bulletin* 21(3): 226–236.

Shugart, H.A. 2003. "She Shoots, She Scores: Mediated Constructions of Contemporary

Female Athletes in Coverage of the 1999 U.S. Women's Soccer Team." *Western Journal of Communication* 67: 1–13.

Shumaker, S.A., C. Legault, L. Thal, R.B. Wallace, J.K. Ockene, S.L. Hendrix, B.N. Jones 3rd, A.R. Assaf, R.D. Jackson, J.M. Kotchen, S.Wassertheil-Smoller, and J. Wactawsk-Wende. 2003. "Estrogen Plus Progestin and the Incidence of Dementia and Mild Cognitive Impairment in Postmenopausal Women: The Women's Health Initiative Memory Study: A Randomized Controlled Trial." *JAMA* 289(20): 2651–2652.

Shulman, S., and I. Seiffge-Krenke. 2001. "Adolescent Romance: Between Experience and Relationships." *Journal of Adolescence* 3: 417–428.

Shumsky, E. 2001. "Transforming the Ties That Bind: Lesbians, Lovers and Chosen Family." In *Sexualities Lost and Found*, eds. E. Gould and S. Kiersky: 57–69. Madison, CT: International Universities Press.

Shute, R., and K. Charlton. 2006. "Anger or Compromise? Adolescents' Conflict Resolution Strategies in Relation to Gender and Type of Peer Relationship." *International Journal of Adolescence and Youth* 13(1–2): 55–69.

Sidanius, J., and U. Pena. 2003. "The Gender Nature of Family Structure and Group-Based Anti-Egalitarianism: A Cross-National Analysis." *Journal of Social Psychology* 143(2): 243–251.

Signorella, M. L. 1999. "Multidimensionality of Gender Schemas: Implications for the Development of Gender-Related Characteristics." In *Sexism and Stereotypes in Modern Society*, eds. W.B. Swann, Jr., J.H. Langlois, and L.A. Gilbert: 107–128. Washington, DC: American Psychological Association.

Signorella, N. 1991. *A Sourcebook on Children and Television*. New York: Greenwood.

Signorielli, N., and S. Kahlenberg. 2001. "Television's World of Work in the Nineties." *Journal of Broadcasting and Electronic Media* 45(1): 4–22.

Silliman, B., and W.R. Schumm. 1995. "Client Interests in Premarital Counseling: A Further Analysis." *Journal of Sex & Marital Therapy* 21(1): 43–56.

Silva, E.B. 2002. "Time and Emotion in Studies of Household Technologies." *Work, Employment and Society* 16(2): 329–340.

Silverman, I.W. 2003. "Gender Differences in Resistance to Temptation: Theories and Evidence." *Developmental Review* 23(2): 219–259.

Silverman, R., and L. Kennedy. 1993. *Deadly Deeds*. Scarborough: Nelson Canada.

Simon, W., and J.H. Gagnon, eds. 1970. "Psychosexual Development." In *The Sexual Scene*, 23–41. Chicago: Trans-action Books.

Simono, R.B. 2002. "Heterosexual Men as Targets: The Shadow Side of Sexual Harassment." In *The Psychology of Sex, Gender and Jobs*, eds. L. Diamant and J.A. Lee: 103–121. Westport, CT: Praeger.

Simons, R.L., K. Lin, and K.C. Gordon. 1998. "Socialization in the Family of Origin and Male Dating Violence: A Prospective Study." *Journal of Marriage and the Family* 60(2): 467–478.

Simpson, M. 2003. "Metrosexual? That Rings a Bell?" *Independent on Sunday*, June 22.

Sinclair, C. 1996. *Net Chick*. New York: Henry Holt.

Singley, S.G., and K. Hynes. 2005. "Transitions to Parenthood: Work-Family Policies, Gender and the Couple Context." *Gender & Society* 19(3): 376–397.

Sinnott, J.D. 1998. *The Development of Logic in Adulthood*. New York: Plenum Press. 1995. "The Development of Complex Reasoning: Postformal Thought." In *Perspectives on Cognitive Changes in Adulthood and Aging*, eds. F. Blanchard-Fields and T. Hess: 151–164. New York: McGraw-Hill.

Sinnot, J.D., D. Rogers, and F. Spencer. 1996. "Reconsidering Sex Roles and Aging: Preliminary Data on Some Influences of Context, Cohort, Time." ERIC, Document_#ED 391 139/CG 026 796.

Sinnott, J.D., and K. Shifren. 2001. "Gender and Aging: Gender Differences and Gender Roles." In *Handbook of the Psychology of Aging*, 5th ed., eds. J.E. Birren and K. W Shaie: 454–476. San Diego: Academic Press.

Sivard, R.L. 1995. *Women,* 2nd ed. Washington, DC: World Priorities.

Six, B., and T. Eckes. 1991. "A Closer Look at the Complex Structure of Gender Stereotypes." *Sex Roles* 24(1–2): 57–71.

Skelton, C. 2003. "Male Primary Teachers and Perceptions of Masculinity." *Educational Review* 55(2): 195–209.

Skolnick, A.S. 1996. *The Intimate Environment*, 6th ed. New York: HarperCollins.

Skolnick, S. 2006. "Beyond the 'M' Word: The Tangled Web of Politics and Marriage." *Dissent* 53(4): 81–87.

Slater, A., and M. Tiggemann. 2002. "A Test of Objectification Theory in Adolescent Girls." *Sex Roles* 46: 343–349.

Slavkin, M.L. 2001. "Gender Schematization in Adolescents: Differences Based in Rearing in Single-Parent and Intact Families." *Journal of Divorce and Remarriage* 34(3–4): 137–149.

Sloane, E. 1993. *Biology of Women*. New York: Delmar.

Sloop, J.M. 2000. "Disciplining The Transgendered: Brandon Teena, Public Representation, and Normativity." *Western Journal of Communication* 64(2): 165–189.

Small, S.A., and D. Riley. 1990. "Toward a Multidimensional Assessment of Work Spillover in Family Life." *Journal of Marriage and the Family* 52: 51–61.

Smith, C. 2002. "'They're Ordinary People, Not Aliens from Planet Sex!': The Mundane Excitements of Pornography for Women." *Journal of Mundane Behavior* 3(1).

Smith, D.B., and P. Moen. 1998. "Spousal Influence on Retirement: His, Her, and Their Perceptions." *Journal of Marriage and the Family* 60: 734–744.

Smith, G. 2004. "Boy Raised as a Girl Suffered Final Indignity." *Globe and Mail*, May 11: A1.

Smith, H.L. 2001. "'Age': A Problematic Concept for Women." *Journal of Women's History* 12(4): 77–86.

Smith, J.L., C. Sansone, and P.H. White. 2007. "The Stereotyped Task Engagement Process: The Role of Interest and Achievement Motivation." *Journal of Educational Psychology* 99(1): 99–114.

Smith, K. 2005. "Prebirth Gender Talk: A Case Study in Prenatal Socialization." *Women and Language* 28(1): 49–53.

Smith, K.B. 1999. "Clean Thoughts and Dirty Minds: The Politics of Porn." The *Policy Studies Journal* 27(4): 723–734.

Smith, P.M. 1985. *Languages, the Sexes and Society*. New York: Blackwell.

Smith, R.A. 2002. "Race, Gender and Authority in the Workplace: Theory and Research." *Annual Review of Sociology* 28: 509–542.

Smith, R.B., J. Davidson, and P. Ball. 2001. "Age-Related Variations and Sex Differences in Gender Cleavage During Middle Childhood." *Personal Relationships* 8(2): 153–165.

Smyth, J. 2003. "Sweden Ranked as Best Place to Have a Baby: Canada Places Fifth on Maternity Leave, 15th for Benefits." *National Post*, January 17: 3.

Smolak, L., and J.A. Stein. 2006. "The Relationship of Drive for Muscularity to Sociocultural Factors, Self-Esteem, Physical Attributes, Gender Role and Social Comparison in Middle School Boys." *Body Image* 3: 121–129.

Smyth, R., G. Jacobs, and H. Rogers. 2003. "Male Voices and Perceived Sexual Orientation: An Experimental and Theoretical Approach." *Language in Society* 32(3): 329–350.

Snodgrass, S. 1985. "Women's Intuition: The Effect of Subordinate Role on Interpersonal Sensitivity." *Journal of Personality and Social Psychology* 49: 146–155.

Snooks, M.K., and S.K. Hall. 2002. "Relationship of Body Size, Body Image, and Self-Esteem in African American, European American, and Mexican American Middle-Class Women." *Health Care for Women International* 23(5): 460–466.

Snyder, M. 2001. "Self-Fulfilling Stereotypes." In *Self and Society*, ed. A. Branaman: 30–35. Malden, MA: Blackwell Publishers.

Sobieraj, S. 1998. "Taking Control: Toy Commercials and the Social Construction of Patriarchy." In *Masculinities and Violence*, ed. L.H. Bowker: 15–28. Thousand Oaks, CA: Sage Publications.

Sokoloff, H. 2001. "Wealth Affects Test Scores." *National Post*, 5 December: A17.

Solomon, S.E., E.D. Rothblum, and K.F. Balsam 2004. "Pioneers in Partnership: Lesbian and Gay Male Couples in Civil Unions

Compared with Those Not in Civil Unions and Married Heterosexual Siblings." *Journal of Family Psychology* 18(2): 275–286.

Somers, M.D. 1993. "A Comparison of Voluntarily Childfree Adults and Parents." *Journal of Marriage and the Family* 55(3) 643–650.

Sommers-Flanagan, R., J. Sommers-Flanagan, and B. Davis. 1993. "What's Happening on Music Television? A Gender Role Content Analysis." *Sex Roles* 28: 745–753.

Sonnet, E. 1999. "'Erotic Fiction by Women for Women': The Pleasures of Post-Feminist Heterosexuality." *Sexualities* 2(2): 167–187.

Sontag, S. 1972. "The Double Standard of Aging." *Saturday Review* 23 September: 29–38.

South, S.J. 1991. "Sociodemographic Differentials in Mate Selection Preference." *Journal of Marriage and the Family* 53: 928–940.

Spade, J.Z., and C.A. Reese. 1991/1995. "We've Come a Long Way, Maybe: College Students' Plans for Work and Family." *Sex Roles* 24: 309–321. Reprinted in *Gender in the 1990s*, eds. E.D. Nelson and B.W. Robinson: 142–153. Toronto: Nelson Canada.

Spain, D. 1992. *Gendered Spaces*. Chapel Hill, NC: University of North Carolina.

Spees, J.M.G., and T.S. Zimmerman. 2002. "Gender Messages in Parenting Magazines: A Content Analysis." *Journal of Feminist Family Therapy* 14(3–4): 73–100.

Spence, J.T., and C.F. Buckner. 1998. "Instrumental and Expressive Traits, Trait Stereotypes, and Sexist Attitudes: What Do They Signify?" *Psychology of Women Quarterly* 24(1): 44–62.

Spence, J.T., and Hall, S.K. 1996. "Children's Gender-Related Self-Perceptions, Activity Preferences, and Occupational Stereotypes: A Test of Three Models of Gender Constructs." *Sex Roles* 35: 659–692.

Spencer, S.J., C.M. Steele, and D.M. Quinn. 1999. "Stereotype Threat and Women's Math Performance." *Journal of Experimental Social Psychology* 31(1): 4–38.

Spender, D. 1995. *Nattering on the Net*. Toronto: Garamond Press Ltd.

Spitzberg, B.H. 1999. "An Analysis of Empirical Estimates of Sexual Aggression Victimization and Perpetration." *Violence & Victims* 14(3): 241–260.

Spitze, G., and K.A. Loscocco. 2000. "The Labour of Sisyphus? Women's and Men's Reactions to Housework." *Social Science Quarterly* 81(4): 1087–1100.

Spitzer, B.L., K.A. Henderson, and M.T. Zivian. 1999. "Gender Differences in Population versus Media Body Sizes: A Comparison Over Four Decades." *Sex Roles* 40(7–8): 545–565.

Spivak, G. 1990. *The Post-Colonial Critic*. London: Routledge.

Sport, K. 2007. "Below the Belt and Bleeding Fingertips: Feminist and Lesbian Music in the Late 1970s." *Australian Feminist Studies* 22(53): 343–360.

Sprecher, S., A. Barbee, and P. Schwartz. 1995. "Was It Good for You, Too? Gender Differences in First Sexual Intercourse Experiences." *Journal of Sex Research* 32(1): 3–15.

Sprecher, S., and D. Felmlee. 1997. "The Balance of Power in Romantic Heterosexual Couples Over Time from 'His' and 'Her' Perspectives." *Sex Roles* 37(5–6): 361–379.

Sprecher, S., and P.C. Regan. 2002. "Liking Some Things (in Some People) More than Others: Partner Preferences in Romantic Relationships and Friendships." *Journal of Social & Personal Relationships* 19(4): 463–481; 1996. "College Virgins: How Men and Women Perceive their Sexual Status." *Journal of Sex Research* 33(1): 3–15.

Sprecher, S., and M. Toro-Morn. 2002. "A Study of Men and Women from Different Sides of Earth to Determine if Men Are from Mars and Women Are from Venus in their Beliefs About Love and Romantic Relationships." *Sex Roles* 46(5–6): 131–147.

Squires, J. 2001. "Representing Groups, Deconstructing Identities." *Feminist Theory* 2(1): 7–27.

Stagnitti, K., S. Rodger, and J. Clarke. 1997. "Determining Gender-Neutral Toys for Assessment of Preschool Children's Imaginative Play." *Australian Occupational Therapy Journal* 44(3): 119–131.

Stainton, M.C. 1985. "The Fetus: A Growing Member of the Family." *Family Relations* 34(3): 321–326.

Stanko, E.A. 1993. "Ordinary Fear: Women, Violence and Personal Safety." In *Violence Against Women*, eds. P.B. Bart and E.G. Moran: 155–164. Thousand Oaks, CA: Sage.

Stanley, J.L., K. Bartholomew, T.Taylor, D. Gram, and M. Landolt. 2006. "Intimate Violence in Male Same-Sex Relationships." *Journal of Family Violence* 21(1): 31–41.

Stanley, L. 2005. "A Child of Its Time: Hybrid Perspectives on Othering." *Sociological Research Online* 10(3). **www.socresonline. org.uk/10/3/stanley.html**

Stark, R. 1992. *Sociology*. 4th ed. Belmont, CA: Wadsworth.

Starkman, R. 1997. "Cashing in on Success." *Toronto Star*, March 30: B6; 1994. "Tragedy of Women's Gymnastics: Athlete's Death Reveals Grim Toll of Eating Disorders." *Toronto Star*, 5 October: C3.

Stapleton, K., and J. Wilson. 2004. "Gender, Nationality and Identity: A Discursive Study." *European Journal of Women's Studies* 11(1): 45–60.

Starrels, M.E., B. Ingersoll-Dayton, D.W. Dowler, and M.B. Neal. 1997. "The Stress of Caring for a Parent: Effects of the Elder's Impairment on an Employed, Adult Child." *Journal of Marriage and the Family* 59: 860–872.

Statistics Canada. 2008a. "Study: Female Offenders, 2005." *The Daily*, January 24. **www.statcan.ca/Daily/English/080124/ d080124a.htm**

———. 2008b. "Study: Organized Sports Participation Among Children." *The Daily*. June 3. **www.statcan.ca/Daily/English/ 080603/d080603a.htm**

———. 2008c. "Study: Participation in Sports." *The Daily*. February 7. **www.statcan.ca/ Daily/English/080207/d080207b.htm**

———. 2008d. "Canadian Internet Use Survey, 2007." *The Daily*, June 12. **www.statcan.ca/ Daily/English/080621/d080621b.htm**

———. 2008e. "Most Prevalent Occupations for Men and Women, Canada, 2006." April 2. **www.statcan.ca/english/census06/analysis/ labour/tables/table3.htm**

———. 2008f. "Canada's Changing Labour Force, 2006 Census, Census Year 2006." Catalogue no. 97-559-X, March. Ottawa: Minister of Industry.

———. 2008g. "Legal Marital Status, Common-Law Status, Age Groups and Sex for the Population 15 Years and Over of Canada, 2006 Census—100% data." Catalogue no. 97-552-XCB2006009.

———. 2008h. "Study: Life Expectancy in the Inuit-Inhabited Areas of Canada, 1989 to 2003." *The Daily*, January 23. **www. statcan. ca/Daily/English/080123/d080123d.htm**

———. 2008i. "Deaths, 2005." *The Daily*, January 14. **www.statcan.ca/Daily/English/ 080114/d080114b.htm**

———. 2008j. "Study: Health Care Use Among Gay, Lesbians and Bisexuals." *The Daily*, March 19. **www.statcan.ca/Daily/English/ 060319/d060319b.htm**

———. 2008k. "Topic-Based Tabulations, Legal Marital Status, Age Groups and Sex for the Population 15 Years and Over of Canada, 2006 Census—100% Data."

———. 2008l. "University degrees, diplomas and certificates awarded, 2005." The Daily, February 7. **www.statcan.ca/Daily/English/ 080207/d080207c.htm**

———. 2007a. "2006 Census: Families, Marital Status, Household Dwelling Characteristics." *The Daily*, September 12. **www.statcan.ca/ Daily/English/070912/d070912a.htm**

———. 2007b. "Study: Sports Participation Among Aboriginal Children, 2006." *The Daily*, July 10. **www.statcan.ca/Daily/ English/070710/d070710b.htm**

———. 2007c. "Educational Portrait of Canada, 2006 Census, Census Year 2006." Catalogue no. 97-560-X, March. Ottawa: Minister of Industry.

———. 2007d. "Study: Why Most University Students are Women." *The Daily*, September 20. **www.statcan.ca/Daily/English/070920/ d070920b.htm**

———. 2007e. "Study: Doctorates in Science and Engineering, 2001." *The Daily*, October 24. **www.statcan.ca/Daily/English/071024/ d071024a.htm**

———. 2007f. "Education Indicators in Canada: Report of the Pan-Canadian Education Indicators Program." Catalogue no. 81-582-XIE, December 12, no. 5.

————. 2007g. "Women in Canada: Work Chapter Updates, 2006." Catalogue no. 89F0133XIE, April. Ottawa: Minister of Industry.

————. 2007h. "Participation and Activity Limitation Survey, 2006." *The Daily*, December 3 **www.statcan.ca/Daily/ English/071203/d071203a.htm**

————. 2007i. "Study: Gender Differences in Quits and Abstenteeism, 1983 to 2003." *The Daily*, February 23. **www.statcan.ca/Daily/ English/070223/d070223b.htm**

————. 2007j. "Family Violence in Canada: A Statistical Profile 2007." Catalogue no. 85-2240XIE, October. Ottawa: Minister of Industry.

————. 2007k. "General Social Survey: Navigating Family Transitions." *The Daily*, June 13. **www.statcan.ca/Daily/English/ 070613/d070613b.htm**

————. 2007l. "Marriages, 2003." *The Daily*, January 17. **www.statcan.ca/Daily/English/ 070117d070117a.htm**

————. 2007m. "Marital Breakdown and Subsequent Depression, 1994/1995 to 2004/ 2005." *The Daily*, May 22. **www.statcan.ca/ Daily/English/070522/d070522a.htm**

————. 2007n. "Births, 2005 (correction)." *The Daily*, September 21. **www.statcan.ca/Daily/ English/070921b.htm**

————. 2007o. "Returning to Work After Childbirth, 1983 to 2004." *The Daily*, December 19. **www.statcan.ca/Daily/ English/071219/d071219e.htm**

————. 2007p. "Maintenance Enforcement Survey: Child and Spousal Support 2005/ 2006." *The Daily*, January 11. **www.stat- can.ca/Daily/English/070111/ d070111b.htm**

————. 2007q. "Study: Frequency of Contact Between Separated Fathers and their Children, 1994 to 1997." *The Daily*, October 29. **www.statcan.ca/Daily/English/071029/ d071029b.htm**

————. 2007r. "Portrait of the Canadian Population in 2006, by Age and Sex, 2006 Census." Catalogue no. 97-551-XIE, July. Ottawa: Minister of Industry.

————. 2007s. "Morality, Summary List of Causes, 2004." *The Daily*, April 27. **www.statcan/Daily/English/070427/ d070427b.htm**

————. 2007t. "Mortality, Summary List of Causes." Catalogue no. 84F0209XIE, April. Ottawa: Minister of Industry.

————. 2007u. "Young Pensioners, 1989 to 2004." *The Daily*, February 21. **www.statcan.ca/ Daily/English/070221/d070221d.htm**

————. 2007v. "Residential Care Facilities 2004/2005." *The Daily*, May 30. **www.statcan.ca/Daily/English/070530/ d070530d.htm**

————. 2006a. "Child Care: An Eight-Year Profile, 1994–1995 to 2002–2003." *The Daily*, April 5. **www.statcan.ca/Daily/ English/060425/d060425a.htm**

————. 2006b. "Trends in the Teaching Profession, 1999 to 2005." *The Daily*, December 1. **www.statcan.ca/Daily/ English/061201/d061201b.htm**

————. 2006c. "Education Matters: Profile of Canada's School Principals 2004/2005." *The Daily*, June 26. **www.statcan.ca/Daily/ English/060626/d060626a.htm**

————. 2006d. "Study: Wage Differences Between Male and Female University Professors, 1970 to 2001." *The Daily*, November 8. **www.statcan.ca/Daily/ English/060802/d060802a.htm**

————. 2006e. "Women in Canada, 5th edition: A Gender-Based Statistical Report." Catalogue no. 89-503-XPE, March. Ottawa: Minister of Industry.

————. 2006f. "University Degrees, Diplomas and Certificates Awared, 2004." *The Daily*, November 7. **www.statcan.ca/Daily/ English/061107/d061107c**

————. 2006g. "Television Viewing, Fall 2004." *The Daily*, March 31. **www.statcan.ca/ Daily/English/060331/d060331b.htm**

————. 2006h. "Study: Changing Patterns of Women in the Canadian Labour Force, 2005." *The Daily*, June 15. **www.statcan.ca/ Daily/English/060615/d060615c.htm**

————. 2006i. "General Social Survey: Paid and Unpaid Work, 2005." *The Daily*, July 11. **www.statcan.ca/Daily/English/ 060719d/060719b.htm**

————. 2006j. "Measuring Violence Against Women: Statistical Trends 2006." Catalogue no 85-570-XIE, October. Ottawa: Minister of Industry.

————. 2006k. "Study: Returning to the Parental Home, 2001." *The Daily*, October 3.

www.statcan.ca/Daily/English/061003d06100a.htm

———. 2006l. "The Risk of First and Second Marriage Dissolution, 2001." *The Daily*, June 29. www.statcan.ca/Daily/English/060628/d060628b.htm

———. 2006m. "Deaths, 2004." *The Daily*, December 20. www.statcan.ca/Daily/English/061220/d061220b.htm

———. 2006n. "Study: New Frontiers of Research on Retirement." *The Daily*, March 27. www.statcan.ca/Daily/English/060327/d060327b.htm

———. 2006o. "Study: The Death of a Spouse and the Impact on Income, 1993 to 2003." *The Daily*, July 10. www.statcan.ca/Daily/English/060510/d060510a.htm

———. 2006p. "Health Reports: Predictors of Death in Seniors, 1994–95 to 2002–03." *The Daily*, February 9. www.statcan.ca/Daily/English/060209/d060209a.htm

———. 2005. "Family Violence in Canada: A Statistical Profile." *The Daily*, July 14. www.statcan.ca/Daily/English/050714/d050714a.htm

———. 2004a. "Canadian Community Health Survey, 2003." *The Daily*, June 15. www.statcan.ca/Daily/English/040615/d040615b.htm

———. 2004b. "Sports Involvement, 1998." www.statcan.ca/english/Pgdb/arts18.htm

———. 2004c. "Women in Canada: Work Chapter Updates." Catalogue no. 89F0133, March.

———. 2004d. "Reasons for Part-Time Work." www.statcan.ca/english/Pgdb/labor63b.htm

———. 2004e. "Divorces, 2001 and 2002." *The Daily*, May 4. www.statcan.ca/Daily/English/040504/d040504a.htm

———. 2004f. "Study: Workers' Knowledge of Retirement Plans." *The Daily*, January 23. www.statcan.ca/Daily/English/040123/d040123b.htm

———. 2004g. "Deaths, 2002." *The Daily*, September 27. www.statcan.ca/Daily/English/040927/d040927a.htm

———. 2004h. "Births, 2002." *The Daily*, April 19. www.statcan.ca/Daily/English/040419/d040419b.htm

———. 2003a. "Earnings of Canadians: Making a Living in the New Economy."

The Daily, March 11. www12.statcan.ca/census01/Products/Analytic/companion/earn/contents.cfm

———. 2003b. "School Enrolments and Teaching Staff, 1999/2000." *The Daily*, September 18. www.statcan.ca/Daily/English/030918/d030918e.htm

———. 2003c. "Women in Canada: Work Chapter Updates." Statistics Canada Housing, Family and Social Statistics Division, Target Groups Project. Catalogue no. 89F0133XIE, May.

———. 2003d. "Education in Canada: Raising the Standard." Catalogue 96F0030XIE2001012. www12.statcan.ca/english/census01/products/Analytic/companion/educ/contents.cfm

———. 2003e. "Part-Time Work and Family-Friendly Practices." *The Daily*, June 26. www.statcan.ca/Daily/English/030626/d030626g.htm

———. 2003f. "The Changing Profile of Canada's Labour Force." www.statcan.ca/english/census01/Products/Analytic/companion/paid/tables/child

———. 2003g. "Life Expectancy, 2001." *The Daily*, September 25. www.statcan.ca/Daily/English/030925//d030925.htm

———. 2003h. "Self-Rated Health, by Age Group and Sex, Household Population Aged 12 and Over, Canada, 2003." www.statcan.ca/english/ freepub/92-221 XIE/00604/tables/html/1117_03.htm

———. 2003i. "Family Violence." *The Daily*, June 23. www.statcan.ca/Daily/English/030623/ d030623c.htm

———. 2003j. "Marriages, 2000." *The Daily*, June 2. www.statcan.ca/Daily/English/03062/ d030623a.htm

———. 2003k. "Marriages, 2001." *The Daily*, November 20. www.statcan.ca/Daily/English/031120/d031120c.htm

———. 2003l. "Benefitting from Extended Parental Leave, 2001." *The Daily*, March 21. www.statcan. ca/Daily/English/030321/d03021b.htm

———. 2003m. "Registered Retirement Savings Plan Contributions, 2002." *The Daily*, October 23. www.statcan.ca/Daily/english/031023/ d031023b.htm

————. 2002a. "A Profile of Disability in Canada, 2001. Tables, Participation and Activity Limitation Survey, December." Catalogue 89-F79-XIE. **www.statcan.ca:8096/bsolc/english/bsolc?catno=89-579-X**

————. 2002b. "Total Income of Adults Without Disabilities, by Sex and Age Groups, Canada, 2001." **www.statcan.ca/english/freepub/89-F87-XIE/tables/html/table6/can6.htm**

————. 2002c. "Total Income of Adults with Disabilities, by Sex and Age Groups, Canada, 2001." **www.statcan.ca/english/freepub/89-587-XIE/tables/html/table5/can5.htm**

————. 2002d. "Disability Supports in Canada, 2001: Difficulties with Transportation." **www.statcan.ca/english/freepub/89-580-XIE/difficulties.htm**

————. 2002e. "Survey of Self-Employment, 2000." *The Daily*, January 29. **www.statcan.ca/Daily/English/020129/d020129d.htm**

————. 2002f. "Childcare Services Industry, 1999." *The Daily*, April 26. **www.statcan.ca/Daily/English/020426/d020426a.htm**

————. 2002g. "Setting Up Shop: Self-Employment Amongst Canadian College and University Graduates." **www.stacan.ca:8096/bsolc/english/bsolc?catno=11F0019M2002183**

————. 2002h. "Trends in Immigrant Self-Employment, 1981 to 1996." *The Daily*, December 9. **www.statcan.ca/Daily/English/021209/ d021209a.htm**

————. 2002i. "Impact of Income on Mortality in Urban Canada, 1971 to 1996." *The Daily*, September 26. **www.statcan.ca/Daily/English/020926/d020926a.htm**

————. 2002j. "Approaching Retirement, 1993 to 1997." *The Daily*, September 26. **www.statcan.ca/Daily/English/020926/d020926h.htm**

————. 2002k. "Retirement Income." *The Daily*. October 23. **www.statcan.ca/Daily/English/021023/d021023h.htm**

————. 2002l. "Unionization and Fringe Benefits." *The Daily* April 29. **www.statcan.ca/Daily/English/020429/d020429j.htm**

————. 2001. "The Health Divide: How the Sexes Differ." *The Daily*, April 26. **www.statcan.ca/Daily/English/010426/d010426a.htm**

————. 1999a. "Survey of Labour and Income Dynamics, 1993–1997." *The Daily*. September 1. **www.statcan.ca/Daily/English/990901/ d990901.htm**

————. 1999b. "Work Absence Rates, 1987 to 1998." July 1999. Labour and Household Surveys Analysis Division. Catalogue 71-535-MPB, no. 10.

————. 1999c. "Survey of Labour and Income Dynamics: The Wage Gap Between Men and Women, 1997." *The Daily*. December 20. **www.statcan.ca/Daily/English/991220/ d991220.htm**

————. 1998. *Canada Yearbook.* Ottawa: Minister of Industry.

————. 1997. "Divorce, 1997." Catalogue 84-213-XMB. Ottawa: Minister of Industry.

————. 1983. *Historical Statistics of Canada.* 2nd edition. Catalogue 11-516. Ottawa: Ministry of Supply and Services.

————. 1972. "Population Sex Ratios. 1971 Census of Canada." Catalogue 92-714. Ottawa: Ministry of Supply and Services.

Steel, F. 1987. "Alimony and Maintenance Orders." In *Equality and Judicial Neutrality*, eds. S.L. Martin and K.E. Machoney: 155–167. Toronto: Carswell.

Steele, J. 2003. "Children's Gender Stereotypes About Math: The Role of Stereotype Stratification." *Journal of Applied Social Psychology* 33(12): 2587–2606.

Steele, J., J. B. James, and R.C. Barnett. 2002. "Learning in a Man's World: Examining the Perceptions of Undergraduate Women in Male-Dominated Academic Areas." *Psychology of Women Quarterly* 26(1): 46–50.

Steinem, G. 1994. *Moving Beyond Words*. New York: Simon & Schuster; 1978. "Erotica and Pornography: A Clear and Present Difference." *Ms* Magazine: 53–4, 75, 76.

Steinpreis, R.E., K.A. Anders, and D. Ritzke. 1999. "The Impact of Gender on the Review of the Curriculum Vitae of Job Applicants and Tenure Candidates: A National Empirical Study." *Sex Roles* 41: 509–528.

Stenberg, C., and J. Campos. 1990. "The Development of Anger Expressions in Infancy." In *Psychological and Biological Approaches to Emotion*, eds. N. Stein, B. Leventhal, and T. Trabasso: 247–282. Hillsdale, NJ: Lawrence Erlbaum Associates.

Stephan, C.W., W.F. Stephan, K.M. Demitrakis, A.M. Yamada, and D.L. Clason. 2000. "Women's Attitudes Toward Men: An Integrated Threat Theory Approach." *Psychology of Women Quarterly* 24(1): 63–78.

Stephen, J.D. 1991. "Sexing the Fetus." *Lancet* 338(8778): 1336.

Sternglanz, S.H., and L.A. Serbin. 1974. "Sex Role Stereotyping in Children's TV Programs." *Developmental Psychology* 10: 710–715.

Stern, B.B. 2003. "Masculinisms and the Male Image: What Does It Mean to Be a Man?" In *Sex in Advertising*, eds. T. Reichert and J. Lambiase: 215–228. Mahwah, NJ: Lawrence Erlbaum.

Stets, J. 1993. "Control in Dating Relationships." *Journal of Marriage and the Family* 55: 673–685; 1993. "The Link Between Past and Present Intimate Relationships." *Journal of Family Issues* 14(2): 236–266.

Stets, J.E., and P.J. Burke. 2005. "Identity Verification, Control and Aggression in Marriage." *Social Psychology Quarterly* 68(2): 160–178.

Stets, J., and D.A. Henderson. 1991. "Contextual Factors Surrounding Resolution while Dating: Results from a National Study." *Family Relations* 40: 29–36.

Stets, J.E., and M. Pirog-Good. 1990. "Interpersonal Control and Courtship Aggression." *Journal of Social and Personal Relationships* 7: 371–394.

Stetson, D.M., and A.G. Mazur. 2000. "Women's Movements and the State: Job-Training Policy in France and the U.S." *Political Research Quarterly* 53(3): 597–623.

Steuter, E. 1992/1995. "Women Against Feminism: An Examination of Feminist Social Movements and Anti-Feminist Countermovements." In *Canadian Review of Sociology and Anthropology* 29(3): 288–306. Reprinted in *Gender in the 1990s*, eds. E.D. Nelson and B.W. Robinson: 537–552. Toronto: Nelson Canada.

Stevens, R. 1983. *Law School*. Chapel Hill, NC: University of North Carolina Press.

Stewart, D.E., and K. Boydell. 1993. "Psychologic Distress During Menopause: Associations Across the Reproductive Life Cycle." *International Journal of Psychiatry & Medicine* 23: 57–62.

Stewart, D.E., E. Gucciardi, and S.L. Grace. 2003. "Depression." In *Women's Health Surveillance Report*: 39–40. Ottawa: Canadian Institute for Health Information.

Stewart, L.P., A.D. Stewart, S.F. Friedley, and P.J. Cooper. 1990. *Communication Between the Sexes*. Scottsdale, AZ: Gorsuch Scarisbrick.

Stillion, J.N., and E.E. McDowell. 2001–2002. "The Early Demise of the "Stronger" Sex: Gender-Related Causes of Sex Differences in Longevity." *Omega* 44(4): 301–318; 2001. "Living and Dying in Different Worlds: Gender Differences in Violent Death and Grief." *Illness, Crisis & Loss* 9(3): 247–259.

St. Lawrence, J.S., and D.J. Joyner. 1991. "The Effects of Sexually Violent Rock Music on Males' Acceptance of Violence Against Women." *Psychology of Women Quarterly* 15(1): 49–63.

Stockard, J., and M.M. Johnson. 1980. *Sex Roles*. Englewood Cliffs, NJ: Prentice-Hall.

Stohs, J.H. 2000. "Multicultural Women's Experience of Household Labor, Conflicts and Equity." *Sex Roles* 42(5–6): 339–362; 1995. "Predictors of Conflict Over the Household Division of Labor Among Women Employed Full-Time." *Sex Roles* 33(3–4): 257–275.

Stokowski, P.A. 2000. "Exploring Gender." *Journal of Leisure Research* 32(1): 161–165.

Stolenberg, J. 2000. *The End of Manhood*. London: UCL.

Stoller, R. 1985. *Observing the Erotic Imagination*. New Haven: Yale University Press.

Storms, M.D. 1981. "A Theory of Erotic Orientation Development." *Psychological Review* 88: 304–353; 1981. "Sexual Scripts for Women." *Sex Roles* 7: 699–708.

Stouffer, S. 1949. *The American Soldier*. New York: Wiley.

Stout, M. 2000. "Aboriginal Canada: Women and Health." **www.hc-sc.gc.ca/canusq/ papers/ canada/english/indigen.htm**

Stovkis, P.R. 2001. "Housewives' Work: Technology and Labour Saving Services Since the Second World War." *Sociologisch Tijdschrift* 28(3): 350–376.

Strand, E.A. 1999. "Uncovering the Role of Gender Stereotypes in Speech Perception." *Journal of Language and Social Psychology* 18(1): 86–99.

Strassberg, D.S., and S. Holty. 2003. "An Experimental Study of Women's Internet Personal Ads." *Archives of Sexual Behavior* 32(3): 253–260.

Straus, M.A. 1993. "Physical Assaults by Wives: A Major Social Problem." In *Current Controversies on Family Violence*, eds. R.J. Gelles and D.R. Loseke: 67–87. Newbury Park, CA: Sage; 1979. "Family Patterns and Child Abuse in a Nationally Representative American Sample." *Child Abuse and Neglect* 3: 213–225.

Straus, M.A., and R. Gelles. 1990. *Physical Violence in American Families*. New Brunswick, NJ: Transaction; 1988. "How Violent Are American Families? Estimates from the National Family Violence Survey and Other Studies." In *Family Abuse and its Consequences*, eds. G.T. Hotaling, D. Finkelhor, John T. Kirkpatrick, and M.A. Straus: 25–26. Newbury Park: Sage Publications, Inc.

Straus, M., R. Gelles, and S. Steinmetz. 1980. *Behind Closed Doors*. New York: Doubleday.

Strazdins, L., and D.H. Broom. 2004. "Acts of Love (and Work): Gender Imbalance in Emotional Work and Women's Psychological Distress." *Journal of Family Issues* 25(3): 356–378.

Street, A.E., J.L. Gradus, J. Stafford, and K. Kelly. 2007. "Gender Differences in Experiences of Sexual Harassment: Data from a Male-Dominated Environment." *Journal of Consulting and Clinical Psychology* 75(3): 464–474.

Stro, S. 2002. "Unemployment and Gendered Divisions of Domestic Labour." *Acta Sociologica* 45(2): 89–106.

Strub, T., B. McKimmie, R. Schuller, and D. Terry. 2006. "Sugar and Spice and All Things Nice: The Role of Gender Stereotypes in Juror's' Perceptions of Criminal Defendants." *Australian Journal of Psychology* 56: 5–60.

Struckman-Johnson, C., and D. Struckman-Johnson. 1997. "Men's Reactions to Hypothetical Forceful Sexual Advances for Women: The Role of Sexual Standards, Relationship Availability and the Beauty Bias." *Sex Roles* 37(5–6): 319–333.

Struckman-Johnson, C., D. Struckman-Johnson, and P.B. Anderson. 2003. "Tactics of Sexual Coercion: When Men and Women Won't Take No for an Answer." *Journal of Sex Research* 40(1): 76–86.

Sturgeon, N. 1997. *Ecofeminist Natures*. New York: Routledge.

Such, E. 2006. "Leisure and Fatherhood in Dual-Earner Families." *Leisure Studies* 25(2): 185–199.

Suh, E.J., D.S. Moskowitz, M.A. Fournier, and D.C. Zuroff. 2004. "Gender and Relationships: Influences on Agentic and Communal Behaviors." *Personal Relationships* 11(1): 41–59.

Suitor, J.J. 1991. "Marital Quality and Satisfaction with the Division of Household Labor Across the Family Life Cycle." *Journal of Marriage and the Family* 53: 221–230.

Suitor, J.J., and K. Pillemer. 2007. "Mothers' Favoritism in Later Life: The Role of Children's Birth Order." *Research in Aging* 29(1): 32–55.

Suizzo, M., and M.H. Bornstein. 2006. "French and European American Child-Mother Play: Culture and Gender Considerations." *International Journal of Behavioral Development* 30(6): 498–508.

Suizzo, M., C. Robinson, and E. Pahlke. 2008. "African American Mothers' Socialization Beliefs and Goals with Young Children: Themes of History, Education and Collective Independence." *Journal of Family Issues* 29(3): 287–316.

Sullins, E.S. 1992. "Interpersonal Perception Between Same-Sex Friends." *Journal of Social Behavior & Personality* 7(3): 395–414.

Sullivan, G., and W. Losberg. 2003. "A Study of Sampling in Research in the Field of Lesbian and Gay Studies." *Journal of Gay & Lesbian Social Services* 5(1–2): 147–162.

Sullivan, O. 2000. "The Division of Domestic Labour: Twenty Years of Change?" *Sociology* 34(3): 437–456.

Sussman, D., and S. Bonnell. 2006.."Wives as Primary Breadwinners." *Perspectives on Labour and Income, Statistics Canada,* Catalogue no. 75-001-XIE, 7(8): 10–17.

Suter, E.A. 2004. "Tradition Never Goes Out of Style: The Role of Tradition in Women's Naming Practices." *The Communication Review* 7: 57–87.

Suter, E.A., K.L. Daas, and K.M. Bergen. 2008. "Negotiating Lesbian Family Identity Via Symbols and Rituals." *Journal of Family Issues* 29(1); 26–47.

Suter, E.A., and R.F. Oswald. 2003. "Do Lesbians Change Their Last Names in the Context of a Committed Relationship?" *Journal of Lesbian Studies* 7(2): 71–83.

Swabb, D.F., W.C.J. Chung, F.P.M. Kruijver, M.A. Hofman, and A. Hestiantoro. 2003. "Sex Differences in the Hypothalamus in the Different Stages of Human Life." *Neurobiology of Aging* 24: S1–S16.

Swain, S. 1989. "Covert Intimacy: Closeness in Men's Friendships." In *Gender in Intimate Relationships*, eds. B.J. Risman and P. Schwartz: 71–86. Belmont, CA: Wadsworth.

Swearinghen-Hilker, N., and J.D. Yoder. 2002. "Understanding the Context of Unbalanced Domestic Contributions: The Influence of Perceiver's Attitudes, Target's Gender, and Presentational Format." *Sex Roles* 46(3–4): 91–98.

Sweeney, B. 2004. "Trans-Ending Women's Rights: The Politics of Trans-Inclusion in the Age of Gender." *Women's Studies International Forum* 27(1): 75–89.

Sweeney, M.M., and M. Cancian. 2004. "The Changing Importance of White Women's Economic Prospects for Assortative Mating." *Journal of Marriage and Family* 66: 1015–1028.

Sweeny, J., and M.R. Bradbard. 1988. "Mothers' and Father's Changing Perceptions of Their Male and Female Infants Over the Course of Pregnancy." *Journal of Genetic Psychology* 149(3): 394–404.

Swigonski, M.E. 2001. "Human Rights, Hate Crimes, and Hebrew-Christian Scripture." *Journal of Gay & Lesbian Social Services* 13(1–2): 33–45.

Swimm, J.K., and L.L. Hyers. 1999. "Excuse Me—What Did You Just Say? Women's Public and Private Responses to Sexist Remarks." *Journal of Experimental Social Psychology* 35: 68–88.

Symons, D. 1979. *The Evolution of Human Sexuality*. New York: Oxford University Press.

Szatmary, D. 1996. *A Time to Rock*. New York: Schirmer Books.

Szinovacz, M.E. 2000. "Changes in Housework After Retirement: A Panel Analysis." *Journal of Marriage and the Family* 62: 78–92.

Szymanski, L.A., and J.C. Chrisler. 1990/1991. "Eating Disorders, Gender-Role, and Athletic Activity." *Psychology* 27(4): 20–29.

Szymanski, M., and T.F. Cash. 1995. "Body-Image Disturbances and Self-Discrepancy Theory: Expansion of the Body Image Ideals Questionnaire." *Journal of Social and Clinical Psychology* 14: 134–146.

Takiff, H.A., D.T. Sanchez, and T.L. Stewart. 2001. "What's in a Name? The Status Implications of Students' Terms of Address for Male and Female Professors." *Psychology of Women Quarterly* 25(2): 134–144.

Talbani, A., and P. Hasanali. 2000. "Adolescent Females Between Tradition and Modernity: Gender Role Socialization in South Asian Immigrant Culture." *Journal of Adolescence* 23(5): 615–627.

Tam, T. 1997. "Sex Segregation and Occupational Gender Inequality in the United States: Devaluation or Specialized Training?" *American Journal of Sociology* 102(6): 1652–1692.

Tanenbaum, L. 2000. *Slut!* New York: Seven Stories Press.

Tannen, D. 1994a. "Gender Gap in Cyberspace." *Newsweek*, May 16: 54–55; 1994b. *Talking from 9 to 5*. New York: William Morrow; 1990. *You Just Don't Understand*. New York: William Morrow; 1990. "Gender Differences in Topical Coherence: Creating Involvement in Best Friends' Talk." *Discourse Processes* 13(1): 73–90.

Tantleff-Dunn, S. 2002. "Biggest Isn't Always Best: The Effect of Breast Size on Perceptions of Women." *Journal of Applied Social Psychology* 32(11): 2253–2265.

Tantlett-Dunn, S., and J.K. Thompson. 2000. "Breast and Chest Size Satisfaction: Relation to Overall Body Image and Self-Esteem." *Eating Disorders* 8(3): 241–246.

Tavris, C. 2005. "Brains, Biology, Science and Skepticism: On Thinking About Sex Differences (Again)." *Skeptical Inquirer*, June 1; 1992. *The Mismeasure of Women*. New York: Simon and Schuster.

Tavris, C., and C. Wade. 1984. *The Longest War*, 2nd ed. San Diego: Harcourt Brace Jovanovich.

Taylor, E. 1995. "The Stress of Infertility." *Human Ecology Forum* 23(4); 12–20.

Taylor, M.G. 1996. "The Development of Children's Beliefs About Social and Biological Aspects of Gender Differences." *Child Development* 67: 1555–1571.

Taylor, M.H. 2000. "The Potential Impact of Gender Role Socialization on Welfare Policy Formation." *Journal of Sociology & Social Welfare* 27(3): 135–151.

Taylor, P. 2003. "Not Tonight Dear." *Globe and Mail*, October 25. **www.globeandmail.com/servlet/ArticleNew/TPStory/LAC/20031025/VIAGRA25.**

Teachman, J.D. 2000. "Diversity of Family Structure: Economic and Social Influences." In *Handbook of Family Diversity*, eds. D.H. Demo and K.R. Allen: 32–58. London: Oxford University Press.

Tebbutt, M. 1995. *Women's Talk*. Aldershot: Scholar Press.

Tenenbaum, H.R., and C. Leaper. 2003. "Parent-Child Conversations about Science: The Socialization of Gender Inequities?" *Developmental Psychology* 39(1): 34–47; 2002. "Are Parents' Gender Schemas Related to their Children's Gender-Related Cognitions? A Meta-Analysis." *Developmental Psychology* 38(4): 615–630.

Tepper, C.A., and K.W. Cassidy. 1999. "Gender Differences in Emotional Language in Children's Picture Books." *Sex Roles* 40: 265–280.

Thayer, S. 1988. "Encounters." *Psychology Today*. March: 31–36.

Thiessen, V., and C. Nickerson. 1999. "Canadian Gender Trends in Education and Work." Otawa: Applied Research Branch, Strategic Policy, Human Resources

Development. Canada (T-00-4E). Catalogue MP32-30/00-4E.

Tholander, M. 2002. "Cross-Gender Teasing as a Socializing Practice." *Discourse Processes* 34(3): 311–338.

Thomas, A.J., R.M. Witherspoon, and S.L. Speight. 2004. "Toward the Development of the Stereotypic Roles for Black Women Scale." *Journal of Black Psychology* 30(3): 426–442.

Thomas, M.D., T.B. Henley, and C.M. Snell. 2006. "The Draw a Scientist Test: A Different Population and a Somewhat Different Story." *College Student Journal* 40(1): 140–148.

Thomas, V.G., and S.E. Miles. 1995. "Psychology of Black Women: Past, Present and Future." In *Bringing Cultural Diversity to Feminist Psychology*, ed. H. Landrine: 303–330. Washington, DC: American Psychological Association.

Thomas, W.I., with D.S. Thomas. 1928. *The Child in America*. New York: Alfred A. Knopf.

Thompson, C. 1995. "A New Vision of Masculinity." In *Race, Class and Gender in the United States*, 3rd ed., ed. P.S. Rothenberg: 475–481. New York: St. Martin's Press.

Thompson, E.H. 1991. "The Maleness of Violence in Dating Relationships: An Appraisal of Stereotypes." *Sex Roles* 24(5–6): 261–278.

Thompson, L. 1993. "Conceptualizing Gender in Marriage: The Case of Marital Care." *Journal of Marriage and the Family* 55: 557–569.

Thompson, L., and A.J. Walker. 1991. "Gender in Families." In *Contemporary Families*, ed. A. Booth: 76–102. Minneapolis, MN: National Council on Family Relations; 1995. "The Place of Feminism in Family Studies." *Journal of Marriage and the Family* 57: 847–865.

Thompson, M. 1987. *Gay Spirit*. New York: St. Martin's.

Thompson, M.J. 2000. "Gender in Magazine Advertising: Skin Sells Best." *Clothing & Textiles Research Journal* 18(3): 178–181.

Thompson, R.B., and K. Moore. 2000. "Collaborative Speech in Dyadic Problem

Solving: Evidence for Preschool Gender Differences in Early Pragmatic Development." *Journal of Language and Social Psychology* 19(2): 248–255.

Thompson, S.H., A.C. Rafiroiu, and R.G. Sargent. 2003. "Examining Gender, Racial and Age Differences in Weight Concern Among Third, Fifth, Eighth, and Eleventh Graders." *Eating Behaviors* 3(4): 307–323.

Thompson, T.L., and E. Zerbinos. 1995. "Gender Roles in Animated Cartoons: Has the Picture Changed in 20 Years?" *Sex Roles* 32(9–10): 651–673.

Thomson, E., S.S. McLanahan, and R.B. Curtin. 1992. "Family Structure, Gender, and Parental Socialization." *Journal of Marriage and the Family* 54: 368–378.

Thomson, K. 1977. *To Be a Man*. Los Angeles: Tarcher.

Thornburg, H.D. 1982. *Development in Adolescence*. 2nd ed. Monterey, CA: Brooks/Cole.

Thorne, B. 1993. *Gender Play*. Buckingham: Open University Press; 1992. "Girls and Boys Together But Mostly Apart: Gender Arrangements in Elementary Schools." In *Men's Lives*, 2nd ed., eds. M.S. Kimmel and M.A. Messner: 108–123. New York: Macmillan; 1982. "Feminist Rethinking of the Family: An Overview." In *Rethinking the Family*. eds. B. Thorne and M. Yalom: 1–24. New York: Longmans.

Thorne, B., and N. Henley (eds.). 1975. *Language and Sex*. Rowley, MA: Newbury.

Thorne, T. 1990. *The Dictionary of Contemporary Slang*. New York: Pantheon.

Tichenor, V. 2005. *Earning More and Getting Less*. New Brunswick, NJ: Rutgers University Press; 2005. "Maintaining Men's Dominance: Negotiating Identity and Power When She Earns More." *Sex Roles* 53(3/4): 191–205; 1999. "Status and Income as Gendered Resources: The Case of Marital Power." *Journal of Marriage and the Family* 61: 48–60.

Tiger, L. 1969. *Men in Groups*. London: Thomas Nelson and Sons.

Timmer, E., C. Bode, and F. Dittmann-Kohli. 2003. "Expectations of Gains in the Second Half of Life: A Study of Personal Conceptions of Enrichment in a Lifespan Perspective." *Aging and Society* 23(1): 3–24.

Tomaskovic-Davey, D. 1993. "The Gender and Race Compositions of Jobs and the Male/Female, White/Black Pay Gap." *Social Forces* 72(1): 48–76.

Tomiak, M., J.M. Berthelot, E. Guimond, and C.A. Mustard. 2000. "Factors Associated with Nursing-Home Entry for Elders in Manitoba, Canada." *Journals of Gerontology* 55A(5): M279–M287.

Tomson, S., and G. Mason. 2001. "Engendering Homophobia: Violence, Sexuality and Gender Conformity." *Journal of Sociology* 37(3): 257–273.

Tong, R. 1989. *Feminist Theory*. Boulder, CO: Westview.

Toronto Star. 2001. "Riverdale Keeps It Sweet and Simple." August 19: D1, D10.

Torres, J.B., V.S. Solberg, and A.H. Carlstrom. 2002. "The Myth of Sameness Among Latino Men and Their Machismo." *American Journal of Orthopsychiatry* 72(2): 163–181.

Totten, M. 2003. "Girlfriend Abuse as a Form of Masculinity Construction Among Violent, Marginal Male Youth." *Men & Masculinities* 6(1): 70–92.

Townsend, A.L., and M.M. Franks. 1997. "Quality of the Relationship Between Elderly Spouses: Influence on Spouse Caregivers' Subjective Effectiveness." *Family Relations* 46(1): 33–39.

Townsend, J.M. 1999. "Mate Selection Criteria: A Pilot Study." *Ethology and Sociobiology*, 10: 241–253; 1998. *What Women Want, What Men Want*. New York: Oxford University Press.

Townsend, J.M., and G.D. Levy. 1990. "Effects of Potential Partners' Physical Attractiveness and Socioeconomic Status on Sexuality and Partner Selection." *Journal of Sexual Behavior* 19: 149–164; 1990. "Effects of Potential Partners' Costume and Physical Attractiveness on Sexuality and Partner Selection." *Journal of Psychology* 124: 371–389.

Townsend, J.M., and T. Wasserman. 1998. "Sexual Attractiveness: Sex Differences in Assessment and Criteria." *Evolution & Human Behavior* 19(3): 171–191.

Townson, M. 1995. *Women's Financial Futures*. Ottawa: Canadian Advisory Council on the Status of Women.

Traustadottir, R. 1997. *Women with Disabilities*. Syracuse, NY: Center of Human Policy.

Treise, D., and A. Gotthoffer. 2002. "Stuff You Couldn't Ask Your Parents: Teens Talking About Using Magazines for Sex Information." In *Sexual Teens, Sexual Media*, eds. J.D. Brown and J.R. Steele: 173–189. Mahwah, NJ: Lawrence Erlbaum Associates.

Trendex Sports Vision. 2004. Sports Participation Study. **www.sportsvision.info/ sports_ participation.htm**

Trexler, R.C. 2002. "Making the American Berdache: Choice or Constraint?" *Journal of Social History* 35(3): 613–633.

Troll, L.E. 1975. *Early and Middle Adulthood*. Monterey, CA: Brooks/Cole.

Trostle, L.C. 2003. "Overrating Pornography as a Source of Sex Information for University Students: Additional Consistent Findings." *Psychological Reports* 92(1): 143–150.

Trovato, F. 2001. "Aboriginal Mortality in Canada, the United States and New Zealand." *Journal of Biosociological Sciences* 33(1): 67–86.

Trovato, F., and N.M. Lalu. 1996. "Causes of Death Responsible for the Changing Sex Differential in Life Expectancy Between 1970 and 1990 in Thirty Industrialized Nations." *Canadian Studies in Population* 23(2): 99–126.

Trudgill, P. 1972. "Sex, Covert Prestige and Linguistic Change in the Urban British English of Norwich." *Language in Society* 1: 179–195. Reprinted in *Language and Sex*, eds. B. Thorne and N. Henley: 88–104. Rowley, MA: Newbury House Publishers.

Tsang, D. 2001. "Gay Pride, Asian Proud." *Banana* 1(1) 24–25.

Tuchman, G. 1978. *Making News*. New York: Free Press.

Tuchman, G., A.K. Daniels, and J. Benet. 1978. *Hearth and Home*. New York: Oxford University Press.

Tuck, B., J. Rolfe, and V. Adair. 1994. "Adolescents' Attitudes toward Gender Roles within Work and its Relationship to Gender, Personality Type and Parental Occupations." *Sex Roles* 31(9–10): 547–558.

Tuggle, C.A., and A. Owen. 1999. "A Descriptive Analysis of NBC's Coverage of the Centennial Olympics." *Journal of Sport and Social Issues* 23(2): 171–182.

Tunley, J.R., S. Walsh, and P. Nicolson. 1999. "'I'm Not Bad for My Age': The Meaning of Body Size and Eating in the Lives of Older Women." *Aging and Society* 19(6): 741–759.

Turkle, S. 1984. *The Second Self*. London: Granada.

Turner, B.F., and C.B. Turner. 1991. "Bem Sex-Role Inventory Stereotypes for Men and Women Varying in Age and Race Among National Register Psychologists." *Psychological Reports* 69: 931–44.

Turner-Bowker, D.M. 1996. "Gender Stereotyped Descriptors in Children's Picture Books: Does 'Curious Jane' Exist in the Literature?" *Sex Roles* 35: 461–468.

Twenge, J.M. 1997. "Mrs. His Name: Women's Preferences for Married Names." *Psychology of Women Quarterly* 21: 417–430.

Twiggs, J.E., J. McQuillan, and M.M. Ferree. 1999. "Meaning and Measurement: Reconceptualization Measures of the Division of Household Labor." *Journal of Marriage and the Family* 61: 712–724.

Twitchell, J.B. 2003. "Adcult and Gender." In *Sex in Advertising*, eds. T. Reichert and J. Lambiase: 181–193. Mahwah, NJ: Lawrence Erlbaum Associates.

Tye, M.C. 2003. "Lesbian, Gay, Bisexual, and Transgender Parents: Special Consideration for the Custody and Adoption Evaluation." *Family Court Review* 41(1): 92–103.

Tylka, T.L., D. Bergeron, and J.P. Schwartz. 2005. "Development and Psychometric Evaluation of the Male Body Attitudes Scale (MBAS)." *Body Image* 2: 161–175.

Uchalik, D.C., and D.D. Livingston. 1980. "Adulthood: Women." In *On Love and Loving*, eds. K.S. Pope et al.: 89–103. San Francisco: Jossey Bass.

Udry, J.R. 2000. "Biological Limits of Gender Construction." *American Sociological Review* 65(3): 443–457; 1994. "The Nature of Gender." *Demography* 31: 561–573; 1971. *The Social Context of Marriage*. 2nd ed. Philadelphia: J.B. Lippincott; 1968. "Sex and Family Life." *Annals of the American Academy of Political and Social Science* 376: 25–35.

Underhill, P. 1999. *Why We Buy*. New York: Simon & Schuster.

Underwood, M.R. 2003. *Social Aggression Among Girls*. New York: Guilford Press.

Unger, R.K. 1993. "Alternative Conceptions of Sex (And Sex Differences)" in *The Development of Sex Differences and Similarities in Behavior*, eds. M. Haug, R.F. Whalen, C. Aron and K.L. Olsen: 457–476. Netherlands: Kluwer Academic Publishers; 1979. "Toward a Redefinition of Sex and Gender." *American Psychologist* 34: 1085–1094.

United Nations Development Programme. 2008. *Human Development Report 2007/2008*. New York: Oxford University Press; 2003. *Human Development Report 2003*. New York: Oxford University Press; 2000. *Human Development Report 2000*. New York: Oxford University Press; 1997. *Human Development Report 1997*. New York: Oxford University Press; 1995. *Human Development Report 1995*. New York: Oxford University Press.

Updegraff, K.A., S.M. McHale, and A.C. Crouter. 2000. "Adolescents' Sex-Typed Friendship Experiences: Does Having a Sister Versus a Brother Matter?" *Child Development* 71(6): 1597–1610.

Upitis, R. 2001. "Girls (and Boys) and Technology (and Toys)." *Canadian Journal of Education* 26(2): 164–182.

Ussher, J.M. 1999. "Commentary: Eclecticism and Methodological Pluralism: The Way Forward for Feminist Research." *Psychology of Women Quarterly* 23(1): 41–46.

Vago, S., and A. Nelson. 2008. *Law and Society*, 2nd edition. Toronto: Pearson Educational Publishing.

Valverde, M. 1991. *The Age of Light, Soap and Water*. Toronto: McClelland & Stewart.

Van Bakel, H.J.A., and J.M. Riksen-Walraven. 2002. "Parenting and Development of One Year-Olds: Links with Parental, Contextual and Child Characteristics." *Child Development* 73(1): 256–273.

Vance, C.S., ed. 1984. *Pleasure and Danger*. Boston: Routledge & Kegan Paul.

Vande Berg, L.H., and D. Streckfuss. 1992. "Prime-time Television's Portrayal of Women and the World of Work: A Demographic Profile." *Journal of Broadcasting and Electronic Media* 36: 195–208.

Vandell, D.L., K. McCartney, M.T. Owen, C. Booth, and A. Clarke-Stewart. 2003. "Variations in Child Care by Grandparents During the First Three Years." *Journal of Marriage & Family* 65(2): 375–381.

Van den Hoonaard, D. 2001. *The Widowed Self*. Waterloo, Ontario: Wilfred Laurier University Press.

van de Rijt, A., and M.W. Macy. 2006. "Power and Dependence in Intimate Exchange." *Social Forces* 84(3): 1455–1470.

Van der Lippe, T., K. Tijdens, and E. De Ruijter. 2004. "Outsourcing of Domestic Tasks and Time-Saving Effects." *Journal of Family Issues* 25(2): 216–240.

Vander Ven, T.M., F.F. Cullen, M.A. Carrozza, and J.P. Wright. 2001. "Home Alone: The Impact of Maternal Employment on Delinquency." *Social Problems* 48(2): 236–257.

VanEvery, J. 1995. *Heterosexual Women Changing the Family*. London: Taylor & Francis.

Vandewater, E.A., M. Shim, and A.G. Caplovitz. 2004. "Linking Obesity and Activity Level with Children's Television and Video Game Use." *Journal of Adolescence* 27(1): 71–85.

Vanier Institute of the Family. 2000. *Profiling Canada's Families II*. Nepean, ON: Vanier Institute of the Family.

Van Wie, V.E., and A.M. Gross. 2001. "The Role of Women's Explanations for Refusal on Men's Ability to Discriminate Unwanted Sexual Behavior in a Date Rape Scenario." *Journal of Family Violence* 16(4): 331–344.

Van Willigen, M., and P. Drentea. 2001. "Benefits of Equitable Relationships: The Impact of Sense of Fairness, Household Division of Labor, and Decision-Making Power on Perceived Social Support." *Sex Roles* 44(9–10): 571–597.

Vassilious, D., and G.F. Cartwright. 2003. "The Lost Parents' Perspective on Parental Alienation Syndrome." *American Journal of Family Therapy* 29(3): 181–191.

Veenhof, B. 2006. "The Internet: Is It Changing the Way Canadians Spend Their Time?" Statistics Canada Catalogue no. 56F0004MIE, no. 013, Science, Innovation and Electronic Information Division, August. Ottawa: Minister of Industry.

Venkatesan, M., and J. Losco. 1975. "Women in Magazine Ads: 1959–71." *Journal of Advertising Research* 15: 49–54.

Verberg, N., E. Wood, S. Desmarais, and C. Senn. 2000. "Gender Differences in Survey Respondents' Written Definitions of Date Rape." *Canadian Journal of Human Sexuality* 9(3): 181–190.

Verdun-Jones, S. 2004. "Criminal Law." In *Criminology*, 5th ed., ed. R. Linden: 55–87. Toronto: Nelson Thomson.

Verhoeven, M., M. Junger, C. Van Aken, M. Dekovic, and M.A.G. Van Aken. 2007. "Parenting During Toddlerhood: Contributions of Parental, Contextual, and Child Characteristics." *Journal of Family Issues* 28: 1663–1691.

Verkuyten, M., and B. Kinket. 1999. "The Relative Importance of Ethnicity: Ethnic Categorization Among Older Children." *International Journal of Psychology* 34(2): 107–118.

Vescio, T.K., and M. Biernat. 2003. "Family Values and Antipathy Toward Gay Men." *Journal of Applied Social Psychology* 33(4): 833–884.

Viano, C.E. 1992. *Intimate Violence.* Washington, DC: Hemisphere Publishing Company.

Vincent, C., and S.J. Ball. 2007. "'Making Up' the Middle-Class Child: Families, Activities and Class Dispositions." *Sociology* 41(6): 1061–1077.

Vincent, R.C., D.K. Davis, and L.A. Boruszkowski. 1987. "Sexism on MTV: The Portrayal of Women in Rock Videos." *Journalism Quarterly* 64(4): 750–755.

Vincent, S. 2003. "Preserving Domesticity: Reading Tupperware in Women's Changing Domestic, Social, and Economic Roles." *Canadian Review of Sociology and Anthropology* 40(2): 171–196.

Viss, D.C., and S.M. Burn. 1992. "Divergent Perceptions of Lesbians: A Comparison of Lesbian Self-Perceptions and Heterosexual Perceptions." *Journal of Social Psychology* 132(2): 169–177.

Vissandjee, B., M. DesMeules, Z. Cao, S. Abdool, and A. Kazanjiam. 2005. "Integrating Ethnicity and Migration as Determinants of Canadian Women's Health." *Women's Health Surveillance Report* 4(Supplement 1): S32–S38.

Vogel, D.L., and B.R. Karney. 2002. "Demands and Withdrawal in Newlyweds: Elaborating on the Social Structure Hypothesis." *Journal of Social & Personal Relationships* 19(5): 685–701.

Vogel, D.L., M.J. Murphy, and R.J. Werner-Wilson. 2007. "Sex Differences in the Use of Demand and Withdraw Behavior in Marriage: Examining the Social Structure Hypothesis." *Journal of Counseling Psychology* 54(2): 165–177.

Vogel, D.L., S.R. Wester, M. Heesacker, and S. Madon. 2003. "Confirming Gender Stereotypes: A Social Role Perspective." *Sex Roles* 48 (11–12): 519–528.

Vogels, J. 2002. *The Secret Language of Girls.* Toronto: Thomas Allen Publishers.

Vogt, A. 1997. "Even in Virtual Reality, It Is Still a Man's World." *Chicago Tribune,* August 24 sec. 13.1.

Vonk, R., and R.D. Ashmore. 2003. "Thinking About Gender Types: Cognitive Organization of Female and Male Types." *British Journal of Social Psychology* 42(2): 257–280.

Vosko, L.F. 2002. "The Pasts (and Futures) of Feminist Political Economy in Canada: Reviving the Debate." *Studies in Political Economy* 68: 55–83.

Voss, K., D. Markiewicz, and A.B. Doyle. 1999. "Friendship, Marriage and Self-Esteem." *Journal of Social & Personal Relationships* 16(1): 103–122.

Voydanoff, P., and B.W. Donnelly. 1999. "The Intersection of Time and Activities and Perceived Unfairness in Relation to

Psychological Distress and Marital Quality." *Journal of Marriage and the Family* 61: 739–751.

Wada. M. 2001. "Effects of Gender and Physical Distance with an Old Friend on Same-Sex Friendship." *Japanese Journal of Psychology* 72(3): 186–194.

Wade, M.L., and M.B. Brewer. 2006. "The Structure of Female Subgroups: An Exploration of Ambivalent Stereotypes." *Sex Roles* 54(11–12): 753–765.

Waite, L.J. 1995. "Does Marriage Matter?" *Demography* 32(4): 483–507.

Waite, L., and M. Gallagher. 2000. *The Case for Marriage*. New York: Doubleday.

Waites, M. 2005. "The Fixity of Sexual Identities in the Public Sphere: Biomedical Knowledge, Liberalism and the Heterosexual/Homosexual Binary in Late Modernity." *Sexualities* 8(5): 539–569.

Wajcman, J. 1991. *Feminism Confronts Technology*. University Park, PA: Pennsylvania State University Press.

Walcott, D.D., H.D. Pratt, and D.R. Patel. 2003. "Adolescents and Eating Disorders: Gender, Racial, Ethnic, Sociocultural and Socioeconomic Issues." *Journal of Adolescent Research* 18(3): 223–243.

Waldron, I. 1991. "Effects of Labour Force Participation on Sex Differences in Mortality and Morbidity." In *Women, Work and Health*, eds. M. Frankenhhaeuser, U. Lundberg, and M. Chesney: 17–38. New York: Plenum Press.

Walker, A.J. 1996. "Couples Watching Television: Gender, Power, and the Remote Control." *Journal of Marriage and the Family* 58: 813–823.

Walker, A.J., and C.C. Pratt. 1991. "Daughters' Help to Mothers: Intergenerational Aid versus Caregiving." *Journal of Marriage and the Family* 53(1): 3–12.

Walker, G. 1990. *Family Violence and the Women's Movement*. Toronto: University of Toronto Press.

Walker, K. 2002. "'I'm Not Friends the Way She's Friends': Ideological and Behavioral Constructions of Masculinity in Men's Friendships." In *Readings in the Psychology of Gender*, eds. A.E. Hunter and C. Forden: 151–166. Needham Heights, MA; Allyn & Bacon; 1994. "Men, Women

and Friendship: What They Say, What They Do." *Gender Society* 8(2): 24–265.

Walker, L. 1979. *The Battered Woman*. New York: Harper Perennial.

Wall, G., and S. Arnold. 2007. "How Involved Is Involved Fathering? An Exploration of the Contemporary Culture of Fatherhood." *Gender & Society* 21(4): 508–527.

Wallace, H. 1996. *Family Violence*. Needham, MA: Allyn & Bacon.

Wallace, S.R., and S. Koerner. 2003. "Influence of Child and Family Factors on Judicial Decisions in Contested Custody Cases." *Family Relations* 52(2): 180–188.

Waller, M. 2005. "'His' and 'Her' Marriage Expectations: Determinants and Consequences." *Journal of Marriage and Family* 67(1) February: 53–67.

Waller, W. 1938. *The Family*. New York: Dryden.

Walsh, A. 1991. *The Science of Love*. Buffalo, NY: Prometheus Books.

Walsh, C., and C.L. Cepko. 1992. "Widespread Dispersion of Neuronal Clones Across Functional Regions of the Cerebral Cortex." *Science* 255: 434–440.

Walster, E., and G.W. Walster. 1978. *A New Look at Love*. Reading, MA: Addison-Wesley.

Walter, B.J. 2003. "Lesbian Mediation: Resolving Custody and Visitation Disputes When Couples End Their Relationships." *Family Court Review* 41(1): 104–121.

Walters, K.S., T. Evans-Campbell, J.M. Simoni, T. Ronquillo, and R. Bhuyan. 2006. "'My Spirit in My Heart': Identity Experiences and Challenges Among American Indian Two-Spirit Women." *Journal of Lesbian Studies* 10(1–2): 125–149.

Walters, V. 2003. "The Social Context of Women's Health." In *Women's Surveillance Report*: 1–2. Ottawa: Canadian Institute for Health Information.

Walters, V., J.Y. Aubtriand, and N. Charles. 2003. "'Your Heart Is Never Free': Women in Wales and Ghana Talking About Distress." In *Situating Sadness*, eds. J.M. Stoppard and L.M. McMullen: 163–206. New York: New York University Press.

Walz, T. 2002. "Crones, Dirty Old Men, Sexy Seniors: Representations of the Sexuality of Older Persons." *Journal of Aging and Identity* 3 October: 112.

Walzer, S. 2008. "Redoing Gender Through Divorce." *Journal of Social and Personal Relationships* 25(1): 5–21.

Ward, L.M., B. Gorvine, and A. Cytron-Walker. 2002. "Would That Really Happen? Adolescents' Perceptions of Sexual Relationships According to Prime-Time Television." In *Sexual Teens, Sexual Media*, eds. J.D. Brown and J.R. Steele: 95–123. Mahwah, NJ: Lawrence Erlbaum Associates.

Ward, L.M., A. Merriwether, and A. Caruthers. 2006. "Breasts Are for Men: Media, Masculinity Ideologies and Men's Beliefs About Women's Bodies." *Sex Roles* 55(9–10): 703–714.

Ward, L.M., and R. Rivadeneyra, R. 2002. "Dancing, Strutting and Bouncing in Cars: The Women of Music Videos." Paper presented at the annual meeting of the American Psychological Association, Chicago, August.

Ward, S.K., K. Chapman, E. Cohn, S. White, and K. Williams. 1991. "Acquaintance Rape and the College Social Scene." *Family Relations* 40: 65–71.

Warren, T. 2007. "Conceptualizing Breadwinning Work." *Work, Employment and Society* 21(2): 371–336.

Waters, V., P. McDonough, and L. Strohschein. 2002. "The Influence of Work, Household Structure and Social, Personal and Material Resources on Gender Differences in Health: An Analysis of the 1994 Canadian National Population Health Survey." *Social Science Medicine* 44: 773–787.

Watkins, P.L., and D. Whaley. 2000. "Gender Role Stressors and Women's Health." In *Handbook of Gender, Culture and Health*, eds. R.M. Eisler and M. Hersen: 43–62. Mahwah, NJ: Lawrence Erlbaum Associates.

Watts, R.J., J.K. Abdul-Adil, and T. Pratt. 2002. "Enhancing Critical Consciousness in Young African American Men: A Psychoeducational Approach." *Psychology of Men & Masculinity* 3(1): 41–50.

Waxman-Fiduccia, B.F. 1999. "Sexual Imagery of Physically Disabled Women: Erotic? Perverse? Sexist?" *Sexuality & Disability* 17(3): 277–282.

Weigel, D.J., K.K. Bennett, and D.S. Ballard-Reisch. 2006. "Influence Strategies in Marriage: Self and Partner Links Between Equity, Strategy Use, and Marital Satisfaction and Commitment." *Journal of Family Communication* 6(1): 77–95.

Weinstein, E. 1996. "'I Thought It Was Our Turn: Therapeutic Considerations in Mid-Life Families." In *Family Scripts,* ed. J.D. Atwood: 271–298. Washington, DC: Accelerated Development.

Weiser, E.B. 2000. "Gender Differences in Internet Use Patterns and Internet Application Preferences: A Two-Sample Comparison." *CyberPsychology & Behavior* 3(2): 167–177.

Weisman, L.K. 1992. *Discrimination by Design.* Chicago: University of Chicago Press.

Weiss, D. 2005. "Constructing the Queer 'I': Performativity, Citationality and Desire in Queer Eye for the Straight Guy." *Popular Communication* 3(2): 73–95.

Weiss, R.S. 1990. *Staying the Course.* New York: Fawcett.

Weitzman, L.J. 1985. *The Divorce Revolution.* New York: Free Press.

Weitzman, L.J., D. Eifler, E. Hokada, and C. Ross. 1972. "Sex Role Socialization in Picture Books for Pre-School Children." *American Journal of Sociology* 77: 1125–1150.

Welch, R.L., A. Huston-Stein, J.C. Wright, and R. Plehal. 1979. "Subtle Sex-Role Cues in Children's Commercials." *Journal of Communication* 29: 202–209.

Wenner, L.A. 2008. "Super-Cooled Sports Dirt: Moral Contagion and Super Bowl Commercials in the Shadows of Janet Jackson." *Television & New Media* 9(2): 131–154.

West, C. 1994. "Rethinking 'Sex Differences' in Conversational Topics." In *The Women and Language Debate*, eds. C. Roman, S. Juhasz, and C. Miller. New Brunswick, NJ: Rutgers University.

West, C., and D. Zimmerman. 1987. "Doing Gender." *Gender & Society* 1: 125–151.

West, C.M. 2002. "Lesbian Intimate Partner Violence: Prevalence and Dynamics." *Journal of Lesbian Studies* 6(1): 121–127.

West, R. 1993. "Jurisprudence and Gender." In *Feminist Legal Theory*, ed. D. Kelly Weisberg: Philadelphia: 75–98. Temple University Press.

Westerfelhaus, R., and C. Lacrois. 2006. "Seeing 'Straight' Through Queer Eye: Exposing the Strategic Rhetoric of Heteronormativity in a Mediated Ritual of Gay Rebellion." *Critical Studies in Media Communication* 23(5): 426–444.

Wherrett, J. 2002. "Indian Status and Band Membership Issues." In *Women, Law and Social Change*, 4th ed., ed. T. B. Dawson: 179–182. Concord, ON: Captus Press.

Whipple, B. 2000. "Beyond the G Spot." *Scandinavian Journal of Sexology* 3(2): 35–42.

Whipple, T. W., and M. K. McManamon. 2002. "Implications of Using Male and Female Voices in Commercials: An Exploratory Study." *Journal of Advertising* 31(2): 79–91.

Whisman, M.A., L.M. Weinstock, and N. Tolejko. 2006. "Marriage and Depression." in *Women and Depression*, ed. by C.L. Keyes and S.H. Goodman,: 219–240. New York: Cambridge University Press.

Whissell, C. 2001. "Cues to Referent Gender in Randomly Constructed Names." *Perceptual & Motor Skills* 93(3): 856–858.

White, E. 2002. *Fast Girls*. New York: Scribner.

White, H.R., and P. Chen. 2002. "Problem Drinking and Intimate Partner Violence." *Journal of Studies on Alcohol* 63(2): 205–214.

White, J.M. 1992. "Marital Status and Well-Being in Canada: An Analysis of Age-Group Variations." *Journal of Family Issues* 13: 390–409.

White, J.W., B. Bondurant, and C.B. Travis. 2000. "Social Constructions of Sexuality: Unpacking Hidden Meanings." In *Sexuality, Society, and Feminism*, ed. C.B. Travis and J.W. White: 11–33. Washington, DC: American Psychological Association.

White, J.W., and P.H. Smith. 2004. "Sexual Assault Perpetration and Reperpetration: From Adolescence to Young Adulthood." *Criminal Justice & Behavior* 31(2): 182–202.

White, K., and R.M. Kowalski. 1994. "Deconstructing the Myth of the Nonaggressive Woman: A Feminist Analysis." *Psychology of Women Quarterly* 18(4): 487–508.

White, L. 1996. "No Boys Allowed in This Class." *Oshawa Whitby This Week*, November 17: 3.

White, L., and J.N. Edwards. 1990. "Emptying the Nest and Parental Well-Being: An Analysis of National Panel Data." *American Sociological Review* 55(2): 235–242.

White, L.E. 1991. "Subordination, Rhetorical Survival Skills, and Sunday Shoes: Notes on the Hearing of Mrs. G." In *Feminist Legal Theory*, eds. K.T. Bartlett and R. Kennedy: 404–428. Boulder, CO: Westview Press.

Whitesell, N., and S. Harter. 1996. "The Interpersonal Context of Emotion: Anger with Close Friends and Classmates." *Child Development* 67: 1345–1359.

Whitla, W. 1995. "A Chronology of Women in Canada." In *Feminist Issues*, ed. N. Mandell: 315–353. Scarborough, ON: Prentice Hall Canada.

Whittle, S. 1998. "The Trans-Cyberian Mail Way." *Social & Legal Studies* 7(3): 389–408; 1996. "Gender Fucking or Fucking Gender? In *Blending Genders*, eds. R. Ekins and D. King. London: Routledge.

Whorf, B.L. 1956. *Language, Thought and Reality*. Cambridge: MA: Technology Press of MIT.

Wickrama, K.A., S.F.O. Lorenz, R.D. Conger, and G.H. Elder. 1997. "Marital Quality and Physical Illness: A Latent Growth Curve Analysis." *Journal of Marriage and the Family* 59(1): 143–155.

Wiederman, M.W. 2001. "Gender Differences in Sexuality: Perceptions, Myths and Realities." *Family Journal—Counseling & Therapy for Couples & Families* 9(4): 468–471; 1997a. "Pretending Orgasm During Sexual Intercourse: Correlates in a Sample of Young Adult Women." *Journal of Sex & Marital Therapy* 23(2): 131–139; 1997b. "The Truth Must Be in Here Somewhere: Examining the Gender Disparity in Self-Reported Lifetime Number of Sex Partners." *Journal of Sex Research* 34(4): 375–386.

Wiederman, M.W., and S.R. Hurst. 1998. "Physical Attractiveness, Body Image and Women's Sexual Self-Schema." *Psychology of Women Quarterly* 21(4): 567–580.

Wiederman, M.W., and T. Pryor. 1997. "Body Dissatisfaction and Sexuality Among Women with Bulimia Nervosa." *International Journal of Eating Disorders* 21(4): 350–365.

Wikan, U. 1977. "Man Becomes Woman: Transsexualism in Oman as a Key to Gender Roles." *Man*, New Series 12: 304–319.

Wilcox, E., W.M. Finlay, and J. Edmonds. 2006. "'His Brain Is Totally Different': An Analysis of Care-Staff Explanations of Aggressive Challenging Behaviour and the Impact of Gendered Discourses." *British Journal of Social Psychology* 45(1): 197–216.

Wilkins, A.C. 2004. "Puerto Rican Wannabes: Sexual Spectacle and the Marking of Race, Class, and Gender Boundaries." *Gender & Society* 18(1): 103–121.

Wilkins, K. 1996. "Causes of Death: How the Sexes Differ." *Canadian Social Trends* 41: 11–17.

Wilkins, R., J.M. Berthelot, and E. Ng. 2002. "Trends in Mortality by Neighbourhood Income in Urban Canada From 1971–1996." *Health Reports* 2002(13) (supplement): 45–71.

Wilkinson, H. 1999. "The Androgynous Generation." In *Rewriting the Sexual Contract*, ed. G. Dench: 238–246. New Brunswick, NJ: Transaction.

William, W. 2001. *Linguistic Evidence*. New York: Academic Press.

Williams, C.L. 2005. "Shopping as Symbolic Interaction: Race, Class, and Gender in the Toy Store." *Symbolic Interaction* 28(4): 459–472; 1995. *Still a Man's World* Berkeley: University of California Press; 1992/2001. "The Glass Escalator: Hidden Advantages for Men in the 'Female' Professions." *Social Problems* 39: 253–267. Reprinted in *Men's Lives*, cds. M.S. Kimmel and M.A. Messner: 211–224. Boston: Allyn and Bacon.

Williams, D.G., and G.H. Morris. 1996. "Weeping or Tearfulness in British and Israeli Adults." *British Journal of Psychology* 87: 479–505.

Williams, Jr., J.A., 1987. "Sex Role Socialization in Picture Books: An Update." *Social Science Quarterly* 68: 148–156.

Williams, J.C. 1991. "Deconstructing Gender." In *Feminist Legal Theory*, eds. K.T. Bartlett and R. Kennedy: 95–123. San Francisco: Westview.

Williams, J.E., and S.M. Bennett. 1975. "The Definition of Sex Stereotypes via the Adjective Checklist." *Sex Roles* 1: 327–337.

Williams, J.E., R.C. Satterwhite, and D.L. Best. 1999. "Pancultural Gender Stereotypes Revisited: The Five Factor Model." *Sex Roles* 40(7–8): 513–525.

Williams, L.S. 2002. "Trying on Gender, Gender Regimes and the Process of Becoming Women." *Gender & Society* 16(1): 29–52.

Williams, R., and M.A. Wittig. 1997. "'I'm Not A Feminist But...' : Factors Contributing to the Discrepancy Between Pro-Feminist Orientation and Feminist Social Identity." *Sex Roles* 37(11–12): 885–904.

Willinger, R. 1993. "Resistance and Change: College Men's Attitudes Toward Family and Work in the 1980s." In *Men, Work, and Family*, ed. J. Hood: 108–130. Newbury Park, CA: Sage.

Wilson, E.O. 1978. *On Human Nature*. Cambridge, MA: Harvard University Press; 1975. *Sociobiology*. Cambridge, MA: Harvard University Press.

Wilson, M. 2002. "'I am the Prince of Pain, for I am a Princess in the Brain': Liminal Transgender Identities, Narratives and the Elimination of Ambiguities." *Sexualities* 5(4): 425–448.

Wilson, M.A., and S. Leith. 2001. "Acquaintances, Lovers and Friends: Rape within Relationships." *Journal of Applied Social Psychology* 31(8): 1709–1726.

Wilson, S.J. 1996. *Women, Families & Work*. 4th ed. Toronto: McGraw-Hill Ryerson; 1991. *Women, Families, and Work*. 3rd ed. Toronto: McGraw-Hill Ryerson.

Windebank, J. 2001. "Dual-Earner Families in Britain and France: Gender Divisions of Domestic Labour and Parenting Work in Different Welfare States." *Work, Employment and Society* 15(2): 269–290.

Winter, S., and N. Udomsak. 2002. "Gender Stereotype and Self Among Transgenders: Underlying Elements." *International Journal of Transgenderism* 6(2).

Wise, E.A., D.D. Price, C.D. Myers, M.W. Heft, and M.E. Robinson. 2002. "Gender Role Expectations of Pain: Relationship to Experimental Pain Perception." *Pain* 96(3): 335–342.

Wise, S., and L. Stanley. 2003. "Looking Back and Looking Forward: Some Recent

Feminist Sociology Review." *Sociological Research Online* 8(3). **www.socresonline. org/uk/8/3/wise.html**

Witt, S.D. 2000. "The Influence of Peers on Children's Socialization to Gender Roles." *Early Child Development and Care* 162: 1–7.

Wittig, M. 1992. *The Straight Mind and Other Essays*. Boston: Beacon Press.

Wizeman, T., and M.L. Pardue (eds.). 2001. *Exploring the Biological Contribution to Human Health*. Institute of Medicine, National Academy of Science, Washington, DC.

Woldeguiorguis, I.M. 2003. "Racism and Sexism in Child Welfare: Effects on Women of Color as Mothers and Practitioners." *Child Welfare* 82(2): 273–288.

Wolf, N. 2001. *Misconceptions*. New York: Doubleday; 1998. *Power Feminism*. New York: Random House; 1994. *Fire with Fire*. New York: Random House; 1990. *The Beauty Myth*. Toronto: Vintage Books.

Wolfmark, J., ed. 1999. *Cybersexualities*. Edinburgh: Edinburgh University Press.

Wolin, L.D. 2003. "Gender Issues in Advertising: An Oversight Synthesis of Research, 1970–2002." *Journal of Advertising Research* 43(1): 111–129.

Wong, O.M. 2003. "Postponement or Abandonment of Marriage? Evidence From Hong Kong." *Journal of Comparative Family Studies* 34(4): 531–554.

Wood, E., S. Desmarais, and S. Gugula. 2002. "The Impact of Parenting Experience on Gender Stereotyped Toy Play of Children." *Sex Roles* 47(1–2): 39–49.

Wood, J. 2009. *Gendered Lives*, 9th ed. Boston, MA: Woodsworth Cengage Learning; 1997. *Gendered Lives*, 2nd ed. Belmont, CA: Wadsworth; 1994. "Engendered Identities: Shaping Voice and Mind Through Gender." In *Interpersonal Communication*, ed. D.R. Vocate: 145–167. Hillsdale, NJ: Lawrence Erlbaum Associates.

Wood, J.T., and K. Dindia. 1998. "What's the Difference? A Dialogue About Differences and Similarities Between Men and Women." In *Sex Differences and Similarities in Communication*, eds. D.J. Canary and K. Dindia: 19–39. Mahwah, NJ: Lawrence Erlbaum.

Wood, J.T., and C. Inman. 1993. "In a Different Mode: Recognizing Male Modes of Closeness." *Journal of Applied Communication Research* 21: 279–295.

Wood, P.B., and J.P. Bartkowski. 2004. "Attribution Style and Public Policy Attitudes Towards Gay Rights." *Social Science Quarterly* 85(1): 58–74.

Wood, W., F.Y. Wong, and J.G. Cachere. 1991. "Effects of Media Violence on Viewers' Aggression in Unconstrained Social Interaction." *Psychological Bulletin* 109: 371–383.

Woolf, V. 1978. *Books and Portraits*. New York: Harcourt, Brace Jovanovich.

Wootton, B. 1997. "Gender Differences in Occupational Employment." *Monthly Labour Review*: 15–24.

Worell, J. 1996. "Feminist Identity in a Gendered World." In *Lectures on the Psychology of Women*, eds. J.C. Chrisler, C. Golden, and P.D. Rozee. New York: McGraw-Hill.

Wozniak, S. 2003. "Identity and the Case for Gay Rights: Race, Gender, Religion as Analogies." *Archives of Sexual Behavior* 32(5): 475–477.

Wren, B. 2002. "'I Can Accept My Child Is Transsexual But If I Ever See Him in a Dress I'll Hit Him': Dilemmas in Parenting a Transgendered Adolescent." *Clinical Child Psychology & Psychiatry* 7(3): 377–397.

Wright, B.W. 2001. *Comic Book Nation*. Baltimore: John Hopkins University Press.

Wright, E.O., J. Baxter, and G.E. Birkelund. 1995. "The Gender-Gap in Workplace Authority: A Cross-National Study." *American Sociological Review* 60: 407–435.

Wright, P.H. 1982. "Men's Friendships, Women's Friendships and the Alleged Inferiority of the Latter." *Sex Roles* 8: 1–20.

Wright, P.H., and M.P. Scanlon. 1991. "Gender Role Orientations and Friendship: Some Attenuation, But Gender Differences Abound." *Sex Roles* 24(9–10): 556–566.

Wright, S.K. 2006. "Phonological Cues Influence Sex Decisions About Novel Names." *Psychological Reports* 99(2): 315–321.

Wu, Z. 2000. *Cohabitation*. Don Mills, ON: Oxford University Press; 1995. "Remarriage after Widowhood: A Marital History Study of Older Canadians." *Canadian Journal on Aging* 14(4): 719–736.

Wu, Z., and T.R. Balakrishnan. 1992. "Attitudes Towards Cohabitation and Marriage in Canada." *Journal of Comparative Family Studies* 22(1): 1–12.

Wylie, M. 1995. "No Place for Women." *Digital Watch* 4(8).

Wyndol, F. 2002. "The Emerging Field of Adolescent Romantic Relationships." *Current Directions in Psychological Science* 11(5): 177–180.

Yancey, A.K., S.D. Cochran, H.L. Corliss, and V.M. Mays. 2003. "Correlates of Overweight and Obesity Among Lesbian and Bisexual Women." *Preventive Medicine* 36(6): 676–683.

Yanowitz, K.L., and K.J. Weathers. 2004. "Do Boys and Girls Act Differently in the Classroom? A Content Analysis of Student Characters in Educational Psychology Textbooks." *Sex Roles* 51 (1–2): 101–107.

Yates, R.A., R.W. Yates, and P. Bain. 2000. *Introduction to Law in Canada.* 2nd ed. Scarborough, ON: Prentice Hall Allyn and Bacon Canada.

Yato, Y. 2000. "Maternal Attention-Directing Behavior and Mother-Infant Joint Attention During Toy Play." *Japanese Journal of Developmental Psychology* 11(3): 153–162.

Yee, M. 1993. "Finding the Way Home Through Issues of Gender, Race and Class." In *Returning the Gaze*, ed. H. Bannerji: 3–44. Toronto: Star Vision Press.

Yeh, S.J., S.K. Lo, and S.J Yeh. 2004. "Living Alone, Social Support, and Feeling Lonely Among the Elderly." *Social Behavior Personality* 32(2): 129–138.

Yelland, C., and M. Tiggemann. 2003. "Muscularity and the Gay Ideal: Body Dissatisfaction and Disordered Eating in Homosexual Men." *Eating Behaviors* 4(2): 107–116.

Yllo, K.A. 1993. "Through a Feminist Lens: Gender, Power and Violence." In *Current Controversies on Family Violence*, eds. R.J. Gellese and D. Loseke: 47–62. Beverly Hills, CA: Sage.

Yogis, J.A., R.R. Duplak, and J.R. Trainor. 1996. *Sexual Orientation and Canadian Law*. Toronto: Emond Montgomery Publications Limited.

Young, A. 2000. *Women Who Become Men*. New York: Berg.

Young, R.M., and E. Balaban. 2006. "Psychoneuroindoctrinology." *Nature* 443(12): 634.

Youngblade, L.M. 2003. "Peer and Teacher Ratings of Third- and Fourth-Grade Children's Social Behavior as a Function of Early Maternal Employment." *Journal of Child Psychology & Psychiatry & Allied Disciplines* 44(4): 477–488.

Youngblut, J.M., D. Brooten, L.T. Singer, T. Standing, H. Lee, and W.L. Haejung. 2001. "Effects of Maternal Employment and Prematurity on Child Outcomes in Single Parent Families." *Nursing Research* 50(6): 346–355.

Yowell, C.M. 1997. "Risks of Communication: Early Adolescent Girls' Conversations With Mothers and Friends About Sexuality." *Journal of Early Adolescence* 17(2): 172–196.

Zahn-Waxler, C., P. Cole, and K. Barrett. 1991. "Guilt and Empathy: Sex Differences and Implications for the Development of Depression." In *The Development of Emotion*, eds. J. Garber and K. Dodge: 43–272. Cambridge: Cambridge University Press.

Zarbatany, L., P. McDougall, and S. Hymel. 2000. "Gender-Differentiated Experiences in the Peer-Culture: Links to Intimacy in Preadolescence." *Social Development* 9(1): 62–79.

Zaretsky, E. 1976. *Capitalism, the Family, and Personal Life*. New York: Harper & Row.

Zebrowitz, L.A., J.A. Hall, N.A. Murphy, and G. Rhodes. 2002. "Looking Smart and Looking Good; Facial Cues to Intelligence and Their Origins." *Personality & Social Psychology Bulletin* 28(2): 238–249.

Zilbergeld, B. 1992. *The New Male Sexuality*. New York: Bantam Books.

Ziegler, A., and K.A. Heller. 2000. "Conditions for Self-Confidence Among Boys and Girls Achieving Highly in Chemistry." *Journal of Secondary Gifted Education* 11(3): 144–151.

Zipp, J.F., A. Prohaska, and M. Bemiller. 2004. "Wives, Husbands and Hidden Power in

Marriage." *Journal of Family Issues* 25(7): 933–958.

Zucker, K.J., D.N.W. Wilson-Smith, J.A. Kurita, and A. Stern. 1995. "Children's Appraisal of Gender-Typed Behavior in Their Peers." *Sex Roles* 33: 703–725.

Zucker, K.J., and R. Blanchard. 2003. "Birth Order in the Fakafefine." *Journal of Sex & Marital Therapy* 29(3): 251–253.

Zumhagen, B. 2004. "A Timeline of Barbie's History." **www.adiosbarbie.com/bology/ bology_timeline.html**

Zuo, J. 2004. "Shifting the Breadwinning Boundary: The Role of Men's Breadwinner Status and Their Gender Ideologies." *Journal of Family Issues* 25: 811–832.

Zuo, J., and S. Tang. 2000. "Breadwinner Status and Gender Ideologies of Men and Women Regarding Family Roles." *Sociological Perspectives* 43: 29–44.

Zurbriggen, E.L., and E.M. Morgan. 2006. "Who Wants to Marry a Millionaire? Reality Dating Television Programs, Attitudes Toward Sex and Sexual Behaviors." *Sex Roles* 54: 1–17.

Zurbriggen, E.L., and A.M. Sherman. 2007. "Reconsidering 'Sex' and "Gender': Two Steps Forward, One Step Back." *Feminism & Psychology* 17(4): 475–480.

Zvonkovic, A.M., K.M. Greaves, C.J. Schmiege, and L.D. Hall. 1996. "The Marital Construction of Gender Through Work and Family Decisions: A Qualitative Analysis." *Journal of Marriage and the Family* 58: 91–100.

Zvonkovic, A.M., C.R. Solomon, A.M. Hunble, and M. Manoogian. 2005. "Family Work and Relationships: Lessons From Families of Men Whose Jobs Require Travel." *Family Relations* 54(3): 411–422.

Name Index

Subject Index